RECORDS OF JASPER COUNTY, GEORGIA

From the Georgia Department of Archives and History

By
Robert Scott Davis, Jr.

Please direct all correspondence and orders to:

SOUTHERN HISTORICAL PRESS, Inc.
PO BOX 1267
375 West Broad Street
Greenville, SC   29601

ISBN: 978-0-89308-626-8

DEDICATED to my pen-pals

Cathy Warren, Jess Shelander, and Isaac C. Asare

CONTENTS

INTRODUCTION

I.   ORIGINAL (UNBOUND) MARRIAGE RECORDS, 1816-1914.
              Record Group 179-2-2.

II.   ORIGINAL (UNBOUND) WILLS, 1809-1907.
              Record Group 179-2-4.

III. ESTATE (UNBOUND RECORDS) FILES, 1809-1907.
              Record Group 179-2-3.

IV.   MISCELLANEOUS PENSION RECORDS, 1812-1920.
              Record Group 179-2-13.

V.   SUPERIOR COURT CASE FILES, 1809-1922.
              Record Group 179-1-1.

VI.   INFERIOR COURT CASE FILES, 1804-1902.
              Record Group 179-2-7.

VII. COUNTY COURT CASE FILES, 1860-1913.
              Record Group 179-3-5.

VIII. JUSTICE OF THE PEACE COURT CASE FILES, 1802-1935.
              Record Group 179-4-9.

IX.   PONEY HOMESTEAD (DEBT AND TAX EXEMPTIONS) RECORDS, 1867-
      1907.
              Record Group 179-2-11.

X.   LAND GRANT RECORDS, 1799-1823.
              Record Group 179-2-12.

XI.   ORIGINAL (UNBOUND) DEEDS, 1808-1903.
              Record Group 179-1-6.

XII. MISCELLANEOUS UNBOUND RECORDS, 1808-1935.
              Record Group 179-12-10.
          Amnesty Oaths.
          Apprenticeships.
          Citizenship Oaths.
          Correspondence.
          Estays.
          Inquests.
          Merchant's Invoices.
          Defaulting Jurors.
          Jurors.
          Court of Ordinary.
          Deeds--Slaves.
          Miscellaneous Deeds.
          Notes, Mortgages etc.
          Defaulting Administrators etc.
          Interrogatories
          Registrations - Free Persons of Color

XIII. BOUND ORIGINAL RECORDS AT THE GEORGIA ARCHIVES.
              Various Record Groups.

XIV. OTHER RECORDS (INCLUDING MICROFILM) AT THE GEORGIA
      ARCHIVES: AN INVENTORY.

      PERSONAL NAME INDEX.

INTRODUCTION

Jasper County, Ga. was created by act of December 10, 1807 from original Baldwin County, which was created from Indian land cessions of 1802 and 1805. The area that became Jasper County was initially granted to lucky Georgia residents through the 1807 land lottery. Originally Jasper County was named Randolph County. The name was changed by act of December 10, 1812 and present-day Randolph County (created December 20, 1828) and the city of Jasper (in Pickens County) should not be confused with Jasper County. In 1815 a small area of northeast Jasper County was transfered to Morgan County and in 1821 a small area of northwest Jasper County was used to create Newton County. An act of November 23, 1814 extended the judicial boundaries of Jasper County to include the Indian lands north of the "road leading from Zachariah Philip's, sen'r. on the Ocmulgee" and "up to the Cherokee line, or a path leading from the High Shoals of the Appalatchee to the Standing Peach Tree, on the Chattahochee, called the Hightower Trail, including said Trail."

The inventories reproduced here were made by the staff of the Georgia Department of Archives and History from Jasper County records open to researchers at the Georgia Archives. The records were brought into the Archives and processed largely through the work of Beatrice Lang, former head of the Government Records Office. For more information on Jasper County families, see:

Jewel Moates Lancaster, Jasper County, Georgia Cemetery and Bible Records (n.p., 1969).

Jasper County Historical Foundation, History of Jasper County, Georgia (Monticello: The Author, 1976).

Georgia Chapter, DAR, Historical Collections (1926; rep. ed. Easley, SC: Southern Historical Press, 1968) 1: 35-43, lists of wills, appraisors, jurors, and marriages.

Silas E. Lucas, Jr., Some Georgia County Records (Easley, SC: Southern Historical Press, 1977) 2: 42-82, includes miscellaneous estate records 1810-1815, and county court minutes and wills, 1813-1822.

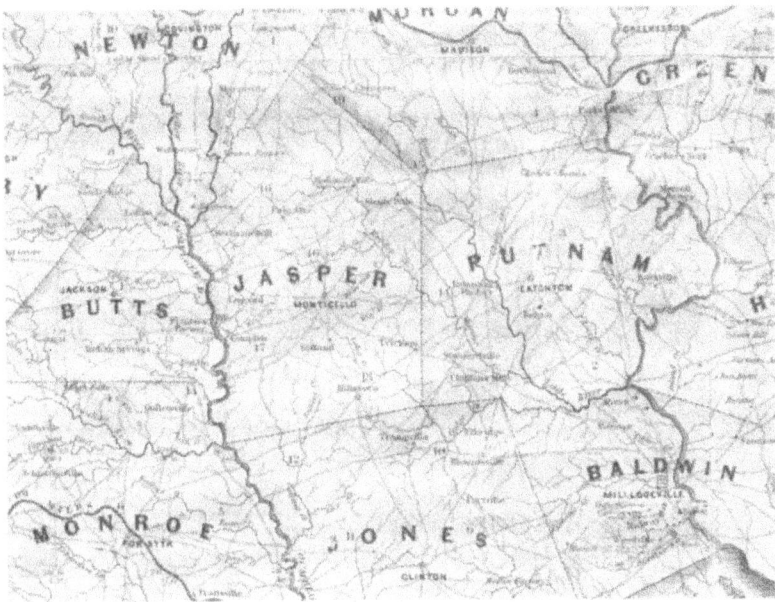

Jasper County from an 1847 map of Georgia by William G. Bonner,
courtesy Georgia Surveyor General Department.

CHAPTER I

ORIGINAL (UNBOUND) MARRIAGE RECORDS, 1816-1914
Record Group 179-2-2

DESCRIPTION OF SERIES AND ITS CONTENTS

This series contains original unbound marriage records which consist of both licenses and certificates included on the same document. Information on the licenses includes name of the groom, name of the bride and date license was issued. The certificates give the date of the marriage, some of the Ordinary and name of the person performing the wedding ceremony. On the back of most of the records is the book and page where the records are recorded although no effort has been made to compare the completeness of this file with the recorded copies in the Marriage Record volumes of the county. The records have been flattened, cleaned and placed in folders. They are arranged chronologically by timespan of considerable length and thereunder alphabetically by surname of the groom. There is a cross-reference index located in Box 3. The following shelf list merely shows the general contents of each box.

Aaron, James A.	Anna Cheek	4/19/1888
Aaron, James C.	Mrs. Mary B. Cunard	12/19/1863
Aaron, James C.	Mrs. Susan Pulliam	3/16/1869
Aaron, John L.	Sarah W. Lawson	7/24/1864
Aaron, John M.	Rebecca F. Cunard	2/27/1873
Aaron, John M.	Emma Moon	10/2/1887
Aaron, Paul S.	Lessie Harris	3/3/1892
Aaron, Robert	Rebecca Osburne	1/12/1888
Aaron, W. A.	Eliza A. Savage	5/7/1891
Aaron, William A.	Solona Shaw	5/20/1860
Abbott, Peter I.	Amanda Dillon	3/26/1818
Acree, W. B.	Mrs. M. S. Plummer	7/25/1864
Aiken, Kimball	Lilly Harvey	8/27/1893
Aikin, John C.	Robbie A. Thompson	12/12/1876
Aken, Daniel	Harriet R. Slagle	12/22/1842
Aken, Isaac	Nancy Fears	12/28/1885
Akens, Ransom H.	Sallie J. Hamilton	12/8/1864
Akin, Robert S.	Carrie A. Benford	4/3/1860
Akins, Patrick H.	Jinnie K. Malone	10/28/1873
Akins, Thomas J.	Julia A. Allen	5/26/1859
Alexander, George T.	Sallie Andrews	1/13/1890
Alexander, Green (col)	Litha Goolsby (col)	10/4/1874
Alexander, James T.	Mary L. Turner	12/23/1885
Alexander, Jeff (col)	Mittie Johnston (col)	12/1/1901
Alexander, Jeff	Mary Jordan	1/11/1897
Alexander, John (col)	Charlotte Humphrey (col)	12/1/1894
Alexander, John	Patience George	1/27/1888
Alexander, John J.	Lelia B. Perkins	1/7/1886
Alexander, Joseph	Roxie Ann Turner	2/28/1888
Alexander, Major (col)	Mary Lou Morgan (col)	12/28/1898
Alexander, Robert W.	Mattie Blackwell	10/23/1892
Alexander, Simon (col)	Eliza Jane Peurifoy (col)	2/4/1894
Alexander, Will (col)	Mattie Gay (col)	12/26/1889
Alexander, William	Martha Cook	10/26/1876
Allen, Aubie	Laura Polk	7/28/1907
Allen, Bob	Evaline Glover	12/23/1886
Allen, Charles	Sarah Tinsley	11/7/1885
Allen, Charly (col)	Amanda Bryant (col)	12/29/1873
Allen, Clark	Adaline Jones	12/18/1887
Allen, Daniel	Sarah Benton	9/20/1877
Allen, Dennis	Sarah Downey	1/6/1818
Allen, Green	Oney Smith	6/18/1877
Allen, Green	Eliza Benton	4/29/1887
Allen, Harris N.	Mary J. Price	11/14/1861

Allen, Herschel W. B.	Mary S. Thompson	1/9/1889
Allen, J. Shadric	C. Zippoah Cunard	2/27/1873
Allen, Jack	Annie Kate Flourney	9/12/1886
Allen, Jefferson D.	Maria C. Deason	2/21/1884
Allen, John	Mary Branham	4/6/1819
Allen, John	Martha Roach	11/27/1886
Allen, John M.	Laura J. Harvey	10/16/1859
Allen, Sam	Caroline Banks	3/31/1866
Allen, Sam (col)	Matilda Ozborn (col)	8/18/1867
Allen, Squire (col)	Mary Driskell (col)	12/4/1892
Allen, Wiley (col) (alias Holland)	Cornelia Porter (col)	12/24/1873
Allen, William F.	Sarah Brooks	?/?/1819
Allison, Hamp (col)	Lizzie Griggs (col)	11/28/1895
Alliston, Charles W.	Margarett K. McDowell	12/15/1858
Almonds, William (col)	Narcis Barron (col)	12/29/1898
Anchors, Joseph B.	Leola Wilson	2/1/1892
Anderson, Anthony	Mary Fitzpatrick	12/21/1888
Anderson, George	Mittie Russell	2/15/1894
Anderson, John F.	Ada Gordon	1/23/1889
Anderson, Newton Z.	Robertine Franklin	7/13/1892
Andrews, Thomas (col)	Fannie Hurt (col)	12/27/1901
Andrews, William	Mrs. Georgia Waits	12/20/1883
Andrews, William P.	Martha F. Goolsby	10/22/1868
Anglin, Samuel	Annie Smith	10/9/1899
Annis, Charles S.	Elizabeth H. Freeman	7/18/1865
Annis, Jesse M.	Martha Fish	9/28/1865
Annis, W. J.	Lula Cook	12/16/1896
Arington, William	Elizabeth C. Sansom	2/3/1859
Ashmore, Pointon	Frances Right	7/1/1818
Askew, James E.	Sarah A. Goolsby	5/26/1846
Athon, Terrell	Florence Mozelle Walker	1/1/1908
Atkinson, William F.	Mrs. Martha Lewis	11/5/1865
Atkisson, Jesse N.	Rebecca H. Ansley	11/4/1858
Ausbern, George	Martha White	6/1/1817
Avent, Henry	Susan Jones	12/17/1872
Averheart, John W.(col)	Corine Allen (col)	4/24/1897
Avery, Joe (col)	Frances Turner (col)	no certification
Avery, Samuel	Rose Ann Bogan	11/26/1865
Aycock, James	Sarah White	1/23/1817
Backum, Richard (col)	Mary George (col)	4/8/1893
Bacon, Summer W.	Sallie J. Jordan	11/8/1870
Bailey, Elisha	Amelia Jumstrom	9/11/1883
Bailey, James	Caroline Wilson	4/24/1872
Bailey, Joe (col)	Lula Kelly (col)	4/13/1895
Bailey, John	Mary Smith	3/12/1893
Bailey, John W.	Rhoda A. Lane	10/27/1870
Bailey, Lee (col)	Margaret Winfrey (col)	12/8/1892
Bailey, Robert L.	Annie E. Cardell	1/1/1896
Bailey, W. T.	M. A. Niblett	11/26/1885
Bailey, William Harrison (col)	Jane McGough (col)	12/28/1888
Bailey, Willis (col)	Mary Belle (col)	11/?/1895
Bailey, Zachariah	Jane Zelemer Key	12/26/1880
Baker, Joseph	Agnes Kenneday	3/28/1819
Ballard, William E.	Katie Dozier	2/11/1886
Banks, Alf (col)	Mima Robinson (col)	12/27/1888
Banks, Anderson	Mollie Robinson	8/6/1885
Banks, Anderson (col)	Matilda Smith (col)	3/8/1895
Banks, Anderson (col)	Carrie Smith (col)	9/18/1898

Banks, Columbus	Jennie Leath	4/8/1888
Banks, Columbus (col)	Annie Jeffries (col)	4/19/1892
Banks, Daniel	Telitha Smith	12/30/1872
Banks, Dennis(col)	Lida Bearden (col)	1/2/1898
Banks, Dennis (col)	Janis Rickerson (col)	2/28/1891
Banks, Ed (col)	Cora Thompson (col)	5/29/1898
Banks, Eli (col)	Mary Lucas (col)	9/24/1892
Banks, Frank	Laura Smith	3/6/1881
Banks, George	Georgia Ann Thornton	1/3/1883
Banks, Green	Indianna Gilstrap	1/15/1885
Banks, Henry (col)	Louisa Malone (col)	12/24/1867
Banks, Henry	Davis Kelly	10/4/1877
Banks, Isaac (col)	Ellen Fears (col)	3/11/1892
Banks, Jeff	Mariah Robinson	12/15/1882
Banks, Joe (col)	Matilda Henderson (col)	11/28/1868
Banks, John	Susan Norman	2/1/1874
Banks, John	Alice Morgan	12/31/1884
Banks, John (col)	Mattie Phillips (col)	9/22/1895
Banks, John C.	Martha A. Henderson	8/15/1857
Banks, Juke (col)	Epsie Jeffries (col)	1/6/1898
Banks, Lucius (col)	Mattie Smith (col)	1/31/1897
Banks, Olinious O.	Sallie Kate Blackwell	12/24/1891
Banks, Richard (col)	Sena Arnold (col)	3/12/1899
Banks, Samuel (col)	Ada Wright (col)	9/16/1893
Banks, Thomas (col)	Emma Moss (col)	10/2/?
Banks, Thomas (col)	Cathrin Tuggle (col)	no certi.
Banks, Walton	Ella Jeffries	3/11/1883
Barber, Daniel (col)	Matilda Holt (col)	12/11/1892
Barber, Daniel	Nancy Phillips	10/24/1872
Barber, Gus (col)	Parthenia Thomas (col)	8/27/1895
Barber, Gustus (col)	Jennett Hanford (col)	1/25/1873
Barber, John (col)	Eliza Minter (col)	1/15/1898
Barber, Peter (col)	Melvina Blan (col)	11/11/1869
Barber, Randal (col)	Julia McKissack (col)	6/19/1881
Barber, Samuel	Rachel Goolsby	4/1/1884
Barker, A. B.	F. M. Hickman	1/16/1873
Barker, John W.	Mattie Johnston	12/24/1884
Barker, Thomas Jefferson	Emma Wheeler	12/14/1893
Barker, Wyatt P.	Luella Evans	12/28/1892
Barnes, Albert	Anna Smith	1/28/1875
Barnes, Berry	Eliza Robinson	11/15/1873
Barnes, Charlie	Annie Blackwell	12/31/1884
Barnes, Charlie	Henrietta Smith	8/21/1889
Barnes, Dave (col)	Betsey Polk (col)	11/20/1898
Barnes, David (col)	Mary J. Conner (col)	4/12/1868
Barnes, Early (col)	Alice Dunn (col)	10/5/1890
Barnes, Henry	Mary Jane Polk	12/25/1891
Barnes, J. H. L.	Lemma S. Leverett	12/15/1896
Barnes, Jim	Easter Pope	11/10/1883
Barnes, John Henry	Adaline Pope	10/10/1885
Barnes, Mathew	Lucinda Harris	12/29/?
Barnes, Phillip (col)	Fanny Stanford (col)	1/9/1897
Barnes, Thomas G.	Maud Campbell	2/17/1892
Barnett, Green D.	Elvira A. Stone	2/15/1849
Baron, William	Sallie Johnson	7/29/1894
Barr, James W.	Mary A. Stanford	5/3/1896
Barr, John	Leathy Sparks	10/18/1882
Barr, Marcus	Patsy Johnson	12/23/1886
Barr, Mitchel (col)	Lizzie Thomas (col)	12/21/1893
Barr, William (col)	Willie Ann Campbell (col)	3/27/1898
Barr, William	Harriet Cook	4/8/1869
Barrett, Richard	Mary A. Ramey	8/29/1867
Barron, Adam (col)	Ann Kelly	12/23/1891

4

Barron, James H.	Adella Gordon	11/20/1884
Barron, John (col)	Anna Jordan (col)	12/18/1893
Barron, Kinchen (col)	Frances Hodge (col)	6/27/1892
Barron, Lewis (col)	Dorah Herd (col)	12/22/1897
Barron, Luther (col)	Hattie Kate McDowell(col)	12/22/1901
Barron, Major	Mattie Vaughn	12/25/1906
Barron, Willie (col)	Cornelia Gardner (col)	1/3/1891
Bartlett, Scott (col)	Addie Joe Jordan (col)	12/27/1891
Basley, William (col)	Willie Standifer (col)	2/23/1876
Baswell, Wesley	Sylvania Gant	3/31/1886
Bayne, Robert R.	Martha L. A. Dunn	3/31/1857
Baynes, Floyd (col)	Margarett Johnson (col)	2/2/1890
Baynes, Mack (col)	Genie Cargile (col)	12/7/1893
Baynes, Robert A.	Mayroe Ward	11/14/1895
Baynes, Sidney R.	Mrs. Lizzie Leverett	5/15/1887
Baynes, Sidney R.	Mrs. Mamie J. McDowell	2/5/1892
Baynes, Wat, Jr.(col)	Eliza Derice (col)	4/3/1901
Beall (Bell), John	Mary M. Crow	11/24/1859
Bearden, Alfred (col)	Manda Wade (col)	?/?/1868
Bearden, Alfred (col)	Easter Marks (col)	no certi.
Bearden, Bob	Sallie Moore	3/10/1873?
Bearden, Wiley	Polly Parish	9/9/1817
Beauhannon, John H.	Rebecca L. Yancy	11/19/1885
Bebee, Henry (col)	Eva Odom (col)	6/23/1907
Bebee, Jefferson	Cora Jordan	4/5/1883
Bebee, Reuben	Susan Smith	1/6/1882
Beckwith, William B.	Sarah F. Jones	12/20/1883
Beebe, Early (col)	Mattie Mullins (col)	8/7/1894
Beebe, Jefferson	Fannie Holt	11/6/1884
Beebe, Joseph (col)	Elizabeth Gordon (col)	1/4/1894
Beebe, Richard (col)	Dinah Brown (col)	11/7/1889
Beebe, Ned	Luiza Peacock	1/16/1873
Belcher, Authar Clifton	Nina Belle Barnes	6/1/1899
Belcher, Green B.	Catherine J. Cornwell	no certi.
	License issued	3/20/1858
Belcher, James L.	Mary E. Kelly	12/13/1863
	License issued	12/16/1863
	Consent	12/16/1863
Belcher, John	Nancy Hardin	11/13/1817
Belcher, John	Mary Ann Lane	12/20/1857
Belcher, O. R.	Martha L. Slaughter	10/31/1865
Belcher, O. R., Jr.	Bettie Daugherty	7/19/1874
Belcher, Warren	Caroline Vickram	1/8/1877
Belcher, Warren (col)	Lizzie Wimbush (col)	8/15/1887
Belcher, William D.	Susan C. McDowell	10/31/1865
Belcher, William Lee(col)	Nancy Shy (col)	6/24/1899
Belew, James C.	Susannah Allen	11/15/1817
Bell, Ab	Nora Dumas	12/28/1876
Bell, Cary (col)	Mary Thurman (col)	4/26/1874
Bell, Charley	Patsey Bell	2/25/1882
Bell, James	Charlotte Toland	10/29/?
	License issued	10/26/1872
Bell, Jim (col)	Katie Reid (col)	4/10/1897
Bell, Nelson (col)	Linie Whitfield (col)	11/9/1901
Bell, Perry (col)	Mamie Preston (col)	6/3/1894
Bell, Thomas	Lucy Ann Goolsby	11/30/1888
Bell, Tom	Joanna White	1/4/1887
Bell, William (col)	Mary Cochran (col)	3/7/1869
Bell, William (col)	Mollie Winbush (col)	12/28/1888
Bell, York (col)	Patsey Reid (col)	1/25/1868
Benford, Allen (col)	Mollie Fears (col)	3/20/1890
Benford, John (col)	Hattie Gotier (col)	3/29.1889
Benton, Abba	Martha E. Harris	8/23/1882

5

Benton, Abe	Mollie Harris	1/5/1877
Benton, Albert	Harriet Williams	12/30/1886
Benton, Alfred (col)	Sallie Powell (col)	3/4/1890
Benton, Anderson (col)	Rosie Blackwell (col)	12/30/1875
Benton, Benjamin	Ellen Walker	12/29/1885
Benton, Coleman (col)	Parthene Robinson (col)	5/12/1895
Benton, Davis (col)	Cora Perry (col)	1/23/1901
Benton, Dock (col)	Cora Smith (col)	11/10/1895
Benton, Elisha	Creacy Goodman	1/6/1859
Benton, Genus (col)	Maggie Hurd (col)	1/3/1897
Benton, George	Sallie Hutchison	10/2/1887
Benton, George (col)	Ida Smith	1/10/1889
Benton, George (col)	Josie Pheny (col)	9/22/1890
Benton, Green (col)	Lucy Benton (col)	4/5/1869
Benton, Harvey (col)	Addie Lou Banks (col)	12/29/1907
Benton, Henry (col)	Susan Tucker (col)	10/31/1874
Benton, Jim Bennie	Lucy Cheek	4/28/1896
Benton, Joseph	Delia Shy	8/13/1892
Benton, Levi	Katie Burney	1/24/1874
Benton, Lucian	Willie Flournoy	2/4/1874
Benton, Milton (col)	Lucy Humphry (col)	3/8/1894
Benton, Monroe (col)	Meeksie Binford (col)	12/27/1895
Benton, Phib	Beir (?) Carter	
	License issued	12/23/1872

Certificate signed, not completed

Benton, Shelton (col)	Lemma Lynch (col)	3/6/1890
Benton, Squire	George Ann Barnes	10/27/1877
Benton, Thomas (col)	Charity Malone (col)	12/29/1870
Benton, Thomas (col)	Susie Blackwell (col)	11/2/1889
Benton, Travis (col)	Lizzie Malone (col)	1/5/1890
Benton, Turner	Adaline Lewis	7/17/1886
Benton, Wiley (col)	Ollie Fears (col)	1/4/1890
Benton, William (col)	Mrs. Sarah Malone (col)	12/29/1895
Benton, Willie (col)	Florence Thomas (col)	1/6/1894
Berner, William R.	Mrs. Frances Gordon	12/20/1865
Berry, Alfred (col)	Mary Wills Rickerson(col)	5/26/1895
Berry, Bill (col)	Mrs. Hester Jackson(col)	5/26/1895
Berry, Howard (col)	Rose Ann Freeman (col)	11/5/1907
Berry, Kiah (col)	Catharine Ball (col)	10/4/1896
Berry, Lewis T.	Patsey Hadley	12/22/1816
Bias, Joe (col)	Mattie Lou Glover (col)	1/5/1898
Bias, William	Maggie Price	1/10/1898
Binford, Augustus	Sabrina Speers	12/8/1870
Binford, Cicero S.	Carrie Tuggle	5/7/1891
Binford, Elbert	Hattie Wyatt	1/11/1883
Binford, T. S.	N. A. Spears	2/22/1866
Birch, James A.	Mattie Lou Spears	3/14/1897
Bird, Joe (col)	Love Hudson (col)	12/27/1896
Bird, John (col)	Matilda Robinson (col)	12/30/1896
Bird, William (col)	Lena Thomas (col)	12/29/1898
Blackwell, Alfred (col)	Adaline Walker (col)	12/18/1869
Blackwell, Alfred	Mahala Pou	4/8/1882
Blackwell, Ben	Eadie Goolsby	12/31/1887
Blackwell, Benjamin	Ann Smith	3/24/1866
Blackwell, C. I.	Jesse Malone	12/25/1907
Blackwell, D. C.	Fannie A. Lane	3/5/1874
Blackwell, Ed	Annie Kemp	1/1/1888
Blackwell, Edward (col)	Lula Clark (col)	3/27/1892
Blackwell, Elbert	Mittie Nix	12/23/1876
Blackwell, Franklin J.	Anna Kelly	6/14/1883
Blackwell, Greene (col)	Mary Jane Franklin (col)	1/27/1894
Blackwell, Henry F.	Mary Shields	12/8/1868
Blackwell, Isaac (col)	Amanda Watters (col)	12/25/1868

Blackwell, Isaac (col)	Amanda Goolsby (col)	10/21/1897
Blackwell, J. H., Jr.	Carrie Belle Wyatt	6/3/1897
Blackwell, James M.	Emma Lane	1/30/1873
Blackwell, John (col)	Georgia Benton (col)	12/31/1901
Blackwell, John P.	Leila Hyatt	4/29/1894
Blackwell, John Warren	Alice Blackwell	12/23/1894
Blackwell, Mack	Angie Green	4/16/1889
Blackwell, Robert M.	Mary K. Akin	10/30/1873
Blackwell, Samuel	Georgia Doster	10/15/1876
Blackwell, Samuel E.	Minnie Reeves	1/3/1892
Blackwell, Samuel S.	Mattie Spearman	1/24/1861
Blackwell, Thomas G.	Nancy Davidson	11/22/1866
Blackwell, W. S.	Clara C. Parker	1/8/1899
Blackwell, Wesley (col)	Elizabeth English (col)	12/31/1870
Blackwell, William F.	Salina W. Shaw	2/26/1861
Blackwell, Willie (col)	Indianna Robinson (col)	12/29/1890
Blackwell, Willis	Dora Roby	9/7/1876
Blizzard, James	Mrs. Savannah Raynor	3/18/1894
Blizzard, William	Frances Freeman	12/23/1883
Bogan, Thomas	Comfort Reid	5/10/1884
Bogan, Tom (col)	Bell Baynes (col)	12/3/1895
Bohannon, James B.	Lula Lindsey	12/26/1895
Boling, Albert (col)	Carrie Humphrey (col)	1/18/1896
Bonner, Eli (col)	Comfort Jackson (col)	1/2/1897
Bonner, Giles	Mary Lou Childs	8/5/1886
Bonner, Gordon L.	Kate Binford	4/18/1898
Bonner, Gordon Lee	Annie J. Tucker	12/15/1895
Bonner, Thomas R.	Leila L. Newton	1/14/1891
Bonner, William (col)	Mattie Sparks (col)	4/16/1891
Boon, Thomas (col)	Jane Freeman (col)	12/17/1874
Boone, George W.	Genia Hawk	7/14/1887
Boriss, I. D.	Sadie Hecht	11/5/1899
Borough, James	Delilah Yarborough	11/13/1817
Bosstick, Isaac (col)	Josie Broughton (col)	11/6/1889
Bostick, Isaac	Jennie Shy	10/17/1882
Boston, John H., Jr.	Nannie B. Smith	9/10/1889
Bowden, Daniel H.	Mollie P. Binford	1/16/1890
Bowden, James H.	Ann G. Johnston	11/4/1857
Bowden, Joe	Emma Toland	1/18/1877
Bowden, Nathan T.	Melissa Park	3/30/1884
Bowden, Robert	Rebecca Couch	12/21/1886
Bowden, Robert T.	Cyntha Hickman	7/13/1893
Bowdoin, John Thomas	Mrs. Nancy Ann C. Spearman	5/10/1864
Boyd, Richard Franklin	Mary Floyd	12/27/1894
Boyett, Eli E.	Martha C. Reeves	6/1/1854
Boykin, David	Talitha Digby	1/6/1887
Boykin, Henry	Charity Goolsby	12/30/1867
Boykin, Henry (col)	Georgia Smith (col)	3/28/1899
Boykin, Joe	Elizza Robinson	12/27/1876
Bozeman, Leonard	Mattie Folds	12/31/1883
Braddy, William E.	Lucy F. Niblett	1/7/1894
Bradley, John W.	Mollie Greer	1/18/1876
Brandon, A. M.	Caro L. Adgate	9/18/1899
Brandon, Green H.	Sarah Ann Cardell	1/16/1851
Brandon, Green V.	Rebecca J. Dawkins	11/18/1869
Brandon, Green V.	Eliza I. Gilmore	1/18/1872
Brandon, James	Lizzie Thompson	12/22/1874
Brandon, John J.	Lucy J. Hatcher	12/11/1860
Brandon, Thomas J.	Amanda Gilmore	3/14/1872
Brandon, William J.	Lucy J. Brandon	1/23/1868
Brandon, William S.	Charlotte C. Millen	12/23/1860
Branham, Joe	Lucy Collier	7/10/1886

Branham, Joe (col)	Sarah Wyatt (col)	12/9/1894
Branham, Wesley (col)	Katie Griggs (col)	12/30/1896
Brannon, Willis (col)	Emiline Davis (col)	12/27/1877
Brawner, Charlie	Emma Brown License Issued 11/18/1881	
Brazil, Wesley (col)	Mary Risby (col)	11/29/1868
Brazile, Green	Catharine Fuller	5/29/1881
Brewer, Henry (col)	Mancy Williams (col)	12/19/1889
Brewer, Henry (col)	Vinie Hart (col)	4/31/1893
Brewer, Oscar (col)	Mary Francis (Lewis)	
	Lucas (col)	1/7/1908
Brice, R. Y.	F. N. Whitehead	9/30/1869
Bridges, Cooper (col)	Ginnie Kelly (col)	12/31/1891
Bridges, Frank M.	Lucy E. Goggans	10/15/1891
Bridges, John M.	Nannie L. McKinley	9/3/1885
Bridges, William	Mollie Goodman	12/6/1888
Briggs, Jesse F.	Julia A. Colton	12/29/1866
Britain, Sanford(Britton)	Jane (Jenney) Clay	2/25/1819
Broddus, Charley (col)	Lucy Ridley (col)	8/9/1887
Broddus, Charlie (col)	Mattie Walker (col)	1/29/1893
Broddus, Edward (col)	Sophia Epps (col)	12/25/1906
Broddus, Elbert S.	Janie Harwell	5/18/1892
Broddus, Isaac (col)	Dily Thomas	9/17/1876
Broddus, Luke (col)	Essie Allen (col)	12/29/1907
Broddus, Luke (col)	Lizzie Johnson (col)	12/30/1907
Broddus, Nelson (col)	Susie Shy (col)	3/24/1897
Broddus, Thomas (col)	Anna Singleton (col)	4/24/1898
Broddus, William (col)	Delia Reddick (col)	7/3/1870
Brooks, Green (col)	Mary Russell (col)	1/13/1898
Brooks, John H.	Mary Henderson	8/7/1885
Brooks, Lafayett	Malessa Ann Blakeley	8/26/1859
Brooks, Robert	Susan McKissack	1/15/1873
Brooks, S. I.	Mrs. E. K. Aven	8/13/1876
Brooks, Sidney (col)	Ruth Pearl Walker (col)	11/16/1897
Brooks, Thomas	Prudy Story	9/20/1818
Brooks, Thomas J.	Nancy A. Gaston	6/4/1857
Broughton, Anderson(col)	Julia Ann Shy (col)	12/29/1897
Broughton, John (col)	Mattie Kelly (col)	1/24/1890
Brown, Austen	Missouri Jordan	1/4/1884
Brown, Charles D.	Mattie A. Barnet	2/10/1884
Brown, Charles D.	Genie Millen	8/29/1896
Brown, Doc	Sidney James	3/19/1882
Brown, Dunk	Anna Whitfield	
	Lincense Issued	3/2/1875
Brown, Frank (col)	Julia Hix (col)	3/13/1890
Brown, Frank (col)	Sarah Rease (col)	9/14/1907
Brown, George	Georgia V. Holland	11/8/1854
Brown, George F.	Lilie Belle Grubbs	5/16/1897
Brown, Henry (col)	Sarah Turk (col)	12/26/1875
Brown, Irwin W.	Mary F. Pennington	8/17/1870
Brown, James Richard(col)	Mrs. Rose Rooks (col)	1/15/1891
Brown, James Wesley	Addie Miss Underwood	
Davis (col)	(col)	2/10/1898
Brown, Jim (col)	Mary Wade (col)	11/6/1892
Brown, John	Anna Whiten	12/5/1818
Brown, John A. (col)	Fannie Kate Tilman (col)	7/29/1897
Brown, Seaborn S.	Georgia C. Freeman	3/15/1866
Brown, Sim (col)	Angie Hill (col)	2/15/1894
Brown, Tekoah J.	Julia Hunter Blackwell	2/19/1885
Brown, W. D.	Sallie McDonough	10/2/1870
Brown, Woodie (col)	Ophelia Pope (col)	1/22/1899
Brunson, Willie (col)	Emma Kate Watson (col)	11/3/1901
Bryan, Willis (col)	Adaline Smith (col)	12/26/1906
Bryant, C. N.	Susan E. Smith	2/1/1876

Bryant, James R.	Henrietta Martin	6/23/1868
Bryant, Johnie	Ella Smith	1/6/1887
Bryant, Lee	T. A. Spears	1/19/1877
Buis, Elbert	Elizabeth Robnett	2/18/1819
Bullard, J. H.	Alice Leverett	6/6/1877
Bullard, W. M.	Mattie Lou Jordan	6/14/1887
Burk, David G.	Annie E. Rowe	12/1/1891
Burner, William	Ada Loyd	1/13/1901
Burnes, William J.	Rebecca Ann Cheek	12/23/1857
Burnett, Julian D.	Salina V. Preston	5/23/1888
Burnett, Peter (col)	Margaret Walker (col)	11/17/1894
Burney, Arthur	Sylvia Alexander	12/20/1877
Burney, Augustus H.	Clara Beaton	11/29/1894
Burney, C. R.	Allice V. Faulkner	12/29/1898
Burney, Elbert (col)	Nora Nolly (col)	12/27/1896
Burney, George	Martha Nolly	11/16/1876
Burney, George (col)	Mrs. Margarett Lynch(col)	12/22/1889
Burney, J. H.	Mattie C. King	12/27/1868
Burney, Jack (col)	Sarah Glover (col)	2/4/1875
Burney, James L.	Cora L. Malone	2/26/1890
Burney, Jim (col)	Cora Goolsby (col)	3/22/1893
Burney, Joseph (col)	Francis Clay (col)	12/22/1870
Burney, Joseph H.	Margarett A. Henderson	11/14/1860
Burney, Sylvanus	Diana Ward	1/22/1886
Burney, Will (col)	Lizzie Brazel (col)	1/17/1895
Burney, William (col)	Mary Roberts (col)	2/18/1892
Burney, William J.	Cynthia Letson	8/24/1876
Burrow, Phillip	Masey Tedards	12/3/1818
Burton, Henry W.	Mamie E. King	1/12/1896
Burton, Isaih	Jane Benton	1/31/1873
Bussey, Jim (col)	Adaline Williams (col)	8/27/1893
Bussey, Moses	Lucy Toney	6/18/1894
Butler, Dennis (col)	Viny Harvey (col)	5/22/1873
Butler, Lewis (col)	Senetta Williams (col)	7/25/1892
Byars, John	Susan Driskell	2/22/1882
Byars, Miles (col)	Manda Goolsby (col)	10/16/1868
Byas, John (col)	Lizzie Pounds (col)	2/9/1901
Byington, Bud (col)	Sarah Crawford (col)	12/27/1894
Byington, Joshua	Rhoda Cooper	12/6/1882
Byrom, Henry (col)	Emma Moreland (col)	12/31/1896
Byrom, Manuel	Leah Shropsy	12/13/1873
Byrom, Matt	Berthie Allen	2/26/1884
Byrom, Matt	Jennie Standifer	12/27/1888

Callaway, J.C. (col)	Lucinda Bailey (col)	
	Lincense issued	11/14/1896
Callaway, James	Nancy Farley	12/10/1818
Cameron, William H.	Alice E. Watley	1/17/1875
Camp, Carlton (col)	Pauline Dunn (col)	4/15/1893
Campbell, Bill (col)	Lizzie Nickols (col)	11/10/1894
Campbell, Bill C.	Letha Meriwether	12/6/1888
Campbell, Calvin (col)	Linda Wyatt (col)	11/13/1894
Campbell, Charles G.	Clementina L. McMichael	6/4/1860
Campbell, E. D.	Martha E. Edwards	2/1/1876
Campbell, Evan (col)	Lucy Chapman (col)	2/24/1907
Campbell, George (col)	George Ann Glover (col)	3/6/1869
Campbell, John (col)	Mrs. Jennie Driskell(col)	1/16/1893
Campbell, John J.	Sarah A. McDonald	2/3/1861
Campbell, John V. E.	Maria C. Shy	11/10/1864
	Consent to issue license	11/10/1864
Campbell, Johnie (col)	Sallie Chatman (col)	1/17/1889
Campbell, Lewis (col)	Anaka Tinsly (col)	12/26/1894

9

Campbell, Mat	Mary Thomas Weaver	1/25/1864
	(consent)	1/25/1864
Campbell, R. D.	Mary Lizzie Blackwell	1/5/1899
Campbell, Richard	Lena Marks	12/30/1906
Campbell, William (col)	Lizzie Jordan (col)	12/30/1868
Campbell, William	Emiline Akin	9/5/1872
Cannon, Thomas L.	Marilla A. Tomlin	5/30/1868
Canon, John (col)	Lonie Smith (col)	7/5/1892
Card, Noah	Rachael Hardwick	1/14/1887
Card, Preston (col)	Mary Jane Branham (col)	1/3/1895
Cardell, Calvin E.	Ludie Roberts	8/31/1892
Cardell, Charles E.	Annie May Roberts	8/28/1898
Cardell, John J.	Sallie B. Bailey	8/19/1884
Cardell, Joseph B.	Virginia Lee Niblett	12/4/1887
Cardell, Peter	Milly Crawford	5/8/1861
Cardell, William	Sarah C. Seymore	2/13/1858
Cardell, William I.	Mary Lou Bailey	7/17/1887
Carey, Edward J.	Aura Odell	12/17/1893
Carey, Henry	Matilda Johnson	12/23/1881
Carey, Henry	Emily Gordon	12/30/1886
Cargel, Lucius (col)	Sarah Benton (col)	8/30/1901
Cargile, Henry N.	Ada Noles	9/27/1892
Cargile, John (col)	Easter Lamar (col)	9/1/1892
Cargile, John W.	Laura Knowles	1/6/1881
Cargile, Kelly (col)	Rosa Gilmore (col)	10/6/1893
Cargile, Micajah	Margaret Cargile	2/15/1814
Cargile, Zeb	Ellen Jordan	12/16/1885
Cargile, Zep (col)	Sally Clay (col)	12/29/1868
Cargle, John (col)	Hattie Jordan (col)	12/28/1898
Carman, J. Q. M.	Laura V. Lane	10/4/1865
Carr, Dock (col)	Mrs. Jennie Wade (col)	4/7/1901
Carr, John (col)	Louisa Fish (col)	11/2/1901
Carr, Samuel	Emily C. Freeman	4/25/1850
Carroll, E. W.	Willie V. Harvey	6/28/1899
Carroll, Joseph T.	Mrs. Emily W. Brewer	11/26/1874
Carter, Abraham (col)	Emily Park (col)	12/30/1868
Carter, Adolphus	Lou Goolsby	1/18/1887
Carter, Anderson	Katie Dougherty	12/7/1889
Carter, Berry (col)	Hannah Fears (col)	12/30/1868
Carter, Berry Lee (col)	Mattie Lou Price (col)	8/17/1898
	Letter asking for license	8/14/1898
Carter, Burke (col)	Kate Carter (col)	12/17/1891
Carter, Ellis (col)	Mary Jane Smith (col)	12/28/1870
Carter, Frank	Eady Maddux	2/18/1866
Carter, Lawson	Mattie Cook	12/27/1872
Carter, Marcus E.	Lydia Williams	12/22/1817
Carter, Martin	Polly Allen	12/31/1884
Carter, Martin (col)	Hattie Thomas (col)	10/23/1892
Carter, Randol (col)	Ann McDowell (col)	1/24/1869
Carter, Thomas Hector (col)	Easter Compton (col)	2/2/1867
Carter, W. M.	Mrs. M. E. Brown	4/27/1876
Cash, Jim	Darkis Garland	1/12/1874
Catchings, Bart (col)	Mrs. Margaret Jordan (col)	2/16/1896
Catchings, Barton	Mary Gordon	9/19/1889
Catchings, Charles (col)	Delia Speights (col)	9/9/1887
Catchings, David (col)	Josephine Davis (col)	2/10/1890
Chaffin, Henry	Katie Bell	5/5/1889
Chaffin, Hiram F.	Kizzie E. Polk	9/11/1888
Chaffin, J. W.	Martha Goggins	2/5/1885
Chaffin, John W.	Viola Hodge	12/17/1884
Chaffin, Thomas L.	Mary J. Noles	12/18/1872
Chafin, R. G.	R. A. Akins	8/27/1874
Chafin, Tyre	Frances McAllister	8/21/1817

Chamberlin, Robert (col)	Rhoda Rodgers (col)	12/30/1890
Chambers, John	Sarah M. McMichael	9/21/1869
Champion, J. W.	Mrs. M. L. Kitchens	6/18/1899
Champion, Jesse	Elizabeth Briers	1/14/1817
Chaney, Earvin (col)	Leila Comer (col)	2/20/1898
Chapman, Aaron	Jane Goolsby	12/18/1884
Chapman, Abner	Lucy Lumpkin	9/25/1817
Chapman, Andrew	Angeline Byars	9/28/1884
Chapman, Crawford (col)	Maria Powell (col)	12/26/1868
Chapman, Will	Lizzie Pritchett	1/10/1889
Charles, Richard (col)	Dora Chatman (col)	5/29/1892
Charles, Willie (col)	Ida Pou (col)	1/1/1898
Charping, Preston S.	Mary G. Folds	7/22/1888
Chatham, Henry (col)	Anna Lou Brown (col)	3/10/1898
Chatman, Eli (col)	Lucinda Jordan (col)	6/28/1896
Chatman, Frank (col)	Matilda Standifer (col)	2/1/1890
Chatman, H. H.	L. A. Long	4/23/1873
Chatman, James (col)	Georgia Ann Jordan (col)	12/28/1890
Chatman, Lewis (col)	Carrie Thurmond (col)	5/3/1890
Chatman, Lewis (col)	Hattie Maxey (col)	2/8/1894
Chatman, Lucius (col)	Rosa Eason (col)	10/16/1898
Chatman, Walter (col)	Sallie Holland (col)	12/23/1897
Chatman, William (col)	Sarah Jane Campbell (col)	12/28/1892
Cheek, Frank	Cenie Elizabeth Duke	8/10/1890
Cheek, John W.	Mary Lou Bell	12/19/1876
Cheek, Lafayett	Elizabeth Burnes	9/2/1857
Cheek, Mallory S.	Artexas C. Allen	11/27/1862
Cheek, Moses	Miranda J. McKinley	7/28/1884
Cheek, Walter P.	Amanda J. Hardman	12/22/1866
Cherry, John Henry (col)	Sallie Lou Gilstrap (col)	3/27/1899
Cherry, L. H.	Mrs. Nannie McGhee	12/22/1895
Childs, Charley	Elisebeth Johnston	12/10/1874
Childs, Henry	Mariah Gilstrap	12/20/1888
Childs, Jacob	Julia Goolsby	12/25/1886
Childs, John (col)	Mattie Jackson (col)	2/23/1890
Childs, John (col)	Pearl Newby (col)	10/31/1901
Childs, N. G.	Mary Elizabeth McMichael	
	License issued	5/20/1864
Childs, Walter W.	Annie Belle Berry	1/4/1899
Chunn, H. F. (col)	Onie Thomas (col)	12/30/1899
Churchil, Isaac (col)	Harriet M? (col)	
	License issued	2/15/1875
Claiborne, T. B.	Susie E. Laurence	6/8/1898
Claiborne, Thomas B.	Indiana Spears	4/21/1887
Clark, Alex	Anna Flournoy	1/1/1886
Clark, Alfred (col)	Rebecca Smith (col)	12/25/1894
Clark, Allen	Catharine Cochran	1/17/1866
Clark, David (col)	Ida Pope (col)	12/25/1891
Clark, Edmond (col)	Mary Ann Pope (col)	12/20/1896
Clark, George (col)	Mrs. Amanda Thomas (col)	7/9/1895
Clark, Green	Ida King	12/25/1887
Clark, John (col)	Fannie Matthews (col)	12/25/1890
Clark, Martin	Pearl Duffy	12/27/1906
Clark, Robert (col)	Annie Blackwell (col)	12/27/1893
Clark, Thomas F.	E. Caroline McNair	?/30/1849
Clark, Warren (col)	Katie Humphrey (col)	2/17/1890
Clark, William (col)	Lillie Flowers (col)	9/6/1893
Clay, Charles Augustus	Effie Liela Malone	9/11/1898
Clay, Chris (col)	Emma White (col)	3/22/1897
Clay, Dave (col)	Missouri Barnes (col)	2/15/1896
Clay, Jessy	Emily R. McMichel	12/21/1876
Clay, W. C. (col)	Ella Reese (col)	1/21/1894
Clayton, Charlie	Emma Humphries	3/12/1881

Cleaveland, Early (col)	Bell Farrow (col)	10/11/1868
Clements, Bennie H.	Mattie A. Smith	12/16/1891
Clements, Evan (col)	Mrs. Renda Penn (col)	12/5/1895
Clements, George (col)	Evaline Shields (col)	12/26/1896
Clements, Harvey (col)	Irine Holloway (col)	8/15/1907
Clements, Isaac (col)	Lina Patterson (col)	12/19/1896
Clements, Jacob (col)	Roberta Glover (col)	10/30/1890
Clements, Mose (col)	Mary Underwood (col)	12/5/1889
Clements, Moses	Sarah Taylor	4/28/1881
Clements, Oliver (col)	Mary Jane Jeffries (col)	12/25/1897
Clements, Simon	Ellen Thomas	6/16/1888
Clements, Simor, Jr.	Harriet Jordan	10/25/1885
Clements, Walter M.	Ida L. Clements	2/10/1885
Clemonts, Wilson (col)	Jane Thomas (col)	12/29/1868
Coach, Sam	Tilla Driskell	6/13/1887
Coats, Earnest	Mattie Thomas	10/17/1907
Coats, J. R.	Lou L. Allen	1/2/1876
Cochran, Charles	Arlee Greer	1/15/1888
Cochran, Dudley (col)	Ella Showers (col)	1/5/1899
Cochran, Joe (col)	Annis Hardrick (col)	12/4/1892
Cochran, Simeon (col)	Madora Ward (col)	1/28/1875
Cochran, W. D.	Mary E. Goolsby	11/22/1877
Cockran, Benjamin (col)	Louisa Holland (col)	7/2/1874
Cody, W. C.	Susan Connelly	8/9/1874
Cofer, J. E.	Cola Binford	12/3/1893
Cofer, J. T.	Nettie Cardell	3/15/1891
Cofer, James A.	Lee Honeycutt	9/10/1891
Cofer, Robert	Sarah M. Fincher	5/16/1875
Cole, George (col)	Matilda Harwell (col)	8/24/1894
Coleman, Thomas (col)	Nancy Fears (col)	1/15/1891
Collier, Howard (col)	Amanda Hix (col)	1/7/1892
Collier, Vines	Eleanor Peal	1/16/1817
Collins, John	Raney Jeffries	12/29/1880
Collins, John (col)	Mrs. Lou Fears (col)	3/19/1899
Collins, John (col)	Mamie Branch (col)	12/30/1901
Collins, Lucius (col)	Julia Drischal (col)	6/12/1875
Combs, Nathan	Lucea Hood	10/15/1818
Comer, Allen	Phoebe Thurmond	6/9/1886
Comer, Jere	Mariah Ridley	10/14/1886
Comer, Jim (col)	Annie Brazel (col)	10/1/1892
Comer, Mitchell (col)	Ada Brown (col)	1/11/1896
Comer, Thomas J.	Sarah L. Simms	1/21/1857
Comer, Wash (col)	Elvira Billings (col)	1/14/1901
Comer, Wiley (col)	Victoria Gant (col)	1/2/1896
Comer, William (col)	Mattie Catchings (col)	10/5/1898
Compton, Drape	Katie Jordan	9/13/1885
Compton, Draper (col)	Mary Edmonds (col)	7/25/1892
Conley, Emmet	Sallie V. Cornwell	9/8/1889
Connelley, James	Susan E. Martin	12/18/1860
Connelly, Gustavus H.	Georgia E. Lane	5/5/1867
Conner, George	Harriet Jeffries	1/2/1878
Conner, William	Washie Goggans	12/22/1895
Conner, David Richard	Katie Pope	2/12/1907
Coogler, Auborn E.	Beulah H. Campbell	12/6/1892
Coogler, Eddie	Sallie Herring	12/18/1898
Coogler, Jesse	Bell Floyd	8/8/1895
Cook, Benjamin W.	Micha A. Noles	11/5/1863
	Consent to marry	11/4/1863
Cook, Braz (col)	Ida Carter (col)	6/9/1891
Cook, Callie F.	Susie L. Leverett	10/5/1890
Cook, George (col)	Eliza Hunt (col)	10/2/1892
Cook, George A.	Janie Hodge	7/12/1896
Cook, J. D.	Tempie Richie	1/31/1897

12

Cook, James W.	Lucy Elder	8/5/1891
Cook, John M.	Josephine Womack	12/11/1887
Cook, John S.	M. L. Whitten	2/26/1882
Cook, John W.	Georgia A. Noles	3/4/1875
Cook, John W., Sr.	Mrs. Mary Gaston	10/19/1884
Cook, Johnny (col)	Annie Tuggle (col)	?/?/1897
Cook, Madison	Roney D. White	12/3/1890
Cook, N. G.	Malissa Turner	1/9/1873
Cooper, Eli	Rebecca May	2/5/1819
Cooper, Prince	Emaline Edwards	1/28/1888
Cook, Robert L.	Katie Thompson	9/27/1892
Cook, Sandy	Lucy Jackson	8/25/1872
Corbit, Charles	Cleminy McMichael	4/28/1875
Cornwell, D. L.	Sallie B. Hardy	7/31/1866
Cornwell, E. C.	Elizabeth Mathews	11/1/1899
Cornwell, Elijah	Elizabeth Edwards	8/10/1854
Cornwell, Franklin	Mary E. Leverett	8/27/1873
Cornwell, G. H.	Louise C. Reese	7/25/1854
Cornwell, G. L.	Ophelia Leverett	1/27/1897
Cornwell, George C.	L. W. Head	1/15/1888
Cornwell, Gibson H.	Cora D. Hardy	12/25/1887
Cornwell, Hugh M.	Mrs. Mary M. Johnson	5/6/1886
Cornwell, Hugh M.	Sarah Leverett	8/27/1873
Cornwell, Lonie (col)	Alberta Lynch (col)	1/13/1898
Cornwell, William (col)	Claudie Nolly (col)	2/24/1895
Cornwell, William D.	Elmina S. Hardy	7/9/1863
Cosby, Marcus (col)	Caroline Robinson (col)	11/25/1892
Cosby, S. T.	Frances A. Freeman	1/31/1858
Couch, Charley (col)	Kate Jordan (col)	2/4/1897
Couch, Crawford (col)	Hattie Jordan (col)	4/7/1909
Couch, Ebenezer (col)	Mary Cleveland (col)	3/10/1870
Couch, George	S. A. Niblett	12/9/1875
Couch, Jefferson	Annie J. Greer	10/8/1893
Couch, Joseph	Sallie Smith	12/23/1899
Coursey, Monroe D.	Bethia O. Edwards	7/18/1871
Cox, Charles G.	Maud McElhenney	12/16/1897
Cox, Henry (col)	Ada Jones (col)	11/17/1896
Cox, Henry (col)	Lyda Fears (col)	6/11/1899
Cox, Presley	Bethany Jackson	10/28/1818
Cox, William S.	Emily Lovejoy	6/12/1898
Crabb, Samuel	Malbary Richards	3/26/1818
Crabtree, Maliciah	Nancy Parker	1/26/1853
Crabtree, Thomas	Martha Powell	4/14/1850
Crane, Burrel (col)	Mary Lou Maning (col)	12/17/1891
Crane, Nathan	Elizabeth Kelly	6/12/1884
Crawford, Berry	Louisa Freeman	9/7/1877
Crawford, Ebbeheart(col)	Mary Jane Parks (col)	1/16/1889
Crawford, Jefferson	Milley Jones	10/6/1853
Crawford, Jeremiah	Nancy Lunsford	4/20/1816
Crawford, M. N.	Mrs. Mary A. B. Perry	3/1/1874
Crawford, Umphrey (col)	Rachael Williams (col)	1/3/1869
Crawford, Will (col)	Pearl Preston (col)	10/13/1897
Crawley, J. H.	Mattie Lou Lane	7/1/1894
Crittenden, George (col)	Mamie Lee (col)	4/4/1897
Crowell, Alfred H.	Mary C. Vickers	11/18/1860
Crumby, Judge (col)	Mattie Bradley (col)	9/6/1898
Crutchfield, Benjamin	Martha A. E. King	11/10/1867
Crutchfield, Jefferson	Mary Russell	1/10/1875
Crutchfield, Jerry (col)	Mrs. Genie Holland (col)	4/2/1893
Crutchfield, Jerry	Patience Penn	12/31/1874
Culberson, John P., Jr.	Genie Watson	3/7/1894
Cullen, George	Susan Shy	1/11/1887
Cullens, Robert	Susan Brown	12/13/1888

Cullens, Robert (col)	Ann Awfrey	1/7/1892
Cullum, James J.	Carrie Dennis	8/13/1893
Cunard, Alfred C.	Cora Lee Lewis	1/6/1890
Cunard, Charles	Maggie May Dooly	1/9/1895
Cunard, Elbert	Exie Aaron	7/6/1865
Cunard, James Clark	Nanie McClendon	8/26/1894
Cunard, John C.	Leila Harris	11/24/1892
Cuttrell, Joshua	Dysey Akridge	10/15/1816
Daniel, Dan	Harriet Glover	1/4/1877
Daniel, Fredrick	Mary Jane Pope	3/6/1848
Daniel, David (col)	Emily Glover (col)	10/16/1870
Daniel, Isaac (col)	Mollie Goolsby (col)	8/18/1887
Daniel, Jerry (col)	Precious Munroe (col)	11/6/1887
Daniel, Jim	Emma Pye	12/30/1886
Daniel, John (col)	Jane Wilson (col)	7/13/1876
Daniel, John (col)	Mary Ann Standifer (col)	12/23/1896
Daniel, Lee (col)	Davie Jane Clements(col)	1/2/1899
Daniel, Richard	Matilda Freeman	12/25/1872
Daniel, Robert (col)	Cora Williams (col)	12/22/1897
Daniel, Warren	Angeline Glover	2/3/1873
Daniel, Warren	Clara Clark	3/12/1887
Daniel, William (col)	Anna Griggs (col)	2/5/1893
Danielly, Thomas F.	Elizabeth C. A. Malone	9/13/1847
Daniels, Anthoney (col)	Mary Jones (col)	10/20/1897
Darden, Anderson (col)	Patsey Holloway (col)	2/27/1869
Darden, Clark	Sarah McElheney	2/10/1867
Darden, Eugene (col)	Willie Maddox (col)	9/7/1907
Dardy, William (col)	Lucy Fish (col)	6/23/1898
Davidson, Alfred (col)	Bettie Gates (col)	7/23/1893
Davidson, B. M.	Lillie Aiken	11/10/1889
Davidson, Benjamin (col)	Georgia Shy (col)	3/?/1896
Davidson, Hilyard	Ann Loften	12/24/1868
Davidson, John R.	Mattie O. Preston	12/19/1883
Davis, Anderson (col)	Peggy Ann Clements (col)	1/2/1896
Davis, David	Mary Kelly	2/10/1877
Davis, Drury M.	Mary Jane Spear	12/28/1869
Davis, Fletcher	Lizzie Wilks	10/2/1894
Davis, Foster (col)	Lucinda Herd (col)	3/31/1907
Davis, Frank	Emma Smith	12/28/1876
Davis, George	Sarah Spears	1/15/1873
Davis, George H.	Annie C. Smith	3/15/1896
Davis, Henry	Cora Odum	9/19/1883
Davis, James (col)	Louanga Doughtie (col)	11/17/1898
Davis, John	Francina Norris	3/25/1819
Davis, John Abner (col)	Florence Barber (col)	4/8/1895
Davis, Joseph E. F.	Mary J. Price	12/19/1867
Davis, Richard	Lena Williams	1/20/1877
Davis, William (col)	Mattie Griffin (col)	1/5/1898
Davis, William L.	Jennie B. Campbell	12/15/1887
Davis, William P.	Alice C. Newton	6/30/1891
Davis, Willie (col)	Anna Eliza Barber (col)	3/26/1898
Davis, Woodson (col)	Matilda Blackwell (col)	10/4/1892
Dawkins, Samuel A.	Lula J. Smith	12/5/1885
Dawkins, Uriah G.	Mary Ann Thornton	2/7/1869
Dawson, Andy (col)	Lou Digby (col)	1/23/1890
Denham, D. B.	Cora Wagner	12/19/1895
Dennis, D. W.	Effie Montgomery	1/24/1901
Dennis, J. H.	Mrs. Selina Elder	7/19/1896
Dennis, John (col)	Emma Rowland (col)	12/24/1895
Dennis, John T.	Annie M. Folds	2/20/1895
Dennis, Jordan (col)	Rena Pou (col)	12/30/1868

Dennis, William	Mary Lizzie Sheffield	1/28/1893
Derico, Dock	Creasy Alison	
(Request for license to be mailed to R. A. Baynes 1/5/?)		
DeVane, Patrick S.	Lavice Gay	12/29/1818
Devant, R. P.	E. V. Dosier	1/28/1858
Devany, John S.	Sarah M. Shaw	12/31/1865
Diamond, H. M.	Sallie J. Davidson	8/20/1874
Diamond, Henry M.	Emma G. Davidson	4/27/1871
Dick, Levi	Rebecca Smith	4/10/1870
Digby, Abraham	Lula Linn	5/3/1885
Digby, Amos	Arbella Mullen	1/7/1897
Digby, Benjamin	Lorrissa Morgan	10/1/1885
Digby, Berry M.	Georgia Womack	11/18/1883
Digby, Charley	Lula Jordan	10/3/1888
Digby, Charlie (col)	Nancy Stokes (col)	12/24/1891
Digby, Dennis	Jane Smith	1/17/1877
Digby, Ellidge (col)	Ione Whitfield (col)	2/13/1896
Digby, Everett W.	Lizzie Wilson	1/7/1900
Digby, George	Easter Tinsley	12/8/1881
Digby, Ike (col)	Janie Jeffries (col)	12/10/1891
Digby, Ike (col)	Mattie Jones (col)	9/18/1898
Digby, James H.	Roxy Ann Tyson	1/30/1868
Digby, Lawrence	Sallie Freeman	1/19/1882
Digby, Lee	Litha Ann Blackwell	12/27/1888
Digby, Wesley	Carrie Lou Hunnicutt	4/4/1897
Digby, William B.	Fannie L. Fears	12/16/1886
Digby, William Berry	N. E. Pully	9/20/1881
Dillard, George	Jane Cunard	6/12/1864
Dillard, Thomas	Nancy E. Aaron	1/23/1859
Dillard, W. C.	Mrs. Fannie Ozburn	10/29/1884
Dismukes, Jepthah V.	Amelia King	12/10/1818
Dixon, Sandy (col)	Cresey Compton (col)	1/28/1874
Dobbins, Jacob	Narcisa Carter	4/19/1877
Dobbins, Warren	Jennie Goolsby	3/31/1877
Dodson, Leroy	Ida Tyler	8/25/1901
Doss, Azariah	Elvira Harrall	7/2/1818
Doster, James C.	Minnie M. Grimes	9/21/1898
Doster, James W.	Susan Wagner	1/21/1872
Doster, John	Sarah Ann Ellis	1/5/1854
Doster, John	Elizabeth M. Jeffries	12/29/1881
Doster, Thomas	N. N. Blackwell	10/15/1876
Dougherty, Clark	Lona Holland	12/23/1886
Dougherty, Clark (col)	Malissa Blackwell (col)	8/19/1899
Dougherty, James Madison	Mattie Parks	3/14/1886
Dougherty, Jim (col)	Roxie Showers (col)	11/18/1894
Dougherty, Joe	Launa Beaton	3/2/1889
Dougherty, Willie (col)	Mary Mullens (col)	12/25/1895
Dowdle, Pierce	Laura Holt	5/22/1876
Downs, James A.	May Agnes Bradley	2/7/1893
Downs, Shelly P.	Ella Cary A. Vaughn	10/14/1858
Downs, Thomas P.	Annie S. Penn	2/13/1898
Dozier, A. A.	Mollie I. Lane	2/9/1886
Dozier, George R.	India Kelly	4/4/1865
Dozier, W. B.	Sallie M. Flournoy	11/12/1873
Dozier, Washington (col)	Georgia Ann Washington (col)	3/2/1896
Drew, John M.	Mason Smith	12/2/1816
Drichal, Thomas	Katie Glover	11/2/1876
Driscol, Alex (col)	Sallie Pounds (col)	12/23/1897
Driskell, Henry H.	Minnie L. Webb	8/4/1895
Driskell, James	Lucy Jordan	12/4/1884
Driskell, John Thomas (col)	Carrie Henderson (col)	8/9/1873

15

Driskell, Reese (col)	Eliza Jane Roby (col)	12/29/1895
Driskell, Tom	Emily Thomas	9/26/1885
Driskell, Tom (col)	Sarah McCoy (col)	10/22/1893
Driskell, William (col)	Lou Ella Driskell (col)	12/28/1890
Driskell, William (col)	Mila Vaughn (col)	12/?/1896
Drummer, Sam	Emma Jenkins	3/1/1888
Drummer, Sam (col)	Dora Jackson (col)	10/5/1896
Dudley, James (col)	Camilla Folds (col)	10/14/1894
Duke, Eldridge	Jane McDonald	11/20/1818
Duke, Joseph	Jane Coal	6/23/1818
Duke, Joseph T.	Mary Hinsey	2/17/1859
Duke, Marion	Talitha Willson	7/25/1861
Duke, Mordecai	Elizabeth Dent	3/22/1818
Duke, O. M.	Susie Harden	2/14/1897
Duke, Stephen H.	Priscilla Miller	3/4/1819
Duke, Thomas M.	Mary Jane Redd	4/2/1889
Duke, William	Essemon Clark	4/25/1816
Duke, Richard	Allice Lewis	8/15/1897
Dukes, Thomas M.	Amanda I. Speers	1/27/1870
Dumas, Cincinattus	Anna Harris	3/5/1873
Dumas, Cincinnatus	Madora Glover	7/13/1876
Dumas, Cooley (col)	Lucy Singleton (col)	2/16/1897
Dumas, Henry (col)	Indiana Glover (col)	12/2/1869
Dumas, Henry	Hester Odom	1/5/1875
Dumas, Richard (col)	Rebecca Louise Singleton (col)	8/23/1892
Dumas, Weyman (col)	Rosa Jackson (col)	12/15/1907
Dumas, William (col)	Elizabeth Glover (col)	12/23/1869
Dunn, Barney	Hannah Storey	10/29/1818
Dunn, Byrom (col)	Sarah Digby (col)	1/12/1870
Dunn, William G.	Martha Freeman	1/2/1854
Durden, L. W.	Mary Ozburn	12/15/1874
Durdin, Walt	Charity Perkins	5/17/1889
Durdin, Walter B.	Amarintha Jackson	12/29/1899
Durdin, Wiley T.	Henrietta M.B.A. Skinner	4/30/1854
Dyer, Henry (col)	Lucy Kelly (col)	4/6/1890
Early, Columbus (col)	Betsey Ann Stewart (col)	2/7/1899
Earsry, Jim (col)	Estell Seagraves (col)	2/5/1898
Eason, Allen	Sofa Nix	1/9/1874
Eason, Allen (col)	Malinda Holt (col)	1/29/1876
Eason, Henry (col)	Lizzie Thomas (col)	2/1/1897
Eddy, Samuel	Levina Hancock	6/25/1818
Edge, James (col)	Addie Fish (col)	12/10/1896
Edwards, C. L.	Ada Tyler	12/29/1895
Edwards, C. M.	Bittie Smith	1/9/1898
Edwards, Henry F.	Eugenia Adams	1/25/1881
Edwards, James B.	Bobbie Lane	1/25/1881
Edwards, John	Adaline Smith	1/11/1883
Edwards, John	Mrs. Ellen Ricketts	6/18/1899
Edwards, Joseph B.	Mamie B. King	9/15/1885
Edwards, Lawrence (col)	Mittie Russell (col)	12/4/1898
Edwards, Lee	Emma Aikens	1/27/1888
Edwards, Richard	Burmah Ann Pritchett	9/14/1867
Edwards, Richard M.	Martha E. Hardy	10/19/1865
Edwards, Robert	Martha J. Campbell	1/9/1873
Edwards, Samuel	Elizabeth Carden	12/5/1867
Edwards, Samuel B.	Daley Ann Goodman	5/14/1873
Edward, W. A.	Eula Pinnell	11/26/1899
Edwards, W. C.	Nannie Lee Hooper	5/21/1895
Edwards, William C.	Leila Moore	8/9/1896
Edwards, William S.	Nancy A. Johnson	12/31/1874

Groom	Bride	Date
Elder, Benjamin F.	Selina C. Tuggle	8/12/1869
Elder, Charles N.	Lou T. Williams	10/15/1882
Elder, Henry (col)	Bettie Greer (col)	10/19/1876
Elder, James E.	Martha E. Yarborough	12/23/1884
Elder, John Henry (col)	Nannie Myrick (col)	12/31/1901
Elder, Turner	Eliza Glover	10/20/1876
Elder, William S.	Ella Wilson	1/26/1887
Elliott, Ross (col)	Mandy Flemister (col)	2/6/1907
Ellis, Edgar C.	Katie L. Thomason	12/2/1885
Ellis, John	Tommie Jones	1/31/1884
Ellis, Samuel	Sarah Smith	12/24/1850
Ellis, Samuel W.	Jennie B. Thomason	9/6/1894
Epps, Alf (col)	Genie Jordan (col)	6/16/1907
Epps, Benjamin, Sr.(col)	Mrs. Jeanette Park (col)	10/7/1894
Epps, Burrell (col)	Lizzie Vaughn (col)	4/13/1893
Epps, Edom (col)	Clara Showers (col)	12/14/1892
Epps, Eugene (col)	Maggie Morgan (col)	12/22/1907
Epps, Jimmie Lee (col)	Mittie Thomas (col)	1/3/1897
Epps, John Clark (col)	Maggie Maddux (col)	8/23/1891
Epps, Morgan	Betsy Ann Chapman	2/25/1886
Epps, Thomas (col)	Caroline Glawson (col)	12/31/1896
Epps, Zachariah	Mary Williams	12/24/1870
Evans, A. Y.	Emily Jeffries	4/26/1859
Evans, Charlie	Maggie Barker	12/7/1887
Evans, Henry	Nora Middlebrooks	9/16/1895
Evans, Patrick	Lillian Kelly	7/24/1898
Evans, Walter	Florence Chaffin	12/22/1907
Evans, William	Polly Patterson	11/26/1818
Ezell, C. T.	Mary D. Hearn	1/13/1878
Ezell, Cullen R.	Augusta Beall	8/20/1861
Ezell, Henry L.	Nannie Middlebrooks	10/31/1891
Ezell, James R.	Carrie Lee Goolsby	12/17/1895
Ezell, John H.	Emily G. Powell	12/19/1849
Ezell, W. B.	L. G. Meriwether	10/15/1884
Ezell, William P.	Julia Roberts	6/20/1884
Ezell, William P.	Kate W. Lee	12/18/1887
Fair, Ned	Victoria Franklin	11/6/1889
Fallen, William	Missouri Greer	2/5/1888
Farler, David (col)	Mrs. Melvina Ridley (col)	1/8/1889
Farrar, Abel	Mary J. Turk	11/22/1876
Farrar, Otis	Mary Kate Leverett	2/24/1907
Farrill, Erasmus W.	Nona Green	6/11/1893
Farrow, Tinch	Jane (Wray) Ray	8/4/1818
Faulkner, Charles M.	Ida Tyler	12/2/1886
Faulkner, Hartwell D.	Mary Virginia Pope	11/21/1883
Faulkner, Hilton James	Alice Lane	12/23/1890
Faulkner, Homer	Emma Nolan	11/12/1889
Faulkner, J. P.	Hattie Lewis	11/18/1876
Faulkner, John P. (col)	Jane Dixon (col)	12/?/1870
Faulkner, John T.	Sallie E. Slaughter	2/17/1876
Faulkner, Maston R.	Mary Cornwell	7/5/1866
Fears, Claiborn (col)	Elizabeth Hardy (col)	3/29/1868
Fears, Edgar	Emma Ezell	6/9/1897
Fears, Freeman (col)	Celia Hurd (col)	12/25/1895
Fears, Jesse R.	Emma Binford	8/31/1898
Fears, Jonah	Mahala Jeffries	12/29/1880
Fears, Peter (col)	Hala Mitchell (col)	12/26/1894
Fears, Robert (col)	Elizabeth Dougherty(col)	2/28/1888
Fears, Wesley (col)	Mattie May Jackson (col)	?/?/1907
Fears, Wesley (col)	Lillie Banks (col)	3/?/1907
Fears, Will (col)	Leila Jeffries (col)	9/29/1907

Fears, William	Lou Kelly	12/9/1886
Ferguson, P. H.	M. E. Weems	5/20/1868
Fincher, Herman	Mattie Goodman	8/17/1907
Fincher, James D.	Fannie Morris	12/18/1875
Fincher, Joe	Mrs. Claudia May O'Rear	11/16/1890
Fincher, John E.	Sarah A. Polk	12/27/1865
Fincher, John L.	Annie Dearing	2/27/1862
Fincher, William J.	Caroline Z. Horton	11/10/1868
Fincher, William J.	Sarah M. Horton	8/21/1877
Finney, William (col)	Caroline Johnson (col)	5/5/1891
Fish, Aaron (col)	Mattie Middlebrooks (col)	10/21/1893
Fish, Charlie (col)	Eliza Ann Barber (col)	11/23/1890
Fish, John (col)	Katie Hill (col)	8/4/1907
Fish, N. N.	Emma Waltz	12/8/1889
Fish, Nathan C.	Elmyra F. Kelly	9/20/1866
Fish, Pryor (col)	Emma Moten (col)	12/28/1898
Fish, Rejes (col)	Lancy Robinson (col)	2/16/1867
Fish, Russell	Margaret Eliza Curry	10/10/1833
Fish, William T.	Wilmoth Greer	2/12/1857
Fish, William T.	Mrs. Mary Ann Bridges	1/5/1897
Fitzpatrick, Richard	Mary Stephens	12/20/1883
Fitzsimmons, O. P.	Emma Jordan	12/8/1875
Flemister, Isaac	Mariah Malone	12/20/1875
Florence, William A.	Nannie L. Hardy	12/2/1896
Flournoy, Frank	Jennie Barnes	12/23/1882
Flournoy, Green (col)	Caroline Digby (col)	3/27/1869
Flournoy, Otis (col)	Mary Thompson (col)	12/29/1898
Flournoy, Samuel (col)	Georgia Allen (col)	12/13/1894
Freeman, Isaac H.	Cyntha A. Wyatt	3/10/1853
Freeman, Jesse (col)	Laura Smith (col)	1/19/1896
Freeman, King (col)	Margaret Bryant (col)	10/25/1869
Freeman, Lee	Nancy Tilmon	12/28/1882
Freeman, Mose (col)	Frances Griggs (col)	7/9/1887
Freeman, Richard	Maud Hardeman	3/28/1894
Freeman, Robert (col)	Cora Harris (col)	1/5/1907
Freeman, Samuel	Hattie E. Jones	2/25/1896
Freeman, Thomas	Henrietta Phillips	12/22/1874
Freeman, Thomas (col)	Indiana Harris (col)	10/11/1877
Freeman, Thomas (col)	Hattie Gilstrap (col)	4/9/1898
Freeman, Tom (col)	Lemma Barnes (col)	5/13/1890
Freeman, Warner (col)	Hattie Elder (col)	5/24/1894
Freeman, Wesley (col)	Nancy Moton (col)	2/16/1876
Freeman, William (col)	Mollie Johnson (col)	7/3/1887
Freeman, William (col)	Pearl Barnes (col)	7/18/1897
Freeman, William M.	Maggie Lynch	12/23/1880
Fuller, Step	Aggie Standifer	12/27/1885
Fuller, Thomas (col)	Sarah Smith (col)	5/19/1889
Funderburk, Thomas B.	Elizabeth A. Huff	12/18/1884
Funderburk, William A.	Matilda F. Waldrep	1/5/1893
Furse, Robert L.	Mrs. Fannie Rebecca Mobley	4/13/1887
Gaither, Charley (col)	Maud Smith (col)	12/26/1907
Gaither, James (col)	Genie Durham (col)	1/23/1880
Gallaway, James M.	Annie J. Price	2/5/1896
Gallman, James	Nancy Stanley	12/2/1818
Gannt, John Wesley	Emily Guy	1/10/1897
Gant, Henry	Chenney Johnson	5/12/1884
Gant, Jefferson (col)	Florence Card (col)	11/25/1891
Gant, Jim (col)	Mattie Marks (col)	1/16/1896
Gant, Levi (col)	Tabitha King (col)	11/15/1889
Gant, Lewis (col)	Love Allen (col)	1/12/1896
Gant, Ridley (col)	Levina Byars (col)	1/23/1897
Gant, Singleton (col)	Vera Hodge (col)	12/16/1906

Gardiner, Cain (col)	Kizzie Whiting (col)	2/6/1870
Gardner, Ben (col)	Eugene Thomas (col)	12/21/1895
Gardner, Benjamin (col)	Creasy Lawrence (col)	12/29/1898
Gardner, Dennis (col)	Anna Jane Wright (col)	8/31/1907
Gardner, James (col)	Mary Lizzie Whiten (col)	9/20/1897
Gardner, Ned	Ella Hardrick	12/23/1886
Garison, James D.	Martha J. Dean	12/27/1873
Garland, Crawford	Mary Eliza Johnson	2/20/1883
Garland, Harry (col)	Eliza Odom (col)	3/6/1892
Garland, William J.	Lucy Harden	12/22/1881
Garner, John W.	Frances Reynolds	3/23/1854
Garrett, Robert M.	Julia F. Hardy	5/6/1877
Gaston, C. A.	Mrs. Fannie Powell	10/27/1868
Gaston, C. A.	Elizabeth Hardman	9/17/1873
Gates, Charles (col)	Sarah Johnson (col)	2/15/1894
Gates, Daniel (col)	Sallie Daniel (col)	
	License issued	1/7/1875
Gates, Henry (col)	Mary Wade (col)	1/18/1894
Gates, John (col)	Annie Belle Robinson(col)	12/29/1898
Gates, Lewis (col)	Mrs. Cinda Cargile (col)	7/16/1899
Gates, Lewis (col)	Nealy Alexander (col)	7/16/1899
Gates, Major (col)	Margarett Glover (col)	12/26/1907
Gates, Milledge (col)	Lula Jordan (col)	9/30/1897
Gates, Sameul (col)	Fannie Johnson (col)	1/7/1895
Gates, William	Martha Nix	3/16/1888
Gault, Robin, Jr. (col)	Charity Fears (col)	1/10/1877
Gautier, Peter W.	Lucy Woddey	9/14/1817
Gay, Henry	Eliza Hicks	7/31/1873
Gay, Jerry	Martha Banks	1/1/1868
Gay, John (col)	Amanda Walker (col)	1/10/1889
Gay, Thomas (col)	Silvia Thomas (col)	3/6/1875
Geiger, Freeman (col)	Ellen Gay (col)	5/3/1898
Geiger, James M.	Leonora M. Bailey	6/2/1867
Geiger, Jere	Launie Harwell	7/25/1896
Geiger, John H.	Lula Wilson	5/24/1877
Geiger, Randal H.	Sallie T. Cox	6/10/1883
Geiger, Tony (col)	Sarah Hawk (col)	1/29/1870
George, Franklin	Emily Frances Holland	11/14/1848
Ghaston, Charley R.	Lucy F. Tomlinson	7/28/1864
Giles, Felix	Carrie Patterson	5/20/1887
Giles, Jettie (col)	Amanda Emory (col)	12/26/1907
Giles, Thomas J.	Laura A. Beall	12/4/1883
Gilliam, John (col)	Rosetta Meriwether (col)	11/21/1895
Gillstrap, Rubin	Cora Thomas (Thomson)	1/2/1878
Gilstrap, Alexander	Liddie Hames	
	License issued	11/12/1878
Gilstrap, Anthony, Jr.	Alice Compton	12/6/1883
Gilstrap, David (col)	Nannie Carter (col)	9/30/1892
Gilstrap, Davis (col)	Mattie Lou Smith (col)	12/29/1887
Gilstrap, George	Emma Gaither	1/5/1873
Gilstrap, James (col)	Renda Epps (col)	11/19/1870
Gilstrap, John B.	Mary Ann Cunard	12/24/1868
Gilstrap, Otis (col)	Julia Smith (col)	1/23/1895
Gilstrap, Reuben (col)	Sallie Epps (col)	8/10/1873
Gilstrap, William (col)	Emily Banks (col)	1/4/1870
Gilstrap, William (col)	Addie Bryant (col)	12/28/1899
Glass, James P.	Elma Peck	10/13/1895
Glass, Thomas	Cely Car	8/6/1872
Glass, Tom (col)	Lucy Jones (col)	7/8/1892
Glass, William W.	Margaret D. Roberson	2/9/1893

(Letter in regard to marriage from F. M. Swanson to
L. L. Middlebrooks)

Glover, Aaron (col)	Katie Goolsby (col)	10/2/1874

19

Glover, Anderson (col)	Louisa Spears (col)	4/29/1889
Glover, Anderson (col)	Randa Cullens (col)	12/28/1896
Glover, Charley	Mollie Rivers	12/15/1886
Glover, Charlie (col)	Julia Crawford (col)	4/19/1897
Glover, David R.	I. Kate Maddux	6/29/1887
Glover, Dennis (col)	Sallie Robinson (col)	12/19/1869
(Name on certificate is Gellia Roberson (col))		
Glover, Dennis (col)	Susan Broddus (col)	11/26/1906
Glover, Edenborough	Nancy Whitfield	7/16/1885
Glover, Elbert (col)	Lucy Anderson (col)	12/25/1890
Glover, Eugene (col)	Emma Peacock (col)	12/22/1901
Glover, George (col)	Mary Handcock (col)	4/29/1897
Glover, George (col)	Cathrien Carr (col)	12/16/1897
Glover, Henry	Willie Ann McMichael	12/31/1885
Glover, Henry	Julia Ann Smith	12/8/1886
Glover, Henry (col)	Jane Solomon (col)	10/2/1896
Glover, Henry (col)	Sallie Thomas (col)	10/17/1897
Glover, Isaac (col)	Trudie Walker (col)	3/24/1894
Glover, Jake (col)	Sarah Ramey (col)	1/18/1896
Glover, Jefferson	Nancy Jackson	3/21/1889
Glover, Jim (col)	Lizzie Sherman (col)	12/26/1894
Glover, John	Jennett Goolsby	12/31/1873
Glover, John J.	Sarah M. Middlebrooks	12/20/1870
Glover, Joseph (col)	Elmina Hansford (col)	2/7/1874
Glover, Lewis	Ednie Campbell	8/28/1869
Glover, Lewis (col)	Leah Roberts (col)	1/4/1870
Glover, Lewis (col)	Ellen Brown (col)	1/4/1875
Glover, Lewis	Lilie Powell	12/30/1884
Glover, Mitchel (col)	Rose Williams (col)	3/4/1891
Glover, Peter (col)	Addie Allen (col)	2/6/1895
Glover, Richard	Amanda Benton	12/15/1884
Glover, Robert (col)	Angeline Standifer (col)	1/31/1869
Glover, Robert	Ida Jones	1/10/1897
Glover, Solomon (col)	Lucinda Malone (col)	4/5/1894
Glover, Tom E. (col)	Viola Belcher (col)	11/30/1898
Glover, W. P.	Mary L. Middlebrooks	12/14/1876
Glover, Walter (col)	Minnie Benton (col)	10/13/1907
Glover, Wash (col)	Lucy Jordan (col)	12/31/1896
Glover, William	Celia Glover	12/28/1882
Glover, William	Ella Orange	12/27/1883
Glover, William (col)	Ginsie Kitte Moreland (col)	12/31/1891
Glover, William (col)	Georgia Belcher (col)	12/25/1901
Goddard, W. T.	Martha M. Brown	11/10/1867
Goggans, Middleton	Annie McKinley	8/1/1892
Goggans, William W.	Sarah M. Tyner	1/14/1886
Goldsley, William	Sarah Powell	3/4/1819
Goodman, Andrew	Bannie (?) Clark	11/7/1906
Goodman, Elisha N.	Fannie M. Pope	12/24/1888
Goodman, George W.	Florence Jeffries	12/7/1895
Goodman, James E.	Janie L. Cardell	9/10/1896
Goodman, Jerry	Dora Pritchet	12/28/1876
Goodman, John	Maud Farthing	12/4/1898
Goodman, John W.	Martha C. Dawkins	11/28/1872
Goodman, Richard H.,Jr.	Mattie Couch	10/7/1883
Goodrum, Tom (col)	Victoria Wethersby (col)	1/20/1901
Goolsby, Abe (col)	Delphy Ridley (col)	10/9/1890
Goolsby, Albert (col)	Mattie Rooks (col)	12/25/1892
Goolsby, Alfred (col)	Winny Goolsby (col)	1/22/1870
Goolsby, Alick (col)	Caroline Jordan (col)	1/2/1869
Goolsby, Anderson (col)	Emma Tinsley (col)	10/3/1889
Goolsby, Bob (col)	Jane Campbell (col)	12/30/1868
Goolsby, C. R.	Francisco B. Peddy	12/10/1862

20

```
Goolsby, C. R.              Annie E. Kennon           1/23/1895
Goolsby, Caleb (col)        Jane King (col)           3/14/1868
Goolsby, Carden L.          Gertrude Glawson          12/21/1897
Goolsby, Charley,Jr.(col)   Ione Haines (col)         11/15/1889
Goolsby, Charlie (col)      Katie Jeffries (col)      3/10/1895
Goolsby, Clark (col)        Sallie Sanders (col)      12/30/1896
Goolsby, Clayton            Ella Bradley              12/16/1872
Goolsby, Corl (col)         Carrie Jackson (col)      12/30/1891
Goolsby, Crit (col)         Tisshy Standifer (col)    12/29/1896
Goolsby, Crit (col)         Narcis Barron (col)       3/2/1901
Goolsby, Daniel             Victoria Gordon           1/6/1883
Goolsby, Davis L.           Mattie Wooten             5/4/1892
Goolsby, Dee                Lidia Standifer           10/16/1889
Goolsby, Dennis             Sylla Card                8/16/1884
Goolsby, Edenborough(col)   Ella Clark (col)          12/31/1891
Goolsby, Frank (col)        Aida Whiten (col)         9/26/1897
Goolsby, Frank (col)        Elizabeth Clark (col)     2/15/1898
Goolsby, Frank Walker       Anna Cora Powell (col)    6/14/1893
  (col)
Goolsby, Gabe (col)         Eula Clark (col)          3/2/1907
Goolsby, General            Amarintha Smith           12/?/1887
Goolsby, Genus              Amelia Davis              10/7/1907
Goolsby, George (col)       Rachael Card (col)        12/29/1892
Goolsby, Grant              Martha Tilmon             4/9/1889
Goolsby, Ira                Berta L. Waits            3/18/1901
Goolsby, James B.           Martha A. Daniel          5/2/1854
Goolsby, Jim (col)          Eliza Cargile (col)       10/17/1894
Goolsby, John (col)         Eliza Jane Powers (col)   10/23/1898
Goolsby, John Henry(col)    Nancy Robertson (col)     12/8/1890
Goolsby, Johnie (col)       Mary Lou Overton (col)    12/24/1893
Goolsby, Johnie (col)       Sarah White (col)         1/13/1895
Goolsby, Johnie (col)       Aggie Rooks (col)         12/27/1896
Goolsby, Lee (col)          Lucy Pye (col)            1/1/1893
Goolsby, Lemon              Judar Ann White           12/31/1873
Goolsby, Levi (col)         Essie Jackson (col)       9/17/1896
Goolsby, M. C.              Daisie Phillips           8/7/1898
Goolsby, McClendon (col)    Sallie White (col)        12/29/1890
Goolsby, Merridy,Jr.(col)   Irene Goolsby (col)       3/14/1897
Goolsby, Milledge (col)     Mrs. Lettie Stanford(col) 1/12/1893
Goolsby, Mitchel            Dilly Boykin              12/29/1868
Goolsby, Mitchel            Emma Jones                5/5/1885
Goolsby, N. B. (col)        Annie Tinsly (col)        2/22/1894
Goolsby, Nelson             Emma Sims                 3/7/1884
Goolsby, Peter (col)        Mary Walker (col)         9/30/1877
Goolsby, Peter E.           Mary Ann Avant            9/17/1868
Goolsby, R. P.              Annie Phillips            1/8/1896
Goolsby, Rich H.            Agnes Nolan               5/2/1889
Goolsby, Reuben             Loula Gordon              12/27/1883
Goolsby, Reuben (col)       Rachel Tyler (col)        3/17/1907
Goolsby, Richard            Mandy Thompson            3/2/1876
Goolsby, Richard (col)      Ada Holloway (col)        5/17/1891
Goolsby, Rufus (col)        Sopha Wilson (col)        1/1/1875
Goolsby, Scott              Martha Powell             12/13/1888
Goolsby, Spencer (col)      Hannah Johnson (col)      1/9/1897
Goolsby, Stephen            Mattie Moreland           11/17/1887
Goolsby, Thomas H.          Mary A. Steele            10/2/1887
Goolsby, W. B.              M. R. Cook                5/8/1876
Goolsby, Wade B.            Mrs. Ann G. Middlebrooks  1/23/1890
Goolsby, Wiley L.           Mattie E. Cheek           12/19/1876
Goolsby, William (col)      Anna Vincent (col)        5/24/1891
Goolsby, William (col)      Annie Gordon (col)        5/26/1898
Gordon, Aaron (col)         Lillie Petty (col)        1/17/1900
Gordon, David               Winnie Barron             8/27/1881
```

Gordon, Edman J.	Mrs. Easter Cargile	11/5/1874
Gordon, Edmond J., Jr.	Medora J. Jordan	11/1/1883
Gordon, George O. (col)	Susie Jordan (col)	9/12/1894
Gordon, Hugh	Martha A. Tilmon	2/3/1859
Gordon, Isaac (col)	Josephine Reese (col)	8/26/1889
Gordon, Jim (col)	Mary Jane Thurman (col)	12/26/1895
Gordon, John	Elizabeth Gordon	3/7/1858
Gordon, John (col)	Silvia Ann Micken (col)	1/25/1890
Gordon, John J.	Annie L. Crutchfield	12/18/1895
Gordon, John Wesley	Willie Ann Johnson	12/26/1888
Gordon, Reuben	Willie Benton	9/17/1907
Gordon, Robert	Mary Ann Tillman	5/23/1858
Gotier, Martin (col)	Mary Lou Williams (col)	9/9/1898
Gotier, Wesley (col)	Nicie Pope (col)	12/31/1868
Gotier, William (col)	Fannie Preston (col)	12/7/1892
Grant, Alonzo (col)	India Johnson (col)	1/8/1891
Grant, Charley (col)	Cora Griggs (col)	9/29/1907
Grant, John	Nancy Nubie	12/11/1872
Graves, Floyd	Ida White	12/22/1888
Gray, Adam	Adaline Dudley	12/23/1886
Gray, Cheter (col)	Pat Saddler (col)	11/8/1898
Gray, L. C.	Fannie Kate Parks	3/10/1901
Green, Andrew J.	Elizabeth Patterson	3/8/1859
Green, Austin	Elizabeth Robinson	1/28/1866
Green, Crawford	Margaret Brown	11/23/1869
Green, Franklin (col)	Julia Windbush (col)	5/6/1877
Green, Joe	Aggie Broddus	2/11/1886
Green, Samuel	Rebeccah White	1/22/1817
Green, William	Sallie Williamson	11/22/1817
Greer, Aaron (col)	Georgia Ann Gordon (col)	10/28/1875
Greer, Adam (col)	Mary Frances Goolsby(col)	12/30/1892
Greer, Andrew Jackson	Emily Roby	4/1/1883
Greer, Cannon (col)	Rena Newby (col)	12/30/1875
Greer, Crawford H.,Jr.	India Malone	12/28/1890
Greer, Dick	Celia Jackson	12/29/1886
Greer, Felix (col)	Maria Gotier (col)	9/21/1890
Greer, George	Susan Hughes	5/10/1885
Greer, George	Sylvia Brown	1/12/1887
Greer, George (col)	Easter Digby (col)	12/14/1887
Greer, George (col)	Jennie Kelly (col)	12/25/1889
Greer, Gilbert	Ann Fish	7/23/1882
Greer, Gilbert D.	Mattie M. Middlebrooks	11/18/1863
Greer, Gilbert D.	Ada Clay	1/29/1892
Greer, Greene (col)	Ada Glover (col)	12/30/1901
Greer, Griffin	Mila Meriwether	8/28/1890
Greer, James (col)	Ophelia Sands (col)	1/19/1899
Greer, John	Ida M. Grubbs	3/10/1881
Greer, John (col)	Sarah Holloway (col)	6/1/1890
Greer, John (col)	Mary Broddus (col)	3/19/1893
Greer, John (col)	Sarah Ragsdale (col)	8/21/1898
Greer, John Anderson (col)	Catherine Broddus (col)	12/30/1901
Greer, Joseph (col)	Roberta Hunt (col)	9/28/1908
Greer, Lewis (col)	Victoria Minion (col)	6/2/1892
Greer, Madison	Ione Jordan	1/6/1887
Greer, Nathan H.	Eliza Holloway	12/26/1867
Greer, Rufus (col)	Sarah Martha Clark (col)	3/18/1896
Greer, Thomas F.	Cora Goins	1/7/1894
Greer, W. G.	Lizzie Malone	12/17/1874
Greer, Washington (col)	Adaline Kelly (col)	2/13/1893
Greer, William (col)	Millie Smith (col)	3/14/1889
Greer, William (col)	Emma Cleveland (col)	1/17/1891
Greer, William (col)	Aggie Glover (col)	10/5/1893

Greer, William (col)	Annie Kate Tindsley (col)	4/11/1898
Greer, William G., Jr.	Lula Niblett	1/11/1894
Greer, William (col)	Mrs. Mollie Usry (col)	11/1/1893
Greer, Womack (col)	Alice Greer (col)	12/15/1869
Greer, Womack	Delia Watters	4/7/1887
Gresham, William (col)	Rachael Montgomery (col)	11/12/1892
Griffin, Dick (col)	Gena Fish (col)	9/28/1895
Griffin, I. L. P.	W. P. McKinly	12/13/1877
Griffin, J. J.	Bettie Funderburk	12/24/1895
Griffin, Morris (col)	Mary Ann Thomas (col)	12/14/1893
Griggs, Albert (col)	Bettie Griggs (col)	12/30/1897
Griggs, Augustus	Delia Cole	12/18/1886
Griggs, Felix (col)	Roxie Morton (col)	11/15/1892
Griggs, Field (col)	Lugene Smith (col)	9/22/1895
Griggs, Frederick (col)	Frances Henderson (col)	1/21/1869
Griggs, James (col)	Mrs. Susie Johnson (col)	11/17/1899
Griggs, Sack	Annie Munroe	1/1/1888
Griggs, Sack (col)	Nettie Jackson (col)	10/19/1896
Griggs, Warren	Rachael Reid	1/24/1885
Grimes, William C.	Flora Montgomery	12/12/1817
Griswold, Abraham	Annie Chapman	7/21/1907
Grubbs, Joseph	Susan Harden	1/11/1887
Grubbs, Joseph S.	Anna Edwards	2/6/1883
Grubbs, Richard (col)	Julia Fish (col)	2/24/1890
Grubbs, Richard S.	Sarah E. Dorsett	1/24/1858
Grubbs, Sam	Jane Goodman	12/7/1887
Grubbs, Wiley B.	M. M. Waldrep	2/16/1869
Gunn, Thomas	Eliza Buias	2/5/1818
Gunnells, Thomas	Carrie Parker	8/26/1873
Guy, Charles	Bettie Jackson	10/19/1884
Guy, Charley (col)	Emma Gates (col)	4/10/1898
Guy, Lewis (col)	Carrie Holland (col)	1/9/1876
Guy, Miles	Cornelia Malone	9/9/1886
Hackaness, Bill (col)	Caroline Thomas (col)	12/31/1896
Hackney, Ben (col)	Rhoda Holland (col)	3/26/1896
Hackney, Davd (col)	Mary A. Billingslea (col)	12/?/1899
Hackney, Jasper	Rebecca Drischal	9/22/1872
Hadley, Anderson	Sarah Marks	11/23/1883
Hafner, Adam	Corrina Johnson	9/22/1872
Haitley, John	Polley Gross	5/27/1816
Haitly, Henry	Frances Chissam	3/25/1818
Hales, John H.	Clifford Q. Green	5/24/1885
Hall, Wiley	Patience Ridley	1/1/1887
Hames, Wesley	Lucretia Ward	5/24/1873
Hamilton, James	Caroline Holt	1/18/1878
Hamilton, John	Lucy Ann Fears (col)	12/23/1874
Hamilton, John	Mollie Showers	12/30/1885
Hamilton, Julius A.	Maggie E. Traywick	6/28/1892
Hammock, William	Polly Luker	12/27/1816
Hammons, John	Hannah Dodson	8/19/1817
Hampton, Willie (col)	Sallie Collier (col)	11/13/1898
Hamrick, Seburn	Sarah Ann Dodson	1/12/1819
Hancock, James W.	Lucy Jordan	12/26/1874
Hancock, John (col)	Carrie Cargile (col)	4/2/1896
Hancock, W. H.	Emma S. Purse	4/12/1899
Hand, John C.	Sally Smith	8/17/1818
Hand, William	Delilah Brooks	7/23/1818
Hanly, C. C.	Mrs. S. F. Kilgore	3/10/1907
Hanson, Edward	Odessa Few	3/29/1893
Hardage, William	Ellen H. Bogan	2/11/1874
Hardeman, Hunter	Kate Blackwell	12/27/1898

23

Hardeman, William P.	Nola Mae Smith	11/20/1907
Harden, Peter	Chaney Vaughn	1/10/1877
Hardman, Charley	G. A. Shepherd	3/8/1875
Hardrick, Reuben (col)	Jinnie Goolsby (col)	12/23/1891
Hardwick, John (col)	Susan Clark (col)	12/3/1891
Hardwick, John W.	Mary R. Nolly	10/13/1818
Hardy, Alfred D.	Eliza A. Price	12/24/1857
Hardy, C. M.	Mrs. L. J. Hooks	9/29/1870
Hardy, Cornelius	Araminta J. McDaniel	4/21/1863
Hardy, James D.	Madora A. Hooks	9/30/1869
Hardy, James G.	Lela Florence Allen	11/15/1891
Hardy, James P.	Sophronia B. Smith	12/13/1863
Hardy, James P.	Carrie D. Cornwell	1/13/1889
Hardy, John H.	Bell Carmon	12/23/1886
Hardy, John L.	Lorena S. Cornwell	2/14/1384
Hardy, John P.	Josephine Allen	1/23/1862
Hardy, Lewis	Mollie Thomas	12/28/1882
Hardy, Lewis (col)	Ella Thomas (col)	9/17/1887
Hardy, William G.	Elmina S. Deason	2/14/1889
Harper, Thomas L.	Haseltine Allen	12/16/1860
Harrell, Gethro	Nancy Phillips	6/4/1818
Harrell, Samuel M.	Elizabeth Mabry	7/21/1818
Harris, Azariah	Indiana Flemister	4/15/1869
Harris, Buck (col)	Sarah Will (col)	9/16/1898
Harris, Esco (col)	Evelina Clemmons (col)	1/23/1898
Harris, John G.	Martha Fannie Whitaker	8/31/1865
Harris, Joseph H.	Laura E. White	8/31/1865
Harris, Melton	Mrs. Belinda Beckwith	9/20/1870
Harris, Monroe (col)	Cornelia Blackwell (col)	9/17/1893
Harris, Nelson (col)	Emma Ross (col)	12/24/1896
Harris, Pon (col)	Mattie Jackson (col)	3/10/1907
Harris, Shedrack (col)	Phoebe Penn (col)	3/10/1875
Harris, Simeon	Harriet Trayler	4/8/1877
Harris, Solomon	Jane Benton	12/29/1872
Harris, Wesly	Amanda Smith	3/16/1874
Harrison, Augustus W.	Mary F. Adams	8/26/1858
Harrison, James	Lula Dawkins	12/16/1886
Harrison, Richard	Mary T. Tompkins	2/24/1857
Harrison, William	Sarah Edwards	9/21/1862
Hart, Will (col)	Sydnie Benton (col)	11/7/1897
Harvey, James D.	Addie P. Dozier	5/14/1891
Harvill, John T.	Frances R. McElhenney	5/28/1897
Harwell, Armor	Bessie Spearman	
	Recorded date	12/12/1904
Harwell, Frank	Selina Brown	2/25/1874
	No certification	
Harwell, Joe	Alley Kelly	1/18/1886
Harwell, London	Indiana Freeman	11/23/1866
Harwell, Robert	Mary Jackson	12/24/1818
Hataway, G. W.	Elizabeth Thomaston	1/23/1873
Hatcher, Uriah	Jane Britton	11/5/1857
Hattaway, W. H.	Annie E. Waits	1/13/1881
Hawk, Anthony	Savanah Davis	9/28/1877
Hawk, Calhoun (col)	Viola Griggs (col)	12/31/1907
Hawk, Wade (col)	Vena Hurt (col)	7/14/1867
Hawkins, John W.	Cora Cardell	10/27/1887
Hawkins, John W. H.	Minnie Wagner	12/12/1897
Hay, Thomas H.	Nancy Webb	4/15/1869
Hayden, Sylvester	Allie Jane Reeves	4/28/1892
Haynes, G. W.	Eugenia Holloway	2/10/1875
Hays, Henry C.	Annie B. Oxford	9/26/1897
Head, Jack (col)	Frances Hawkins (col)	3/19/1898
Head, William	Missouri Ann Johnson	12/29/1857

Head, William B.	Mary L. Tilmon	10/30/1884
Head, William R.	Jane Bickerstaff	4/1/1818
Head, Wilson F.	Ella Meeks	12/15/1887
Heard, Clark (col)	Lucinda Manage (col)	11/10/1901
Heard, Daniel (col)	Milly Fears (col)	12/21/1877
Heard, Lee	Mary Ann Shy	12/18/1884
Heard, W. M.	M. A. Thompson	11/22/1898
Heard, Wesley (col)	Nettie Turner (col)	1/31/1874
Hearn, Robert L.	Lula M. Tolleson	1/10/1899
Hearn, Samuel	Carrie T. Wyatt	11/14/1872
Heath, Richard	Nancy Terrell	8/10/1815
Hecht, J. J.	Harriet N. Talmadge	12/25/1870
Heflin, James S.	Maggie H. Webb	12/27/1870
Height, Matthew	Lula Jewel	2/27/1897
Henderson, Berry	Mollie Banks	1/1/1887
Henderson, Charles L.	Rebecca J. Jordan	9/19/1893
Henderson, Charley	Lou Henderson	1/27/1873
Henderson, G. B.	Mary A. McWilliams	11/23/1898
Henderson, Isham (col)	Manerva Peurifoy (col)	11/2/1867
Henderson, J. P.	Marie H. Dyer	9/24/1877
Henderson, J. W.	Ida E. Thomas	5/11/1898
Henderson, Jake A.	Mattie H. Bonner	4/23/1890
Henderson, James (col)	Sarah Martha Clark (col)	12/30/1892
Henderson, James, Jr.	Maranda Sparks	11/16/1853
Henderson, James P.	Mrs. Sarah A.V. Dodson	11/14/1865
Henderson, John (col)	Della Henderson (col)	6/15/1889
Henderson, John (col)	Emma Johnson (col)	11/14/1898
Henderson, John P.	Mattie Banks	12/26/1876
Henderson, Joseph	Lissie Jeffries	2/7/1878
Henderson, Lewis (col)	Annie Perry (col)	
	Date issued	6/14/1876
Henderson, Lewis	Mattie Bryant	1/30/1883
Henderson, Lewis (col)	Dee Purington (col)	8/7/1901
Henderson, Richard W.	Amanda J. Wammack	8/19/1877
Henderson, Samuel J.	Susan F. Davis	1/17/1866
Henderson, Wood	Ollie Letson	12/18/1892
Hensey, Richard	Nancy Wilson	3/20/1863
Hensly, Thomas	Kittie T. Spear	12/15/1895
Herridge, John	Polly Coggin	11/29/1818
Herring, John	Mattie L. Langston	12/26/1890
Hester, Augustus	Shadie Ann Rutland	10/16/1884
Hester, George (col)	Mandy Preston (col)	12/29/1874
Hester, Henderson (col)	Mrs. Laura Beebe (col)	9/27/1891
Hester, Michal	Polly Mosely	3/17/1819
Hester, Obadiah	Abbie Pearson	4/1/1888
Hickman, H. W.	Mary Jones	7/23/1873
Hickman, L. J.	T. A. Roberts	7/31/1872
Hickman, O. P.	Elizabeth Turner	11/23/1873
Hickman, Oliver P.	Mattie Turner	11/16/1890
Hickman, W. S.	M. F. Turner	2/6/1873
Hickman, Walter H.	Alice Niblett	5/6/1894
Hicks, Moses (col)	Frances King (col)	6/13/1869
Hicks, Richard	Penny Dunn	4/2/1818
Higgason, Philemon C.	Polly Hudspeth	9/13/1818
Hight, Stephen	Lucinda Brown	6/11/1818
Hill, Charley (col)	Florence Williams (col)	1/5/1908
Hill, Henry	Sallie Malone	12/20/1883
Hines, J. R.	Anna Malone	10/24/1899
Hinsey, James A.	Mary E. Murphey	2/22/1861
Hix, George (col)	Tempe Nash (col)	12/20/1889
Hock, Eli (col)	Laura Jordan (col)	1/3/1898
Hodge, Amos (col)	Ellen Goolsby (col)	12/29/1889
Hodge, C. L.	Mary F. Aaron	11/18/1869

Hodge, Cincinnatus L.	Lola McClendon	12/7/1893
Hodge, Easley	Mary Burney	2/10/1868
Hodge, James D.	Georgia A. Floyd	12/10/1893
Hodge, John (col)	Lizzie Maxey (col)	1/11/1893
Hodge, John (col)	Lucy Flournoy (col)	3/29/1898
Hodge, Lee (col)	Minton Stanton (col)	12/29/1897
Hodge, Richard (col)	Alice Hodge (col)	12/31/1891
Hodges, James J.	Addie D. Kelly	10/23/1895
Hogan, Cimeon	Phebee Holt	6/22/1873
Hogan, David E. (col)	Willie Malone (col)	11/17/1897
Hogan, Ellis	Emma Barker	4/28/1889
Hogan, Mansfield	Delphie McMichael	7/22/1883
Hogan, Squire	Jennett Davis	1/4/1873
Hoil, William B.	Frances Lumpkin	12/27/1846
Holder, John M.	Beulah G. Ferguson	9/20/1887
Holland, Abraham	Amma Brooks	3/3/1881
Holland, Alexander S.	Adeline N. Lowery	4/14/1859
Holland, Andrew	Tabitha Standifer	5/4/1872
Holland, Charley	Lou Greer	12/13/1883
Holland, Charley (col)	Lucy McDowell (col)	1/2/1899
Holland, Dave (col)	Margarette Hames (col)	1/26/1893
Holland, Ed (col)	Mattie Howard (col)	11/15/1896
Holland, F. B.	Mary Jane Nelms	12/7/1897
Holland, J. A.	Alice P. Kirkpatrick	2/26/1861
Holland, J. W.	C. C. Holland	9/21/1864
Holland, Jack (col)	Caroline Jackson (col)	9/18/1890
Holland, Jackson (col)	Susie Gordon (col)	1/1/1899
Holland, James (col)	Clarissa Jeffries (col)	2/4/1892
Holland, James Adolphus	America T. Kinard	3/3/1886
Holland, Jesse (col)	Martha Dawson (col)	8/15/1869
Holland, Littleton (col)	Clara Marks (col)	6/28/1873
Holland, Scott (col)	Lucy Buckner (col)	9/27/1891
Holland, Thomas R.	Catherine Hines	11/11/1857
Holland, Walter J.	Mary A. Roberts	12/13/1885
Holland, Walter (Walton) F.	Sarah Binford	6/26/1861
Holloway, Alonzo	Alice McElhenney	12/22/1895
Holloway, Joe (col)	Mary Mason (col)	11/7/1895
Holloway, Joe (col)	Mrs. Sudie Jackson (col)	1/8/1897
Holloway, John	Annie Goodman	11/23/1887
Holloway, Joseph	Caroline Ussery	11/12/1881
Holloway, Joseph	Mittie Spears	12/25/1893
Holloway, Maston	Ella Tyler	12/25/1890
Holloway, R. B.	R. S. Holloway	11/18/1885
Holloway, Randal	Nancy Goolsby	12/22/1887
Holloway, William (col)	Josie Jordan (col)	10/14/1899
Holmes, James (col)	Florence Vincent (col)	12/26/1899
Holmes, Plumer (col)	Minnie Franks (col)	12/24/1901
Holmes, Sam (col)	Agnes Underwood (col)	12/25/1892
Holmes, Warren (col)	Lutisa Jordan (col)	12/27/1907
Holmes, William (col)	Ola Lee Preston (col)	3/18/1893
Holms, Elbert H. (col)	Vinie Jeffries (col)	11/19/1893
Holms, Howard (col)	Matilda Vaughn (col)	8/18/1895
Holms, Isham (col)	Adeline Coles (col)	2/6/1875
Holsenbeck, Alexander	Lula Goolsby	2/5/1863
Holsenbeck, M. R.	Annie Jacobson	11/26/1899
Holsenbeck, P. R.	Bernice Oxford	10/11/1899
Holstin, Alexander	Lula Viola Crain	12/9/1894
Holt, Billie (col)	Hastie Goolsby (col)	12/22/1889
Holt, David (col)	Sarah Turner (col)	1/3/1871
Holt, Eli (col)	Sallie Jordan (col)	5/10/1890
Holt, Frank (col)	Hannah Greer (col)	5/18/1890
Holt, John Wesley (col)	Anna Daniel (col)	12/27/1892

Holt, Owen (col)	Ednie McDaniel (col)	3/13/1875
Holt, Owen (col)	Rachel Whitfield (col)	8/23/1899
Holt, Peter	Lou Kelly	3/29/1885
Holt, Peter	Sylvia Michael	2/2/1887
Holt, Richard	Mahala Paschal	4/30/1818
Holt, Will (col)	Lizzie Clements (col)	1/13/1898
Holt, William Alex (col)	Catharine Glover (col)	7/8/1894
Honeycutt, Thomas J.	Susie Cofer	1/8/1891
Hooks, Charles D.	Louisa J. Lane	9/1/1861
Hooks, David I.	Nancy Jane Rodden	10/16/1849
Hooks, Farra M.	Clara J. Price	7/25/1886
Hooten, D. W.	Lelia Anderson	1/13/1895
Hopper, William (col)	Mrs. Anna Harris (col)	3/25/1894
Hopson, Berry (col)	Annie Shropshire (col)	2/23/1873
Horsley, James	Elizabeth Bullard	1/21/1819
Horsley, William G.	Mrs. Salina H.J. Walton	8/26/1863
Horton, Columbus	Nancy Horton	4/15/1883
Horton, James P.	Martha Ozburn	12/24/1867
Horton, Robert	Mary (Mollie) Dawkins	12/3/1874
Horton, Wesley	Frances Isaac	12/28/1882
Howard, James B.	Catharine A. Maddux	3/24/1861
Howard, John (col)	Lula Nelson (col)	4/16/1890
Howard, Thomas T.	Susan T. Moreland	11/8/1859
Howard, William S.	Martha E. Lynch	4/20/1890
Howard, Willis (col)	Mattie Kelly (col)	12/19/1898
Hudson, Charlie (col)	Carrie Simon (col)	3/31/1889
Hudson, John F.	Emma Lancaster	10/7/1896
Hudson, Nelson (col)	Mrs. Eliza Wright (col)	3/21/1896
Hues, Bob (col)	Annie Fuller (col)	9/7/1876
Huff, Bartlett D.	Alice A. Funderburk	12/21/1886
Huff, Clayton W.	Mary Jane Marks	12/20/1881
Huff, George W.	Martha A. Campbell	11/7/1865
Huff, J. T.	Addie Toles	3/1/1898
Huff, James D.	Addie Jane Funderburk	2/10/1883
Huff, John	Emeliza Noles	8/22/1861
Huff, Oscar G.	Alice McMichael	1/18/1883
Huff, William Thomas	Julia Frances Waits	2/3/1907
Hughes, Jack (col)	Davie Jane Reese (col)	8/28/1892
Hughs, Allen (col)	Nettie Dumas (col)	12/30/1897
Hughs, Wesley (col)	Fannie Glover (col)	7/24/1892
Hughs, Wilson	Polly Greer	7/15/1883
Humphrey, Edmond	Jane Singleton	10/21/1882
Humphrey, Edmond	Lucy Goolsby	1/28/1886
Humphrey, Evan (col)	Cinda Jackson (col)	1/9/1897
Humphrey, Joshua (col)	Emma Kelly (col)	11/22/1896
Humphry, Howard (col)	Nancy Glover (col)	11/23/1898
Hunt, A. J.	M. E. Noles	12/4/1865
Hunt, Ed (col)	Matilda Alexander (col)	3/30/1901
Hunt, Elbert	Ella Banks	2/19/1881
Hunt, John (col)	Georgia Ella Moore (col)	11/9/1897
Hunt, Robert Henry	Lucy I. Garland	12/21/1893
Hunt, William (col)	Amanda Barron (col)	4/19/1896
Hunter, Cornua (col)	Laura Driscal (col)	5/12/1898
Hunter, Gip	Mary Brown	11/11/1889
Hunter, Green	Rebecca Williams	2/21/1888
Hunter, Henry	Georgia Ann Ward	1/2/1883
Hunter, Jackson (col)	Lula Goolsby (col)	12/31/1896
Hunter, Reuben (col)	Annie Kelly (col)	8/31/1891
Hunter, William A. (col)	Susie Arnold (col)	12/23/1897
Hurd, Clark (col)	Ellen Benton (col)	12/28/1893
Hurst, John N.	Lucretia J. Pace	1/12/1847
Hutchings, Phillip P.	Annie M. Freeman	4/14/1870
Hutchings, Walter (col)	Sallie Ponder (col)	2/13/1907

```
Hutchinson, T. A.          T. C. Smith              2/9/1888
Hutchinson, Thomas L.      Sarah Lewis              4/23/1850


Ike, John                  Adaline Benton           10/27/1896
Ingram, Andrew             Nannie Kate Faulkner     1/13/1886
Irwin, Charles             Melinda Echols           7/2/1818
Isaac, Dennis (col)        Allie Howard             12/14/1896
Isaac, Reese (col)         Lizzie Bearden (col)     9/21/1894
Isaacs, Dennis             Lina Derico              11/6/1886
Ivins, Josiah              Martha Newton            12/17/1875
Ivy, Flournoy              Martha Noles             1/22/1867
Ivy, Reese (col)           Emma Lewis (col)         1/27/1901
Ivy, William H.            Mrs. Emily Brooks        2/5/1868
Ivory, Sam                 Sallie Nash              7/11/1886


Jackson, Alfred            E. F. Dillard            12/25/1877
Jackson, Anderson          Savannah Witt            12/29/1889
Jackson, Ben (col)         Mary Pace (col)          9/25/1876
Jackson, Berry (col)       Mrs. Matilda Thomas(col) 12/14/1895
Jackson, Bose (col)        Annie Kate Branch (col)  1/7/1894
Jackson, Bose (col)        Fannie Johnson (col) (No Certifica-
                                                    tion)
Jackson, Charley (col)     Milly Henderson (col)    4/4/1874
Jackson, Charley (col)     Susie Jackson (col)      12/30/1899
Jackson, Charlie (col)     Mattie Lou Rogers (col)  1/3/1898
Jackson, Clark (col)       Sallie Zinnaman (col)    4/1/1894
Jackson, Claud (col)       Claud (?) Benton (col)   12/1/1907
Jackson, Doc               Alice Collier            10/25/1885
Jackson, Fed (col)         Delia Glover (col)       3/12/1870
Jackson, George (col)      Sue Lee Ridley (col)     1/17/1891
Jackson, Green             Mary Brown               12/20/1888
Jackson, Henry             Rebecca Daniel           11/4/1882
Jackson, Hiram             Jeanette Jackson         1/10/1897
Jackson, Ivy (col)         Susan Cargile (col)      6/5/1870
Jackson, James             Mary Lawrence            12/24/1888
Jackson, Jim (col)         Carrie McMichael (col)   12/25/1896
Jackson, John (col)        Anna Meriwether (col)    12/28/1889
Jackson, King (col)        Matilda Alexander (col)  3/23/1907
Jackson, Lewis             Nettie Usry              12/27/1882
Jackson, Peter             Jennett Williams         8/24/1872
Jackson, Peter             Delia Whitfield          1/13/1878
Jackson, Peter (col)       Charity Hurd (col)       3/5/1893
Jackson, Price             Comfort Hames            5/19/1887
Jackson, R. F.             A. E. Lane               11/30/1882
Jackson, Richard (col)     Carrie Thomas (col)      5/27/1891
Jackson, Richard          Mary Lawrence            12/22/1907
Jackson, Robert (col)      Sarah Folds              1/18/1877
Jackson, Robert Lee(col)   Susan Ann Marks (col)    12/30/1897
Jackson, Spencer           Caroline Roberts         1/8/1873
Jackson, Thomas (col)      Genie Walker (col)       10/4/1896
Jackson, Thomas (col)      Lilie Mitchell (col)     12/24/1897
Jackson, Wade (col)        Pauline Jackson (col)    1/16/1907
Jackson, Will (col)        Elmira Williams (col)    12/5/1898
Jackson, William (col)     Rebecca Moreland (col)   12/4/1899
Jackson, Willie Flem(col)  Pearler Pou (col)        12/26/1901
Jacob, Jack                Burmey Pritchett         12/26/1883
Jacob, Nathan              Sarah Marks              12/2/1882
Jacobson, Charlie          Belle Hitchcock          8/23/1899
James, Andrew (col)        Sallie Kelly (col)       6/4/1894
James, Charlie Lee (col)   Amanda Jackson (col)     11/8/1899
James, John (col)          Roman Bonuer (col)       7/3/1875
```

James, Marshall (col)	Parthie Sluder (col)	9/4/1887
James, Michel	Harriet Byram	2/15/1874
James, Wesley (col)	Susan Relaford (col)	11/18/1875
James, Wesley (col)	Sallie Meriwether (col)	11/16/1896
James, Willie (col)	Ellen Glover (col)	12/26/1894
Jeffers, Cordy	Sarah Josephine Spears	12/14/1859
Jefferson, Thomas	Lucy Raney	12/29/1888
Jeffries, Aurelius (col)	Lula Mitchel (col)	5/24/1896
Jeffries, Billy	Harriet Seats	11/29/1877
Jeffries, Billy	Easter Fears	10/21/1886
Jeffries, Calvin	Caroline McElhenney	12/28/1886
Jeffries, Charlie (col)	Frances Wyatt (col)	12/25/1889
Jeffries, Colbert	Nancy T. Smith	12/2/1883
Jeffries, Dan (col)	Mattie Gay (col)	12/29/1897
Jeffries, Elijah (col)	Elmyra Harwell (col)	9/26/1894
Jeffries, Frank (col)	Ida Gay (col)	8/19/1894
Jeffries, Henry	Silla Tuggle	1/23/1873
Jeffries, Henry (col)	Marie R. Barnes (col)	12/26/1889
Jeffries, Henry (col)	Mollie Walker (col)	12/20/1893
Jeffries, Henry, Jr.	Margarett Walker Date issued	1/11/1889
Jeffries, James	Margarett Smith	1/1/1874
Jeffries, Jessie (col)	Sylvia Binford (col)	12/16/1890
Jeffries, John (col)	Manda Jeffries (col)	1/18/1875
Jeffries, John (col)	Annie Chamberlain (col)	12/24/1890
Jeffries, John (col)	Lou Simmons (col)	12/31/1896
Jeffries, Lee (col)	Rachael Brown (col)	1/6/1892
Jeffries, Milton	Mary Cook	5/8/1887
Jeffries, Naz (col)	Alice Kelly (col)	2/13/1890
Jeffries, Oscar (col)	Ella Reves (col)	12/28/1899
Jeffries, Payton (col)	Sarah Broughton (col)	12/25/1890
Jeffries, Rollin	Miranda Fair	3/27/1881
Jeffries, Rowland	Lany Smith	12/31/1873
Jeffries, Samuel	Blanche Hurts	12/27/1888
Jeffries, Thomas	Johnie Aiken	6/29/1888
Jeffries, Thomas J.	Pearl Jeffries	12/11/1896
Jeffries, Tom (col)	Catharine Hurt (col)	6/11/1894
Jeffries, Tooms (col)	Eddie Johnson (col)	10/17/1889
Jeffries, Wesley	Emma Greer	12/30/1889
Jeffries, Will (col)	Henrietta Wright (col)	12/25/1892
Jeffries, William (col)	Ida Williams (col)	7/11/1896
Jeffries, Zach	Ella Wyatt	8/29/1889
Jenkins, B. W.	Annie Grubbs	12/24/1901
Jenkins, Francis	Elizabeth Pye	12/24/1844
Jenkins, Frank E.	Sallie H. Harden	1/16/1872
Jenkins, Henry (col)	Rhoda Walker (col)	1/31/1875
Jenkins, M. B. (col)	Carrie Carter (col)	12/28/1894
Jewel, Diamond (col)	Ella Smith (col)	1/31/1896
Jewel, Dimond	Fannie Tompkins	1/5/1886
John, E. D.	Mary P. Allen	12/18/1866
John, Enoch D.	Martha S. Allen	8/11/1870
Johnson, Aaron (col)	Mrs. Amanda Thomas (col)	8/5/1894
Johnson, Alfred (col)	Sylvia Newby (col)	12/22/1892
Johnson, Allas	Margaret Ann J. Hillsman	7/11/1860
Johnson, Alonzo (col)	Josia Shannon (col)	2/3/1907
Johnson, Andrew	Nancy Shy	12/25/1883
Johnson, Bennie D.	Julia Binford	8/8/1897
Johnson, Benjamin	Lucy Turner	8/13/1816
Johnson, Bryant	Aimey Williams (Wilson)	6/8/1876
Johnson, Burrel	Mollie Kelly	12/28/1883
Johnson, Charley	Hattie Jackson Date Issued	9/7/1907
Johnson, Charlie (col)	Pink Maxey (col)	8/5/1893

Johnson, Cicero	Carrie Tanner	3/22/1883
Johnson, Eli (col)	Sultana Banks (col)	1/4/1870
Johnson, Eli (col)	Alice Johnson (col)	12/19/1895
Johnson, Ephraim (col)	Emily Glover (col)	7/19/1892
Johnson, Ervin	Hattie Johnson	12/19/1895
Johnson, George (col)	Sallie Wyatt (col)	12/23/1892
Johnson, George (col)	Josie Billingsly (col)	10/23/1898
Johnson, Henry (col)	Eliza Cargile (col)	12/30/1869
Johnson, Henry (col)	Carrie Goolsby (col)	1/11/1891
Johnson, Jack	Eliza Glover	12/17/1885
Johnson, James (col)	Hattie Williams (col)	3/13/1892
Johnson, James (col)	Cinda Smith (col)	5/29/1892
Johnson, James (col)	Savanah Simmons (col)	10/22/1892
Johnson, James (col)	Susie Baynes (col)	12/21/1893
Johnson, James H.	Polly Ann Tomlin	1/2/1868
Johnson, James M.	Irene Jordan	12/8/1898
Johnson, John	Kittie Greer	12/30/1884
Johnson, John	Mattie Banks	2/3/1887
Johnson, John	Roxie Greer	1/5/1889
Johnson, John (col)	Mollie Bridges (col)	1/31/1897
Johnson, John (col)	Nancy Binford (col)	12/20/1899
Johnson, John C.	Mynona Elder	10/15/1899
Johnson, John W.	Elisabeth Moore	12/19/1872
Johnson, Johnnie (col)	Queen Driscoll (col)	9/23/1899
Johnson, Jonas (col)	Susie Thomas (col)	12/31/1895
Johnson, Joseph H. (Johnston)	Mary M. Leverett	12/23/1875
Johnson, Joseph S.	Winiford Hill	8/16/1895
Johnson, M. F.	S. J. Brooks	12/30/1877
Johnson, Martin	Adeline Moore	12/12/1871
Johnson, Moses (col)	Mrs. Bettie Banks (col)	12/25/1894
Johnson, Ned	Mary Broddus	2/21/1897
Johnson, Oliver	Dora Campbell	9/27/1888
Johnson, Oliver H.	Diana Jackson	3/27/1886
Johnson, Reuben	Sarah Glover	12/28/1882
Johnson, Rosser M.	Judith Eugene Howard	10/2/1888
Johnson, Samuel	Winney C. Kitchings	12/3/1860
Johnson, W. S. (col)	Georgia Banks (col)	11/4/1899
Johnson, William	Jennie Turner	12/19/1884
Johnson, William (col)	Mattie Myrick Date issued	11/14/1888
Johnson, William	Fanny Goolsby	4/12/1889
Johnston, Henry	Crisie Williams	6/29/1873
Johnston, Henry	Elisebeth Ridley	12/19/1873
Johnston, Isaac	Emily Johnston	1/11/1877
Johnston, James H.	Ellie J. Malone	12/22/1885
Johnston, James S.	Emma Binford	1/21/1885
Johnston, Pollard	Minnie Johnston	3/10/1877
Johnston, William A.	Jane L. Price	9/2/1847
Jones, A. L.	Lucy Moss	2/2/1862
Jones, Francis P.	Margarett Jane Hubbard	7/8/1847
Jones, Green	Callie Turk	1/4/1888
Jones, Harry Hill	Stella Benton	7/10/1907
Jones, Isaac	Cornelia Hurt	7/?/1872
Jones, J. J.	Lissie Avant	8/12/1875
Jones, James M.	Mrs. Tresa Benton	12/20/1874
Jones, James R.	Alice Holsenbeck	10/29/1863
Jones, John D.	Leila Minter	1/10/1894
Jones, Mitchell	Tildy Jackson	12/29/1873
Jones, Phillip	Anna Glover	3/7/1888
Jones, Rial A.	Sallie R. Greer	1/15/1885
Jones, Thomas R.	Leontine Durden	4/21/1895
Jones, Tommie (col)	Rhoda Perry (col)	12/31/1895

Jones, Wesley (col)	Lina Brown (col)	1/12/1896
Jones, Wiley Oscar	Mattie Fannie Elliot	7/27/1892
Jones, Wiley R.	Virginia Freeman	3/19/1866
Jones, William (col)	Ida Hunter (col)	7/19/1896
Jones, William C.	Mary I. Kelly	2/19/1885
Jones, William H.	Lizzie Edwards	1/4/1891
Jordan, Aaron (col)	Georgia Ann Gant (col)	10/6/1873
Jordan, Aaron (col)	Caroline Thomas (col)	9/25/1895
Jordan, Alex Hunter	Hattie N. White	8/3/1887
Jordan, Charles (col)	Ada Clark (col)	3/28/1897
Jordan, Charles (col)	Pennie Thomas (col)	1/11/1898
Jordan, Charles A. (col)	Medora Eberhart Compton (col)	5/28/1891
Jordan, Charles H.	Lizzie Kate White	9/19/1893
Jordan, Charles Lee (col)	Mrs. Kate Ann Flanders (col)	1/5/1896
Jordan, Charlie (col)	Carrie Glawson (col)	6/22/1889
Jordan, Charlie (col)	Leona Bias (col)	12/30/1897
Jordan, Chris (col)	Mrs. Annie Grubbs (col)	11/21/1894
Jordan, Christopher	Georgia Ann Standifer	10/17/1875
Jordan, Daniel	Martha Wilson	2/4/1875
Jordan, Edward (col)	Frances Henderson (col)	1/5/1869
Jordan, Edward (col)	Frances Hogan (col)	12/29/1892
Jordan, Edward (col)	Mrs. Lula Thornton (col)	2/1/1894
Jordan, Erasmus H.	Rebecca M. Glover	5/18/1869
Jordan, Fleming, Jr.	N. H. Dillon	3/4/1862
Jordan, Fleming B. (col)	Georgia Kate Smith (col)	11/14/1897
Jordan, George (col)	Adaline Williford (col)	11/19/1893
Jordan, George	Bertha Brazel	3/24/1897
Jordan, Gus (col)	Ada Jackson (col)	12/26/1895
Jordan, Henry (col)	Amey Holland (col)	9/6/1899
Jordan, Hilliard	Anna Olivia Witt	2/6/1887
Jordan, Howard (col)	Martha Jordan (col)	12/31/1869
Jordan, Howard	Rosetta Pickens	2/16/1873
Jordan, Jack (col)	Mary Hill (col)	12/31/1888
Jordan, Jack (col)	Beatris Roberts (col)	1/5/1899
Jordan, James (col)	Georgia Smith (col)	2/28/1892
Jordan, Janty (col)	Sarah Lofton (col)	4/10/1869
Jordan, Jewett (col)	Mariah Goolsby (col)	12/25/1866
Jordan, Jim (col)	Lula Penn (col)	4/17/1898
Jordan, Jimmie (col)	Ella Marks (col)	2/5/1890
Jordan, Joe (col)	Millie Epps (col)	12/27/1901
Jordan, John (col)	Annie Johnson (col)	9/17/1893
Jordan, John (col)	Anna Shields (col)	2/27/1898
Jordan, L. (col)	Mrs. Anna Freeman (col)	3/2/1899
Jordan, Loot (col)	Rebecca Gordon (col)	1/12/1876
Jordan, May (col)	Rebecca Goolsby (col)	1/5/1868
Jordan, Moses	Cilla Jackson	1/14/1883
Jordan, Randal (col)	Susan Robertson (col)	8/7/1898
Jordan, Robert	Harriet Penn	12/24/1886
Jordan, Robert (col)	Eliza Standifer (col)	1/7/1889
Jordan, Rufus L. (col)	Polly Hughes (col)	12/28/1890
Jordan, Scott	Martha Ann Allen	1/15/1885
Jordan, Sim T. (col)	Mrs. Sallie Fears (col)	8/6/1893
Jordan, Singleton (col)	Lou Genie Michael (col)	12/27/1889
Jordan, Thomas	Rhoda Goolsby	1/7/1866
Jordan, Thomas M.	Elizabeth Powell	12/8/1881
Jordan, V. A.	M. L. Geiger	9/7/1870
Jordan, Wesley (col)	Kittie Ann Byars (col)	2/27/1890
Jordan, Wesley (col)	Carrie Holt (col)	10/9/1898
Jordan, William (col)	Frances Powell (col)	7/7/1881
Jordan, William (col)	Mattie Thomas (col)	11/2/1898
Jordan, William, Jr.	Anna Holloway	4/21/1888

31

Jordan, William F., Jr.	Lena M. Barnes	6/8/1898
Jordan, Wyatt	Amanda Moreland	4/13/1867
Jordan, Zach	Betsy Tilman	9/21/1882
Joseph, Alex (col)	Eveline Sanders (col)	12/27/1897
Kaigler, Alexander	Milly Linsey	3/4/1869
Keeland, Ike (col)	Jane Freeman (col)	4/15/1889
Keith, Whitten	Sally McDonald	2/3/1816
Keith, William F. T.	Jeanette H. Jordan	5/23/1854
Kello, Robert (col)	Allice Daniel (col)	12/8/1876
Kellor, Everett (col)	Levie Jackson (col)	3/21/1901
Kelly, Amos	Ellen Robinson	2/17/1873
Kelly, Amos (col)	Lucinda Price (col)	6/21/1891
Kelly, Archie	Silvie Glover	1/14/1877
Kelly, Burney (col)	Kittie Johnston (col)	12/30/1874
Kelly, Burton (col)	Sarah Digby (col)	12/14/1887
Kelly, Crawford H.	Annie F. Thompson	11/22/1883
Kelly, Eaton H.	Margaret Jane Greer	1/13/1859
Kelly, Eaton Digby	Sallie A. Smith	6/6/1886
Kelly, Ephraim (col)	Matilda Allen (col)	4/4/1869
Kelly, Everett (col)	Mandy Reid (col)	
	Date issued	4/26/1875
Kelly, Henry	Lucy Walker	6/27/1885
	Permission to issue license	6/27/1885
Kelly, Henry (col)	Mollie Epps (col)	1/19/1896
Kelly, Henry (col)	Masoury Smith (col)	10/16/1907
Kelly, Isaac T.	Mollie Blackwell	12/24/1885
Kelly, Jacob (col)	Mrs. Mima Gant (col)	11/10/1893
Kelly, James	Sophronia Shy	12/8/1886
Kelly, Jim	Margarett Wyatt	12/6/1883
Kelly, Jim (col)	Cora Benton (col)	1/6/1895
Kelly, John (col)	Helon Kelly (col)	12/29/1887
Kelly, John (col)	Fronie Hurt (col)	12/27/1894
Kelly, John A.	Mellie Robinson	12/22/1889
Kelly, John H.	Sallie H. Barron	2/1/1887
Kelly, John R., Jr.	Caroline S. McMichael	12/21/1864
Kelly, Julian	Mattie Clyde Gaston	8/17/1896
Kelly, Lewis (col)	Corine Pitts (col)	8/26/1898
Kelly, M. C.	Ruby Ellis	12/22/1907
Kelly, Samuel (col)	Mattie Smith (col)	8/30/1897
Kelly, Seaborn J.	L. A. Shaw	10/14/1869
Kelly, Seaborn J.	Mattie C. Downs	3/12/1891
Kelly, Tom (col)	Margarett Smith (col)	1/3/1889
Kelly, W. G.	Sophia W. Shaw	10/8/1874
Kelly, W. G.	Eula Malone	1/13/1901
Kelly, Wallis	Carrie Tuggle	6/20/1885
Kelly, Walter	Nannie Williams	12/14/1893
Kelly, William	Anna George	12/31/1873
Kelly, William	Sophronia Johnson	3/10/1898
Kelly, William	Inies Cook	12/26/1901
Kelly, William (col)	Ora Digby (col)	1/9/1898
Kendall, Paul	Annie S. White	10/28/1896
Kendrick, Willis E.	Angeline Cheek	12/27/1888
Key, Asa (col)	Lula Redmond (col)	10/6/1891
Key, Burney (col)	Ophelia Howard (col)	12/26/1901
Key, Eli (col)	Lema Smith (col)	11/13/1890
Key, Freeman (col)	Lizzie Brown (col)	11/1/1898
Key, John C.	P. A. S. Allen	7/28/1857
Key, Lawrence (col)	Lula Goteer (col)	12/29/1901
Key, Osh (col)	Charity Ann Kelly (col)	2/9/1893
Key, Thomas C.	Lucy May Thompson	12/29/1895
Kilgore, E. C.	Mrs. Emaliza Huff	12/31/1865

Kilgore, James A.	Elmyra C. Ellis	9/27/1864
Kilgore, W. C.	Sarah F. Niblett	1/1/1889
Kilgore, William I.	Florence Barker	11/29/1887
Killgore, Isaac C.	Sarah J. Doster	11/7/1865
Kimbell, J. H.	Anna C. Cofer	4/4/1888
Kinard, Joseph C.	Kate Clark	10/3/1896
Kindrick, Major W. E.	Elizabeth L. Morgan	10/3/1869
King, George	Sallie Curry	2/5/1885
King, Jake (col)	Lula Jackson (col)	12/30/1897
King, Jim (col)	Frances Brazel (col)	2/17/1890
King, Joe	Caroline Tilmon	11/15/1883
King, John	Rebecca Price	3/21/1888
King, William	Ellen Maddux	12/16/1868
Kitchens, Benjamin	Delphi Yancy	11/9/1817
Kitchens, George	Parthena Roby (date iss.)	12/28/1873
Kitchens, Joel	Adaline F. Warren	7/4/1869
Kitchens, Nelson	Nancy J. Parker	11/24/1870
Kitchings, C. W.	M. L. Oxford	10/29/1885
Knight, John	Mary Kettner	7/3/1892
Knight, Warren	Ann Adams	1/12/1847
Lackey, Albert	Cynthia Smith	12/26/1885
Lamar, Robert (col)	Easter Carter (col)	9/3/1875
Lancaster, James	Catharine Leverett	11/15/1859
Lane, Augustus G.	Mary A. M. Shipp	7/16/1867
Lane, Augustus W.	Mary I. Leverett	9/25/1860
Lane, Ben (col)	Silva Holland (col)	2/15/1899
Lane, Charles Q.	Mary E. Park	5/19/1853
Lane, Elbert	Evelina Slaughter	11/11/1874
Lane, Elijah D.	Nancy E. White	3/20/1859
Lane, Floyd	Lucy Standifer	3/6/1873
Lane, James O.	M. V. Kimbell	10/17/1865
Lane, John F.	Frances E. Pope	10/22/1882
Lane, L. A.	Susan Greer	9/28/1865
Lane, Lawson	Rose Benton	6/28/1888
Lane, R. L.	Lillie Thomason	5/22/1898
Lane, Robert M.	George Ann Adams	10/25/1860
Lane, William D.	Mrs. Sarah A. Smith	10/15/1865
Lane, William L.	C. M. Pope	12/15/1881
Langston, D. M.	Susie A. Brazille	1/6/1897
Langston, Isaac M.	Annie L. Cardell	10/28/1894
Langston, James J.	Annie L. Niblett	8/20/1884
Langston, Thomas W.P.	Martha J. Barr	10/6/1867
Langston, Warren A.	Matilda Morgan	12/30/1885
Lassetter, V. T.	Mary Jane Minter	11/26/1872
Laurence, James L.	Biddie Lane	1/4/1888
Laurence, Jeff (col)	Ginnie Phillips (col)	11/9/1893
Laurence, Robert (col)	Dora Davis (col)	11/22/1890
Lavender, David M.	Matilda Wise	11/10/1889
Lawrence, Anthony (col)	Hattie Jordan (col)	12/6/1899
Lawrence, Ben (col)	Annis Roby (col)	1/8/1891
Lawrence, Bennie (col)	Irene Ursery (col)	12/26/1907
Lawrence, Charles	Cora Jenkins	2/23/1893
Lawrence, Francis C.	Annie D. Jenkins	1/19/1892
Lawrence, Frank (col)	Josie Woodley (col)	12/22/1897
Lawrence, Harvey P.	Mattie Hearn	12/8/1901
Lawrence, J.A.C.S.	Sarah F. Barclay	10/18/1858
Lawrence, Overton	Lee Idus Sigman	10/20/1907
Lawrence, Robert (col)	Victoria Preston (col)	12/25/1896
Lawrence, Seaborn	Martha Stewart	11/10/1863
Lawson, Ivey	Peggy Carr	5/30/1817
Lawson, Thomas J.	Margaret J. Varnom	5/14/1882

Lay, L. A.	Nannie Couch	3/31/1892
Layfield, James M.	Annie C. Spears	11/3/1896
Layson, William A.	M. B. Cardell	12/12/1872
Lazenby, Micheal	Nettie Johnston	1/24/1877
Leach, Hiram	Janie Yancy	3/5/1897
Leach, J. R.	Mollie McMichael	11/7/1886
Leach, John W.	Emily C. Gilstrap	10/3/1869
Leath, Jesse	Martha Brown	12/25/1882
Leath, John	Emma Thompson	12/23/1884
Leath, John (col)	Izora Banks (col)	8/15/1899
Leath, Jordan	Caroline Shy	1/11/1883
Leathy, Allen (col)	Charlott Shy (col)	11/25/1897
Lee, Adam (col)	Kate Driskell (col)	11/27/1895
Lee, Allen	Fannie Fears	12/21/1877
Lee, Berry	Eliza Cullen	11/18/1881
Lee, Jesse (col)	Willie Mary Slack (col)	5/26/1907
Leith, Richard (col)	Mariah Thomas (col)	8/13/1873
Leonard, Reubin	Lucy Pierce	6/7/1818
Letson, George A.D.	Elizabeth R. Faulkner	11/13/1867
Letson, Robert F.	Cinthia Clara Chaffin	4/28/1889
Leven, Edgar Lee (col)	Lola Burney (col)	12/25/1899
Leverett, Andrew J.	Julia E. Martin	9/1/1870
Leverett, Bee	Bradley Ward	4/12/1896
Leverett, D. F.	Beulah Kate Chaffin	2/17/1901
Leverett, James H.	Julia R. Freeman	12/11/1884
Leverett, Reid (col)	Martha Tinsley (col)	12/4/1890
Leverett, Thomas G.	Martha C. Leverett	10/1/1861
Leverett, William (col)	Carrie Wood (col)	12/26/1895
Leverette, E. T.	M. T. King	12/5/1889
Lewis, E. F.	Mrs. Rhoda Stone	3/10/1867
Lewis, George (col)	C. B. Walker (col)	11/8/1897
Lewis, J. W.	Lucy M. Meriwether	1/27/1874
Lewis, James T.	Martha Digby	12/15/1870
Lewis, Ned	Elvira Williams	6/2/1872
Lewis, Phillip	Mrs. Edney D. Grubbs	7/28/1850
Lewis, R. W.	Lola Tedders	1?/3/1891
Lewis, Taylor (col)	Fannie Williams (col)	1/8/1874
Limbrick, James (col)	Rose Smith (col)	11/18/1868
Lindsey, David (col)	Millie Clay (col)	10/16/1870
Lindsey, Emanuel	Sarah A. Steel	1/12/1875
Lindsey, Frank	Alice Smith	10/27/1889
Lindsey, Thomas	Sallie Nash	12/29/1892
Lindsey, Will (col)	Lizzie Harris (col)	12/24/1898
Little, Reuben	Sarah Jane Johnson	2/1/1883
Little, Sid, Jr. (col)	Lilly Williams (col)	2/17/1907
Little, Sidney (col)	Fanny Turk (col)	9/23/1893
Lloyd, W. D.	Mollie Polk	11/23/1899
Lofton, William A.	Catherine T. Burney	8/17/1854
Long, Alexander (col)	Mary Pye (col)	10/24/1874
Long, James	Mollie Niblett	
	(Consent to issue license)	1884
Long, John J.	Louisa E. Goodman	12/15/1867
Long, Tommie (col)	Mollie Johnson (col)	7/24/1892
Love, John	Catherine Kelly	7/4/1816
Lovejoy, Coleman B.	Lizzie Henderson	5/2/1889
Loyd, G. P.	J. C. Persons	10/22/1874
Loyd, James I.	Clemmie L. McMichael	12/18/1884
Loyd, James M.	Mary Smith	2/10/1870
Loyd, John (col)	Aggie Heard (col)	6/2/1896
Loyd, John D.	Frances Ramey	3/6/1859
Loyd, Lewis (col)	Mattie Lou Smith (col)	12/28/1897
Loyd, Pleasant B.	Allie Henderson	1/13/1868
Luke, Thomas M.	Annie Wyatt	3/30/1907

Lummus, William M.	Nellie Lynch	7/17/1884
Lumpkin, Judge (col)	Dora Crawford	
	Date Issued	2/5/1874
Lumsden, Charles T.	Althea Ophelia Cook	12/24/1890
Lunsford, J. R.	Sevesta Shepherd	7/24/1889
Lunsford, J. W.	Ally B. Lunsford	11/19/1868
Lynch, Ben (col)	Martha Kelly (col)	2/20/1868
Lynch, Benjamin (col)	Nancy Stone (col)	3/2/1899
Lynch, Charles C.	Susie Andrews	1/2/1887
Lynch, Fleetwood	Etta Thomson	10/28/1894
Lynch, Gried	Sarah Ann Thompson	8/13/1868
Lynch, James (col)	Dinah Glover (col)	1/29/1896
Lynch, Jarrett	Frances A. Brandon	12/28/1862
Lynch, John (col)	Katie Mary Barber (col)	3/27/1901
Lynch, Monroe (col)	Anna Hamilton (col)	7/4/1877
Lynch, Philip	Lee Ann Johnson	7/17/1881
Lynch, Phillip (col)	Jossie Glover (col)	8/30/1894
Lynch, Pleasant T.	Martha A. Barnett	10/26/1865
Lynch, William H.	Melissie Faulkner	12/21/1893
Lyon, Rufus M.	Lizzie Gordon	11/7/1888
Mabray, Rezin	Elizabeth Benton	6/11/1818
Maddox, Charley (col)	Mrs. Annie Kelly (col)	5/7/1899
Maddox, Green (col)	Frances Sands (col)	7/17/1897
Maddox, James Henry(col)	Sarah Morton (col)	3/8/1894
Maddox, John	Ella Moore	11/16/1892
Maddox, Joseph (col)	Corine Jackson (col)	2/24/1898
Maddox, Tillman (col)	Julia Wyatt (col)	3/14/1897
Maddux, Abe (col)	Margaret Kelly (col)	10/1/1893
Maddux, Abram (col)	Jeanette Pritchett (col)	2/26/1888
Maddux, Ambrose	Angelina Dixon	8/5/1866
Maddux, Arthur	Mrs. Ann Carter	10/20/1883
Maddux, Barney F.	Nancy S. Waldrep	1/3/1867
Maddux, Billie (col)	Pauline Preston (col)	2/2/1899
Maddux, John (col)	Nancy Smith (col)	12/22/1870
Maddux, John	Martha Smith	4/12/1887
Maddux, John	Mollie Hodge	12/22/1889
Maddux, John C.	H. E. Malone	1/19/1888
Maddux, Sawney (col)	Minnie James (col)	10/14/1901
Maddux, Washington	Retta Mason	4/22/1886
Maddux, Washington	Annie Brown	10/11/1888
Maddux, Washington(col)	Eliza Thomas (col)	4/6/1901
Maddux, William (col)	Clara Butts (col)	1/28/1899
Magby, Hiram	Susannah Wooten	10/6/1816
Mahon, John Henry (col)	Charlotte Stewart (col)	11/19/1899
Malone, Allen M.	Mrs. Mattie L. Kelly	1/15/1874
Malone, Amos	Emeline Tolan	3/16/1887
Malone, Cade	Margaret Smith	1/8/1838
Malone, Charles (col)	Lucy Preston (col)	2/22/1891
Malone, Charles R.	Clifford E. Downs	12/27/1894
Malone, Clarence O.	Addie Kate Kelly	11/27/1895
Malone, Eli T.	Clara Persons	1/27/1889
Malone, Eugene B.	Bessie Spears	5/6/1894
Malone, F. J.	Emma J. Lane	11/26/1868
Malone, Floyd	Mrs. Catharine J.Belcher	11/16/1865
Malone, Frank (col)	Carrie Kelly (col)	1/1/1891
Malone, George	Sylva A. Hogans	1/5/1882
Malone, George (col)	Kate Hempfield (col)	12/17/1899
Malone, Henry	Emily McGinnis	4/13/1881
Malone, Henry	Jeanette Sanders	5/11/1890
Malone, Isham P.	Pearla V. Malone	12/4/1894
Malone, J. S.	Mattie T. Ezell	12/16/1875

Malone, John (col)	Carrie Usher (col)	1/26/1894
Malone, John B.	Mattie Blackwell	12/24/1885
Malone, Jordan	Clara Fears	8/17/1883
Malone, Josiah P.	Ella C. Downs	12/22/1891
Malone, Persey W.	Willie Kelly	7/9/1893
Malone, Peter (col)	Ida Baynes (col)	1/23/1898
Malone, Sheroa (col)	Sarah Comer (col)	11/4/1886
Malone, Sidney	Maria Preston	9/24/1883
Malone, Stephen F.	India V. Freeman	12/18/1884
Malone, Thomas (col)	Annie Jones (col)	12/28/1899
Malone, Thomas S.	Sarah A. Kelly	3/11/1850
Malone, Walker B.	Annis Phillips	2/14/1892
Malone, Wash	Sarah Malone	1/2/1877
Malone, William F.	Hattie O. Walker	12/21/1876
Malone, Willis	Josie Sims	12/27/1883
Maning, Bert (col)	Janie Crawford (col)	6/15/1895
Maning, Simeon	Linda Freeman	12/30/1888
Maning, William (col)	India Blackwell (col)	5/20/1894
Manings, Siman (col)	Georgia Ann Williams(col)	12/18/1897
Manins, Simon (col)	Mollie Harris (col)	3/21/1874
Mann, A. V.	Georgia E. E. Watters	9/5/1854
Mann, Claiborn S.	Mrs. Elizabeth Z. White	9/23/1888
Manning, Aaron	Drucilla Glenn	12/27/1886
Manning, Berry	Louiza Carter	3/?/1877
Manning, Berry (col)	Mrs. Mariah Freeman (col)	12/28/1893
Manning, Berry (col)	Ida Ross (col)	3/4/1897
Manning, Billy	Emma Brown	10/21/1885
Manning, Dock (col)	Ella Wright (col)	12/27/1871
Manning, Gus	Ednie Minter(Date issued)	1/27/1877
Manning, Richard	Alice Williams	1/5/1885
Mannings, George	Diana Glover	2/20/1884
Mannings, James (col)	Cindy Smith (col)	12/26/1876
Manuel, Ed	Pearl Key	11/10/1907
Mapp, Benjamin H.	Julia Turk	11/22/1866
Marberry, James Newton	Rosa Wynn	1/1/1894
Marchman, John	Lillie Wilson	12/29/1907
Marks, Arnold (col)	Lucy Ann Smith (col)	12/26/1895
Marks, Billy (col)	Caroline Goolsby (col)	12/5/1868
Marks, Brack (col)	Ida Thomas (col)	12/26/1899
Marks, Dozier (col)	Dewby Thomas (col)	11/3/1907
Marks, Edenborough (col)	Mary Ann Harris (col)	3/13/1892
Marks, Edinbourough	Luch Beebee	11/16/1893
Marks, Henry (col)	Caroline Kelly (col)	11/21/1893
Marks, Horace	Eliza Elder	6/18/1882
Marks, I. H.	Sarah Jane Tyler	2/14/1882
Marks, James	Lethe Pritchett	1/20/1884
Marks, James (col)	Ione Haynes (col)	6/4/1893
Marks, Jeff	Anna Jones	1/8/1873
Marks, John T.	Mary Virginia Dawkins	1/20/1882
Marks, Levi	Adaline Flemister	1/13/1888
Marks, Levi (col)	Phebia Hight (col)	3/7/1899
Marks, Lige (col)	Katie Goolsby (col)	4/22/1894
Marks, Lucius	Dilcie Hartrick	3/17/1886
Marks, Nelson	Jennie Pou	6/4/1881
Marks, Samuel J.	Martha M. Adams	9/13/1859
Marks, Scott (col)	Emma Sheilds (col)	1/1/1895
Marks, Tom (col)	Mattie Warren (col)	12/29/1891
Marks, Walace (col)	Ella Avery (col)	12/29/1894
Marks, Will (col)	Frances Clay (col)	10/12/1895
Marks, William (col)	Lorena Goolsby (col)	9/11/1897
Marsh, R. L.	Mattie Lou Florence	11/10/1901
Marshall, Andrew J.	Mattie L. Funderburk	2/19/1889
Martin, Jerry P.	Henrietta Edwards	12/20/1851

Martin, Thomas	Martha Burton	8/13/1818
Mashburn, John H.	Josephine Holloway	11/1/1874
Mason, Dempsy	Cassie Chaffin	4/6/1895
Mason, Henry Turner	Kittie Ann Allen	10/16/1884
Mason, James	Allace Brooks	3/12/1876
Mason, James	Emma Jones (date issued)	12/5/1900
Mason, Turner (col)	Malinda Brown (col)	3/18/1890
Mason, William	Mattie Mooneyham	11/24/1898
Mathis, Davis (col)	Emma Daniel (col)	10/14/1899
Matthews, Edgar (col)	Lina Cullen (col)	11/15/1893
Matthis, John T.	Carrie T. Driskell	2/10/1890
Maxey, Adolphus	Mary Reid	1/5/1883
Maxey, Dock	Betsy Kelly	1/1/1886
Maxey, Isham	Harriet Barnes	12/17/1885
Maxey, Jim (col)	Louisa Smith (col)	2/24/1896
Maxey, Mabe	Randa Banks	5/12/1872
Maxey, Mabron (col)	Amanda Bearden (col)	10/26/1890
Maxey, Sid (col)	Mrs. Caroline Johnson (col)	10/22/1899
May, Charles F.	Sallie V. Spearman	12/6/1892
Meadows, P. W. L.	Nora B. Wagner	11/15/1896
Meeks, Bennie B.	Sallie Lee Adams	10/9/1888
Menefee, Thomas H.	Bessie C. Jordan	11/14/1872
Mercer, D. T.	Edney E. Phillips	3/5/1863
Mercer, Daniel T.	Sue Phillips	11/19/1889
Mercer, L. A.	Mrs. Ginnie Straiton	1/3/1898
Mercer, Luke B.	Susan Lawrence	9/8/1870
Mercer, Thomas W.	Ada Goolsby	11/16/1892
Mercer, William	Sallie Waits	10/6/1881
Mercer, William F.	Frances Green	12/31/1849
Meriwether, Charles(col)	Annie Johnson (col)	10/9/1889
Meriwether, Dawson (col)	Emily Walker (col) Date issued	3/22/1868
Name on Certificate:		
Pearson, Auston	Julia Whitfield	3/22/1868
Meriwether, George (col)	Martha Clements (col)	12/27/1897
Meriwether, George	Lena Hempfield (Laura)	10/20/1907
Meriwether, Humphry	Mariah Roberts	1/24/1892
Meriwether, James	Dinah Lazenby	12/31/1869
Meriwether, Julius (col)	Elisebeth Griggs (col)	9/13/1874
Meriwether, Nelson	Emily Thomas	3/4/1876
Meriwether, Thomas	Miranda Walker	9/18/1860
Meriwether, Walter (col)	Emma Kate Singleton (col)	12/31/1895
Meriwether, Willie Flem (col)	Annie Goolsby (col)	2/23/1898
Merrit, Madrick	Barbara Cavender	3/12/1818
Middlebrooks, Batch (col)	Mrs. Rachael Goolsby (col)	1/24/1895
Middlebrooks, C. F.	Sallie Beck Persons	11/15/1892
Middlebrooks, Clark	Sally Sailor	2/24/1884
Middlebrooks, Jacob	Joseph Hunter	1/5/1882
Middlebrooks, James	Carrie Barker	10/21/1876
Middlebrooks, L. H.	L. A. King	11/4/1875
Middlebrooks, Robert (col)	Anna Perry (col)	12/30/1896
Middlebrooks, Robert L.	Mary C. Goodman	12/21/1890
Middlebrooks, Walter P.	Aurie I. Fullerton	12/15/1891
Middlebrooks, William H.	Biddie S. Malone	9/14/1865
Middlebrooks, William H., Jr.	Mollie E. Persons	12/4/1894
Mike, Monroe	Julia Freeman	12/30/1886
Millen, Henry D.	Nancy Jane Noles	11/28/1876
Millen, Henry D.	Lucy Allen	1/10/1888

```
Millen, Samuel              Cheney Tinsley            10/20/1877
Miller, A. J. (col)         Fannie Jordan (col)       11/2/1892
Miller, Jacob               Georgia Ann Pitts         3/30/1877
Miller, John (col)          Frances Tilman (col)      2/17/1907
Minter, Andrew (col)        Georgia Ann Smith (col)   8/28/1869
Minter, Andrew J.           Sarah E. Dougherty        1/15/1878
Minter, Collins (col)       Elizabeth Parks (col)     2/2/1889
Minter, Edmond (col)        Callie Maddux (col)       3/25/1894
Minter, Jeremiah P.         Jane E. Bailey            10/31/1848
Minter, John W.             Annie Lane                3/6/1890
Minter, Olin J.             Mary A. Driskell          12/16/1886
Minter, R. A.               Susan Letson              3/19/1865
Minter, R. A.               Mrs. A. J. Freeman        1/9/1896
Minter, Richard A.          Frances B. Byars          9/25/1887
Minter, Robert              Sarah Jane Steel          10/1/1857
Minter, Samuel              Mattie Davis              10/22/1901
Minter, Thomas              Elizabeth Goolsby         2/22/1885
Minter, Vincent (col)       Kate Pope (col)           2/27/1892
Minter, Wallace (col)       Ada Freeman (col)         9/24/1898
Minter, Warner (col)        Mary Morgan (col)         1/8/1898
Mitcheal, Richard           Mattie Wilson             10/4/1873
Mitchel, Davis (col)        Mary Fort (col)           3/12/1893
Mitchel, Henry (col)        Rena Lewis (col)          12/8/1868
Mitchel, Robert             Leah Henderson            1/8/1874
Mitchel, Tom (col)          Kattie Pou (col)          8/14/1892
Mitchell, Charlie (col)     Ida Varner (col)          11/18/1901
Mitchell, George            Amanda Jackson            12/25/1892
Mitchell, Henry (col)       Mariah Nash (col)         11/26/1891
Mitchell, Homer (col)       Betsy Jeffries (col)      2/6/1898
Mitchell, Isaac (col)       Cresie Howard (col)       5/5/1907
Mitchell, Wess (col)        Corer Evans (col)         10/14/1897
Mitchell, Will (col)        Julia Johnson (col)       9/22/1896
Mitchem, Byron E.           Addie Belle Doster        10/29/1901
Mohorn, Henry (col)         Matilda Hunter (col)      12/29/1867
Moleman, Stephen            Ellen Williams            1/3/1874
Monroe, Madison (col)       Genie Banks (col)         12/30/1898
Montgomery, David F.P.      Catherine F. Adams        12/19/1848
Moody, F. M.                Sarah Henderson           6/16/1914
(Request for marriage license to be mailed to F. M. Moody)
Moon, Bud (col)             Susie Dumas (col)         12/20/1896
Mooneyham, Charley Lee      Fannie Lou Meredith       12/26/1895
Moore, J. B.                Lelia Estell Cunard       8/19/1885
Moore, Jack (col)           Carrie Bell Hogans (col)  8/23/1898
Moore, William H.           Lucy T. Waits             11/17/1889
Moreland, G.W. (col)        Malinda Roberts (col)     12/6/1876
Morgan, Berry (col)         Georgia Goolsby (col)     1/19/1896
Morgan, James E.            Lula V. McKinley          12/18/1898
Morgan, Jefferson P.        Georgia Ann McClure       12/6/1865
Morgan, Jim (col)           Sallie Clark (col)        12/7/1893
Morgan, John (col)          Dollie Bell (col)         10/31/1896
Morgan, Newton Charles      Sallie A. Evans           8/2/1888
Morgan, Nix                 Margarett Allen           1/10/1889
Morgan, William             Polley Cross              2/19/1818


McDade, J. W.               Jennie Lane               11/1/1883
McDaniel, Adam (col)        Mandy Hales (col)         8/23/1877
McDaniel, Benjamin F.       Lucy F. McGahee           9/2/1869
McDaniel, W. T.             Haney E. Thornton         8/5/1873
McDonald, Alex G.           Balzona Chambers          11/12/1844
McDowell, Starling (col)    Maggie Morgan (col)       9/23/1898
McElheney, Barney F.        Nannie O. Pye             3/4/1869
McElheney, Judge (col)      Sarah Channel (col)       12/30/1897
```

McElhenney, Albert	Mary Jane Victrum	9/23/1885
McElhenney, Greene (col)	Sarah Preston (col)	1/3/1897
McElhenney, Hezekiah(col)	Lucy Fears (col)	12/28/1893
McElhenney, J. M.	Nancy J. Willingham	3/15/1870
McElhenney, James W.	Kate Tyler	12/15/1895
McElhenney, John H.	Rebeca A. Vincent	1/22/1867
McElhenney, John H.	Lucy N. Loyd	1/21/1870
McElhenney, John M.	Amie B. Eubanks	12/8/1886
McElhenney, Lee M.	Carrie Faulkner	7/19/1899
McElhenney, M. T.	M. A. Holloway	1/23/1877
McElhenney, Martin	Mattie Holloway	12/22/1885
McElhenney, Robert V.	Ada King	12/14/1892
McElhenney, Vincent H.	Mary E. Wise	10/20/1861
McElhenney, William	Catharine Kinard	1/6/1831
McElhenney, William H.	Mollie Willingham	12/12/1895
McElhenney, William J.	Mary Ramey	4/14/1870
McElhenny, George W.	M. F. Wise	12/20/1868
McGahee, W. H.	Mollie F. Whatley	9/2/1869
McGaughee, William R.	Eliza E. Perdue	12/18/1862
McGaughey, Benjamin F.	Elizabeth Smith	5/20/1860
McGhee, T. W.	Mary J. Cook	12/26/1893
McGinnis, Hamilton	Emma Z. Clark	12/24/1868
McGough, W. T.	Addie May Goolsby	12/22/1895
McGuire, Rich (col)	Delia Aiken (col)	12/30/1899
McInis, A.	Emma K. Goolsby	11/11/1891
McIntyre, J. W.	Genie Thompson	11/20/1892
McKinley, E. C.	Pearl Niblett	12/24/1899
McKinley, Eli B.	Emily Greer	11/19/1854
McKinley, Eli B.	Sarah Braddy	12/15/1884
McKinley, M. M.	Emma Leverett	10/28/1884
McKinley, William T.	Nannie J. Waldrep	12/24/1896
McKissack, Isaac	Louisa Avent	2/28/1883
McMichael, Charlie (col)	Mary Jane Patterson (col)	8/16/1890
McMichael, Ed (col)	Liza Ann Fish (col)	1/4/1902
McMichael, Emmit	Emmie Lee Wilks	2/10/1901
McMichael, Green L.	Elizabeth Hill	12/3/1817
McMichael, Griffin	Mollie Morgan	9/28/1898
McMichael, J. H.	Noma Ginc	10/16/189?
McMichael, Joe (col)	Rosa Waters (col)	12/29/1899
McMichael, John G.	Catherine McKissack	3/4/1852
(Certification of marriage by Ordinary)		
McMichael, John L.	R. E. A. Starr	9/28/1862
McMichael, John Lee	Flora Pearson	12/27/1891
McMichael, Lewis	Martha Alexander	10/5/1892
McMichael, P. B., Jr.	Mattie A. Chambers	5/13/1869
McMichael, P. B., Jr.	Alice S. Roberts	2/26/1885
McMichael, S. J.	Nancy Hensey	10/3/1872
McMichael, Shadrach I., Jr.	Zilla A. Almand	2/8/1893
McMichael, Vines Fish	Lenora Cornwell	12/21/1869
McMichael, W. G.	M. C. French	11/3/1885
McMichael, W.J., Jr.	Lela Griffin	3/21/1897
McMichael, W. S.	Addie B. Goolsby	11/5/1899
McMichael, Warren	Dealy Lynch (date iss.)	9/12/1872
McMichael, William J.	Emily J. Stewart	6/26/1873
McMichael, William J.	Lizzie McMichael	11/20/189?
McMichael, Zachariah W.	Charity Powell	11/12/181?
McNair, I. L.	Julia B. Hilton	4/5/1895
McNeal, Alfred (col)	Genie Kelly (col)	12/8/1892
Napier, James (col)	Sarah Reynolds (col)	12/27/186?
Napier, Mose	Adaline Williams	5/27/1883

Napper, Dock (col)	Leona Vinson (col)	5/15/1907
Nash, Boston (col)	Mittie Bell (col)	12/31/189?
Nash, James F.	Lula Aaron	12/26/188?
Nash, Lee	Sallie Humphrey	3/3/1883
Nash, Lee (col)	Judy Carter (col)	4/21/1890
Nash, Peter (col)	Lizzie Rodgers (col)	11/20/1891
Nash, Titus	Adaline Blackwell	1/31/1884
Nelson, John (col)	Mary Appling (col)	12/19/1867
Nelson, King (col)	Susie Waters (col)	12/28/189?
Nelson, Walter	Lenaan Holloway	1/10/1877
Nesby, Hiram	Croenlia Aslin (date iss)	12/2/1873
Newby, Hiram	Hannah Ridly	3/16/1887
Newman, William Frank	Ada Elder	11/11/189?
Newton, Aris	Cornelia Smith	10/6/1898
Newton, Arthur R.	Victoria A. Lane	10/2/1889
Newton, Charles Aris	Minnie Blackwell	1/6/1897
Newton, Emett	Elizabeth Farrar	7/21/1897
Newton, George W.	Mary J. Bogan	11/30/187?
Newton, O. H.	A. J. Cook	2/11/1874
Newton, Peter (col)	Fannie Smith (col)	12/26/189?
Niblett, Charlie	Mattie E. McClure	1/20/1876
Niblett, Charlie	Judson Couch	5/24/1896
Niblett, Eli (col)	Emma Williams (col)	8/25/1907
Niblett, H. M.	India McClure	12/23/1899
Niblett, J. H.	Martha Jane Edwards	3/2/1876
Niblett, James E.	Martha J. Morgan	12/20/1868
Niblett, James H.	Matilda D. Tyner	9/7/1865
Niblett, James I.	Mittie L. Waldrep	12/23/1897
Niblett, James L.	Jennie Turner	12/22/1901
Niblett, James M.	Lillie Cardell	5/5/1894
Nichols, Tom Jeff	Harriet Dennis	10/21/1886
Nickols, Richard	Mollie Williams	1/3/1889
Nicks, Frank (col)	Mary Jane Norwood (col)	4/5/1897
Night, Wiley	Cara F. Lewis	10/23/1876
Nix, Adam	Mintie Wilson	12/19/1872
Nix, Berry (col)	Hannah Smith (col)	12/28/1869
Nix, Julius (col)	Georgia Smith (col)	12/19/1890
Nix, Richard (col)	Georgia Ann Nash (col)	12/25/1892
Nolan, Thomas	Elizabeth Barr	12/12/1883
Nolen, John W.	Sarah Merriett	6/10/1888
Noles, Alfred	Clara Kilgore	11/29/1883
Noles, David G.	Mary Ann Parker	9/10/1860
Noles, J. H.	Mrs. Carrie L. Binford	12/16/1894
Noles, John	Annie Smith	6/23/1897
Noles, William A.	M. L. Edwards	11/9/1876
Noles, William D.	Mary E. Lovejoy	12/20/1860
Nolley, Alfred (col)	Mary Key (col)	12/18/1873
Nolley, George (col)	Mattie Benton (col)	12/25/1873
Nolley, Otis (col)	Labora Parks (col)	12/31/1899
Nolly, Isaac	Margarett Hightower	1/3/1874
Nolly, Isaac	Annie Pitcher	1/5/1888
Nolly, John (col)	Addie Barnes (col)	12/23/1891
Nolly, Troy (col)	Sallie Shy (col)	1/2/1907
Norman, Charley	Martha Pitts	1/1/1885
Norrid, Eli	Nettie Loftin	8/28/1872
Norris, James	Catharine Love	11/20/1817
Norris, Joel D.	Virginia L. Cardell	3/5/1890
Norris, Samuel G.	Mary Stone	11/25/1818
Norsworthy, James	Lottie Andrews	2/24/1896
Norwood, John	Peggy Loyd	3/9/1819
Odom, Dock (col)	Josie Vaughn (col)	12/12/1894

Odom, Luke	Fannie Strozier	4/11/1872
Odom, Taylor	Eliza Sanders	12/27/1883
O'Kelly, Francis M.	Mary A. Harris	4/26/1864
Oliver, Burrell (col)	Lizzie Goolsby (col)	1/25/1896
Oliver, John (col)	Lessie Branch (col)	3/21/1907
Orange, Titus (col)	Genie Holms (col)	4/15/1894
Orear, James F.	Claudie M. Faulkner	9/16/1886
Osburn, J. M.	Sallie Aaron	12/11/1873
Owens, Anderson (col)	Loudell Epps (col)	11/30/1899
Owens, J. M.	Marthena Cunard	
	(Consent to marry)	5/13/1864
Owens, Robert P.	Mattie Waggoner	1/1/1887
Oxford, Edward I.	Kittie Malone	4/8/1888
Ozburn, E. C.	Lessie Lewis	4/7/1901
Ozburn, William M.	Gertrude Turner	12/20/1893
Also see Ausbern, George		
Paine, T. M.	Nannie Persons	1/24/1884
Park, Quedallous S.	Celestia E. Dennis	8/26/1888
Parker, A. J.	E. A. Wilson	11/26/1874
Parker, Chris	Ella Thomas	6/19/1892
Parker, Jacob	Lizzie Benton	1/4/1874
Parker, James	Sarah J. Pope	11/26/1874
Parker, James M.	Jemimah C. Polk	12/15/1853
Parker, John H.	Mattie I. Tucker	12/29/1895
Parker, Sidney R.	Isabel Fincher	7/6/1847
Parker, Thomas M.	Martha Ann Kitchens	7/25/1869
Parks, Jack	Frances Wyatt	1/16/1877
Parks, Thomas (col)	Ophelia Carter (col)	3/3/1895
Parks, William W.	Margarett A. Maddux	12/22/1846
Parker, Jesse	Polly McDaniel	11/12/1818
Parnell, John W.	Sallie B. Cornwell	11/7/1876
Parr, Jasper N.	Carrie McMichael	1/14/1875
Paton, Levi (col)	Fannie Glover (col)	12/18/1897
Patrick, Anthony (col)	Henrietta Moss (col)	5/29/1868
Patrick, Charly (col)	Silva Ann Williams (col)	2/14/1898
Patterson, Rich (col)	Lela Fears (col)	8/31/1899
Patterson, Wade (col)	Sallie Morton (col)	6/26/1875
Patton, Matthew	Pulley Bennett	12/24/1818
Peacock, Aaron (col)	Lucy Jane Meriwether(col)	11/29/1893
Peacock, Dudley	Penney Jackson	4/18/1869
Peacock, Gill (col)	Georgia Stewart (col)	2/10/1898
Peacock, Joe (col)	Louisiana Holland (col)	9/10/1891
Pearson, Austin (col)	Julia Whitfield (col)	3/22/1868
Pearson, Ellis	Mollie Glover	12/27/1883
Pearson, George (col)	Lucy Hogan (col)	9/17/1896
Pearson, John W.	Eliza Wilson	8/12/1868
Pearson, Reese (col)	Abbie Roberts (col)	12/25/1873
Pearson, William (col)	Harriet Holloway (col)	5/25/1890
Pearsons, Andrew J.	Annie Dougherty	12/18/1884
Peddie, Moses	Sallie Rivers	9/3/1875
Peddy, Morris (col)	Betsy Ann Allen (col)	12/25/1890
Peddy, Mort (col)	Lula Pounds (col)	12/30/1897
Pendergrass, H. N.	Hattie E. Geiger	3/5/1873
Penn, A. A.	Salina Penn	2/24/1873
Penn, Aaron	Alice Byars	12/28/1881
Penn, Andrew Jackson (col)	Mary Jane Price (col)	2/12/1887
Penn, F. L.	Leona Bullard	6/29/1899
Penn, Henry	Martha Humphries	1/11/1878
Penn, J. A.	M. T. Grubbs	11/11/1875
Penn, Russell J.	Maud Phillips	2/28/1874
Penn, Thomas	Patience Pritchett	10/31/1872

Penn, William J.	Miranda White	12/4/1888
Pennamon, Morris	Patsy Billingsly	12/26/1872
Pennell, John O.	Sarah C. Stone	7/20/1876
Penniman, Morris	Mary J. Franklin	1/6/1877
Pennington, G. F.	Vallie D. Malone	5/16/1897
Pennington, Samuel S.	Mrs. Almeta M. Wynens	9/3/1892
Pennington, William B.	Mary Phillips	6/15/1817
Pennyman, John Wesley (col)	Lillie Carter (col)	10/1/1896
Penton, John	Elizabeth Brooks	12/4/1816
Perkins, J. O.	Berta Malone	2/2/1898
Perkins, John	Cheney Coleman	3/7/1891
Perkins, William J.	Laney Hitchcock	11/20/1893
Perry, Bose (col)	Ida Banks (col)	12/29/1898
Perry, Daniel	Manda Henderson	1/4/1874
Perry, Green	Martha Smith	12/23/1886
Perry, Jerry	Susie Ann Smith	12/29/1884
Perry, Joe (col)	Josie Brittain (col)	1/8/1891
Perry, Joseph (col)	Nancy Robinson (col)	12/27/1867
Perry, Moses (col)	Liza Spears (col)	2/5/1873
Perry, Thomas (col)	Elmira Kelly (col)	9/24/1893
Perry, Wayman W.	Lizzie Lee Kelley	3/24/1907
Persley, George T.	Mrs. Ardecie Stewart	3/8/1865
Persons, Burrell (col)	Annie Crain (col)	4/6/1899
Persons, Jeff (col)	Martha Darden (col)	8/11/1887
Persons, John (col)	Carrie Minter (col)	3/19/1894
Persons, R. F.	Mollie Banks	1/31/1884
Persons, Thomas B.	Kittie Middlebrooks	4/11/1895
Persons, William P.	Mary A. Kelly	12/22/1853
Persons, Willie F.	Lena Harris	12/6/1892
Petrie, C. B.	Ina Maud Kelly	6/7/1893
Peurifoy, Bragg	Mollie Roby	6/10/1888
Peurifoy, Bragg (col)	Annie Walker (col)	12/18/1894
Peurifoy, Gus (col)	Mattie Fears (col)	9/25/1887
Peurifoy, Henry	Harriet Odum	12/18/1884
Peurifoy, James	Oda Middlebrooks	6/7/1893
Phelps, Charly (col)	Hattie Jefferson (col)	12/26/1895
Phelps, Oliver (col)	Katie Bray (col)	11/17/1894
Phelps, William N.	Elizabeth Skiner	7/7/1853
Phillips, Charley	Hannah Greer	10/5/1837
Phillips, Clem (col)	Mattie Walker (col)	1/10/1898
Phillips, Floyd (col)	Caroline Brooks (col)	5/1/1869
Phillips, Henry	Sidney Glover	2/16/1888
Phillips, John B. M.	Catharine B. Freeman	2/9/1847
Phillips, John B. M.	Mrs. Mary E. McDowell	12/16/1869
Phillips, John W.	Mary Lane	12/19/1815
Phillips, John W.	Mattie Watters	4/10/1887
Phillips, Lewis I.	Sarah Ann Dukes	4/5/1850
Phillips, Scott (col)	Tempy Nash (col)	11/1/1887
Phillips, Stephen J.	Matilda Comer	4/12/1866
Phillips, Webster	Mrs. Martha Watters	11/17/1889
Phillips, Wiley H.	Emma E. Pulley	3/11/1869
Phillips, Wiley J.	Maggie Lee Fish	3/27/1892
Phillips, Wiley J.	Corine Fish	12/27/1896
Phillips, William S.	Annie Dawkins	11/28/1895
Phillips, Willie (col)	Callie Gill (col)	12/26/1893
Pickens, Thomas (col)	Lucy Polk (col) (date issued)	12/24/1907
Pickens, Tilman (col)	Laura Phelps (col)	12/17/1899
Pickens, Tilmon (col)	Evaline Minter (col)	12/29/1887
Pickett, Leroy	Emma Thompson	1/21/1889
Pickins, William	Polley Williams	11/13/1817
Pierce, Banley	Phoebe Luckie	1/26/1817

42

Pierce, John (col)	Kittie Simonds (col)	1/20/1901
Pinckard, Thomas C.	Susan Crane	6/24/1818
Pinnell, Lee	Lou Hardy	1/13/1889
Pioer, J. O.	Minnie Ritchey	11/17/1897
Piper, John	Amande Moss	11/14/1868
Piper, Thomas R.	Lemma Anne J. Johnson	4/23/1868
Piper, Zadock	Victoria Scott	2/5/1863
Pitmon, Dudley (col)	Mrs. Ann Freeman (col)	11/3/1894
Pitmon, Ezell (col)	Mattie Lou Campbell (col)	6/9/1895
Pitts, Chaney	Sally Colwell	4/19/1818
Pitts, Charles N.	Julia Bowdoin	1/6/1876
Pitts, Eugene (col)	Annie Kelly (col)	12/29/1908
Pitts, Henry	Laney Shy	7/14/1872
Pitts, Henry	Susan Thomas	11/28/1874
Pitts, J. A.	Fannie L. Cardell	11/22/1877
Pitts, J. E.	Nora E. Curry	12/12/1901
Pitts, James (col)	Lizzie Carr (col)	12/26/1889
Pitts, M. W.	Elizabeth Bowden	1/6/1878
Pitts, Manson	Annie Robinson	12/28/1881
Pitts, Pleas (col)	Lizzie Heard (col)	3/3/1901
Pitts, Thomas (col)	Margaret Brown (col)	11/13/1892
Pitts, Wesley (col)	Malissa Hogan (col)	10/2/1898
Pitts, Will (col)	Amanda McGuire (col)	1/17/1895
Pitts, William (col)	Florence Banks (col)	9/24/1899
Plowmale, Thomas	Lizzie Long	8/27/1899
Plymale, T. W.	Isabella Speear	
	(date issued)	4/9/1872
Plymale, W.	S. K. Letson	12/9/1875
Polk, Frank	Georgia Thomas	11/4/1896
Polk, J. A.	S. M. Key	1/8/1874
Polk, J. K.	Frances Caroline Minter	11/5/1867
Polk, James T.	Lela A. Moore	11/13/1887
Polk, John	Carl Thomas	11/17/1898
Polk, William H. A.	Harriet A. Chaffin	10/9/1884
Polk, William O.	Nancy E. Fisher	12/11/1860
Pon, Nuck	Jane McGuire	7/6/1867
Ponder, S. M.	A. F. Aiken	12/6/1894
Pope, A. H.	Ella Waits	1/18/1888
Pope, Andrew (col)	Emma Liza Nolley (col)	12/24/1897
Pope, Burwell	Sarah Harrison	10/5/1865
Pope, Charles W.	Mollie E. Hunter	12/19/1877
Pope, Daniel (col)	Susan Barber (col)	9/17/1890
Pope, Doc	Laura Gotier	10/28/1882
Pope, Hopson J.	Harriet E. Clark	8/14/1849
Pope, J. E. (col)	Ida Heard (col)	10/9/1892
Pope, James J.	Indiana Talmadge	12/22/1869
Pope, Josiah P.	Catharine Giles	9/19/1889
Pope, L. L.	Mattie Lewis	11/30/1899
Pope, Laurance L.	Florence Couch	11/26/1882
Pope, Lucius (col)	Carrie Burney (col)	12/28/1896
Pope, Miller W.	Charlotte E. Faulkner	10/20/1868
Pope, Miller W.	Mary J. Hooks	1/20/1869
Pope, Rufus (col)	Mattie Johnson (col)	12/29/1897
Pope, S. M.	Annie Baldwin	12/16/1875
Pope, Thomas C.	Annie M. Willson	2/17/1870
Pope, Wash	Sarah Blower	2/3/1883
Pope, Willie	Vesta Williams	11/5/1907
Porter, Henry (col)	Fannie Gates (col)	1/7/1892
Porter, John Henry (col)	Mrs. Lula Turner (col)	12/26/1897
Portwood, Howard	Lucy Polk	10/23/1901
Portwood, John H.	Mary E. Cornwell	12/28/1892
Portwood, Montgomery	Hattie C. Dyar	11/25/1888
Portwood, Thomas J.	F. J. Hodges	11/9/1875

Potts, Stephen	Nancy Colley	2/22/1818
Pou, Carey	Lucinda Whitfield	9/16/1886
Pou, Carie (col)	Lizzie Watters (col)	2/19/1874
Pou, Edmond	Tomie Mitchel	5/1/1884
Pou, John W. (col)	Sylvester Cooper (col)	12/28/1867
Pou, Turner	Mary Roswell	12/30/1886
Pou, Wesley	Jomima Ridley	1/22/1887
Pound, Eli E.	Sallie A. Leverette	10/4/1859
Pound, Eli E.	Susie F. Conner	12/16/1896
Pound, Paul P.	Alma J. McNair	6/1/1898
Pounds, John	Della Walker	12/31/1897
Pounds, Tommie (col)	Janie Hancock (col)	2/10/1894
Powell, Albert	Eliza Ann Jackson	10/26/1884
Powell, Augustus W.	Cornelia Millen	12/23/1866
Powell, Benjamin W.	Ester M. Geiger	7/30/1862
Powell, Cornelius (col)	Frances White (col)	3/13/1875
Powell, Davis	Carrie Smith	10/8/1885
Powell, Evan H.	Mary Davis Jordan	12/19/1893
Powell, James (col)	Ida Kelly (col)	12/14/1889
Powell, John (col)	Susan White (col)	12/12/1874
Powell, John (col)	Mrs. Frances Penn (col)	4/6/1889
Powell, Lewis (col)	Carrie Lou Jordan (col)	
	(Date issued)	2/3/1903
Powell, Norborne	Eliza Holmes	12/10/1818
Powell, William R.	Fannie Folds	11/3/1859
Powell, William R.	Agnes C. Webb	11/16/1893
Powell, Woody (col)	Ellen Benton (col)	12/27/1890
Power, Charles G.	Eva E. Elder	12/31/1888
Preston, Aaron (col)	Nice Barnes (col)	3/3/1895
Preston, Charley (col)	Emma Holland (col)	10/3/1891
Preston, Elbert (col)	Leila Blackwell (col)	1/1/1891
Preston, John	Amanda Persons	12/27/187?
Preston, John (col)	Lula Ben (col)	12/26/189?
Preston, Johnie (col)	Mary Doster (col)	10/16/190?
Preston, Joseph W.	Victoria V. Leverett	10/3/1865
Preston, Riley	India Kelly	2/1/1885
Preston, T. G.	Mary T. Pulley	5/25/1876
Preston, W. J. M.	Bessie Malone	11/24/1886
Preston, William B.	Mary A. Blackwell	12/29/1881
Preston, William J. M.	Angeline N. Pou	12/18/186?
Price, Calhoun	Jennie Waits	3/27/1890
Price, Crawford (col)	Mary Jane Williams (col)	1/30/1890
Price, Isaac	Harriet Preston	11/26/188?
Price, John (col)	Miranda Smith (col)	1/3/1892
Price, Oscar D.	Addie Stone	6/9/1907
Price, Robert (col)	Dora Freeman (col)	12/26/189?
Price, Robert W.	Sophia C. Hardy	3/28/1865
Price, Stephen (col)	Mattie Shropshire (col)	1/21/1897
Price, Turner	Ardena Worthy	2/17/1877
Price, Wash (col)	Lucinda Thomas (col)	11/3/1885
(Certification of marriage by Ordinary)		
Prince, Reuben	Ginnie Smith	2/14/1892
Pritchett, Abraham	Henrietta Barker	12/28/1871
Pritchett, Alexander	George Ann Smith	1/23/1873
Pritchett, Alfred M.	Drucilla Lowe	4/13/1858
Pritchett, Thomas (col)	Ellen Jackson (col)	1/2/1891
Pritchett, William	Cheney Nichols	9/14/1867
Pritchett, William (col)	Babe Banks (col)	
	(Date issued)	1/28/1875
Proctor, Henry	Harriet Watson	12/31/1888
Proctor, Joseph J.	Carrie Hardy	1/1/1885
Pullam, Bluford	Susan A. Cunard	1/24/1858
Purington, William	Delia Maxey	12/18/1886

Pye, Burrell J.	Martha J. Malone	6/9/1857
Pye, Edward H.	Lucy A. Kimbell	9/23/1860
Pye, Stephen (col)	Ellen Brown (col)	4/16/1868
Pye, Thomas W.	Sarah P. Allen	1/17/1888
Pye, Wade (col)	Elizabeth Smith (col)	2/13/1893
Pye, William H.	Adella Thomson	11/21/189?
Pue, William	Mat Brown	5/18/1873
Quaker, Alexander (col)	Angerona Goolsby (col)	2/13/1890
Radford, Charles (col)	Georgia Bearden (col)	8/23/1894
Radford, Mose (col)	Patience Rivers (col)	9/25/1887
Ragan, Berry (col)	Rhoda Pearson (col)	10/9/1891
Ragland, Milledge	Delia Darden	12/23/188?
Ragland, Milledge (col)	Mariah McElhenney (col)	12/23/189?
Raglin, Jack	Kissiah Reagen	10/2/1875
Ramey, Ike (col)	Mary J. Rutledge (col)	12/26/1891
Ramey, Nathaniel H.	Mary Ann Garrett	11/17/1853
Randal, Richmond (col)	Lucy Jane Goolsby (col)	12/27/1891
Ray, Joseph (col)	Jane Vaughn (col)	11/?/1870
Rea, David A.	Mary E. Wilson	7/24/1892
Redman, Charles (col)	Maggie Minter (col)	1/29/1901
Reece, William (col)	Mary Jackson (col)	3/9/1901
Reese, Albert	Emeline Cargill	1/2/1877
Reese, Allen	Joanna Broddus	1/18/1873
Reese, America (col)	Mary Glover (col)	2/6/1869
Reese, Charlie (col)	Sallie White (col)	10/24/1898
Reese, Jim	Emaline Thomas	11/18/1887
Reese, Peter (col)	Charlotte Gardner (col)	12/25/1890
Reese, Sam	Ann Hughes	1/1/1888
Reese, Samuel (col)	Anna Bird (col)	1/11/1894
Reese, Samuel, Jr.	Joanna Fuller	6/27/1885
Reese, Thornton	Henrietta Barron	11/1/1887
Reese, Titus	Josephine Byran	12/29/1869
Reese, William (col)	Minnie Vincent (col)	10/12/1893
Reeves, Ben	Mollie Greer	3/27/1883
Reeves, Benjamin F.	Casand Smith	11/25/1869
Reeves, Joseph	Allah H. Wade	7/6/1848
Reeves, Warner (col)	Mrs. Alice Jackson (col)	1/11/1896
Reid, Alfred	Emma Williams	1/16/1886
Reid, Augustus (col)	Nancy Cheek (col)	8/9/1893
Reid, Ben (col)	Hattie Brooks (col)	10/29/1893
Reid, Charlie, Jr.(col)	Dilla Williams (col)	11/20/1890
Reid, Dennis (col)	Minnie Johnson (col)	10/29/1892
Reid, George W.	Mary Reynolds	4/22/1852
Reid, John (col)	Nancy Humphry (col)	6/22/1896
Reid, Lilburn H.	Eileen McNair	10/15/1899
Reid, Nathan (col)	Martha Roswell (col)	8/21/1887
Reid, Robert Robinson	Ruth Hill	10/17/1907
Reid, Willie (col)	Emma Roberts (col)	3/4/1892
Renfoe, James T.	Martha P. Lane	3/23/1854
Ressan, Evan	Carrie Phillips	12/27/1895
Ressean, George M.	Minnie Lee Jones	3/22/1894
Reynolds, Jule (col)	Mattie Smith (col)	12/30/1907
Reynolds, Patrick	Martha Jasters	11/27/1886
Rhimes, Littlejohn	Miram Clowers	12/17/1815
Richard, John	Augusta Jordan	12/18/1886
Richards, Duke (col)	Mary Brazel (col)	5/8/1896
Richards, Gabriel (col)	Margaret Jeffries (col)	12/10/1891
Richards, George (col)	Jane Whitfield (col)	10/2/1890
Richards, Jerre (col)	Sallie Meriwether (col)	12/27/1896

Richards, John (col)	Ida Gates (col)	3/3/1895
Richards, Robert	Margarett Taylor	3/17/1887
Richards, Seaborn (col)	Beatrice Broddus (col)	12/29/1892
Richards, William (col)	Chaney Walker (col)	8/20/1893
Richardson, James	Amanda Hale	5/13/1876
Rickerson, Harman	Mary Manes	6/5/1897
Rickett, C. A.	Lilian Piper	12/23/1897
Ricketts, John M.	Ellen Nolen	8/4/1881
Ricketts, Tilman O.	Cynthia M. Nolan	3/18/1886
Ridley, Charles (col)	Matilda Thurman (col)	12/29/1896
Ridley, Frank (col)	Lou Morgan (col)	12/28/1882
Ridley, Marshall (col)	Eliza Myrick (col)	12/27/1890
Ridley, Steve (col)	Lena Morgan (col)	12/31/1897
Ridley, William (col)	Mrs. Mason Walton (col)	10/4/1888
Ridley, William Thom	Grace Robinson	12/12/1907
Ridley, Willie (col)	Mattie Ross (col)	11/22/1897
Riggins, John	Henrietta Smith	1/10/1897
Riggins, Scott (col)	Lula Thompson (col)	12/31/1899
Ritchey, Edward, Jr.	Berta May Cargle	9/30/1898
Ritchie, Spencer	Florida Alexander	12/30/1886
Rivers, C. K.	Julia Standifer	1/2/1906
Rivers, Cary (col)	Henrietta Thomas (col)	2/28/1868
Rivers, Lee (col)	Mary Hunter (col)	12/29/1897
Rivers, William (col)	Lavina Ridley (col)	3/26/1896
Rivers, Willis	Aggie Clements	12/2/1869
Roach, John Lee	Mary Ann Banks	3/8/1885
Roberson, Elbert	Mary George	1/29/1886
Roberson, George (col)	Annis Benton (col)	1/12/1890
Roberson, John H.	Zipporah Spears	11/7/1876
Roberson, S. A. (col)	Millie Jordan (col)	12/18/1898
Roberson, Sam (col)	Mary Kate Davis (col)	12/30/1897
Roberts, Brown (col)	Mattie Thurmond (col)	4/10/1890
Roberts, Charley (col)	Minnie Boykin (col)	12/30/1907
Roberts, Daniel A.	Sallie Tyner	12/31/1885
Roberts, Elias W.	Blakeley S. Shy	1/7/1867
Roberts, Eugenius R.	Blandina E. Mullins	4/14/1859
Roberts, Guilford	Tex Maddux	12/29/1881
Roberts, Harvey	Cora Wormley	1/12/1897
Roberts, Henry (col)	Terrill Cooper (col)	12/28/1868
Roberts, J. A.	Maud Faulkner	3/10/1898
Roberts, J. R.	Mattie F. Childers	5/31/1896
Roberts, J. W.	Anna M. Nolen	5/2/1876
Roberts, James (col)	Amanda Scarver (col)	9/1/1889
Roberts, John (col)	Mary Jackson (col)	1/26/1893
Roberts, Joseph	Sallie F. Gordon	9/22/1887
Roberts, Laurence W.	Minnie G. Newton	9/8/1886
Roberts, Leander	Mary Frances Fears	10/13/1883
Roberts, Lucious (col)	Aray Hawkins (col)	12/30/1890
Roberts, Peyton	Florence Harper	3/26/1899
Roberts, W. V.	Lula Kennon	1/12/1898
Roberts, William O.	Lura Adams	7/19/1891
Robertson, Samuel (col)	Charlott Davis (col)	12/26/1897
Robertson, Willis	Julia Ridley	5/10/1884
Robinson, Alex (col)	Lizzie Waters (col)	4/6/1893
Robinson, Burt (col)	Mattie Lou Perry (col)	7/28/1894
Robinson, Cary (col)	Lucy Rossel (col)	11/10/1895
Robinson, Charles (col)	Adline Nelson (col)	9/4/1875
Robinson, Clark S. (col)	Ada Maxey (col)	1/5/1899
Robinson, Earnest	Betsy Smith	10/19/1882
Robinson, Hartwell	Martha Digby	1/6/1887
Robinson, Hiliard	Hannah Malone	4/27/1873
Robinson, Ike (col)	Carrie Roswell (col)	12/25/1897
Robinson, Isaac,Jr.(col)	Mrs. Sallie Broddus(col)	9/14/1893

Robinson, Isham (col)	Tilda Bryant (col)	8/18/1876
Robinson, Jep (col)	Anna White (col)	3/5/1874
Robinson, Jerry (col)	Louraney Odum (col)	11/9/1890
Robinson, Jim (col)	Sarah Digby (col)	3/2/1897
Robinson, Jim (col)	Carrie Blackwell (col)	3/14/1899
Robinson, John (col)	Lizzie Goolsby (col)	3/31/1898
Robinson, John L.	Sarah Cornelia Smith	2/22/1849
Robinson, Josiah	Rose Smith	2/20/1883
Robinson, Kinion (col)	Sallie Smith (col)	7/21/1887
Robinson, Perry	Frances Howard	12/28/1881
Robinson, Peter (col)	Florence Roby (col)	11/10/1907
Robinson, Sherman (col)	Beckie Gaither (col)	5/27/1894
Robinson, Solomon (col)	Lula Hutchison (col)	1/18/1890
Robinson, Wallace	Jane Gilstrap	4/4/1881
Robinson, Wallace	Sarah Lovejoy	12/26/1888
Robinson, William C.	Sarah F. Morgan	7/6/1848
Robinson, Willie (col)	Mattie Smith (col)	1/17/1891
Robinson, Willia (col)	Mrs. Susan Ann Perry(col)	3/12/1889
Roby, George (col)	Martha Jackson (col)	7/1/1875
Roby, James (col)	Ida Bell (col)	12/27/1888
Roby, James R.	Lucy A. Ledbetter	1/15/1863
Roby, John (col)	Kittie Ann Peurifoy (col)	2/6/1893
Roby, John (col)	Harriet Holloway (col)	7/23/1893
Roby, Walter L.	Adel L. Wilson	12/10/1876
Roby, Walter L.	Addie L. McMichael	7/2/1891
Roby, William (col)	Emma Couch (col)	12/31/1896
Roby, Willie (col)	Mary Davis Jordan (col)	12/30/1892
Rock, Philip (col)	Nancy Pope (col)	7/21/1873
Rodgers, Charles (col)	Ollie Nash (col)	2/5/1891
Rodgers, Robert Y.	Mrs. Martha E. Carter	5/30/1888
Rodgers, Vincent (col)	Celia Hicks (col)	11/13/1891
Rodgers, Vincent (col)	Catharine Glover (col)	2/24/1894
Rogers, George	Mollie Jeffries	9/26/1885
Rogers, Wiley S.	Florine Flournoy	1/16/1901
Roland, A. P.	Carrie Roberts	8/26/1875
Rooks, Alex (col)	Lula Moorhon (col)	7/6/1895
Rooks, Alexander (col)	Louisa Chugs (col)	6/1/1870
Rooks, Alexander	Frazier Allen	5/19/1873
Rooks, Dudley (col)	Matilda Goolsby (col)	12/29/1898
Rooks, Joe (col)	Maria Maddox (col)	1/6/1898
Rooks, Johnnie (col)	Zadie Clements (col)	4/10/1907
Rooks, Simon (col)	Carrie Glawson (col)	3/13/1898
Rooks, William	Amanda Standifer	12/20/1883
Rooks, William (col)	Bula Clements (col)	12/1/1907
Ross, Berny	Sally Pitts (Date Iss.)	1/2/1877
Ross, George,Jr.(col)	Eugene Baynes (col)	1/8/1897
Ross, Henry (col)	Juliann Hawkins (col)	10/27/1887
Ross, John (col)	Genie Brown (col)	12/12/1893
Ross, Rich (col)	Sue Sellers (col)	10/7/1907
Ross, Thomas (col)	Sena Baynes (col)	12/7/1892
Ross, William	Betsey Compton	7/7/1818
Roswell, John (col)	Elizabeth Broddus (col)	1/23/1898
Roswell, Robert (col)	Titt Branch (col)	12/26/1889
Rowe, J. C.	Seliency Tomerson	12/14/1850
Rowland, G. W.	Julia Jordan	8/7/1884
Rowland, O. P.	A. V. Shy	12/1/1874
Rozell, Joe	Caroline Badger	11/16/1884
Russel, Ben (col)	Henrietta Barber (col)	6/11/1891
Russel, Henry (col)	Mollie Johnson (col)	10/6/1895
Russel, Jesse	Georgia Fears	10/28/1884
Russel, Monroe (col)	Anna Smith (col) Issued	12/24/1874
Russel, Richard (col)	Adaline Goolsby (col)	12/9/1892
Russell, Albert (col)	Viola Shaw (col)	12/15/1907

Russell, Jordan (col)	Ida Jackson (col)	11/12/1899
Russell, Major (col)	Lizzie Spearman (col)	12/28/1897
Russell, William (col)	Lucy Jordan (col)	7/27/1889
Saddler, Sam (col)	Onie Johnson (col)	1/26/1901
Saddler, Samuel	Dora Tuggle	11/29/1898
Saddler, Willie (col)	Sarah Walker (col)	1/10/1901
Saffold, Ben (col)	Amarintha Preston (col)	12/25/1892
Saffold, Dexter	Lizzie Kelly	9/3/1882
Saffold, Eberhart (col)	Hattie Ann Jenkins (col)	1/3/1892
Sandefer, Thomas B.	Martha Ann M. Kinard	6/21/1881
Sandefer, Isaac (col)	Berta Penn (col)	6/4/1898
Sanders, Allen	Clarra Holoway	12/29/190?
Sanders, B. H.	Anna E. Leverett	1/23/1873
Sanders, Clifford B.	Ida Johnson	1/26/1897
Sanders, Hardy (col)	Mattie Toland (col)	10/22/189?
Sanders, Jim (col)	Sylvia Toland (col)	3/28/1891
Sanders, Pleasant (col)	Mariah Holt (col)	3/27/1875
Sanders, R. W.	Mrs. Mary Ann Bryant	8/16/1868
Sanders, Robert (col)	Cora Wright (col)	6/9/1890
Sanders, Wash	Canthia Cochran	2/4/1877
Sands, James	Leila Middlebrooks	2/6/1897
Sands, Tom	Mollie Broddus	3/11/1883
Satterwhite, W. D.	Carrie Head	11/25/1888
Saunders, Clifford B.	Addie Leverett	10/5/1890
Sawyer, King	Loney Key	12/29/1884
Scott, Jacob	Patsey Chafin	6/24/1817
Scott, Levi (col)	Nannie Dougherty (col)	12/5/1901
Scott, William R.	Ruby Holland	1/22/1895
Scroggins, Fielder	Anny Bender	1/3/1817
	(Date on License)	12/29/1818
Seymore, A. H.	Luvana Doster	7/15/1873
Seymore, L. R.	Cynthia M. Lane	2/18/1849
Shackleford, Collin	Mary (Polley) Hodge	7/17/1861
Shannon, James M.	Mary Ann Freeman	7/17/1861
Shaver, Henry	Nancy Price	8/25/1816
Shaw, C. A.	Jennie McMichael	4/11/1897
Shaw. J. S.	Anna Newton	10/7/1874
Shaw, James N.	Serena C. Kelly	1/25/1872
Shaw. Joseph S.	Wadie Allen	12/21/1899
Shaw, Ned	Ann Jackson	12/1/1872
Shaw, Willie K.	Irma Kennon	6/13/1899
Sheilds, Augustus	Isabella McKissack	3/8/1879
Shepherd, Hence (col)	Tack Walker (col)	3/29/1896
Shepherd, John M.	Mrs. Minerva E.Shepherd	9/1/1870
Shepherd, Wash	Grace Ann Fagan	1/27/1888
Shepherd, Weldon K.	Elizabeth Thompson	2/28/1893
Sherman, Wiley (col)	Annie Pounds (col)	5/2/1897
Shields, Harvey (col)	Fannie Wise (col)	1/21/1897
Shields, Thomas (col)	Lucy White (col)	3/13/1897
Shockley, George W.	Mrs. Elizabeth Grubbs	5/5/1861
Shoners, Elias	Georgia Ann Freeman	
	(Date issued)	6/28/1873
Short, William T.	Parthena Harding	3/12/1817
Showers, Eldridge (col)	Fannie Gordon (col)	1/25/1893
Shropshire, Charles H.	Annie Smith	9/27/1896
Shropshire, John W.	Rebecca Waits	12/24/1868
Shropshire, W. D.	Annie L. Turner	1/1/1891
Shropshire, Wiley (col)	Matilda Goolsby (col)	2/12/1891
Shropshire, William W.	Emily Holloway	10/13/1867
Shy, Anderson (col)	Indiana Carter (col)	1/16/1896
Shy, Chess (col)	Lovie Bryant (col)	11/22/1894

48

```
Shy, Ephraim (col)        Mitta Smith (col)          5/11/1867
Shy, Frank (col)          Adaline Washington (col)   2/2/1896
Shy, Freeman (col)        Randa Showers (col)        12/22/1870
Shy, Joe (col)            Rachael James (col)        11/27/1898
Shy, John (col)           Ella Akens (col)           11/15/1868
Shy, John Wesley (col)    Mary Cullen (col)          9/1/1895
Shy, Joseph (col)         Cora Smith (col)           12/22/1870
Shy, Joseph (col)         Charlotte Cargile (col)    1/1/1891
Shy, Lewis                Georgia A. Smith           12/26/1872
Shy, Lucius (col)         Mary Vaughn (col)          1/9/1890
Shy, Milas (col)          Amanda Preston (col)       12/30/1894
Shy, Peter                Carry Showers              12/21/1876
Shy, Peyton R.            Elizabeth Jane Green       7/3/1864
                           (Consent to marry)        7/1/1864
Shy, Pleas                Delia Robinson             12/26/1885
Shy, Robert L.            Annie Ella Honeycutt       3/25/1889
Shy, Sidney (col)         Ella Ivy (col)             2/18/1893
Shy, Thaddeus P.          Mary A. Binford            4/21/1864
Shy, W. V.                Lizzie King                6/29/1897
Shy, William              Maggie Hunt(Name on cert)12/30/1897
     Name on license     Liney Broughton
(Oath of T. Shy, asking to change name of bride on license)
                                                     2/10/1898
Shy, William R.           Mary L. Fitzpatrick        11/8/1893
Shy, William V.           Florence Tucker            10/25/1885
Shy, Willie (col)         Mrs. Mattie Malone (col)   1/18/1894
Shy, Wyatt (col)          Jennie Jeffries (col)      1/25/1893
Sillivant, George         Winney Harris              8/?/1818
(Name on license, Johnson Sillivant)
Simens, Dock (col)        Eva Lofton (col)           1/11/1868
Simmons, Allen G.         Nancy Germany              11/13/1817
Simmons, G. M.            Sarah J. Jenkins           2/6/1864
(Consent from Guardian)
Simmons, John             Juda Goodrum               10/27/1894
Simon, Frank              Emily Rodgers              11/1/1888
Simpson, Charles Robert   Louvora Dukes              8/28/1883
Singleton, Charley (col)  Clara Bell Smith (col)     4/10/1898
Singleton, Elisha (col)   Dolly Seaborn (col)        11/10/1896
Singleton, Henry (col)    Amanda Smith (col)         12/26/1897
Singleton, Lee            Emaline Malone             3/22/1883
Singleton, Monroe         Elizabeth Cooper           12/31/1872
Singleton, Monroe (col)   Carrie Bird (col)          10/25/1896
Singleton, Tom (col)      Fannie Kate Goolsby (col)  1/31/1907
Skinner, Robert           Polley Downey              8/7/1818
                           (Date on License)         8/7/1817
Slack, Ambrose            Carrie Patterson           11/23/1877
Slack, William (col)      Mary Mitchell (col)        9/4/1890
Slaughter, Henry (col)    Mary Tanner (col)          10/31/1894
Slaughter, Jacob          Marier Minter              1/1/1873
Slaughter, Robin          Lucy Fears                 3/1/1876
Slaughter, Tom Allen      Martha Ann Proctor         12/6/1891
  (col)                     (col)
Slaughter, Wilkins        Elizabeth Elder            5/6/1883
Slocumb, John E.          Jennie M. Spearman         12/6/1892
Sluder, John H.           Anna Jeffries              12/13/1877
Sluter, A. L.             Carry H. Tuggle            4/28/1872
Smith, A. F.              E. C. Kitchens             9/12/1865
Smith, Aaron (col)        Sallie Kelly (col)         2/3/1867
Smith, Abe (col)          Willie Coop (col)          10/17/1891
Smith, Alex (col)         Lucy Walker (col)          10/21/1893
Smith, Allen C.           Amanda Binford             12/21/1875
Smith, Allen Eugene       Lula McElhenny             12/23/1894
Smith, Alonzo (col)       Carrie Johnson (col)       3/13/1899
```

Smith, Anderson	Lucinda Vickers	1/22/1876
Smith, B. L.	Mattie Hardin	1/30/1907
Smith, Basil	Elizabeth Abbett	6/23/1818
Smith, Berry	Belle Hill (date issued)	8/7/1874
Smith, Berry	Adline Banks	1/11/1874
Smith, Boykin	Betsy Thurmond	12/30/1881
Smith, Boykin (col)	Dora Reid (col)	5/17/1891
Smith, Boykin R.	Lizzie Flournoy	11/26/1865
Smith, Bunk (col)	Dolly Driscoll (col)	1/23/1898
Smith, C. E.	Rebecca Goodman	11/18/1896
Smith, Carl E. (col)	Mary Robinson (col)	2/17/1907
Smith, Cart (col)	Susie Marks (col)	2/27/1907
Smith, Caught (col)	Carrie Burney (col)	12/14/1898
Smith, Chatman (col)	Mattie Alexander (col)	12/29/1907
Smith, Chyde (col)	Annie Lee (col)	6/16/1907
Smith, Cooley (col)	Juno Epps (col)	10/18/1868
Smith, Cornelius	Melissa Jane Jackson	2/12/1887
Smith, Coy (col)	Ada Maning (col)	4/1/1894
Smith, Coy (col)	Lizzie White (col)	12/26/1895
Smith, Dan (col)	Lizzie Jeffries (col)	1/14/1896
Smith, David	Patsey Hardin	5/30/1818
Smith, Doc (col)	Bettie Smith (col)	1/10/1889
Smith, Durrell	Annie Kate Malone	12/13/1894
Smith, Earl (col)	Fannie Kelly (col)	1/5/1898
Smith, Ed	Nannie Freeman	8/6/1889
Smith, Elbert (col)	Harriet Manuel (col)	9/28/1875
Smith, George (col)	Lona Kelley (col)	12/30/1875
Smith, George	Anna Cheek	12/30/1883
Smith, George	Jane Banks	7/10/1884
Smith, George (col)	Mattie Lou Gilstrap (col)	1/6/1890
Smith, George (col)	Mariah Thompson (col)	1/5/1902
Smith, Grant (col)	Emma Banks (col)	12/27/1896
Smith, Green (col)	Hanna Nash (col)	5/24/1873
Smith, Hampton	Belle Pennington	12/18/1898
Smith, Henry (col)	Hannah Cox (col)	11/25/1867
Smith, Henry	Lou Cooper	8/23/1872
Smith, Henry	Zipporah Malone	12/21/1876
Smith, Henry (col)	Mattie Benton (col)	1/9/1893
Smith, Hollis	Mattie Smith	2/4/1883
Smith, Homer	Nancy Dillard	12/5/1881
Smith, Horace	Ella Winkfield	3/4/1873
Smith, James (col)	Lizzie Singleton (col)	11/17/1889
Smith, James (col)	Lizzie Blackwell (col)	2/23/1899
Smith, James	Liddy Broadus (col)	12/29/1898
Smith, James J.	Sarah E. Jones	12/27/1866
Smith, James T.	Georgia Slack	10/26/1859
Smith, Jim	Matilda Fears	2/20/1875
Smith, Jim Bolden (col)	Annie Davidson (col)	8/14/1896
Smith, Joe (col)	Beckie Smith (col)	5/6/1896
Smith, John	Angeline Thomas	2/26/1885
Smith, John	Jane Gay	3/11/1888
Smith, John (col)	Belle Jeffries (col)	5/20/1899
Smith, John Henry (col)	Mary Jane Howard (col)	1/8/1891
Smith, John Wesley (col)	Ada Card (col)	12/21/1907
Smith, Johnie (col)	Mary Turk (col)	11/3/1892
Smith, Joseph	Elizabeth Ramsey	12/3/1818
Smith, Joseph H.	Sarah Jane Lawson	11/9/1873
Smith, Joseph H. S.	Rhoda Ann Williams	10/18/1897
Smith, Joseph Henry S.	Annie R. Peurifoy	8/16/1892
Smith, Levi (col)	Dora Malone (col)	12/28/1892
Smith, Lewis (col)	Laura Gotier (col)	3/23/1890
Smith, Lewis (col)	Maggie Dougherty (col)	8/30/1895
Smith, Lewis (col)	Amanda Truit (col)	12/23/1906

Smith, Lucius (col)	Emma Epps (col)	1/19/1890
Smith, Marcus (col)	Ossie Pearl Smith (col)	6/16/1907
Smith, Martin	Celia P. Toland	12/22/1870
Smith, Matt (col)	Emma White (col)	12/2/1897
Smith, Monroe (col)	Ida Harris (col)	12/25/1896
Smith, Nestor P.	Maggie I. Perry	1/31/1883
Smith, Niles L.	Emma Kelly	2/23/1888
Smith, Orilious (col)	Harriet Benton (col)	1/30/1890
Smith, Ranisome (col)	Fannie Whiting (col)	11/20/1907
Smith, Richard	Sallie Lindsey	12/2/1883
Smith, Rufus H.	Adeline Harris	9/20/1870
Smith, Sam	Viney Walker	1/3/1874
Smith, Sam (col)	Drucilla Ridley (col)	4/9/1893
Smith, Samuel (col)	Nancy Jeffries (col)	9/30/1877
Smith, Samuel	Lela Smith	1/27/1885
Smith, Samuel (col)	Harriett Powell (col)	7/30/1890
Smith, Samuel (col)	Beckie Thomas (col)	7/1/1894
Smith, Scott (col)	Delie Williams (col)	2/6/1875
Smith, Sherman (col)	Lucy Gotell (col)	3/22/1899
Smith, Swanson (col)	Clemie Gilstrap (col)	2/5/1895
Smith, T. A.	S. E. Davis	2/3/1873
Smith, Thomas	Susan Elizabeth Henderson	2/26/1873
Smith, Thomas E.	Nancy Ann McCullars	1/18/1865
Smith, Thomas Edgar	Mrs. Sarah Jones	1/5/1882
Smith, Walton	Delia Ann Benton	12/28/1868
Smith, Will (col)	Virginia Green (col)	7/3/1892
Smith, Will (col)	Eliza Jane Felphs (col)	1/1/1899
Smith, William	Sarah Hathhorn	7/20/1818
Smith, William	Ellen Thomas	3/13/1886
Smith, William (col)	Mary Jane Harris (col)	1/5/1888
Smith, William (col)	Corine Ridley (col)	1/6/1892
Smith, William (col)	Alsey Freeman (col)	3/31/1892
Smith, William (col)	Lucy Washington (col)	11/5/1891
Smith, William F.C.	E. S. McNair	2/19/1850
Smith, William H.	Lemma Johnson	1/9/1890
Smith, William Henry	Harriet Gates	1/21/1886
Smith, Willie	Ida Key	1/4/1887
Smith, Willie (col)	Eliza Tuggle (col)	12/30/1890
Smith, Willie (col)	Carrie Kelly (col)	11/27/1892
Smith, Willie (col)	Mollie Pearson (col)	2/3/1897
Smith, Woodie (col)	Rony Smith (col)	1/20/1901
Smith, Wyatt (col)	Patience Jordan (col)	11/29/1896
Smith, Zachairah P.	India A. Key	1/9/1873
Spain, William	Milley Catrel	5/7/1818
Sparks, Alex (col)	Hattie Barron (col)	4/13/1898
Sparks, Nap (col)	Candy Braswell (col)	1/9/1898
Sparks, William	Willie Ann Rooks (Date issued)	1/2/1876
Spear, Francis M.	Sarah L. Marsh	7/24/1869
Spear, William T.	Sallie Ophelia Blackwell	1/25/1887
Spearman, Albert (col)	Emma Whitfield (col)	1/24/1897
Spearman, Amos M.	Lucinda Shy	11/30/1888
Spearman, Fleming (col)	Martha Miller (col)	12/19/1895
Spearman, J. C.	L. J. Robinson	10/27/1870
Spearman, James (col)	Mrs. Caroline Shy (col)	1/3/1895
Spearman, James (col)	Magnolia Preston (col)	10/29/1896
Spearman, John	Nancy Blackwell	2/11/1858
Spearman, John	Dee Blackwell	7/6/1892
Spearman, John (col)	Evalyne Shy (col)	12/29/1897
Spearman, M. W.	J. S. Geiger	9/7/1870
Spearman, W. S. (col)	Hattie J. Brawner (col)	9/22/1907
Spearman, William	Harriett B. Leverett	2/28/1858
Spears, A. M.	Mary Banks	9/11/1872

Spears, Caleb P.	Mattie Binford	7/14/1891
Spears. Cicero M.	Martha Tuggle	1/9/1877
Spears, Cicero M.	Narcissa L. Wagner	5/11/1882
Spears, Columbus A.	Easter L. Jeffries	1/4/1860
Spears, J. B.	Loy Smith	11/3/1907
Spears, John N.	Ada Chaffin	8/19/1886
Spears, John W.	J. W. Davis	2/12/1874
Spears, Joseph (col)	Mary Digby (col)	10/30/1870
Spears, Oscar H.	Annie Lee Greer	6/8/1895
Spears, Sidney	Betsie Jeffries	3/5/1885
Speer, Thomas Eugene	Essie Hall Preston	6/2/1907
Speights, Dave (col)	Linda White (col)	9/23/1891
Speights, John C.	S. J. Dozier	3/6/1877
Speller, Dave (col)	Laura Sheilds (col)	5/14/1893
Speller, Frank (col)	Lissie Ann Simmons (col)	9/1/1889
Speller, Lewis (col)	Lizzie Brown (col)	1/12/1893
Speller, Oliver	Nancy Johnson (Johnston)	4/13/1877
Spellers, Joshua (col)	Adaline Griggs (col)	12/30/1898
Spellers, Oliver (col)	Mrs. Adaline Brooks (col)	4/8/1894
Spikes, Ananias (col)	Sallie Freeman (col)	10/2/1897
Spiller, Frank (col)	Rosa Jordan (col)	3/17/1897
Spivy, Thomas (col)	Lizzie Montgomery (col)	4/18/1896
Stallings, Simeon W.	Lettice W. Reeves	3/18/1819
Standifer, Adolphus (col)	Mrs. Louisiana Peacock (col)	10/11/1893
Standifer, Allen (col)	Malissa Tilman (Tiglman) (col)	1/15/1873
Standifer, Boby (col)	Lizzie Tillman (col)	12/26/1901
Standifer, Byrom	Lina Brown	1/20/1887
Standifer, General(col)	Corine Bartlett (col)	10/13/1907
Standifer, Jack	Sallie Standifer	1/24/1888
Standifer, John (col)	Dorah Mohon (col)	12/31/1901
Standifer, John,Jr.(col)	Lou Zelia Goolsby (col)	12/31/1889
Standifer, Lollie	Carry Phillips	12/28/1907
Standifer, Robert (col)	Roxy Ann Braswell (col)	12/29/1907
Standifer, Sam (col)	Jane Glawson (col)	3/30/1898
Standifer, Silas (col)	Leithe Barron (col)	7/29/1887
Standifer, Walker	Adaliza Chapman	12/31/1885
Standifer, Willis W. (col)	Mary Eliza Glawson (col) (issued)	3/21/1901
Standifer, Willis W.(col)	Emma Wyatt (col)	11/9/1901
Standifer, Zachairah(col)	Janie Finney (col)	7/16/1893
Standifur, William (col)	Malissa Gordon (col)	12/25/1898
Stanford, Joe (col)	Georgia Ann Fears (col)	12/12/1874
Stanford, Joe	Lucy Walker	12/23/1886
Stanford, Obadiah	Annie Meridy	12/12/1894
Stanley, Caleb	Sarah Hubbard	7/12/1818
Starr, S. H.	Nannie Childs	4/4/1888
Steadham, John	Laura McMichael	11/8/1896
Steele, G. A.	Ellen King	10/22/1893
Steele, Jonas (col)	Amanda Jeffries (col)	1/27/1903
Steele, Tom M. (col)	Nancy Minter (col)	7/1/1891
Steele, William H.	Mollie A. Jones	1/8/1885
Stephen, Peter (col)	Marina Harris (col)	12/31/1874
Stephens, Abner	Delia Benton	12/4/1890
Stephens, Burl	Delphy Roberts	12/27/1877
Sterling, Wiley G.	Bethany Bonner	1/28/1819
Stewart, Floyd (col)	Matilda Kelly (col)	1/31/1891
Stewart, James T.	Sarah F. Speer	2/2/1859
Stewart, John	Nicey White	8/8/1810
Stewart, Leroy	Angeline Phillips (Date issued)	10/5/1876
Stokes, Edward (col)	Bella Bell (col)	12/6/1893

52

Stone, Gus (col)	Lizzie Lynch (col)	4/30/1896
Stone, Jeff (col)	Martha Ann Barnes (col)	12/29/1892
Stone, M. P.	Viola J. Smith	5/31/1877
Stone, Philip	Georgia Ann McElhenney	1/16/1890
Stone, W. M.	Opie Cunard	11/9/1896
Stone, William M.	Levora E. White	7/26/1891
Stonewall, Walter (col)	Silie Durdin (col)	12/20/1888
Story, James	Elizabeth Lambert	9/27/1818
Stovall, Richard (col)	Saby Digby (col)	12/26/1867
Strickland, E. S.	Alice L. Cornwell	11/29/1885
Strickland, Eli	Celia Kelly (date iss.)	1/7/1816
Strickland, Nathan M.	Mary M. Edwards	10/8/1861
Strong, Bagger (col)	Cornelia Roberts (col)	3/9/1907
Strozier, James W.	Sarah E. Nowell	7/2/1866
Sullivan, Otis H.	Florence N. Hardy	8/7/1887
Sullivan, William	Uldine Bullard	6/28/1895
Sutton, Jesse (col)	Carrie Richards (col)	3/13/1898
Swanson, Frank J.	Telula J. Preston	11/18/1874
Swift, Bart	Queen Crawford	12/31/1880
Swift, Berry (col)	Silvey Holland (col) (date issued)	1/24/1874
Swift, Hiram	Susan Prophett	12/28/1886
Swift, James	Sultana Smith	12/26/1872
Swift, Jim, Jr. (col)	Rosetta Hopson (col)	9/28/1891
Swift, Sam (col)	Mollie Cofer (col)	5/14/1899
Swift, Will (col)	Delphia Gordon (col)	2/3/1901
Swift, William	Annie Goolsby	12/23/1886
Talmadge, Clovis A.	Sallie F. Flournoy	6/28/1891
Talmadge, Herbert	Maggie Kelly	8/14/1884
Talmadge, J. E.	M. Gertrude Alexander	6/27/1900
Tanner, Link	Sarah Carter	2/19/1882
Taylor, George A.	Margarett A. Steel	1/8/1854
Taylor, James	Anna Penn	11/1/1883
Taylor, James J.	Mattie V. Rowe	12/28/1886
Taylor, John (col)	Louvinia Smith (col)	12/16/1891
Taylor, Jordan	Elizabeth Jordan	2/5/1883
Taylor, Lewis	Mat Lou Goolsby	1/6/1897
Tedderds, Walker	Belle Davis	8/7/1898
Tedders, George W.	Zimma Campbell	1/30/1866
Teel, Henry	Patsey Young	7/6/1815
Teller, James (col)	Vora Burney (col)	12/1/1907
Thaxton, John (col)	Rindy Price (col)	12/7/1897
Thomas, Albert (col)	Laura Jackson (col)	3/19/1907
Thomas, Ben (col)	Nettie Campbell (col)	12/26/1896
Thomas, Benjamin (col)	Eliza Benton (col)	11/8/1873
Thomas, Charles (col)	Sibilitie Dumas (col)	9/25/1893
Thomas, Charley (col)	Emma Jordan (col)	7/17/1898
Thomas, Eli (col)	Mrs. Julia Jackson (col)	12/27/1888
Thomas, Fleetwood	Lizzie Davis	10/6/1907
Thomas, Hilliard (col)	Louisiana Brown (col)	4/3/1892
Thomas, Jim (col)	Mary Tinsley (col)	12/15/1890
Thomas, Jim (col)	Patience Benton (col)	1/18/1894
Thomas, Joe (col)	Mary Peurifoy (col)	12/27/1896
Thomas, Joe (col)	Sallie George Cargile (col)	6/26/1907
Thomas, John	Maggie Lee Clay	8/25/1907
Thomas, John (col)	Beula Shannon (col)	12/31/1907
Thomas, John H.	Mrs. L. M. Ivey	10/1/1872
Thomas, John H. (col)	Sallie Goolsby (col)	12/31/1890
Thomas, Joseph	Amanda Binford	5/9/1889
Thomas, Lewis, Jr.	Della Walker	6/16/1887

Thomas, Lucius (col)	Ella Baynes (col)	6/10/1899
Thomas, Oliver (col)	Mary Glover (col)	10/8/1896
Thomas, Oliver (col)	Easter Marks (col)	4/7/1907
Thomas, Oliver,Jr.(col)	Ellen Driskell (col)	1/29/1894
Thomas, Richard (col)	Mattie Goolsby (col)	5/18/1894
Thomas, Scott (col)	Martha George (col)	1/4/1868
Thomas, Scott	Hattie Williams	2/21/1884
Thomas, Tobe (col)	Lara Whitfield (col)	12/23/1874
Thomas, William (col)	Eliza Alexander (col)	12/28/1873
Thomas, William (col)	Lizzie Seaborn (col)	1/5/1891
Thomas, William (col)	Josie Card (col)	12/12/1907
Thomas, William (col)	Catharine Benton (col)	12/23/1907
Thomas, William T.	Mary Jane Jackson	3/6/1884
Thomas, Willie (col)	Lou Morris (col)	12/9/1898
Thomas, Wyatt (col)	Elizabeth Jordan (col)	2/24/1894
Thomason, Andrew J.	Sallie U. Digby	3/17/1881
Thomason, Davis Clark	Lee P. Kelly	2/10/1887
Thomason, J. C.	Zaydee Thompson	4/28/1907
Thomason, James (col)	Mollie Jordan (col)	5/16/1869
Thomason, Joe (col)	Sallie B. Glover (col)	7/23/1876
Thomason, Oscar	Pearl Lane	8/18/1899
Thomason, Samuel E.	Nancy A. Burns	12/7/1869
Thomason, William J.	Zou Ella Evans	11/28/1886
Thomerson, Jackson	Elizabeth Parker	12/19/1850
Thompkins, Mason	Hannah Nash	11/12/1873
Thompson, David (col)	Mrs. Jane Smith	8/13/1876
Thompson, Ed	Carrie Robinson	12/19/1886
Thompson, Ed N.	Althea Price	5/26/1895
Thompson, Edward J.	Mrs. Burnetta Lane	6/7/1866
Thompson, Edwin J.	Martha M. Crow	12/21/1854
Thompson, Elbert (col)	Sarah Walker (col)	
	(date issued)	8/17/1876
Thompson, Evan	Della Spears	6/2/1907
Thompson, George (col)	Mary Flournoy (col)	8/5/1892
Thompson, George M.	Laura Rickets	3/19/1885
Thompson, H. T.	N. J. Bryant	4/9/1874
Thompson, Harrison (col)	Mattie Thompson (col)	12/22/1888
Thompson, Henry	Franky Banks	4/20/1866
Thompson, Henry T.	Johnnie Christian	8/17/1898
Thompson, J. M., Jr.	Emma Kate Malone	5/23/1897
Thompson, J. T.	Willie C. Farris	3/14/1897
Thompson, Jim (col)	Lottie Allen (col)	3/14/1897
Thompson, Joe	Amelia Chapman	3/23/1882
Thompson, John F.	Sarah C. Waits	3/2/1876
Thompson, John F.	Angeline D. Slocum	5/24/1891
Thompson, Matthew J.	Emeliza Turk	12/23/1866
Thompson, Pink (col)	Ann Walker (col)	1/20/1869
Thompson, Pink (col)	Millie Peddy (col)	1/3/1897
Thompson, Samuel (col)	Emma Bell (col)	12/31/1893
Thompson, Thomas W.	Lessie Hudson	1/18/1894
Thompson, Thommy (col)	Lonie Preston (col)	7/26/1897
Thompson, Tom (col)	Minnie Kelly (col)	1/8/1894
Thompson, Turner H.(col)	Susie A. Jordan (col)	5/17/1891
Thompson, Turner H.(col)	Mary Jane Clements (col)	10/24/1897
Thompson, William (col)	Janie Benton (col)	12/31/1901
Thompson, William D.	Mattie Edwards	10/25/1888
Thompson, William F.	Gertrude M. Hardy	9/13/1891
Thompson, William L.	Sarah J. Goolsby	11/19/1868
Thornton, Anthony (col)	Lula Lee (col)	6/10/1891
Thornton, Cullen	Polley Banks	10/5/1817
Thornton, Handy	Rachael Ross	11/21/1884
Thornton, James	Gittie McMichael	11/22/1896
Thornton, Solomon	Elizabeth Mize	3/13/1816

Thurman, Aaron	Eliza Johnston	2/19/1875
Thurman, Augustus (col)	Janie Garland (col)	1/22/1898
Thurman, Joe	Biana Greer	1/1/1873
Thurman, Mitch (col)	Julia Brown (col)	11/13/1898
Thurman, Phillip (col)	Annie Card (col)	12/10/1907
Thurmond, Aaron (col)	Sarah Meriwether (col)	12/16/1867
Thurmond, Benjamin (col)	Emily Pye (col)	12/27/1873
Thurmond, Jim	Carrie Thrash	12/28/1883
Thurmond, Mannie (col)	Mattie Sanders (col)	1/2/1890
Thurmond, Sydney	Miranda Goolsby	12/28/1882
Thurmond, Stephen	Theodosia Bebee	2/3/1883
Thurmond, Willie (col)	Lizzie Moreland (col)	1/20/1893
Thurmond, Wilson	Queen Chapman	7/7/1885
Tillery, Hudson	Elizabeth Beller	10/16/1817
Tillman, Henry	Alice Couch	2/7/1892
Tillman, John	Drucilla Fesset	2/26/1866
Tillman, Robert	Sallie Willingham	12/23/1897
Tilman, Elijah L.	Dora Kate Couch	12/23/1890
Tilman, George	Kittie Pye	10/7/1896
Tilmon, John	Phebe Perkins	2/9/1847
Tilmon, Richard	Leila Morgan	12/25/1888
Tilmon, William H.	Emma Waits	1/17/1884
Tindsley, Frank (col)	Fannie Marks (col)	12/18/1898
Tindsley, Homer (col)	Daisey Bebee (col)	10/27/1907
Tindlsey, James (col)	Enley Smith (col)	3/6/1898
Tindsley, Lewis (col)	Sudie Chatman (col)	2/14/1898
Tingle, Steven G.	Addie L. Campbell	12/1/1884
Tinsley, Arch (col)	Mary Jane Walker (col)	12/16/1897
Tinsley, Charles (col)	Julia Boykin (col)	12/2/1866
Tinsley, Charles (col)	Clarissa Robertson (col)	2/4/1894
Tinsley, Charles (col)	Fannie Lou Goolsby (col)	12/27/1896
Tinsley, Daniel	Angyline Whitfield	12/12/1877
Tinsley, Henry	Cass Ann Thurman	11/28/1874
Tinsley, James (col)	Penny Allen (col)	4/5/1890
Tinsley, Joe (col)	Mamie Hutchison (col)	12/23/1896
Tinsley, Lewis (col)	Allie Reid (col)	2/11/1894
Tinsley, Wiley (col)	Addie Showers (col)	11/25/1894
Tinsley, William	Frances Perry	12/28/1886
Tinsley, William (col)	Julia Glover (col)	12/14/1890
Todd, Ira D.	Ida Burney	11/4/1888
Toland, Bob (col)	Rhoda Middlebrooks (col)	9/14/1868
Toland, Lewis (col)	Lara Comer (col)	1/2/1876
Toland, Thyers J.	Nancy Ann McDonald	4/4/1847
Tomlinson, J. D.	Nancy A.E. Holsomback	2/26/1874
Tomlinson, Jack J.	Mary Jane Polk	1/1/1882
Tomlinson, James Lee(col)	Josephine Allen (col)	12/28/1899
Tomlinson, Stephen D.	Jennie F. Lane	1/17/1882
Tompkins, Ed	Harriet Vaughn	1/3/1884
Tompkins, Ed	Mamie Edwards	10/2/1897
Torrence, George W.	Annie Lee Spears	10/24/1899
Traylor, Mark (col)	Bettie Kelly (col)	7/8/1875
Trimble, Charlie (col)	Cintha Clark (col)	4/22/1894
Trip, Emanuel (col)	Ella Ridley (col)	1/19/1892
Truitt, J. T. (col)	Mary Jeffries (col)	3/7/1895
Trussell, Green B.	Caroline Hatcher	9/6/1849
Trussell, William H.	Mary L. Hatcher	8/26/1849
Tucker, Allen	Nancy Paschal	8/27/1818
Tucker, George A.	Octavia Baynes	2/24/1901
Tuggle, Alfred F.	Nora Tyler	9/29/1895
Tuggle, Carlton	Mariah Jane Taylor	12/11/1889
Tuggle, Crayton	Mollie Barker	12/19/1883
Tuggle, Elmore D.	Annie Fish	11/15/1888
Tuggle, Frank (col)	Bettie Smith (col)	4/27/1895

Tuggle, Henry	Lizzie Kelly	12/25/1873
Tuggle, Henry	Emma Thomas	9/9/1886
Tuggle, Henry (col)	Sis Murphy (col)	10/31/1889
Tuggle, James (col)	Lizzie Smith (col)	2/5/1891
Tuggle, Joseph	Adeline Harrison	3/25/1854
Tuggle, Phillip	Callie Hawkins	12/30/1886
Tuggle, Samuel (col)	Frances Smith (col)	11/27/1889
Tuggle, Washington (col)	Fannie Bryant (col)	11/29/1868
Tuggle, William R.	Louisa S. Hardy	12/19/1867
Turk, Avington	Emaliza Leverett	11/22/1848
Turk, Charles (col)	Mrs. Mary Nichols (col)	1/14/1893
Turk, Edward B.	A. B. Wilson	12/6/1893
Turk, Frank	Lou Williams	12/14/1882
Turk, Jeff (col)	Lizzie Watters (col)	8/24/1894
Turk, Joe (col)	Gussie Jordan (col)	6/4/1893
Turk, Jonathan	Phoeba M. Baynes	8/28/1859
Turk, Oscar (col)	Louangie Thomason (col)	12/26/1907
Turk, Swan	Annie Lee Grant	12/1/1907
Turk, Will (col)	Puss Johnston (col)	6/25/1898
Turk, William (col)	Mary Simon (col)	3/2/1893
Turner, Anderson	Aggie Davis	2/1/1877
Turner, Benjamin H.	Hattie Lou Ozburn	1/2/1890
Turner, Esom	Polley Mabray	12/4/1817
Turner, James	Jane Spear	2/14/1819
Turner, James (col)	Lula Nix (col)	11/1/1893
Turner, Joel Will	Mittie Mozelle Anderson	12/24/1891
Turner, John	Mary Lou Ella Kelly	11/2/1893
Turner, John D.	M. F. Harden	1/20/1883
Turner, John W.	Mary M. Lumsden	7/2/1882
Turner, L. W.	Anna A. Greer	10/15/1875
Turner, Thomas	Fannie Glover	12/27/1877
Turner, Willie (col)	Lizzie Kate Walker (col)	8/6/1899
Tyler, Albert A.	Oteila Oxford	12/20/1887
Tyler, Andrew L.	Leila Jenkins	12/21/1898
Tyler, F. M.	Emily C. Chapman	2/2/1863
Tyler, Francis M.	Ida M. Goolsby	12/12/1882
Tyler, Job	Mary J. McElhenney	12/10/1872
Tyler, John J.	Brazoria T. Ramey	11/14/1867
Tyler, John J.	Nannie Polk	5/12/1892
Tyler, John J., Jr.	Gussie Lane	12/21/1886
Tyler, Samuel B.	Clara Waits	10/25/1884
Tyner, Charles J.	Nannie D. Baxley	12/10/1890
Tyner, David	M. A. Funderburk	10/24/1865
Tyner, David M.	Ann Elizabeth Niblett	10/3/1882
Tyner, David M.	Martha S. Turner	1/3/1884
Tyner, Martin V.	Mary M. Lane	7/26/1860
Tyner, R. J.	Martha M. Lane	8/26/1858
Usery, Jackson	Laura Proctor	12/22/1881
Usry, Jordan	Mary Fish	12/28/1888
Usry, Mose	Jane Hudson	1/4/1887
Vannerson, J. H.	Mrs. M. F. Coxe	9/10/1872
Varner, David	Jane Bebee	11/16/1872
Varner, Harvey (col)	Emma Tuggle (col)	7/6/1899
Varner, Milas (col)	Vila Shy (col)	3/21/1874
Varner, Reuben (col)	Aurie Richards (col)	11/22/1896
Vaughn, Albert	Syna Pou	1/18/1883
Vaughn, Andrew (col)	Lucy Swift (col)	1/5/1895
Vaughn, William	Lou Edwards	4/18/1885
Vaughn, William (col)	Sallie Brown (col)	12/26/1899

Veal, Wiley King	Martha Sansom	1/1/1854
Vickers, H. H.	Ollie Tyler	12/11/1898
Vickerson, Wash (col)	Vera Poarch (Ponds)(col)	12/25/1907
Vickram, William	Georgia Ann Johnston	8/4/1877
Vickrum, Adolphus (col)	Carrie Mack (col)	2/4/1890
Vickrum, Reese (col)	Carrie Barnes (col)	2/9/1890
Vicram, Thomas L.	Mary J. Johnson	10/27/1872
Victrum, Andrew (col)	Elizabeth Roach (col)	12/26/1893
Victrum, Woody (col)	Ever Gene Pope (col)	1/2/1898
Vincent, Jim (col)	Letha Marks (col)	12/21/1893
Vincent, Rance (col)	Allice Holland (col)	9/13/1897
Vincent, Ransom (col)	Mattie Thomas (col)	11/19/1891
Vincent, Tom (col)	Mary Dickey (col)	9/19/1895
Vincent, Turner (col)	Lizzie Singleton (col)	12/26/1897
Vincient, James (col)	Lula Porter (col)	1/27/1907
Vining, James F.	Sophia N.M.B. Lewis	11/28/1869
Vinson, J. W. (col)	Nancy Jones (col)	12/25/1901
Wade, Elijah	Ellen Cooper	11/20/1884
Wade, Gus (col)	Hattie Peacock (col)	2/26/1893
Wade, Joel (col)	Aggie Robinson (col)	11/14/1877
Wade, Sam (col)	Angeline Drischal (col)	6/17/1876
Wagner, T. L.	Mary O. Loyd	12/4/1907
Waits, Alex Milton	Lilie Thurmand	1/27/1901
Waits, Alexander	Sarah F. Jones	9/24/1868
Waits, Assian	Florence P. Goolsby	7/15/1894
Waits, Charles	Mollie Waldrep	8/12/1894
Waits, Edgar	Susie Waits	11/24/1895
Waits, Harvey	Annie M. Brandon	12/23/1894
Waits, Henry	Ann Eliza Evans	8/2/1888
Waits, Isaac N.	Sarah Ann Freeman	4/22/1868
Waits, John A. C.	Willie McMullins	10/29/1894
Waits, John R.	Lucinthia C. White	4/13/1890
Waits, Joshua	Callie Hunnicut	12/6/1875
Waits, Leroy	Sarah E. Grubbs	6/4/1857
Waits, Levi	Ann Eliza Fisher	4/18/1869
Waits, Levi Fleming	Angie McMichael	4/1/1894
Waits, Nathaniel	Elvada McKinly	5/7/1876
Waits, Thomas	Hattie Pinnell	12/1/1889
Waits, W. J.	Martha Lilian Goodman	12/23/1894
Waits, William	Sallie Standford	1/4/1877
Waits, William	Kissie Strickland	11/19/1899
Waldrep, Elihu N.(Elisha)	Frances C. Holloway	2/2/1869
Waldrep, James	Lady Baxley	12/25/1907
Waldrep, John S.	C. E. Tyler	1/17/1866
Waldrop, John W.	Telitha Clementine Leverett	10/12/1870
Waldrup, G. W.	C. L. Goodman	1/28/1877
Waldrup, J. T.	Rebecca McElhenney	12/8/1875
Walker, Albert Sidney	Minnie M. Henderson	2/21/1889
Walker, Allen (col)	Fanny Lou Bryant (col)	4/13/1889
Walker, Bartley	Mary E. Roby	4/2/1850
Walker, Berry (col)	Lear Matthews (col)	2/28/1901
Walker, Elige (col)	Addie Roby (col)	12/19/1898
Walker, Fed (col)	Silla Nash (col)	10/29/1901
Walker, Green (col)	Lucy Jane George (col)	12/24/1868
Walker, Henry (col)	Nealie Gilstrap (col)	1/12/1890
Walker, Henry W.	India E. Robinson	12/22/1868
Walker, J. B.	Delona S. Thomason	12/28/1854
Walker, J. B.	Annie Greer	2/28/1888
Walker, James (col)	Silvey Goolsby (col)	1/22/1877
Walker, James	Hannah Glover	5/10/1885

Walker, Jim	Nancy Aaron	11/12/1886
Walker, Jim	Mary Jane Mullins	1/6/1889
Walker, Jim (col)	Mollie Digby (col)	7/13/1889
Walker, Joseph (col)	Effie Franklin (col)	10/28/1866
Walker, Lewis	Dilla Barnes	5/13/1883
Walker, Nix (col)	Mary Frances Jordan (col)	11/14/1896
Walker, Reese (col)	Anna Cargle (col)	8/25/1874
Walker, Reese (col)	Nora Nix (col)	2/24/1907
Walker, Rowland (col)	Lila Benton (col)	1/4/1896
Walker, Taswell (col)	Susan Robinson (col)	9/7/1867
Walker, Thomas	Cornelia Bryant	12/28/1876
Walker, Tom (col)	Mattie Smith (col)	12/30/1897
Walker, Troup (col)	Edna Belcher (col)	10/28/1898
Walker, Willie (col)	Mary Singleton (col)	12/2/1897
Walker, Willie (col)	Dorah Jester (col)	12/2/1897
Wallen, Jarratt L.	Telitha Ellen Brogdon	1/16/1853
Waller, Arnold Winkelried	Georgia Inez Pye	11/26/1898
Waller, Christopher C.	Mason Jackson	11/14/1881
Waller, Jonathan S.	Mary H. Letson	11/10/1867
Waller, Robert D.	Annie Bailey	12/20/1896
Walton, Columbus (col)	Nancy Jones (col)	1/15/1895
Waltz, Elsworth	Addie Fish	5/19/1889
Waltz, James L.	Mrs. Eliza A. Aken	10/6/1864
Wammack, James	Laney Lumsden	12/15/1850
Wammack, James	Evaline Pitts	1/25/1876
Wammack, John W.	M. A. Cardell	8/13/1874
Wammack, Linton	Julia A. Stone	9/4/1877
Wammack, Thomas K.	Tresa Horton	12/19/1872
Wammock, Sid	Lee Hunnicutt	12/27/1899
Ward, Davis (col)	Amey Ann Standifer (col)	12/26/1897
Ward, Ed (col)	Larcenie Thomas (col)	4/13/1897
Ward, Edmond (col)	Cornelia P. Gant (col)	3/22/1891
Ward, Francis M.	Susan Hensey	2/17/1859
Ward, George	Patsy Bell	3/6/1884
Ward, Thomas	Caroline Ross	1/15/1873
Ward, Thomas	Kittie Hancock	4/20/1884
Ward, Tommie	Louisa Brown	12/29/1882
Ward, Tommie (col)	Lou Glawson (col)	1/19/1896
Ward, Willie (col)	Ada Nix (col)	12/26/1901
Ware, Oscar	Medora Jordan	1/3/1887
Ware, Willis (col)	Randa Phagin (col)	1/22/1875
Warren, John	Eliza Ann Losson	2/8/1847
Warren, John (col)	Sallie More (col)	6/1/1877
Warren, John H.	Emeline Parker	12/27/1868
Warren, John H.	Mary E. Smith	5/12/1895
Warren, Robert J.	Lula G. Connor	11/23/1888
Warren, William	Sallie Key	11/5/1876
Washington, Frank (col)	Lizzie Green (col)	1/5/1908
Washington, George (col)	Lizzie Waters (col)	1/17/1897
Waters, Ernest (col)	Safronia Colquitt (col)	10/10/1897
Waters, Hudson (col)	Mrs. Sarah Greer (col) (issued)	12/17/1901
Waters, Richard (col)	Adelphia Goolsby (col)	12/15/1899
Waters, Warren (col)	Elizabeth Jenkins (col)	7/3/1890
Waters, William (col)	Easter Persons (col)	11/21/1895
Watkins, Kinman	Harriet Johnson	6/29/1889
Watson, Charley	Cordelia Underwood	7/12/1886
Watson, Farrar	Florence Harvey	9/6/1885
Watson, Henry	Rhoda Ann Pearson	12/24/1887
Watson, Martin (col)	Maria Henry (col)	11/25/1871
Watters, William (col)	Cordelia Powell (col)	2/5/1875
Watters, William	Rhoda Lane	1/17/1877
Watters, William (col)	Laura Butler (col)	6/18/1893

58

Watters, Wyatt	Fannie Coleman	1/20/1873
Watts, John	Sarah Hunt	11/1/1816
Watts, Wade (col)	Mollie Appling (col)	12/27/1891
Weathers, S. R.	Mary C. Weathers	9/2/1858
Weathersbee, John F.	C. M. Toland	12/10/1885
Weaver, George	Bettie Whitfield	12/10/1885
Weaver, W. M.	Mary E. Roberts	7/25/1897
Weaver, Wesley (col)	Amelia Jeffries (col)	12/3/1897
Webb, Austin, Jr. (col)	Maggie Jackson (col)	9/12/1898
Webb, Frank G.	Mollie G. Preston	6/29/1892
Webb, George W.	Martha C. Davidson	10/16/1866
Webb, James F.	Florence E. Pope	10/12/1893
Webb, Lane	Sallie Freeman	4/4/1869
Webb, William W.	Lizzie Ozburn	9/12/1894
Weeks, James	Anne Jane Stpehens (Stevens)	12/2/1817
Weldon, A. W.	Manda A. Portwood	11/22/1877
Weldon, Abram	Frances Arrington	4/6/1885
Weldon, James	Doratha Williams	3/12/1818
Wellington, Charles E.	Mary F. Talmadge	12/22/1881
Wesby, Jim (col)	Sallie Greer (col)	1/5/1901
West, Jeremiah	Sarah Williams	7/30/1818
West, Lucius	Sarah Jane Brown	1/13/1889
Weyman, Taylor	Carrie Harris	12/26/1906
Whitaker, John B.	Rachael Douglas	10/20/1818
White, A. F.	Mattie Lawrence	11/31/1877
White, Aaron (col)	Louisa Thomas (col)	?/?/1894
White, Albert (col)	Mary Bell Russell (col)	12/13/1896
White, Alford (col)	Lucinda Allen (col)	3/27/1875
White, Andrew (col)	Cresa Proctor (col)	1/7/1894
White, Archa B.	Rhoda A. Hooks	7/26/1870
White, Ben (col)	Lizzie Cargile (col)	5/27/1896
White, Cato (col)	Letha Johnston (col) (Johnson)	12/25/1875
White, Cato	Sallie Gordon	2/20/1886
White, Dennis	Sophia Wilson	5/22/1886
White, George	Delia Gill	12/27/1876
White, J. A.	Lena M. Edwards	3/15/1896
White, James F.	Martha J. Leverett	4/19/1870
White, Jimmie (col)	Daisy Greer (col)	12/1/1907
White, John J.	Mary Jane Grubbs	1/17/1849
White, John Walton (col)	Emaline Barber (col)	5/18/1891
White, Monroe (col)	Sallie Michael (col)	12/29/1890
White, William (col)	Nannie Glover (col)	3/7/1894
White, William A.	Lovie Allen	12/21/1892
Whitehead, Eugene S.	Berta Anderson	6/22/1898
Whitehead, Jack (col)	Mary Jane Wilson (col)	11/1/1891
Whitehead, Robert	Charity Smith	5/15/1887
Whitehead, Samuel	Mrs. Elizabeth A. Mullens	10/16/1864
Whitehead, William A.	Addie E. Lovejoy	5/3/1877
Whitfield, Clovis (col)	Sarah Pitts (col)	12/11/1897
Whitfield, George	Susan Williams	11/19/1874
Whitfield, Henry	Rachael Banks	10/2/1887
Whitfield, Jacob (col)	Sarah Pou (col)	10/29/1891
Whitfield, Jake (col)	Mrs. Easter Bearden (col)	12/22/1896
Whitfield, Jordan (col)	Sallie Griggs (col)	10/21/1899
Whitfield, Lewis	Nancy Sanders	12/26/1885
Whitfield, Louis	Rebecca Edwards	1/25/1883
Whitfield, Matthew	Mrs. Martha A.Walton	8/12/1847
Whitfield, Samuel	Martha Sanders	12/24/1872
Whiting, Shade (col)	Ida Lee (col)	12/27/1901
Whitten, George F.	Christianna Holston	11/10/1886

Whitten, Henry W.	Nancy Cook	11/9/1881
Whitten, James A.	Zoro Morrow	12/13/1885
Whitten, Scott	Jane Ross	9/8/1872
Whittle, Joseph L.	Sarah M. Aaron	11/15/1863
Wideman, Henry	Penny Teel	2/13/1818
Wilburn, John (col)	Mary Eliza Robertson(col)	1/4/1898
Wilburn, Leonidas C.	Dora Davidson	12/21/1882
Wilburn, William H.	Etta Benton	1/24/1882
Wilder, Larkin	Elizabeth Horton (Houghton)	3/11/1819
Williams, Alonzo (col)	Ada Clay (col)	7/30/1892
Williams, Anderson (col)	Harriett Maddox (col)	3/26/1899
Williams, Beverly	Laura Sanders	1/19/1878
Williams, Cage (col)	Celie Baynes (col)	9/4/1887
Williams, Charles (col)	Jane Price (col)	5/22/1896
Williams, D. M.	Lucy E. McElhenney	3/6/1901
Williams, David (col)	Marinda Persons (col)	10/8/1866
Williams, Dick (col)	Mariah Avery (col)	12/24/1873
Williams, Durham	Elsi Reed	5/9/1873
Williams, Esquire	Lou Reed	12/27/1885
Williams, Evan	Mary Johnston	12/9/1874
Williams, Francis H.	Elizabeth Cardell	3/21/1861
Williams, Hampton (col)	Mattie Clay (col)	12/30/1897
Williams, Henry	Winny Hardwick	8/3/1872
Williams, Henry	Nettie Heard	10/23/1886
Williams, Henry	Mattie Vaughn	12/8/1886
Williams, Henry (col)	Sallie McMichael (col)	9/18/1892
Williams, Henry (col)	Angie Campbell	1/10/1895
Williams, Jack	Jane Whitfield	12/23/1875
Williams, James E.	Emma Maddux	6/6/1886
Williams, Jefferson D.	Eliza Flemister	12/1/1881
Williams, Jock (col)	Martha Nash (col)	9/24/1892
Williams, John	Polly Coleman	4/7/1819
Williams, John (col)	Anna Kelly (col) (Date issued)	6/19/1875
Williams, John	Emma Little	2/8/1888
Williams, John P.	Willie E. Malone	9/12/1889
Williams, John S.	Lucy Lane	1/21/1890
Williams, Oblire (col)	Mary Ann Jones (col)	9/22/1898
Williams, Pleasant M.	Nancy P. Waller	1/5/1854
Williams, Reese	Harriet Wilson	1/25/1873
Williams, Richard	Nora Allen	1/27/1888
Williams, Roe (col)	Josie Redmond (col)	4/4/1895
Williams, Samuel (col)	Estelle Belcher (col)	1/12/1896
Williams, Solomon	Mary Morris	6/26/1884
Williams, Thomas R.,Sr.	S. E. Minter	12/18/1895
Williams, W. S.	Minnie Maddux	10/18/1899
Williams, Wesley	Elvira Shy	3/18/1881
Williams, Wesley	Jane Williams	12/13/1883
Williams, William	Martha Howard	10/8/1854
Williams, William (col)	Aurie Vaughn (col)	11/20/1898
Williams, William S.	Mrs. Margaret Cook	9/11/1883
Williams, Willie (col)	Cora Maddux (col)	1/2/1890
Williamson, Thomas J.	Ninnie Thornton	12/17/1891
Willingham, Theophalus	Susan Hatcher	1/1/1861
Willingham, W. N.	Katie McElhenney	3/24/1895
Willis, Jonathan	Polly Wallis	9/14/1818
Wilson, Abraham V.	Sarah J. Fisher	12/19/1867
Wilson, Allen	Polly McKissack	11/16/1872
Wilson, Augustus	Lizzie Tuggle	10/26/1886
Wilson, Charles (col)	Jennie Turk (col)	3/6/1890
Wilson, Charles M.	Lilla Jones	4/25/1883
Wilson, Dave	Lizzie Horton	12/17/1885

Wilson, David (col)	Mattie Walker (col)	4/11/1889
Wilson, Dawson (col)	Susie Daniel (col)	11/11/1896
Wilson, Elick (col)	Angeline Fort (col)	12/29/1868
Wilson, Elijah	Martha Gamage	11/5/1818
Wilson, Fulton	Mollie Guy	1/21/1884
Wilson, George (col)	Sallie Griggs (col)	1/17/1897
Wilson, Irwin W.	Lena E. Whitfield	1/21/1892
Wilson, James	Elizabeth Goodman	10/12/1884
Wilson, James H.	Anna Tuggle	9/11/1883
Wilson, John	Mollie Clark (date iss.)	3/11/1874
Wilson, John (col)	Frances Rooks (col)	2/9/1896
Wilson, John H. L.	Ora Bay Ellis	11/8/1896
Wilson, Lucious	Minnie L. Reynolds	10/6/1898
Wilson, Lum (col)	Jane Wilson (col)	5/23/1897
Wilson, Robert	Susan Whitfield	1/14/1886
Wilson, Fufus	Annie Green	2/21/1877
Wimberly, Elijah (col)	Florence Davis (col)	3/24/1901
Wimbish, Sam (col)	Martha Ann Glawson (col)	3/23/1895
Wimbush, Samuel	Jane Standifer	5/7/1876
Wimbush, William (col)	Martha Wilson (col)	1/4/1898
Wimbush, William (col)	Poggie Rivers (col)	1/22/1899
Winn, Hartwell	Elizabeth Colbert	10/12/1816
Wisborn, Eilga (col)	Clara Hardwick (col)	12/24/1898
Wise, Dave (col)	Alice Williams (col)	9/12/1895
Wise, Henry	Laura Thomas	6/17/1883
Wise, James (col)	Emma Greer (col)	12/30/1887
Wise, Joseph A.	Martha Jane Edwards	11/27/1859
Wise, Patton	Amanda Trammell	3/12/1854
Womack, John H.	Mattie I. Niblett	10/8/1897
Womack, Seaborn	Tabitha Tucker	12/22/1859
Womack, Seaborn	Bessie Henderson	11/17/1895
Womack, Sidney	Mattie Lewis	2/10/1894
Wood, James B.	Cornelia S. Devaney	7/25/1860
Wood, Jim (col)	Georgia Nolly (col)	1/24/1892
Woodley, William	Telitha McMichael	10/3/1816
Woodruff, Clifford	Priscilla G. Spillards	?/?/1819
Woods, J. L. G.	S. Virginia Barnes	11/12/1874
Woody, James	Emma Maxey	1/3/1884
Wooten, Richard J. T.	Martha Jane Bowden	9/14/1884
Wooton, James	Nancy Elizabeth Wooton	11/11/1875
Wooton, William	M. F. Wooton	3/5/1875
Wright, Anderson (col)	Lula James (col)	9/17/1897
Wright, George W.	Mrs. Lizzie Cheek	12/28/1890
Wright, Henry (col)	Mattie Jackson (col)	10/3/1907
Wright, James	Mattie Niblett	11/30/1886
Wright, Robert (col)	Susan Mahon (col)	9/5/1907
Wyatt, Azariah	Eliza Rogers	1/19/1884
Wyatt, Barton	Matilda Fears	3/3/1881
Wyatt, Coalman	Lucy Humphreys	12/30/1875
Wyatt, Henry (col)	Dora Thompson (col)	12/24/1891
Wyatt, Henry (col)	Lizzie Mabry (col)	12/28/1897
Wyatt, Henry J.	Lula Sheppered	1/9/1873
Wyatt, Isaac T.	Mary Ann Sullivan	9/14/1854
Wyatt, Jesse (col)	Katie Jackson (col)	3/4/1899
Wyatt, John (col)	Josie Carr (col)	3/16/1907
Wyatt, Pleas (col)	Lessie Shy (col)	11/20/1889
Wynn, Edward	Anna L. Ezell	12/11/1889
Wynn, James C.	Dessa C. Hodge	9/15/1893
Yancey, Benjamin	Clara Polk	2/19/1899
Yancey, Louis H.	Estelle V. Price	1/9/1898
Yancy, George	Mary B. Deason	8/21/1884

```
Yancy, James                Martha Kitchens         12/24/1818
Young, William (col)        Mary Smith (col)        8/12/1875


Zachry, Abner S.            Juliet A. Comer         10/7/1847
Zachry, W. L.               Mrs. Lula Bankston      12/14/1899
Zachry, Walter L.           Florance Price          3/18/1875
```

JASPER COUNTY MARRIAGES
SUPPLEMENTAL INDEX

```
Hogan, Lofton               Lemma Robinson          8/24/1877


Shy, Iverson (col)       Beatrice Jeffries (col) 12/27/1903
   (Letter ordering marriage license signed by W. A. Wagner)


?                           ? Thompson             11/6/1883
   (Letter of consent from J. Mat Thompson)


?                           ? Winans               12/20/1892
   (Letter of consent from Chester A. Winans)
```

CHAPTER II

ORIGINAL (UNBOUND) WILLS, 1809-1907

Record Group 179-2-4

This series contains original copies of probated wills. Usually, the case files on the administration of the estates are found in Series 3, "Estate Case Files," but in some instances there are variations in the spelling of the names between the two series. No effort has been made to compare the completeness of this file with the recorded copies in the Will Records volumes of the county. The file is arranged alphabetically by the name of the testator. The list below shows the names of the testators and the year the will was probated.

Aaron, Mitchel, 1881
Adams, James, 1857
Aken, James, 1871
Akins, Samuel S., 1851
Akins, Thomas, 1853
Alexander, Jane, 1822
Allen, Harris, 1854
Allen, Samuel, 1857
Allen, Susan, 1854
Allen, William, 1858
Armstrong, William, 1834
Avant, Henry, 1873
Avery, Samuel, 1883

Bailey, William H., 1855
Bailey, Williamson, 1857
Ballard, Mrs. W. E., 1903
Banks, Benjamin W., 1857
Banks, John C., 1861
Banks, Josiah C., 1859
Banks, Mary, 1859
Banks, Nancy, 1857
Barnes, Nancy, 1861
Barnett, Nathaniel, 1824
Bartlett, Eugene S., 1879
Bartlett, George T., 1885
Bartlett, Mary, 1851
Baynes, Elbert W., 1886
Baynes, John H., 1842
Benton, Abba, 1852
Binford, E. A., 1906
Blackwell, Samuel H., 1894
Bogan, John, 1868
Borum, George, 1823
Bowden, Nancey, 1853
Boyd, Richard, 1822
Brandon, John, 1859
Bridges, Bennett R., 1865
Broddus, Thomas, 1854
Byars, Obadiah, 1875

Campbell, Richard, 1851
Carter, Temperance, 1849
Chapman, Asa W. F., 1851
Cheek, William, 1868
Clark, Allen, 1884
Clark, George, 1846
Clark, Gilbert, 1885
Clark, John, 1861
Clark, Leama, 1907
Clay, Martha, 1851
Comer, Mary B., 1867
Comer, Thomas J., 1865

Compton, Jordan, 1863
Compton, Pleasant, 1822
Cornwell, George W., 1861
Couch, N. H., 1905
Couch, Nancy, 1884
Cox, Sarah, 1834
Cox, Wiley J., 1833
Crawford, Andrew, 1876
Crawman, Mary, 1843
Cross, John, 1823
Cunard, John, 1869
Cunard, John, Jr., 1861
Cunard, Jumina, 1872
Curry, Thompson, 1857

Daniel, Isaac, 1856
Digby, Berry T., 1879
Doggett, John, 1813
Doster, James C., 1863
Downs, John, 1817
Dozier, Abner C., 1869
Dozier, Adaline B., 1888
Driskell, Julia G., 1882
Dunn, William G., 1886
Dyer, Anthony, 1849

Edmonds, Rachel, 1824
Edwards, Reuben, 1864
Ellis, Henry, 1881
Ellis, Radford, 1811

Faulkner, John, 1861
Faulkner, Maston, 1849
Fears, Ailsey, 1859
Fish, Calvin, 1861
Fish, Emily B., 1871
Franklin, John Carter, 1877
Freeman, Cynthia A., 1879
Freeman, Floyd, 1905
Freeman, James, 1848
Freeman, Josiah, 1824
Freeman, Mary C., 1865

Gay, Sherrod H., 1859
Geiger, Elizabeth, 1853
Geiger, Harman H., 1868
Glover, Eli, Sr., 1858
Goode, James Henderson, 1857
Goode, Jesse, 1833
Goode, John C., 1862
Goolsby, Carden, 1882
Goolsby, Cincinnatus L., 1890
Goolsby, Jacob, 1862

Goolsby, William, 1872
Gordon, Louise, 1855
Gregory, Lewis, 1824
Grier, Thomas 1849

Hardman, Alphonso, 1864
Hardwick, Charity, 1886
Hartsfield, Middleton, 1851
Hawk, Henry, 1903
Henderson, Charles, 1885
Henderson, James, 1856
Henderson, Samuel, 1850
Hines, James, 1845
Hodge, D. R., 1879
Holloway, Dabney P., 1879
Holloway, Jesse, 1822
Horton, Elisha, 1853
Houghton, Josiah
Howard, J. B., 1897
Howard, Stephen, 1860
Hunter, Alexander A., 1864
Hunter, James T., 1860

Jackson, Pleasant, 1860
Jenkins, Francis, 1862
Jenkins, William, 1864
Johnston, James M., 1851
Johnston, John, 1844
Johnston, Martha M., 1875
Johnston, Thomas, 1844
Jones, David C., 1864
Jones, William, 1850
Jordan, Fleming, Sr., 1864
Jordan, Reuben, 1857

Keene, Ann T., 1852
Kelly, John R., 1878
Kelly, John W., 1875
Kennedy, Jane, 1823
Key, B. P., 1870
King, Dolly, 1849
Kitchens, Charles, 1864

Lane, William D., 1882
Langston, John E., 1862
Lawrence, Leroy, 1864
Lawrence, William, 1846
Lazenby, Mary A., 1886
Leverett, Martha Caroline, 1905
Long, George, 1858
Lowry, Ann, 1858
Lowry, Elizabeth, 1869
Lunsford, Leonard L., 1823
Lynch, Jarrett, 1863

Macon, Martha Williamson, 1809
Maddux, John, 1870
Maddux, John C., 1859
Maddux, William D., 1898
Malone, Anna B., 1888
Massey, Enos, 1880
Maxey, William, 1873
Meriwether, David, 1866

Meriwether, Sallie A., 1905
Minter, Jeremiah P., 1863
Mitchell, Richard, 1818
Montgomery, James N., 1866
Moreland, Frances, 1833
Norris, Benjamin F., 1859
Morris, Sarah M., 1884
Moseley, Henry, 1822

McClendon, Isaac, 1821
McClendon, Stephen W., 1857
McDowell, Daniel, 1860
McGlaughlin, James, 1889
McKee, John F. M., 1849
McKissack, Thomas, 1888
McMichael, Elijah H.L., 1863
McMichael, Shadrach, 1861
McMury, John, 1829

Newton, Aristarchus, 1869
Nolan, Elizabeth C., 1902

Oxford, Washington, 1891

Parker, Urania Elizabeth, 1853
Pearson, Jeremiah, 1855
Penn, Joseph, 1863
Penn, Martha A., 1883
Penn, Thomas R., 1906
Perkins, Moses, 1816
Peurifoy, Avaline, 1882
Peurifoy, B. W., 1896
Phelps, Aquilla, 1853
Phillips, Lewis, 1847
Phillips, Mary E., 1866
Phillips, Wiley, 1869
Porter, Matilda M., 1857
Post, Samuel, 1840
Pou, John T., 1880
Powell, A. L., 1892
Powell, Evan H., 1857
Powell, Rachel, 1879
Preston, William H., 1863
Price, Mary, 1858
Pye, James, 1854
Pye, Jordan, 1856
Pye, Theophilus, 1868

Ragland, Mary R., 1893
Ratcliff, Moses, 1837
Reese, Cuthbert, 1853
Reid, Samuel, 1836
Reid, William A., no date
Rivers, Benjamin, 1866
Robey, Nathan, 1826
Robey, Timothy, 1825
Robinson, William C., 1857
Roby, Williamson, 1834
Rogers, Dread, 1820
Ross, William, 1857

Satterwhite, Dawson, 1854
Shaw, John, 1868

Shepherd, Eleazer W., 1863
Shepherd, Sarah, 1862
Showers, Paschal, 1879
Shropshire, James W., 1866
Shropshire, Olivia J., 1873
Shy, Seaborn J., 1858
Smith, Abraham H., 1887
Smith, Charles S., 1856
Smith, David, 1865
Smith, Henry T., 1854
Smith, Henry T., 1906
Smith, John, 1826
Smith, John W. A., 1887
Smith, William G., 1863
Speairs, Caleb W., 1879
Spearman, G. T., 1868
Spearman, John, 1862
Spearman, Martha, 1883
Spears, Columbus A., 1863
Spears, Creed A., 1864
Spears, John, 1855
Spears, William H., 1881
Speights, James, 1872
Standifer, Archibald, 1867
Stanley, Martin, 1823

Talmadge, Stephen C., 1873
Taylor, Leonard, 1812
Thomas, William, 1907
Thomason, Thomas, 1850
Thompson, Henry, 1817
Toland, Michael M., 1857
Tompkins, Lucy Ann, 1849
Towns, John G., 1823

Traylor, Champion T., 1817
Traylor, Thomas, 1811
Tuggle, Elizabeth, 1854
Tuggle, William J.L., 1864
Turk, John, 1875
Turner, S. W., Jr., 1896

Vaughn, Stephen H., 1864

Wade, Benjamin, 1824
Waits, Benjamin, 1839
Waits, Leroy, 1863
Waldrep, Leecil J., 1883
Walker, Hackey, 1853
Walker, Henry, 1874
Ware, Henry, 1822
Watters, John C., 1854
Watters, Robert P., 1859
West, Andrew, 1851
White, Ann H., 1856
White, John, 1824
Whitfield, Matthew, 1864
Wilkins, Drury, 1834
Williams, James M., 1887
Wilson, Arkillis, 1831
Wilson, Joseph, 1822
Wilson, Rachael, 1879
Wooten, Elizabeth, 1828
Wyatt, Mary Ann, 1904
Wyatt, Thomas, 1853

Yancy, Lewis D., 1843
Yancy, Nancy, 1887

CHAPTER III

ESTATE (UNBOUND RECORDS) FILES, 1809-1907

Included in this series are all the papers generated in the settlement of the estate of a deceased person except that wills are in Series 4 rather than here. Also included are, in some instances, papers relating to the appointing of guardians for the minor children of the deceased. Often, if there was a civil court case connected with the administration or execution of the estate, the court case file is interfiled with the estate case file in this series.

No effort has been made to compare the completeness of these files with the estate papers recorded in the county's various volumes of estate records.

The files are arranged alphabetically by the surname of the deceased. A list of the folders is included below.

Aaron, James C.
Aaron, John L.
Aaron, John M.
Aaron, Mitchel
Abbott, Ezekiel
Adams, David L.
Adams, Elizabeth L.
Adams, George W.
Adams, James
Adams, Jonathan
Adams, Meridith
Aiken, Charles P.
Aiken, John C.
Aikens, James
Akens, Daniel
Akins, Samuel S.
Akins, Thomas
Alexander, Abden
Alexander, Eliza
Alexander, George
Alexander, Robert J.
Allen, David
Allen, Harris
Allen, John
Allen, Macon
Allen, Phoebe
Allen, Robert A.
Allen, Samuel
Allen, W. W.
Allen, William
Ambrose, Warren
Anderson, S. M.
Anderson, Samuel
Andrews, Davis R.
Andrews, Greene
Andrews, Robert
Annis, Emerson B.
Annis, Martha G.
Anthony, James
Antony, Milton
Appling, Otho H.
Armor, James
Armstrong, John
Armstrong, William
Arnold, William W.
Arrington, Elizabeth
Ashurst, Josiah T.
Askew, William
Atcheson, James A.

Avant, Henry
Averett, James
Avery, Asa G.
Avery, Herbert
Avery, Rose Ann
Avery, Samuel
Avery, William

Bailey, William H.
Bailey, Williamson
Baldwin, John
Baldwin, Marcus A.
Ballard, W. E.
Banks, Benjamin W.
Banks, Charles
Banks, Christopher C.
Banks, Dunstan
Banks, Eaton
Banks, James
Banks, John C.
Banks, John T.
Banks, Josiah C.
Barbee, Joseph
Barclay, Leroy P.
Barclay, William
Barkley, William
Barnes, Nancy
Barnett, Elijah F.
Barnett, Eliza
Barnett, Nathaniel
Barnwell, Elizabeth A.
Barr, Harriett N.
Barr, William J.
Barron, Andrew J.
Bartlett, Abner
Bartlett, Eugene S.
Bartlett, George T.
Bartlett, Mary
Bartlett, Samuel Eugene
Bass, Mitchel
Bass, William A.
Baynes, Alfred J.
Baynes, Elbert W.
Baynes, Gene
Baynes, John H.
Baynes, Sarah Elizabeth
Baysden, Mary
Beach, James
Beal, Elizabeth

Beall, James D.
Beasley, Robert C.
Beasley, Stephen W.
Beckwith, W. B.
Beckwith, William S.
Belcher, Green B.
Belcher, Isham S.
Belcher, Obadiah R.
Belcher, William D.
Bell, John
Bender, John S.
Benson, James M.
Benton, Abba
Benton, James
Benton, Jeremiah
Benton, John
Benton, Lucian
Benton, Otis M.
Benton, Sarah J.
Berner, William R.
Berry, A. T.
Berry, Anderson
Betts, Abraham
Binford, Cicero S.
Binford, Henry W.
Binford, Joseph T.
Binford, Josephine S.
Binns, Burwell
Birdsong, Benajah
Blackwell, J. H.
Blackwell, Samuel H.
Blackwell, Samuel S.
Blizzard, Henry
Blount, John
Blount, Susan
Bogan, John
Bond, William S.
Bonner, Whitmill
Boon, Exum
Boon, Jacob
Boram, George
Boram, John
Boswell, Henry
Bowden, Amanda M.
Bowden, Nancy
Boyd, Samuel
Boykin, Francis
Boykin, Jesse W.
Boykin, William P.
Boynton, Stewart
Bozeman, Samuel
Bradford, Edmund
Brady, Thomas
Brandon, James
Brandon, John
Brantley, Green D.
Branum, Harris
Brazil, Samuel
Brazil, William
Brazwell, Aaron
Breedlove, Ann
Brewer, Elisha W.
Bridges, Bennett

Bridges, Wiseman
Briers, John
Britt, Willis
Broddus, Edward A.
Broddus, Edward S.
Broddus, Thomas
Brooks, Iverson S.
Brooks, James, Sr.
Brooks, Russell
Brooks, William
Broughton, Belitha
Broughton, Charles
Brown, Bartlett
Brown, Edward
Brown, George A.
Brown, James
Brown, Jeremiah
Brown, John W.
Brown, Josiah
Brown, Robert
Brown, Russel J.
Brown, Sucky
Bryant, Artemus
Bryant, John
Buchanan, Benjamin
Buchannan, Alexander N.
Buchannon, James, Sr.
Buchannon, John
Buis, John
Bullard, James, Sr.
Bullard, Wiley
Bullard, William
Burney, Charles C.
Burney, J. H.
Burney, John W., Sr.
Burney, Tom
Butler, Thomas
Butts, Samuel
Byars, Obadiah
Byrom, John
Byrom, Seymore S.

Caldwell, William D.
Callaway, James C.
Callaway, John
Callaway, Joshua
Calvert, Susan E.
Campbell, Charles E. F. W.
Campbell, Charles G.
Campbell, Cooley
Campbell, Dorcas
Campbell, James L.
Campbell, Jarrett
Campbell, Richard
Campbell, Richard S.
Campbell, William C.
Cardel, John C.
Cardell, Peter
Carden, James
Cardin, William
Cargile, Charles
Cargile, John
Cargile, Thomas

Carlisle, Mary
Carmichael, John
Carter, Kissiah
Carter, Landon
Carter, Richard
Case, Wiley J.
Castellow, John B., Sr.
Castleberry, Thomas
Catchings, Elbert G.
Chaffin, Beverly
Chaffin, John T.
Champion, Moses
Chapman, Abner
Chapman, Asa W. F.
Chapman, Edmond
Chapman, John
Cheek, John W.
Cheek, LaFayette
Cheek, William
Cheney, William R.
Cherry, Jesse
Childs, Henry
Childs, Jack
Clark, Emily
Clark, Francis A.
Clark, George W.
Clark, Gilbert
Clark, John
Clark, Joseph
Clark, Joshua
Clark, Joshua R.
Clark, Lindsey
Clark, Thomas
Clark, Thomas
Clay, Hezekiah
Clay, James C.
Clay, Jesse, Sr.
Clay, Martha S.
Cleckley, Jacob
Clements, Allen
Clements, Peyton
Coats, James
Cochran, Cheadle
Cochran, John
Cochran, Jubil
Cole, Elizabeth L.
Cole, Rene
Cole, William
Collier, John
Collier, William
Colquit, John Terry
Comer, Lydia
Comer, Mary B.
Comer, Thomas J.
Compton, John W.
Compton, Jordan
Compton, Pleasant
Compton, Polly Ann
Conner, John W.
Cook, Benjamin W.
Cook, John W.
Cornwell, Elijah
Cornwell, George W.

Cornwell, Gibson H.
Cornwell, Obadiah
Cornwell, William D.
Couch, Moses
Couch, N. H.
Couch, Nancy
Cousins, John
Cousins, Thomas
Cox, Jesse
Cox, Wiley J.
Crain, Spencer, Sr.
Crall, James
Crawford, Andrew
Crawford, Samuel
Crawman, Mary
Creagh, Thomas B.
Crenshaw, Jarrell
Cross, George
Cross, John
Crow, Elisha
Crow, John M.
Culbertson, Samuel
Cunard, John
Cunard, Jumina
Curry, John
Curry, Thompson
Cuthbert, Alfred

Dabney, Anderson
Dabney, Hannah
Daniel, Alexander
Daniel, Isaac
Daniel, John W.
Daniel, Levi
Daniel, Moses
Daniel, Thomas
Danielly, Nancy
Darden, James M.
Darden, John
Darden, John B.
Davidson, John, Sr.
Davidson, Robert
Davis, Thomas
Dawkins, George
Dawkins, Partheny
Deadwilder, Eva
Deal, William
Deane, Nathaniel
Deane, Thomas
Dennis, Jesse
Dickinson, Henry A.
Digby, Benjamin
Digby, Berry T.
Digby, John
Digby, John B.
Dillard, John A.
Dillard, Thomas
Dillon, John
Dingler, William
Dismukes, Martha D.
Dodson, Elijah
Doggett, Garner
Doggett, John

Dorsett, Palemon W.
Doster, James C.
Doster, James W.
Dougherty, William
Downs, S. P.
Downs, Skelly
Dozier, Abner C.
Dozier, George R.
Dozier, Woody
Driskell, James B.
Driskell, John
Driskell, Julia G.
Duke, Isham
Duncan, Thomas
Dunn, Albert G.
Dunn, Gatewood
Dunn, William G.
Durden, Stephen J.
Dyer, Anthony
Dyer, John P.

Echols, Elizabeth
Edmonds, Rachel
Edmondson, Benjamin C.
Edmondson, Crawford
Edmondson, Samuel
Edwards, Herbert
Edwards, James
Edwards, Joel J.
Edwards, John
Edwards, Reuben
Edwards, Robert S.
Edwards, William J.
Egnew, William
Elder, Edward A.
Elder, Susan
Elder, Turner
Ellis, Henry
Ellis, James
Ellis, John B.
Ellis, Radford
English, Augustus
Epps, Joseph
Eubanks, Magers
Evans, Henry W.
Evans, Jesse, Sr.
Evans, Josiah J.
Ezell, Braxton R.
Ezell, John
Ezell, Robert

Farley, John
Farrar, William G.
Faulkner, James Hilton
Faulkner, John
Faulkner, Maston
Faulkner, Zachariah
Favors, Joseph C.
Fears, Alsea
Fears, Benjamin Franklin
Fears, Ezekiel
Fears, William Q.
Fears, Wyly

Featherston, Richard
Fincher, Leonard C.
Fish, Calvin
Fish, Nathan
Fitzpatrick, Bouth
Fitzpatrick, William
Fitzsimmons, Emma
Flemister, Ellender G.
Flemister, James C.
Florence, A. S.
Flournoy, Josiah
Flournoy, Samuel A.
Flournoy, William F.
Folds, Charles J.
Folds, Grandason
Folds, Jacob
Folds, John
Ford, Washington
Foreman, Jacob
Franklin, John C.
Frazier, Andrew
Freeman, Bailey
Freeman, Benjamin B.
Freeman, Daniel
Freeman, George
Freeman, Hartwell W. B.
Freeman, Hopson
Freeman, Isaac H.
Freeman, James
Freeman, Josiah
Freeman, Mary C.
Funderburk, William A.

Gallman, John C.
Gardner, Ethelred
Garland, John
Garrett, Blunty
Garrett, George S.
Gaston, Catharine
Gaston, Nancy A.
Gaston, P. F.
Gaston, Thomas
Gay, Sherrod H.
Geiger, Elizabeth
Geiger, Harmon H.
Geiger, Randal H.
Geiger, Washington
George, James
Gholston, Anthony
Gibson, John C.
Gilstrap, John B.
Glenn, Thornton I.
Glover, Eli
Glover, Eli S.
Glover, Henry S., Sr.
Glover, John
Glover, John E.
Goggins, Madison
Good, Sterling
Good, Theophilus
Goode, James H.
Goode, Jesse
Goode, John C.

Goode, William
Goodman, Barney
Goolsby, Cardin
Goolsby, Cincinattus L.
Goolsby, Dennis
Goolsby, Jacob
Goolsby, James B.
Goolsby, John, Sr.
Goolsby, Levi
Goolsby, Wade B.
Goolsby, William
Gordon, Charles P.
Gordon, Louisa
Gordon, Mary D.
Gordon, Thomas A.
Grace, John
Graham, James
Grant, Samuel
Grant, Thomas
Graves, Lewis
Gray, A. T.
Green, Pleasant
Green, William, Sr.
Greene, Burwell
Greer, Aaron
Greer, Abraham
Greer, Crawford H., Sr.
Greer, Hattie
Greer, Jefferson
Greer, John R.
Greer, Robert S.
Greer, Thomas L.
Gregory, Lewis
Gregory, Matthew
Grier, Aaron W.
Griggs, John J.
Grimmett, James T.
Grimmett, Sarah E.
Grimmett, William
Grinnell, Benjamin
Grinnell, Charles
Gross, John
Grubbs, Elisha C.
Grubbs, Wiley B.
Guinn, Franklin
Gunn, Gabriel

Hadley, Thomas
Hairston, Moses B.
Hairston, Thomas
Hale, Josey
Hall, James N.
Hall, John
Hamilton, Thomas P.
Hamilton, Winney
Hammel, G. A.
Hancock, William
Hardman, Alphonzo
Hardin, John S.
Hardin, Silas M.
Hardwick, William
Hardy, Benajah
Hardy, Cornelius

Hardy, William P.
Harral, James
Harris, David
Harris, Isham
Harris, John
Harris, Mary
Harrison, Epthpatha
Harrison, Henry
Hartsfield, Middleton
Harvey, Zepheniah
Harwell, Mason
Hatcher, Uriah
Hawk, Seaborn J.
Hawkins, John W.
Hay, Edmond
Hay, Stephen
Hay, Washington
Hay, William T.
Hays, Rebecca
Heath, Richard
Henderson, Charles
Henderson, Frankie
Henderson, Isaac W.
Henderson, James
Henderson, Jane L.
Henderson, John
Henderson, Joseph
Henderson, Samuel
Henderson, William
Henly, Abijah
Hester, William
Hicks, John
Hicks, John J.
Hicks, Joseph
Higginbotham, Jacob
Higginbotham, Joseph
Higginbotham, Robert
Hill, Isaac
Hill, James
Hill, Lawrence
Hill, Theophilus
Hill, William
Hines, Elias
Hines, James, Sr.
Hines, John
Hitchcock, Matthew
Hitchcock, William
Hobson, Christopher
Hobson, John
Hodge, Duke R.
Hodge, James
Hodge, William
Hodnett, Benjamin
Holifield, Polly
Holifield, Wiley
Holland, Henry J.
Holland, J. L.
Holland, James W.
Holland, Jonas H., Sr.
Holland, Lawson S.
Holland, Levinia
Holland, Lewis C.
Holland, Margarett

Holland, Mary A.
Holland, William T.
Holloway, Alsey
Holloway, Dabney P.
Holloway, Elizabeth
Holloway, Isam
Holloway, James M.
Holloway, Jesse
Holloway, Samuel
Holsenbeck, Alfred
Holsey, George
Hood, Wiley
Hooks, John W.
Hooten, James
Horton, Elisha
Horton, James
Horton, Mary Jane
Horton, Seaborn R.
Houghton, Josiah
Howard, James B.
Howard, Samuel
Howard, Stephen
Hubbard, Samuel
Huff, Clayton W.
Huff, Ralph
Huff, Thomas
Hungerford, Anson, Jr.
Hunt, James
Hunt, Jesse
Hunt, W. H.
Hunter, Henry
Hunter, James T.
Hunter, S. A.
Hunter, T. P.
Hurt, William
Huson, David
Hutchings, Richard S.
Hutchison, M. H.
Hutchison, Thomas L.

Ivey, Lot
Ivy, Henry
Ivy, Robert W.
Ivy, Wenney

Jackson, Eliza
Jackson, Isaac
Jackson, John
Jackson, Pleasant
Jackson, Thomas
Jeffries, B. S.
Jeffries, Colbert
Jeffries, Cordial D.
Jeffries, Georgia Ann
Jeffries, Thomas
Jeffries, William R.
Jenkins, Cyrus R.
Jenkins, Francis
Jenkins, John H.
Jenkins, William
Jewett, Martha
Johns, Thomas
Johnson, Alexander

Johnson, Alfred
Johnson, Annis T.
Johnson, Felix
Johnson, Haney
Johnson, James M.
Johnson, John
Johnson, Snellen
Johnson, Thomas M.
Johnson, Walter
Johnson, William, Sr.
Johnston, Martha M.
Johnston, Nathan
Johnston, Thomas
Johnston, William A.
Johnston, William H.
Jones, David C.
Jones, Edward
Jones, Joseph
Jones, Mary
Jones, Vincent
Jones, William, Sr.
Jones, William L.
Jordan, Benjamin
Jordan, Bill
Jordan, Fleming, Sr.
Jordan, Jack
Jordan, Reuben, Sr.
Jordan, Spencer
Jordan, Sterling
Jordan, Thomas M.
Jordan, William P., Sr.

Keeling, William
Keene, Ann T.
Keene, Benjamin F.
Kello, Samuel B.
Kelly, Allen
Kelly, Daniel
Kelly, Eaton S.
Kelly, Jane E.
Kelly, Jarrett B.
Kelly, John C.
Kelly, John H., Sr.
Kelly, John R.
Kelly, John W.
Kelly, Mary
Kelly, Seaborn C.
Kendrick, Shadrack
Kendrix, Angie
Kennedy, David
Key, B. P.
Key, Mary G.
Kilby, William
Kilgore, William
Kimball, Benjamin
Kimble, David
Kinard, Francis M.
Kinard, John H.
Kinebrew, Shadrack
King, B. G.
King, Cattel
King, Dolly
King, John Mitchel

King, Mitchel
King, Richard D.
King, William
Kieby, David D.
Kitchens, Charles
Knight, John, Sr.

Lacey, Philemon
Landrum, Thomas
Lane, Augustus W.
Lane, Davis
Lane, John T.
Lane, L. A.
Lane, William D.
Langston, David M.
Langston, Isaac L.
Langston, Jefferson F.
Langston, John E.
Lanier, William
Lasetter, Elisha
Lawrence, James
Lawrence, Leroy
Lawrence, Seaborn
Lawrence, William, Sr.
Lawrence, William, Jr.
Laws, Martin
Lawson, David
Lawson, Mary
Lawson, Sarah A.
Lawson, William
Layson, C. C., Sr.
Lazenby, Ellender
Lazenby, John
Lazenby, William
Ledbetter, Henry
Lee, William
Leggett, C. R.
Letson, Robert
Leverett, Jesse
Leverett, William C.
Lewis, James B.
Lewis, Mary Ann
Lewis, Phillip
Lindsey, John L.
Lindsey, Samuel
Littlejohn, Thomas
Lloyd, Edmund
Lockwood, James
Long, George
Lovejoy, Colman B.
Lovejoy, Eleazer
Lovejoy, John D.
Lovejoy, Pleasant P.
Lowery, Ann
Lowery, Kirby D.
Lowry, Elizabeth
Loyall, Jesse
Loyd, Thomas, Jr.
Lucas, John
Luckie, William F.
Lumpkin, John
Lumpkin, Mary
Lumsden, Jeremiah

Lunsford, Leonard L.
Lynch, Jarrett
Lyon, John

Macon, Nathaniel G.
Maddux, John
Maddux, William D.
Malay, James
Malone, Allen M.
Malone, Annie B.
Malone, Cader
Malone, Floyd
Malone, Francis
Malone, Frank, Sr.
Malone, Jarrel
Malone, Jarrett
Malone, Jeptha
Malone, Mary Lucy
Malone, Sherod
Malone, W. B.
Malone, William
Mapp, Jeremiah
Marks, James K.
Martin, Hugh M.
Mashburn, Jefferson
Massey, Enos
Mathews, Jefferson
Maxey, Garland
Maxey, William
Mayberry, Adam P.
Mays, Abney
Medford, George
Medlock, George
Melton, Timothy
Mercer, William
Meriwether, Charles
Meriwether, David, Sr.
Meriwether, George M.
Meriwether, Lula
Meriwether, Matilda A.
Meriwether, Sallie A.
Messer, William
Middlebrooks, Joseph A.
Millen, George D.
Millen, Henry
Millen, John
Miller, Daniel
Miller, William
Minter, F. B.
Minter, Jeremiah P.
Minter, Joe
Minter, John W.
Minter, Richard
Minter, Robert J.
Minter, Thomas C.
Minter, William S.
Miser, Joseph
Mitchel, Daniel
Mitchell, Richard
Mize, James
Mobley, Stephen
Montgomery, Benjamin H.
Montgomery, David

Montgomery, James H.
Moore, Augustus C.
Moore, Hiram
Moore, John
Moore, Palatine
Moreland, Francis
Moreland, John
Moreland, Thomas
Morgan, Charles
Morgan, Milton
Morgan, Stokley
Morgan, William J.
Morris, Benjamin F.
Morris, John G.
Morris, Sarah M.
Morris, Stephen
Morris, William
Mosely, Henry
Mosely, W. R.
Moses, John
Moss, Archibald
Moss, Susannah C.
Moye, Thomas W.
Mygatt, George
Myles, William H.

McAfee, Greene
McAfee, Robert
McBean, Henry L.
McClelland, David
McClendon, Ethelred
McClendon, Isaac
McClendon, Joel
McClendon, Jonathan
McClendon, Moses J.
McClendon, Stephen W.
McClendon, Washington
McClendon, Wiley F.
McCormack, James
McCune, Thomas B.
McDaniel, Jacob
McDaniel, George F.
McDonald, William A.
McDowell, Daniel
McDowell, James M.
McDowell, John M.
McDowell, Mary Ann
McDowell, Michael A.
McDowell, William
McElhenney, G. W.
McElhenney, John
McElhenney, Vincent H.
McEncroe, William
McGahee, Benjamin
McGehee, Edward
McKee, Lewis W.
McKemie, James
McKemie, John
McKinley, Lula
McKissack, Duncan
McKissack, John
McKissack, Thomas
McKissack, William T.

McLaughlin, James
McLemore, Catherine
McLendon, Francis M.
McLeroy, James
McMichael, David
McMichael, Elijah
McMichael, Elijah H. L.
McMichael, Greene L.
McMichael, James
McMichael, John L.
McMichael, Shadrack
McMichael, William
McMichael, William T.
McMichael, Zachariah
McMurrin, John
McMurry, John
McNeil, Daniel F.

Nall, Nathan
Newby, John
Newton, Aris
Newton, Julia
Newton, Lucien B.
Newton, Mark L.
Newton, Martha B.
Newton, Mary F.
Newton, O. H. P.
Newton, Oliver H.
Newton, Willis
Nichols, Jeff
Noles, Elinor
Noles, J. H.
Noles, John W.
Noles, William D.

Odoms, Mrs. S. E.
Odum, Winburn
Organ, Matthew
Orr, Allen
Osborne, William
Owens, Jacob
Owens, Stewart
Owens, Susannah C.
Oxford, James W.
Oxford, R. L.
Ozborn, James

Paine, Thomas
Parham, Polly
Parker, Ann Eliza
Parker, Isaac L.
Parker, Lewis S.
Parker, William C.
Parks, John B.
Parks, William
Parnell, John
Parrot, Henry
Paschall, Samuel
Patterson, Jesse
Payne, John
Peacock, Daniel
Peacock, John
Peacock, William

Pearson, Austin
Pearson, Jeremiah
Pearson, John W.
Pearson, Reese
Peddy, Wiley
Peeler, Anthony
Pelot, S. C.
Penn, Joseph
Penn, Martha A.
Penn, Stephen A.
Penn, William
Penn, William C.
Pennington, Thomas
Pennington, William B.
Penson, James
Perkins, David A.
Perkins, Moses
Perkins, Paul
Perry, Elvira
Perry, James
Perry, William
Persons, Benjamin
Peurifoy, Arrington
Peurifoy, Avoline
Peurifoy, B. W.
Peurifoy, McCarroll
Peurifoy, Silas M.
Phelps, Aquilla, Sr.
Phelps, Aquilla, Jr.
Phelps, Washington
Phillips, Augustus C.
Phillips, Bryant G.
Phillips, Hillery
Phillips, Isaac
Phillips, John B. M.
Phillips, Lewis
Phillips, Mary E.
Phillips, Richard
Phillips, Wiley H.
Phillips, William L.
Phinizee, William
Pinchard, James
Piper, Thomas L.
Pitts, John D.
Pitts, Joseph A.
Pitts, Nester
Pitts, Permelia
Platt, George
Plummer, Samuel
Polk, Charles E.
Polk, Joshua F.
Pollard, Richard
Pon, John T.
Pon, Taylor
Poole, Abram
Poole, Thomas
Pope, Annie J.
Pope, John C.
Pope, Josiah
Pope, Miller W.
Pope, William K.
Porter, Catharine
Porter, Elizabeth

Porter, Matilda M.
Porter, William
Portwood, Catherine
Post, Samuel
Potter, Adam C.
Potter, Pleasant
Potts, Stephen
Powell, Allie Laura
Powell, Evan H.
Powell, John G.
Powell, Moses
Powell, Whit
Powell, William R.
Preston, Charles T.
Preston, William H., Jr.
Price, Edward
Price, John
Price, Robert
Prtichett, Alfred M.
Pritchett, T. J.
Pritchett, William H.
Puckett, Martin
Purkins, Daniel
Pye, Bartheny
Pye, Griffin L.
Pye, Harmon W.
Pye, James
Pye, Jordan
Pye, Thadeus
Pye, Theophilus
Pye, Thomas W.

Radcliff, Moses
Radden, David
Ragan, Asa
Ragland, Pettus
Rainey, Matthew
Rainey, Nathaniel H.
Rainey, William
Ramey, Absalom
Ramey, Allice
Ramey, Clarissa
Ramey, Daniel M.
Ramey, Elizabeth P.
Reddick, George
Reddick, Henry
Reese, Cuthbert
Reeves, Joel A.
Reeves, Joseph
Reid, Samuel
Reid, Virgil
Reid, William A.
Repass, Churchwell
Rhodes, Samuel P.
Richardson, George
Richey, Edward J.
Ricketts, Richard S.
Ridley, Archibald B.
Rivers, Benjamin
Rivers, Fred
Rivers, James
Robert, Lawrence Wood
Roberts, Bartholomew G.

Roberts, Daniel
Roberts, James H.
Roberts, Sarah
Robertson, Isaac E.
Robertson, John
Robey, Eliza Jane
Robinson, Cornelius
Robinson, James F.
Robinson, James T.
Robinson, Jerry
Robinson, John
Robinson, Thomas
Robinson, William C.
Roby, Milledge
Roby, Nathan
Roby, Thomas L.
Roby, Timothy
Roby, Walter L.
Roby, Williamson
Roby, Williamson B.
Rodgers, James H.
Rogers, Enoch
Rogers, Robert
Ross, William
Rowe, John C.
Russel, David
Ryan, Lewis

Sanders, Ephraim P.
Sansom, Richard
Satterwhite, Dawson
Seymore, John R.
Seymore, Martha
Shard, Cornelius
Sharman, James
Sharp, James
Sharpe, William
Shaw, John
Shaw, Watson
Sheffeld, Barnabee
Shepherd, Abraham
Shepherd, Eleazer W.
Shepherd, William L.
Shepherd, Winburn R.
Shipp, Gustavus V.
Shockley, George W.
Shorter, Oliver
Showers, Elridge
Showers, Paschal
Shropshire, James E.
Shropshire, James W.
Shropshire, Mrs. M. G.
Shy, Frank
Shy, Peyton
Shy, Samuel
Shy, Seaborn J.
Siler, William D., Sr.
Simmons, Sanders W.
Simms, Richard S.
Simonton, Gilbraith
Simpson, John
Simpson, John J.
Sistrunk, Samuel

Slaughter, Andrew G.
Slaughter, Elizabeth T.
Slaughter, Henry
Slaughter, John B.
Slaughter, Nathan T.
Slaughter, Sarah
Slaughter, Thomas K.
Sluder, John
Smart, Elisha
Smart, Francis B.
Smith, Abraham H.
Smith, Alexander
Smith, Andrew
Smith, Charles L.
Smith, David
Smith, Edgar T.
Smith, Edward B.
Smith, Fanny
Smith, Francis
Smith, Harrison J.
Smith, Henry T.
Smith, Jacob E.
Smith, Jeff
Smith, Jesse
Smith, Jesse H.
Smith, John H.
Smith, John T.
Smith, John W. A.
Smith, Lucy B.
Smith, Mattie A.
Smith, Richard B.
Smith, Rolin
Smith, Samuel R., Sr.
Smith, Thomas
Smith, Thomas J.
Smith, Thomas R.
Smith, Thomas W.
Smith, William G.
Smith, William H.
Smith, Wyatt R.
Smith, Zachariah A.
Smith, Zipporah A.
Spear, Harry
Spearman, Gabriel T.
Spearman, John F.
Spears, Augustus
Spears, Columbus A.
Spears, Creed E.
Spears, Eaton
Spears, James T.
Spears, Jesse
Spears, John
Spears, John Wesley
Spears, Joshua B.
Spears, Josiah C.
Spears, Sidney
Spears, Thomas J.
Spears, William
Spears, William H.
Speights, James
Spence, Paul
Spencer, Jesse M.
Standifer, Archibald

Stanford, Joel
Stanford, Jordan
Steel, Francis M. W.
Steel, William F. M.
Stevens, Tucker I.
Stewart, Francis M.
Stewart, James
Stokes, Ignatius
Stokes, William B.
Stone, John W.
Stone, Mahala Ann
Strickland, Solomon, Sr.
Stringfellow, George W.
Stringfellow, James
Stubbs, James, Sr.
Swanson, F. M.
Swinney, Ransom

Talmadge, John
Talmadge, John H.
Talmadge, Stephen C.
Taylor, Francis N.
Taylor, Leonard
Taylor, William H.
Teddars, C. M.
Tedders, Samuel
Terrell, Thomas
Thomas, William
Thomason, Jackson C.
Thomason, Thomas
Thompson, Alexander
Thompson, Hannah
Thompson, Jacob M.
Thompson, James
Thompson, Jeremiah
Thompson, Robert M.
Thompson, Sallie
Thurman, Phillip
Thurmond, Fountain M.
Tillman, John
Tillman, Phoebe
Tindill, Jonathan
Toland, Michael M.
Toland, Sally
Toland, Samuel
Tomlinson, John D.
Tompkins, Lucy Ann
Towns, John G.
Towns, John T. C.
Traylor, Champion T.
Traylor, William H.
Trippe, William
Truit, Riley
Truitt, John
Trussell, Charles H.
Tucker, Allen
Tucker, Sarah
Tuggle, Elizabeth
Tuggle, Junie A.
Tuggle, Robert
Tuggle, William J. L.
Tuggle, William R.
Tuggle, Willie

Turk, John
Turk, Jonathan
Turk, William C.
Turner, John G.
Turner, Thomas M.
Turner, Toliver A.
Turney, P. F.
Tyler, Francis M.
Tyler, Job
Tyler, John
Tyler, Marcus H.
Tyler, Samuel B.
Tyner, R. John
Tyson, Henry F.

Urquhart, Alexander
Urquhart, Mary V.
Vardeman, William
Varner, William
Vaughan, Benjamin T.
Vaughn, James M.
Vaughn, Stephen H.
Vaughn, Thomas J.
Vaughn, William
Vickers, Elijah

Wade, Benjamin
Wade, Elizabeth L.
Wade, H.
Wade, James
Wade, Mary A. E.
Wagner, Sampson
Wagoner, Hiram
Waits, Alexander
Waits, Amy
Waits, Benjamin
Waits, John
Waldrep, Leecel
Waldrop, Delphia A.
Waldrop, Johnson
Waldrop, Solomon
Walker, Hackey
Walker, Henry
Walker, James
Walker, Magers
Walker, Moses
Walker, William W.
Walthall, Edward
Walton, Bluford M.
Walton, Henry B.
Walton, Hiram
Walton, Robert J.
Wammack, James
Wammack, Williamson L. B.
Ward, James D. S.
Ward, John E.
Ware, Henry
Ware, Joseph H.
Warren, Bray
Warren, Edmond
Warren, Edward
Waters, Robert P.
Watkins, Alexander

Watson, James
Watters, Jane
Watters, John C.
Watters, Mary C.
Weathersbee, Owen
Webb, Annie J.
Webb, Eliza
Webb, James
Webb, P. A.
Webb, Thomas P.
Weights, John
Weldon, Andrew
Weldon, Isaac (see Wilder,
           Isaac)
Weldon, Mary
Wellborn, William T.
West, J. A. J.
Wethersbee, Charlott M.
Whatley, Willis
Whitaker, John P.
White, Ann H.
White, John
White, Joseph
White, Lucius
White, Nehemiah B.
White, Samuel
White, Thomas
Whitfield, John B.
Whitfield, Matthew
   (2 folders)
Whitfield, Matthew C.
Wiggins, Wade
Wilburn, Herman H.
Wilburn, Leonidas C.
Wilder, Dred
Wilder, Isaac
Wilkerson, Harmon
Wilkins, Drury
Wilkins, William
Willard, Roswell
Willaims, Alfred
Williams, Augustus L.
Williams, Francis M.
Williams, James M.
Williams, N. M.
Williams, Thomas R.
Williams, William L., Sr.
Williams, Zachariah
Williamson, Isaac
Willingham, William
Willis, Arthur
Willis, Jonathon
Willson, George
Willson, James E.
Willson, John
Wilson, A. J.
Wilson, Adell S.
Wislon, Arkillis
Wilson, Elijah
Wilson, George J.
Wilson, Jenkins
Wilson, Joseph A.
Wilson, Rachael

Wilson, Sarah
Wilson, Thomas S.
Wilson, William S.
Wimbush, Mary Jane
Wise, Barney
Wise, Isaiah
Wise, James C.
Wise, Patton
Wiseners, Thomas
Wolfe, William
Wood, John
Wooten, Elizabeth
Wooten, James
Wright, George W.
Wright, Thomas
Wyatt, G. W.
Wyatt, Isaac T.
Wyatt, John W.
Wyatt, Mary A. F.
Wyatt, Thomas
Wyatt, William H.
Wynens, Elisha S.
Wynn, William

Yancey, Lewis D.
Yancey, Nancy
Yancey, Sarah
Yancey, Ellender
Yancy, Layton
Yates, James
Young, Ernest L.

Zachary, Abner S.

CHAPTER IV

MISCELLANEOUS PENSION RECORDS, 1812-1920

Record Group 179-2-13

NOTE: The Georgia Department of Archives and History has Civil War pensions of Georgia residents who served in the Southern Cause. For Federal Pensions for other wars, write to Military Service Records, National Archives, Washington, DC 20408.

This series contains original unbound pension records involving:

    (1)   Applications for business licenses and issuances of same.
    (2)   Applications for pensions.
    (3)   Commissioner's of Pensions correspondence.
    (4)   Confederate soldiers' pensions.
    (5)   Miscellaneous correspondence.
    (6)   Deceased veterans lists.
    (7)   Pre-Civil War pensions.
    (8)   Widows' pensions.
    (9)   Miscellaneous

These papers deal primarily with the early bureaucratic workings of the pension board in providing welfare to war veterans. There are a few records that go back as far as the Indian War and War of 1812. It should be noted that in no case are these records complete. They have been flattened and placed in folders. Box 1 has been arranged alphabetically by subject and thereunder alphabetically by surname. Box 2 is unarranged.

Applications for Business Licenses & Licenses Issued
-Barnes, George S., 1902
-Bartlett, Robert E., 1893
-Blackwell, Samuel S., 1899
-Burney, J. H., 1894
-Cox, William M., 1898
-Craine, Marcus L., 1897
-Elliott, James H., 1898
-Fish, William T., 1893
-Folds, George W., 1897
-Grantham, William R., 1888
-Holsenbeck, Alexander, 1899
-Jones, Robert B., 1899
-Loftin, E. M., 1889
-Murphy, James F., 1896
-McClendon, J. A., 1896
-McElhenney, Barney F., 1901
-Pitts, Carrinton, 1897
-Ritchey, Edward J., 1897
-Rodgers, Bud, 1896
-Shropshire, William W., 1898
-Smith, John C. C., 1896
-Waller, J. S., 1900
-Water, William B., 1897

Applications for Pensions
-Burney, John W., 1898
-Cox, A. L., 1901
-Dennis, John M., 1900
-Dukes, Joseph T., 1897
-Faulkner, John H., 1897
-Fears, Wiley M., 1894
-Hardy, Cornelius, 1873
-Jackson, John F., 1900
-Key, M. B., 1895
-Morgan, Henry, 1897

-Niblett, Tilman, 1894
-Noles, David G., 1896
-Parker, William, 1899
-Pope, James J., 1900
-Price, John W., 1875
-Shropshire, John W., 1893
-Tugle, Lee, 1873
-Waldrop, John S., 1893

Commissioner's of Pensions correspondence, 1898-1919
Confederate soldiers' pensions, 1898-1920
Correspondence, miscellaneous
-Boyer, W. H., 1901
-Miller, James, 1866

Deceased Veterans, 1919
Soldiers' Pensions (Pre-Civil War)
-Goff, Nathaniel, 1830
-Hobbs, Robert, 1843
-Jones, William, 1829
-Wright, John, 1831

Widow's pensions, 1892-1920
Miscellaneous
-1815 Arms & Equipment Report
-Indian War (letter seeking veterans)
-Goolsby, William (claim against Southern Claims
   Commission, 1874)
-Murphy, James S. (admission to Soldiers Home, 1901)
-War of 1812 (David Cook and Frederick Dukes)

Box 2:
Civil War Pension Papers
1903-1922

CHAPTER V

SUPERIOR COURT CASE FILES, 1809-1922

Record Group 179-1-1

NOTE: Not included below are some interrogatories in
Record Group 172-12-10, Box 13. See page 469.

These Civil and Criminal case files of the Superior Court
are very often incomplete. In many instances only portions of
the papers that should be found on a given case are actually in
the file. The type of documents that are included are not con-
sistent from one case to another. Contrary to the normal manner
of citing cases by listing the plantiff first and then the defendant, these are arranged and listed by the name of the defendant. All names on the list below are spelled as they appeared
on the documents.

Aarant, Mitchel vs. The State
Aaron, Green and Clarissa Aaron vs. James M. Williams
Aaron, James C. and William H. Aaron vs. George T. Bartlett
Aaron, John vs. Samuel B. Ewing
Aaron, John and Thomas Dillard vs. William H. Goodrich
Aaron, john vs. The State
Aaron, John L. vs. Francis M. Swanson and Elbert G. Catchings
Aaron, Mitchel, Jesse Cliatt and James Buchannon vs.
    Anthony Dyer
Aaron, Mitchell vs. Reuben Lawson
Aaron, Mitchell and Sarah Aaron vs. James Pate
Aaron, Mitchell vs. Nahemiah B. White and Lucius White
Aaron, R. A., J. C. Aaron and Joseph Lemmonds vs. Linton
    Cheney
Aaron, R. A., J. C. Aaron and Joseph Lemons vs. Officers of
    Court
Aaron, Richard vs. The State
Aaron, Richard A. vs. George T. Bartlett
Aaron, W. A. vs. The State
Aaron, William H., and Gilbert W. Shaw vs. William S. Hurd
    Anson Hungerford
Aaron, William H. and James C. Aaron vs. John C. Watters,
    Dyer C. Bancroft, Executor, and Andrew J. Watters, Executor
Abbet, Goodwin W. vs. The State
Abbett, Ezekiel vs. Graham Sellbeck
Abbett, Peter J. vs. Adam McClendon
Abbett, Peter J. vs. John Owen
Abbett, Goodwin vs. Henry Jordan
Abbott, Goodwin W. vs. Peter Jaillet and Peter F. Jaillet
Abbott, Goodwin W. vs. Thomas F. Nolan
Abbott, Peter A. vs. John Carden
Abbott, Peter I. vs. Thomas Grier
Abernathy, Caleb vs. James Johnson and Thomas W. Harris
Abernathy, Caleb vs. The State
Abernethy, Caleb vs. Thomas P. Carnes
Abernethy, Caleb vs. Liberty Holmes
Abernethy, Caleb vs. Charles Stewart for use of George W.
    Dillard
Acree, W. B. vs. Joseph W. Preston
Adair, Hiram and Edmund Jenkins vs. Lewis Peacock
Adams, Caleb B. vs. Jonathan Adams, John G. Mangham and
    Richard S. Walker
Adams, Caleb B. vs. Dyer C. Bancroft and Lindsey H. Durham
Adams, Caleb B., Thomas Slaughter, James H. Miller and
    John A. Dillard vs. Central Bank of Georgia
Adams, Caleb B. vs. Pleasant M. Compton
Adams, Caleb B., James C. Wilkins and Nathaniel Barnes vs.
    James Griggs
Adams, Caleb B. vs. Seaborn J. Hendrick for use of Joshua
    Hill

Adams, Caleb B. vs. William B. Johnson and Allen L. Lace
Adams, Caleb B. vs. Jesse Loyall
Adams, Caleb B. vs. Charles F. Newton and William V. Burney
Adams, Caleb B. vs. Aquilla Phelps
Adams, Caleb B. vs. James J. Ross and William Ross,
  Administrator
Adams, Caleb B. vs. Henry C. Seymore
Adams, Caleb B. vs. Thomas K. Slaughter
Adams, Caleb B. vs. The State
Adams, Caleb B. and David Adams vs. James Whitfield
Adams, Caleb B., Jefferson Adams and W. H. C. Mickelberry
  vs. Samuel J. Wilborn
Adams, David vs. Milton Antony for use of Edward Wallthrall
Adams, David vs. James Armor
Adams, David vs. John Ashurst and John F. Ashurst, Executor
Adams, David vs. Abba Benton
Adams, David vs. Thomas Butler
Adams, David vs. James H. Darden
Adams, David vs. William Folk
Adams, David vs. Thomas Gaston
Adams, David vs. Monticello Academy
Adams, David vs. Alexander McDonald
Adams, David vs. Jeremiah Pearson
Adams, David vs. John Pitkin
Adams, David vs. William Sanford
Adams, David vs. Joshua Strickland
Adams, David vs. Hugh Taylor
Adams, David vs. William H. Traylor
Adams, David vs. Martin Yeomans
Adams, David L., David A. Reese, Administrator and Leroy
  Lawrence, Administrator vs. Silas Harden
Adams, Davis S. and Jefferson Adams vs. Hampton Smith and
  James E. Morgan
Adams, George vs. Samuel Goggans
Adams, George W. vs. Jubil Cochran
Adams, George W. vs. William Johnson
Adams, Jefferson vs. Martin Cochran
Adams, Jefferson vs. William H. Crane and Abraham Crane
Adams, Jefferson, Stephen Mobley and J. R. Clark vs. David
  Epps
Adams, Jefferson vs. Thomas B. Erwin
Adams, Jefferson vs. William Freeman
Adams, Jefferson and Stephen McLendon vs. Franklin Gwinn
  and Joel Sturdevant
Adams, Jefferson vs. William Johnson
Adams, Jefferson vs. Daniel Parish, Jasper Corning, Thomas
  Parish and Joseph Kernochan
Adams, Jefferson, John C. Gibson and David A. Reese vs.
  James Whitfield
Adams, Jefferson, Garland Maxey, John McMichael and William
  Vaughn vs. James Whitfield
Adams, Jefferson, John McMichael and Martin Cochran vs.
  James Whitfield
Adams, Jefferson, Lucas Powell and Jacob McClendon vs.
  James Whitfield
Adams, John vs. Jonathan Benton
Adams, John vs. The State
Adams, Jonathan, Sr. vs. Woody Dozier, Jr.
Adams, Jonathan, Sr. vs. William W. Smith
Adams, Jonathan, Sr. vs. Isaac R. St. Johns
Adams, Richard vs. Jesse Gallman
Adams, Richard vs. Stephen Hackney
Adams, Richard and Meridith Adams vs. David Lynn

Adams, Richard vs. Michael Whatley, Jr.
Adkinson, William F. vs. Charles L. Flint
Aiken ? vs. ? Broughton
Aiken, C. P. and E. H. Aiken, Administrator vs. Mary K.
Blackwell, L. A. J. Roseberry and Hattie L. Cofer
Aiken, Charles A. E. vs. Augustus Benford for use of Offi-
cers of Court
Aiken, Hamp vs. The State
Aiken, J. J. vs. Matthew Whitfield and J. A. Billups,
Administrator
Aiken, Jeff T. vs. Warren Wallace & Co.
Aiken, R. H. vs. Foster & Ackerman
Aiken, R. H. vs. Jacob Wolf
Aiken, Sarah vs. S. S. Blackwell for use of Officers of
Court
Aiken, Thomas J. vs. The State
Aiken, W. A. vs. A. S. Aiken
Aikens, Carrie, Augustus Benford, James Benford, Porter
Benford and Emma Cole vs. Joseph T. Benford, Cicero S.
Benford, Minor and Cicero M. Spears, Guadian
Aikens, James vs. Matthew Whitfield
Aikens, Maria (Sheppard) vs. Seaborn S. Aikens
Akens, Samuel S. vs. Benjamin King, William Farrar, Adminis-
trator, Robert T. C. Tucker, Administrator and John W.
Hardaway, Administrator
Akeridge, Moses and Alfred Kelly vs. The State
Akins, Samuel S. and John C. Akins, Executor vs. Burwell
C. Clark
Akins, Thomas J. and A. C. Mixon vs. John C. Akins
Alexander, Abden vs. William Nelson and William Knight
Alexander, Adam vs. Peter F. Boisclair
Alexander, Adam vs. Elijah N. Hascall and David N. Hascall
Alexander, Adam vs. William McMath
Alexander, Adam vs. Aquilla Phelps
Alexander, Adam, James H. Morrow, Albert Alexander and
Charles Morgan vs. Francis B. Smartt, John Hill, Adminis-
trator and Eliza Smartt, Administrator
Alexander, Albert vs. John W. Houghton for use of Silas
Alden, Jr.
Alexander, Albert and Asa E. Stratton vs. Augustus Owen
Alexander, Albert vs. George W. Smith and Elisha Robbins
Alexander, Albert vs. Hansford Smith, William Wright and
George Huston
Alexander, Albert vs. James Whitfield
Alexander, Albert vs. Asa Wood
Alexander, Buck vs. The State
Alexander, Casandra vs. Lawrence P. Alexander
Alexander, Charles T. vs. Robert C. Beasley and Palemon L.
Weeks
Alexander, Eliza and George Alexander, Administrator vs.
William Campbell
Alexander, Ella vs. The State
Alexander, G. W. vs. L. O. Benton & Brother
Alexander, George and Asa E. Stratton vs. James A. Blanton
Alexander, George vs. Martin Cochran
Alexander, George vs. Luther Faulkner and John T. Reid
Alexander, George vs. Andrew E. Small
Alexander, George vs. William H. Turpin
Alexander, Henry vs. The State
Alexander, Ike vs. The State
Alexander, John J. vs. L. O. Benton & Brothers
Alexander, John J. vs. The State
Alexander, Lawrence P. vs. George Alexander

Alexander, Leila vs. W. G. Greer and C. H. Greer
Alexander, Martha, Lawrence T. Alexander and Albert
  Alexander vs. Anthony Dyer
Alexander, Newton O. vs. Wyatt R. Smith
Alexander, Newton O. vs. Eben T. White
Alexander, Paul vs. The State
Alford, Holcut and Robert Brown vs. Thomas Brown
Alford, Holcut vs. Hardy Crawford
Alford, Jeptha and James Scroggin vs. Henry Head
Alfriend, A. H. vs. The State
Alison, Clayton (alias Clayton Cargile) vs. The State
Allen, A. J. vs. The State
Allen, Alexander, Penelope Allen, Executor, Jane Allen,
  Executor, Robert Allen, Executor, and Edmund Allen,
  Executor vs. Stephen W. Beasley
Allen, Alexander vs. Thomas Black and James Black
Allen, Alexander vs. Zenos Bronson
Allen, Alexander vs. Thomas P. Gwyn and James Gwyn
Allen, Alexander and Robert C. Beasley vs. David Hunter
Allen, Alexander vs. Robert Williams
Allen, Alexander vs. Philo Woodruff
Allen, Alexander M. vs. Officers of Court
Allen, Andrew I. vs. J. C. Franklin for use of Officers of
  Court
Allen, Arthur vs. The State
Allen, Ben vs. The State
Allen, Columbus vs. The State
Allen, Dan vs. The State
Allen, David, Armstead Dodson, Administrator and Elijah
  Dodson, Administrator vs. Rufus Broom
Allen, David vs. Thomas Buttrell
Allen, David, Armstead Dodson, Administrator and Elijah
  Dodson, Administrator vs. Willoby Hammock and John B.
  Garrett, Administrator
Allen, David vs. John W. Pitts, James M. Finley and John
  Edgar
Allen, David vs. The State
Allen, David vs. Isaac Strickland
Allen, David vs. Samuel Thompson
Allen, Dennis vs. John Cargile
Allen, Dennis and James W. Morgan vs. Alston H. Greene and
  Joseph Buchannon
Allen, Dennis vs. William Mulkey
Allen, Dennis vs. Hardy Perry
Allen, Drury vs. Joshua Callaway
Allen, Ebben E. vs. The State
Allen, Edward M. and Isaac C. W. T. McKissack vs. Jesse
  Cherry and Johnson Springer, Executor
Allen, George and John Allen vs. The State
Allen, Greene vs. The State
Allen, J. D. vs. The State
Allen, Jeff vs. The State
Allen, John and Micajah Hendrick vs. Aimey Pinson
Allen, John vs. The State
Allen, Jordan vs. The State
Allen, Lemuel vs. John F. Evans
Allen, Mack vs. The State
Allen, O. C. vs. Willcox, Gibbs and Co.
Allen, R. C. vs. Griffin, Monticello and Madison Railroad Co.
Allen, R. C. and B. T. Digby vs. William S. Minter
Allen, Robert A. and Edward M. Allen vs. James Johnston
Allen, Robert A. vs. Wiley Peddy
Allen, Robert A. vs. Thomas I. Smith and William M. Broddus

Allen, Robert C. vs. The State
Allen, Robert C. and Leroy M. Price vs. Robert P. Watters,
  Minor and Maxamillian H. Hutchison, Guardian
Allen, Sam vs. The State
Allen, Samuel, John C. Key Administrator, William C. Penn,
  John W. A. Smith, Robert C. Barnes, Morris Knowles and
  George T. Bartlett vs. Joseph E. Brown for use of
  Maximilian H. Hutchinson
Allen, Samuel and Robert A. Allen vs. Harry Camp
Allen, Samuel and John A. Allen vs. Newton Manufacturing Co.
Allen, Sarah vs. William Hazeltine
Allen, Sid vs. The State
Allen, Thomas vs. The State
Allen, W. W. vs. J. C. Johnson
Allen, Walker vs. The State
Allen, Walker C. vs. George T. Bartlett
Allen, Walker C. vs. Faithey Huff
Allen, Walker C. vs. James M. C. Robinson, Thomas Leslie
  and Alexander Ragland
Allen, Walker C. vs. John M. Stephens and Moses Allmond,
  Administrator
Allen, William vs. Elizabeth Allen
Allison, Alexander vs. Charles Squire and Gold L. Silliman
Allison, Alexander H. vs. John T. Boykin
Allison, Alexander H. vs. John Howard
Allison, Isham L. vs. The State
Allison, Isham S. F. vs. Elias Landrum
Allison, Isham S. F. vs. Thomas J. Parmelee
Allmond, Burwell vs. Caleb Abernathy
Almund, William vs. John W. Compton
Alewine, David and George H. Buchanan vs. Champion T.
  Traylor
Ambrose, Martha vs. The State
Ambrose, Warren, Martha E. Bowden, Administrator, James T.
  Renfroe and James F. Renfroe vs. Jubil Cochran and
  Mildred Cochran, Administrator
Amos, Milton and James H. Rogers vs. John Abercrombie
Amos, Milton vs. E. N. Hascall and D. Hascall
Amos, Milton vs. Henry K. Jones
Amos, Milton vs. William Nelson and William Knight
Amos, Milton vs. Cuthbert Reese and Joseph Reese
Amos, Milton vs. John F. Simpson for use of William Whatley
Amos, Milton and John C. Rodgers vs. Francis B. Smith, John
  Hill, Administrator and Eliza Smartt, Administrator
Amos, Savannah vs. The State
Anderson, George vs. The State
Anderson, James vs. Zachariah Hall
Anderson, James vs. Andrew Miller
Anderson, James and Henry B. Cabiness vs. Alexander Smith
Anderson, John vs. Artemus Gould
Anderson, John vs. John Nisbet
Anderson, John vs. Sheldon Smith and William Wright
Anderson, John vs. Pleasant Stovall
Anderson, John, Jr. vs. Betsey Hunt
Anderson, Jonathan vs. The State
Anderson, William W. vs. Edward A. Broddus and Thomas C.
  Broddus
Anderson, William W. vs. John W. Burney
Anderson, William W. vs. Jonas H. Holland
Anderson, William W. vs. William S. Hurd, Anson Hungerford,
  Jr., Nehemiah B. White and Lucius White
Anderson, William W. vs. Davis Lane and John F. Patterson
Anderson, William W. vs. John C. Maddux

Anderson, William W. vs. William D. Maddux
Anderson, William W. vs. John Pope
Anderson, William W. vs. William C. Robinson, James C.
  Robinson, Executor and John L. Robinson, Executor
Anderson, William W. vs. Lewis Ryan
Anderson, William W. vs. Thomas J. Smith
Anderson, William W. vs. Francis M. Swanson and Elbert G.
  Cathcings
Anderson, William W. vs. E. T. White
Andrews, Davis R. vs. Elias Benham
Andrews, Davis R. vs. A. B. Small
Andrews, James G., Oliver H. P. Bonner and Richard W.
  Bonner vs. Andrew J. Stewart
Andrews, James G. and Nancy C. Andrews vs. Oliver H. P.
  Bonner and Richard W. Bonner
Andrews, James G. and Davis R. Andrews vs. Crawford Greer
Andrews, James G. vs. Thomas Hardeman and James Griffin
Andrews, James G. and Andrew Q. Stewart vs. Thomas Holcombe,
  John R. Johnson and James H. Johnson
Andrews, James G. vs. John Lasenby
Andrews, James G. and Thomas G. Andrews vs. B. B. Odom
Andrews, James G. vs. Wiley Peddy
Andrews, James G. vs. Paul Perkins
Andrews, James G. and Richard S. Grubbs vs. George T.
  Rogers and Charles Rogers
Andrews, James G., O. H. P. Bonner and R. W. Bonner vs.
  Stephen C. Talmadge
Andrews, Pauline vs. The State
Andrews, Samuel and John Hill vs. Anthony Dyer
Andrews, Samuel B. vs. Robert Humber and Mary E. Humber
Andrews, Samuel R. and William Phillips vs. Davis Andrews
Andrews, Samuel R. vs. James Brady and William Shivers,
  Administrator
Andrews, William vs. William Clark and Milton A. Cooley
Annis, J. P., Charles Annis and Jesse Annis vs. Beverly A.
  Kelly
Annis, Jesse M., Bundy A. Kelly, Jarrett B. Kelly, John B.
  Webb, George F. Bartlett, Dawson B. Wynn, ? Peacock,
  Felix B. Martin, Asher Levy, and N. Goodhue vs. Isaac H.
  Freeman and C. L. Bartlett, Administrator
Ansley, Gilbert D. vs. Henry Gasset and Richard W. Bailey
Ansley, Gilbert D., Thomas P. Gwynn and James Wynn vs.
  Warren Phelps
Anthony, Anne vs. Reubin Blakey
Anthony, John vs. Hugh Porter
Anthony, Joseph and Abner Chapman vs. Alston H. Greene and
  Joseph Buchannon
Anthony, Joseph vs. Jonathan Sell for use of Peyton Baker
  and Chappel Heith
Anthony, Milton vs. Nathaniel Allen
Anthony, Milton vs. Drury Spain
Antony, Milton vs. Robert R. Billups and James C. Cook
Antony, Milton and William Cook vs. John W. Devereux
Antony, Milton vs. Eli Glover and John Cashin
Antony, Milton vs. Lemuel Greene
Antony, Milton, Benjamin C. Edmondson and John Slappy vs.
  The State
Appling, Flora vs. The State
Appling, William vs. The State
Armor, James vs. Cyrus Billingslea
Armor, James vs. William Cook for use of James Butts, John
  Lucas, Administrator and William Lee, Administrator
Armor, James vs. John Cox

Armor, James vs. Anthony Dyer
Armor, James vs. Henry Glover
Armor, James vs. Edmund Greene
Armor, James vs. Thomas Lyon
Armor, James vs. Robert McAfee
Armor, James vs. Thomas Napier
Armor, James vs. Robert Owen for use of Jacob Owen
Armor, James vs. William Park
Armor, James vs. Reuben Wade
Arms, Lucius vs. Artemus Gould
Arms, Lucius vs. Erastus Graves
Arms, Lucius and John Hall vs. Robert B. Haviland and
  Daniel G. Haviland
Arms, Lucius vs. John W. Houghton
Arms, Lucius vs. John McKenzie and Peter Bennoch
Arms, Lucius vs. John Ward
Arms, Seth vs. Lucius Arms and Stephen Crane
Arms, Seth vs. Hiram Glazer and Woody Dozier
Arms, Seth and John Compton vs. The State
Arms, Seth vs. John Sweet
Armstead, Ajax vs. John Baldwin
Armstrong, John and William Armstrong vs. Ephraim Sanders
Armstrong, William and Jacob McClendon vs. Green McAfee,
  Green McAfee, Minor, Nancy G. McAfee, Minor and Jonathan
  Anderson, Guardian
Armstrong, William vs. Eli S. Shorter
Arnold, Will vs. The State
Aron, John L. and Thomas Dillard vs. Lamback and Cooper
Arrington, William vs. The State
Arthur, James vs. Samuel Butts and John Lucas, Administrator
Ascue, Perry vs. Thomas C. Pinckard and John Baldwin
Ashmore, John, Sarah Ashmore, Polly Barron and Matilda
  Malear vs. The State
Ashmore, William vs. Alston H. Greene and Joseph Buchannan
Askew, John vs. Jeremiah Pearson
Askew, John vs. Cornelius D. Terhune
Askew, Patsey vs. David Askew
Askew, Perry and John Askew vs. James S. Weekes
Askew, William and Aris Newton vs. Anthony Dyer
Askew, William and Halcut Alford vs. Andrew Low, Robert Low,
  and John McHenry
Askew, William vs. The State
Askew, William vs. Pleasant Stovall
Askew, William H. and James Shropshire vs. Andrew J. Varner
Aspinwall, George vs. Isaac Bailey
Aspinwall, George vs. John Ely and Horace Ely
Aspinwall, George vs. Reid and Woodruff
Aspinwall, George vs. Allen P. Rice
Atchinson, Arnold vs. Isaiah Browning
Atchinson, James A. vs. The State
Atkinson, Martha vs. The State
Atkinson, Samuel C. vs. John Davis and Hezekiah W. Cater
Atkisson, Job vs. Wiley Thornton
Auston, Joe vs. The State
Avant, Eli and Antoinette Lofton vs. The State
Avant, Eliza vs. Eli Avant
Avary, Asa G., Robert Sharman and Crawford H. Greer vs.
  Central Bank of Georgia
Avary, James C. vs. Marcus A. Franklin
Avary, James C. vs. John L. Jones and Chandler Smith
Avary, James C. vs. Sterling W. Smith
Averett, James and Samuel Crockett vs. Moses Hartfield
Avery, Asa G. and Edward Varner, Administrator vs. Thomas

J. Smith

Avery, Herbert, James C. Avery, Executor, and James W.
  Shropshire, Executor vs. Thomas Grant, Daniel Grant,
  Executor, Thomas Grant, Executor, and Peter Grinnell,
  Executor
Avery, James and Orpha Avery vs. William Avery and James
  Price, Administrator
Avery, James C. vs. Robert C. Beasley and Palemon L. Weeks
Avery, James C. vs. Hamilton Brown
Avery, James C. vs. Daniel Parish, Jasper Corning, Thomas
  Parish and Joseph Kernochan
Averyt, Henry vs. Barnett Gresham

Bacon, S. W. vs. John Merryman and Co.
Bacon, Sumner W. vs. Sarah J. Bacon
Bacon, Sumner W. vs. Francis C. Jordan
Bacon, Sumner W. vs. Thomas J. Smith
Bacon, Sumner W. vs. Warren Wallace and Co.
Baer, ? vs. ? Berg
Bagley, Moore vs. John Hand
Bagley, Robert A. vs. William Hurd and Anson Hungerford
Bailey, Charles vs. Hamlin Freeman and Mary Freeman
Bailey, Charles and John Donaldson vs. Alston H. Greene
  and Joseph Buchannon
Bailey, Charles vs. John E. Stallings for use of Jesse
  Mosely
Bailey, Isaac vs. Alexander Atkinson
Bailey, Isaac and Stephen D. Crane vs. Thomas Grant
Bailey, Isaac and James Smith vs. William L. Miller, John
  H. McCall and Timothy Olmsted
Bailey, Isaac and Stephen D. Crane vs. William Pritchett
Bailey, Isaac vs. John Thomas
Bailey, Isaac and Stephen D. Crain vs. Hosea Webster and
  Thomas J. Parmelee
Bailey, James vs. The State
Bailey, Jane Z. L. vs. Equitable Mortgage Co.
Bailey, Joe vs. The State
Bailey, Joel vs. Andrew Kerr, Alexander Graham and John
  Kerr
Bailey, Joel vs. James Richards, and James Mercer for use
  of Shadrach Bogan
Bailey, John vs. Mary Sauls Millen, Jacob Waldburg, Trustee
  and Cornelius M. Millen, Trustee
Bailey, John M. vs. The State
Bailey, John R. vs. The State
Bailey, Judson vs. The State
Bailey, Press vs. The State
Bailey, Robert vs. The State
Bailey, William and Williamson Bailey vs. Michael Barnes
Bailey, William vs. Moses Brightwell
Bailey, William vs. Samuel Henderson
Bailey, William vs. Jonas H. Holland
Bailey, William vs. Felix Martin
Bailey, William vs. George D. Millen
Bailey, William and Isaac L. Parker vs. Martin Puckett and
  James Vaughn, Administrator
Bailey, William, John W. Wyatt and Williamson Bailey vs.
  Martin Puckett and James W. Vaughn, Administrator
Bailey, William and Craton A. J. Flemister vs. William S.
  Roberts and Thomas Roberts
Bailey, William vs. Henry L. Roosevelt and Samuel G. Barker
Bailey, William vs. Gilbraith Simonton and William V. Burney
Bailey, William vs. The State

93

Bailey, William vs. Jacob Walburg, Cornelius M. Miller,
   Grustee and Robert Tolefree, Attorney
Bailey, Williamson vs. James L. Burney
Bailey, Williamson vs. Thompson Curry
Bailey, Williamson vs. Elizabeth Dabney and Tyre G. Dabney,
   Guardian
Bailey, Williamson vs. Lindsey H. Durham and Dyer C. Bancroft
Bailey, Williamson, William Bailey, Executor, John R. Kelly
   and Wiley Phillips vs. Anthony Dyer and John R. Dyer,
   Executor
Bailey, Williamson and William Bailey vs. William Goolsby
Bailey, Williamson and William Y. Harris vs. Artemas Gould,
   Justus R. Bulkley and Alpheus H. Stone
Bailey, Williamson and William Bailey, Executor vs. Frizell
   M. Hardwick, Elisha Hardwick, Elijah Hardwick and Robert
   M. Hardwick
Bailey, Williamson vs. James R. McCord
Bailey, Williamson vs. Ephraim Miller and Charles V.
   Chamberlain
Bailey, Williamson and William Bailey vs. Officers of Court
Bailey, Williamson vs. Weekly I. Pearman
Bailey, Williamson, John C. Watters and Shadrack McMichael
   vs. Jeremiah Pearson
Bailey, Williamson and William Harris vs. Andrew Rankin,
   Archibald Boggs and Peter W. Auter
Bailey, Williamson and Henry T. Smith vs. James H. Roberts
Bailey, Williamson vs. John Robson
Bailey, Williamson and Jeremiah P. Maye vs. Robert Tolefree
Bailey, Williamson and William Bailey vs. Milton P. Walthall
Bailey, Zachariah vs. Matthew Rainey
Baily, Stephen vs. Henry Pearson
Baines, Robert vs. The State
Baker, Henry vs. The State
Baker, James, Thomas Davis and Gabrail Colley vs. The State
Baker, Jorden vs. Daniel Scott
Baker, Joseph vs. Benjamin Garrett
Baker, Joseph vs. Henry Keller
Baker, Joseph vs. Burrel Richards
Baker, Joseph vs. The State
Baker, Kit vs. Richard McManus
Baker, Thomas vs. William Cook and Robert J. Walton
Baker, Thomas, Jacob Laughridge, William Lynn, Jonathan
   Benton and Samuel Teders vs. The State
Baldwin, Edmund and Moses Maxcy vs. The State
Baldwin, Frederick vs. William Chisolem
Baldwin, Frederick vs. Thomas Huson
Baldwin, John vs. John W. Cook
Baldwin, John and Colman Allen vs. Thomas Goolsby
Baldwin, John and Thomas C. Pinckard vs. John Heard
Baldwin, John vs. John Hill
Baldwin, John vs. Clement Molliere
Baldwin, John vs. Robert B. Porter
Baldwin, John vs. James Richards
Baldwin, John, Nelson Colley and James Hunt vs. John Sharp
   and Reason D. Bealle
Bales, Daniel D. vs. Thomas Moore
Baley, Elisha vs. The State
Baley, Joel vs. Ashbael Cone
Baley, Joel, John Brownfield and Joseph Buchannan vs.
   Whitson H. George
Baley, Joel vs. Archibald H. Scott
Baley, Joel vs. The State
Ball, Jonathan vs. Allen H. Ryland

94

Ballard, James and Simeon Durham vs. Andrew Low, James
  Taylor and John Low
Ballard, R. W., Frank D. Ballard and J. T. Connally vs.
  Margarett Price
Ballard, W. A. vs. D. C. Bancroft
Ballard, William and Sarah J. Watters vs. William Hurd and
  Anson Hungerford
Ballard, William A. vs. The State
Bancroft, Dyer C. vs. Samuel P. Hudson
Bancroft, Dyer C. vs. Richard J. Loyall and John E. Langston
Bancroft, Dyer C. vs. Creed T. Wise
Bandin, Jesse vs. Reuben Knott
Banes, Elbert vs. Hamilton B. Ridley
Banks, Agie and Nilia Banks vs. The State
Banks, Alford, Jr. vs. The State
Banks, Anderson vs. The State
Banks, Armstead vs. The State
Banks, Benjamin vs. James McClure
Banks, Benjamin vs. Officers of Court
Banks, Benjamin E. vs. C. A. Baldwin
Banks, Benjamin W. vs. Jeremiah Boggus
Banks, Benjamin W. vs. John Doster
Banks, Benjamin W. and John Durden vs. Jesse W. Fears and
  James F. Swanson
Banks, Benjamin W. vs. Cordy Fellows
Banks, Benjamin W. vs. John Hudson
Banks, Benjamin W. vs. Jarrett B. Kelley
Banks, Benjamin W. vs. John Sheffield
Banks, Benjamin W., William H. Wyatt, Vines Fish and Newton
  Turner vs. The State
Banks, Benjamin W. vs. Francis M. Swanson and Thomas J.
  Comer
Banks, Benjamin W. and Jarrell B. Kelly, Executor vs.
  Augustus H. Trammell
Banks, Bettie vs. The State
Banks, Burton vs. The State
Banks, Dean vs. The State
Banks, Dennis vs. The State
Banks, Eaton, Josiah Banks and William G. Smith vs. Stephen
  M. Bennet
Banks, Ed and Pon Harris vs. The State
Banks, Edmond vs. Alston H. Greene and Joseph Buchannon
Banks, Edmond vs. Cornelius Robinson
Banks, Green vs. The State
Banks, H. D., Mrs. H. E. Banks and D. M. Davis vs. Officers
  of Court
Banks, Henry vs. Fleming Jordan
Banks, Henry vs. Robinson, Kelly and Co. and Jane L. Smith
Banks, Henry vs. The State
Banks, Henry D. vs. Eaton Banks and Jarrett B. Kelly,
  Administrator
Banks, Henry D. vs. William G. Smith
Banks, Henry D. and John W. Wyatt vs. The State
Banks, James P. vs. The State
Banks, John vs. The State
Banks, John C. vs. William C. Gathright
Banks, John C. and Berry T. Digby, Administrator vs.
  Joseph Henderson
Banks, John C. vs. William Maxey, Charles S. Jordan and
  John R. Dyer
Banks, John C. vs. Stephen C. Talmadge
Banks, John C. and Berry T. Digby, Administrator vs. Hugh
  White

Banks, John C. and John S. Robinson vs. Mathew Whitfield
Banks, John C. N. and Berry T. Digby, Administrator vs.
    Samuel R. Smith
Banks, Lee vs. The State
Banks, Mary vs. V. H. Crawley
Banks, O. O. vs. Thomas C. Spivey
Banks, Priscilla vs. Richard J. Loyall and William C. Andrews
Banks, Priscilla vs. Washington Poe
Banks, Ralph and Charles D. Bostick vs. Thomas Reynolds
Banks, Samuel H. vs. The State
Banks, Scott vs. The State
Banks, Simeon D. vs. Russel J. Brown
Banks, Simeon D. vs. William Dukes
Banks, Simeon D. vs. Martin Folds
Banks, Simeon D. vs. Thomas M. Harkness
Banks, Simeon D. vs. Davis Lane
Banks, Simeon D. and Simeon Scales vs. William Maxey and
    Charles S. Jordan
Banks, Simeon D. vs. William A. McDonald
Banks, Simeon D. vs. The State
Banks, Simeon D. and Priscilla Banks vs. L. C. Talmadge
Banks, Thomas G. vs. John W. Hughs
Bankston, Abner vs. Thomas Cargile
Bankston, Elijah vs. Jonathan Belton
Bankston, Elijah vs. Jordan Bonner
Bankston, Elijah vs. Hugh Hamill
Barantine, John vs. The State
Barber, Ben vs. The State
Barber, Buster vs. The State
Barber, Herbert vs. The State
Barber, Hub vs. The State
Barber, Matilda vs. The State
Barber, Moses vs. The State
Barber, Thomas L. vs. Sylvester G. Lusk
Barclay, William and William Jenkins, Administrator vs.
    Elizabeth Barclay
Barclay, William and William Ramey vs. Edward Y. Hill
Barclay, William vs. John Hill, Augustin Slaughter and
    Charles Labuzan
Barclay, William vs. Uriah Morris for use of Alexander
    McGregor
Barclay, William vs. The State
Barifield, William vs. Christian Isham
Barker, Joseph G. and Banks Ledbetter vs. Shotwell B.
    Clarkson
Barker, William H. H. and Tobe Barker vs. The State
Barkesdale, Jeffery and Wright Hill vs. William McMichael,
    Elizabeth McMichael, Executor, Richard Carter, Executor
    and John McMichael, Executor
Barnes, Anna vs. Albert Barnes for use of Officers of
    Court
Barnes, Charlie vs. The State
Barnes, David vs. The State
Barnes, Homer vs. The State
Barnes, James vs. The State
Barnes, Jethro vs. Benjamin Sanford and John G. Lumsden
Barnes, Jethro vs. Thomas Stanford
Barnes, Jim vs. The State
Barnes, John vs. The State
Barnes, Lewis A. vs. The State
Barnes, Matthew vs. Cinda (Jordan) Barnes
Barnes, Michael, Harris Allen and Samuel Allen vs. Thomas
    Wright, William B. Wright, Administrator, Robert A.

Wright, Administrator, John S. Weaver, Administrator, and
  Mary Wright, Administrator
Barnes, Nathaniel vs. John G. Waters
Barnes, Sallie E. vs. Eugene Benton
Barnett, E. F. vs. William H. Preston
Barnett, E. F. vs. Coswell Ethridge
Barnett, Green D. and William B. Stone vs. Thomas Ingram
  and John Bartish
Barnett, James H. vs. William B. Pryor
Barnett, John, Dallas Barnett and Thomas Lynch vs. The State
Barnett, John S. vs. Thomas Black
Barnett, Joseph and John Barnett vs. Elijah N. Hascall and
  David Hascall
Barnett, Joseph L. vs. Reubin Braselton
Barnett, Nathaniel and Daniel McDowell, Administrator vs.
  William Barnett, James Peede, Administrator, Hezekiah
  Spears and Eli Garnett, Administrator
Barnett, Nathaniel and Daniel McDowell, Administrator vs.
  William Crawford and Susan Crawford
Barnett, Sion vs. Alexander and Morrow
Barnett, Sion vs. John Buis
Barnett, Sion vs. William Harper
Barnett, Sion vs. David Smith and Adam McKravin
Barnwell, Henry and Edward Young Hill vs. Milledge Bartlett
  Roby and Abner Bartlett
Barnwell, Henry vs. The State
Barr, William J. vs. William Maxey, Charles S. Jordan and
  John R. Dyer
Barr, William J. vs. The State
Barran, Silas vs. James Callaway
Barrett, Erasmus D. vs. Thomas J. Smith and William M.
  Broddus
Barrett, James H. vs. Boswell B. DeGraffenreidt
Barrett, James H. vs. Clement Molliere
Barrett, James H. vs. Newton H. Sample
Barron, Benjamin vs. P. W. Dorsett, C. H. Greer, Adminis-
  trator and James Dorsett, Administrator
Barron, Benjamin vs. W. H. Head for use of Officers of
  Court
Barron, Benjamin vs. Mobley and Cabiness
Barron, Carrie vs. The State
Barron, Louis vs. The State
Barron, Mannie vs. The State
Barron, Thomas vs. John Randle
Barrott, James H. and David A. Reese vs. James Whitfield
Bartlett, Abner vs. Thomas Carter
Bartlett, Abner and James C. Bartlett, Executor vs. Henry
  A. Dickinson and Sarah A. Dickinson
Bartlett, Abner vs. The State
Bartlett, George C. vs. The State
Bartlett, George T. vs. Bennett Bridges and Mary Ann
  Bridges, Executor
Bartlett, George T. vs. William Maxey, Charles S. Jordan
  and John R. Dozier
Bartlett, George T. and Pleasant T. Lovejoy vs. The State
Bartlett, George T. vs. Matthew Whitfield, Pleasant Willson,
  Executor, John F. Patterson, Executor, William H. Mathis,
  Executor, and Leroy Wilson, Executor
Bartlett, James C., George L. Bartlett and Mary Bartlett vs.
  Thomas J. Bartlett, William A. Bartlett and John E.
  Bartlett
Bartlett, James C. vs. John R. Dicken
Bartlett, James C. vs. Henry A. Dickenson

Bartlett, Joe vs. The State
Bartlett, Thomas I., John E. Bartlett and Isaac Langston vs.
The State
Bartlett, William A., Henry R. McKay, Administrator, William
Maxey and Joel C. McDowell vs. Sarah Dickinson, Henry A.
Dickinson, Trustee and Cicero A. Thorp, Trustee
Barwell, Lion vs. Alexander Morrow
Beasley, Aron vs. The State
Bass, Allen and James Mitchell vs. John McCrary
Bass, Allen vs. Henry Mitchell and James H. Jones
Bass, Allen vs. Henry F. Simmons for use of Sterling Acree
Bass, Hartwell vs. The State
Bass, Jarett vs. Patsey Nichols
Bass, Thomas vs. Thomas Baldwin and Co.
Bass, Thomas vs. George Clower for use of John Mumford
Bass, Thomas vs. Jesse Loyal
Bass, Thomas vs. Jacob Mercer
Bass, Thomas vs. Roger McCarthy
Bass, Thomas and John Hill vs. Thomas Napier
Bass, Thomas vs. Jacob Owen
Bass, Thomas vs. James Richards
Batchelor, Algie vs. The State
Bates, Asa vs. Elisha Barnard
Bates, Daniel D. and Caleb C. Dibble vs. Simon P. Hadly and
John W. Compton
Bates, James and Presley Dodson vs. Maguire and Leprestree
for use of Nathan Carter
Bates, Luzan vs. The State
Battle, Arthur vs. The State
Baugh, William C. vs. George W. Holland and Hugh P.
Kirkpatrick
Baugh, William C. vs. The State
Baxley, Aaron vs. Allen McClendon
Baxley, Aaron vs. The State
Baxley, Aron vs. William W. Smith
Baxley, W. D. vs. N. S. Glover
Baynes, Alfred J. vs. John P. Force
Baynes, Alfred J. vs. William H. Howard
Baynes, Alfred J. and John Baynes, Administrator vs. John
Spearman
Baynes, Caroline vs. Samuel Baynes for use of Officers of
Court
Baynes, E. W. vs. B. F. Adams for use of Officers of Court
Baynes, E. W. vs. Barrett and Caswell
Baynes, E. W. vs. Foster, Wright and Co.
Baynes, E. W. vs. Griffin, Monticello and Madison Railroad
Co.
Baynes, E. W. vs. Hamp Ridley for use of Officers of Court
Baynes, E. W. vs. Henry Seymour for use of Officers of
Court
Baynes, E. W. vs. Thomas J. Smith
Baynes, E. W. vs. Warren Wallace and Walter Scott
Baynes, E. W. vs. W. D. Wynn for use of Officers of Court
Baynes, Elbert vs. The State
Baynes, Elbert W. vs. Baldwin and Co. for use of Officers
of Court
Baynes, Elbert W., John Baynes and James Y. Baynes vs.
James Barrott
Baynes, Elbert W., John Baynes and James Y. Baynes vs.
James Y. Baynes, Fally Mariah Baynes and Judith P. Baynes,
Guardian
Baynes, Elbert W., John Baynes and James Y. Baynes vs. John
H. Baynes and Mathew Whitfield, Executor

98

Baynes, Elbert W. vs. Thomas H. Cosby and Green Allen,
Administrator
Baynes, Elbert W. vs. Thomas M. Darnall
Baynes, Elbert W. vs. Joel Davis
Baynes, Elbert W. vs. John R. Greer
Baynes, Elbert W., Edward Hicks and Joel Baley vs. James T.
Hays and Henry Hays, Administrator
Baynes, Elbert W. vs. William Hearn
Baynes, Elbert W. vs. Joshua Hill
Baynes, Elbert W. vs. James Hutsel and John Bowles
Baynes, Elbert W. vs. F. S. Jenkins and James L. Reid
Baynes, Elbert W. vs. J. M. Johnson and Co.
Baynes, John vs. Ephraim Miller and Charles V. Chamberlain
Baynes, Elbert W. vs. M. A. McDowell
Baynes, Elbert W. vs. The State
Baynes, Elbert W. vs. Matthew Whitfield and J. A. Billups,
Administrator
Baynes, Harry vs. The State
Baynes, Henry vs. The State
Baynes, James Y. and Mary (Johnson) Baynes vs. Benjamin T.
Lowe
Baynes, James Y. vs. The State
Baynes, James Y., John Baynes and Elbert W. Baynes vs.
Avington Turk and Elizabeth Turk
Baynes, John, E. W. Baynes, C. W. McMichael and S. McMichael
vs. George T. Bartlett
Baynes, John vs. Judith Baynes, Fally Mariah Baynes and
James Y. Baynes
Baynes, John A., Elbert W. Baynes and Harry J. Dennis vs.
Evan Harvey and William B. Carter
Baynes, John H. vs. Martha Edmondson
Baynes, John H. vs. Robert Flournoy
Baynes, John H. vs. Charles Forbes
Baynes, John H. vs. David Johnson
Baynes, John H. vs. James Mize
Baynes, John H., James A. Atchinson and John Turk vs. The
State
Baynes, John H. and Elbert Baynes, Executor vs. Lewis D.
Yancey
Baynes, R. A. vs. Mrs. S. L. Martin
Baynes, S. R. vs. C. T. Ezell
Baynes, T. and Judith Baynes vs. William Maxey and Charles
Jordan
Baynes, W. E. and Aris Newton vs. Officers of Court
Baynes, W. E. vs. The State
Baysmore, Marion vs. The State
Baysmore, Paulina vs. The State
Beach, James vs. George Dawson
Beach, James, Catharine Beach, Administrator and Sanders
Vann, Administrator vs. James Fears
Beall, Doctor H. vs. Tilmon D. Oxford
Beall, James D. and Andrew H. Beall, Administrator vs.
Franklin Hervey and Cornelius D. Terhune
Beall, Thomas vs. Caleb Woodly
Bean, John vs. David Lynn
Bean, John, Walter Bean, James Fincher and Bount (?) Kannard
vs. James Turner
Bean, John vs. Elisha Vinson
Beard, Walter and John Beard vs. James Turner
Bearden, Wiley, William Jeffries and John McMichael vs.
The State
Beasley, James, Matthew Kilgore, Absalom Kilgore, Lewis
Kilgore and Edmond Wilkerson vs. The State

Beasley, Jarrel vs. Hamilton Brown, Thomas P. Gwynn and
  James Gwyn
Beasley, Jarrel vs. Commissioners of Randolph County for
  use of Stokly Morgan
Beasley, Jarrel vs. David A. Reese
Beasley, Jarrel vs. John Watson and Thomas Watson, Adminis-
  trator
Beasley, Jarrell vs. James Whitfield
Beasley, Jarrel vs. Robert Williamson, Mary Williamson,
  Administrator and Willis Williamson, Administrator
Beasley, Robert, Wesley Griggs and Jarrel Beasley vs.
  James Dowdell
Beasley, Robert vs. Elisha Smart for use of Francis Irwin
Beasley, Robert and Palemon L. Weekes vs. Pleasant Stovall
  and Greenesville Simmons
Beasley, Robert and Jarrell Beasley vs. Leroy M. Wiley and
  Thomas W. Baxter
Beasley, Robert C. vs. Hamilton Brown
Beasley, Robert C. and Jarrel Beasley vs. Thomas Carrel
  and Susan Carrel
Beasley, Robert C. vs. Thomas Erwin and James Cowan
Beasley, Robert C. and Palemon S. Weekes vs. John E. Glover
Beasley, Robert C. and Palemon L. Weekes vs. Simeon Hyde
  and George Cleveland
Beasley, Robert C. vs. Benjamin Marshall
Beasley, Robert C. and Palemon L. Weeks vs. Daniel Parish
  and Thomas Parish
Beasley, Robert C. vs. Aquilla Phelps
Beasley, Robert C. vs. Jordan Pye
Beasley, Robert C. vs. Isaac G. Seymour
Beasley, Robert C. vs. Eli S. Shorter
Beasley, Robert C., Jarrel Beasley, Administrator and
  Palemon L. Weekes, Administrator vs. Joseph Stovall
Beasley, Robert C. vs. James Whitfield
Beasley, Robert C. vs. Asa Wood and Ezekiel Wood
Beasley, William vs. John Hardwick and Cornelius Hardwick,
  Administrator
Beavers, John F. vs. Phineas Kill
Beavers, Joshua, Thomas Marks and Henry Kelly vs. The State
Beavers, Thomas, John Towns and Jane Ray vs. William Gartrell
Bebee, Early vs. The State
Bebee, Flem vs. The State
Bebee, Henry vs. The State
Beck, Absalom vs. Thomas Cheeves
Beck, Absalom vs. Jeremiah Clark
Beck, Absalom vs. Irby Hudson and Gabriel R. Thomas
Beck, Absalom vs. The State
Beck, John vs. William P. Buis
Beckwith, William B. vs. The State
Beebe, Ben vs. The State
Beebe, Cooley vs. The State
Beebe, Harvey vs. The State
Beebe, Joe vs. The State
Beebee, Wesley vs. The State
Beeland, James vs. Thomas Grant
Beeland, James vs. Williamson B. Roby, Elbert W. Baynes,
  Administrator and Elizabeth Roby, Administrator
Beeland, James vs. The State
Beeland, James vs. Matthew Whitfield
Beeland, James vs. Arthur Willis, David Henderson, Executor
  and Jimey (June) Willis, Executor
Beer, Jonathan S. vs. John Head
Beland, James M. and Sarah Beland vs. James L. Maddux

Belcher, Collins H. vs. Joel Baley and Parham P. Mabry
Belcher, Elijah C. vs. Nathan H. Garten for use of John
  Allen
Belcher, Elijah C. vs. James Glass
Belcher, Elijah C. vs. Isiah Purse
Belcher, Elijah C. vs. Francis Spear
Belcher, Elijah C. vs. John Spearman
Belcher, Elijah C. vs. Amos S. Vail
Belcher, Green L. and Obediah R. Belcher vs. William C.
  Jessup, Barack F. Nichols and Edgar Sherman
Belcher, Isham L., Ransome Harwell, Administrator and Eliza
  D. Belcher, Administrator, vs. Obadiah Belcher and Obadiah
  R. Belcher, Executor
Belcher, Isham L. and Obadiah R. Belcher vs. George H.
  Metcalf
Belcher, Joe and Grant Belcher vs. The State
Belcher, John vs. George Hannah
Belcher, John vs. Sebron Moore
Belcher, O. R. vs. N. M. Williams
Belcher, O. R., Jr. vs. Susan C. Belcher
Belcher, Obadiah and Polly Belcher vs. James H. Shy and
  Mary C. (Kirby) Shy
Belcher, Oabdiah vs. The State
Belcher, Obediah vs. Joseph Heard
Belcher, Obediah vs. Josiah M. Lyon
Belcher, Obediah, Sr. vs. Stephen D. Mobley and Henry H.
  Cabiniss
Belcher, Obediah R. vs. Nehemiah B. White and Lucius White
Belcher, Thomas vs. The State
Belcher, Warren vs. The State
Belcher, William vs. Lovick Persons for the use of Officers
  of Court
Belcher, William vs. The State
Belcher, William vs. Archibald R. Turk
Belcher, William D. vs. David Dixon and Capers Dixon,
  Administrator
Belcher, Wyatt vs. The State
Belk, Norman A. vs. Officers of Court
Bell, Bailey vs. Thomas Arrington
Bell, Bailey, John G. Morris and Samuel Barker vs. Central
  Bank of Georgia
Bell, Ed vs. The State
Bell, Garfield vs. The State
Bell, George vs. Zedock Cook
Bell, George vs. Benjamin Darnall
Bell, George vs. Young Gresham and Edward Paine
Bell, Ida vs. The State
Bell, James vs. The State
Bell, Simon vs. The State
Bell, William vs. The State
Bellamy, Alexander vs. Jarrel W. Crenshaw
Bellamy, Alexander vs. Samuel Drewry
Bellamy, Alexander vs. George Ingram and Elizabeth Ingram
Bellamy, Alexander and Thomas Rivers vs. John D. Kirkpatrick
Bellamy, Alexander vs. Palemon Weekes and John Hunt
Bences, William vs. Robinson and Pabodie
Bender, John vs. Burwell Allmond and Polly Allmond
Bender, John vs. Gresham Selleck
Bender, John vs. The State
Bender, John S. vs. John P. Coles for use of Isaac Harvey
Benford, Boss vs. The State
Benford, Henry W. vs. Mathew Whitfield
Benford, Joe vs. Carrie F. B. Benford

Benford, Joseph, John Fears and James Kelly vs. The State
Benham, Elias vs. Shuback Foot and Corydon Dyer
Benham, Elias vs. The State
Benham, Elias vs. Robert Wasson and George Nichols
Bennett, J. C. vs. Charles F. Harvey
Bennett, J. F. vs. T. J. Brian for use of Officers of Court
Bennett, William and Green Pennell vs. John Luckie
Benson, Eli vs. Archibald Batchelor
Benson, Eli vs. The State
Benson, James M. vs. Nehemiah Stanford
Bentley, John vs. Jeremiah Pearson
Benton, Abel vs. The State
Benton, Ben, Lewis Walker and Henry Malone vs. The State
Benton, Eugene vs. The State
Benton, George vs. The State
Benton, Herschel vs. The State
Benton, James vs. William G. Horsley
Benton, James B. and William Philips vs. The State
Benton, Jeremiah vs. Reason E. Mabry and Co. for use of
  Samuel Lovejoy
Benton, Jeremiah vs. William Pabodie
Benton, Jesse and Robert Benton vs. James L. Burks
Benton, Joe vs. The State
Benton, John H. and H. O. Benton vs. William R. Parker
Benton, John Henry vs. The State
Benton, Jonathan, James Sansom and John McAllister vs.
  United States of America
Benton, Joseph, Jr. vs. William Bowen
Benton, L. O. and Eugene Benton vs. T. M. Singleton
Benton, L. O., Ed Benton and Charles Henderson vs. The State
Benton, Lucian vs. Wilks Walker for use of Officers of Court
Benton, Monk vs. The State
Benton, Oscar vs. The State
Benton, Philip vs. The State
Benton, Robert vs. James Whitfield
Benton, Shelton vs. The State
Benton, Wiley vs. The State
Benton, William vs. The State
Berg, Rosa vs. W. D. Nottingham
Berner, William R. vs. William C. Courtney and Gilbert B.
  Tennet
Berner, William R. vs. James Speights
Berner, William R. vs. E. B. Stoddard and Co.
Berry, A. T. vs. Benjamin Askew
Berry, Alfred, Howard Berry, Mose Clements, Will Clements,
  Harrison Miller and (alias Harris Miller) vs. The State
Berry, Augustine T. vs. Thomas J. Smith
Berry, Augustine T. vs. Napolean B. Atkinson
Berry, Augustine T. vs. F. M. Swanson for use of Jasper
  Lodge #50
Berry, Augustine T. vs. Mathew Whitfield, John F. Patterson,
  Executor, William Mathis, Executor, Leroy M. Willson,
  Executor and Pleasant Willson, Executor
Berry, E. P. vs. The State
Berry, John D. and Beverly Daniel vs. James Adams
Berry, Lewis T. vs. Davis Smith
Bertram James vs. William Robinson and Albert Pabodie
Betts, Abraham vs. William R. Russel
Bevens, Thomas H. vs. James H. Bennett
Bevens, Thomas H. vs. Elbert Dickson
Bevens, Thomas H. vs. Luther Roll
Bevers, Joseph vs. William H. Crane and Joseph Kopman
Bickerstaff, Robert vs. James Alexander

Bickerstaff, Robert vs. Benjamin Jordan
Bill (col) vs. The State
Billings, Bardwell vs. William Biscoe and James N. Hall
Billings, Bardwell vs. Hardy Crawford
Billings, Bardwell vs. Benjamin Irvine
Billings, Bardwell and John McMichael vs. Eli Shorter
Billings, Christopher and Mary Stokes vs. The State
Binford, Oliver vs. The State
Bird, Harvey, Isiah Bird and Monroe Singleton vs. The State
Bird, Isaiah vs. The State
Birdson, George L. F. vs. John G. Slaughter
Biscoe, William and James N. Hall vs. Jonas H. Holland
Biscoe, William, James N. Hall and Charles S. Jordan vs.
  William S. Pritchett
Bishop, Philip vs. Thomas Goolsby
Bishop, Phillip vs. John Hobson and Christopher Hobson
Bivens, Christopher H. vs. James Whitfield and Anthony Dyer
Black, James vs. Milton Antony
Black, James vs. Thomas Beall
Black, James vs. Anthony Dyer
Black, James vs. Willis Grady, Augustin Slaughter and
  Charles Labuzan
Black, James vs. Alston H. Green and Joseph Buchannon
Black, James vs. Robert Grierson
Black, James vs. Samuel Hale and Gilbert Shearer
Black, James, Unice Dean and Crawford Edmondson vs. Abraham
  Hester
Black, James vs. John Hill and Co.
Black, James, John P. Nall and Unicey Deane vs. Christopher
  Hobson, Harriet H. Hobson, Administrator and John Willson,
  Administrator
Black, James vs. Joseph Johnson
Black, James and Sally Black vs. Andrew Low
Black, James, John P. Nall and Unicey Deane vs. Sanders
  Stallings
Black, James, Samuel Crockett, Fountain M. Thurmond and
  Sahdrick McMichael vs. The State
Black, James vs. William Watson
Black, John vs. Handy Waller
Black, Thomas and James Black vs. Andrew Low, Robert Isaac,
  Alexander Low and James Henry
Blackburn, Benjamin vs. The State
Blackwell, Ben and Sarah Blackwell vs. The State
Blackwell, Betsey vs. The State
Blackwell, Emuel vs. The State
Blackwell, H. F. vs. J. H. Broughton
Blackwell, Isaac vs. The State
Blackwell, James F. vs. Griffin, Monticello and Madison
  Railroad
Blackwell, James F. vs. William D. Maddux and John F.
  Patterson
Blackwell, James F. vs. Spencer Preston
Blackwell, James F., James Benton, Aris Newton, E. W.
  Baynes, I. H. Freeman, S. C. Kelly, Robert Y. Ezell,
  Samuel H. Blackwell and Mitchell Aaron vs. Sheriff of
  Jasper County
Blackwell, James F. vs. The State
Blackwell, James F. vs. V. B. White and L. White
Blackwell, James F. and Samuel H. Blackwell vs. Matthew
  Whitfield, Leroy M. Willson, Executor, Pleasant Willson,
  Executor, John F. Patterson, Executor and William H.
  Mathis, Executor
Blackwell, John vs. The State

Blackwell, John H. vs. Amanda I. Fitts
Blackwell, Robert M. vs. J. A. Broughton
Blackwell, Robert M. vs. Pollard and Company
Blackwell, S. H. and R. W. Blackwell vs. W. G. High
Blackwell, S. H. and R. M. Blackwell vs. W. F. Martin
Blackwell, S. S. vs. Sarah Aken for use of Officers of
   Court
Blackwell, S. S. vs. Matthew Whitfield
Blackwell, Samuel H. vs. Alphonso Hardman and Berry T.
   Digby, Administrator
Blackwell, Samuel H. vs. William D. Maddux
Blackwell, Samuel H. vs. The State
Blackwell, Samuel H. vs. Matthew Whitfield
Blackwell, T. G. and Jack Blackwell vs. The State
Blackwell, Francis vs. William A. Cowen
Blake, Joseph vs. Alston H. Greene and Joseph Buchannon
Blake, Joseph vs. William Holebrooks
Blake, Joseph vs. Tandy D. King
Blake, Joseph vs. Archibald McNeal
Blake, Joseph vs. Zachary Pope
Black, Joseph vs. Gresham Selleck
Blan, Thomas, William Ramey and Shadrach McMichael vs.
   Central Bank of Georgia
Blan, Thomas and Fleming Jordan vs. Erby Hudson and Davis
   R. Adams, Executor
Blan, Thomas vs. Freeman McClendon
Blan, Thomas vs. Jeremiah Pearson
Blan, Thomas and William Ramey vs. Robert Tolefree
Blan, Thomas vs. James S. Weekes
Blan, Thomas vs. John Wood and William F. Mapp, Administra-
   tor
Blanchard, Frederick vs. The State
Blankenship, Daniel vs. John Belcher
Blankenship, Daniel vs. The State
Blankenship, Reuben vs. Isham Thornton for use of Thomas
   Napier
Blann, William vs. James D. Head
Blanton, Benjamin vs. Bennet M. Ware
Bledsoe, J. J. vs. The State
Bloodworth, John vs. Benjamin Kitchens
Bloodworth, John D. and John Bloodworth vs. Junius Bloodworth
Bloodworth, Thomas F. and John Bloodworth vs. Joseph Bacon
Blosson, Simon G. vs. William Cunningham
Blossom, Simeon G. and John Clute vs. Ludwick H. Levingston,
   Israel G. Lash and Thomas Lash
Blossom, Simeon G. and John H. Clute vs. John C. Reid
Blossom, Simon G. vs. John T. Loyd
Blount, Alfred G. P. vs. Joseph Day
Blount, Alfred W. G. T. vs. Lucinda Blount
Blow, Will vs. The State
Blunt, Alfred W. G. P. and Theolphilus Pye vs. James D. Head
Blunt, Alfred W. G. P. and Richard Carter vs. John M. King
Blunt, Alfred W. G. P. vs. Thomas J. Smith and William M.
   Broddus
Blunt, Alfred W. G. P. vs. The State
Blunt, John vs. John Owen
Blurton, John and James Cannon vs. Bedford Shorter for use
   of John P. Coles
Boen, John and William H. Wyatt vs. Abram A. Heard
Bogan, Caswell P. vs. William C. Thompson and William S.
   Townsend
Bogan, Charles and Isham Mitchell vs. The State
Bogan, Tom vs. The State

Bohanan, Alexander vs. Joel Towns
Bohannan, John vs. Wingfield Shropshire
Bond, Edward, David Sims and Harmon Runnels vs. James
  Spurlock and Drury Spurlock, Administrator
Bond, William S. vs. George F. Buchanan
Bond, William S. vs. James Cameron, William Cameron and
  James Hawthorn, Sr.
Bond, William S., William Cameron, James Cameron and James
  Hawthorne, Sr. vs. Alston H. Green, Henry H. Cook and
  James C. Cook
Bond, William S. vs. John Hill, Augustin Slaughter and
  Charles Labuzan
Bond, William S. vs. Robert V. Marye
Bond, William S. vs. William Morgan and Fielding Bradford
Bonner, Edward vs. The State
Bonner, George vs. William Spence
Bonner, George W. vs. Elijah McMichael
Bonner, Jerry vs. Stephen C. Talmadge
Bonner, Jonathan vs. George W. Bonner for use of Augustin
  Slaughter and Charles Labuzan
Bonner, Jones and Henry Cox vs. Benjamin Chapman, Britain
  Chapman, Minor and Abner Chapman, Guardian
Bonner, Josiah M. and James King vs. David Hascall
Bonner, Josiah M. vs. Amory Sibley
Bonner, Thomas C. vs. James W. Vaughn
Bonner, Thomas R. and Bedford F. Leverett vs. Sidney R.
  Baynes
Bonner, Whitmell, Jonathan Bonner, Administrator and Ally
  Bonner, Administrator vs. Thomas Hardeman
Bonner, Whitmill vs. Shadrach McMichael
Boon, James vs. Anthony Dyer
Boone, Spencer vs. The State
Boozer, O. R. vs. The State
Boram, John and Thomas J. Burney, Administrator vs. James
  Long
Borland, Andrew and Abram Borland, Administrator vs. John
  Graves
Born, John (alias J. P. Alexander) vs. The State
Borum, George and Benjamine Borum, Executor vs. Beverly
  Daniel
Borum, George and Benjamin Borum, Executor vs. William Pye
Borum, Margaret vs. Daniel Parish, Jasper Corning, Henry
  Parish, Joseph Kernochan and Ephraim Holbrook
Borum, Nathaniel, John M. Sims and Paschal Murphy vs. Elias
  Wallen and Joseph Pope McKinney
Bostic, Dave vs. The State
Bostick, Charles D. vs. John C. Curd and Whitfield D.
  Carhart
Bostick, Charles D. vs. William B. Grubbs
Bostick, Charles D. vs. Gasaway D. Lamar
Bostick, Charles D. and Lawson G. Chambliss vs. Augustus W.
  Lane
Bostick, Charles D. vs. Joseph C. Little
Bostick, Charles D. vs. Richard J. Loyall
Bostick, Charles D. vs. William Maxey, Charles S. Jordan
  and John R. Dyer
Bostick, Charles D. vs. John Powell
Bostick, Charles D. vs. Thomas P. Reynolds
Bostick, Charles D. vs. Henry Solomon, Larkin Griffin and
  James Land
Bostick, Charles D. vs. The State
Bostick, Charles D. vs. William D. Williams, Wilson Pope
  and Gideon Pope

Bostick, Thornton P. and Charles D. Bostick vs. William
  Cleland and Jesse Pitts, Administrator
Bostick, Thornton P. vs. John Hines
Bowden, Algie vs. The State
Bowden, Dumas vs. The State
Bowden, I. vs. The State
Bowden, J. T. vs. The State
Bowden, Jesse vs. Milton Anthony
Bowden, Jesse vs. Samuel Post
Bowden, John W. vs. Sherrod H. Gay
Bowden, Mattie Lou vs. The State
Bowdin, James vs. Richmond Bledsoe
Bowdin, James and William A. Slaughter vs. Bird Goolsby
Bowdin, James vs. William A. Slaughter
Bowdin, James vs. John Warren, Abner Turner and Matthew R.
  Evans
Bowen, Christopher C. and Charles S. Jordan vs. John W.
  Check
Bowers, J. N. vs. The State
Boyd, George, John Boyd and Elias Boyd vs. Levi Stokes
Boyd, John vs. The State
Boyet, John vs. Hugh Johnson
Boyet, William vs. Elijah N. Hascall
Boyet, William and Samuel Clay vs. Thomas Moffit
Boykin, Ellen vs. Henry Boykin
Boykin, Francis vs. Thomas J. Casey
Boykin, Francis, John T. Boykin, Executor and William
  Williams, Executor vs. Thomas Grant
Boykin, Francis vs. Jeremiah Harvey and Michael Dennis
Boykin, Francis vs. James Hollaway
Boykin, Francis, John T. Boykin, Executor and William
  Williams, Executor, vs. Edwin H. Macon
Boykin, John T. vs. The State
Boykin, John T. vs. John Warren, Abner Turner and Mathew
  R. Evans
Boykin, M. V. and C. M. Boykin vs. John W. Wyatt
Boyles, Thomas W. vs. The State
Bradford, Edmund vs. Wiseman Bridges
Bradford, Edmund vs. Elijah N. Hascall and David Hascall
Bradford, Edmund vs. Abraham Warren
Bradford, Edmund vs. Joseph White, Avarilla B. (White)
  Traylor, Administrator and Thomas White, Administrator
Bradford, John vs. The State
Bradley, Bunk vs. The State
Bradley, James and Reuben Jordan, Executor, vs. Trustees of
  Methodist Episcopal Church
Bradley, Mollie vs. The State
Bradley, William vs. Mathew Reed
Branch, Taylor vs. The State
Branche, John vs. The State
Brandon, James and James L. Brandon, Administrator vs.
  J. P. Brandon
Brandon, Rebecca J. (Dawkins) vs. Green V. Brandon
Branham, Edmund vs. The State
Branham, Henry vs. Officers of Court
Branham, Horace vs. The State
Brannan, Russell vs. John Holland
Brantley, Greene D., Alsea Holifield and John Baldwin vs.
  Anthony Dyer
Brantley, Greene D. vs. Seaborn Jones
Brantley, John H. vs. Gilbert Ansley
Brantley, John H. vs. Robert C. Beasley and Palomon S.
  Weekes

Brantley, John H. and James W. Morgan vs. William V. Burney
Brantley, John H. vs. Elizabeth Echols
Brantley, John H. vs. Robert Germany, William Germany,
  Executor and James Germany, Executor
Brantley, John H. vs. Thomas Hairston
Brantley, John H. vs. John Knight
Brantley, John H. vs. John McBryde and James McBryde
Brantley, John H. vs. Joseph May for use of Birdsong Burnes
Brantley, John H. vs. John B. McDaniel
Brantley, John H. vs. John E. Morgan
Brantley, John H. vs. Hardeman Owens
Brantley, John H. vs. John Payne
Brantley, John H. vs. Earnest L. Young and Jeremiah Pearson
Brantley, John W. vs. Thomas W. Baxter, Robert W. Fort and
  Laird H. Wiley
Brantley, John W. vs. George W. Carhart
Brantley, John W. vs. Jeremiah H. Clarke and Neal Holland
Brantley, John W. vs. Anthony Dyer
Brantley, John W. vs. The State
Brantly, John H. vs. John Baldwin and Alfred Shorter
Brantley, John H. vs. James Dickson, William Dickson,
  Donald McLeod and Charles Rockwell
Brantly, John H. vs. The State
Brantly, John H. vs. John G. Webb
Brantly, John H. vs. James Whitfield
Braswell, Caeser vs. The State
Braswell, Eselene (alias New Rag) vs. The State
Braswell, John vs. John L. Pennington
Bray, Henry vs. The State
Bray, Thomas H. and Gilbert E. Thigpen vs. Officers of Court
Brazeal, William, Jr. vs. The State
Brazel, Martha vs. Lawson H. Brazel
Brazil, Mose vs. The State
Brazile, Bettie and Barbara Brazile vs. The State
Brewer, Benjamin and Thomas Smith vs. The State
Brewer, Benjamin W. and Susanna Brewer vs. William C. Baugh
Brewer, Benjamin W. vs. Jacob Roll and Sanford Clark
Brewer, Benjamin W. and Susanna Brewer vs. Thomas Wyatt
Brewer, Clark vs. Drewry Brewer, Ethan Brewer, Executor,
  and Elisha Brewer, Executor
Brewer, Clark vs. William Broughton and John A. Broughton,
  Executor
Brewer, Clark vs. Banjamin B. Freeman
Brewer, Clark vs. Robert C. Rankin
Brewer, Clark vs. The State
Brewer, Clark vs. Parminas Thomson and Drury Evans
Brewer, Clark vs. Parminas Thomason and Thomas D. Hollings-
  worth
Brewer, Cofe, Willis Swift and Henry Fort vs. The State
Brewer, Elisha vs. Pettus Ragland
Brewer, John J. vs. Charles Strong
Brewer, Mary vs. Eli Glover
Brewer, Oliver and Samuel Clay vs. William Keener
Brewer, Susanna vs. William Maxey
Brewer, Susanah vs. The State
Brewer, W. J. vs. Ella J. Brewer for use of Officers of
  Court
Bridges, Bennett vs. Stephen W. McClendon
Bridges, Cooper vs. The State
Bridges, Daniel vs. Samuel Johnson
Bridges, Frank vs. The State
Bridges, Henry vs. The State
Bridges, John vs. The State

Bridges, Johathan F. vs. James Cowan and Thomas B. Erwin
Bridges, Johathan F. vs. Isaac Hill
Bridges, Johathan F. vs. Cuthbert Reese and Joseph Reese
Bridges, William vs. John C. Gibson
Britton, George vs. James L. Weekes
Broadus, Charley vs. The State
Broadus, Robert vs. The State
Broddus, Charlie vs. The State
Broddus, E. S. vs. J. D. Thornton for use of Officers of
Court
Broddus, Edward A. and John W. Jones vs. Joshua C. Garrett
Broddus, Edward A. vs. The State
Broddus, Elbert S. vs. Janie L. Broddus for use of Officers
of Court
Broddus, Thomas C. vs. Wiley W. Bullard
Broddus, Thomas C. vs. Lindsey H. Durham
Broddus, Thomas C. vs. Lindsey H. Durham
Broddus, Thomas C. and Joshua Hill vs. Charles M. Furlow
Broddus, Thomas C. vs. Officers of Court
Broddus, Thomas C. vs. James C. Wise, Henry Hendrick,
Administrator, Emily Wise, Minor, Cyntha Wise, Minor and
William Wise, Minor
Broddus, Tom and Aaron Smith vs. The State
Broddus, William M. vs. Hubbard W. Cozart
Brogden, Peterson G. vs. Amos Martin
Brogden, Peterson G. vs. Garland Maxey and William Maxey,
Administrator
Brogden, Peterson G. vs. Grief Smith
Brogden, Peterson G. vs. Thomas G. Smith
Bronson, Zenos vs. John Huddleston
Bronson, Zenos and Claiborn Mills vs. The State
Brooke, Joseph vs. Joseph Johnson
Brooke, Joseph vs. George Lewis for use of Felix Lewis
Brookes, William and William Bennett vs. Allen McClendon
Brooks, Aaron, Thomas C. Russell and William Hitchcock vs.
James Whitfield
Brooks, Aaron, Jr., John W. Burney and Hamlin Truman vs.
Officers of Court
Brooks, Ashley, W. J. Oxford and Richard Newton vs. The
State
Brooks, Baley C. vs. James Martin
Brooks, George vs. The State
Brooks, Greene vs. The State
Brooks, Guss vs. The State
Brooks, Hiram vs. Jonas H. Holland, Eunice Holland, Admin-
istrator and William W. Holland, Administrator
Brooks, Hiram vs. William S. Hurd and Anson Hungerford
Brooks, Hiram vs. Maximilian H. Hutchinson
Brooks, Hiram vs. Thomas J. Pritchett, Alfred Pritchett and
George Pritchett
Brooks, James vs. Ebenezar T. Hearne
Brooks, James vs. Samuel Maddox
Brooks, James vs. John Peacock, Lewis Peacock, Executor and
William Peacock, Executor
Brooks, James, Sr., Paschal Brooks, Administrator and
Bivings Brooks, Administrator vs. Eli Glover
Brooks, James, Sr. vs. John McKenzie and Peter Bennock
Brooks, Moses vs. The State
Brooks, Paschal and James Brooks vs. Eli S. Shorter
Brooks, Paschal and John B. Slaughter vs. James Whitfield
Brooks, S. I. vs. Mrs. L. E. Holland
Brooks, Silas vs. Rufus Broom
Brooks, Silas vs. Robert Leak for use of Joseph Moss

Brooks, Thomas J. vs. Thomas J. Prtichett, Alfred Pritchett
  and George Pritchett
Broom, William vs. Bennedick Jetton
Broswell, Teat vs. The State
Broughton, ? and ? Broddus (alias) vs. The State
Broughton, Belitha vs. Daniel Melson
Broughton, Dock vs. The State
Broughton, John A. and James H. Weathersbee vs. Harrison
  Smith, John C. Smith, Guardian
Broughton, W. A. and N. B. Brown vs. The State
Broughton, William vs. Edward Castleberry
Brown, Agnes and Jonas R. Brown vs. Seaborn Jones
Brown, Alfred H. vs. Thomas Broadus
Brown, Alfred H. vs. Alston H. Greene and Joseph Buchannon
Brown, Alfred H. vs. William O. Kelley
Brown, Alfred H. vs. Allen McClendon
Brown, Alfred H. and James Pye vs. William Pabodie
Brown, Alfred H. vs. Robert Robey and Timothy Robey,
  Administrator
Brown, Amos vs. Thomas Hester
Brown, Amos vs. Welcom C. Lovejoy
Brown, Anderson vs. John Nellams
Brown, Andrew M. vs. Hugh Brown
Brown, Austin vs. The State
Brown, Bartlett and James Brown vs. Jenkins D. Weathers and
  Archibald H. Sneed
Brown, Bedford vs. Howell W. Runnels
Brown, Benjamin vs. Robert Reed and Joseph Fitzpatrick
Brown, Benjamin vs. The State
Brown, Christopher vs. The State
Brown, Daniel C. vs. Anthony Dyer
Brown, David vs. Samuel Butts and John Lucas, Administrator
Brown, David vs. William Sharp
Brown, David vs. The State
Brown, David vs. Jesse Thurmond
Brown, David vs. West Whitaker
Brown, David vs. William Whitfield
Brown, Dink vs. The State
Brown, Edward vs. Abner Bartlett
Brown, Edward, Edward A. Broddus, Executor, Josias R. Brown,
  Executor and Thomas Broddus vs. Seaborn Jones
Brown, Edward vs. John Lanier
Brown, Edward vs. Francis Wisdom
Brown, Fielding vs. Edward Coxe and James Gillespie
Brown, Francis vs. The State
Brown, Henry vs. M. S. Benton and L. O. Benton
Brown, Henry vs. Abner Chapman and Betsey Chapman
Brown, Henry vs. The State
Brown, Isbel vs. Robert Robey and Timothy Robey, Adminis-
  trator
Brown, Isham vs. The State
Brown, James and Drewcilla Brown vs. Erastus Graves and
  Rufus R. Graves
Brown, James E. vs. John Baldwin
Brown, James E. vs. Anthony Dyer
Brown, James E. vs. Alston H. Greene
Brown, James E. and James McKemie vs. William Jewett
Brown, James E. vs. Thadeus Moynihan
Brown, James E. vs. Reuben C. Shorter
Brown, James E. and James McKemie vs. Augustin Slaughter
  and Charles Labuzan
Brown, James E. vs. Pleasant Stovall
Brown, John vs. Thaddeus Beall, Elias Beall & Thomas Beall

Brown, John vs. Samuel Downey
Brown, John vs. Otis Dyer
Brown, John vs. John Ferrell
Brown, John vs. Alston H. Green and Joseph Buchannon
Brown, John and James E. Brown vs. William Shaw
Brown, John vs. The State
Brown, John G. vs. William Whipple and James O. Whipple
Brown, John G. W. vs. David Myrick
Brown, Joseph E. vs. The State
Brown, Kitt vs. The State
Brown, Levy and Jack Willis vs. The State
Brown, Richmond vs. Charles Cargile
Brown, Richmond vs. Thomas Napier
Brown, Robert vs. John Conduit
Brown, Robert vs. James Cowan and Thomas B. Erwin
Brown, Robert and William Hitchcock vs. John E. Glover
Brown, Robert vs. Crawford H. Greer and Amy Greer
Brown, Robert vs. Jonas H. Holland
Brown, Robert vs. Hurd and Hungerford
Brown, Robert vs. James Jenkins
Brown, Robert and Francis Jenkins vs. High P. Kirkpatrick
Brown, Robert vs. Isaac L. Parker and Maxmillian H.
  Hutchinson, Administrator
Brown, Robert, Moses B. Hairston and Eliza M. C. Hairston,
  Administrator vs. David A. Reese
Brown, Robert vs. Joseph Straus
Brown, Robert vs. Francis M. Swanson
Brown, Robert vs. Stephen C. Talmadge
Brown, Robert vs. Asa P. Toland
Brown, Robert vs. Thyers J. Toland
Brown, Robert vs. Mary A. Trussell
Brown, Robert and George T. McDaniel vs. Albert B. Vaughn
Brown, Robert, William Willingham and Stephen W. McClendon
  vs. Henry Vaughn
Brown, Robert vs. John Walker
Brown, Robert C. vs. James Lucus
Brown, Robert C. vs. William Robinson
Brown, Russell J. vs. Aley A. Flemister
Brown, Simon vs. The State
Brown, T. J. vs. The State
Brown, T. W. and Mrs. J. H. Brown vs. J. F. Bennett
Brown, Thomas vs. John Abercrombie
Brown, Thomas vs. Jeremiah Pearson and Allan McClendon
Brown, Thomas vs. Armsted Taler and John Laine, Administrator
Brown, Thomas, Jr. vs. James S. Weeks
Brown, William, James Lanier and John Donaldson vs. Thomas
  J. Casey
Brown, William vs. Alston H. Greene and Joseph Buchannon
Brown, William vs. Moses Rosser
Brown, William and James M. Beeland, Administrator vs.
  Mathew Whitfield
Brown, William vs. William Woods
Brown, Willis and Andrew M. Hamilton vs. Major Barkwell
Brownfield, John vs. James A. Atcheson and Williamson Roby
Brownfield, John vs. Central Bank of Georgia
Bruce, John vs. Armstead Dodson
Bryan, Bartram vs. James Smith
Bryan, Bartrum vs. William Watson
Bryan, Bartrum vs. John Wilson
Bryant, Bird vs. William C. Jessup, Barak F. Nichols and
  Edgar Sherman
Bryant, Bird and Jefferson E. Bryant vs. William Maxey
Bryant, E. L. and Benjamin Jordan vs. Joseph Anderson

110

Bryant, Henry vs. Fannie Bryant
Bryant, Hilliard vs. The State
Bryant, James vs. The State
Bryant, Jarrott and Stephen Bailey vs. The State
Bryant, John vs. William Maxey
Bryant, John vs. The State
Bryant, Josh vs. The State
Bryant, Lee, Aug Spears, Lum Bryant and Columbus Bryant vs.
  The State
Bryant, Nancy and Alice Jeffries vs. The State
Bryant, Needham vs. Isaac Foreman
Bryant, Temp vs. The State
Bryant, William vs. Warren Ambrose
Bryant, William vs. Charles P. Gordon
Bryant, William vs. Zorobabel Williamson, William William-
  son, Administrator and Green Williamson, Administrator
Bryant, Willie vs. The State
Buchanan, James E. and Isaac Moore vs. James Herring and
  Samuel Hall
Buchanan, James E. and Isaac Moore vs. Jesse Lane
Buchanan, John W. vs. Benjamin B. Buchanan
Buchannan, Alexander N. vs. Abner Chapman
Buchannon, Alexander N. and William Tolefree, Administrator
  vs. Edward A. Broddus
Buchannon, Alexander N. vs. Edward T. Hill
Buchannon, George F. vs. John Fluker
Buchannon, George H. vs. George F. Buchannon for use of
  Benjamin H. Willson
Buchannon, James vs. Anthony Dyer
Buchannon, James vs. Robert Robey
Buchannon, James P. vs. David Montgomery
Buchannon, Joseph vs. The State
Buchanon, James vs. Daniel Tomlinson
Buck, John vs. George Buchannan
Buck, John vs. John Ferguson
Buck, John vs. The State
Buckhannon, John vs. Wingfield Shropshire
Buckner, Daniel vs. Wiley Abercrombie
Buckner, John vs. The State
Buice, John, Woodmoreland Richardson, Executor, and James
  E. Richardson, Executor vs. Daniel Wilson
Buis, Elbert vs. Warren Hopson
Buis, Elbert vs. Jonathan Parrish
Buis, Elbert vs. John J. Smith
Buis, Elbert vs. Lewis Wynn and William Johnson
Buis, John vs. Augustin Slaughter and Charles Labuzan
Buis, Zachariah vs. Andrew McBryde
Bullard, J. H. vs. The State
Bullard, James vs. Jenkins D. Weathers
Bullard, James, Jr., William Hudson and James Bullard, Sr.
  vs. William Shaw and John Talbert, Administrator
Bullard, Thomas and William Stephens vs. Joseph Gunnels
Bullard, Thomas vs. Henry Slaughter
Bullard, Thomas vs. The State
Bullard, Wiley W. vs. Nancy Ann Bullard
Bullard, Wiley W. vs. Stephen C. Talmadge and Samuel Plummer
Bullock, Richard vs. James Patterson
Burdett, Samuel L. B. vs. The State
Burg, John (alias John Bird) vs. The State
Burge, John and Hugh Wise vs. Wylie B. Ector
Burgess, Thomas vs. Gresham Selleck
Burgess, Thomas vs. The State
Burke, Francis, Richard V. Gregory and Theophilus Freeman

vs. The State
Burke, William B. vs. Eliza L. Newton
Burke, William B. vs. Charles M. Sledge
Burkes, William vs. James Digby for use of William Bowen
Burkes, William vs. William Pekens
Burks, James S. vs. James Phillips
Burks, William and William Bennett vs. Allen McClendon
Burks, William vs. William P. Yonge
Burnett, Anthony, Richardson Pennington and William R.
   Russell vs. Archer Willingham
Burnett, John vs. William Ferrell for use of Thomas Butler
Burnett, William vs. Alford Shepherd
Burney, Bob vs. The State
Burney, C. C. vs. Griffin, Monticello and Madison Railroad
   Co.
Burney, C. C. and John W. Burney vs. William H. Preston
   and James H. Preston, Executor
Burney, Charles C. and John W. Burney vs. George T. Bartlett
Burney, Charles C. vs. Loyall and Andrews
Burney, Charles C. and John W. Burney, Jr. vs. Samuel C.
   Weems and Francis M. Swanson
Burney, Charles C. vs. Ebenezar T. White
Burney, Ella vs. The State
Burney, Eugene vs. The State
Burney, G. W. vs. The State
Burney, James vs. The State
Burney, Jeff vs. The State
Burney, Jim vs. The State
Burney, John vs. Crawford H. Greer
Burney, John W. vs. Nancy Antony
Burney, John W. vs. William Bailey
Burney, John W. and Thomas M. Jordan vs. Benjamin Barrow
Burney, John W., John Randolph Dyer and Charles S. Jordan
   vs. Central Bank of Georgia
Burney, John W. and Charles C. Burney vs. Berry T. Digby
Burney, John W. and Seaborn J. T. Whatley vs. Anthony Dyer
Burney, John W. vs. Reese Goolsby
Burney, John W. and Francis M. Swanson, Administrator vs.
   Thomas M. Jordan
Burney, John W. and Martha L. Burney vs. David M. Langston
Burney, John W. vs. Monticello Academy
Burney, John W. vs. Nehemiah B. White and Lucius White
Burney, John W. vs. John Willson
Burney, John W., Jr. vs. Joshua Hill
Burney, John W., Jr. vs. Felix B. Martin
Burney, John W., Sr. and John W. Burney, Jr., Administrator
   vs. Augustus M. Jenkins
Burney, Joseph H. and John W. Burney, Jr. vs. John R. Greer
Burney, Thomas J., John W. Stark, Silvanus W. Burney,
   William V. Burney and John W. Burney vs. John M. Adams,
   Joseph C. Fargo and William T. Adams
Burney, Will vs. The State
Burney, William (alias Buck) vs. The State
Burney, William V., John W. Burney and Thomas J. Smith vs.
   Central Bank of Georgia
Burney, William V. vs. Eureal H. Doolittle
Burney, William V. vs. John Robinson
Burney, William V. vs. Neal Strahan
Burney, Zeb vs. The State
Burns, Cornelius vs. The State
Burns, Thomas H. vs. James H. Bennett
Burns, W. J. vs. The State
Burr, S. B. and Bolling Whitfield vs. James A. Damour

Burton, Patsey W. vs. William Christian
Burton, Sarah and William Burton vs. John Greer, Guardian
and Ira Foreman, Minor
Bush, John vs. The State
Bussey, Charles L. vs. Bank of Augusta
Bussy, Charles L. and Alexander S. Holland vs. Giles Bowers
and Martha Bowers
Butler, David vs. William Simmons
Butler, James vs. James Patterson
Butler, John vs. The State
Butler, Thomas vs. Elijah N. Hascall and David Hascall
Butram, James and Andrew Butram vs. James Richards
Butrell, Burwell and John Sharman vs. Ernest L. Young and
Jeremiah Pearson
Butts, Bell vs. The State
Butts, Henry vs. John G. Towns and John Martin, Executor
Byas, Walker vs. The State
Byram, Mat vs. The State
Byrom, Henry C. and William H. Byrom vs. Jackson Fitzpatrick
and Edward Varner, Administrator
Byrom, John, Edward Varner, Executor, and Cynthia (Byrom)
vs. Edward A. Broddus
Byrom, John vs. Eliza Byrom and Jarrel Beasely, Guardian
Byrom, John and Jackson Fitzpatrick, Executor vs. James
Fretwell
Byrom, John, Cynthia Byrom, Executor and Jackson Fitzpatrick
Executor vs. Thomas E. Rogers
Byrom, John L. D. vs. Lamack Hines
Byrom, John L. D. vs. The State
Byrom, John S. D. vs. Augustin Slaughter and Charles Labuzan
Byrom, Seymore S. and John Byrom, Administrator vs. Eliza
P. Byrom and Jarrel Beasley, Guardian
Byrom, Seymour S. and Jarrel Beasley, Administrator vs.
William Byrom
Byrom, William vs. Nathaniel Barnes
Byrom, William and John Byrom, Executor vs. John Rudisille
and Henry Graybill, Executor
Byrom, William H. vs. James C. Bartlett
Byrom, William H. vs. Henry C. Byrom
Byrom, William H. vs. Hollis Cooley and James H. Robinson
Byrom, William H. vs. James D. Head
Byrom, William H. vs. William S. Hurd and Anson Hungerford
Byrom, William H. vs. Robert Kellam and William Maxey
Byrom, William H. and Edward Price vs. John Thurmond
Byrum, William vs. James Wright

Cabaness, Henry B. vs. Abner Chapman
Cabaness, Henry B. and Jarrel Beasly vs. John Cargile, John
Martin, Joseph Carter and Solomon Strickland for use of
Stokely Morgan
Cabiness, Henry B. vs. Thomas Davis
Cabiness, Henry B. vs. John Fannin for use of Eli S. Shorter
Caldwell, Creed bs. Aquilla Phelps
Caldwell, David vs. James Hines
Callaway, Elizabeth vs. Milton P. Walthall
Callaway, Jabez G. and James Callaway vs. Joshua Callaway
and Elizabeth Callaway, Administrator
Callaway, Jabez G. vs. Asa Ragan
Callaway, James and Elmore Callaway, Executor vs. Elisha
Perryman
Callaway, James C., Elmore Callaway, Administrator,
Williamson B. Robey and Elbert W. Baynes, Administrator
vs. Elizabeth Callaway

113

Callaway, Jobe vs. Messon Academy
Callaway, Jonathan, William W. Callaway and Noah Callaway
   vs. Evan H. Powell
Callaway, Joshua vs. Samuel Butts, John Lucas, Administra-
   tor and William Lee, Administrator
Callaway, Joshua vs. James Manning
Callaway, Joshua vs. John Robinson
Callaway, Joshua vs. Robert Williamson
Callaway, Tobe vs. Ferdinand Phinizy, Son and Shields
Calloway, Elmore and Elbert W. Baynes vs. Milton Roby and
   Mark S. Newton
Calloway, Peter vs. James Paramore
Calvert, John vs. Thomas McGehee
Calvert, John M. vs. George Alexander
Calvert, John M. vs. Thomas B. Erwin and James Cowan
Calvert, John M. vs. Daniel Guinn and Thomas A. Brown
Calvert, John M. vs. James T. J. Orr
Cameron, James vs. Alston H. Green and Henry H. Cook
Cameron, James vs. Samuel Shields
Cameron, James vs. John Willson
Cameron, James H. vs. Anthony Dyer
Cameron, William vs. Banjamin H. Willson
Camp, Arch vs. The State
Camp, Thomas vs. Henry Jordan
Campbell, Andrew G. vs. The State
Campbell, C. G. vs. Charles Merriwether, Oscar Bergstrom
   and John Cargile
Campbell, Mrs. C. L. vs. B. Whitfield for use of Officers
   of Court
Campbell, Charles, Charles E. F. W. Campbell and George T.
   Bartlett vs. George W. Stringfellow and Riley S. Fears,
   Administrator
Campbell, Charles A., Edward Calloway, Horace T. Shaw and
   Noel Mixon vs. Andrew Craver
Campbell, Charles E. F. vs. Thomas F. Danielly
Campbell, Charles E. F. W. vs. Georgia Railroad and Banking
   Co.
Campbell, Charles G. vs. Hardeman and Sparks
Campbell, Charles G. vs. W. S. McComb
Campbell, Charles G. vs. Shropshire and Thomas for use of
   William R. Phillips
Campbell, Charles G. vs. George W. Susong
Campbell, Charles G. vs. William D. Terrell
Campbell, Charles G. and Pollard B. McMichael vs. Matthew
   Whitfield, Leroy M. Willson, Executor, Pleasant Willson,
   Executor, John F. Patterson, Executor and William H.
   Mathis, Executor
Campbell, Cooley vs. George T. Bartlett
Campbell, Cooly vs. William Maxey, Charles S. Jordan and
   John R. Dyer
Campbell, Cooly vs. The State
Campbell, Duncan, Zarobabel Williamson, Administrator,
   Green Williamson, Administrator, and William Williamson,
   Administrator vs. William D. Garland and Robert Morris,
   Administrator
Campbell, E. L. and Elvira Campbell vs. Franklin H. Gay
Campbell, James, William Campbell, James Dupree, James
   Blizzard and J. G. Lazenby vs. The State
Campbell, James H. vs. The State
Campbell, James M. and Adaline Gray vs. The State
Campbell, Jeff vs. The State
Campbell, John vs. John Garner
Campbell, Lum vs. The State

Campbell, Nelse vs. The State
Campbell, Richard vs. William Nelson
Campbell, Richard vs. The State
Campbell, Richard S. vs. The State
Campbell, William (alias Bill Campbell) vs. The State
Canant, Jerry vs. William Hindman
Canant, Jerry vs. Isaac Hughes and John Lucas
Canant, William L. vs. John Allen
Canatt, William L. vs. John Hooper and William Ezzard
Candle, James vs. Edward M. Allen
Cannafax, Benjamin vs. James Powers
Cannon, Henry and George Bell vs. Alston H. Green and Henry
    H. Cook
Cannon, Henry and George Bell vs. Robert Leak for use of
    Bedford Brown, Peter Mosely and Sally (Brown) Mosely,
    Administrator
Cannon, Henry vs. The State
Cannon, James and Rice P. Knowles vs. Elijah N. Hascall
    and David Hascall
Cannon, James vs. Bedford Shorter
Cannon, Mureler (Tomlin) vs. John C. Pope
Cannon, Nathaniel vs. John Kinard
Cape, William B. vs. The State
Caps, Eli vs. The State
Card, Peter vs. The State
Cardell, Aaron vs. William B. Carhart, James D. Carhart,
    John B. Stow and Elijah Carhart
Cardell, John vs. The State
Cardell, Peter vs. The State
Cardell, William and Elbert W. Baynes vs. John Baynes
Cardell, William, Elbert W. Baynes and John Baynes vs.
    Robert Bledsoe and Nathan Bass, Executor
Cardell, William vs. Hugh T. Inman and Co.
Cardell, William vs. Whitfield and Beeland
Cardelle, Peter vs. John G. Lumsden and William B. Carter,
    Administrator
Cardin, John vs. Owen H. Kenan
Cargil, Carrie vs. The State
Cargil, Ozroe vs. The State
Cargile, Augustus and John W. Burney vs. Anthony Dyer and
    John R. Dyer, Executor
Cargile, Augustus vs. J. H. Roberts
Cargile, Charles vs. Henry Buchannon and Fleming Jordan
Cargile, Charles, John W. Burney and John R. Cargile vs.
    Joseph K. Kilburn
Cargile, Charles, John R. Cargile and William H. Cargile
    vs. Thomas Napier
Cargile, Charles vs. The State
Cargile, Charles, Jr. vs. William H. Crane
Cargile, Dan vs. The State
Cargile, Dave vs. The State
Cargile, James vs. Griffin Bender
Cargile, James and James Williamson vs. Oren D. Carstarphen
Cargile, James vs. John P. Coles
Cargile, James and Tandy D. King vs. Garland Dawkins
Cargile, James vs. Isaac Hill
Cargile, James and William Barclay vs. Parham P. Mabry,
    Jordan Thornton and Esom Turner for use of Andrew Kerr,
    John Kerr and Alexander Graham
Cargile, James vs. Gresham Selleck
Cargile, Jason vs. William Scott
Cargile, John, Robert Williamson, Administrator, James
    Cargile, Administrator and William Cargile, Administrator

115

vs. Jarrel Beasley, John McMichael, Magers Henderson,
    Robert Germany, Lavina Cargile, Guardian, Joseph J. W.
    Cargile, Minor, and Runno B. M. Cargile, Minor
Cargile, John, Solomon Strickland and Charles Crawford vs.
    John Moore, Hiram Glazier, John W. Compton, Bennet Craw-
    ford and John Rivers
Cargile, John vs. Officers of Court
Cargile, John, Joseph J. W. Cargile, Minor and Lewis C.
    Holland, Guardian vs. Gilbraith Simonton and Ransom H.
    Smith
Cargile, John, Sr. vs. William Robinson
Cargile, John R., Charles Cargile and John W. Burney vs.
    Adna Rowe
Cargile, John R. vs. The State
Cargile, John R. vs. Zachariah White for use of Anthony Dyer
Cargile, Joseph J. W. vs. Hamilton Atchison and Samuel B.
    Hunter, Administrator
Cargile, Joseph J. W. and John F. Rivers vs. James C.
    Bartlett and William Maxey
Cargile, Joseph J. W. vs. Simon G. Blossom and John H.
    Clute
Cargile, Joseph J. W. vs. Hollis Cooley and James H.
    Robinson
Cargile, Joseph J. W. and Henry Dillon vs. James D. Head
Cargile, Joseph J. W., Eugenia T. Cargile and Joseph C.
    White, Administrator vs. Joseph L. Holland
Cargile, Joseph J. W. and Runno B. M. Cargile vs. Lawson
    S. Holland, Jonas H. Holland and Joseph L. Holland
Cargile, Joseph J. W. and John R. Dickin vs. James McBryde,
    John McBryde and Alexander Wallace
Cargile, Joseph J. W. vs. Alfred Shaw
Cargile, Joseph J. W. vs. Stephen C. Talmadge
Cargile, Kelly vs. The State
Cargile, Micajah vs. Abyhugh Sewell
Cargile, Monroe B. and Lewis C. Holland, Guardian, vs.
    Hollis Cooley and James C. Robinson
Cargile, Rufus vs. The State
Cargile, Thomas vs. John Owen
Cargile, Thomas vs. Reuben C. Shorter
Cargile, Thomas and Phineas Whatley vs. The State
Cargile, Thomas vs. John Waits
Cargile, Thomas vs. Adam Wilie
Cargile, William and Thomas Wynn vs. The State
Cargile, William H. and Garland Maxey vs. John Baldwin
Cargile, William H. vs. Zenos Bronson and Claiborne Mills
Cargile, William H. and William Hitchcock vs. William V.
    Burney
Cargile, William H. vs. Lewin Cohen
Cargile, William H. and John R. Cargile vs. Eli Glover
Cargile, William H. vs. Franklin Harvey
Cargile, William H. vs. John Hawkins
Cargile, William H. vs. Edward Hicks and Joel Baley
Cargile, William H. vs. Robert Kellam and William Maxey
Cargile, William H. vs. John Kendrick
Cargile, William H. vs. Officers of Court
Cargile, William H. vs. Stephen Stephens
Cargile, William H. vs. Nathan Warner
Cargile, William H. vs. John Willson, John Hill, Executor,
    Fleming Jordan, Executor, and David A. Reese, Executor
Caril, Thomas and John Byrom vs. Thomas Greer
Carlile, John R. and Albert Pabodie vs. Elias Bliss, George
    Charter and Ammi (?) Williams
Carlisle, George W. and Reubin Lawson vs. The State

116

Carmon, John Q. A. vs. Laura V. Carmon
Carol, David vs. Robert Stewart
Carrell, Jesse vs. Russel Branum
Carrell, Richmond vs. John Turner
Carrol, Susannah vs. Robert C. Beasley
Carroll, Redman vs. The State
Carroll, Thomas vs. John S. Murphy
Carsell, Jim and Lee Minter vs. The State
Carswell, Neal vs. The State
Carter, ? vs. ? Turnell
Carter, Amanda vs. The State
Carter, John vs. Agness Beck
Carter, John vs. Zachariah Cox for use of James Zabriskee
   (?) and John Parsons
Carter, John, George Varner, Matthew Whitfield and James
   Whitfield vs. James Dickson, William Dickson and Donald
   McCloud
Carter, John vs. William Kennedy
Carter, John, George Varner, Matthew Whitfield and James
   Whitfield vs. Andrew Low, Robert Isaac and James McHenry
Carter, John vs. Green Perry
Carter, John vs. David B. Perryman
Carter, John vs. Robert Phelps for use of Washington Phelps
Carter, John vs. John Walker
Carter, John vs. Matthew Whitfield and James Whitfield
Carter, John A. and Willingham vs. Thomas J. Davis
Carter, Joseph vs. James Beaty
Carter, Joseph vs. George Hargraves
Carter, Joseph and Zacheus Phillips vs. Warner L. Kennon
   for use of S. Wingfield
Carter, Joseph vs. Stephen Lawrence
Carter, Joseph vs. John Michael
Carter, Joseph vs. Henry Simmons for use of Samuel Alexander
Carter, Joseph vs. William Singuefield
Carter, Joseph vs. The State
Carter, Joseph and Gabriel Colley vs. The United States of
   America
Carter, Josiah and Thomas Carter vs. Solomon Rountree, Hugh
   Taylor, Executor, and William Terrell, Executor
Carter, Landon vs. Hardy T. Humphreys
Carter, Langdon vs. William S. Hurd and Anson Hungerford
Carter, Richard vs. John Baldwin
Carter, Richard vs. Isham Berry
Carter, Richard vs. Hamilton Brown
Carter, Richard vs. Samuel Butts, John Lucas, Administrator
   and William Lee, Administrator
Carter, Richard and William Armstrong vs. Washington C.
   Cleveland and Edna (McClendon) Cleveland
Carter, Richard vs. Anthony Dyer
Carter, Richard, Richard V. Carter, Administrator, Temper-
   ance Carter, Administrator, Betsey (Carter) McMichael,
   May C. Carter, Elisha M. Carter, Minor, Joseph McMichael,
   Guardian and John A. Carter vs. John W. Frith, John W.
   Collier, Temperance A. (Faith) Collier, Francis Marion
   Frith, Minor, Mary F. Frith, Minor and Nathan Miller,
   Guardian
Carter, Richard, Temperance Carter, Administrator and
   Richard V. Carter, Administrator vs. William L. Hurd and
   Anson Hungerford
Carter, Richard vs. Charles L. Kennon
Carter, Richard, David McCoy and Avington Williams vs. Joel
   Lockhart
Carter, Richard and Richard V. Carter, Administrator vs.

117

Joseph McMichael and Eliza A. M. McMichael
Carter, Richard vs. Davis W. McRee
Carter, Richard and John Paine vs. John Rees
Carter, Richard and Joseph McMichael vs. The State
Carter, Richard vs. Avington Williams
Carter, Richard V. vs. Samuel W. Brooks
Carter, Richard V. and Dyer C. Bancroft vs. Newdeyate Ousley
Carter, Thomas vs. The State
Cary, J. A., D. T. Mercer and R. B. Phillips vs. A.
   Standifer and H. V. Standifer, Executor
Cary, Job A. and Daniel T. Mercer vs. Thomas Hardeman and
   O. G. Sparks
Cary, Job A. vs. William Little
Cary, Jobe A. vs. M. H. Morton
Cary, Jobe A. vs. Wiley Peddy
Cary, Jobe A. vs. Stephen C. Talmadge and A. J. Talmadge
Cary, Tom vs. The State
Case, Midleton W. vs. Simonton and Burney
Castellow, John vs. Eli Glover and John Cashin
Castellow, William H. vs. Moses B. Hairston and E. H.
   Walker, Administrator
Castillow, Amy and Flemming Mobley vs. John B. Castillow
   and John B. Castillow, Administrator
Castillow, John vs. The State
Castleberry, Edward vs. Jeremiah Smith
Caswell, W. C. vs. The State
Catchings, Asberry vs. The State
Catchings, Asbury vs. Griffin, Monticello and Madison
   Railroad Co.
Catchings, Bart vs. The State
Catchings, Charles vs. The State
Catchings, David vs. Josephine Catchings
Catchings, Mitchel vs. The State
Cate, James vs. Jourdan Gay
Cathy, James and Edward Price vs. Charles Tinsley and Young
   F. Tignor, Guardian
Central Bank and Burney and Dyer vs. Officers of Court
Central Georgia Power Co. vs. Lucy Millen
Chaffin, Green vs. The State
Chaffin, Jeptha J. and Lewis L. Lane vs. Jonas H. Holland
Chaffin, Jeptha J. vs. James Ravenel
Chaffin, John vs. William Maxey, Charles S. Jordan and John
   R. Dozier
Chaffin, Moses vs. William Phillips
Chaffin, Moses vs. Francis M. Swanson, Thomas G. Pritchett
   and Alfred Pritchett
Chaffin, Thomas vs. The State
Chaffin, Thomas P. vs. Joseph R. High and John H. Baker
Chaffin, Thomas P. vs. William H. Howard and James P.
   Gardner
Chaffin, Thomas P. vs. William C. Robinson, John Robinson,
   Executor and James Robinson, Executor
Chaffin, Thomas Perry and Moses Chaffin vs. John G. Morris
Chaffin, William F. C. vs. The State
Chafin, John D. and Pleasant J. Mullins vs. William P.
   Farrar
Chafin, Joshua and Sherod Malone vs. George L. Bird
Chafin, Joshua vs. Elizabeth Calloway
Chafin, Joshua and Thomas Pennington vs. Thomas Grant
Chafin, Moses and Lewis McKee vs. Justices of Court for use
   of Richard Sisson, William Sisson, Jacob Smith, Guardian
   and Linsey Smith
Chafin, Nathan vs. John McCoy

Chafin, Nathan vs. Elijah Phillips
Chafin, Thomas P. vs. Washington Pope
Chafin, Thomas P. vs. Officers of Court
Chafin, Thomas P. vs. Marcus A. Pharr and Henry D. Snellings
Chamberlain, Benjamin vs. The State
Chambers, C. G. vs. Griffin, Monticello and Madison Railroad
    Co.
Champion, Elizabeth vs. The State
Champion, Elizabeth G. vs. Central Bank of Georgia
Champion, Elizabeth G. vs. George H. Kelsey
Champion, Jesse vs. Leonard Wilson
Champion, Moses, Joseph L. Holland, Administrator, William
    H. White and Robert V. Hardeman vs. William Fuller,
    Alexander M. Ragland and Matthew Whitfield
Champion, Moses vs. Hudson Kirk
Chance, Allen vs. Ezekiel Abbett
Chandler, John vs. James Harper and William Harper
Chapman, Abner vs. John Baldwin
Chapman, Abner vs. Charles Cargile
Chapman, Abner vs. William Cook
Chapman, Abner vs. Hollis Cooley and Dyer C. Bancroft
Chapman, Abner vs. Samuel Crockett for use of Elijah N.
    Hascal, Jr.
Chapman, Abner vs. Artemas Gould, Justus R. Bulkley and
    Alpheus H. Stone
Chapman, Abner and William Penn vs. Terrel Higdon
Chapman, Abner and Thomas J. Dozier vs. Augustus B.
    Longstreet
Chapman, Abner vs. James L. Maddux
Chapman, Abner vs. Eli S. Shorter and Charles P. Gordon
Chapman, Abner, Jr. vs. Caleb B. Adams
Chapman, Abner, Jr. and William Morgan vs. John E. Hide
    and Robson Bielley
Chapman, Abner, Jr. vs. Dana Hungerford
Chapman, Abner, Jr. and Abner Chapman vs. Robert Minter
Chapman, Abner, Jr. vs. William Penn
Chapman, Abner, Jr. vs. James Richards and Willis Richards
Chapman, Abner, Jr. vs. George N. Selleck
Chapman, Abner, Jr. and Harrison Lumpkin vs. The State
Chapman, Abner, Sr. vs. William V. Burney
Chapman, Asa and Abner Chapman vs. Brittain Chapman,
    William Penn, Guardian and Martha Penn, Guardian
Chapman, Asa vs. The State
Chapman, Britton W. and Abner Chapman vs. The State
Chapman, Solomon vs. Robert F. Sessions
Chapman, Will vs. The State
Chapman, William vs. Hollis Cooley and Robert Kellam
Clark, Joshua R. vs. Thomas P. Gwyn
Clark, Joshua R. vs. Sterling Harrison
Clark, Joshua R. vs. Daniel Hightower
Clark, Joshua R. vs. John I. Smith
Clark, Lewis vs. Thomas J. Pritchett, Alfred Pritchett and
    George Pritchett
Clark, Martin vs. The State
Clark, Micajah vs. Abraham Jones, Seaborn Jones, Executor
    and John A. Jones, Executor
Clark, Micajah vs. Nathan Smith
Clark, Samuel vs. George H. Traylor
Clark, William, Robert E. Richard and Henry Peddy vs.
    Abden Alexander
Clark, William vs. Isaac H. Webb
Clarke, George and Thomas J. Alexander, Administrator vs.
    John G. Slaughter for use of Officers of Court

119

Clarke, George and Thomas J. Alexander, Administrator vs.
  George A. Weaver for use of Officers of Court
Clarke, Josephus vs. William M. Burnett
Clarke, Josephus vs. Joseph R. High
Clarke, Will vs. The State
Clay, Ada vs. The State
Clay, Dave vs. The State
Clay, Hezekiah vs. Hollis Cooley
Clay, Hezekiah vs. Richard Edmondson
Clay, Hezekiah vs. Henry George
Clay, Hezekiah and Joshua Hill vs. Pollard B. McMichael and
  Byrum P. Kennymore
Clay, Hezekiah and Jesse F. Clay vs. Elijah Miller
Clay, Hezekiah vs. The State
Clay, James vs. Lucrecy Sharp
Clay, Jefferson vs. Abba Benton
Clay, Jefferson vs. Thomas Broddus
Clay, Jefferson vs. Erwin Brown
Clay, Jefferson vs. Martha Clay
Clay, Jefferson vs. Richard Flemister for use of Fielding
  Flemister
Clay, Jefferson vs. Levi Goolsby
Clay, Jefferson vs. Jonas H. Holland
Clay, Jefferson vs. Jesse Loyall
Clay, Jefferson vs. Simeon Scales
Clay, Jefferson, Samuel Clay and Noah S. Drummond vs. The
  State
Clay, Jefferson, Hezekiah Clay, Jesse F. Clay, Graves S.
  Wilson and Arkiles Wilson vs. The State
Clay, Jesse vs. William V. Burney and Gilbraith Burney
Clay, Jesse vs. John Hendrick
Clay, Jesse F. vs. Central Bank of Georgia
Clay, Jesse F. vs. Hollis Cooley
Clay, Jesse F. vs. Henry George
Clay, Jesse F. and William Ramey vs. Jonas H. Holland
Clay, Jesse F. and Charles McMichael vs. Jacob Owen
  (Orphans) and Mary Owen, Guardian
Clay, Jesse F. and Jefferson Clay vs. Alfred Shorter
Clay, Mary Lee vs. The State
Clay, Royall, Samuel Clay and Thomas Finch vs. Thomas I.
  Davis
Clay, Samuel vs. Bartlett Brown
Clay, Samuel, James C. Holland (?) and Pascal Murphy vs.
  Martin Cochran
Clay, Samuel vs. Rutherford Mays
Clay, Samuel vs. John Moore
Clay, Samuel, Pleasant G. Clay and Nathaniel B. Hornbuckle
  vs. James Whitfield
Clay, Thomas, Hezekiah Clay, Executor, Jesse F. Clay,
  Executor, Jefferson Clay, Executor and Jesse S. Sharman,
  Executor vs. William V. Burney
Clay, William vs. Archibald H. Scott
Clayton, Charles vs. The State
Clayton, George R. and Jesse Evans vs. Abraham Betts
Clayton, Richard C. vs. Thomas M. Ellis, Jacob Shotwell,
  Harvey Shotwell, Henry Haddock and Robert Haddock
Clayton, Richard C. vs. Baldwin Fluker and Robert Collins
Clayton, Richard C. vs. William Freeman
Clayton, Richard C. and Benjamin F. Keene vs. James C.
  Haviland, Robert B. Haviland, Theodore Keese, Hubbel W.
  Risley, James Harral and Samuel L. Allen
Clayton, Richard C. vs. Charles Marshall
Clayton, Richard C. vs. Ammi Williams

Clayton, Robert vs. John J. Smith
Clayton, Robert vs. Lewis Wynn and William Johnson
Clayton, Willie and Thomas Clayton vs. The State
Clegg, Jonathan H. vs. Colonel M. Dickenson
Clegg, Jonathan H. vs. Kindsay H. Durham and Dyer C. Bancroft
Clegg, Narcis W. vs. A. L. Prophett
Clegg, Narcissas M. and Jackson C. Thomason vs. Stephen C.
   Talmadge and Albert J. Talmadge
Clements, Allen vs. Thomas B. White and Simeon Durham
Clements, Charlie vs. The State
Clements, G. C. vs. The State
Clements, Ida L. vs. N. B. White and Co.
Clements, J. H., B. F. Keene, Mary Clements, A. C. Morrison
   and A. G. Morrison vs. Henry Branham
Clements, Jacob and Peyton Clements, Administrator vs. Hugh
   W. Ector
Clements Jacob and Peyton Clements, Administrator vs. John
   Posey and Josiah Flournoy, Executor
Clements, Jacob and Peyton Clements, Administrator vs.
   Benjamin Wright (Orphans) and John H. Fannin, Guardian
Clements, Jeptha and Peyton Clements vs. William Barker,
   David Thrash, Administrator, Edwin Barker, Administrator
   and Dorothy Barker, Administrator
Clements, Jeptha H. and Alexander C. Morrison vs. John
   Thurmond
Clements, Major vs. The State
Clements, Mariah vs. Allen Clements
Clements, Mary vs. Wiley L. Clements
Clements, Mary vs. William Freeman
Clements, Mary vs. William McGehee
Clements, Mary and Jeptha H. Clements vs. John Thurmond
Clements, Mose vs. The State
Clements, Oliver vs. The State
Clements, Peyton and Adam Carson vs. David Wessons, Andrew
   Wessons and Alanson Trask
Clements, Peyton R. and Adam Carson vs. Theodore F. Brett
   and Francis Doremus
Clements, Peyton R. and Adam Carson vs. Robert Fort, Everard
   Hamilton and Laird H. Wiley
Clements, Peyton R. vs. William B. Johnston
Clements, Peyton R. and James A. Merriwether vs. Officers
   of Court
Clements, Peyton R. and Adam Carson vs. Aquila G. Stout,
   Felix Ingoldsby, James E. Boissean and James C. Comly
Clements, Peyton R., Mary Clements and Jeptha H. Clements
   vs. John Thurmond
Clements, Riley vs. Cinda Clements
Clements, Simon vs. The State
Clements, Wiley and Edmond Jenkins vs. Horatio N. Spencer
   Ira Gooddard for use of Abram Jewett
Clements, Wiley L. vs. Erasmus Marable
Clements, Will vs. The State
Clemmons, Mose vs. The State
Clemons, Jeptha and Thomas Gore vs. William Freeman
Clemonts, Isaac vs. The State
Cleveland, Larkin and Joshua Hagerty vs. Stephen Heard
Cleveland, William vs. Lewis H. Pye
Cliatt, Jesse vs. William Pate
Cline, T. R. vs. The State
Clower, George vs. Jacob Mercer
Clower, Jacob vs. Anthony Dyer
Clower, Jonathan vs. Samuel Butts and John Lucas,
   Administrator

Clute, John H., William Galloway, Eurial H. Doolittle and
   William Burney vs. Shadrach McMichael
Coats, John vs. James Richards
Cobb, Britt vs. The State
Cobb, Lee vs. The State
Cobb, Silla vs. The State
Cochran, James vs. The State
Cochran, James (alias Jenes Cochran) and Otis Greer vs.
   The State
Cochran, Jeff and William Appling vs. The State
Cochran, Joe, Berry Cochran and Louis Cochran vs. L. O.
   Benton and Brothers
Cochran, John vs. The State
Cochran, John S. vs. James Whitfield
Cochran, Marion and Nelson Cochran vs. A. H. Colquit
Cochran, Marshall and Dudley Cochran vs. The State
Cochran, Martin vs. Catharine Hirl (?)
Cochran, Martin vs. Robert R. Minter
Cochran, Martin, James W. McGehee and Justices of Court
   vs. Thomas T. Nolan
Cochran, Martin vs. James Patterson
Cochran, Martin vs. Alfred Shorter and John Baldwin
Cochran, Martin and Edmund B. Darden vs. The State
Cochran, Martin vs. William G. Tyus
Cochran, Martin vs. Matthew Whitfield
Cochran, Martin and Jarrel Beasley vs. Alexander Wilkinson
Cochran, Robert vs. The State
Cochran, William, Moses Butt, Administrator, and John Robson,
   Administrator vs. Aris Newton
Cochrane, Corbin vs. The State
Cockran, Allen and Jubal Cockran, Executor vs. Mary J. Baldy
Cockran, Allen, Jubal Cockran, Executor, John Neal, H.
   Crutchfield and Garnett Andrews vs. Benjamin M. Polhill,
   Mary J. (Cockran) Polhill and Medora (Cockran) Wade
Cogswell, Matilda vs. The State
Cohen, Sam, R. Cohen, L. Cohen and H. Cohen vs. Coleman,
   Burden and Warthen Co., A. M. Robinson and Co., M. A.
   Freidman and Co., Saffer Brothers, S. Goldin, Gray and
   Landrum, Manier and Co., Romaine, Barham Co., United Shoe
   Co., C. E. Graham and Co., Greenewald and Co., American
   Tailors, Leiberman and Kaufman, Elial Loucheim and Hass,
   J. and H. Mann and Co., M. and M. Hornik and Co. and I.
   Leokouicz
Cohen, W. G. and (alias George W. Eberhart) vs. The State
Colbert, Thomas vs. Stephen Thurman
Colbert, William vs. Isaac Humphries
Colbert, William vs. The State
Cole, John P. vs. William Bowen
Cole, Robert vs. Joseph Sutton
Cole, William vs. Daniel Mosely for use of William Cook
Coleman, Frank vs. The State
Coleman, James vs. The State
Coles, John P. vs. Absalom Echols
Coles, John P. vs. James Harrison
Coles, John P. vs. Solomon Kneeland
Coles, John P. vs. Joseph Reed
Coles, Patsy vs. The State
Colley, Gabriel vs. Caleb Abernethy
Colley, Gabriel and Zachariah Faulkner vs. Joseph Carter
Colley, Gabriel and Milton Antony vs. Abner Chapman
Colley, Gabriel vs. John Colley
Colley, Gabriel vs. John W. Compton
Colley, Gabriel vs. Eli Glover and John Cashin

Colley, Gabriel vs. Caleb Abernethy
Colley, Gabriel and Zachariah Faulkner vs. Joseph Carter
Colley, Gabriel and Milton Antony vs. Abner Chapman
Colley, Gabriel vs. John Colley
Colley, Gabriel vs. John W. Compton
Colley, Gabriel vs. Eli Glover and John Cashin
Colley, Gabriel vs. Edmund Greene
Colley, Gabriel vs. Henry Jordan
Colley, Gabriel vs. Bartley Sadler
Colley, Gabriel vs. The State
Colley, Gabriel vs. James Wiggins
Colley, Gabriel vs. Daniel Wilson
Colley, Nelson vs. William Gill, Jeremiah Davis and John
  Malpass
Colley, Nelson vs. William Penn
Colley, Nelson G. and John Hamil vs. Stephen G. Heard
Collier, Charles P. vs. Alston H. Greene and Joseph
  Buchannon
Collier, Charles P. vs. John Hill, Augustin Slaughter and
  Charles Labuzan
Collier, Charles P. vs. William Jewett
Collier, Charles P. vs. James Richards for use of Miles
  Beach and Edward Thomas
Collier, John vs. Erastus Armes and Dennis Armes
Collier, John, Crawford Edmondson vs. Thomas Beall, Elias
  Beall and Thaddeus Beall
Collier, John vs. John F. Beavers
Collier, John vs. Noah Butt
Collier, John vs. Anthony Dyer
Collier, John vs. John Hough and Henry Wyche, Administrator
Collier, John, Thomas W. Collier, Executor, and William L.
  Collier, Executor vs. Reazen E. Mabry
Collier, John vs. William McDowell, Daniel McDowell,
  Executor and Isaac Baley, Executor
Collier, John, James Prigden and Jack Collier vs. Jeremiah
  Pearson
Collier, John and Bennett Crawford vs. Elizabeth Porter,
  Philemon Owen, Administrator and Robert Owen, Administra-
  tor
Collier, John, William L. Collier, Executor and Thomas W.
  Collier, Executor vs. William L. Wilson and Simeon L.
  Lovejoy
Collier, Lucy vs. The State
Collier, Robert vs. John F. Beavers
Collier, Robert vs. William Jewett
Collier, Thomas and William Collier vs. Drusilla Lumpkin
Collier, Thomas W. vs. Solomon Perteet and Jeremiah Pearson,
  Guardian
Colliers, John vs. The State
Colliers, John vs. The State
Collins, Henry vs. The State
Collins, James vs. The State
Collings, John M. and Stephen McClendon vs. Moses Collins,
  Nicholas G. Barksdale, Administrator and Gibson Collins,
  Administrator
Colquit, John T. vs. James Simmons
Colvert, John M. vs. Hamilton Brown, Thomas P. George, and
  James George
Colvert, John M. and John O. Daniel vs. Eli S. Shorter
Colwell, Edward vs. William Colwell
Colwell, Edward and John Paine vs. Garland Dawkins
Colwell, Edward vs. James Griggs
Colwell, Edward and John Paine vs. Earley Harris

123

Colwell, Edward and John Paine vs. William Walker
Combs, John vs. The State
Comer, George W. vs. Orren W. Massey
Comer, Thomas J. vs. Abner Bartlett
Comer, Thomas J. vs. Frederick Dukes for use of William
  Dukes
Comer, Thomas J. vs. John M. King
Comer, Wash vs. The State
Comer, William vs. The State
Compton, John and Jourdan Compton vs. John Lucas, Jr.
Compton, John vs. The State
Compton, John and Jordan Compton vs. Charles D. Stewart
Compton, John W. and Jordan Compton vs. John Aspinall
Compton, John W. vs. Augusta Baldwin and John Baldwin
Compton, John W. vs. Daniel D. Bates and Caleb C. Dibble
Compton, John W. vs. Thadeus Beall, Elias Beall and Thomas
  Beall
Compton, John W. and Mary Compton vs. Farish Carter and
  Andrew McDougall for use of Andrew McDougall
Compton, John W. and Thomas Hadley vs. John Crowell
Compton, John W. vs. Anthony Dyer
Compton, John W., Jordan Compton and James Garlington vs.
  John Ector, Robert Freeman, Executor and Hugh W. Ector,
  Executor
Compton, John W. vs. Hananiah Gillcoatt
Compton, John W., Asa Pye and Crawford Edmondson vs. Eli
  Glover
Compton, John W. vs. Minton Graves
Compton, John W. vs. Alston H. Greene and Joseph Buchannon
Compton, John W., John Graves and David Shoulders vs.
  Stephen W. Harris, Eli S. Shorter, Executor, Seaborn Jones,
  Executor, William Wilkins, Executor and Sarah H. Harris,
  Executor
Compton, John W. vs. David Hascall
Compton, John W. vs. John Hill, Augustin Slaughter and
  Charles Labuzan
Compton, John W. vs. William Hillard
Compton, John W. vs. John Hobson
Compton, John W. and George Cross vs. Lewis C. Holland
Compton, John W. and Jordon Compton vs. Jeremiah Pearson
Compton, John W. vs. James Smith
Compton, John W. vs. James Whitfield
Compton, Jordan vs. Samuel Butts
Compton, Jordan vs. John Compton for use of Jonathan Jewett
Compton, Jordan vs. Moses Moore
Compton, Jordan vs. Thomas Robinson
Compton, Jorden, Sr. vs. John Graves
Compton, Jorden and John W. Compton vs. John Lucas, Jr.
Compton, Kate vs. The State
Compton, Pleasant M. vs. Stephen B. Marshall
Compton, Pleasant M. vs. Officers of Court
Cone, Benjamin and Samuel G. Stanley vs. The State
Conger, Eli vs. John F. Beavers
Conley, Augustus vs. The State
Conley, Emmett vs. The State
Conley, James, Joe Cornwell and Edgar Thompson vs. The State
Connel, John and William Connel vs. Champion T. Traylor
Connell, William vs. William Askew
Connell, William vs. John Hobson and Christopher Hobson
Connell, William vs. Thomas Moore
Connell, William vs. James Richards
Connell, William vs. Ely Strickland for use of Jesse Evans
Conner, Boly vs. Ransom Whatley

Conner, Charles D. and Francis Irvin vs. James Dickson,
  William Dixon and Donald McLeod
Conner, Charles D. vs. Phillip Thurman
Conner, Charles D. vs. Thomas Walton, Charles W. Rockwell
  and Thomas C. Hayward
Coogler, A. C. vs. The State
Cook, ? vs. Case Threshing Machine and Co.
Cook, Asstadge vs. Timothy McGuire
Cook, Augustin and Thomas P. Hamilton vs. George Stovall
Cook, Augustin vs. John Wilson and Thomas Smith
Cook, Augustus vs. Eli Glover and John Cashin
Cook, Ben vs. The State
Cook, David R. vs. Joseph May
Cook, Dawson vs. The State
Cook, George vs. The State
Cook, Green vs. The State
Cook, H. E. vs. The State
Cook, Hardy vs. The State
Cook, Hardy vs. William Turk
Cook, Henry H. and Samuel Fulton vs. Francis H. Cone
Cook, J. M. vs. Rosser, Harvey and Davis
Cook, James and William M. Cook vs. Hugh Wise
Cook, Jim, Walter Roberts, Fulton Freeman and Johnnie Jordan
  vs. The State
Cook, John W. vs. John Baynes
Cook, John W. vs. Robert Kellam and William Maxey
Cook, John W. vs. Officers of Court
Cook, Martin vs. John Baldwin
Cook, Martin vs. Lewis Lanier
Cook, Martin and Theophilus Freeman vs. Henry Pennington
Cook, N. G. vs. Robert Childs
Cook, William vs. John Abercrombie
Cook, William vs. William Armstrong
Cook, William and Allen McClendon vs. Beach and Thomas
Cook, William vs. Robert Bledsoe
Cook, William vs. William Bowen
Cook, William vs. Thomas Butler
Cook, William vs. David Cande
Cook, William vs. William Christie
Cook, William vs. John Digby, William Penn, Administrator
  and Belinda Digby, Administrator
Cook, William vs. John Fluker
Cook, William vs. Solomon Kneeland
Cook, William and Allen McClendon vs. Andrew Knox for use
  of Matthews Wills and George G. Mathews
Cook, William vs. Edward Lee
Cook, William and Henry C. Hutchison vs. John McKenzie,
  Peter Bennoch and Thomas McDonald
Cook, William vs. David McKinney
Cook, William vs. Alexander Mobley for use of Moses Mulky
Cook, William vs. Monticello Academy
Cook, William vs. William Penn
Cook, William vs. Zachariah Phillips
Cook, William vs. Gideon Pott and Joseph McKinne
Cook, William vs. Raymond and Lockwood
Cook, William vs. James Rea
Cook, William vs. Benjamin W. Rogers and Co.
Cook, William vs. Lemuel B. Skaggs
Cook, William vs. The State
Cook, William vs. Charles D. Stewart and George Hargraves
Cook, William vs. Samuel H. Stockhouse for use of Thomas
  Cumming
Cook, William vs. Lucy Traylor

Cook, William vs. William F. Walker for use of Kenneth McKenzie
Cook, William vs. Elias Wallen and Joseph P. McKinne
Cook, William and William Hitchcock vs. John Willson
Cook, William vs. James Woodrew, Andrew Low, Robert Isaac and James McHenry
Cook, William A. vs. John J. Smith
Cook, William A. vs. Lewis Wynn and William Johnson
Cook, William M. and James Cook vs. Daniel Dawkins
Cook, William M. and Nathaniel B. Hornbuckle vs. William Goolsby
Cooke, Martin vs. Robert Ashurst, Matthew C. Farley, Executor and Martha Ashurst, Executor
Cooke, Martin vs. James R. Gray
Cooke, Martin vs. Gilbraith Simonton, William Simonton and Alexander R. Buchannon
Cooley, Briant vs. Josiah Perry
Cooley, Bryant vs. Jeremiah Bogguss
Cooley, Bryant vs. John G. Willis
Cooley, Hollis and James H. Robinson vs. Thomas Blan
Cooly, Bryant vs. The State
Cooper, Charles H. vs. James Patterson
Cooper, Howel vs. Allen Morgan
Cooper, Howell vs. Hamilton Brown, Peyton Gwyn and James Gwyn
Cooper, India vs. The State
Cooper, Robert vs. Beverly Daniel
Cooper, William H., Joshua Pinkston and William Hitchcock vs. Zenos Bronson
Cooper, Willis vs. The State
Coopper, Benjamin and Hardy Bennett vs. The State
Coots, John vs. Henry Walker
Coppage, Oliver H. vs. John Paty
Corbin, John vs. William Chapman and William Ross
Cornels, Alexander vs. Carter B. Harrison
Cornwall, Eli and Kitty Cornwall vs. The State
Cornwell, Mrs. ? vs. Central Georgia Power Co.
Cornwell, Elijah vs. Mathew Duncan
Cornwell, Elijah and Gilbert Gay vs. The State
Cornwell, Elijah, John Echols and Jacob Laughridge vs. Jason Warner
Cornwell, George vs. The State
Cornwell, George W. vs. William Bartlett for use of Abner Bartlett
Cornwell, George W. vs. John H. Baugh
Cornwell, George W. vs. Crawford H. Greer
Cornwell, Gibson H. and Lucius L. Reese, Administrator vs. Jonas H. Holland
Cornwell, Gibson H. and Lucius L. Reese, Administrator vs. William S. Hurd and Anson Hungerford
Cornwell, Hiram vs. John R. Cargile
Cornwell, John Henry vs. The State
Cornwell, L. C. vs. Officers of Court
Cornwell, Obediah and George Cornwell vs. James H. Roberts
Cornwell, Obediah vs. The State
Cornwell, W. D. vs. Smith and Ethridge
Corsy, George vs. The State
Cosby, Thomas H. vs. John McBryde and James McBryde
Cotton, Abner vs. Rene Fitzpatrick
Couch, Bessie and Mary Couch vs. The State
Couch, Charlie vs. The State
Couch, Drury vs. John Couch
Couch, Drury vs. Henry Hardin

Couch, Drury vs. Abram Pool
Couch, Drury and Nancy Couch vs. The State
Couch, Hilliard, James Couch and George Couch vs. The State
Couch, Jeff vs. The State
Couch, John vs. The State
Couch, John vs. William Tommerson
Couch, Nathaniel H. vs. Adam Toland
Couch, Nathaniel H. vs. Rhody Walker
Courcey, Monroe D. vs. The State
Coursey, Vinson R. vs. Hiram Geasland, Matilda Geasland,
   Matilda Ann Geasland, Minor, Hiram Geasland, Minor and
   Edmond Coursey
Courtney, James vs. Peter Prow
Cousby, Johnnie vs. The State
Cousins, Betsy vs. The State
Covington and Macon Railroad Co. vs. Merchant M. McKinley
Cowan, James vs. Nathaniel Coggershall
Cowen, James vs. John Hill
Cowan, James vs. Russel Hoyt, Eli T. Hoyt and David H.
   Boughton
Cowan, James and Thomas B. Erwin vs. The State
Cowan, James and Thomas B. Erwin vs. Giles Whitney and
   Edward Bement
Cowles, W. T. vs. The State
Cowthron, Minnie vs. The State
Cox, Cary vs. Nathan B. Knapp
Cox, Cary vs. Solomon B. Murphy
Cox, Jesse vs. Elhanan Gibbs
Cox, Jesse vs. Robert Trippe
Cox, Middleton W. vs. Gilbraith Simonton and William V.
   Burney
Cox, Pressley M. vs. Barnet Powell for use of Thomas Napier
Cox, Rube vs. The State
Cox, Tom vs. The State
Cox, Wiley J. vs. Sarah Cox and John Griggs, Executor
Cox, Will vs. The State
Cox, Zachariah vs. James Cooper
Crab, Asa and Samuel Crab vs. Asa Hill
Crab, Burton vs. John Morris, Rebecca Morris, Executor and
   Hardy Gregory, Executor
Crabtree, Ezekiel and Moses B. Hairston vs. Martin R.
   McDaniel
Crabtree, Exekiel vs. David Michael
Crabtree, Ezekiel vs. George Raglin
Crabtree, Ezekiel vs. Aaron M. Smith
Crabtree, Ezekiel vs. Henry Vaughn
Crabtree, Malachi vs. William Maxey and Co.
Crabtree, Thomas M. and Ezekiel Crabtree vs. Aquilla Phelps
   and William Johnson, Executor
Craddock, John and Richardson Pennington vs. Dinwodda Dosure
   (alias Woody Dozier)
Craig, Andrew vs. Thomas J. Davis
Craig, Andrew vs. William Gill, Jeremiah Davis and John
   Malpass
Craig, Andrew vs. John Gresham
Crain, George vs. Alston H. Greene and Joseph Buchannon
Crain, George vs. John Norwood
Crain, Spencer vs. Willis Dent
Crain, Spencer vs. John Emmons for use of Thomas Napier
Crain, Spencer vs. Tarlton Sheets, Joseph Luker, John Orr
   and Elisha Ogden
Crain, Stephen D. vs. James Whitfield
Crain, William vs. Bedford Brown, Peter Mosely, Executor

and Sally (Brown) Mosely, Executor
Crain, William and George Crain vs. William Cook
Crain, William, Levi Daniel and Edward Flowers vs. Reuben
   Goolsby
Crain, William vs. Thomas Hixon
Crane, Burrell vs. The State
Crane, Spencer vs. Milton Antony
Crane, Spencer vs. James Armor and William Armor
Crane, Spencer vs. Andrew H. Bell
Crane, Stephen D., Abner Chapman, Robert Tuggle vs. Zenos
   Bronson
Crane, Stephen D., Abner Chapman, Luke Williams and Greene
   B. Hill vs. Gilbert Cleland
Crane, Stephen D., Abner Chapman, Sr., Robert Tuggle and
   John Robinson vs. James W. Crews
Crane, Stephen D. vs. Robert B. Haviland, David G. Haviland,
   James C. Haviland and Alfred Ashfield
Crane, Stephen D., John Robinson, Lawrence Galiagan and
   Benjamin F. Tucker vs. Hezekiah M. Scovill
Crane, Stephen D. vs. Alfred Shorter
Crane, Stephen D. vs. The State
Crane, Stephen D. and Magers Henderson vs. Nathan Warner
   for use of Thomas Grant
Crane, Stephen D. and Robert Tuggle vs. Sanford Wellborn
Crane, William, Edward Flowers and Levi Daniel vs. Jesse
   Cox
Crane, William vs. Stephen G. Heard
Crane, William vs. John Walton
Crange, Eliza vs. The State
Crawford, Amy (Ann) vs. The State
Crawford, Ann vs. James A. Hascall
Crawford, Bennet vs. Alphanus Beall and Thomas Beall
Crawford, Bennett vs. Elijah N. Hascall
Crawford, Bennett vs. Elizabeth Porter, Philemon Owen,
   Administrator and Robert Owen, Administrator
Crawford, Charles vs. Nathan Williams
Crawford, Eberhart vs. The State
Crawford, Elias vs. John McKinne
Crawford, Elisha G. vs. Thomas Hollis
Crawford, Joel and Stokely Morgan vs. John Elliot
Crawford, Joel vs. Archibald Stokes
Crawford, John W. vs. The State
Crawford, Leonard vs. The State
Crawford, Marshall vs. The State
Crawford, Meshach N., John L. Robinson and John A. Allen
   vs. George T. Bartlett
Crawford, Meshack N. vs. John Campbell
Crawford, Meshanc N. vs. Griffin, Monticello and Madison
   Railroad Co.
Crawford, Meshack N. vs. Hugh P. Kirkpatrick
Crawford, Meshack N., William Y. Harris and Thomas Wyatt
   vs. John Sheffield
Crawford, Walter vs. The State
Crawford, William vs. George Ramsay
Crawford, William vs. The State
Crawford, William H., Mary H. Crawford and Samuel H.
   Crawford vs. James Harkness
Crawl, Mary, Samuel Crawl and Elizabeth Crawl vs. Samuel
   Knox
Crawley, James vs. William Cook
Crawley, James vs. Thomas W. Harris for use of Henry Walker
Crawley, James and Kiziah Sanders vs. William Harrison
Crawley, James vs. James Shackleford

Crawman, Mary vs. Joshua Hill
Crawman, Mary vs. G. W. Wyatt
Creagh, Thomas B. vs. The State
Crenshaw, Jarrel W. vs. Burwell Green, Jr.
Crenshaw, Jarrel W. vs. Palemon Weekes and John Hunt
Crenshaw, Joseph vs. William Crane
Crenshaw, Joseph vs. Eli Glover
Crenshaw, Joseph vs. Alston H. Greene and Joseph Buchannan
Crenshaw, Joseph vs. Avington Williams
Crenshaw, Micajah and Joseph Crenshaw vs. Benjamin Fudge
Crenshaw, William F. vs. William F. Mapp
Crews, Joseph bs. Thomas W. Harris
Critchfield, Nichols and Nehemiah Harvey vs. John Moses,
    Ann Moses, Administrator, Samuel Moses, Administrator
    and Moses Perkins, Administrator
Crocket, Samuel vs. Milton Antony
Crockett, James W. vs. John Baldwin
Crockett, Joseph, Jr. and Joseph Crockett, Sr. vs. The State
Crockett, Samuel vs. Henry Crow and William D. Crow, Guard-
    ian
Crockett, Samuel vs. John Digby, William Penn, Administra-
    tor and Belinda Digby, Administrator
Crockett, Samuel vs. Bedford Shorter
Crockett, Samuel vs. The State
Crockett, Samuel vs. John Sweet
Croll, James, Hezekiah Luckie, Executor, Champion T. Luckie,
    Executor, and Mary Croll, Executor vs. Joseph Wilson
Cross, George vs. Robert Estes and Baxter Estes, Adminis-
    trator
Cross, George, William Morgan, Administrator, Harris Cross,
    Administrator and Richard Cross, Administrator vs. Eli
    Glover
Croww, George W. S., Palemon Cross, Nathan Lanier and
    Thomas Dillon vs. The State
Cross, Harris and Richard Cross vs. John Hill
Cross, Perlemon vs. Nazro Smith
Cross, Pleasant P. vs. The State
Cross, Richard vs. Anthony Dyer
Cross, Richard vs. Charles Lowrey
Crossly, R. J. vs. James L. Tucker
Crouch, George vs. Harris Lunsford and Evan H. Powell
Crouch, John vs. Joshua Broughton
Crow, Elisha and John Hudson vs. Betsey Adams and Jonathan
    Adams, Executor
Crow, Elisha and Robert Hudson vs. Jarral Beasley for use
    of John E. Morgan
Crow, Elisha and Robert Hudson vs. Jarral Beasley for use
    of John E. Morgan
Crow, Elisha vs. William Biscoe and James N. Hall
Crow, Elisha vs. John Hill, Augustin Slaughter and Charles
    Labuzan
Crow, Elisha vs. Hartwell Jones
Crow, Elisha vs. Edward Price
Crow, Isaac vs. James Prigin
Crow, Isaac vs. James Richards
Crowder, George W. and John D. Segur vs. The State
Croxton, Gideon H. vs. John W. Cook
Croxton, Gideon H. vs. Alston H. Greene and Joseph
    Buchannon
Croxton, Gideon H. vs. William Maxcey
Cruce, Catharine and John Shaw vs. The State
Crutchfield, William vs. The State
Cubage, J. vs. Griffin, Monticello and Madison Railroad Co.

Cubbage, John vs. John F. Patterson
Cullens, Will vs. The State
Culpepper, Robert and Hezekiah Clay vs. Hollis Cooley
Culpepper, Robert vs. Officers of Court
Cunard, J. C. vs. J. P. Henderson for use of Officers of
  Court
Cunningham, George vs. Zachariah Jordan
Cunningham, William vs. Dyer C. Bancroft
Cureton, John vs. John P. Speir, Augustin Slaughter and
  Charles Labuzan
Curry, Dennis vs. The State
Curry, Eliza vs. The State
Curry, Fanny vs. Mose Curry
Curry, James, Sherod H. Gay, Nathaniel M. Bachelor, Elbert
  Gay, Milledge Gay, Sarah Gay, Elvira Gay, Mary Curry vs.
  The State
Curry, Willie vs. The State
Cuthbert, Alfred vs. John Baynes
Cuthbert, Alfred vs. Charles A. Burnett
Cuthbert, Alfred vs. Central Bank
Cuthbert, Alfred vs. William Cook and Jonathan Vanwagenen
Cuthbert, Alfred vs. Thomas Hunt
Cuthbert, Alfred vs. James L. Maddux
Cuthbert, Alfred vs. Edmund Molyneux, Jr.
Cuthbert, Alfred vs. Charles W. Sadler and James A. Davis
Cuthbert, Alfred vs. Alfred Shorter
Cuthbert, Alfred vs. William G. Skillman
Cuthbert, Alfred vs. Joseph Stark
Cuthbert, Alfred vs. The State
Cuthbert, Alfred vs. Alfred Sturtz
Cuthbert, Alfred vs. Josiah Tatnall
Cuthbert, Alfred vs. Thomas Walker and Eli H. Walker,
  Executor
Cuthbert, Alfred vs. William T. Williams

Dabney, Anderson, Hannah Dabney, Administrator and Tyre G.
  Dabney, Administrator vs. Churchill Mason
Dabney, Anderson vs. John T. Sankey
Dabney, Anderson vs. William Williams
Dabney, Garland vs. Eli Denson
Dabney, Garland vs. John Fairchild and William Fairchild
  for use of William Scarbrough
Dabney, Garland vs. Robert Martin, Christopher Brown,
  Administrator, and William Woods, Administrator
Dabney, Garland vs. Hezekiah Terrell
Dale, Andrew C. vs. Isham Kelly
Dale, Samuel vs. George W. Moore
Dalton, E. W. vs. The State
Daniel, Anthony vs. The State
Daniel, Beverly vs. John Black
Daniel, Beverly and Thomas Kennedy vs. David Kerlon
Daniel, Daniel vs. The State
Daniel, Edna vs. The State
Daniel, Egbert and James Johnson vs. James W. Y. Walton
Daniel, Ephraim vs. Joseph Ledbetter
Daniel, Hopkins vs. Henry Pearson, Jr., William G. Gilbert
  and Felix H. Gilbert
Daniel, Isaac vs. William Giles
Daniel, Isaac vs. The State
Daniel, isaac, Frederick Daniel and William Giles vs.
  The State
Daniel, Isaac and Thomas Hickson vs. Edward Varner
Daniel, James G. vs. L. D. Moore and Robert T. Saunders

130

Daniel, James J. vs. The State
Daniel, John vs. The State
Daniel, John O. vs. Jacob Faulkner
Daniel, Lee vs. The State
Daniel, Mollie vs. The State
Daniel, Obadiah E. and James F. Robinson vs. Ambrose A.
  Phillips
Daniel, Pig vs. The State
Daniel, Richard vs. William Mitchell and Edward Coxe
Daniel, Robert H. vs. Nathaniel Barnes for use of John R.
  Dicken
Daniel, Robert H. vs. Henry L. Cook and David Flanders
Daniel, Robert H. vs. Hollis Cooley
Daniel, Robert H. vs. William H. Crane
Daniel, Robert H. vs. Hugh N. Crawford
Daniel, Robert H. vs. William M. D'Antignad and John Hill
Daniel, Robert H. and Nathaniel Barnes vs. James Griggs
Daniel, Robert H. vs. Fleming Jordan and Henry Buchannon
Daniel, Robert H. vs. Isaac Kendrick
Daniel, Robert H. vs. William Maxey
Daniel, Robert H. vs. Robert Myrick
Daniel, Robert H. vs. Caleb Ross
Daniel, Robert H. vs. Simeon Scales
Daniel, Robert H. vs. Ebenezer Skinner
Daniel, Robert H. vs. The State
Daniel, Robert H. vs. John Thurmond
Daniel, Robert H. vs. Hosea Webster and Thomas J. Parmelee
Daniel, Viney vs. Officers of Court
Daniel, Will vs. The State
Danielly, Thomas F., Williamson Bailey and William Dukes
  vs. Robert Davidson and James M. Newton, Administration
Darden, Augustus vs. The State
Darden, Bedford H. and Edmund B. Darden vs. Pleasant
  Stovall and William P. Ford
Darden, Edmond B. and James M. Darden vs. James L. Burney
Darden, Edmond B. vs. Benjamin H. Reed
Darden, Edmond B. and George Darden vs. John Robinson
Darden, Edmond B. vs. The State
Darden, Edmond B., Jr. vs. Francis M. Swanson and Thomas B.
  Comer
Darden, George W. and Allen Martin vs. Alston H. Greene
  and Joseph Buchannan
Darden, George W., Augustus H. Kenan and Joseph Williams
  vs. Edmund Puckett
Darden, George W., Jr. vs. Abraham Betts, James Betts,
  Executor, and John C. Gibson, Executor
Darden, George W., Jr. vs. Robert H. Musgrove
Darden, Richmond vs. The State
Dardin, James W. vs. Robert Williamson
Darnall, Thomas M. and Joshua Hill vs. Officers of Court
Darnell, James J. vs. John Ashmore and Sally Ashmore
Darnell, James J. vs. Cyrus Barron and Polly Barron
Dasher, Thomas J. and Joseph Stovall vs. The State
Daughtery, Mat vs. The State
Davenport, John vs. Alexander Garden
Davenport, John vs. The State
Davidson, Elijah vs. Jesse Allen
Davidson, Elizabeth and Gilbert W. Shaw vs. Robert C.
  Barnes
Davidson, John vs. Elijah Law
Davidson, John, Jr. vs. Watson Shaw, William N. Kirkpatrick,
  Guardian and Mary Ann Shaw, Minor
Davidson, Reid vs. The State

Davidson, Richard vs. The State
Davidson, W. T. vs. The State
Davis, Arthur vs. The State
Davis, Baby vs. The State
Davis, Benjamin and John Davis, Jr. vs. John Davis, Sr.
Davis, Benjamin and Martha Davis vs. Susanah Hicks
Davis, Benjamin vs. Allen McClendon
Davis, Benjamin vs. James Richards for use of James McDonald
Davis, D. M. and H. D. Banks vs. B. T. Montgomery
Davis, David and Greene B. Hill vs. James Davis
Davis, Finch vs. Robert Freeman
Davis, George B. vs. Thomas Wilson
Davis, George R. vs. Oldby S. Prophitt
Davis, Henry vs. The State
Davis, James vs. Elijah N. Hascall and David Hascall
Davis, Jeremiah vs. Joseph C. Bryant
Davis, Jeremiah and John Malpass vs. John W. Burney
Davis, Jeremiah vs. William Harris
Davis, Jeremiah vs. The State
Davis, Jeremiah vs. William W. Woolsey, Abraham M. Wollsey,
    John M. Woolsey and William C. Woolsey
Davis, Joel vs. Thadeus B. Rees and William H. Gilliland
Davis, John, Jr. and Molley Mitchell vs. The State
Davis, Kate vs. The State
Davis, Mary Lou vs. The State
Davis, Matthew vs. Thomas Davis
Davis, Robert and Thomas Davis vs. The United States of
    America
Davis, Robert H. and Thomas Davis vs. Anthony Dyer
Davis, Robert H. and Wesley Glazier vs. William A. Moore
Davis, Sarah and George R. Davis vs. David Allen and W. W.
    Allen, Administrator
Davis, Thomas, Hannah Davis, Administrator and Robert H.
    Davis, Administrator vs. Thomas S. Bonner
David, Thomas, Robert Richards and Philip Fitzpatrick vs.
    Anderson Comer, Leonard Abercrombee, Administrator,
    Robert Baldwin, Administrator and Nancy Comer, Administra-
    tor
Davis, Thomas vs. George Hargraves
Davis, Thomas vs. Walden Lewis
Davis, Thomas vs. Phillip Mulky
Davis, Thomas, Hannah Davis, Administrator and Robert H.
    Davis, Administrator vs. James Richards
Davis, Thomas vs. Hiram Storrs
Davis, Thomas B. vs. Gilbert Cleeland
Davis, Wiley vs. John Donaldson
Davis, William O., Thomas P. Gwyn and James Gwyn vs. Warren
    Phelps
Davis, Wink vs. The State
Dawes, Joel vs. William Maxey, Charles S. Jordan and John
    R. Dyer
Dawes, Joel vs. Marshall McKavett and Co.
Dawkins, Daniel vs. Thomas Kennedy
Dawkins, Daniel vs. Samuel Reed
Dawkins, George, John Spears, Administrator and William
    Jones vs. William Evans and Drury S. Patterson
Dawkins, George and George W. Dawkins vs. Moses B. Hairston
Dawkins, George vs. Jesse Loyall
Dawkins, George vs. Jeremiah Pearson
Dawkins, George W. vs. R. J. Brown
Dawkins, William H. and George Dawkins vs. Daniel Gunn and
    Thomas A. Brown
Dawkins, William H. vs. Rebecca McClendon

132

Daws, Joel vs. Thomas I. Bartlett
Daws, Joel vs. Charles D. Pearson and Lewis P. Harwell for
use of John Williams
Daws, Joel vs. The State
Daws, Joel, Samuel Carr and Elbert W. Baynes vs. James W.
Vaughn
Daws, Joel, Elbert W. Baynes and Augustus C. Freeman vs.
Matthew Whitfield and Joel A. Billips, Administrator
Daws, Joel vs. John Wingfield
Dawson, Armstead B. vs. Anthony Dyer
Dawson, John vs. John Doby
Dawson, Thomas vs. George L. Holmes
Dawson, Thomas vs. Charles Roe and Charles P. Merriman
Dawson, Thomas and William C. Dawson vs. Thomas Victory
Deadwilder, Chrisley vs. Deverauz Jarratt
Deadwilder, Christopher vs. Sanders Brown
Deadwilder, Christopher vs. James Oliver
Deadwilder, William and Christopher C. Deadwilder vs. Jonas
H. Holland
Deane, George vs. John R. Cargile
Deane, George vs. Joseph Johnson
Deane, Nathaniel vs. Milton Antony
Deane, Nathaniel, Sanders Stallings and James Black vs.
Sally Brown and B. Brown
Deane, Nathaniel vs. Jack F. Cocke, Aaron Biggs, Sherwood
Strong, Administrator, Sherwood Strong and Munford Stokes
Deane, Nathaniel, John P. Nall, James Black and Unicey
Deane vs. Henry C. Hutchinson
Deane, Nathaniel and Burket Deane vs. James Mitchell
Deane, Nathaniel, Paschal Murphey and William Jeffries vs.
Matthew Mitchell
Deane, Nathaniel vs. Edward Paine
Deane, Nathaniel and Sanders Stallings vs. Robinson and
Pabodie
Deane, Nathaniel vs. Charles Smith
Deane, Nathaniel and Sanders Stallings vs. George Stovall
Deane, Nathaniel and George Deane vs. United States of
America
Deane, Nathaniel, Majers Henderson and James Black vs.
William Watson
Dearing, Simeon vs. The State
Dearing, Simon vs. Ephraim Pennington
Deason, Joseph vs. Thomas Bass
Deason, Michael vs. William Cook
Deason, William vs. William Brawner
Deason, William vs. Officers of Court
Deason, William and Zachariah Chaffin vs. The State
Dedwilder, Christopher vs. Robert Kellam and William Maxey
Dedwilder, Christopher vs. Albert B. Vaughn
Derring, Abner F. vs. James Richards and Willis Richards
Denham, Dumas vs. The State
Denham, James C. and John Merryman and Co. vs. Mary F.
Newton for use of Officers of Court
Denier, Clement and Albert Alexander vs. James Whitfield
Denis, Wilse vs. The State
Dennis, George W., Jr. vs. Robert F. Ezell
Dennis, Nat vs. The State
Dennis, Tom vs. The State
Dennis, W. E. vs. The State
Denson, Edmond vs. The State
Denson, Eli vs. Lewis C. Holland
Denson, Elkanah vs. Eli Glover and John Cashin
Denson, Elkanah vs. James Shearer, James Rutledge and

William Shearer
Denson, John, Burwell McCullars and William Connaway vs.
  John Maxey
Denson, John H. vs. James Richards for use of Miles Beach
  and Edward Thomas
Denson, John W. C. vs. Washington L. Walton
Denson, Obediah vs. The State
Derico, Eliza (alias Eliza Ridley) vs. The State
Deshazo, Wilkins vs. Isaac Kendrick
Deshazo, Wilins vs. Hosea Webster and Thomas J. Parmelee
Deupree, Drury vs. George M. Meriwether, David A. Reese,
  Administrator, David Meriwether, Administrator, Charles
  M. Reese, Administrator and Lucy (Meriwether) Reese,
  Administrator
Devany, William vs. The State
Dewberry, Giles vs. Williamson Roby for use of Thomas
  Willborn
Dewberry, Hopson vs. James Richards and Willis Richards
Dewberry, John and John B. Sisson vs. Anthony Dyer
Dewberry, Richard vs. Robinson and Pabodie
Dewberry, T. D. vs. W. B. Sparks
Diamond, William vs. Harris Walton and Edward R. Sely
Dibble, Caleb C. vs. John Hill, James Willson, Fleming
  Jordan, John Willson and David A. Reese
Dicken, John R. and Nathan H. Williams vs. Edmond Haviland
  and David Haviland
Dickens, Charles vs. The State
Dickens, John R. vs. The State
Dickenson, Henry A. vs. James H. George
Dickerson, Henry A., William W. Anderson, William Kirk-
  patrick, Alexander O'Daniel and Davis Lane vs. The State
Dickin, John R. vs. Philip H. Mantz
Dickin, John R. and Lucas Powell vs. Enoch W. Spofford
Dickin, John R. and Nathan H. Williams vs. James Wemple
Dickinson, Henry A. and George W. Kunze vs. Joseph L.
  Holland
Dickinson, Henry A. vs. Joseph Washburn
Dickson, Elbert and J. Hill vs. Officers of Court
Dickson, Thomas vs. John Heard
Diemer, Clement vs. Peter F. Boisclair
Diemer, Clement vs. Thomas P. Gwynn and James Gwyn
Diemer, Clement vs. John R. Pitkin
Digby, Alex (alias Bum Digby) vs. The State
Digby, Annie vs. The State
Digby, B. T. vs. James F. Blackwell
Digby, B. T. vs. Griffin, Monticello and Madison Railroad
Digby, B. T. and Ann Loyall vs. Maxey Jordan and Co.
Digby, Berry T. and James T. Lewis, Executor vs. Eliza
  Allen and W. W. Allen, Administrator
Digby, Berry T. vs. Tyree G. Finly
Digby, Berry T. vs. David M. Langston
Digby, Berry T. vs. The State
Digby, Berry T., George W. Allen and Bryant Allen vs.
  Layton Yancy
Digby, Charles vs. The State
Digby, Clinton and William Dukes vs. The State
Digby, James vs. The State
Digby, James H. vs. Griffin, Monticello and Madison
  Railroad Co.
Digby, James H. vs. S. C. Talmadge
Digby, James M. vs. E. S. Strohicker
Digby, John, William Penn, Administrator, and Belinda
  Digby vs. Charles Crawford for use of Samuel Crockett

Digby, John B. vs. Samuel Blackwell
Digby, John B. vs. Russel J. Brown
Digby, John B. and Berry T. Digby vs. Crawford H. Greer
Digby, John B. vs. Griffin Monticello and Madison Railroad
  Co.
Digby, John B. vs. Hurd, Hungerford and Co.
Digby, John B. vs. William Lawrence, Leroy Lawrence,
  Executor and Allen Lawrence, Executor
Digby, John B. vs. J. D. Maddux for use of W. D. Maddux
Digby, John B. and Russel J. Brown vs. Martin Puckett and
  James W. Vaughn, Administrator
Digby, John B. vs. William Van Anwerp
Digby, John B. and William C. Penn vs. Thomas Walker and
  Eli H. Walker, Executor
Digby, John C. and William B. Digby vs. The State
Digby, Scott vs. The State
Digby, W. B. vs. The State
Digby, Whit vs. The State
Digby, William (alias Dash) vs. The State
Dike, Isaac R. vs. The State
Dillard and Pye, Francis Jenkins, J. P. Holland and John W.
  Clark vs. Gustavus Shipp
Dillard, John A. vs. Tilman Niblett
Dillard, John A. vs. Ephraim Sanders
Dillard, Mary vs. James H. Robinson and Augustus M. Robinson
Dillard, Thomas and John L. Aaron vs. Elisha Grubbs and
  George M. Shockley, Administrator
Dillard, Thomas vs. Wiley B. Grubbs
Dillard, Thomas vs. The State
Dillon, Henry vs. William Biscoe
Dillon, Henry vs. Alfred Boren
Dillon, Henry and Samuel Crockett vs. Jacob R. Brooks
Dillon, Henry and John W. Burney, Executor vs. James B.
  Camp
Dillon, Henry and William Maxey vs. Central Bank of Georgia
Dillon, Henry vs. Walter T. Colquit
Dillon, Henry vs. George W. Darden
Dillon, Henry vs. Simeon Deloach
Dillon, Henry vs. Samuel Fulton and Henry H. Cook
Dillon, Henry and Hamlin Freeman vs. Jonas H. Holland
Dillon, Henry vs. Horatio N. Spencer
Dillon, Henry vs. The State
Dillon, Henry vs. Thomas Tuggle
Dillon, Henry and Parham P. Mabry vs. James Whitfield
Dillon, Henry and Lucas Powell vs. James Whitfield, Hollis
  Cooley, William Strozier, Abraham B. Dale and George W.
  Holland
Dillon, Thomas and Jerry Terry vs. Isaac Hill
Dillon, Thomas vs. John Owen
Dillon, Thomas vs. Gresham Selleck
Diamond, Abel vs. John Hobson
Dimon, Abel and Stephen D. Crane vs. Isaac Hutchins
Dimon, Abel vs. John Hutchins
Dimon, Abel vs. Alexander MacKenzie and Dimas Ponce
Dingler, Jonathan B. vs. Jarrett Malone and James Malone,
  Administrator
Dingler, Jonathan B. and Nancy Dingler vs. The State
Dingler, T. P. vs. C. M. Parsons and William Whitley
Dingler, Thomas B. vs. The State
Dingler, William vs. Thomas Powell
Dingler, William vs. The State
Diomatarie, John vs. The State
Dismukes, James vs. Wyly Rogers

135

Dismukes, Jeptha V. vs. John Butt for use of N. B. Williams
Dismukes, Jeptha V. vs. Lawson S. Holland
Dismukes, Jeptha V. vs. Pleasant Stovall and William P. Ford
Dismukes, Jeptha V. vs. Richard Turner
Dismukes, John F. and Abel P. Willson vs. James C. Bartlett
Dismukes, John F., Egbert P. Daniel and Thomas K. Slaughter
  vs. Anthony Dyer
Dismukes, John F. and James C. Flemister vs. Samuel Hender-
  son
Dismukes, John F. vs. William S. Hurd and Anson Hungerford
Dismukes, John F. and Abel P. Wilson vs. Hugh P. Kirkpatrick
Dismukes, John F. vs. Lane and Patterson
Dismukes, John F. vs. John C. Maddox and Co.
Dismukes, John F. vs. Shatteen C. Mitchell
Dismukes, John F. and Silas Grubbs vs. Aquilla Phelps and
  William Johnson, Executor
Dismukes, John F. vs. Planters Manufacturing Co.
Dismukes, John F. and Abel P. Wilson vs. Martin Puckett and
  James W. Vaughn, Administrator
Dismukes, John F. vs. Gilbreath Simonton and William V.
  Burney
Dismukes, John F. vs. Thomas J. Smith and John C. Maddux
Dismukes, John F. vs. Stephen C. Talmadge
Dixon, Henry, John Ramy and Jacob Carter vs. Benjamin Knox
Dobbins, Warren vs. The State
Doby, Waitus, Durrell Doby and Beverly Chafin vs. The State
Dodd, James and Cunningham D. Reid vs. Anthony Dyer
Dodd, James and Jarrel Beasley vs. John Kendrick
Dodds, James vs. Nathan Warner, John Baldwin, Administrator
  and Benjamin F. Ward, Administrator
Dodson, Armsted and Elijah Dodson vs. William Nelson
Dodson, Elijah, Leah Dodson, Administrator and Joel W.
  Dodson, Administrator vs. James Cammeron and Joshua Hill
Dodson, Elijah, Leah Dodson, Administrator and Joel Dodson,
  Administrator vs. Edward Castleberry and James Cameron,
  Executor
Dodson, Elijah, Joel W. Dodson, Administrator and Leah
  Dodson, Administrator vs. James P. Glover
Dodson, Elijah, Joel W. Dodson, Administrator and Leah
  Dodson, Administrator vs. Officers of Court
Dodson, Joel W. vs. Eaton Banks
Dodson, Joel W. vs. John Smith and James H. Shi
Dodson, John P. vs. The State
Dodson, Presley vs. Charles L. Matthews
Dodson, Presley vs. Henry Pearson and Co.
Dodson, Presley vs. Obediah Slayton
Dodson, Presley vs. John Watson
Dodson, W. A. vs. L. O. Benton for use of Officers of
  Court
Donaldson, John vs. Thomas Beall
Donaldson, John vs. Woody Dozier
Donaldson, John vs. Andrew Jeter
Donaldson, John vs. David Shepherd
Donaldson, John vs. Eli Shorter
Dorsett, Andrew vs. William Ramey
Dorsett, James vs. Martha Alexander
Dorsett, James vs. The State
Dorsett, Palemon vs. The State
Dorsette, James and Marcus D. Vance vs. Jesse Short
Doss, Claborn vs. James Callaway
Doss, Claborn vs. John Evans
Doster, Burney vs. The State
Doster, James C. vs. Sean B. Robson and Robert C. Robson

Doster, Pleas vs. The State
Doster, William vs. The State
Dougherty, E. C. vs. N. M. Williams
Dougherty, Ed vs. The State
Dougherty, Grover vs. The State
Dougherty, John vs. The State
Dougherty, William vs. Lane and Patterson
Dougherty, William, Augustus W. Lane and Pleasant M. Compton
  vs. James Pye and Harmon W. Pye, Administrator
Dougherty, William vs. Ferdinand Straus and Joesph Straus
Douglas, Martin vs. Milton Antony
Dowdel, Lewis vs. The State
Dowdell, James vs. The State
Dowdell, Lewis vs. Augustin Cook
Dowdell, Lewis vs. Starkey Hill
Dowdle, Pierce vs. The State
Downey, Calvin vs. Thomas Broadus
Downey, Charles C. P. vs. Robert B. Camfield
Downey, Charles P. and James McLemore vs. Lucius Arms
Downey, Charles P. vs. William Gill, Jeremiah Davis and
  John Malpass
Downey, Charles P. vs. Hosea Webster and Thomas J. Parmelee
Downey, James vs. James Moon
Downey, Samuel and Peter Downey vs. James Crawley
Downey, Samuel and James Downey vs. Benjamin Hawkins for
  use of Presley W. Smith
Downey, Samuel, James Downey and Peter Downey vs. The State
Downs, James vs. Elisha Lake
Downs, James vs. The State
Downs, James, Jr. vs. James Patterson
Downs, John, John Bentley and Sherod H. Gay vs. The State
Downs, Shelly P. vs. William J. L. Tuggle and James M.
  Williams, Executor
Dozier, Ed vs. The State
Dozier, Thomas J. and Abner Chapman vs. Eli Glover
Dozier, Thomas J. vs. Ellison Gross
Dozier, Tom vs. The State
Dozier, Woody vs. Thomas R. Barker
Dozier, Woody and Jeremiah Pearson vs. James B. Bishop
Dozier, Woody, Hiram Glazier and William Hitchcock vs.
  Clending and Bulkley
Dozier, Woody vs. Anthony Dyer
Dozier, Woody and Garland Maxcey vs. Artemus Gould
Dozier, Woody vs. William Harris
Dozier, Woody vs. Elijah N. Hascall
Dozier, Woody vs. Russell Hoyt, Eli T. Hoyt and David H.
  Broughton
Dozier, Woody vs. Jonathan Jewett and James N. Codwise
Dozier, Woody vs. Justices of Court
Dozier, Woody vs. Joseph K. Kilburn
Dozier, Woody vs. John T. Lamar
Dozier, Woody and Abner Chapman vs. Jethro Mobley
Dozier, Woody vs. Charles F. Moulton
Dozier, Woody vs. Daniel Parish, Jasper Corning, Henry
  Parish, Joseph Kernochan and Ephraim Holbrook
Dozier, Woody and Stokely Morgan vs. William Roberts
Dozier, Woody vs. James Robertson and William Walker
Dozier, Woody vs. Eli S. Shorter
Dozier, Woody vs. Joseph Stovall
Drew, John L. vs. John Logan and Peter Primrose
Driggons, John and Abner Chapman vs. John Willson, James
  Willson, Executor, John Hill, Executor, Fleming Jordan,
  Executor and David A. Reese, Executor

Driskell, Christopher vs. James H. Roberts
Driskell, James T. vs. Griffin, Monticello and Madison
Railroad Co.
Driskell, N. N. vs. The State
Driskill, Christopher, Luke Williams and James M. Spurlin
vs. Burwell Ragland
Driskill, Christopher vs. James Stratton and Asa E. Stratton
Duck, Timothy vs. Eli Glover and John Cashin
Duck, Timothy vs. Edmond Greene
Duck, Timothy vs. Hugh G. Johnson
Duck, Timothy vs. Henry Walker for use of Zachariah
Phillips, Jr.
Dugger, Sampson vs. James Simmons
Duke, Bartholomew H. and John West vs. The State
Duke, Frederick vs. Thomas L. Ross
Duke, Frederick vs. William Underhill and Charles Underhill
Duke, Hardy vs. The State
Duke, Jane (cole) vs. Joseph Duke
Duke, Joseph and Jane Duke vs. John Rainey
Duke, Joseph G. and Jane Duke vs. William Cook
Duke, Joseph G. and Jane Duke vs. James Griggs
Duke, Stephen vs. Airs Hudspeth
Duke, Stephen vs. John Rainey
Duke, Stephen H. and Elihu V. Waldrup vs. John Hunt
Duke, Stephen H. vs. Hosea Webster and Thomas J. Parmelee
Dukes, Frederick vs. Hamilton Brown, Peyton Gwyn and James
Gwynn
Dukes, Frederick and John Griggs, Jr. vs. Pleasant Bonner,
Minor and William Hunter, Guardian
Dukes, Frederick vs. Eli S. Shorter
Dukes, Frederick and Thomas H. B. Rivers vs. The State
Dukes, Hardy H. vs. John G. Morris and James B. Bell
Dukes, Ransom H. vs. The State
Dukes, Robert W. and Hardy H. Dukes vs. Hamilton Atchison
and Samuel B. Hunter, Administrator
Dukes, Robert W. vs. Stephen W. Beasley
Dukes, Robert W. and Robert A. Allen vs. Walker I. Brooks
and Iverson L. Brooks, Guardian
Dukes, Robert W. and Stephen W. Beasley vs. Wesley Griggs
Dukes, Robert W. vs. Cuthbert Reese
Dukes, Stephen and Sarah Dukes vs. Polly Junior
Dukes, Stephen H. vs. John Hurst
Dukes, William and Tilmon Niblet vs. William S. Roberts and
Thomas H. Roberts
Dukes, William and Thomas Moreland vs. The State
Dukes, William and Tilmon Nibblet vs. The State
Dukes, William and Tilmon Niblett vs. Andrew J. Varner and
Jefferson M. Varner
Dumas, Cincinatus vs. John Cargill
Dumas, Cooley vs. The State
Dumas, Jack vs. The State
Dumas, James vs. The State
Dumas, John C., Martin V. Tyner and Reubin J. Tyner vs.
E. P. Beauchamp
Dumas, Steve vs. The State
Duncan, James vs. Abba Benton
Duncan, James, Abba Benton and Bailey Freeman vs. Central
Bank of Georgia
Duncan, James vs. Cardin Goolsby
Duncan, James vs. George Moore
Duncan, James vs. Jeremiah Pearson
Duncan, James vs. The State
Duncan, Mathew vs. Jesse Evans for use of James Black

138

Duncan, Mathew vs. Alexander Mackey
Duncan, Mathew and Jesse Evans vs. Harmon Runnels, Peter
   Randolph and Robert McGowen
Duncan, Mathew and Elizabeth Duncan vs. The State
Duncan, Mathew vs. Solomon Strickland
Duncan, Matthew vs. William Cook
Duncan, Matthew vs. Eli Glover and John Cashin
Duncan, Matthew vs. Henry Walker for use of Michael Moore
Duncan, Matthew vs. William D. Wright
Dunlap, David vs. Elijah Dodson, Joel W. Dodson, Adminis-
   trator and Leah Dodson, Administrator
Dunn, Byron vs. The State
Dunn, Ed vs. The State
Dunn, Gatewood and Albert Dunn vs. John Portwood and Nathan
   Williams, Administrator
Dunn, William vs. Luke J. Morgan
Dunn, William G. vs. Jacob Hass and Company
Dunom, Thomas I. vs. Peter Cauble
Dunom, Thomas I. vs. William H. Crane
Dunom, Thomas I. vs. John M. Roberts and Benjamin F. Maldin
Dunom, Thomas J. vs. Henry George
Durden, Bill Graft (alias W. D. Durden) vs. The State
Durden, Joe C. vs. The State
Durden, John vs. Isaac L. Parker
Durden, Rona vs. The State
Durham, Lindsey H., Dyer C. Vancroft and John E. Watters
   vs. Anthony Dyer
Durham, Lola vs. The State
Durham, Simeon vs. John Baldwin
Durham, Simeon vs. Sally Cabiness
Durham, Simeon vs. James Cowan and Thomas B. Erwin
Durham, Simeon vs. Israel Dissoway
Durham, Simeon vs. John Greer
Durham, Simeon vs. Martin King
Durham, Simeon vs. Daniel Lord and Jeremiah Pierson
Durham, Simeon vs. Ralph Olmsted
Durham, Simeon vs. Daniel Parish, Jasper Corning, Henry
   Parish, Joseph Kernochan and Ephraim Holbrook
Durham, Simeon vs. William Peddy
Durham, Simeon vs. Eli S. Shorter
Durham, Simeon vs. David Walker
Durham, Simeon vs. Joseph Welden
Durr, Michael vs. Joel Baley
Durr, Michael vs. Sarah Kilbee
Dyer, Edmund Walker and Susan (Smith) Walker
Dyer, Anthony vs. Edward Y. Hill and Joshua Hill
Dyer, Anthony, John Hill, Fleming Jordan, James Dodson,
   David A. Reese and Mathew Phillips vs. William Hitchcock
Dyer, Anthony and Otis Dyer vs. John Ragan and William C.
   Watson
Dyer, Anthony vs. William Robinson
Dyer, Anthony and William Cochran vs. The State

Eagerton, Mary and Edward D. Barrow vs. Leroy Napier
Eagerton, Zachariah B. vs. Louzia C. Flewellen and Charles
   P. Gordon, Guardian
Eagerton, Zachariah B. and Jason Shingleton vs. James Long
Eagerton, Zachariah B. and Charles McLemore vs. James Pinkard
Earley, A. L. vs. Mat Whitfield
Earley, Anslem L. and Caleb Earley vs. Seaborn B. Watts
Earley, Anslem L. vs. Hosea Webster and George Webster
Earley, Caleb and Anslem L. Earley vs. Eli S. Shorter and
   Charles P. Gordon

Earley, Caleb vs. The State
Earley, Caleb vs. John Wingfield
Earley, Joseph vs. William Robinson
Earley, Joseph vs. Williamson Roby
Earley, Joseph vs. Matthew Whitfield
Early, Anselem, Crawford Edmondson and Joseph Early vs.
  James Turner
Early, Anselm L. vs. Joseph Early
Early, Anselm L. vs. John C. Watters
Early, Anslem and Joseph Early vs. William Askew
Early, Anslem L. vs. Raymond Davenport
Early, Anslem L. vs. James T. Hayes
Early, Anslem L. vs. Augustus Hayward
Early, Anslem L. vs. Elizabeth Heard
Early, Anslem L. vs. Leroy Napier
Early, Anslem L. vs. Thomas B. Peet
Early, Anslem L. and James F. Robinson vs. Frederick
  Pennington for use of Hannah Dabney
Early, Anslem L. vs. Richard Pollard
Early, Anslem L. vs. James F. Robinson
Early, Anslem L. vs. Carter Shepherd
Early, Anslem L. vs. The State
Early, Caleb, Joseph Early and Charles Smith vs. Thaddeus
  Beall, Elias Beall and Thomas Beall
Early, Caleb vs. Edward Delona
Early, Caleb vs. James B. Randall
Early, Joseph vs. Francis Edmondson
Early, Joseph vs. William B. Gregory for use of William
  Stock
Early, Joseph vs. Eli S. Shorter
Easco, Nancy (Pledger) vs. John Eascoe
Easco, Nancy M. vs. The State
Eason, Whitmel vs. Samuel Butts, John Lucas, Administrator
  and William Lee, Administrator
Easter, Champion vs. John Easter for use of Reuben Ransom
Easter, Champion vs. William Jones
Easter, Champion vs. Robert Thompson for use of Thomas Bibb
Easter, John C. vs. Stephen C. Crane
Easter, John C. vs. Asa E. Stratton
Easter, John C. vs. William Woods
Easter, Baxter vs. The State
Easter, Catharine, Leroy Napier, Administrator, and John
  T. C. Towns, Administrator vs. Elbert J. Easters
Eastes, Zachariah vs. Richard Carter
Eastes, Zachariah vs. John Miles
Eastes, Zachariah and Nancy M. Eastes vs. The State
Eastes, Zachariah vs. Abednego Wright
Eaves, Bartlett vs. John C. Gibson
Eaves, Buckner vs. Isaac McClendon
Eaves, Buckner vs. The State
Eaves, Buckner vs. Isaac McClendon
Eaves, Buckner vs. Edward Walthall
Echols, Absalom and Nathan Williams vs. Bedford Brown,
  Sally Moseley, Executor and Peter Moseley
Echols, Absalom vs. William Cleveland
Echols, Absalom vs. Benjamin Cone
Echols, Absalom vs. William Connell
Echols, Absalom vs. Lawson S. Holland
Echols, Absalom vs. Joseph Moss
Echols, Absalom vs. William Pabodie
Echols, Absalom vs. John T. Swann
Echols, Absolem vs. James Richards
Echols, John vs. The State

Echols, Obadiah vs. Alston H. Greene and Joseph Buchannon
Echols, Obadiah vs. Seaborn Jones
Echols, Obadiah vs. Elisha Kindall
Echols, Obadiah vs. Stokely Morgan
Echols, Obadiah and Jeptha V. Dismuke vs. Archibald Perkins,
    Abraham Perkins, Executor, Alexander Perkins, Executor,
    Bennett W. Ware, Executor, Bennett Crawford, Executor and
    Frances Coleman
Echols, Obadiah vs. Abel P. Wilson
Echols, Richard vs. Henry Walker
Echols, William vs. Isaac Bailey
Echols, William and Garret Clark vs. John Cargile, Robert
    Williamson, Administrator, James Cargile, Administrator,
    William Cargile, Administrator and Lavina Cargile,
    Administrator
Echols, William, Magers Henderson and Isaac Bailey vs.
    Justice of Inferior Court
Echols, William vs. Robert B. Porter
Echols, William vs. The State
Echols, William vs. James Whitfield
Ector, Martha vs. Charles Webb
Edelman, David and Moses Edelman vs. Barnabas Peace
Edge, Allen and John Edge vs. Isaac Hill
Edge, Jake vs. The State
Edge, John vs. Edmond Bradford
Edge, Obadia vs. James Lamkin
Edmonds, Amos vs. Robert Therman
Edmonds, John vs. Early Harris and Rowland Thurmond
Edmonds, John and Nichols Critchfield vs. William McMichal,
    Elizabeth McMichal, Administrator, John McMichal,
    Administrator and Richard Carter, Administrator
Edmonds, John vs. Jesse Thurmond for use of Abner McGehee
Edmondson, Benjamin C. vs. Milton Antony
Edmondson, Benjamin C. vs. Samuel Crockett
Edmondson, Benjamin C., William Cook, Administrator and
    John Willson, Administrator vs. John Fluker
Edmondson, Benjamin C., John Willson, Administrator and
    William Cook, Administrator vs. George Stringfellow
Edmondson, Crawford vs. John Willson
Edmondson, Crawford, Humphrey Edmondson, Administrator,
    William A. Moore, Administrator and Hannah Edmondson,
    Administrator vs. John Baldwin
Edmondson, Crawford vs. Anthony Dyer
Edmondson, Crawford, William A. Moore, Administrator,
    Humbhrey Edmondson, Administraotr, Hannah Edmondson,
    Administrator, and Alexander R. Buchannon vs. Samuel
    Edmondson and Martha Edmondson, Administrator
Edmondson, Crawford vs. Alston H. Greene and Joseph
    Buchannon
Edmondson, Crawford vs. William Shropshire
Edmondson, Crawford vs. Alexander Smith
Edmondson, Crawford and Charles Pearson vs. The State
Edmondson, Crawford vs. George Stovall
Edmondson, Crawford vs. William Thompson
Edmondson, Hannah vs. Alsea Holifield
Edmondson, Hannah vs. James Whitfield
Edmondson, Henry D. C. and Richard Flemister vs. William
    C. Edmondson
Edmondson, Henry D. C. and William O. Edmondson vs. James
    N. Hall, Lucius Mansfield, Administrator and David
    A. Reese, Administrator
Edmondson, Henry D. C., William A. Edmondson, Silas
    Grubbs, John Maxey, John Maxey and Wiley Phillips vs.

Ransom H. Smith for use of Gilbraith Simonton, Hugh P.
Kirkpatrick, Administrator and Agnes T. Simonton,
Administrator
Edmondson, Henry D. C. vs. The State
Edmondson, Richard vs. John H. Baynes
Edmondson, Richard and Martha Edmondson vs. Fleming Jordan
and Henry Buchannon
Edmondson, Richard vs. The State
Edmondson, Thomas vs. Robert Williamson
Edmondson, William B., Stith B. Malone vs. Artemus Goolsby
Edmondson, William O. vs. John Horton
Edmondson, William O. vs. William Maxey and Joshua Hill
Edward, James and John Edward vs. John Buchannon
Edwards, H. L. vs. The State
Edwards, Herbert vs. The State
Edwards, James vs. John Armstrong
Edwards, John vs. William L. Brien
Edwards, John and Williamson A. Roby vs. Charles Cargile
Edwards, John vs. Peter Farrar and William Reed
Edwards, John vs. George Fitzgerald
Edwards, John and James Edwards vs. Moses Martin
Edwards, John vs. John Sessions
Edwards, John W. and Williamson A. Roby vs. Thornton Barlough
Edwards, John W. vs. Jubal Cochran and Mildred Cochran,
Administrator
Edwards, John W. vs. W. L. Lampkin and Co.
Edwards, John W. vs. Wiley Peddy
Edwards, Reuben vs. James Ravenel
Edwards, Reuben vs. James Richards for use of John McKinne
Edwards, Reuben and Pinton Tucker vs. John Spearman
Edwards, Susan and Fanny Smith vs. Benjamin White
Edwards, Walter C. vs. The State
Edwards, William and Fleming McFall vs. William A. Black
Egnew, Francis and Harrison Mobley vs. The State
Egnew, William vs. The State
Elder, Benjamin F. vs. Griffin, Monticello and Madison
Railroad Co.
Elder, Benjamin F., Edward A. Elder, Thomas M. Jordan,
William Maxey, F. M. Swanson and J. W. Burney, Jr. vs.
The State
Elder, David, Augustus Elder and Turner Elder vs. The State
Elder, Edward and Polly Elder vs. John H. Brantley
Elder, Edward and James Elder vs. Jonas H. Holland
Elder, Edward, Sr. vs. Mathew Whitfield
Elder, Edward A. and Williamson A. Roby vs. Thornton
Barlough
Elder, Edward A. and James Elder vs. The State
Elder, Edward A. and Mary Elder vs. The State
Elder, Edward A., James Wilson, Graves Wilson and George
N. Carlile vs. The State
Elder, George B. and Jefferson Pope vs. Carden Goolsby
Elder, Harbert B. vs. Samuel Clay
Elder, Herbert B. vs. J. Boon, Hiram Glazier, Administra-
tor and Marnoch Glazier, Administrator
Elder, James E. vs. C. and M. Railroad Co. for use of
Officers of Court
Elder, John G. and Edward A. Elder vs. Henry J. Lamar
Elder, John G. vs. The State
Elder, W. A. vs. The State
Elder, William A. and Edward A. Elder vs. William V. Burney
Elliott, J. H. vs. The State
Elliott, Patsey vs. The State
Ellis, Daniel vs. William Glass

142

Ellis, Radford vs. William Hammett
Ellis, Radford, Elizabeth Ellis, Executor, James Ellis,
   Executor and William Ellis, Executor vs. Archy McKissack
   and Lucy McKissack
Ellis, Radford, Sr. vs. William Wallace
Emmons, John vs. Jeremiah Pitman
Emory, Samuel vs. Elizabeth Callaway
Emory, Samuel vs. Washington C. Cleveland
English, Augustus and Turner Elder vs. The State
Epps, Alfred vs. The State
Epps, Andrew vs. The State
Epps, Berry (alias Took Epps) vs. The State
Epps, Burrell vs. The State
Epps, Jimmie L. vs. The State
Epps, Madison vs. W. A. Loftin
Epps, Madison vs. R. A. Malone
Epps, Madison vs. Nettie Miller
Epps, Madison vs. The State
Epps, Madison vs. James A. Stone
Erwin, Thomas B. vs. Nathaniel Coggeshell
Erwin, Thomas B. and James Cowan vs. Rullel Hoyt, Eli Hoyt
   and David H. Boughton
Erwin, William vs. The State
Eskew, Jim vs. The State
Esters, Philip and James Esters vs. Thomas Akins
Estes, John A. Compton and James H. Roberts vs. Thomas
   R. S. Holifield
Estes, Winston vs. Thomas B. Erwin and James Cowan
Estes, Winston vs. Edward Price
Estes, Winston C. vs. Robert C. Beasley
Estes, Zachariah, Alsea Holifield and Bartlet Eaves vs.
   The State
Eubanks, Majers and Thomas J. Hadley vs. The State
Evans, Charles vs. The State
Evans, David vs. Thaddeus Beall and Elias Beall
Evans, David vs. Henry Walker, Abner Chapman and Michael
   Moore
Evans, Henry W. vs. Thomas Barrett
Evans, Jesse vs. Samuel Butts, John Lucas, Administrator
   and William Lee, Administrator
Evans, Jesse vs. David Cande
Evans, Jesse vs. James Cunningham
Evans, Jesse vs. William G. Gilbert and Felix Gilbert
Evans, Jesse and Timothy Duck vs. Eli Glover and John Cashin
Evans, Jesse and Abner Chapman vs. Thomas Harris
Evans, Jesse and Stokely Morgan vs. Thomas Harris
Evans, Jesse and Stokely Morgan vs. Mathew Hawkins
Evans, Jesse and Jesse Evans, Jr. vs. Alsea Holifield
Evans, Jesse vs. John Maxwell
Evans, Jesse vs. Moses Mulkey
Evans, Jesse vs. John McKinne
Evans, Jesse and Hutson Rose vs. Alexander Steel and Samuel
   Harper, Administrator
Evans, Jesse vs. Samuel Walker
Evans, Jesse, Jr., Jesse Evans, Sr., Johnson Strong and
   Abel Pennington, Sr. vs. Obed Baker
Evans, Jesse, Jr. vs. James Dickson and William Dickson
Evans, Jesse, Jr., Jesse Evans, Sr., Abel Pennington, Sr.
   and Johnson Strong vs. Francis Doyle
Evans, Jesse, Jr. and Jesse Evans, Sr. vs. Thomas Fitch
Evans, Jesse, Jr., Jesse Evans, Sr., Abel Pennington, Sr.
   and Johnson Strong vs. Thomas Scott and Martha Scott,
   Administrator

Evans, Jesse, Jr., Jesse Evans, Sr., Abel Pennington, Sr.
and Johnson Strong vs. The State
Evans, Jesse, Jr., Jesse Evans, Sr., Abel Pennington, Sr.
and Johnson Strong vs. Stevens Thomas
Evans, John P. vs. High and Baldwin
Evans, John P. vs. Frederick Lamback and William H. Cooper
Evans, John P., Meshack N. Crawford vs. The State
Evans, John P. vs. Francis M. Swanson
Evans, S. C. vs. The State
Evans, Walter vs. The State
Evans, William vs. Mary Crawman
Evans, William vs. John W. Mays
Evans, William and William H. Wyatt vs. Ransom Smith
Evans, William vs. Thomas Smith
Evans, William, John P. Evans, Francis Evans and Asbury
Evans vs. The State
Everett, Wiley N. H., Nathan P. Lee and William B. Allred
vs. Charles A. Griener and Frederick B. Griener
Everett, Wiley N. H. vs. Lewis H. Hoard
Everett, Wiley N. H. and William Pope vs. Mary McCollum
Everett, Woley N. H. vs. The State
Evers, Jasper vs. James McLeroy
Eves, Bartlet vs. Joseph Price
Ezell, Braxton R. vs. Robert P. McEvoy
Ezell, Braxton R. vs. Mathew Whitfield, Leroy M. Willson,
Executor, Pleasant Willson, Executor, John F. Patterson,
William H. Mathis, Executor
Ezell, Braxton R., Jr., vs. William H. Thompson for use of
William S. Townsend
Ezell, Harry G. vs. Lewis King and James Freeman, Guardian
Ezell, Henry G. vs. Charles L. Kennon and Howell Kennon
Ezell, John H. vs. George B. Hallock
Ezell, John H. and Aris Newton vs. Almeda Wammack
Ezell, L. D. vs. The State
Ezell, Levi D. vs. William H. Thompson for use of William
S. Townsend
Ezell, Robert F. vs. John Otis
Ezell, Robert F. vs. William H. Thompson for use of William
S. Townsend

Fails, Arthur, Stephen Stephens, Administrator and Tully
Choice vs. Reuben Fails
Falkner, James, John Falkner, Executor, James Falkner,
Patsey (Falkner) Fipps and Lewis Fipps vs. Isaac Suttle
Falkner, John and John Stephenson vs. Jacob Peeler
Falkner, John H. vs. George J. Rogers and William Rogers
Fall, John H. vs. Edward Collier
Fall, John N. vs. Hosea Webster, Thomas I. Parmalee and
Edwin B. Webster
Fall, John N. vs. William P. White
Farley, James vs. Hezekiah Bussey
Farley, James, Jr. vs. Joshua Callaway and Elizabeth
Callaway, Administrator
Farley, Jim vs. The State
Farley, John vs. Robert B. Camfield
Farley, John vs. Ralph Olmsted
Farley, Russ vs. The State
Farmer, Jimie vs. The State
Farmers State Bank of Sparks vs. National Surety Company
Farrar, Charlie vs. The State
Farrar, G. W. and Isaac H. Freeman vs. James Pennington
Farrar, George, Isaac Freeman and Gabriel Harrison vs.
Matthew Whitfield

Farrar, George W. vs. Pleasant M. Compton for use of
  Benjamin T. Bethune
Farrar, George W. vs. William A. Reid
Farrar, George W. and William H. Pogg vs. Permenius R.
  Thomason
Farrar, Will vs. The State
Farrer, Benjamin K. vs. The State
Farrow, Absalom and John C. Reese vs. Jordan Reese
Farrow, Finch vs. Eli Glover
Farrow, Finch and Jane (Ray) Farrow vs. William Johnston
Farrow, Nich vs. The State
Farthing, Joe vs. The State
Faulkner, Floyd vs. The State
Faulkner, J. P. vs. L. O. Benton and Brothers
Faulkner, John vs. Albert Jones and Gabriel Harrison,
  Administrator
Faulkner, John H. vs. Mitchell Parker
Faulkner, John M. vs. James M. Spurlin
Faulkner, Ruckner and Mastin R. Faulkner vs. The State
Faulkner, Thomas H. vs. The State
Faulkner, Zachariah vs. Joseph Carter
Faulkner, Zachariah vs. Thomas Grant, Daniel Grant, Execu-
  tor, Thomas Grant, Executor and Peter Grinell, Executor
Faulkner, Zachariah vs. William Hurt
Faulkner, Zachariah vs. Charles D. Ramey for use of John D.
  Ramey
Faulkner, Zachariah vs. Henry T. Smith
Feagin, William H. and Tilman D. Oxford vs. William D.
  Ethridge
Fears, Alsey and Ezekiel P. Fears, Administrator vs. George
  W. Stringfellow and Riley S. Fears, Administrator
Fears, Claborn vs. The State
Fears, Colsby vs. The State
Fears, James S. vs. Stephen W. Beasley
Fears, John P. vs. William Jones, James R. Jones, Carrie
  Thornton and Ginie Jones
Fears, Jonah vs. The State
Fears, Riley S. vs. Archibald B. Ridley and Robert A. T.
  Ridley, Executor
Fears, Riley S. vs. The State
Fears, Wiley and Berry Digby vs. The State
Fears, Will vs. The State
Fears, William vs. The State
Fears, William T. and Riley S. Fears vs. William Kangleton
Fears, William T. vs. James M. Knight and David Thompson,
  Administrator
Fee, Jobe (Shy) vs. The State
Fergason, Neal vs. The State
Fergerson, Alfred W. and Abner Chapman vs. Randal Robinson
Fergerson, Neil vs. Bartley Wooten
Fergerson, Neill vs. David Urquhart for use of John Bethune
Fergerson, Neill vs. Abraham Waldrop
Ferguson, Neill vs. Alston H. Greene and Joseph Buchannon
Ferrel, William vs. Samuel Harrel
Ferrell, Cuthbert vs. James Cowan and Thomas B. Erwin
Ferrell, Cuthbert and Amos Jones vs. Snellen Johnson
Ferrell, Cuthbert, William Ferrell and Henry T. Smartt vs.
  Winburn Odom
Fielder, James M. and Obadiah M. B. Fielder vs. Cornelius
  Atkinson
Fielder, James M., James S. McClure and James R. McCord vs.
  John Bones and Samuel Bones
Fielder, James M. and Obadiah M. B. Fielder vs. John Hendrick

Fielder, James M. and James S. McClure vs. Andrew Kerr,
  John Kerr and James Hope
Fielder, James M., James L. McClure and Obadiah M. B.
  Fielder vs. Thomas C. Taylor
Fielder, Obadiah M. B. vs. Central Bank of Georgia
Fielder, Obadiah M. B. and Burton J. McMichael vs. Anthony
  Dyer
Fielder, Obadiah M. B. vs. Sidney Few for use of John R.
  Hubbard
Fielder, Obadiah M. B. vs. William Hightower
Fielder, Thomas B. vs. George W. Gilleland
Fielder, Obadiah M. B. vs. Albert O. Parmelee
Fielder, Thomas B. vs. Joseph R. High and John H. Baker
Fields, Lemuel H. vs. James Shearer, William Shearer,
  Executor, James Rutledge, Executor and Richard Smith
Fields, Martin vs. Paschal Murphy
Fields, William B., Jr. vs. James W. Oxford
Finch, Mose vs. The State
Fincher, Angeline (Angelira) vs. Moses Fincher
Fincher, James vs. Lewis C. McKey
Fincher, James, Barnett Kinard, Walter Bean and John Bean
  vs. James Turner
Fincher, Mary (McCurdy) vs. Christopher Fincher
Finley, Harriott and Celia Finley vs. The State
Finley, Jacob vs. The State
Finley, John vs. Drury Deupree
Finley, Quinton, Cullen Finley and John Lindsey vs. The
  State
Finley, Riley and William Askew vs. The State
Fish, Bernhard and Isaac Fish vs. Henry Grossmayer
Fish, Charles vs. The State
Fish, Nathan vs. Anthony Dyer
Fish, Nathan and Naomy Fish vs. Nathan Phillips and Amy
  Phillips (Ann, Nancy)
Fish, Nathan vs. David Ralston
Fish, Nathan vs. The State
Fish, Ridges vs. The State
Fish, Russell vs. The State
Fitzpatrick, Booth W. vs. The State
Fitzpatrick, Jackson vs. Charles W. Rockwell, Thomas
  Walton and Thomas C. Hayward
Fitzpatrick, Jackson and James Cowan vs. James Stephens,
  and John Rivers, Executor for use of Jesse Stephens
Fitzpatrick, Joseph, Jesse Evans and Philip Fitzpatrick
  vs. Thomas Lamar
Fitzpatrick, Joseph, Phillips Fitzpatrick and Jesse Evans
  vs. Moses Perkins
Fitzpatrick, Joseph and Henry Walker vs. The State
Fitzpatrick, Philip vs. James Billingslea
Fitzpatrick, Philip vs. Samuel Butts, John Lucas, Adminis-
  trator and William Lee, Administrator
Fitzpatrick, Philip vs. Rene Fitzpatrick
Fitzpatrick, Philip vs. Nicholas Waggoner
Fitzpatrick, Philip and John Huston vs. Thomas T. Walker
Fitzpatrick, Rene vs. William Baldwin
Fitzpatrick, Rene vs. Thomas Grant and Joseph McBride
Fitzpatrick, Rene, Joseph Phillips, James Patterson and
  David McCoy vs. Alexander McMillan
Fitzpatrick, Rene vs. Joel Marton
Fitzpatrick, Rene vs. Robert Roby for use of Anthony Dyer
Fitspatrick, William and Joseph Fitzpatrick vs. Booth
  Fitzpatrick
Fitzpatrick, William and Joseph Fitzpatrick, Administrator

vs. Thomas Hide
Flake, William vs. Charles Marshall
Flake, William and Richard C. Clayton vs. Cuthbert Reese
Flanegin, Joel vs. Anthony Dyer
Flanegin, Joel vs. The United States of America
Flannagan, James vs. Otis Dyer and Anthony Dyer
Flanniken, David vs. John C. Gibson
Flat, John vs. The State
Flatau, Moris vs. S. Aronhimer
Flemister, Alse vs. Robert Tolefree
Flemister, Craten A. J., Henry Camp, Administrator, John
   W. Wyatt and William Bailey vs. Henry Brehm and John
   Foster
Flemister, Craton A. J. vs. Theodore Franklin
Flemister, Craton A. J. vs. Thomas J. N. Osborne
Flemister, Craton A. J. vs. Isaac L. Parker and Maximillan
   H. Hutchison, Administrator
Flemister, Craton A. J. vs. William S. Roberts and Thomas
   H. Roberts
Flemister, Craton A. J. vs. John W. A. Smith
Flemister, Craton A. J. vs. The State
Flemister, Craton A. J., William Bailey and John W. Wyatt
   vs. David A. Vason
Flemister, Creighton A. J. vs. George M. Cunningham
Flemister, Elleanor, Jeremiah M. Gilstrap, Administrator,
   Lewis Flemister and John Lindsey vs. John Robinson
Flemister, Horance vs. The State
Flemister, James C. and Alsy Flemister, Executor vs. Samuel
   Dllis
Flemister, James C. vs. William S. Hurd and Anson Hunger-
   ford, Jr.
Flemister, James C. vs. Anderson F. Thompson
Flemister, James C. and Abel P. Wilson vs. Thomas Smith,
   John C. Smith, Administrator and Asa Smith, Administrator
Flemister, Jeff vs. Lucian L. Turk
Flemister, Jeff, Jr. vs. The State
Flemister, John and Jim Flemister vs. The State
Flemister, John M. vs. William C. Leverett
Flemister, John M. vs. The State
Flemister, Lewis W., John Robinson and John Lindsey vs.
   Central Bank of Georgia
Flemister, Lewis W. and John Lindsey vs. Ephraim S. Hopping
Flemister, Lewis W. vs. William H. Vaughn
Flemister, Richard vs. Henry A. Dickinson
Flemister, Richard vs. William Maxey and James C. Bartlett
Flemister, Richard vs. The State
Flemister, William C. and William L. Flemister vs. The State
Flemister, William L. vs. Williamson Bailey and William
   Bailey
Flemister, William L., Abel P. Wilson and John Robinson vs.
   The Central Bank of Georgia
Flemister, William L. vs. Thompson Curry
Flemister, William L. vs. James C. Haviland, Robert B.
   Haviland, Theodore Keese, Hubbell W. Risley, James Harral
   and Samuel L. Allen
Flemister, William L., Abel P. Willson, James C. Flemister
   and John Lindsey vs. William Hitchcock and David A.
   Reese, Administrator
Flemister, William L. vs. Jonas H. Holland
Flemister, William L. vs. James H. Hollingsworth, Albert
   Smith and Joseph J. Scranton
Flemister, William L. vs. William Hurd and Anson Hungerford
Flemister, William L. and Green Trussell vs. Hugh P.

Kirkpatrick
Flemister, William L. vs. James L. Maddux
Flemister, William L. vs. William Maxey and Joshua Hill
Flemister, William L. and Abel P. Wilson vs. Miller W.
  Pope and William K. Pope, Guardian
Flemister, William L. vs. Thomas J. Smith and John C. Maddux
Flemister, William L. and Abel P. Wilson vs. Thomas Smith,
  John C. Smith, Administrator and Asa Smith, Administrator
Flemister, William S. and Abel P. Wilson vs. Martin Puckett,
  James W. Vaughn, Administrator
Flemister, Willson L. vs. Lewis Ryan
Flemister, Willson L. vs. Henry C. Sizmour
Flemming, James vs. Jesse Oneal
Flenniken, Samuel vs. Isaac McClendon
Flenniken, Samuel vs. Henry Walker
Fletcher, Charles vs. William Freeman
Fletcher, Charles vs. The State
Fletcher, Thomas vs. John Byrom
Flewellen, Lovewell C. vs. Joshua Hill
Flewellen, Lovewell C. vs. Pleasant Stovall and Robert D.
  Hamlin
Florence, William H. vs. The State
Flornoy, Joseph vs. The State
Flournoy, George vs. The State
Flournoy, Samuel, Aris Newton, Administrator and Elizabeth
  G. Flournoy, Administrator vs. John A. Ellis
Flournoy, William vs. The State
Flournoy, Willis vs. Griffin, Monticello and Madison Rail-
  road Co.
Flowers, Edward, Edward Crain and Levi Dannel vs. Jesse Cox
Flowers, Edward vs. Joseph Johnson
Flowers, Edward vs. James Waits
Flowers, Theophilus vs. James Smith, Thomas J. Smith and
  Charles McLemore
Flowers, William and Thomas Carter vs. David Myrick, Robert
  Myrick, Guardian, Thomas Mosley, Guardian and Irby Hudson,
  Guardian
Flowers, William vs. Reuben C. Shorter
Floyd, Jim vs. The State
Floyd, John vs. The State
Floyd, Richard vs. William H. Crane
Floyd, Richard vs. James Smith, Thomas J. Smith and Charles
  McLemore
Floyd, William vs. The State
Fluelen, Lovewell C. vs. Robbin Grant and Robert Kellam,
  Guardian
Fluker, John vs. Waters Briscoe
Fluker, John vs. Allen McClendon
Fluker, John vs. Jeremiah Pearson
Fluker, John vs. Reuben C. Shorter
Fluker, John and Owen H. Kenan vs. The State
Fluker, John vs. Henry Walker, Abner Chapman and Michael
  Moore
Folds, John J. vs. Spencer Carrell and Robert A. Johnston
Folds, John J. vs. James L. Daniel
Folds, John J. vs. Robert F. Ezell
Folds, Mary and Z. K. Folds vs. S. C. Talmadge and A. J.
  Talmadge
Folds, William vs. Charles Saunders
Fooshee, Jepthah vs. Robert B. Porter
Forbes, Charles vs. Eaton Banks
Forbes, Charles and David Johnson vs. John H. Baynes
Forbes, Charles vs. John Glover

Forbes, Charles vs. Thomas Hoxey and Edward Dudley
Forbes, Charles vs. Mary Johnson
Forbes, Charles vs. Osborne G. Ogetree
Forbes, Charles vs. James Whitfield and Anthony Dyer
Forbes, Wesley vs. Smallwood P. Allison
Forbes, Wesley vs. William Ledbetter
Forbs, Charles vs. The State
Foreman, Edmund vs. Jonas Lawson, Sr. and James Lawson, Executor
Foreman, Edmund, Isaac Foreman, Jesse Foreman, Gilbert Greer, Jacob Foreman, Thomas Mangham, Thomas Greer and John Greer vs. The State
Foreman, Isaac vs. John Towson for use of Steven Hackney
Forte, Alexander vs. The State
Foster, Andrew vs. The State
Foster, Granville W. and Martha Foster vs. Alexander Garden
Foster, Granville W. vs. Rodah Haston for use of Robertson Brewer
Foster, Jake vs. The State
Foster, Martha vs. Alexander T. Harper
Foster, Polley (alias Polley Yancey) vs. The State
Foster, Richard vs. Gideon G. Mintor
Foster, William vs. John Dunn for use of William Askew
Fowler, William R. vs. Norborne B. Powell
Fowler, William R. vs. John Willson
Franklin, Ernest vs. The State
Franks, Britton J. and William L. Franks vs. William H. Crane
Franks, Britton J. vs. George Stovall
Frazer, Ely vs. Avington P. Williams
Frazier, Eli vs. Chesley Cannant for use of John T. Swann
Freeman, B. B. and Isaac H. Freeman, Administrator vs. James M. Shannon and Mary E. Shannon
Freeman, Bailey vs. The State
Freeman, Benjamin B., Shelly P. Downs, Administrator, Nathan C. Fish, Administrator and Isaac H. Freeman, Administrator vs. John Benton
Freeman, Benjamin B. vs. Alfred S. Franklin
Freeman, Bob vs. The State
Freeman, Brown vs. The State
Freeman, Daniel, James Freeman, Executor, W. M. Lambeth and Thompson and Fleming Jordan vs. Edward A. Broddus
Freeman, Daniel and George Freeman vs. Reuben Freeman and Charles Freeman, Administrator
Freeman, Daniel and James Freeman, Executor vs. Fleming Jordan
Freeman, Daniel and James Freeman, Executor vs. Mary Pye
Freeman, Ed vs. The State
Freeman, George H., Jr. vs. A. J. Talmadge and Co.
Freeman, Harriett vs. The State
Freeman, Hawkins vs. John P. Force
Freeman, Hawkins vs. Robert Leak
Freeman, Hawkins and Franklin George vs. Jesse Loyall
Freeman, Hawkins vs. John C. Smith
Freeman, Hawkins and Bennett Crawford vs. William E. Wade and Robert C. Dale
Freeman, Henry H. and Benjamin B. Freeman vs. Jenkins Wilson and Alfred G. Wilson, Executor
Freeman, Hopson vs. Isaac Newell
Freeman, Isaac H. vs. Jane P. Annis, Jesse Annis, Charles Annis and Annie E. Weems
Freeman, Isaac H. and James B. Goolsby vs. Chichester and Co.

Freeman, Isaac H. vs. William H. Graham
Freeman, Isaac H. vs. Lovice P. Jordan
Freeman, Isaac H. vs. James M. Shannon
Freeman, Isaac H. vs. Matthew Whitfield, John F. Patterson,
  Executor, Leroy M. Wilson, Executor and Pleasant Wilson,
  Executor
Freeman, Jabez vs. The State
Freeman, James vs. John Hill, Augustin Slaughter and Charles
  Labuzan
Freeman, James vs. William P. Rathbone
Freeman, James and Dorcas Campbell vs. The State
Freeman, James vs. James Stratton and Asa E. Stratton
Freeman, James, George Freeman, Executor and Jabez Freeman
  vs. Richmond Waits
Freeman, Jesse vs. The State
Freeman, Joe, Ed Freeman, John Freeman, Ed Clay, Bud Persons
  and Stewart Minter vs. The State
Freeman, John vs. Thomas J. Davis
Freeman, John vs. Thomas Gaston
Freeman, John vs. Hugh Williams
Freeman, John F. vs. Eliza Freeman
Freeman, Levi vs. William Biscoe and James N. Hall
Freeman, Phillip vs. The State
Freeman, Sam vs. The State
Freeman, Theophilus vs. Jarrel Beasley
Freeman, Theophilus and John Freeman vs. John S. D. Byrom
Freeman, Theophilus vs. Samuel Fulton
Freeman, Theophilus and Robert C. Beasley vs. James S. Jones
Freeman, Theophilus vs. William M. Lambeth and William E.
  Thompson
Freeman, Theophilus vs. William McDowell
Freeman, Theophilus vs. Henry Pennington
Freeman, Theophilus and John Freeman vs. James Whitfield
Freeman, Thomas vs. N. B. White
Freeman, Timothy and Solomon Strickland, Administrator vs.
  Absalom Rhodes
Freeman, Tom and Andrew Epps vs. The State
Fretwell, James vs. James Anderson
Fretwell, James and Micajah H. Fretwell vs. John and William
  Byrom
Fretwell, James and Macajah H. Fretwell vs. William Clark
Fretwell, James vs. William Edwards
Fretwell, James vs. Tomerlane Jones
Fretwell, James vs. Joseph Nixon
Fretwell, James vs. Randolph Rutland, Walter Hamilton,
  Administrator and James McNeel
Fretwell, Micajah vs. John Chaffin
Fretwell, Micajah vs. John Haggin
Fretwell, Micajah H. vs. Charles Crawford Thurmond
Fretwell, Micajah H. vs. Charles Crawford
Fretwell, Micajah H. vs. William Edwards
Fretwell, Micajah H. vs. Peter Franciscoe
Fretwell, Micajah H. vs. Daniel Henry
Fretwell, Micajah H. vs. Samuel Johnson
Fretwell, Richard vs. Thomas Foard and John Lucas
Fretwell, Richard and John Moreland vs. John Hubert and
  Hubert Reynolds
Fretwell, Richard vs. William Hurt
Fretwell, Richard and Charles Williams vs. The State
Frith, Thomas vs. Clarisa C. Boyd
Fry, Dave vs. The State
Fry, Lodowick vs. Jeremiah Pearson
Fry, Lodowick vs. Robert Williamson

Fudge, Benjamin vs. John Nisbet
Fuller, Sam vs. The State
Fuller, Stephney and Jesse Rooks vs. The State
Fuller, Thomas vs. Zadoc McGruder
Fuller, William, Alexander M. Ragland and Matthew Whitfield
    vs. Charles J. Baldwin
Fuller, William, Alexander M. Ragland and Matthew Whitfield
    vs. Moses Champion and Joseph L. Holland, Administrator
Fuller, William, Alexander M. Ragland and Matthew Whitfield
    vs. Henry St. J. Hillsman
Fuller, William, Alexander M. Ragland and Matthew Whitfield
    vs. Stephen C. Talmadge
Fullerton, James vs. The State
Fullerton, Samuel vs. L. O. Benton and Bros.
Fulton, Samuel and William F. Jordan vs. Nancy T. Davis and
    Grant D. Carter, Administrator
Fulton, Samuel vs. Griffin, Monticello and Madison Railroad
    Co.
Fulton, Samuel vs. John P. Setze
Funderburk, G. R. vs. H. C. McClure and N. B. White
Furgason, Julius vs. The State

Gaither, Bob vs. The State
Gaither, Georgia vs. The State
Gaither, Rob vs. The State
Gaither, Robert vs. Henderson and Brothers
Gant, Levi vs. The State
Gant, Oliver vs. The State
Gant, Ridley vs. The State
Gant, Tabitha vs. Levi Gant
Gardner, James vs. The State
Gardner, John E. and William Patrick vs. James J. Ross and
    William Ross, Administrator
Gardner, Patrick H. vs. Joseph Moss
Garland, Crawford vs. The State
Garland, John, Edward Garland, John Garland, Jr., Louisa
    Gordon, Hastings Garland, Thomas Garland, William Lott
    and Susan Lott vs. James Peddy, Jane Peddy, Sanders Lott
    and Elizabeth Lott
Garlington, James vs. John Baldwin
Garlington, James vs. Matilda Bonner, Minor and John Selman
Garlington, James and Samuel Crockett vs. Thomas Broadus
Garlington, James vs. Alston H. Greene and Joseph Buchannon
Garlington, James vs. Pouncey Maxey
Garner, John vs. Nancy (Smith) Garner
Garner, John vs. John Smith, Sr., Nancy (Smith) Garner,
    William Smith, Silas Gammon, Sarah (Smith) Gammon,
    Joseph Smith, Asa Smith, Cynthia Smith and John Smith,
    Executor
Garner, John W. vs. Samuel G. Cannon
Garner, Richard and William Cook vs. John Ector, Hugh W.
    Ector, Executor and Robert Freeman, Executor
Garner, Stephen vs. The State
Garret, Miles vs. Robert Mitchell
Garrett, Benjamin vs. Bartlett Brown
Garrett, Benjamin vs. Matthew Whitfield and James Whitfield
Garrett, Eleazar vs. James Edmonds
Garrett, George vs. Hamilton Brown, Peyton Gwyn and James
    Gwyn
Garrett, George S. and Talitha Garrett, Administrator vs.
    William S. Minter
Garrett, Jesse and Blount L. Garrett vs. Thomas F. Nolan
Garrett, Jesse H. and Robert Mitchell vs. Miles Garrett

151

Garrett, Jonathan and Benjamin Jordan vs. Charles Cargile
Garrett, Miles and Robert Mitchell vs. Augusta Baldwin and
  John Baldwin
Garrett, Miles vs. Alston H. Greene and Joseph Buchannon
Garrett, Miles vs. Thomas T. Walker
Garrett, Miles vs. Hugh Wyllie
Garrett, Thomas vs. Miles Garrett for use of Jones Adair
Garrett, Thomas, Jefferson Garrett and Thomas C. Garrett
  vs. The State
Garrett, Thomas C. vs. Elisha Crow
Garrett, Thomas C. vs. Richard Flemister
Garrett, Thomas C. vs. Henry George
Garrett, Thomas C. vs. Thomas Greer
Garrett, Thomas C. vs. Thomas J. Pritchett, Alfred
  Pritchett and George Pritchett
Garrett, Thomas C. vs. G. W. Shaw
Garrett, Thomas C. vs. Thomas J. Smith and William M. Broddus
Garrett, Thomas C., Shadwick McMichael, James M. Williams,
  Robert Brown, Pleasant M. Compton, Nathan T. Slaughter,
  Maximillian H. Hutchinson, S. J. McMichael, Silas Grubbs,
  John E. Langston, Hartwell W. B. Freeman, Bird Bryant,
  Francis M. Swanson and Isaac Langston vs. The State
Garrett, William and Stephen W. McClendon vs. Hammond and
  Alexander
Gary, Matthias G. vs. Alexander Herren
Gary, William vs. Garland Dawkins
Gary, William vs. Robert Gordon
Gaston, Charles B. vs. The State
Gaston, Charles R., Leonidas R. Price, Clifton Whitfield
  and Fleming Ward vs. The State
Gaston, George M. T. and Elizabeth Gaston vs. William Maxey
Gaston, George M. T. vs. Charles H. Stilwell
Gaston, George M. T. vs. Charles W. C. Wright
Gaston, Henry W. vs. James C. Bartlett
Gaston, Henry W. and Richard Flemister vs. Thomas M. Darnall
Gaston, Henry W. vs. George W. Holland and Hugh P.
  Kirkpatrick
Gaston, Henry W., William J. Goolsby, Cincinnatus L. Goolsby,
  and William O. Edmondson vs. Jonas W. Holland
Gaston, Hudson and Thomas Gaston vs. The State
Gaston, James vs. William Hammet
Gaston, James vs. Shadrach McMichael
Gaston, Kate (alias Kate Brazeal) vs. The State
Gaston, Lizzie and Charley Gaston vs. J. C. Porter and F. R.
  Porter
Gaston, Thomas vs. The State
Gates, Carney vs. The State
Gathright, Wilson, Benjamin F. Keene and Thomas Redding vs.
  Hosea Johnson
Gauther, Peter, Jeremiah Pearson, Eli Glover, Jesse Loyall
  and Norborne B. Powell vs. Thomas Grant, Daniel Grant,
  Executor, Thomas Grant, Executor and Peter Grinnell,
  Executor
Gautier, Peter vs. John Michael
Gay, Elbert vs. Michael Barry
Gay, Elbert H., John Webb and Mathew Whitfield vs. Anthony
  Dyer and John R. Dyer, Executor
Gay, Elbert H. vs. Samuel Rollins
Gay, F. H. and M. Louisa Gay vs. John W. Lindsey
Gay, Franklin H., Isaac L. Parker and Wiley Phillips vs.
  Abner Bartlett
Gay, Gilbert vs. Benjamin Barnes
Gay, Gilbert vs. Isaac Phillips

Gay, Hilliard M. vs. Jackson Graham
Gay, Hilliard M. vs. The State
Gay, J. W. and E. H. Gay vs. W. H. Thompson
Gay, John W. vs. Isham Kelly
Gay, Jordan vs. Henry W. Evans
Gay, Milledge M., Sherrod H. Gay and Charles E. F. W.
   Campbell vs. Anthony Dyer and John R. Dyer, Executor
Gay, Sherod H. vs. William H. Capers
Gay, Sherod H. vs. Francis H. Cone
Gay, Sherod H. vs. John Graves and John Donaldson
Gay, Sherod H. vs. Mary Harrell
Gay, Sherod H. vs. Robert J. Henderson
Gay, Sherod H. vs. Christopher Hobson, John Willson,
   Administrator and Harriet H. Hobson, Administrator
Gay, Sherod H. vs. John Hutchins
Gay, Sherod H. vs. Bolin L. Jeffers
Gay, Sherod H. vs. Henry Mitchell
Gay, Sherod H. vs. Valentine Nash
Gay, Sherod H. and Fleming Jordan vs. Isaac L. Parker and
   Maximillian H. Hutchison, Administrator
Gay, Sherod H. vs. Henry Pennington
Gay, Sherod H. vs. Charles D. Ramey
Gay, Sherrod H. vs. Benjamin W. Banks
Gay, Sherrod H. vs. Samuel Butts, John Lucas, Administrator
   and William Lee, Administrator
Gay, Sherrod H. vs. William Cook and William A. Moore
Gay, Sherwood H. vs. Richard Strother
Gearrett, Jesse vs. Matthew Wells for use of Banjamin Smith
Geiger, Freeman vs. The State
Geiger, Harman H. vs. Henry Boon
Geiger, Harmon H. vs. Isaac L. Walton
Geiger, James W., Harman H. Geiger and Lewis W. Pon,
   Executor vs. Mathew Whitfield, John F. Patterson,
   Executor, Leroy Willson, Executor and Pleasant Willson,
   Executor
Geiger, Man vs. The State
Geiger, Margaret C. vs. Lewis W. Pou
Geiger, Randal C. and Margaret Wardlow vs. Charles E. Aiken
George, America vs. The State
George, Franklin vs. Elliott R. Chamberlain
George, Franklin vs. Braxton R. Ezell
George, Franklin vs. Jeremiah Nute
George, Franklin vs. William H. Preston
George, Franklin vs. David A. Vason
George, Franklin vs. James H. Wiley
George, Henry vs. Mary Harris
George, Henry vs. James Patterson
George, Henry vs. William A. Reid
George, Henry and Hugh Wise vs. The State
George, Henry vs. George Stringfellow
George, Jeptha V., John Reid and Hugh Porter vs. Pleasant
   Stovall
George, Merina vs. Henry George
George, William vs. Zachary Pope
Georgia Printing Co. vs. Benjamin Conley
Germain, William vs. Cross Harris
Germain, William vs. Henry Kirby
Gibbs, Elhanan vs. John Buchannon, Joseph Buchannon,
   Administrator and Priscilla Buchannon, Administrator
Gibbs, Elhanan vs. Boze Maxey
Gibbs, Pheolus, Zachery Gibbs, Achsah (?) Gibbs, Elhannon
   Thomas Philpot, William Keener and Bastiti Keener vs.
   The State

153

Gibson, Eliza vs. Davis McCoy
Gibson, John C. vs. Moses Alexander
Gibson, John C. vs. Pointun Ashmore for use of Jesse Jeter
Gibson, John C., Henry Walker and Fleming Jordan vs.
  William V. Burney
Gibson, John C. vs. Jeremiah Callahan
Gibson, John C. vs. Central Bank of Georgia
Gibson, John C. and Henry Barnwell vs. Jonas H. Holland
Gibson, John C. and Marnock Glazier vs. John McEntire
Gibson, John C. and Marnoch Glazier vs. James Pollard
Gibson, John C. vs. John C. H. Reid
Gibson, John C., James L. Maddux and William D. Maddux vs.
  Mary E. Robey (Minor) and Wiley Phillips, Guardian for
  use of Bartley Walker
Giles, John J. vs. The State
Giles, R. C. vs. The State
Giles, Robinson vs. The State
Giles, Thomas, Jr. vs. Thomas Giles, Richard Whatley,
  Administrator and John Giles, Administrator
Gill, George vs. The State
Gill, William vs. Fielding W. Arnold
Gill, William vs. William Biscoe for use of Edwin Chambers
Gill, William vs. Daniel Coleman
Gill, William vs. James K. Daniel and John W. Porter for
  use of James Kirkpatrick
Gill, William vs. Alston H. Greene and Henry H. Cook
Gill, William vs. John Hill, Augustin Slaughter and
  Charles Labuzan
Gill, William vs. Joseph Johnson
Gill, William, Jeremiah Davis and John Malpass vs. John
  T. Lawrence, Daniel Rapelye and William R. Smith
Gill, William and William Cook vs. Edmond Loyd, Margaret
  (Loyd) Norwood, Administrator, John S. Drew, Administra-
  tor and John Norwood, Administrator
Gill, William and John Malpass vs. Robert Malone
Gill, William, Jeremiah Davis and John Malpass vs. Benjamin
  Marshall
Gill, William vs. Thomas McCarten
Gill, William and John Malpass vs. McKinzie and Bennoch
Gill, William vs. Joseph P. Penick
Gill, William, Jeremiah Davis and John Malpass vs. Andrew
  Rankin
Gill, William vs. Samuel Shy
Gill, William, Jeremiah Davis and John Malpass vs. William
  Sims and Charles D. Williams
Gill, William vs. The State
Gill, William, Jeremiah Davis and John Malpass vs. Phillip
  Thurmond
Gill, William vs. Richard Wade
Gill, William, Jeremiah Davis and John Malpass vs. Giles
  Whitney
Gill, William and John Malpass vs. Charles Williamson,
  Seaborn Jones and Tomlinson Fort
Gill, William, Jeremiah Davis and John Malpass vs. William
  W. Woolsey, Abraham M. Woolsey, John M. Woolsey and
  William C. Woolsey
Gillam, John vs. The State
Gillcoat, Hannamah, Azariah Gillcoat, John Robinson and
  James Ellis vs. John Hardwick
Gilleland, Thomas vs. William Bennett and William Burks for
  the use of John Woodall
Gilleland, Thomas vs. Isaac Carter
Gillespie, John vs. Samuel Shields

Gillis, Kenneth vs. Anthony Dyer
Gilmore, John and Brice Miller vs. Jeremiah W. Ray and
  Charles Labuzan
Gilmore, John vs. John J. Smith
Gilmore, Natley vs. James Smith
Gilmore, Notley and Robert Gilmore vs. John Smith and
  Maliciah Murden
Gilmore, Robert vs. John Lucas
Gilmore, Samuel, Elizabeth Gilmore, Executor, David Gilmore,
  Executor and Sanford M. Gilmore, Executor vs. Mathew
  Whitfield
Gilmore, Thomas vs. The State
Gilmore, Wilie vs. Abner Bartlett
Gilmore, Wilie vs. Henry George
Gilmore, Willis vs. Wilson Gilbert
Gilstrap, Jeremiah M. and Shelly F. Downs vs. James B.
  Howard and Lewis Lynch
Gilstrap, John vs. The State
Gilstrap, Lee vs. The State
Gilstrap, Love vs. The State
Glascock, Thomas and Peter Donaldson vs. Arthur L. Simms
Glass, Hubeard vs. Nimrod Vinson
Glass, James vs. Hardy Lassiter
Glass, James vs. Henry Walker
Glass, James L. vs. John Durdin
Glawson, Joseph, William Little, Jeremiah Miller and Joseph
  Meeks vs. The State
Glawson, L. C. vs. The State
Glazier, Wesley vs. Absalom Kennedy
Glenn, Little P. vs. The State
Glenn, Matthew H. vs. Thomas Beal
Glenn, Matthew H. vs. William Biscoe
Glissen, John vs. The State
Glover, Adaline vs. The State
Glover, Allen vs. John W. Pitts
Glover, Augustus L. vs. The State
Glover, Bill vs. The State
Glover, Bob vs. The State
Glover, Charles vs. The State
Glover, Christopher vs. The State
Glover, Dennis vs. The State
Glover, Ebenezer vs. Sarah Glover
Glover, Ebenezer I. and Henry Glover vs. Alfred Shorter
Glover, Edenborough vs. The State
Glover, Eli vs. Michael Kennymore
Glover, Eli vs. Clement Molliere for use of Jeremiah Pearson
Glover, Eli, Benjamin Edmondson, Joseph McBride, Edmond
  Green, Robert Roby, Thomas Higginbotham, William Robert-
  son, Allen McClendon and Thomas Brown vs. The State
Glover, Eli S. vs. John R. Dyer
Glover, Eveline vs. The State
Glover, Frances vs. The State
Glover, Frank and Genie Benton vs. The State
Glover, Gena vs. The State
Glover, George vs. The State
Glover, Henry vs. John M. Adams, William P. Adams and
  James C. Fargo
Glover, Henry vs. William S. Hurd and Anson Hungerford, Jr.
Glover, Henry vs. Wilie Peddy
Glover, Henry vs. The State
Glover, Henry vs. Leroy M. Wiley, William G. Lane and Hugh
  R. Bank
Glover, Henry S. and David Merriwather vs. Benjamin Barron

Glover, Henry S. vs. David Meriwether, Sr., David Meriwether, Jr., Executor and Matilda Meriwether, Executor
Glover, James vs. The State
Glover, James P. vs. Reuben C. Shorter
Glover, James P. vs. Edwin Snyder
Glover, Jenette vs. The State
Glover, John vs. James H. Shy and Mary C. (Kirby) Shy
Glover, John J. vs. Jonas H. Holland
Glover, Lewis vs. The State
Glover, Louis vs. W. W. Holland
Glover, Mary Jane vs. The State
Glover, Mathew vs. The State
Glover, Mathew, B. T. Digby and James T. Lewis, Administrator vs. W. D. Wynn
Glover, Mattie vs. The State
Glover, Milton P. vs. Joel Daws
Glover, Mitchell vs. The State
Glover, Peter vs. The State
Glover, Reese vs. The State
Glover, Rich vs. The State
Glover, Richard vs. The State
Glover, Robert (alias Blute Glover) vs. The State
Glover, Roy vs. The State
Glover, Sol and Mollie Goodman vs. The State
Glover, Tom vs. M. E. Campbell
Glover, Tom vs. The State
Glover, Will and Mack Allen vs. The State
Glover, William Henry vs. The State
Goddard, Austin and Charles G. Murdock vs. Cheeves Newhall and Joseph Eveleth
Goodard, Austin and Charles G. Murdock vs. William Tuckerman and Gustavus Tuckerman
Goddard, Austin vs. James Wade and John Knight, Administrator
Godkin, John R. vs. William Ingraham
Godkin, John R. vs. Loyall and Andrews
Godkin, John R. and William M. Holland vs. P. P. Lovejoy and John D. Lovejoy, Administrator
Godkin, John R., John C. Gibson and James M. Williams, Executor vs. Jeremiah Pearson and Samuel H. Dean, Administrator
Godley, James vs. William Cook
Godley, James vs. Nathaniel Deane
Godley, James vs. Caleb Woodley
Godley, James M. and John Willson vs. Burton B. Hill
Godley, James M. vs. John Hill
Godwin, Mary H. vs. James A. Meriwether
Godwin, Samuel vs. Honor Odom
Goff, Garlin vs. John Dent
Goggans, J. M. vs. A. M. Williams
Goggans, Samuel vs. The State
Goggins, Samuel vs. William Melrose
Goodman, Isaac and Wesley A. Snell vs. John B. Ross and Co.
Goodman, John T. and A. F. White vs. John Head for use of Officers of Court
Goodman, Richard H. vs. The State
Goodman, Wiley vs. David M. Langston
Goodwin, William H. and Henry Haynes vs. Henry Pearson, Jr., William Gilbert and Felix H. Gilbert
Goolsby, Allen vs. Simeon Hyde and George Cleveland
Goolsby, Amarintha vs. The State
Goolsby, Anderson vs. The State
Goolsby, Artemus vs. Jonas H. Holland

156

Goolsby, Artemus vs. Samuel D. Varner
Goolsby, Braxton E., Carden J. Goolsby and Sarah Campbell
  vs. L. A. Mercer
Goolsby, Carden R. vs. R. J. Brown and Martha E. Brown,
  Administrator
Goolsby, Carden R. vs. P. W. Dorsett, Crawford H. Greer,
  Administrator and James Dorsett, Administrator
Goolsby, Cardin vs. Francis Burke
Goolsby, Cardin vs. Mary Hollifield
Goolsby, Cardin R., Sr. vs. George H. Knapp
Goolsby, Charles vs. The State
Goolsby, Charley vs. The State
Goolsby, Cincinattus L. vs. Samuel Hall
Goolsby, Crit vs. The State
Goolsby, Dan vs. The State
Goolsby, Eberhart and F. C. Goolsby vs. John B. Gordon
Goolsby, Edenboro vs. The State
Goolsby, F. C. vs. Mrs. M. E. Cochran
Goolsby, F. C. vs. W. T. Holland and Walter L. Zachry,
  Administrator
Goolsby, F. C. vs. The State
Goolsby, Grant vs. The State
Goolsby, J. B. vs. W. F. Jordan
Goolsby, J. B. and James Henderson vs. William S. McMichael
Goolsby, J. K. vs. D. J. Baer
Goolsby, James vs. James L. Maddux
Goolsby, James vs. The State
Goolsby, James B., Cardin Goolsby, Administrator and
  Kirby Goolsby, Administrator vs. Stephen W. Beasley
Goolsby, James B. and Carden Goolsby vs. The State
Goolsby, John vs. John Hill, Augustin Slaughter and Charles
  Labuzan
Goolsby, John and John R. Dyer vs. Fleming Mobley
Goolsby, John vs. The State
Goolsby, John Henry vs. The State
Goolsby, John K. vs. W. T. Holland and W. L. Zachry,
  Administrator
Goolsby, John K. vs. Warren Wallace and Co.
Goolsby, John K. vs. Wilcox, Gibbs and Co.
Goolsby, John N. vs. Abner Chapman, Augustus W. Lane,
  Executor and Abner C. Dozier, Executor
Goolsby, Julia E. and John K. Goolsby vs. James Watson and
  Felix Walker
Goolsby, Kirby, Leroy F. Jarrel and Joseph Philips vs.
  William A. Banister
Goolsby, Kirby and James Johnston vs. James W. Y. Walton
Goolsby, Mat and Charles Goolsby vs. The State
Goolsby, Mollie vs. The State
Goolsby, Ned vs. The State
Goolsby, Oliver vs. The State
Goolsby, Richard vs. Elizabeth Goolsby
Goolsby, Richard and William Nelson vs. Isaac Scott, James
  D. Carhart and William Carhart
Goolsby, Rick vs. The State
Goolsby, Ross vs. The State
Goolsby, Samuel, Joshua Goolsby and Pleasant Goolsby vs.
  Joseph C. Glenn
Goolsby, Seely vs. Martha Thomas
Goolsby, Sherman vs. The State
Goolsby, Simon vs. The State
Goolsby, Thomas vs. Strong and Herbert
Goolsby, Thomas vs. Ellemander Warbington
Goolsby, Tom vs. The State

Goolsby, Tom Alf vs. The State
Goolsby, Trump vs. The State
Goolsby, Wade B. vs. W. T. Holland and Walter L. Zachery
Goolsby, Will vs. The State
Goolsby, William vs. John Freeman
Goolsby, William vs. John C. H. Reid
Goolsby, William vs. William Simmons
Goolsby, William J. vs. Artemus Goolsby
Goolsby, William J. vs. Cardin Goolsby
Goore, Thomas vs. William R. Wheeles
Gordan, John vs. The State
Gordan, Lawyer vs. The State
Gordon, Arthur vs. The State
Gordon, Clayt vs. The State
Gordon, George Dyer vs. The State
Gordon, N. W. vs. Smith and Broddus
Gordon, Nathaniel W., John T. C. Towns, Richard C. Clayton
   and Thomas J. Knight vs. Justices of Court for use of
   Garner Doggett (Orphans of)
Gordon, Reuben, Sr. vs. Charles H. Stilwell, Robert Kellam
   and Alfred Brewer
Gordon, Robert, Fish McMichael and Mitchael Tomlinson vs.
   The State
Gordon, Thomas vs. The State
Gore, Thomas and Rice P. Knowles vs. Lewis Gibson
Gore, Thomas vs. James Gunn
Goss, Benjamin vs. John H. Mallory
Goss, Churchwill C. vs. Rufus Broom
Gould H. S. vs. W. C. Clark
Grace, James and Richard Lowell vs. Thaddeus Holt,
   Thaddeus G. Holt, Executor and Macerniss Goode, Executor
Grace, James and Uriah Taylor vs. Henry Stephens
Grace, James vs. Leroy M. Wiley and Thomas W. Baxter
Grace, Joshua and Joseph Heard vs. James Beaty
Grace, Joshua vs. Leonard Burford
Grace, Joshua and John Moore vs. Thomas P. Carnes
Grace, Joshua vs. Lee Griggs
Grace, Mary (Bollinger) vs. James Grace
Graham, James and Richmond Williamson Wynn vs. Joel Towns,
   Ann Towns, Administrator and Carter B. Harrison,
   Administrator
Grant, Alonzo vs. The State
Grant, Earnest vs. The State
Grant, Fannie vs. The State
Grant, Ridley vs. The State
Grant, Samuel, Talitha Grant, Cornelius Grant, Nathaniel
   Grant and William Avington vs. The State
Grant, Thomas vs. Jonathan Ellis, Jr.
Grant, Thomas vs. Howel Tatum
Graves, Davenport and James Bunyard vs. Tandy W. Key
Graves, J. B. and Sumner W. Bacon vs. Francis A. Leverett
Graves, John and John Donaldson vs. Charles Cargile
Graves, John vs. Abner Chapman, Jr.
Graves, John vs. John Ector, Robert Freeman, Executor
   and Hugh W. Ector, Executor
Graves, John vs. Sherod H. Gay
Graves, John vs. Absalom Hearne for use of Richard Whitehead
Graves, John vs. Peter Laurens
Graves, John vs. James Lewis
Graves, John vs. William Mason
Graves, John vs. Richard Morgan
Graves, John and John W. Compton vs. The State
Graves, John vs. James L. Weekes

Graves, John vs. James L. Weekes
Graves, John, John W. Compton and James Garlington vs.
  Leroy M. Wiley and Thomas W. Baxter
Gray, Mrs. A. T. vs. Kelly Robinson and Co.
Gray, A. T. and T. M. Jordan vs. W. A. Kelly
Gray, Adaline vs. The State
Gray, Mrs. Annie C. vs. Mrs. S. L. Lannin
Gray, John, Jr. vs. John Rainey
Graybill, Henry vs. Commissioners of Milledgeville
Graybill, Henry vs. John Dawson, Benjamin Talliferro,
  Administrator and Ann Dawson, Administrator for use of
  Noe Dodridge
Graybill, Henry vs. Allen Greene
Graybill, Henry vs. Elijah N. Hascall and David Hascall
Graybill, Henry vs. Jesse James
Graybill, Henry vs. Merrill and Parkhurst
Graybill, Henry vs. Thomas Smith, William Smith, Alton
  Pemberton, Administrator and Susan M. Smith, Administrator
Graybill, Henry, Jr., Lewis Gregory and Royal Clay vs. John
  Knight for use of Thomas Bullard
Graybill, James S. vs. James D. Carhart, William B. Carhart
  and John B. Storr
Grear, Thomas vs. The State
Greaves, Joseph D. vs. Daniel McDowell
Green, Bolden vs. The State
Green, Burrell vs. Milton Antony
Green, Burwell vs. Gilbert Longstreet
Green, G. F. vs. The State
Green, Gilbert vs. The State
Green, J. M. vs. S. D. Smith
Green, James vs. Joseph Henderson
Green, James M. vs. The State
Green, Lucinda vs. The State
Green, Lucinda vs. The State
Green, Raleigh vs. James T. Hays
Green, Thomas vs. Anthony Dyer
Green, Thomas and Charles Crawford vs. Elisha Brothers
Green, Thomas vs. Aaron Morgan
Green, Thomas vs. James Speir and John W. Bridges
Green, Wayman vs. The State
Green, Will vs. The State
Green, William M. vs. James M. Beeland for use of
  Frederick D. Fanning
Green, William M. vs. Franklin George
Green, William M. vs. Reuben T. Sanders
Green, William M. vs. John Stewart
Green, William M. and William W. J. Lowrey vs. Matthew
  Whitifeld, John F. Patterson, Executor, Leroy M. Wilson,
  Executor and Pleasant Wilson, Executor
Greene, Bowling, Wiley Clayton and Thomas Clayton vs. The
  State
Greene, Burwell and James Greene vs. Jesse Stephens
Greene, Edmund vs. Thomas J. Black
Greene, George vs. Lucius T. Cadwell
Greene, John vs. The State
Greene, Raleigh vs. John N. Birch
Greene, Raleigh vs. James Irwin and Felix Bryan
Greene, Raleigh vs. Benjamin M. Peeples
Greene, Robert vs. The State
Greene, Thomas vs. Thomas G. Gordon
Greene, William vs. The State
Greene, William M. and William W. J. Loury vs. Matthew
  Whitfield

Greene, William P. vs. Eli Glover
Greene, William P. vs. Aaron Talmadge
Greenwood, John vs. The State
Greer, Adam vs. The State
Greer, Benjamin and Armstead Dodson, Executor vs. Stephen
  Potts and Moses Potts, Administrator
Greer, Benjamin vs. James S. Trimble
Greer, C. H. and John McCullough vs. James B. Goolsby
Greer, Frank and John Hazelip vs. The State
Greer, G. D. vs. The State
Greer, George vs. The State
Greer, Gilbert D. and John Greer vs. Sarah (Foreman) Burton
Greer, Gilbert D. vs. Isaac Foreman
Greer, Gilbert D., James Digby and Richard Barret vs. The
  State
Greer, Gilbert D. vs. Avington Williams
Greer, Mrs. Ida and W. F. Jordan, Administrator vs. J. H.
  Kelly
Greer, Jack, Clark Greer, Andrew Greer and Jonas Greer vs.
  The State
Greer, James vs. The State
Greer, James A. vs. Isaac Hill
Greer, James A. vs. Carrington Knight
Greer, James A. and Thomas F. Nolan vs. Bedford Shorter
  for use of Gilbert Longstreet
Greer, Jim vs. The State
Greer, Joe vs. The State
Greer, John vs. Robert Brown
Greer, John vs. Anthony Dyer and Otis Dyer
Greer, John vs. Theophilus Pye
Greer, John vs. The State
Greer, John R., Thomas Greer and Hezekiah Clay vs. The State
Greer, Leroy vs. The State
Greer, Lowell vs. The State
Greer, Mat vs. The State
Greer, Pep vs. The State
Greer, Robert vs. The State
Greer, Thomas vs. Anthony Dyer and Otis Dyer
Greer, Thomas vs. Simon H. Saunders
Greer, Thomas vs. The State
Greer, Will vs. The State
Greer, William vs. The State
Gregg, Jacob and Henry Heald vs. Evan P. Taylor
Gregory, Lewis vs. John Dawson and Allen Green
Gregory, Mathew vs. Champion Easter
Gregory, Mathew and Pleasant Williamson vs. William Griggs
  for use of Wilie Abercrombie
Gregory, Mathew vs. Burwell Jourden
Gregory, Matthew vs. James Dupree
Gregory, Matthew vs. Elizabeth Gregory for use of John
  Middlebrooks
Gregory, Matthew and Pleasant Williamson vs. John Stephens
Gregory, Richard V. vs. John Hill, Augustin Slaughter and
  Charles Labuzan
Georgory, Richard V. and Charles Morgan vs. Abram Jewett
Gregory, Richard V., James M. Gregory and John Freeman vs.
  Daniel Lloyd
Gregory, Richard V., Yancy Thornton, James W. Morgan,
  Thomas C. Taylor, Matthew Gregory, William Morgan and
  Charles Morgan vs. The State
Gregory, Richard V. vs. Cornelius D. Terhune
Gregory, William B. and Thomas J. Burney, Administrator vs.
  Benjamin Mosely for use of Thomas L. Bonner

Gresham, David vs. Jesse Bledsoe
Gresham, David vs. William Gill, Jeremiah Davis and John
  Malpass
Gresham, Isham, James Gresham, Jonathan Benton and Allen
  McLean vs. The State
Gresham, James vs. James Mullins
Gresham, Sellers vs. The State
Grier, Benjamin vs. Rufus Broom
Grier, G. D. vs. The State
Grier, George vs. The State
Grier, Giles vs. The State
Grier, John vs. The State
Grier, John Anderson vs. The State
Grier, Sue vs. The State
Grierson, Robert vs. Henry Walker
Griffin, Banjamin vs. David Bates and Randolph Bates,
  Administrator for use of Andrew Shepherd
Griffin, Benjamin vs. Aaron Formby
Griffin, Benjamin vs. John Griffin and Sally Griffin,
  Executor
Griffin, D. R. vs. The State
Griffin, David vs. The State
Griffin, John and Reuben Edwards vs. The State
Griffin, Lydia vs. The State
Griffin, Milledge vs. The State
Griffin, Richard vs. The State
Griffins, Dick vs. The State
Griffith, Jonathan and Daniel Phillips vs. Cartley Johnson
Griffith Jonathan and Nathan Fish vs. William T. Short
Griffith, Jonathan vs. Edward White
Griggs, Bob vs. The State
Griggs, Cincinatus W. vs. William T. Lightfoot
Griggs, Cincinatus W. vs. George Raglin
Griggs, Cincinatus W. vs. Robert J. Wynn
Griggs, Cincinnatus and Wesley Griggs vs. Jeptha J. Hammock
Griggs, Cincinnatus W. vs. Lindsey H. Durham and Francis
  M. Swanson for use of George G. Gaines
Griggs, Cincinnatus W. vs. John H. Hancock and Richard Kolb
Griggs, Cincinnatus W. vs. Richard J. Loyall and John E.
  Langston
Griggs, Cincinnatus W. vs. William Maxey and Charles S.
  Jordan
Griggs, Cincinnatus W. vs. Andrew J. Miller
Griggs, Cincinnatus W. vs. Ebenezer T. White and John H.
  Hancock
Griggs, Cincinnatus W. vs. Ebenezer T. White and William
  D. Johnson
Griggs, Frank vs. The State
Griggs, Frederick vs. The State
Griggs, Gene vs. The State
Griggs, Gus vs. The State
Griggs, J. W. vs. Robert Coleman
Griggs, J. W. vs. A. B. Small
Griggs, John vs. Norvell Billingsley, Urbun Billinglsey
  and Henry Rumble
Griggs, John vs. Middleton W. Cox and Alexander Oden,
  Guardian
Griggs, John vs. Thomas Morton
Griggs, John I. vs. Deborah M. Disbow
Griggs, John J. vs. William Dukes and Thomas Danielly
Griggs, John J. vs. Thomas B. Harwell
Griggs, Levy vs. The State
Griggs, Robert vs. James Dowdell

Grigs, Hughs vs. Elijah N. Hascall and David Hascall
Grimett, Seaborn B. vs. John Warren
Grimmet, Seaborn B. and Ambrose Phillips vs. The State
Grinnell, Peter and William V. Burney vs. William P.
  Rathbone and Alfred Baker
Grisham, David vs. Thomas Stone
Grisham, Joseph, Claborn Trussell and Daniel Trussell vs.
  The State
Groathouse, Archibald vs. John S. McCurdy
Gromet, Joseph vs. James Dickson and Co.
Gromet, Joseph vs. William Hitchcock
Gross, Ellison vs. John Singer
Gross, John and Joseph C. Post, Administrator vs. Willis
  Little
Gross, John and Joseph C. Post, Administrator vs. Grief
  Lynch
Groves, Jasper B. vs. Francis A. Leverett
Grubb, Conrad and Zachariah H. Goss vs. James Dickson
Grubb, Conrad vs. William Grubb for use of John James
Grubb, Conrad vs. Thomas Jones
Grubb, Conrad vs. David Macarrel
Grubb, Conrad vs. James Newland
Grubb, Conrad vs. William Sheets
Grubbs, Elijah C. and George W. Shockley, Administrator vs.
  William W. Grubbs
Grubbs, Elisha and Elizabeth Grubbs, Administrator vs.
  John R. Godkin
Grubbs, Elisha and Elizabeth Grubbs, Administrator vs.
  William A. Lofton
Grubbs, Elisha and George W. Shockley vs. William D. Stanton
Grubbs, Elisha c., William W. Grubbs, Administrator and
  George W. Shockley, Administrator vs. Silas Grubbs
Grubbs, John W. vs. Hugh P. Kirkpatrick
Grubbs, John W., Mildred A. Grubbs and Silas Grubbs vs.
  Stephen C. Talmadge
Grubbs, Mildred A. vs. British and American Mortgage Co.
Grubbs, Richard vs. The State
Grubbs, Silas vs. James P. Couch
Grubbs, Silas vs. Ezekiel Crabtree
Grubbs, Silas vs. John Hines
Grubbs, Silas vs. Hugh P. Kirkpatrick
Grubbs, Silas vs. Planters Manufacturing Co.
Grubbs, Silas and Craton A. J. Flemister vs. Mauris
  Wilkinson
Grubbs, Thomas E. and Joseph Grubbs vs. The State
Grubbs, Wiley B. vs. The State
Guin, John vs. Micajah Williamson
Gun, Gabriel vs. The State
Gunn, Gabriel vs. Micajah N. Fretwell
Gunn, Gabriel vs. Micajah Harris
Gunn, Gabriel vs. George Mathews, Jr.
Gunn, James vs. The State
Gunn, Thomas and John Buis vs. Augustin Slaughter and
  Charles Labuzan
Gunnels, Alsea (alias Aley Gunalds) and John W. Wyatt vs.
  William Carter
Gunnels, Joseph vs. William Nelson and William Knight
Gunnels, Pittman vs. Robert Owen
Gunter, M. A. vs. The State
Guy, Charles and Lewis Thompson vs. B. H. Sanders and Co.
Gwyn, Bailey vs. John Billups, William Billups, Executor
  and Susannah Billups, Executor

Hackney, Emmett vs. The State
Hackney, James B. and Sarah S. Hackney vs. James Whitfield
Hackney, Stephen, William Gill, John Gill and Eli S. Shorter
vs. William Williams
Hadaway, Lizzie vs. George W. Hadaway for use of Officers
of Court
Hadley, Anderson vs. The State
Hadley, Thomas and John W. Compton, Administrator vs. John
Crowell
Hadley, Thomas, John W. Compton, Administrator and Mary C.
Compton, Administrator vs. William Greene for use of
William Armstrong
Hadley, Thomas, John W. Compton, Administrator and Mary
Compton, Administrator vs. Simon Hadley
Hadley, Thomas vs. Thomas Jones
Hadley, Thomas J. vs. Mary C. Compton
Hairston, Charles A. and Eli H. Walker, Guardian vs. James
M. Johnston and Michael Roberts
Hairston, Charles C. and Moses B. Hairston vs. Cardin
Goolsby
Hairston, Charles C. and Moses B. Hairston vs. The State
Hairston, Hugh B. and John Hairston vs. Samuel Clay
Hairston, Moses B. and Elisa M. C. Hairston, Administrator
Vs. Exekiel Crabtree
Hairston, Moses B. and Thomas K. Slaughter vs. Jubil C.
Cochran
Hairston, Moses B. vs. Edmond B. Darden
Hairston, Moses B., Thomas K. Slaughter, Charles C. Hairston
and Lucretia Hairston vs. John Folds, George Folds,
Administrator and Thomas Folds, Administrator
Hairston, Moses B. vs. Stephen B. Marshall and Henry
McKavitte
Hairston, Moses B. vs. William S. Hurd and Anson Hungerford
Hairston, Moses B. vs. Joseph W. Slaughter
Hairston, Moses B. and Eliza Hairston, Administrator vs.
William Maxey and Joshua Hill
Hairston, Moses B. and Elizabeth Hairston vs. Thomas K.
Slaughter
Hairston, Moses B., Lewis Worten, Administrator and Eliza
M. C. Hairston, Administrator vs. Anthony Storr
Hairston, Thomas vs. William A. Redd
Hales, Thomas vs. The State
Hall, Elizabeth D. and William O. Edmondson vs. Martin
Puckett and James W. Vaughn, Administrator
Hall, Elizabeth N. and C. W. C. Wright vs. Simeon Scales
Hall, James N. and David A. Reese, Administrator vs. Samual
S. Farrar and John K. Hays
Hall, James N. vs. Jonas H. Holland
Hall, James N. and David A. Reese, Administrator vs. David
Meriwether
Hall, James N. and William Goolsby vs. Bluford M. Walton
Hall, John H. vs. The State
Hall, Seaborn L. vs. The State
Hallmark, John vs. Alford King
Ham, Stephen and Daniel Dossey vs. Joshua Callaway and
Elizabeth Callaway, Administrator
Ham, William and John Ham vs. Andrew Low, Robert Isaacs
and James McHenry
Hamel, James, Jonathan Reeves and Hugh Hamel vs. Edward
Echols
Hamel, John vs. William Stevens
Hames, Joshua vs. Charles Bailey
Hames, Joshua vs. Robert Beasley and Palemon L. Weekes

163

Hames, Joshua vs. Hamilton Brown
Hames, Joshua vs. Thomas B. Erwin
Hames, Joshua vs. Thomas Grant, Daniel Grant, Executor,
Thomas Grant, Executor and Peter Grinnell, Executor
Hames, Joshua vs. Thomas Johnson
Hames, Joshua vs. Julius C. B. Mitchell for use of Uriah
G. Mitchell
Hames, Joshua and Caleb W. Key vs. Jane B. Moreland, Minor
and Thomas Hightower, Guardian
Hames, Joshua and Walter H. Mitchell vs. John G. Nelson,
Charles G. Carleton and William H. Stewart
Hames, Joshua vs. Jeremiah Pearson
Hames, Joshua vs. Warren Phelps
Hames, Joshua vs. James Whitfield
Hames, Joshua vs. Wiley Wilson
Hames, Joshua vs. William T. Young
Hamil, Hugh and John Hamil vs. Thomas Eckles
Hamil, Hugh vs. Greene McAfee, Jonathan Anderson, Adminis-
trator, Phebe (McAfee) Downey, Administrator and Calvin
Downey, Administrator
Hamilton, Amos vs. Bardwell Billings
Hamilton, Andrew M. vs. John McKinne
Hamilton, Andrew M. vs. The State
Hamilton, Andrew M. vs. William F. Steele
Hamilton, Andrew M. vs. John Willson
Hamilton, David vs. Robert Allen
Hamilton, David vs. Alfred Shepherd
Hamilton, George vs. The State
Hamilton, James vs. Seth Nims
Hamilton, John vs. The State
Hamilton, Thomas P. vs. Augusta Baldwin and John Baldwin
Hamilton, Thomas P. vs. John Brown
Hamilton, Thomas P. vs. Samuel Butts and John Lucas,
Administrator
Hamilton, Thomas P. vs. George Clower
Hamilton, Thomas P. vs. Thomas Napier
Hamilton, Thomas P. vs. William Penn
Hamilton, Thomas P. vs. George Powell
Hamilton, Thomas P. vs. Robert Roby and Timothy Robey,
Administrator
Hamilton, Thomas P. vs. James Waits
Hamilton, Thomas P. vs. Matthew Whitfield and James Whit-
field
Hamilton, Thomas P. vs. John Willson
Hammel, Simeon vs. The State
Hammer, Wingfield and Richardson Hammer vs. The State
Hammett, Absalom and James Armor vs. Gabriel Colley for use
of George Hughs
Hammett, James vs. John Jones
Hammett, James vs. Patton Wise, William Traylor, Executor,
Parham Lindsay, Executor and Elizabeth Wise, Executor
Hammett, William vs. James Dickson and Co.
Hammett, William vs. William Harris
Hammett, William vs. John H. Lowe
Hammett, William and Zacheus Phillips vs. Harrison Young
Hammock, Asa C. and Benjamin Hammock vs. Job Chandler,
Aaron B. Marvin and Henry Waldeon
Hammock, Asa C. and Benjamin Hammock vs. Edward Y. Hill
Hammock, Asa C. and Benjamin Hammock vs. Joshua Hill
Hammock, Asa C. vs. Jack A. Johnson
Hammock, Benjamin vs. John Baldwin
Hammock, Benjamin vs. Thomas Carter
Hammock, Benjamin vs. Hardy Crawford

Hammock, Benjamin vs. Thomas Doles
Hammock, Benjamin vs. James D. Head
Hammock, Benjamin vs. William Johnston and Lancetor Johnston
Hammock, Benjamin vs. Kellam and Maxey
Hammock, Benjamin and Thomas H. B. Rivers vs. Wyatt Smith
Hammock, Benjamin vs. John Walker for use of Callan and
   Robson
Hammock, John vs. Elisha Lake
Hammock, Willoughby vs. Henry Lane
Hammond, Mortimore L. and Nancy W. (Puckett) Hammond vs.
   William Wilson
Hammond, Nancy W. (Puckett) and Mortimore L. Hammond vs.
   John W. Pitts
Hammond, Thomas L. vs. William H. Beeland and Thomas Beeland
Hammons, Jesse J. and Joseph L. Holland vs. Thomas J.
   Middlebrooks
Hamp, Zeb (alias Zeb Hamilton) vs. The State
Hampton, George vs. James Cowan for use of Thomas B. Erwin
Hampton, George vs. James A. Grier and Nathaniel H. Grier
Hampton, George vs. Mary Henderson, Andrew Henderson,
   Executor and Ezekiel Alexander, Executor
Hampton, George and Littleberry Smartt vs. John Owen
Hampton, George and Littleberry Smartt vs. Reuben C. Shorter
Hamrick, James vs. Alsea Holifield
Hamrick, James vs. William Jones
Hamrick, James and Samuel Steagall vs. Robert McAfee
Hamrick, Seburn vs. James L. Weekes
Hancock, Antony vs. The State
Hancock, Isham vs. Jeremiah Pearson
Hancock, Isham vs. Burton Rucker
Hancock, William H. and William Goolsby vs. Anthony Dyer
   and John R. Dyer, Executor
Hann, James and John Hann vs. The State
Hansford, John M. and Isaac McGehee vs. John McCarter and
   George W. Henry
Hansford, John M. and Isaac McGehee vs. James M. Dunn and
   Jeremiah Clark
Hansford, John M. vs. Thomas McGehee
Hansford, John M. vs. James Myrick
Hansford, John M. vs. Jonathan Richardson
Hansford, John M. vs. William Scarbrough
Hansford, John M. vs. The State
Hansford, John M. vs. Thomas B. Stubbs
Hansford, John M. and George W. Hansford vs. Benjamin A.
   White
Hardeman, Daniel vs. The State
Hardeman, Henry vs. The State
Hardeman, Jim vs. The State
Hardeman, John Henry vs. The State
Hardeman, Will vs. The State
Harden, Silas vs. The State
Harden, William B. and Thomas Crabtree vs. James H. Roberts
Hardin, Henry vs. George Thompson
Hardin, William R. vs. William R. Mathis
Hardman, Samuel vs. The State
Hardwick, Ben vs. The State
Hardwick, Garland vs. Warren Bunn
Hardwick, Garland vs. James Holt
Hardwick, Garland and Richard Carter vs. Benjamin Keaten
Hardwick, Garland and Steth Daniel vs. Hugh McCullough
   and John Osgood, Executor
Hardwick, Garland vs. James Richardson
Hardwick, Garland vs. John Stewart

Hardwick, Garland and George Hardwick vs. Lewis B.
  Taliaferro
Hardwick, George vs. William Germany
Hardwick, George vs. Wiley Rogers
Hardwick, John vs. Gustavus Hendrick
Hardwick, John vs. The State
Hardwick, William vs. Echols Daniel
Hardy, Aquilla vs. John Jinks
Hardy, Aquilla vs. Samuel Lancaster
Hardy, Cornelius vs. Araminta Hardy
Hardy, Cornelius, William P. Hardy, Administrator and
  William P. White, Administrator vs. Susan Hardy
Hardy, D. vs. The State
Hardy, Dora A. vs. Equitable Mortgage Co.
Hardy, J. G. vs. The State
Hardy, James and Benajah Hardy vs. The State
Hardy, James and Benajah Hardy vs. William J. L. Tuggle and
  James M. Williams, Executor
Hardy, John T. vs. Davis Lane and John F. Patterson
Hardy, Miles vs. William Wallace
Hardy, Robert M., John A. Sharman, Elbert W. Baynes and
  James W. Lillard vs. The State
Hardy, William B. vs. Thomas Beall
Hardy, William B., Hugh McDonald and Henry T. Truitt vs.
  Bennet Crawford, Woody Dozier and John Heard for use of
  James Robertson and William Walker
Hardy, William B. vs. Moses Daniel
Hardy, William B. vs. Andrew Jeter
Hardy, William B. and John Robinson vs. Samuel Knox, Sr.
Hardy, William B. and Samuel Lovejoy vs. Angus Martin
Hardy, William B. and Hugh MacDonald vs. John McKenzie,
  Peter Bennoch and Thomas McDowell
Hardy, William B. vs. John Tomkins
Hardy, William P. vs. Berry T. Digby
Hardy, William P. and James Duncan vs. Allen McClendon and
  William F. Mapp, Administrator
Hargrove, Robert T. vs. John Van Wagenin
Harkness, Jonathan and Woody Dozier vs. James McClure
Harman, John and Frances Steedman vs. The State
Harmon, William vs. William Gibson
Harper, Alexander T. vs. Elizabeth Echols and Charles A.
  Dickens, Administrator
Harper, Samuel vs. Isaac Sullivant
Harper, Sarah (alias Sarah Cox) vs. Abyhugh Sewell
Harper, William and John Robertson vs. Burwell Greene and
  Nancy Green, Administrator
Harper, William vs. The State
Harper, William vs. Nicholas B. Williams
Harrel, Jethro vs. Alston H. Greene and Joseph Buchannan
Harrel, Samuel and Josiah Yarbrough vs. Robert Stacy
Harrell, Joseph vs. Jethrow Harrell
Harrell, Joseph vs. Collin Shackleford for use of Sherod
  H. Gay
Harrell, Mary and Joseph Harrell vs. James Buchanan
Harrell, Samuel and Mary Harrell vs. James Callaway
Harrell, Samuel vs. Tarlton Sheets
Harrey, William vs. The State
Harris, David vs. John Baynes
Harris, David vs. Abraham Smith and John H. Smith,
  Administrator
Harris, David vs. Matthew Whitfield, Leroy M. Willson,
  Executor, Pleasant Willson, Executor, John F. Patterson,
  Executor and William H. Mathis, Executor

Harris, Isham vs. Lemuel P. Skaggs
Harris, James (alias Jack) vs. The State
Harris, Jesse vs. Thadeus Beall and Elias Beall
Harris, Jesse vs. The State
Harris, Joel N. vs. The State
Harris, John vs. Alston H. Greene and Joseph Buchannon
Harris, Leah vs. Henry Pearson, Jr., William G. Gilbert and
    Felix H. Gilbert
Harris, Micajah and Micajah H. Fretwell vs. Redick Sims
Harris, Peter vs. William Gilbert and Felix Gilbert
Harris, Peter vs. John F. Pope
Harris, Pon vs. The State
Harris, Pugh vs. The State
Harris, Thomas vs. William Stroud
Harris, Will vs. The State
Harris, William G. vs. Willis Newton
Harris, William Y. vs. William Hannah
Harrison, Jacob vs. Felix Lewis
Harry, John and William Harry vs. Adam G. Saffold
Harry, William vs. Benjamin Jenkins
Hartsfield, Allen vs. William H. House
Hartsfield, Allen vs. Leroy Pope
Hartsfield, Moses vs. John McLea and Jackson Fitzpatrick
Hartsfield, Moses vs. Josiah Newton
Hartsfield, Warren vs. Owen Weathersbee, Richard Homes,
    Administrator and Sarah Weathersbee, Administrator
Harvel, Mason vs. Sherrod H. Gay
Harvel, Mason and Sherod H. Gay vs. John Mays
Harvell, Mason vs. The State
Harvey, Elizabeth vs. The State
Harvey, Evan J. vs. John M. Adams, William L. Adams and
    John C. Fargo
Harvey, Evan P. vs. William Maxey
Harvey, Evans J. vs. Richardson R. Stevens
Harvey, H. H. vs. Nathan H. Leverett
Harvey, James P., James Smith and Zenepheniah Harvey vs.
    Otho H. Appling and John Brown for use of John Hill
Harvey, James P. and Evan H. Powell vs. John Brown
Harvey, James P. vs. Thomas T. Napier
Harvey, Nehemiah vs. Samuel Devereaux, John W. Devereaux
    and Samuel S. Steel
Harvey, Nehemiah vs. Aron Fagan
Harvey, Nehemiah vs. Angus Morrison
Harvey, Nehemiah vs. John Moses, Ann Moses, Administrator,
    Samuel Moses, Administrator and Moses Perkins, Adminis-
    trator
Harvey, Nehemiah vs. John Roe
Harwell, Amos vs. The State
Harwell, Ernest (alias Isaac Harwell) vs. M. Benton
Harwell, J. L. vs. The State
Harwell, Joe vs. The State
Harwell, Thomas B. vs. William H. Wyatt, Jr.
Hascal, David vs. William Spence
Hascall, Elijah N. vs. Alexander Bryan
Hascall, Elijah N. vs. Joseph Buchannon
Hascall, Elijah N. vs. Abner Chapman
Hascall, Elijah N. and James A. Hascall vs. Horace
    Cunningham
Hascall, Elijah N. and Charles Cargile vs. James Godfrey
Hascall, Elijah N. vs. John Hill, Augustin Slaughter and
    Charles Labuzan
Hascall, Elijah N. and Adam Alexander vs. Lawrence Hill
    and James Reed, Administrator

Hascall, Elijah N. vs. Monticello Academy
Hascall, Elijah N., David Hascall and Joseph Johnson vs.
  Elijah Nichols, Jr. for use of William Godfrey
Hascall, Elijah N. vs. Thomas B. Peet
Hascall, Elijah N., James Hascall and David Hascall vs.
  Thomas Post
Hascall, Elijah N., David Hascall and Joseph Johnson vs.
  James Rea
Hascall, Elijah N. vs. Benjamin W. Rodgers and Co.
Hascall, Elijah N. vs. Reuben Slaughter
Hascall, Elijah N., James A. Hascall and David Hascall vs.
  Robert Walton
Hascall, J. A., David Hascall and Elijah N. Hascall vs.
  Collins and Hanah and Moses Marsh
Hascall, J. A. and D. Hascall vs. George Gilbert
Hascall, James A. vs. Armstead Atkinson
Hascall, James A. vs. John Cargile for use of John McKee
Hascall, James A. and David Hascall vs. Elisha Dyer
Hascall, James A. and David Hascall vs. George Gilbert
Hascall, James A. and Elijah N. Hascall vs. Alston H.
  Greene and Joseph Buchannon
Hascall, James A., Elijah N. Hascall and David Hascall vs.
  Alston H. Greene and Henry H. Cook
Hascall, James A., Lawson S. Holland and Elijah N. Hascall
  vs. David Henderson
Hascall, James A. and David Hascall vs. John Hill,
  Augustin Slaughter and Charles Labuzan
Hascall, James A., David Hascall, Willard Bradley and
  Israel Beckworth vs. Ralph Ketchum for use of James
  Emerson
Hascall, James A. and David Hascall vs. Thomas Lawrence,
  John J. Lawrence and Thomas G. Casey
Hascall, James A. vs. James Rea
Hascall, James A. and David Hascall vs. David Silden
Hascall, James A. vs. John K. Simmons
Hascall, James A. and Elijah N. Hascall vs. Littleberry
  Watts, Pleasant Watts, Administrator and John Bailey,
  Administrator
Hatcher, Josiah vs. Anthony Dyer
Hatcher, Josiah vs. Robert Robey and Timothy Robey,
  Administrator
Hatcher, Martin vs. The State
Hatcher, Maston vs. Thomas Dickson
Hatcher, Samuel C. and Mastin Hatcher vs. The State
Hatcher, Uriah vs. Jesse Loyall and John Andrews,
  Administrator
Hatcher, Uriah and Lawson Adams vs. The State
Harfield, Will vs. The State
Hathcock, John vs. Wiley Jones
Hattaway, Frank vs. The State
Hawk, Andrew vs. Isaac Bailey
Hawk, Andrew vs. Alston H. Greene and Joseph Buchannan
Hawk, Andrew vs. John Hill, Augustin Slaughter and
  Charles Labuzan
Hawk, Andrew vs. Lawson S. Holland
Hawk, Andrew vs. Williamson Roby and Henry Boswell
Hawk, Andrew vs. James Stratton and Asa E. Stratton
Hawk, Jacob vs. James Richards and Willis Richards
Hawk, Jacob vs. Mary Williamson
Hawk, John and Peter Hawk vs. Alston H. Greene and Joseph
  Buchanan
Hawk, John vs. Lawson S. Holland
Hawk, Peter and Andrew Hawk vs. Jeremiah Pearson

Hawk, Peter vs. James Richards and Willis Richards
Hawk, Will vs. The State
Hawkins, John W., Obadiah Belcher, Administrator and Exey
    Hawkins, Administrator vs. Alexander Hawkins
Hawkins, John W. vs. Greene B. Turner
Hawkins, Thomas vs. The State
Hawks, Peter and Jacob Hawks vs. Augusta Baldwin and John
    Baldwin
Hawthorn, Benjamin vs. Robert Galley
Hawthorn, Benjamin, Elizabeth Hawthorn, Administrator,
    Arthur Herring, Administrator, Cyril Herring, Administra-
    tor and Henry Sharp, Administrator vs. John B. Parks and
    Welcom Parks
Hawthorn, James vs. Jonathan Anderson for use of Abraham
    McAfee
Hawthorn, James vs. William L. Bond
Hay, Chesley vs. Samuel Clay
Hay, Chesley vs. Levy Newton
Hay, Leonard B. vs. The State
Hay, Stephen, Beverly Chaffin and Isaac L. Parker vs. Thomas
    H. Tuggle
Hayes, James T. and Henry Hayes, Administrator vs. James
    F. Robinson
Hayes, James T. and James F. Robinson vs. Joseph W. Walton
Hayes, James T., Nancy R. Robinson and Richard Robinson vs.
    Joseph W. Walton
Hayes, James T. vs. William Whitfield
Hayes, Martin vs. The State
Hayes, Albert G. vs. Anthony Dyer
Haynes, Henry vs. Samuel Butts, William Lee, Administrator
    and John Lucas
Haynes, Henry vs. Ebenezar H. Cummins for use of James C.
    Campbell
Haynes, Henry vs. Thomas Fitch
Haynes, Henry vs. Eli Glover and John Cashin
Haynes, Henry vs. Joel Newsom
Haynes, Henry vs. The State
Haynes, Henry vs. Jonathan Vasser
Haynes, Thomas vs. Abner Chapman
Haynes, Thomas vs. Henry D. Paine
Hays, ? vs. The State
Hays, James and Nancy Hays, Executor vs. Osborn Wilkes for
    use of Edmond Baldwin
Hays, John vs. The State
Hays, Stephen, John Robinson, John C. Watters and Isaac L.
    Parker vs. Central Bank of Georgia
Head, George vs. John E. Glover
Head, Henry and Gatewood Dunn vs. William Phelps
Head, Henry vs. Alfred Shorter
Head, Henry, George Head and John M. Pearson vs. James
    Whitfield
Head, John vs. Cornelius Atkinson
Head, John and William Head vs. James L. Beers
Head, John, William Head and James Hammett vs. Jonathan
    S. Beers
Head, John vs. James Smith for use of Daniel Lord and
    Jeremiah Pierson
Head, Lee vs. The State
Head, Richard vs. Edward Jordan for use of David Terrell
Head, W. H. and Mary A. Bridges vs. Thomas J. Bridges
Head, William vs. Abner Chapman
Head, William vs. Hawkins Huff
Head, William vs. The State

Head, William H. vs. James T. Moore for use of Richard
D. Byars
Heald, Jeremiah vs. The State
Heald, Samuel vs. The State
Heald, Samuel vs. John Thomas
Heard, Annis, Bennett Crawford and Woody Dozier vs.
Thomas Grant
Heard, Annis vs. Daniel Parish, Jasper Corning, Henry
Parish, Joseph Kernochan and Ephraim Holbrook
Heard, John vs. Thomas J. Davis
Heard, John vs. Thomas Grant
Heard, John vs. The State
Heard, Joseph vs. The State
Heard, Samuel vs. A. Husson
Heard, Samuel vs. Robert McAfee
Heard, Samuel vs. Edward Paine for use of Thomas Fitch
Heard, Samuel vs. Job Springer
Heard, Stephen vs. The State
Heard, Stephen G. vs. James Abercrombie for use of John
Abercrombie
Heard, Stephen G. vs. Levi H. Echols and Simeon Echols for
use of Ragland Beasley
Heard, Stephen G. vs. Isaac Hill
Heard, Stephen G. and William Echols vs. Allen McClendon
Heard, Thomas and Henry Benford vs. The State
Hearn, Asa vs. Charles N. Rice
Hearn, Asa vs. Emanuel Sandusky
Hearn, C. C. vs. Griffin, Monticello and Madison Railroad
Co.
Hearn, C. C. vs. Stephen C. Talmadge
Hearn, Christopher C. vs. John C. Aiken
Hearn, Christopher C. vs. William D. Maddox and John G.
Patterson
Hearn, Christopher C. and William Hearn vs. Matthew
Whitfield, Leroy M. Willson, Executor, Pleasant Willson,
Executor, John F. Patterson, Executor and William H.
Mathis, Executor
Hearn, Columbus C. and William Hearn vs. John C. Akins
Hearn, Columbus C. and Ebenezer T. White vs. James Logan
Hearn, Columbus C. vs. The State
Hearn, Ferdinand L. and Lewis McKee vs. William P. Roby
Hearn, George vs. Reuben Lockett
Hearn, George and John Hearn vs. Reuben C. Shorter
Hearn, Isaac vs. Baker Hobson
Hearn, John vs. John H. Gilmore
Hearn, Oscar vs. The State
Hearn, Priscilla vs. Zabed Hearn
Hearn, Selby vs. Gilum Scogan
Hearn, Zabad and Curtis Conaway vs. William B. Meson
Heartfield, Moses vs. The State
Heath, Abel F. vs. The State
Heath, Van vs. The State
Hecht, Samuel vs. Mary Hecht
Heflin, John and Cincinatus W. Griggs vs. Ann Keene, Henry
W. Tindall, Executor and William D. Redding, Executor for
use of Samuel M. Farrar
Height, Phoebie (alias Amanda Height) vs. The State
Heldebrand, David and William Spence vs. Isaac Fincher
Heldebrand, David vs. The State
Helms, Lloyd vs. The State
Henderson, ? vs. D. L. Patrick, Jr.
Henderson, Brockman W. and Majers Henderson vs. Lewin Cohen
Henderson, Brockman W. and Magers Henderson vs. Hollis Cooly

for use of Bronson and Mills
Henderson, Charles vs. William Maxey, Charles S. Jordan and
  John R. Dyer
Henderson, Charles vs. The State
Henderson, Charles vs. Stephen C. Talmadge and A. J. Tal-
  madge
Henderson, Charles vs. William P. Truitt
Henderson, Francis vs. William W. Walker
Henderson, George vs. Allen W. Coleman
Henderson, Isaac W. vs. Crawford H. Greer
Henderson, Isaac W. vs. George B. Hallock
Henderson, Isaac W. vs. Stephen Howard, Lewis Linch,
  Executor and James B. Howard, Executor
Henderson, Isaac W. vs. Seaborn S. Mimms
Henderson, James and Wesley Henderson vs. Charles Cargile
Henderson, James vs. Matthew H. Glenn
Henderson, James vs. John F. Gray
Henderson, James vs. Griffin, Monticello and Madison
  Railroad Co.
Henderson, James vs. William H. Thompson for use of William
  S. Townsend
Henderson, James P. vs. Virginia Henderson
Henderson, John, Beverly Allen, Administrator, William
  Whitfield, Administrator and Matilda J. (Henderson)
  Whitfield, Administrator vs. Seth Ward
Henderson, Joseph vs. Hollis Cooley
Henderson, Joseph and John Johnson vs. Thomas Moore
Henderson, Joseph vs. William P. Truitt
Henderson, Lewis vs. The State
Henderson, Magers vs. John Baldwin
Henderson, Magers vs. William Barker
Henderson, Magers vs. William H. Crane
Henderson, Magers vs. James Henderson
Henderson, Magers vs. Lawson S. Holland
Henderson, Magers vs. Richard Loyall
Henderson, Magers vs. Benjamin Reed
Henderson, Magers vs. James Smith and Thomas I. Smith
Henderson, Magers vs. Mary Williamson
Henderson, Majers vs. Joseph Johnson
Henderson, Majers vs. John Brown
Henderson, Majers vs. Ralph Olmsted
Henderson, Majers vs. James Stratton and Asa E. Stratton
Henderson, S. F., S. J. Henderson and D. M. Davis vs. Dora
  Vaughn
Henderson, S. J. vs. J. D. Kilpatrick
Henderson, S. J. vs. J. L. Pitts
Henderson, S. J. vs. J. B. Robinson, W. M. Robinson, C. C.
  Robinson and J. R. Mobley
Henderson, Sam, Sr., Sam Henderson, Jr., Dubon Henderson,
  Flem Henderson, Sid Womack, John Bailey, Charles Bailey,
  Jud Bailey and Charles Williams vs. The State
Henderson, Samuel vs. Bryant Cooley
Henderson, Samuel vs. John Wall
Henderson, Samuel L., Samuel R. Smith and Pleasant E.
  Banks vs. Richard W. Henderson
Henderson, Thomas vs. Francis Comer
Henderson, Thomas vs. The State
Henderson, Tony vs. The State
Henderson, Wesley and John T. Henderson vs. Jefferson Adams
Henderson, Wesley and James Henderson vs. Susan Hill
Henderson, Wesley and Lewis Smith vs. The State
Henderson, William vs. Joseph Moss
Henderson, Wood vs. The State

Hendrick, Micajah vs. David Anderson
Hendrick, Micajah vs. Fouche Cleveland
Hendrick, Micajah vs. Thomas W. Harris
Hendrick, Macajah and Mary Magdaline Hendrick vs. William
  Johnson
Hendrick, Nancy vs. William Cook
Hendrick, Seaborn J. and William Maxey vs. Edward A. Broddus
Hendrick, Seaborn J. and Edward Y. Hill vs. Artemas Gould
Hendrick, Seaborn J., Edward Y. Hill, William Maxey and
  Charles W. C. Wright vs. Josiah Perry
Hendrick, Seaborn J. and Edwin W. Pearson vs. Josias Pope
Hendricks, John H. vs. The State
Hendricks, Seaborn I. and William H. Byrum vs. James
  Hulbert and Luther Roll
Hendricks, Seaborn I. vs. Thomas Morton
Hendricks, Seaborn J. vs. Abner Chapman
Hendricks, Seaborn J. vs. Edward Y. Hill
Hendricks, Seaborn J. and Caleb B. Adams vs. Simeon Scales
Hendricks, Seaborn J. vs. The State
Henry, George W. vs. The State
Henry, James vs. Charles P. Gordon, James H. Gordon,
  Executor and George M. Gordon, Executor
Henry, James vs. The State
Hensey, Richard vs. Nancy Hensey
Hensley, Thomas vs. Gilbert Longstreet
Henson, Joe vs. The State
Henson, Robert vs. Mathew Whitfield
Herbert, William vs. The State
Herrage, Benjamin vs. Lewis C. Holland and Lawson S. Holland
Herren, Alexander vs. James S. Weekes
Herrin, Alexander vs. Thomas Hairston
Herrin, Alexander vs. John Howard for use of Daniel Dawkins
Herrin, Alexander vs. John Powell
Herrin, Alexander vs. James Richards and Willis Richards
Herrin, Alexander and Larkin Turner vs. Williamson Robey
  and Henry Boswell
Herrin, James and Zachariah White vs. Alston H. Greene and
  Joseph Buchannan
Herrin, James vs. Reuben C. Shorter
Herring, Alexander vs. John H. Baines
Herring, Alexander vs. Samuel Butts, John Lucas, Administra-
  tor and William Lee, Administrator
Herring, Arthur vs. Stephen Anderson
Herring, Arthur vs. Joseph Johnson
Herring, Arthur vs. Jesse Lane
Herring, Arthur vs. Robert V. Marye
Herring, Arthur vs. John McMurrain, Sr.
Herring, Arthur vs. Welcom Parks
Herring, Arthur vs. Coleman M. Roberts
Herring, Arthur vs. The State
Herring, Arthur vs. Benjamin H. Wilson
Herron, David vs. Henry Lane
Hershfeld, Jacob vs. Ebinezer T. White
Hervey, Franklin and Cornelius D. Terhune vs. James D. Bell
  and Andrew H. Bell, Administrator
Hervey, Franklin and Cornelius D. Terhune vs. James Hines
Hervey, Franklin and John Catlin vs. Joseph Kopman
Hervey, Franklin and Cornelius D. Terhune vs. William S.
  Miller and John H. McCall
Hervey, Franklin vs. Seth Nims
Hervey, Franklin and John Catlin vs. Hosea Webster and
  Thomas J. Parmalee
Hervey, Franklin and John Catlin vs. James Wells and

172

Charles Redfield
Hester, Henry vs. The State
Hester, Robert vs. Joseph Brown
Hester, Robert vs. James Head
Hickman, Joseph vs. John F. Beavers
Hickman, Joseph and John Armstrong vs. Levy Daniel and
   Robert McGinty, Executor
Hickman, Joseph, Joseph Hickman, Sr. and Thomas Carter vs.
   Elijah N. Hascall
Hickman, Joseph vs. John Hill
Hickman, Joseph vs. James Richards
Hickman, Joseph, Jr. and Joseph Hickman, Sr. vs. Thomas
   Carter
Hicks, Edward vs. William Biscoe and James N. Hall
Hicks, Edward and Joel Baley vs. William Cook and Samuel
   Painter
Hicks, Edward and Joel Baley vs. Ebenezer M. Cowles
Hicks, Edward and Joel Baley vs. Simeon G. Glenn
Hicks, Edward and Joel Baley vs. Thomas Grant, Daniel Grant,
   Executor, Thomas Grant, Executor and Peter Grinell,
   Executor
Hicks, Edward and Joel Baley vs. John Lepper
Hicks, Edward and Joel Baley vs. Benjamin Marshall
Hicks, Edward and Joel Baley vs. Garland Maxey
Hicks, Edward and Joel Baley vs. Lemuel Newcomb
Hicks, Edward, Joel Baley and Rolin Smith vs. Solomon
   Perteet and Jeremiah Pearson, Guardian
Hicks, Edward and Joel Baley vs. John T. Rowland
Hicks, Edward and Joel Baley vs. Marcus A. Starr
Higgason, Philemon C. vs. James Downs
Higgason, Richard and Alexander Avery vs. James Richardson
Higginbotham, Burras and Joseph Higginbotham vs. John
   Cunningham
Higginbotham, Ephraim, Robert Higginbotham and William
   Coggin vs. The State
Higginbotham, Joseph, Frederick Ward, Executor, Williamson
   Robey, Executor, Robert Higginbotham, Executor and
   William Higginbotham vs. The State
Higgins, Joe vs. The State
Higgins, Palmer A. vs. Henry W. Conner
Higgins, Palmer A. vs. Robert W. Fort, William H. Townsend,
   Robert C. Townsend and Marmaduck Mendenhall
Higgins, Wiley I. vs. The State
Hightower, Daniel vs. The State
Hightower, Elizabeth vs. The State
Hights, Mathis vs. The State
Hildebrand, David vs. Royal Clay
Hill, Asa vs. Josiah Flourney
Hill, Asa vs. Benjamin Sanford and John Lumsden
Hill, Asa vs. John Simmons
Hill, Benjamin and Obadiah Echols vs. John Ector, Hugh W.
   Ector, Executor and Robert Freeman, Executor
Hill, Benjamin and Joseph Hill vs. Lawson Holland
Hill, Benjamin vs. Leroy Napier and Thomas Napier
Hicks, Edward and Joel Baley vs. Benjamin Stiles and
   Abraham B. Fannin
Hicks, Edward and Joel Baley vs. William H. Turpin and
   William D'Antignac
Hicks, Ephraim and Henry Jones, Sr. vs. James J. Callaway
   for use of Thomas Holloway
Hicks, Joseph vs. Alston H. Greene and Joseph Buchannon
Hicks, Joseph vs. John Hill
Hicks, John Kennaday

173

Hicks, Joseph vs. Stephen Kirk
Hicks, Joseph vs. Solomon Phillips for use of Jeremiah
  Peddy
Hicks, Joseph, Garland Dawkins, Administrator and William
  Phillips, Administrator vs. Jesse Ricks
Hicks, Joseph vs. The State
Hicks, Joseph vs. Joseph Westmoreland
Hicks, Marcus vs. The State
Hicks, Mark vs. Aaron Smith
Hicks, Rich vs. The State
Hickson, Thomas vs. James Dowdell
Hickson, Thomas vs. William Paty
Hickson, Thomas vs. Cary Wood
Hide, Samuel vs. Alston H. Greene and Joseph Buchannon
Higgason, Larkin vs. Sherwood H. Gay
Higgason, Larkin vs. James Richards
Hill, Benjamin vs. Thomas W. Scott
Hill, Benjamin vs. James Whitfield
Hill, George A. vs. James C. Flemister
Hill, George A. vs. Lawson S. Holland
Hill, Gordon vs. The State
Hill, Green B. vs. Luke Reid, Luther Goble and Frederick
  S. Thomas
Hill, Green B. vs. The State
Hill, Green B. vs. David Treadwell
Hill, Green B. vs. James Whitfield
Hill, Henry vs. The State
Hill, Isaac vs. Cheadle Cochran
Hill, Isaac, Martha (Hill) Cobb, Seth Cobb, Polly (Hill)
  Jackson, William Jackson, Susanna Hill, Henry Peddy and
  Penny (Hill) Peddy vs. Isaac Hill, John Hill, Guardian,
  Ashley Hill and Lucinda Hill
Hill, Isaac vs. The State
Hill, Isaac, Sr. vs. Francis Doyle
Hill, Jesse vs. Hamilton Brown, Peyton Gwyn and James Gwyn
Hill, Jesse vs. Edward Kellogg and David T. Baldwin
Hill, John vs. Gilbert Clealand
Hill, John vs. Charles Coursey
Hill, John vs. Thomas Grant, Daniel Grant, Executor, Thomas
  Grant, Executor and Peter Grinnell, Executor
Hill, John vs. Thomas Greer
Hill, John and Edward Hill vs. William Hitchcock and
  Matthew Phillips
Hill, John vs. Thomas Napier
Hill, John vs. James Robinson
Hill, John vs. Daniel H. Willis
Hill, Joseph vs. Royall Clay
Hill, Joseph vs. Edward Hicks and Joel Baley
Hill, Joseph vs. Thomas Napier
Hill, Joshua vs. Bank of the State of Georgia
Hill, Lydia and Moses Speirs vs. Chadlea Cochran
Hill, Middleton and John F. Beavers vs. Phineas Hill
Hill, Peter vs. The State
Hill, Theophilus, Isaac McClendon, Administrator, John
  Castellow, Administrator and Amey (Hill) Castellow vs.
  James Edwards and William G. Gilbert
Hill, Theophilus, Isaac McClendon, Administrator, John
  Castilow, Administrator and Amy (Hill) Castilow,
  Administrator vs. Francis McClendon
Hill, Wright vs. John Robertson
Hillsborough Academy vs. Aaron W. Kitchel
Hillsborough Academy vs. Mary Ann Palmer
Hindsley, Michael vs. The State

Hines, James vs. Elias Hines
Hines, James vs. Maramia (?) Hines
Hines, James, John Hines and Littleberry Hines vs. The State
Hines, John vs. Sherod H. Gay and Gilbert W. Shaw
Hinsey, Nancy vs. Shadrack J. McMichael
Hitchcock, Jesse vs. Samuel Butts and John Lucas,
  Administrator
Hitchcock, Jesse vs. Eli Glover and John Cashin
Hitchcock, Jesse and Thomas W. Harris vs. Charles Kennon
  and Christopher Baker
Hitchcock, Jesse vs. James Robertson and William Walker
Hitchcock, Jesse vs. James Stratton and Asa F. Stratton
Hitchcock, John, William Hitchcock and Matthew Phillips vs.
  James Whitfield
Hitchcock, Matthew and William Hitchcock vs. Samuel Johnson
  for use of John Lucas
Hitchcock, William and William H. Cargile vs. John Baldwin
Hitchcock, William vs. Richard Banks
Hitchcock, William and David A. Reese, Administrator vs.
  John G. Bird
Hitchcock, William vs. Charles L. Bolton
Hitchcock, William vs. David Carrol and George Vegal,
  Administrator
Hitchcock, William vs. Robert M. Cleveland and Jesse F.
  Cleveland
Hitchcock, William and Overton Hitchcock vs. David Clopton
Hitchcock, William vs. William Cooke and John Van Wagenin
Hitchcock, William and David A. Reese, Administrator vs.
  Thomas Copelin
Hitchcock, William vs. John Cormick
Hitchcock, William vs. William S. Crayton and Thomas Smith
Hitchcock, William vs. Thomas I. Davis
Hitchcock, William vs. Joseph Duncan and Moses G. Towles
Hitchcock, William vs. Joel Flennekin
Hitchcock, William vs. Benjamin W. Force, John P. Force
  and Lewis M. Force
Hitchcock, William vs. Benjamin Fudge for use of Isaac
  Bailey
Hitchcock, William vs. Eli E. Gaither
Hitchcock, William vs. Eli Glover
Hitchcock, William vs. Artemas Goolsby
Hitchcock, William vs. Cardin Goolsby
Hitchcock, William vs. Thomas Grant, Daniel Grant, Executor,
  Thomas Grant, Executor and Peter Grinnell, Executor
Hitchcock, William vs. Edwin Graves and Rufus R. Graves
Hitchcock, William vs. Samuel Griswold
Hitchcock, William and Evan I. Harvey vs. John W. Hardaway
Hitchcock, William vs. Lewis P. Harwell
Hitchcock, William vs. James D. Head
Hitchcock, William vs. Edward Hicks and Joel Baley
Hitchcock, William vs. Turner Hunt
Hitchcock, William vs. Francis Irwin
Hitchcock, William vs. Theron Lancaster
Hitchcock, William vs. Hiram Lewis
Hitchcock, William vs. Elizabeth Low for use of Norborne
  P. Powell
Hitchcock, William, Luke Williams and James Black vs.
  Edmund Loyd, John L. Drew, Administrator and John Norwood,
  Administrator
Hitchcock, William vs. James G. Lyle
Hitchcock, William vs. William Maxey and James Bartlett
Hitchcock, William vs. Joshua S. Mitchell for use of
  Joseph T. Camp

Hitchcock, William vs. Turner Moreland
Hitchcock, William vs. Luke J. Morgan and John H. Morgan
Hitchcock, William and William Flowers vs. David Myrick,
    Irby Hudson, Guardian, Thomas Moseley, Guardian and
    Robert Myrick, Guardian
Hitchcock, William vs. John McKee
Hitchcock, William vs. Leroy Napier
Hitchcock, William vs. John North, John Manning and
    William Hoyt
Hitchcock, William and David A. Reese, Administrator vs.
    Thomas Norton
Hitchcock, William vs. Solomon Perteet and Jeremiah
    Pearson, Guardian
Hitchcock, William vs. Warren Phelps
Hitchcock, William vs. Benjamin H. Reed
Hitchcock, William and James W. Morgan vs. David A. Reese
Hitchcock, William and Evan J. Harvey vs. Williamson Robey,
    Mariah Robey, Guardian, Aquilla Marcus DeLayfayette
    Robey, (minor) and Mary Evaline Robey (minor)
Hitchcock, William vs. William C. Rutter and Loyal Scranton
Hitchcock, William vs. James Shaw
Hitchcock, William vs. Augustin Slaughter and Charles
    Labuzan
Hitchcock, William vs. George Smith and Joseph Kingsley
Hitchcock, William vs. The State
Hitchcock, William vs. Green Stephens
Hitchcock, William and Peter M. Hughes vs. Pleasant Stovall
    and William P. Ford
Hitchcock, William vs. Charles Strong
Hitchcock, William and David A. Reese, Administrator vs.
    Matthew Anderson Thomas, Humphrey W. Tomlinson,
    Administrator and Amanda Melvina Tomlinson, Administrator
Hitchcock, William vs. Edmund B. Thompson for use of
    George W. Persons and Amos J. Persons
Hitchcock, William vs. Philip Thurman
Hitchcock, William, David A. Reese, Administrator and Sally
    Cooper, Administrator vs. Humphrey W. Tomlinson
Hitchcock, William and David A. Reese, Administrator vs.
    Alexander Waits
Hitchcock, William vs. Henry Walker
Hitchcock, William vs. Hosea Webster and Thomas J. Parmalee
Hitchcock, William vs. John Wood
Hix, Rick vs. The State
Hobson, Baker vs. Anthony Dyer and Otis Dyer
Hobson, Baker vs. Jeremiah Pittman
Hobson, Christopher, John Wilson, Administrator and
    Thomas W. Harris, Administrator vs. John Hobson, Sr.
Hobson, Christopher and John Willson vs. William Meriwether,
    Howard Beal, Elias Beall and Thadeus Beall
Hobson, Christopher, John Wilson, Administrator and Thomas
    W. Harris, Administrator vs. Jeremiah Pearson
Hobson, Hardy vs. Jordan Ivy and Sarah (Williams) Ivy
Hobson, John vs. Thomas Grant
Hobson, John vs. William H. Hobson
Hobson, John vs. James B. Patterson and John Patterson
Hobson, John and Christopher Hobson vs. Edward Quin
Hobson, John and Christopher Hobson vs. Benjamin W. Rogers
Hobson, John vs. John Willson
Hodge, Andrew vs. Phebe (McClendon) Hodge
Hodge, Jesse vs. The State
Hodge, Lee vs. The State
Hodge, Lon L. vs. H. H. Ezell
Hodge, Nathaniel vs. The State

Hodge, Paul vs. The State
Hodge, Willis vs. The State
Hodges, Addie vs. The State
Hodges, Andrew vs. Thomas J. Davis
Hodges, Andrew vs. Robert Sturdevant, Jeremiah Pearson and
   James Griggs
Hodges, Harvey vs. The State
Hodnett, Benjamin vs. Gilbert Gay
Hodnett, Benjamin vs. John Smith
Hodnett, Henry W. vs. Joseph Bacon
Hoff, William vs. Smith and Morgan
Hogan, Andrew J. vs. James B. Goolsby
Hogan, Dave vs. The State
Hogan, Ellis vs. The State
Holbrook, William vs. Martin Nall
Holifield, Alsea vs. Jordan Abott and William Usry
Holifield, Alsea vs. Milton Antony
Holifield, Alsea and John L. S. Foster vs. Thomas Grant
Holifield, Andrew J. vs. John R. Dickin
Holifield, Andrew J. vs. Thomas C. Garrett
Holifield, Andrew J. vs. High P. Kirkpatrick and George
   W. Holland
Holifield, Andrew J. vs. William Maxey
Holifield, Andrew J. vs. Charles W. C. Wright
Holland, Alexander and William N. Kirkpatrick vs. William
   Maxey and Charles S. Jordan
Holland, B. W. and E. A. Holland vs. Bastley Walker
Holland, Bus vs. The State
Holland, Dave, William Ambers and Brock Marks vs. The State
Holland, Dave vs. W. T. Tucker
Holland, Deille C. vs. S. L. Adgate for use of Officers of
   Court
Holland, George W. vs. Anthony Dyer
Holland, George W. vs. Thomas Grant, Daniel Grant, Executor,
   Thomas Grant, Executor and Peter Grinnell, Executor
Holland, George W., Jonas H. Holland and James McKemie vs.
   Mortimer Jordan
Holland, George W. vs. James Keath
Holland, George W. and Hugh P. Kirkpatrick vs. Henry B.
   Walker
Holland, George W. vs. James Whitfield
Holland, Harvy vs. The State
Holland, Henry J. vs. James Henderson
Holland, J. A. vs. The State
Holland, J. H. vs. Officers of Court
Holland, J. H. vs. Bolling Whitfield
Holland, James A. vs. Druscilla Pritchett
Holland, James W. vs. Wilkin Powel, Sr. and Berry T. Digby,
   Administrator
Holland, Jane M. vs. George T. Holland
Holland, Jim vs. The State
Holland, Jonas H. vs. Bank of Darien
Holland, Jonas H. vs. Bank of the State of Georgia
Holland, Jonas H. and George W. Holland vs. William Banks
Holland, Jonas H. vs. Alphaus Beall and Thomas Beall
Holland, Jonas H. vs. Thadeus Beall, Elias Beall and Thomas
   Beall
Holland, Jonas H. vs. Thomas Beall for use of Andrew Jeter
Holland, Jonas H. vs. Hamilton Brown, Payton Gwyn and
   James Gwyn
Holland, Jonas H., Lawson S. Holland and Joseph L. Holland
   vs. Runno B. M. Cargile
Holland, Jonas H. and George W. Holland vs. John A. Carter

Holland, Jonas H. vs. Thomas Clay
Holland, Jonas H. vs. Thomas B. Erwin
Holland, Jonas H. vs. A. G. Foster and F. C. Foster, Executor
Holland, Jonas H. vs. Henry Gaston
Holland, Jonas H. vs. Nathaniel W. Jordon
Holland, Jonas H. vs. James Henderson
Holland, Jonas H. vs. John Hobson, Francis Hobson, Adminis-
    trator, Alsea Holifield, Administrator and James Whitfield
    Administrator
Holland, Jonas H. vs. James B. Howard
Holland, Jonas H. vs. John Kendrick
Holland, Jonas H., Lawson S. Holland and George W. C.
    Holland vs. Gazaway B. Lamar
Holland, Jonas H. vs. James D. Malone
Holland, Jonas H. and William G. Swanson vs. Allen
    McClendon and William F. Mapp, Administrator
Holland, Jonas H. vs. John Moore
Holland, Jonas H. vs. James Robertson and William Walker
Holland, Jonas H. vs. David Shoulders
Holland, Jonas H. vs. The State
Holland, Joseph L. vs. Charlotte Holland
Holland, Judge vs. The State
Holland, Lawson S. vs. John Baldwin
Holland, Lawson S. vs. Bank of Darien
Holland, Lawson S. vs. Thomas Beall
Holland, Lawson S. vs. Hollis Cooley and Dyer C. Bancroft
Holland, Lawson S., George W. Holland, Lewis C. Holland,
    Joel Baley and Jonas H. Holland vs. John Extor, Robert
    Freeman, Executor and Hugh W. Ector
Holland, Lawson S. vs. Robert Freeman
Holland, Lawson S. vs. Thomas Grant, Daniel Grant, Execu-
    tor, Thomas Grant, Executor and Peter Grinnell, Executor
Holland, Lawson S. vs. William Harris
Holland, Lawson S., Lewis C. Holland and Jonas H. Holland
    vs. John Hill
Holland, Lawson S. vs. Eli T. Hoyt and David H. Boughton
Holland, Lawson S. and Mathew Whitfield vs. Absalom Jones
Holland, Lawson S. vs. Justices of Court
Holland, Lawson S. vs. Nathan Lanier
Holland, Lawson S. vs. George McIntire, Ralph McIntire,
    William McIntire, Charles Kelsey and Charles W. Rockwell
Holland, Lawson S., Lewis C. Holland and Jonas H. Holland
    vs. Benjamin Marshall
Holland, Lawson S. and Matthew Whitfield vs. Adiel Sherwood
Holland, Lawson S. vs. Eli S. Shorter
Holland, Lawson S. vs. The State
Holland, Lewis C. vs. William Armor
Holland, Lewis C. and Lawson S. Holland vs. Thomas Bass
Holland, Lewis C. vs. Simon G. Blossom and William
    Cunningham
Holland, Lewis C. vs. Jonas Brown
Holland, Lewis C. and Lawson S. Holland vs. James Callaway
Holland, Lewis C., William Jeffries and Daniel McDowell vs.
    John Clendening, Jr. and Horace Bulkley
Holland, Lewis C., Pascal Murphey and Samuel Clay vs.
    Martin Cochran
Holland, Lewis C. vs. William H. Crane and Joseph Kopman
Holland, Lewis C. and Lemuel O. Lawrence vs. Hardy Crawford
Holland, Lewis C. vs. Bank of Darien
Holland, Lewis C. vs. Caleb C. Dibble
Holland, Lewis C. and William Hitchcock vs. Anthony Dyer
Holland, Lewis C. and Henry J. Holland vs. John Ector,
    Robert Freeman, Executor and Hugh W. Ector, Executor

Holland, Lewis C. vs. James Germany
Holland, Lewis C. vs. Stephen Gilmore
Holland, Lewis C. vs. Eli Glover
Holland, Lewis C. and Andrew Johnson vs. John E. Glover
Holland, Lewis C. vs. Alston H. Greene and Joseph Buchannan
Holland, Lewis C., Alsea Holifield, Jonas H. Holland, Lawson
  S. Holland and Elijah Dodson vs. Garry Grice, Thomas C.
  Russell, Wade H. Turner, William Griffin and Joseph P.
  Greene
Holland, Lewis C. vs. Edward Hicks and Joel Baley
Holland, Lewis C. and Lawson S. Holland vs. John Hobson,
  Francis Hobson, Administrator, Alsea Holifield, Adminis-
  trator and James Whitfield, Administrator
Holland, Lewis C. vs. William S. Hurd and Anson Hungerford
Holland, Lewis C. vs. William S. Hurd and Alfred Shorter
Holland, Lewis C. vs. Thomas D. Johnson and William L.
  Crayton
Holland, Lewis C. vs. Justices of Court
Holland, Lewis C. vs. Gazaway B. Lamar
Holland, Lewis C. vs. Lemuel O. Lawrence
Holland, Lewis C. and Jonathan Reeves vs. Edmund Lloyd,
  John S. Drew, Executor, John Norwood, Executor and
  Margaret Norwood, Executor
Holland, Lewis C. vs. Augustus B. Longstreet
Holland, Lewis C. vs. Jesse Loyall
Holland, Lewis C. vs. Richard Loyall
Holland, Lewis C. vs. David Lynn
Holland, Lewis C. and Lawson S. Holland vs. Adam P. Mabry,
  Jordan Thornton, Administrator, Parham P. Mabry, Adminis-
  trator and Esom Turner, Administrator
Holland, Lewis C. vs. Seaborn J. Mays and William Daring
Holland, Lewis C. and John R. Dickin vs. James McBryde,
  John McBryde and Alexander Wallace
Holland, Lewis C. and Lawson S. Holland vs. David McKinney
Holland, Lewis C. and Lawson S. Holland vs. John Miller
Holland, Lewis C. vs. Samuel Parks
Holland, Lewis C. vs. James Robertson and William Walker
Holland, Lewis C. and Lawson S. Holland vs. Eli S. Shorter
Holland, Lewis C. vs. Reuben C. Shorter for use of Pleasant
  Stovall
Holland, Lewis C. and Lawson S. Holland vs. William Simmons
Holland, Lewis C., Lawson S. Holland and William H. Parker
  vs. William Sims and Co.
Holland, Lewis C. vs. Augustin Slaughter and Charles Labuzan
Holland, Lewis C. and Lawson S. Holland vs. John Spears, Jr.
Holland, Lewis C. vs. William Spears
Holland, Lewis C. vs. Pleasant Stovall and David Stanford
Holland, Lewis C. vs. William G. Swanson
Holland, Lewis C. and Lawson S. Holland vs. Jordan Thornton
Holland, Lewis C. vs. Richard Turner
Holland, Lewis C., Mathew Hitchcock and Jonas H. Holland
  vs. The United States of America
Holland, Lewis C., Lawson S. Holland and John High vs.
  Elijah C. Walker
Holland, Lewis C. and Lawson S. Holland vs. Nathan Warner,
  John Baldwin, Administrator and Benjamin F. Ward,
  Administrator
Holland, Lewis C., Lawson S. Holland and Jonas H. Holland
  vs. John Warren
Holland, Lewis R. and Lawson S. Holland vs. Thomas Smith,
  John C. Smith, Administrator and Asa Smith, Administrator
Holland, Margaret vs. Benjamin M. Cargile
Holland, Margaret vs. William S. Hurd and Anson Hungerford

Holland, Margaret vs. William N. Kirkpatrick
Holland, Margaret vs. William Maxey and Charles S. Jordan
Holland, Mary vs. The State
Holland, R. L. vs. The State
Holland, Thomas R. vs. John L. McMichael and Fleming Mobley,
  Administrator
Holland, Thomas R. vs. The State
Holland, Tom vs. The State
Holland, W. T. vs. Francis S. Johnson
Holland, W. T. and Walter L. Zachry vs. R. C. Marks and
  F. C. Marks
Holland, W. T. vs. John L. Robinson
Holland, W. T. vs. N. B. White and S. White
Holland, Zeltner vs. The State
Hollaway, Maston vs. Kellam and Maxey
Holliman, William vs. The State
Hollis, James vs. Hardy Crawford
Hollis, Thomas vs. Jordan Thornton and Jemima Thornton
Hollis, William and Joseph M. Post vs. Samuel W. Pearson
  and Robert Pearman
Holloway, Alonzo vs. The State
Holloway, Charles D. vs. Benjamin Maroney
Holloway, Chesley D. vs. Alston H. Greene and Joseph
  Buchannon
Holloway, Chesley D. and John Brownfield vs. Matthew Ozburn
Holloway, D. P. and Seab Lawrence vs. George B. Hallock
Holloway, Dan vs. The State
Holloway, Daniel vs. Rosalie (Cook) Holloway
Holloway, Francis E. vs. Officers of Court
Holloway, Jesse and James Heard, Administrator vs. Little-
  berry B. Phillips
Holloway, Jesse and William Holloway vs. L. B. Watts,
  Pleasant Watts, Administrator and John Bailey,
  Administrator
Holloway, Joe vs. The State
Holloway, John W. vs. The State
Holloway, Joseph vs. The State
Holloway, Martin vs. The State
Holloway, Robert W. vs. The State
Holloway, Rosalea vs. Officers of Court
Holloway, Samuel vs. John R. Skag
Holloway, William, Burrell Leverritt and Stephen Baley,
  Administrator vs. Anderson Dabney, Tyre G. Dabney,
  Administrator and Hannah Dabney, Administrator
Holloway, William vs. Eli Denson
Holmes, James P. vs. Henry Slappy
Holmes, John vs. William Farrington and Luther Cummings
Holmes, Norman vs. The State
Holmes, Pleas vs. The State
Holmes, Thomas J. vs. The State
Holmes, Will vs. The State
Holsenback, Alexander vs. Marcus L. D. Luson
Holsenback, Marshall, Elisha S. Wynens and Wesley Goolsby
  vs. Pleaman W. Dorsett
Holsenbeck, Marshall vs. Thomas J. Lane and Davis Lane
Holsenbeck, Marshall and James B. Goolsby vs. William P.
  Middlebrooks
Holsenbeck, R. L. and W. A. Holsenbeck vs. The State
Holt, Asa vs. Rolan Taylor
Holt, D. S. vs. E. L. Strochacker and Co.
Holt, Dave vs. The State
Holt, Gus (alias Henry Holt; alias William Holt) vs. The
  State

Holt, Matilda vs. The State
Holt, Peter vs. The State
Holt, Russel vs. Russel J. Penn
Holt, Will, Jr. vs. The State
Holt, William vs. James Morris
Holt, William vs. Hampton Smith and John E. Morgan
Honeycut, John vs. Eli Glover and John Cashin
Honeycut, Solomon vs. W. T. Young
Hood, Ichabod vs. Ephraim Ivey
Hood, Ichabod vs. George Owen
Hood, Ichabod vs. Solomon Perteet and Jeremiah Pearson,
   Guardian
Hood, Ichabod and George W. Stringfellow vs. The State
Hood, Wiley vs. Charles Stewart, David Meriwether, Executor,
   and John Stewart, Executor
Hood, Wiley and Micajah Stinson vs. Anna Thomson
Hood, William vs. Alston H. Greene and Joseph Buchannon
Hooper, N. W., Sr., N. W. Hooper, Jr. and Thomas Hooper vs.
   The State
Hooten, Amos vs. Joel Baley and Parham P. Mabry
Hooton, D. W. vs. Sidney L. (Anderson) Hooton
Hooton, James vs. Robert Kellam and William Maxey
Hopsom, Warren vs. William H. Oakman
Hopson, Hardy vs. Nathaniel Sturges and Samuel Sturges
Hopson, Warren vs. James Cargile
Hopson, Warren vs. Thomas Cunningham and John Cunningham
Hopson, Warren vs. Andrew Kerr, John Kerr and Alexander
   Graham
Hopson, William vs. Garland Dawkins
Horn, Joseph vs. The State
Horn, Thomas and Emily Jordan vs. The State
Hornbuckle, Nathaniel vs. Jonathan Bonner
Hornbuckle, Nathaniel vs. The State
Hornbuckle, Nathaniel B. vs. Eli Glover
Hornbuckle, Nathaniel B. vs. Eli S. Shorter
Hornbuckle, Nathaniel B. vs. James Smith and Thomas Smith
Hornbuckle, Richard B. vs. Joseph Moss
Horne, Joseph and Jesse Glawson vs. The State
Horsley, Thomas vs. Jeremiah Pearson
Horsley, William G. vs. H. C. Seymore
Horton, James vs. The State
Horton, James A. vs. The State
Horton, James A. vs. John Steward
Horton, John, James Knight and John Clark vs. Central Bank
   of Georgia
Horton, John vs. Samuel A. Flournoy for use of William
   Maxey
Horton, John vs. Jonas H. Holland
Horton, Mary Ann (Thompson) vs. Stephen Horton
Horton, Turner vs. The State
House, James vs. Officers of Court
House, William H. and John Watson vs. The State
Hudson, William, James Bullard, Sr. and John Knight vs.
   William Shaw and John Talbert, Administrator
Hudspeth, Airs vs. Robert Bain
Hudspeth, Airs vs. John Carmichael and William C. Ware
Hudspeth, Airs and Phillemon C. Higgason vs. James Downs
Hudspeth, Airs vs. John Logan
Hudspeth, Airs vs. Edward Quin and John Campbell
Hudspeth, Airs vs. Christopher Rush
Hudspeth, Airs vs. James Shivers
Hudspeth, Airs vs. Isham Thompson
Hudspeth, Airs vs. Elijah Willson

Hudspeth, Airs vs. Fields Willson
Hudspeth, Ares, Mark Hudspeth and Crawford Edmondson vs.
  James Edwards
Hudspeth, Ares vs. Thomas Williams, Sr.
Hudspeth, Aris vs. Archelaus Moore
Hudspeth, Aris vs. The State
Hudspeth, Mark and Leonard Wilson vs. The State
Huey and Catlin vs. Webster and Parmalee
Huff, Adda vs. The State
Huff, Andrew vs. The State
Huff, Davis vs. The State
Huff, Frank vs. The State
Huff, Henry B. vs. William Maxey and Charles S. Jordan
Huff, Henry B. vs. Planters Manufacturing Co.
Huff, Henry B. vs. Henry C. Seymour
Huff, J. D. vs. The State
Huff, James vs. P. P. Lovejoy
Huff, Lucinda E. vs. N. B. White
Huff, James vs. P. P. Lovejoy
Huff, Lucinda E. vs. N. B. White
Huff, Lundy vs. Robert C. Beasley and Palemon L. Weekes
Huff, Lundy vs. Hamilton Brown
Huff, Lundy, James Huff and William Lawrence vs. Anthony
  Dyer
Hovater, Jacob vs. James Lanear
Howard, Coradon H. vs. Henry Branham
Howard, Coradon H. vs. William L. Hurd and Anson Hungerford
Howard, Coradon H. vs. William Maxey and James C. Bartlett
Howard, Coredon (?) H. vs. Eatonton Manufacturing Co.
Howard, Coryden H. vs. Richardson Black and John Linch,
  Administrator
Howard, Corydon H. vs. Joseph Whitney
Howard, Henry vs. The State
Howard, Joseph vs. Williamson Bailey
Howard, Pleas vs. The State
Howard, Will and Annie Howard vs. A. O. Johnson
Howard, William vs. Thomas Wilborn
Howel, Byrum vs. The State
Howell, Weston and Nancy Howell vs. Joseph Bacon
Howle, Thomas T. vs. Jubel Cochran
Howle, Thomas T. and Richard C. Clayton vs. William Freeman
Howle, Thomas T. vs. James Layless and Samuel Drewry
Hozey, James vs. The State
Huckaby, Charles vs. Elijah N. Hascall and David Hascall
Huckaby, David vs. Joseph Gunnels
Huckaby, Isham vs. Anthony Dyer
Huckaby, Isham vs. Thadeus Moynihan
Huddleston, John F. N. and Wiley Phillips vs. George W.
  Holland and Hugh P. Kirkpatrick
Hudson, Isum vs. Reuben C. Shorter
Hudson, John and Sarah Slaughter vs. William H. Vaughn
Hudson, Lewis vs. The State
Hudson, Richard vs. Thomas Grant
Hudson, Richard vs. James Hines and James Hines, Executor
Hudson, Richard vs. John J. Smith and Thomas Hardeman
Hudson, Richerson, William Hudson and Obadiah Echols vs.
  Central Bank of Georgia
Hudson, Rolan vs. The State
Hudson, Thomas vs. Nathan Spence
Huff, Lundy vs. Thomas Hairston
Huff, Lundy and John Reid vs. Pleasant Stovall
Huff, Ralph vs. Morton N. Birch
Huff, Ralph vs. Hamblin Huff

Huff, Tabitha vs. Bailey Goddard
Huff, Whitfield vs. Richard Williams
Hughes, Jerry vs. George T. Bartlett and Bolling Whitfield
Hughes, Peter M. and Fleming Jordan vs. Thomas Cooper
Hughes, Peter M. vs. Thomas Grant, Daniel Grant, Executor,
  Thomas Grant, Executor and Peter Grinnell, Executor
Hughes, Peter M. vs. Mary Williamson
Hull, Francis M. vs. William Maxey and James C. Bartlett
Humber, Robert vs. Jonathan Clower
Humber, Robert vs. William Cole
Humber, Robert vs. John Fluker
Humber, Robert vs. James Smith
Humburg, Sabra vs. John Wooten
Humphrey, Thomas vs. The State
Humphreys, Edmund, Jr. vs. The State
Humphries, George W. vs. Uriah Humphries, Stevens Thomas,
  Executor and Edward Paine, Executor
Humphries, Milton vs. Richard Newton
Humphry, Edmond and Wesley Smith vs. S. B. Bailey
Hunneycut, Thomas vs. Eli Glover and John Cashin
Hunnicutt, E. P. vs. Lewis P. Harrell and William Fort
Hunnicutt, Thomas vs. Benjamin Echols, Sr.
Hunnicutt, Thomas vs. John Sparks
Hunt, Aaron vs. John Hill, Augustin Slaughter and Charles
  Labuzan
Hunt, Aaron vs. John McKinne
Hunt, Aaron vs. The State
Hunt, Catherine and Mary Ann Hunt vs. The State
Hunt, Henry and James Barintine vs. The State
Hunt, Jack and James Clemm vs. The State
Hunt, James vs. John H. Green
Hunt, John, Guardian vs. Angelina P. (Smartt) Fambrough and
  Allen G. Fambrough
Hunt, John and Earnest Wood vs. The State
Hunt, John R. and George Alexander vs. C. W. Alexander
Hunt, Judkins and Appleton Hunt vs. George Lamar for use of
  John D. Lamar
Hunt, Judkins vs. John Nisbet
Hunt, Randall vs. The State
Hunt, William H. vs. William H. Crane
Hunt, William H., Charles W. C. Wright and Eli Glover vs.
  The Central Bank of Georgia
Hunter, Henry vs. The State
Hunter, Idus vs. The State
Hunter, James vs. Augusta Baldwin and John Baldwin
Hunter, James F., Wyatt R. Smith, Executor, Alfred Goolsby,
  Executor and Alexander Hunter, Executor vs. Jonas H.
  Holland
Hunter, Reubin vs. Annie Hunter
Hunter, Reubin vs. The State
Hunter, Sylla vs. The State
Hunter, William vs. The State
Hurston, John vs. James Moore
Hurt, Mason, Joe Ike and Lewis Ike vs. The State
Hurt, William and Phillip Stroud vs. James Dickson and
  William Dickson
Hurt, William and Thomas Banckston vs. James Johnston
Hurt, William vs. Zachariah Maddux and Leonard Maddux
Hurt, William vs. James Taylor
Huson, David, Levi Martin, Executor, and Judy Huson,
  Executor vs. William Cameron
Huson, John vs. Benjamin Darnall
Huson, Judy vs. John Baldwin

Husting, John vs. The State
Huston, John vs. Mary Ann Cook
Huston, John vs. George Twitty for use of Mordecai
  Shackelford
Huston, Samuel vs. Pleasant Stovall
Hutchens, William vs. The State
Hutcheson, Henry C. vs. Augusta Baldwin and John Baldwin
Hutcheson, Henry C. vs. William Echelberger and Joseph E.
  Clemm for use of Alexander McDonald and Nicholas G.
  Ridgley
Hutcheson, Henry C. vs. James House
Hutcheson, Henry C. vs. Hugh G. Johnson
Hutcheson, Henry C. and William Hutcheson vs. The State
Hutcheson, Henry C. vs. Nathaniel Truesdale and James
  Jarvis for use of L. C. Cantelow and Co.
Hutcheson, Henry C. vs. William H. Turpin
Hutcheson, Henry C. vs. James Woodrow, Andrew Lowe, Robert
  Isaac and James McHenry
Hutcheson, John C. vs. William Cook for use of Allen
  McClendon
Hutcheson, John C. vs. Eli Glover
Hutcheson, William vs. Jesse Loyall and William H. Pritchett
Hutchinson, Alfred vs. Lamech H. Hines
Hutchinson, Henry C. vs. Hosea Willis
Hutchinson, M. H. vs. John Andrews
Hutchinson, M. H. and John H. Kelly vs. Berry T. Digby
Hutchison, Richard and William Hutchinson vs. Robert
  Buchannon
Hutchison, John C. vs. Joseph Johnson
Hutson, John vs. John C. Reese
Hyatt, L. P. and H. C. Hyatt vs. J. O. Shepherd
Hyde, Samuel vs. David Carson
Hyde, Simeon and George Cleveland vs. Officers of Court

Ike, Joseph vs. The State
Ike, Lewis vs. The State
Ingram, Preslly vs. John Lang
Irby, Anthony vs. The State
Irven, John vs. Eli S. Shorter
Irvin, Absalom and John Greer vs. Jesse Crawford
Irvin, Absalom vs. John Owen
Irvin, Christopher vs. Adam Alexander and James H. Morrow
  for use of David Hascall
Irvin, Christopher vs. Richard Dicken
Irvin, Christopher and Joseph Carter vs. Isaac Phillips,
  William Hammett, William Phillips, Jenny Phillips and
  John Jones
Irvin, Christopher vs. James Randle and Washington Randle
Irvin, Christopher and Cyrus Parnell vs. The State
Irvin, James vs. Thomas B. Erwin and James Cowan
Irvin, John vs. Eli S. Shorter
Irvin, John vs. Hardy Wheales
Irvin, William, Benjamin Irvin and John Irvin vs. George
  R. Jessup
Irwin, Benjamin vs. Jonathan Gibson
Irwin, Christopher vs. Alexander and Morrow
Irwin, Francis vs. Abner Abercrombie
Ivey, Fannie vs. The State
Ivey, Robert W. vs. David Dixon (Dickson) and Capers
  Dickson, Administrator
Ivey, Sam and Rich Hicks vs. The State
Ivins, John vs. W. R. Moseley

Jackson, Alice (alias Alice Collins) vs. The State
Jackson, Anthony vs. The State
Jackson, Bunk vs. The State
Jackson, Celia vs. Horatio N. Spencer for use of Jeremiah
  Pierson and Daniel Lord
Jackson, Charley vs. The State
Jackson, Clarence (alias Brad Proctor) vs. The State
Jackson, Claude vs. The State
Jackson, Delie vs. The State
Jackson, Dock vs. The State
Jackson, Garfield vs. The State
Jackson, Greene B. vs. Isaac R. Jackson
Jackson, Isaac R. and Pleasant Cokes vs. The State
Jackson, John vs. Jesse Cherry and Johnson Springer,
  Executor
Jackson, John and William A. Lane, Administrator vs. G. H.
  Cornwell and Charles L. Smith
Jackson, John vs. Thomas Hardeman
Jackson, John and Nathaniel Raines vs. Americus C. Mitchell
Jackson, John vs. Thomas W. Scott
Jackson, John and William A. Lane, Administrator vs. Charles
  S. Smith and James Dorsett, Administrator
Jackson, John vs. The State
Jackson, Lucy vs. The State
Jackson, Luke vs. The State
Jackson, Plass vs. The State
Jackson, Pleasant vs. Andrew J. Crawford
Jackson, Pleasant and Isaac H. Freeman vs. A. C. Potter,
  Minor and James C. Robinson, Guardian
Jackson, Pleasant, Isaac H. Freeman, Executor and Seaborn
  Kelly vs. O. S. Phrophitt
Jackson, Pleasant vs. The State
Jackson, Pleasant and Isaac H. Freeman, Executor vs. Mathew
  Whitfield
Jackson, Seneca vs. Keverett and Ezell
Jackson, Stephen D. vs. Thomas H. Bray
Jackson, Thomas vs. Peyton Gwyn, Hamilton Brown and James
  Gwyn
Jackson, Thomas vs. Isaac McGehee
Jackson, Wallace vs. The State
Jackson, Warren vs. The State
Jackson, Wilkins vs. William J. Bullard
Jackson, Wilkins, John Jackson, Administrator and Nathaniel
  Raines, Administrator vs. John Jones
Jackson, Will vs. The State
Jackson, William vs. James Cowan and Thomas B. Erwin
Jackson, William vs. John Jackson
Jackson, William (alias Buddy Jackson) vs. The State
Jacobs, John vs. Daniel Kilcrease
Jacobs, John, Joshua Jacobs and Richard J. Loyd vs. The
  State
Jacobs, John vs. Zachariah White
Jacobs, Joshua vs. John Beck
Jacobs, Joshua vs. William Bowen
Jacobs, Joshua vs. Daniel Kilcrease
Jacobson, Charlie vs. The State
James, Dovie vs. The State
James, John P. and Joel A. Reeves vs. Anthony Dyer
James, Scott (alias Jim James) vs. The State
James, Wesley vs. The State
James, West vs. The State
James, Willie Lee vs. The State
Jamison, Arthur and Jonathan Griffith vs. Cortley Johnson

Jarrel, Leroy F. vs. Miller, Ripley and Co.
Jarrel, Leroy F., Hiram Johnson and James Johnson vs.
  William H. Townsend, Isaac Townsend, Robert C. Townsend
  and Marmaduke T. Mendenhall
Jasper, Academy vs. Thomas Grant, Daniel Grant, Executor,
  Thomas Grant, Executor and Peter Grinnell, Executor
Jasper, County vs. James Benton
Jasper County vs. George R. Dozier
Jay, William vs. The State
Jeffers, Berry vs. Roberts and Peurifoy
Jeffers, Frank vs. The State
Jeffers, Grady vs. The State
Jeffers, Lee vs. James Richards and Willis Richards
Jeffers, Lee vs. The State
Jeffries, Albert vs. The State
Jeffries, Alice, Lane Jeffries, S. R. Smith, Jr., J. L.
  Robinson and Colbert Jeffries vs. Officers of Court
Jeffries, Bolin S. vs. William Duke and Tilman Niblet
Jeffries, Boling vs. Micajah Pitman
Jeffries, Boling vs. The State
Jeffries, Boling S. vs. Franklin George
Jeffries, Boling S. and Charles E. F. W. Campbell vs. John
  Kissinger
Jeffries, Boling S. vs. P. P. Lovejoy
Jeffries, Boling S. vs. James Robinson
Jeffries, Boling S. and Sherrod H. Gay vs. The State
Jeffries, Bolling and Green McMichael vs. The State
Jeffries, Bolling S. vs. William L. Shepherd
Jeffries, Burkett M. vs. Joseph R. High
Jeffries, Burkett W. and Thomas Jeffries vs. Graves E.
  Wilson
Jeffries, Colbert, Isaac T. Wyatt and John W. Wyatt vs.
  George T. Bartlett
Jeffries, Colbert and Minerva Smith vs. The State
Jeffries, Cordial, Sarah Jeffries, Administrator and Cicero
  M. Spears vs. Thomas Jeffries and Colbert Jeffries,
  Executor
Jeffries, George vs. William B. Barnett
Jeffries, George vs. Thaddeus Beall, Elias Beall and
  Thomas Beall
Jeffries, George vs. Samuel Crocket
Jeffries, George vs. Thomas J. Davis
Jeffries, George vs. Anthony Dyer
Jeffreis, George vs. Thomas Grant
Jeffries, George vs. Daniel Parish, Jasper Corning, Henry
  Parish, Joseph Kernochan and Ephraim Holbrook
Jeffries, George, William Jeffries and B. Crawford vs.
  Reuben C. Shorter
Jeffries, Grady vs. The State
Jeffries, Henry and Thomas Jeffries vs. The State
Jeffries, Hill vs. Bill Wilson and Jim Wilson
Jeffries, J. P. vs. Heard, White and Thompson
Jeffries, James vs. The State
Jeffries, John and Col. Jeffries vs. The State
Jeffries, Lee vs. Abner Chapman, Sr.
Jeffries, Lee vs. The State
Jeffries, Lelar and Geary Jeffries vs. The State
Jeffries, Mollie and Henry Jeffries vs. The State
Jeffries, Murf vs. The State
Jeffries, Norman vs. The State
Jeffries, Richard vs. The State
Jeffries, Sarah and Mollie Jeffries vs. The State
Jeffries, T. J. vs. The State

Jeffries, Thomas and Burket Jeffries vs. Thomas Grant,
  Daniel Grant, Executor, Thomas Grant, Executor and Peter
  Grinnell, Executor
Jeffries, Thomas and Colbert Jeffries vs. Benjamin F. Taylor
Jeffries, Tom vs. The State
Jeffries, William vs. James Daniel
Jeffries, William vs. Thomas Grant, Daniel Grant, Executor,
  Thomas Grant, Executor and Peter Grinnel, Executor
Jeffries, William vs. John Gwyne
Jeffries, William vs. Archibald Perkins, Bennet M. Ware,
  Executor, Abraham Perkins, Executor, Alexander Perkins,
  Executor, and Frances Perkins, Executor
Jeffries, William vs. John Willson, John Hill, Executor,
  James Willson, Executor, Fleming Jordan, Executor and
  David A. Reese, Executor
Jenkins, Benjamin vs. Charles P. Gordon
Jenkins, Clem vs. The State
Jenkins, Edmond vs. Isham Huckeby
Jenkins, Edmond vs. The State
Jenkins, F. E. vs. J. B. English and Co.
Jenkins, Francis vs. John Hines
Jenkins, Francis vs. Wiley Peddy
Jenkins, Francis vs. Swanson, Pritchett and Co.
Jenkins, Francis vs. Francis M. Swanson and Thomas J. Comer
Jenkins, Isham vs. The State
Jenkins, John H. vs. William Head
Jenkins, L. O. vs. The State
Jenkins, William vs. Elizabeth Barclay
Jenkins, Willie vs. The State
Jennings, David C. vs. Anna (Lovejoy) Jennings
Jeter, Andrew vs. James Holsey, Duke Hamilton, Executor and
  William Terrell, Executor
Jeter, Andrew vs. Jesse Lanford and William Lanford
Jeter, Andrew and George Stovall vs. John McKinnie and
  Henry Shultz
Jiles, R. E. vs. The State
Jinks, Matthew vs. Dempsey Portwood
Johnson, Ahab vs. William D. Grimes
Johnson, Ahab P. vs. Isaac R. Hall
Johnson, Ahab P. vs. James H. Roberts
Johnson, Albert vs. The State
Johnson, Alexander vs. Hollis Cooley
Johnson, Alfred vs. John M. Bruce
Johnson, Alfred, Snelling Johnson, Administrator and
  LaFayette Johnson vs. W. C. Clement
Johnson, Alfred vs. James Whitfield
Johnson, Allen vs. Anderson and Lumsford
Johnson, Allen vs. A. L. Sluder for use of Officers of
  Court
Johnson, Allen vs. The State
Johnson, Andrew vs. Anthony Dyer
Johnson, Andrew vs. Harman Geiger
Johnson, Andrew and Lewis C. Holland vs. Thomas Grant
Johnson, Andrew vs. Edward Hicks and Joel Baley
Johnson, Andrew vs. The State
Johnson, Andrew and Lewis C. Holland vs. John Willson
Johnson, Anthony vs. The State
Johnson, Brice C. and Polly Q. Johnson vs. Allen McClendon
Johnson, Brice C. vs. John McKenzie and Peter Bennoch
Johnson, Brice C. vs. The State
Johnson, Bryant vs. The State
Johnson, Cleavland vs. The State
Johnson, Cornelius and Henry S. Strickland vs. The State

Johnson, Daniel vs. The State
Johnson, David vs. Henry Bailey for use of Robert Freeman
Johnson, Ed vs. The State
Johnson, Eli vs. The State
Johnson, Flemming vs. George W. Adams and William Johnson,
    Administrator
Johnson, Frank vs. The State
Johnson, Gabriel and William P. Ford vs. John Baldwin
Johnson, Gip vs. The State
Johnson, Hannah vs. The State
Johnson, Henry vs. Peter Crawford
Johnson, Henry vs. Thomas Gibson for use of John Gibson
Johnson, Henry vs. The State
Johnson, Hugh G. vs. John W. Bridges
Johnson, Hugh G. vs. Martin Cochran
Johnson, Hugh G. vs. Edward W. Collier and William P.
    Dearmond
Johnson, Hugh G. vs. Adam Lee, Henry H. Lee and Jonathan
    Squire
Johnson, Hugh G. vs. Rufus Lord and Ralph Olmstead
Johnson, Hugh G. vs. John Owen
Johnson, Hugh G. and William Cook vs. Randolph Paine
Johnson, Hugh G. vs. Edward Quin and John Campbell
Johnson, Hugh G. vs. David Stanford and Pleasant Stovall
Johnson, Hugh G., Henry Stevens and William Cook vs.
    Charles D. Stewart and George Hargraves
Johnson, Hugh G. vs. Hosea Webster and George Webster
Johnson, Hugh P., Osborn R. O'Neal, James C. Johnson and
    Abraham Pyle vs. James C. Bartlett
Johnson, Hugh P. vs. Littleton T. P. Harwell
Johnson, Jack A. vs. Nancy Couch
Johnson, Jack A. vs. William McDonald
Johnson, James, Lewis Lane, Jackson Mobley and Hiram
    Johnson vs. Zacheriah Roe
Johnson, James vs. The State
Johnson, James C. vs. Josiah Davis and Orville Barbour
Johnson, James H. vs. Jesse Pitts
Johnson, John vs. Artemus Gould
Johnson, John vs. The State
Johnson, John vs. Cornelius D. Terhune for use of Luther
    Goble, Frederick L. Thomas and Luke Reid
Johnson, Joseph vs. Stephen W. Beasley
Johnson, Joseph vs. William I. Brewington
Johnson, Joseph and Hungerford and Woodruff vs. William
    Godfrey
Johnson, Joseph vs. Joseph K. Kilburn
Johnson, Joseph vs. Monticello Academy
Johnson, Joseph vs. Thomas J. Smith and William M. Broddus
Johnson, Joseph vs. Charles D. Stewart and George Hargraves
Johnson, Joseph vs. Christian Zabriskie
Johnson, Legree vs. The State
Johnson, Lewis and John Johnson vs. The State
Johnson, Minor W. S. vs. Zachariah Arnold
Johnson, Minor W. S. vs. Isaac Holeman
Johnson, Minor W. S. vs. John Walton
Johnson, Nicholas and Manson Turner vs. Anslem L. Earley
Johnson, Nicholas and Manson Turner vs. Henry Hepburn and
    Charles Price
Johnson, Nicholas vs. Allen McClendon
Johnson, Nicholas vs. Alfred Shepherd
Johnson, Nicholas vs. The State
Johnson, Nicholas vs. Pleasant Stovall
Johnson, Nicholas vs. Nathaniel and Samuel Sturges

Johnson, Nicholas and Mason Turner vs. Levi Trapp
Johnson, Peter vs. Nathaniel Deane
Johnson, Polly O. vs. Martin Yeoman
Johnson, Sam vs. The State
Johnson, Samuel and Charles Forbes, Administrator vs. John
  H. Baynes
Johnson, Sithy (Dukes) vs. George Johnson
Johnson, Snellen and Alfred Johnson vs. Benjamin Barron
Johnson, Snellen vs. Benjamin Marshall
Johnson, Snellen and Alfred Johnson vs. Isaac C. W. T.
  McKissack
Johnson, Snellen vs. Hezekiah W. Scovill
Johnson, Snellen, Alfred Johnson and Reuben Dawkins vs.
  James Whitfield, Hollis Cooley, William Strozier,
  Abraham B. Dale and George W. Holland
Johnson, Snelling vs. John H. Brantley for use of John
  Greer
Johnson, Snelling vs. Hamilton Brown, Peyton Gwyn and
  James Gwyn
Johnson, Snelling vs. Charles Kelsey, Alfred M. Hobby and
  Charles McIntire
Johnson, Snelling and Jarrel Beasley vs. George Stephens,
  Steven Stephens, Administrator and William Stephens,
  Administrator
Johnson, Snelling vs. John T. C. Towns
Johnson, Stephen H. vs. W. W. Fisher
Johnson, Thomas vs. The State
Johnson, Vince vs. The State
Johnson, Will (alias Chief) vs. The State
Johnson, William vs. Abner Bartlett, James C. Bartlett,
  Executor, William A. Bartlett, Executor, John E. Bartlett,
  Executor and George T. Bartlett, Executor
Johnson, William vs. Jeremiah Clark
Johnson, William and J. Wilkerson, Administrator vs.
  Charles P. Gordon
Johnson, William and Jeptha Wilkerson, Administrator vs.
  Thomas Grant, Executor, Daniel Grant, Executor, Thomas
  Grant, Executor and Peter Grinnell, Executor
Johnson, William and Jeptha Wilkerson vs. William Grimmett
  for use of Hosea Webster and George Webster
Johnson, William and Zachariah White vs. John Hill,
  Augustin Slaughter and Charles Labuzan
Johnson, William vs. Thomas Hoxey and Edward Dudley
Johnson, William vs. Seaborn Jones
Johnson, William and Pleasant Greene vs. John M. King
Johnson, William vs. Wilson Pope, Gideon Pope and William
  D. Williams
Johnson, William and Nicholas Johnson vs. Samuel Post
Johnson, William vs. The State
Johnson, William vs. Peter Wyche
Johnson, William, Jr. vs. Hiram Whatley
Johnson, William, Sr., Polly O. Johnson, Executor,
  Nicholas Johnson, Executor, and William Johnson, Sr.,
  Executor vs. Anthony Dyer
Johnson, William, Sr., William Johnson, Executor and Polly
  O. Johnson vs. James McGehee
Johnson, William, Sr. vs. Pearce Stevens
Johnson, William A. and John W. A. Smith, Administrator
  vs. William W. Bliss
Johnson, William D. vs. Elison E. Carhart and Aaron A. Raff
Johnson, William S. vs. Cyrus Holmes
Johnson, Willis vs. Jonathan Jewett, Gordon Abel and James
  N. Codwise

Johnson, Willis, Alfred. Johnson, Snellen Johnson, Jeptha
  Clements and John Grier vs. James Whitfield
Johnston, Fleming and James H. Johnston vs. Thomas J.
  Comer, Jr.
Johnston, Fleming and George W. Comer vs. James H. Roberts
Johnston, Fleming and James H. Johnston vs. James M.
  Williams
Johnston, Isaac vs. The State
Johnston, Jack A. and John W. Burney, Jr. vs. James H.
  Johnston
Johnston, James vs. Noah Butt and Eldridge Butt, Administra-
  tor
Johnston, James, Reuben Dawkins and William Phillips vs.
  Zachariah Roe, Minor Children of Z. Roe and Nathaniel
  G. Gordon, Guardian
Johnston, James vs. The State
Johnston, James and Martha Johnston, Guardian vs. Jackson
  Thadaway
Johnston, James H. vs. James Benton
Johnston, James H. vs. Robert Berry
Johnston, James H. vs. Elbridge G. Cabiness
Johnston, James H. and William Barclay vs. Edwin Graves
Johnston, James H. vs. John Hines
Johnston, James H. vs. Davis Lane and John F. Patterson
Johnston, James H. and Charles O. Bostick vs. James H.
  Roberts
Johnston, James H. vs. Williamson A. Roby
Johnston, James H. and Thomas R. King vs. Rachel Stagner
Johnston, Martha and Stephen H. Johnston vs. John Garland
Johnston, Martha vs. W. D. Maddox
Johnston, Nathan and William M. Johnston, Executor vs.
  James M. Clower
Johnston, Reese vs. Officers of Court
Johnston, Richard vs. Jacob Faulkner
Johnston, S. H. vs. W. S. Minter
Johnston, Snelling vs. James Cowen and Thomas B. Erwin
Johnston, Stephen H. vs. Matt Pritchett for use of Officers
  of Court
Johnston, William D. vs. Carhart and Ross
Johnston, William L. vs. Amos Moore
Johnston, William M., John F. Moreland, Executor, Patsey
  Maria Johnston, Franklin Malone, Guardian, Littleton
  Johnston, Minor, Margaret Johnston, Minor, James J.
  Johnston, Minor, Stephen H. Johnston, Steth Malone, Biddy
  Malone, Harriet E. Malone, William L. Phillips and Nancy
  A. Phillips vs. John Johnston and Lewis L. Lane
Johnston, William S. and Joseph Holland vs. Thomas
  Middlebrooks
Johnstone, Fleming vs. William S. Hurd and Anson Hungerford
Johnstone, James H. vs. Edgar Sherman, Basak Nichols and
  William C. Jessup
Jones, Abram D. and Stephen W. McLendon vs. Isaac Willingham
Jones, Amos vs. Isaac Hill
Jones, Amos vs. James Reed
Jones, Efford H. vs. William S. Hurd and Anson Hungerford,
  Jr.
Jones, Ephraim vs. Drury Davis
Jones, Evans vs. Elijah N. Hascall
Jones, Francis P. vs. James Doster
Jones, Hardy vs. John W. Bridges and James Speir
Jones, Harold vs. The State
Jones, Hartwell vs. Jefferson Adams
Jones, Hartwell vs. Thaddeus Beall and Elias Beall

190

Jones, Hartwell vs. Hamilton Goss and George Hargraves
Jones, Hartwell vs. Simeon Hyde
Jones, Hartwell vs. Pearce A. Lewis
Jones, Hartwell vs. John Newby
Jones, Hartwell vs. James Rousseau
Jones, Hartwell, Jr. and Hartwell Jones, Sr. vs. James C.
  Hearn
Jones, Henry vs. James Hines
Jones, Henry vs. Pope and Stilwell
Jones, Henry, Sr. vs. James J. Callaway and Thomas Holloway
Jones, J. R. vs. The State
Jones, Jack (alias Shack Jones) vs. James B. Goolsby
Jones, James vs. Rene Fitzpatrick
Jones, Jeff vs. The State
Jones, Joel and Kiziah Orr vs. The State
Jones, John vs. James Adams, Robert Adams, Administrator
  and Shearly Sledge, Administrator
Jones, John vs. Etheldred Jelks
Jones, John vs. Jesse Loyall
Jones, John vs. Allen McClendon
Jones, John vs. Andrew McKelroy
Jones, John vs. Jeremiah Pearson
Jones, John vs. Barnett Powell
Jones, John vs. Marlow Pryor
Jones, John vs. Thomas Wooten
Jones, John J. vs. Isaac McClendon
Jones, John J. vs. Reuben C. Shorter
Jones, Joseph W. vs. Henry Slaughter
Jones, Joseph W. and Charles Murran vs. Henry Walker for
  use of Michael Moore
Jones, Matthew and James Jones vs. Jesse Evans
Jones, Nancy vs. The State
Jones, Neal vs. The State
Jones, Phillip, Jr. vs. William Peddy
Jones, Reuben vs. Mary Findlay
Jones, Reuben vs. Harmon H. Geiger
Jones, Reuben vs. James Mitchell, Hamilton Burge for use of
  Alvah Wilson
Jones, Reuben, Sr. vs. John N. Williamson
Jones, Robert vs. Isaac Bailey
Jones, Robert vs. Richmond Brown
Jones, Robert vs. Hollis Cooley
Jones, Robert vs. John Fluker
Jones, Robert vs. Eli Glover
Jones, Robert and John Hill vs. Goodrich Jonas
Jones, Robert and John Hill vs. Justice of Court
Jones, Robert vs. Joseph Kopman
Jones, Robert vs. Jordan Pye
Jones, Robert vs. Edward Quinn and John Campbell
Jones, Robert vs. Benjamin Wagner
Jones, Russell vs. Ferdinand Phinizy for use of Thomas
  Terrell
Jones, Russell vs. Joseph Smith
Jones, Seaborn vs. John S. D. Byrom
Jones, Seaborn vs. Daniel Parish, Jasper Corning, Henry
  Parish, Joseph Kernochan and Ephraim Holbrook
Jones, Seaborn vs. Elias Windham
Jones, Thomas vs. Oliver Whyte
Jones, Thomas B. vs. Thomas Black and James Black
Jones, Vincent vs. Mathew Whitfield
Jones, W. H. vs. The State
Jones, Whit vs. The State
Jones, William, George Dawkins, Administrator and John

191

Spears, Administrator vs. William Evans and Drury S.
  Patterson
Jones, William vs. Isaac Hill
Jones, William, John Spears, Administrator and George
  Dawkins, Administrator vs. John Spears, Sr.
Jones, William, Jr. and John Spears, Sr. vs. Christian
  Lewis, Wilson Daniel, James Daniel and Iby Hill
Jones, William B. and James H. Morrow vs. Anthony Dyer
Jones, William B. and James H. Morrow vs. Joseph B. Week,
  David M. Benedict and Frederick D. Fanning
Jones, Wood, Joe Thomas, Eva Moon, Joe Davis, Wink Davis
  and Sam Henderson vs. The State
Jordan, ? vs. ? Weathersby
Jordan, Abram vs. The State
Jordan, Addie Joe vs. The State
Jordan, Anna vs. William Jordan
Jordan, Benjamin vs. George L. Bird
Jordan, Benjamin vs. Peter F. Boisclair
Jordan, Benjamin vs. Littleberry Bostick
Jordan, Benjamin vs. Francis Boykin
Jordan, Benjamin vs. Peter Bray
Jordan, Benjamin and Henry Dillon vs. Zeno Bronson
Jordan, Benjamin vs. Isaac Carter
Jordan, Benjamin vs. Gabriel Colley
Jordan, Benjamin vs. Samuel Connally for use of George
  Harris, Jr.
Jordan, Benjamin vs. D. Dixon
Jordan, Benjamin vs. John Farley
Jordan, Benjamin and Henry Jordan vs. Ephraim Hudson
Jordan, Benjamin vs. Amos W. Langdon
Jordan, Benjamin vs. Thomas Napier
Jordan, Benjamin vs. James Phillips
Jordan, Benjamin vs. John R. Pitkin
Jordan, Benjamin vs. John Raiford, John S. Raiford,
  Executor, Baldwin Raiford, Guardian and Lucry Raiford
Jordan, Benjamin vs. William Robinson
Jordan, Benjamin vs. James Speir and John W. Bridges
Jordan, Benjamin vs. Pleasant Stovall and William P. Ford
Jordan, Benjamin vs. Reuben Turner
Jordan, Benjamin vs. John Twiggs, Abraham Twiggs, Executor
  and George Twiggs, Executor
Jordan, Benjamin, Stephen D. Crane and Magers Henderson vs.
  Nathan Warner for use of Thomas Grant
Jordan, Benjamin vs. Peter Wigins
Jordan, Benjamin and Henry Dillon vs. Caleb Woodley
Jordan, Bill vs. The State
Jordan, Bob vs. The State
Jordan, C. W. vs. Griffin, Monticello and Madison Railroad
  Co.
Jordan, C. W. vs. William C. Leverette
Jordan, C. W. vs. Officers of Court
Jordan, C. W. vs. Matthew Whitfield and J. A. Billips,
  Administrator
Jordan, Charles S. and Fleming Jordan vs. William N. Reid,
  Sr., Mrs. E. W. Reid, Samuel T. Reid and William N. Reid
Jordan, Charles S., Jr. vs. Davis Lane and John R.
  Patterson
Jordan, Charley Scott vs. The State
Jordan, Charlie vs. H. B. Jordan, E. H. Jordan, A. H.
  Jordan and D. R. Glover
Jordan, Charlie, Singleton Jordan and Gill Peacock vs.
  The State
Jordan, Doll vs, The State

192

Jordan, E. H. and O. G. Jordan vs. Mrs. Callie Pounds
Jordan, Emily and Thomas Horn vs. The State
Jordan, Mrs. F. C. vs. W. A. Kelly and Brothers
Jordan, Fleming vs. Marine and Fire Insurance Bank of
  Georgia
Jordan, Fleming vs. Joseph Stark
Jordan, Fleming vs. The State
Jordan, Fleming vs. Edward Thomas
Jordan, Floyd vs. The State
Jordan, Genty vs. Officers of Court
Jordan, George vs. The State
Jordan, Gus vs. The State
Jordan, Hardy vs. William A. Kelly and Brothers
Jordan, Harry vs. The State
Jordan, Harry vs. The State
Jordan, Henry vs. Milton Antony
Jordan, Henry vs. Andrew Ervin, James Ervin, Jared E. Grace,
  Andrew Ervin, Jr. and Walter Crenshaw
Jordan, Henry vs. Ephraim Hudson
Jordan, Henry and Thomas Lewis vs. Joel Randolph and John
  Rucker
Jordan, Henry vs. John Sparks
Jordan, Henry vs. Charles Spear
Jordan, Henry vs. The State
Jordan, Henry vs. Samuel Sturges and Nathaniel L. Sturges
Jordan, J. F. vs. Monticello Merchandise Co.
Jordan, Jack vs. Peyton Clements, A. E. Clements, Adminis-
  trator, W. C. Clements, Lizzie Clements and Thomas
  Clements
Jordan, Jack vs. W. A. Kelly and Brothers
Jordan, Jack vs. The State
Jordan, Jacob vs. Hardy Cook for use of Officers of Court
Jordan, John vs. The State
Jordan, John F. vs. The State
Jordan, Lott vs. Mrs. H. N. White
Jordan, Mortimer vs. Adam Alexander for use of George
  Simmons
Jordan, Nathaniel vs. The State
Jordan, Pitman vs. The State
Jordan, Randall vs. The State
Jordan, Reuben vs. J. H. Freeman and C. L. Bartlett,
  Administrator
Jordan, Reuben vs. Jonas H. Holland
Jordan, Reuben vs. Insurance Bank of Columbus
Jordan, Reuben vs. Matthew Whitfield and John F. Patterson,
  Executor
Jordan, Sarah vs. Gentry Jordan for use of Officers of
  Court
Jordan, Seneca vs. Warren Wallace and Co.
Jordan, Starling and Henry Jordan, Administrator vs. John
  Powell
Jordan, Starling and Henry Jordan, Administrator vs. John
  Pugsley
Jordan, T. M. and F. C. Jordan, Administrator vs. N. B.
  White
Jordan, Thomas M. and Mrs. F. C. Jordan, Administrator vs.
  William C. Leverett
Jordan, Thomas M. and Reuben Jordan vs. Francis Ward,
  Flemming Jordan, Sr., Fleming J. Ward, Trustee, Martha
  Ward, S. B. Ward and R. C. Ward
Jordan, Thomas M. vs. Matthew Whitfield, Leroy M. Willson,
  Executor, Pleasant Willson, Executor, John Patterson,
  Executor and William H. Mathis, Executor

Jordan, Vic vs. The State
Jordan, W. H. (alias Will Maxey) and Wiley H. Jordan and
   G. O. Gordan vs. The State
Jordan, W. J. vs. J. F. Webb
Jordan, Wash vs. The State
Jordan, Will vs. The State
Jordan, William vs. William A. Kelly and Brothers
Jordan, William vs. The State
Jordan, William F. vs. Russel J. Brown
Jordan, William F. vs. Mathew Whitfield, John F. Patterson,
   Executor, William Mathis, Executor, Leroy M. Wilson,
   Executor and Pleasant Wilson, Administrator
Jordan, Willie vs. The State
Justices of Court vs. Norman A. Belk
Justices of Court vs. Armistead Dodson
Justices of Court vs. David Dunlap
Justices of Court vs. Anslem L. Earley, Caleb Earley, James
   Robinson and Abram Pyle
Justices of Court vs. James Farley
Justices of Court vs. Craton A. J. Flemister
Justices of Court vs. Isham Kendrick
Justices of Court vs. Irvine Lawson and John Bogan
Justices of Court vs. John H. Marks
Justices of Court vs. Isaac L. Parker
Justices of Court vs. William Pope
Justices of Court vs. Armstead Richardson
Justices of Court vs. Barnabas Strickland
Justices of Court vs. William H. Taylor
Justices of Court vs. Edward Varner

Keeling, William, Thomas Worthy, Administrator and
   Leonard Keeling, Administrator vs. Susannah Poindexter
Keene, B. K. vs. W. W. Chapman and William A. Ross
Keene, Benjamin F., James Freeman, and George Freeman,
   Administrator vs. Haviland, Keese and Co.
Keene, Benjamin F. vs. William M. Broddus and Edward A.
   Broddus, Executor
Keene, Benjamin F. vs. Drury M. Cox
Keene, Benjamin F. vs. David Flanders
Keene, Benjamin F. and Nelson Gathright vs. Henry K.
   Harrell, Harford Lyon and William Wright
Keene, Benjamin F. vs. James Johnston
Keene, Benjamin F. vs. John H. Powers
Keene, Benjamin F. vs. Thomas I. Smith
Keene, Benjamin J. vs. William Harper
Keith, Jeremiah and Arthur Herring vs. Welcom Parks
Keith, John and Stephen Tyner vs. Jesse L. Long
Kellam, Robert vs. John Robinson
Keller, Everett vs. The State
Kelley, Croff vs. The State
Kelley, Jacob, Jr. vs. George Osbern
Kelley, John vs. The State
Kelley, John R., Beverly A. Kelley and James H. Robinson
   vs. Robert Wright
Kellogg, Andy vs. The State
Kellum, Henry and William B. Hardy vs. Elizabeth Callaway
Kelly and Phillips vs. Herbert Talmadge for use of
   Officers of Court
Kelly, Alfred vs. The State
Kelly, Allen vs. Williamson Bailey
Kelly, Allen, Jarrett B. Kelley, Administrator and Beverly
   A. Kelly, Administrator vs. Frances (Kelly) Blount, James
   Blount and James G. Blount, Administrator

194

Kelly, Allen, J. B. Kelly, Administrator and B. A. Kelly,
   Administrator vs. Matilda (Kelly) Redd and Joel A.
   McClendon
Kelly, Allen vs. The State
Kelly, Amos vs. Officers of Court
Kelly, Anthony vs. Griffin, Monticello and Madison Railroad
   Co.
Kelly, B. vs. The State
Kelly, B. A. vs. Emily Cunard
Kelly, B. A. vs. Alfred Goolsby
Kelly, Bee and Will Kelly vs. The State
Kelly, Beverly and Colbert Jeffries vs. Earley W. Thrasher
Kelly, Buddie vs. The State
Kelly, Burt and Charles Digby vs. The State
Kelly, C. H. and C. E. Cordell vs. The State
Kelly, Crawford vs. The State
Kelly, Daniel and Greene Pernell, Administrator vs. John B.
   Slaughter
Kelly, Ebin H. vs. Carter and Cutcher
Kelly, Eden vs. The State
Kelly, Eden H., C. H. Kelly, Administrator and Eden H.
   Kelly, Jr., Administrator vs. Mattie Lou Malone
Kelly, Ezekiel B. vs. Nathan Mossy
Kelly, Francis O. and Thomas Gaston vs. The State
Kelly, Geila (alias Geila Jeffers) vs. The State
Kelly, George vs. The State
Kelly, Hamp and Pink Kelly vs. The State
Kelly, J. H. vs. Lawrence and Pope
Kelly, J. R. vs. Emiline Johnson
Kelly, Jacob vs. James Richards
Kelly, James vs. James Holt
Kelly, James and Abner T. Deering vs. Robinson and Pabodie
Kelly, Jarrett B. vs. Benjamin Banks
Kelly, Jarrett B. vs. Henry D. Banks and Pleasant E. Banks,
   Guardian
Kelly, Jarrett B. vs. Griffin, Monticello and Madison
   Railroad Co.
Kelly, Jarrett B. vs. O. S. Prophitt
Kelly, John C. and Jarrett B. Kelly, Administrator vs.
   Eaton H. Kelly
Kelly, John R. vs. Littleberry B. Phillips
Kelly, John R. vs. Alexander Smith and John C. Gibson,
   Administrator
Kelly, John Thomas vs. Thomas Nolen
Kelly, Lela (alias Lela Jeffers) vs. The State
Kelly, Lewis vs. The State
Kelly, Lucy vs. The State
Kelly, Marvin vs. The State
Kelly, Michael vs. Saban Horton
Kelly, Michael and John C. Watters vs. Martin Puckett and
   James W. Vaughn, Administrator for use of William Maxey
   and Joshua Hill
Kelly, Michael vs. Abel P. Wilson
Kelly, S. J. vs. John H. Kelly
Kelly, S. J. vs. Officers of Court
Kelly, Seaborn C. vs. Drury P. Evans
Kelly, Seaborn J. vs. Seaborn W. Shy
Kelly, Thomas vs. The State
Kelly, Tire and Anthony Lewis vs. Harly Attaway
Kelly, Type vs. The State
Kelly, W. A. vs. The State
Kelly, W. G. and A. J. Kelly vs. The Waxelbaum Co.
Kelly, William vs. Thomas Beall

Kelly, William A. and Leroy R. Price vs. The State
Kelly, William A. and Brothers vs. O. G. Roberts, L. A.
    Roberts and V. F. McMichael
Kelly, William M. vs. The State
Kelton, B. T. vs. The State
Kenan, Owen H. vs. David Beach
Kenan, Owen H. and Hardy H. Kenan vs. The State
Kenan, Owen H. vs. William F. Steele
Kenan, Owen H. vs. George Stovall and Betsy Stovall
Kenan, Owen H. vs. Leroy M. Wiley and Thomas W. Baxter
Kendrick, Benjamin B. vs. The State
Kendrick, Burks vs. The State
Kendrick, James vs. The State
Kendrick, James vs. Green B. Williamson
Kennady, Thomas and Woody Dozier vs. Jonas Clark
Kennedy, John vs. Abden Alexander
Kennedy, John, Garland Hardwick, Abdon Alexander vs. Burrel
    Green
Kennedy, John vs. Elijah N. Hascall and David Hascall
Kennedy, John vs. William McMath
Kennedy, John vs. William Nelson and William Knight
Kennedy, Thomas vs. John Donaldson
Kennedy, Thomas vs. The State
Kennedy, Thomas and Samuel Harper vs. John B. Whitaker for
    use of Joseph Johnson and John Baldwin
Kennon, Charles vs. John Cowan
Kennon, Charles vs. Moses Hill
Kennon, Charles vs. Charles W. Smith
Kennon, Isham and Robert F. Benton vs. Reason E. Mabry and
    George H. Cook
Kennon, James vs. The State
Kennon, Richard vs. Hezekiah Terrel
Kennon, William W. vs. David S. Cherry
Kennon, William W. vs. John Cowan
Kennon, William W. and Stokely Morgan vs. John M. Dooley
Kennon, William W. vs. Eli Glover and John Cashin
Kennon, William W. and Horatio Gartrell vs. Greene and
    Buchannon
Kennon, William W. vs. William Hitchcock
Kennon, William W. vs. Joseph Johnson
Kennon, William W. vs. Warner L. Kennon
Kennon, William W. vs. Charles Lewis for use of William
    Lewis
Kennon, William W. and Stokeley Morgan vs. Thomas Napier
Kennon, William W. vs. Joseph Williams for use of John
    Williams
Kennon, William W. vs. Thomas Williams and Co.
Kennymore, Byrum P. vs. The State
Kennymore, Michael vs. Elizabeth Callaway
Key, Abraham vs. William Barron
Key, Abraham and Littleberry B. Phillips vs. John W. Hawkins
Key, Abraham vs. Norborne B. Powell
Key, Abraham and Eldred Wilkerson vs. Pleasant Stovall and
    William P. Ford
Key, Abraham and John K. Benford vs. Bennet M. Ware
Key, Abraham vs. John Willson, John Hill, Executor, James
    Willson, Executor, Fleming Jordan, Executor and David A.
    Reese, Executor
Key, Burney vs. The State
Key, Burrell vs. William Hodges
Key, Burrell and Aron Brooks vs. John Williams
Key, Burwell P. vs. Joseph Godard
Key, Burwell P. (Burrell) and Thomas Key vs. Robert B.

Haviland, Daniel G. Haviland, James C. Haviland and
   Alfred Ashfield
Key, Burwell P. vs. Shadrach J. McMichael
Key, Burwell P. vs. The State
Key, F. C. vs. The State
Key, George M. vs. Joseph J. Spencer
Key, Jim vs. The State
Key, John C. vs. Joseph E. Brown (Governor)
Key, John C. vs. S. H. Kelly
Key, Joseph vs. Robert Crenshaw for use of William Crenshaw
Key, M. B., Charles Turner and O. G. Roberts vs. Mayor and
   Council
Key, Micajah B., John C. Key, John R. Greer, Joseph W.
   Preston and John B. Webb vs. County Commissioners
Key, Micajah B. vs. The State
Key, Tandy W. vs. John McQueen
Key, Thomas vs. Henry Summerlin
Key, William H. and John Edwards vs. Dunlap and Harris
Key, Willie vs. The State
Kidd, Anderson R. vs. William Ross
Kidd, James H. vs. David Evans
Kidd, James H. and Timothy Freeman vs. Robert Rogers for
   use of Thomas W. Harris
Kight, Samuel vs. John Simms
Kight, Samuel, Sr. vs. The State
Kilgore, John vs. Robert Roby, William V. McGehee, Adminis-
   trator and Nancy Roby, Administrator
Kilgore, Joseph, Ephram Higginbotham and Robert Higginbotham
   vs. The State
Killgore, John and Robert L. Willis vs. Sarah A. Kirby
Kilpatrick, James vs. William Bowen
Kimbro, John vs. Reuben Shorter
Kimbrough, Shadrach vs. Charles D. Williams and Abraham
   Woolsey
Kimbrough, William H. and Shadrick Kimbrough vs. George
   Ralph, Charles McIntire, Charles W. Rockwell and Charles
   W. Kelsey
Kinard, Barney C. and Michael Kinard vs. Robert Brown
Kinard, J. and James M. Williams, Administrator vs. Theresa
   Maddox
Kinard, Jesse vs. The State
Kinard, M. J. vs. The State
Kinard, Martin J. vs. T. W. Pye
King, Benjamin and Winburn Odom vs. Edward Beaird
King, Benjamin vs. Lewin Cohen
King, Benjamin and Elisha Mathis vs. Robert Owsly and
   Isaac T. Moreland, Administrator
King, Benjamin vs. William Thames
King, Benjamin vs. Benjamin Williamson
King, Dock vs. The State
King, Edward and Marcus Vance vs. Alexander Allen
King, Edward vs. Joseph Duncan for use of James R. Jones
King, Edward vs. Robert D. Potter
King, Edward D. vs. The State
King, Jacob vs. The State
King, Jim vs. The State
King, John vs. The State
King, John M. vs. Benjamin Bennett
King, John M. vs. William Goolsby
King, John M. vs. The State
King, John M., Jr. vs. William Maxey and Charles S. Jordan
King, Nancy vs. John Tilman
King, Richard vs. Thomas Broddus

King, Richard vs. Hamilton Brown
King, Richard vs. Daniel Parish, Thomas Parish, Joseph
  Kernochan, Henry Parish and Jasper Corning
King, Richard vs. James S. Walker
King, Richard D. vs. Thomas B. Erwin
King, Tandy D. vs. William P. Buis
King, Tandy D. vs. Lewis C. Cantelou and Benjamin H. Warren
King, Tandy D. and Jeremiah Davis vs. Charles Kelsey,
  Charles McIntire and Alfred M. Hobby
King, Tandy D. and Zachariah Phillips vs. Arnold Johnson
King, Tandy D. vs. Stephen Norris
King, Tandy D. vs. Abner Radden
King, Tandy D. vs. Richard Richardson, John Bolton, Curtis
  Bolton and Durham T. Hall
King, Thomas vs. The State
King, Thomas vs. John Webb
King, Thomas R. and John M. King vs. Berry T. Digby
Kinman, Samuel vs. James A. Greer
Kinnard, Barney vs. George D. Millen
Kinnon, Richard vs. Robert Culbertson
Kirby, Jesse vs. Edmund S. Williams
Kirk, Hudson and John Jones vs. James Sumter
Kirkpatrick, Hugh P. and George W. Holland vs. Jeremiah
  Pearson
Kirkpatrick, Hugh P. vs. Henry S. Roosevelt and Samuel G.
  Barker
Kirksey, Elisha vs. John F. Dismukes
Kirksey, Elisha S. and Robert Goen vs. Pleasant M. Compton
Kirksey, Elisha S. vs. Alfred D. Kerr
Kirksey, William, James H. Westmoreland and William H.
  Taylor vs. George Foalds
Kirtley, Lemma vs. Beach and Thomas
Kirtley, Lemma vs. William O. Eichelberger and Joseph E.
  Clemm
Kiser, Newt vs. The State
Kitchen, Charles vs. Clark Brewer
Kitchen, Charles vs. The State
Kitchens, Brant vs. The State
Kitchens, Charles vs. Alford Brewer
Kitchens, Charles vs. Ethan Brewer
Kitchens, Charles vs. Lewis H. Hoard
Kitchens, Charles vs. Archibald L. Polk
Kitchens, Elizabeth and Barthena Wilson vs. William A.
  Lofton
Kitchens, Joel, J. H. Connally and William Pope vs.
  Elizabeth Kitchens
Kitchens, Joel, Henry Kitchens, Nelson Kitchens and Aaron
  Parker vs. The State
Kitchens, Oscar vs. The State
Kitchens, W. H. vs. The State
Kitchens, Will vs. The State
Knight, Carrington vs. William McMath
Knight, Carrington vs. William H. Oakman
Knight, Carrington vs. Nathaniel L. Sturges and Samuel
  Sturges
Knight, Elisha vs. Stokely Lambert
Knight, James P. vs. Matthew Whitfield
Knight, John vs. James Bryan
Knight, John vs. John Carrington, Sr. and John J.
  Carrington, Administrator
Knight, John vs. William Freeman
Knight, John vs. Joshua Holcomb
Knight, John vs. The State

Knight, John vs. William Tyler
Knight, John and James Irvin vs. James Whitfield
Knight, John, Jr., Thomas J. Smith and James Knight vs.
Central Bank of Georgia
Knight, John, Sr. vs. Robert A. Beall and Stephen T. Miller
Knight, John, Sr. and Marcus Vance vs. John Buck
Knight, John, Sr., Robert A. Ridley and R. C. Clayton vs.
Central Bank of Georgia
Knight, John, Sr. vs. Charles P. Gordon, James H. Gordon,
James H. Gordon, Executor and George W. Gordon, Executor
Knight, John, Sr. vs. James Kendrick
Knight, John, Sr. vs. Horatio Spencer for use of Daniel
Lord and Jeremiah Pierson
Knight, John, Sr. vs. William Wade and Robert O. Dale,
Executor
Knight, John, Sr. vs. John G. Webb
Knight, T. P. vs. The State
Knight, Warren v. and Richard W. Henderson vs. Nancy Speer
for use of John W. Speer
Knight, Wiley vs. The State
Knight, William vs. The State
Knowles, Benjamin E. vs. William C. Johnson for use of
Samuel Johnson
Knowles, Charles vs. Frederick Freeman
Knowles, Rice P. vs. Alston H. Green
Kolb, David, John Bass and Elias Ozburn vs. Williamson
Bailey and William Bailey, Executor

Lacy, William vs. Jacob Sansom
Lamar, Bob vs. The State
Lamar, John P. vs. The State
Lambert, Stokeley vs. Barney Dunn for use of Larkin Dunn
Lambert, William vs. James Perry
Lamberth, Edwin vs. Thomas Napier
Lamberth, John and Eden Lamberth vs. Thomas Cargile
Lambeth, James vs. The State
Lambright, William vs. Joseph Beven
Lambright, William vs. John Bolton
Lamkin, Robert (alias Frank Allen) vs. The State
Lamsden, Jeremiah C. vs. John Hobson
Lancer, Nathan S. vs. The State
Land, Hiram vs. The State
Landrum, Elias vs. The State
Landrum, Timothy vs. James Richards and Willis Richards
Lane, A. W. vs. William V. Burney
Lane, Alexander vs. Christopher Killbee
Lane, Augustus W., William A. Lane and Davis Lane vs.
Benjamin F. Cunningham and Sarah L. Cunningham
Lane, Carlton vs. The State
Lane, Davis, John F. Patterson, Stephen C. Talmadge and
Ebenezer T. White vs. James L. Maddux
Lane, Davis, Thomas Bartlett, George T. Bartlett, Henry A.
Dickensen, Richard Loyall and Miles Perry vs. The State
Lane, Edward W. and John Holmes vs. James Duncan
Lane, Henry vs. Emelina J. Flemister and Willson L.
Flemister, Guardian
Lane, James vs. The State
Lane, James M. vs. R. B. Phillips
Lane, James M. and John F. Lane vs. F. M. Swanson
Lane, John B. vs. The State
Lane, Lewis, Hiram Johnston and Jackson Mobly vs. The State
Lane, Lewis L. vs. George T. Bartlett
Lane, Lewis L. and Stephen Johnston vs. Joseph E. Brown for

use of Mathew Whitfield
Lane, Lewis L. vs. Russel Brown
Lane, Lewis L. vs. Crawford H. Greer
Lane, Lewis L. and Maximilian H. Hutchison vs. John R. Greer
Lane, Lewis L. and Stephen H. Johnston vs. Alfred Johnson
Lane, Lewis L. vs. Thomas J. Lawrence
Lane, Lewis L. and James H. Johnston vs. John C. Maddux and
  James L. Maddux, Executor
Lane, Lewis L. vs. William T. Maddux
Lane, Lewis L. vs. Isaac T. Robinson
Lane, Sampson and James Flood vs. Boley Conner
Lane, Samuel vs. John Hinson and Reuben Radford
Lane, Samuel, Jeremiah Lumsden and Joseph M. Post vs. John
  B. Parks
Lane, Samuel, William Spears and John M. Patrick vs. Welcom
  Parks
Lane, Samuel, William Shaw, Peter Randolph, Administrator
  and Margaret Shaw, Administrator
Lane, W. B. vs. Wiley Peddy
Lane, W. D. vs. Griffin, Monticello and Madison Railroad Co.
Lane, William D. and Augustus W. Lane vs. Hurd, Hungerford
  and Co.
Lane, William D. and Augustus W. Lane vs. Matthew Whitfield,
  Leroy M. Willson, Executor, Pleasant Willson, Executor,
  John F. Patterson, Executor and William H. Mathis,
  Executor
Lang, John vs. Nehemiah Schogen and Benjamin Wallace
Langham, Elias vs. The State
Langham, James vs. William Cook
Langham, James vs. William Martin and Lucy Martin
Langston, D. M. vs. Henry Roby
Langston, Isaac vs. Jonas H. Holland and James C. Bartlett
Langston, Isaac vs. David M. Langston
Langston, Isaac vs. William Lightfoot and Davis Flanders
Langston, Isaac vs. Isaac L. Parker and Maximillian H.
  Hutchison, Administrator
Langston, Isaac vs. Planters Manufacturing Co.
Langston, Isaac and John Langston vs. Thomas K. Slaughter
Langston, Isaac, John Bartlett and Thomas Bartlett vs. The
  State
Langston, James vs. The State
Langston, John E. and David M. Langston, Executor vs. John
  T. Marks, Nathan T. Marks, Guardian, Amarintha P. Marks,
  Martha E. Smith and Thomas Langston
Langston, John E. vs. The State
Langston, Warren vs. The State
Lanier, Frances (Boyd) vs. Nathan S. Lanier
Lanier, James vs. Joel Baley for use of Alston H. Greene
  and Joseph Buchannon
Lanier, James vs. Jonathan Ellis, Jr.
Lanier, James vs. Jonathan Ellis, Jr.
Lanier, James and William Brown vs. John Hill, Augustin
  Slaughter and Charles Labuzan
Lanier, James and John Donaldson vs. Christopher Hobson,
  John Willson, Administrator and Harriet H. Hobson,
  Administrator
Lanier, James vs. John Kinard
Lanier, James vs. Henry Walker
Lanier, John vs. Thomas C. Pinkard
Lanier, Nathan S. vs. The State
Lard, Adam and James Splawn vs. Zachary Pope and John
  Stilwell
Lasiter, Benjamin vs. Edward McGehee

Lassiter, Jacob vs. Elias Sinclair for use of Jeremiah
   Powell
Laurence, Lemuel O. vs. Bank of Darien
Lawrence, Abraham vs. The State
Lawrence, Frank vs. The State
Lawrence, George vs. William Hardwick
Lawrence, George W. vs. Jethro Mobley
Lawrence, George W. vs. The State
Lawrence, James and William K. Pope, Administrator vs.
   George T. Bartlett
Lawrence, James vs. Jonas H. Holland
Lawrence, James and Leroy Lawrence, Administrator vs.
   Augustus W. Lane
Lawrence, Lemuel O., Lewis C. Holland and John R. Dickin
   vs. James C. Bartlett
Lawrence, Lemuel O. and Lewis C. Holland vs. Stephen W.
   Beasley
Lawrence, Lemuel O. vs. Thomas R. S. Holifield
Lawrence, Lemuel O. vs. Burwell Jordan
Lawrence, Lemuel O. and Lewis C. Holland vs. James Robinson
Lawrence, Lemuel O. vs. Alfred Shorter
Lawrence, Lemuel O. vs. Bennett M. Ware
Lawrence, Lemuel O. and Lewis C. Holland vs. Hosea Webster
   and Thomas J. Parmelee
Lawrence, Lemuel O. vs. James Whitfield
Lawrence, Leroy and David A. Reese vs. Abner Bartlett,
   James C. Bartlett, Executor, William A. Bartlett,
   Executor, John E. Bartlett, Executor and George T.
   Bartlett, Executor
Lawrence, Leroy vs. Andrew J. Chisson
Lawrence, Leroy, William K. Pope, Administrator and Seaborn
   Lawrence, Administrator vs. Crawford H. Greer
Lawrence, Leroy and Seaborn Lawrence, Executor and William
   K. Pope, Executor vs. Nancy Lawrence
Lawrence, Leroy vs. Jesse Loyall
Lawrence, Leroy vs. George Stringfellow and Riley S. Fears,
   Administrator
Lawrence, S. C. and C. W. Pope vs. Major and Council of
   Monticello
Lawrence, Seaborn, S. C. Lawrence, Administrator, Lucien B.
   Newton, John R. Grier, Nathan C. Fish and Mattie M.
   Lawrence vs. County Commissioners
Lawrence, Seaborn vs. George P. Hallock
Lawrence, Seaborn and Stephen C. Lawrence, Administrator vs.
   William Middlebrooks
Lawrence, Stewart vs. The State
Lawrence, William and Leroy Lawrence, Guardian vs. Andrew
   I. Chipon
Lawrence, William vs. George W. Daniel
Lawrence, William vs. Neill Ferguson
Lawrence, William vs. Susan Rivers and John P. Lamar,
   Trustee
Lawrence, William vs. Hezekiah Smith
Laws, Alexander vs. Rene Fitzpatrick
Laws, Isham and Spencer Laws vs. Joshua Grace
Laws, Joseph and Stephen Laws vs. Joshua Grace
Laws, Joseph vs. John Rieves
Laws, Joseph vs. Charles D. Stewart
Laws, Spencer vs. Nathan Fish
Laws, Spencer and Joseph Laws vs. Early Harris
Laws, Spencer vs. The State
Laws, Thomas vs. P. P. Vincent
Lawson, Arther vs. Benajah Birdsong and George Clark, Executor

Lawson, Arthur vs. John Greer
Lawson, Arthur vs. Allen McClendon
Lawson, Arthur vs. Martin Yeomans
Lawson, David, Irvine Lawson, Administrator and Matilda
   Lawson, Administrator vs. Benjamin Layton for use of
   Charles S. Ridley
Lawson, David vs. Matthew Mitchell
Lawson, Francis vs. William Murray
Lawson, Francis and Irvine Lawson vs. Allen Ryland
Lawson, Irvine vs. William Hitchcock
Lawson, Irvine vs. John Hobson, Francis Hobson, Administra-
   tor, Alsea Holifield, Administrator and James Whitfield,
   Administrator
Lawson, Irvine vs. Lawson S. Holland
Lawson, Reuben vs. D. C. Bancroft
Lawson, Reuben, Samuel D. Varner and William J. Goolsby vs.
   Henry Vaughn
Lawson, Thomas R. vs. Peyton R. Clements
Lawson, Thomas R. and James Calloway vs. Elisha Perryman
Layson, Ann N. vs. C. W. Jordan and B. Whitfield for use of
   Officers of Court
Layson, Berry vs. The State
Layson, C. C. vs. Davis R. Andrews, Jr.
Layson, C. C., Jr. vs. The State
Layson, J. N. vs. The State
Lazenby, Bob, Jordon Stanford, Paten Lazenby and Aaron
   Purifoy vs. The State
Lazenby, Dan vs. The State
Lazenby, J. G. vs. Officers of Court
Lazenby, J. G. vs. The State
Lazenby, Jefferson and Sarah E. Lazenby vs. John Lazenby
   and Francis M. Swanson, Administrator
Lazenby, William and Francis M. Swanson, Administrator vs.
   Martha E. Lazenby
Leach, Mollie vs. John H. Kelly
Leake, Robert vs. William Bryson and Harper Bryson
Leake, Robert vs. The State
Ledbetter, Banks, Joseph G. Barker and Thomas W. O'Neal vs.
   John T. Boykin
Lee, Adam vs. The State
Lee, John vs. Thomas Richardson
Lee, William and Peter William Gautier vs. Commissioners of
   Monticello for use of Stokely Morgan
Lee, William vs. Carton A. J. Flemister
Leffman, Lee and Frederick Green vs. Robert Adams
Leonard, William P. W. vs. William W. Chapman and William
   A. Ross
Letson, Robert vs. Griffin, Monticello and Madison Railroad
   Co.
Leveret, John, Betsey Reison (Paschal) and Benjamin Reison
   vs. Elizabeth Parks
Leverett, Bee vs. The State
Leverett, Burrel and Thomas Jester vs. James Gresham for
   use of John Hays
Leverett, Burrel vs. James Whitfield
Leverett, Charles P. vs. The State
Leverett, Edward A. vs. Leroy M. Seymore
Leverett, Henry vs. E. W. Baynes
Leverett, J. H. vs. The State
Leverett, Jack vs. The State
Leverett, James vs. The State
Leverett, Jeremiah and Andrew McElroy vs. The State
Leverett, John and Jesse Leverett vs. Noah Ramsay

Leverett, N. H. vs. Obediah Cornwell
Leverett, N. H., Thomas Leverett and James Leverett vs.
  The State
Leverett, Nancy Jane vs. Edward Leverett and Wilkins Lynch,
  Administrator
Leverett, Thomas vs. Joseph Price
Leverett, Thomas vs. The State
Leverett, W. C. vs. Sarah Hawk
Leverett, William C. vs. Benjamin Barron and Samuel Barron,
  Administrator
Leverett, William C. vs. M. V. Urquhart
Leverett, William C. vs. Matthew Whitfield, Leroy M. Willson,
  Executor, Pleasant Willson, Executor, John F. Patterson,
  Executor and William H. Mathis, Executor
Leverette, B. F. vs. The State
Leverette, N. H. vs. J. W. Burney and W. H. Malone for use
  of Officers of Court
Leverette, N. H. vs. Christopher Fincher for use of Officers
  of Court
Leverette, Nathan, Elias G. Langham, Executor and James
  Baggett, Executor vs. Jesse Matthews
Leverette, W. C., Aristarchus Newton, J. H. Bullard, H. W.
  Bullard, S. H. Bullard, Thomas Spivey and O. H. Arnol vs.
  Emily F. Adams (2 folders)
Leverette, W. C. Jordan vs. Thomas M. Jordan
Leverette, W. C. vs. Mrs. Sid C. Newton
Leverette, William C. vs. Joseph Favors and Hardy Cook,
  Administrator
Leveritt, Burrel vs. James Gresham for use of John Hays
Leverrett, Ambros vs. The State
Leverrett, David vs. The State
Leverrett, Mrs. Em W. vs. The State
Levy, Lewis vs. Mein and Mackay
Lewis, George vs. The State
Lewis, James B. and Edmund B. Darden, Administrator vs.
  Jesse Lambeth, William Fain, Joseph Watters, Thomas H.
  Cliatt and Robert Ware for use of William Hitchcock
Lewis, John vs. The State
Lewis, Lon vs. The State
Lewis, Philip vs. George Seago
Lewis, Sallie vs. The State
Lewis, Willis vs. The State
Lin, Fergus C. and Samuel J. Milburn vs. Mordica Shackelford
Lin, Rees H. and Samuel J. Wilburn vs. Peter Grinnell
Lin, Rees H. and Samuel J. Wilburn vs. John Harris
Lin, Rees H. and Samuel J. Wilburn vs. Charles B. Hitt and
  John C. Green
Lin, Rees H. and Samuel J. Wilborn vs. Andrew S. Hodge
Lin, Rees H. and Samuel J. Wilburn vs. Joseph Newland
Lin, Rees H. and Samuel J. Wilburn vs. Robert O. Usher and
  Joseph S. Anderson
Lin, Reese H. and Samuel J. Willburn vs. Isaac P. Henderson
Linch, Jones vs. The State
Lindsay, Will vs. The State
Lindsey, Emanuel vs. The State
Lindsey, James H. vs. Edwin Graves, Thomas Wood and John M.
  Kibbee
Lindsey, John, Lewis W. Flemister and William Conaway vs.
  Central Bank of Georgia
Lindsey, John vs. Samuel Griswold
Lindsey, John vs. Robert J. Henderson
Lindsey, John vs. Charles D. Ramey
Lindsey, John, Guardian vs. Creed E. Spears and Susannah C.

(Moss) Spears
Lindsey, John vs. James A. Stark
Lindsey, John vs. John White
Lindsey, John, Sr. and Isaac Parker vs. David Meriwether
Lindsey, John A. and Nancy Jeffries vs. Hugh P. Kirkpatrick
Lindsey, Lemuel W. vs. The State
Lindsey, Lewis and John Lindsey vs. Isaac C. Moore and
  Franklin Moore
Lindsey, Mrs. S. A. vs. S. J. Steele and G. H. Cornwell
Lindsey, Sarah vs. Officers of Court
Lindsey, Sarah A. (Jeffries) vs. John A. Lindsey
Little, John vs. The State
Little, Sydney vs. The State
Little, Thomas vs. John Robson
Little, William, Jeremiah Miller, J. H. Meeks and Joseph
  Glawson vs. The State
Littlejohn, Thomas vs. Thomas Grant, Daniel Grant, Executor,
  Thomas Grant, Executor and Peter Grinnell, Executor
Lloyd, Daniel M. and Smith Davenport vs. John Norwood
Lloyd, Edmond, John S. Drew, Administrator and John Norwood,
  Administrator vs. John Heard
Lloyd, Edmund vs. Drew Alston for use of William Wilcox
Lloyd, Edmund vs. Henry Pearson, Jr., William G. Gilbert
  and Felix H. Gilbert
Locket, Benjamin vs. Alston H. Greene and Joseph Buchannan
Locket, Benjamin vs. Jesse Lovall and William H. Pritchett
Locket, Benjamin vs. Joseph Turner for use of Hardy Pou
Lockett, Benjamin vs. John Carmichael
Lockett, Benjamin and John Martin vs. Thomas Grant
Lockett, Benjamin vs. Augustus Hayward
Lockett, Benjamin vs. John McLea, Peter Bennock and John
  McKenzie
Lockett, Benjamin vs. Thomas T. Napier
Lockett, Benjamin vs. James Smith
Lockett, Benjamin vs. Philip Thurmon
Lockwood, William and Henry Walker vs. James S. Weekes
Lockwood, William vs. John Willson
Loftin, Riley vs. The State
Lofton, William A. vs. E. G. Cabaness
Lofton, William A. vs. Early Cleaveland
Lofton, William H. vs. Jonas H. Holland
Long, Coulbron vs. Elizabeth Long
Long, David vs. Thomas Webb
Long, H. H. vs. The State
Long, L. B., D. T. Long and J. C. Thomason vs. William S.
  Minter
Looser, John C. vs. Peter F. Boisclair
Looser, John C. vs. Jesse Cherry
Looser, John C. vs. Daniel Parish, Jasper Corning, Thomas
  Parish and Joseph Kernochan
Looser, John C. vs. Marcus Vance
Loughridge, Jacob vs. John Lane, Jr. for use of Vincent
  Garner
Love, Ed vs. The State
Love, Jackson vs. The State
Love, James vs. The State
Love, James vs. David Witt
Love, John vs. Lucy Flanningham
Love, John and Michael Wright vs. Armstead Richardson
Love, John vs. Henry Stovall
Lovejoy, C. B. vs. S. A. Lovejoy
Lovejoy, Crawford vs. The State
Lovejoy, Edward vs. Maxey Brooks

Lovejoy, Edward vs. Joseph A. Wilson
Lovejoy, Eleazer vs. James Blaylock
Lovejoy, Eleazer vs. Anthony Dyer
Lovejoy, Eleazer vs. Thomas Grant, Daniel Grant, Executor,
    Thomas Grant, Executor and Peter Grinnell, Executor
Lovejoy, Eleazer vs. Henry T. Smith
Lovejoy, John vs. The State
Lovejoy, John D. vs. Nehemiah B. White and Lucius White
Lovejoy, P. P. and John D. Lovejoy, Administrator vs.
    Maximillian H. Hutchison for use of Eliza Allen
Lovejoy, S. A. vs. The State
Lovejoy, Samuel vs. Riley Finley
Lovejoy, Samuel vs. Angus Martin
Lovejoy, Welcom C. and Vines Fish vs. Anthony Dyer and John
    R. Dyer, Executor
Lovejoy, Welcom C. vs. John D. Lovejoy
Lovejoy, Welcom C. and Pleasant P. Lovejoy vs. Jesse
    Loyall and John Andrews, Administrator
Lovejoy, Welcom C. vs. The State
Lovejoy, Welcom C. vs. Francis M. Swanson and Thomas J.
    Comer, Sr.
Lovejoy, Welcome C. vs. Benjamin Banks
Lovejoy, Welcome C. and Boling S. Jeffries vs. Jackson Cheney
Lovejoy, Welcome C. vs. Maximilian H. Hutchinson
Lovejoy, Welcome C. vs. Richard J. Loyall
Lovejoy, Welcome C. vs. Gilbert W. Shaw
Lovejoy, William, Hampton Lovejoy, Edmond Banks, Samuel
    Lovejoy, Eleazer Lovejoy and Crawford Lovejoy vs. Joseph
    Moss
Lovejoy, William C. vs. Charles C. Norton
Lovejoy, William H. vs. James B. Randall
Lovejoy, William H. vs. The State
Low, Tom vs. P. P. Vincent
Lowery, Elisha vs. Jeremiah Pearson
Lowry, Kirby D., Charles F. Preston, Administrator and
    William H. Preston, Sr. vs. Rachael Wilson and Elizabeth
    Lowry
Lowry, William W. J. vs. Jesse Loyall
Loyall and Boynton vs. John B. M. Phillips
Loyall, Richard J. vs. James S. Boynton
Loyall, Richard J. vs. Bryant W. Collier
Loyall, Richard J. vs. John McCullough vs. James Hazlett
    and Co.
Loyall, Richard J. vs. William Maxey, Charles S. Jordan and
    John R. Dyer
Loyall, Richard J. and William Andrews vs. William S.
    Roberts and Thomas W. Craskey
Loyall, Richard J. vs. The State
Loyall, Richard J. and John McCullough vs. Gassard S. Watts,
    Fleming J. Haviland and ? Coulter
Loyall, William vs. The State
Loyd, Edmund vs. Archibald Hatcher, Mary Hatcher, Adminis-
    trator, James Meriwether, Administrator and Littleberry
    Bostick, Administrator for use of John Walton
Loyd, Nancy and Thomas Loyd vs. Reuben C. Shorter
Loyd, R. W. vs. The State
Loyd, Richard Jay vs. Allen Braswell
Loyd, Richard T. vs. Joseph Price
Loyd, Thomas vs. Timothy Freeman
Loyd, Thomas vs. Edward Webster
Loyd, Thomas, Jr. and Nancy Loyd, Administrator vs.
    Matthew Duncan
Loyd, Thomas, Jr. and Thomas Loyd, Sr. vs. The State

Loyd, William P. and George W. Wyatt vs. Stephen C.
    Talmadge
Luckett, Thomas H. vs. Maria Luckett
Lumpkin, Dickinson vs. John P. Spier and Co.
Lumpkin, George vs. Stokely Morgan
Lumpkin, George vs. The State
Lumpkin, Harrison vs. Thomas Hooks
Lumpkin, Harrison vs. James Richards and Willis Richards
Lumpkin, Harrison and Abner Chapman, Jr. vs. The State
Lumpkin, Robert vs. Samuel Butts, John Lucas, Administrator
    and William Lee, Administrator
Lumpkin, Robert vs. Marnock Glazier
Lumpkin, Robert and Stokely Morgan vs. Thomas Greer for use
    of William Varner and George Varner
Lumpkin, Robert vs. John Jones
Lumpkin, Robert vs. George Lumpkin for use of Jesse Evans
Lumpkin, Robert and Johnson Strong vs. William McKree
Lumpkin, Robert and Stokely Morgan vs. Daniel Miller
Lumpkin, Robert, Jr. vs. Francis Mison, George Phillips,
    Executor, William H. Crawford, Executor and Robert
    Allison, Executor
Lumpkin, W. vs. Thomas Carter
Lumpkin, Walter vs. James Richards and Willis Richards
Lumpkin, Walter vs. David Shepherd
Lumpkin, Walter vs. The State
Lumpkin, Walter and Fields Wilson vs. Isaac Fincher
Lumsden, John vs. William Sparadlin
Lumsden, John vs. The State
Lumsford, Leonard, Cyrus White, Executor, Christopher
    Driskell, Executor, Luke Williams, Executor and Elijah
    Rivers, Executor vs. John Parks and Welcom Parks
Lyle, Noah vs. Abel Dimon
Lynch, D. F. vs. Robinson, Kelly and Co.
Lynch, D. F. vs. The State
Lynch, Greif vs. George W. Holland
Lynch, James N. and Elizabeth vs. The State
Lynch, John vs. Riley S. Fears
Lynch, Josie vs. The State
Lynch, Sackville and Daniel McDowell vs. William H. Crane
    and Henry O. Cook
Lynch, Thomas vs. The State
Lynn, Asa vs. John McMurrain
Lynn, David vs. Gidian Easterwood
Lynn, David vs. Clement Molliere
Lynn, David vs. The State
Lynn, William vs. Benjamin Wade
Lynn, James M. vs. John W. Barkwell
Lyon, James M., James L. Barks and John W. Burney vs.
    Henry Solomon
Lytte (?), Thomas vs. The State

Mabry, Adam, Easum Turner, Administrator, Thornton Mabry,
    Administrator and Parham P. Mabry, Administrator vs.
    Daniel Mabry, Ledford Mobley, Executor and Louiza Mabry,
    Executor
Mabry, Parham P. vs. Andrew Kerr, John Kerr and Alexander
    Graham
MacDonald, Hugh, William B. Hardy and Drury Wilkins vs.
    Thomas Baskin
MacDonald, Hugh vs. Abner Bidwell and Henry Cowles
MacDonald, Hugh vs. Benjamin Cook
MacDonald, Hugh vs. Richard J. Easter, Isaac Mines and
    John P. Henry

MacDonald, Hugh vs. Gilbert Longstreet
MacDonald, Hugh vs. Abel Pearson
Machen, E. C. vs. Munford W. Hayward
Madden, Toliver vs. David Madden
Maddox, Billie vs. The State
Maddox, John vs. Sanders Vann
Maddox, Troy vs. The State
Maddox, Wash, Jr. vs. The State
Maddox, Will vs. The State
Maddux, Benjamin W. vs. Robert Weddington, Zeno Weddington,
    Administrator, Charity Weddington, Administrator and John
    J. Smith, Administrator
Maddux, Ellen vs. The State
Maddux, Washington and Martha Maddux vs. W. A. Reid
Maddux, William D. vs. Mary Comer
Mahone, Boling, Washington Ross and Benjamin Williamson vs.
    The State
Malden, Henry vs. Allen Orr
Malone, Cade vs. The State
Malone, Cader vs. John Benton
Malone, Cader vs. Hugh P. Kirkpatrick
Malone, Clarence vs. The State
Malone, E. B., J. B. Malone, Administrator and Bessie Malone,
    Administrator vs. Benton Supply Co.
Malone, Eli vs. The State
Malone, Felix vs. Crawford Edmondson
Malone, Felix vs. Alston H. Greene and Joseph Buchannan
Malone, Felix vs. Francis Lawson
Malone, Felix vs. Jonathan McDougall
Malone, Felix vs. Drury Patterson
Malone, Felix vs. Jesse J. Roan and Willis J. Roan
Malone, Felix, Sherrod Malone, Francis Malone and Gilbert
    Malone vs. The State
Malone, Felix and Mary Martin vs. The State
Malone, Floyd vs. Griffin, Monticello and Madison Railroad
    Co.
Malone, Floyd vs. Anson Hungerford, William S. Hurd and
    Lucius White
Malone, Francis vs. John L. D. Byrom
Malone, Francis vs. The State
Malone, Frank, William Malone and John L. McMichael vs.
    Isaac Langston
Malone, Franklin vs. James Adams and William Adams, Executor
Malone, Franklin vs. George T. Bartlett
Malone, Frankoin vs. Robert L. Duke
Malone, Franklin vs. George B. Hallock
Malone, Franklin, William Malone and John L. McMichael vs.
    Isaac Langston
Malone, Franklin, John L. McMichael, William Malone and
    Thomas Malone vs. The State
Malone, Franklin, William Malone and Floyd Malone vs.
    Matthew Whitfield, John F. Patterson, Executor, William
    Mathis, Executor, Leroy M. Willson, Executor and Pleasant
    Willson, Executor
Malone, George vs. William V. Burney
Malone, George vs. Hollis Colley
Malone, George vs. William B. Roby, Elbert W. Baynes,
    Administrator and Elizabeth Roby, Administrator
Malone, George and Tom Dennis vs. The State
Malone, Gilbert and William Bennet vs. The State
Malone, Henry vs. The State
Malone, James and Benjamin J. Wilson vs. Jesse Loyall
Malone, James and James M. Beeland, Administrator vs.

Sherrod Malone, George Malone, Administrator and Nancy
Malone, Administrator
Malone, James vs. Lucias Mansfield
Malone, James D. vs. Elbert W. Baynes
Malone, James D. vs. Thomas M. Darnall
Malone, James D. and Nancy Wilson vs. John R. Dicken
Malone, James D. vs. Richard Flemister
Malone, Jarrel vs. John C. H. Reid
Malone, Jarrell vs. James Barr for use of George W. Holland
and Hugh P. Kirkpatrick
Malone, Jarrett vs. William Biscoe and James N. Hall
Malone, Jarrett and James Beeland, Administrator vs.
William V. Burney
Malone, Jarrett and James Beeland, Administrator vs. Hollis
Cooley
Malone, Jarrett and James Beeland, Administrator vs.
Artemas Gould
Malone, Jarrett and James Beeland, Administrator vs. Alfred
J. Huntington
Malone, Jarrett and James Beeland, Administrator vs. Alfred
D. Kerr
Malone, Jarrett and James Beeland, Administrator vs. Sherod
Malone, George Malone, Administrator and Nancy Malone,
Administrator
Malone, Jarrett and James Beeland, Administrator vs. Robert
Prophitt
Malone, Jarrett and James Beeland, Administrator vs.
Williamson Roby, Elizabeth Roby, Administrator
Malone, Jesse vs. Lawson S. Holland
Malone, Jesse and Sherrod Malone vs. Hardy Lasiter
Malone, Lush vs. The State
Malone, Matt vs. The State
Malone, Nancy vs. Thomas M. Darnall
Malone, Nancy vs. James D. Head
Malone, Nancy vs. Lawson S. Holland
Malone, Nancy vs. John Spearman
Malone, Sherod vs. John Baldwin
Malone, Sherod vs. Lawson S. Holland
Malone, Stephen vs. The State
Malone, Stith B. vs. Nehemiah B. White and Lucius White
Malone, Thomas S. vs. John Eckles, Brewer A. Abercrombie
and John Hinton
Malone, Thomas vs. William A. Kelly
Malone, Thomas S. and James M. Williams vs. A. Pharr and
M. A. Pharr, Administrator
Malone, Thomas S. vs. The State
Malone, W. H. vs. Griffin, Monticello and Madison Railroad
Co.
Malone, Walker B. vs. The State
Malone, West vs. The State
Malone, Will vs. The State
Malone, William vs. I. W. Brown
Malone, William vs. The State
Malpass, John, William Gill and Levi Daniel vs. Thomas
Grant
Malpass, John and Andrew Craig vs. Edmund Lloyd, John G.
Drew, Administrator and John Norwood, Administrator
Malpass, John vs. Daniel McCook
Malpass, John vs. James Smith
Malpass, John vs. The State
Mangham, Thomas vs. Benjamin Carroll
Mangham, Thomas vs. Anthony Dyer and Otis Dyer
Mangham, Thomas vs. Alston H. Greene and Joseph Buchannon

Mangham, Thomas vs. Robert Robey
Mangham, Thomas vs. Joseph White, Thomas White, Administrator and Simeon Durham, Administrator
Mangham, Thomas vs. Reuben Williamson
Mangham, Thomas vs. Robert Williamson
Mann, Americus V. vs. John Richardson
Mann, John and Polly Mann, Executor vs. John Lofton
Manning, James (alias Jemes Manning) vs. The State
Manning, Troy vs. The State
Manning, Will vs. The State
Mansfield, Lucas and Reuben Jordan vs. Williamson Roby
Mansfield, Lucius vs. Levi Eckley
Manuel, Mack and Ed Manuel vs. The State
Manuel, Walter vs. The State
Mapp, Jeremiah and Isaac McClendon vs. Eli Harris and Co.
Marable, Robert vs. Lea and Armstrong
Marable, Thomas C. vs. The State
Marks, Brock vs. The State
Marks, Clarra vs. The State
Marks, Dozier vs. The State
Marks, F. C. and C. H. Marks vs. Peoples National Bank Seesburgh
Marks, Fernando C. vs. Callie F. Skinner
Marks, George vs. The State
Marks, Henry vs. The State
Marks, Horace vs. The State
Marks, J. H. and D. M. Langston vs. C. W. Jordan, W. W. Anderson and B. Whitefield
Marks, James K. vs. William Maxey and Charles S. Jordan
Marks, Jennie vs. The State
Marks, Jim B. vs. The State
Marks, Job vs. The State
Marks, John vs. Officers of Court
Marks, John H. vs. William Wayne and James Berry, Administrator
Marks, John T. vs. D. M. Langston for use of Officers of Court
Marks, Nathan T. vs. David M. Langston
Marks, Scott vs. The State
Marks, Sherman vs. The State
Marks, Thomas vs. The State
Marks, W. A. vs. Berry T. Digby
Marks, Wallace vs. The State
Marks, Will vs. The State
Marks, Sarah vs. Joseph Marsh
Marshall, Benjamin vs. William L. Wade
Marshall, John vs. Joel Baley
Martin, Allen vs. John S. D. Byrom
Martin, Allen vs. Peter W. Gautier
Martin, Allen vs. Stephen Holland
Martin, Allen vs. Stephen Morris, Henrietta Morris and Henry M. Macy, Guardian
Martin, Elijah, William Martin, Thomas Smith, Henry Neely and William Smith vs. David Darnall
Martin, Elijah vs. The State
Martin, F. P. and B. F. Barnett vs. William H. Preston
Martin, Francis S. vs. Alston H. Green
Martin, Francis S. vs. Jeremiah Pearson and Warren Phelps
Martin, Francis S. vs. William Pickens
Martin, Francis S. vs. Eli S. Horter and Alfred Iverson
Martin, George W. vs. The State
Martin, Isaac N. D. vs. The State
Martin, J. B. vs. The State

Martin, James vs. William Barnett
Martin, James vs. James Downey
Martin, James vs. Gilbert Malone
Martin, James vs. The State
Martin, James L. and Alexander Smith vs. Eli Cleveland for use of William Penn
Martin, James L. and Joseph Hill vs. Thomas Grant
Martin, James S. and Wyatt R. Smith vs. Hardy Crawford
Martin, John vs. The State
Martin, John vs. Jacob Thrash
Martin, Joseph R. vs. Jeremiah Pearson
Martin, Mahalah vs. The State
Martin, Martha vs. Thomas Martin
Martin, Oliver H. vs. Sacville Lynch
Martin, P. K. vs. The State
Martin, Thomas vs. James T. Hays
Martin, Thomas vs. Samuel Williams
Martin, Tolliver and Samuel Braswell vs. George Bell and B. Brown
Martin, William A. vs. John Hobson and Christopher Hobson
Martin, William W. vs. Henry Hepburn and Charles Prince
Martin, William W. vs. Henry Pennington
Martin, William W. vs. James Walker
Martin, William W. vs. Matthew Williams
Martin, Yearby vs. Thaddeus Beall, Elias Beall and Thomas Beall
Martin, Yearby vs. Stephen Gilmore
Martin, Yearby vs. Eli Glover
Martin, Yearby vs. John Hobson and Christopher Hobson
Martin, Yearby vs. Sanders Walker
Mason, A. M. vs. Thomas R. Penn
Mason, Alfred vs. The State
Mason, Lofton vs. The State
Mathis, James (alias James Matthews) vs. Theophilus Freeman
Maton, Joe vs. James H. Campbell and Brothers
Maxcey, Moses vs. The State
Maxcey, Walter vs. James Daniel, Drury Towns, Ann (Lankey) Towns and John T. Lankey
Maxcey, William vs. Thomas Davis, Robert H. Davis, Administrator and Hannah Davis, Administrator
Maxcey, Yelverton and Thomas Maxcey vs. Pincney Parsons
Maxcey, Yelverton (Yerton) vs. Henry Pennington
Maxcy, Yelverton vs. Thomas McGehee
Maxey, Babe vs. The State
Maxey, Boze vs. Polley Williams
Maxey, Garland and William Maxey, Administrator vs. William F. Flournoy, William A. Ellis and Simeon D. Maddux
Maxey, Garland and John Maxey vs. William S. Hurd and Anson Hungerford, Jr.
Maxey, Greene vs. The State
Maxey, James vs. The State
Maxey, James E. vs. Cary Wood and Lambeth Hopkins
Maxey, John and James W. Faulkner vs. Charles Cargile
Maxey, John vs. Hollis Cooley and James H. Robinson
Maxey, John vs. Fielding Flemister
Maxey, John vs. Joshua Hill and William Maxey
Maxey, John vs. Charles D. Ramey, Lindsey H. Durham, Dyer C. Bancroft and William G. Swanson
Maxey, John vs. James Ravenel
Maxey, John vs. Henry C. Seymour
Maxey, John vs. The State
Maxey, Jordan and Co. vs. John R. Dyer
Maxey, Mabe and Kinion Maxey vs. The State

210

Maxey, Mayburn and Henry Kelly vs. The State
Maxey, Mayburn and Kenan Maxey vs. The State
Maxey, Pouncey vs. Kethrin Edmonds for use of Thomas Grant,
    Daniel Grant, Executor, Thomas Grant, Executor and Peter
    Grinnell, Executor
Maxey, Pouncey vs. Allen McClendon
Maxey, Robert vs. The State
Maxey, Sid vs. The State
Maxey, Will vs. The State
Maxey, William and Charles S. Jordan vs. William W. Clark
Maxey, William, Charles S. Jordan and Eli S. Glover, vs.
    James C. Haviland, Willington Stevenson, Thomas W.
    Chichester, Hamilton S. Sheltin and George B. Olmstead
Maxey, Yelberton vs. Cornelius D. Terhune
Maxwell, Nathan vs. The State
Maxwell, William B. vs. William Cook and Jerry Cowles
Maxwell, William B. vs. Amos Greene
Maxwell, William B. vs. Riley Potter
May, James vs. Henry Clem
Mayfield, Lewis vs. Lawson S. Holland
Mays, John vs. The State
Mays, Moses J. vs. Henry Branham
Mealer, Thompson vs. Henry Gasset and Richard W. Bailey
Medaris, John S. vs. Jonas H. Holland
Medaris, John W. vs. Isaac N. Johnson
Medaris, John W. vs. Isaac L. Parker, William J. L. Tuggle
    and Jonas H. Holland
Medford, George vs. John M. Patrick
Medlock, Charles, Ezekiel Smith, Executor, John Smith,
    Executor and Thomas T. Walker, Executor vs. Richard D.
    Shackelford and Susannah H. (Medlock) Shackleford
Medlock, George, Ferrebee (Medlock) Walker, Executor,
    George DeLafayette Medlock, Executor, William Smith,
    Executor, John Smith, Executor, Ezekiel F. Smith, Execu-
    tor and Thomas T. Walker vs. Zachariah Phillips and Polly
    (Medlock) Phillips
Medlock, George D. F. vs. Reuben C. Shorter
Medlock, George D. F. vs. Lawrence S. Slaughter
Medlock, George D. F. vs. Charles D. Stewart and George
    Hargraves
Medlock, George DeLafayette and Thomas L. Walker vs. Andrew
    Erwin, James Erwin, William H. Oakman, Walter Crenshaw
    and Jane Groce (?)
Medlock, George D. Lafayette and Thomas T. Walker vs.
    Elijah N. Hascall and David Hascall
Medlock, George F. vs. Luke Reid, David Woodruff and David
    W. Luther
Mercer, Charles and Daniel Penn vs. The State
Mercer, Daniel T. vs. David Flanders and David M. Flanders
Mercer, Daniel T. vs. Jonas H. Holland
Mercer, Jacob and James Walden vs. Ransom Swenney
Mercer, Jacob vs. Charles Walden
Mercer, William vs. Thomas Loyd
Meriwether, Charles vs. W. A. Kelly
Meriwether, Charles vs. Officers of Court
Meriwether, Charles vs. J. R. Sparks
Meriwether, David vs. William Russel
Meriwether, David, Sr. and Matilda A. Meriwether, Executor
    vs. William C. Penn
Meriwether, Dawson vs. The State
Meriwether, Doner vs. The State
Meriwether, Dorman vs. The State
Meriwether, George F. vs. Griffin, Monticello and Madison

Railroad Co.
Meriwether, George F. vs. William H. Head
Meriwether, James A. vs. William Cleland and Jesse Pitts,
  Administrator
Meriwether, Joe vs. The State
Meriwether, Queen vs. Charles Meriwether for use of
  Officers of Court
Meriwether, Will vs. The State
Merk, Howard vs. The State
Merrit, Thomas vs. Snelling Johnston
Merrits, Thomas vs. The State
Merritt, Benjamin vs. Elijah N. Hascall and David Hascall
Merriwether, Aaron vs. The State
Merriwether, Charles vs. Missouri Smith
Merriwether, David vs. Thomas W. Huson
Merriwether, George F. vs. Russel J. Brown
Merriwether, M. A. and Charles Merriwether, Administrator
  vs. W. C. Bailey
Messer, John vs. Mason Howel
Middlebrooks, Aaron vs. The State
Middlebrooks, Alfred vs. The State
Middlebrooks, Joe vs. The State
Middlebrooks, W. H. vs. George B. Hallock
Middlebrooks, William H. and John K. Goolsby. vs. Wilcox,
  Gibbs and Co.
Middlebrooks, Williamson P. vs. George T. Bartlett
Middlebrooks, Williamson P. vs. The State
The Middle Georgia and Atlanta Railroad Co. vs. J. J. Aken
Middle, Georgia and Atlantic Railway Co. vs. E. B. Turk for
  use of John Turk
Milam, Benjamin vs. James Turner
Milam, Thomas vs. John Milner
Milam, Thomas F. vs. Alfred Findley
Milam, Wiley vs. James Buchannan and Henry Buchannan,
  Executor
Milam, Wiley vs. The State
Milburn, William B. vs. The State
Miles, Elijah vs. Alfred Shepherd
Miles, John and Lewis Miles vs. The State
Miles, William vs. Charles Lanos
Miles, William vs. Jonathan Phillips
Miles, William vs. Ellemander Warbington
Millen, Cornelia M. vs. The State
Millen, Elizabeth vs. The State
Millen, George D. vs. Officers of Court
Millen, George D. vs. Andrew Plymale
Millen, George D. vs. The State
Millen, Henry D. and Alfred C. Millen vs. Joel C. McDowell
  for use of Justices of Court
Millen, Mary vs. Officers of Court
Millen, Mary S. and Grief Lynch, Trustee vs. Joseph Pittman
  and William Hodges
Millen, Mary Sauls and Grief Lynch, Trustee vs. Robert
  Tolefree
Miller, David and Abraham Waldrop vs. Thomas Greer
Miller, Edwin W. and John H. Ezell vs. Stephen Howard, J. B.
  Howard, Executor and Lewis Lynch, Executor
Miller, Elijah and Robert Burks vs. The State
Miller, Elijah, Lewis Pye and Asa Pye vs. The State
Miller, George, Horation Miller, ? Ripley, John W. Burney
  and Hamlin Freeman vs. Officers of Court
Miller, Harris vs. The State
Miller, Harrison, Mose Clemons and Will Clemons vs. The State

Miller, Ike vs. The State
Miller, Jake vs. The State
Miller, James H. vs. Eli Glover
Miller, John vs. Jarrel Beasley
Miller, Mark vs. David Caldwell
Miller, Sam vs. The State
Miller, Stephen vs. The State
Miller, William vs. Gilbert Longstreet
Miller, William vs. William Morgan
Millon, Mary vs. The State
Mills, William and Jeptha Wilkerson vs. Nathan S. Dent for
    use of Williamson Boswell
Milner, Dudley and Samuel Huston vs. Richard Loyall
Milner, Hopson vs. Samuel Huston
Milner, Hopson vs. William Pabodie
Milner, Hopson vs. Thomas Walker
Milner, Matilda (alias Matilda Wilkerson) vs. The State
Minter, A. J. vs. Sam Cohen
Minter, A. J. vs. K. P. Greer
Minter, A. J. vs. J. H. Kelly
Minter, Ada vs. The State
Minter, Andrew J. vs. The State
Minter, Calhoun vs. The State
Minter, Gideon G. and Samuel Plummer vs. Permemus R.
    Thomaston and Thomas D. Hollingsworth
Minter, J. P. and Jane E. Minter, Administrator vs. Nehemiah
    B. White and Lucius White
Minter, J. W. vs. Griffin, Monticello and Madison Railroad
    Co.
Minter, John vs. The State
Minter, John W. vs. William Maxey and James C. Bartlett
Minter, John W. vs. Mary A. Minter
Minter, Pat vs. The State
Minter, R. J. vs. Atlanta Mutual Life Insurance
Minter, R. J. and John W. Minter vs. The State
Minter, Rachel vs. The State
Minter, Robert vs. William S. Hurd and Anson Hungerford
Minter, Robert vs. James H. Morrow
Minter, Robert vs. The State
Minter, Robert vs. John A. Steele
Minter, Robert vs. Lucinda Stone
Minter, Robert vs. N. B. White and L. White
Minter, Robert R. vs. Jarrel Beasley for use of Burwell
    Ragland
Minter, Robert R., James H. Morrow and John Hill vs. Anna
    Ann Birdsong
Minter, Robert R., James H. Morrow and John Hill vs. James
    Blaylock
Minter, Robert R. vs. Elias Bliss
Minter, Robert R. vs. Hamilton Brown, James Gwyn and Thomas
    P. Gwyn
Minter, Robert R. vs. Josiah R. Brown
Minter, Robert R. vs. Abiel Camfield and William Longstreet
Minter, Robert R. vs. George Clark
Minter, Robert R. vs. John O. Daniel
Minter, Robert R. vs. Stephen W. Harris, Eli S. Shorter,
    Executor, Seaborn Jones, Executor, William W. Wilkins,
    Executor and Sarah H. Harris, Executor
Minter, Robert R. vs. Franklin Heard and Henry H. Cook
Minter, Robert R. vs. William Hitchcock
Minter, Robert R. and John Hill vs. Seaborn Jones
Minter, Robert R. vs. Charles Kelsey, Alfred M. Hobby and
    Charles McIntire

Minter, Robert R. vs. Lodowick Lord
Minter, Robert R. and Eli Glover vs. Cullen Lockett
Minter, Robert R. vs. William McCane
Minter, Robert R. vs. Thomas Napier
Minter, Robert R. vs. Nathaniel Perry and Edward Perry
Minter, Robert R. vs. John R. Pitkin and Jeremiah Pearson
Minter, Robert R. vs. William Porter
Minter, Robert R. vs. Samuel Rockwell
Minter, Robert R. vs. William B. Rodgers and Co.
Minter, Robert R. vs. David Shepherd, Ashley Parker and
  Robert Parker
Minter, Robert R., James H. Morrow and John Hill vs. John
  M. Taylor
Minter, Robert R. vs. William Tuckerman and Gustavius
  Tuckerman
Minter, Robert R. vs. William Underhill and Charles
  Underhill
Minter, Rufus vs. The State
Minter, Sol vs. The State
Minter, Thomas C. vs. Thornton Carter
Minter, Thomas C. vs. Jackson Merchandise Co.
Minter, Thomas C. vs. Francis M. Swanson, Thomas J.
  Pritchett and Alfred Pritchett
Minter, Thomas C. vs. James M. Williams
Minter, W. S. and Charles Ellis vs. H. C. McClure and N. B.
  White
Minter, W. S. vs. Elira Pearson for use of Officers of
  Court
Minter, Warner vs. The State
Minter, William vs. The State
Minter, William S. and Jefferson Aiken vs. Tabitha Garrett
Minter, William S. vs. Joseph B. Groves
Minter, William S. vs. Simeon Scales
Mitchel, Melvin and Mira Mitchel vs. The State
Mitchell, Bob, Jr. vs. The State
Mitchell, Elizabeth and Richard Mitchell vs. Robert
  Davidson and James M. Newton, Administrator
Mitchell, George vs. The State
Mitchell, Homer vs. The State
Mitchell, Joel vs. William Hollaway
Mitchell, John F. M. and Jefferson Mitchell vs. William
  Barclay
Mitchell, Joshua S. vs. James Robertson and William Walker
Mitchell, Levin and Elisha S. Wynens vs. Wiley S. Clements
Mitchell, Levin vs. James H. Holland
Mitchell, Levin vs. Wesley A. Snell
Mitchell, Richard and Burrell Green vs. Benjamin Keaton
Mitchell, Richard and Robert Davidson vs. Matthew Whitfield
Mitchell, Robert vs. James Richards
Mitchell, Sam vs. The State
Mitchell, Thomas J. vs. Charles D. Ramey, Lindsey H. Durham
  and Dyer C. Bancroft
Mitchell, Thomas J. vs. The State
Mitchell, William vs. Lawson S. Holland
Mitchell, William and Joshua Hill vs. Officers of Court
Mitchell, William vs. The State
Mize, James vs. Powel and Griggs
Mize, Stacy and James B. Mize vs. James P. Holmes
Moats, John and Edward Lovejoy vs. Maxey Brooks
Mobley, Albert vs. The State
Mobley, Eleazer, Gideon Easterwood, John Easterwood and
  Lawrence Easterwood vs. John McMurrain
Mobley, Nathan vs. Thomas Sparks

Mobley, Stephen vs. The State
Mobley, Stephen vs. Andrew Woodly
Mobley, Stephen H. vs. John M. Adams, William P. Adams and
   James C. Fargo
Mobley, Stephen H. vs. William S. Hurd and Anson Hungerford
Mobley, Stephen H. vs. Lewis Ryan and Ann Ryan, Administra-
   tor
Mobley, William vs. Central Bank of Georgia
Mobley, William and James S. Fears vs. William D. Grimes
Mobley, William vs. Nancy Huddleston
Mobley, William and Alexander C. Morrison vs. Leroy F.
   Jarrell and Hiram E. Johnston
Mobley, William vs. Hugh G. Johnson
Mobley, William vs. William Mitchell
Mobley, William and Lucy Mobley vs. Officers of Court
Mobley, William and Stephen Mobley vs. Smith and Broddus
Mobley, William vs. William G. Swanson
Mobley, William and James S. Fears vs. Francis M. White
Moleman, Stephen (alias Stephen Norman), Squire Walker and
   Dick Davidson vs. The State
Mollier, Clement vs. Henry Peebles
Mollier, Clement and Ephraigen (Ephraim) Ivey vs. G.
   Simonton and Co.
Mollier, Clement vs. Joseph White
Molliere, Clement vs. The State
Molliere, Clement vs. James Pye
Monk, Thomas vs. George W. Owens
Monticello Academy vs. James Cowan
Monticello Academy vs. John Norwood
Monticello Academy vs. Hosea Webster and George Webster
Moody, Greene vs. Jeremiah Pearson
Moody, Joel vs. James Smith
Moon, John, Sr. and Rebecca Whatley vs. The State
Moon, Mary vs. William H. Moon
Mooney, Valentine vs. James Johnston, Jr.
Mooneyham, Charlie vs. The State
Moore, A. L. vs. The State
Moore, Aaron vs. Snellen Johnson
Moore, Benjamin L. vs. Edward Williams
Moore, Benjamin S. and Leonard Roon vs. Valentine Nash
Moore, Elbert vs. The State
Moore, Emmett and Odus Moore vs. The State
Moore, Franklin vs. The State
Moore, George vs. The State
Moore, Isaac vs. Isaac Bailey
Moore, Isaac and John Moore vs. John Hobson
Moore, Isaac vs. William Osborne
Moore, Jackson vs. The State
Moore, Jacob vs. Zacheus Powell
Moore, Jacob and Patsey Sheffield vs. The State
Moore, James vs. Samuel Alexander
Moore, James vs. Champion Easter and Robert Moore
Moore, James vs. Seaborn Jones
Moore, James vs. William Scott
Moore, James and Elizabeth Lord vs. The State
Moore, James, William Moore and Stephen Venters vs. The
   State
Moore, John vs. Thomas Broddus
Moore, John vs. James Caston
Moore, vs. James Curlee
Moore, John vs. Anthony Dyer
Moore, John vs. William Flowers
Moore, John vs. Richard Garner

Moore, John vs. Gill, Davis and Malpass, Kerr and Graham
and Sanders Walker
Moore, John vs. Eli Glover
Moore, John vs. Jacob Hinton
Moore, John vs. William Howard
Moore, John, Crawford Edmondson and David Adams vs. William
D. Jarrott
Moore, John vs. Owen H. Kenan
Moore, John vs. John Mercer
Moore, John vs. Monticello Academy
Moore, John and James Moore, Administrator vs. Jane Moore,
John Moore and James B. Moore, Guardian
Moore, John vs. Matthew Phillips
Moore, John vs. The State
Moore, John vs. John Stayner
Moore, John vs. Stephen Thomas
Moore, John and John W. Compton vs. William Trailer
Moore, John vs. Henry Walker and Michael Moore
Moore, John vs. Handy Waller
Moore, John vs. John Willson
Moore, Jonas, Samuel Walker, Executor and James Walker,
Executor vs. James Bridon, Peggy Bridon, Ignatious Moore,
Prudence Moore, Asa Moore and Polly Moore
Moore, Josiah J. vs. William V. Burney
Moore, Michael vs. Anthony Dyer and Otis Dyer
Moore, Michael vs. Elbert Jones
Moore, Michael vs. Russell Jones
Moore, Michel vs. The State
Moore, Morning vs. Jeremiah Phips and Robert Grainger
Moore, Moses vs. Ishmael Stewart
Moore, Seth H. vs. The State
Moore, William vs. Charles F. Wall
Moore, William A. vs. Thadeus Beall, Elias Beall and Thomas
Beall
Moore, William A. vs. William Biscoe and James N. Hall
Moore, William A. vs. Alston H. Greene and Joseph Buchannon
Moore, William A. vs. Christopher Hobson and John Aspinwall
Moore, William A. vs. Alsea Holifield
Moore, William A. vs. William D. Jarrott
Moore, William A. vs. Joseph Johnson
Moore, William A. vs. William H. Myles
Moore, William A., John Moore and William Cook vs. Charles
D. Stewart and George Hargraves
More, Consadie vs. The State
More, Lilly vs. The State
Moreland, Francis vs. Jesse Ivey
Moreland, Gus vs. The State
Moreland, Henry vs. The State
Moreland, John and Robert McGehee vs. Beal Baker
Moreland, John vs. David Clark
Moreland, Salena vs. The State
Moreland, Wesley vs. The State
Moreland, William and Samuel C. Atkinson vs. Nicholas
Wagner
Moreland, Wood vs. Jesse Matthews
Morgan, A. H. vs. Richard King
Morgan, A. H. vs. Thomas Willy and James Zimmerman
Morgan, Asa and Burwell P. Key, Guardian vs. Charles D.
Ramey and Samuel D. Varner
Morgan, Asa H. vs. George Cosgroves
Morgan, Asa H. vs. Durham and Swanson
Morgan, Asa H. vs. Benjamin McCay and Gideon Norman
Morgan, Asa H. vs. Joseph H. Murrell

Morgan, Asa H. vs. Joseph H. Murrell
Morgan, Asa H. vs. Officers of Court
Morgan, Asa H. vs. William H. C. Pace and McCormick Neal
Morgan, Asa H. vs. William C. Robinson
Morgan, Asa H. vs. The State
Morgan, Asa H. vs. William F. Stodghill and William O. Robinson
Morgan, Asa H. vs. Francis M. Swanson and Thomas J. Comer
Morgan, Asa H. vs. Francis M. Swanson and Alexander O'Daniel
Morgan, Asa H. vs. Isaac Willingham
Morgan, Asa H. vs. Mary Wright and Nancy L. Wright
Morgan, Bethena (Kitchens) vs. Miniard Morgan
Morgan, Charles and Sarah N. Morgan, Administrator vs. John J. Bennett
Morgan, Charles vs. William Biscoe
Morgan, Charles vs. Samuel Butts, John Lucas, Administrator and William Lee, Administrator
Morgan, Charles and Sarah N. Morgan vs. Central Bank of Georgia
Morgan, Charles vs. Richard Garner
Morgan, Charles and Sarah Morgan, Administrator vs. James P. Glover
Morgan, Charles vs. John Hill, Augustin Slaughter and Charles Labuzan
Morgan, Charles vs. Isaac Kendrick
Morgan, Charles vs. John McBryde and James McBryde
Morgan, Charles and Josias R. Brown vs. Andrew Pye
Morgan, Charles and Thomas C. Taylor vs. Alfred Shorter
Morgan, Charles and Clark McLemore vs. The State
Morgan, Frank vs. The State
Morgan, Isaac N. vs. Ann Easter Cross
Morgan, Isaac N. vs. Job Tyler
Morgan, James vs. Lowe Brothers and Small
Morgan, James H., John W. Burney, Jr. and John E. Langston vs. Stephen C. Talmadge and Albert J. Talmadge
Morgan, James W., Samuel Barber and Shadrach McMichael vs. George M. Crawford for use of Richard Flemister
Morgan, James W. vs. William Hitchcock and David A. Reese, Administrator
Morgan, James W. vs. Robert Kellam
Morgan, James W. vs. Jesse Loyall
Morgan, James W. and Isaac L. Parker vs. William Maxey for use of James C. Bartlett
Morgan, James W., Lucius Mansfield vs. Stephen C. Talmadge
Morgan, James W. vs. James E. Wilson
Morgan, John and Herriman Pounds vs. Edward Young Hill
Morgan, John vs. Jesse Loyall
Morgan, John vs. William McMichael
Morgan, Jumima vs. The State
Morgan, Luke J. vs. John F. Dismukes
Morgan, Mineard vs. Officers of Court
Morgan, Miniard and Sally Morgan vs. The State
Morgan, Minyard vs. Charles Kitchens
Morgan, Sarah N. vs. James P. Glover
Morgan, Sarah N. vs. Milton P. Walthall
Morgan, Stokeley vs. Irwin Bird
Morgan, Stokeley vs. James Bird
Morgan, Stokeley and William Hitchcock vs. Anthony Dyer and Otis Dyer
Morgan, Stokeley vs. John Hendrick
Morgan, Stokeley vs. William McLellan
Morgan, Stokeley vs. Hastings Marks
Morgan, Stokeley vs. Williamson Wynn

Morgan, Stokely vs. Rufus Brown
Morgan, Stokely vs. Anson W. Langdon
Morgan, Stokely and William Hitchcock vs. Gabriel Colley
Morgan, Stokely vs. John Hill, Augustin Slaughter and
  Charles Labuzan
Morgan, Stokely, John Price, Administrator and Mary (Morgan)
  Price, Administrator vs. Stokely Lambert
Morgan, Stokely vs. Winfrey Lockett
Morgan, Stokely vs. Moses Mathews for use of James P. McKee
Morgan, Stokely vs. William Penn
Morgan, Stokely vs. The State
Morgan, Stokely and James Garlington vs. Tabitha Wood and
  Obediah Echols
Morgan, Will vs. The State
Morgan, William vs. Eli Glover
Morgan, William vs. John Hill
Morgan, William vs. The State
Morgan, Wooddie vs. The State
Morris, Alexander vs. Henry Cook
Morris, B. F., Braxton R. Ezell, Executor and Robert A. T.
  Ridley, Executor vs. Jonas H. Holland, Eunice A. Holland,
  Administrator and William W. Holland, Administrator
Morris, Benjamin vs. Thomas B. Erwin and James Cowan
Morris, Benjamin and Isham Morris vs. Josiah Newman
Morris, Burrell vs. The State
Morris, Cyrus vs. The State
Morris, Edmund and Henry Morris vs. Richard W. Fon
Morris, George vs. Abner Bankston
Morris, Henry vs. Joseph Blake for use of Thomas McGehee
Morris, Henry vs. John W. Bridges and James Speir
Morris, Henry, Stephen Satterwhite, Executor and Thomas
  Morris, Executor vs. Henry Cook
Morris, Henry vs. William H. Crenshaw and Jacob Barrow
Morris, Henry vs. Thomas McGhee
Morris, Henry vs. Alexander McGrigor
Morris, Henry vs. Aaron Morgan
Morris, Henry vs. David Wright
Morris, Thomas and James H. Morrow vs. John W. Hereford
Morris, Thomas vs. Jeptha Hill
Morris, Thomas vs. Charles L. Kennon for use of Asa Hill
Morris, Thomas vs. Augustin Slaughter and Charles Labuzan
Morris, Thomas vs. The State
Morris, Thomas vs. Thomas Williams
Morris, Uriah C. and Joshua L. Clark vs. Augustus Hayward
Morris, Uriah C. vs. James Spier and John W. Bridges
Morrison, Alexander and Jeptha Clements vs. Nathaniel G.
  Slaughter
Morrison, Alexander C. vs. William Biscoe
Morrison, Alexander C. vs. James P. Heartwell
Morrison, Alexander C., Angus G. Morrison and Moses I. Mays
  vs. John Thurmond and Henry Branham
Morrison, Angus and Alexander Morrison vs. Joel Stanford
Morrison, Angus G. and Alexander C. Morrison vs. Uriah I.
  Bullock
Morrison, Angus G. vs. Daniel Gunn and Thomas A. Brown
Morrow, James and John Wynens vs. Samuel Lowther and
  Elizabeth (Billingslea) Lowther
Morrow, James H. and James Cowen vs. Anthony Dyer
Morrow, James H., Thomas Morris and David S. Thomas vs.
  Anthony Dyer
Morrow, James H. vs. David Epps
Morrow, James H., Robert Lawson and Arthur Lawson vs.
  Thomas B. Erwin

Morrow, James H., Rebeckah Morrow and Robert R. Minter vs. John Hunt
Morrow, James H. vs. Charles Morgan
Morrow, James H. vs. John North
Morrow, James H. vs. Winburn Odum and William A. Slaughter, Administrator
Morrow, James H., Thomas P. Gwyn and James Gwyn vs. Warren Phelps
Morrow, James H. and Samuel R. Andrews vs. Eli S. Shorter
Morrow, James H. vs. Robert Smith
Morrow, James H. and James McClendon vs. Thomas Smith, Asa Smith, Administrator and John C. Smith, Administrator
Morrow, James H. vs. Horatio Spencer and Ira Goddard
Morrow, James H. vs. Pleasant Stovall and William P. Ford
Morrow, James H. vs. Philip Thurmond
Morrow, James H. and Robert Smith vs. William Weekes
Morrow, James H. and John T. C. Towns vs. James Whitfield
Morrow, James H. vs. Leroy M. Wiley and Thomas W. Baxter
Morrow, William H. vs. James Magavirk
Morrow, William H. vs. The State
Morton, Erotas vs. The State
Moseley, A. F. vs. The State
Moseley, Alansom vs. Greene R. Turner
Moseley, Elisha vs. James Boone
Moseley, Elisha and David J. Britt vs. Charles D. Stewart and George Hargraves
Moseley, William R. vs. John Kerr and James Hope
Mosely, Elisha and John A. Fairchild vs. Josiah Newton for use of John McKinne
Mosely, Elisha vs. Matthew Whitfield and James Whitfield
Moses vs. The State
Mothershed, William vs. Jonas H. Holland
Mothershed, William H., Thomas J. Howard and Tilman Niblet vs. Berry T. Digby
Mothershed, William H. and Eleanor Mothershed vs. Lindsey A. Durham and Francis M. Swanson
Mothershed, William H. vs. Elleanor F. Mothershed
Mothershed, William H. vs. William R. Phillips
Mothershed, William H. vs. The State
Moye, Jeremiah P. and William Bailey vs. The State
Moye, Wiley and Thomas W. Moye vs. William M. Broddus and Thomas J. Smith
Moye, Wilie vs. Nathan Johnston, John Johnston, Executor and William M. Johnston, Executor
Muckelroy, James S. vs. The State
Muckleroy, Andrew vs. John Jones
Muckleroy, Jacob vs. Francis H. Cone
Muckleroy, James and William Head vs. Thomas Wootten
Mulkey, Madison J. vs. Nathaniel W. Gordon
Mulkey, Madison J. vs. Angus G. Morrison
Mullens, James vs. Daniel Gunn and John Gunn
Mullens, Pleasant I. vs. Nathan Ward
Mullens, Pleasant J. vs. John Hines
Mullins, Pleasant I. vs. Daniel Slade
Mullins, Pleasant J. and Thomas R. King vs. John Barry
Mullins, Pleasant J. vs. James A. Ethridge
Mullins, Pleasant J. vs. Thomas Hobbs
Mullins, Pleasant J. and Charles D. Bostick vs. Pleasant P. Lovejoy
Mullins, Pleasant J. and J. M. King vs. James H. Roberts
Mullins, Pleasant P., G. W. Comer and Elise Cheak vs. John Castelow
Murdock, Joseph vs. James Beggs and John B. Barnes for use

of Anderson Watkins
Murdock, Joseph vs. John Huston
Murdock, Joseph vs. William Lawrence
Murdock, Joseph vs. The State
Murphey, Mastin W., William H. Wills and George H. Traylor
    vs. James A. Hascall and David Hascall for use of John
    Spainwall
Murphey, Mastin W. vs. William Meriwether, Howard Beall,
    Elias Beall and Thadeus Beall
Murphey, Mastin W. and Beverly Daniel vs. Reuben C. Shorter
Murphey, Paschal vs. Thomas Beall, Thaddeus Beall and Elias
    Beall
Murphey, Paschal, Mastin W. Murphey and Thomas Dillon vs.
    John McKinne and James Lamkin
Murphey, Paschal and William Cook vs. Daniel Sanford and
    Benjamin Sanford
Murphy, Paschal vs. Robert Allison
Murphy, Paschal vs. John W. Bridges
Murphy, Paschal, Robert Robey and Mastin Murphy vs. Martin
    Cochran
Murphy, Paschal vs. West Harris
Murphy, Paschal and Charles Cargile vs. John Hobson and
    Christopher Hobson
Murphy, Paschal vs. Harrison Smith
Murphy, Paschal vs. Elias Wallen and Co.
Murrah, Charles vs. Elijah N. Hascall and David Hascall
Murrah, Charles vs. Isaac Hill
Murray, Henry vs. Daniel Kilcrise
Murrelle, Mrs. Eliza N. and C. W. Aiken vs. S. R. Baynes
Mygatt, William G. and James E. Wood vs. David A. Ambler
Mygatt, William G. and James E. Wood vs. William Bailey
Mygatt, William G. and James E. Wood vs. Edward W. Bancroft,
    Andrew F. Browning, James B. Betts, William W. Leman and
    Edward W. Marshall
Mygatt, William G. and James E. Woods vs. Nathan A. Cohen
    and Leopold Cohen
Mygatt, William G. and James E. Wood vs. Samuel C. Dunn
Mygatt, William G. and James E. Wood vs. Benjamin W. Force,
    John P. Force and Benjamin Conley
Mygatt, William G. vs. Pleasant P. Lovejoy
Mygatt, William G. and James E. Wood vs. Loyal and Langston
Mygatt, William G. vs. John C. Maddux and William D. Maddux
Mygatt, William G. and James E. Wood vs. Simeon Scales
Mygatt, William G. and James E. Wood vs. Henry Thayer and
    John Butt
Myles, Isham vs. Richards and Mercer
Myles, William H., William Jeffries, Elijah Myles and
    Avington Williams vs. The State
Myrick, David and Thomas Wright vs. Robert Brown and Robert
    Sharp, Executor
Myrick, William vs. The State

McAlister, John vs. The State
McAllister, Margaret vs. Green McAfee and Robert McAfee
McArthur, John vs. Thomas I. Davis
McArthur, John vs. Dread Warren
McArthy, Charles E. vs. Thomas Hardeman and O. G. Sparks
McBean, Daniel vs. John Hill, Augustin Slaughter and
    Charles Labuzan
McBean, Daniel vs. Christopher Hobson and John Hobson
McBean, Daniel vs. McCarter and Henry
McBean, Daniel vs. Reuben C. Shorter
McBride, Andrew vs. John Patterson

McBride, Andrew vs. John Patterson
McBryde, Andrew vs. William Caldwell
McBryde, Andrew and Francis B. Smartt vs. George Duesan
McBryde, Andrew and Francis B. Smartt vs. Young J.
  Harrington and James Fernanders
McBryde, Andrew vs. Elijah N. Hascall
McBryde, Andrew vs. Joseph Johnson
McBryde, Andrew vs. Levi Lee
McBryde, Andrew and Francis B. Smartt vs. Jefery Pitts
McBryde, Andrew and Henry T. Smartt vs. Daniel Sanford and
  Benjamin Sanford
McBryde, Andrew vs. John T. Swan
McCain, Hugh vs. William Stroud
McCalister, Henry vs. The State
McCane, William vs. Francis McClendon
McCarter, John B. and George W. Henery vs. Nathaniel B.
  Pass, Jr.
McCarthy, C. E. vs. Benier Pye and W. A. Pye
McCleland, A. P. vs. The State
McClendon, Allen vs. John Cargile, Robert Williamson,
  Administrator, William Cargile, Administrator and Lavinia
  W. Cargile, Administrator
McClendon, Allen vs. Nathaniel Coggeshell
McClendon, Allen vs. Thomas J. Davis
McClendon, Allen vs. Jonathan McClendon (minor of),
  Washington C. Cleveland, Guardian
McClendon, Allen vs. The State
McClendon, Amos vs. Reuben Blakey
McClendon, Amos vs. Charles Cargile
McClendon, Amos vs. George Clower
McClendon, Amos vs. James Hines
McClendon, Amos and Stephen McClendon vs. John Owen
McClendon, Charlie vs. The State
McClendon, Frances vs. Benjamin Hill
McClendon, Francis vs. John M. Dooly and Micajah Henley
McClendon, Francis vs. Caleb Woodley
McClendon, Jacob vs. Hamilton Brown
McClendon, Jacob vs. Richard C. Clayton
McClendon, Jacob vs. John L. Cochran
McClendon, Jacob vs. James Cowen and Thomas B. Erwin
McClendon, Jacob vs. William H. Crane and Abram Crane
McClendon, Jacob vs. George W. Darden
McClendon, Jacob and William Armstrong vs. Thomas Grant,
  Daniel Grant, Executor, Thomas Grant, Executor and
  Peter Grinnell, Executor
McClendon, Jacob and Richard C. Clayton vs. James S.
  Graybill, Jonas N. Holland and James Dorsatt
McClendon, Jacob vs. William M. Green
McClendon, Jacob vs. Thomas Hairston
McClendon, Jacob vs. Everard Hamilton and John R. Hays
McClendon, Jacob vs. James Hunter
McClendon, Jacob vs. John McKenzie and Peter Bennoch
McClendon, Jacob vs. Eli Shorter
McClendon, Jacob vs. James Smith, Thomas J. Smith and
  Charles McLemore
McClendon, Jacob vs. Ignatius Stokes
McClendon, Jacob and William Armstrong vs. James Whitfield
McClendon, Jacob and Jarrel Beasley vs. James Whitfield
McClendon, James vs. Alfred Shorter
McClendon, Jesse vs. The State
McClendon, Joel vs. Elijah Bradshaw
McClendon, Joel vs. John S. D. Byrom
McClendon, Joel vs. Samuel Clay

McClendon, Joel and Samuel Clay vs. John Hobson, Francis
Hobson, Administrator, Alsea Holifield, Administrator and
James Whitfield, Administrator
McClendon, Joel vs. Ichabod Hood
McClendon, Joel vs. James Whitfield and Anthony Dyer
McClendon, Joseph vs. George L. Holmes
McClendon, Judah vs. Edward Hicks
McClendon, Pheba E. and John Thurmond vs. The State
McClendon, Stephen vs. Charles Cargile
McClendon, Stephen vs. Wylie B. Ector
McClendon, Stephen vs. Oliver Huston
McClendon, Stephen and Amos McClendon vs. William Meriwether,
Howard Beall, Elias Beall and Thaddeus Beall
McClendon, Stephen and William Barclay vs. Thomas F. Nolan
McClendon, Stephen, Amos McClendon and George Hardwick vs.
Joseph White, Thomas White, Administrator and Averilla B.
Durham, Administrator
McClendon, Stephen and Jefferson Adams vs. James Whitfield
McClendon, Thomas vs. Gideon Berry
McClendon, Thomas vs. James Gafford
McClure, H. C., N. B. White and H. N. White, Executor vs.
Charles Ellis
McClure, H. C. vs. W. J. McClure
McClure, H. C. Merchandising Co. vs. Georgia Farmers Oil
and Fertilizing Co.
McClure, Thomas A. vs. The State
McComb, R. A. vs. W. H. Whitfield
McCord, William vs. William Cook
McCord, William vs. Jeremiah Pearson
McCord, William vs. John Pinkard
McCorkle, James K. vs. Susan Hodges
McCorkle, William vs. John H. Brantley
McCorkle, William vs. John Hill, Augustin Slaughter and
Charles Labuzan
McCorkle, William vs. William Penn
McCormick, Edward and John F. Spearman vs. William Terry
and Samuel Smith
McCormick, John and John Reid vs. Thomas F. Noland
McCoy, David and William Head vs. John Cargile
McCoy, David vs. William Colbert
McCoy, David vs. John Cormick
McCoy, David vs. John Farley
McCoy, David vs. Benjamin Gresham
McCoy, David vs. Duke Hamilton
McCoy, David and Robert Garmany vs. Richard Hudson
McCoy, David, John West, Sr. and James Turner vs. Walter
Johnson
McCoy, David vs. Richard Knight
McCoy, David and Airs Hudspeth vs. Samuel Lovejoy
McCoy, David vs. John Moore
McCoy, David, Thomas Davis and Fields Wilson vs. Joseph
Watters
McCoy, Nealey vs. James M. Laws
McCullers, Freeman, Bradford McCullers and Charles Ozborn
vs. Isaac L. Parker and Maximilian H. Hutchinson,
Administrator
McCullers, Freeman and Bradford McCullers vs. Henry Walker
McCullough, Bradford vs. The State
McCullough, John vs. The State
McCune, William, Thomas B. McCune, Administrator, Jane
McCune, Administrator and Moses Haynes, Administrator vs.
Alexander Patterson
McDade, J. W. vs. The State

McDaniel, Daniel vs. William Magruder
McDaniel, George T. and Robert Brown, Guardian vs.
  Elizabeth J. Phelps for use of Hurd and Hungerford
McDaniel, George T., Nancy McDaniel, Martha A. McDaniel and
  Robert Brown, Guardian vs. Michael Toland
McDaniel, Jacob, George McDaniel, Nancy Ann McDaniel and
  Robert Brown, Guardian vs. Aquilla Phelps
McDaniel, Samuel and Jacob McDaniel vs. Edward Clark for
  use of Thomas Grant, Sr., Daniel Grant, Executor, Thomas
  Grant, Executor and Peter Grinnell, Executor
McDaniel, Samuel vs. The State
McDaniel, W. S. and G. T. Bartlett, Administrator vs. T. C.
  Broddus
McDavid, John vs. Claborn Foster
McDonald, Alexander vs. Nathaniel Coggeshell
McDonald, Alexander vs. Charles F. V. Reeve
McDonald, Thomas vs. Alston H. Greene and Joseph Buchannon
McDonald, Thomas vs. Henry C. Hutcheson
McDonald, W. A. and Gus T. Bartlett, Administrator vs.
  Davis Lane and John F. Patterson
McDonald, William A. and George T. Bartlett, Administrator
  vs. Daniel Marshall and William Rice
McDonald, William A. vs. Joseph Penn
McDonald, William A. and Gus T. Bartlett, Administrator vs.
  Samuel Prudden
McDonnel, Hugh vs. William Powel
McDougal, Jonathan vs. Joel Baley and Parham P. Mabry
McDougall, Thomas vs. James Reid
McDowell, Charles and Daniel McDowell vs. Joseph Johnson
McDowell, Charles vs. John Mann and Edward B. Brooking
McDowell, Daniel and Sackville Lynch vs. Greenberry Bankston
McDowell, Daniel vs. James S. Bankston
McDowell, Daniel vs. Burrell P. Key
McDowell, Daniel vs. Benjamin F. Tidwell
McDowell, Daniel and John M. McDowell vs. John C. Watters,
  Cornelius Hardy and B. P. Key
McDowell, Daniel, Miller W. Pope, William H. Preston,
  James M. McDowell and Margaret R. McDowell vs. William
  T. Welborn
McDowell, Daniel vs. Leroy M. Wiley, Thomas Parish, Henry
  Parish, Daniel Parish, John R. Marshall and Thomas P.
  Norris
McDowell, George (alias George Cook) vs. The State
McDowell, J. C. and Martha C. McDowell vs. Saulsbury Respess
McDowell, Joel C. vs. George W. Holland and Hugh P.
  Kirkpatrick
McDowell, Joel C. vs. Jennie C. Nelson
McDowell, Joel C. and Daniel McDowell vs. William H. Preston
McDowell and Jones vs. J. H. Bullard for use of Officers
  of Court
McDowell, Levi vs. The State
McDowell, M. A. vs. Daniel McDowell and T. B. Williams,
  Executor
McDowell, William, Daniel McDowell, Executor and Isaac
  Baley, Executor vs. Monticello Academy
McDowell, William vs. Avery Reeves
McDowell, William, Jr. vs. John McLemore, John Martin,
  Administrator and John Drew, Administrator
McDowell, William T. vs. Sanford C. Warrill
McElhany, John and W. F. Jordan, Administrator vs. Mary J.
  Tyler
McElhenney, G. W. vs. The State
McElhenney, John vs. William S. Hurd and Anson Hungerford

223

McElroy, Andrew and Hugh Grigs vs. Lysander Burdick for use
 of Alexander Herring
McElroy, Henry vs. Alfred Shepherd
McElroy, Isaac vs. Richard Hudspeth
McElroy, Isaac W. vs. Thomas Hudspeth
McElroy, James vs. Abner Chapman
McElroy, John J. vs. Joseph Price for use of Wesley Glazier
McFall, Fleming vs. Robert Kellam and William Maxey
McFalls, W. F. vs. The State
McGaughey, Benjamin and William R. McGaughey vs. William
 Maxey and Charles S. Jordan
McGee, John vs. John Robson
McGee, Robert vs. Fields Pruit
McGehee, Edward vs. The State
McGehee, Jacob vs. William L. Middlebrooks
McGehee, John W. vs. Thomas McGehee
McGehee, Robert vs. Beal Baker
McGehee, Thomas vs. The State
McGehee, Thomas and John W. McGehee vs. Alfred Y. Walton,
 John W. Y. Walton, John T. Murrell and Robert Edger
McGehee, Thomas, Sr., Thomas McGehee, Jr. and John W.
 McGehee vs. Joseph B. Weed, David M. Benedict and
 Frederick D. Fanning
McGinnis, Will vs. The State
McGuirk, John, Jr. and John McGuirk, Sr. vs. Solomon
 Phillips and James Mobley
McIntosh, William vs. Loyall and Pritchett
McKee, Lewis vs. Lawson S. Holland
McKee, Lewis vs. Hugh P. Kirkpatrick
McKee, Lewis and James Fincher vs. Charity McCray
McKee, Lewis vs. The State
McKee, Lewis vs. Barnabas Strickland
McKeen, Hugh vs. Thomas Grant
McKeen, Hugh vs. Josiah Hardy
McKeen, Hugh vs. John Hill, Augustin Slaughter and Charles
 Labuzan
McKeen, Hugh vs. William Stroud
McKelroy, James vs. John Baldwin
McKemie, James, James Pye and Alsea Holifield vs. Thomas
 I. Davis
McKemie, James vs. Eli S. Shorter
McKinley, E. B. vs. Wily Peddy
McKinley, Eli B. vs. Jonathan T. Holmes
McKinley, Eli B. vs. Edward S. Riley for use of Joseph Banks
McKissack, Dunkin vs. James Barnes
McKissack, Isaac C. W. T. and John McKissack vs. Joseph Day
McKissack, John vs. Francis S. Johnson
McKissack, John vs. Telitha Joice and Johnson Springer,
 Executor
McKissack, John vs. The State
McKissack, John vs. Joseph C. White and Ada C. White,
 Executor
McKissack, John vs. Robert Woodall
McKissack, John F. vs. Wiley Peddy
McKissack, Thomas vs. Neil C. Berry
McKissack, Thomas vs. Alfred Johnson
McKissack, William T. vs. Gambell, Beck and Co.
McKissack, William T. and John McKissack vs. Mary A. Goolsby
McKissack, William T. and Thomas McKissack vs. J. H. Holland
McKissack, William T. vs. Wiley Peddy
McKissack, William T. and Richard L. Grubbs vs. Stephen C.
 Talmadge
McKlanckling, James vs. Isaac L. Walton

McKnight and Davison Mercantile Co. vs. Everett, Ridley, Ragan Co.
McKree, William vs. Giles Tompkins
McLamore, Franklin vs. Thomas J. Davis
McLaughlin, James vs. Maximillian H. Hutchison
McLaughlin, James vs. Isaac L. Walton
McLea, John and Jackson Fitzpatrick vs. Joseph Cummings and Humphrey B. Gwathney
McLean, Allen vs. James J. Darnell
McLean, Allen vs. Airs Hudspeth
McLean, Cochran and Co., J. J. Johnson and Co. and Kelly adn McDowell vs. Sarah H. Ward
McLear, Robert H. vs. William Cook
McLear, Robert H. vs. James Richards
McLelland, Elijah vs. The State
McLemore, Charles and James McLemore, Guardian vs. Jarrel Beasley
McLemore, Charles vs. The State
McLemore, Franklin vs. John Baldwin
McLemore, Franklin vs. John Hill, Augustin Slaughter and Charles Labuzan
McLemore, Franklin vs. Gilbraith Simonton and William Simonton
McLemore, James vs. Edward Hicks and Joel Baley
McLemore, James vs. Thomas J. Holmes
McLemore, James vs. Simeon Hyde and George Cleveland
McLemore, James vs. Joseph Kopman
McLendon, Amos vs. Israel Gamble
McLendon, Amos, Stephen McLendon and Edmond Jenkins vs. James Griggs
McLendon, Amos vs. Tandy D. King
McLendon, Amos vs. James Mullins
McLendon, Amos vs. David Smith and Green Whatley
McLendon, Francis vs. Theophilus Hill
McLendon, Joel vs. William Biscoe and James N. Hall
McLendon, Joel vs. The State
McLendon, Stephen and Edmond Jenkins vs. Reuben Blakey
McLendon, Stephen and Amos McLendon vs. Jeremiah Pearson
McLendon, Stephen W. vs. William Johnson
McLeroy, Andrew vs. Thomas Camp for use of James Henderson
McLeroy, James vs. Thomas Beall
McLeroy, William H. vs. Joel Branham and Simeon Fuller, Jr.
McLeroy, William T. vs. James M. Denson
McLeroy, William T., Mary E. McLeroy, Sarah T. Denson, Rebecah Denson and Lee Ann Denson vs. Maxey, Jordan and Co.
McMahan, William vs. The State
McMath, John H. vs. Samuel Bennett
McMath, John H. vs. Thomas B. Erwin
McMichael, B. H. vs. The State
McMichael, B. J. vs. N. G. Childs and Lizzie Childs for use of Officers of Court
McMichael, B. J. and E. W. Baynes vs. Berry T. Digby
McMichael, Brown vs. The State
McMichael, Burton J. vs. George B. Hallock
McMichael, Burton J. and William Pope vs. Green B. Turner
McMichael, C. W. and Pollard B. McMichael vs. John Straiton
McMichael, Catherine vs. John McMichael
McMichael, Charles vs. Edward A. Broddus
McMichael, Charles vs. Hamilton Brown, Peyton Gwyn and James Gwyn
McMichael, Charles vs. Jeremiah Pearson
McMichael, Charles and James Rivers vs. James Whitfield

225

McMichael, Clark W. and Shadrach McMichael vs. Anthony
  Dyer and John R. Dyer, Executor
McMichael, Clark W. and Shadrick J. McMichael vs. Crawford
  H. Greer
McMichael, D. and Alsey McLean vs. James I. Darnall
McMichael, David and Mary Brewer vs. Eli Glover
McMichael, E. H. S. vs. Loyal McCullough
McMichael, Elijah vs. Whitmill Bonner
McMichael, Elijah and Shadrach McMichael, Executor vs.
  Greene L. McMichael and Elizabeth McMichael, Administrator
McMichael, Elijah H. L., Clark W. McMichael, Executor and
  Pollard B. McMichael vs. John D. Butt and Joshua W. Butt
McMichael, Elizabeth vs. Isham Berry
McMichael, C. J. (?) vs. Mrs. Nancy Hines
McMichael, G. L. vs. Griffin, Monticello and Madison
  Railroad Co.
McMichael, George vs. The State
McMichael, Green vs. John Campbell
McMichael, Green and Simeon Scales vs. William Malone
McMichael, Green L. vs. Stephen Childers
McMichael, Green L. and Nancy Wilson vs. J. H. Holland
McMichael, Green L. and John McMichael, Jr. vs. Henry Howard
McMichael, Green L. and John McMichael, Jr. vs. John T.
  Howard
McMichael, Green L. vs. John H. Lawson
McMichael, Green L. vs. Maxey, Jordan and Co.
McMichael, Green L. vs. Griffin L. Pye
McMichael, Green L. vs. The State
McMichael, James, Margaret (Peggy) McMichael, Administrator
  and William Armor, Administrator vs. John Piper and Jane
  Piper
McMichael, James vs. The State
McMichael, John vs. Zenos Bronson
McMichael, John vs. Thomas Cargile and Robert Germany,
  Executor
McMichael, John and David McMichael vs. Eli Glover
McMichael, John and Isaac N. D. Martin vs. Joseph Johnson
McMichael, John vs. Pleasant Stovall and William P. Ford
McMichael, John vs. George W. Wright
McMichael, John, Jr. vs. William Penn
McMichael, John, Sr. vs. Jeremiah Pearson
McMichael, John B. vs. The State
McMichael, John L., Fleming Mobley, Frank Malone, Benjamin
  Lane and Martin Tyner vs. George T. Bartlett
McMichael, John L., Shadrick McMichael and William Ramey
  vs. Central Bank of Georgia
McMichael, John L. vs. Henry H. Chapman
McMichael, John L. and Fleming Mobley, Administrator vs.
  Jonas H. Holland
McMichael, John L. vs. Adam W. Jones
McMichael, John L. vs. Amos Marshall
McMichael, John L. vs. Edward Paine, John H. Low, Executor
  and William James, Executor
McMichael, John L. and Isaac H. Slaughter vs. William A.
  Slaughter
McMichael, John L. vs. The State
McMichael, John L. and Leroy Lawrence vs. George W. Walker
McMichael, John L. vs. Moses Ward
McMichael, John Lee and Robert L. Bowdoin vs. The State
McMichael, John S. vs. William S. Hurd and Anson
  Hungerford, Jr.
McMichael, Joseph vs. William Pryor
McMichael, Joseph vs. The State

McMichael, Mathew vs. John Cimbrough for use of John McKinne
McMichael, Mathew vs. John Fluker
McMichael, Mathew, Zachariah Estes and David McCoy vs.
  The State
McMichael, N. D. vs. Jesse Clay
McMichael, N. A. vs. Sarah A. Waits
McMichael, P. Brown vs. The State
McMichael, Peter vs. The State
McMichael, Pollard vs. The State
McMichael, Pollard B. and Byrum P. Kennymore vs. John M.
  Adams, Albert O. Parmelee and Hosea Webster
McMichael, Pollard B. and Byrum P. Kennymore vs. Hezekiah
  Clay
McMichael, Pollard B. vs. William S. Hurd and Anson
  Hungerford, Jr.
McMichael, Pollard B. vs. Samuel B. Kello
McMichael, Pollard B. vs. Emily R. McMichael
McMichael, Pollard B. vs. John L. McMichael
McMichael, Pollard B. and P. W. McMichael, Executor vs.
  John I. Straton
McMichael, Pollard B. vs. Kenneth M. Urquhart
McMichael, R. L. vs. W. F. Jordan
McMichael, Reuben vs. The State
McMichael, Robert vs. The State
McMichael, S. I., Sr. vs. The State
McMichael, S. J. vs. P. B. McMichael
McMichael, S. L. and John L. McMichael vs. H. C. McClure
  and N. B. White
McMichael, Sally vs. James Black
McMichael, Shade, Jr. vs. The State
McMichael, Shadrach vs. Bank of Darien
McMichael, Shadrach vs. George W. Bonner
McMichael, Shadrach vs. Justices of Court for use of Joel
  McClendon, Deceased, Francis McClendon, Minor, Caroline
  McClendon, Minor, Susan McClendon, Minor and William
  Maxey, Guardian
McMichael, Shadrach and John McMichael vs. Elijah McMichael
  and Merina McMichael, Administrator
McMichael, Shadrach vs. The State
McMichael, Shadrach and Crawford Edmondson vs. The State
McMichael, Shadrach, Elijah McMichael and John McMichael
  vs. The State
McMichael, Shadrach I. vs. Amos W. Hammond
McMichael, Shadrach I. and Naney McMichael vs. Matilda
  Persons
McMichael, Shadrach I. and Nancy (Hinsey) McMichael vs.
  Thomas J. Pritchett
McMichael, Shadrack vs. John W. Brantley
McMichael, Shadrack vs. Joshua Broughton
McMichael, Shadrack vs. James H. Miller and Elizabeth Miller
McMichael, Shasrick I. and Nancy Hensey vs. The State
McMichael, W. J. vs. The State
McMichael, Walter vs. The State
McMichael, Zachariah vs. Alston H. Greene and Joseph
  Buchannon
McMichal, John vs. Jacob Finley
McMurray, John vs. James Butram
McMurray, John vs. John Spear
McMurray, John, Jr. vs. Eleazer Mobley
McMurry, John, David McMichael and Thomas Steedman vs.
  Isaac N. D. Martin and Edy (Steedman) Martin
McNeal, Fred vs. The State
McNeil, Alfred vs. The State

227

McNeil, Alfred vs. The State
McNeill, Archibald vs. Thomas Broadus for use of Charles
  McDowell

Nall, James vs. Thomas Napier
Nall, John P. vs. William Jones and Harrison Smith
Nall, Martin vs. Obed Baker
Nall, Martin vs. Thomas Colbert
Nall, Martin vs. Pope and Stilwell
Nall, Martin vs. John J. Smith
Nall, Martin and Thomas Colbert vs. The State
Nall, Martin and Matthew Duncan vs. The State
Nall, Martin vs. Stevens Thomas
Nall, Martin vs. Lewis Wynn and William Johnson
Nall, Willis B. vs. Peter Harris
Napier, Jesse vs. The State
Napier, Thomas vs. The State
Nash, Dan, Simeon Harris and Aaron Meriwether vs. The State
Nash, King vs. The State
Nash, Matilda vs. The State
Neal, David and Samuel Townsend vs. Gabriel Green
Neal, John vs. The State
Nelson, Thomas vs. Turner Chapman
Nelson, Thomas and Richard D. King vs. Jonathan Jewett,
  Gordon Abell and James M. Codwise
Nelson, William vs. Robert C. Beasley and Palemon L. Weekes
Nelson, William vs. Reuben Dawkins
Nelson, William and William Knight vs. John Kerr and
  Alexander Graham
Nelson, William and William Knight vs. Alexander Russell
Nelson, William and Richard Goolsby vs. Isaac Scott,
  James D. Carhart and William Carhart
Nelson, William and William Knight vs. Archibald H. Sneed
  and Jenkins D. Weathers
Nelson, William and Riley Nelson vs. The State
Newby, Mike vs. The State
Newby, Will vs. The State
Newell, Leonard vs. William Bradley and Joseph T. Camp
Newton, ? vs. ? Roby
Newton, Aris vs. Mercer Babb
Newton, Aris, Richard Newton, Joseph Shaw, John Davidson
  and W. J. M. Preston vs. Pollard and Co.
Newton, Aris vs. The State
Newton, Aris, Jr. vs. Griffin, Monticello and Madison
  Railroad Co.
Newton, Aristachus and Elizabeth G. Flournoy vs. John A.
  Ellis and Phebe W. (Cheatham) Ellis
Newton, George W. vs. Barrett and Caswell
Newton, George W. vs. Griffin, Monticello and Madison
  Railroad Co.
Newton, L. B. vs. Griffin, Monticello and Madison Railroad
  Co.
Newton, Lucian B. vs. Thomas Johnson
Newton, Mary F. vs. Navassa Guano Co.
Newton, Richard vs. Officers of Court
Newton, Seaborn vs. The State
Newton, Willis vs. C. H. Phinezy and P. B. Phinezy
Niblet, Tilman vs. Thomas F. Danielly
Niblet, Tilmon and John Langston vs. William S. Roberts
  and Thomas H. Roberts
Niblet, Tilmon vs. Simeon Scales
Niblet, Tilmon and John E. Langston vs. Henry C. Seymore,
  Jesse Ansly and John G. McHenry

Niblett, Ed vs. The State
Niblett, James H. vs. Silas Grubbs
Niblett, James H. vs. William Maxey and Co.
Niblett, James H. vs. Stephen C. Talmadge
Niblett, Tilman and Elbert W. Baynes vs. Matthew Whitfield
Niblett, Tilmon and Elbert W. Baynes vs. Amos Martin
Niblett, Tilmon vs. Jacob B. Rosenfield for use of Stephen
  C. Talmadge
Nichols, Catherine vs. John Nichols
Nichols, Jeff vs. John R. Greer
Nichols, Simon W., Daniel McCloud and Bailey Bell vs. Jonas
  H. Holland
Nichols, Tom vs. The State
Nichols, Travis vs. James McInvale
Niles, Ambrose, Horatio R. Spencer and Ira Goddard vs.
  Barney Shivers
Nix, David vs. Ferdinand Phinizy
Nix, Jacob vs. Moris Flatan
Nix, McKendin T. vs. David Dickson
Nix, Sarah A. vs. Officers of Court
Nix, Thomas L. vs. William Maxey and Charles S. Jordan
Nix, Washington and Dick Jordan vs. The State
Nixson, Joseph and James Fretwell vs. Randolph Rullas (?),
  Walter Hamilton, Administrator and James McNeil
Noble, Stephen vs. John Floyd and Richard Stewart
Nolan, Thomas F. vs. Thomas Richards
Nolan, Thomas F. vs. Bedford Shorter for use of Gilbert
  Longstreet
Nolan, Thomas F. vs. Isham Thompson and James A. Black
Noles, John W. and Morris Noles vs. Thomas S. Smith and
  John W. A. Smith, Guardian
Noles, Zachariah and Sherod H. Gay vs. William V. Burney
Nolan, Thomas F. vs. Alexander Bonner
Nolley, Ada vs. The State
Nolley, John vs. The State
Nolley, Nathan vs. Alston H. Greene and Joseph Buchannon
Nolly, Fed vs. The State
Nolly, Nathan vs. Elijah Shores for use of Matthew Whitfield
  and James Whitfield
Norman, Stephen, Comer Early, Richard Davidson, and Squire
  Walker vs. The State
Norris, Needham vs. William Norris
Norris, William vs. John Aler
Norris, William and Rigdon Norris vs. Robert Bledsoe
Norris, William vs. Moses Powell
Norris, William vs. Moses Watkins
Norsworthy, James vs. The State
Norsworthy, Samuel vs. Stephen Hackney
Norton, Robert S. vs. Horace I. Bates
Norton, Robert S. vs. William D. Luckie
Norton, Thomas vs. The State
Norwood, James vs. Jane Jones
Norwood, John vs. Thomas Grant
Norwood, Ned vs. The State
Nova, William vs. William Hodges
Nowland, George vs. The State
Nunnally, Moses vs. William P. Culbertson
Nutt, Andrew vs. Isaac Bailey
Nutt, Andrew vs. Henry Duke
Nutt, Andrew vs. Henry Robinson
Nutt, Samuel vs. Jesse Grice

O'Conner, Patrick vs. Thomas Dawson

O'Conner, Patrick B. vs. The State
O'Daniel, Alexander vs. The State
O'Daniel, Wilson and John O'Daniel vs. Wood Moreland
Oden, Alexander vs. James Dupee
Odom, B. B. and S. E. Odom vs. J. W. Griggs for use of
    Officers of Court
Odom, Gus vs. The State
Odom, Roland vs. The State
Oglesby, James and William L. Gwinn vs. The State
Ogletree, Joseph H. and Thomas Watts vs. John G. Colbert
Ogletree, Joseph H. and Gabriel Johnson
O'Hara, Charles vs. Hollis Cooley and Dyer C. Bancroft
Oliver, Love vs. The State
O'Nail, Jesse and Daniel Saffold vs. William Crain
Onail, Jesse vs. James Fleming
O'Nail, Jesse vs. Robert McAfee
Onail, Jesse vs. William H. Miles
Onail, Jesse vs. James Richards
Onail, Jesse vs. John Underwood
Onail, Jesse vs. William S. Underwood
Onail, Jesse vs. William Woods
Oneal, Bartlet vs. Hiram Brown
Oneal, Edmund vs. Jeremiah Clark and Munford Lawson
Oneal, Osban vs. Gilbert T. Snowden and William Shear
Oneal, Thomas W. vs. Eli S. Shorter
Oneal, Thomas W. and Absalom Beck vs. Gilbert T. Snowden
    and William Shear
Orange, Eliza vs. The State
Organ, Matthew, Howell Tatom, Administrator and William
    Copland, Administrator vs. George Cabaness, Henry B.
    Cabaness, Administrator, Harrison Cabaness, Administrator,
    Robert McGough, Administrator and Palatier Cabaness,
    Administrator
Orr, Allen vs. Daniel Bridges
Orr, Allen vs. Noah Butt
Orr, Allen and Jacob McClenden vs. Elisha Cain
Orr, Allen vs. Stephen D. Crane
Orr, Allen vs. Joseph Ferguson
Orr, Allen vs. Alston H. Greene and Joseph Buchannon
Orr, Allen vs. John Maddox
Orr, Allen vs. Royal Sibly, Amory Sibly and Orray Taft
Orr, Allen vs. The State
Orr, James and Allen Orr vs. James Cowan
Orr, Sample vs. James Cowan and Thomas B. Erwin
Orr, Sample vs. William Foster
Orr, Sample vs. James Locke
Orr, Sample vs. John Nesbit
Orr, Sample vs. Absalom Simonton
Osborn, Benjamin and James Osborn vs. The State
Osborn, Lazerous vs. Dona A. Beatie
Osborn, Charles vs. Oliver P. Fonts
Osborn, Charles vs. John S. Weaver
Osborn, J., C. A. J. Flemister and Charles Osburn vs. James
    F. Marshall and William M. Estes
Osborn, Thomas O. and Franklin O. Fielder vs. John H. Moss
Owen, Bracket and Thomas Moreland vs. Henry Gassett and
    Henry W. Bailey
Owen, Hardaman vs. James Cowen and Thomas B. Erwin
Owen, Hardaman vs. Jonathan Jewett, Gordon Abel and James
    N. Codwise
Owen, Hardaman vs. Henry Trippe
Owen, Hardeman vs. Peyton Clements, Polly Clements,
    Executor, Wiley L. Clements, Executor and Peyton R.

Clements, Executor
Owen, Hardeman vs. William McGar
Owen, Hardeman vs. Lewis Wynn and William Johnson
Owen, Polly vs. Stephen Wood
Owen, Robert and Burwell Greene vs. William Rabun for use
of William Woods
Owens, Elijah M. vs. Susannah C. Owens
Owens, Hardaman vs. John J. Smith
Owens, Hardaman, Robert Beasley and William Peddy vs.
Thomas T. Walker
Owens, Hardeman vs. John E. Morgan
Owens, Hardeman vs. The State
Owens, Hardiman, John C. Rogers and Jacob Lindsey vs.
John A. Ellis
Owens, John N. vs. J. T. Corley
Owens, Robert vs. Charles W. Rockwell
Owens, William vs. The State
Owensby, Francis vs. The State
Oxford, J. W. vs. James Benton and M. S. Benton, Adminis-
trator
Ozburn, Charles vs. Berry T. Digby
Ozburn, Charles vs. The State
Ozburn, Matthew and Elias Ozburn vs. Williamson Bailey and
William Bailey, Executor

Pabodie, Albert vs. Elias Bliss and Co.
Pace, Stephen vs. Williamson Robey and Henry Boswell
Pace, Stephen vs. Thomas Willingham for use of Williamson
Robey
Pace, William vs. David Taylor, Jr.
Pace, William T. vs. Gibson H. Cornwell and Lucian Reese
Pace, William T. and John Durdin vs. Jesse W. Fears and
James F. Swanson
Pace, William T. and Agatha Montgomery vs. William Maxey
and Co.
Pace, William T. and Josephus Clark vs. The State
Paine, Henry D. and John Farley vs. Joshua Callaway and
Elizabeth Callaway, Administrator
Paine, Henry D. vs. John Hobson and Christopher Hobson for
use of William Pabodie
Paine, Henry D. vs. The State
Paine, John vs. Edward McGehee and James McGehee,
Administrator
Paine, Randal and Paschal Murphy vs. The State
Palmer, Chaney vs. The State
Palmer, David E. vs. The State
Pane, Randolph vs. John Pane and Thomas Binges
Parker, Aaron, Joel Kitchens, Henry Kitchens, and Nelson
Kitchens vs. The State
Parker, Andrew J. vs. The State
Parker, Chris vs. The State
Parker, Ed vs. The State
Parker, Isaac H. vs. David Peck
Parker, Isaac L. vs. Seth Arms
Parker, Isaac L. and Maximilian Hutchinson, Administrator
vs. Williamson and William Bailey, Executor
Parker, Isaac L. vs. James C. Bartlett
Parker, Isaac L. vs. Henry G. Blunt, Joel Colly and Thomas
Freeman
Parker, Isaac L. vs. John W. Burney and John R. Dyer
Parker, Isaac L. vs. Mary Cargile
Parker, Isaac L., John Robinson, William H. Wyatt and
Edward A. Broddus vs. Central Bank of Georgia

Parker, Isaac L., Elbert W. Baynes, William H. Wyatt,
   Maximilian H. Hutchinson, Welcome C. Lovejoy and Sherrod
   H. Gray vs. Hollis Colley
Parker, Isaac L., Shadrack McMichael, Edward A. Broddus,
   John C. Watters, John Robinson, Robert Kellam, Fleming
   Jordan, Thomas Greer, William H. Wyatt, Lucas Powell and
   Williamson Bailey vs. George W. Crawford (Governor) for
   use of James B. Lewis and Edmund B. Darden, Administrator
Parker, Isaac L. vs. Lemuel Culpepper and Daley Culpepper,
   Executor
Parker, Isaac L. vs. Gordon Davis
Parker, Isaac L. vs. William O. Edmondson
Parker, Isaac L. vs. Porter Fleming
Parker, Isaac L. vs. Isaac Goodman
Parker, Isaac L. vs. Cincinnatus L. Goolsby
Parker, Isaac L. vs. William J. Goolsby
Parker, Isaac L. vs. Samuel Griswold
Parker, Isaac L. vs. Daniel Gunn and William Gunn
Parker, Isaac L. vs. James W. Horne
Parker, Isaac L. vs. John Horton
Parker, Isaac L. and J. C. Thomason, Administrator vs. M. H.
   Hutchison
Parker, Isaac L. and M. A. Hutchison, Administrator, Vinis
   Fish, Robert Brown, P. J. McMichael, Leroy M. Price,
   William Bailey, Silas Grubbs, W. C. Lovejoy and J. W. A.
   Smith vs. Herschel V. Johnson (Governor) for use of
   Wiley Banks and Co. and John L. McMichael
Parker, Isaac L. vs. Nathan Massey and Hurd and Hungerford
Parker, Isaac L. vs. William Maxey and Joshua Hill
Parker, Isaac L. vs. William P. Moore
Parker, Isaac L. vs. Officers of Court
Parker, Isaac L. vs. Jonathan Parish
Parker, Isaac L. vs. Gilbraith Simonton, Hugh P. Kirkpatrick,
   Administrator and Agnes I. Simonton, Administrator
Parker, Isaac L. vs. James Smith
Parker, Isaac L. vs. Thomas I. Smith
Parker, Isaac L. vs. Francis Spears
Parker, Isaac L. and Lewis Dowdell vs. The State
Parker, Isaac L., James D. Malone and Nancy Malone vs. The
   State for use of George W. Holland and Hugh P. Kirkpatrick,
   Administrator
Parker, Isaac L. and Edward Price vs. The State
Parker, Isaac L. and Samuel G. Stanley vs. The State
Parker, Isaac L. vs. Anderson F. Thompson
Parker, Isaac L. and John C. Watters vs. John Thurmond
Parker, James vs. Thomas McGehee
Parker, John G. vs. William Richards
Parker, John G. vs. James Tatum
Parker, Rowe vs. The State
Parker, William vs. Michea C. Ferndon
Parker, William, Landford Parker and Charles Parker vs.
   The State
Parker, William C. and Richard Hudson vs. Robert Beasley
Parker, William C. and Maximillian H. Hutchinson vs. Richard
   W. Henderson
Parker, William C. and M. H. Hutchison vs. S. C. Talmadge
   and H. J. Talmadge
Parker, William H. vs. Thaddeus Beall, Elias Beall and
   Thomas Beall
Parker, William H. vs. George Clower
Parker, William H., Hiram Glazier and Richard Hudson vs.
   Spencer Crain
Parker, William H. vs. Anthony Dyer

Parker, William H. vs. Alston H. Greene and Joseph
  Buchannan
Parker, William H. vs. John Hough and Henry Wyche,
  Administrator
Parker, William H. vs. Owen H. Kenan
Parker, William H., Hiram Glazier and Richard Hudson vs.
  William H. Kenan
Parker, William H. vs. James Mare
Parker, William H. vs. John McCurdy
Parker, William H. vs. Paschal Murphy for use of Samuel
  Weems
Parker, William H. vs. James Phillips
Parker, William H. and Crawford Edmondson vs. Benjamin
  Sanford and John G. Lumsden
Parker, William H. and Richard Hudson vs. Hosea Webster and
  George Webster
Parker, William H., Hiram Glazier and Richard Hudson vs.
  James Weekes
Parker, William S. vs. Benjamin Flowers
Parks, Clayborn vs. The State
Parks, Luther vs. The State
Parks, Thomas vs. The State
Parks, Welcom vs. James Whitfield
Parmer, Jesse vs. John McLea and Jackson Fitzpatrick
Parmer, Jesse vs. The State
Parnell, James and Celia Ann Leverett vs. The State
Parrot, George, Jeremiah Lumsden and Samuel Thompson vs.
  The State
Parrot, William H., Owen H. Kenan, Norborne B. Powell and
  John C. Watters vs. The State
Parrott, William H. vs. Fleming Jordan
Paten, Fannie vs. The State
Patilloe, Delilah vs. Benjamin B. Freeman
Patrick, Charlie vs. The State
Patrick, John M. vs. John J. Darnell
Patrick, John M. vs. Joseph Delk
Patrick, John M., Ethelred Gardner and Jordan Thornton vs.
  John Ector, Hugh Ector, Executor and Robert Freeman,
  Executor
Patrick, John M. vs. Gabriel Gunn
Patrick, John M. vs. Robert Hardwick McLear
Patrick, John M. vs. Robert Mitchell
Patrick, John M. vs. Thomas McCarten
Patrick, John M. and Wiley Hood vs. Peter Randolph, Harmon
  Runnels, Zadock Cook, Stephen Crow, Jonathan Melton, John
  Strother, Benjamin Haygood, William Wright and Thomas Hill
Patrick, John M. and John Graves, Sr. vs. Hosea Webster and
  George Webster
Patrick, John W. and Leonard Worthy vs. Emily Lloyd and
  John Norwood, Guardian
Patrick, John W. vs. The State
Patrick, John W. vs. Thomas Watts
Patrick, Jonathan vs. Samuel Lane
Patrick, William vs. Lodowick Laird
Patterson, Henry vs. The State
Patterson, John C. and William D. Maddox vs. Edwin Bates
  and Co.
Patterson, John F. and William D. Maddux vs. Russel J. Brown
Patterson, John F. and Richard D. Maddox vs. John P. Jenkins
Patterson, John F. and William D. Maddux vs. John F.
  Stillwell
Patterson, William vs. Lucas Powell
Pattillo, David vs. John Durden

Paty, Elijah and George Clifton vs. George Powell
Paty, Henry vs. Thomas Grant
Paul, W. E. and James Benton vs. Thomas C. Broddus
Payne, John vs. Daniel D. Bates
Payne, John vs. Thomas Hairston
Payne, John and Henry D. Payne vs. Franklin Hervey
Peacock, Alice vs. The State
Peacock, Gilbert vs. The State
Peacock, John vs. The State
Pearce, James vs. Joel Baley
Pearman, Robert vs. Anthony Dyer and Otis Dyer
Pearson, Charles vs. Thomas Hardeman and Irby Hudson
Pearson, Charles vs. John McKenzie and Peter Bennock
Pearson, Charles vs. Winborn Odom
Pearson, Edwin W. vs. James N. Hall and David A. Reese,
    Administrator
Pearson, Edwin W. and Seaborn J. Hendrick vs. Alsa Pope and
    Josias Pope, Administrator
Pearson, Francis vs. The State
Pearson, Green vs. The State
Pearson, Jeremiah and Allen McClendon vs. John W. Compton
    for use of William Ross
Pearson, Jeremiah vs. Jesse Loyall
Pearson, Jeremiah vs. Thomas Mason, Asia M. Caston, Eliza
    (Mason) Caston and Araminta Mason
Pearson, Jeremaih and Artemus Goolsby vs. Caroline Varner
    and Samuel D. Varner, Guardian
Pearson, John W. vs. Russel J. Brown
Pearson, John W. vs. C. M. Meriwether
Pearson, S. S. vs. The State
Pearson, Simeon vs. Elisha Smartt
Pearson, Thomas G. and Allen Martin vs. John S. D. Byrom
Pearson, W. A. vs. William C. Leverette
Pearson, W. A. vs. The State
Peavy, Allen vs. James Cowan and Thomas B. Erwin
Peavy, Allen and David Peavy vs. Anthony Dyer
Peavy, Allen and William Lawrence vs. George Foreman
Peavy, Allen and David Peavy vs. John Hunt
Peavy, Allen and David Peavy vs. William Lawrence
Peavy, Allen and David Peavy vs. John Reid
Peavy, David vs. Hamilton Brown, Peyton Gwyn and James Gwyn
Peavy, David and William Lawrence vs. John W. Cook
Peddy, Henry vs. Garland Dawkins
Peddy, Henry vs. Thomas B. Erwin and James Cowan
Peddy, Henry, Cornelius Robinson and Robert Beasley vs.
    Jonathan Richardson
Peddy, Henry and William Peddy vs. Willie Robinson and
    Allen Robinson, Administrator
Peddy, Wiley vs. Mrs. Mary Bell
Peddy, Wiley vs. James C. Haviland, Willington Stevenson,
    Thomas W. Chichester and Hamilton L. Shelton
Peddy, William vs. Zachariah Booth
Peddy, William and Henry Peddy vs. Willis Robinson and
    Alan Robinson, Administrator
Peel (Peale), John vs. Milton Antony
Peel, William vs. William Foyil for use of John Allison
Peel, William vs. William Jones
Peeples, James D. vs. Isham S. Fannin
Peeples, James D. vs. Nathaniel G. Foster
Peeples, James D. vs. John Jackson
Peeples, James D. and Lewis Smith vs. The State
Pegg, William H. and J. T. Benford vs. T. Byrne
Pegg, William H. vs. Elijah C. Jones

Pegg, William H. vs. William R. Kitchen
Pegg, William H. and John W. Wyatt vs. W. H. C. Pace,
   George T. Carr and Jeptha M. Cody
Pegg, William H. and John W. Wyatt vs. Carter Shepherd,
   Thomas J. Swanson and William B. Fitzpatrick
Pegg, William H. vs. Kinchin Strickland and Andrew J.
   Monday, Administrator
Pegg, William H. and William H. Speer vs. Jonas Thomas
Pegg, William H. vs. Thomas Willy and James Zimmerman
Pelot, J. J. vs. Julius Gerding
Pemberton, Joshua and Jane Pemberton vs. Sally Downey and
   James Downey
Penman, Wess vs. The State
Penn, A. A. vs. W. C. Penn
Penn, A. A. vs. The State
Penn, Annie P., Thomas R. Penn and Russel J. Penn vs.
   William Y. Harris
Penn, Bill vs. The State
Penn, Daniel and Charles Mercer vs. The State
Penn, Henry vs. The State
Penn, J. A. vs. The State
Penn, Joseph and B. T. Digby, Executor vs. B. W. Chapman
Penn, Joseph vs. Isham S. Fanning
Penn, Joseph, Berry T. Digby, Administrator, Russel J.
   Brown and Stephen C. Talmadge vs. Cynthia Henderson and
   Eli S. Glover, Trustee
Penn, Joseph and Berry T. Digby vs. John E. Langston and
   David M. Langston, Executor
Penn, Joseph and Berry T. Digby, Executor vs. Nehemiah B.
   White and Lucius White for use of Stephen A. Penn
Penn, Lewis and Peter Penn vs. The State
Penn, Lula vs. The State
Penn, Russel J. vs. James W. Young
Penn, Stephen A. vs. Thomas J. Smith and John C. Maddux
Penn, T. R. vs. Russel J. Brown
Penn, Thomas R. vs. Claghorn and Herring
Penn, Thomas R. vs. George R. Dozier
Penn, Thomas R. and Russel J. Penn vs. William Smith
Penn, Thomas R. and William C. Penn vs. Stephen C. Talmadge
   for use of A. J. Talmadge
Penn, Thomas R. vs. B. W. Whitfield
Penn, Thomas R. vs. Matthew C. Whitfield
Penn, Tom vs. The State
Penn, W. C. vs. Griffin, Monticello and Madison Railroad Co.
Penn, W. C. vs. Selina Penn
Penn, William vs. Charles Cargile
Penn, William vs. Asa Chapman, Abner Chapman, Executor,
   Solomon Lockett, Executor, Henry Lockett, Executor and
   Cynthia Chapman, Executor
Penn, William vs. Anthony Dyer
Penn, William vs. William Echols
Penn, William vs. Ephraim Gordon
Penn, William vs. Stephen W. Harris, Eli S. Shorter,
   Executor, Sarah H. Harris, Executor and William Wilkins,
   Executor
Penn, William vs. Monticello Academy
Penn, William vs. Isaac Pennington
Penn, William vs. John Robinson, Sr.
Penn, William vs. The State
Penn, William vs. Robert Taylor
Penn, William C. vs. Cardin Goolsby
Penn, William C. vs. John N. Goolsby
Penn, William C. vs. William W. Holland

Penn, William C. vs. William Maxey
Penn, William C. vs. M. Whitfield and J. A. Billups,
  Administrator
Pennington, Abraham vs. William Askew
Pennington, Abraham vs. John Moreland for use of Eli S.
  Shorter
Pennington, Henry vs. Lewis Lanier
Pennington, Henry vs. Charles Oliver
Pennington, Isaac and James Richards vs. John Mitchell
Pennington, Isaac vs. Elizabeth Pool and William Pentecost
Pennington, Isaac vs. Thomas Preston
Pennington, Isaac vs. William T. L. Robinson
Pennington, Isaac vs. The State
Pennington, J. C. vs. Thomas M. Clarke and Co.
Pennington, John vs. William Miller
Pennington,. John L. vs. Anthony Dyer
Pennington, John L. vs. Henry Walker
Pennington, Richardson vs. John Cradrick
Pennington, Richardson vs. John Hill, Charles Labuzan and
  Augustin Slaughter
Pennington, Richardson vs. Thomas Hutson
Pennington, Richardson vs. The State
Pennington, Thomas vs. Allen McClendon
Pennington, Thomas vs. Thomas W. Shivers for use of Edward
  Godwin
Pennington, William B. R. and James L. Maddux vs. Samuel
  W. J. Steele
Pennyman, George vs. The State
Penton, William and Samuel S. Norris vs. Stephen Norris
Perdell, Jackson vs. Francis H. Cone
Perdue, Penelope (alias Ellander McAlister) and John
  McAlister vs. The State
Perkins, Francis vs. Asa Bates
Perkins, John, Sr. vs. Hezekiah W. Scovill
Perkins, Moses and Samuel Moses vs. Drury Mays
Perkins, Moses vs. John Perkins
Perkins, Paul vs. Wesley A. Snell
Perry, Burrell vs. Chapman and Moore
Perry, Edward vs. William Freeman
Perry, Edward vs. Robert Stoodly
Perry, Edward N. vs. Horatio Bowen
Perry, Edward N. vs. Charles Hutchings and Joseph Winship
Perry, Edward N. vs. Daniel Tye
Perry, James vs. Baker Hobson
Perry, James vs. John Loyd
Perry, James vs. Thomas Loyd
Perry, James vs. The State
Perry, James vs. Solomon Strickland
Perry, James and Sherod H. Gay vs. Green B. Turner
Perry, James vs. John Wilson and Sherrod H. Gay
Perry, Jerry vs. The State
Perry, Malvina (Trammel) vs. James Perry
Perry, Miles M. vs. Lewis Ryan and Huldah Ann Ryan
Perry, Tom vs. The State
Persley, Crawford vs. The State
Persons, George W. vs. The State
Persons, J. B. vs. The State
Persons, J. D. vs. The State
Persons, Thomas, Thadeus B. Reese and John Reese vs. John
  McKenzie, Peter Bennock and Thomas McDowell
Persons, Thomas vs. Robert Russel
Perteet, Solomon vs. James Whitfield
Peterson, Jake vs. The State

Petter, Anson L. vs. Gabriel Harrison
Pettie, Anson L. vs. Stephen C. Talmadge and Albert L.
  Talmadge
Pettie, W. B. vs. The State
Petty, Job (alias Job Shy) vs. The State
Peurifoy, Alice vs. The State
Peurifoy, B. W., Jr. vs. William H. Thompson for use of
  William H. Townsend
Peurifoy, Gus vs. The State
Phelps, Aquilar vs. Elijah Berry
Phelps, Aquilar vs. John Moore
Phelps, Aquilla and Thomas M. Childs vs. Elizabeth Childs
  and Robert Brown
Phelps, Aquilla vs. The State
Phelps, Aquilla, Jr. vs. James McLendon
Phelps, Oliver vs. The State
Phelps, Thomas vs. James Buchanan
Phelps, Washington, Woody Dozier and Ezekiel Fears vs.
  Thomas J. Davis
Phelps, Washington vs. Robert Haynes
Phelps, William vs. Blount S. Garrett
Phelps, William vs. Tabitha Phelps
Phelps, William vs. The State
Phenesee, William and Moses Potts, Guardian vs. Jefferson
  E. Spears
Philips, Robert B. vs. James H. Roberts and Willis Little
Phillips, ? vs. The State
Phillips, Ambrose vs. The State
Phillips, Blewford vs. John Warren
Phillips, Charles vs. The State
Phillips, Dempsey vs. George Hargraves
Phillips, Edmund, Blewford Phillips and Abraham Pyles vs.
  Mark A. Cooper
Phillips, Elbert and Daniel Goodman vs. The State
Phillips, Floyd vs. The State
Phillips, Frank vs. The State
Phillips, Hillery vs. John M. Pearson
Phillips, J. B. M. vs. Griffin, Monticello and Madison
  Railroad Co.
Phillips, J. B. M. vs. Mobley and Cabiness
Phillips, James vs. Edmund Stone
Phillips, Jeremiah vs. John Dorsey
Phillips, John vs. The State
Phillips, John B. M. vs. William S. Minter
Phillips, John B. M. vs. Mathew Whitfield, John F. Patterson,
  Executor, William Mathis, Executor, Leroy M. Wilson,
  Executor and Pleasant Wilson, Executor
Phillips, John P. vs. Elizabeth Henderson
Phillips, Lewis vs. The State
Phillips, Lewis Q. vs. The State
Phillips, Littleberry and Abraham Key vs. Pleasant Watts
  for use of Felise Bryan
Phillips, Mathew and Jacob McClendon vs. Tunstall B. George
Phillips, Matthew and William D. Phillips vs. John Baldwin
  and Martha Baldwin, Administrator
Phillips, Matthew and John Hill vs. Abner Bartlett
Phillips, Matthew vs. Martin Cochran
Phillips, Matthew, William Hitchcock and Josias R. Brown
  vs. Edward Y. Hill
Phillips, Matthew, William Hitchcock and William B. Stokes
  vs. Solomon Perteit and Jeremaih Pearson, Guardian
Phillips, Matthew vs. The State
Phillips, Monroe vs. Central of Georgia Railroad Co.

Phillips, N. A., William L. Phillips and James Lawrence,
  Trustee vs. Michael Plymail
Phillips, Nathan vs. The State
Phillips, Nimrod vs. The State
Phillips, Palmer R. vs. The State
Phillips, Phil vs. The State
Phillips, R. B. vs. W. C. Clark and Co.
Phillips, Richard B. vs. Equitable Mortgage Co.
Phillips, Richard B. vs. Sherman Jessup and Co.
Phillips, Richard B. vs. C. O. Minter
Phillips, Scott vs. The State
Phillips, Wiley vs. Holland and Kirkpatrick
Phillips, William vs. Nathaniel W. Gordon
Phillips, William vs. John Hobson and Christopher Hobson
Phillips, William vs. The State
Phillips, William L. vs. John C. Gibson
Phillips, William L. vs. Eli Glover
Phillips, William L. vs. Crawford H. Greer
Phillips, William L. vs. Lawson S. Holland
Phillips, William L. vs. Hugh P. Kirkpatrick
Phillips, Z. and Patton Wise vs. A. Steel
Phillips, Zachariah vs. Jacob Clower for use of Joseph
  Wilson
Phillips, Zachariah vs. Bird Fitzpatrick
Phillips, Zachariah and Washington Randle vs. Lemuel Gresham
Phillips, Zachariah, Washington Randle and Henry Walker vs.
  Richard Lawrence, John T. Lawrence and Simeon Rensen
Phillips, Zachariah, James Woodruff and Thomas T. Walker vs.
  John Paine for use of William Sims and Co.
Phillips, Zachariah vs. Jeremiah W. Ray
Phillips, Zachariah, Jr. and Washington Randle vs. William
  Bryce
Phillips, Zachariah, Sr. vs. Thomas Terrell
Phillips, Zacheus and Joseph Carter vs. Abraham Betts
Phillips, Zacheus vs. William Hamett
Phillips, Zacheus vs. George Medlock, John C. Smith,
  Executor, Fereby (Medlock) Walker, Executor and Thomas T.
  Walker, Executor
Phillips, Zacheus and Patton Wise vs. William Scott
Phillips, Zacheus and Joseph Carter vs. The State
Phinise, William and John Winfrey vs. Jackson Chaney
Phinise, William vs. John Durden
Phinisee, William vs. William C. Dawson
Phinisee, William vs. Butler B. King
Phinizee, C. H. and Co. vs. Officers of Court
Phinnisee, William vs. John W. Pitts for use of John Edgar
Pickens, William vs. Joel F. Randolph
Pickett, W. H. vs. The State
Pickins, William vs. Aaron Miller
Piles, Abraham vs. John Watten, Abner Turner and Mathew B.
  Evans
Pinckard, Thomas C. and John Baldwin vs. John Sharp, Richard
  Mason and Reason D. Bealle
Pinkard, John vs. William Byars
Pinkard, John vs. Betsey Cooper and James G. Randle for use
  of Thomas Greer
Pinkard, John and William McDowell vs. Elijah Patey
Pinkerton, Davis vs. Thomas Hearn
Pinkston, Joshua and William Hitchcock vs. Zenos Bronson
Pinnell, Green and William Bennett vs. Pleasant Compton,
  John Compton, Executor and Elizabeth Compton, Executor
Pinnell, Green vs. Jesse Loyall
Piper, John vs. The State

238

Piper, Thomas L. vs. John C. Pope
Piper, W. E. vs. J. H. Kelly Co.
Pitkin and Pearson vs. Peter W. Gautier
Pitman, Barns vs. Thomas Tatum
Pitman, Jess vs. The State
Pitman, Jesse, Daniel C. Heard and William A. Pitman vs.
  Thomas Floyd and Richard B. Wootten
Pitman, Jesse vs. William Hamrick and William Saffold,
  Administrator
Pitman, Jesse vs. William S. Mires
Pitman, Jesse vs. Joel Smith
Pitman, Jesse vs. Joseph Watkins for use of Robert S. Sayre
Pitman, William vs. James W. Yarbrough
Pittard, Jim vs. The State
Pittman, Joseph vs. William V. Burney
Pitts, Dick vs. The State
Pitts, Isaac vs. Eatonton Mfg. Co.
Pitts, Julius vs. The State
Platt, George and Richard Boyd, Administrator vs. Benjamin
  Thurman
Plummer, Samuel vs. Abner Bartlett, James E. Bartlett,
  Executor, William A. Bartlett, Executor, John E. Bartlett,
  Executor and George T. Bartlett, Executor
Plummer, Samuel vs. John Maddux
Plummer, Samuel and William Y. Harris vs. Skelton Napier
Plummer, Samuel vs. Thomas Rivers
Plummer, Samuel vs. James W. Vaughn
Pluncket, J. F. vs. The State
Polk, Dan vs. The State
Polk, Lush vs. The State
Pollard, Major A. vs. Jesse Coxe
Pollard, Major A. vs. Eaton Fluellen
Pollard, Major A. vs. Thomas B. Peck
Pollard, Richard vs. James Clark and William Clark
Pon, E. and Rebecca C. Pon vs. John Merriman and Co.
Pon, Ed vs. The State
Pon, Giles vs. The State
Ponder, Rosco vs. The State
Poole, Adam and John Hudspeth vs. Samuel Huston
Poole, Frederick, James Kelley and Abner F. Derring vs.
  William Robinson and Albert Pabodie
Pope, ? vs. The State
Pope, Andrew vs. The State
Pope, Annie M. and John H. Blackwell vs. B. C. Kelly for
  use of Officers of Court
Pope, C. H. and C. H. Ballard vs. ? Greer
Pope, C. W. vs. William T. Fish for use of Frederick Vaughn
Pope, Clarance vs. The State
Pope, Cohen vs. Griffin, Monticello and Madison Railroad Co.
Pope, Dan vs. The State
Pope, Daniel W. vs. The State
Pope, Dock vs. The State
Pope, E. C. and Mrs. S. H. Pope vs. John Merryman and Co.
Pope, E. C. and S. H. Pope vs. Walton Whann and Co.
Pope, Edgar C. vs. W. A. Kelly and Brothers
Pope, J. J. vs. James Benton and M. S. Benton, Administrator
Pope, J. J. vs. John A. Broughton
Pope, Jane vs. The State
Pope, Josiah P. vs. Griffin, Monticello and Madison Rail-
  road Co.
Pope, Josiah P. vs. Charles D. Ramey for use of John D. Ramey
Pope, Josiah P. vs. Francis M. Swanson, Thomas G. Pritchett
  and Alfred Pritchett

239

Pope, Lucius vs. The State
Pope, Miller W. and Charles G. Campbell vs. Jonathan
  Collins and Son
Pope, Miller W. vs. Robert G. Duke
Pope, Miller W. and Mary Pope vs. William H. Head
Pope, Miller W. vs. William D. Maddux and John F. Patterson
Pope, Miller W. vs. Daniel McDowell and Thomas B. Williams,
  Executor
Pope, Miller W. vs. S. C. Talmadge
Pope, Miller W. vs. Nehemiah B. White and Lucius White
Pope, Miller W. and William K. Pope vs. Matthew Whitfield,
  Leroy M. Willson, Executor, Pleasant Willson, Executor,
  John F. Patterson, Executor and William H. Mathis, Executor
Pope, William and Luke L. Morgan vs. John F. Dismukes
Pope, William vs. Charles Kitchens
Pope, William vs. Officers of Court
Pope, William K. and Seaborn Lawrence, Executor vs.
  Crawford H. Greer
Pope, William K. vs. J. L. Maddux
Porter, Archibald, Hugh Griggs, Abraham Alexander and Hardy
  Hopson vs. Daniel Dawkins
Porter, Archibald, Hugh Grigs, Abner Alexander, Hardy Hopson,
  and Bennet Lawrence vs. John Hobson and Christopher Hibsib
Porter, Archibald, Hugh Grigs, Abraham Alexander and Hardy
  Hopson vs. Thomas F. Nolan
Porter, Dennis vs. E. H. Jordan
Porter, Edward R. and James M. Finley vs. William G. Smith,
  Sr.
Portwood, Benjamin vs. Thomas Kennady
Portwood, Benjamin vs. John Portwood
Portwood, Sam vs. The State
Posey, Francis vs. Thomas Huston
Posey, Francis vs. Henry Walker
Post, Joseph vs. James L. Brown
Post, Joseph and John R. Cargile vs. Archibald Perkins,
  Bennet M. Ware, Executor, Abraham Perkins, Executor and
  Alexander Perkins, Executor
Post, Joseph C., John Robinson and Berry T. Digby vs.
  Central Bank of Georgia
Post, Joseph C. vs. Willie Little
Post, Joseph C. and Isaac L. Parker vs. Luke J. Morgan,
  Minor and Luke J. Morgan, Guardian
Post, Joseph C. vs. William B. Stone
Post, Joseph M. vs. Henry H. Cook and James C. Cook
Post, Joseph M. and William Hollis vs. Norman McLeod
Post, Joseph M. vs. Stephen Smith
Post, Marian vs. The State
Post, Samuel, Joseph C. Post, Executor, William P. Walthall,
  Executor and Ephraim Lynch, Executor vs. Mary Walthall
Post, Samuel vs. Isaac Wells
Post, Samuel vs. Aron Williams
Post, Samuel G. and William M. Post vs. Mary Chaffin
Post, Samuel B. vs. Jesse Loyall
Post, Samuel G. vs. The State
Post, Samuel M. and Nathaniel G. Slaughter vs. James
  Whitfield
Post, William M., Ephraim Lynch and Samuel G. Post vs.
  Joshua Hill
Post, William M. vs. Jesse Loyall
Post, William M., Samuel G. Post and Welcome C. Lovejoy vs.
  John L. Robinson
Post, William M., Samuel G. Post and Thomas K. Slaughter vs.
  Stephen C. Talmadge

240

Potter, A. C. vs. James J. McClelland
Potter, Riley and Pleasant Potter vs. Norborne B. Powell
Potts, James vs. Joseph M. Evans and John P. Evans
Potts, James vs. David Peck
Potts, Moses, Jenkins Wilson and David Harris vs. Jefferson
  E. Spears
Potts, Moses vs. The State
Pou, Lewis W. vs. John Baynes
Pou, Lewis W. vs. Matthew Whitfield, Leroy M. Willson,
  Executor, Pleasant Willson, Executor, John F. Patterson,
  Executor and William H. Mathis, Executor
Pounds, Bill vs. The State
Pounds, Frank vs. The State
Pounds, Merriman vs. Cardin Goolsby
Powel, Zacheus vs. Christopher Orr
Powell, Albert vs. The State
Powell, Barnet R. vs. George H. Williams
Powell, Christopher W. vs. John Routon (Roudon)
Powell, John vs. John Bennett
Powell, John vs. Harfery Holland
Powell, John vs. Alexander Huson
Powell, John and Edmond Deens vs. Isaac Phillips
Powell, John vs. James S. Weekes
Powell, John G., Isaac L. Parker and Thomas K. Slaughter
  vs. Central Bank of Georgia
Powell, John G. vs. Jesse Loyall
Powell, Johnson vs. William Cabaness
Powell, Johnson vs. Gresham Selleck
Powell, Lewie vs. The State
Powell, Lucas, John W. Burney and William Maxey vs. Central
  Bank of Georgia
Powell, Lucas vs. James D. Head
Powell, Lucas vs. Holland and Kirkpatrick
Powell, Lucas vs. William S. Hurd and Anson Hungerford
Powell, Lucas vs. William K. Kitchen
Powell, Lucas vs. Williamson Robey, Mariah Robey, Guardian,
  Williamson Aquilla Marcus, D'Lafayette Robey, Minor and
  Eveline Robey, Minor
Powell, Norbin B. vs. The State
Powell, Norborne B. and James Griggs vs. Isham Thompson and
  James A. Black
Powell, Reuben vs. The State
Powell, Sammy Davis vs. The State
Powell, Simeon and William Riley vs. The State
Powell, Thomas vs. The State
Powell, Tom vs. The State
Powell, W. R., B. T. Digby, Administrator, William Powell,
  Evan Powell, Alfred Goolsby, Guardian, Elizabeth Powell,
  McCarrol Purifoy, Guardian, Emma Powell and Beverly A.
  Kelly, Guardian vs. John H. Ezell
Powell, William vs. The State
Powell, Woody vs. The State
Powers, Francis vs. John Willson
Powers, John H., John W. Burney and John R. Dyer vs.
  Officers of Court
Powers, Robert vs. Jonathan VanWagenen
Presley, Joe vs. The State
Preston, Amos vs. The State
Preston, Archibald and Obadiah Echols vs. Thaddeus Beall,
  Elias Beall and Thomas Beall
Preston, Archibald vs. William W. Woolsey, Abram M.
  Woolsey and John C. Woolsey
Preston, C. T. vs. Central Railroad and Banking Co.

241

Preston, Charles vs. The State
Preston, Essick vs. The State
Preston, Gilliam and Armstid Dodson vs. Joel Haile, Jr.,
  John Selman, Administrator, Lydia Haile, Administrator
  and Hosea Haile, Administrator
Preston, Gilliam, Archibald Preston and Asa Gardner vs.
  Green Hill
Preston, Lee vs. The State
Preston, Lony vs. The State
Preston, Mary T. and Thomas G. Preston vs. A. L. Sluder
Preston, Thomas G. vs. Frances J. Swanson
Preston, Tildy vs. The State
Preston, W. J. M., W. C. Leverett, W. H. Preston and T. W.
  Thompson vs. John B. Gordon for use of Martha E. Rodgers
Preston, Willis vs. The State
Price, Charles vs. The State
Price, Crawford vs. The State
Price, Edward and Wiley Griggs vs. James Dowdell
Price, Edward and Ann Price, Administrator vs. William
  Harper
Price, Edward and Ann Price, Administrator vs. Lewis M.
  Harris
Price, Edward vs. John Settle
Price, John vs. John L. Calhoun
Price, John vs. Abner Dozier
Price, John, Mary (Morgan) Price, John C. Watters, Cornelius
  Hardy and Burwell P. Key vs. Justices of Court for use of
  Stokely Morgan and Asa H. Morgan, Minor
Price, John and John Key, Administrator vs. Mary Price
Price, Joseph and John J. Ferrill vs. Cornelius Blankinbaker
Price, Joseph vs. John W. Bridges
Price, Joseph vs. Hollis Dunton
Price, Joseph vs. William Scott and William Maxey
Price, Leroy and John W. A. Smith vs. The State
Price, Leroy M., Cooley Campbell and Jefferson Pye vs.
  The State
Price, R. W. vs. Corley and Dorsett
Price, Robert and James W. Faulkner vs. Milledge R. Robey
  and Abner Bartlett, Guardian
Price, Robert vs. The State
Price, Robert W. vs. John W. A. Smith
Price, Robert W., James Hardy and Cornelius M. Hardy vs.
  The State
Price, Sterling vs. Isaac McClendon
Price, Starling vs. Paschal Murphy
Price and Steele vs. L. M. Price
Price, Thomas R. vs. Robert G. Duke and Charles H. Nutting
Price, Thomas R. and John W. H. Smith vs. James H. Roberts
Price, Wash vs. The State
Price, Will vs. The State
Prickett, David vs. William Mahoney and Dennis Mahoney
Pridgen, James vs. William Burks
Pridgen, James vs. Jonathan Reeves
Prie (Prye), James vs. The State
Prince, Joseph vs. John King
Prince, William vs. Thomas B. White and Henry Kirby
Prior, John vs. Jess Loyall and William H. Pritchett
Pritchet, William vs. Anthony Dyer and Otis Dyer
Pritchett, Abraham vs. The State
Pritchett, E. H. vs. Griffin, Monticello and Madison
  Railroad Co.
Pritchett, E. H. and Sarah L. Pritchett vs. Thomas Hardeman
  and O. G. Sparks

Pritchett, E. H. vs. H. J. Lamar
Pritchett, E. H. and S. L. Pritchett vs. William S. Minter
Pritchett, E. H. vs. Arch Tanner and Robert Whitfield
Pritchett, Edward H. and George W. Pritchett vs. Aris
  Newton, Jr.
Pritchett, George W., Thomas J. Pritchett and Richard
  Bonner vs. Jonas H. Holland
Pritchett, Loyall J. vs. John Digby, Belinda Digby, Adminis-
  trator and William Penn, Administrator
Pritchett, Mary vs. Zachariah Sims
Pritchett, T. J. vs. George Jones and John Baxter
Pritchett, Thomas J. vs. Jonas H. Holland and Bolling
  Whitfield
Pritchett, Thomas J. and George W. Pritchett vs. J. M.
  DeLoach
Pritchett, Thomas J. and Shadrack J. McMichael vs. William
  E. Newell, James Newell and William M. Newell
Pritchett, Thomas J. and Shadrach I. McMichael vs. John B.
  Ross and Son
Pritchett, Thomas J. and Shadrach J. McMichael vs. Henry K.
  Sheldon, William J. Hoyt, Samuel A. Busick, Edward Lynes
  and Erastus Sheldon
Pritchett, Thomas J. vs. H. K. Thurber and Co.
Pritchett, Thomas J. vs. Whittle and Gustin
Pritchett, Thomas L. vs. Oglesby Prophitt
Pritchett, William vs. Abraham Betts
Pritchett, William vs. Green and Buchannon
Pritchett, William vs. Thomas Hannah
Pritchett, William vs. Dotson Harville
Pritchett, William vs. David Henderson
Pritchett, William vs. Littleton Ivy for use of James Smith
Pritchett, William and Thomas Pritchett vs. Gabriel Johnson
Pritchett, William vs. William Mason
Pritchett, William vs. James Nall for use of Andrew Welden
Pritchett, William vs. Solomon Strickland
Pritchett, William H. vs. William Eichelberger and Joseph
  Clemm
Proctor, Henry vs. The State
Prophitt, George vs. The State
Pryer, William vs. Thomas Humphrey
Pryor, William vs. Jonathan Bonner
Pryor, William vs. Alsea Holifield
Pryor, William vs. Allen McClendon
Pucket, Martin vs. The State
Puckett, John C. I. A. W. vs. The State
Puckett, Martin and Nancy Puckett, Executor vs. Absalom
  Casils
Puckett, Martin and James W. Vaughn, Administrator vs.
  Robert L. Puckett
Puckett, Martin vs. James F. Robinson
Puckett, Nancy W. and Robert L. Puckett vs. John Digby
Puckett, Nancy W. vs. William Wilson
Puckett, Robert L. vs. John W. Pitts
Pughe, Edward vs. Benjamin Conley, Foster Blodgett, John
  M. Rice, John E. Bryant and Charles H. Prince
Purcy, John L. vs. Eli Glover and John Cashin
Purifoy, Benjamin, Sr. vs. S. C. Talmadge and A. J.
  Talmadge for use of James L. Maddux
Pye, Asa vs. John Hill
Pye, Asa and Lewis Pye vs. Allen McClendon
Pye, Eli vs. The State
Pye, Elizabeth and Zifford Mann vs. The State
Pye, Griffin L. vs. The State

Pye, Harman vs. Green McMichael
Pye, Harman W. vs. The State
Pye, Harmon W. vs. James D. Head
Pye, James vs. Abner Bankston
Pye, James vs. James Duncan
Pye, James vs. Jeremiah Pearson
Pye, John E. vs. Lottie E. Pye
Pye, Jordan vs. Elijah McMichael
Pye, Lewis vs. Hollis Cooley
Pye, Lewis vs. Samuel Fulton
Pye, Lewis vs. Green Holifield
Pye, Lewis vs. James J. Ross and William Ross, Administrator
Pye, Lewis vs. James Whitfield
Pye, Lewis vs. Eady Wright
Pye, Lewis H. vs. John C. Gibson
Pye, Lewis H. vs. William Reeves for use of Palemon Weekes
Pye, Lewis H. vs. Jesse H. Sharman
Pye, Lumpkin vs. The State
Pye, Theophilus, Alsea Holifield and James Pye vs. Thomas
    I. Davis
Pye, Theophilus and Lundy Huff vs. Austin Goddard for use
    of David Epps
Pye, Theophilus vs. Thomas Grant, Daniel Grant, Executor,
    Thomas Grant, Executor and Peter Grinnell, Executor
Pye, Theophilus vs. George W. Holland, Mary Ann Holland and
    Hugh P. Kirkpatrick, Guardian
Pye, Theophilus and Harman W. Pye vs. David M. Langston
Pye, Theophilus vs. Jeremiah Pearson
Pye, Theophilus vs. Jonathan Reeves
Pye, Thomas vs. The State
Pye, Tom vs. The State
Pye, W. Tom and E. W. Cardell vs. L. O. Benton and Eugene
    Benton
Pye, W. Tom vs. The State

Radden, Abner and John Byrom vs. Thomas Gamage
Radden, Abner vs. William Towns
Radford, Charles vs. The State
Ragan, Asa vs. Thadeus Beall, Elias Beall and Thomas Beall
Ragan, Asa, Moses Smith, Lawson S. Holland, Charles Webb,
    Robert Tuggle, Alexander Dale and Obediah Echols vs. John
    Brownsfield
Ragan, Asa vs. Magers Henderson for use of John Willson
Ragland, Drayton vs. The State
Ragland, Fererick vs. David Parish, Thomas Parish, Jasper
    Corning, Leroy M. Wiley and Joseph Kernochan
Ragland, Ferderick W. vs. Alston H. Green and Joseph
    Buchannon
Ragland, Ferderick W. and John A. Ragland vs. Jeremiah
    Pearson
Ragland, Fuller and Co. and Mathew Whitfield vs. Moses
    Champion and Joseph L. Holland
Ragland, Fuller and Co. vs. Stephen C. Talmadge
Ragland, John vs. Abner Chapman
Ragland, John A. vs. Pouncey Maxey for use of Alston H.
    Green and Joseph Buchannan
Raines, Josiah vs. William Broughton
Rainey, Ann and Elizabeth Rainey vs. Lewis and Bailey
Rainey, John vs. Officers of Court
Rainey, Mary E. vs. William H. Rainey
Rainey, Matthew vs. Lancy Bailey
Rainey, Matthew vs. Andrew M. Brown
Rainey, Reuben M. vs. Hartwell Bass

Rainey, Reuben M. and John R. Russel vs. Peter M. Hughes
Rainey, Reuben M. vs. Lewis Lanier
Rainey, Reuben M. vs. Elijah Patey
Rainey, Reuben M. vs. Norborne B. Powell
Rainey, Reuben M. vs. James Whitfield and Anthony Dyer
Rainey, William vs. Allen McClendon
Rainey, William vs. Aquilla Phelps
Rainey, William vs. The State
Ramey, Charles D. and Samuel D. Varner vs. John Lee McMichael
Ramey, Charles D. and John L. McMichael vs. John C. Ramey
Ramey, Charles D. vs. The State
Ramey, N. H., Richard Barret, Executor, Mary H. Barrett,
   Executor, John W. Burney and J. H. Talmage vs. Thomas J.
   Smith
Ramey, Nathaniel and William Ramey vs. William H. Crane
Ramey, Nathaniel and Burton J. McMichael vs. Aquilla Phelps
   and William Johnson, Executor
Ramey, William vs. John Bransford for use of John C. Goode
Ramey, William, Garland Maxey and John W. Burney vs.
   Central Bank of Georgia
Ramey, William vs. Hollis Cooley and James H. Robinson
Ramey, William and David A. Rees vs. John Edmondson
Ramey, William vs. Richard Flemister
Ramey, William vs. James B. Lewis and Edmund B. Darden,
   Administrator
Ramey, William vs. Jeremiah Pearson
Ramey, William and Simeon Scales vs. Martin Puckett and
   James W. Vaughn, Administrator
Ramey, William vs. Charles D. Ramey, Lindsey H. Durham and
   Dyer C. Bancroft
Ramey, William vs. David A. Reese
Ramey, William vs. The State
Ramsay, Alexander and Thomas Ramsay vs. John Collier
Ramsey, Noah and Jeremiah Harrison vs. Aron Springfield
Ramsey, Thomas and Jacob Laughridge vs. Absalom Hammett
Ramsey, Thomas and Jacob Laughridge vs. George Rogers
Ramsey, W. A. vs. The State
Ramy, Ike vs. The State
Ranay, Mathew and John W. Ranay vs. George Ranay and Mary
   E. Ranay
Randall, James B. vs. James Smith and Thomas J. Smith
Randall, James B. vs. Moses Tremble
Randall, John Henry vs. The State
Randle, Benjamin J. vs. John Walker
Randle, Newton vs. Lewis Stanley
Raney, Elizabeth vs. The State
Raney, George vs. The State
Raney, Harriet vs. The State
Rankin, Robert C. vs. Joseph Riley
Ransom, James B. and John S. D. Byrom vs. Joseph Nichols,
   Charles Nichols and Frederick Nichols
Ransom, Joseph vs. John Lucas and William Lee
Rasberry, William vs. Jesse Mathews
Rasseter, White vs. Joseph Longworth
Ratliff, Elizabeth vs. The State
Ray, Clark vs. Hezekiah Palmer
Ray, Mark vs. Richard Gregory
Ray, P. J. vs. John P. Fears
Ray, Thomas vs. Andrew H. Beall
Ray, Thomas vs. James D. Beall
Ray, Thomas and Magers Henderson vs. John Brown
Ray, William vs. John Meacham
Ray, William vs. The State

Reddick, George and Ernest Waters vs. The State
Redman, Charlie vs. The State
Redman, Stephen vs. Miller W. Pope
Reed, Peter vs. Thomas White, Cuthbert Reese and Joseph
    Reese
Rees, Jordan vs. Bryan Lee for use of Elias Kennedy
Reese, America vs. The State
Reese, Cuthbert vs. John W. Bridges
Reese, Cuthbert vs. John L. D. Byrom
Reese, Cuthbert vs. Francis Irwin
Reese, Cuthbert vs. George Low, Norman Wallace and William
    Smith
Reese, Cuthbert vs. John Thurmond
Reese, David A. and Jonas H. Holland vs. John Arnold
Reese, David A. vs. Henry H. Chapman
Reese, David A. vs. Eaton Manufacturing Co.
Reese, David A. vs. Francis Irvin
Reese, David A. vs. Reuben Jordan and Fleming Jordan
Reese, David A. vs. William Maxey and Joshua Hill
Reese, David A., Wiley Phillips, Augustus W. Lane, James
    M. Williams and Robert Kellam vs. Stephen C. Talmadge
Reese, David A. vs. Henry Vaughn
Reese, Hamp vs. The State
Reese, Harriett vs. The State
Reese, Hamp vs. The State
Reese, Harriett vs. The State
Reese, Jordan vs. Pascal Brooks for use of Palemon Weekes
Reese, Jordan and Cuthbert Reese vs. John S. D. Byrom
Reese, Jordan vs. James Cowan and Thomas B. Erwin
Reese, Jordan and John Reese vs. Abselem Farrar
Reese, Jordan vs. Stephen W. Harris, Eli S. Shorter,
    Executor, William Wilkins, Executor and Seaborn Jones,
    Executor
Reese, Jordan vs. John C. Rodgers for use of Elisha Smartt
Reese, Joseph and Cuthbert Reese vs. William Porter
Reese, Lucien L. vs. Crawford H. Greer
Reese, Lucien L. vs. Paul Perkins
Reese, Williamson H. and Thomas Hunt vs. Charles A. Nutting
Reeves, Asa vs. John Huston
Reeves, Asa, Thomas Moreland and Davis R. Andrews vs.
    Justices of Inferior Court
Reeves, Avery vs. Proser Horton for use of Early Harris
Reeves, Ben vs. The State
Reeves, Cap vs. The State
Reeves, G. W. and O. S. Profitt vs. Joseph Winship, C. A.
    Pitts and G. W. D. Cook
Reeves, James vs. James McLeroy
Reeves, James vs. The State
Reeves, Joel A., Burkett M. Jeffries, Executor and Joseph
    Reeves vs. Matthew Whitfield
Reeves, John vs. Augusta Baldwin and John Baldwin
Reeves, John W. L. vs. William S. Hurd and Anson Hungerford
Reeves, John W. L. vs. James C. McAlister
Reeves, John W. L. vs. John Spearman
Reeves, John W. L. vs. Anderson F. Thompson
Reeves, John W. L. vs. James W. Vaughn
Reeves, John W. S. vs. Officers of Court
Reeves, Jonathan and Hugh Hamel vs. Edward Echols
Reeves, Jonathan vs. Wyatt Reeves for use of Alston H.
    Greene and Joseph Buchannon
Reeves, Jonathan vs. Henry Teel
Reeves, Joshua vs. Henry Walker
Reeves, P. W. vs. Starkey Perry

Reeves, Pleasant W. vs. Matthew Whitfield
Reeves, Prior vs. Joel Baley
Reeves, Prior and Jonathan Reeves vs. Thaddeus Beall, Elias
  Beall and Thomas Beall
Reeves, Prior vs. Anthony Dyer
Reeves, Robert T. vs. Stephen Clower
Reeves, Thomas K. and Wiley Reeves vs. William Pressley,
  Edmund Jennings and John Bailey
Reeves, Thomas K. vs. William Thomason
Reeves, Thomas K. vs. Osborne Wilks
Reeves, Warner vs. The State
Reeves, Willey vs. Freeman McClendon
Reeves, William vs. Armsted Dodson
Reeves, William vs. Tandy D. King
Reeves, Wyatt vs. John Tison
Reeves, Zeb vs. The State
Reid, Cunningham D. vs. Isham Woodward and John Williamson
Reid, George W. vs. James J. Weaver
Reid, Gus vs. The State
Reid, Harriet vs. The State
Reid, James vs. The State
Reid, John vs. George Clower
Reid, John vs. Jacob Danforth
Reid, John vs. Anthony Dyer
Reid, John and Samuel Mayes vs. Isaac Hill
Reid, John vs. Hartwell Jones
Reid, John and Andrew Reid vs. John Reid (heirs) and
  Elizabeth Chandler, Guardian for use of Henry Chandler
Reid, John vs. Gresham Selleck
Reid, Lish vs. The State
Reid, Samuel vs. James Reid and John S. Lacie, Administrator
Reid, Samuel T. vs. John C. McCullough
Reid, Samuel T. vs. Officers of Court
Reid, Samuel T. vs. Officers of Court
Reid, Samuel T. vs. Ebenezar T. White
Reid, Samuel T. vs. Nehemiah B. White and Lucius White
Reid, W. A. and Samuel T. Reid vs. Benjamin Grinnell
Reid, W. A. and C. S. Jordan, Executor vs. Dave Slade
Reid, Washington vs. The State
Reid, William A., Charles S. Jordan, Executor, Samuel Reid
  and William Reid vs. James C. Denham and Josiah C. Denham
Reid, William A., Charles G. Thompson and James W. Vaughn
  vs. Wiley T. High
Reid, William A. vs. Charles S. Jordan
Reid, William A., Joshua Hill, Executor, Charles S. Jordan,
  Executor and Fleming Jordan, Executor vs. J. W. A. Smith,
  Samuel R. Smith and J. S. Robinson
Reid, William A. and Charles S. Jordan, Executor vs.
  Stephen C. Talmadge
Reid, William A. and Charles S. Jordan, Executor vs.
  Stephen C. Talmadge
Reid, William A. vs. William Warren, Andrew J. Land and
  John Wallace
Reid, William A. vs. George W. Webster
Reid, William A. and Charles S. Jordan, Executor vs.
  Nehemiah B. White and Lucius White
Renfroe, Stephen, Jr. and Elisha Renfroe vs. Allen Greene
Reynolds, John vs. The State
Reynolds, Thomas vs. John Hines
Reynolds, Thomas vs. James D. Oats and William H. Oats
Reynolds, Thomas vs. Joseph Pittman
Reynolds, Thomas vs. Benjamin F. Ross
Reynolds, Thomas vs. The State

Rhodes, Samuel vs. Nancy Bailey
Rhodes, Samuel T. vs. Hampton S. Smith and John E. Morgan
Rice, James vs. William Askew
Rich, George and Bud Giles vs. The State
Richards, Green M. vs. John Fluker
Richards and Hudspeth vs. Hungerford and Johnson
Richards, James vs. John Bogan
Richards, James vs. David Brown
Richards, James vs. Abner Chapman
Richards, James vs. William Cook, John Willson and Martin
  Cochran
Richards, James vs. Joseph Crockett
Richards, James vs. Richard Garner
Richards, James and James Mercer vs. Thomas Grant
Richards, James and Airs Hugspeth vs. John Logan
Richards, James vs. John Mitchell for use of James Mitchell
Richards, James vs. Levi Newton
Richards, James vs. J. S. Oliver
Richards, James vs. Elias Reed for use of Jeremiah Pearson
Richards, James and Willis Richards vs. John C. Rodgers and
  Thomas E. Rodgers
Richards, James vs. Moses Speer
Richards, James vs. The State
Richards, James and Willis Richards vs. William F. Steele
Richards, James vs. Isham Thompson
Richards, James vs. Charles Walden
Richards, James and James Mercer vs. William C. Ware for
  use of John Carmichael
Richards, James vs. John Wooton for use of Bedney Franklin
Richards, William vs. Winfrey Lockett
Richards, William B. vs. Robert Kellam and William Maxey
Richards, William B. vs. William Richards and Abram B.
  Elliott
Richardson, Daniel vs. Tandy D. King
Richardson, George and Samuel Harrel, Administrator vs.
  Thomas J. McGehee and Mahaley McGehee
Richardson, Jonathan vs. Isaac McGehee
Richardson, Jordan and Claxton Ray vs. Robert Thompson
Richardson, Moses, Jacob Richardson, Theophilus Pye and
  Charles S. Morgan vs. James Whitfield
Richardson, Peter B. vs. Phillip Stroud
Richardson, Robert E. vs. Rebecca Matthews
Richardson, William G. W. and William P. Beasley vs.
  Benjamin B. Amos
Rickerson, Benjamin vs. The State
Rickerson, Ed and L. H. Cranford vs. The State
Richerson, R. A. and B. A. Rickerson vs. R. F. Dick
Ridgeway, Hays vs. The State
Ridley, Charles vs. Iverson S. Brooks
Ridley, Charles B., Robert Ridley, John Ridley, Francis M.
  Ridley and Robert A. F. Ridley, Guardian vs. Benjamin F.
  Morris, Crawford H. Grier, Executor and Wiley Peddy,
  Executor
Ridley, Charles L. vs. Joshua B. Clark
Ridley, Crissy vs. The State
Ridley, Gus and John Bostwick vs. The State
Ridley, Hamilton B. vs. Georgia H. Whitfield
Ridley, Hannibal vs. Hamilton B. Ridley
Ridley, Howard vs. A. B. Small
Ridley, John vs. The State
Ridley, Peter vs. The State
Ridley, Stephen, Jr. vs. The State
Riece, Sam vs. The State

Rines, Joseph, Benjamin F. Chamberlin and James D. Peoples
  vs. The State
Ritchey, E. J., Jr. vs. The State
Ritchie, E. J. vs. J. M. Tyner
Rivers, Claude vs. The State
Rivers, Elijah vs. William Scott
Rivers, James and Thomas Rivers vs. James P. Holmes
Rivers, James and Thomas Rivers, Sr., Administrator vs.
  Walter H. Mitchel
Rivers, James and Thomas Rivers vs. Effingham H. Warner
Rivers, John and Thomas Rivers vs. Hugh P. Kirkpatrick
Rivers, John, Thomas Rivers, Administrator and James Rivers,
  Administrator vs. Philip Thurmond
Rivers, John and Thomas Rivers, Administrator vs. James
  Whitfield
Rivers, John F., Thomas Rivers and John R. Dickin vs. John
  Bones
Rivers, John F. vs. Edwin Delano and Joel B. Delano
Rivers, John F. vs. George W. Holland and Hugh P. Kirkpatrick
Rivers, John F. vs. William S. Hurd and Anson Hungerford
Rivers, John F. vs. Jesse Loyall
Rivers, John F., Thomas H. B. Rivers and Thomas Rivers vs.
  William Maxey and James C. Bartlett
Rivers, John F. and Thomas Rivers vs. Williamson Robey,
  Mary Eveline Robey, A. M. Williamson, DeLafayette Robey
  and Maria Robey, Guardian
Rivers, John F. vs. Gilbraith Simonton
Rivers, John F. vs. Thomas I. Smith
Rivers, John W. L. vs. Anderson F. Thompson
Rivers, Robert T. vs. Robert C. Bealsey and Palemon L.
  Weeks
Rivers, Robert T. vs. Norvell Billingsley, Urban Billingsley
  and Henry Ramble
Rivers, Robert T. and Thomas Rivers vs. William Bostwick
  and Benjamin Baird
Rivers, Robert T. vs. Charles Cargile
Rivers, Robert T. vs. Jeremiah Clark
Rivers, Robert T. vs. Peyton R. Clements
Rivers, Robert T. vs. Stephen Clower
Rivers, Robert T. vs. William H. Crane and Abraham Crane
Rivers, Robert T. vs. Thomas B. Erwin
Rivers, Robert T. vs. Jacob Faulkner
Rivers, Robert T. and Thomas H. B. Rivers vs. Thomas B.
  Harwell
Rivers, Robert T. vs. Jonas H. Holland
Rivers, Robert T. vs. William B. Jones and James H. Morrow
Rivers, Robert T. and Thomas Rivers vs. Isaac Kendrick
Rivers, Robert T., Susan Rivers and John P. Lamar, Trustee
  vs. Jones Kendrick
Rivers, Robert T. vs. Wiley M. Mason and John S. Randle
Rivers, Robert T., Susan Rivers and John P. Lamar, Trustee
  vs. David Reid
Rivers, Robert T. vs. Susan (Thurmond) Rivers
Rivers, Robert T. and Philip Thurmond vs. Thomas Rivers
Rivers, Robert T. vs. Thomas L. Ross
Rivers, Robert T. vs. Robert Sharman
Rivers, Robert T., James C. Avery and James H. Morrow vs.
  Reuben C. Shorter
Rivers, Robert T. vs. The State
Rivers, Robert T. and Thomas Rivers vs. John Thurmond
Rivers, Robert T. vs. Philip Thurmond
Rivers, Robert T. vs. Edward Varner
Rivers, Robert T. vs. Blewford M. Walton

Rivers, Robert T. and John Hill vs. Joseph C. Weekes
Rivers, Robert T. vs. James Whitfield
Rivers, Sam vs. The State
Rivers, Susan vs. The State
Rivers, Thomas vs. Cassandra L. Alexander
Rivers, Thomas vs. Hamilton Atchison and Samuel B. Hunter,
    Administrator
Rivers, Thomas, Leroy Jarrel and Joseph Phillips vs. William
    A. Banister
Rivers, Thomas and Thomas H. B. Rivers vs. Jesse Cherry
Rivers, Thomas and Thomas H. B. Rivers vs. Henry L. Cook
    and David Flanders
Rivers, Thomas and Thomas H. B. Rivers vs. Hollis Cooley
    and Dyer C. Bancroft
Rivers, Thomas vs. Hollis Cooley and James H. Robinson
Rivers, Thomas, Thomas H. B. Rivers and John M. King vs.
    Anthony Dyer
Rivers, Thomas vs. Thomas B. Erwin
Rivers, Thomas and William C. Dawson vs. Stephen Felker
Rivers, Thomas vs. John E. Glover
Rivers, Thomas vs. Burgess Goolsby
Rivers, Thomas vs. William Harwell
Rivers, Thomas vs. James L. Maddux
Rivers, Thomas vs. Felix B. Martin and Francis C. McKinley
Rivers, Thomas vs. John G. Morris and James B. Bell
Rivers, Thomas vs. Thomas Napier
Rivers, Thomas vs. William C. Penn
Rivers, Thomas and Thomas H. B. Rivers vs. William C.
    Powell and Charles Powell
Rivers, Thomas and Thomas H. B. Rivers vs. Edward Price
Rivers, Thomas and Thomas H. B. Rivers vs. Nathaniel A.
    Rivers, Burwell G. Rivers and Milly Rivers, Guardian
Rivers, Thomas and Thomas H. B. Rivers vs. Susan Rivers and
    John P. Lamar, Trustee
Rivers, Thomas vs. David F. Sanders and Henry L. Cook
Rivers, Thomas, James Rivers and John Rivers vs. Philip
    Thurmond
Rivers, Thomas vs. Bluford M. Walton
Rivers, Thomas vs. Maurice Wilkinson
Rivers, Thomas and John Rivers vs. Daniel H. Willis
Rivers, Thomas, Sr. vs. James D. Head
Rivers, Thomas, Sr. and William W. Rivers vs. Francis
    Malone, John Malone, Administrator and Cader Malone,
    Administrator
Rivers, Thomas H. vs. Luther Roll
Rivers, Thomas H. B., Thomas Rivers and William W. Rivers
    vs. John Banks
Rivers, Thomas H. B. and Thomas Rivers vs. Abner Bartlett,
    James C. Bartlett, Executor, William A. Bartlett, Execu-
    tor, John E. Bartlett, Executor and George T. Bartlett,
    Executor
Rivers, Thomas H. B. and William W. Rivers vs. Stephen W.
    W. Beasley
Rivers, Thomas H. B. vs. Joseph Betts
Rivers, Thomas H. B. vs. John Caldwell and James Williamson
    for use of Jonas H. Holland
Rivers, Thomas H. B. and Leroy Waits vs. Mary Cargile
Rivers, Thomas H. B. vs. Central Bank of Georgia
Rivers, Thomas H. B. vs. Benjamin S. Collins, Stacy B.
    Collins, John Keese, George B. Collins, Robert Collins
    and William B. Collins
Rivers, Thomas H. B. vs. Hollis Cooley and James H.
    Robinson

Rivers, Thomas H. B. vs. Scott Craz
Rivers, Thomas H. B. and Thomas Rivers vs. Robert O. Dale
Rivers, Thomas H. B., John F. Rivers, Thomas J. Stanford,
  James M. Wesson and Littleberry Moody vs. Benjamin H.
  Field
Rivers, Thomas H. B. vs. Philemon Frost and John Dickerson
Rivers, Thomas H. B. vs. John Gordon
Rivers, Thomas H. B. vs. Isaac G. Graham, George J. W.
  Mabee and Isaac N. Plum
Rivers, Thomas H. B. vs. James N. Hall and David A. Reese,
  Administrator
Rivers, Thomas H. B. vs. Burwell Jackson
Rivers, Thomas H. B. vs. William Lawrence, Allen Lawrence,
  Executor and Leroy Lawrence, Executor
Rivers, Thomas H. B. vs. William Maxey and James C. Bartlett
Rivers, Thomas H. B. vs. William Maxey and Joshua Hill
Rivers, Thomas H. B. vs. John S. McMichael
Rivers, Thomas H. B. vs. Dwight B. Perry
Rivers, Thomas H. B. and Thomas Rivers vs. George Sharp,
  James N. Trittle and William C. Evanson
Rivers, Thomas H. B. vs. The State
Rivers, Thomas H. B. and Thomas Rivers vs. Hezekiah Thompson
Rivers, Thomas H. B. vs. John Thurmond
Rivers, Thomas H. B. vs. Robert Tolefree
Rivers, Thomas H. B., William W. Rivers and Thomas Rivers,
  Sr. vs. Benjamin H. Wright
Rivers, William W., Thomas A. Rivers and Thomas Rivers vs.
  Cardin Goolsby
Roach, David K. vs. Thomas Holland
Roach, James and John Simons vs. William Williams
Roan, Leonard vs. Thomas Crawford for use of Joseph Reese
Robenett, Jesse vs. Littleberry Champion
Roberson, Duffie vs. The State
Roberts, Charles and Alford Burner vs. Reuben Jordan
Roberts, E. R. vs. C. E. McCarthy
Roberts and Gay vs. Augustus B. Sharp
Roberts, Gus vs. The State
Roberts, J. W. vs. J. H. Kelly
Roberts, James H. vs. Sarah Roberts
Roberts, Jordan vs. Hardy Cook
Roberts, Lex (alias Lex Robinson) vs. The State
Roberts, Lucius vs. The State
Roberts, Lydia vs. The State
Roberts, Marsh vs. The State
Roberts, O. G. vs. W. H. Head
Roberts, O. G. vs. Mayor and Council of Monticello
Roberts, Paul vs. The State
Roberts, Richard vs. John M. Patrick
Roberts, Samuel M. vs. Thomas B. White, Henry Kirby and
  C. J. Baldwin
Roberts, Sue vs. The State
Roberts, Tilman W. vs. The State
Roberts, Will vs. The State
Roberts, William M. vs. Adam G. Saffold and William Porter
Robertson, George B. and James C. Avary vs. Jonathan
  Parrish for use of Shadrick F. Slatter
Robertson, Isaac vs. The State
Robertson, Jesse vs. Anthony Dyer
Robey, James R. vs. John T. Howard and Alexander H. Howard
Robey, Milledge B., Mary Bartlett, Henry A. Dickinson,
  Sarah A. Dickinson, William H. White, Elizabeth T. White,
  William A. Bartlett, John E. Bartlett, Thomas J. Bartlett,
  George T. Bartlett, John W. Boswell, William P. Robey,

Charles N. Horn, Amanda J. Horn, Henry A. Bartlett, Lucy
M. Bartlett, and Medora C. Bartlett vs. Eliza Jane Robey
and James C. Bartlett, Executor
Robey, Nathan, Williamson Robey, Executor and John E.
Glover, Executor vs. James Robey
Robey, Robert vs. Alston H. Greene and Joseph Buchannon
Robey, Robert vs. Joseph Johnson
Robey, Robert and Timothy Robey, Administrator vs. Jesse
Loyall for use of Thomas A. Brewer and George Aspinwall
Robey, Robert and Timothy Robey, Administrator vs. William
Ross
Robey, Robert vs. Charles D. Stewart and George Hargraves
Robey, Robert vs. John Towns
Robey, Robert vs. William H. Turpin
Robey, Robert and Timothy Robey vs. James Woodruff
Robey, Williamson vs. John Hamilton
Robinett, Allen vs. Eli S. Shorter and Seaborn Jones
Robinett, Allen vs. John I. Smith
Robinett, Allen vs. John P. Speir, Augustin Slaughter and
Charles Labuzan
Robinett, Jesse vs. Jonathan Gibson
Robinett, Jesse vs. Aron Moore
Robinett, Jesse vs. John Owen
Robinett, Jesse vs. John Richardson
Robinett, Jesse vs. Henry T. Russel
Robinett, Jesse vs. Matthew Whitfield and James Whitfield
Robinett, Jesse vs. Lewis Wynn, Green Wynn and Henry
Johnson
Robinson, Berry vs. Griffin, Monticello and Madison Rail-
road Co.
Robinson, Bert vs. The State
Robinson, Cornelius vs. Joshua Callaway and Elizabeth
Callaway, Administrator
Robinson, Cornelius vs. Jacob Lassiter
Robinson, Cornelius vs. William Lovejoy
Robinson, Cornelius vs. William Penn
Robinson, Cornelius vs. Luke Reid, David Woodruff and
Luther Goble
Robinson, Cornelius vs. Benager Saxon
Robinson, Cornelius R. vs. Nathan Williams
Robinson, Ellen vs. The State
Robinson, George vs. The State
Robinson, Henry vs. The State
Robinson, Henry Jeff vs. The State
Robinson, Isaac E. vs. The State
Robinson, James vs. The State
Robinson, James vs. John Wilson, John Hill, Executor, James
Wilson, Executor, Fleming Jordan, Executor and David A.
Reese, Executor
Robinson, James C. vs. George W. Cornwell
Robinson, James C. vs. Charles D. Ramey for use of John D.
Ramey
Robinson, James C. vs. Henry C. Seymour
Robinson, James C. vs. Matthew Whitfield
Robinson, James F. vs. Bank of Darion
Robinson, James F. vs. Lazarus Battle, William Porter,
Executor and Thomas S. King, Executor
Robinson, James F. and Caleb Early vs. Henry H. Cook and
James C. Cook
Robinson, James F. vs. Tyre G. Dabney
Robinson, James F. vs. Raymond Davenport
Robinson, James F. vs. James Delay
Robinson, James F., James T. Hays and Caleb Early vs. John

A. Ellis for use of Levi Newton
Robinson, James F. vs. Henry Hannahan for use of Joseph
  Billups
Robinson, James F. vs. Lewis P. Harwell
Robinson, James F. and Abraham Pyle vs. Daniel Johnson for
  use of Joseph W. Walton
Robinson, James F. vs. Joshua D. Martin
Robinson, Frank F. vs. Joshua G. Moore
Robinson, James F. vs. Ambrose Phillips and Seaborn B.
  Grimmett
Robinson, James F. vs. Adam G. Saffold and William Porter
Robinson, James F. and Martin Pucket vs. The State
Robinson, James T. vs. James Richards and James Mercer
Robinson, Jerry and Mason Robinson vs. The State
Robinson, Jesse vs. Anthony Dyer
Robinson, John vs. David Hamilton
Robinson, John vs. Ransom H. Smith
Robinson, John vs. The State
Robinson, John, James C. Robinson, Executor and John S.
  Robinson, Executor vs. Samuel J. Welborn
Robinson, John vs. Joseph Whedbee
Robinson, John L. vs. Stillman Ilsley
Robinson, John L. vs. Matthew Whitfield
Robinson, Osborn vs. Samuel I. Thomas for use of Humphrey
  Edmondson
Robinson, Richard and Nancy R. Robinson vs. James T. Hayes
Robinson, Richard vs. The State
Robinson, Sam vs. The State
Robinson, Sarah F., Samuel H. Blackwell, John C. Key, W. W.
  Clark and John J. Floyd vs. William C. Robinson, John L.
  Robinson, Executor and James C. Robinson, Executor
Robinson, Seth vs. William Vaughn
Robinson, Sol vs. The State
Robinson, Wallace vs. The State
Robinson, William vs. Anson Blake
Robinson, William and Albert Pabodie vs. John Byrom, Jackson
  Fitzpatrick, Executor and Cynthia Byrom, Executor
Robinson, William vs. William Crawford
Robinson, William and John Robinson vs. Thomas Grant
Robinson, William, Albert Pabodie, John R. Carlile and
  Hugh MacDonald vs. Samuel Greenlee
Robinson, William vs. Reuben C. Shorter
Robinson, William C. vs. John W. Attaway
Robinson, William C. vs. Wallace Burke
Robinson, William C. vs. Lindsey H. Durham and Dyer C.
  Bancroft
Robinson, William C. vs. Henry Jones
Robinson, William C. and James C. Robinson vs. Hugh P.
  Kirkpatrick
Robinson, William C. vs. Morgan Phelps
Robinson, William C. and James C. Robinson vs. Charles D.
  Ramey for use of John D. Ramey
Robinson, William C., James C. Robinson, Executor and John
  L. Robinson, Executor vs. Jesse J. Robinson and Eluno
  Harper, Administrator
Robinson, William T. L. vs. Eli S. Shorter
Roby, Adel vs. W. L. Roby
Roby, Charles W., Eliza Ann Roby, Richard R. Roby, Guardian,
  Lucius T. Boswell, John W. Boswell, John T. Sims, William
  Roby, Malachi Roby, Charles N. Horne, Amanda J. Horne,
  James M. Williams, Guardian, Williamson A. L. D. Roby,
  Wiley Phillips, Guardian, Mary E. Roby, Henry A. Bartlett,
  Mary L. Bartlett and Medora C. Bartlett vs. James C.Bartlett

Roby, Eddie vs. The State
Roby, Frank vs. The State
Roby, George vs. The State
Roby, Gus vs. The State
Roby, Henry vs. The State
Roby, Henry W. vs. Elmore Callaway
Roby, Henry W. vs. Francis M. Swanson and Thomas J. Comer
Roby, Mariah vs. Milledge Roby, Abner Bartlett, Executor
  and James C. Bartlett, Executor
Roby, Nathan and Williamson B. Roby, Executor vs. Elizabeth
  Higginbotham
Roby, P. M. vs. Aris Newton
Roby, Paul M. vs. J. G. Elder
Roby, W. L. vs. The State
Roby, Walter, Cohen Pope and Sherod Pope vs. The State
Roby, William A. vs. Amos Stiles
Roby, Williamson and John N. Roby vs. Alonzo B. Bigelow
Roby, Williamson, Milledge Roby, Abner Bartlett, Executor
  and James C. Bartlett, Executor vs. William John W.
  Boswell, Elizabeth Boswell and Charles W. Roby, Guardian
  for use of James A. Meriwether
Roby, Williamson vs. Thomas Butler and Charles Hartridge
Roby, Williamson vs. Thomas Cooper
Roby, Williamson vs. Hugh Cox
Roby, Williamson and John N. Roby vs. Jacob Danforth
Roby, Williamson vs. William Dearing
Roby, Williamson vs. Thomas Grant
Roby, Williamson vs. George R. Hamilton
Roby, Williamson and James A. Atcheson vs. Franklin Heard
  and Henry H. Cook
Roby, Williamson vs. Alfred Iverson
Roby, Williamson vs. John W. McCowen
Roby, Williamson vs. Joshua S. Penniman
Roby, Williamson and John N. Roby vs. Luke Reid, Luther
  Goble and Frederick S. Thomas
Roby, Williamson vs. Eli S. Shorter
Roby, Williamson vs. James Whitfield
Roby, Williamson vs. William Williams
Roby, Williamson A. vs. William M. Boon
Roby, Williamson A. vs. Thomas C. Davis
Roby, Williamson A. vs. Samuel Dunlap and John J. Allen
Roby, Williamson A. and Charles D. Bostick vs. George Gayer
Roby, Williamson A. vs. Pleasant P. Lovejoy
Roby, Williamson A. and William T. McDaniel vs. James H.
  Roberts
Roby, Williamson A. vs. Stephen C. Talmadge
Roby, Williamson B. and Elbert W. Baynes, Administrator vs.
  Green Allen, Susan Allen, Robert Edwards, Guardian, Eliza
  Edwards and George Roby
Rock, Frank vs. The State
Rock, Shade vs. The State
Rockwell, Samuel vs. The State
Rodgers, B. vs. The State
Rodgers, Cathren vs. The State
Rodgers, John vs. Jesse Gallman
Rodgers, John vs. George Laurence
Rodgers, John C. and Thomas E. Rodgers vs. Adam Alexander
Rodgers, John C. vs. William Blount
Rodgers, John C., Hardaman Owen and Thomas E. Rodgers vs.
  Elijah Boynton
Rodgers, John C. and Thomas E. Rodgers vs. Isaac Hill
Rodgers, John C. vs. John Hill for use of Malachi Lawrence
Rodgers, John C. and Thomas E. Rodgers vs. James Peoples

Rodgers, John C. vs. John Poe for use of John Carter
Rodgers, John C. vs. Wyley Rodgers
Rodgers, John C. and Thomas E. Rodgers vs. Eli S. Shorter
Rodgers, John C. and James H. Rodgers vs. Walter Shropshire
  for use of Burnet Moore
Rodgers, John C. vs. Mary Stephens
Rodgers, John C. and Thomas E. Rodgers vs. David L. White
Rodgers, Thomas E. vs. Adam Alexander and James H. Morrow
Rodgers, Thomas E. vs. Edmund W. Barker, James McGehee and
  John H. Brantley
Rodgers, Thomas E. and John C. Rodgers vs. William Blount
Rodgers, Thomas E. vs. James Cowan and Thomas B. Erwin
Rodgers, Thomas E. vs. Jackson Fitzpatrick
Rodgers, Thomas E. vs. John Hill
Rodgers, Thomas E. and John C. Rodgers vs. John C. Reese
Rodgers, Thomas E. vs. John C. Rodgers, James Anthony,
  Henry T. Smartt and Owen H. Kenan
Rodgers, Thomas E. vs. Alexander Smith
Rodgers, Thomas E. vs. David S. White
Roe, Early vs. Robert R. Bostwick, Samuel T. Beecher and
  John H. Brown
Roe, Early vs. William G. Lane
Roe, Early vs. James H. Shahan, Jeremiah Beall and
  Benjamin H. Reynolds
Roe, James vs. Richard Carter
Roe, Richard and David Adams vs. John Doe and Walton Harris
Roe, Richard, John Allen and Micajah Hendrick vs. John Doe
  and James Pinson
Roe, Richard and Azariah Bailey vs. John Doe and John Dees
Roe, Richard, Richard Bird, Ransom Whatley, Amos Jones
  and Richard Bird, Sr. vs. William Styles and Boley Conner
Roe, Richard, Joseph Carter, Presley Sanford, Christopher
  Irvine, Zacheus Phillips, Francis Winn and Nancy Heard vs.
  John Dow and David Smith
Roe, Richard and John W. Compton vs. John Doe and David
  Kennedy
Roe, Richard and William Cook vs. John Doe and George W.
  Hardwick
Roe, Richard, Samuel Crabb and Jesse Cox vs. John Doe and
  Robert Trippe
Roe, Richard and William D. Crow vs. John Doe and William
  Bird
Roe, Richard and Nathaniel Deane vs. John Doe and Magers
  Henderson
Roe, Richard and Tabitha A. Doster vs. John Doe and James
  W. Doster
Roe, Richard, John Dunn and John Dunn, Jr. vs. John Doe and
  George W. Hardwick
Roe, Richard and Anthony Dyer vs. John Doe and William Penn
Roe, Richard and Henry W. Evans vs. John Doe and John M.
  Patrick
Roe, Richard, Micajah H. Fretwell and Richard Daniel vs.
  John Doe and Wylie Burge
Roe, Richard and Joseph Funderburk vs. John Doe and Hattie
  A. Sanders
Roe, Richard, George Hampton and Richard Carter vs. John
  Doe and Abijah Henly
Roe, Richard and William Holt vs. John Doe and James Morris
Roe, Richard and Joshua Jones vs. John Doe and Sampson Lane
Roe, Richard and Fleming Jordan vs. John Doe, William A.
  Davis and John C. Davis
Roe, Richard, Thomas F. Key and Burrell P. Key vs. John
  Doe and Daniel McDowell

Roe, Richard and Elisha S. Kirksey vs. John Doe and David
  Dawkins
Roe, Richard, John Lang, Sr. and Robert Lang vs. John Doe
  and Nehemiah Schogen
Roe, Richard and James Lanier vs. John Doe and Lawson S.
  Holland
Roe, Richard, Hardy Lassiter and Abner Durham vs. John Doe,
  Joseph Sessions and Elizabeth Sessions
Roe, Richard and Gilbert Longstreet vs. John Doe and John
  P. Coles
Roe, Richard and Green McAfee vs. John Doe and Richard
  Wheeler
Roe, Richard, Levi Mercer and Nancy Hendrick vs. John Doe
  and John McKinne
Roe, Richard, Isaac Moore, Sr., Isaac Moore, Jr., John
  Moore, Joshua Moore and Jacob Moore vs. John Doe and
  William McDonald
Roe, Richard and Nicholes Morgan vs. John Doe and Sampson
  Lane
Roe, Richard and David McCoy vs. John Doe and George Walker
Roe, Richard and William Nelson vs. John Doe and Garland
  Dawkins
Roe, Richard and William Phinisee vs. John Doe, Moses Potts
  and William L. Potts, Administrator
Roe, Richard and Abel L. Robinson vs. John Doe and William
  P. Henry
Roe, Richard and John Selfridge vs. John Doe and William
  Wallace
Roe, Richard and James T. Simons vs. John Doe, Robert T.
  Allen, Mary P. Allen and Sophia Allen
Roe, Richard, Thomas Stamps and Judith Huson vs. John Doe
  and Charles Forbes
Roe, Richard, Thomas Steedman and Cyntha Steedman vs. John
  Doe, Isaac N. D. Martin and Edy Martin
Roe, Richard, Robert Trippe, Asa Stewart, Burton Crabb and
  Taylor Burris vs. John Doe and Samuel Jackson
Roe, Richard and William G. Tyus vs. George Clark
Roe, Richard and Thomas Webb vs. John Doe and David Long
Roe, Richard and Matthew Whitfield vs. John Doe, Reid Smith,
  Charlie Smith and Andrew Smith
Roe, Richard and Richard Yancy vs. John Doe, Nancy Allen,
  Mathew Allen and Elizabeth Allen
Roe, Zachariah and Matilda G. Roe vs. Garner Doggett, Mary
  Ann Doggett, Elizabeth Doggett and Nathaniel W. Gordon,
  Guardian
Roe, Zachariah vs. Leroy F. Jarrel
Roe, Zachariah vs. Amasa Wood
Rogers, Dread vs. Eaton Bass
Rogers, Dread vs. Stephen Dunn for use of William Phillips
Rogers, Ellis and Burrell P. Key vs. Isaac Benham
Rogers, Ellis vs. Sanders W. Durham
Rogers, Ellis vs. Singleton Durham
Rogers, Ellis vs. John Nisbet
Rogers, Ellis vs. Edward Price
Rogers, James A. and John C. Rogers vs. John B. Gorman and
  William B. Rogers
Rogers, W. and J. Boswell vs. T. Jordan
Rogers, Wiley vs. The State
Rooks, John and Stepney Fuller vs. C. H. Greer
Rooks, John Ben vs. The State
Rooks, Pearla vs. The State
Rooks, Tom, Oscar Bell and Howard Cargile vs. The State
Rooks, William vs. The State

Rose, L. vs. Johnson P. Lee, Ulysses B. Brewster and Henry
B. Hall
Ross, James vs. John Raney
Ross, Richard vs. The State
Ross, William and Lawson S. Holland vs. William Bostwick
Rosser, Ada S. vs. W. R. Ingram
Rosser, Benjamin vs. Samuel Lovejoy
Rosser, Isaac vs. William Williams and David Sholders
Roswell, Bob, Felix Childs, Sam Mitchell, Ben Moten and Joe
Moten vs. The State
Roswell, Fredrick and Charles Guy vs. The State
Routon, John vs. Joseph Carter
Routon, John vs. William Pritchett
Routon, John, Sr. vs. Anthony Dyer
Routon, Talbot vs. George Stinson for use of Joel Baley
Routon, William vs. Green L. McMichael
Routon, William vs. Hosea Webster and George Webster
Routon, William vs. Joseph Wooten
Rowden, Laban vs. The State
Rowden, Lot vs. The State
Rowland, Eliza N. vs. James Dunn and Uriah Dunn
Rowley, Ansel and John T. Lloyd vs. William Garrett
Ruarks, William vs. The State
Rucker, Burton vs. Thomas Carter
Rucker, Burton vs. Samuel Clay
Rucker, Burton vs. Burkett Deane
Rucker, Burton vs. John Echols
Rucker, Burton vs. James Henderson
Rucker, Burton vs. Jonas H. H. Holland
Rucker, Burton vs. Allen McClendon for use of Nathaniel L.
Sturges and Samuel Sturges
Rucker, Burton vs. Welcom Parks
Rucker, Burton vs. Demsey Phillips
Rucker, Burton vs. John Pinkard, Jr.
Rucker, Burton vs. Joel F. Randolph
Rucker, Burton vs. Wiatt Reeves
Rucker, Burton vs. Jesse Ricks
Rucker, Burton vs. Wiley Rogers
Rucker, Burton vs. William Sims
Rucker, Burton vs. Moses Speir
Rucker, Burton vs. John C. Willis
Rucker, Fielding vs. Henry C. Hutchison and Co.
Rucker, Fielding and Robert Sharman vs. William C. Redding
Rucker, Mastin vs. Thomas Napier
Runnels, George and James G. Sims vs. John A. Bradley
Runnels, Howell W. vs. William D. Crow
Runnels, Howell W. vs. Peter Randolph, Harmon Runnels,
Zadock Cook, John Strother, Stephen Crow, William George,
Gilbert Gay, Jonathan Melton, Benjamin Hagood, Thomas
Hill and William Wright
Runnels, Preston vs. Benjamin Haygood
Runnels, Preston vs. Abraham Heard
Runnels, Preston vs. Amos Welborn
Rushin, Bryant vs. Sophia Runnells
Rushing, Bryant vs. William Cunningham
Rushing, Bryant and Joseph Dixon vs. Gabriel Stalnaker for
use of Thomas P. Hamilton
Rushing, Bryant vs. The State
Russel, Bill vs. The State
Russel, Eleanor and Ignatius Russel vs. The State
Russel, John R. vs. John Kendrick
Russel, John R. vs. James Whitfield
Russel, William R. vs. John Hill

Russel, William R. vs. Isham Thompson
Russell, John vs. William L. Durk
Russell, John R. vs. Elijah Paty
Russell, Lee vs. The State
Russell, Wiley vs. The State
Russell, William and Thomas Blan vs. Edward Y. Hill
Russell, William vs. The State
Russell, Willie vs. The State
Rutledge, Alvah H. vs. Bennett M. Ware
Ryan, Hiram vs. Milton Anthony
Ryan, Hiram vs. Sarah Ryan

Saffold, Cooley and Will Clark vs. The State
Saffold, Daniel vs. Hiram Bird
Saffold, Caniel and Wiley Holifield vs. Thomas Grant, Daniel
   Grant, Executor, Thomas Grant, Executor and Peter Grinnell,
   Executor
Saffold, Daniel vs. Jesse Pye
Saffold, David and Cornelius D. Terhune vs. Soloman Perteit
   and Jeremiah Pearson, Guardian
Saffold, Ellen vs. M. L. Duke and Co.
Saffold, Heard vs. The State
Salinger, Levi and Julius Salinger vs. Jacob L. Scixas (?)
Salter, Benjamin vs. The State
Samples, Eli vs. The State
Sanders, Albert vs. The State
Sanders, Brown vs. The State
Sanders, Daniel vs. Israel Beckwith and Frizzell W. Hardwick
Sanders, Daniel vs. Edward Hicks and Joel Baley
Sanders, Daniel vs. William Stocks
Sanders, James vs. The State
Sanders, Kesiah and James Crawley vs. Grief Carriel for use
   of Thomas Broaddus
Sanders, Mary A. vs. James W. Doster and W. F. Jordan,
   Administrator
Sanders, Mattie vs. Charlotte Wethersby
Sanders, Moses vs. The State
Sanders, Richard W. vs. Peyton R. Clements
Sanders, Richard W. and Atkinson T. Harding vs. Matthew
   Whitfield
Sanders, Robert vs. The State
Sanders, Rossie vs. The State
Sanders, S. B. vs. The State
Sanders, Wyatt E. vs. Mattie A. Sanders
Sandford, Presley vs. The State
Sansom, James vs. Joel Bailey
Sansom, James, John Wright and William Wright vs. Thomas
   Whitaker
Sansom, Peter vs. Joseph Hickman
Sansom, Richard and Jeremiah Smith, Executor vs. Benjamin
   Jones
Sansom, Richard and Anna Cox vs. The State
Sansom, Robert vs. Alphaus Beall and Thomas Beall
Sansom, Robert vs. Thomas Grant
Sansom, William vs. William Baldwin, Sr.
Sansom, William vs. B. Brown and Peter Mosely, Executor
Sardis Academy vs. John H. Booker
Satterwhite, Stephen vs. Jacob Faulkner
Satterwhite, Stephen vs. John Greene
Saunders, Simon H., Nancy Saunders, Alexander Saunders, and
   George T. Bartlett vs. Matthew Whitfield, John F.
   Patterson, Executor, William Mathis, Executor, Leroy M.
   Willson, Executor and Pleasant Willson, Executor

Saunders, Tony vs. The State
Scales, Joe vs. The State
Scales, Simeon, Dyer C. Bancroft and C. D. Bostick vs.
  William M. Boon
Scales, Simeon vs. Edward A. Broddus and Thomas C. Broddus,
  Administrator
Scales, Simeon vs. Thomas F. Danielly
Scales, Simeon vs. Edward A. Elder
Scales, Simeon vs. Thomas C. Garrett
Scales, Simeon vs. John Jackson and William A. Lane,
  Administrator
Scales, Simeon vs. Richard J. Loyall and John E. Langston
Scales, Simeon vs. William Maxey and Charles S. Jordan
Scales, Simeon vs. Officers of Court
Scales, Simeon vs. Susannah C. Owens and William Phillips,
  Trustee
Scales, Simeon and Berry T. Digby vs. Wiley P. Phillips
Scales, Simeon and Priscilla Banks vs. Reuben T. Sanders
Scales, Simeon and Priscilla Banks vs. William Scales
Scales, Simeon vs. Stephen C. Talmadge
Scoggin, Gillam vs. James Richards and Willis Richards
Scoggin, Gilliam vs. Thomas Pennington
Scoggin, Nehemiah vs. Elizabeth Palmer
Scoggin, Philip vs. John Towns
Scogin, Nehemiah vs. Howel W. Runnels for use of Sally
  Griffin
Scogin, Benjamin vs. David Myrick
Scott, Benjamin C. vs. Felix Bryan
Scott, Sandy vs. The State
Scott, Stephen P. vs. Elisha Osborne
Scott, William and Albert G. Haynes, Administrator vs.
  James B. Bishop and Adam Lee
Scott, William and Albert G. Haynes, Administrator vs.
  Joseph K. Kilburn
Scott, William vs. William Leverit
Scott, William, Albert G. Haynes, Administrator, Bailey
  Freeman and Pouncy Maxey vs. Robert A. Scott, Christopher
  Thompson, Harriet Thompson, Sidney W. Blackburn and
  Martha Blackburn
Scott, Wilson vs. The State
Scroggin, George vs. Tandy D. King
Scroggin, George vs. Andrew Satterwhite for use of John
  Wadsworth and Anson W. Langdon
Scoggins, Fielding vs. Joshua R. Clark
Scroggins, Fielding vs. Anderson Scroggins
Scroggins, Fielding, Gilliam Nicholson, William Bennet,
  Bardwell Billings, William Williams and Manson Turner vs.
  The State
Scroggins, Phillip vs. John Towns
Seats, Ann vs. The State
Seavors, Henry and Orb Smith vs. The State
Segreese, Walter vs. The State
Self, William vs. The State
Selffrage, Robert vs. John Hodges
Sellars, Silas vs. Christopher Fincher
Semore, James vs. John M. Taylor
Semore, Richard H. vs. Henry Madders
Semore, Richard H. vs. Edward Price
Semore, Richard H. vs. Benjamin Wates
Semour, Richard H. vs. Luke Harp for use of Isaac Hill
Sentell, Joseph vs. John Barifield
Sentell, Joseph vs. Isaac Carter
Sentell, Joseph vs. Daniel Dawkins

Sentell, Joseph vs. Alston H. Greene and Joseph Buchannon
Sentell, Joseph vs. David Henderson
Sentell, Joseph vs. John Hill, Augustin Slaughter and
  Charles Labuzan
Sentell, Joseph vs. John Robinson and Lydia Robinson,
  Executor
Sentell, Joseph vs. William Robinson and Jesse J. Robinson
Sentell, Joseph and Alexander Herren vs. William White
Sentill, Joseph and Alexander Herren vs. Zachariah White
  for use of Jeremiah Pearson
Sessions, Robert F. vs. Welcome Allen
Sessions, Robert F. and Jerry Canant vs. John R. Welborn
Sewell, Abihu vs. Bailey C. Brookes and Shadrach McMichael
Sewell, Abihugh vs. James Smith for use of Thomas Whitaker
Sewell, Abyhugh vs. Thomas Gaston
Sewell, Abyhugh vs. David Nix
Sexton, Yancey vs. William Morgan and Fielding Bradford
Sexton, Yancey vs. The State
Sexton, Zadock vs. John R. Dickin
Sexton, Zadock vs. William Maxey and James C. Bartlett
Sexton, Zadocke vs. Willis Randle
Seymore, Henry and William W. Anderson vs. Officers of Court
Seymore, Leroy P. and David A. Reese vs. Jackson Cheney
Seymore, Leroy P. vs. Hugh P. Kirkpatrick
Seymore, Leroy P. vs. William N. Kirkpatrick
Seymore, Leroy P. vs. William A. McDonald
Seymore, Leroy P. and Wyatt R. Smith vs. Simeon Scales for
  use of Abel Johnson
Seymore, Leroy P. vs. Henry C. Seymore
Seymore, Leroy P. and William C. Penn vs. Thomas J. Smith
Seymore, Richard H. vs. Terrell Barksdale
Seymore, Richard H. vs. James Layless
Seymour, Richard vs. Robert Seymour
Seymour, William A. vs. William W. O'Neal
Seymour, William H. vs. William A. Davis
Seymour, William H. vs. William Maxey, Charles S. Jordan
  and John R. Dyer
Seymoure, William H. vs. The State
Shackleford, James vs. William Porter and Thomas J. Burney
Shamtitle, William and Charles Forbes vs. William Hay,
  John Landworthy, Elizabeth (Hay) Malone, Edward D. Malone,
  Jacob Early and Melissa (Hay) Early
Shannon, John vs. Michael A. Roberts
Sharman, John and James F. Robinson vs. Eleazer M. Hearn
Sharman, John A. vs. William Butler
Sharman, John A. vs. John North, John Manning and William
  S. Hoyt
Sharman, John A., Abram Pyle, James F. Robinson, Aris Newton,
  William Ware, Matthew Whitfield, Seaborn B. Grimmett and
  Joseph Prince vs. The State
Sharman, John A. vs. William Stokes
Sharman, John A. vs. Henry Turk
Sharman, Robert vs. Central Bank of Georgia
Sharman, Robert vs. Tunstall B. George
Sharman, Robert vs. James Goddard and Amos Langdon
Sharman, Robert vs. Robert Hudson and Charles McDowell,
  Administrator
Sharman, Robert vs. John G. Morris and James B. Bell
Sharman, Robert vs. John G. Morris and James Bell
Sharman, Robert vs. Aquilla Phelps
Sharman, Robert and Cardin Goolsby vs. George Turnball
Sharp, James vs. The State
Sharp, Lucrecy vs. William Varner

Sharp, Samuel vs. Alston H. Greene and Joseph Buchannon
Sharp, Thomas and Samuel Sharp vs. Robert Hughes for use of
  Isaac Hughes
Sharp, William vs. James Steele
Sharpe, Augustus vs. The State
Shaw, Caleb T. and Alexander N. Buchanan vs. Abner Chapman
Shaw, Caleb T. vs. Lawson S. Holland and Lewis McKee
Shaw, Caleb T. vs. Nathaniel F. Townson
Shaw, Cathren and John Shaw vs. Joel Towns
Shaw, Eli vs. Zachariah Sims
Shaw, Eli D. and Garland Maxcey, Administrator vs. James B.
  Clark
Shaw, Gilbert vs. John Allen
Shaw, Gilbert H. vs. John Durdin
Shaw, Gilbert W. vs. John Brackin
Shaw, Gilbert W. vs. J. H. Hollingsworth and T. D.
  Hollingsworth
Shaw, Gilbert W. vs. William P. Ingram and Nimrod D. Ingram
Shaw, Gilbert W. vs. John F. Patterson and William D. Maddux
Shaw, Gilbert W. vs. The State
Shaw, J. W. vs. Pollard and Co.
Shaw, James vs. The State
Shaw, James W. vs. Burrell C. Clark
Shaw, Joel and Warren Dozier vs. The State
Shaw, Robert A. vs. The State
Shepherd, Abraham vs. William S. Hurd and Anson Hungerford
Shepherd, Abraham and James C. Flemister vs. Matthew
  Whitfield
Shepherd, Alfred vs. The State
Shaw, Gilbert W. vs. John F. Patterson and William D. Maddux
Shaw, Gilbert W. vs. The State
Shaw, J. W. vs. Pollard and Co.
Shaw, James vs. The State
Shaw, James W. vs. Burrell C. Clark
Shaw, Joel and Warren Dozier vs. The State
Shaw, Robert A. vs. The State
Shepherd, Abraham vs. William S. Hurd and Anson Hungerford
Shepherd, Abraham and James C. Flemister vs. Matthew
  Whitfield
Shepherd, Alfred vs. The State
Shepherd, Carter and Thomas J. Shepherd vs. Officers of
  Court
Shepherd, Carter vs. James F. Robinson
Shepherd, David vs. The State
Shepherd, Eleazer W. vs. The State
Shepherd, Eleazer W. vs. Cannon Worsham
Shepherd, J. M. vs. The State
Shepherd, John vs. O. J. Durden
Shepherd, John vs. The State
Shepherd, John C. vs. Malissa Ann Shepherd and Lucinda A.
  Brown
Shepherd, Thomas vs. Joseph Howard
Shepherd, Thomas vs. Nathan Massey and Susan Massey
Shepherd, Thomas and William Campbell vs. William B. Mott
Shepherd, Thomas vs. Susan L. C. Ware
Shepherd, W. K. vs. The State
Shepherd, Weldon vs. The State
Shepherd, William L. vs. Rufus Howel
Shepherd, William L. vs. The State
Shi, Augustus C. vs. John R. Godkin
Shipp, G. V., C. H. Shipp and Mitchell Aaron vs. Thomas
  Curry and Berry T. Digby, Executor
Shipp, Gustavus V. and Mitchel Aaron vs. Russel J. Brown

Shirling, Isom W. vs. William T. Shields
Sholar, Edward and John Moore vs. Beach and Thomas
Sholar, Edward vs. Abner Chapman
Short, William T. vs. Thaddeus Beall, Elias Beall and
   Thomas Beall
Shorter, Alfred vs. Britton W. Chapman
Shorter, Alfred vs. The State
Shorter, Reuben C. vs. The State
Showers, Lucius vs. The State
Shropshire, H. C. vs. Asher Ayre
Shropshire, Henry C. and Richard T. Grubbs vs. Stephen C.
   Talmadge
Shropshire, James E. vs. The State
Shropshire, James E. vs. Andrew J. Varner
Shropshire, James W. vs. Central Bank of Georgia
Shropshire, James W. and James H. Morrow vs. Thomas Napier
Shropshire, John W., Silas Grubbs and Thomas K. Slaughter
   vs. The State
Shropshire, Walter vs. James H. Ravens for use of Young D.
   Allen
Shropshire, William vs. The State
Shurlock, Sam vs. The State
Shy, Caroline F. vs. Mathew Whitfield, John F. Patterson,
   Executor, William Mathis, Executor, Leroy M. Wilson,
   Executor and Pleasant Wilson, Executor
Shy, Joe vs. The State
Shy, P. R. vs. The State
Shy, Peyton R. vs. O. R. Belcher
Shy, Peyton R. and Caroline F. Shy vs. Corley and Dorsett
Shy, Samuel C. vs. Alfred Shaw
Shy, Seaborn and Samuel C. Shy, Executor vs. John F.
   Spearman
Shy, Seaborn vs. The State
Shy, Seaborn J., Caroline F. Shy, Executor and Samuel C.
   Shy, Executor vs. John Campbell and M. C. Campbell
Shy, Seaborn J. and Samuel C. Shy, Executor vs. Alexander
   Proudfit (?)
Shy, Seaborn J. and Samuel C. Shy, Executor vs. Roberts
   and Gay
Shy, Seaborn J. and Samuel C. Shy, Executor vs. Thaddeus
   P. Shy
Shy, Seaborn J. and Samuel C. Shy, Executor vs. Matthew
   Whitfield, John P. Fears, P. R. Thomaston, A. G. Foster,
   John W. Kelly, Mary Belcher, Samuel C. Shy, Leroy M.
   Wilson and William D. Stanton
Shy, Seaborn W. vs. William Belcher
Shy, Seaborn W. vs. Robert L. Duke
Shy, Seaborn W. and John W. H. Gunn vs. J. R. Pininex and
   Lea
Shy, Seaborn W. and Samuel C. Shy, Executor vs. Mat Whitfield
Shy, Seaborn W. vs. Melford N. Williams
Shy, Smaley vs. The State
Shy, T. P. vs. Robert Childs
Shy, Thaddeus P. and Samuel C. Shy vs. William H. Spears
Shy, William vs. The State
Simmons, Allen vs. Robert Beasley
Simmons, Allen vs. James Cowan and Thomas B. Erwin
Simmons, James vs. Henry Brown
Simmons, John vs. The State
Simmons, John K. vs. Alston H. Greene and Joseph Buchannon
Simmons, William and Aris Newton vs. Edward Young Hill
Simmons, William vs. Ambrose A. Phillips
Simms, Joshua vs. The State

262

Simms, Reddick P. vs. The State
Simms, Thomas vs. The State
Simms, William vs. The State
Simons, James G. vs. Lucius Arms
Simons, James T. and Allen Orr vs. Jarrel Beasley
Simons, James T. vs. John McLea and Jackson Fitzpatrick
Simons, James T. vs. John M. Taylor
Simons, Pleas vs. The State
Simons, Thomas vs. The State
Simonton, Gilbraith vs. Bank of the State of Georgia
Simonton, Gilbraith vs. Thomas W. Baxter
Simonton, Gilbraith vs. David Meriwether
Simonton, Gilbraith and Burney and Dyer vs. Officers of
  Court
Simonton, Gilbraith, Agnes J. Simonton, Administrator and
  Hugh P. Kirkpatrick, Administrator vs. Isaac L. Parker
Simonton, Gilbraith, William Simonton and James Buchannon
  vs. Oliver C. Raymond and Abraham K. Allison for use of
  Smallwood Allison
Simonton, Gilbraith, Hugh P. Kirkpatrick, Administrator and
  Agnes J. Simonton, Administrator vs. John C. H. Reid
Simonton, Gilbreath and James Buchanan vs. John North, John
  Manning and William S. Hoyt
Simonton, Robert vs. Robert Williamson
Simpson, Jack vs. The State
Simpson, John and Berry T. Digby, Administrator vs. Alameda
  Wammack
Simpson, John J. and Asbury T. Evans vs. The State
Simpson, John P. vs. The State
Simpson, Pete vs. The State
Simpson, Thomas vs. The State
Simpson, William vs. The State
Sims, Allen J. vs. William Farrington and Luther Cummings
Sims, James G. vs. James K. Daniel
Sims, James G. vs. Norborn B. Powell
Sims, James G., John Towns, Administrator, and George W. B.
  Towns, Administrator vs. Robert Robey and Timothy Robey,
  Administrator
Sims, James C. vs. The State
Sims, Perry vs. The State
Sims, Thomas W. and William Sims vs. William C. Davis
Sims, Thomas W. vs. William Haines, Jr.
Singleton, Bob vs. M. A. Reid
Singleton, David vs. William B. Allison
Singleton, Owen, Jr. vs. The State
Singleton, T. W. vs. L. O. Benton and Brother
Sission, Edwin S., Moses Chalin, Administrator and Lewis
  McKee, Administrator vs. Richard Sisson, William Sisson
  and Jacob Smith, Guardian
Sisson, Richard vs. John Cartwright, Martha Cartwright,
  Administrator and Thomas Johnson, Administrator
Sisson, Richard M. vs. Jonathan Battelle
Sisson, Richard M. and James Beland vs. The State
Sistrunk, Samuel and James Pou vs. Thomas C. Pinckard for
  use of John Pinckard
Skaggs, Henry M. vs. Alansom Mosely
Skelton, John T. vs. Goodwin W. Abbett
Skelton, John T. vs. Martha E. (Abernathy) Skelton
Skinner, Robert vs. George N. Selleck
Slack, Henry vs. The State
Slack, Joseph and William H. Wyatt vs. Edward W. Collier
  and John Hill
Slack, Joseph and William H. Wyatt vs. Henry W. Conner

Slack, Joseph and William H. Wyatt vs. Nathaniel Hayden
Slack, Joseph and William H. Wyatt vs. Joseph B. Weed,
  David M. Benedict and Frederick D. Fanning
Slack, Joseph B. and William H. Wyatt vs. James H. Shi
Slack, William vs. The State
Slagle, Jacob vs. Gilbraith Simonton and William Simonton
Slappy, Henry vs. Thaddeus Beall, Elias Beall and Thomas
  Beall
Slappy, Henry vs. Alexander Chambers
Slappy, Henry vs. Spencer Crain
Slappy, Henry vs. John Dreghorn and Co.
Slappy, Henry vs. Anthony Dyer
Slappy, Henry vs. Robert Echols
Slappy, Henry vs. Thomas Gaston
Slappy, Henry vs. John C. Gibson
Slappy, Henry vs. Benjamin Harvey
Slappy, Henry vs. Richard Holmes
Slappy, Henry vs. Joseph Johnson
Slappy, Henry vs. William T. Jones
Slappy, Henry vs. Owen H. Kenan
Slappy, Henry vs. David Kerling for use of Alston H. Greene
  and Joseph Buchannon
Slappy, Henry vs. Jesse Loyall and William H. Pritchett
Slappy, Henry vs. Robert Malone and James C. Campbell
Slappy, Henry vs. John Malpass
Slappy, Henry vs. Allen Martin
Slappy, Henry, John G. Slappy, Executor and Anne Slappy,
  Executor and Robert H. Musgrove
Slappy, Henry vs. Jeremiah Pearson
Slappy, Henry vs. Henry Pope
Slappy, Henry vs. Robert Rutherford
Slappy, Henry vs. Reuben C. Shorter
Slappy, Henry vs. Augustin Slaughter and Charles Labuzan
Slappy, Jacob and John W. Compton, Administrator vs.
  William R. Boote
Slappy, Jacob and John Compton, Administrator vs. Thomas
  Butler for use of John Crowell
Slappy, Jacob and John W. Compton, Administrator vs. Carter
  and McDougall for use of Kendrick McDougall
Slaton, Obadiah vs. Peter Downey
Slaton, Obadiah vs. Samuel Downey
Slaughter, Andrew J. and William P. Ramey vs. Stephen C.
  Talmadge
Slaughter, Henry and Frances (Fanny) Slaughter, Administra-
  tor vs. Isaac Hill, Benjamin Hill, Executor and Isaac
  Hill, Executor
Slaughter, Henry P. vs. The State
Slaughter, Isaac H. vs. Pleasant M. Compton
Slaughter, Isaac H. vs. William Doritz
Slaughter, Isaac H. vs. Durham and Bancroft
Slaughter, Isaac H. vs. Flemming Mobley
Slaughter, Isaac H. vs. Simeon Scales
Slaughter, Isaac H., Isaac Langston, E. W. Baynes, B. T.
  Digby and William C. Lovejoy vs. The State
Slaughter, Isaac H. and Jefferson Taylor vs. The State
Slaughter, Isaac H. and Francis Slaughter vs. Francis M.
  Swanson
Slaughter, Isaac H. vs. Creed T. Wise
Slaughter, Isaac L., Jefferson Barnett, Jordan Reynolds and
  James Reynolds vs. The State
Slaughter, John vs. Elisha Cook
Slaughter, John and William Gill vs. Samuel Shy for use of
  David Hodge

Slaughter, Joseph vs. Green H. Breazial
Slaughter, Joseph W. and Lemuel O. Lawrence vs. Jonas H.
  Holland
Slaughter, Joseph W. vs. William S. Hurd and Anson Hungerford
Slaughter, Joseph W. vs. James H. Roberts
Slaughter, Joseph W. vs. Ignatius Russell
Slaughter, Joseph W. and William Ramey vs. Alfred Shorter
Slaughter, Mason vs. The State
Slaughter, Moses B. vs. The State
Slaughter, Nathaniel G. vs. Joel Stanford
Slaughter, Robert vs. The State
Slaughter, Sarah and Thomas K. Slaughter, Executor vs.
  Andrew R. Bickerstaff
Slaughter, Sarah vs. William S. Hurd and Anson Hungerford
Slaughter, Sopha vs. Frederick Slaughter
Slaughter, T. K., Matilda Slaughter, Administrator and
  James M. Williams, Administrator vs. Francis M. Swanson
  and Thomas J. Comer
Slaughter, Thomas K., William Ramey and Isaac L. Parker vs.
  Central Bank of Georgia
Slaughter, Thomas K. vs. Littleton Johnston
Slaughter, Thomas K. and Carter C. Hairston vs. Aquilla
  Phelps
Slaughter, Thomas K., James M. Williams, Administrator and
  Matilda Slaughter, Administrator vs. Francis Slaughter
Slaughter, Thomas K. vs. The State
Slaughter, Wilkins vs. The State
Slaughter, William A. vs. Dennis Maddux
Slaughter, William A. vs. John S. McMichael and Isaac H.
  Slaughter
Slaughter, William A., John Burge and Lemuel O. Lawrence
  vs. Samuel Plummer
Slaughter, William A., Isaac Langston and Francis Jenkins
  vs. The State
Slickheel, Jim (alias Pleasant Burton) vs. The State
Sluder, A. L. and James P. Hardy vs. Martha A. Spears
Sluder, Augustus L. vs. The State
Small, Archie vs. The State
Smart, Elisha, J. H. Morrow and John Wynen vs. Eli Foreman
Smart, Elisha vs. Wiley and Baxter
Smart, Osborne vs. Jonathan Jewett, Gordon Abel and James
  N. Codwise
Smartt, Elisha vs. John Baldwin and Augusta Baldwin
Smartt, Elisha vs. Theophilus Fowler
Smartt, Elisha and Henry Smartt vs. Alston H. Greene and
  Joseph Buchannan
Smartt, Elisha vs. Joseph Johnson
Smartt, Elisha, Henry T. Smartt and John Wynens vs. James
  Morrow for use of James Cowan and Thomas B. Erwin
Smartt, Elisha vs. Thomas G. Polk
Smartt, Elisha and Allen Wynens vs. The State
Smartt, Elisha and Henry Smartt vs. David L. White
Smartt, Francis B. and Elisha Smartt vs. George Duesan
Smartt, Francis B., Eliza (Smartt) Hunt, Administrator and
  John Hill, Admininstrator vs. Allen G. Fambrough and
  Angelina P. (Smartt) Fambrough
Smartt, Francis B., Elisha Smartt vs. Harrington and
  Fernanders
Smartt, Francis B., Thomas B. Smartt, Eliza (Smartt) Hunt,
  Administrator and John Hill, Administrator vs. Reuben
  Phillips and Mary B. (Smartt) Phillips
Smartt, Henry T., Yancy Thornton and Jesse Hill vs. John
  Brown

Smartt, Henry T. and John Wynen vs. John L. D. Byrom
Smartt, Henry T. vs. Lewis Gibson
Smartt, Henry T. vs. Lewis Gregory
Smartt, Henry T. and Osborne Smartt vs. E. N. Hascall and
D. Hascall
Smartt, Henry T. and Cuthbert Harrell vs. James Hascall
Smartt, Henry T. vs. Franklin C. Heard and Henry H. Cook
Smartt, Henry T. vs. Jeptha McClendon
Smartt, Henry T. and John Wynens vs. Francis B. Smartt,
John Hill, Administrator and Eliza Smartt, Administrator
Smartt, Henry T. vs. The State
Smartt, Littleberry vs. Hamilton Brown, Peyton Gwyn and
James Gwyn
Smartt, Littleberry vs. Lewis Gregory
Smartt, Littleberry vs. Elijah N. Hascall and David Hascall
Smartt, Littleberry vs. Edward Kellogg and David T. Baldwin
Smartt, Littleberry vs. Charles Marshall
Smartt, Littleberry vs. James Reid for use of William Nelson
and William Knight
Smartt, Littleberry and Henry T. Smartt vs. Elisha Smartt
for use of Nathaniel S. Sturges and Samuel Struges
Smartt, Littleberry vs. Asa E. Stratton
Smartt, Osbon vs. Adam Alexander and James H. Morrow
Smartt, Osborn vs. William Flake
Smartt, Osborne vs. Thomas Fletcher
Smartt, Osborne and Henry T. Smartt vs. John Wynens for use
of Joseph Reese
Smith, A. H., Thomas H. Ellis, Emily F. Hickman and Nancy
Brooks vs. J. C. Gibson and James M. Williams, Executor
Smith, Abner vs. John Willson, John Hill, Executor, James
Willson, Executor, Fleming Jordan, Executor and David A.
Reese, Executor
Smith, Albert vs. The State
Smith, Alex and Guy Smith vs. The State
Smith, Antony W. vs. H. C. McClure
Smith, Bazil vs. William P. Rathbone
Smith, Benjamin vs. Daniel Holderfield
Smith, Benjamin vs. Aaron Morgan
Smith, Bill vs. The State
Smith, Bowling vs. The State
Smith, Boyken vs. The State
Smith, Boykin, Richard Smith, Joseph Smith, Homer Smith,
Abram Yancey and John Maddox vs. The State
Smith, Boykin R. and James H. Robinson vs. Russel J. Penn
Smith, Boykin R. vs. William C. Penn for use of Officers of
Court
Smith, Boykin R., Kesiah Smith, Jesse F. Mixon and Georgia
E. Mixon vs. Henry T. Smith
Smith, Carrie vs. Polly Jordan
Smith, Cell vs. The State
Smith, Charles vs. Thomas Carter
Smith, Charles vs. Robert Dillon
Smith, Charles vs. William Fairchild
Smith, Charles, Ann R. Smith, Administrator and Hyram Hayes,
Administrator vs. Samuel Murril
Smith, Charles vs. Edward Paine
Smith, Charles vs. John H. Richardson
Smith, Charles vs. The State
Smith, Clara (Clary) vs. James Griffin
Smith, David vs. William Huckaby
Smith, David vs. James Mullins
Smith, David vs. James Patterson
Smith, David vs. Zachary Pope

Smith, David vs. John I. Smith
Smith, Delia Ann and Alex Smith vs. The State
Smith, Drury vs. James Mitchell and Hamilton Burge
Smith, Ed vs. The State
Smith, Edward, Dudley Smith and Mary Smith vs. The State
Smith, Edward B. vs. Hattie H. Marshall
Smith, Elbert and Sidney Malone vs. The State
Smith, Ernest vs. The State
Smith, Fanny vs. The State
Smith, Farrar vs. The State
Smith, Francis (Fanny) vs. John Bean for use of William
  Askew
Smith, Francis vs. The State
Smith, Gene vs. The State
Smith, George vs. The State
Smith, Guy vs. The State
Smith, Harrison J. vs. William S. Hurd and Anson Hungerford,
  Jr.
Smith, Harrison J. vs. Benjamin King for use of William B.
  Johnston and Co.
Smith, Harrison J. and John C. Smith, Guardian vs. John W.
  Pitts and James M. Finley
Smith, Henry vs. The State
Smith, Henry T. and William G. Smith vs. Azariah Baily
Smith, Henry T. and James Callaway vs. Joshua Callaway and
  Elizabeth Callaway, Administrator
Smith, Henry T. vs. Royal Clay for use of Thomas I. Davis
Smith, Henry T. vs. William Pabodie
Smith, Henry T. vs. John Robson
Smith, Henry T. vs. Thomas C. Strickland for use of George
  Jeffries
Smith, Henry T. vs. Daniel H. Wilcox, Leonard G. Gibbs and
  W. G. MacMurphy
Smith, Henry W. vs. William Crawford
Smith, Henry W. vs. Anthony Dyer
Smith, Henry W. vs. John Hill
Smith, Homer vs. The State
Smith, J. H. S. vs. The State
Smith, J. W. A. vs. William C. Leverett
Smith, J. W. A. vs. D. A. Wilcox for use of Officers of
  Court
Smith, James vs. David Allison
Smith, James vs. Anselm Bugg and John Tanner
Smith, James vs. Thomas Carter
Smith, James vs. Henry Cosnard
Smith, James and William Freeman vs. Franklin Hervey and
  John Catlin
Smith, James vs. Joseph K. Kilburn
Smith, James vs. John A. King
Smith, James vs. George W. Lawrence
Smith, James vs. Stephen Mobley
Smith, James vs. Monticello Academy
Smith, James vs. Cornelius Robinson
Smith, James vs. The State
Smith, James J. vs. The State
Smith, James L. and William W. Smith vs. Evan H. Powell
Smith, Jefferson vs. The State
Smith, Jesse and Cornelius Johnson vs. The State
Smith, John, Lucius Pope and Ed Dunn vs. The State
Smith, John C. vs. Milton Antony
Smith, John C. and William Campbell vs. Pitts and Finly
Smith, John C. vs. Hartwell Wynn
Smith, John G. vs. The State

Smith, John Henry vs. The State
Smith, John J. vs. John Hobson and Christopher Hobson
Smith, John J. and Cyrus White vs. Levi Lestin
Smith, John W. vs. Zenos Bronson
Smith, John W. A. and Charles Camp vs. Lucinda Camp
Smith, John W. A. vs. Colbert Jeffries
Smith, John W. A. and Berry T. Digby vs. James L. Maddux
Smith, John W. A. vs. Matthew Whitfield, Leroy M. Willson,
  Executor, Pleasant Willson, Executor, John F. Patterson,
  Executor and William H. Mathis, Executor
Smith, Jonathan vs. The State
Smith, Jonathon vs. Pleasant Stovall and William P. Ford
Smith, Joseph vs. Nathaniel S. Glover
Smith, Joseph vs. Alston H. Greene and Joseph Buchannon
Smith, Joseph vs. The State
Smith, Levi vs. George Simmons
Smith, Levi vs. The State
Smith, Lewis vs. Thomas Walton and John H. Walton,
  Administrator
Smith, Lot vs. Jeremiah Harvey and Michael Dennis
Smith, Lot vs. James Lamkin
Smith, Lot vs. John McLea, John McKenzie and Peter Bennoch
Smith, Lot vs. Cornelius Robinson
Smith, Lou vs. The State
Smith, Lucius and Fuller Benton vs. R. J. J. Greer
Smith, Martha (Appling) vs. Warner Smith
Smith, Maxey vs. The State
Smith, Missouri and Joe Mosely vs. S. C. Laurence for use
  of Officers of Court
Smith, Missouri vs. Charles Meriweather
Smith, Monroe (alias Dick Smith) vs. The State
Smith, Nancy and Henry Hays vs. James Howard for use of
  Noel Pace
Smith, Nancy R. vs. Norborn B. Powell
Smith, Nathan vs. James Huling
Smith, Nathan, Nancy Smith, Executor and James Bagget,
  Executor vs. Jesse Mathews
Smith, Nevel G. vs. John Heard, John S. Drew, Executor,
  Spencer Heard, Executor and Anna Heard, Executor
Smith, Nezro vs. Pleasant P. Cross
Smith, Nezro vs. The State
Smith, Peyton Thomas and James Pinckard, Executor vs.
  Peyton Smith
Smith, Pollie vs. The State
Smith, Presley Wheeler vs. John Burgess
Smith, Ransom H. vs. Bank of The State of Georgia
Smith, Ransom H. vs. James Betts
Smith, Ransom H. vs. Lewis F. Harris and Philip Reilly
Smith, Ransom H. and John Hill vs. Hervey S. Hoadley
Smith, Ransom H. vs. George W. Holland and Hugh P.
  Kirkpatrick
Smith, Ranson, Sarah A. Smith and William Reid, Trustee
  vs. Benjamin Russell
Smith, Rich vs. The State
Smith, Richard vs. The State
Smith, Richard, Green McAfee and Robert McAfee vs. William
  Stiles and Margaret McCollister
Smith, Richard, Jeremiah Phips and Robert Granger vs.
  William Stiles and Moring Moore
Smith, Richard and Fields Wilson vs. William Stiles and
  Joseph Watters
Smith, Rolin vs. Gazaway B. Lamar
Smith, Rollin and Hanniah Smith vs. James Dodds

Smith, Sam vs. The State
Smith, Samuel vs. Elijah Law
Smith, Samuel vs. Jeremiah C. Lumsden
Smith, Samuel vs. Stephen Smith
Smith, Samuel R. vs. Russel J. Brown
Smith, Samuel R. vs. John L. Robinson
Smith, Samuel R. vs. Milton T. Roby
Smith, Samuel R. vs. H. D. Stanton
Smith, Samuel R. vs. The State
Smith, Samuel R. vs. Nehemiah B. White and Lucius White
Smith, Samuel R., and Isaac H. Freeman vs. Matthew Whitfield,
   Leroy M. Willson, Executor, Pleasant Willson, Executor,
   John F. Patterson, Executor and William H. Mathis, Executor
Smith, Samuel R., Jr., Guy Smith and Henry Smith vs. E. H.
   Kelly for use of Officers of Court
Smith, Samuel R., Sr. vs. Josiah C. Banks and C. L.
   Bartlett, Administrator
Smith, Shop vs. The State
Smith, Sidney, Jane Leverett and Francis Leverett vs. Joel
   Dawes
Smith, Stephen vs. Stephen W. Harris
Smith, Sterling vs. The State
Smith, Thomas vs. Fanny Smith (Frances)
Smith, Thomas vs. John Smith and James H. Shi
Smith, Thomas vs. The State
Smith, Thomas and Vinson R. Coursey vs. Amos Ward
Smith, Thomas and Fanny Smith vs. William Whorton
Smith, Thomas J. vs. Stephen W. Beasley
Smith, Thomas J. vs. Matilda G. Dogget and Richard C.
   Clayton, Trustee
Smith, Thomas J. and Samuel H. Blackwell vs. Edward Varner
Smith, Thomas R. and William G. Smith, Administrator vs.
   Charles H. Thompson, Amarintha A. Thompson and Charles
   J. Thompson, Guardian
Smith, Thomas W. vs. James Edwards
Smith, Tom vs. The State
Smith, Turner vs. Jesse Loyall
Smith, Turner, John P. Lamar and William H. Byrom vs. The
   State
Smith, W. G. and A. H. Burney vs. A. H. Burney
Smith, W. G. vs. The State
Smith, W. R. and Olinious O. Banks vs. Bank of Monticello
Smith, W. R. vs. H. N. Phillips for use of J. A. Shepherd
Smith, Wes vs. The State
Smith, Will vs. The State
Smith, William (Buck) vs. John Flemming
Smith, William vs. The State
Smith, William vs. Green Wynn, Richmond W. Wynn, Executor
   and William W. Wynn
Smith, William vs. Green Wynn, Executor and William W.
   Wynn, Executor
Smith, William B. vs. William P. Henry and Beverly Allen,
   Administrator
Smith, William G., Boykin R. Smith, Kesiah Smith, Jesse F.
   Mixon and Georgia Mixon vs. Henry O. Smith, Emma Clark,
   Alice Clark, Charles H. Thompson, William C. Penn, Selma
   Penn, Russel Penn, Henry F. Penn, Thomas Penn, Martha
   Penn, and Henry T. Smith
Smith, William W. vs. Allen McClendon
Smith, William W. and Fleming Jordan vs. The State
Smith, Willie vs. The State
Smith, Willis and Joshua Beavers vs. The State
Smith, Wyatt B. vs. Russell B. Brown

Smith, Wyatt R. vs. George W. Kelly
Spears, Jefferson E., Welcome Spears, Thomas Spears, Eton
  Spears and Cicero Spears vs. The State
Spears, John vs. William S. Bond for use of Officers of
  Court
Spears, John vs. Samuel Butts, John Lucas, Administrator
  and William Lee, Administrator
Spears, John vs. John Hobson and Christopher Hobson
Spears, John, Charles Finch, Thomas Wooten and William
  Spears vs. Robert Pope and Miles Hill
Spears, John vs. William Robertson for use of Jacob
  Danforth
Spears, John, Jr. and James Spears vs. Henry Boyd
Spears, Joseph vs. The State
Spears, Joshua C. vs. Jefferson C. Spears
Spears, Josiah C. vs. Cicero M. Spears
Spears, Martha A. vs. Cicero M. Spears for use of Officers
  of Court
Spears, Robert vs. Isaac L. Walton
Spears, Thomas vs. The State
Spears, Wash vs. The State
Spears, Moses vs. Bank of United States
Speer, Moses vs. John Meliss, David Taylor, Jr. and
  Andrew Meliss
Speer, Moses and William Furlow vs. University of Georgia
Speers, Hezekiah vs. John Richardson
Speight, Dave vs. The State
Speight, George vs. The State
Speight, Jutson vs. The State
Spence, Malachi vs. The State
Spence, William vs. James A. Hascall
Spence, William vs. John McKinne
Spence, William vs. Fields Wilson
Spence, Horatio N. vs. Artemas Gould
Spencer, Horatio N. and Ira Goddard vs. Chervir (?)
  Newhall and Joseph Codbeth
Spencer, Jesse M., Charles L. Ridley, Administrator and
  Elijah M. Owens vs. Susannah C. (Spencer) Owens
Spencer, Thomas F. vs. Oglesbay S. Prophitt
Spencer, Thomas F., Jesse M. Spencer and Josiah Bowdoin vs.
  The State
Spencer, Thomas F. vs. John T. C. Towns
Spiller, Ike vs. The State
Spivy, Joab vs. Zachariah Sims
Splawn, James vs. Zachary Pope and John Stillwell
Spon, James and John Guin vs. Jesse J. Rhymes, Wilkins
  Jackson, Executor and Joseph Fergerson, Executor
Spradlin, James vs. Alston H. Greene and Joseph Buchannan
Spradling, William vs. Joshua Reeves
Springer, McCullars vs. The State
Spurlin, James M. vs. Bedford H. Darden and Edmund B.
  Darden for use of George W. Wright
Spurlin, James M. vs. John M. Pearson
Spurlin, James M. vs. The State
Spurlin, John vs. Eli Glover
Stagner, James vs. The State
Stallings, J. P. vs. Wilcox, Gibbs and Co.
Stallings, Jeremiah W. vs. James Hunter
Stallings, Jesse and Sanders Stallings vs. John R.
  Anderson and Thomas Anderson, Administrator
Stallings, Sanders and Nathaniel Deane vs. Milton Antony
Stallings, Sanders vs. William Armstrong
Stallings, Sanders vs. Thaddeus Beall, Elias Beall and

Thomas Beall
Stallings, Sanders and Nathaniel Deane vs. Anthony Dyer
Stallings, Sanders vs. Jepthah George
Stallings, Sanders vs. Henry C. Hutchison
Stallings, Sanders and Robert Sharman vs. William Johnson,
  Nicholas Johnson, Executor, William Johnson, Executor and
  Polly O. Johnson, Executor
Stallings, Sanders vs. John H. Pope
Stallings, Sanders vs. Guy Smith
Stallings, Sanders vs. Sanders Walker
Stallings, Sanders vs. Moses Williams
Stamps, Timothy vs. Samuel Hale and Gilbert Shearer
Standifer, Adolphus vs. The State
Standifer, General vs. The State
Standifer, H. V. vs. Wiley Peddy
Standifer, Joel and Martha Standifer, Administrator vs.
  Wiley Peddy
Standifer, Luke vs. The State
Standifer, Milly vs. The State
Standifer, Pres vs. The State
Standifer, Sam vs. F. M. Swanson
Standifer, Silas and John Standifer vs. Mobley and Cabiness
Standifer, Thomas vs. The State
Standifer, Tomie vs. The State
Standiford, Archibald, Thomas Bullard and William Stephens
  vs. Henry Slaughter
Stanford, Joel vs. Stephen Mobley
Stanford, Obadiah vs. The State
Stanford, Phillip vs. The State
Stanley, Caleb vs. Dennis Allen
Stanley, Caleb and Martin Stanley vs. Reuben C. Shorter
Stanley, James vs. Molly Brooks
Stanley, Samuel G. vs. The State
Starks, Tom vs. The State
Stedevent, John vs. William Brown
Steed, A. S. vs. The State
Steedman, Mary vs. Henry C. Hutcheson
Steedman, Thomas vs. The State
Steele, James and Edward W. Lane vs. The State
Steele, James vs. Richard D. Wheeler
Steele, James and Nathan Williams vs. James Whitfield
Steele, W. H. and Obadiah Williams vs. The State
Steele, William vs. The State
Steene, Thomas vs. George Ramsay
Stegall, Samuel vs. William Brown
Stegall, Samuel vs. Bedford M. Darden
Stegall, Samuel vs. Reuben C. Shorter
Stephens, Andrew vs. Peter M. Hughs
Stephens, Ben vs. The State
Stephens, Henry vs. Thomas Grant
Stephens, John vs. Isaac McGehee
Stephens, John vs. William Morgan and Fielding Bradford
Stephens, John vs. John J. Smith
Stephens, Pierce vs. The State
Stevens, Henry vs. Otis Dyer
Stevens, Henry vs. The State
Stevens, John vs. Joseph Moss
Stevens, Pearce vs. John A. Jones
Stevens, Pearce and Marshall Smith, Jr. vs. John W. Kendrick
Stevens, Pearce vs. Gilbert Longstreet
Stevens, Pierce vs. John Stephens
Stevens, Sherman vs. The State
Stevens, T. I. and A. S. Florence, Administrator vs. J. H.

271

Bullard

Stevens, William vs. Henry Slaughter
Stevenson, John and Henry A. Dickinson vs. Fielding Flemister
Steward, Absalom vs. Robert Blakely
Stewart, Absalom and Elizabeth Stewart vs. David McCroy
Stewart, Ben vs. The State
Stewart, Charles vs. William Bird
Stewart, Hugh vs. Lemuel Skaggs
Stewart, Hugh B. vs. Hollis Cooley
Stewart, Hugh B. vs. Martha Morris for use of John H. Minter
Stewart, Hugh B. vs. The State
Stewart, Hugh B. and Thomas H. B. Rivers vs. Hezekiah
 Thompson
Stewart, James vs. The State
Stewart, John and John Duke vs. Thomas Greer for use of
 Early Harris
Stewart, John vs. John P. Jones
Stewart, John P. vs. Samuel Butts, John Lucas, Administra-
 tor and William Lee, Administrator
Stewart, Phillip vs. The State
Stewart, Sylvanus vs. David Peevy
Still, John vs. Alston H. Green and Joseph Buchannon
Stinson, Burrel vs. Robert Freeman
Stokes, Ignatius vs. Bernard Baker
Stokes, Ignatius and Pheby (Gordon) Stokes vs. John H. Baugh
Stone, Henry N. and Nancy Wammack vs. The State
Stone, J. A. vs. The State
Stone, John W. and William B. Stone vs. Hollis Cooley
Stone, John W. vs. James Davis
Stone, John W. vs. The State
Stone, Lucinda E. vs. Griffin, Monticello and Madison
 Railroad Co.
Stone, Susan J. vs. John W. Stone
Stone, Thomas vs. Miller Fleming, Mary Fleming, Administra-
 tor and John Fleming, Administrator
Stone, Thomas vs. Edward D. Malone, Elizabeth (Hay) Malone,
 Jacob Early and Melissa (Hay) Early
Stone, William B. vs. Jeremiah Pearson
Stone, William B. vs. Mathew Whitfield
Storrs, Hiram vs. Samuel Hale
Stovall, George vs. Orville Atkins
Stovall, George vs. Thomas Beall, H. G. Webster and
 Andrew Jeter
Stovall, George vs. John Fluker
Stovall, George vs. Alston H. Greene and Joseph Buchannon
Stovall, George vs. John Hill, Augustin Slaughter and
 Charles Labuzan
Stovall, George vs. Lawson S. Holland
Stovall, George vs. Joseph Johnson
Stovall, George vs. Robert Malone
Stovall, George vs. Edward Quin and John Campbell
Stovall, George, John Fluker, Charles Cargill, John Malpris,
 William Penn and Jeremiah Davis vs. The State
Stovall, George vs. Philip Thurman
Stovall, George vs. Hosea Webster and George Webster
Stovall, George vs. Matthew Whitfield
Stovall, Henry vs. William Hitchcock
Stratten, Asa E. vs. George Alexander
Stratton, A. E. vs. Lundy Huff
Stratton, Acee E. and George Alexander vs. Thomas Campbell
Stratton, Andrew vs. Brooks Aaron, Jr.
Stratton, Asa E. vs. George Adams and Stephen Fessender
Stratton, Asa E. vs. Joseph Cumming

272

Stratton, Asa E. vs. Luther Faulkner and John T. Reed
Stratton, Asa E. and Albert Alexander vs. Artemus Gould
Stratton, Asa E. vs. James O. Parshall
Stratton, Asa E. vs. William Sims, Charles D. Williams and
  Abraham M. Woolsey for use of Freeman Allen
Stratton, Asa E. vs. Ebenezer J. White and Edward S. White
Stratton, Asa E. vs. Abraham M. Woolsey and John M. Woolsey
Stratton, Asa E. vs. Abraham M. Woolsey and John M. Woolsey
Stratton, James vs. The State
Stratton, Jesse, Asa Stratton and Robert R. Minter vs.
  William B. Rodgers
Stratton, Jesse vs. James Smith
Straus, Joseph vs. The State
Strickland, Barnabas vs. Wiley J. Bridges
Strickland, Barnabas vs. Central Bank of Georgia
Strickland, Barnabas vs. Josie Dunn
Strickland, Barnabas vs. Obadiah M. B. Fielder
Strickland, Barnabas vs. Alexander Morris
Strickland, Barnabas vs. Officers of Court
Strickland, Barnabas vs. Reddick Smith
Strickland, Isaac vs. William Harrison
Strickland, James vs. The State
Strickland, Solomon vs. William Diamond
Stringfellow, George W. vs. The State
Stringfellow, John W. vs. The State
Strong, Charles vs. John J. Brewer
Strong, Johnson vs. Peter Brookes
Strong, Johnson vs. Joseph Brown and Bedford Brown
Strong, Johnson vs. Charles L. Mathews
Stroud, Philip vs. James Perry
Stroud, Phillip vs. James Steele
Stroud, Wiley vs. The State
Stroud, Wiley vs. James Steele
Stroud, William vs. John Fluker
Stroud, William and Richard D. Wheeler vs. The State
Strouse and Brothers vs. J. H. Kelly
Strozer, William vs. David Terrel
Strozier, John W. vs. The State
Strozier, William vs. Andrew H. Beall
Strozier, William vs. James Whitfield
Stuart, James vs. The State
Stubbs, James vs. D. S. Holt
Stubbs, James vs. Mathew Whitfield
Sturdevant, Edwin vs. Thomas Bass
Sturdivant, James and Mary Williams vs. The State
Sturdivant, James vs. John Law, Jr.
Sullivan, William vs. The State
Sumter, James M. vs. Joel Dailey
Suttle, Bill vs. The State
Suttle, George vs. Jepthah Harrington
Suttle, George vs. James M. Spurlin
Suttles, George vs. James H. Roberts
Suttles, George W. vs. Comfort Belcher
Suttles, George W. vs. Mastin D. Hendrick
Sutton, Jesse vs. The State
Sutton, Joseph and James Lanier vs. John Hill, Augustin
  Slaughter and Charles Labuzan
Swann, John T. vs. Thaddeus Beall, Elias Beall and Thomas
  Beall
Swann, John T. vs. William Bowen
Swann, John T. vs. Anthony Dyer
Swann, John T. vs. John Hobson and Christopher Hobson
Swann, John T. vs. James Sansom

Swann, John T. vs. Reuben C. Shorter
Swann, John T. vs. Jesse Tucker
Swann, John T. vs. John M. Whitlock
Swann, John T. vs. Thomas Williams and Samuel W. Butler for
   use of Joseph Johnson
Swann, Stewart and Thompson vs. Alfred Cunard for use of
   Officers of Court
Swann, William and John P. Nall vs. Matthew Whitfield and
   James Whitfield
Swanson, F. M. vs. Griffin, Monticello and Madison Railroad
   Co.
Swanson, F. M. vs. O. W. Massey
Swanson, Francis M. vs. John R. Grier
Swanson, Francis M. and John W. Burney vs. Sarah M. Morris
Swanson, William G. vs. The State
Sweeney, E. Ray vs. The State
Sweet, John vs. The State
Swift, Adam vs. The State
Swift, Hiram vs. The State
Swift, Millie vs. The State
Swinney, John vs. Robert Reynolds
Swinney, Ransom, Polly Swinney, Administrator and Benjamin
   Walker, Administrator vs. Thomas B. Greene

Talmadge, A. J. vs. M. Block
Talmadge, Albert I. vs. William W. Holland
Talmadge, Emily C., Stephen C. Talmadge and William C. Penn
   vs. Shadrach McMichael
Talmadge, S. Flourine (Flournoy) vs. Clovis A. Talmadge
Talmadge, Stephen C. vs. James C. Bartlett
Talmadge, Stephen C. vs. A. C. Barstow
Talmadge, Stephen C. vs. Justices of Court
Talmadge, Stephen C. vs. James L. Maddux
Talmadge, Stephen C. vs. Francis M. Swanson for use of John
   Greer
Talmadge, Stephen C. vs. James A. Turner
Tankesley, Carter vs. Joseph M. Evans and John P. Evans
Tanner, William vs. The State
Tarva, Henry vs. The State
Tatum, Howell vs. Augustine Slaughter and Charles Labuzan
Tatum, Organ vs. John Huston
Tatum, Peter vs. Samuel Paschal, Burwell Greene, Administra-
   tor and Betsey Paschal, Administrator
Taylor, Absalom vs. Robert Kellam
Taylor, Absalom vs. Daniel Saffold
Taylor, Alfred vs. The State
Taylor, Benjamin F. vs. William S. Hurd and Anson Hungerford
Taylor, Frances N., Leonard Taylor, John Weathersby,
   Administrator and William Whithead vs. Lucy Whitehead
   and Leonard T. Whithead
Taylor, Frances N. and William H. Taylor vs. Daniel Whitsley
Taylor, Frances W. vs. William W. Smith
Taylor, Francis N. and William H. Taylor vs. William Barclay
Taylor, Francis N. vs. David Michiell for use of Jonas H.
   Holland
Taylor, Francis P. and William H. Taylor vs. Nathan Brewer
Taylor, Hardy vs. The State
Taylor, Henry R., Charles G. Murdock and Theodore Nims vs.
   George Alexander
Taylor, Henry R., Charles G. Murdock and Theodore Nims vs.
   Thomas Evans
Taylor, Henry R., Charles G. Murdock and Theodore Nims vs.
   Henry Gassett and Richard W. Bailey

Taylor, Henry R., Charles G. Murdock and Theodus Nims vs. Joseph Whitney and Froman Allen
Taylor, Jack vs. The State
Taylor, Stephen S. and William B. Taylor vs. Ebenezer Caldwell
Taylor, Uriah vs. Bailey Gwyn
Taylor, Uriah vs. Joshua Holcombe
Taylor, Uriah vs. Henry Peddy
Taylor, William vs. Officers of Court
Taylor, William H. vs. Robert Bleakly
Taylor, William H. vs. Abraham G. Goggins
Taylor, William H. vs. Samuel Goggins
Taylor, William H. vs. William M. Harman
Taylor, William H. vs. William H. Haseltine
Taylor, William H. vs. John F. Martin
Taylor, William H. vs. Officers of Court
Taylor, William H. vs. Aquilla Phelps
Taylor, William H. vs. Adam T. Scott
Taylor, William H. and Frances Taylor vs. Alfred Shorter
Taylor, William H., William Whitehead, Priscilla Whatly and Priscilla Wynn vs. The State
Taylor, William H. vs. Robert O. Usher, William P. Anderson and Nicholas P. Hunter
Teal, Henry and Lodowick Teal vs. The State
Teal, Jesse vs. The State
Teal, William and John Wamack vs. The State
Tedard, Samuel vs. Thomas Williams, Samuel W. Butler and Otho W. Callis
Tedders, Samuel vs. Isaac Bailey
Tedders, Samuel vs. Elijah Dodson
Teel, Meshack vs. John P. Moate
Teel, Milley vs. The State
Teel, Thomas and Meshic Teel vs. The State
Terhune, Cornelius D. vs. James B. Bishop and Adam Lee
Terhune, Cornelius D. vs. Thomas W. Harris
Terhune, Cornelius D. vs. Luke Reid, Luther Gobel and Frederick S. Thomas
Terhune, Cornelius D. vs. Augustin Slaughter and Charles Labuzan
Terhune, Cornelius D. vs. The State
Terhune, Cornelius D. vs. William W. Williamson
Terrell, Elizabeth, Louisa Gordon and Edward Garland vs. Hugh Brown and Myrna (Gordon) Brown
Terrell, Joel L. vs. Starkey Perry
Terrell, Joel L. vs. John Wingfield and Alfred M. Wingfield
Terry, Garland B. vs. James A. Atchison for use of Williamson Roby
Terry, Jeremiah vs. Goodwin W. Abbott
Terry, Jeremiah and Thomas McGehee vs. Jesse Evans
Terry, Jeremiah vs. James A. Hascall and David Hascall
Terry, Jeremiah vs. John Kennady
Terry, Jeremiah vs. Gilbert Longstreet
Terry, Jerry vs. William G. Gilbert
Terry, Jerry and Absalom Irvin vs. Isaac Hill
Terry, Jerry vs. John Owen
Terry, Jerry vs. Jeremiah Pearson
Thames, Joseph, Mary (Thames) Gilmore, John Thames Gilmore, Charles McAllister, Executor and William Robinson, Executor vs. Stephen Gilmore
Thermon, John vs. McCullars Springer
Thomas, Buck and Mary Thomas vs. The State
Thomas, C. C. vs. E. S. Broddus for use of M. S. Benton
Thomas, David S. and Henry Murray vs. Martin Cochran

Thomas, David S. vs. John R. Pitkin
Thomas, David S. vs. William Tuckerman and Gustavus Tuckerman
Thomas, Douglas vs. The State
Thomas, Elbert vs. The State
Thomas, Frank vs. The State
Thomas, G. Wash vs. The State
Thomas, Govenor vs. The State
Thomas, Gus vs. The State
Thomas, Harper vs. The State
Thomas, Jack (alias John Thomas) vs. The State
Thomas, Joe and Thomas Marks vs. The State
Thomas, Lewis vs. The State
Thomas, Olin vs. The State
Thomas, Oliver (Tar) vs. The State
Thomas, Scott vs. The State
Thomas, Wiley and Safrona Thomas vs. The State
Thomas, William and John Martin vs. Alston H. Greene and
   Joseph Buchannan
Thomas, William vs. Irby Hudson
Thomas, William and William R. Russel vs. Daniel M. Lloyd
   and John Norwood, Guardian
Thomas, William vs. The State
Thomason, Amelia vs. Richard S. Thomason
Thomason, Clark vs. The State
Thomason, Isaac vs. The State
Thomason, J. C. vs. B. P. Bailey
Thomason, J. C. vs. Griffin, Monticello and Madison
   Railroad Co.
Thomason, J. C. vs. Samuel Griswold and Ebenezer C. Greer,
   Executor
Thomason, J. C. vs. The State
Thomason, Jackson C. vs. Francis M. Swanson, Thomas J.
   Pritchett and Alfred Pritchett
Thomason, Martha vs. Artemus Goolsby
Thomason, Martha M. vs. Nancy Boyd
Thomason, Martha M. and Maximillian H. Hutchison vs. Amos
   Farrer
Thomason, Martha M. and Richard S. Thomason vs. Lane and
   Patterson
Thomason, Martha M. (alias Tomerson), Richard S. Thomason
   and Martin A. Thomason vs. Mathew Whitfield
Thomason, Richard vs. The State
Thomason, Richard S. vs. Lemuel Dean
Thomason, S. E. vs. John Tilman
Thomason, T. J. and J. G. Roe vs. The State
Thomason, Thomas vs. William T. Short
Thomason, William vs. William Askew
Thomason, William and William Askew vs. William Broughton
Thomason, William vs. Jesse Evans
Thomason, William and Alexander Smith vs. Jeremiah Pearson
Thomason, William vs. The State
Thomason, William S. vs. John Willson, John Hill, Executor,
   James Willson, Executor, Fleming Jordan, Executor and
   David A. Reese, Executor
Thomasson, Aaron and James Wilson vs. The State
Thomasson, William S. vs. William H. Cargile
Thomaston, Jackson vs. The State
Thomaston, William L. vs. The State
Thompson, Boot (John Henry) (alias George Williams) vs.
   The State
Thompson, Brooking vs. The State
Thompson, Daniel vs. The State
Thompson, Ed vs. The State

Thompson, Edward J. vs. Francis H. Swanson, Thomas J.
   Pritchett, Alfred Pritchett and George Pritchett
Thompson, G. M. vs. The State
Thompson, George vs. Eshmel Davis
Thompson, George and Richard Madocks vs. William McGee for
   use of Burrel Perry
Thompson, George vs. William Megee and William Harden
Thompson, Henry vs. John J. Corley and Brother
Thompson, Henry vs. John M. Crow and William D. Crow,
   Administrator
Thompson, Henry vs. Harris and Warner
Thompson, Hiram vs. The State
Thompson, J. R. vs. The State
Thompson, J. Matt vs. The State
Thompson, Jacob M. vs. The State
Thompson, James and Lewis Whitfield vs. The State
Thompson, Jannie vs. The State
Thompson, Jeremiah vs. John Bender
Thompson, Joe vs. The State
Thompson, John and Samuel Thompson vs. Herod Bridges
Thompson, John vs. The State
Thompson, John F. vs. Officers of Court
Thompson, John F. and Lewis McKee vs. George Thomas
Thompson, John F. vs. Matthew Whitfield and James G. Beeland
Thompson, John F., Jr. vs. The State
Thompson, Joseph and Crawford Edmondson vs. Allen McClendon
Thompson, Lewis vs. The State
Thompson, M. H. and D. F. Gunn vs. Wiley Fears
Thompson, Pink vs. The State
Thompson, Robert vs. Thomas Grant, Daniel Grant, Executor,
   Thomas Grant, Executor and Peter Grinnell, Executor
Thompson, Robert, Harman H. Geiger, Administrator and John
   R. Seymour vs. Harriet Seymour and Joshua Hill
Thompson, Robert vs. Reuben C. Shorter
Thompson, Robert M. vs. The State
Thompson, S. E. vs. John Tilman
Thompson, Stephen vs. The State
Thompson, Tete vs. The State
Thompson, Thomas vs. The State
Thompson, William vs. The State
Thompson, William H., Micajah B. Key and Seaborn Lawrence
   vs. John Turk and William C. Turk, Executor
Thompson, William L. vs. Richard Johnston
Thornton, Archibald and Mahala Thornton, Executor vs. Bailey
   Goddard
Thornton, Archibald and Mahala Thornton, Executor vs.
   Elliot Reed
Thornton, Frank vs. The State
Thornton, John vs. The State
Thornton, Jordan W. vs. James Spears
Thornton, Meahalah vs. Aaron Brooks
Thornton, Noble vs. Thomas E. Erwin and James Cowan
Thornton, Thomas vs. William Morgan and Fielding Bradford
Thornton, Thomas vs. Eli S. Shorter and Seaborn Jones
Thornton, Thomas vs. John L. Smith
Thornton, William vs. Nevel Smith
Thornton, William vs. Fountain M. Thurmond
Thornton, Yancey vs. Edward Kellogg and David T. Baldwin
Thornton, Yancy, Jarrell Beasley and Martin Cochran vs.
   John Forsyth (Governor) for use of Peter W. Gautier, Sr.
Thornton, Yancy vs. Bailey Goddard
Thornton, Yancy vs. William M. White
Thorp, Green vs. The State

Thrash, Martin vs. Thomas I. Davis
Thrower, Thomas vs. Elijah Clark for use of Moses Fort
Thrower, Thomas vs. John Lucas
Thrower, Thomas vs. James McGehee
Thurman, Aaron vs. The State
Thurman, Arnold vs. The State
Thurman, C. D. and J. H. Holland vs. W. B. Fitzpatrick
Thurman, Charlie, Edward Thurman and Joshua Waits vs. The
  State
Thurman, James vs. Thomas Duncan
Thurman, James vs. Calvin Dunning
Thurman, James vs. John Hobson
Thurman, James vs. Jeremiah Pearson
Thurman, John, Mary Clements, Jeptha H. Clements, Angus G.
  Morrison and Alexander Morrison vs. Cuthbert Reese
Thurman, Mitchel vs. The State
Thurman, Philip vs. Samuel B. Head
Thurman, Wilkes vs. The State
Thurmon, Fountain M. vs. James Griggs
Thurmon, James vs. James S. Weekes
Thurmond, Charles and Jesse Thurmond vs. John Bowie, Jr.
Thurmond, Clint vs. The State
Thurmond, Edmond vs. The State
Thurmond, Fountain M. vs. Robert B. Camfield
Thurmond, Fountain M. vs. Gilbert Cleeland
Thurmond, Fountain M. vs. Samuel Crocket for use of John
  Hill, Augustin Slaughter and Charles Labuzan
Thurmond, Fountain M. vs. Nathan Lyon
Thurmond, Fountain M. and Parthenia Tatum vs. Reuben Shorter
Thurmond, Fountain M. vs. The State
Thurmond, Fountain M. vs. Willis Watley
Thurmond, Fountain M. vs. John Willson
Thurmond, Jack vs. Augustus McGehee
Thurmond, James, Gus Goolsby and Moses Clemmons vs. The
  State
Thurmond, John vs. Thomas B. Erwin and James Cowan
Thurmond, John vs. Augustus McGehee
Thurmond, Phillip vs. Thomas A. Foster
Thurmond, Phillip vs. Samuel Hill, Sr. for use of Goodrich
  Jones
Thurmond, Thomas and Joel McClendon vs. Pleasant Clay
Thurmond, Thomas vs. The State
Thurmond, William, Phillip Thurmond, Administrator and James
  Thurmond, Administrator vs. Joseph Brown
Thurmond, William, James Thurmond and Phillip Thurmond vs.
  William McCree
Tidwell, John G. vs. The State
Tiller, Ephraim and Mason Tiller vs. William Dennis
Tiller, Ephraim E. vs. Daniel Slade
Tiller, Paul H. vs. The State
Tiller, Sam vs. The State
Tillery, John vs. Robinson and Pabodie
Tillett, George and Moses Fort, Guardian vs. George Street
Tillman, Bob Lee vs. The State
Tillman, Dan vs. The State
Tillman, Dave vs. The State
Tillman, George vs. The State
Tillman, James vs. The State
Tillman, Penelope vs. James H. Gordon, Zachariah H. Gordon
  and Charles P. Gordon
Tillman, Walter vs. The State
Tilman, Bob vs. Thomas C. Spivey
Tilman, Henry vs. Lewis Wynn and William Johnson

Tindol, Samuel, Alexander Wilkerson, Madison Morris and
    John Wilkerson vs. The State
Tiner, Reuben vs. Robert Woodall
Tingle, Joseph vs. Benjamin Brantley
Tingle, W. A. vs. The State
Tinnan, David vs. Isaac Bailey
Tinsley, Allancen R., Warren J. Tucker and Joseph Buse vs.
    Stephen Felker
Tinsley, Emma vs. The State
Tinsley, Mary vs. The State
Tinsley, William vs. The State
Toland, Adam vs. The State
Toland, Mariah vs. Richard Toland
Toland, Michael vs. The State
Toland, T. L. vs. W. E. Paul
Toland, Thyus J., Robert McCord, Rebecca McCord, Iverson L.
    Toland, William Pitts and Nancy A. Pitts vs. Michael M.
    Toland and Asa P. Toland, Executor
Tolefree, Robert, William Y. Harris and William Tolefree
    vs. David Harris
Tolefree, Robert vs. William Y. Harris
Tolefree, Robert and David Meriwether vs. Jonas Holland
Tolefree, Robert vs. The State
Tolefree, William and Robert Tolefree vs. Jonas H. Holland
Tollerson, J. G. vs. W. M. Robinson
Tomlin, Dave vs. The State
Tomlin, Rufa vs. The State
Tomlinson, John, Jr. and James Smith vs. Brittain Grant
    and William A. Slaughter, Executor
Tompkins, Eubanks and Lewis W. Pon vs. Alfred Cuthbert
Tompkins, Giles vs. The State
Tompkins, John vs. Alexander McDonald
Tompson, John F. vs. William H. Whitfield
Touchstone, Christopher vs. Hartwell Willyford for use of
    Adam G. Saffold
Tourney, Jesse vs. Russell J. Penn
Tourney, Jesse vs. William C. Penn
Towns, Henry C. and Bartley Towns vs. Michael Durr
Towns, Henry C. vs. William Simmons
Towns, J. T. C., Robert A. Ridley and Thomas Rivers vs.
    Central Bank of Georgia
Towns, Joel vs. George Clower
Towns, Joel, Anna Towns, Administrator and Carter B.
    Harrison, Administrator vs. James Graham and Williamson
    Wynn, Administrator
Towns, John vs. Horace Ames, David Mitchell and George B.
    White
Towns, John vs. Andrew Cragg
Towns, John vs. Samuel Drowry
Towns, John vs. William Foxey
Towns, John vs. Richard Loyall
Towns, John and George W. B. Towns vs. Robert Roby and
    Timothy Roby, Administrator
Towns, John vs. William Spratlin and John Burney, Executor
Towns, John vs. Joseph B. Swan
Towns, John G. vs. Henry H. Cook and James C. Cook
Towns, John G. and John Martin, Executor vs. John Towns for
    use of James Whitfield
Towns, John G. vs. John Warren
Towns, John T. C. vs. Garrett Clark
Towns, John T. C. vs. Zachariah Cox and John Carter
Towns, John T. C. vs. John J. Griggs
Towns, John T. C., Lucy I. Holly, Bartley Towns, Henry C.

Towns and Mary Esters vs. William Holt
Towns, John T. C. vs. James Larkin
Towns, John T. C. vs. Leroy Napier
Towns, John T. C. vs. John Sturdivant
Towns, John T. C. vs. Isaac B. Williamson
Towns, Marlen vs. Robert Robey
Towns, Marlin vs. James K. Daniel, Sr.
Towns, Simon and Jack Hurd vs. The State
Townsend, George vs. Fielding Flemister
Townsend, Jesse vs. Gabriel Gunn
Townsend, William vs. James Tredwell
Trammel, A. A. vs. William C. Johnston
Trammel, A. A. vs. Beverly A. Kelly
Trammell, Augustus A. vs. Benjamin W. Banks and Jarrott B. Kelly, Executor
Traweck, Robert vs. The State
Trawick, Robert vs. Joshua Callaway
Trayler, Thomas G. and James L. Standifer vs. Crawford H. Greer
Trayler, Thomas G. vs. William Maxey and Charles S. Jordan
Traylor, John W. vs. Alexander S. Reid
Traylor, Mark vs. The State
Traylor, Mason, Willis Broddus and Nancy Waters vs. The State
Traylor, Mijamin B. vs. Andrew Frasier and Shadrach McMichael, Guardian
Traylor, Thomas G. vs. Jonas H. Holland, Eunice A. Holland, Administrator and W. W. Holland, Administrator
Traylor, Thomas G. vs. Wiley Peddy
Trice, Thomas C. vs. Josiah David and Orvil Barber
Trimble, Henry vs. The State
Triplett, John vs. Dyer C. Bancroft and Hollis Cooley
Tripp, Robert vs. Jesse Cox, Fleming Jordan, Executor and Sarah Cox, Executor
Trippe, Henry vs. Gilbraith Simonton
Trippe, Henry W. vs. Hiram Gilbert
Trippe, Henry W. vs. Isaac Kendrick
Trippe, Henry W. vs. Henry Maddera
Trippe, Henry W. vs. The State
Trippe, Henry W. and Joseph T. Moreland vs. James Whitfield
Trippe, Robert vs. Hugh Taylor
Trippe, William and Robert Trippe vs. Alston H. Greene and Joseph Buchannon
Trippe, William vs. Justice of Court for use of James Trippe
Trippe, William vs. Palemon Weekes and John Hunt
Truit, Jack vs. The State
Truitt, John and Watson Shaw, Administrator vs. James Beeland and Sarah Beeland
Trussel, Daniel and James McLeroy vs. James Whitfield
Trussell, Green B. and James L. Trussell vs. Hugh P. Kirkpatrick
Trussell, Green B. vs. Thomas J. Smith and John C. Maddux
Trussell, James vs. The State
Trussell, William H., James Trussell and Berry T. Digby vs. Jeremiah Pearson for use of John W. Pearson
Tucker, George vs. The State
Tucker, Green C. vs. G. T. Bartlett
Tucker, Joel vs. Pleasant Stovall and Greensville Tucker
Tucker, John vs. Hosea Webster and George Webster
Tucker, Reddick vs. The State
Tucker, Thomas vs. James Richards and Willis Richards
Tucker, W. E. vs. George W. Newton

Tucker, Warren vs. Nathan Massey and Susan L. C. (Ware)
  Massey
Tucker, Warren vs. Amos Ward
Tucker, Warren J. vs. Robert C. Philips
Tucker, William vs. Alfred I. Huntington and Alfred S.
  Huntington
Tucker, William vs. Ephraim Pennington
Tucker, William vs. The State
Tucker, William G. vs. James Hill
Tuggle, Benjamin F. and George Jeffries vs. John Hill
Tuggle, Benjamin F. and Freeman McCullough vs. The State
Tuggle, Benjamin F., Obediah E. Cavender, Frances Cavender,
  Coby R. Jackson, Nancy Jackson, John W. Smith and Eliza-
  beth Smith vs. Elizabeth Tuggle and William J. L. Tuggle,
  Executor
Tuggle, Catherine vs. Thomas Banks
Tuggle, Ed vs. The State
Tuggle, F. M. and J. A. Tuggle vs. Walton County Guano Co.
Tuggle, F. N. vs. T. J. Nash
Tuggle, Hugh vs. The State
Tuggle, John vs. The State
Tuggle, Lee and Robert Tuggle vs. Eleazer Mobley
Tuggle, Lee vs. The State
Tuggle, Lewis, Alf Tuggle and Bob Tuggle vs. The State
Tuggle, Lodowick vs. Joel Bailey
Tuggle, Lou S. vs. The State
Tuggle, Phil and Carrie Tuggle vs. The State
Tuggle, Robert vs. Thomas Grant, Daniel Grant, Executor,
  Thomas Grant, Executor and Peter Grinnell, Executor
Tuggle, Robert vs. The State
Tuggle, Thomas vs. Charles Labuzan
Tuggle, Thomas and Leonard Tuggle vs. Allen McClendon
Tuggle, Thomas and Richmond Brown vs. William Penn
Tuggle, Thomas H. and William J. L. Tuggle vs. William S.
  Hurd and Anson Hungerford
Tuggle, Thomas H. vs. The State
Tuggle, W. R. vs. Cosley and Dorsett
Tuggle, W. R. and P. C. Bennett vs. O. S. Prophitt
Tuggle, W. R. vs. A. L. Sluder for use of Officer of Court
Tuggle, William vs. The State
Turk, Adolphus A. vs. The State
Turk, E. B. vs. O. H. Arnold
Turk, E. B. vs. J. C. Peteet
Turk, E. B. vs. J. M. Thompson
Turk, John vs. Stephen Durdan
Turk, John vs. Thomas Hardeman, Matthew Whitfield and James
  Whitfield
Turk, John vs. James Lamkin
Turk, T. J., R. W. Malone, J. P. Malone, Jake Thompson and
  J. H. Lane vs. J. D. Kilpatrick, W. F. Jenkins and Son
  and Foster and Butler
Turk, T. J., Lucius Turk and Will R. Turk vs. The State
Turnell and Lasseter vs. E. W. Baynes for use of Officers
  of Court
Turner, Allen vs. The State
Turner, Anderson vs. The State
Turner, B. S. vs. J. H. Kelly
Turner, Charles, M. B. Key and O. G. Roberts vs. Mayor and
  Council of Monticello
Turner, Crawford vs. The State
Turner, George Ann vs. The State
Turner, Greenbury H. vs. William Penn and William C. Penn
Turner, Henry G. vs. Nathaniel H. Wildman and Starr Nichols

Turner, J. W. and A. Newton, Jr. vs. John A. Broughton
Turner, J. W. vs. James Turner, George Turner, Sue Norman
  and Francis Trayler
Turner, James vs. Elisha G. Crawford
Turner, James vs. John M. Dooly
Turner, James vs. Jacob Finley
Turner, James vs. Anthony Lewis
Turner, James vs. John Mays
Turner, James vs. The State
Turner, James F. vs. John Ashmore
Turner, James N. and Toliver B. Turner vs. William Shields
Turner, James N., Toliver B. Turner, William H. Smith,
  William Mosely, Henry McCullers, Culpepper McCullers and
  John Vinings vs. The State
Turner, John (alias John Fears) vs. The State
Turner, Larkin vs. Thomas Pennington
Turner, Larkin vs. James Richards and Willis Richards
Turner, Larkin vs. Williamson Roby and Henry Boswell
Turner, Mamsom (Manson) vs. Woody Dozier
Turner, Manson vs. Edward Hicks and Joel Baley
Turner, Manson vs. Allen McClendon
Turner, R. Newton vs. The State
Turner, Richard vs. The State
Turner, Roberson H. vs. Eleazer Shepherd
Turner, Samuel vs. The State
Turner, Shadrach vs. The State
Turner, Tom vs. The State
Turney, Jesse vs. Thomas R. Penn and John C. Pope for use
  of Officers of Court
Tweedell, Alexander W. H. vs. James L. Standifer
Tyler, Albert vs. The State
Tyler, B. F. vs. Maggie Price for use of Officers of Court
Tyler, Barney and George Tyler vs. The State
Tyler, Barney F. vs. H. W. Pye and W. L. Zachry, Adminis-
  trator
Tyler, Ed vs. The State
Tyler, F. M. vs. Griffin, Monticello and Madison Railroad Co.
Tyler, J. J. vs. The State
Tyler, Job, Jr. vs. The State
Tyler, Samuel, Thomas Tyler, Richard Goodman, Jr. and
  James Greer vs. The State
Tyler, William vs. John Hill
Tyler, William vs. The State
Tyler, William P. vs. Thomas M. Darnall
Tyner, David M. vs. Wiley Peddy
Tyner, R. J. vs. John McCullough
Tyner, Reuben vs. Thomas G. Pritchett, Alfred Pritchett
  and George Pritchett
Tyner, Reuben J. vs. Jubil Cochran and Milford A. Cochran,
  Administrator
Tyner, Reuben J. vs. John Hines
Tyner, Reuben J. vs. Henry J. Marshall
Tyner, Reuben J. vs. Francis M. Swanson and Thomas J. Comer
Tyner, Reuben J. vs. Francis M. Swanson, Thomas J. Prit-
  chett and Alfred Pritchett
Tyner, Stephen vs. Hartwell Jones
Tyson, Henry F. and D. M. Langston vs. William C. Leverette
Tyson, Henry F. vs. Wiley Peddy
Tyus, William G. vs. Warren Ambrose
Tyus, William G. vs. George Clark
Tyus, William G. vs. Benajah Birdsong and George Clark,
  Executor
Tyus, William G. vs. Thomas B. Erwin and James Cowan

Tyus, William G. vs. David Gunn and John Gunn
Tyus, William G. vs. Hugh G. Johnson
Tyus, William G. vs. Rice P. Knowles
Tyus, William G. vs. Aman W. Langdon
Tyus, William G. vs. Charles S. Lewis
Tyus, William G. vs. Thomas Lundy
Tyus, William G. vs. Thomas Napier
Tyus, William G. vs. Jeremiah Pearson
Tyus, William G. vs. Zachary Pope
Tyus, William G. vs. John Prewitt
Tyus, William G. vs. Litte Sims
Tyus, William G. vs. John I. Smith
Tyus, William G. vs. Robert H. Strong
Tyus, William G. vs. John Tyus and Lewis Tyus, Administrator
Tyus, William G. vs. Abraham S. Write for use of Tandy D. King
Tyus, William G. vs. Green Wynn, Richmond W. Wynn, Executor and William Wynn, Executor

Underwood, William vs. Nathaniel Stattham
Urquhart, Alexander and Samuel Harrell vs. Daniel Parish, Jasper Corning, Thomas Parish and Joseph Kernochan
Urquhart, Alexander vs. Philo D. Woodruff
Urquhart, Henry vs. Eli McKinney
Urquhart, Henry and Yancey Thornton vs. George Stephens, Steven Stephens, Administrator and William Stephens, Administrator
Urqueheart, Alexander vs. Benjamin May
Usher, Sarah A. and Cornelius D. Terhune vs. Jarrel Beasley

Valentine, Thomas and John S. Scott vs. Solomon Worrill for use of Alexander Sloan
Van, Sanders and Enos Merchon vs. Abner Locket
Vanbibber, Henry vs. Joseph Moss
Vance, Marcus vs. Hamilton Brown, Thomas P. Gwyn and James Gwyn
Vance, Marcus and Jarrel Beasley vs. Jesse Cherry
Vance, Marcus vs. James Cowan
Vance, Marcus vs. John Fletcher
Vance, Marcus vs. William R. Fowler
Vance, Marcus vs. Reuben C. Shorter
Vance, Marcus vs. James Smith, Thomas J. Smith and Charles McLemore
Vance, Marcus vs. George W. Willingham
Vance, Marcus vs. John Wood
Vance, Marcus vs. Davis Woodruff and Isaac Brant
Vance, Marcus D. vs. Robert C. Beasley and Palemon L. Weeks
Vance, Marcus D. vs. John W. Bridges and Lewis Gibson
Vance, Marcus D. vs. James Bullard, Sr., Jarmoney G. Bullard, Executor, Albert Alexander, Executor and Thomas B. Erwin, Executor
Vance, Marcus D. vs. Henry W. Dorsey
Vance, Marcus D. vs. Jacob Faulkner
Vance, Marcus D. vs. Samuel Fulton
Vance, Marcus D. and John Bradley vs. Bailey Goddard
Vance, Marcus D. vs. James Jones
Vance, Marcus D. vs. William B. Jones and James H. Morrow
Vance, Marcus D. vs. Jacob McDaniel for use of John W. McGehee
Vance, Marcus D. vs. Larkin Reynolds
Vance, Marcus D. vs. Thomas Smith, John C. Smith, Administrator and Asa Smith, Administrator
Vance, Marcus D., Anthony Johnson and Samuel McDaniel vs.

The State
Vance, Marcus D. vs. James Whitfield
Vandegrift, John vs. Benjamin Kitchens
Vandergrief, John vs. Willie Milam
Vardeman, Henry W. and Wyly Traylor vs. Martin Nall and
    Frances Nall
Vardeman, William, Brice Miller, Benjamin Smith and Israel
    Gambol vs. The State
Varnam, W. C. and Eliza Ann Warren vs. J. C. Watters, D. C.
    Bancroft, Executor, and A. J. Watters, Executor
Varner, Amos and Pierce Varner vs. The State
Varner, Andrew J., Jefferson M. Varner and Clinton L.
    Varner vs. James B. Carhart, William B. Carhart, John B.
    Storr and Elijah H. Carhart
Varner, Andrew J. vs. Berry T. Digby
Varner, Andrew J., Edward Varner and Samuel D. Varner vs.
    Hopson Freeman
Varner, Andrew J. and Jefferson M. Varner vs. Joshua Hill
Varner, Andrew J., Clinton L. Varner and Samuel D. Varner
    vs. Hugh P. Kirkpatrick
Varner, Andrew J. and Jefferson M. Varner vs. Tilmon Niblett
    and John E. Langston
Varner, Andrew J. vs. Charles D. Ramey and John D. Ramey
Varner, Andrew J. and Jefferson M. Varner vs. Lewis Ryan,
    Administrator
Varner, Andrew J., Clinton L. Varner and Jefferson M.
    Varner vs. James M. William and Thomas Minter
Varner, Earley vs. William Maxey and James C. Bartlett
Varner, Early and Edward Varner vs. John Marsh
Varner, Early, Levin J. Stewart and Frederick A. Varner
    vs. Isaac C. W. T. McKissack
Varner, Edward vs. Byran Allen
Varner, Edward vs. Bank of Darien
Varner, Edward, Andrew J. Varner, Clinton Varner and Brax-
    ton R. Ezel vs. Robert Bledsoe and Nathan Bass, Executor
Varner, Edward, Cynthia H. (Byron) Varner, Jarrel Beasley
    and Jackson Fitzpatrick vs. John Byron, William H. Byron
    and Edward Price, Guardian
Varner, Edward vs. Hollis Cooley and Dyer C. Bancroft
Varner, Edward vs. Richard Duryee (?) and Cornelius Heyer
Varner, Edward and Cynthia H. Varner vs. Jackson Fitzpatrick
Varner, Edward and William Varner vs. Daniel Freeman and
    James Freeman, Executor
Varner, Edward vs. Evenard Hamilton, John R. Hayes and
    Robert Hart
Varner, Edward vs. William S. Hurd and Anson Hungerford
Varner, Edward vs. Robert Kellam and William Maxey
Varner, Edward and James Griggs vs. George L. Kilpatrick
    and Bushead W. Sanford, Guardian
Varner, Edward vs. Henry J. Lamar
Varner, Edward vs. William Maxey and John Hill
Varner, Edward vs. John McKinne and James Lamkin
Varner, Edward vs. John McNeil
Varner, Edward vs. Cuthbert Reese
Varner, Edward vs. Henry C. Seymour
Varner, Edward and Robert H. Daniel vs. James W. Shropshire
Varner, Edward vs. William Sims and Charles D. Williams
Varner, Edward and William Maxey vs. Thomas J. Smith and
    William M. Broddus
Varner, Edward vs. Charles Squire and Gold S. Selleman
Varner, Edward and William H. Byrom vs. Patrick M. Stevens
Varner, Edward and Samuel D. Varner vs. Levin J. Stewart
Varner, Edward vs. John Thurmond

284

Varner, Edward vs. William H. White and Hendley Varner
Varner, Edward, Isaac Bailey and John W. Burney vs. James
  W. Whitfield
Varner, Edward vs. Henry F. Young
Varner, Frederick A. vs. William Maxey and Charles S. Jordan
Varner, Hendley and Robert C. Beasley vs. George Lee
Varner, Hendley and Robert C. Beasley vs. Green Lee
Varner, Hendley and George W. Harvey vs. Nathainiel
  Truesdell
Varner, Henley vs. Isaac B. Williamson
Varner, Jefferson vs. Tilmon Niblett and John G. Langston
Varner, Jefferson M., Andrew J. Varner, Clinton L. Varner
  and Edward Varner vs. Henry Dillon
Varner, Jefferson M. vs. Louden Willis
Varner, Samuel D. vs. Benjamin M. Cargile
Varner, Samuel D. vs. William Hannah
Varner, Samuel D. and Edward Warner vs. William S. Light-
  foot and David Flanders
Varner, Samuel D. vs. Jesse Loyall
Varner, Samuel D. vs. Ananias D. Martin
Varner, Samuel D. and Edward Varner vs. William Maxey and
  James C. Bartlett
Varner, Samuel D. vs. Charles D. Ramey
Varner, Samuel D. vs. Matthew Whitfield
Varner, William vs. The State
Varner, William G. vs. William Dukes and Thomas F. Danielly
Varnum, Margarett vs. The State
Vaughn, Andrew vs. The State
Vaughn, Benjamin T. vs. Moses B. Hairston
Vaughn, Benjamin T., Berry T. Digby, Administrator and
  William H. Mothershed vs. Ellen F. Mothershed
Vaughn, Benjamin T. vs. Henry C. Seymour
Vaughn, Berry vs. The State
Vaughn, Georgia (Missie) vs. The State
Vaughn, Horace vs. The State
Vaughn, Isham vs. The State
Vaughn, James W. vs. Joseph A. Holland
Vaughn, James W. vs. Jesse Loyall
Vaughn, James W. vs. William Maxey and James C. Bartlett
Vaughn, James W. vs. Robert L. Puckett
Vaughn, Milton vs. The State
Vaughn, Will vs. The State
Vaughn, William and John Vaughn vs. Richard Garner
Vaughn, William vs. James A. Meriwether
Vaughn, William, Sr., George Tucker and Benjamin T. Vaughn
  vs. The State
Vawn, William vs. Isham Huckeby
Veal, and Brother vs. Officers of Court
Veal, Joseph vs. The State
Venters, Stephen vs. The State
Vickers, Elijah vs. Thomas Bivins
Vickers, John vs. James Richards for use of Jonathan
  Battelle
Vickery, Middleton vs. The State
Vickrum, Walter vs. The State
Victrum, Carrie vs. The State
Vincent, Caroline and Thomas Lowe vs. Powel P. Vincent
Vincent, Henry and Wesley A. Snell vs. John B. Ross,
  William A. Ross and George W. Ross
Vincent, Jim vs. The State
Vincent, Nathaniel and Thomas Vincent vs. James B. Howard
Vincent, Nathaniel and Thomas Vincent vs. James B. Howard
Vincent, Thomas G. and Wesley A. Snell vs. John B. Ross,

William A. Ross and George W. Ross
Vincent, William L. vs. Richard J. Loyall and John G.
  Langston
Vineable, ? vs. The State
Vining, Shadrach vs. Irby Hudson

Waddill, Marshall H. vs. Thomas Hairston
Waddill, Marshall H. vs. William S. Middlebrooks
Waddill, Marshall H. vs. John Payne
Wade, James and John Knight, Administrator vs. Thomas B.
  Erwin and James Cowan
Wade, James and John Knight, Administrator vs. Haratio
  Spencer
Wade, Richard vs. John Emmerson
Wade, Richard vs. Bennett Fitzpatrick
Wagner, James and Jeremiah Wagner vs. The State
Wagner, John W. vs. The State
Wagoner, Jerry vs. The State
Waits, Addie vs. The State
Waits, G. W. T. vs. Pritchett Brothers
Waits, Gurley vs. The State
Waits, Henry vs. The State
Waits, John vs. Isaac Mills
Waits, Joshua vs. Alexander Waits and W. L. Zachry,
  Administrator
Waits, Leroy vs. Davis Lane and John L. Patterson
Waits, Leroy vs. Maxey, Jordan and Co.
Waits, Leroy vs. Thomas J. Pritchett, Alfred Pritchett and
  George Pritchett
Waits, Leroy and William B. Waits vs. James M. Williams
Waits, Levi vs. James L. Maddux
Waits, Levi, Seaborn Lawrence and S. C. Lawrence, Adminis-
  trator vs. William J. McMichael
Waits, Levi and Edward Y. Griggs vs. Evan H. Powell, John
  Ezell, Executor and William R. Powell, Executor
Waits, Levi vs. Arch W. Tanner and Robert Whitfield
Waits, William vs. Alexander Waits and W. L. Zachry,
  Administrator
Waits, William W. vs. Pritchett Brothers
Walden, Alexander vs. John Booker
Walden, Alexander, James Dick and George Parrot vs. John
  Donaldson
Walden, Alexander vs. Elijah N. Hascall
Walden, Alexander vs. Clement Molliere
Walden, Alexander and William H. Walden vs. Reuben C.
  Shorter
Walden, Charles vs. Thomas Hutson
Walden, Daniel vs. Edward Castleberry and James Cameron,
  Executor
Walden, Daniel vs. Maurice Wilkinson
Walden, Henry vs. James Richards for use of Miles Beach
  and Edward Thomas
Walden, James vs. Abner Chapman, Jr.
Walden, James vs. James Richards and Willis Richards
Waldin, Charles vs. The State
Waldrep, Leescol J. vs. Lewis Gilstrap
Waldrop, David vs. Benjamin Harrison
Waldrop, John W. (Isaac) vs. The State
Waldrop, Solomon vs. James Richards
Waldrop, Solomon vs. The State
Waldrup, Kirby vs. The State
Walker, Asa vs. The State
Walker, Asa vs. Edee Walker

Walker, Bartley vs. Stephen W. McLendon and Sterling Jenkins, Executor
Walker, Berry vs. The State
Walker, Burney vs. The State
Walker, Charles and Bill Johnson vs. The State
Walker, Charlie vs. The State
Walker, Cornelius vs. The State
Walker, Eady vs. The State
Walker, Elijah C. vs. Zenos Bronson and Claiborne Mills
Walker, Elijah C. vs. Daniel Parish, Jasper Corning, Henry Parish, Joseph Kernochan and Ephraim Holbrook
Walker, Ernest (alias Ernest Porter) vs. The State
Walker, F. Elijah vs. The State
Walker, Fred vs. The State
Walker, Henry vs. Thomas Barrett and Benjamin Sims
Walker, Henry vs. Thomas Collins
Walker, Henry vs. Thomas Fitch
Walker, Henry and John W. Burney, Administrator vs. Benjamin Fitzpatrick
Walker, Henry vs. Stephen W. Harris
Walker, Henry vs. Richard Lawrence, John T. Lawrence and Simeon Remsen
Walker, Henry vs. Thomas Napier
Walker, Henry vs. Thomas Sexton
Walker, James vs. James Richards for use of Jonathan Battelle
Walker, Jeff vs. The State
Walker, Jeremiah S. and Adam Alexander vs. James Jones, Jonathan Parish and Samuel Lowther
Walker, Jeremiah S. vs. Aquilla Phelps
Walker, Jeremiah S. and James H. Morrow vs. James Whitfield
Walker, Jim vs. The State
Walker, Joe vs. The State
Walker, John vs. Anson Blake
Walker, John vs. Benjamin Camfax
Walker, John vs. John Cox
Walker, John vs. Jesse Lane
Walker, John vs. The State
Walker, John vs. Lemuel Wynn
Walker, Lewis vs. The State
Walker, Reese vs. The State
Walker, Samuel and Henry Haynes vs. Eleazar Early
Walker, Samuel vs. James Peddy
Walker, Samuel vs. Aquilla Phelps
Walker, Samuel, Jr. vs. Gilbert Longstreet
Walker, Samuel, Jr. vs. John Reed
Walker, Samuel, Jr. vs. John C. Rodgers
Walker, Sanders vs. James Irwin and Felix Bryan
Walker, Sanders vs. Milus C. Nisbet and Alfred M. Nisbet
Walker, Sanders vs. William H. Sayre
Walker, Sanders vs. John G. Smith
Walker, Sanders and Simeon Walker vs. Archibald Stokes
Walker, Sanders and John R. Anderson vs. Simon Walker
Walker, Scott vs. The State
Walker, Sylva vs. James Walker for use of Officers of Court
Walker, Thomas and David Walker vs. Chappel Sledge
Walker, Thomas T. vs. Erwin, Oakman and Co. for use of William Sims and Co.
Walker, Thomas T., George D. F. Medlock and Zachariah Phillips vs. Elijah N. Hascall and David Hascall
Walker, Thomas T. vs. John Huston
Walker, Thomas T. vs. John Lucas
Walker, Thomas T. vs. Michael Moore

Walker, Thomas T. vs. Stokely Morgan
Walker, Thomas T. vs. Aquilla Phelps
Walker, Thomas T. vs. Hosea Webster and George Webster
Walker, Tobe vs. The State
Walker, Warren vs. The State
Walker, Will vs. The State
Walker, William vs. The State
Walker, Wilson vs. The State
Walker and Wynn vs. Penn and Jackson
Wall, Evan vs. The State
Wallace, Benjamin and Nehemiah Schogin vs. John Lang
Wallace, Benjamin vs. Rolan Taylor
Wallace, Warren and Co. vs. Officers of Court
Wallace, William C. vs. The State
Wallace, William W. vs. The State
Waller, C. C. vs. Mason Waller
Waller, David vs. The State
Waller, David L. vs. Amos Marshall
Waller, David S. and Ezekiel P. Fears vs. John Herring
Waller, James B. and Magers Henderson vs. James D. Beall
Waller, James B. vs. Elbert Davis
Waller, Nat vs. Reuben C. Shorter
Waller, Nathaniel G. and Ransom R. Smith vs. Nathaniel
  Waller
Wallis, William C. vs. The State
Walls, John vs. William W. Boyett
Walters, William and David Kennedy vs. John W. Compton and
  John Graves
Walter, William vs. Thomas F. Foster and Augustus B.
  Longstreet
Walthal, Richard vs. The State
Walthall, Charles F. vs. John Robinson
Walthall, Edward vs. John Hanson
Walthall, Edward vs. Hugh Taylor
Walthall, Edward vs. Johnson Wellborn
Walton, Edmond J. vs. Georgia Brown and Eunice A. Holland,
  Guardian
Walton, Edmund J. vs. John Broughton and William Fitzpatrick
Walton, Edward J. vs. John Baynes
Walton, Edward J. vs. Charles M. Furlow
Walton, Edward J. vs. James H. Porter
Walton, Edward J. and John U. Boon vs. G. W. Walker, H. W.
  Clark, Administrator and Allen Lawrence, Sr., Administra-
  tor
Walton, Edward P. vs. James A. Wade
Walton, Guano Co. vs. M. A. Wyatt
Walton, Henry B. vs. Simeon N. Brown for use of Peter W.
  Walton and Harman H. Geiger, Executor
Walton, Hiram vs. Charles N. Horn and James L. Horn
Walton, Isaac L. vs. Thomas P. Chaffin
Walton, Isaac L. and Thomas P. Chaffin vs. James McLaughlin
Walton, Peter W. and Harman H. Geiger, Executor vs. Benjamin
  M. Peeples
Walton, Serena R. vs. John Nolan
Walton, Serina R. vs. Adam G. Saffold for use of Robert D.
  Martin
Wamack, Edmond and Mordecai Shackleford vs. Eli Glover
Wamack, John E. and Edmund Wamack vs. The State
Warbington, Elemander vs. John L. D. Byrom
Warbington, Elemander vs. Thomas Carter
Warbington, Elemander vs. Allen W. Coleman
Warbington, Elemander vs. Robert Ashurst
Warbington, Elemander vs. Isaac Williams

Warbington, Ellimander vs. Stephen Heard
Warbington, Jacob B. vs. Nathaniel Hill
Warbington, Jacob and Allemander Warbinton vs. John
  Griffin and Sally Griffin, Executor
Ward, Amos vs. Alford Clopton
Ward, Amos vs. The State
Ward, Benjamin vs. Burwell Almond
Ward, Benjamin vs. Thomas Greer
Ward, Benjamin vs. The State
Ward, Charlie vs. The State
Ward, F. J. vs. W. T. Repess
Ward, F. J. vs. The State
Ward, Fleming and James Henderson vs. William J. McMichael
Ward, Fleming and E. C. Pope vs. W. A. Pye
Ward, Fleming J. vs. William H. Adams and David R. Adams
Ward, Fleming J. vs. The State
Ward, Francis and Thomas J. Pritchett vs. Jonas H. Holland
Ward, Franklin vs. Whitmel L. Sterling
Ward, James D. S. and Archibald C. Standifer vs. Dunlap
  and Harris
Ward, John E. and Amos Ward, Administrator vs. Mark Thornton
Ward, Nathan F. vs. Elijah N. Hascall
Ward, Nathan F. vs. John Lucas and Walter Lucas
Ward, Nathan F. vs. Appleton Rosseter
Ward, Thomas vs. Hosea Webster and Thomas I. Parmelee
Wardlow, Margaret vs. Middle Georgia and Atlantic Railway
Ware, Allen, Alfred Johnson and John O'Daniel vs. James
  Whitfield
Ware, Clifford vs. The State
Ware, Henry, James Ware, Executor, Wilson Whatley, Executor,
  John K. Binford, Executor and Mary (Ware) Binford vs.
  Samuel McDougal and Mary (Robinson) McDougal
Ware, John vs. William Henderson for use of P. McKeen
Wares, John vs. Nathan L. Hutchens
Warner, N. and Benjamin F. Ward, Administrator vs. McKenzie
  and Bennock
Warner, Nathan and Benjamin F. Ward, Administrator vs.
  Sanders Walker
Warner, Thomas vs. Joseph Hicks
Warner, Thomas vs. Solomon Philips
Warren, Bray vs. Joel Towns
Warren, James vs. William Maxey, Charles S. Jordan and
  John R. Dyer
Washington, George vs. The State
Washington, Richard vs. The State
Waters, Bill (alias Bill Glover) vs. The State
Waters, Lane vs. The State
Waters, William vs. The State
Watkins, Charity, James M. Denson, Administrator and James
  S. Thompson, Administrator vs. William Walker and
  Charity Walker
Watson, Charlie vs. The State
Watson, Gideon vs. Mark Ray
Watson, James vs. W. B. Brightwell
Watson, James and Neill Urquhart vs. Allen Heeth
Watson, James and James F. Walker, Administrator vs. John
  A. Kelly
Watson, James H. vs. The State
Watson, Kate vs. The State
Watson, Nannie vs. The State
Watson, Robert (Bob) vs. The State
Watters, Andrew and Dyer C. Bancroft vs. Thomas J. Smith
Watters, Andrew J. vs. William Bailey and Craton A.J.Flemister

Watters, Andrew J. vs. Wiley W. Barron
Watters, Andrew J., Dyer C. Bancroft and John W. A. Smith
  vs. Russell J. Brown
Watters, Andrew J. vs. William Dukes and Tilmon Niblett
Watters, Andrew J. vs. Henry Horn
Watters, Andrew J. vs. William S. Hurd and Anson Hungerford
Watters, Andrew J. vs. James D. Johnson
Watters, Andrew J. vs. Barthenia Morgan (alias Barthenia
  Kitchens)
Watters, Andrew J., Dyer C. Bancroft and John W. A. Smith
  vs. Thomas J. Smith
Watters, Andrew J. vs. The State
Watters, Andrew J. vs. Swanson and Comer
Watters, Andrew J., Simeon Scales and P. P. Lovejoy vs.
  Francis Swanson, Thomas J. and Alfred M. Pritchett
Watters, Andrew J. vs. Stephen C. Talmadge
Watters, Andrew J. and Sarah J. Watters vs. Robert P.
  Watters and Maximilian H. Hutchison, Guardian
Watters, Andrew J. vs. Worham W. Woodruff, Moris C. Green
  and James H. Green
Watters, Andrew J. vs. Cannon Worsham
Watters, John vs. William B. Taylor
Watters, John C. vs. Joseph S. Anderson
Watters, John C., Dyer C. Bancroft, Executor and Andrew J.
  Watters, Executor vs. Thomas H. Callaway for use of
  Martin W. Stamps
Watters, John C. vs. Central Bank of Georgia
Watters, John C. vs. John Clark
Watters, John C. vs. Doctor F. Compton
Watters, John C. vs. Ransom Cooly for use of Murchison
  Finley
Watters, John C. vs. Durham and Swanson
Watters, John C. vs. Joseph Early
Watters, John C. vs. Christopher Fincher
Watters, John C. vs. William Foster
Watters, John C. and Sherrod H. Gay vs. Daniel Freeman and
  James Freeman, Executor
Watters, John C., Dyer C. Bancroft, Executor and Andrew J.
  Watters, Executor vs. Thomas Hardeman
Watters, John C. vs. Nathan S. Lanier
Watters, John C. vs. John Neal
Watters, John C., Dyer C. Bancroft, Administrator and
  Andrew J. Watters, Administrator vs. W. H. C. Pace,
  George T. Carr and Jeptha M. Cody
Watters, John C., Dyer C. Bancroft, Executor and Andrew J.
  Watters, Executor vs. John U. Price
Watters, John C. vs. Nathan C. Sayre
Watters, John C. vs. Hezekiah Smith
Watters, John C., Andrew J. Watters, Executor and Dyer C.
  Bancroft, Executor vs. Thomas J. Smith
Watters, John C. vs. Davis A. Vason
Watters, John C. and Reuben Jordan, Sr. vs. Benjamin Waits,
  Carden Goolsby, Executor and Evan H. Powell, Executor for
  use of James H. Robinson and James C. Bartlett
Watters, John C. vs. Joseph Washburn, Robert A. Lewis and
  John R. Wilder
Watters, John C. vs. Hugh Wise, Barnabas Wise and Benjamin
  Harrison
Watters, John C., Jr. vs. William Bailey and Craton A. J.
  Flemister
Watters, John C., Jr. vs. Hugh P. Kirkpatrick
Watters, John C., Jr. vs. Tilmon Niblet and John E. Langston
Watters, John C., Jr. vs. John C. Watters

Watters, John C., Sr. vs. Gibson Cornwell
Watters, John C., Sr. vs. Lindsey H. Durham and Francis M.
  Swanson
Watters, John C., Sr., Andrew J. Watters, John C. Watters,
  Jr., James McClure and James Elder vs. The State
Watters, John C., Sr., Andrew J. Watters, John C. Watters,
  Jr., William D. Watters and Levi Q. Phillips vs. The State
Watters, John C., Sr., Dyer C. Bancroft, Executor and
  Andrew J. Watters, Executor vs. Stephen C. Talmadge
Watters, Sarah J. vs. James H. Bryant
Watters, Sarah J. vs. George Comb
Watters, Sarah J. vs. John T. Henderson and Isaac T. Cashing
Watters, Sarah J. vs. Americus V. Mann
Watters, Sarah J. and Americus V. Mann vs. Robert P.
  Watters and Maximilian H. Hutchison, Guardian
Watters, Warren and Alfred Kelly vs. The State
Watters, William vs. John Graves
Watters, William D. vs. William Bailey
Watters, William D., Andrew J. Watters and Gipson H.
  Cornewell vs. Russel J. Brown
Watters, William D. vs. Charles Camp and John R. Camp
Watters, William D. vs. Cornwell and Rodaham
Watters, William D. vs. Edward G. Foster
Watters, William D., Andrew J. Watters and Dyer C. Bancroft
  vs. William S. Hurd and Anson Hungerford
Watters, William D. vs. Richard King
Watters, William D. vs. William Maxey, Charles S. Jordan
  and John R. Dyer
Watters, William D. and Americus vs. Mann vs. Nathan C.
  Munroe
Watters, William D. vs. Thomas Scarborough
Watters, William D. vs. The State
Watters, William D. vs. Edward Varner, Andrew J. Varner
  and Clinton L. Varner
Watters, William D. vs. E. T. White and A. H. Hancock
Watts, Ab vs. The State
Watts, Ludwell vs. William Martin
Watts, Ludwell vs. Pilgrim Williams
Weathersbee, James H. vs. John A. Broughton
Weathersbee, James H. vs. Matthew Whitfield
Weathersbee, John F., Jr., Charlotte Weathersbee, E. H.
  Toland and Isaac Langston vs. J. E. Langston and David
  M. Langston, Administrator
Weathersbee, John F., Jr. vs. Charlotte M. Weathersbee
  (Toland)
Weathersbee, John G., Jr. vs. Joseph Smith
Weathersby, Owen vs. Henry Thomas
Weathersby, Owen, Edward Lovejoy, Administrator and Richard
  Holmes, Administrator vs. Joseph A. Wilson
Weaver, George vs. The State
Weaver, John S. and John B. Davis vs. Green B. Turner
Webb, John vs. Isaac Bailey
Webb, John vs. Hollis Cooley
Webb, John vs. Thomas B. Erwin and Co.
Webb, John vs. Eli S. Shorter
Webb, John vs. The State
Webb, John vs. Desbrew S. Webb
Webb, John B. vs. L. C. Slade
Webb, John B. vs. Lucy Smith
Webb, P. A. vs. E. A. Green
Webb, Thomas, Maxey Smith, James Stagner, John Griffin and
  Reuben Edwards vs. The State
Webb, Thomas P. and Ezekiel Crabtree vs. Aquilla Phelps

Webb, Thomas P. vs. Archibald W. Tanner
Webb, Wyatt V. vs. Caleb Abernethy
Weed, Daniel A., Lurany (Green) Weed and Leroy P. Seymore
  vs. Jacob McDaniel (Minors of) and Robert Brown, Guardian
Weed, Daniel A. vs. Luraney (Green) Weed
Weekes, James vs. Thomas A. Brewer and George Aspinwall
Weekes, James S. and George Stovall vs. Alexander Chambers
Weekes, James S. and David A. Reese vs. James Hines
Weekes, James S. vs. Archibald Stokes
Weekes, James S. vs. Bardwell Billings vs. Joseph F. Wachob
Weekes, James S. vs. John Willson
Weekes, John C. and Benjamin Irvine vs. Abram Jewett
Weekes, Joseph C., Benjamin Irwin vs. John H. Brantley
Weekes, Joseph C. and John O'Daniel vs. Anthony Dyer
Weekws, Joseph C. and James Irvin vs. James Whitfield
Weekes, Joseph C. vs. Nathaniel H. Wildman and Starr Nichols
Weekws, Palemon and Benjamin Amos vs. Charles McIntire,
  Charles W. Rockwell, Charles Kelsey and George A. Kelsey
Weekes, Palemon L. and Benjamin B. Amos vs. Richard Allen
Weekes, Palemon L. vs. Robert C. Beasley and Jarrel
  Beasley, Administrator
Weekes, Palemon L. and Philip B. Pritchett vs. Thomas Cooper
Weekes, Palemon L. vs. Francis M. George
Weekws, Palemon L. vs. John E. Glover
Weekes, Palemon L. vs. Jacob Higinbotham for use of William
  Kilgore
Weekes, Palemon L. vs. Irby Hudson for use of Lewellen W.
  Hudson
Weekes, Palemon L. and Isaac Kendrick vs. Miller Ripley
  and Co.
Weekes, Palemon L. vs. Pleasant Stovall
Weekes, Palemon S. vs. Alexander M. Allen
Weekes, Palemon S. vs. Benjamin Barron
Weekes, William and John Knight, Jr. vs. Robert C. Beasley
  and Jarrel Beasley, Administrator
Weekes, James S. vs. Mark A. Cooper for use of John Nesbit
Weekes, Palemon S. vs. John Nesbit
Weems, John and Timothy Duck vs. Samuel Butts, John Lucas,
  Administrator and William Lee, Administrator
Weems, Samuel and John Weems vs. John Briant
Weems, Samuel vs. William Penn
Weichselbaum, Ed vs. The State
Welborn, Samuel J. vs. William M. Boone
Welborn, Samuel J. vs. Daniel H. Wilcox
Welburn, Samuel J. vs. Bank of The State of Georgia
Welch, Gus vs. The State
Welch, Jack vs. The State
Welch, James R. vs. William Maxey and Stephen C. Talmadge
Welch, James R. vs. Francis M. Swanson
Welch, John and Samuel Hide vs. Alston H. Greene and Joseph
  Buchannon
Welch, William vs. Reuben Jackson
Welch, William vs. The State
Welden, John W. vs. Crawford H. Greer
Welden, John W. vs. William S. Hurd, Anson Hungerford,
  Nehemiah White and Lucius White
Welden, John W. vs. Thomas P. Lane
Welden, John W. vs. Wiley Peddy
Welden, John W. vs. Thomas J. Smith
Welden, John W. vs. John Thomas
Weldon, Andrew vs. Elijah Dodson
Weldon, Asa vs. Elijah N. Hascall
Weldon, Isaac, Andrew Weldon, Executor and Jacob McClendon,

Executor vs. Catharine Weldon
Weldon, Jane vs. James W. Holland
Weldon, Mary, Anna Adams, Administrator and John W. Weldon,
    Administrator vs. David L. Adams, David A. Reese,
    Administrator and Leroy Lawrence, Administrator
Wells, John D. vs. Hamilton Atcheson
Wells, John D. vs. Thompson Curry
Wells, William vs. Charles B. Bowen
Wells, William vs. James Callaway
Wells, William vs. Gilbert Gay, Jr. for use of John Mitchell
Wells, William and Gilbert Gay vs. Sherod H. Gay
Wells, William vs. Christopher Hobson
Wells, William vs. William Pabodie
Wells, William vs. James Pickett
Wells, William vs. James Richards and Willis Richards
Wells, William vs. Hope H. Slatter and Thomas P. Chaires
Wells, William H. vs. Joel Baley
Wells, William H. vs. Thomas Beall and Co.
Wells, William H. and Paschal Murphy vs. John Cole for use
    of George Swain, Jr.
Wells, William H. vs. Robert Robey and Timothy Robey,
    Executor
Weltch, James R. vs. Broddus and Maddox
Weltch, James R. vs. John W. Burney
West, J. A. A. and Emma Walker, Executor vs. Birmingham and
    Atlantic Air Line Railroad, Banking and Navigation Co.
West, J. A. A. and Emma Walker, Executor vs. Eugenia J. Brown
West, John vs. The State
West, L. W. vs. The State
Wester, Edward and William Terry vs. The State
Wester, John R. vs. The State
Westmoreland, John vs. John Carrell
Whaley, Charles vs. John Wall
Whatley, John B. vs. John Wingfield
Whatley, John H. vs. Hamilton Brown and Thomas P. Gwyn
Whatley, John H. vs. Robert B. Camfield
Whatley, John H. and Fleming Jordan vs. Richard Carter
Whatley, John H. vs. William Porter
Whatley, John H. vs. The State
Whatley, Michael and Isaac McClendon vs. Polly Saffold for
    use of Daniel Freeman
Whatley, William B. vs. The State
Whatley, Willis vs. Aquilla Phelps
Whatley, Willis vs. John P. Speir, Charles Labuzan and
    Augustin Slaughter
Whatly, Willis vs. James Smith and Son
Whealas, Joab vs. William Cinguefeld
Wheatley, Jesse, Lucy Wheatley, Sarah Prince and Mary
    Prince vs. The State
Whedbee, Joseph vs. John Black
Whedbee, Joseph vs. Henry C. Hutcheson
Whedbee, Joseph vs. William Penn
Wheeler, William vs. Isaac C. W. T. McKissack
Wheeler, William and John McKissack vs. William A. Slaughter,
    Peyton Holt, Administrator and Sarah Slaughter, Adminis-
    trator
Wheeler, William vs. The State
Wheeles, Isam vs. Robert A. Allen
Wheeles, Littleberry vs. The State
Wheeless, Drury vs. Lewis Wynn and William Johnson
Wheelus, Isom vs. William Maxey
Wheelus, William R. vs. William Freeman
Whitaker, John B. vs. Lawson S. Holland

Whitaker, John B. vs. Hosea Putman
Whitaker, Rachel (Douglass) vs. John B. Whitaker
White, Albert vs. The State
White, Albert vs. The State
White, Anne vs. George W. Owen
White, Clifford vs. The State
White, Cyrus vs. Samuel Butts, John Lucas, Administrator
    and William Lee, Administrator
White, Cyrus, Elijah Dodson and James Willson vs. Anthony
    Dyer
White, Cyrus vs. William Farrington and Luther Cummings
White, Cyrus, Jesse Conner and Jesse Travis vs. William
    Flournoy and William B. Flournoy
White, Cyrus, Lewis C. Holland and James Reeves vs. Arthur
    Ginn
White, Cyrus vs. William J. Hobby
White, Cyrus vs. Edmund Lloyd, John S. Drew, Administrator,
    John Norwood, Administrator and Margaret Norwood,
    Administrator
White, Cyrus vs. Archibald Turner
White, Cyrus and James Trussell vs. Allen McClendon
White, Cyrus and Richard Gray vs. Clark D. Parks and
    Welcom Parks, Guardian
White, Cyrus vs. Edward Smith
White, David vs. Joel Crawford
White, E. T. vs. Braxton Ezell
White, E. T. vs. Charles Goldsborough and James E. Yate
White, Ebenezer T. vs. Joel C. Barnett
White, Ebenzer T. vs. John W. Cheek
White, Ebenezer T. vs. The State
White, Edward vs. John Thurmond
White, George vs. The State
White, Henry vs. The State
White, Henry B. and William F. Flournoy vs. Levicy Bailey
White, Henry B. vs. Hollis Cooley
White, Jacob vs. The State
White, John vs. The State
White, Joseph vs. John Hobson and Christopher Hobson
White, Joseph and John White vs. James King and Thomas
    Sparks, Guardian
White, Joseph vs. Joel Towns
White, Joseph E. and Joshua White vs. Samuel Huston
White, Martin vs. The State
White, Mich vs. The State
White, Moses D. vs. Thomas Black and James Black
White, N. B. and Lucius White vs. Benjamin L. Brittain
White, N. B., H. C. McClure, Executor and H. N. White,
    Executor vs. William S. Minter
White, N. B., H. N. White, Executor and H. C. McClure,
    Executor vs. H. M. Robinson and Co.
White, Valentine vs. Joseph Henderson
White, Valentine vs. John Lasseter for use of James Baldwin
White, Valentine vs. Pope and Stilwell
White, Valentine vs. John P. Speir, Charles Labuzan and
    Augustin Slaughter
White, William H. vs. Bank of The State of Georgia
White, William H. and Thomas J. Bartlett vs. James C.
    Bartlett and George T. Bartlett, Administrator
White, William H. vs. Simon G. Blossom and John H. Clute
White, William H., Jonas H. Holland and John Knight vs.
    Central Bank of Georgia
White, William H. vs. Hollis Cooley and James H. Robinson
White, William H. vs. Henry A. Dickinson

White, William H. and David Knott vs. Samuel C. Elliott and
   John Brownfield
White, William H. vs. Spence M. Grayson
White, William H. vs. David Meriwether and Cincinnatus S.
   Goolsby
White, William H. vs. Gilbraith Simonton, Hugh P. Kirkpatrick,
   Administrator and Agnes J. Simonton, Administrator
White, Zachariah vs. John W. Bridges
White, Zachariah vs. John H. Broadnax
White, Zachariah vs. Benjamin Cook and George Horton
White, Zachariah and Matthias E. Gray vs. Daniel Dawkins
White, Zachariah and David Adams vs. Seaborn Jones
White, Zachariah vs. Robert Melton
White, Zachariah, Joseph Sentell and William Johnson, Jr.
   vs. William H. Parker
White, Zachariah vs. William Penn
White, Zachariah vs. Augustine Slaughter, Charles Labuzan
   and John Hill
White, Zachariah vs. Stephen Tyner
White, Zifford vs. The State
Whitehead, Lucinda and Leonard J. Whitehead, Trustee vs.
   George T. Bartlett
Whitehead, Lucinda and Leonard Whitehead, Trustee vs.
   Madison Goggans
Whitehead, Lucinda, Leonard T. Whitehead and James H.
   Johnston vs. Bryce C. Johnson
Whitehead, Thomas vs. The State
Whitfield, Bolling and Jonas H. Holland vs. James L. Maddux
Whitfield, Clifton vs. The State
Whitfield, Diamond vs. The State
Whitfield, Gaston vs. The State
Whitfield, Georgia and Bolling Whitfield vs. M. A. McDowell
Whitfield, Henry vs. The State
Whitfield, India C. vs. John B. Whitfield
Whitfield, Jacob vs. Griffin, Monticello and Madison
   Railroad Co.
Whitfield, James and Matthew Whitfield vs. Thomas R. Smith,
   Robert Hyslop and William R. Smith
Whitfield, John B. and Elbert W. Baynes vs. Richmond A. Reid
Whitfield, John P. vs. Griffin, Monticello and Madison
   Railroad Co.
Whitfield, Lewis vs. The State
Whitfield, M. C. vs. Jacob Mosteller
Whitfield, M. C. vs. Richmond A. Reid
Whitfield, M. C. vs. M. Whitfield and Leroy M. Wilson,
   Executor
Whitfield, M. C. vs. S. J. Wilborn
Whitfield, Mathew vs. George Hargraves
Whitfield, Mathew vs. Justices of Court
Whitfield, Mathew vs. Hiram Walton and Isaac L. Walton,
   Administrator
Whitfield, Mathew C. vs. Willis P. Chisolem
Whitfield, Matthew vs. Moses Champion and Joseph S.
   Holland, Administrator
Whitfield, Matthew and James Whitfield vs. John Godley and
   Elijah Walker, Executor
Whitfield, Matthew and John Davidson vs. John Hawk
Whitfield, Matthew vs. Jacob Thompson
Whitfield, William H. vs. Linton Cheney
Whitfield, William H. vs. Otis Childs
Whitfield, William H. vs. Joseph Miller
Whitfield, William H. vs. Robert A. McCombs
Whitfield, William H. vs. The State

Whitfield, William H. vs. Zeno D. E. Swinney and William
  M. Day
Whitfield, William H. vs. Joseph E. Veal and Thomas C. Veal
Whitfield, William H. vs. John H. Walker
Whiting, Moses vs. The State
Wiatt, Samuel vs. Robert Guthrie
Wiggins, Lemuel G. R. vs. William V. McGehee
Wilbern, Dr. T. R. vs. The State
Wilborn, Amos and James Glass vs. Tollefair Martin
Wilborn, Amos vs. West Whitaker
Wilborn, Samuel J. vs. Permedus Reynolds and Richard S.
  Simms
Wilborn, Samuel J. vs. Nancy Shepherd
Wilburn, Jack, Elizabeth Wilburn, Executor and Samuel J.
  Wilburn vs. Joseph Bishop and William Brown, Administrator
Wilburn, Jack and Elizabeth Wilburn vs. Nester Pitts
Wilburn, Leonidas C. vs. The State
Wilburn, S. J. and James C. Robinson vs. M. Whitfield and
  J. A. Billips, Administrator
Wilburn, Sam vs. The State
Wilburn, Samuel vs. Wilkinson and Pierce
Wilburn, Samuel C. and William H. Wilburn vs. Jesse Turney
Wilburn, Samuel J. vs. John Bass
Wilburn, Samuel J. vs. McAllen Batts, Larence Baker,
  Administrator and John J. Floyd, Administrator
Wilburn, Samuel J. vs. Hamilton Burge, Alfred Shorter,
  Administrator and Augustus W. Evans, Administrator
Wilburn, Samuel J. vs. Central Bank of Georgia
Wilburn, Samuel J. vs. Sherrod H. Gay
Wilburn, Samuel J. vs. Griffin, Monticello and Madison
  Railroad Co.
Wilburn, Samuel J. vs. Peter Grinnell
Wilburn, Samuel J. vs. Charles B. Hill and John C. Greene
Wilburn, Samuel J. vs. Isaac W. Langston
Wilburn, Samuel J. vs. William D. Luckie
Wilburn, Samuel J. vs. Joseph Newland
Wilburn, Samuel J. vs. William A. Perry
Wilburn, Samuel J. and Elizabeth Wilburn vs. Nester Pitts
Wilburn, Samuel J. vs. Robert O. Usher and Joseph S.
  Anderson
Wilburn, Samuel J. vs. Isham Weaver
Wilburn, Samuel J. and Rees H. Lin vs. James R. Wilbourn
Wilburn, William H., H. H. Wilburn, Administrator, L. O.
  Benton, Eugene Benton and H. V. Robinson vs. F. C. Goolsby
  for use of W. Eugene Wilburn
Wilburne, Thomas vs. Officers of Court
Wilder, John, William Jeffries and Larkin Wilder vs. Bennet
  Crawford
Wilder, Joseph vs. Jesse Curlee
Wilder, Larken vs. Jonathan McDougal
Wilder, Larkin vs. John Baldwin
Wilder, Larkin vs. Elizabeth Calloway
Wilding, James vs. Reuben C. Shorter
Wilkerson, Jeptha vs. William Gresham
Wilkerson, Lemuel vs. The State
Wilkerson, Simeon vs. William Blossomgame
Wilkes, Osborne vs. William Penn
Wilkes, Reuben vs. James D. Head
Wilkins, Cynthia (Youngblood) vs. Aladin Wilkins
Wilkins, Drury and Alexander McDonald vs. Thomas Cargile
  and Robert Germany, Executor
Wilkins, Drury vs. Thomas Gay
Wilkins, Drury vs. Lawson S. Holland

Wilkins, Drury vs. William Jeffries
Wilkins, Drury and Michael Kenimore vs. Thomas Jones
Wilkins, Drury, William Jeffries and William B. Hardy vs.
  Zachariah Phillips
Wilkins, Drury vs. James Robertson and William Walker
Wilkins, Drury vs. James Stratton and Asa E. Stratton
Wilkins, Drury vs. Thomas C. Strickland for use of George
  Jeffries
Wilkins, Drury vs. John Willson
Wilkins, F. P. vs. The State
Wilkinson, Archibald vs. Zacheriah Faulkner
Wilkinson, John vs. William Brown
Wilkinson, John vs. Gustavus Hendrick
Wilkinson, John, James Brown and Elias Landrum vs. Isham
  Hollaway, Judith Hollaway, Administrator
Wilkinson, John vs. Pointon Tucker
Wilkinson, John and Martin Stanly vs. John Wallace, Jr. and
  Owen Woodard, Executor
Wilkinson, John, Sr. vs. Henry T. Smith
Willard, Roswell and Theodore Nims, Administrator vs. James
  Morris
Williams, Aaron vs. Zacheous Gibbs
Williams, Aaron and Christopher Deadwilder vs. Archelas
  Nunnally for use of William Johnson
Williams, Arthur vs. The State
Williams, Asberry vs. The State
Williams, Avington vs. Thomas W. Grimes and Andrew Knox
Williams, Avington, Aaron Williams and Alexander Waldon
  vs. Isaac Hill
Williams, Avington, Benjamin Baldwin and Douglas Watson vs.
  Cary W. Pope, Nancy Pope, John Duke, Polly Duke, David
  Ray and Sally Ray
Williams, Charles vs. The State
Williams, Charles vs. Richard Thurmond
Williams, Charlie vs. The State
Williams, Clinton and Nathan Williams vs. The State
Williams, Daniel vs. Allen W. Coleman
Williams, David M. vs. The State
Williams, Elizabeth and Burney and Dyer vs. Officers of
  Court
Williams, G. P. vs. Ossian Benton
Williams, Henry vs. The State
Williams, Isaac and William Colbert vs. Karsten Peterson
  and John Christian Burkard
Williams, Jacob vs. William H. Pritchett
Williams, James M. vs. William T. Fears and Frances E.
  Fears
Williams, James M. and Matilda Slaughter vs. Francis
  Slaughter
Williams, Jesse vs. The State
Williams, John vs. Charles Cates
Williams, John vs. Jeremiah Pearson
Williams, John vs. The State
Williams, John Dempsy vs. The State
Williams, Joseph vs. The State
Williams, Joseph P. vs. John A. Broughton
Williams, Joseph P. and Charles S. Jordan, Jr. vs. Alfred
  S. Franklin
Williams, Joseph P. vs. James J. Pope for use of Officers
  of Court
Williams, Joseph P. and George W. Winburn vs. Lewis W. Pou
Williams, Luke and Isaac Rosser vs. Eli S. Shorter
Williams, Luke vs. The State

Williams, Luke vs. Earnest S. Young and Jeremiah Pearson
Williams, Mark vs. The State
Williams, Missie vs. The State
Williams, Moses vs. The State
Williams, N. M. vs. Anderson and Hunter
Williams, N. M. vs. W. D. Belcher
Williams, N. M. vs. Joseph Dougherty
Williams, N. M. vs. W. W. Fisher
Williams, N. M. and T. R. Williams vs. The State
Williams, Nathan vs. James Armor and William Armor
Williams, Nathan and Lewis Spear vs. John Baldwin
Williams, Nathan and John Huston vs. Samuel Butts and John
    Lucas, Administrator
Williams, Nathan vs. Joseph Carter
Williams, Nathan vs. Thomas Cooper
Williams, Nathan vs. William D. Crow
Williams, Nathan vs. Thomas J. Davis
Williams, Nathan vs. Richard Garner
Williams, Nathan vs. John Hagan
Williams, Nathan vs. Owen H. Kenan
Williams, Nathan vs. Wyly Rogers
Williams, Ned vs. B. H. Sanders and Co.
Williams, Prince (alias Prince Meriwether) vs. The State
Williams, Rowland, Robert Williams, Executor, Rowland
    Williams, Executor, and John Faver, Executor vs. Baker
    Harris, Wilery Harris, (Orphan), Albus Harris (Orphan),
    Lard Harris, Guardian and Sarah (Harris) Jones (Orphan)
Williams, Samuel vs. Gilbert Longstreet
Williams, Thomas vs. Otho W. Callis
Williams, Thomas vs. Daniel Kilchrist
Williams, Thomas vs. Robert Russell
Williams, Thomas and Samuel Butler vs. William Sims and
    Benjamin Sims
Williams, Thomas vs. The State
Williams, Thomas vs. Amos Warner
Williams, Thomas R. vs. Jonathan Collins and Son
Williams, Thomas R. vs. W. D. Cornwell and N. M. Williams
Williams, Thomas R. and James M. Williams vs. Thomas R.
    Holland
Williams, Thomas R. vs. Henry B. Huff
Williams, Thomas R. vs. Lewis Linch
Williams, Thomas R. and A. W. Land vs. William S. Minter
Williams, Thomas R. and James M. Williams vs. William S.
    Minter
Williams, W. S. vs. Griffin, Monticello and Madison Rail-
    road Co.
Williams, Wesley vs. The State
Williams, William and Rufus W. Phillips vs. William
    Davenport
Williams, William S. and Luke Williams vs. John R. Dickin
    for use of George T. Treadway and Hosea B. Blain
Williams, William S. vs. Gould and Bulkley
Williams, William S. vs. Joseph S. Holland
Williams, William S. vs. William Maxey and James C. Bartlett
Williams, William S. vs. Catharine Portwood for use of John
    R. Jones
Williams, William S. vs. Henry C. Seymore
Williams, William S. and James H. Williams vs. Joseph
    Stovall
Williams, William S. vs. Elizabeth Williams
Williams, William S. vs. James M. Williams
Williams, William T., Luke Williams and Benjamin Persons
    vs. Central Bank of Georgia

Williams, Zachariah vs. John Robinson
Williamson, Isaac, Nathan Williams, Executor and Stokely
  Morgan, Executor vs. Adolphus H. Gibson and William Gilbert
Williamson, James and James Cargile vs. James H. Gordon
Williamson, James vs. Joseph Johnson and John Baldwin
Williamson, James and James Cargile vs. John Owen
Williamson, James vs. Jeremiah Pearson
Williamson, James vs. Thomas Smith
Williamson, James H. vs. Woody Dozier
Williamson, Micajah vs. The State
Williamson, Pleasant vs. Lyman Benham
Williamson, Pleasant vs. Wesley Glazier
Williamson, Pleasant vs. Mathew Gregory
Williamson, Pleasant vs. Thomas McGehee
Williamson, Pleasant vs. Pope and Stilwell
Williamson, Richard vs. James Mullins
Williamson, Robert, Mary Williamson, Executor and Willis
  Williamson, Executor vs. Jarrel Beasley
Williamson, Robert vs. John Buchannon, Priscilla Buchannon,
  Administrator and Joseph Buchannon, Administrator
Williamson, Robert vs. Elizabeth Calloway
Williamson, Robert and Mary Williamson, Executor vs. John
  Cargile, Lavinia M. Cargile, Joseph J. W. Cargile, Runno
  B. M. Cargile, Henry Dillon, Nancy (Cargile) Dillon and
  Charles Cargile
Williamson, Robert and Francis McClendon vs. William G.
  Gilbert and Felix H. Gilbert
Williamson, Robert vs. Stephen W. Harris, Eli S. Shorter,
  Executor, Seaborn Jones, Executor, William Wilkins,
  Executor and Sarah H. Harris, Executor
Williamson, Robert vs. David Hascall
Williamson, Robert vs. Matthew Hawkins
Williamson, Robert vs. John Heard, Annis Heard, Executor,
  John S. Drew, Executor, Stephen Heard, Executor and
  Spencer Heard, Executor
Williamson, Robert vs. Isaac Hill
Williamson, Robert vs. John Hobson and Christopher Hobson
Williamson, Robert vs. George Humphreys
Williamson, Robert vs. Seaborn Jones
Williamson, Robert, James Cargile and William Cargile vs.
  Charles Morgan
Williamson, Robert vs. James Mullens
Williamson, Robert vs. Francis McClendon
Williamson, Robert vs. The State
Williamson, Robert vs. John Stephens and Johnson Wellborn
Williamson, Robert vs. Philip Thurmond
Williamson, Robert vs. Zadock Woolley
Williamson, William, James Callaway and Hugh MacDonald vs.
  Joshua Callaway and Elizabeth Callaway, Administrator
Williamson, William vs. John Hobson and Christopher Hobson
Williamson, William vs. Henry C. Hutchison
Williamson, William vs. James Richards
Williamson, William vs. The State
Williamson, William and James Callaway vs. John Willson
Williamson, William T. vs. The State
Williamson, William W. vs. Bank of Darien
Williamson, William W. and Reuben Jordan vs. Central Bank
  of Georgia
Williamson, William W. vs. Martin Cochran and John S.
  Cochran, Administrator
Williamson, William W. vs. James Cunningham and Robert
  Cunningham, Administrator
Williamson, William W. vs. John R. Dickin

Williamson, William W. vs. Samuel Fulton
Williamson, William W. vs. Insurance Bank of Columbus
Williamson, William W. vs. David Merriwether
Williamson, William W. vs. Henry Mims
Williamson, William W. vs. Burton Mullens for use of Israel
Beckwith
Williamson, William W. and William Ramey vs. Simeon Scales
Williamson, William W. and Davis A. Reese vs. Isaac G.
Seymour
Williamson, William W. vs. Gilbraith Simonton and William
V. Burney
Williamson, William W. vs. Thomas J. Smith and William M.
Broddus
Williamson, William W. vs. Alex M. Sparks
Williamson, William W. vs. The State
Williamson, William W. vs. Charles W. C. Wright
Williamson, Zorobabel, Green Williamson, Administrator and
William Williamson, Administrator vs. Robert Norris and
William D. Garland, Administrator
Williford, David vs. John Robertson
Willingham, Archibald and Majers Henderson vs. James
Whitfield
Willingham, Isaac vs. Thornton Bostick
Willingham, Jeremiah vs. Thomas Wellborn and Williamson
Robey
Willingham, Joe vs. The State
Willingham, William vs. Thomas J. Davis
Willingham, William vs. Hugh P. Kirkpatrick
Willingham, William and Albert B. Vaughn vs. Aquilla Phelps
Willingham, William, Isaac Willingham, Administrator,
Charles D. Bostick and John Edwards vs. John Powell
Willis, John C. and Francis Wisdom vs. James Bradley
Willis, Robert vs. John Willson, John Hill, Executor, James
Willson, Executor, Fleming Jordan, Executor and David A.
Reese, Executor
Willis, Robert L. vs. William Cargile
Willis, Robert L. vs. Thomas Carter
Willis, Robert L. and Charles H. Webb vs. Robert Germany
Willis, Robert L. vs. Edward Hicks and Joel Baley
Willson, Abel P. and Thomas H. B. Rivers vs. John Marrow
Willson, Abel P. and John F. Dismukes vs. Martin Puckett
and James W. Vaughn, Administrator
Willson, Alford G. and John P. Moats vs. Cary Wood
Willson, Arcillis vs. The State
Willson, Benjamin, David Cameron and John Willson vs.
William Robinson and Jesse J. Robinson
Willson, Benjamin H. and James Willson vs. Anthony Dyer
Willson, Benjamin H., James Willson and Elijah Dodson vs.
James Whitfield
Willson, Colonel John vs. Isaac Hart
Willson, Fields vs. Cyrus White
Willson, Frank vs. The State
Willson, George vs. The State
Willson, Hiram vs. James E. Willson
Willson, James, Willima Russell and Thomas Blair vs.
Jarrett Lynch
Willson, John vs. William Broughton
Willson, John, John Hill, Executor, Fleming Jordan,
Executor, David A. Reese, Executor and James Willson,
Executor vs. Thomas Cargile and Robert Germany, Executor
Willson, John, John Hill, Executor, David A. Reese,
Executor, Fleming Jordan, Executor and James Willson,
Executor vs. Gilbert Cleland

Willson, John, Fleming Jordan, Executor, John Hill, Executor
James Willson, Executor and David A. Reese, Executor vs.
William H. Crane and Joseph Kopman
Willson, John, John Hill, Executor, Fleming Jordan, Executor,
David A. Reese, Executor, James Willson, Executor and
Robert L. Willis vs. Robert Germany
Willson, John vs. Buckner Harris for use of Early Harris
Willson, John, John Hill, Executor, Fleming Jordan, Executor
John Hill, Executor, Davis, James Willson and David A.
Reese vs. Alsea Holifield
Willson, John and John Hill, Executor vs. Andrew Kerr, John
Kerr and Alexander Graham
Willson, John vs. Green McAfee and William Armstrong,
Administrator
Willson, John, John Hill, Executor, James Willson, Executor,
Fleming Jordan, Executor and David A. Reese, Executor vs.
Clark D. Parks and Welcom Parks, Guardian
Willson, John, John Hill, Executor, James Willson, Executor,
Fleming Jordan, Executor, and David A. Reese, Executor
vs. Lewis Peacock
Willson, John and John Hill, Executor vs. Solomon Perteet
and Jeremiah Pearson, Guardian
Willson, John vs. David Silden
Willson, John, James Willson, Executor, John Hill, Executor,
David A. Reese, Executor and Fleming Jordan, Executor vs.
Martha Turner, Willson Pope, Administrator and Gidion
Pope, Administrator
Willson, Joseph and Sally Willson, Executor vs. Lawson S.
Holland
Willson, Joseph vs. Rezin E. Mabry
Willson, Joseph vs. John Willson
Willson, Lawrence L. vs. Charles Pearson
Willson, Leroy M. vs. John Baldwin and Martha Baldwin,
Administrator
Willson, William L., Simon Lovejoy and Allen McClendon vs.
Jonathan Jewett, Gordon Abell and James N. Codwise
Wilson, Abe vs. The State
Wilson, Abel P. and William S. Flemister vs. Moses Bright-
well
Wilson, Abel P. vs. Central Bank of Georgia
Wilson, Abel P. vs. John F. Comer
Wilson, Abel P. vs. Samuel Griswold
Wilson, Abel P. and Benjamin J. Wilson vs. V. Haralson and
Robert M. Echols, Administrator
Wilson, Abel P. vs. Thomas Hardeman
Wilson, Abel P. and I. L. Parker vs. William S. Hurd and
Anson Hungerford
Wilson, Abel P. vs. James S. Johnson
Wilson, Abel P. vs. William Maxey and Joshua Hill
Wilson, Abel P. and Sarah Wilson vs. Jethro Mobley
Wilson, Abel P. vs. Evan H. Powell
Wilson, Abel P. vs. Thomas G. Sanford
Wilson, Abel P. vs. Gilbreath Simonton and William V. Burney
Wilson, Abel P. vs. Thomas I. Smith and William M. Broddus
Wilson, Abel P. vs. Robert Tolefree
Wilson, Abel P. vs. Thomas H. Tuggle
Wilson, Abel P. and John F. Dismukes vs. William J. L.
Tuggle
Wilson, Abel P. and William L. Flemister vs. Henry Vaughn
Wilson, Abel P., William H. Wyatt and Moses Chafin vs.
James Ware, Joseph A. Ware, Minor, and Nathan Massey,
Guardian
Wilson, Andrew J. vs. Jesse Loyall

Wilson, Andrew J. vs. William Maxey and Joshua Hill
Wilson, Andrew J. and Nancy Wilson vs. Thomas Traylor
Wilson, Arkillis vs. Humphry Edmondson
Wilson, Benjamin J. and Abel P. Wilson vs. John Murrow
Wilson, Bethenia vs. Elizabeth Kitchens
Wilson, Charles John vs. The State
Wilson, Dave vs. The State
Wilson, Fields vs. Eli Glover and John Cashin
Wilson, Fields vs. Joseph Johnson
Wilson, Fields vs. Joseph Johnson
Wilson, Fields vs. John McCulloch
Wilson, Fields vs. Thomas Napier
Wilson, Fields vs. Henry Walker for use of Michael Moore
Wilson, Fields vs. Joseph Watters
Wilson, Fields vs. Robert Williamson
Wilson, George J. vs. Tilmon Niblet and John E. Langston
Wilson, Graves, James Wilson and Edward A. Elder vs. The
    State
Wilson, Graves S. vs. Richard J. Loyall and William Andrews
Wilson, Hugh vs. Thomas J. Casey
Wilson, James vs. Edward Bird for use of Felix Gilbert
Wilson, James vs. David Witt
Wilson, James W. vs. The State
Wilson, James W. vs. William G. Swanson
Wilson, Jim vs. The State
Wilson, John, John Hill, Executor, James Wilson, Executor,
    Fleming Jordan, Executor and David A. Reese, Executor vs.
    Caleb Woodley
Wilson, John L. and Leonard Wilson vs. James Grier
Wilson, John L. vs. William Scott
Wilson, Joseph vs. Elias Benham
Wilson, Joseph vs. Jeremiah Pearson
Wilson, Joseph vs. Charles Wood
Wilson, Larkin, Henry Kellam and W. M. Wilder vs. Thomas J.
    Davis
Wilson, Lawrence L., John Mitchell and John N. Carter vs.
    The State
Wilson, Leonard and John P. Wilson vs. Moses E. Bates
Wilson, Leonard and William A. Moore vs. Charles F. V.
    Reeves
Wilson, Martha vs. The State
Wilson, Mrs. Mary E. vs. James F. Blackwell
Wilson, Nelson vs. John R. Skeggs
Wilson, Nelson vs. The State
Wilson, Pat vs. The State
Wilson, Rachel (Lowry) vs. William L. Wilson
Wilson, Randol P. vs. The State
Wilson, Robert vs. The State
Wilson, Sarah vs. Willis Whatley and Jefferson Adams
Wilson, Sarah vs. Eaton P. Wilson for use of John Reid
Wilson, Thomas vs. Isaac Bailey
Wilson, Thomas vs. Jarrel Beasly
Wilson, Thomas vs. John Reaves
Wilson, Thomas vs. The State
Wilson, Thomas vs. Robert Williamson
Wilson, William and Burney and Dyer vs. James W. Vaughn
Wilson, Willie and Grant Goolsby vs. The State
Wimbush, William vs. The State
Winfrey, John vs. John Bones
Winfrey, John vs. Porter Fleming
Winfrey, John vs. Benjamin Peavy
Winfrey, John vs. James H. Shi
Winfrey, John vs. Thomas Wyatt

Winn, Francis, James Edwards, Peter Douglass and John
Douglass vs. John Allen
Winn, Francis and James Edwards vs. John Armstrong
Winne, Francis vs. Larkin Clark
Winslett, John C. and Rice B. Nowles vs. Nathaniel Gordon
for use of Charles P. Gordon
Winsted, Samuel vs. James Richards
Winstell, John C. vs. Hamilton Brown, Peyton Gwyn and
James Gwyn
Winstell, John C. vs. Eli Peavy
Wisdom, Elenor and Hamilton Wisdom vs. The State
Wisdom, Francis vs. Mathew Mitchell
Wise, Hugh, Augustus Wise, Barnabas Wise, William Vickers,
David Johnson and Nicholas Johnson vs. The State
Wise, Joel vs. Willie Alford
Wise, Joel vs. William P. Culbertson
Wise, Joel vs. Nicholas Johnson
Wise, Joel vs. William Sanders
Wise, Joel vs. The State
Wise, John vs. The State
Wise, Joseph A. vs. William Maxey and Charles S. Jordan
Wise, Patton vs. Smith Rumley
Wise, Patton, William Traylor, Executor, Piram Linsey,
Executor, Betsey Wise, Executor and Zaccheus Phillips
vs. William Scott
Wise, Patton vs. The State
Wise, Patton and Z. Phillips vs. Alexander Steed
Wise, Patton, William Traylor, Executor, Parham Lindsay,
Executor and Elizabeth Wise, Executor vs. Henry Walker,
Abner Chapman and Michael Moore for use of Zachariah
Phillips, Jr.
Wise, Patton vs. Joel Wise
Wise, William, Isaac H. Slaughter, Moses Slaughter and
William Slaughter vs. The State
Wiseman, William vs. Robert Germany
Womack, James and Alsey Hodge vs. The State
Wommack, Edward vs. James Lumpkin
Wood, Amasa and James Smith vs. Officers of Court
Wood, James E. and Shadrach G. McMichael vs. William W.
Anderson
Wood, James E. vs. William Bailey and Crayton A. J.
Flemister
Wood, James E. vs. Henry A. Dickinson
Wood, James E. vs. Artemus Goolsby
Wood, James E. vs. William S. Hurd and Anson Hungerford
Wood, James E. vs. John C. Maddux and William D. Maddux
Wood, James E. vs. William Maxey and Charles S. Jordan
Wood, James E. and William Williams vs. Josiah Newman
Wood, James E. vs. Tilmon Niblett and John E. Langston
Wood, James E. vs. Francis M. Swanson
Wood, James M., Lucinda Wood and Georgianna Wood vs. The
State
Wood, John vs. Jeremiah Beall
Wood, John vs. Samuel Butts and John Lucas, Administrator
Wood, John vs. Eli Glover and John Cashin
Wood, John and Job Bird vs. Mattox Mays
Wood, John vs. Thomas Napier
Wood, John and Nancy Wooton vs. The State
Wood, Joshua J. vs. Martha Egnew for use of William Egnew
Wood, Thomas vs. Hamilton Brown, Thomas P. Gwyn and James
Gwyn
Wood, William vs. William Hodges
Wood, Woody vs. The State

Woodfin, Moses and John K. Binford vs. Jesse Loyall
Woodfin, Moses and John K. Benford vs. Reuben C. Shorter
Woodfin, Moses vs. The State
Woodruff, Clifford vs. Alston H. Greene and Joseph Buchannan
Woodruff, Clifford, Jr. vs. George Phillips for use of
  John K. Benford
Woodruff, David, Isaac Brant and Charles Murdock vs. George
  Alexander and Asa E. Stratton
Woodruff, James vs. John Abercrombie
Woodruff, James vs. Winkfield Bagwell
Woodruff, James vs. Samuel Butts and John Lucas, Administra-
  tor
Woodruff, James and Joseph Price vs. William H. Crawford
Woodruff, James and William W. Kennon vs. John M. Dooley
Woodruff, James vs. Anthony Dyer and Otis Dyer
Woodruff, James vs. John Fluker
Woodruff, James vs. Wesley Glazier
Woodruff, James vs. Eli Glover
Woodruff, James vs. Owen H. Kenan for use of Willis Grady
  and Augustus Slaughter
Woodruff, James vs. Jesse Loyal
Woodruff, James vs. John Nesbit
Woodruff, James vs. Robert Robey
Woodruff, James and Agatha Woodruff vs. Ezekiel Smith,
  Thomas T. Walker, Executor, Ferebee Walker, Executor,
  John C. Smith, Executor, George D. F. Medlock, Executor,
  Exekiel F. Smith, Executor and William Smith, Executor
Woodruff, James vs. John Willson
Woodruff, James vs. Joseph Woodruff
Woolsey, William W., Abraham M. Woolsey, John M. Woolsey
  and William C. Woolsey vs. Eli Glover
Wooten, Bartly vs. The State
Wooten, John vs. Officers of Court
Wooten, Riley vs. The State
Wooten, William vs. Samuel Butts, John Lucas, Administrator
  and William Lee, Administrator
Wooton, John vs. The State
Wooton, William vs. Anthony Dyer
Worsham, James C., Priscilla Banks and Simeon Scales vs.
  Jonas H. Holland
Worthy, Leonard vs. Alston H. Greene and Joseph Buchannon
Worthy, Leonard vs. Matthew Williams
Wosshum, John vs. John R. Anderson
Wright, Benjamin M., John W. Crabtree, Silas Grubbs and
  Ezekiel Crabtree vs. Aquilla Phelps
Wright, Charles W. C., John C. Gibson, and Lovewell C.
  Flewellen vs. Central Bank of Georgia
Wright, Charles W. C. vs. William W. Chapman and William
  A. Ross
Wright, Charles W. C. vs. Otis Childs
Wright, Charles W. C. and Samuel A. Flournoy vs. Commercial
  Bank of Macon
Wright, Charles W. C. vs. James Fellows, John Wadsworth and
  Richard S. Fellows
Wright, Charles W. C. vs. Jonas H. Holland
Wright, Charles W. C. and John C. Gibson vs. Frances
  Johnston
Wright, Charles W. C. vs. Jeremiah Pearson
Wright, Charles W. C. vs. Francis Tomes, Sr., William H.
  Miller and Francis Tomes, Jr.
Wright, David vs. William H. Crenshaw and Joseph Barrow
Wright, James vs. The State
Wright, James B. vs. James Richards

Wright, John E. vs. Mary Cargile
Wright, Mary and Artemus Goolsby, Trustee vs. Smith and
  Ezzard
Wright, Michael vs. Caleb Abernethy
Wright, Michael vs. Jarrel Beasley
Wright, Michael and Presley Dodson vs. William Evans,
  Thomas Evans, Administrator and Charles Evans, Administra-
  tor
Wright, Michael vs. Elijah N. Hascall
Wright, Michael, Wright Hill and Jacob Warbington vs.
  Fleming Jourden
Wright, Michael vs. John T. Lankey, Drury Towns, Adminis-
  trator, Ann (Lankey) Towns and James Daniel, Administrator
Wright, Michael and John Love vs. William McMichael, Richard
  Carter, Executor, John McMichael, Executor and Elizabeth
  McMichael, Executor
Wright, Michael and Alsea Holifield vs. Samuel Paschall,
  Burwell Greene, Administrator and Elizabeth Paschall,
  Administrator
Wright, Michael, Wright Hill and Jacob Warbington vs.
  William Swanson
Wright, Michael vs. Henry Walker and Michael Moore
Wright, Robert A., John S. Weaver and William B. Wright vs.
  Green B. Turner
Wright, William vs. The State
Wyatt, George W. vs. Thomas B. Baldwin and Benjamin Harris,
  Executor
Wyatt, Ike vs. The State
Wyatt, Isaac T. and John W. Wyatt vs. George T. Bartlett
Wyatt, Isaac T. vs. V. H. Crawley and John T. Eckles
Wyatt, Isaac T., John A. Broughton, W. A. Broughton,
  Executor and Lessie Speer, Executor vs. A. G. Foster and
  F. C. Foster, Executor
Wyatt, Isaac T. and John W. Wyatt vs. Jonas H. Holland
Wyatt, Isaac T. vs. Officers of Court
Wyatt, Isaac T. vs. Permenus R. Thomason
Wyatt, Isaac T. vs. Joseph Vason and James M. Few
Wyatt, Isaac T. vs. Daniel H. Wilcox, Leonard Y. Gibbs and
  William C. McMurphy
Wyatt, J. T. vs. Augustus B. Sharp
Wyatt, John vs. Jonas Hail
Wyatt, John vs. Thomas Stamps
Wyatt, John W. and Crayton A. J. Flemister vs. Horace J.
  Bates
Wyatt, John W. and A. C. Freeman vs. John Baynes
Wyatt, John W., J. T. Wyatt and G. W. Wyatt vs. C. M.
  Boykin and M. V. Boykin
Wyatt, John W. vs. Jackson Chany
Wyatt, John W. vs. William W. Clark
Wyatt, John W. vs. Michael L. Colbert
Wyatt, John W. vs. Thomas J. Comer, Jr.
Wyatt, John W. vs. Hollis Cooley and Dyer C. Bancroft
Wyatt, John W. vs. Artemeous Gould, William H. Bulkley and
  John T. Bulkley
Wyatt, John W. vs. William S. Hurd and Anson Hungerford, Jr.
Wyatt, John W. vs. Sherman Jessup and Co.
Wyatt, John W. and Samuel J. Wilborn vs. Adam W. Jones
Wyatt, John W. vs. William D. Maddux
Wyatt, John W. vs. William Mascey and Charles Jordan
Wyatt, John W. vs. Joel C. McDowell
Wyatt, John W. vs. Merchants and Planters Bank
Wyatt, John W. vs. Marcus A. Pharr and Henry D. Snelling
Wyatt, John W., William Bailey and William V. Seat vs.

Martin Puckett and James W. Vaughn
Wyatt, John W. and William H. Wyatt, Jr. vs. Martin
  Puckett and James W. Vaughn, Administrator
Wyatt, John W. vs. William Ross
Wyatt, John W. vs. Albert Rowan
Wyatt, John W. vs. William A. Sidwell
Wyatt, John W. vs. Uriah Smith
Wyatt, John W. vs. The State
Wyatt, John W. vs. George B. Stovall
Wyatt, John W. vs. Robert Tolefree
Wyatt, John W. vs. John Truit and Watson Shaw, Administrator
Wyatt, John W. and Crayton A. J. Flemister vs. Cary Wood
Wyatt, Pleas vs. The State
Wyatt, Thomas vs. John Combs
Wyatt, Thomas, John W. Wyatt, Executor, Nancey Wyatt,
  Executor, George W. Wyatt, Executor, Joseph B. Slack,
  Executor and Isaac L. Walton vs. Guy Smith and Lucius T.
  Campbell, Administrator
Wyatt, William H. vs. William R. Berner
Wyatt, William H. vs. Hollis Cooley and Dyer C. Bancroft
Wyatt, William H. and John W. Wyatt vs. Elijah Dodson, Joel
  W. Dodson, Administrator and Leah Dodson, Administrator
  for use of James Cameron
Wyatt, William H. vs. Joseph M. Evans and John P. Evans
Wyatt, William H. vs. Catharine Fannin and John W. Porter
Wyatt, William H. vs. Porter Fleming
Wyatt, William H. vs. Thomas Harwell
Wyatt, William H. vs. Charles F. Hoffman for use of Daniel
  Hand
Wyatt, William H. vs. Holland and Kirkpatrick
Wyatt, William H. vs. Lawson S. Holland
Wyatt, William H. and John W. Wyatt vs. James H. Hollings-
  worth, Albert Smith and Joseph J. Scranton
Wyatt, William H. vs. Launcelot Johnston and John Robson
Wyatt, William H., John H. Wyatt and Jefferson E. Spears
  vs. Elijah E. Jones
Wyatt, William H. vs. Robert Kellam and William Maxey
Wyatt, William H. vs. Oliver H. Lee
Wyatt, William H. vs. John C. Smith and James H. Shi (Shy)
Wyatt, William H. vs. Ransom H. Smith
Wyatt, William H. vs. Thomas I. Smith and William M. Broddus
Wyatt, William H. vs. Francis Spears
Wyatt, William H., T. Wyatt, Administrator and C. Wyatt,
  Administrator vs. J. E. Speer
Wyatt, William H. vs. Stephen C. Talmadge
Wyatt, William H., Jr. and John W. Wyatt, Jr. vs. Nathan
  Massey
Wyatt, William H., Jr. vs. Watson Shaw
Wyatt, William H., Jr. vs. Madison B. Snellings for use of
  John Wingfield and Alfred W. Wingfield
Wyatt, William H., Jr. vs. John Spearman
Wyatt, William H., Jr. vs. Green B. Turner
Wyatt, William H., Jr. vs. Matthew Whitfield
Wynens, Allen vs. Jackson Fitzpatrick and John McLane
Wynens, Elisha vs. Matthew Whitfield, John F. Patterson,
  Executor, Leroy M. Willson, Executor and Pleasant Willson,
  Executor
Wynens, Elisha L. and Paul Perkins vs. Thomas I. Smith
Wynens, Elisha S., Charles T. Willson and James L. Standifer
  vs. Crawford H. Greer
Wynens, Elisha S., James L. Standifer and Charles T.
  Willson vs. John R. Greer
Wynens, John vs. Andrew H. Beall

Wynens, John vs. Stephen W. Beasley
Wynens, John, Jarrel Beasley and Stephen W. Beasley vs.
  Central Bank of Georgia
Wynens, John, John Hill and Stephen W. Beasley vs. Central
  Bank of Georgia
Wynens, John and Robert C. Beasley vs. Jesse Cherry
Wynens, John and James H. Morrow vs. Jesse Cherry
Wynens, John vs. Carleton B. Cole
Wynens, John vs. Thomas B. Erwin
Wynens, John vs. Jackson Fitzpatrick
Wynens, John vs. Carden Goolsby
Wynens, John vs. Francis Irwin
Wynens, John vs. William G. Lane
Wynens, John and Stephen W. Beasley vs. James T. I. Orr
Wynens, John vs. Albert W. Smith
Wynens, John, John Beck and Samuel McDaniel vs. Richard
  Tankersly
Wynens, John and Warren Jourdan vs. John Thomas
Wynens, John and Elisha S. Wynens vs. Thomas J. Walton
Wynens, John and Robert H. Daniel vs. James Whitfield
Wyning, John vs. Joseph B. Green
Wynn, Lemuel vs. Gabriel Gunn
Wynn, Lemuel and George Bell vs. The State
Wynn, Lewis and R. W. Wynn vs. Giles Griswold
Wynn, Richmond W. vs. James M. Dunn and Jeremiah Clark
Wynn, Richmond W. vs. Josiah King
Wynn, Richmond W. vs. James P. Knowles
Wynn, Richmond W. vs. Joshua Lundy
Wynn, Richmond W. vs. Thomas McGehee
Wynn, Richmond W. vs. John P. Speer, Charles Labuzan and
  Augustin Slaughter
Wynn, Robert B. vs. The State
Wynn, Thomas vs. William H. Cargile
Wynn, Thomas and John W. Melson vs. The State
Wynn, W. D. vs. S. R. Baynes for use of Officers of Court
Wynn, W. D. vs. W. A. Broughton and A. M. Spear
Wynn, Williamson vs. Isaac Hill
Wynne, Lemuel vs. Thomas Crowder and James Crowder

Yancey, Layton vs. Russell J. Brown for use of Sherrod H.
  Gay
Yancey, Layton, Robert C. Barnes and Jeremiah M. Gilstrap
  vs. The State
Yancey, Richard D. vs. Josiah Newman
Yancey, Thomas vs. The State
Yancy, Benjamin vs. The State
Yancy, Benjamin D. vs. William S. Hurd and Anson Hungerford
Yancy, Benjamin D. vs. Coleman R. Reynolds
Yancy, Benjamin D. vs. Richard Yancy
Yancy, George and Robert Watley vs. The State
Yancy, James vs. The State
Yancy, Layton vs. William F. Davis for use of Newton
  Manufacturing Co.
Yancy, Layton vs. Christopher Fincher for use of Newton
  Manufacturing Co.
Yancy, Layton vs. William S. Hurd and Anson Hungerford
Yancy, Layton and Pheba Yancy vs. Gilbert W. Shaw
Yancy, Layton vs. Ebenezer T. White
Yancy, Layton vs. Richard D. Yancy
Yancy, Lewis vs. The State
Yancy, Lewis D. vs. John W. Burney and John R. Dyer
Yancy, Lewis D. vs. John C. Gibson
Yancy, Lewis D. and John C. Watters vs. Cardin Goolsby

Yancy, Phoebe vs. Cornelius Johnston
Yancy, Polly vs. William Hill
Yancy, Richard vs. Officers of Court
Yancy, Richard D. vs. William S. Hurd, Anson Hungerford,
  Lucius White and Nehemiah B. White
Yancy, Thomas and Gilbert W. Shaw vs. John B. Pickett
Yancy, Thomas J. vs. Nancy Yancy
Yancy, Thomas Y. vs. James L. Epps and Josiah B. Epps,
  Administrator
Yarbrough, James W. and Jacob J. Hollingsworth vs. John
  Bones and Samuel Bones
Yarbrough, James W. and Jacob J. Hollingsworth vs. Andrew
  Kerr, John Kerr and James Hope
Yarbrough, James W. and Jacob J. Hollingsworth vs. John
  Moore and Joseph Davis
Yarbrough, Joseph vs. Henry Strickland
Yeomans, Martin vs. Jonathan Jewett and James N. Codwise
Yeomans, Martin vs. Jeremiah Pearson
Yonge, William P. vs. Henry Kirby
Young, Earnest L. and Jeremiah Pearson, Administrator vs.
  George T. Young and Robert Tolefree
Young, Ernest L. and Jeremiah Pearson vs. David Meriwether
  and Matilda Ann Meriwether
Young, Gasham and John Rivers, Guardian vs. Robert Trippe
Young, Green vs. Abner Chapman, Michael Moore and Henry
  Walker
Young, Greene and Stephen Hawkins vs. Samuel Harper and
  Polley Steele
Young, Greene vs. Alexander Steel
Young, Harrison vs. Henry Walker for use of Michael Moore
Young, John vs. Lindsay H. Durham and Dyer C. Bancroft
Young, John and Isaac H. Slaughter vs. Josiah Newman
Young, John N. vs. Jarrel O. Towns
Young, William vs. The State
Young, William P. vs. John Walton
Youngblood, Abemilich vs. Hamilton Brown, Peyton Gwyn and
  James Gwyn
Youngblood, Abimeleck vs. Susannah Perminter
Youngblood, Abimilech and Asa O. Stratten vs. John H.
  Brantly
Youngblood, Abimilech vs. The State

Zinn, Edwin vs. Edward Hicks and Joel Baley
Zinn, Jacob vs. Abbe Benton
Zinn, Jacob and Edwin Zinn vs. Hollis Cooley
Zinn, Jacob vs. William Fincher
Zinn, Jacob vs. John Henderson
Zinn, Jacob vs. Edward Hicks and Co.
Zinn, Jacob vs. John Hill, Augustin Slaughter and Charles
  Labuzan
Zinnamon, Charles vs. The State

CHAPTER VI

INFERIOR COURT CASE FILES, 1804-1902
Record Group 179-2-7

This series contains original unbound papers which formed
portions of civil and criminal case files involving, but not
limited to, (1) bail bonds, (2) misdemeanors, (3) debts, (4)
fi fas, (5) attachments and (6) assumsits. The records have
been flattened, cleaned and placed in folders. They are grouped
chronologically by time span of considerable length and arranged
alphabetically by name of defendant. There is a cross-reference
available in Box 1 that lists the surnames of the plaintiffs
alphabetically.

Aaron, James C. (def.) vs. Robert Bayne (plf.)
Aaron, Mitchel (def.) vs. William H. Bailey (plf.), James
    H. Robinson (exor.) and Mary Ann Bailey (exrx.)
Adams, Caleb B. (def.) and Mark H. Mickelberry (def.) vs.
    Jonas H. Holland (plf.)
Alexander, Adam (def.), Elijah N. Hascall (def.) and James
    H. Morrow (def.) vs. William P. Beers (plf.)
Alexander, Adam (def.) vs. John McKenzie (plf.) and Peter
    Bennoch (plf.)
Allen, Dennis (def.) vs. Isaac Bailey (plf.)
Allen, Dennis (def.) vs. Eli Glover (plf.)
Anderson, John (def.) vs. Amory Sibley (plf.)
Andrews, Davis R. (def.) and Wesley A. Snell (def.) vs.
    John B. Ross (plf.), William A. Ross (plf.) and George
    W. Ross (plf.)
Andrews, James G. (def.) vs. William Lightfoot (plf.) and
    David Flanders (plf.)
Andrews, James G. (def.) vs. William Maxey (plf.), Charles
    S. Jordan (plf.) and John R. Dyer (plf.)
Andrews, James G. (def.), Oliver H. P. Bonner (def.) and
    Richard W. Bonner (def.) vs. Andrew J. Stewart (plf.)
Andrews, Thomas G. (def.) and James G. Andrews (def.) vs.
    John C. Dumas (plf.)
Armor, James (def.) vs. Thomas Kennon (plf.) for use of
    Thomas Bird
Arms, Seth (def.) vs. Erastus Arms (plf.) and Dennis Arms
    (plf.)
Arms, Seth (def.) vs. Lewis Arms (plf.)

Bailey, Williamson (def.) vs. William Maxey (plf.) and
    Joshua Hill (plf.)
Bailey, Zachariah (def.) vs. William Shaw (plf.)
Baker, Joseph (def.) and Norborn Powell (def.) vs. Shadrach
    McMichael (plf.)
Baley, Joel (def.) vs. Shadrack Bogan (plf.)
Baley, Joel (def.) vs. Peter L. Jackson (plf.)
Baley, Joel (def.) vs. Reuben C. Shorter (plf.) for use of
    John Aspinwall
Baley, Joel (def.) vs. Thomas C. Strickland (plf.) for use
    of Armstead Dodson
Banks, Benjamin W. (def.) vs. Solomon Dewald (plf.)
Banks, Benjamin W. (def.) vs. William G. Dunn (plf.)
Banks, Benjamin W. (def.) vs. Elbert H. Gay (plf.)
Banks, Benjamin W. (def.) vs. Richard King (plf.)
Banks, Benjamin W. (def.) vs. William Maxey (plf.) and
    Charles S. Jordan (plf.)
Banks, Benjamin W. (def.) and James M. Williams (def.) vs.
    Robert O. Usher (plf.), William P. Anderson (plf.) and
    Nicholas P. Hunter (plf.)
Banks, John C. (def.) vs. Richard J. Loyall (plf.) and
    William Andrews (plf.)
Banks, Priscilla (def.) vs. Thomas C. Davis (plf.)
Banks, Samuel H. (def.) vs. Richard J. Loyall (plf.)

Banks, Simeon D. (def.) vs. E. G. White (plf.) and J. H. Hancock
   (plf.)
Barkley, William (def.) vs. Washington Phelps (plf.)
Barrett, James H. (def.) vs. John C. Gibson (plf.)
Baynes, John (def.) vs. James H. Hollingsworth (plf.) and Thomas
   D. Hollingsworth (plf.)
Beach, James (def.) vs. Ezekiel Fears (plf.)
Beardin, Jesse K. (def.), John Thurmond (def.) and Aquilla
   Beardin (def.) vs. Edward Y. Hill (plf.) and Joshua Hill (plf.)
Bell, George (def.) vs. Elijah Thompson (plf.)
Bickerstaff, Robert (def.) vs. William Gay (plf.)
Blan, Thomas (def.) vs. James L. Maddus (plf.) and Colley &
   Robinson (plf.)
Bond, William S. (def.), James Hawthorne, Sr. (def.), James
   Cameron (def.) and William Camerson (def.) vs. James Richards
   (plf.) for use of James Potts, Sr.
Bowen, Josiah M. (def.) vs. Monticello Academy (plf.)
Brantley, John (def.) vs. James Ellis (plf.)
Brantley, John H. (def.) vs. Asa E. Stratton (plf.)
Briant, George (def.) vs. John M. Dooly (plf.)
Brooks, Bailey (def.) and Shadrack McMichael (def.) vs. Abihugh
   Sewell (plf.)
Brooks, Hiram (def.) vs. Richard J. Loyall (plf.) and William
   Andrews (plf.)
Brooks, James (def.) vs. Jesse Loyall (plf.)
Brown, Ervin (def.) vs. George D. Millen (plf.)
Brown, James E. (def.) vs. Isaac Bailey (plf.)
Brown, James E. (def.) vs. Elisha Crow (plf.)
Brown, John G. W. (def.) vs. John Boyd (plf.)
Brown, Robert (def.), George Long (def.) and William T. McDowell
   (def.) vs. Charles Cargile (plf.)
Brown, Robert (def.) vs. David A. Vason (plf.)
Bullard, Wiley W. (def.) vs. James M. Bullard (plf.)
Bullard, Wiley W. (def.) vs. William S. Hurd (plf.) and Anson
   Sungerford (plf.)
Bullard, Wiley W. (def.) vs. J. P. Moye (plf.) and L. H. Durham
   (plf.)
Bullard, Wiley W. (def.) vs. Thomas Nix (plf.)
Burgay, John M. (def.) and Pleasant J. Mullens (def.) vs. James
   S. Gholston (plf.)
Burgess, John (def.) vs. Presley W. Smith (plf.)
Butts, Henry (def.) vs. Thomas Broudus (plf.)

Calaway, Elmore (def.), Mathew Whitfield (def.) and Joshua Hill
   (def.) vs. Pleasant P. Lovejoy (plf.) for use of Henry R. Roby
Campbell, John (def.) vs. Tilmon Niblet (plf.) and John Langston
   (plf.)
Cargile, James (def.) vs. William Holbrooks (plf.) for use of
   Zachariah White
Cargile, Jason (def.) vs. Paschal Murphy (plf.)
Cargile, Thomas (def.) vs. Isaac Hill (plf.)
Cargile, Thomas (def.) vs. James Jackson (plf.)
Cargile, Thomas (def.) vs. Robert McGowen (plf.)
Cargile, William H. (def.) vs. Nathaniel Hornbuckle (plf.)
Carrell, William (def.) vs. John Henderson (plf.)
Carter, Richard (def.), Richard V. Carter (adm.) and Temperance
   Carter (admx.) vs. William J. Dawson (plf.)
Carter, Richard (def.) and Richard V. Carter (adm.) vs. Orrin
   W. Massey (plf.)
Carter, Richard V. (def.) vs. James H. Roberts (plf.)
Chaffin, Moses (def.) vs. William N. Kirkpatrick (plf.)
Chaffin, Moses (def.) vs. William Maxey (plf.), Charles S.
   Jordan, Sr. (plf.) and John R. Dyer (plf.)

Chaffin, Moses (def.) vs. Whitfield & Beeland (plf.)
Chafin, John O. (def.) vs. Edgar Sherman (plf.), William C.
  Jessup (plf.) and Basak Nichols (plf.)
Chafin, Thomas P. (def.) vs. David A. Vason (plf.)
Chapman, Abner (def.) vs. George Selleck (plf.)
Chapman, Asa (def.) and Wiley T. High (exor.) vs. William P.
  Anderson (plf.) and Nicholas P. Hunter (plf.)
Clark, George (def.) and Benjamin Jordan (adm.) vs. Joseph S.
  Holland (plf.)
Clark, Josephus (def.) vs. John Wingfield (plf.) and Marcellus A.
  Wingfield (plf.)
Clay, James J. (def.) vs. Martin J. Kinard (plf.)
Clements, Jeptha (def.) vs. Aquilla Phelps (plf.)
Clements, Payton R. (def.) vs. John Edmondson (plf.)
Cole, Robert (def.) vs. Amory Sibley (plf.)
Coles, John P. (def.) vs. William Bostwick (plf.)
Compton, John W. (def.) vs. William Cleavland (plf.)
Compton, John W. (def.) and Jourdan Compton (def.) vs. Early
  Harris (plf.) and Rowland Thurmond (plf.)
Compton, John W. (def.) vs. Daniel Stagner (plf.) for use of
  Jesse Loyall
Compton, John W. (def.) vs. John Walton (plf.)
Connell, William (def.) vs. Joseph Moss (plf.)
Conner, Charles D. (def.) vs. John McKenzie (plf.) and Peter
  Bennoch (plf.)
Cook, Augustin (def.) vs. Samuel Butts (plf.) and John Lucas
  (adm.)
Cook, James (def.) vs. Sylvanus Walker (plf.)
Cook, Martin (def.) vs. Randolph Blackwell (plf.)
Cook, William (def.) and Benjamin C. Edmondson (def.) vs.
  Milton Antony (plf.)
Cook, William (def.) vs. Benjamin S. Collins (plf.), Joseph B.
  Collins (plf.) and Samuel Hannay (plf.)
Cook, William (def.) vs. James Taylor (plf.)
Cornwell, George W. (def.) and John Clark (def.) vs. William
  Maxey (plf.) and Joshua Hill (plf.)
Cornwell, Gibsen H. (def.) and Lucien L. Reese (adm.) vs.
  Crawford H. Greer (plf.)
Cornwell, Gibson H. (def.) and Lucien L. Reese (adm.) vs. Davis
  Lane (plf.) and John F. Patterson (plf.)
Cornwell, Hiram (def.) vs. Thomas Johnston (plf.)
Cornwell, Hiram (def.) vs. James Webb (plf.)
Cowan, James (def.) vs. Robert R. Minter (plf.)
Cowan, John (def.) and James Turner (def.) vs. Thomas Walton
  (plf.) and John H. Walton (adm.)
Crabtree, Ezekiel (def.) and Thomas K. Slaughter (def.) vs.
  Riley S. Fears (plf.)
Crabtree, Ezekiel (def.) and William P. Ramey (def.) vs. Madison
  S. Holoway (plf.)
Crabtree, Ezekiel (def.) and Mary A. (Trussell) Crabtree (def.)
  vs. William Maxey (plf.) and Charles S. Jordan (plf.)
Crabtree, Ezekiel (def.) and Charles D. Bostick (def.) vs.
  Aquilla Phelps (plf.) and William Johnson (exor.)
Crabtree, Ezekiel (def.) and Thomas Crabtree (def.) vs. Simeon
  Scales (plf.)
Crabtree, Ezekiel (def.) vs. David A. Vason (plf.)
Crabtree, Ezekiel (def.), John Edwards (def.) and Silas Grubbs
  (def.) vs. Eli H. Walker (plf.)
Crabtree, Thomas (def.) and Ezekiel Crabtree (def.) vs. Clark
  W. McMichael (plf.)
Crawford, Meshack N. (def.) vs. John Goodman (plf.)
Crawford, Meshack N. (def.), John S. Robinson (def.), John A.
  Allen (def.) and Samuel Allen (def.) vs. William Maxey (plf.)

and Charles S. Jordan (plf.)
Criswell, David (def.) vs. Richard Revere (plf.)
Crow, Elisha (def.) vs. Alston H. Greene (plf.) and Joseph
  Buchannon (plf.)
Crow, Henry (def.) and Moses Hartsfield (def.) vs. John S. D.
  Byrom (plf.) and Henry Byrom (plf.)
Crow, John M. (def.) and William L. D. Crow (adm.) vs. Aquilla
  Phelps (plf.) and William Johnson (exor.)

Davis, Michael (col) (def.) and William Maxey (guard.) vs.
  Simeon Scales (plf.)
Davis, William G. (def.) vs. Benjamin F. Tuggle (plf.)
Dawkins, Garland (def.) vs. Allen Orr (plf.)
Daws, Joel (def.) and Elbert W. Baynes, Sr. (def.) vs. Samuel
  Allen (plf.) and John C. Key (exor.)
Daws, Joel (def.) and Elmore Calloway (def.) vs. James B.
  Moseley (plf.)
Daws, Joel (def.) vs. John Spearman (plf.) and John A. Boon (plf.)
Dean, Robert (def.) vs. Hardy Crawford (plf.)
Deane, Nathaniel (def.) vs. Anthony Dyer (plf.)
Deane, Nathaniel (def.) and James Black (exor.) vs. Abraham
  Hester (plf.)
Deane, Nathaniel (def.) vs. John Hill (plf.), Augustin Slaughter
  (plf.) and Charles Labuzan (plf.)
Ceane, Nathaniel (def.) and Elisha Brewer (def.) vs. James
  Richards (plf.)
Deane, Nathaniel (def.) and Elisha Brewer (def.) vs. Benton
  Rucker (plf.) for use of William Williamson
Deane, Robert (def.) vs. Joseph Moss (plf.)
Denson, James M. (def.) vs. Fears & Swanson (plf.)
Dillard, Thomas (def.) and Joseph Penn (def.) vs. John B. M.
  Philips (plf.)
Dillon, Thomas (def.) vs. Joel McClendon (plf.)
Dingler, Thomas P. (def.) vs. Charles S. Jordan (plf.) and
  William Maxey (plf.)
Dodds, Caroline E. (def.) and James Dodds (adm.) vs. Rollin
  Smith (plf.) and Hannah Smith (plf.)
Dowdell, Lewis (def.) vs. Matthew Whitfield (plf.)
Dozier, Woody (def.) vs. Soloman Kneeland (plf.)
Dozier, Woody (def.) vs. Jeremiah Pearson (plf.)
Dukes, Frederick (def.) vs. John S. D. Byrom (plf.) and Henry
  Byrom (plf.)
Durham, Simeon (def.) vs. Allen McClendon (plf.)
Durham, Simeon (def.) vs. Hiram P. Troutman (plf.)

Earley, Caleb (def.) vs. Joseph Bays (plf.)
Early, Caleb (def.), Armstead Carter (def.) and James F.
  Robinson (def.) vs. William Bradley (plf.)
Echols, Absalom (def.) vs. James D. Cole (plf.)
Echols, Absalom (def.) vs. Thomas Grant (plf.)
Edmondson, William O. (def.) and Josiah P. Pope (def.) vs.
  James E. Wilson (plf.)
Edwards, John W. (def.) vs. Henry G. Lamar (plf.) and Osburn S.
  Lochrane (plf.)
Eeds, John (def.) and Conrad Walls (def.) vs. John Pugsley (plf.)
Elder, Herbert B. (def.) vs. Greene & Buchannon (plf.)
Evans, David (def.) vs. Anthony Dyer (plf.) and Otis Dyer (plf.)
Evans, Jesse (def.) vs. Lewis Prudhomme (plf.)

Farley, John J. (def.) vs. Elizabeth M. A. Holland (plf.)
Farley, John J. (def.) vs. William N. Kirkpatrick (plf.)
Faulkner, Zachariah (def.) vs. Wiley McClendon (plf.), Allen
  McClendon (adm.) and Nancy McClendon (admx.)

Favors, Nisbet (def.) vs. The State (plf.)
Fears, John P. (def.), Joseph T. Benford (def.) and James Kelly
   (def.) vs. Pleasant Jackson (plf.) and Isaac H. Freeman (exor.)
Fitzpatrick, Jackson (def.) vs. William Cook (plf.)
Fitzpatrick, Rene (def.) and Andrew Baxter (def.) vs. Nathaniel
   Cocke (plf.)
Fitzpatrick, Rene (def.) vs. John Hill (plf.)
Fitzpatrick, Rene (def.) vs. Hiram Storrs (plf.)
Fleming, William (def.) vs. B. C. Johnson (plf.)
Flemister, Crayton A. J. (def.) vs. Russell J. Brown (plf.)
Flemister, Elsie (def.) vs. William Maxey (plf.) and Joshua
   Hill (plf.)
Flowers, Edward (def.) vs. Eli Glover (plf.) and John Cashin
   (plf.)
Flowers, Edward (def.) vs. John Heard (plf.)
Flowers, William (def.) and Yearby Martin (def.) vs. Churchwill
   Respass (plf.), John Heard (adm.) and George Powell (adm.)
Forbes, Charles (def.) vs. Samuel Edmondson (plf.)
Fowler, Theophilus (def.) vs. Charles Pearson (plf.) for use of
   Thomas Hardeman and Irby Hudson
Freeman, Andrew J. (def.), Hartwell M. B. Freeman (def.) and
   Abner C. Dozier (def.) vs. Levi Freeman (plf.)
Freeman, Hamlin (def.) vs. Charles Bailey (plf.)
Freeman, Isaac H. (def.) and Cintha (Wyatt) Freeman (def.) vs.
   John Durdin (plf.)
Freeman, Isaac H. (def.) vs. John Mayo (plf.)
Freeman, Theophilus (def.) vs. Edward A. Broddus (plf.)
Fretwell, Micajah H. (def.) vs. Charles Humphreys (plf.) for
   use of John Rhymes

Garrett, Mials (def.) vs. Nathaniel Cooper (plf.)
Gary, William (def.), Andrew Gordon (def.) and Matthias E. Gary
   (def.) vs. Ker Boyce (plf.) and Bert Harrington (plf.)
Gaston, Henry W. (def.) vs. William Maxey (plf.), Charles S.
   Jordan, Sr. (plf.) and John R. Dyer (plf.)
Gay, Hilliard M. (def.) vs. Rufus L. Graves (plf.) for use of
   L. W. Earnest
George, Franklin (def.) vs. Joseph R. High (plf.) and John H.
   Baker (plf.)
George, Franklin (def.) vs. Hugh P. Kirkpatrick (plf.)
George, Franklin (def.) and William W. Kirkpatrick (def.) vs.
   Thomas Rivers (plf.)
Gibson, John C. (def.) vs. Zachariah Williams (plf.)
Gibson, Robert B. (def.) and Samuel Lovejoy (def.) vs. Benjamin
   Darnell (plf.)
Gill, William (def.), Jeremiah Davis (def.), John Malpass (def.)
   and Robert Williamson (def.) vs. David J. Boyd (plf.) and
   Richard Suydom (plf.)
Gilstrap, Jeremiah M. (def.) vs. Charles W. Parker (plf.) and
   William Lewis (plf.)
Glass, James (def.) vs. Presley W. Smith (plf.)
Glass, Thomas (def.) vs. The State (plf.)
Glover, Eli (def.) vs. William W. Woolsey (plf.)
Glover, John J. (def.) vs. Jonas H. Holland (plf.)
Godkin, John R. (def.) vs. Stephen C. Talmadge (plf.)
Goolsby, John N. (def.) and Jarrell Malone (def.) vs. Maurice
   Wilkinson (plf.)
Grace, Joshua (def.) vs. John Willson (plf.)
Grant, William (def.) vs. James Grant (plf.)
Green, William M. (def.) vs. William Maxey (plf.) and Charles
   S. Jordan (plf.)
Greer, James A. (def.) and Thomas F. Nolan (def.) vs. John Owen
   (plf.)

Gregory, Lewis (def.) vs. Lewellyn W. Hudson (plf.)
Gresham, Ellison (def.) vs. Jonathan VanWagenen (plf.)
Griggs, Cincinattus W. (def.) vs. Russel J. Brown (plf.)
Griggs, Cincinatus W. (def.) vs. B. B. Odom (plf.)
Griggs, Cincinnattus W. (def.) and Robert H. Daniel (def.) vs.
  Jesse Loyall (plf.)
Grubbs, John W. (def.) vs. Moses Jones (plf.)
Grubbs, John W. (def.) vs. Lightfoot, Flanders & Co. (plf.)
Grubbs, John W. (def.) vs. Berner Pye (plf.)
Grubbs, Richard J. (def.) and Silas Grubbs (def.) vs. Ashur
  Ayres (plf.)
Grubbs, William (def.) and James Grubbs (def.) vs. Ezekiel
  Crabtree (plf.) and John W. Crabtree (plf.)

Haggerthy, Joshua (def.) vs. Larkin Dunn (plf.)
Hairston, John (def.) vs. Allen McClendon (plf.)
Hairston, Thomas (def.) vs. Susan Egnew (plf.)
Hammer, Wingfield (def.) and Richard Hammer (def.) vs. The
  State (plf.)
Hamrick, James (def.) and John G. Hammock (def.) vs. Davis
  Bostick (plf.)
Hamrick, James (def.) vs. Allen Tucker (plf.) and Nancy Tucker
  (plf.)
Hanks, Thomas (def.) and John Fleming (def.) vs. Allen McClendon
  (plf.)
Hardwick, John W. (def.) vs. John W. Ranay (plf.)
Hardy, William B. (def.) and Nathaniel Coggeshall (def.) vs.
  Abner Bidwell (plf.)
Hardy, William B. (def.) and Drury Wilkins (def.) vs. Abner
  Bidwell (plf.)
Hardy, William B. (def.) vs. John L. D. Byrom (plf.)
Hardy, William B. (def.) vs. Eli Glover (plf.)
Hardy, William B. (def.) vs. John Hall (plf.) and Lucien Arms
  (adm.)
Hardy, William B. (def.) vs. Middleton Hartsfield (plf.) for use
  of William Sims and Charles D. Williams
Hardy, William P. (def.) vs. John Goodman (plf.)
Hardy, William P. (def.) vs. William Shaw (plf.)
Harris, William Y. (def.) vs. Jeremiah Boggers (plf.)
Harvey, Nehemiah (def.) vs. Samuel Lancaster (plf.)
Hascall, Elijah N. (def.), David Hascall (def.) and Joseph
  Johnson (def.) vs. Benjamin S. Collins (plf.), Joseph B.
  Collins (plf.) and Samuel Hannah (plf.)
Hascall, Elijah N. (def.), James A. Hascall (def.) and David
  Hascall (def.) vs. Nicholas Ware (plf.)
Hascall, James A. (def.) vs. James H. Bell (plf.)
Hascall, James A. (def.) and David Hascall (def.) vs. Oliver H.
  Hicks (plf.) and Thomas Lord (plf.)
Hascall, James A. (def.) vs. John P. Nall (plf.)
Hascall, James A. (def.) vs. Thomas Napier (plf.) and William
  B. Ector (plf.)
Hascall, James A. (def.) and David Hascall (def.) vs. Gardner
  Tufts (plf.)
Hatcher, Uriah (def.) vs. William Maxey (plf.) and Charles S.
  Jordan (plf.)
Heard, Stephen G. (def.) vs. Robert Robey (plf.) and Timothy
  Robey (adm.)
Heldebrand, David (def.) vs. Royal Clay (plf.)
Henderson, Samuel L. (def.) vs. William Maxey (plf.) and Charles
  S. Jordan, Sr. (plf.)
Hendrick, S. I. (def.) and G. Simonton (def.) vs. John C. H.
  Reid (plf.)
Herring, Arthur (def.), John Hill (def.) and Samuel Lane (def.)

315

vs. William Lovejoy (plf.)

Hicks, Joseph (def.), Garland Dawkins (adm.) and William
Philips (adm.) vs. John Cargile (plf.), Robert Williamson
(adm.), James Cargile (adm.), William Cargile (adm.) and
Levina W. Cargile (admx.)

Hickson, Thomas (def.) vs. Allen Goolsby (plf.)

Hickson, Timothy (def.) vs. James Henry (plf.)

Higginbotham, Joseph (def.) vs. John Gresham (plf.)

High, Joseph R. (def.), John H. Baker (def.) and John W. L.
Reeves (def.) vs. Officers of Court (plf.)

Hill, Asa (def.) vs. Whitmell Hill (plf.)

Hines, James (def.) and John Hines (exor.) vs. Gilbert W. Shaw
(plf.) and Martha Ann (Lovejoy) Shaw (plf.)

Hitchcock, Jesse (def.) vs. Thadeus Beall (plf.), Elias Beall
(plf.) and Thomas Beall (plf.)

Hobson, Christopher (def.), John Wilson (adm.) and Thomas W.
Harris (adm.) vs. John Hobson (plf.)

Hobson, Christopher (def.) and John Willson (adm.) vs. Matthew
Hobson (plf.)

Hobson, John (def.) vs. Charles Cargile (plf.)

Hobson, John (def.) and Christopher Hobson (def.) vs. Abner
Chapman, Sr. (plf.)

Hobson, John (def.) and Christopher Hobson (def.) vs. John T.
Lawrence (plf.), Daniel Rapelye (plf.) and William R. Smith
(plf.)

Hobson, John (def.) and Christopher Hobson (def.) vs. Robert
H. Musgrove (plf.) for use of Benjamin S. Collins, Joseph B.
Collins and Samuel Hannah

Holeman, Joseph (def.), William Phillips (def.) and William
Hammett (def.) vs. Eleazer Jeter (plf.)

Holland, Alexander S. (def.) vs. Mathew Whitfield (plf.)

Holland, Henry J. (def.) and Lawson S. Holland (adm.) vs. Alston
H. Greene (plf.) and Joseph Buchannon (plf.)

Holland, Jonas H. (def.) vs. John Cargile (plf.), Robert
Williamson (adm), James Cargile (adm.), William Cargile (adm.)
and Lavina W. Cargile (admx.)

Holland, Lawson S. (def.) vs. Joseph L. Holland (plf.)

Holland, Lewis C. (def.) vs. Joshua Hill (plf.)

Holland, Lewis C. (def.) vs. Robert Kellam (plf.) and William
Maxey (plf.)

Holland, Lewis C. (def.) vs. James King (plf.)

Holland, Lewis C. (def.) vs. Jesse Loyall (plf.) and William H.
Pritchett (plf.)

Holland, Lewis C. (def.) vs. Richard I. Nichols (plf.) and
George Atkinson (plf.)

Holland, Stephen (def.) vs. Allen Martin (plf.)

Holmes, James P. (def.) vs. John P. Nall (plf.)

Holmes, John (def.) vs. Hardy Doyle (plf.) and William Brittain
(plf.)

Holt, James (def.) vs. Harrison Cabiness (plf.)

Hopson, William (def.) vs. John Gunn (plf.)

Horton, James A. (def.), John Horton (def.) and James T. Barrett
(def.) vs. Thomas J. Smith (plf.) and John C. Maddux (plf.)

Howard, Corodon H. (def.) and George H. Luckett (def.) vs. Jesse
King (plf.)

Howell, Vines (def.) vs. William Gay (plf.)

Huckeby, Isham (def.) vs. Reuben C. Shorter (plf.)

Hudson, Thomas (def.) vs. William Penn (plf.)

Hudspeth, Airs (def.) vs. Hungerford J. Johnson (plf.)

Hughes, Peter M. (def.) vs. James Whitfield (plf.)

Hunicutt, Thomas (def.) vs. Samuel P. Smith (plf.)

Hurt, William C. (def.), Frederick Thompson (def.) and Presley
Seurlock (def.) vs. Samuel Thompson (plf.)

Huston, David (def.) and Judy Huston (exrx.) vs. William Morgan (plf.) and Fielding Bradford (plf.)
Hutcheson, Henry C. (def.) vs. Bresie & Motte (plf.)

Irvin, Christopher (def.) and David Bates (def.) vs. Lewis Hogg (plf.)

Jeffries, Boling L. (def.) vs. William Bailey (plf.) and Crayton A. J. Flemister (plf.)
Jenkins, Benjamin (def.) and Armsted Dodson (def.) vs. James Whitfield (plf.)
Jenkins, Charlie (def.) vs. The State (plf.)
Jenkins, Francis (def.) vs. William Maxey (plf.), Charles S. Jordan (plf.) and John R. Dyer (plf.)
Jenkins, John P. (def.) vs. Riley Potter (plf.)
Johnson, Arthur (def.) vs. Aaron Williams (plf.)
Johnson, Cornelius (def.) vs. William Maxey (plf.) and James C. Bartlett (plf.)
Johnson, Hugh G. (def.) vs. Henry Stephens (plf.) and William Cook (plf.)
Johnson, Hugh G. (def.) vs. Charles D. Stewart (plf.) and George Hargraves (plf.)
Johnson, Jack A. (def.) vs. William Maxey (plf.) and Charles S. Jordan, Sr. (plf.)
Johnson, Jackson A. (def.) vs. George F. Gerald (plf.)
Johnson, James W. (def.) vs. Isaac Bailey (plf.)
Johnson, Nicholas (def.) vs. John R. Cargile (plf.) for use of Charles Cargile
Johnson, William (def.) vs. Elizabeth Rosser (plf.)
Johnson, William (def.) vs. Isaac R. Walton (plf.)
Johnston, James H. (def.) and Franklin Malone (def.) vs. John Goodman (plf.)
Jones, Gideon L. (def.) vs. Allen McClendon (plf.)
Jones, John (def.) vs. Bedford H. Darden (plf.)
Jones, Robert (def.) vs. Jeremiah Pearson (plf.)
Jordan, Benjamin (def.) vs. Jonas Skinner (plf.)
Jordan, Benjamin (def.) vs. Zachariah White (plf.)
Jordan, Charles S., Jr. (def.) and Joseph J. W. Cargile (def.) vs. William H. Whitfield (plf.)
Jordan, Fleming (def.) vs. Francis Johnston (plf.) and Moses B. Hairston (adm.)
Jordan, Henry (def.) vs. James Grace (plf.)
Hustices of Court (def.) vs. William Dougherty (plf.)

Kennedy, Absalom (def.) vs. Thomas Carter (plf.)
Key, Abraham (def.) vs. James H. Kirkpatrick (plf.)
Key, Thomas (def.) and John Hunter (def.) vs. Littleberry Watts (plf.), Pleasant Watts (adm.) and John Bailey (adm.)
King, Tandy D. (def.) vs. Henry Kelley (plf.)
Kirkpatrick, William N. (def.) and Mathew Whitfield (def.) vs. Justices of Court (plf.)
Kirtley, Lemma (def.) vs. John Fluker (plf.)

Lambright, William (def.) vs. Oliver Sturges (plf.)
Lane, Lewis L. (def.) vs. Davis Lane (plf.) and John F. Patterson (plf.)
Lane, Lewis L. (def.) and Artemus Goolsby (def.) vs. William Maxey (plf.)
Lane, Lewis L. (def.) vs. James H. Roberts (plf.)
Lane, Samuel (def.) vs. John Baldwin (plf.)
Langston, Isaac (def.) vs. William Macey (plf.), Charles S. Jordan (plf.) and John R. Dyer (plf.)
Lanier, James (def.) vs. Joseph Johnson (plf.) for use of James

Garlington

Lassitter, John (def.) vs. John Thurmond (plf.)
Lawrence, James (def.) vs. William Maxey (plf.), Charles S.
  Jordan, Sr. (plf.) and John R. Dyer (plf.)
Lawrence, James (def.) and Leroy Lawrence (adm.) vs. William H.
  Reese (plf.)
Lawrence, Lemuel O. (def.) and Jonas H. Holland (def.) vs. John
  Cargile (plf.), Robert Williamson (adm.), James Cargile (adm.),
  William Cargile (adm.) and Lavinia Cargile (admx.)
Lawson, Arthur (def.) vs. Aaron Baxley (plf.)
Lee, John (def.) vs. Ephraim Herring (plf.) for use of Moses
  Herring
Lemon, Abraham (def.) vs. Thomas Beall (plf.) and Alphaus Beall
  (plf.)
Lewis, Thomas (def.) and Robert W. Bickerstaff (def.) vs. Thomas
  Brown, Sr. (plf.)
Littlejohn, Thomas (def.) vs. Stephen G. Heard (plf.)
Lloyd, Edmond (def.) vs. Paschal Murphy (plf.)
Lovejoy, Samuel (def.), Felix Hardman (def.) and Edmund Banks
  (def.) vs. Anthony Dyer (plf.)
Lovejoy, Welcom C. (def.) vs. William Maxey (plf.), Charles S.
  Jordan (plf.) and John R. Dyer (plf.)
Lovejoy, Welcome C. (def.) vs. George F. Gerold (plf.)
Lovejoy, Welcome C. (def.) and John W. Wyatt (def.) vs. Pleasant
  Lovejoy (plf.) and John D. Lovejoy (adm.)
Loyall, Richard J. (def.) and George T. Bartlett (def.) vs. John
  H. Ezell (plf.) and William R. Powel (plf.)
Loyall, Richard J. (def.) vs. Davis Lane (plf.) and John F.
  Patterson (plf.)
Loyd, Thomas (def.) vs. Isaac Rolls (plf.)
Lynch, Grief (def.) vs. William Maxey (plf.), Charles S. Jordan,
  Sr. (plf.) and John R. Dyer (plf.)
Lynch, John (def.) vs. Riley Fears (plf.)
Lynch, Sackville (def.) and Daniel McDowell (def.) vs. Artemas
  Gould (plf.) and Justus R. Buckley (plf.)
Lynn, David (def.) vs. Lodowick Teal (plf.) for use of Jordan
  Teal

Malone, George (def.) vs. William S. Hurd (plf.) and Alfred
  Shorter (plf.)
Mann, Americus V. (def.) vs. Thomas DeGraffenreid (plf.) and
  William Coleman (plf.)
Martin, Yearby (def.) vs. Thomas Grant (plf.)
Maxey, Yelverton (def.) vs. Isaac Bailey (plf.)
Melvin, Joseph B. (def.) vs. Gabriel Colley (plf.)
Millen, Mary S. (def.), Grief Lynch (trustee) and Joel C.
  McDowell (def.) vs. Thomas Holland (plf.)
Miller, James H. (def.) and James W. Morgan (def.) vs. Thomas
  Grier (plf.)
Mobley, Stephen H. (def.) vs. Joshua Hill (plf.)
Molliere, Clement (def.) vs. Warren Phelps (plf.) and Jeremiah
  Pearson (plf.)
Moore, Aaron (def.) vs. Jesse Robinett (plf.)
Moore, Franklin (def.) vs. Thomas R. Price (plf.)
Moore, John (def.) vs. John Bryant (plf.)
Moore, John (def.) vs. Christopher Hobson (plf.) and John
  Aspinwall (plf.)
Moore, John (def.) vs. Vincent Sandford (plf.)
Morgan, Asa H. (def.) vs. William Bailey (plf.) and Crayton
  A. J. Flemister (plf.)
Morgan, Asa H. (def.) vs. Pleasant Banks (plf.)
Morgan, Asa H. (def.) vs. James T. Barrett (plf.)
Morgan, Asa H. (def.) vs. William Dukes (plf.) and Thomas F.

Danielly (plf.)
Morgan, Asa H. (def.) vs. John Durden (plf.)
Morgan, Asa H. (def.) vs. Isaac H. Freeman (plf.)
Morgan, Asa H. (def.) vs. Jonas H. Holland (plf.)
Morgan, Asa H. (def.) vs. Thomas Jones (plf.)
Morgan, Asa H. (def.) vs. Richard King (plf.)
Morgan, Asa H. (def.) and John L. Robinson (def.) vs. Hugh P.
  Kirkpatrick (plf.)
Morgan, Asa H. (def.) vs. Richard J. Loyall (plf.) and John E.
  Langston (plf.)
Morgan, Asa H. (def.) vs. John Maddux (plf.)
Morgan, Asa H. (def.) vs. Tilmon Niblett (plf.) and John E.
  Langston (plf.)
Morgan, Asa H. (def.) and William C. Robinson (def.) vs. James
  H. Roberts (plf.)
Morgan, Asa H. (def.) vs. William Rodgers (plf.)
Morgan, Asa H. (def.) and William C. Robinson (def.) vs. Stephen
  C. Talmadge (plf.) for use of Hugh P. Kirkpatrick
Morgan, Luke I. (def.) vs. John F. Dismukes (plf.)
Morgan, Sarah N. (def.) vs. Hiram Brooks (plf.) and John Morgan
  (plf.)
Morgan, Stokely (def.) vs. Isack Mooney (plf.)
Morgan, William (def.) and Charles Morgan (def.) vs. John L. D.
  Byrom (plf.)
Moss, Henry (def.) vs. George Hargraves (plf.)
Mothershed, William H. (def.), Tilmon Niblet (def.) and Thomas
  J. Howard (def.) vs. Berry T. Digby (plf.)
Mullins, Pleasant J. (def.) and Thomas V. King (def.) vs. Carden
  Goolsby (plf.)
Mullins, Pleasant J. (def.) and Thomas R. King (def.) vs.
  Cincinnatus Goolsby (plf.)
Mullins, Pleasant J. (def.) vs. William Lightfoot (plf.) and
  David Flanders (plf.)
Myles, William H. (def.) vs. John Bogan (plf.)

McCane, Alexander (def.) vs. McKenzie & Bennoch (plf.)
McClendon, Jacob (def.) and William Armstrong (def.) vs. Isaac
  Foreman (plf.)
McClendon, Stephen (def.) vs. John Cargile (plf.)
McCorkle, William (def.) and William B. Hardy (def.) vs. James
  S. Biers (plf.)
McCorkle, William (def.) and William B. Hardy (def.) vs. John
  Hobson (plf.) and Christopher Hobson (plf.)
McDonald, Alex (def.) vs. John Cargile (plf.)
McDonald, William A. (def.) vs. James D. Minton (plf.)
McDowell, Daniel (def.) and John M. McDowell (def.) vs. Artemas
  Gould (plf.) and Justus R. Bulkeley (plf.)
McDowell, Daniel (def.) vs. James L. Shaffer (plf.)
McIntosh, William (def.) vs. James Hammett (plf.)
McKee, Robert (def.) vs. John McKenzie (plf.) and Peter Bennoch
  (plf.)
McKenzie, William C. (def.) vs. Airs Hudspeth (plf.)
McLaughlin, James (def.) vs. William Maxey (plf.) and Charles
  S. Jordan, Sr. (plf.)
McLea, John (def.) and Jackson Fitzpatrick (def.) vs. T. C.
  Hayward (plf.)
McLemore, Charles (def.) and James McLemore (def.) vs. Mary
  Estes (plf.)
McLemore, Franklin (def.) vs. William C. Dawson (plf.)
McLeroy, James (def.) vs. Henry G. Smithson (plf.)
McMichael, David (def.) and John McMichael (def.) vs. William
  Cleveland (plf.)

Newton, Aris (def.) and William H. Pritchett (def.) vs. Moses
  Butts (plf.)
Niblett, Tilman (def.) vs. Simeon Scales (plf.)
Nolan, Thomas F. (def.) and Greene D. Brantley (def.) vs.
  Chelsea Johnson (plf.)
Nolley, Nathan (def.) vs. Daniel Nolley (plf.)
Norris, John (def.) and Nathaniel Goff (def.) vs. Allen
  McClendon (plf.)

O'Hara, Charles (def.) vs. William H. Byrom (plf.)
Onail, Jesse (def.) and Thomas Hooks (def.) vs. Benjamin Johnson
  (plf.)
Orr, Allen (def.) vs. Jacob Julin (plf.)
Orr, Allen (def.) vs. Nathan Orr (plf.)
Orr, Allen (def.) vs. John Payne (plf.)
Osburn, Thomas O. (def.) and Elias Osburn (def.) vs. Creed E.
  Spears (plf.)
Oxford, Tilman D. (def.) vs. Doctor H. Beall (plf.)

Pace, William T. (def.) vs. James Adams (plf.) and William M.
  Adams (exor.)
Pace, William T. (def.) vs. George W. Finley (plf.)
Pace, William T. (def.) vs. Artemus Gould (plf.), William H.
  Bulkley (plf.) and John T. Bulkley (plf.)
Pace, William T. (def.) vs. Loyall & Langston (plf.)
Pace, William T. (def.) vs. Lucy Seat (plf.)
Pace, William T. (def.), John E. Langston (def.) and Simeon
  Scales (def.) vs. Thomas J. Smith (plf.)
Parker, Isaac (def.) vs. Burton Mullins (plf.)
Parker, Isaac L. (def.) vs. William Vaughn, Sr. (plf.)
Parker, William H. (def.) and William R. Marchman (def.) vs.
  Woody Dozier (plf.) and Burwell Ragland (plf.)
Parker, William H. (def.) and William R. Marchman (def.) vs.
  Joseph Johnson (plf.)
Parnall, Cyrus (def.) and Daniel Parnall (def.) vs. Shaler
  Hillyer (plf.)
Parrott, William H. (def.) vs. Leverett Pardu (plf.)
Peddy, Wiley (def.) vs. Mary Bell (plf.)
Pegg, William H. (def.) vs. Lucien P. Cook (plf.) and Alvarez
  Hart (plf.)
Pegg, William H. (def.) vs. John Wingfield (plf.) and Marcellus
  A. Wingfield (plf.)
Pendarvis, James (def.) vs. William H. Parker (plf.)
Perkins, Archibald (def.) and Reuben C. Shorter (def.) vs.
  William H. Beatty (plf.)
Peurifoy, Silas M. (def.), Benjamin W. Peurifoy (adm.) and John
  Peurifoy (def.) vs. Isaac Brant (plf.) and David Woodruff (plf.)
Phillips, Wiley (def.) vs. Jonas H. Holland (plf.)
Pollard, Richard (def.) vs. Thomas T. Walker (plf.)
Pope, Josiah P. (def.) vs. Richard J. Loyall (plf.)
Post, Joseph M. (def.) vs. Russel Jones (plf.)
Potts, Stephen, Jr. (def.) vs. John Pearce (plf.)
Preston, Charles T. (def.) and William H. Preston, Sr, (def.)
  vs. George Mygatt (plf.)
Pridgen, William (def.) vs. James Crosson (plf.)
Prince, Joseph (def.) vs. Thomas Mackie (plf.)
Pritchett, T. J. (def.) vs. Thomas J. Swanson (plf.)
Pye, Jefferson (def.) vs. Green L. McMichael (plf.)
Pye, Jordan (def.) and John M. McDowell (def.) vs. Riley S.
  Fears (plf.)
Pye, Jordan (def.) and Augustus W. Lane (exor.) vs. James Pye
  (plf.) and Harmon W. Pye (adm.)
Pye, Thadeous (def.) vs. Loyall and Langston (plf.)

Pye, Theophilus (def.) vs. Stephen J. Heard (plf.)

Raddeh, Abner (def.) and David Radden (def.) vs. Edward Walthall
(plf.), Turman Walthall (adm.) and Charles F. Walthall (adm.)
Ragan, Asa (def.) vs. John L. D. Byrom (plf.)
Rainey, Matthew (def.) vs. Isaac Bailey (plf.)
Ramey, Charles D. (def.) and William O. Edmondson (def.) vs. John
Campbell (plf.)
Ramey, Charles D. (def.) and John T. High (def.) vs. John Camp-
bell (plf.)
Ramey, Charles D. (def.) vs. Henry A. Dickinson (plf.)
Ramey, Charles D. (def.) vs. Simeon Scales (plf.)
Ramey, Nathaniel H. (def.) and David A. Reese (def.) vs. Allen
Kelly (plf.) for use of Joel McClendon
Ramey, William (def.) vs. John A. Dillard (plf.)
Ramsey, Henry (def.) and John Pennington (adm.) vs. James Luckey
(plf.)
Reaves, William (def.) vs. Nathaniel Coggershall (plf.) and
James C. Coggershall (plf.)
Reaves, William (def.) vs. William Penn (plf.)
Reese, David A. (def.) vs. John Pearson (plf.)
Reeves, John W. L. (def.) vs. Lindsey H. Durham (plf.) and
Francis W. Swanson (plf.)
Reeves, John W. L. (def.) vs. High & Baker (plf.)
Reeves, Pleasant W. (def.) and George T. Bartlett (def.) vs.
Thomas Broddus (plf.) and Thomas C. Broddus (exor.)
Reeves, P. Wyatt (def.) vs. Sion B. Robson (plf.) and Cornelius
Robson (plf.)
Reid, John (def.) and William Willingham (def.) vs. Zachariah
W. McMichael (plf.), Charles McMichael (adm.) and Moses Powell
(adm.) for use of William R. Marchman
Reid, John (def.) vs. John Winans (plf.)
Richards & Hudspeth (def.) vs. Hungerford & Johnson (plf.)
Richards, James (def.) and Airs Hudspeth (def.) vs. Horace
Kirby (plf.)
Richardson, Thomas (def.) vs. Hezekiah Spires (plf.) and Martha
Spires (plf.)
Rivers, Robert T. (def.) vs. David D. Bostick (plf.)
Rivers, Robert T. (def.), Thomas Rivers (def.), Susan Rivers
(def.) and John P. Lamar (trustee) vs. Jarrel, Johnson & Co.
(plf.)
Rivers, Susan (def.) and John P. Lamar (trustee) vs. William
Larrence (plf.)
Rivers, Thomas (def.) vs. John L. Woodward (plf.)
Rivers, Thomas H. B. (def.), Thomas Rivers (def.) and William
W. Rivers (def.) vs. Jonas H. Holland (plf.)
Rivers, Thomas H. B. (def.), Thomas Rivers (def.) and William
W. Rivers (def.) vs. Littleton Johnston (plf.)
Rivers, Thomas H. B. (def.) and Thomas Rivers (def.) vs. Jesse
Loyall (plf.)
Robinson, Cornelius (def.) vs. Abner Bidwell (plf.) and Peter
Curtis (plf.)
Robinson, Cornelius (def.) vs. John Hardwick (plf.)
Roby, William A. (def.) vs. William Macey (plf.) and Charles
S. Jordan, Sr. (plf.)
Roby, Williamson A. (def.) vs. Newton Mfg. Co. (plf.)
Roby, Williamson A. (def.) vs. James H. Roberts (plf.)
Rodgers, John C. (def.) and James H. Rodgers (def.) vs. Henry
Maulden (plf.)
Rodgers, Thomas E. (def.) vs. John Byrom (plf.)
Rodgers, Thomas E. (def.), John C. Rodgers (def.) and James H.
Rodgers (def.) vs. Robert Tucker (plf.) for use of David Hascall
Rucker, John T. (def.) vs. John McKenzie & Peter Bennoch (plfs.)

Runnels, Howel W. (def.) vs. Culbert & Hays (plf.)
Runnels, Preston (def.) vs. Abraham Heard (plf.)
Runnels, Preston (def.) vs. John Taylor (plf.)
Russell, Ignatius (def.) and Ellender Russell (def.) vs. Achsah Gibbs (plf.) and Phebe Gibbs (guard.)
Ryan, William (def.) vs. William Mygatt (plf.) and James E. Wood (plf.)

Sansom, Robert (def.) vs. Jesse Loyall (plf.)
Satterwhite, Stephen (def.) vs. Hiram B. Troutman (plf.)
Scales, Simeon (def.) vs. Joshua Hill (plf.)
Scales, Simeon (def.) vs. John C. Maddux (plf.) and William D. Maddux (plf.)
Scales, Simeon (def.) and Joshua Hill (def.) vs. John H. Phillips (plf.)
Scales, Simeon (def.) vs. David A. Vason (plf.)
Scisson, Edwin S. (def.), Moses Chafin (adm.) and Lucy Scisson (exrx.) vs. Alexander Sledge (plf.)
Shackelford, Edmund (def.) vs. John Cargile (plf.), James Cargile (adm.), Robert Williamson (adm.) and Lavina W. Cargile (admx.)
Shaw, Gilbert W. (def.) vs. John Brackin (plf.)
Shaw, Gilbert W. (def.) vs. Asa H. Morgan (plf.)
Shaw, Gilbert W. (def.) and Welcome C. Lovejoy (def.) vs. Josiah Newman (plf.)
Shaw, William (def.), Peter Randolph (adm.) and Margaret Shaw (admx.) vs. Sherwood Strong (plf.)
Sheffield, John (def.) vs. Joseph R. High (plf.) and John H. Baker (plf.)
Shepherd, Abram (def.) vs. John Hobson (plf.) and Christopher Hobson (plf.)
Shepherd, E. W. (def.) and Morris Noles (def.) vs. John C. Banks (plf.)
Shepherd, Eleazer W. (def.) and Charles F. Preston (def.) vs. John W. A. Smith (plf.)
Shepherd, William (def.) vs. Joseph Moss (plf.)
Shipp, G. V. (def.) and Mitchel Aaron (def.) vs. Russel J. Brown (plf.)
Simmons, Allen (def.) vs. Charles Pearson (plf.) for use of Thomas Hardeman and Irby Hudson
Sims, James G. (def.) vs. Ansalum Earley (plf.)
Slaughter, Francis (def.) and Isaac H. Slaughter (def.) vs. Thomas R. Slaughter (plf.), James M. Williams (adm.) and Matilda Slaughter (admx.)
Slaughter, Thomas K. (def.) and Charles C. Hairston (def.) vs. Anthony Dyer (plf.)
Slaughter, William A. (def.) and John Burge (def.) vs. Josiah Newman (plf.)
Smart, Elisha (def.) vs. Bank of Darian (plf.)
Smartt, Francis B. (def.), John Hunt (adm.) and Eliza (Smartt) Hunt (admx.) vs. Ker Boyce (plf.)
Smartt, Henry T. (def.) vs. John McKinzie (plf.)
Smartt, Henry T. (def.) vs. Simon Pearson (plf.) for use of Thomas Hardeman and Irby Hudson
Smith, Charles (def.), Hyram Hays (adm.) and Nancy R. Smith (admx.) vs. Samuel Murril (plf.)
Smith, David (def.) vs. Gabriel Colley (plf.)
Smith, John J. (def.) vs. Alston H. Greene (plf.) and Joseph Buchannon (plf.)
Smith, John W. A. (def.) vs. Russel J. Brown (plf.)
Smith, Jonathan (def.) vs. James M. Flowers (plf.)
Smith, Lewis D. M. (def.) vs. The State (plf.)
Smith, Samuel R. (def.) vs. William Maxey (plf.) and Charles S.

Jordan, Sr. (plf.)
Smith, Thomas W. (def.), David M. Langston (def.) and Welcome
C. Lovejoy (def.) vs. Caswell P. Bogan (plf.)
Smith, Thomas W. (def.) vs. John Maddus (plf.) and William D.
Maddux (plf.)
Stallings, Jeremiah (def.) vs. William Cook (plf.)
Stallings, Sanders (def.) vs. Joseph B. Swann (plf.)
Standifer, Archibald C. (def.) vs. William Maxey (plf.) and
Charles S. Jordan, Sr. (plf.)
Steedman, Thomas (def.) vs. Eli Glover, Benjamin C. Edmondson,
Joseph McBride, Thomas Higginbotham, Allen McClendon, William
Robinson and Edmund Green (plfs.)
Steele, James (def.) vs. Thomas Nealey (plf.)
Stephenson, John (def.) and John Faulkner (def.) vs. Thomas
Barnes (plf.)
Stovall, George (def.) vs. Eli O. Cooly (plf.)
Stovall, George (def.) vs. Woody Dozier (plf.) and Burrel
Ragland (plf.)
Stovall, George (def.) and John W. Compton (def.) vs. Amanda
Ector (plf.), Jane L. Ector (plf.), Robert Freeman (guard.)
and Hugh W. Ector (guard.)
Stubbs, John W. (def.) and James H. Stubbs (def.) vs. Thomas P.
Stubbs (plf.)
Sweet, John (def.) vs. Isaac Bailey (plf.)

Talmadge & Kirkpatrick (def.) vs. Harrison & Breese (plf.)
Taylor, James (def.) and Thomas W. Harris (def.) vs. Solomon
Strickland (plf.) and Timothy Freeman (adm.)
Taylor, Stephen S. (def.) vs. James H. Halbert (plf.) and
Robert A. Collins (plf.)
Taylor, William H. (def.) vs. Robert Blakely (plf.) and Robert
Mays (plf.)
Taylor, William H. (def.) vs. Joseph H. Cargile (plf.)
Taylor, William H. (def.) vs. J. H. Hollingsworth (plf.) and
T. D. Hollingsworth (plf.)
Terry, Jeremiah (def.) vs. Zachariah H. Gordon (plf.)
Terry, Jerry (def.) vs. Lewis Franklin (plf.)
Thompson, Henry B. (def.) vs. Ephraim A. Alexander (plf.) and
Clayton Lawrence (plf.)
Thompson, Henry B. (def.) vs. John L. Lindsay (plf.) and Elisha
C. Grubbs (adm.)
Thompson, Henry B. (def.) vs. Thomas J. Pritchett, Alfred M.
Pritchett and George W. Pritchett (plfs.)
Thompson, Jacob M. (def.) vs. William Marks (plf.)
Thrash, Martin (def.) vs. Joshua Callaway (plf.)
Thurmond, Benjamin (def.) vs. Robert Williamson (plf.)
Towns, John T. C. (def.) vs. John Goodman (plf.)
Towns, Marlin (def.) vs. William Spratlin (plf.) and John
Burney (exor.)
Trammel, Mark D. (def.) vs. Thomas K. Slaughter (plf.)
Trayner, James (def.) vs. William Gilbert (plf.) and Felix
Gilbert (plf.)
Turner, James F. (def.) vs. Henry Mims (plf.)

Urquhart, Henry (def.) vs. John Hill (plf.)

VanAntwerp, William (def.) vs. Colbert Jeffries (plf.)
Varner, Andrew J. (def.) vs. Stephen C. Talmadge (plf.)
Varner, Edward (def.) vs. William H. Byrom (plf.)
Varner, Frederick A. (def.) vs. William Maxey and Joshua Hill
(plfs.)
Varner, Joseph W. (def.) vs. Edward Varner (plf.)
Varner, Samuel (def.) vs. Edward Varner (plf.)

Varner, Samuel D. (def.) and Edward Varner (def.) vs. Wiley
  Banks & Co. (plf.)
Varner, Samuel D. (def.) and William A. Byrom (def.) vs. John L.
  McMichael (plf.)
Vaughn, James W. (def.) vs. John Goodman (plf.)
Vincent, Henry (def.) vs. Charles Campbell and Asher Ayres (plfs.)
Vincent, Henry (def.) vs. Wesley A. Snell (plf.)
Vining, James F. (def.) and James C. Aaron (def.) vs. John C.
  Watters (plf.), Dyer C. Bancroft (exor.) and Andrew J.
  Watters (exor.)

Walker, James (def.) vs. John L. Childs (plf.) for use of
  Kinchen P. Tison
Walker, James (def.), John Walker (def.) and Samuel Walker (def.)
  vs. Benjamin Glover & Co. (plf.)
Waller, James B. (def.) and James M. Flowers (def.) vs. John
  L. D. Byrom (plf.)
Walthall, William (def.) vs. Benjamin Davis (plf.)
Warner, Nathan (def.) and Benjamin F. Ward (adm.) vs. Sanders
  Walker (plf.)
Waters, John C. (def.) vs. Daniel D. Bates (plf.) and Caleb C.
  Dibble (plf.)
Watters, Andrew J. (def.) vs. Davis Lane (plf.)
Watters, Andrew J. (def.), Simeon Scales (def.) and P. P. Love-
  joy (def.) vs. Richard J. Loyall (plf.)
Watters, John C., Sr. (def.) vs. Cornelius Lummus (plf.)
Watters, Sarah J. (def.) vs. David M. Bell (plf.)
Watters, Sarah J. (def.) vs. Sarah Yancey (plf.) and Thomas
  Yancey (adm.)
Watters, W. D. (def.) vs. Connell & Rodaham (plf.)
Watters, William D. (def.) vs. Eudoxcess Swift (plf.) and Henry
  Anderson (plf.)
Weathersby, John F., Jr. (def.) vs. John W. Edwards (plf.)
Webb, Thomas P. (def.) vs. Albert C. Garlington (plf.)
Webb, Thomas P. (def.) vs. William Maxey (plf.) and Charles S.
  Jordan (plf.)
Wells, John (def.) and Lot Smith (def.) vs. Edward Varner (plf.)
Wells, William H. (def.) vs. Alston H. Greene (plf.) and Joseph
  Buchannon (plf.)
West, Jeremiah (def.) vs. Joseph Williams (plf.)
West, Jeremiah D. (def.) vs. Thomas Williams (plf.)
Whatley, Willis, Def.) and John McArthur (def.) vs. Daniel
  McDowell (plf.)
Wheelus, Isem (def.) vs. Thomas J. Smith (plf.) for use of
  John Goodman
Wheelus, Isom (def.) vs. Jesse Loyall (plf.)
White, Cyrus (def.) vs. Nancy Simons (plf.)
White, Hugh (def.) vs. John McKenzie (plf.) and Peter Bennoch
  (plf.)
White, William H. (def.) vs. John C. Watters (plf.)
White, Zachariah (def.) vs. Francis B. Smartt (plf.), Eliza
  Smartt (admx.) and John Hill (adm.)
Whitfield, William H. (def.) vs. William G. Mygatt (plf.) and
  James E. Wood (plf.)
Wilborn, Sam (def.) vs. William J. Dunn (plf.) and James C.
  Aaron (exor.)
Wilburn, Samuel J. (def.) vs. Alfred Shorter (plf.)
Wilkins, Drury (def.) vs. Phillip Barnes (plf.) and Ransalier
  Upson (plf.)
Wilkins, Drury (def.) vs. James Smith (plf.)
Williams, William (def.) vs. S. C. Talmadge (plf.)
Williamson, Isaac (def.), Nathan Williams (exor.) and Stokely
  Morgan (exor.) vs. Richard J. Willism (plf.)

Willis, Robert L. (def.) vs. Elizabeth Eubanks (plf.)
Willson, John (def.) and Thomas B. Davis (def.) vs. Charles D.
  Stewart (plf.) and George Hargraves (plf.)
Wilson, Elijah (def.) vs. John Warren (plf.)
Wilson, George I. (def.) and L. S. Holland (def.) vs. Burrell P.
  Key (plf.)
Wilson, James D. (def.) vs. Jarrel Beasley (plf.)
Wilson, Joseph (def.) and Sarah Wilson (def.) vs. Jeremiah
  Benton (plf.)
Wilson, Nancy S. (def.) vs. George F. Meriwether (plf.)
Wilson, William (def.) vs. Robert Howe (plf.)
Wommack, Edmond (def.) vs. James Lumpkin (plf.)
Woodruff, James (def.) vs. Whitmell Hill (plf.)
Wright, Michael (def.) vs. Thomas Grant (plf.)
Wright, Michael (def.) vs. Welcome Parks (plf.)
Wyatt, Isaac T. (def.), John W. Wyatt (def.) and George W.
  Wyatt (def.) vs. James H. Roberts (plf.)
Wyatt, John W. (def.) vs. John Baynes (plf.)
Wyatt, John W. (def.) vs. Stephen J. Durden (plf.) and John
  Durden (adm.)
Wyatt, John W. (def.) vs. High & Baker (plf.)
Wyatt, William H. (def.) and Meshack N. Crawford (def.) vs.
  Abner Bartlett (plf.), James C. Bartlett, William A. Bartlett,
  John C. Bartlett and George T. Bartlett (exors.)
Wyatt, William H. (def.) vs. Thomas G. Fish (plf.)
Wyatt, William H. (def.), Thomas Wyatt (adm.) and Cynthia
  Wyatt (admx.) vs. James M. Reeves (plf.) and William Watt
  (exor.)
Wyatt, William H. (def.) vs. John J. Wyatt (plf.)

Yancy, Jackonias (def.) vs. John C. Bancroft (plf.) for use of
  John Lovell
Yancy, Layton (def.) vs. Francis M. Swanson (plf.) and Thomas
  J. Pritchett (plf.)
Yancy, Polly (def.) vs. John Butler (plf.)
Yonge, Henry (def.) and William P. Yonge (def.) vs. Thadeus
  Moynihan (plf.)
Yonge, William P. (def.) vs. William H. Pritchett (plf.)

Zinn, Jacob (def.) vs. John Anderson (plf.)
Zinn, Jacob (def.) vs. Gilbraith Simonton and William Simonton
  (plfs.)

CHAPTER VII

COUNTY COURT CASE FILES, 1860-1913
Record Group 179-3-5

Most of the civil cases are suits for debt, foreclosure actions, suits for damages and other cases where the amount of money involved was not large enough to require the case to be tried in Superior Court. The criminal cases are misdemeanors, mostly assault and battery, theft, larceny and similar crimes. The types of documents included vary from one case to another, but frequently included are complainant's petitions, evidence, bail bonds, accusations, arrest warrant, defendant's petitions, fi fas, judgments, verdicts, sentences and similar documents. In many cases some of the documentation appears to be missing. The cases are arranged alphabetically by name of defendant. The folder labels show the names of the parties to the suit and the date the case was filed.

Aaron, Green (col) vs. Clasey Aaron
Aaron, Green vs. Key & Preston
Aaron, J. C. vs. J. C. R. Boyed and J. R. Kelley
Aaron, John L. and H. V. B. Allen vs. Jumima Cunard and J. S. Cunard
Aaron, John L. vs. W. A. Kelly & Bros.
Aaron, Mitchel and Sarah F. Aaron vs. Stewart, Swan & Thompson
Aaron, S. A. F. vs. N. B. White and H. C. McClure
Acre, William B. vs. Keely & McDowell
Acree, W. B. vs. Frank Leverett
Acree, W. B. vs. Augustus Mosely
Acree, William vs. E. Newton
Acree, William B. vs. F. M. Lester
Acree, William B. vs. The State
Adams, Edward H. vs. Julia A. Adams
Adams, Leaven vs. The State
Adgate, C. F. and Sarah L. Adgate vs. John Flannery & Co.
Adgate, C. F. & Co. vs. Athens Manufacturing Co.
Adgate, C. F. & Co. vs. Rockmore & Barnett
Adgate, C. F. & Co. vs. Walton Guano Co.
Aiken, C. P. vs. Robert Childs
Aiken, E. S. vs. Mrs. Floyd Pennington
Aiken, I. A. vs. O. H. Arnold, Jr.
Aiken, J. J. vs. Harris Bros.
Aiken, Jeff vs. B. F. Adams
Aiken, Jeff, S. R. Baynes and E. W. Baynes vs. C. Aultman & Co.
Aiken, Jeff vs. E. H. Cohen
Aiken, Jeff vs. James T. Davis
Aiken, Jeff vs. C. W. Jordan
Aiken, Jeff vs. Mapes Formula & Peruvian Co.
Aiken, Jeff vs. J. Wolfe
Aiken, Jeff and W. W. Baynes vs. Nichols, Shepherd & Vo.
Aiken, Jefferson vs. J. R. High and P. S. Burney
Aiken, Jefferson F. and E. W. Baynes vs. Charles Gerding & Co.
Aiken, Jefferson J. vs. Charles Griggs
Aiken, Jefferson J. vs. B. Rice
Aiken, R. H. vs. Childs, Harwell & Bonner
Aiken, R. H. vs. J. T. Corley
Aiken, R. H. vs. William E. Simmons
Aiken, R. S. vs. R. S. Stewart
Aiken, Mrs. S. J. vs. P. S. Burney
Aiken, Mrs. T. A. vs. Benton Supply Co.
Aiken, Mrs. T. A. vs. Frank E. Block Co.
Aiken, Mrs. T. A. vs. A. B. Small
Aiken, T. A. vs. Walton Guano Co.
Aiken, T. A. & Son vs. L. E. Sullivan
Aikens, T. A. & Son vs. H. Y. McCord Co.

Aikin, J. J. vs. John J. Broughton
Aikin, J. J. vs. W. A. Houghton
Aikin, J. Jeff vs. E. T. Alling
Aikin, J. Jeff vs. Frank Leverett
Aikin, Jeff vs. Kelly & McDowell
Aikin, Jeff vs. Talmage & Tolleson
Aikin, Jeff J. and Senica Jackson vs. F. M. Lester
Aikin, Jeff J. vs. John L. Wright and James K. Wright
Aikin, Jefferson vs. Franklin George
Aken, Jefferson vs. W. E. Tucker
Akens, J. J. vs. Howard & Soule
Akens, R. H. vs. S. A. Burney and P. S. Burney
Akens, R. H. vs. J. R. High & Son
Akens, Thomas J. vs. Burnett, Broughton & Co.
Akens, Thomas J., exor. vs. J. P. Fears
Akin, Jefferson vs. I. T. Bryson
Alexadner, Mrs. A. W. and G. W. Alexander vs. M. S. Benton
Alexander, Alfred vs. H. J. Lamar
Alexander, George vs. Kelly & Price
Alexander, George vs. John H. Talmadge
Alexander, Green vs. Major Alexander
Alexander, Jerry and Batch Middlebrooks vs. J. P. Malone
Alexander, N. O. vs. Griffin, Monticello & Madison Railroad Co.
Alexander, R. W. vs. W. C. Kincaid
Alexander, R. W. vs. F. M. Lawson & Bros.
Alexander, T. J. vs. Berud & Brothers
Alexander, Thomas J. vs. J. L. Holland and B. L. Holland
Alfriend, A. H., Mrs. A. H. Alfriend and W. F. Jordan vs. John
   F. Goodman
Alfriend, Edmond vs. A. S. Holland
Allen, A. J. vs. James Corley
Allen, A. J. vs. Day, Crew and Conner
Allen, A. J. vs. B. T. Digby and James L. Lewis
Allen, A. J. vs. J. C. Johnson
Allen, Jack vs. The State
Allen, John A. vs. T. J. Shepherd and Son
Allen, R. C. vs. Corley and Dorsett
Allen, R. C. vs. D. C. Ridnour and Silas Ridnour
Allen, Robert C. vs. Thomas J. Kitchens
Allen, W. W. vs. Continental Gin Co.
Allen, W. W. vs. Marietta Fertilizer Co.
Allen, Walker vs. Carey Frances Knight
Allen, Walker W. vs. Flawainer (?) N. Tuggle
Ambrose, George and Delia Ambrose vs. Ellick Johnson
A. M. E. Church of Monticello vs. John Cargyle for use of F.
   Walker
Amos, John (alias James Henson) vs. The State
Anderson, Antony vs. Mary Anderson
Anderson, George vs. The State
Anderson, John T. (col) vs. The State
Anderson, William W. vs. Hurd and Hungerford
Andrews, D. R. and R. R. Andrews vs. J. M. Cox and Co.
Andrews, D. R. vs. Roberts and Roberts
Andrews, David vs. Price and Steele
Andrews, David R. vs. C. C. Layson
Andrews, Davis R. vs. The State
Andrews, W. A. and T. P. Andrews vs. Doris R. Andrews, Rebecca
   P. Andrews for use of Jordan Brothers
Andrews, William A. and Thomas P. Andrews vs. J. M. Cox & Co.
Annis, Barbara vs. The State
Annis, Jesse vs. Isaac H. Freeman
Annis, Jesse M. vs. C. H. Andrews and Co.
Annis, Jesse M. vs. The State

Appling, Henry and William Appling vs. D. B. Benton
Arnold, O. H., Jr. vs. National Cash Register Co.
Atkinson, H. A. vs. J. K. Orr Shoe Co.
Atkinson, William F. vs. Corley and Dorsett
Atkinson, William F. vs. James M. Dawson
Atkinson, William F. vs. H. N. Phillips
Atkinson, William F. vs. Augustus L. Sluder
Atkinson, William F. vs. John H. Sluder
Avent, Alvas vs. B. H. Ray
Avent, Alves vs. David J. Baer
Avent, Alves vs. Rodgers, Worsham and Co.

Bacon, S. W. vs. James L. Campbell
Bacon, S. W. and Mrs. S. W. Bacon vs. Willis Fields
Bacon, S. W. vs. Charles Gaston
Bacon, Sumner W. vs. Ann E. Mygatt
Bailey, C. A. vs. J. S. Pursley
Bailey, C. T. vs. J. E. Pitts
Bailey, Elisha J. vs. Newton O. Alexander
Bailey, J. Z. L. and Z. Clark Bailey vs. James Benton
Bailey, R. S. vs. E. H. Carrol and Co.
Bailey, R. S. vs. Georgia Chemical Works
Bailey, R. S. vs. W. A. Kelly and Bros.
Bailey, R. S. vs. S. and E. Weichselbaum
Bailey, W. C. vs. George F. Merriwether
Bailey, W. C. vs. William C. Penn
Bailey, W. C. and S. B. Bailey vs. Temple Pump Co.
Bailey, W. T. vs. Bullard Bros.
Bailey, Zachariah vs. Corley and Dorsett
Banks, Alford vs. John W. A. Smith
Banks Alfred (col) and John W. A. Smith vs. Obadiah R. Belcher
  and William D. Belcher
Banks, Alfred vs. W. A. Kelly and Bros.
Banks, Alfred vs. John Merryman
Banks, Alfred vs. John H. Sluder
Banks, Anderson vs. Mary Francis Reeves
Banks, Arilious O. and Olinious O. Banks vs. Mack, Stadler & Co.
Banks, Columbus vs. The State
Banks, Dan vs. The State
Banks, Hen vs. Cornelia Newton
Banks, Henry D. and Harveil Banks vs. F. M. Davidson
Banks, Henry D., Bill Banks and Ransom Jeffries vs. Sarah J.
  Jeffries
Banks, Henry D. vs. F. M. Swanson
Banks, James vs. George Thompson
Banks, John vs. A. S. Holland
Banks, John vs. Kelly and McDowell
Banks, John C. and Berry T. Digby vs. Samuel R. Smith
Banks, Mary vs. Freeman and Wyatt
Banks, Mary vs. Howard and Soule
Banks, Mary vs. Samuel R. Smith, Jr.
Banks, Olinious O. vs. A. H. Seymour
Banks, Polly vs. Charles Meriwether (col)
Banks, Randal and S. R. Smith, Sr. vs. B. P. Bailey
Banks, William vs. W. R. Tuggle
Barber, Amos and Will Benton vs. The State
Barber, Charlie vs. The State
Barber, George vs. N. B. White
Barber, Mary vs. The State
Barber, Sam, Jr. vs. The State
Barker, Bill vs. The State
Barker, J. R. vs. Griffin, Monticello and Madison Railroad Co.
Barker, J. R. vs. A. M. Robinson and Co.

330

Barker, J. R. vs. Travers, Snead and Co.
Barker, John vs. N. L. Walker
Barker, John R. vs. West Bros.
Barkley, Minnie vs. The State
Barnes, Green vs. The State
Barnes, Lewis (col) (alias Lewis Kelley) vs. The State
Barnes, Lon (alias Lon Smith) vs. The State
Barnes, R. C., G. P. Loyd and Joseph Williams vs. E. J. Lindsey
Barnes, Tom (col) (alias Tom Vaughn) vs. County Commissioners
Barnwell, B. F. vs. The State
Barr, James W. vs. Nannie M. Barr
Barr, John vs. The State
Barr, W. J. vs. J. H. Holland
Barr, William vs. Griffin Greer and Mary Jane Greer
Barr, William J. vs. Lawton and Willingham
Barr, William J. vs. Reid and Lazenby
Barrett, J. M. vs. Sallie H. Kelly and J. H. Kelly
Barron, B. vs. South. Bank and Trust Co.
Barron, Ben and Thomas C. Spivey vs. Bank of Monticello
Barron, Ben vs. M. S. Benton
Barron, Benjamin vs. Samuel Barron
Barron, Benjamin vs. W. B. Dozier
Barron, Benjamin and Julia W. Shropshire vs. Mary E. Goodson
Barron, Benjamin and Ida Barron vs. W. A. Kelly and Bros.
Barron, Benjamin vs. Shipp and Webb
Barron, Benjamin vs. Francis M. Swanson
Barron, Benjamin vs. A. J. Talmadge and Co.
Barron, Benjamin vs. M. V. Tyner
Barron, Elza vs. Sallie Kelly and J. H. Kelly
Barron, Elzy vs. The State
Barron, J. H. vs. Thomas L. Swift and Co.
Barron, Jim vs. Cindy White
Barron, Peter vs. The State
Barron, Silas vs. Charles G. Campbell
Baxley, W. D. vs. Bramlett and Bros.
Baynes, Albert vs. The State
Baynes, Becky vs. W. A. Pearson
Baynes, Bill vs. John W. Morgan
Baynes, E. W., Aris Newton and Joseph W. Preston vs. Charles L.
  Bartlett
Baynes, E. W. vs. J. A. Baynes, Susan McMichael and Martha
  Baynes
Baynes, E. W. vs. John A. Broughton, W. H. Broughton and A. M.
  Speer
Baynes, E. W. vs. Charping and Chaffin
Baynes, E. W. vs. L. W. Davidson
Baynes, E. W. vs. Davis Brothers
Baynes, E. W. vs. P. Fell and Sons
Baynes, E. W. vs. Flanegan, Abell and Co.
Baynes, E. W. vs. Charles Gerding and Benjamin F. Gerding
Baynes, E. W. vs. High and Foster
Baynes, E. W. vs. Hogan and Lembrick
Baynes, E. W. vs. W. A. Kelly and Bros.
Baynes, E. W. vs. Key and Preston
Baynes, E. W. vs. C. V. Lenard
Baynes, E. W., Eliza Baynes and S. R. Baynes vs. Frank Leverett
Baynes, E. W. vs. F. M. Luster
Baynes, E. W. vs. Berien Rice
Baynes, E. W. vs. A. M. Robinson and Co.
Baynes, E. W., S. R. Baynes and Eliza Baynes vs. George W. Scott
Baynes, E. W. vs. Shipp and Webb
Baynes, E. W. vs. J. W. Thompson
Baynes, E. W. vs. Robert Young and Robert Adams

331

Baynes, Elbert vs. Kelly and Price
Baynes, Elbert W. vs. Asher Levy
Baynes, Elbert W. vs. P. C. Sawyer
Baynes, Elbert W. vs. F. M. Swanson
Baynes, Elbert W. vs. Bolling Whitfield
Baynes, Harry vs. The State
Baynes, Mrs. M. J. vs. Louis Thompson
Baynes, Peter and B. Baynes vs. McDade and Paschal
Baynes, R. A. vs. L. Mohr and Sons
Baynes, R. A. vs. Talmage Bros. and Co.
Baynes, R. A. vs. Taylor and Bolling Co.
Baynes, Rebecca vs. John P. Harris
Baynes, S. R. vs. M. J. Baer
Baynes, S. R. vs. Elbert W. Baynes
Baynes, S. R. vs. John A. Broughton, W. A. Broughton and H. M.
   Speer
Baynes, S. R. vs. Stephen C. Lawrence
Baynes, S. R. vs. Frank Leverett
Baynes, S. R. vs. E. Y. Mallary, F. L. Mallary and J. S. Lester
Baynes, S. R. vs. Mapes Formula and Peruvian Guano Co.
Baynes, S. R. vs. Purse and Thomas
Baynes, S. R. vs. Reid and Dennis
Baynes, S. R. vs. Nancy Roby
Baynes, S. R. vs. J. H. Smith for use of S. P. Smith
Baynes, S. R. vs. J. W. Smith
Baynes, S. R. vs. Talbott and Sons
Baynes, S. R. vs. J. R. Webster
Baynes, S. R. vs. N. B. White
Baynes, Sidney vs. William J. M. Preston
Baynes, Sidney R. vs. Robert Childs
Baynes, Sidney R. vs. Michael McDowell
Baynes, W. E. vs. Jefferson Aiken
Baynes, W. E. vs. E. H. Cohen
Baynes, W. E. vs. Frank Leverett
Baynes, W. E. vs. John W. Morgan
Baynes, W. E. vs. Swift Fertilizer Works
Baynes, W. E. vs. N. B. White
Baynes, Watt and Mrs. E. N. Murrell vs. J. P. Harris
Baynes, Watt, Peter Baynes and Ned Baynes vs. John J. Tyler
Baynes, William vs. Franklin George
Baynes, William vs. W. A. Houghton
Baynes, William E. vs. J. W. Ashby
Baynes, William E. vs. Evan Harvey, J. C. Allen and E. T. Mathis
Baynes, William E. vs. A. J. Talmadge and Co.
Baynes, William E. vs. W. W. Turnell and R. M. Lassiter
Baynes, William E. vs. Charles Turner
Bearden, Alfred vs. W. W. Evans
Bebe, John vs. A. B. Small
Bebee, Bob vs. Jordan Bros. and Co.
Bebee, Wesley vs. R. E. Hutchings
Bebee, Westley vs. A. M. Robinson and Co.
Bebee, Bob vs. Carter and Cutcher
Beebe, Dick and James Henderson vs. W. C. Leverett
Beebe, John W. vs. Charles Gerding and Co.
Belcher, George vs. The State
Belcher, James vs. The State
Belcher, O. R. vs. Griffin, Monticello and Madison Railroad Co.
Belcher, O. R. vs. Samuel Griswold
Belcher, O. R. vs. Prior and Booth
Belcher, O. R., Jr. vs. Stephen D. Mobley and George A. Cabaness
Belcher, O. R., Sr., John M. Belcher, William D. Belcher, O. R.
   Belcher, Jr. and J. L. Belcher vs. John Maddox and Abraham B.
   Maddox

Belcher, Susan C., W. D. Belcher and William C. Belcher vs.
  Schaefer and Mallet
Belcher, W. C. vs. M. V. McKibben
Belcher, W. D. vs. Stephen D. Mobley and George A. Cabaniss
Belcher, William D. vs. Joel C. McDowell
Belcher, William D. vs. William H. Preston and James A. Preston
Bell, Carrie vs. The State
Bell, Garfield, S. C. Lawrence, Aaron Bell and Henry Bell vs.
  A. D. Candler
Bell, George Ann vs. The State
Bell, John West vs. The State
Benford, Michell vs. Wynn and Clack
Benford, P. P. vs. J. S. Dell
Benton, Alf vs. The State
Benton, Ben vs. The State
Benton, Dave and Herschel Benton vs. L. O. Benton and Bros.
Benton, Dock vs. The State
Benton, Feb vs. Benton Supply Co.
Benton, Henry vs. The State
Benton, L. and D. B. Benton vs. Lawrence Digby
Benton, L. O. and Bro. vs. George C. Clements
Benton, L. O. and Eugene Benton vs. E. B. Warren Co.
Benton, Oscar vs. The State
Benton, Ossian vs. Griffin, Monticello and Madison Railroad Co.
Benton, Ossian vs. Howard and Soule
Benton, Ossian vs. Amos Kelly
Benton, Ossian vs. Ellen C. Middlebrooks
Benton, Will vs. The State
Benton, Will (col) vs. The State
Bergstrom, Oscar vs. Feb Cargile
Bergstrom, Oscar vs. Willis Flournoy
Berner, W. R. and N. B. White vs. William S. Minter
Berner, William R. vs. James M. McMichael
Berry, A. B. and R. C. Berry vs. W. F. Jordan
Berry, A. T. vs. S. J. McMichael
Berry, Adolphus vs. M. A. Goolsby
Berry, Dock, Frank Foster and Jake Foster vs. A. S. Thurman and
  W. S. Florence
Berry, E. P. vs. Cheney Sanders
Berry, J. M. vs. James T. Lewis and B. P. Bailey
Berry, Kiah vs. The State
Vines, Joe vs. The State
Binford, Augustus vs. The State
Binford, E. A. vs. Sim Jordan and Sally Lordan
Binford, E. A. vs. A. Shaw
Binford, E. A. vs. Jacob Wolfe
Binford, H. W. vs. W. B. White and L. White
Binford, Ike W. vs. T. A. Hutchinson and R. W. Hutchinson
Binford, J. S. vs. J. C. Pennington
Binford, Joseph T. vs. Burnett, Broughton and Co.
Binford, Joseph T. vs. F. M. Swanson
Binford, Joseph T. vs. Nehemiah B. White and Lucius White
Binford, Mitchell vs. Printup Bro. and Pollard
Binford, Seab and Herbert Talmadge vs. Kelly and Phillips
Bius, Miles vs. Morris Flatan
Blackwell, Adeline vs. W. M. Robinson
Blackwell, Alfred vs. Dealey Glover
Blackwell, Ben vs. The State
Blackwell, C. D. vs. L. O. Benton and Eugene Benton
Blackwell, D. C. vs. A. W. Foster and Co.
Blackwell, D. C. vs. W. A. Kelly and Bros.
Blackwell, D. C. vs. McCormick Neal
Blackwell, Elbert vs. William C. Bailey

Blackwell, Elbert (col) vs. J. G. Elder
Blackwell, Elbert vs. Frank Leverett
Blackwell, Elbert and Adda C. White vs. Martin V. Tyner
Blackwell, Elbert and Thomas Blackwell vs. John B. Webb
Blackwell, F. vs. John H. Blackwell
Blackwell, H. F. vs. Clark, Rosser and Co. for use of W. C.
  Clark and Co.
Blackwell, H. F. vs. Eliza Elder
Blackwell, H. F. vs. S. Lewy and Co.
Blackwell, H. F. vs. W. D. Wynn
Blackwell, Henry vs. Francis M. Swanson
Blackwell, Henry vs. A. J. Talmadge and Co.
Blackwell, Henry F., J. Madison Blackwell and William Malone
  vs. John T. Brown
Blackwell, Henry F. vs. Corley and Dorsett
Blackwell, Henry F. vs. Morris Flatan
Blackwell, Henry F. vs. William L. High
Blackwell, Henry F. vs. Printup Bros. and Pollard
Blackwell, Henry F., Samuel L. Henderson, Mary Banks, and John
  L. Robinson vs. N. B. White
Blackwell, Isaac vs. Amanda Blackwell
Blackwell, Isaac vs. Roberts and Roberts
Blackwell, J. H. vs. A. Horton
Blackwell, J. M. vs. John A. Broughton
Blackwell, J. M. vs. McCormick Neal
Blackwell, J. M. vs. Printup Bros. and Pollard
Blackwell, J. M. vs. T. Spearman
Blackwell, J. M. and Samuel H. Blackwell vs. Francis M. Swanson
Blackwell, J. M. and S. S. Blackwell vs. W. D. Wynn
Blackwell, James F. vs. John H. Blackwell
Blackwell, James F. vs. Claghorn, Herring and Co.
Blackwell, James F., James C. Aaron, Samuel H. Blackwell, Robert
  F. Ezell, Elbert W. Baynes, James Benton, Aris Newton, Jr.,
  Seaborn C. Kelly and Isaac H. Freeman vs. John R. Dyer
Blackwell, James F., T. S. Blackwell and S. S. Blackwell vs.
  Printup Bros. and Pollard
Blackwell, James F. vs. John B. Webb
Blackwell, James F. vs. Mary Wilson
Blackwell, James F. vs. Wynn and Clack
Blackwell, John H. vs. W. H. Beach
Blackwell, John H. vs. Claghorn, Herring and Co.
Blackwell, John H. vs. Clark, Rosser and Co. for use of W. C.
  Clark and Co.
Blackwell, John H. vs. Corley and Dorsett
Blackwell, John H. vs. A. W. Foster and James K. Wright
Blackwell, John H. vs. W. A. Kelly and Brothers
Blackwell, John H. vs. Price and Steele
Blackwell, John H. vs. N. B. White
Blackwell, R. M. vs. James L. Campbell
Blackwell, R. M. and Isaac Malone vs. J. S. Dell
Blackwell, Robert vs. Spencer Preston
Blackwell, Robert vs. Jacob Wolfe
Blackwell, Robert M. and S. H. Blackwell vs. John Benton
Blackwell, S. E. vs. O. H. Arnold
Blackwell, S. H. vs. John A. Broughton
Blackwell, S. S. vs. W. B. Beckwith and J. T. Kelly
Blackwell, S. S. and J. M. Blackwell vs. Goldsmith Brothers
Blackwell, S. S. vs. Jacob Wolfe
Blackwell, S. W. vs. T. A. Hutchinson and R. W. Hutchinson
Blackwell, S. W. vs. Robinson, Kelly and Co.
Blackwell, Samuel H. vs. W. C. Bailey
Blackwell, Samuel H. vs. William D. Belcher
Blackwell, Samuel H. vs. S. C. Talmadge, A. J. Talmadge for use

of James L. Maddux
Blackwell, Samuel H. vs. W. D. Wynn
Blackwell, Samuel H., Sr. vs. W. A. Kelly, John H. Kelly and
 Pleasant P. Kelly
Blackwell, Samuel S. vs. Martha Whitfield
Blackwell, Sarah vs. The State
Blackwell, T. L. vs. Price and Steel
Blackwell, Thomas G. vs. S. T. Reid
Blackwell, Thomas S. vs. Daniel H. Wilcox, Leonard Y. Gibbs and
 William C. MacMurphy
Blackwell, W. Frank vs. Mrs. A. L. Powell
Blackwell, Wesley vs. The State
Blackwell, Wess, E. B. Malone and W. J. S. Tuggle vs. Jasper
 County Bank
Blackwell, Will vs. Mat Goolsby
Blackwell, Willis vs. The State
Bogan, Comfort vs. The State
Bogan, M. B. vs. F. M. Lester
Bogan, M. B. vs. A. M. Robinson and Co.
Bohannon, J. A. and S. W. Garrett vs. J. H. Allen
Bonner, Jerry vs. Madison Epps
Bonner, Jerry vs. O. P. Fitzsimons
Bonner, Jerry vs. Charles Gerding and Co.
Bonner, Jerry vs. William A. Kelly and Bros.
Bonner, Jerry vs. William D. Maddux
Bonner, Jerry vs. J. O. Shepherd
Bostwick, Henry vs. The State
Boswell, Jerry vs. The State
Bowden, Caleb, Dumas Bowden and Fannie Bowden vs. The State
Bowden, D. H. vs. S. P. Speairs
Bowdin, John T. and John H. Blackwell vs. B. F. Johnson and Co.
Bowers, Will L. and Lessie Bowers vs. W. P. Cosby
Boykin, Dave vs. R. Jordan
Bradley, L. C. vs. Mrs. Mary Lou Smith
Bradley, Lee vs. The State
Bradley, W. F. and L. C. Bradley vs. James T. Corley, J. J.
 Corley, and L. L. Middlebrooks for use of Clark Banking Co.
Branch, Robert vs. The State
Brandon, A. M. vs. A. D. Adair and McCarty Bros. for use of
 Greer Bros. and Garland
Brandon, A. M. vs. Monticello Cotton Oil Co.
Branham, Sid vs. The State
Brannom, Horace, Tom Ross, Charles Wilson and Felix Chiles vs.
 The State
Branson, Will vs. The State
Brantley, William N. vs. The State
Braswell, Anthony vs. The State
Bray, Henry and John G. Barron vs. David M. Langston
Brazill, William (col) vs. Rheuben J. Tyner
Brewer, Nelson vs. L. O. Benton and Eugene Benton
Bridges, Mary A. vs. Coleman and Ray
Briscoe, J. M. vs. Bowker Fertilizer Co. and J. D. Weld
Briscoe, J. M. vs. L. W. Pon and Caroline Pon
Broddus, Edmund M., Thomas J. Smith, James L. Maddux, Emery M.
 Maddux and Thomas C. Broddus vs. Wiley Moye and Thomas W. Moye
Broddus, Lizzie vs. The State
Broddus, M. C. vs. H. B. Jordan, E. H. Jordan, A. H. Jordan and
 D. R. Glover
Broddus, Thomas C. vs. R. H. Hutchings and Cornelia Hutchings
Broddus, Thomas C. vs. Silas Newman
Broddus, Thomas C. vs. Columbus H. Webb
Bronson, Sim vs. J. M. Dawson
Brooks, Eugenia A. and Eunice A. Holland vs. Albert J. Talmadge,

Samuel C. Charping and Joseph G. Tolleson
Brooks, Hiram, P. B. Brooks and William Lawrence vs. S. J. Brooks
Brooks, Hiram vs. Griffin, Monticello and Madison Railroad Co.
Brooks, P. B. and W. H. Lawrence vs. Roberts and Roberts
Brooks, Shade vs. Albert J. Talmadge, Samuel C. Charping and
  Joseph G. Tolleson
Broughton, Ed vs. The State
Broughton, Wash vs. The State
Brown, George Y. vs. The State
Brown, J. W. vs. The State
Brown, Levi vs. The State
Brown, Mary vs. The State
Brown, Otis vs. The State
Brown, Richard (col) vs. E. W. Baynes
Brown, T. J. and J. H. Brown vs. J. F. Bennett
Brown, Tucker (col) vs. The State
Bryant, Cody vs. Turner Vinson
Bryant, John vs. Barberella Bryant
Bryant, Susan vs. Reed Henderson
Bullard, Francis (col) vs. The State
Bullard, James M., Jr. vs. Early W. Thrasher
Bullard, Samuel vs. The State
Burk, Walter vs. The State
Burney, C. C. vs. Anderson and Hunter
Burney, C. C. vs. L. M. Price
Burney, C. C. vs. The State
Burney, J. W. vs. A. J. Talmadge
Burney, Jack (col) vs. The State
Burney, Jim vs. The State
Burney, John W. vs. W. F. Fitch
Burney, Joseph (col) vs. Russel Belcher
Burney, Joseph (col) vs. George McKey
Burney, Joseph (col) vs. Price and Steele
Burney, Man (col) vs. The State
Burney, William (col) and William Dickson (col) vs. William R.
  Berner
Burney, William (col) and William Dixon (col) vs. Lee Crane (col)
Burton, Henry and Charlie Marks vs. The State
Busby, M. A. vs. W. A. Kelly and Bros.
Busby, M. C. vs. Charping and Chaffin
Butler, Lewis vs. Andrew T. Lewis
Butler, Umphry vs. The State
Butner, C. A. vs. Dempsey and Fennel
Butner, Charles A. vs. Jack Whitehead
Butter, Jack vs. The State
Butts, Bill vs. Sophy Hester
Butts, Charles vs. The State
Butts, Mat vs. The State
Byars, Gabe (col) and Leah Byars (col) vs. The State
Byers, Miles vs. Morris Flatan
Byington, Joshoway vs. Kelly and Price
Byram, Silas vs. James Turner
Byron, Mat vs. Jennie Byron
Byron, Matt vs. The State

Calvert, J. F. and S. W. Calvert vs. J. O. Shepherd
Campbell, Amanda (col), India Campbell, Gus Campbell and Kate
  Campbell vs. The State
Campbell, Bill vs. F. M. Swanson
Campbell, C. G. vs. Griffin, Monticello and Madison Railroad Co.
Campbell, C. G. and C. G. Chambers vs. William P. Persons
Campbell, C. G. vs. M. W. Pope
Campbell, C. G. vs. J. H. Roberts

Campbell, C. G. vs. Bolling Whitfield
Campbell, Charles G. vs. Solomon Cohen
Campbell, Charles G. vs. Madison Epps
Campbell, Charles G. vs. Harriett Gardner (col)
Campbell, Charles G. and Clemmie Campbell vs. The State
Campbell, Charles G. vs. Seymour, Tinsley and Co.
Campbell, Charles G. vs. N. M. Williams
Campbell, Mrs. Clemmie vs. Martha Gilstrap
Campbell, Cooley, Reuben Jordan and George T. Bartlett vs.
  George Alexander (col)
Campbell, George vs. The State
Campbell, J. L. vs. Griffin, Monticello and Madison Railroad Co.
Campbell, J. M. vs. M. S. Benton
Campbell, J. M. vs. Dannenberg Co.
Campbell, J. M. vs. T. L. Furse
Campbell, James H. vs. Benton Supply Co., J. G. Pope, H. A.
  Allen and L. M. Price
Campbell, James H. vs. J. R. Carmichael
Campbell, James H. vs. Charley Jackson
Campbell, James H. vs. J. H. Kelly
Campbell, James L., Jr. vs. The State
Campbell, James M. vs. L. O. Benton and Bro.
Campbell, Jasper vs. S. R. Baynes
Campbell, Jasper vs. Thomas M. Leverett
Campbell, John vs. William C. Campbell and H. C. Hill
Campbell, M. O. vs. A. M. Robinson and Co.
Campbell, R. S. vs. Robinson and Son
Campbell, William vs. S. I. McMichael
Capers, S. E. vs. Mrs. W. F. Jordan
Carbine, P. V. vs. E. V. Carey for use of Officers of Court
Cardell, Aaron vs. Kelly and McDowell
Cardell, Aaron vs. Willis Newton
Cardell, C. E. vs. W. E. Baynes
Cardell, C. E. vs. Jasper County Bank
Cardell, Ed. W. vs. The State
Cardell, Mrs. Fannie and P. D. Cardell vs. J. T. Smith and Mrs.
  Mary B. Smith
Cardell, J. J. vs. L. O. Benton and Bro.
Cardell, J. J. and William Cardell vs. Elliott Estes
Cardell, John vs. Kelly and McDowell
Cardell, John vs. John W. Morgan
Cardell, John vs. Augustus Moseley
Cardell, John and Early Davis vs. W. J. M. Preston
Cardell, John vs. N. S. Walker
Cardell, John vs. Bolling Whitfield
Cardell, John and William G. Horsley vs. W. D. Wynn
Cardell, M. F. vs. W. D. Wynn
Cardell, Mary E. vs. High and Foster
Cardell, P. D. vs. O. H. Arnold, Jr.
Cardell, P. D. vs. Medina Turk, Claudius Turk and W. F. Jordan
Cardell, Peter vs. Key and Preston
Cardell, Peter vs. F. M. Lester
Cardell, Peter vs. John W. Morgan
Cardell, Peter D. vs. Franklin George
Cardell, Peter D. vs. W. D. Wynn
Cardell, William vs. Commercial Nurseries
Carey, J. A., J. W. Barr, A. L. Johnson and Snelling Johnson vs.
  Reuben Hunter
Carey, Job A. vs. Collins, Flanders and Co.
Carey, Job A. vs. Wesley Griggs
Cargile, Brisco and Joe Shy vs. Bank of Monticello
Cargile, John and P. M. Roby vs. Allen D. Candler for use of
  Officers of Court

Cargile, John vs. Cincinnatus Dumas
Cargile, John vs. Corey Freeman
Cargile, John and H. B. Jordan vs. Solomon Penn
Cargile, John vs. Shipp and Webb
Cargile, Shade vs. Kelly and McDowell
Carr, John vs. N. B. White
Carter, Alex vs. The State
Carter, Alexander vs. James Oxford
Carter, Frank vs. John Edwards
Carter, Frank vs. The State
Carter, George vs. James Thomas Smith
Carter, Hector vs. The State
Carter, Lawson and Eli Carter vs. George W. McKlehaney
Carter, W. M. vs. Anderson, Starr and Co.
Carter, W. M. vs. Bernd Brothers
Carter, W. M. and Son vs. M. C. Kiser and J. F. Kiser
Carter, W. M. and Son vs. Remington Sewing Mach. Co.
Cary, D. T. and C. A. Cary vs. Mayer and Watts
Cary, J. A. vs. Clark, Rosser and Co.
Cary, Job A. vs. S. C. Talmadge
Cary, Jobe A. vs. Howe Machine Co.
Cary, Tom vs. The State
Catchings, Asbury vs. Thomas C. Broddus
Catchings, Asbury, Dave Catchings and Stephen Catchings vs.
   The State
Catchings, Bart vs. The State
Catchings, Eliza vs. The State
Central of Georgia R. R. Co. vs. Thomas G. Blackwell
Central of Ga. R. R. Co. vs. N. B. Goolsby
Central of Ga. R. R. Co. vs. V. F. McMichael
Central of Ga. R. R. Co. vs. J. W. Sammons
Chaffin, Greene vs. L. O. Benton and Bro.
Chaffin, Henry vs. The State
Chaffin, T. S. and Ellender Noles vs. Thomas Camp
Chaffin, Virgil vs. Mrs. Jane Jordan
Chambers, J. W. and C. G. Chambers vs. Georgia Chemical Works
Chapman, Allen vs. N. B. White
Charping, S. C. vs. Virginia L. Bartlett
Charping, S. C. and V. A. Chaffin vs. A. O. M. Gay
Charping, S. C. vs. W. A. Kelly
Charping, S. C. vs. N. B. White
Chatman, Bobbie vs. The State
Chatman, Janie vs. The State
Chatman, Lewis vs. County Commissioners
Cherry, James vs. J. H. Kelly
Childers, E. D., J. R. Roberts and T. J. Smith vs. L. O. Benton
   and Bro.
Childs, John vs. G. T. Powers
Childs, Robert vs. J. W. Oxford
Clark, Alex vs. The State
Clark, Alf. vs. L. O. Benton and Eugene Benton
Clark, Allen and Henry Appling vs. Dr. S. M. Anderson
Clark, Martin (col) vs. The State
Clark, William (col) vs. The State
Clay, J. J. vs. S. C. Talmadge and Berry T. Digby
Clay, James J. vs. William Andrews
Clay, Lawton vs. The State
Clay, Mary Lee vs. The State
Clem (col) vs. Elbert Baynes
Clements, Dave vs. Robert Whitfield
Clements, Evan vs. The State
Clements, Jeptha vs. Henry Branham
Clements, Phineas vs. The State

338

Clements, Simon and Moody Thurman vs. J. W. Holland
Clements, Willie vs. K. P. Greer and Co.
Clemons, David vs. John W. Morgan
Clemons, Mose vs. The State
Cochran, Berry vs. L. O. Benton and Bro.
Cochran, James and Thomas S. Hammond vs. Wiley B. Grubbs
Cochran, Joe vs. Thomas W. Pye
Cochran, John vs. The State
Cochran, Thomas vs. Richmond Darden
Cochran, Thomas vs. Doctor Johnson
Cofer, J. Thomas vs. John L. Cofer
Cohen, Sam vs. Anderson Shoe and Leather Co.
Cohen, Sam vs. B. Light and Co.
Cohen Samuel vs. David Greenwald and Samuel Greenwald
Cohen, Samuel and E. H. Cohen vs. Harrett Hawk
Coleman, Levie vs. Arnold Grocery Co.
Collier, Isaac vs. Asher Levy
Comer, Lewis and Ad Blackwell vs. W. D. Maddux
Comer, Lewis vs. Roberts and Peurifoy
Comer, Lydie (col) vs. The State
Compton, Dora vs. The State
Connelly, H. E. vs. L. O. Benton and Eugene Benton
Connelly, James and G. H. Connelly vs. The State
Cook, Aaron vs. The State
Cook, Hardy vs. Dick Davidson
Cook, Hardy vs. W. C. Turk
Cook, J. B. vs. Mattie Folds
Cook, J. W. vs. W. E. Ballard
Cook, J. W. vs. L. O. Benton and Bro.
Cook, J. W. vs. Thomas Camp
Cook, J. W. vs. The State
Cook, John W. vs. Key and Preston
Cook, John Wesley vs. Partheney Dawkins
Cook, L. E. vs. John Bogan and C. P. Bogan
Cook, L. E. vs. F. M. Lester
Cook, Lawrence E. vs. Aug Mosely
Cook, N. G. and J. W. Cook vs. Boykin R. Smith
Cook, N. G. and B. Barron vs. South. Bank and Trust Co.
Cook, Thomas vs. The State
Cook, Thomas L. vs. J. H. Lane
Cornwell, G. M. vs. The State
Cornwell, H. M. vs. Richard Graham
Cornwell, Henry (col) vs. George M. Key
Cornwell, J. C. vs. Carmichael and Co.
Cornwell, Lee vs. The State
Cornwell, W. D. vs. W. B. Sparks
Cornwell, William D. vs. Griffin, Monticello and Madison Rail-
  road Co.
Cornwell, William D. and J. C. Cornwell vs. M. M. McKinley and Co.
Couch, Croff vs. L. O. Benton and Eugene Benton
Couch, Ede vs. The State
Couch, Mollie vs. The State
Couch, N. H. vs. Gilbert Greer (col)
County of Jasper vs. ? Smith
Covington and Macon R. R. Co. vs. James K. Polk
Cowan, Edwin vs. The State
Cox, Tom vs. The State
Cox, W. M. vs. D. T. Singleton
Cox, W. M. vs. Robert Young
Cox, William vs. Nancy Whitfield, Bryant Johnson and Gaston
  Whitfield
Crane, Lee vs. A. M. Robinson and Co.
Crane, Nathan vs. N. B. White

Crawford, Humphrey and Queen Crawford vs. Pleas Sanders
Crossley, R. J. vs. S. G. Shy
Crossley, R. J. vs. James L. Tucker
Crow, Elisha vs. William Andrews
Cubbage, John vs. E. W. Baynes
Cullens, Charles vs. Robert Whitfield
Cunnard, N. vs. Swan, Stewart and Co.

Daniel, Annie vs. The State
Daniel, Anthony (col) vs. W. W. Evans
Daniel, Anthony vs. W. J. M. Preston
Daniel, Dan vs. Daughtry Brothers
Daniel, Robert vs. Jacob Whitfield
Daniel, Warren vs. Daniel Daniel
Daniel, Warren vs. Mrs. O. J. Jordan
Daniel, William vs. W. W. Evans
Darden, W. W. vs. S. C. Lawrence
Darden, Wiley vs. Shipp and Webb
Darden, William (col), Isham Morgan (col) and Stephen H.
    Johnston vs. John E. Pye
Davidson, Dick vs. The State
Davidson, Rea vs. N. B. White
Davidson, Richard vs. N. B. White
Davidson, T. M. vs. Price and Steele
Davidson, Thomas M. vs. James L. Campbell
Davidson, Thomas M. vs. The State
Davis, Anderson (col) (alias Dick Davidson) vs. W. F. Matthews
Davis, Drew vs. John W. Morgan
Davis, George and Sallie Davis vs. David K. Allen and Walker W.
    Allen
Davis, George H. vs. Mary Baley
Davis, Joe vs. The State
Davis, Marion A. vs. The State
Davis, Mrs. Mollie vs. A. S. Thurman
Davis, S. W. vs. Robert Childs
Davis, S. W. vs. W. W. Davis
Davis, Sarah, I. H. Freeman and C. E. Spears vs. Joel L. Terrell
Davis, Sarah E. vs. J. T. Estes
Davis, Thomas C. vs. Lucius Newton
Davis, Will vs. The State
Dawkins, George W. and Samuel Dawkins vs. John R. Greer
Dawkins, George W. vs. Kelly and Price
Dawkins, George W. vs. A. M. Robinson and Co.
Dawkins, George W. vs. N. B. White
Daws, Joel vs. Broughton and Fitzpatrick
Daws, Joel vs. Franklin George
Dawson, W. R. vs. E. B. Ezell and B. W. Hunt
Dawson, Warren vs. J. T. Smith
Deiter, A. W. vs. Monticello Merchandise Co.
Denham, Lurie J. vs. Willy Denham
Dennis, Annie E. and N. S. Walker vs. Putnam County Banking Co.
Dennis, Frank vs. The State
Dennis, G. W. vs. Frank Leverett
Dennis, G. W. vs. E. Ward
Dennis, G. Wesley vs. W. C. Davis
Dennis, John vs. The State
Dennis, W. E. vs. K. P. Greer and Co.
Dennis, W. E. vs. R. Jordan
Denson, James M. vs. William T. McLeroy
Derica, Dock vs. Sidney Baynes
Derico, Lucien vs. Sidney Baynes
Digby, Abe vs. The State
Digby, B. T., W. W. Baynes, W. P. Hardy and W. F. Jordan vs.

Delia Glover
Digby, B. T. vs. John Turk and W. C. Turk
Digby, Benjamin vs. William H. Arnold
Digby, Berry T. and James T. Lewis vs. Charles L. Bartlett
Digby, Berry T. vs. J. Clisby, H. H. Jones and A. W. Reese
Digby, Berry T. vs. J. H. Connelly, J. Connelly for use of G. H.
Connelly
Digby, Berry T. vs. William A. Reid
Digby, Dennis vs. W. B. Beckwith
Digby, George vs. A. L. Sluder
Digby, J. M. vs. John T. Eckols
Digby, James vs. Holland and Anderson
Digby, James H. vs. Charping and Chaffin
Digby, James H. vs. G. H. Connelly and J. Connelly
Digby, James H. vs. Anderson J. Middlebrooks
Digby, James H. vs. William C. Penn
Digby, James H. vs. G. V. Shipp and J. B. Webb
Digby, James H. vs. N. B. White
Digby, James M. vs. Kelly and Price
Digby, James M. vs. Price and Steele
Digby, James M. vs. Francis M. Swanson
Digby, John B., Sawrence Digby and W. B. Digby vs. James Benton
Digby, John B. vs. William H. Head
Digby, John B. vs. Johnson and Dunlop
Digby, John B. vs. A. I. Sluder
Digby, T. E. vs. L. O. Benton and Eugene Benton
Digby, W. L. vs. Monticello Merchandise Co.
Digby, William and John Digby vs. L. O. Benton and Eugene Benton
Digby, William B. vs. Georgia Chemical Works
Digby, William B. vs. The State
Dillard, Will vs. The State
Dixon, Seaborn vs. J. O. Shepherd
Doster, James W. and William F. Jordan vs. Alphonsus F. Spears
Doster, P. W., L. P. Doster and Mrs. Georgia M. Flemister vs.
Kelly and Beckwith
Doster, Mrs. T. A. vs. John W. Morgan
Dougherty, P. H. vs. Saulsbury Respass and Co.
Dougherty, William vs. William Andrews
Dozier, G. R. vs. Griffin, Monticello and Madison Railroad Co.
Dozier, G. R. and Co. vs. J. C. Ayer and Co.
Dozier, George R. and John G. Elder vs. Barrett and Land
Dozier, Warner vs. Key and Preston
Drew, Franklin vs. Madison Epps
Driscoll, Alex and Mrs. M. C. Broddus vs. D. J. Holsenbeck
Driskel, Mollie and Meridy Driskel vs. W. F. Jordan
Driskell, Jack vs. A. H. Jordan and C. L. Henderson
Driskell, James L. vs. Thomas Camp
Driskell, James T. vs. M. Flatan
Driskell, James T. vs. G. D. Gordon
Driskell, James T. vs. H. J. Lamar
Driskell, James T. vs. F. M. Swanson
Driskell, William vs. The State
Duberry, Thomas vs. J. C. Clark
Dudley, Joe vs. The State
Dukes, F. M. vs. A. M. Robinson and Co.
Dumas, Cincinatus vs. N. B. White
Dumas, Cincinnatus vs. Thomas C. Broddus
Dumas, Frank vs. The State
Dumas, Medora vs. E. S. Broddus
Durden, J. C. vs. L. O. Benton and Bro.
Durden, W. D. vs. E. H. Carroll and Co.
Durden, Wiley vs. Dumas and Allen
Dyer, Henry vs. Albert Barnes

Dyer, John R. vs. Samuel Harris
Dykes, Tom vs. The State
Earley, Comber and Dick Davidson vs. Eaton H. Kelly
Eberhardt, George W. vs. The State
Edwards, Columbus vs. M. A. McDowell
Edwards, Ed vs. The State
Edwards, John vs. Roberts and Roberts
Edwards, Mariah and W. D. Durdin vs. O. H. Arnold, Jr.
Edwards, Richard vs. W. J. M. Preston
Edwards, Richard vs. Roberts and Peurifoy
Edwards, S. B. vs. Mrs. J. A. Adams
Edwards, S. B. vs. R. L. Doughtry, J. G. Doughtry and H. L.
  Doughtry
Edwards, S. J. vs. J. H. Andrews and J. H. Huddleston
Edwards, W. C. vs. J. H. Kelly
Elder, B. F. vs. W. E. Tucker
Elder, Benjamin F. vs. Kelly and Price
Elder, Benjamin F. and Edward A. Elder vs. B. Rice
Elder, Benjamin F. vs. A. L. Sluder
Elder, Benjamin F. vs. The State
Elder, Dave vs. Aris Newton
Elder, Edward A. vs. Scipio Pye (col)
Elder, J. G. vs. H. B. Ridley
Elder, John G. vs. O. P. Fitzsimmons
Elder, Salina C. vs. Newton and Bailey
Elder, W. S. vs. J. H. Smith for use of Bank of Monticello
Epps, Andrew vs. Martha E. Carter
Epps, Andrew and Madison Epps vs. Kelly and Price
Epps, B. J., Jr. and Benjamin Epps, Jr. vs. L. O. Benton and
  Eugene Benton
Epps, Benjamin, Jr. vs. The State
Epps, Edom vs. Monticello Merchandise Co.
Epps, Madison vs. Bank of Monticello
Epps, Madison vs. Obadiah R. Belcher
Epps, Madison vs. Francis B. Davies
Epps, Madison vs. Edward A. Freeman
Epps, Madison vs. Lewis Glover
Epps, Madison and Elizabeth Epps vs. John R. Greer
Epps, Madison vs. Jewett Jordan
Epps, Madison vs. Kelly and Price
Epps, Madison vs. Lawton and Wellingham
Epps, Madison vs. S. Levy and Co.
Epps, Madison and Elizabeth Epps vs. Lewis and Bailey
Epps, Madison vs. Ann E. Mygatt
Epps, Madison vs. Francis M. Swanson
Epps, Madison vs. A. J. Talmadge, Samuel C. Charping and Joseph
  G. Tolleson
Epps, Madison vs. Aaron Thurman, Jr.
Epps, Madison vs. Charles Turner
Epps, Matt vs. Carhart and Curd
Epps, Morgan and Tillman Pickens (col) vs. The State
Evans, S. C. vs. The State
Ezell, John vs. The State
Ezell, John H. vs. J. H. Freeman
Ezell, L. D. vs. J. C. Allen
Ezell, L. D. vs. J. B. English and Co.
Ezell, Robert F. vs. Wheeler and Willson Mfg. Co.
Ezell, W. P. vs. Lucian Benton

Farr, J. M. R. vs. Monticello Merchandise Co.
Faulkner, J. P. vs. Mrs. Alice (Faulkner) Burney
Favers, J. R. vs. The State
Favers, J. R. and E. N. Waldrup vs. J. M. Terrell

Favors, Joe T. vs. John W. Morgan
Fears, Buster vs. The State
Fears, Claiborne vs. Elizabeth Fears
Fears, Ephraim vs. J. L. Campbell
Fears, Ephraim (col) vs. George Gill
Fears, John vs. The State
Fears, Mike vs. Wynn and Clack
Fears, Rhoda, W. R. Smith and Clabe Fears vs. L. O. Benton and
    Eugene Benton
Fish, Henry and E. D. Tuggle vs. L. O. Benton and Bros.
Fish, John vs. The State
Fish, William T. vs. D. A. Gibbs and I. N. B. Spence
Flatan, Morris vs. J. M. Holbrook
Flemister, Mrs. Georgia M. vs. A. D. Adair and McCarty Brothers
Flemister, Georgia M. vs. L. O. Benton and Eugene Benton
Flemister, George M. and J. M. Flemister vs. James H. Campbell
    and Bro.
Flemister, Horace vs. Rose Alexander
Flemister, Horace vs. A. S. Holland
Flemister, J. C. vs. Sally Lewis and Clifford Lewis
Flemister, J. C. vs. Summers and Murphey
Flemister, J. M. vs. Anderson and Lunceford
Flemister, J. M. vs. Hutchinson Company
Flemister, J. M. vs. W. F. Jordan
Flemister, J. M. vs. Miller and Smith
Flemister, J. M. and J. C. Flemister vs. J. R. Mobley and Co.
Flemister, J. M. vs. Robinson, Kelly and Co.
Flemister, Martha vs. James L. Tucker
Flournoy, J. E. vs. Benton Supply Co.
Flournoy, S. A. vs. H. C. Hill
Flournoy, Samuel vs. Mickey Flournoy
Flournoy, Will M. vs. James A. Stone
Flournoy, Willis vs. John W. Morgan
Folds, Boston vs. Elvira Driskell
Folds, J. F. vs. J. H. Kelly
Folds, James and Jane Folds vs. William F. Jordan
Folds, W. L. vs. T. J. Smith and R. L. Davis
Fort, Neal (col) vs. The State
Fort, Sam (Ford) vs. Joseph H. Brooks
Fort, Sam vs. Sealey Dobbins and Pharrer Watson
Fort, Samuel and Nelson Glover vs. Reid and Lazenby
Foster, Abe vs. The State
Foster, Jake vs. The State
Foster, Young vs. J. E. Pitts
Fowler, Stephen and J. M. Briscoe vs. L. W. Pon and Caroline Pon
Franklin, A. S. vs. Jefferson G. Lazenby
Franklin, Hattie vs. The State
Freeman and Goolsby vs. Chichester and Co.
Freeman and Goolsby vs. Day, Hoagland, Steger and Co.
Freeman, A. C. vs. George W. Scott and Co.
Freeman, Ada vs. The State
Freeman, Benjamin B. and Isaac H. Freeman vs. Pleasant P.
    Lovejoy and John D. Lovejoy
Freeman, Brown vs. The State
Freeman, Cynthia A. and Isaac T. Wyatt vs. G. H. Dixon
Freeman, E. and William Jordan vs. H. P. Smith
Freeman, E. A. vs. Daughtry Bros.
Freeman, E. A. and M. A. Freeman vs. J. S. Pursley for use of
    Wheeler and Wilson Mfg. Co.
Freeman, Eliza and Catharine McMichael vs. Silla Hunter
Freeman, Ellie vs. Louisa Smith
Freeman, Floyd vs. Madora Keen and Mrs. T. W. Reese
Freeman, Frank vs. W. W. Evans

Freeman, Frank vs. F. M. Lester
Freeman, George vs. W. A. Kelly and Bros.
Freeman, George, Sr. and John F. Freeman vs. Edgar C. Pope
Freeman, Henry vs. The State
Freeman, I. H. vs. William M. Burnett and G. A. Ray
Freeman, Isaac H. vs. Elisha G. Crawford, Abednego J. Crawford, and William G. Crawford
Freeman, Isaac H., Seaborn Kelly, George Freeman (col), Sam Freeman (col) and Lucky Freeman vs. John W. Wyatt
Freeman, John, King Freeman and Edmund Freeman (alias Horse Freeman) vs. The State
Freeman, John F. and S. M. Pope vs. Georgia Chemical Works
Freeman, John F. vs. The State
Freeman, Lee vs. W. H. Jordan
Freeman, Mollie (col) vs. The State
Freeman, Sam and C. Freeman vs. Benton Supply Co.
Freeman, Silla vs. E. S. Broddus
Freeman, Thomas vs. Madison Epps
Freeman, Thomas (col) vs. A. J. Talmadge and Co.
Freeman, W. M. vs. W. A. Kelly and Bro.
Freeman, Wesley (col) vs. The State
Freeman, William vs. Wiley Phillips, Green M. Phillips, John B. Phillips and Andrew J. Freeman
Fry, Dave vs. The State
Funderburg, J. C. and J. W. Crow vs. Lawton and Willingham

Gaither, Morris vs. The State
Gant, John vs. Leverett and Co.
Gant, Lewis vs. Ida Barron and Benjamin Barron
Gant, Lewis and Elmira Gant vs. R. B. Holloway
Gant, Lewis vs. The State
Gant, Louis vs. Robert Coleman and Boliver H. Ray
Gantt, Cicero vs. A. J. Talmadge and J. G. Tolleson
Gantt, Henry (alias Bob Gantt) vs. The State
Gantt, Jim vs. Greer Bros. and Garland for use of S. E. Lazenby and Charles L. Henderson, exor.
Garrett, R. M. vs. Thomas Camp
Garrett, R. M. vs. Frank Wright
Garrett, S. W. vs. S. J. Steele and G. H. Cornwell
Gaston, Charles vs. Albert J. Talmadge
Gaston, Charley A. vs. Frank Leverett
Gaston, Elizabeth and William H. Thompson vs. A. C. Perry
Gaston, T. G. vs. J. H. Campbell and S. R. Campbell
Gaston, Tom vs. The State
Gates, Henry, Ben Moreton and Lewis Gates vs. J. H. Bullard and S. H. Bullard
Gautier, Fannie vs. The State
Gay, A. O. M. and Elbert H. Gay vs. John L. Robinson
Gay, Charles vs. Bank of Monticello
Gay, Elbert H. and Augustus O. M. Gay vs. Alexander Bennett, Silas S. Starr for use of James Harvey
Geiger, R. C. vs. L. W. Pon
Geiger, R. C. vs. Francis M. Swanson
George, America (col) vs. Martha Reese (col)
George Berry vs. The State
George, Harriet vs. John W. Morgan
George, Harriet vs. The State
George, Hilliard vs. The State
Ghant, Dora vs. N. B. White
Gibson, Abe (col) vs. Ely Braseal (col)
Giles, John vs. James T. Corley
Gilmore, Thomas vs. F. M. Lester
Gilstrap, George vs. A. J. Talmadge

Gilstrap, J. M. and Shelly P. Downs vs. James Howard and Lewis
  Lynch
Gilstrap, J. M. vs. N. B. White
Gilstrap, Jeremiah M. vs. William P. Anderson and Co.
Gilstrap, Jeremiah M. vs. Shipp and Webb
Gilstrap, Jeremiah M. vs. D. H. Wilcox
Gilstrap, Reuben (col) vs. The State
Gilstrap, Reuben vs. N. B. White
Glass, Henry vs. Printup Bro. and Pollard
Glass, Thomas vs. The State
Glawson, Genus vs. Benton Supply Co.
Glawson, Mary E., Jonas Standifer and J. C. Durden vs. W. E.
  Baynes
Glover, America vs. Elder and Dozier
Glover, Anderson vs. J. P. Hardy
Glover, Brack, Jr. and Mitch Glover vs. The State
Glover, Dennis vs. John B. Webb
Glover, Emily (col) vs. The State
Glover, Frances vs. The State
Glover, Gena vs. The State
Glover, H. S. vs. Russell J. Brown
Glover, H. S. vs. N. B. White and L. White
Glover, Henry vs. Matilda Thomas
Glover, Henry S. and Francis M. Swanson vs. Samuel Griswold
Glover, Henry S. vs. S. C. Talmadge and Bro.
Glover, Henry S. vs. Nehemiah B. White and Lucius White
Glover, J. J. vs. James H. Campbell and S. R. Campbell
Glover, Jessie vs. The State
Glover, Lewis (col) vs. Jonas H. Holland
Glover, Mathew (col) vs. J. L. Campbell
Glover, Matthew (col) vs. W. A. Kelly and Bro.
Glover, Milley vs. James Thomas Smith
Glover, Millie (col) vs. W. F. Jordan
Glover, Millie vs. B. L. Willingham
Glover, Orange vs. A. S. Thurman
Glover, Orange and J. H. Glover vs. W. L. Turner
Glover, Peter vs. A. M. Robinson and Co.
Glover, Stewart vs. The State
Glover, William vs. The State
Godkin, John R. vs. Charles D. Pearson
Goodman, Barney and Aaron Fish vs. L. O. Benton and Eugene Benton
Goodman, Barney and Abram Greer vs. Martha Lane
Goodman, James vs. John R. Greer
Goodman, James T. vs. Key and Preston
Goodman, Mollie vs. The State
Goodwin, Randall vs. The State
Goolsby, Mrs. A. L. vs. L. O. Benton and Eugene Benton
Goolsby, Mrs. A. L. and R. H. Goolsby vs. J. H. Kelly
Goolsby, Alex vs. Talmadge and Tolleson
Goolsby, Alfred (col) vs. Tabitha Goolsby (col)
Goolsby, Alfred vs. J. H. Kelly and W. A. Kelly
Goolsby, Braxton vs. The State
Goolsby, Burrel vs. G. W. Scott and Co.
Goolsby, C. D. vs. F. M. Swanson
Goolsby, C. L. vs. L. O. Benton and Eugene Benton
Goolsby, C. R. vs. A. H. Coates
Goolsby, C. R. vs. Georgia Farmers Oil and Fertilizer Co.
Goolsby, C. R. vs. John Merryman and Co.
Goolsby, C. R. vs. Sarah Ann Waits
Goolsby, C. R. vs. Walton Guano Co.
Goolsby, C. R. vs. S. Waxelbaum and Son
Goolsby, C. R., Sr. vs. J. D. Anchors
Goolsby, Carden R. vs. Nehemiah B. White and Henry C. McClure

Goolsby, Charles vs. Dr. J. C. Clark
Goolsby, Charles vs. Francis Goolsby
Goolsby, Charles vs. A. M. Robinson and J. R. Robinson
Goolsby, Charles vs. The State
Goolsby, Charley and Mary Goolsby vs. J. G. Lazenby
Goolsby, Cincinnatus L. vs. Nehemiah B. White and Henry C.
   McClure
Goolsby, Clayton D. vs. Allen Eason (col)
Goolsby, Clayton D. vs. Francis M. Swanson
Goolsby, F. C. vs. J. C. Clark
Goolsby, F. C. and M. C. Goolsby vs. T. A. Hutchinson and R. W.
   Hutchinson
Goolsby, F. C. vs. Napes Formula and Peruvian Guano Co.
Goolsby, F. C. vs. J. O. Mathewson
Goolsby, F. C., J. C. Goolsby and J. K. Goolsby vs. W. M.
   Robinson and Co.
Goolsby, Frank vs. Fannie Rebecca Jordan
Goolsby, Frank vs. Shipp and Webb
Goolsby, Frank vs. N. B. White
Goolsby, Frank Walker (alias Coot Goolsby) vs. The State
Goolsby, Freeman vs. A. Gruhn
Goolsby, Gus (col) vs. The State
Goolsby, H. L. vs. Monticello Vehicle Co.
Goolsby, J. C. vs. J. P. Quinn
Goolsby, J. C. vs. F. M. Swanson
Goolsby, J. K. vs. Lucian Benton
Goolsby, J. K. vs. Leo Frank
Goolsby, J. K. vs. Illinois Sewing Machine Co.
Goolsby, J. K. vs. Macon Grocery Co.
Goolsby, J. K. vs. Monticello Grocery Co.
Goolsby, J. K. vs. Ed Weichselbaum
Goolsby, J. K. vs. Wingo, Ellett and Crump Shoe Co.
Goolsby, James vs. G. R. Dozier and Co.
Goolsby, James (col) vs. The State
Goolsby, James B. vs. Howard and Soule
Goolsby, James B. vs. Key and Preston
Goolsby, James B. vs. N. S. Walker
Goolsby, James B. vs. Walter L. Zachry
Goolsby, John K. vs. Henry Christian and R. T. Christian
Goolsby, John K. vs. Loyd and Williams
Goolsby, John K. vs. John Merryman and Co. and James C. Denham
Goolsby, John K. vs. William E. Paul
Goolsby, John K. vs. Shipp and Webb
Goolsby, John K. vs. D. T. Singleton
Goolsby, John K. vs. Francis M. Swanson
Goolsby, John K. vs. C. Taylor
Goolsby, John K. vs. James Turner
Goolsby, John K. vs. J. D. Wild for use of Bowker Fertilizer Co.
Goolsby, John K. vs. W. W. Woodruff
Goolsby, John Walker vs. Jonas H. Holland
Goolsby, Leman vs. S. P. Lane for use of Smith and Etheridge
Goolsby, M. A. vs. O. P. Fitzsimmons
Goolsby, M. C. and F. C. Goolsby vs. L. O. Benton and Eugene
   Benton
Goolsby, M. C. and F. C. Goolsby vs. Napier Bros.
Goolsby, M. C. and F. C. Goolsby vs. Planters Warehouse Co.
Goolsby, Mason vs. C. T. Ezell
Goolsby, Meredy vs. John H. Kelly
Goolsby, N. B. vs. The State
Goolsby, Nat, Jr. vs. J. W. Murrell
Goolsby, R. H. vs. Chemical Co. of Canton
Goolsby, R. H. vs. Spring and Co.
Goolsby, Rufus vs. A. H. Jordan and C. L. Henderson

Goolsby, Squire vs. Mary Goolsby
Goolsby, Tom vs. Robert F. Ezell
Goolsby, W. B. and R. H. Goolsby vs. C. Masterson and Wallace
  Masterson
Goolsby, W. B. vs. A. M. Robinson and Co.
Goolsby, Wade B. vs. James L. Campbell
Goolsby, Wade B. vs. G. W. Dozier and Co.
Goolsby, Wade B. vs. Madison Epps
Goolsby, Wade B. vs. Mrs. E. A. Mygat
Goolsby, Wade B. vs. Reid and Lazenby
Goolsby, Wade B. vs. Francis M. Swanson
Goolsby, William vs. The State
Goolsby, Willie vs. G. F. Greene for use of L. O. Benton and
  Bros.
Gollsby, Willie vs. The State
Gordon, Clayton vs. Lawton and Willingham
Gordon, G. O. vs. K. P. Greer and T. A. Hutchinson
Gordon, George vs. Roberts and Peurifoy
Gordon, George D. vs. Lawrence and Co.
Gordon, George D. vs. A. A. Penn
Gordon, J. W. and Benjamin Barron vs. L. O. Benton and Bro.
Gordon, W. R. and Julia A. Adams vs. Shipp and Webb
Gordon, W. R. vs. Francis M. Swanson
Gotier, Fannie vs. The State
Gould, H. S. vs. O. H. Arnold, Jr.
Gould, H. S. and J. R. Hightower vs. H. D. Bush
Gould, H. S., Ada Gould and J. R. Hightower vs. Etheridge,
  Trammell and Co.
Gould, H. S. vs. Charlie Kent
Gould, H. S. vs. George Kent
Gould, H. S. vs. Richard Kent
Grant, Lewis vs. Coleman and Ray
Graves, Charley vs. The State
Gray, A. T. and Annie G. Gray vs. The Cable Company
Gray, A. T. and Katie Gray vs. James Thomas Smith
Gray, Adam vs. The State
Green, Ann vs. Rebecca C. Pon
Green, E. A. vs. E. B. Ezell and Co.
Green, E. A. vs. R. S. Jaques, Tinsley Co.
Green, E. A. vs. Kennesaw Guano Company
Green, E. A. vs. Martha E. Rodgers
Green, Elizabeth vs. Charles P. Aiken and E. H. Aiken
Green, G. F. vs. Davis and Leverett
Green, J. A. vs. Commercial Nurseries
Green, James A. vs. W. E. Tucker and Bro.
Green, James M. vs. James Lowery
Green, Joseph vs. George J. Wilson
Green, Nancy J. and W. F. Jordan vs. Kelly and Phillips
Green, R. Jasper vs. Wise and Breed
Green, Randal vs. J. G. Tolleson
Green, Robert vs. Athon Brothers
Green, William vs. Augustus Mosely
Green, William vs. Delphy Penn (col)
Green, William vs. N. S. Walker
Green, William M. and John Cardell vs. F. George
Green, William M. vs. Kelly and McDowell
Green, William M. vs. John W. Morgan
Green, William M. vs. W. D. Wynn
Greene, E. A. vs. S. Cohen
Greene, G. F. vs. H. C. Blackwell
Greene, James vs. Bolling Whitfield
Greer, A. C. and K. P. Greer vs. J. A. Stone
Greer, Aaron vs. John R. Greer

Greer, Andrew and Charles Greer vs. The State
Greer, Annie and Abraham Greer vs. C. M. Davis and Co. for use
   of Putnam County Banking Co.
Greer, Bill (col) vs. The State
Greer, Clark and Andrew Greer vs. The State
Greer, Dick (col) vs. The State
Greer, Dick (col) vs. John P. Webb
Greer, Frances and Frank Greer vs. Benton Supply Co.
Greer, G. D. vs. N. B. White and H. C. McClure
Greer, George (col) vs. Robert L. Berner
Greer, George (col) vs. George M. Key
Greer, Gilbert D. vs. Demerest and Woodruff
Greer, Giles and Willis McMichael vs. Robert J. Warren
Greer, Green vs. The State
Greer, Henry and Richard B. Phillips vs. M. S. Benton and L. O.
   Benton
Greer, J. C. vs. J. A. Kelly
Greer, J. L. vs. M. Kinard and T. J. Kinard
Greer, Jack vs. J. W. Minter
Greer, Jack vs. Charles Wilson for use of Officers of Court
Greer, Jasper vs. J. M. Wise and Thomas Breed
Greer, John C. vs. Sally H. Kelly
Greer, John L. vs. James Aron
Greer, John R. vs. Lewis and Bailey
Greer, John R. vs. The State
Greer, Lucinda and Aaron Kelly vs. L. O. Benton and Eugene
   Benton
Greer, N. H. vs. M. K. Kinard
Greer, N. H. and W. T. Morgan vs. W. T. Maynard
Greer, Nathaniel H. vs. Roberts and Roberts
Greer, Nathaniel H. vs. Talmadge and Tolleson
Greer, R. C. vs. Georgia A. Wilkes
Greer, Richard vs. The State
Greer, Robert vs. Athan and Bros.
Greer, William, Henry Williams, George Davis and Abner Davis vs.
   The State
Greer, Willie vs. James H. Campbell and Bro.
Greer, Willie and E. N. Goodman vs. G. B. Elder
Grier, Giles vs. J. O. Shepherd
Grier, Haly vs. Gilbert D. Grier
Griffin, Alonzo vs. Joe Sands
Griffin, Alonzo vs. The State
Griffin, Bettie and J. J. Griffin vs. R. L. Allen
Griffin, W. A. vs. Joe Sands
Griffin, E. H. vs. J. H. Kelly
Griffin, Everett vs. The State
Griffin, Missouri and Maggie Griffin vs. The State
Griffin, Willie and J. L. P. Griffin vs. M. S. Benton
Griggs, Elbert vs. H. B. Jordan, A. H. Jordan and D. R. Glover
Griggs, Elbert vs. J. H. S. Smith
Griggs, Gus vs. The State
Griggs, J. W. vs. William Hazlehurst
Griggs, J. W. vs. B. B. Odom and S. E. Odom
Griggs, J. W. vs. D. T. Singleton
Griggs, J. W. vs. J. G. Tolleson
Griggs, Mark vs. M. A. McDowell
Griggs, Mark vs. The State
Griggs, Simmons vs. The State
Griggs, Wesley and A. T. Barber vs. James M. Terrell
Grimes, Bishop vs. The State
Grimes, Peter vs. The State
Grits, Sam vs. The State
Groodzuiski, H. M. vs. The State

Groves, Jasper B. vs. John Redding
Grubbs, John W. vs. Giles Greer (col)
Grubbs, Mrs. M. A. vs. John W. Cochran
Grubbs, Mildred A. and Edwin Grubbs vs. James H. Campbell
Grubbs, Mildred A., James M. Jones and J. W. Grubbs vs. William
   H. Head
Grubbs, Wiley vs. J. H. Morgan
Grubbs, Wiley B. vs. Shipp and Webb
Gunn, John T. vs. The State
Gunnels, W. T. vs. H. W. Whitten
Guy, Charles vs. A. S. Holland
Guy, Charles vs. C. W. Jordan
Guy, Charles (col) and Lewis Tompkins (col) vs. Warren, Wallace
   and Co.

Hadaway, W. T. vs. J. H. Kelly
Hailes, Lucious vs. The State
Hale, T. H. vs. The State
Hales, J. F. vs. W. B. Beckwith and J. T. Kelly
Hall, Will vs. The State
Hames, Henrietta vs. The State
Hames, Kitty Ann vs. The State
Hames, Louisiana (col) vs. The State
Hancock, Lum vs. The State
Hancock, Tom vs. A. Gruhn
Hansford, Simeon vs. Middle Georgia Bank of Eatonton
Hardeman, Daniel vs. Cody Bryant
Harden, S. A. vs. R. L. Allen
Hardin, J. M. vs. J. J. Thornton
Hardin, W. S. vs. R. S. Allen
Hardman, Alp and Amanda Hardman vs. William H. Head
Hardman, Alphonso and Amanda Hardman vs. James Lewis
Hardman, Alphonso and Amanda Hardman vs. N. B. White and L. White
Hardman, Alphonzo and Amanda Hardman vs. James C. Aaron
Hardman, Daniel vs. Thomas J. Shepherd and William Shepherd
Hardman, Mollie A. vs. Charley A. Gaston
Hardwick, Thomas, Berry Cochran, Joe Cochran and John Hardwick
   vs. L. O. Benton and Eugene Benton
Hardy, A. D. vs. W. A. Kelly and Bros.
Hardy, Alfred H. vs. Corley and Dorsett
Hardy, C. M. vs. William Andrews
Hardy, C. M. vs. Griffin, Monticello and Madison Railroad Co.
Hardy, J. G. vs. Benton Supply Co.
Hardy, James D. and W. P. Hardy vs. Hugh T. Inman and Co.
Hardy, James D., J. O. Andrews and Turk Barnes vs. The State
Hardy, James P. and John R. Davidson vs. Gibbs and Sterrett Mfg.
   Co.
Hardy, James P. vs. Howard and Soule
Hardy, W. P. vs. Johnson and Lane
Hardy, W. P. vs. H. J. Lamar
Hardy, W. P. vs. M. V. McKibben
Hardy, William P. vs. Joshua Hill
Hardy, William P. vs. N. B. White
Harper, Ella vs. The State
Harris, Butler vs. The State
Harris, Frank vs. County Commissioners
Harris, James vs. Bolling Whitfield
Harris, Milton vs. Zachariah Bailey
Harris, Milton vs. W. B. Beckwith
Harris, Rilious vs. G. T. Powers
Harris, Rilious vs. The State
Harris, Shade (col) vs. Charles M. Meriwether
Harris, Simeon, Dan Nash and Aaron Meriwether vs. The State

Hart, Adam vs. Aris Newton, Jr.
Harvel, Frank vs. Whitfield and Brown
Harvell, James vs. Cinetta Hubbard
Harwell, Amos vs. The State
Harwell, John vs. Kelly and McDowell
Harwell, Marcus vs. Bolling Whitfield
Haschal, Cornelia vs. G. T. Pursley and S. C. Pursley
Hatterway, Martin vs. F. M. Swanson
Hawk, Isaac vs. Madison Epps
Hawk, Peter vs. Alexander L. Holland
Haynes, George W. vs. James F. Barnes
Hays, Chesley vs. J. G. Elder
Hays, Chesley vs. A. J. Talmadge
Head, J. G. vs. Southern Banking and Trust Co.
Head, J. H. vs. J. J. McClelland
Head, J. H. vs, J. H. S. Smith
Head, John H. vs. N. A. Griffitts
Head, William H. vs. Martha Ambrose
Head, Wilson vs. The State
Heard, Clark vs. W. W. Allen
Hearn, C. C. vs. James L. Campbell
Hearn, C. C. vs. Hardy Cook
Hearn, C. c. and W. A. J. Hearn vs. Mrs. F. C. Hearn
Hearn, C. C. vs. Key and Preston
Hearn, C. C. vs. P. C. Sawyer
Hearn, C. C. vs. Sibley and Wheless
Hearn, W. and Ransom H. Aikin vs. Z. J. Fitzpatrick
Hearn, W. S. vs. Georgia Chemical Works
Hempfield, Sarah vs. O. H. Arnold, Jr.
Henderson, Albert vs. The State
Henderson, C. W. vs. Anchors and Middlebrooks
Henderson, C. W. vs. Frank Leverett
Henderson, C. W. vs. W. M. Robinson
Henderson, Charles vs. William Andrews
Henderson, Charles vs. The State
Henderson, Charles, Sr. vs. Thomas M. Davidson
Henderson, Isaac W. vs. W. F. Cannon
Henderson, Isaac W. vs. O. G. Sparks and Son for use of R. W.
  Bonner
Henderson, Lewis and Mattie Henderson vs. McDade and Paschal
Henderson, M. G. vs. Bank of Monticello
Henderson, P. D. vs. O. H. Arnold, Jr.
Henderson, Samuel vs. Manson Pitts
Henderson, Samuel L. and Randal Banks vs. James Robinson,
  Augustus M. Robinson, John Webb and W. F. Davis
Henderson, W. P. vs. A. M. Robinson and J. B. Robinson
Herring, John Henry vs. The State
Hester, Henderson vs. The State
Hickman, H. W. vs. Leverett and Ezell
Hickman, O. P. vs. Thomas Camp
Hickman, Sidney A. J. vs. Francis M. Swanson
Hicks, Moze vs. J. W. Thompson
High, Clem vs. The State
Hightower, Tony vs. The State
Hill, Anthony vs. Bolling Whitfield
Hill, Augustus vs. F. M. Lester
Hill, Jim vs. The State
Hill, Joshua vs. C. W. Jordan
Hill, Sam vs. The State
Hill, W. C. vs. E. R. Black
Hodges, J. J. vs. The State
Hogan, A. J. vs. J. H. Holland
Hogan, A. J. vs. W. A. Kelly and Bros.

Hogan, Ellis vs. Price and Steele
Hogan, Loftin and Wilkes Walker vs. The State
Hogan, Mansfield vs. Mary Roberts
Holand, Mat vs. The State
Holland, A. S. vs. Kelly and McDowell
Holland, Aaron (col) vs. The State
Holland, Dr. Alexander vs. Augustus Moseley
Holland, George vs. A. M. Robinson
Holland, J. W. and W. F. Jordan vs. C. H. Greer
Holland, J. W. vs. F. M. Swanson
Holland, James A. vs. Key and Preston
Holland, James W. vs. W. A. Kelly and Bros.
Holland, James W. vs. Alice Phillips
Holland, John vs. The State
Holland, Judge and Green Wise vs. C. L. Bartlett
Holland, Seymore vs. The State
Holloway, D. P. vs. Griffin, Monticello and Madison Railroad Co.
Holloway, D. P. vs. E. H. Henry
Holloway, John vs. The State
Holloway, Newton vs. James B. Goolsby
Holloway, Oliver vs. The State
Holloway, R. B. vs. J. R. Carmichael
Holmes, Elbert vs. The State
Holsenbake, Alexander vs. John T. McLean
Holsenbeck, Alex vs. John Adams
Holsenbeck, Alex vs. S. R. Lawrence
Holsenbeck, Alex vs. H. C. McClure
Holsenbeck, Alex vs. The State
Holsenbeck, Alexander vs. B. F. Johnson and Co.
Holsenbeck, Alexander vs. John B. Webb
Holsenbeck, J. E. vs. Melia Griggs
Holsenbeck, Marshal vs. Wiley Peddy
Holsenbeck, Will vs. T. A. Hutchinson and Bro.
Holt, David vs. The State
Holt, Ella vs. The State
Holt, Owen vs. Mrs. E. T. Jordan
Holt, Owen vs. The State
Holt, Russel vs. Madison Epps
Holt, Russell vs. Jonas H. Holland
Holt, Susan and Russell Holt vs. The State
Holt, Wes vs. The State
Holt, Will vs. The State
Honeycut, James E. vs. E. Harvey, J. C. Allen and Evan T. Mathis
Horseley, Robert (Bob) vs. Bolling Whitfield
Horseley, W. G. vs. H. T. Inman and Co.
Horseley, William vs. Bolling Whitfield
Horsley, William G. vs. Henry Seymour
Horton, Hal vs. George M. Key
Horton, James vs. M. F. Lester
Horton, James A. and A. J. Horton vs. William E. Tucker
Horton, Jerrie and Willis Preston vs. The State
Horton, Peter vs. The State
Howard, Fed vs. J. P. Matthewson and Co.
Howard, Fed vs. J. B. Reese
Howard, Mandy vs. Rebecca C. Pon
Howard, S. N., Lewis Lynch and James B. Howard vs. Matthew
  Whitfield, John F. Patterson, Leroy M. Willson, Pleasant
  Willson and William H. Mathis
Huff, John and Riley Wooten vs. Alfred S. Franklin
Huff, L. E. and J. F. Huff vs. Georgia Chemical Works
Hughes, Ras vs. The State
Humphrey, Edmond vs. John W. Morgan
Humphrey, Marshall and Elbert Baynes vs. The State

351

Humphrey, Milton vs. W. L. Zachry
Humphries, George vs. T. L. Cook
Humphries, Milton vs. Lawrence C. Cook
Humphry, Anderson vs. C. W. Jordan
Hunt, Abe, Anthony Card, Peter Thurman and George Thurman vs.
   A. D. Candler
Hunt, Harrison vs. G. C. Spearman
Hunt, Randal, Catharine Hunt and Isaac McKissack vs. E. L.
   Bartlett
Hunter, Asbury vs. Roberts and Roberts
Hunter, Cleve vs. The State
Hunter, Quince, Will Hunter, Ben White and Henry Hunter vs. L. O.
   Benton and Eugene Benton
Hunter, Will Frank vs. The State
Hurt, Emily (col) vs. The State
Hurt, Mason vs. W. W. Evans
Hutchings, R. C. vs. A. J. Talmadge and Co.
Hutchings, R. E. vs. L. W. Rasdal
Hutchings, Robert E. vs. Hardy Cook
Hutchins, George and J. W. Wilson vs. C. A. Harwell
Hutchins, P. P. vs. N. B. White
Hutchins, R. E. and P. P. Hutchins vs. Evan Harvey, John C.
   Allen and E. T. Mathis
Hutchins, Robert E. vs. Charles Gerding
Hye, Clem vs. The State

Ivey, H. H. vs. A. J. Talmadge, S. C. Charping and J. G. Tolleson

Jackson, Aaron vs. Asbury Catchings
Jackson, Andy vs. The State
Jackson, Arthur vs. The State
Jackson, Frank vs. Littie Brazil
Jackson, Greene vs. A. H. Jordan and C. L. Henderson
Jackson, Isham and Chris Jordan vs. Clark, Rosser and Co.
Jackson, Jack (col) vs. The State
Jackson, Jack vs. Robert Whitfield
Jackson, John Henry vs. The State
Jackson, Julia Ann and Emily Jordan vs. The State
Jackson, Lothie and Pleas Jackson vs. Henry Jackson
Jackson, Mose vs. G. T. Powers
Jackson, Peter and Robert Whitfield vs. Davis Brothers
Jackson, Peter and Reuben Whitfield vs. Horace Flemister
Jackson, Pleasant and Isaac H. Freeman vs. O. S. Proffit
Jackson, Price vs. The State
Jackson, Racheal vs. The State
Jackson, Seneca vs. W. B. Acree
Jackson, Seneca vs. E. W. Baynes
Jackson, Seneca vs. Kelly and McDowell
Jackson, Stoby vs. The State
Jackson, Thomas vs. Roberts and Roberts
Jacobson, Charlie vs. L. O. Benton and Bro.
James, Wash vs. The State
Jasper County vs. W. R. Waldrop
Jasper County Commissioners vs. John G. Elder
Jeffers, Berry vs. Aris Newton
Jeffers, Thomas vs. The State
Jeffries, A. L. vs. James H. Campbell and Bro.
Jeffries, C. vs. P. R. Thomason and J. T. Henderson
Jeffries, C. vs. Usher Thomason and J. F. Henderson
Jeffries, Colbert vs. J. M. Bryan
Jeffries, Colbert vs. Asher Levy
Jeffries, Colbert vs. John W. Morgan
Jeffries, Colbert vs. W. E. Tucker

Jeffries, Colbert vs. Bolling Whitfield
Jeffries, Coos vs. The State
Jeffries, Dilley vs. Henry Hawk
Jeffries, Henry vs. Banks, Davidson and Kelly
Jenkins, F. E. vs. John H. Jenkins and Walter L. Zachry
Jenkins, F. E. vs. Roper, Adams and Co.
Jenkins, Francis vs. John A. C. S. Lawrence
Jenkins, Isham vs. The State
Johnson, A. E. vs. Roberts and Peurifoy
Johnson, Allen vs. Ceni Jeffries
Johnson, Allis vs. W. A. Kelly and Bros.
Johnson, Bryant (col) vs. William E. Baynes
Johnson, Eli, Rilious Smith and James Robinson vs. The State
Johnson, Elizabeth and Nancy A. Edwards vs. The State
Johnson, Georgia Ann vs. W. B. Beckwith and Co.
Johnson, J. H. and Catharine Johnson vs. A. J. Talmadge and
   J. G. Tolleson
Johnson, Joseph A. vs. The State
Johnson, Margarett vs. Farmer, Douglas and Co.
Johnson, Martha vs. Job Cary
Johnson, Moses vs. The State
Johnson, S. A. vs. D. J. Baer
Johnson, S. H. vs. W. A. Kelly and Bros.
Johnson, Stephen H. vs. Griffin, Monticello and Madison Railroad
   Co.
Johnson, Stephen H. and M. A. McDowell vs. Mrs. E. C.
   Middlebrooks
Johnson, Stephen H. vs. The State
Johnson, Thomas (col) vs. Charles Meriwether (col)
Johnson, Thomas vs. Jacob Wolfe
Johnson, Tom vs. The State
Johnson, Turner vs. The State
Johnson, William vs. William Akridge
Johnson, William vs. Mollie Walker
Johnston, Mrs. Ella vs. L. O. Benton and Eugene Benton
Johnston, Fleming and J. W. Burney, Jr. vs. Robert Bartlett
Johnston, Fleming vs. P. W. Dorsett
Johnston, Martin K. vs. George McKey
Johnston, Stephen vs. T. R. King
Johnston, Stephen H. vs. Francis M. Swanson
Johnston, Stephen H. vs. J. W. Williams
Johnston, William L. vs. Robert M. Blackwell
Johnston, W. S. vs. Shipp and Webb
Johnston, William S. vs. Crawley and Eckles
Johnston, William S. vs. John T. Eckles
Johnston, William S. vs. W. C. Penn
Johnston, William S. vs. The State
Jones, Benjamin vs. The State
Jones, Ike vs. Banks, Davidson and Kelly
Jones, James M., J. W. Grubbs and Oliver Holloway vs. William
   H. Head
Jones, Joseph and Samuel C. Shy vs. Broughton and Fitzpatrick
Jones, Joseph and Samuel C. Shy vs. Burnett, Broughton and Co.
Jones, Joseph vs. P. P. Lovejoy and John D. Lovejoy
Jones, Sallie B. vs. E. S. Broddus
Jones, W. H. vs. Madison Epps
Jones, Walter vs. L. O. Benton and Eugene Benton
Jordan, ? vs. ? Berry
Jordan, Adaline vs. The State
Jordan, Betsy vs. M. S. Benton
Jordan, C. H. vs. H. B. Downing
Jordan, C. H. and Walter M. Clements vs. Mrs. F. C. Jordan
Jordan, C. W. vs. J. L. Campbell

Jordan, C. W. and John F. Spearman vs. R, F. Powell
Jordan, C. W. vs. Shipp and Webb
Jordan, C. W. vs. F. M. Swanson
Jordan, Charles W. vs. W. A. Kelly
Jordan, Charley vs. J. H. Kelly
Jordan, Chris vs. Clark, Rosser and Co.
Jordan, Edmond vs, Morris Flatan for use of M. Newman
Jordan, Edmond vs. James Henderson
Jordan, Elizabeth and Lee Freeman vs. W. H. Jordan
Jordan, Ellen vs. Mary Gaston
Jordan, Emily (col) vs. L. H. Simms
Jordan, Fleming vs. Singer Mfg. Co.
Jordan, Floyd vs. The State
Jordan, Frances C. vs. A. M. Robinson and Co.
Jordan, Francis C. vs. Howard and Soule
Jordan, H. J. vs. Monticello Merchandise Co.
Jordan, Hardy (col) vs. J. L. Campbell
Jordan, Hardy vs. Ellen Cooper
Jordan, Henry B. vs. John F, Elder
Jordan, Isaiah vs. Thomas C. Broddus
Jordan, Jack, W. C. Campbell and H. C. Hill vs. Lucian Benton
Jordan, Jack and C. J. Goolsby vs, Lucian Benton
Jordan, Jack vs. Savannah Guano Co,
Jordan, Jewett vs. The State
Jordan, Liddie vs. Mary Gaston
Jordan, Lot vs. William C. Campbell and H. C. Hill
Jordan, Louis vs. The State
Jordan, R. vs. Griffin, Monticello and Madison Railroad Co,
Jordan, Randal (col) vs. J. L. Campbell
Jordan, Randall vs. Charles Gerding and Co,
Jordan, Randol vs. M, A. McDowell and Alliston
Jordan, Randolph vs. M. Flatan
Jordan, Sam vs. The State
Jordan, Spencer vs. Madison Epps
Jordan, T. M. vs. C. W. Pope
Jordan, Thomas M. and Caroline M. Jordan vs. Bryan and Hunter
Jordan, Thomas M. vs. J. Mon Johnson and Co.
Jordan, Thomas M. and Frances M. Jordan vs. Kelly and Price
Jordan, Thomas M. and Frances C. Jordan vs. J, L. K. Smith
Jordan, W. F. vs. John R. Greer and C, H. Greer
Jordan, W. F. vs, William S. Minter
Jordan, W. H. vs. M. S, Benton
Jordan, W. H. vs. E. S. Broddus
Jordan, W. H. vs. H. G. Lewis
Jordan, William and Hardy Jordan vs. Jonas H. Holland
Jordan, William and S. W, Bacon vs. Francis M. Swanson
Jordan, William F, vs. Russell Brown
Jordan, William F. vs. John D. Butt and Joshua R. Butt
Jordan, William F. vs. Loyall and McCulough
Jordan, William F. and William C. Penn vs. James L, Maddux
Jourden, Mose vs. The State

Keller, Everett vs. L, W. Pon and Caroline Pon
Kelley, James vs. The State
Kelly, Alfred vs. Key and Preston
Kelly, Amos vs. The State
Kelly, Amos vs. N. B. White
Kelly, Anna vs. Jasper County Merchandise Co.
Kelly, Anthony and Jim Holland vs. William T. Fish
Kelly, B. C. vs, Hattie W. Smith
Kelly, C. B. vs. The State
Kelly, E. D. vs. P. W. Warren
Kelly, E. Digby and Mrs. Emily Kelly vs. H. F, Blackwell and

354

Mary Blackwell
Kelly, E. H. and John L. Robinson vs. M. C. Kiser and J. F. Kiser
Kelly, E. H. vs. Mallet and Nutt and W. H. Malone
Kelly, Eaton vs. Mollie Dusenberry
Kelly, Eden H. vs. Lewis and Bailey
Kelly, Erbin H. vs. J. M. Best
Kelly, Erbin H. vs. J. T. Eckles
Kelly, Erbin H. vs. A. L. Sluder
Kelly, F. M. O. vs. W. A. Kelly and Bros.
Kelly, Henry (col) vs. C. M. Meriwether
Kelly, J. H. vs. John L. Aaron
Kelly, J. T. vs. W. S. Minter, Thomas C. Minter and Emma J.
  Minter
Kelly, Jake vs. J. W. Holland
Kelly, John H. vs. Francis C. Jordan
Kelly, Littleton (col) vs. John B. Webb
Kelly, Michael vs. Cornelius Hardy, William P. White and William
  P. Hardy
Kelly, Michael vs. Robert Ivy
Kelly, Michael vs. Luke J. Morgan
Kelly, S. J. and W. G. Kelly vs. John Silvey and Co.
Kelly, Stephen vs. Madison Epps
Kelly, William vs. The State
Kelly, William vs. N. B. White
Kendall, Whit vs. The State
Kennon, T. H. vs. W. B. Fitzpatrick
Ketchens, Nelse vs. George M. Key
Ketchings, Charles vs. George M. Key
Key, Jacob (col) vs. George M. Key
Key, M. B. vs. A. F. Perry
Key, M. D. L. vs. W. A. Kelly and Bros.
Key, Mrs. Mary vs. E. B. Malone
Kiley, M. J. and Mary Watkins vs. Augustus Studdard
Kilgo, Will vs. J. H. Campbell
Kilgore, Charles M. vs. N. B. White
Kinard, John J. vs. O. H. Arnold, Jr.
Kinard, John J. vs. William L. Minter
Kinard, JOhn J. vs. N. B. White
Kinard, T. L. vs. The State
King, B. G. vs. E. B. Ezell and B. W. Hunt
King, B. G. vs. Z. W. Falkner
King, B. G. vs. Griffin, Monticello and Madison Railroad Co.
King, Burl G. vs. O. R. Belcher, Jr.
King, Burrel G. vs. William S. Minter
King, J. E. and T. R. King, Jr. vs. M. S, Benton
King, Jacob vs. The State
King, James vs. The State
King, T. R. and E. R. Roberts vs. William H. Head
Kitchens, Asberry vs. Thomas Broadus
Kitchens, Asbury vs. Obediah Hester
Knight, Warren vs. E. H. Gay
Knowles, W. J. vs. Banks, Davidson and Kelly

Lackey, Albert vs. The State
Lancaster, Kitty vs. Middle Ga. and Atlantic R. W. Co.
Lane, C. Q. vs. W. E. Tucker
Lane, Charles Q. vs. Price and Steel
Lane, E. D. vs. Anderson and Hunter
Lane, E. D. vs. Corley and Dorsett
Lane, E. D. vs. Georgia Chemical Works
Lane, J. H. vs. Frank Leverett
Lane, James M. vs. W. A. Kelly, P. P. Kelly and John H. Kelly
Lane, S. P. vs. M. L. Duke

Lane, William D. vs. Corley and Dorsett
Langston, D. M. and Q. M. Langston vs. H. P. Almond, Sr.
Langston, D. M. vs. J. H. Kelly
Langston, D. M. vs. H. J. Lamarr
Langston, D. M. vs. W. R. Pope
Langston, David vs. E. H. Marks
Langston, David M. vs. J. L. Dickens
Langston, David M. vs. Fannie Thurman
Langston, David M. vs. Jefferson Webb
Langston, I. M., John S. Langston and D. M. Langston vs. M. S.
    Benton
Langston, I. M. vs. Imperial Fertilizer Co. and J. H. Kelly
Langston, Isaac vs. T. J. Lane and D. Lane
Langston, Isaac vs. James R. Minter
Langston, Isaac and David M. Langston vs. Leroy Price
Langston, John E. and David M. Langston vs. William H. Head
Langston, John S. vs. Imperial Fertilizer Co. and J. H. Kelly
Lawrence, James and William K. Pope vs. Cardin Goolsby
Lawrence, John vs. The State
Lawrence, Leroy, William McDowell and Seaborn Lawrence vs. Joel
    J. Edwards and Isaac Langston
Lawrence, Seaborn and S. C. Lawrence vs. W. W. Fisher
Lawrence, Seaborn and S. C. Lawrence vs. John McCullough
Lawrence, Seaborn, William H. Thompson, M. B. Key and S. C.
    Lawrence vs. John W. Pearson
Lawrence, Seaborn and S. C. Lawrence vs. Bolling Whitfield
Lawrence, Stewart vs. The State
Layson, B. T. vs. Mallory Mill Supply Co.
Layson, C. C. vs. Frank Leverett and ? Ezell
Layson, C. C., Sr., J. H. S. Smith and C. C. Layson, Jr. vs.
    The State
Layson, J. N. vs. T. L. Cook and Bros.
Layson, J. N. vs. Mallory Mill Supply Co.
Leach, J. R. vs. Banks, Davidson and Kelly
Leach, J. W. vs. Corley and Dorsett
Leach, J. W. vs. Shipp and Webb
Leach, J. W. and Hiram Leach vs. Thomas C. Swann
Leath, John vs. B. F. Reeves
Lee, Daniel vs. The State
Letson, Robert vs. Claghorn, Herring and Co.
Letson, Robert vs. W. B. Dozier
Leverett, B. and J. A. Cathey vs. King Hardware
Leverett, B. and J. A. Cathay vs. Michael Brothers Co.
Leverett, Caroline vs. George M. Key
Leverett, David vs. The State
Leverett, David D. vs. Susan E. Tucker
Leverett, Frank vs. Officers of Court
Leverett, James vs. The State
Leverett, Thomas J. vs. Tabitha Freeman
Leverett, Thomas J. and Mancefield Leverett vs. The State
Leverett, William C. and Peter Cardell vs. C. W. Jordan and
    J. T. Spearman
Leverette, Jesse vs. George M. Key
Leverette, N. H. vs. Tabitha Gerrett
Lewis (col) vs. Emily (col)
Lewis, Henry and Freeman Gay vs. W. A. Kelly and Bros.
Lewis, Henry vs. Thomas C. Spivey
Lewis, Henry vs. The State
Lewis, James T. vs. Robert Whitfield
Lewis, Phillip vs. W. P. Anderson and Co.
Linch, Henry vs. B. Rice
Lindsey, Frank vs. The State
Lindsey, Mrs. S. A. vs. S. J. Steele and G. H. Cornwell

Lindsey, Will vs. The State
Linze, E. J. vs. Thomas Camp
Loftin, W. A. vs. Early C. Cleveland
Long, Thomas and Thomas Ross vs. The State
Long, Tom vs. The State
Lovejoy, C. B. vs. Aaron Fish
Lovejoy, J. D. vs. Griffin, Monticello and Madison Railroad Co.
Lovejoy, John D. vs. William A. Kelly, John H. Kelly and Pleasant
    P. Kelly
Lovejoy, John D. and Fannie Lovejoy vs. William A. Whitehead,
    Addie E. Whitehead and F. M. Whitehead
Lovejoy, P. P., John D. Lovejoy and Thomas C. Broddus vs.
    Samuel Allen and John C. Key
Lovejoy, S. A. and E. L. Campbell vs. J. W. Davis
Lovejoy, Sidney A. vs. F. A. Lovejoy
Lovejoy, Sidney A. vs. The State
Loyd, M. A. vs. Howard and Soule
Lynch, Ben and Matthew Rany vs. Thomas Camp
Lynch, Ben vs. McCallum and Fennell
Lynch, Charles vs. The State
Lynch, Genus vs. The State
Lynch, Henry vs. Davis Brothers
Lynch, Henry vs. Julius Singleton
Lynch, Melie vs. The State
Lynch, Seab vs. The State

Macarthy, C. E. and A. Mccarthy vs. A. H. Tredwell
Machen Improvement Mfg. Co. vs. H. D. Bush
Mack, Golan vs. The State
Mack, Will vs. The State
Maddox, Ellen vs. The State
Maddux, Annie vs. Cora Morton
Maddux, Arter vs. Mary Johnson for use of Caroline Johnson
Maddux, E. M. vs. D. A. Beattie
Maddux, James L., O. G. Roberts and J. B. Webb vs. James W.
    Wilson
Maddux, Phil vs. The State
Maddux, Troy vs. The State
Maddux, Wash vs. B. R. Ezell, Sr.
Maddux, Wash vs. Reid and Dennis
Maddux, Wash vs. Roberts and Peurifoy
Maddux, Wash (col) vs. John B. Webb
Malone, A. M. and T. S. Malone vs. J. J. Clack
Malone, A. M. vs. Loyd and Williams
Malone, A. M. vs. Mallett and Nutt
Malone, A. M. vs. Warren Wallace and Co.
Malone, Amos vs. James J. M. McClelland
Malone, Augustus vs. A. W. Foster, James K. Wright and W. L. High
Malone, Augustus vs. Roberts and Peurifoy
Malone, C. R. vs. T. A. Hutchinson and Bro.
Malone, Charles vs. R. K. Hoard
Malone, Charles vs. H. C. McClure
Malone, Floyd vs. W. A. Kelly and Bros.
Malone, Franklin vs. R. H. Barron
Malone, Franklin vs. Wesley Griggs
Malone, Franklin and S. C. Lawrence vs. J. W. Grubbs and Co,
    for use of Officers of Court
Malone, Franklin vs. Hardeman and Sparks
Malone, Franklin vs. Martha Johnson and Stephen H. Johnson
Malone, Franklin vs. B. Pye and Son
Malone, Franklin vs. H. W. Pye and W. L. Zachry
Malone, Franklin vs. H. B. Ridley
Malone, Franklin vs. Seymour, Tinsley and Co.

Malone, Franklin vs. Martin V. Tyner
Malone, Franklin vs. Bolling Whitfield and Robert Whitfield
Malone, George vs. W. W. Allen
Malone, George vs. E. W. Baynes
Malone, George vs. Warren Wallace and Co.
Malone, Gus vs. Mrs. Anna B. Malone
Malone, J. R. vs. Printup Bro. and Pollard
Malone, J. R. vs. F. M. Swanson
Malone, J. R. vs. Mary Wilson
Malone, Jim vs. The State
Malone, Jordan vs. Foster, Wright and Co.
Malone, Mattie and William Malone vs. L. O. Benton and Eugene
  Benton
Malone, Obe vs. The State
Malone, P. C. vs. W. F. Jordan
Malone, S. B. vs. Home Sewing Machine Co.
Malone, S. B., John W. Edwards and William P. Lane vs. Benjamin
  Jordan and Jane M. Holland
Malone, S. H. and W. L. Roby vs. M. S. Benton
Malone, Stith B. vs. Martha Jane Johnston
Malone, Stith B. vs. M. V. Tyner
Malone, T. J. vs. Doughtry Bros.
Malone, T. J. vs. W. A. Kelly and Bros.
Malone, T. J. vs. F. M. Swanson
Malone, T. J. vs. N. B. White
Malone, T. L. vs. Corley and Dorsett
Malone, Thomas vs. Mollie Dusenberry
Malone, Thomas vs. W. D. Wynn
Malone, Thomas L. vs. William T. Hollingsworth
Malone, Thomas S. vs. Willis Field
Malone, Thomas S. vs. W. A. Kelly and Bros.
Malone, Thomas S. vs. F. M. Swanson
Malone, Thomas S. vs. Warren, Wallace and Co.
Malone, Thomas S., Jr. and Sarah Malone vs. Dearing and Guinn
Malone, W. H. vs. McCormick Neal
Malone, William vs. Griffin, Monticello and Madison Railroad Co.
Malone, William vs. A. Newton
Malone, William vs. Pollard and Co.
Malone, William, John B. M. Phillips and Bartley Walker vs.
  William C. Robinson, James C. Robinson and John L. Robinson
Malone, William vs. N. B. White
Malone, William vs. Wynn and Clack
Malone, William S. vs. W. A. Kelly and Bro.
Manning, Dick vs. Wiley Phillips, Andrew Freeman, Green M.
  Phillips and John B. Phillips
Manning, Silas vs. Wiley Phillips, Green M. Phillips, John B.
  Phillips and Andrew J. Freeman
Manuel, Dennis vs. The State
Mapp, B. H. vs. John Turk and W. C. Turk
Mapp, Benjamin H. and Julia Mapp vs. W. D. Wynn
Mapp, Julia vs. J. P. Quinn
Marks, Edenboro (col) vs. Morris Flatan
Marks, Edenborough vs. The State
Marks, F. C. vs. John Gordon
Marks, F. C. vs. W. T. McKissack
Marks, F. C. vs. The State
Marks, Horace (col) and James Marks (col) vs. Thomas J. Pritchett
Marks, Horace vs. The State
Marks, I. H. vs. H. C. McClure
Marks, N. T. vs. Berry T. Digby
Marsh, R. L. vs. J. T. Benton
Martin, Allen vs. Stephen Morris (col) and Henry M. Macy
Martin, Ben vs. Childs, Harwell and Bonner

Martin, J. B. vs. Bullard Brothers
Martin, J. B. vs. M. J. Cofer
Martin, S. L. vs. Mrs. Caroline Pon
Mason, Loftin vs. Francis Mason
Maxcy, Randy vs. Henry George
Maxey, Green, Isham Maxey, Lawson Maxey, Jr. and Lawson Maxey,
   Sr. vs. Preston, Giles and Polhill
Maxey, Mabe vs. Caroline Pon
Maxey, W. H. (alias W. H. Jordan) vs. The State
Mayo, J. M. T. vs. John C. McHutchins
M. E. Church vs. C. Banks
Meeks, B. B. and W. A. Mercer vs. Bank of Monticello
Mercer, L. A. vs. S. B. Cohen
Mercer, L. A. and A. L. Mercer vs. Georgia Farmers Oil and
   Fertilizer Co.
Mercer, L. A. vs. Mayer and Watts
Meriwether, Charles vs. C. M. Meriwether
Meriwether, Charles and David Elder vs. The State
Meriwether, Dawson vs. H. B. Jordan, E. H. Jordan, D. R. Glover
   and A. H. Jordan
Meriwether, Dorse vs. The State
Meriwether, Ed vs. The State
Meriwether, Prince vs. Francis M. Swanson
Meriwether, Prince vs. A. J. Talmadge and Tolleson
Meriwether, Thomas vs. Davis, Leverett and Co.
Meriwether, Thomas vs. The State
Merriwether, Aaron vs. L. Lewy and Co.
Merriwether, Charles vs. S. B. Bailey and W. C. Bailey
Merriwether, Charles vs. A. W. Foster and Co.
Merriwether, Charles (col) vs. W. A. Kelly
Merriwether, Charles vs. Wynn and Clack
Merriwether, Thomas vs. W. B. Ezell
Merriwether, Thomas vs. John Merryman and James C. Denham
Merriwether, Thomas vs. W. M. Robinson
Middlebrooks, Alonza vs. The State
Middlebrooks, C. F. vs. L. O. Benton and Eugene Benton
Middlebrooks, F. G. vs. Virgil O. Hardon
Middlebrooks, Joe, Albert Couch and Joe Greer vs. The State
Middlebrooks, Silas vs. The State
Middlebrooks, W. P. vs. L. O. Benton and Eugene Benton
Middlebrooks, Walter vs. M. S. Benton
Millen, Mary and Grief Lynch, Sr. vs. N. B. White and L. White
Miller, Georgia vs. Rebecca C. Pon
Miller, Jake vs. The State
Miller, William vs. William Morgan
Mills, Henry C. vs. The State
Minter, A. J. vs. M. S. Benton
Minter, A. J. vs. Monarch Mfg. Co.
Minter, A. J. vs. Popplein Silicated Phosphate Co.
Minter, A. J. vs. J. B. Settle and Co.
Minter, A. J. vs. T. C. Swann
Minter, A. J. vs. Albert Talmadge, Jr.
Minter, Andrew J. vs. John Merryman and Co. and R. P. Brooks
Minter, Emma, Nannie Minter and Jane Minter vs. Tilman Pickens
Minter, Fleetwood vs. S. R. Campbell
Minter, Judson vs. The State
Minter, Lee vs. N. B. White
Minter, Leroy and M. P. Stone vs. J. W. Stokes
Minter, Mattie vs. The State
Minter, R. J. vs. McCormick Neal
Minter, R. J. vs. The State
Minter, Richard vs. George M. Key
Minter, Rufus vs. The State

Minter, Sam vs. S. R. Campbell
Minter, T. C. vs. L. O. Benton and Bro.
Minter, Thomas C. vs. Griffin, Monticello and Madison Railroad
  Co.
Minter, Thomas C. vs. Mrs. H. N. White for use of Officers of
  Court
Minter, W. S., Thomas C. Minter and Emma Minter vs. Z. M. Faulkner
Minter, Wallace vs. The State
Minter, William L. vs. Tabitha J. Garrett
Minter, William S. vs. Henry J. Lamar
Mitchell, Bob, Jr. vs. The State
Mitchell, Charles vs. John W. Morgan
Mitchell, David vs. W. J. Preston
Mitchell, Dick vs. Bolling Whitfield
Mitchell, Henry and Horace Flemister vs. J. H. Holland
Mitchell, Henry vs. The State
Mitchell, Melvin vs. The State
Mitchell, Richard vs. Warren, Wallace and Co.
Mitchell, Richard and F. Jordan vs. Robert Whitfield
Montgomery, Henry (col) vs. Peter Hill
Montgomery, Henry vs. The State
Montgomery, John vs. W. C. Bailey
Mooney, Snelling S. vs. Charles L. Bartlett
Mooneyham, Charles vs. J. W. Stokes
Moore, B. A. vs. George Davis
Moore, E. B. vs. The State
Moore, Horace vs. The State
Moreland, G. W. vs. N. B. White
Moreland, George vs. The State
Moreland, Henry vs. Emma Holloway
Morgan, Clark vs. L. O. Benton and Eugene Benton
Morgan, H. A. vs. William C. Leverett
Morgan, Isham vs. W. H. Middlebrooks
Morgan, Isham (col) vs. Shipp and Webb
Morgan, James vs. W. P. Glover
Morris, Burrell vs. The State
Morris, Will vs. The State
Morrison, M. A. E. vs. Davis R. Andrews and Rebecca P. Andrews
Morton, Ben and Alice Morton vs. Green F. Johnson and B. F.
  Leverett
Morton, Ben vs. Spivey and Stubbs
Morton, Ben vs. Whitfield and Brown
Morton, Joe and Bob Morton vs. The State
Mosely, Joe vs. The State
Murphy, J. H. and R. G. Murphy vs. Southern Bank and Trust Co.
Murphy, Mrs. R. A. vs. L. O. Benton and Eugene Benton
Murphy, W. E. and J. H. Murphy vs. The State

McAllister, Henry vs. The State
McCarthy, Arthur vs. The State
McClellan, A. P. and T. B. McClellan vs. D. B. Benton and L.
  Benton
McClelland, A. P. vs. T. W. Pye
McClendon, J. A. vs. The State
McClendon, J. A., C. M. Hardy and Robert Shaw vs. W. K. Yateman
McClendon, S. L. vs. James Thomas Smith
McClure and Holt vs. Madison Epps
McClure, T. A. vs. Mrs. Martha Burns
McClure, T. A. vs. J. R. Carmichael
McClure, T. A. vs. The State
McCombs, Otis (alias Bubber Hardaway) vs. The State
McCommons, John vs. The State
McDaniel, Henry and Jordan Roberts vs. Frances M. Tyler

McDonald, Alec G. vs. H. J. Talmadge and Co.
McDonald, Henry vs. Roberts and Peurifoy
McDowell, Isaac vs. J. O. Shepherd
McDowell, Joel C. vs. Russell J. Brown
McDowell, Joel C. vs. Griffin, Monticello and Madison Railroad Co.
McDowell, Joel C. vs. Lucien Newton
McDowell, Mack (col) vs. John B. Webb
McDowell, Michael A. vs. Richard Davidson
McDowell, Wallace vs. The State
McElhaney, V. H., R. V. McElhaney and John M. McElhaney vs.
   J. H. Kelly
McElhaney, Samps vs. H. J. Lamar
McElheney, J. D. vs. L. O. Benton and Eugene Benton
McElheney, John and W. F. Jordan vs. Jane Tyler
McElhenney, Allen vs. Benjamin F. Elder
McElhenney, G. W. vs. R. L. Daughtry, J. G. Daughtry and H. L.
   Daughtry
McElhenney, George W. vs. N. B. White and Co.
McElhenney, H. C. vs. W. L. DuVall
McElheny, J. D., Charlie Niblett and E. T. Grubbs vs. J. T.
   Goodman
McGee, Allie vs. A. M. E. Church
McGee, T. W. vs. S. R. Campbell
McGee, T. W. vs. A. H. Jordan and C. L. Henderson
McGinnis, Tom (col) vs. The State
McGough, W. T. and C. D. Thurmond vs. J. H. Kelly
McGuire, Robert vs. The State
McKey, John C. vs. Sallie H. Kelly
McKinley, M. vs. B. P. Blanton
McKinley, M. vs. M. Codington
McKinley, M. vs. Cordesman Machine Co.
McKissack, Isaac vs. Richmond H. Reid
McKissack, John vs. James G. Barnes
McKissack, John, Isaac McKissack and W. T. McKissack vs. Abram
   Smith
McKissack, John, Isaac McKissack and William T. McKissack vs.
   Talmadge and Charping
McKissack, W. T. vs. Wiley Peddy
McKissack, William vs. William H. Reese
McKissack, William T. vs. Lightfoot, Flanders and Co.
McKissack, William T. vs. Maxey, Jordan and Co.
McKissack, William T. vs. James Murphy
McKissack, William T. vs. Shipp and Webb
McMichael, B. J. vs. Griffin, Monticello and Madison Railroad Co.
McMichael, Burton J. vs. The State
McMichael, Burton J. vs. Mathew Whitfield, John F. Patterson and
   William Mathis
McMichael, C. C. vs. Sallie H. Kelly
McMichael, C. C. vs. N. B. White
McMichael, George Ann and Jeanette McMichael vs. The State
McMichael, Green L. (children of) and Shadrach J. McMichael vs.
   Key and Preston
McMichael, Green L. vs. Shipp and Webb
McMichael, Green L. vs. James A. Turner
McMichael, Green L. vs. N. B. White and L. White
McMichael, Griffin vs. The State
McMichael, J. M. and Ella McMichael vs. J. S. Pemberton and Co.
McMichael, J. S. vs. L. O. Benton and Eugene Benton
McMichael, J. S. vs. Monticello Merchandise Co.
McMichael, J. S. vs. T. C. Spivey
McMichael, James M. vs. Kelly and Price
McMichael, James M. vs. John Wilson
McMichael, John L. and Fleming Mobley vs. Thomas R. Holland

McMichael, L. L. vs. W. E. Baynes
McMichael, L. L., W. J. McMichael and N. H. Greer vs. William
  Godard
McMichael, Mrs. Lily vs. The State
McMichael, N. D. vs. M. S. Benton
McMichael, N. D. vs. H. B. Jordan, E. H. Jordan, H. H. Jordan
  and D. R. Glover
McMichael, Nancy D. vs. N. B. White
McMichael, P. B. vs. N. B. White
McMichael, Peter (col) vs. The State
McMichael, Pollard B. vs. Green L. McMichael
McMichael, R. L. vs. John H. Kelly
McMichael, S. L. vs. Seaborn Lawrence
McMichael, S. L. vs. M. A. McDowell and Jones
McMichael, S. L. vs. Watson and Walker
McMichael, Seaborn vs. Shipp and Webb
McMichael, Seaborn L. vs. William E. Baynes
McMichael, Seaborn L. vs. Francis M. Swanson
McMichael, T. J. vs. Key and Preston
McMichael, V. F. vs. W. A. Kelly and Bros.
McMichael, V. F. vs. The State
McMichael, V. F. vs. N. B. White and Co.
McMichael, W. J. vs. L. O. Benton and Eugene Benton
McMichael, W. J. vs. R. S. Franklin
McMichael, W. S. vs. Robinson, Kelly and Co.
McNair, Mrs Julia vs. J. D. Thornton
McNeal, Charley vs. The State
McNeal, Jacob vs. A. S. Holland
McNeal, Jacob vs. F. M. Swanson

Naper, John vs. O. G. Roberts and B. W. Peurifoy
Napier, John vs. The State
Nash, King vs. Samuel Whitfield
Nash, Matilda vs. Isaiah Jordan
Nash, Matilda vs. The State
Nash, T. J. vs. The State
Nelson, Andrew vs. The State
Newman, S. vs. Thomas C. Broddus
Newton, A. and M. S. Benton vs. Mrs. Eugenia Baynes
Newton, A. vs. Lewis and Bailey
Newton, George W. vs. E. H. Cohen
Newton, George W. vs. Frank Leverett
Newton, George W. vs. John W. Morgan
Newton, George W. vs. Francis M. Swanson
Newton, George W. vs. W. E. Tucker
Newton, Isaac vs. Madison Epps
Newton, Isaac vs. John B. Webb
Newton, Jake vs. Shipp and Webb
Newton, L. B. vs. A. M. Robinson and Co.
Newton, Mary F. and Willis Newton vs. M. A. McDowell
Newton, Mary F. and T. R. Bonner vs. R. W. Newton
Newton, Mollie F. and Willis Newton vs. B. Rice
Newton, Mollie F. vs. J. R. Sparks
Newton, Mollie F. vs. J. G. Tolleson
Newton, Mollie I. and George W. Newton vs. Meyer, Weis and Co.
Newton, Mrs. Neal vs. O. L. Holmes
Newton, O. H. vs. E. H. Cohen and S. B. Cohen
Newton, O. H. vs. J. M. Cox and Co.
Newton, O. H. vs. Kelly and McDowell
Newton, O. H. vs. John W. Morgan
Newton, O. H. vs. W. E. Tucker
Newton, O. H. vs. N. B. White
Newton, O. H. vs. Whitfield and Brown

Newton, Richard vs. A. W. Foster and Co.
Newton, Richard vs. Hilsman and Penick
Newton, Richard vs. W. E. Tucker and J. L. Tucker
Newton, Sidney vs. Aris Newton
Newton, Willis vs. John Q. Adams
Newton, Willis vs. W. A. Kelly and Bros.
Newton, Willis vs. Solomon Lewy and Isaac Herman
Newton, Willis vs. James H. Robinson and Augustus M. Robinson
Newton, Willis vs. Shipp and Webb
Newton, Willis vs. Francis M. Swanson
Newton, Willis vs. W. E. Tucker
Newton, Willis vs. John Turk and William Turk
Newton, Willis vs. Jacob Wolfe
Nrwton, Willis vs. Worth Lumber Co.
Niblet, T. S. vs. W. D. Wynn
Niblett, Charlie, John S. Langston and I. M. Langston vs. M. S.
   Benton
Niblett, J. V. vs. Wynn and Clack
Niblett, James H. vs. W. H. Head
Niblett, James H. vs. Martin V. Tyner
Nichols, Henry vs. The State
Nichols, T. J. and Richard Nichols vs. Joseph H. S. Smith
Nichols, Thomas J. and H. C. Hill vs. Bibb Brick Co.
Nichols, Thomas J. vs. J. A. Stone
Nickols, Jeff vs. Woody B. Dozier
Nix, Berry and Sam Grits vs. The State
Nix, McKendrick T. vs. The State
Nix, Tucker vs. David Dixon
Nix, Wash and Mathew Glover vs. W. D. Wynn
Nix, Washington and Dick Jordan vs. The State
Noles, David G. vs. W. H. Pickett
Noles, Ellander vs. Thomas Camp
Noles, Ellen vs. Childs and Bailey
Noles, Ellender vs. W. H. Pickett
Noles, Morris and C. E. Spears vs. Joel S. Terrell
Norman, Stephen vs. Whitfield and Brown
Nosworthy, D. vs. Key and Preston

Odom, Gus (col) vs. The State
Odom, John Wes vs. The State
Odum, Augustus vs. The State
Odum, Wesley, Sol Pound and Nelson Pound vs. L. O. Benton and
   Bros.
O'Kelly, F. M. vs. F. J. Shepherd and Son
Osborn, Jesse H. vs. Corley and Dorsett
Owens, Jesse and John Aaron vs. A. C. Wyly and B. F. Wyly
Ozburn, B. S. vs. J. L. Campbell
Oaburn, B. S. vs. O. G. Roberts
Ozburn, J. E. vs. Swann, Stewart and Thompson

Park, Henry vs. The State
Parker, Isaac L. vs. Susannah Brewer
Parker, L. B. vs. Sydney R. Parker and Robert W. Ballard
Parker, Rowe vs. The State
Parker, W. C. and M. H. Hutchison vs. O. S. Huson
Parker, William C. vs. Akridge, Alcorn and Co.
Parker, William C. vs. Robert Ivy, Sr.
Parks, Abraham vs. The State
Paul, W. E. vs. H. B. Ridley
Paul, William E. vs. Madison Epps
Paul, William E. vs. Groves and Bacon
Paul, William E. vs. Seaborn McMichael
Paul, William E. vs. Middlebrooks and Co.

Paul, William E. vs. Stephen D. Mobley
Paul, William E. vs. Augustus M. Robinson and James H. Robinson
Paul, William E. vs. John W. Shropshire
Paul, William E. vs. L. H. Simms
Peacock, Cora and Gilbert Peacock vs. L. O. Benton and Eugene Benton
Peacock, Dudley vs. James H. Roberts
Peacock, Frank vs. The State
Peacock, Gil and W. E. Tyler vs. J. M. Ferrell
Peacock, Gil vs. The State
Pearson, Austin vs. Sarah Harwell
Pendergrass, H. N. and H. E. Pendergrass vs. W. T. Lackey
Penn, A. A. vs. L. O. Benton and Eugene Benton
Penn, A. A. and George C. Clements vs. J. T. Benton
Penn, A. A. and Celina Penn vs. Clark, Rosser and Co.
Penn, A. A. vs. J. C. Morgan
Penn, Bill vs. The State
Penn, Daniel, A. A. Penn, J. G. Elder and M. B. Key vs. The State
Penn, Harriett (col) and Adeline Blackwell (col) vs. The State
Penn, Henry vs. The State
Penn, J. A. and M. A. E. Penn vs. D. T. Mercer
Penn, John A. vs. Felker and Anderson
Penn, John A. and M. T. Penn vs. W. A. Kelly and Bros.
Penn, John A. vs. Sallie H. Pope
Penn, L. A. vs. Griffin, Monticello and Madison Railroad Co.
Penn, Lewis vs. The State
Penn, Linwood vs. J. B. Persons
Penn, Louis vs. John G. Elder
Penn, M. A. vs. Griffin, Monticello and Madison Railroad Co.
Penn, M. T. and J. A. Penn vs. H. C. McClure
Penn, Russell vs. J. W. Murrell
Penn, Russel J. vs. Joseph Mosely (col)
Penn, Russell J. vs. Kelly and Price
Penn, Mrs. Salina vs. C. L. Campbell
Penn, Solomon vs. Shipp and Webb
Penn, Solomon vs. The State
Penn, Mrs. T. R. vs. C. H. Jordan
Penn, T. R. vs. J. R. Wilkinson
Penn, Thomas (col) vs. The State
Penn, Thomas R. vs. William Akeridge
Penn, Thomas R. vs. George T. Bartlett
Penn, Thomas R. vs. John S. Downs
Penn, Mrs. Thomas R. vs. C. Harrey Jordan
Penn, Thomas R. vs. Wood and Rogers
Penn, W. C. vs. Kelly and Price
Penn, W. C. vs. Alfred A. Penn
Penn, W. C. vs. T. W. Reese
Penn, W. C. and B. T. Digby vs. A. J. Talmadge
Penn, W. J. and James Taylor vs. J. O. Shepherd
Penn, William C. vs. Madison Epps
Penn, William C. vs. Hunt, Rankin and Lamar
Penn, William C. vs. Lawrence and Pope
Penn, William C. vs. Wiley Phillips
Penn, William C. vs. Shipp and Webb
Pennington, J. C. vs. H. D. Adams and Co.
Pennington, J. C. vs. John B. Daniel
Pennington, J. C. vs. R. O. Medlock
Pennington, J. C., Joe S. Nix and Mrs. Siller Camp vs. M. F. Pennington
Pennington, J. C. vs. Southern Agricultural Works
Pennington, John C. vs. J.O. Medlock
Perry, Nep vs. The State
Persons, A. J. vs. Hugh T. Inman and Co.

Persons, E. E. and Kittie Johnston vs. George H. Hulme
Persons, E. E. and Kittie Johnston vs. Monticello Merchandise Co.
Persons, James vs. Henry McClure
Persons, James vs. W. L. Zachrey
Persons, W. F. and A. L. Malone vs. A. B. Small
Persons, W. F. vs. The State
Persons, William P. vs. Griffin, Monticello and Madison Railroad
  Co.
Peters, George vs. The State
Pettie, Anson L. vs. Hiram Segar
Peurifoy, McCarrol vs. Lewis Penn for use of Leonidas R. Price
Phillips, Mrs. A. L. and W. S. Phillips vs. L. O. Benton and Bro.
Phillips, Fell vs. O. A. W. Stanford
Phillips, Frand vs. The State
Phillips, J. B. M. vs. Anderson and Hunter
Phillips, J. B. M. vs. J. W. Murrell
Phillips, J. B. M. vs. E. B. Smith
Phillips, J. M. B, Andy Freeman, John J. Kinard and George
  Cunningham vs. W. M. Mallett
Phillips, John vs. The State
Phillips, John B. M. vs. William Gilstrap
Phillips, Monroe vs. N. T. Bowden
Phillips, Oscar vs. D. B. Benton
Phillips, R. B. vs. Central Georgia Alliance Warehouse Co.
Phillips, R. B. vs. Collins, Flanders and Co.
Phillips, R. B. vs. John H. Kelly
Phillips, R. B. vs. McClure Merchandise Co.
Phillips, R. B. vs. L. S. Worsham
Phillips, Richard vs. M. Flatan
Phillips, W. H. vs. Lucian Benton
Phillips, W. S. vs. N. B. White and Co.
Phillips, Wiley H. vs. Griffin, Monticello and Madison Railroad
  Co.
Phillips, William vs. Bill Phillips
Phillips, William (col) vs. The State
Phipp, Charles and Rufus Manning vs. D. B. Benton
Pie, Eli, Jacob Hemppiel and T. P. Shy vs. Georgia Chemical Works
Pie, Elizabeth, Ruby Lee Pie and Kitty Pie vs. The State
Pinnell, J. O. vs. James T. Corley
Pinnell, J. O. vs. N. B. White
Pinnell, John O. vs. George Walker
Pinnell, S. C. vs. Harvey and Davis
Piper, John vs. The State
Piper, Thomas L. vs. James C. Aaron
Piper, W. E. and J. O. Piper vs. John H. Kelly
Piper, Zadock vs. James T. Corley
Piper, Zadock vs. Griffin, Monticello and Madison Railroad Co,
Piper, Zadok vs. James H. Campbell
Pitts, C. N. vs. Mrs. J. G. Elder
Pitts, Joseph C. vs. E. B. Ezell and Co.
Plymale, Clem vs. The State
Plymale, Mike vs. The State
Polk, G. W. vs. Frank D. McDowell
Pon, Edgar vs. Patrick S. Burney and Samuel Burney
Pon, Edgar vs. P. V. Carbine
Pon, Edgar vs. Mapes Formula and Peruvian Guano Company
Pon, Edgar vs. John Merryman and Co.
Pon, Edgar vs. The State
Pon, Mrs. Rebecca C. vs. E. C. Buchannon and J, W. Buchannon
Pope, Cohen and Sherod Pope vs. The State
Pope, Danniel W., A. L. Sluder and James Benton vs. The State
Pope, E. C. vs. Luticen Blow and Frank Blow
Pope, Edgar C. vs. John Merryman and Co.

Pope, Edgar C. and J. Otis Pope vs. Walton, Whann and Co.
Pope, J. Otis vs. James W. Points
Pope, Jack vs. C. C. Burney
Pope, James vs. Joseph P. Williams
Pope, Miller W. vs. W. H. Head
Pope, Miller W. vs. Howard and Soule
Pope, Nathan vs. The State
Pope, S. M. vs. Chemical Co. of Canton
Pope, S. M. and George R. Dozier vs. W. C. Clark and Co.
Pope, S. M. vs. Georgia Chemical Works
Pope, S. M. and E. C. Pope vs. Paul Jones
Pope, Mrs. Sarah H. vs. W. J. L. Tuggle
Pope, Thomas C. vs. John Talmadge
Pope, W. R. vs. C. M. Davis and Frank Leverett
Pope, W. R. vs. Samuel Griswold
Porter, Fannie vs. G. T. Powers
Post, Joseph S. and Mary J. Post vs. Benton Supply Co.
Potter, A. C. vs. Downs and Langford
Potter, A. C. vs. Georgia Chemical Works
Potter, A. C. vs. Griffin, Monticello and Madison Railroad Co.
Potter, A. C. vs. J. J. McClelland
Potter, Adam C. vs. Kelly and Price
Powell, Carrie vs. The State
Powell, Charlie vs. The State
Powell, Eliza (col) vs. The State
Powell, James T. vs. Banks, Davidson and Kelly
Powell, John vs. The State
Powell, Louis (col) vs. The State
Powell, Pompey vs. John B. Webb
Powell, W. R. and B. T. Digby vs. Fannie P. (Powell) Gaston
Powers, Butler (alias William Meriwether) and Will Daniel vs.
  The State
Powers, Thomas and Charles Campbell vs. The State
Poynts, J. W. vs. G. W. Wardwell
Preston, Aaron, J. W. Preston and W. J. M. Preston vs. David
  Harris
Preston, Amos vs. The State
Preston, C. T. vs. William Hearn and Ransom Aikins
Preston, C. T. vs. M. A. McDowell
Preston, C. T. vs. W. H. Preston
Preston, C. T. vs. F. M. Swanson
Preston, C. T. vs. A. J. Talmadge, J. G. Tolleson and S. C.
  Charping
Preston, Charles T. and Joseph W. Preston vs. Albert W. Foster,
  James Wright and William L. High
Preston, J. F. vs. James S. Maddux
Preston, J. W. vs. Lewis and Bailey
Preston, Joseph W. vs. Samuel Walker
Preston, Lee vs. The State
Preston, Leila vs. Wesley Blackwell
Preston, Leila vs. Elbert Preston
Preston, Major vs. The State
Preston, Manuel(col) vs. George M. Key
Preston, Spencer vs. Franklin George
Preston, Spencer vs. John W. Morgan
Preston, Spencer vs. F. M. Swanson
Preston, Spencer (col) vs. John B. Webb
Preston, T. G. vs. W. F. Smith
Preston, Thomas G. vs. James L. Campbell
Preston, Thomas G. vs. Frances J. Swanson
Preston, W. B. vs. S. Lewy and Co.
Preston, W. B. vs. Michael A. McDowell and John A. Broughton
Preston, W. J. M. vs. W. A. Kelly and Bros.

Price, L. M. vs. Griffin, Monticello and Madison Railroad Co.
Price, L. R. and John N. Steele vs. Mendleson and Jacob
Price, Leonidas R. and John N. Steele vs. Gustavus H. Connelly
  and James Connelly
Price, R. W. vs. Corley and Dorsett
Price, R. W. vs. John H. Kelly
Price, Richard W. vs. J. R. Carmichael
Price, Robert vs. William P. Anderson and Co.
Price, Robert, Thomas R. Price and John M. Belcher vs. John P.
  Harris
Price and Steele vs. Bonnie and Company
Price and Steele vs. Cole and Gilpin
Price and Steele vs. The State
Price and Steele, A. W. Price and L. M. Price vs. Barney F. Tyler
Price, Thomas R. vs. William P. Anderson and Co.
Price, Thomas R. vs. William Andrews
Price, Thomas R. vs. Russell Brown
Pritchett, Abram vs. Roberts and Peurifoy
Pritchett, E. H. vs. Aris Newton, Jr. for use of Jim Whitfield
Pritchett, E. H. and S. L. Pritchett vs. J. O. Shepherd
Pritchett, Edward H. vs. William C. Bailey
Pritchett, Edward H. vs. Morris Flatan
Pritchett, Mat vs. William T. Fish
Pritchett, Mat vs. The State
Pritchett, Mat vs. David M. Tyner
Pritchett, Matt vs. Madison Epps
Pritchett, Moses vs. Madison Epps
Pritchett, S. L. vs. J. Mon Johnson for use of Ida Comer
Pritchett, S. L. vs. H. J. Lamar
Pritchett, Sarah L. vs. H. B. Jordan, E. H. Jordan, A. H. Jordan,
  and D. R. Glover
Pritchett, Sarah L. (Comer) vs. James L. Maddux
Pritchett, Sarah L. vs. Benjamin Meeks
Pritchett, T. J. and James B. Goolsby vs. Baldwin, Starr and Co.
Pritchett, Thomas J. and James B. Goolsby vs. George P. Trigg,
  Simeon M. Ayers and Henry F. Everson
Pritchett, William (col) vs. Hal Griggs
Prophitt, George vs. Soloman Smith
Prophitt, George vs. The State
Pye, Harman W. vs. J. M. Landers
Pye, Harman W. and Barthena Pye vs. David M. Langston
Pye, Harman W. vs. Thomas Pye
Pye, Rina vs. The State
Pye, Thad B. vs. Key and Preston
Pye, Thaddeus B. vs. I. Salinger
Pye, Thadeus B. vs. Sarah Cardin
Pye, Thadeus B. vs. Pleamon W. Dorsett
Pye, Thomas vs. The State
Pye, W. T. vs. N. B. White

Quarterman, Dave vs. The State

Ragland, Drayton and John Johnson vs. R. L. Allen
Rainy, Ike vs. The State
Ramy, D. M., Lizzie Ramy, Alice Ramy and W. F. Jordan vs. S. R.
  Miller and Co.
Randall, J. C. vs. Mrs. T. A. Aiken
Randall, Richmon vs. J. H. Kelly
Randel, Anderson vs. J. M. Cox and Co.
Reaves, William vs. N. Coggeshall
Reddick, Allen vs. Robert Whitfield
Reddick, George and Robert Whitfield vs. J. T. Davis and C. M.
  Davis

Reed, Dixie (alias Dixie Pon) vs. The State
Reed, Image vs. The State
Reese, Peter, Samuel Reese, Seaborn Reese and C. G. Campbell vs.
  Lawton and Willingham
Reese, Sam, Jr. vs. The State
Reese, Samuel vs. Francis M. Swanson
Reeves, Allie vs. Samuel R. Smith, Jr.
Reeves, B. F. vs. John W. Morgan
Reeves, Ben vs. The State
Reeves, Benjamin F., Mary Banks, J. E. Ferguson and William R.
  Tuggle vs. J. L. McElvany and Co.
Reeves, Warner vs. The State
Reid, Charles, Jr. vs. The State
Reid, Joseph (col) vs. The State
Reid, Joshua (col) vs. A. M. Robinson and Co.
Reid, Mary Jane vs. The State
Reid, S. T. vs. O. H. Arnold
Reid, S. T. and W. R. Berner vs. G. R. Dozier and Co.
Reid, S. T. vs. M. A. McDowell
Reid, S. T. vs. Monroe Singleton
Reid, Samuel vs. William A. Kelly
Reid, Samuel T. vs. James L. Campbell
Reid, Samuel T. vs. Tilda Compton
Reid, Samuel T. vs. W. T. Young and Co.
Reid, W. A. vs. Freeman and Wyatt
Reid, W. A. vs. Officers of Court
Reid, Will vs. P. P. Sanders
Reid, William A. vs. Gustavus H. Connelly and James Connelly
Reid, William A. vs. Freeman and Goolsby
Reid, William A. vs. F. M. Lester
Reid, William A. vs. E. Ward and Co.
Renfroe, James T. vs. W. A. Kelly and Bros.
Renfroe, James T. vs. N. B. White
Reynolds, John vs. James H. Campbell
Reynolds, John vs. S. Lewy and Co.
Reynolds, Jule vs. The State
Reynolds, Willie vs. Robert Childs
Richardson, Cliff vs. The State
Richey, E. J. and Nannie Richey vs. Ida Barron and Benjamin
  Barron
Richey, Spencer vs. The State
Richmond and Danville R. R. Co. vs. C. H. Jordan
Rickerson, Benjamin vs. M. A. McDowell
Rickerson, Benjamin and William Rickerson vs. T. Jeff Smith
Rickerson, Neel vs. The State
Ricket, Dolphus vs. James H. Campbell
Ricketts, Tilman O. and John M. Ricketts vs. Isaac Hardeman
Ridley, C. L. vs. Johnson and Lane
Ridley, Crissy vs. The State
Ridley, Hamp vs. Spivey and Stubbs
Ridley, Hamp vs. Bolling Whitfield
Ridley, Hannibal vs. Key and Preston
Ridley, Howard and L. M. Anderson vs. J. H. Holland
Ridley, Howard vs. Lewis and Bailey
Ridley, Howard vs. James H. Roberts
Ridley, Jesse vs. The State
Ridley, Jumima vs. The State
Ritchey, Will vs. The State
Rivers, C. K. vs. O. H. Arnold, Jr.
Rivers, Dock vs. The State
Robert, L. W. vs. J. H. Kelly
Robert, Minnie N. vs. S. M. Anderson and J. W. Anderson
Roberts, Anthony vs. A. S. Holland

368

Roberts, Anthony vs. Whitfield and Brown
Roberts, Augustus vs. The State
Roberts, Daniel and Mary A. Roberts vs. Roberts and Roberts
Roberts, Daniel and Mary A. Roberts vs. Aaron Thurmond
Roberts, Henry vs. The State
Roberts, Hyder vs. Bolling Whitfield
Roberts, J. R. and E. D. Roberts (children of) vs. L. O. Benton
   and Bros.
Roberts, J. W. and Mary A. Roberts vs. Kelly and Price
Roberts, J. Willie vs. A. M. Robinson and Co.
Roberts, Jordan vs. The State
Roberts, L. H. vs. W. P. Hardy
Roberts, O. G. vs. P. M. DeLeon
Roberts, O. G. vs. B. H. Rawls
Roberts, Spencer and Charles Blackwell vs. J. T. Corley
Robertson, Albert vs. The State
Robinson, Aaron vs. N. B. White
Robinson, Alex vs. Banks, Davidson and Kelly
Robinson, Alex vs. The State
Robinson, Berry vs. N. B. White
Robinson, Ike vs. The State
Robinson, J. H. vs. C. B. Rosser, J. D. Harvey and R. L. Davis
Robinson, Jesse, Jr. vs. The State
Robinson, John L. vs. J. O. Burton for use of Goldsmith Bros.
Robinson, John L. vs. Henry Sloan
Robinson, John S. vs. R. M. Everett
Robinson, Lonie vs. L. O. Benton and Bros.
Robinson, Monroe and Willie Robinson vs. W. W. Allen
Robinson, Monroe vs. Richard I. Davis, C. B. Rosser and J. D.
   Harvey
Robinson, Monroe vs. J. A. Kelly
Robinson, Monroe vs. James Shaw
Robinson, Sam vs. The State
Robinson, William vs. William Malone
Robinson, Willie vs. Baglett and Willett
Roby, Augustus (col) vs. S. R. Baynes
Roby, Henry vs. D. M. Langston
Roby, P. M. vs. Gibbs Drug Co.
Roby, P. M. vs. Medoc Wine Co.
Roby, Paul M. vs. Job Petty
Roby, T. S. vs. John S. Dance
Roby, W. A. vs. Wynn and Clack
Roby, W. L. vs. W. T. Fish
Roby, Mrs. W. L. vs. C. D. Jordan
Roby, Walter vs. Eckels and Abercromby
Roby, Walter L., B. C. Kelly and E. H. Kelly vs. John M. Allen
Roby, Walter L. vs. W. A. Kelly and Bros.
Roby, Walter L. and Eaton H. Kelly vs. The State
Roby, Walter L. vs. Martha A. Wilburn and Samuel C. Wilburn
Roland, Charles vs. W. C. Leverette
Roland, O. P. and T. P. Shy vs. A. W. Foster and Co.
Rooks, Will vs The State
Rooks, William vs. J. B. Dickey
Rosel, Anderson and Phillis Rosel vs. Mrs. E. T. Jordan
Rosell, Anderson and Phillis Rosell vs. A. S. Holland
Ross, Harry vs. Elliott Estes and Co.
Ross, Harry, Mark Griggs, John Ross and Henry Ross vs. Mrs. E.
   Baynes for use of Talbot Sons
Ross, Tom vs. The State
Roswell, John vs. J. T. Davis and C. M. Davis
Roswell, John vs. Pauline Pon and Caroline Pon
Rowe, John C. and J. G. Rowe vs. James Benton
Rowland, O. P. vs. W. H. Howard

Russell, Wiley vs. The State
Rye, Lawrence vs. The State

Saffo, Eberhart and Ben Saffo vs. M. L. Duke and Co.
Samples, Eli vs. W. F. Jordan
Sandefer, T. B. and Mike Kinard vs. Doughtry Brothers
Sanders, Albert vs. The State
Sanders, Cofer and Co. vs. Tolbert Hoyt and Co.
Sanders, Moses vs. The State
Sanders, Pleas and John Carr vs. Lawton and Willingham
Sanders, Pleas vs. W. L. Zachry
Sanders, S. B. vs. The State
Sanders, Wesley vs. Hodge Mercantile Co.
Sands, Tom vs. A. S. Thurman
Satterwhite, Carrie and B. F. Thomas vs. The State
Scales, Joe vs. Moses Peddy
Scott, Levi vs. The State
Scott, Wilson and Arthur Scott vs. The State
Seats, Anderson vs. Wynn and Clack
Seats, Andrew vs. W. D. Wynn
Seats, Thomas and Thomas W. Shy vs. Bolling Whitfield
Self, William vs. The State
Seymore, Henry C. vs. W. E. Baynes
Seymore, Henry C. vs. Webster, Davis and Co.
Seymore, L. V. vs. W. E. Baynes
Seymour, Alice vs. Watson and Walker
Sharpin, Sam vs. The State
Shaver, Sam vs. Clay Tape
Shaw, J. L. vs. N. B. White
Shaw, James vs. The State
Shaw, Milus vs. J. O. Shepherd
Shecut, John F., B. T. Digby and J. A. Broughton vs. W. A. Kelly
Shehee, Cal (alias Cal Andrews) vs. The State
Shelverton, H. N. vs. John B. M. Phillips
Shepherd, John vs. The State
Shepherd, Minerva vs. W. H. Thompson
Sherman, Jefferson vs. The State
Shields, Jermima vs. Thomas Malone
Shipp and Webb vs. The State
Shipp, G. V. and M. Aaron vs. Berry T. Digby
Shockley, G. W. vs. J. H. Freeman
Showers, E. S. vs. Thomas Camp
Showers, Elias vs. Thomas R. Penn
Showers, Lucius vs. Thomas Camp
Showers, Lucius vs. The State
Showers, Paschal and Jeremiah Showers vs. John W. Pearson
Shropshier, Julia W., Martha G. Shropshire and Rebecca E.
   Shropshire vs. Hardeman and Gibson
Shy, Alfred and George Shy vs. Martin Durden
Shy, Alfred vs. Printup Bro. and Pollard
Shy, Anderson vs. J. C. Pennington
Shy, Mrs. C. F. vs. Commercial Nurseries
Shy, Charles vs. A. W. Foster and Co.
Shy, Frank vs. Printup Bro. and Pollard
Shy, J. M. vs. James A. Green
Shy, J. M. vs. William H. Spears
Shy, Jack vs. Pennington and Binford
Shy, Jackson vs. A. S. Hough
Shy, Jackson vs. Printup Bro. and Pollard
Shy, Maranda vs. H. N. White
Shy, P. R. vs. Purse and Thomas
Shy, Peter vs. Paschall Showers and W. F. Jordan
Shy, Reese vs. Bolling Whitfield

Shy, S. C. and Wade B. Goolsby vs. M. N. Williams
Shy, S. G. vs. Bearden Furlow and Co.
Shy, S. J. vs. Printup Bro. and Pollard
Shy, S. W. and William N. Shy vs. James M. Shy
Shy, S. W. vs. N. M. Williams
Shy, Sallie and Jackson Shy vs. G. B. Stovall
Shy, Samuel C. vs. A. L. Hough
Shy, Samuel C. vs. John W. Kelly
Shy, Samuel C. vs. William G. Kelly
Shy, Samuel C. vs. S. W. Shy
Shy, Samuel C. vs. N. B. White and L. White
Shy, Seaborn J., Samuel C. Shy and Caroline C. Shy vs. Burnett, Broughton and Co.
Shy, Sebron W., Samuel C. Shy and Peyton R. Shy vs. Billips and Brobston
Shy, T. P. vs. O. H. Arnold, Jr.
Shy, T. P. and J. M. Shy vs. Lucien Benton
Shy, T. P. vs. J. S. Dell
Shy, T. P. and S. G. Shy vs. J. P. Harris
Shy, T. P. vs. C. A. Harwell
Shy, T. P. vs. P. R. Thomason
Shy, T. P. vs. Jacob Wolf
Shy, T. P. vs. Wright and Crane
Shy, Thad vs. A. S. Hough
Shy, W. N. and R. L. Shy vs. J. H. Bullard, S. H. Bullard and H. W. Bullard
Sigman, Manson vs. The State
Simmons, Jones vs. The State
Simpson, Jack vs. The State
Simpson, Y. A. vs. The State
Singleton, Robert vs. John J. Jones
Slaughter, Delia vs. The State
Slaughter, Fed (col) vs. Nathan C. Fish
Slocumb, H. V. and W. S. Slocumb vs. Goldsmith Bros.
Slute, W. H. and Obadiah Williams vs. The State
Slutter, Ed vs. The State
Smith, Alex vs. The State
Smith, Anthony vs. Alfred C. Millen, Tabethy Showers for use of W. B. Dozier
Smith, Anthony vs. Anthony Pennimon
Smith, B. R. and C. F. Thompson vs. Temperance Cheek and J. W. Grubbs
Smith, Boykin and O. D. Price vs. James M. Terrell
Smith, Caroline vs. The State
Smith, Delia Ann vs. The State
Smith, Ed vs. Robert A. Reid
Smith, Eugene vs. S. R. Campbell
Smith, Eugene vs. T. A. Hutchinson and K. P. Greer
Smith, George vs. G. R. Dozier
Smith, George vs. A. W. Foster and William L. High
Smith, George vs. W. A. Kelly and Bros.
Smith, George vs. A. L. Sluder
Smith, George vs. The State
Smith, George vs. N. B. White
Smith, Guy vs. The State
Smith, H. P. vs. Mary Evans
Smith, H. T. vs. T. C. Spivey
Smith, Hattie W. and J. W. A. Smith, Jr. vs. W. A. Kelly and Bros.
Smith, Henry (col) vs. L. Benton and O. M. Benton
Smith, Henry (col) vs. Lee Rocquemore
Smith, Henry, J. H. Smith, Guy Smith and Cornelia Smith vs The State

Smith, Henry T. vs. Gibbs and Serrett Mfg. Co.
Smith, Henry T. and John C. Key vs. John Merryman and Co.
Smith, Henry T. vs. Pink Thompson
Smith, Horace and Cody C. Bryant vs. R. Jordan and Co.
Smith, J. H. vs. Allen and Dumas Co.
Smith, J. H. and W. G. Smith vs. L. O. Benton and Eugene Benton
Smith, J. H. vs. J. H. Bullard and H. W. Bullard
Smith, J. H. vs. Empire Liquor Co.
Smith, J. H. vs. W. S. Florence
Smith, J. H. vs. The State
Smith, J. H. vs. Thompson and Farmer
Smith, J. H. and W. G. Smith vs. Joseph Thompson
Smith, J. H. and Co. vs. Samuel Evans
Smith, J. H. S. vs. Gramling, Spalding, Kingsbery
Smith, J. Henry vs. E. H. Cohen
Smith, J. Henry vs. Officers of Court
Smith, J. Hinto vs. S. P. Downs
Smith, J. T. vs. The State
Smith, J. W. A. and Sterling Smith vs. The State
Smith, J. W. A., Jr. vs. Schaefer and Mallet
Smith, James J. vs. A. M. Robinson and Co.
Smith, John vs. S. R. Smith
Smith, John C. vs. F. M. Lester
Smith, John C. C. vs. F. M. Park
Smith, John W. A. vs. Griffin, Monticello and Madison Railroad
   Co.
Smith, John W. A. vs. Allen Johnson
Smith, John W. A. vs. Daniel H. Wilcox and Leonard Y. Gibbs
Smith, Lean vs. The State
Smith, Lucy vs. The State
Smith, Mrs. Lucy B. vs. W. L. Zachry
Smith, Manch (col) vs. The State
Smith, Maneb vs. R. J. Warren and W. P. Davis
Smith, Matt vs. Solomon Smith
Smith, Missouri and Anna Barnes vs. William C. Penn
Smith, Orelious vs. The State
Smith, Orilious and Gardner Smith vs. W. H. Phillips
Smith, Ponder vs. The State
Smith, Mrs. Rhoda Ann vs. A. B. Small
Smith, Rhoda Ann vs. Walton Guano Co.
Smith, S. P. vs. Frank E. Block
Smith, S. P. vs. T. A. Crews
Smith, S. P. vs. Everett, Ridley, Ragan and Co.
Smith, S. P. vs. George H. Hulme
Smith, S. P. vs. Oglesby Grocery Co.
Smith, S. P. vs. The State
Smith, S. P. vs. J. B. Taylor Tobacco Co.
Smith, S. R., Jr. vs. James Benton
Smith, S. R., Jr. vs. W. H. Lloyd
Smith, S. R., Jr. vs. N. B. White
Smith, Sam vs. Banks, Davidson and Kelly
Smith, Samuel R., Jr. vs. Shipp and Webb
Smith, Samuel R., Jr. vs. F. M. Swanson
Smith, Sidney, Jane Leverette, and Francis Leverette vs. Joel
   Daws
Smith, Solomon vs. George Newton
Smith, T. P. vs. J. W. Preston and Co.
Smith, Thomas J. vs. Officers of Court
Smith, Tom vs. The State
Smith, W. R. vs. O. H. Arnold, Jr.
Smith, W. R. vs. O. L. Benton and Bro.
Smith, W. R. vs. Fowler Brothers
Smith, W. R. vs. Hodge Mercantile Co.

Smith, Willis (col) and Joshua Beavers (col) vs. The State
Soloway, Abe vs. The State
Speairs, Thomas L. vs. Navassa Guano Co.
Spear, William H. and Elizabeth A. Spear vs. Richard Henderson
Spearman, Andrew vs. Frank Harvill
Spearman, J. S. vs. H. W. Baldwin
Spearman, John and Samuel Blackwell vs. S. C. Talmadge, A. J.
    Talmadge for use of James L. Maddux
Spearman, John F. vs. W. N. Brown
Spearman, John F. vs. Fisher Levy
Spearman, William vs. Bartlett and Caswell
Spearman, William vs. Commercial Nurseries
Spearman, William vs. Braxton R. Ezell, Sr.
Spearman, William vs. James J. Johnston
Spearman, William vs. E. Newton
Spearman, William vs. Temple Pump Co.
Spearman, William vs. John Turk and William Turk
Spearman, William vs. M. P. West
Spearman, William vs. Bolling Whitfield
Spearman, William vs. Whitfield and Brown
Spears, A. M. vs. A. L. Sluder
Spears, Augustus vs. Sidney Spears
Spears, Betsey vs. Sidney Spears
Spears, Creed E. and Catharine Spears vs. Richard Henderson
Spears, Henry (col) vs. Henry Sloan
Spears, J. A. vs. L. S. Kelly and W. J. Phillips
Spears, Jane vs. The State
Spears, Mahala vs. The State
Spears, Martha A. and W. R. Tuggle vs. Eden H. Kelly
Spears, S. C. vs. J. S. Pursley
Spears, Thomas L. vs. Banks, Davidson and Kelly
Spears, Thomas L. vs. Nevassa Guano Co.
Speights, Surania (col) vs. The State
Spellers, Oliver vs. James T. Benton
Spiller, Frank vs. The State
Springfield Baptist Church vs. William Belcher
Springfield Baptist Church vs. Henry B. Jordan
Standerfer, Milley vs. The State
Standifer, Adolphus vs. M. S. Benton
Standifer, Adolphus vs. Crawford Kelly
Standifer, Currin vs. J. A. Cary
Standifer, Silas vs. N. B. White
Standifer, Walker vs. A. H. Jordan and C. L. Henderson
Stanford, Obe vs. The State
Starke, Mary vs. A. S. Holland
Steed, A. S. vs. J. F. Watson
Steel, J. N., W. H. Steel, J. H. Hardy and W. G. Hardy vs. J. W.
    Crum and Co.
Steele, John vs. A. M. Robinson and Co.
Steele, Mollie A. vs. J. H. Kelly
Steele, W. H. and J. N. Steele vs. M. N. McKinly
Stephens, Abna vs. The State
Stephens, Genie vs. The State
Stephens, Sherman vs. The State
Stewart, Henry (col) vs. The State
Stewart, Joseph vs. The State
Stewart, Susan vs. The State
Stokes, C. M. vs. Corley and Dorsett
Stokes, C. M. vs. Anderson V. Hunter
Stokes, J. W. vs. J. A. Taylor
Stone, James vs. Annie Smith (col)
Stone, L. E. vs. Howard and Soule
Stone, M. P. vs. J. W. Stokes

373

Strickland, J. W. vs. Greer Bros. and Garland
Strickland, J. W. vs. A. C. Sanford
Strong, Grant and Cornelia Newton vs. L. O. Benton and Bro.
Strong, William vs. Mrs. M. P. Gaston
Strong, William E. vs. Roberts and Peurifoy
Sullivan, L. E. and A. S. Sullivan vs. Dr. W. M. Durham
Sumners, John T. vs. S. H. Johnson
Swanson, E. Y. vs. J. W. Moran
Swanson, E. Y. vs. J. W. Morgan
Swanson, F. M. vs. Edmond T. Brown
Swanson, Francis M. vs. Russel J. Brown
Swanson, Francis M. vs. Oscar Cheesman
Swanson, Francis M. vs. W. H. Stark and Co.
Swanson, Francis M. vs. Solomon Waxelbaum and Bro.
Swanson, Susan vs. The State
Swift, Jim vs. The State
Swift, Willis vs. The State

Talmadge, C. A. and S. A. Flournoy vs. J. A. Stone
Talmadge, Henry vs. Goldsmith Bros.
Talmadge, Herbert vs. Laura Hester
Talmadge, John H. vs. N. B. White
Talmadge, Robert S. vs. L. O. Benton and Bros.
Talmadge, S. C. and B. T. Digby vs. Clisby, Jones and Reese
Tanner, A. W. vs. Thomas R. Williams vs. J. W. Minter
Taylor, Mark vs. The State
Taylor, Samuel (col) vs. The State
Teddars, G. W. vs. W. C. Clark and Co.
Terhune, Cornelius vs. Joseph Tyler
Thomas, Buck vs. Thomas C. Broddus
Thomas, Buck and J. M. Campbell vs. S. R. Campbell
Thomas, Buck vs. W. A. Kelly and Bros.
Thomas, Buck vs. Talmadge and Tolleson
Thomas, Ednie vs. O. P. Fitsimons, Jr.
Thomas, Hiram vs. The State
Thomas, Jeff vs. The State
Thomas, Lewis vs. Henretta Alfred
Thomas, Lewis vs. Isaac Daniel
Thomas, Lewis vs. J. M. Dawson
Thomas, Lewis vs. Willis Field
Thomas, Lewis vs. The State
Thomas, Mary and Buck Thomas vs. L. O. Benton and Bro.
Thomas, Mat vs. G. W. Scott and Co.
Thomas, Rich vs. The State
Thomas, Scott vs. Clementine Campbell for use of W. B. Dozier
Thomas, Scott vs. W. A. Kelly and Bros.
Thomas, Scott vs. Lewis and Bailey
Thomas, Scott vs. The State
Thomas, Scott (col) vs. Wheeler and Wilson Mfg. Co.
Thomas, Wash (col) vs. The State
Thomas, Will vs. The State
Thomason, A. J. vs. W. F. Jordan
Thomason, Isaac vs. Berry Fears
Thomason, J. C. and W. R. Tuggle vs. Early W. Thrasher
Thomason, Jackson C. vs. W. F. Jordan
Thomason, T. J. vs. Georgia Chemical Works
Thomason, W. vs. The State
Thompson, Abraham vs. The State
Thompson, Charles F. and B. R. Smith vs. J. W. Grubbs
Thompson, E. I. vs. John E. Langston and David M. Langston
Thompson, Henry vs. Banks, Davidson and Kelly
Thompson, J. C. vs. J. D. Thornton
Thompson, J. F. vs. H. Adler

Thompson, J. F. vs. Griffin, Monticello and Madison Railroad Co.
Thompson, J. F., Jr. vs. The State
Thompson, J. M. vs. Wynn and Clack
Thompson, Jackson P. vs. S. A. Flournoy
Thompson, Jacob M. vs. Franklin George
Thompson, Joseph vs. The State
Thompson, Joseph M. vs. Lawrence E. Cook
Thompson, Joseph M. vs. Mapes Formula and Peruvian Guano Co.
Thompson, Joseph R. vs. The State
Thompson, L. L. vs. John B. Webb
Thompson, Mary vs. The State
Thompson, Mat and John Thompson vs. The State
Thompson, Matthew vs. Jacob Whitfield
Thompson, Samuel vs. The State
Thompson, W. D. vs. W. D. Wynn
Thompson, W. H. and Mattie Hardeman vs. Charles Gaston
Thompson, William (col) vs. The State
Thompson, William vs. Bolling Whitfield
Thompson, William, Jr. vs. John W. Morgan
Thompson, William D. vs. W. E. Tucker
Thompson, William H. and Charles F. Thompson vs. Eugene S.
  Bartlett and Charles L. Bartlett
Thompson, William L. vs. Isaiah Jordan
Thompson, William L. vs. Cordelia Minter
Thornton, Handy vs. The State
Thornton, Handy vs. J. W. Williams for use of Officers of Court
Thornton, Joseph D. vs. Enterprise Lumber Co.
Thurman, Aaron vs. Officers of Court
Thurman, Aaron vs. Mrs. L. E. Stancil
Thurman, Aaron, Robert Whitfield and Bolling Whitfield vs.
  George W. Wolf and J. C. Carmichael
Thurman, Arnel vs. The State
Thurman, C. D. vs. The State
Thurman, James vs. The State
Thurman, Joe and Frank Thurman vs. The State
Thurman, Mitchell vs. The State
Thurman, Moody vs. James W. Holland
Thurman, Primus vs. The State
Thurman, Rich vs. The State
Thurman, Sarah vs. Aaron Thurman
Thurman, Wilks vs. The State
Thurmon, Aaron, Sr. vs. Whitfield and Brown
Thurmond, Aaron vs. Madison Epps
Thurmond, Aaron vs. James Turner
Thurmond, Aaron vs. N. B. White
Thurmond, C. D. vs. Benton Supply Co.
Thurmond, Charles H. and Ed H. Thurmond vs. Julia E. Goolsby
Tillman, C. B. and W. S. Simmons vs. Mayer and Watts
Tillman, Robert Lee (col) vs. The State
Tilman, Edny vs. The State
Tilman, George T. vs. L. O. Benton and Bros.
Tingle, W. A. vs. Willis Branham
Tingle, W. A. vs. James H. Campbell and S. R. Campbell
Tinseley, Charles vs. Joshua Hill
Tinsley, Charlie, Jr., Will Tinsley and Dave Boykin vs. R.
  Jordan and Co.
Tinsley, Daniel vs. Wiley Phillips, Green M. Phillips, John B.
  Phillips and Andrew J. Freeman
Tinsley, Mary vs. The State
Tinsley, William vs. The State
Titts, J. E. vs. The State
Todd, Ed vs. The State
Toland, Matilda vs. R. P. Brooks

Toland, T. L. and W. E. Paul vs. Lucy B. Smith
Toland, T. L. vs. F. M. Swanson
Tolleson, J. G. vs. Frank E. Block
Tolleson, J. G. vs. E. W. Ezell and Co.
Tolleson, J. G. vs. Talmadge and Dorsey
Tomlinson, J. T. vs. A. J. Talmadge and J. G. Tolleson
Tomlinson, Jack vs. Roberts and Peurifoy
Tomlinson, John and W. J. Tomlinson vs. Bullard Bros.
Tomlinson, M. W. vs. W. A. Kelly and Bros.
Tomlinson, W. M. vs. W. H. Holsenbeck
Tomlinson, W. M. vs. Seaborn Lawrence and S. C. Lawrence
Tomlinson, W. M. vs. Frank Leverett for use of B. H. Sanders Co.
Tompkins, Mason vs. A. S. Holland
Touggle, W. R. vs. B. T. Lowe
Towns, Lewis (col) vs. James W. Holland
Trayler, Mark (col) vs. The State
Truitt, J. T. vs. The State
Tucker, Alfred vs. H. D. Banks
Tucker, Alfred (col) and John W. Wyatt vs. Thomas K. Wommack
Tucker, B. H. and William Tucker vs. D. Weil, A. Meyers, J. P.
   Givens and S. B. Wolef
Tucker, G. C. vs. John B. Webb
Tucker, Green vs. F. M. Swanson
Tucker, Green C. vs. Corley and Dorsett
Tucker, Green C. vs. Howard and Soule
Tucker, T. C. vs. W. E. Baynes
Tuggle, A. F. vs. L. O. Benton and Eugene Benton
Tuggle, Berry vs. David Belcher
Tuggle, Charlie, Jr. vs. Lucian Benton
Tuggle, Charlie, Jr. vs. The State
Tuggle, E. D. vs. Southern Banking and Trust Co.
Tuggle, E. D. vs. N. B. White and Co.
Tuggle, Earney vs. Benton Supply Co.
Tuggle, F. N. vs. James Knight
Tuggle, F. N. vs. S. P. Smith
Tuggle, Florence N. vs. Shipp and Webb
Tuggle, Harry (col) vs. The State
Tuggle, Henry vs. The State
Tuggle, L. S. vs. W. C. Clark and Co.
Tuggle, L. S. and W. R. Tuggle vs. The State
Tuggle, L. S. vs. N. B. White and Co.
Tuggle, Otis vs. County Commissioners
Tuggle, Robert vs. J. L. Campbell
Tuggle, W. R. and Colbert Jeffries vs. Banks, Davidson and Kelly
Tuggle, W. R. vs. R. C. Harper
Tuggle, W. R. and L. S. Tuggle vs. W. A. Kelly and Bros.
Tuggle, W. R. vs. Mallet and McCandless
Tuggle, W. R. vs. Martin and Stovall
Tuggle, W. R. vs. Printup Bro. and Pollard
Tuggle, W. R. vs. W. T. Vincent
Tuggle, W. R. vs. Wynn and Clack
Tuggle, Wash vs. L. O. Benton and Eugene Benton
Tuggle, William R. vs. Franklin George
Tuggle, William R. vs. Shipp and Webb
Tuggle, William R. vs. Francis M. Swanson
Turk, A. A. vs. W. E. Baynes
Turk, Avington vs. William Spearman
Turk, E. B. vs. J. P. Harris
Turk, E. B. vs. Evan Harvey, John C. Allen and Evan T. Mathis
Turk, Edward B. vs. Clayton Lancaster
Turk, Edward B. vs. W. W. Turnell and R. M. Lassiter
Turk, Medora vs. Spivey and Stubbs
Turk, T. J. vs. H. D. Adams

Turk, T. J. vs. T. A. Crews
Turk, T. J. vs. Everett, Ridley, Ragan and Co.
Turk, T. J. vs. George H. Hulme
Turk, T. J. vs. A. M. Robinson and Co.
Turk, T. J. vs. W. W. Turnell and W. M. Lasiter
Turk, T. J. vs. F. G. Webb
Turk, Thomas I. vs. William Robinson
Turk, Thomas J. vs. Georgia Chemical Works
Turke, John and W. C. Turke vs. Willis Newton
Turke, Thomas vs. Kelly and McDowell
Turner, A. J. vs. Middle Georgia Bank
Turner, Allen vs. The State
Turner, J. W. vs. B. F. Barnwell and E. A. Barnwell
Turner, J. W. vs. Georgia Chemical Works
Turner, J. W. vs. F. M. Lester
Turner, James vs. A. S. Holland
Turner, James vs. Bolling Whitfield
Turner, James A. vs. Crawford H. Greer
Turner, James A. vs. Thomas J. Pritchett
Turner, John vs. Shipp and Webb
Turner, John W. vs. Francis M. Swanson
Turner, Nick vs. The State
Turner, Owen vs. The State
Turner, R. F. and W. T. Turner vs. Dunlap Hardware Co.
Turner, T. A. B. vs. Berry T. Digby
Turner, T. A. B. vs. A. B. Small
Turner, Thomas vs. Martha Carter
Turner, Thomas vs. C. M. Meriwether
Turner, Thomas, Jr. vs. The State
Turner, Toliver A. vs. Key and Preston
Turner, W. T. and R. F. Turner vs. John Silvey and Co.
Turner, W. T. vs. The State
Tyler, Barney vs. The State
Tyler, F. M. vs. Madison Epps
Tyler, F. Marion vs. Nehemiah B. White
Tyler, John and E. T. Swanson vs. J. W. Morgan
Tyler, John J. and F. M. Tyler vs. George T. Bartlett
Tyler, John J. vs. G. R. Dozier and Co.
Tyler, John J. vs. Kelly and McDowell
Tyler, John J. and F. M. Tyler vs. Medora Turk, Claudia Turk,
   and W. F. Jordan
Tyler, John J. vs. Wynn and Clack
Tyler, Martin vs. A. J. Talmadge and J. G. Tolleson
Tyler, Mike vs. R. J. J. Greer
Tyler, Mike vs. The State
Tyler, T. M. vs. Howard and Soule
Tyner, D. M. vs. John A. Allen
Tyner, D. M. and M. A. Tyner vs. Singer Manufacturing Co.
Tyner, D. M. vs. John B. Webb
Tyner, David M. vs. J. W. Turner and V. A. Wilson
Tyner, M. V. and William T. McKissack vs. Richard S. Grubbs
Tyner, Reuben J. vs. Pleasant P. Lovejoy and John D. Lovejoy

Umphrey, Milton vs. Burnett and Co.
Ursry, Mose vs. The State

Varner, Alex and Charlie Rowland vs. The State
Vaughn, Bill vs. The State
Vaughn, Jeff vs. Mrs. E. T. Jordan
Vaughn, Jefferson vs. Lewis W. Pon
Vickrum, Homer vs. The State
Vincent, James vs. Wellington and Hickmon
Vinson, John and J. W. Smith vs. Robinson, Kelly and Co.

Wade, Joe, Andrew Freeman and Monroe Wilson vs. The State
Wadford, Alexander vs. The State
Wadley, Henry vs. The State
Wasley, Isaac vs. The State
Wagner, H. Lee vs. O. O. Banks Bros.
Wagner, J. C. and J. W. Wagner vs. O. H. Arnold, Jr.
Wagner, J. C. vs. Central Georgia Alliance Warehouse Co.
Wagner, J. C., J. M. Wagner and E. Vincent vs. A. B. Small
Waits, Alexander, Jr. vs. Nehemiah B. White
Waits, C. L. vs. The State
Waits, James vs. S. C. Lawrence
Waits, James and E. T. Swanson vs. J. W. Moran
Waits, Jefferson vs. Thomas Holland and Walter L. Zachry
Waits, Jefferson and Joshua Waits vs. W. T. Holland and W. L.
  Zachry
Waits, Levi vs. T. R. King
Waits, Levi vs. A. M. Robinson and J. B. Robinson for use of
  Officers of Court
Waits, Levi (alias Tobe Waits) vs. The State
Waits, Lucinda vs. Hiram Brooks
Waits, Mittie vs. Howe Machine Co.
Waits, T. L. vs. The State
Waits, Thomas vs. The State
Waits, W. J. vs. H. B. Jordan, E. H. Jordan, A. H. Jordan and
  D. R. Glover
Waits, W. J. and W. B. Waits vs. E. W. McGehee
Waits, W. J. vs. Waxelbaum Company
Waits, Wade and Pete Pye vs. The State
Waits, Wade vs. W. L. Zachry
Waits, William, W. B. Goolsby and John B. Webb vs. William A.
  Kelly and Bros.
Waldrup, Clifford vs. The State
Waldrup, J. S. vs. L. O. Benton and Eugene Benton
Waldrup, O. W. and K. J. Waldrup vs. L. O. Benton and Eugene
  Benton
Waldrup, Oscar vs. James H. Campbell and S. R. Campbell
Walker, Emma, Ellen Thomas, Emma Thomas and Rebecca Walker vs.
  The State
Walker, Henry vs. The State
Walker, J. W. and J. L. Aaron vs. David Tiner
Walker, Jack vs. L. O. Benton and Bro.
Walker, Jack (col) vs. Gilbert D. Greir
Walker, John and Mathew Rany vs. Thomas Camp
Walker, John, Henry Penn and Jack Walker vs. The State
Walker, Lewis vs. William T. Fish
Walker, Lewis vs. Edney Thomas
Walker, Lewis vs. Susan Walker
Walker, Mary vs. Nick Walker
Walker, Reese vs. Els Barnes
Walker, Roland vs. The State
Walker, Scott vs. Thomas Meriwether
Walker, Sid vs. J. O. Shepherd
Walker, Sid (col) vs. The State
Walker, Troup (col) vs. The State
Walker, W. H. vs. Price and Steele
Walker, Westley vs. Key and Preston
Walker, Westly vs. The State
Walker, Winfield vs. Francis M. Swanson
Walkins, Jack vs. The State
Wallace, Benjamin vs. Elizabeth Palmer
Walters, Warren vs. The State
Walton, C. W. vs. W. F. Jordan
Walton, E. I. vs. Henry Clack

Walton, E. J. vs. Key and Booth
Walton, Ed vs. William P. Henderson
Wammack, Mrs. E. H. vs. J. H. Kelly
Wammack, James vs. Emily V. Cary
Wammack, James T. vs. Coleman and Newsom
Wammack, James T. vs. Frank Leverett
Wammack, Linton and William Loyd vs. The State
Wammack, T. K. vs. John W. Morgan
Ward, Benjamin vs. Burrell Almond
Ward, F. J. vs. Key and Preston
Ward, Fleming and E. C. Pope vs. William A. Pye
Ward, Fleming J. vs. Evan B. Ezell and George Hunt
Ward, Fleming J. vs. Charles Gerding
Ward, Fleming J. vs. Leverett and Co.
Ward, Fleming J. vs. Willingham and Dunn
Ward and Pope vs. Joe Pitman
Wardlow, M. C. vs. Clark and Pace
Ware, George vs. Martha E. Brown
Ware, George vs. Charles M. Meriwether
Waters, Ernest vs. The State
Waters, Fred vs. The State
Waters, Lane vs. The State
Watson, Charles vs. Bithy Dudley
Watson, Farrer (alias Pig Watson) vs. The State
Watson, Willie vs. The State
Watters, Aaron (col) vs. Lewis W. Pon
Watters, Andrew J. vs. Richard King
Watters, Andrew J. vs. Americus V. Mann
Watters, Dick vs. John R. Greer
Watters, Lane vs. Isaac Daniel
Watters, Warren vs. Key and Preston
Weathersby, James vs. J. H. Kelly
Weaver, John S. vs. Clark and Evans
Weaver, John S. vs. William S. Lee
Weaver, John S. vs. F. M. Morris
Weaver, John S. vs. Oliver S. Porter
Weaver, John S. vs. Franklin Wright
Weaver, Will and Lucy Seift vs. The State
Webb, G. G. vs. Crane, Boylston and Co.
Webb, G. G. vs. M. C. Kiser and J. F. Kiser
Webb, George vs. Nelson Glover
Webb, George G. vs. William E. Paul
Webb, George G. vs. N. B. White
Webb, J. B. vs. L. C. Slade
Webb, P. A. vs. Benton Supply Co.
Webb, Thomas P. vs. William Andrews
Webb, Thomas P. vs. John Hill and William Smith
Webb, Thomas P. vs. Francis M. Swanson
Weldon, Abraham vs. Roberts and Peurifoy
Wellington and Hickman vs. Southern Banking Co.
West, Lucius vs. W. D. Wynn
West, Lush (col) vs. The State
Western Union Telegraph Co. vs. L. O. Benton and Bro.
White, B. A. vs. M. R. Bell
White, B. A. and Dick Mitchell vs. The State
White, Ben vs. C. G. Campbell for use of F. Jordan
White, Benjamin A. vs. J. A. Bybee
White, Charlie vs. The State
White, J. E. vs. The State
White, Joe vs. The State
White, N. B. and Co. vs. B. C. Bibb Stove Co.
White, N. B. vs. Robert J. Minter, Levi Goolsby and William
    Andrews

White, Scott vs. Lowe Bros. and Small
White, T. A. vs. John R. Dickey Drug Co.
White, T. A. vs. Rich Johnson
White, T. A. vs. Solomon and Riley
Whitfield, Alfred vs. John W. Morgan
Whitfield, B. vs. B. B. Odom
Whitfield, Bolling and Robert Whitfield vs. W. J. M. Preston
Whitfield, Bolling vs. Peter C. Sawyer
Whitfield, Bolling vs. John S. Stewart
Whitfield, Bolling vs. Oscar Thomason
Whitfield, Bolling W. vs. George F. Meriwether
Whitfield and Brown vs. Carley, Calder and Co.
Whitfield and Brown vs. James A. Gray
Whitfield and Brown vs. McBride and Co.
Whitfield and Brown vs. A. C. Wiley and B. F. Wiley
Whitfield, Charles vs. John W. Morgan
Whitfield, Eugene vs. Kelly and McDowell
Whitfield, Eugene vs. A. J. Talmadge, S. C. Charping and Joseph
     G. Tolleson
Whitfield, Gaston vs. Robert Childs
Whitfield, Georgia and Bolling Whitfield vs. Kelly and McDowell
Whitfield, India and John B. Whitfield vs. Lawson E. George
Whitfield, India C. vs. J. D. Sparks
Whitfield, Indie vs. Franklin George
Whitfield, Indie and John B. Whitfield vs. William C. Leverett
     for use of Bolling Whitfield
Whitfield, Indie C. vs. Willis Newton
Whitfield, J. B. vs. J. H. Bullard
Whitfield, Jake vs. Shipp and Webb
Whitfield, James and Wesley Blackwell vs. Charles Gerding and Co.
Whitfield, James (col) vs. Henry Montgomery
Whitfield, John B. vs. Samuel S. Blackwell
Whitfield, John B. and Indiana Whitfield vs. Key and Preston
Whitfield, John B. vs. F. M. Luster
Whitfield, John B. and Indiana Whitfield vs. S. C. McDaniel
Whitfield, John B. vs. Willis Newton
Whitfield, John B. vs. Lewis W. Pon
Whitfield, Lewis vs. Mrs. M. J. Baynes
Whitfield, Lewis vs. The State
Whitfield, Nancy vs. George Malone
Whitfield, Reuben vs. Robert Whitfield
Whitfield, Sam vs. John W. Morgan
Whitfield, Sam vs. Whitfield and Brown
Whitfield, Samuel vs. Henry Kelly (col)
Whitten, Levi vs. Mrs. M. P. Gaston
Whitten, Levi vs. Frank Leverett
Whitten, Levi vs. Henry C. McClure
Whitten, Levi vs. Henry C. Mills
Whitten, Levi vs. James H. Robinson and Augustus M. Robinson
Wilburn, Clark vs. County Commissioners
Wilburn, Martha and S. C. Wilburn vs. Lucian Benton and D. B.
     Benton
Wilburn, Martha A. vs. Clark, Rosser and Co.
Wilburn, Polk vs. The State
Wilburn, S. C. vs. T. J. Hunt
Wilburn, S. C. and Martha A. Wilburn vs. W. M. Mallet
Wilburn, S. J. vs. V. H. Wilson
Wilburn, Sam J., S. C. Wilburn and William H. Wilburn vs. A.
     Newton
Wilburn, Samuel vs. J. H. Holland
Wilburn, Samuel C. and Samuel J. Wilburn vs. B. A. Thomas
Wilburn, Samuel J. and Martha A. Winburn vs. Susan C. McMichael
Wilburn, W. H. vs. O. O. Banks and Bro.

Wilburn, W. H. vs. McCormick Neal
Wilburn, William H., Samuel Wilburn and Martha A. Wilburn vs.
   W. B. Dozier
Wilburn, William H. vs. Hugh T. Inman and Co.
Wilburn, William H. vs. Wynn and Clack
Williams, Berry and L. H. Williams vs. C. G. Campbell
Williams, Grady and Dolphus Parks vs. The State
Williams, Handy vs. F. M. Lester
Williams, J. S. vs. W. S. Florence and A. S. Thurman
Williams, J. Westly vs. W. B. Dozier for use of Sallie Dozier
Williams, James vs. The State
Williams, Jeems vs. The State
Williams, Jim vs. The State
Williams, John vs. The State
Williams, John vs. J. S. Tucker
Williams, N. M. vs. Akers, Gorden and Pattillo
Williams, N. M., A. W. Lane, A. W. Tanner, L. A. Lane and Henry
   T. Smith vs. James M. Smith (Governor) for use of Jasper Co.
Williams, N. M. vs. Wilcox, Gibbs and Co.
Williams, Pony vs. John W. Morgan
Williams, Prince vs. Harriett Hetch
Williams, Reese vs. Bolling Whitfield
Williams, Sam vs. John L. Mapp
Williams, Squire vs. B. R. Ezell, Sr.
Williams, Squire vs. The State
Williams, Thomas R. vs. Thomas B. Griffin
Willingham, Theophilus vs. William Andrews
Willingham, W. N. vs. Joseph G. Tolleson
Willington, C. E. and O. P. Hickman vs. S. Alexis Hecht
Wilson, Charles vs. S. I. Brooks
Wilson, Charles vs. O. P. Fitzsimmons
Wilson, Charles vs. Lewis Thomas
Wilson, George vs. Shipp and Webb
Wilson, Henry vs. The State
Wilson, Hiram vs. Edward A. Elder
Wilson, Hiram vs. Grief Lynch
Wilson, J. W. vs. Frank Leverett
Wilson, James, Jr. vs. The State
Wilson, James H. vs. The State
Wilson, James W. vs. W. R. Tuggle for use of J. B. Odor
Wilson, Jim and Ben Wilson vs. Susan E. Jones
Wilson, Milly vs. Mary Gaston
Wilson, Munroe vs. N. B. White
Wilson, Nancy vs. Hiram Brooks
Wilson, R. W. vs. Farmer, Douglas and Co.
Wilson, Texas (alias Texas Sparks) vs. The State
Wilson, V. A. vs. Lewis Comer
Wilson, V. A. vs. T. D. Guinn
Wilson, Vines A. vs. Shipp and Webb
Winans, C. A. vs. L. D. Ezell
Winter and Boss vs. Corfunkle Brothers
Wise, Henry vs. The State
Wolfe, Jacob vs. Mary J. Newton
Womack, Mrs. Eva vs. John H. Kelly
Womack, James T. vs. O. G. Roberts
Womack, T. K. vs. Jacob Wolfe
Wommack, William and James T. Wommack vs. John Merriman and Co.
Wormley, Will vs. The State
Wormly, Eliza vs. Monticello Coal and Lumber Co.
Worthy, George vs. The State
Worthy, Ose vs. The State
Wright, Charles W. C. vs. John Price, Sr.
Wright, G. W. and J. J. Pope vs. Almond and Marbutt

Wyatt, Asriah vs. The State
Wyatt, H. J. vs. L. O. Benton and Bros.
Wyatt, I. T. vs. Broughton and Fitzpatrick
Wyatt, I. T. vs. John A. Broughton, W. A. Broughton and A. M.
  Speer
Wyatt, I. T. vs. A. Shaw
Wyatt, I. T. vs. Jacob Wolfe
Wyatt, Isaac T. vs. John H. Baker and Theodore D. Caswell
Wyatt, Isaac T. vs. Russell J. Brown
Wyatt, J. O. vs. F. M. Swanson
Wyatt, J. T. vs. J. F. Patterson
Wyatt, J. T. vs. Printup Bro. and Pollard
Wyatt, Jeff vs. The State
Wyatt, M. L. and H. J. Wyatt vs. W. A. Kelly and Bro.
Wyatt, Quinn vs. The State
Wyatt, Sam vs. John J. Tyler
Wyatt, Will (col) (alias Will Ivory) vs. The State
Wynens, E. L. and T. A. B. Turner vs. J. M. B. Best
Wynn, W. D. vs. Day and Crew
Wynn, W. D. vs. Frank Drew
Wynn, W. D. vs. J. M. Thompson
Wynn, W. D. vs. Mary C. Walton

Yancey, George vs. The State
Yancy, J. E. vs. A. A. Barfield for use of Nancy J. Floyd
Yancy, J. E. vs. Perry M. DeLeon
Yancy, Thomas vs. Robert Ivy, Sr.
Yeatman, W. K. vs. A. J. Talmadge and Co.

Zimmerman, Charles vs. Roberts and Roberts
Zimmerman, Charles vs. N. B. White

CHAPTER VIII

JUSTICE OF THE PEACE COURT CASE FILES, 1802-1935
Record Group 179-4-9

    This series contains original unbound papers which formed
portions of civil and criminal case files involving, but not
limited to:

(1) Prossessory warrants   (9) Distress for rents
(2) Caveats   (10) Subpoenas
(3) Laborers' liens   (11) Complaints
(4) Magistrates summonses   (12) Judgments
(5) Summonses of garnishment   (13) Receipts for court costs
(6) Actions on accounts   (14) Criminal warrants
(7) Suits on accounts   (15) Claims on property
(8) Attachments   (16) Mortgage notes

The records have been flattened, cleaned and placed in folders.
They are grouped chronologically by time span of considerable
length and arranged alphabetically by surname of the defendant.
There is a cross-reference available in Box 1 that lists the
surnames of the plaintiffs alphabetically.

Aaron, J. L. vs. J. L. Campbell
Aaron, J. L. vs. Dooley and Dick
Aaron, J. T. and Sarah A. F. Aaron vs. Sidney J. Coogler
Aaron, James T. vs. John Boyed
Aaron, John L. vs. J. F. Rodgers and E. F. Edwards
Aaron, Mitchel and Sarah A. F. Aaron vs. T. J. Shepherd and
    Son
Aaron, Sarah F. vs. J. M. Floyd
Acre, W. B. and M. L. Acre vs. J. A. Hawkins
Adams, Caleb B. vs. Littleton Johnston
Adams, Richard vs. David J. Britt
Adgate, H. C. and Fred Adgate vs. Z. E. Holland
Aiken, A. M. vs. The State
Aiken, Kimball vs. The State
Aikens, David vs. The State
Alexander, Floid vs. C. M. McCart
Alexander, George vs. The State
Alexander, Jesse vs. Idus Smith
Allen, A. J. vs. B. T. Digby and James T. Lewis
Allen, Abner, Sarah Allen and Mary Allen vs. W. W. Allen
Allen, Green vs. Alf Banks
Allen, Howard vs. The State
Allen, J. S. vs. W. Whitlock
Allen, John vs. E. Cunard
Allen, Nelly vs. W. W. Allen
Allen, R. C., A. J. Talmadge and W. P. Hardy vs. J. H. Martin
Allen, Squire vs. J. T. Garland
Allen, Squire vs. J. D. McElhenney
Allen, Thomas (col) vs. James S. Burney
Allen, W. W. vs. McDade and Paschal
Allen, W. W. vs. Hampton Smith
Allen, W. W. vs. Martha Thompson
Wllen, Willie vs. The State
Ambers, Hance vs. G. W. McElhenny
Ammus, Sam vs. J. B. Hanson
Anderson, J. T. vs. Lucian Benton
Anderson, John T. vs. Banks, Davidson and Kelly
Andrews, James G. vs. John Gantt
Andrews, Lucious vs. The State
Andrews, William vs. J. H. Campbell
Anis, J. M. vs. Berry Walker
Annis, J. M. vs. J. A. McClendon
Annis, W. J. vs. L. O. Benton and Bros.
Appling, John Henry vs. The State

Arnold, O. H., Jr. vs. T. A. Aikens
Arnold, T. J. vs. S. Elias
Arnold, W. H. vs. Dock Smith
Athens, Joe Mat vs. The State

Bailey, Elisha vs. Bolling Whitfield
Bailey, J. L. vs. M. V. McKibben
Bailey, Mrs. J. Z. L. vs. S. J. Kelly and Bros.
Bailey, John W. vs. L. Benton and D. B. Benton
Bailey, R. L. and W. M. Bailey vs. E. B. Ezell and Co.
Bailey, R. S. vs. L. O. Benton and Bro.
Bailey, William vs. Hugh M. Martin
Bailey, Williamson vs. Thomas Smith
Bailey, Z. L. and J. L. Bailey vs. J. W. Almond
Baldwin, Martin vs. The State
Banks, Alf., Sr. vs. Banks, Davidson and Kelly
Banks, Alfred vs. George W. Scott and Co.
Banks, Anderson vs. Banks, Davidson and Kelly
Banks, Columbus vs. Banks, Davidson and Kelly
Banks, H. D. vs. W. A. Kelly and Bro.
Banks, Henry vs. William H. Thompson
Banks, Henry D. vs. Banks, Davidson and Kelly
Banks, John vs. A. H. Burney
Banks, Len vs. The State
Banks, Leroy vs. The State
Banks, Orilous vs. Will Malone
Banks, Sultana vs. The State
Banks, Thom vs. W. W. Allen
Banks, Thom vs. W. H. Kelly
Banks, Thomas vs. J. R. Mobley and Co.
Banks, Thomas vs. Pennington and Clegg
Banks, Tom vs. James T. Corley
Banks, Walton vs. Banks, Davidson and Kelly
Banks, Wes vs. The State
Barber, Dock vs. The State
Barclay, Clark A. vs. S. H. Stone
Barclay, Jerrie vs. The State
Barnes, Albert vs. The State
Barnes, John Henry vs. The State
Barnes, Mariah vs. W. H. Pickett
Barnes, Richard vs. The State
Barnes, Richard (col) vs. The State
Barnes, William (col) vs. The State
Barnwell, Henry vs. Doctor H. Beall
Barnwell, Henry and Lucius Mansfield vs. Jesse Loyall
Barr, Willie vs. The State
Barrett, Richard vs. The State
Barron, Adam vs. B. R. Ezell
Barron, Elzy vs. F. C. Monks
Barron, Jake vs. The State
Barron, Jesse vs. The State
Barron, John vs. The State
Barron, Will vs. C. D. Jordan
Bartlett, Will (col) vs. The State
Battle, J. P. vs. The State
Baynes, George vs. The State
Beavers, Joshua, Henry Kelly and Thomas Marks vs. The State
Bebee, Bob vs. Oliver Durden
Bebee, John vs. The State
Bebee, Lizzie and Bob Bebee vs. J. H. Kelly Co.
Bebee, Rich vs. L. O. Benton and Bro.
Bebee, Richard vs. T. R. King
Bebee, Susie and Rube (?) Bebee vs. D. J. Holsenbeck

Bebee, Will vs. The State
Beckwith, W. B. vs. Scot Benton (col)
Bee, Willie vs. The State
Beebee, Earl (col) vs. The State
Beebee, Flem (col) vs. The State
Belcher, David vs. Berry W. Tuggle
Belcher, N. B. vs. The State
Belcher, W. D. vs. David Dixon and Capers Dixon
Belcher, William vs. William Tinsley
Belcher, Willie vs. The State
Bell, Jerie (col) vs. The State
Bell, Johnie vs. The State
Benford, J. C. vs. The State
Bennett, William vs. Alfred Shepherd
Benson, Joe Billie vs. The State
Benton, Bill vs. T. J. Nash
Benton, Carrie (col) vs. The State
Benton, Doyle (col) vs. The State
Benton, Herschell vs. The State
Benton, Ida (col) vs. The State
Benton, James vs. B. F. Jones
Benton, Joe vs. Hilliard Jeffries
Benton, John (col) vs. The State
Benton, Lucius vs. The State
Benton, Mat (col) vs. The State
Benton, Robert (col) vs. James M. Jones
Benton, Travis (col) vs. The State
Benton, Willis vs. The State
Berry, William vs. G. T. Powers
Bill (col) vs. The State
Billingslea, Eugene vs. The State
Black, James vs. John Fluker
Blackwell, Emel vs. G. T. Blackwell
Blackwell, Frank vs. L. O. Benton and Bro.
Blackwell, H. F. vs. M. S. Benton and L. O. Benton
Blackwell, H. F. vs. Navassa Guano Co.
Blackwell, H. F. vs. Shipp and Webb
Blackwell, Isaac vs. W. W. Allen
Blackwell, Isaac vs. Farmer, Douglas and Co.
Blackwell, Isaac vs. Patcy Preston
Blackwell, Isaac vs. William Smith
Blackwell, J. F. vs. Banks, Davidson and Kelly
Blackwell, Pate vs. Banks, Davidson and Kelly
Blackwell, S. E. and B. F. Reeves vs. J. H. Kelly
Blackwell, S. H. vs. S. P. Downs
Blackwell, W. F. vs. Madison Epps
Blackwell, W. S. vs. G. W. Murell
Blackwell, Wesley vs. Elbert Preston
Blackwell, Will vs. Alcy Meriwether
Blizzard, G. W. vs. W. J. Tucker
Blossom, Simon G. and John H. Clute vs. Abel P. Wilson
Blunt, Alfred vs. Edward Garland
Bolam, Lula Bell vs. The State
Bonnett, Joe vs. The State
Bowden, Dawson vs. The State
Boy, New vs. The State
Boykin, Charity vs. The State
Boykin, David vs. Manda Blackwell
Boykin, Henry (col) vs. The State
Boykin, Joe, Dave Boykin and Charlie Digby vs. James Kilgore
Boykin, Joe vs. Berry Robinson
Boykin, Joe vs. Walton County Guano Co.
Bradford, John vs. J. T. Pitts and J. W. Pitts

Bradford, Charley vs. F. M. Kinard
Branon, Charlie vs. The State
Brant, Dink vs. Lillian Brant
Brantley, John H. and John W. Burney vs. Abner Bartlett
Barntley, John H. vs. Joseph Brantley
Brantley, John H. vs. Wiseman Bridges
Brantley, John H. vs. Thomas B. Erwin
Brantley, John H. and Thomas C. Taylor vs. Jonas H. Holland
Brewer, Susannah vs. John Spearman
Brewer, William (col) vs. The State
Brewor, Minnie vs. The State
Bridges, Thomas vs. Ephraim Sanders
Brinley, Frank vs. The State
Broadus, Neal vs. The State
Broddus, Earnest vs. The State
Broddus, Luke vs. G. W. McElhaney
Brodus, Thomas C. vs. Henry Hendrick
Brogden, Peterson G. vs. Mathew Farley
Brogden, Peterson G. vs. John Fears
Brookes, Allendel (?) vs. Gip Johnston
Brooks, George vs. The State
Brooks, S. I. vs. J. B. Oder and J. B. Webb
Broudis, Nelson vs. The State
Broughton, J. B. vs. The State
Broughton, Jonnie vs. The State
Brown, Adolphus vs. The State
Brown, Dunk vs. James L. Tucker
Brown, Richmond vs. Robert Flournoy
Brown, T. J. vs. Banks, Davidson and Kelly
Brown, William vs. Mathew Ranay
Bruce, B. F. and T. W. Dooly vs. Talbert, Hoyt and Co.
Bryan, Travis vs. John C. Willis and Aron C. Hickman
Bryant, Alice vs. Columbus Banks
Bryant, Jim vs. Joe Green
Bryant, Jim Henry vs. B. F. Reeves
Bryant, Joe vs. Banks and Davidson
Bryant, Joe vs. James T. Corly
Bryant, Joe and George Lewis vs. J. A. B. Stewart and J. King
  Stewart
Buckner, William vs. The State
Burdette, Samuel L. B. vs. Samuel Gogans
Burdett, Samuel L. B. vs. Robert R. Minter
Burford, Boss vs. The State
Burge, John vs. Jacob Waldrop and Cornelia M. Miller
Burney, C. C. vs. N. B. White
Burney, Charles C. vs. L. M. Price
Burney, Harrison vs. J. C. Durden
Burney, J. H. vs. William S. McHenry
Busby, M. C. vs. Susanna Busby
Bussy, Jim vs. T. R. Bonner
Butner, C. A. vs. Theo Shuman (Schumann)
Butts, Dumas vs. The State
Butts, Redic vs. E. A. Greene
Butts, William vs. The State
Byers, Haddie vs. The State
Byrom, Henry vs. J. D. McElhenney
Byrom, William H. vs. Hurd and Hungerford
Byrom, William H. vs. Johnston and Snell
Byrom, William H. vs. William Maxey
Byrum, Tobe vs. The State

Cabiness, Henry B. and Jarrel Beasley vs. Stokely Morgan
Caldwell, Edward vs. James Griggs

Calvert, J. F. and S. W. Calvert vs. Gibbs and Spence
Cambell, Willie vs. The State
Campbell, James H. vs. R. M. Everitt
Campbell, J. M. vs. Fleming Jordan and Son
Campbell, James M. vs. J. D. Kilpatrick
Campbell, John vs. John Monroe
Campbell, Leroy and Brock Marks vs. International Harvester Co.
Campbell, R. S. and James Benton vs. Patapsco Guano Co.
Campbell, Robert vs. The State
Campbell, Rubin vs. A. O. Johnson
Campbell, S. R. vs. R. M. Everitt
Capers, Amos vs. The State
Capers, Dora vs. The State
Card, Peter vs. The State
Cardelle, Peter vs. William B. Carter
Cargil, Rachael vs. The State
Cargile, Joseph J. W. vs. Fielding Flemister
Cargile, Joseph J. W. vs. Hurd and Hungerford
Cargile, Joseph J. W. vs. James S. Maddux
Cargile, Joseph J. W. and Lewis C. Holland vs. John Wood and
  William F. Mapp
Cargile, Munroe B. vs. John R. Grier
Cargile, Munroe B. and John H. Dickin vs. John L. Manley
Cargol, Oliver vs. Mattie Malone
Carlisle, George M. vs. Cooley and Kellam
Carlisle, George W. vs. H. P. Kirkpatrick
Carr, Calvin George vs. The State
Carr, Lynn vs. The State
Carr, Willie vs. The State
Carrol, Abner vs. Eaton Banks and Asa Smith
Carroll, M. J. vs. The State
Carry, Doyle vs. The State
Carsby, James vs. The State
Carter, Andrew (col) vs. The State
Carter, Booker B. vs. James A. Atchinson
Carter, W. M. and Son vs. H. P. Kennedy
Carter, W. M. vs. J. A. Virgin
Castillow, John vs. Thomas P. Carnes, Owen H. Kennan, Samuel
  Rockwell and William Cook
Cay, Wilson H. vs. C. D. Terhune
Central of Georgia Railway vs. C. T. Willson
Chaffin, J. M. vs. Lucian Benton
Chaffin, Joshua vs. John Baldwin
Chaffin, T. L. vs. Banks, Davidson and Kelly
Chaffin, T. L. vs. L. O. Benton
Chaffin, T. L. vs. N. B. White and Co.
Chaffin, V. A. vs. N. B. White
Champion, Elizabeth G. vs. John M. Beavers
Chance, Allen and Archibald Porter vs. Allen Stokes
Chandler, C. B. vs. The State
Chapman, Asa vs. Erwin Brown
Chapman, Asa W. vs. Moses Mounce
Chapman, Asa W. F. vs. Urban D. Mounce
Chapman, Crof vs. Reuben Bebee
Charping, S. C. vs. William S. McHenry
Chatman, Henry vs. G. W. McElhenney
Chatman, Sallie (col) vs. The State
Chatman, Willie (col) vs. The State
Cheatham, W. D. vs. The State
Cheek, William and J. W. Burney, Jr. vs. C. L. Ridley
Cheney, John vs. The State
Cheney, W. R. vs. Henry T. Stanton
Cheny, J. and J. W. Freeman vs. P. R. Thomason

Cherry, Jim, Jr. vs. The State
Childs, John vs. Maddox and Stubbs
Churchfield, Alford (col) vs. The State
Churchwell, A. P. vs. The State
Clark, Arter vs. The State
Clark, Daniel vs. The State
Clark, Joe vs. G. W. McElhenney
Clark, John (col) vs. The State
Clark, Mack vs. C. W. McElhenney
Clark, Mack vs. The State
Clark, Martin vs. G. W. McElhenney
Clark, Matt vs. The State
Clark, Will vs. The State
Clark, William D. vs. Benjamin Moseley
Clark, Willie B. vs. The State
Clarke, John vs. The State
Clay, Hezekiah vs. The State
Clay, Lawton vs. The State
Clay, Samuel vs. John R. Cargall for use of James Boon
Clay, Samuel, Louis C. Holland and Pascal Murphy vs. Martin
   Cochran
Clay, Willie (Buck) (col) vs. The State
Clemens, Alex vs. The State
Clements, Calvin vs. The State
Clements, George C. vs. A. J. Talmadge
Clements, Riley vs. The State
Clute, John H. and D. R. Blossom vs. John N. Triplett
Cobb, Thomas vs. Wellington and Hickman
Cobb, Tom vs. Jordan Bros. and Co.
Cochran, Dock vs. The State
Cochran, Dudley vs. The State
Cochran, Joe Frank vs. The State
Cochran, Oren vs. The State
Cochron, Bell (col) vs. The State
Cocran, Monroe vs. G. W. McElhenney
Coleman, Francis and Daniel Coleman vs. The State
Comer, John Allen vs. The State
Comer, Pheobe vs. Mrs. E. V. Carey
Compton, John W. and James Garlington vs. James Whitfield
Connell, William, William McCorkel and Mial Turner vs. Sherrod
   H. Gay
Cook, Aubie vs. The State
Cook, B. W. and J. W. Cook vs. Atlanta Guano Co.
Cook, B. W. vs. J. O. Shepherd
Cook, B. W. vs. Spivy and Horne
Cook, J. M. vs. G. W. Garrett
Cook, J. W. vs. J. E. Pitts and Co.
Cook, J. W., Jr. vs. G. W. Scott
Cook, J. W., Sr. vs. Charping and Chaffin
Cook, John W. vs. Heard, White and Thompson
Cook, Mrs. Mary and Tommas Gaston vs. N. G. Cook
Cook, William M. vs. James Smith
Cooley, Charles and Orpha Cooley vs. Harrison Smith
Cornwell, Lon vs. The State
Cornwell, Odis vs. The State
Cosby, Moses vs. T. R. Bonner
Cosby, Will vs. The State
Couch, Charles vs. The State
Couch, G. W. vs. Dozier, Speights and Co.
Couch, George vs. E. L. Campbell
Couthon, John vs. The State
Crabb, John vs. The State
Crabb, Sillia vs. The State

Crabtree, Ezekiel vs. James E. Shropshire
Crabtree, James vs. The State
Crawford, A. W. vs. The State
Crawford, Leonard vs. The State
Crocker, W. J. vs. The State
Croner, Samuel vs. The State
Cross, Paleman P. vs. The State
Crossley, R. J. and J. P. Farris vs. Mrs. Julia A. Spearman and
  M. W. Spearman
Crow, William vs. G. W. McElhenney
Cullin, Will, Jr. vs. The State
Cunard, J. C. vs. J. F. Vining
Cunard, J. S. vs. C. D. Pace and Co.
Cunard, Lucindy and J. S. Cunard vs. W. A. Kelly and Bros.
Cunard, N. vs. W. A. Kelly and Bros.
Cunard, William vs. L. A. Murphy
Cunningham, William vs. Cooley and Robinson
Cunningham, William vs. John F. Zimmerman
Curtis, Tom vs. The State
Cuthbert, A. vs. Bustin and Walker

Daniels, John vs. J. D. McElhenney
Daniels, Lee vs. J. D. McElhenney
Daugherty, Joe vs. E. M. Maddux
Davidson, Thomas vs. The State
Davis, Calvin vs. The State
Davis, G. L. vs. Banks, Davidson and Kelly
Davis, George vs. The State
Davis, Squire vs. The State
Dawkins, George and William Ramey vs. Hugh G. Branon
Dawkins, George vs. Jesse Loyall
Dawkins, George W. vs. Campbell and Jones
Dawkins, Thomas vs. R. G. Bryan
Deason, Ben vs. Henry Letson
Dennis, J. T. and Charlie Meriwether vs. S. D. Edwards
Denson, James vs. William Davis, J. Davis, Davis and Walker and
  P. E. Prichard
Deomatarie, John vs. Clement Diemer
Derby, L. A. vs. The State
Dickey, Raymond (col) vs. The State
Digby, Benjamin vs. W. H. Arnold
Digby, Benjamin and Anderson Banks vs. Banks, Davidson and Kelly
Digby, Benjamin vs. J. H. Smith
Digby, Charles vs. Banks, Davidson and Kelly
Digby, Dennis (col) vs. The State
Digby, Eledge and John Smith vs. The State
Digby, Emeline vs. Isaac Blackwell
Digby, Ike vs. Banks, Davidson and Kelly
Digby, Ike (col) vs. Pitts Brothers
Digby, Isaac vs. Robert Childs
Digby, Isaac vs. Samuel L. Henderson
Digby, Isaac vs. J. T. Pitts and J. W. Pitts
Digby, Isaac vs. W. R. Smith
Digby, Isaac, Jr. vs. L. S. Kelly and W. J. Phillips
Digby, Isham (col) vs. The State
Digby, J. Clinton vs. William A. Kelly and Leroy R. Price
Digby, J. Clinton vs. G. M. Shipp and John B. Webb
Digby, James H. and John B. Digby vs. W. B. Lee
Digby, John vs. Mrs. B. W. Pye
Digby, John B. vs. W. S. Edwards
Digby, John B. vs. George W. Persons
Digby, W. Berry vs. William A. Kelly
Digby, W. L. vs. L. O. Benton and Bros.

Dillard, Arthur and Thomas Tyus vs. The State
Dillon, Thomas vs. The State
Domeney, J. E. vs. The State
Donalson, Clatie Bell vs. The State
Donalson, Lola Butts vs. The State
Dooley and Bruce vs. A. G. Howard and Co.
Dooley and Bruce vs. Swann, Stewart and Co.
Downs, Mark (col) and Henry Kelly (col) vs. The State
Driggers, John vs. Edward Hicks
Driskell, Bob vs. The State
Driskell, C. W. and W. J. Driskell vs. Mrs. M. A. Cochran and
  W. A. Cochran
Driskell, Thomas and Isaac Blackwell vs. Farmer-Douglas and Co.
Dukes, J. L. vs. Mary R. Dukes
Dukes, Joseph and Mary Dukes vs. The State
Dukes, Ransom vs. Jesse Loyall
Dukes, Robert W. vs. James B. Goolsby, Cardin Goolsby and Kirby
  Goolsby
Dukes, Robert W. vs. James L. Maddux
Dukes, Robert W. and Robert Sharman vs. Sarah Slaughter
Dukes, Robert W. vs. Thomas J. Smith and Co.
Dukes, Tobe vs. The State
Dukes, William vs. Millner, Clanton and Co.
Dukes, William vs. Millner, Hazlip and Co.
Dumas, Eula C. vs. The State
Dumas, Frank vs. Bill Tinsley
Dumas, Jenes vs. The State
Dunlap, David vs. Warren Wilkins
Dunn, Albert G. and Gatewood Dunn vs. John Portwood
Dunn, Byron vs. W. B. Beckwith
Dunn, Gatwood vs. W. Andrew Fulwood for use of W. Watson and Co.
Dupree, Drury vs. Abel P. Wilson
Durden, Will vs. J. T. Gray
Durham, Simeon vs. A. Wood and E. Wood

Early, Anslem L. and Armsted Carter vs. A. Dabney and Hannah
  Dabney
Early, Anslem L., Caleb Early, James F. Robinson and Abraham
  Pyle vs. William Simmons
Early, Caleb vs. William Bradley
Easy, William vs. The State
Eavens, A. Y. vs. W. W. Allen
Echols, William vs. Lucius Arms
Edmondson, Benjamin C. vs. Theophilus Freeman
Edmondson, William D. vs. Maxey and Bartlett
Edwards, James vs. John Armstrong
Edwards, James vs. The State
Edwards, L. D. and W. M. Edwards vs. J. H. Campbell and S. R.
  Campbell
Edwards, Leander vs. J. J. Pope
Edwards, S. B. vs. Chesapeake Guano Co.
Edwards, S. B. vs. Jordan Brothers and Co.
Egerton, Zachariah B. vs. James Pinckard, Peyton Pinckard and
  Michael Durr
Elder, B. F. vs. John Webb
Elder, Edward A. vs. The State
Elder, Walter vs. The State
Epps, Ab (col) vs. The State
Epps, Hattie vs. Joe Epps and Madison Epps
Epps, Joe vs. James S. McMichael
Epps, Madison vs. Lucian Benton
Epps, Madison vs. John Carr and Co.
Epps, Matt vs. T. J. Pritchett

Evans, A. Y. vs. William H. Lloyd
Evans, Jim vs. The State

Falley, Abe vs. The State
Farley, James vs. Abel P. Wilson
Farr, W. A. and Will Ritchie vs. W. S. Cox
Faulkner, J. P. vs. J. F. Webb
Faulkner, John vs. The State
Fears, Albert (col) vs. The State
Fears, Clabe vs. Banks, Davidson and Kelly
Fears, Clabe vs. O. O. Banks and Bros.
Fears, Clabe vs. Elbert Smith
Fears, Claborn vs. R. S. Jeffries
Fears, Claborn and O. O. Banks vs. S. A. Lovejoy
Fears, Claborn vs. Mobley, Smith and Co.
Fears, Claiborn vs. S. J. Kelly
Fears, Claiborn vs. Robinson Bros. and Mobley
Fears, Green vs. The State
Fears, Lonnie vs. The State
Fears, Pleas vs. The State
Fears, Rans vs. The State
Fears, Willie (col) vs. The State
Ferrel, Albert vs. The State
Finley, Riley vs. The State
Finney, Ed vs. The State
Fish, Aaron vs. L. O. Benton and Bros.
Fish, Gim vs. G. W. McElhenney
Fish, James vs. Lucy H. Simms
Fish, Prior vs. G. W. McElhenney
Fitzpatrick, Joseph vs. Thomas Pinkard
Flemister, C. A. J. vs. S. H. Starr
Flemister, J. M. vs. Louisa Digby
Flemister, Jeff (col) vs. The State
Florence, Annie (col) vs. The State
Flornoy, Dock vs. The State
Flournoy, Foy vs. The State
Flournoy, Sam vs. The State
Flournoy, Willis vs. W. E. Tucker
Floyd, Nancy J. vs. D. J. Baer
Folds, Eli vs. Rufus Broom
Folds, W. L. vs. Simon Clements
Ford, Richmond (col) vs. The State
Forte, Robert vs. Banks, Davidson and Kelly
Foster, Doe vs. The State
Foster, Jeptha vs. Zachariah Hall
Franklin, Floyed vs. The State
Franklin, Henry vs. The State
Frazier, John vs. W. R. Mosely
Freeman, Carl Lee (col) vs. The State
Freeman, E. A. vs. J. S. Persley
Freeman, Eliza vs. James L. Glawson
Freeman, Frank vs. F. M. Lester
Freeman, Horse (col) vs. The State
Freeman, J. W. vs. The State
Freeman, Jabez and Richmond Waits vs. John R. Dickin
Freeman, John J. vs. The State
Freeman, Josiah M. vs. Alexander Buchannan
Freeman, Josiah M. vs. Fielding Flemister
Freeman, Josiah M. vs. Jesse Loyall
Freeman, Josiah M. vs. Thomas J. Smith
Freeman, Josiah M. vs. Henry Summerlin
Freeman, L. E. vs. The State
Freeman, Lee vs. Emily Roby

Freeman, N. B. vs. Bell Bros. Marble Co.
Freeman, Turner vs. The State
Freeman, William vs. W. B. Dozier
Fretwell, Micajah H. vs. William Byrum
Fulford, O. L. vs. The State
Funderburk, Joseph vs. G. W. McElhenney

Gaither, Harris (col) vs. The State
Gaither, Jim vs. The State
Gaither, Josephine vs. The State
Gaither, Ophelia vs. The State
Gaither, Robert vs. The State
Gaither, Wodin (?) vs. The State
Gant, Elie vs. The State
Gant, James vs. Charles L. Henderson
Gant, Lewis vs. L. O. Benton and Bro.
Gant, Lewis and Jake Kelly vs. Walton Guano Co.
Gantt, Dora and Cicero Gantt vs. N. B. White
Gantt, Eula vs. The State
Garland, Eugene vs. The State
Garrett, W. W. vs. T. C. Swann
Gaston, W. T. vs. Farrar Smith
Gay, Hilliard M. vs. Henry Bond
George (col) vs. The State
Germain, William vs. S. D. Crane
Gibson, John C. vs. The State
Giles, Johnson vs. S. C. Owens
Giles, Tommie vs. The State
Gill, William and John Malpass vs. Caleb Woodley
Gilmore, W. E. vs. The State
Gilstrap, Bill (col) vs. The State
Gilstrap, James vs. The State
Glover, Aaron vs. L. O. Benton and E. C. Benton
Glover, Aaron vs. Kelly and Phillips
Glover, Aaron vs. William H. Wilburn
Glover, Charles vs. Gordon and Co.
Glover, Charlie vs. L. O. Benton and Bro.
Glover, Elbert (col) vs. The State
Glover, Eli vs. Lemuel O. Lawrence
Glover, Fannie vs. The State
Glover, Henry S., Jr. vs. B. F. Barnwell and E. A. Barnwell
Glover, J. J. and Mary Glover vs. C. L. Adgate
Glover, J. J. vs. L. O. Benton and Bro.
Glover, John vs. J. D. McElhenney
Glover, Jonah vs. The State
Glover, William vs. J. H. Kelly
Goggans, J. S. and Madison Goggans vs. Thomas L. Greer and John
    R. Greer
Goodman, Caroline vs. G. W. McElhenney
Goodman, H. A. vs. The State
Goolsby, Bart (col) vs. The State
Goolsby, Ben vs. The State
Goolsby, Benjamin vs. Wade Goolsby
Goolsby, C. R. vs. Isaac McKissack
Goolsby, Caliss vs. G. W. McElhenney
Goolsby, Caroline vs. W. S. McMichael
Goolsby, Charles vs. The State
Goolsby, Clark vs. The State
Goolsby, Crit vs. Samuel Freeman
Goolsby, Gabe vs. The State
Goolsby, George vs. L. D. Edwards and W. M. Edwards
Goolsby, J. B. vs. Howard and Soule
Goolsby, Jim (col) vs. The State

Goolsby, Jodie and Jennie May Goolsby vs. The State
Goolsby, Joe vs. The State
Goolsby, John vs. Jesse Loyall
Goolsby, Johnnie and Spencer Goolsby vs. L. O. Benton and Co.
Goolsby, Levi vs. George M. Key
Goolsby, Mary vs. The State
Goolsby, Merida vs. John R. Greer
Goolsby, Nelson vs. Banks, Davidson and Kelly
Goolsby, Nelson vs. Walton Co. Guanno Co.
Goolsby, Obe vs. Olin J. Minter
Goolsby, R. H. vs. Springe and Co.
Goolsby, W. B. vs. Springe and Co.
Goolsby, W. L. vs. Lawrence and Pope
Gordon, George D. (col) vs. The State
Gorman, H. D. vs. T. A. Hutchinson
Gotier, J. C. (col) vs. The State
Gotier, William vs. The State
Grant, Samuel vs. Stephen C. Talmadge
Green, Aaron vs. S. C. Lawrence
Green, Ira vs. The State
Green, Joe vs. The State
Green, N. H. vs. J. H. Bryant and A. G. Bryant
Green, Randel vs. Gilbert Green
Greene, Jessie vs. The State
Greer, Arthur vs. The State
Greer, Ben vs. Jim Robinson
Greer, Benjamin vs. Rufus Broom
Greer, Griffin vs. D. M. Langston
Greer, J. C. vs. J. R. Greer
Greer, Jasper vs. Wise and Breed
Greer, Jiles vs. G. W. McElhenney
Greer, Manuel vs. The State
Greer, N. H. vs. Hugh T. Inman
Greer, N. H. vs. Lewis and Bailey
Grey, Addam vs. The State
Grier, J. L. vs. The State
Griffin, Benjamin vs. Andrew Shepherd
Griffin, Harvey vs. The State
Griffin, Parker vs. G. W. McElhenney
Griggs, Bully vs. The State
Griggs, Ella vs. The State
Griggs, George vs. E. B. Smith, Jr.
Griggs, Guss vs. W. F. Jordan
Griggs, Julious vs. The State
Griggs, Warren vs. The State
Grimes, Clarence vs. E. B. Smith, Jr.
Grubbs, Elisha C. and George W. Shockley vs. James L. Nisbit
Grubbs, Missouri vs. N. H. Greer
Grubbs, Thomas vs. G. W. McElhenney
Grubbs, Wiley B. and William J. Burns vs. The State
Gunn, Tom (col) vs. The State
Gunnels, Alsea vs. Mathew Raney

Han, Mitchell vs. The State
Hancock, Lum vs. The State
Hanks, John and Thomas Hanks vs. Alex Allison
Hanks, Thomas and John Fleming vs. Allen McClendon
Harden, Silas vs. G. W. McElhenney
Hardin, Monroe vs. G. W. McElhenney
Hardman, Alice and C. J. Hardman vs. D. B. Benton and Bros.
Hardman, Charles and Allis Hardman vs. W. W. Allen
Hardwick, H. V. vs. M. J. Wheeler
Hardy, C. M. vs. Dearing and Grimm

Hardy, C. W. vs. R. W. Price
Harris, Esco vs. The State
Harris, Nels vs. The State
Harvey, Nehemiah vs. Angus Morrison
Harwill, John vs. W. E. Tucker
Hawkins, John vs. The State
Head, John vs. S. C. Lawrence
Head, John H. vs. J. H. S. Smith
Head, T. J. vs. Cabaniss and Bean
Heard, Bartlett vs. The State
Heard, Clark vs. J. D. Tucker
Heard, Clark R. vs. Corley Brothers
Heard, George vs. The State
Hearn, Legare vs. The State
Hearnton, Mack and Guss Hearn vs. The State
Heath, H. H. vs. The State
Henderson, A. R. and S. W. Wommack vs. J. A. Kelly and R. S.
  Talmadge
Henderson, Berry vs. L. C. Spivey
Henderson, Charles vs. C. N. Bryant
Henderson, Isiah vs. The State
Henderson, J. P. vs. M. F. Malsly
Henderson, John vs. The State
Henderson, Lewis vs. The State
Herren, Alexander vs. Thomas Hairston
Herrington, J. C. vs. J. O. Medlock
Hester, Albert vs. The State
Hickman, H. W. vs. Leverett and Ezell
Hickman, Scot vs. M. S. Benton and L. O. Benton
Hicks, Charlie vs. The State
Hill, Joshua vs. John W. A. Smith
Hill, Peter vs. John W. Morgan
Hill, Shadrach (col) vs. David Meriwether
Hill, William, Isaac Hill, Lydia Hill and Moses Speer vs.
  Cheadle Cochran
Hines, Nancy vs. John E. Nolan
Hitchcock, William and William J. Goolsby vs. Thomas B. Barnwell
Hitchcock, William vs. Alexander N. Buchannan
Hitchcock, William vs. Cooley and Robinson
Hitchcock, William vs. Henry A. Dickinson
Hitchcock, William vs. Edward A. Elder
Hitchcock, William vs. Mathew Farley
Hitchcock, William vs. Geiger and Hawk
Hitchcock, William vs. William Maxey
Hitchcock, William, Evan J. Harvey and William Goolsby vs.
  Samuel Plummer
Hitchcock, William vs. G. Simonton and Co.
Hitchcock, William vs. Edmund Walker
Hodge, John (col) vs. The State
Holifield, Andrew J. vs. James N. Hall
Holifield, Mary vs. William Goolsby
Holifield, Thomas vs. Lemuel L. Lawrence
Holifield, Thomas R. vs. Ervin Brown
Holifield, Thomas R. L. vs. John A. Easters
Holifield, William vs. James B. Holifield
Holland, Abe, John Holland, Willis Gay, John Pritchard and
  Elleck Freeman vs. John Flemister
Holland, Lewis C. vs. Wyatt R. Smith
Holloway, Daniel vs. The State
Holloway, John vs. G. W. McElhenney
Holloway, M. vs. A. O. Johnson
Holoway, M. D. vs. J. C. Dunseith (?)
Holoway, Ran vs. The State

Holsenbeck, Alex vs. Clark, Rosser and Co.
Holt, Davie (col) vs. The State
Holt, James vs. Joseph Westmoreland
Holts, Edney vs. S. A. Hecht
Hooks, Robert vs. The State
Hornbuckle, Nathaniel B. vs. Anthony Dyer
Horseley, Morris vs. The State
Howard, Corydon H. vs. Cooley and Bancroft
Howard, Corydon H. vs. Charles Cargile
Howard, Corydon H. vs. George W. Holland
Howard, Corydon H. vs. Jesse Loyall
Howard, Corydon H. vs. Thomas Moreland
Howard, Corydon H. vs. Milas C. Shield
Howard, Corydon H. vs. Thomas J. Smith and Co.
Howard, Jessie vs. The State
Howard, Tell vs. The State
Hubbard, Roy vs. The State
Huff, Bart and Sulervin Huff vs. The State
Huff, Ralph vs. Hamblin Huff
Hughes, Willie vs. The State
Hunt, Obie Dias vs. The State
Hunter, Bud vs. The State
Hunter, Quince (col) vs. The State
Hurt, Lillian vs. The State
Hutchings, Walter vs. The State
Hutchinson, William vs. Harris and Thurmond
Hyatt, L. P. vs. J. O. Shepherd

Isham, Robert (col) vs. The State

Jackson, Albert vs. The State
Jackson, Boss vs. T. R. Bonner
Jackson, Charley vs. J. B. Cook
Jackson, Claude vs. The State
Jackson, Dave vs. Kelly and Phillips
Jackson, Garfield vs. The State
Jackson, Gordon vs. The State
Jackson, Grady (col) vs. The State
Jackson, Henry vs. L. O. Benton and Bros.
Jackson, Mose and Mary Jackson vs. Alex Holsenbeck
Jackson, Mose vs. J. Y. Smith
Jackson, Ran vs. The State
Jackson, Robert vs. The State
Jackson, Wade vs. The State
Jacobson, C. D. vs. James L. Campbell
James, Mitchel vs. The State
James, West vs. The State
Jamison, H. and Garland Hardwick vs. James Holt, Joseph
   Westmoreland and Andrew Moore
Jeffers, Colbert vs. C. R. Hodge and Co.
Jeffers, Rans vs. The State
Jeffries, Alice vs. Laura Butler
Jeffries, Alice L. vs. Airs Newton
Jeffries, Berry vs. J. P. Harris
Jeffries, Berry vs. W. A. Kelly and John H. Kelly
Jeffries, Berry vs. Porter and Kirkpatrick
Jeffries, Berry vs. George W. Scott
Jeffries, Bill vs. Onie Banks
Jeffries, Burkett vs. The State
Jeffries, C. vs. Jacob Wolfe
Jeffries, Charley vs. Banks, Davidson and Kelly
Jeffries, Colbert vs. Banks, Davidson and Kelly
Jeffries, Colbert vs. W. A. Kelly and Bros.

Jeffries, Colbert vs. J. Wingfield
Jeffries, Everett vs. The State
Jeffries, Henry vs. W. W. Allen
Jeffries, Henry vs. Corley Brothers
Jeffries, Henry vs. Colbert Jeffries
Jeffries, Henry vs. T. L. Stevens and A. S. Florence
Jeffries, Henry vs. Wellington and Hickman
Jeffries, Hilliard vs. Banks, Davidson and Kelly
Jeffries, J. P. vs. Farmer and Thompson
Jeffries, J. R. vs. The State
Jeffries, James vs. Robert Childs
Jeffries, Jeanie (col) vs. The State
Jeffries, John vs. Robert Childs
Jeffries, Mary vs. The State
Jeffries, Matilda vs. W. R. Smith
Jeffries, Nat (col) vs. Banks, Davidson and Kelly
Jeffries, Richard and Tom Jeffries vs. L. O. Benton and Bros.
Jeffries, Rowland vs. Banks, Davidson and Kelly
Jeffries, Rowland vs. Heard, White and Thompson
Jeffries, Thomas vs. Banks, Davidson and Kelly
Jenkin, Loften vs. The State
Jenkins, Francis and William Barclay vs. Edmund Bryant
Jenkins, Francis vs. William L. Phillips
Jenkins, Robert (col) vs. The State
Johnson, A. T. vs. J. H. Roberts
Johnson, Anderson vs. Banks, Davidson and Kelly
Johnson, Andrew vs. Banks, Davidson and Kelly
Johnson, Andrew vs. Lucian Benton
Johnson, Andrew vs. J. L. Pitts
Johnson, Andrew vs. T. C. Spivey
Johnson, Bill and Charles Walker vs. The State
Johnson, Cornelius vs. Maxey and Bartlett
Johnson, Eli vs. H. P. Almon
Johnson, Eli vs. Banks, Davidson and Kelly
Johnson, Eli vs. D. B. Benton
Johnson, Eli vs. George W. Person
Johnson, Eli vs. J. H. Smith
Johnson, Ephraim and John Glover vs. L. O. Benton
Johnson, Georgia Ann vs. T. C. Spivey
Johnson, Georgia Ann vs. Edward Wynn
Johnson, Hugh G. vs. Henry Stevens
Johnson, James H. vs. Samuel H. Blackwell
Johnson, James H. vs. James H. Holland
Johnson, Jonas, Jr. (col) vs. The State
Johnson, Lessie (col) vs. The State
Johnson, Martin L. vs. Elbert Cunard
Johnson, Melvin vs. The State
Johnson, Paul and Carl Evans vs. The State
Johnson, Peter vs. James McCoy
Johnson, William D. vs. Aaron A. Roff
Johnston, Andrew vs. Alice Kelly
Johnston, Peter vs. William F. Steel
Johnston, William S. vs. Wiley Peddy
Jones, A. D. vs. William H. Head
Jones, A. D. and Stephen W. McLendon vs. William Jenkins
Jones, Mrs A. D. (col) and Tuck Jones (col) vs. The State
Jones, Abraham D. and Stephen W. McClendon vs. M. M. Toland
Jones, Abram D. vs. Francis N. Taylor
Jones, Hartwell vs. Abner Chapman
Jones, Ike vs. L. S. Kelly
Jones, James, Jr. vs. G. W. McElhenney
Jones, John and Joel Wise vs. Washington Phelps
Jones, John and Martin Thrash vs. The State

Jones, Weaver vs. Marshall C. Goolsby
Jordan, C. H. vs. W. M. Lowrey and R. J. Lowrey
Jordan, Floyd vs. Mrs. M. A. Wilburn and S. C. Wilburn
Jordan, Floyd vs. William H. Wilburn
Jordan, Jeff vs. The State
Jordan Jenty (col) vs. The State
Jordan, Jewell vs. The State
Jordan, Joe vs. Millie Jordan
Jordan, Jonnie vs. The State
Jordan, Shine vs. The State
Jordan, W. J. vs. Frank B. Holland
Jordan, Warren vs. Elzie Barron
Jordan, Warren vs. L. O. Benton and Bro.
Jordan, Warren vs. E. A. Green

Keler, Oscar vs. The State
Keller, Everett vs. James L. Tucker
Keller, Robert vs. The State
Kelley, Bill vs. William H. Pickett
Kelly, Aaron vs. S. W. Anderson
Kelly, Amos vs. Glen Ellis
Kelly, Bill vs. F. H. Franklin and R. S. Franklin
Kelly, Digby and Burton Kelly vs. Crafford H. Greer, Sr.
Kelly, E. H. vs. W. W. Allen
Kelly, E. H. vs. W. H. Pickett
Kelly, Mrs. Emily vs. Banks, Davidson and Kelly
Kelly, George vs. Swan, Stewart and Co.
Kelly, Henry vs. John B. Webb
Kelly, Jack vs. J. H. Conaway
Kelly, Jack vs. Dooley and Nash
Kelly, Jacob vs. W. B. Dozier
Kelly, Jane, L. S. Kelly and James T. Powell vs. B. M. Davidson
Kelly, Jarrott B. vs. Augustus A. Trammel
Kelly, Jim (col) vs. The State
Kelly, John vs. The State
Kelly, Lit vs. W. W. Allen
Kelly, M. K. vs. The State
Kelly, Murry vs. Roberts and Peurifoy
Kelly, Tipe (col) vs. The State
Kelly, W. A. vs. G. R. Dozier
Kelly, William vs. Sidney R. Baynes
Kennedy, John and Thomas C. Richards vs. Henry Walker
Kennon, William W. vs. A. Baldwin
Key, Jerrie vs. The State
Kilgore, J. A. and J. W. Leach vs. Guano Company
Kilgore, James vs. R. D. Coe and Co.
Kilgore, William vs. Pinkney Kelly (col)
Kilgore, William Isaac vs. Ike W. Brown
Killgo, Will vs. J. F. Lunsford
Kindall, Whit vs. The State
Kindrick, W. E. vs. J. L. Greer
King, Elizabeth vs. The State
King, John vs. Cooley and Robinson
King, Mary vs. The State
Kirksey, Elisha S. vs. William Maxey

Lacy, Thomas and Samuel Wilkerson vs. W. R. Moseley
Land, Hiram vs. Avery Reeves and Thomas Hester
Landrum, Dony vs. The State
Lane, J. L., Jr. vs. The State
Langston, Henry vs. The State
Lason, J. N. vs. Wellington and Hickman
Law, Thomas vs. W. G. Maddux

Lawrence, Anthony vs. K. P. Greer
Lawrence, Ben vs. G. W. McElhenney
Lawrence, Frank vs. J. H. Kelly
Lawrence, Lee (col) vs. The State
Laws, John vs. The State
Lawson, Reuben vs. Cunnard and Speer
Lay, Andrew vs. The State
Layson, Eliza and C. C. Layson, Sr. vs. L. O. Benton
Layson, J. N. vs. Davis and Co.
Layson, J. N. vs. N. G. Maddox and Co.
Layson, Lum vs. The State
Leach, J. W. and J. A. Kilgore vs. T. M. Deleon
Leach, J. W. vs. James H. Turner
Leath, Emma vs. Mattie Malone
Leath, John vs. Banks, Davidson and Kelly
Lee, Nathan R. vs. Stephen Nolin
Leggon, John Henry vs. The State
Leverett, William vs. James A. Goodin
Lewis, Ben vs. The State
Lewis, George vs. Mrs. Harriette E. Banks
Lewis, George (col) vs. W. A. Kelly and Bro.
Lewis, George vs. E. D. Tuggle
Lewis, Henry vs. Banks, Davidson and Kelly
Lewis, Henry (col) vs. J. C. Harwell
Lewis, Phillip vs. Thomas P. Chaffin
Lewis, Phillip vs. Beverly A. Kelly
Lindsey, Cornelius vs. The State
Linzie, Will vs. The State
Little, Dan vs. Bank of Shady Dale
Logan, Riley vs. The State
Long, J. L. and J. W. Long vs. The State
Long, L. B. vs. J. C. Chupp
Louis, Henry vs. The State
Love, John vs. Willis Cooper
Lovejoy, C. B. and Nora Lovejoy vs. W. W. Allen
Lovejoy, C. B. vs. H. P. Almon
Lovejoy, C. B. vs. Baldwin Fertilizer Co.
Lovejoy, C. B. vs. W. B. Lee and W. B. Beckwith
Lovejoy, C. B., L. A. Lovejoy and J. D. Lovejoy vs. W. G. Smith
   for use of J. P. Harris
Lovejoy, C. B. vs. Walton Guano Co.
Lovejoy, C. B. vs. Wellington and Hickman
Lovejoy, Colman and J. D. Lovejoy vs. J. C. Franklin
Lovejoy, J. D. and Fannie Lovejoy vs. W. W. Allen
Lovejoy, John D. and C. B. Lovejoy vs. Spence Preston
Lovejoy, S. A., Manson Sigman and C. B. Lovejoy vs. W. W. Allen
Lovejoy, S. A. vs. Banks, Davidson and Kelly
Lovejoy, S. A. vs. J. D. Lovejoy
Lovejoy, S. A. vs. Mattie Malone
Lovejoy, Sidney A. vs. W. C. Clark
Lovejoy, Sidney A. vs. Henry Lewis
Lovejoy, Sidney A. vs. Sarah Lewis
Lovejoy, William vs. Henry Burdett for use of Francis S. Martin
Low, Edmond and John Dumas vs. N. R. Maddox and Co.
Lucas, Duffy vs. The State
Lumpkin, Robert vs. Dillard and Miller
Lynch, Grief vs. Creed T. Wise
Lynch, Ty vs. The State

Macarthy, C. E. vs. George A. Cabaniss
Machmahan, William vs. John Ike
Maddox, Annis vs. The State
Maddox, J. C. (col) vs. Minnie Maddox

Maddox, John vs. R. F. Dick
Maddux, Green vs. T. C. Spivey
Maddux, Sol vs. The State
Maddux, William vs. The State
Malone, A. M. vs. James Benton
Malone, A. M. vs. Ben L. Jones
Malone, Amos (col) vs. The State
Malone, Bill vs. Reese Walker
Malone, Cade (col) vs. Banks, Davidson and Kelly
Malone, Charley and Sidney Malone vs. J. H. Kelly
Malone, Dee (col) vs. The State
Malone and Edwards vs. A. H. Burney
Malone, George vs. James Benton
Malone, George vs. Jimmie Wilson
Malone, James D. vs. Baker S. Binford
Malone, James D. and Nancy Malone vs. George W. Holland
Malone, Jimmie Lee vs. The State
Malone, John vs. The State
Malone, Mat and J. D. Lovejoy vs. Kelly and Phillips
Malone, Matt and William Malone vs. J. H. Smith
Malone, Pete vs. The State
Malone, Sidney vs. Willie B. Malone
Malone, T. S. vs. William Akeridge
Malone, Thomas vs. G. W. McElhenney
Malone, W. F. vs. W. S. Minter
Malone, W. F. vs. George W. Scott and Co.
Malone, Wilis vs. C. M. Wilson
Malone, Will vs. John W. Almand
Malone, Will and Mat Malone vs. John Malone
Malone, Will vs. Jef Nash
Malone, Will vs. Monrow Phillips and W. H. Phillips
Malone, Will vs. Charles B. Rosser, R. L. Davis and J. D. Harvey
Malone, Will vs. Warren and Harris
Manell, Buster (col) vs. The State
Manell, Davis (col) vs. The State
Manell, Ed (col) vs. The State
Manning, George vs. The State
Manning, Pink vs. The State
Mannings, John vs. J. B. Malone and E. B. Malone
Mapp, William vs. Bailey Freeman
Marion (col) vs. The State
Marks, Edenboro vs. Maddox and Stubbs
Marks, F. C. vs. The State
Marks, Harvey vs. William Wayne and James Berry
Marks, Wade vs. The State
Marshall, William vs. Samuel Townsend, Sr.
Marten, L. F. vs. The State
Martin, John B. vs. S. R. Fuller
Martin, John F. vs. William H. Taylor
Martin, Perk vs. The State
Martin, Roman vs. The State
Martin, Yearby vs. Thomas Grant
Masters, Robert vs. George Alexander
Mathis, J. C. vs. The State
Maxey, James E. vs. Isaac L. Parker and John W. Brantley
Maxey, Kage vs. The State
Maxey, Lonnie vs. The State
Maynard, William vs. Jeff Nichols
Merriwether, Charles vs. Robert Childs
Merriwether, William vs. The State
Methodist Church vs. C. L. Bailey
Michael, Arther vs. The State
Middlebrooks, Aron vs. Joe King

Milam, Dudley vs. Samuel Milam
Millbrook, Joe Bell vs. The State
Millen, George D. vs. John Burge
Miller, Abner vs. The State
Miller, James H. vs. Simeon Scales
Miller, John vs. The State
Minter, J. C. vs. J. J. Dearing
Minter, Judson R. vs. George W. Persons
Minter, R. A. vs. Swann, Stewart and Co.
Minter, Robert vs. Berry T. Digby
Minter, Robert vs. William S. McHenry
Minter, Robert R. vs. Nathaniel Perry and Edward Perry
Minter, T. C. vs. J. H. Kelly
Minter, Thomas, Jr. vs. Heard, White and Thompson
Minter, Thomas C. vs. Thomas M. Williams
Mirack, Bill vs. G. W. McElhenney
Mitchal, Wess vs. The State
Monroe, Thomas (col) vs. The State
Moore, B. H. vs. M. L. Johnson
Moore, Newton vs. The State
Moore, Owens vs. A. Livingston
Moore, W. R. vs. J. B. Dickey
Moore, W. R. vs. Martha S. Moore
Moorehorn (?), Henry vs. Phillis Bartlett (col)
Morgan, Asa H. vs. William Maxey and Co.
Morgan, Asa H. vs. Oglesby S. Prophitt
Morgan, Berry vs. The State
Morgan, Grady vs. The State
Morgan, Henry vs. G. W. McElhenney
Morgan, James W. vs. William Hitchcock and David A. Reese
Morgan, James W. vs. Simeon Scales
Morgan, James W. vs. Thomas J. Smith
Morgan, Sarah N. vs. Hurd and Hungerford
Morgan, Sarah N. vs. Thomas J. Smith and Co.
Morgan, W. L. vs. The State
Morgan, William vs. Joel Baley
Morris, Isham vs. W. Maxey and Co.
Morrison, Alexander vs. Henry Branham
Morton, Beatrick (col) vs. The State
Morton, Levi, Ben Morton and Robert Morton vs. W. P. Davis
Moss, Henry and Allen Bass vs. Thomas Napier
Mullins, Fed (col) vs. The State
Mullins, George (col) vs. Mary A. B. Crawford
Mullins, George (col) vs. The State

McCarthy, C. E. vs. B. Pye and Son
McCarthy, Charles vs. H. H. Kelsey
McClelland, Pearce vs. G. W. McElhenney
McClendon, Fill vs. G. W. McElhenney
McClendon, J. A. vs. William G. Smith
McClendon, Jacob vs. William Armstrong
McClendon, Jacob and William Lawrence vs. Aquilla Phelps
McClendon, Joel vs. Anthony Dyer
McClendon, P. T. vs. Dooley and Nash
McClendon, Stephen W. vs. Abraham D. Jones
McCollum, Ben (col) vs. The State
McCoy, Daniel vs. Allen J. Whatley
McCullers, Burwell vs. Bennett Crawford
McDaniel, George vs. The State
McDonald, Daniel vs. Zadoc Megruder
McDonnell, Rachael and Ann Price (col) vs. T. Willingham
McDowell, Brady vs. The State
McDowell, Joel C. vs. Wilcox, Gibbs and Co.

McElheney, Edward vs. The State
McGaughey, Robert vs. The State
McGinnis, Thomas vs. Kelly and Phillips
McGinnis, Tom vs. Pitts Brothers
McGinnis, Tom vs. W. R. Smith
McKinley, Annie Lee vs. The State
McKinley, E. B. vs. W. P. Glover
McKinley, Rufus vs. The State
McKissack, John vs. Hamilton Atchison
McLemore, Charles vs. Alexander H. Allison
McMichael, Catherine vs. James L. Glawson
McMichael, S. L. vs. Banks, Davidson and Kelly

Nall, John P. vs. Thaddeus Beall, Elias Beall and Thomas Beall
Nall, John P. vs. Eli Glover
Nall, John P. vs. Alston H. Greene and Joseph Buchannon
Nall, John P. vs. John Hobson and Christopher Hobson
Nash, Ed vs. The State
Nash, T. J. vs. Rosser, Harvey and Davis
Neil, David vs. Presley W. Smith
Nelson, A. B. vs. The State
Nelson, Sou vs. The State
Newby, J. B. vs. Ashepoo Phosphate Co.
Newby, J. B. vs. William Pope
Newby, S. M., J. L. Coogler and J. B. Newby vs. Mixon and Davis
Newton, Aris vs. Robert C. Barnes
Niblett, James vs. G. W. McElhenney
Nivens, Charlie vs. The State
Nolan, Thomas F. vs. Alex Bonner
Noles, A. P. vs. Banks, Davidson and Kelly
Noles, Elender vs. Eckels and Abercrombie
Noles, Morris vs. Berry T. Digby
Noles, W. A. J. vs. Banks, Davidson and Kelly
Noles, William A. J. vs. O. O. Banks and Bros.
Nooso, Gust vs. The State
Nooso, John vs. The State

Odom, Roland vs. Minor Phillips
Odum, Jim vs. The State
O'Hara, Mary Jane vs. William H. Byrom
O'Neal, Jesse vs. Ector and Napper
Orange, Titus vs. J. C. Durden
Orr, Allen vs. G. Simonton and W. Simonton
Owen, Hardiman vs. The State
Ozborn, E. J. vs. J. T. Aaron
Ozborn, N. B. and H. W. Derden vs. Ashopoo Phosphate Co.
Ozburn, Mrs. E. J. vs. Dooley and Nash
Ozburn, Mrs. M. E. and R. L. Aaron vs. J. T. Aaron

Pace, William T. vs. John P. Evans
Pace, William T. vs. Hurd and Hungerford
Parker, Isaac L. and Richard Flemister vs. George Boyd
Parker, Jodie vs. The State
Parker, Johnnie vs. The State
Parker, William R. vs. Wyatt Smith and Berry T. Digby
Paschal, Scott vs. The State
Pass, Arthor vs. The State
Patillo, David vs. High and Baker and John Wingfield
Patilloe, David vs. James A. Campbell
Patilloe, David and Delilah Patilloe vs. John Durdin
Patilloe, David vs. R. P. Zimmerman
Patilloe, Delilah and David Patilloe vs. Bryant Cooley
Peacock, Aden vs. The State

Peacock, Charly vs. The State
Peacock, Dub (col) vs. The State
Peacock, Scot vs. The State
Penn, Giles vs. The State
Penn, M. T. vs. Rainy Odum
Penn, T. R. vs. T. J. Bell and Son
Penn, Thom (col) vs. The State
Penn, William vs. John Cane
Pernell, Green and Joel Edwards vs. William W. Pearson
Perry, Joe vs. Banks, Davidson and Kelly
Perry, Joe vs. J. E. Hoard
Perry, Joe vs. N. B. White
Perry, Joseph vs. Vines A. Wilson
Perry, Morris vs. Henry Malone
Persons, W. F. vs. The State
Pettie, George vs. The State
Phelps, Carter vs. The State
Phill (col) vs. The State
Phillips, R. B. vs. Jordan Bros. and Co.
Phillips, Zacheus vs. William Hammett
Phinisee, William, Jr. vs. Thomas I. Hays, Jr.
Phinisee, William J. P., Hiram Phinisee and John H. Phinisee vs.
    Jefferson E. Spears
Pinkey, James (col) vs. The State
Pinnell, Green vs. Joseph C. Little
Piper, Thomas L. vs. A. W. Powell
Pitts, Coy vs. The State
Pitts, Manse vs. Banks, Davidson and Kelly
Polk, George vs. The State
Polk, George W. and W. L. Folds vs. Earnest McMichael and R. L.
    McMichael
Polk, Grover C. vs. The State
Polk, Julian B. vs. Lucian Benton
Polk, R. A. vs. Benton Supply Co.
Polk, Will H. A. vs. G. R. Dozier and Speights and Dozier
Ponder, Tom (alias Tom Waters) vs. The State
Pone, Zell vs. The State
Pope, C. W. vs. B. F. Elder
Pope, Edgar C. vs. J. B. Cook
Pope, Gim vs. G. W. McElhenney
Pope, Tannis (Polk) vs. The State
Pope, W. M. vs. Solon F. Wilder and Elijah Boyles
Portwood, Howard vs. The State
Portwood, Lucy vs. The State
Post, Jim vs. The State
Pounds, Sarah Bell (col) and Sallie Pounds (col) vs. The State
Powell, James T. vs. Banks, Davidson and Kelly
Powell, Lucas vs. James Barr
Powell, Lucas vs. Joseph J. Marsh
Powers, G. T. vs. John Childs
Powers, J. B. vs. The State
Preston, Aaron vs. Banks, Davidson and Kelly
Preston, Aaron vs. James H. Smith
Preston, Amos vs. Banks, Davidson and Kelly
Preston, Charlie vs. The State
Preston, Childs vs. W. H. Smith
Preston, Spencer vs. Thomas Wilburn
Preston, W. B. vs. Banks, Davidson and Kelly
Preston, W. B. vs. W. C. Clark and Co.
Price, Calhoun vs. D. B. Benton and Bros.
Price, Robert vs. Thomas Camp
Pritchett, T. J. vs. James Harral, H. W. Risley, C. H. Tompkins,
    James Harral, Jr. and C. T. Risley

Pritchett, Thomas J. and James B. Goolsby vs. Charles L. Chovey
  and Theodore Hopping
Pritchett, Thomas J. vs. Jackson C. Thomason
Purcell, Robert vs. Thomas Williams
Pye, Asa and Joel McClendon vs. Cornelius D. Terhune
Pye, Pete and Wade Waits vs. The State

Qarterman, Florence vs. The State
Queen, Will vs. The State

Ramey, Charles D. vs. John Lee McMichael
Randall, Annie vs. The State
Reaves, Warner and Robert Richards vs. B. M. Davidson
Redick, Dave vs. The State
Reed, Lizzie vs. The State
Reed, Will vs. The State
Reeves, Allie H. vs. J. T. Eckols
Reeves, B. F. vs. H. P. Almon
Reeves, B. F. vs. M. E. Farmer
Reeves, B. F. vs. J. E. Pitts
Reeves, Ben (col) vs. Joe Thompson (col)
Reeves, Joel vs. Amos Brown
Reeves, Sherman vs. John M. Shepherd
Reeves, Wiley vs. Anthony Dyer
Reid, Dennis and Minnie Reid vs. S. B. Sanders
Reid, S. T. vs. B. F. Barnwell and E. A. Barnwell
Reid, Sam vs. William S. McHenry
Reid, William A. vs. William S. McHenry
Rhods, Lula vs. The State
Richards, James vs. Jesse Loyall and William Pritchett
Richards, James and Willis Richards vs. James McDonald (3 folders)
Richardson, Thomas vs. Hezekiah Speers
Rickerson, J. C. vs. Pauline Pou Adams
Ridley, Charlie vs. E. A. Green
Ridley, Tom (col) vs. The State
Ridley, William vs. Jacob Wolfe
Rivers, Charley vs. S. G. Shy
Rivers, John F., Thomas Rivers and Thomas H. B. Rivers vs.
  Dunston Banks and Simeon Scales
Rivers, John F., Thomas Rivers and Thomas H. B. Rivers vs. Moses
  Champion and Joseph S. Holland
Rivers, John F. vs. Lawson S. Holland
Rivers, Sam vs. W. S. Conner
Roach, Floyd vs. The State
Roberts, Dora vs. The State
Roberts, John vs. The State
Roberts, Rufus vs. H. B. Ridley
Roberts, Spencer and Charles Blackwell vs. J. T. Corley
Roberts, William vs. The State
Robinson, Berry vs. Justice Court
Robinson, Berry vs. The State
Robinson, Burton vs. The State
Robinson, Hartwell vs. Banks, Davidson and Kelly
Robinson, James C. vs. Toombs Spearman
Robinson, Jess (col) vs. Banks, Davidson and Kelly
Robinson, Monroe vs. W. W. Allen
Robinson, R. M. vs. The State
Robinson, Tolitha vs. L. O. Benton and Brothers
Robinson, Tolitha vs. Imperial Fertilizer Co.
Robinson, Wallace vs. Allen Shoats
Robinson, Willis vs. Allis L. Powell
Roby, Hill vs. G. W. McElhenney
Roby, John vs. The State

Roby, Milledge, Abner Bartlett and James Bartlett vs. James
  Shepherd, Carter Shepherd and Thomas J. Shepherd
Roby, Thomas L. vs. B. B. Odom
Roby, Tom vs. The State
Rockmore, Ziek vs. The State
Rogers, John C. vs. Henry Maulden
Rooks, George (col) vs. The State
Rooks, Hilard vs. The State
Rooks, Jim (col) vs. The State
Rooks, S. T. vs. The State
Rooks, William and Adolphus Standifer vs. M. S. Benton
Ross, George vs. W. C. Leverette
Ross, John vs. The State
Roswell, John vs. L. W. Pon
Rowe, Matilda G. vs. Morris and Bell
Runnells, Preston vs. Abraham Hears
Runnells, Preston vs. Uriah Humphries
Runnells, Preston vs. Amos Wheeler
Russel, Rich vs. The State
Russell, Pete vs. The State
Rutledge, Robert vs. A. Atkins and R. Atkins
Rutlin, Lewis vs. W. R. Cheek
Rye, Buss vs. The State

Saffold, Deck vs. Banks, Davidson and Kelly
Saffold, Deck vs. The State
Saffold, Dexter vs. J. H. Smith
Sailor, Ernest vs. The State
Sanders, Addeline vs. The State
Sanders, Claborn vs. Thomas Sullivant
Sanders, Daniel vs. Robert Curry
Sanders, Dave (col) vs. The State
Sanders, P. P. vs. Jordan Bros. and Co.
Sanders, Pleas vs. N. A. Hardees, Son and Co.
Saunders, Troy S. and Isaac J. Slaughter vs. Lewis and Bailey
Sanders, Walter vs. The State
Scales, Pompey vs. John Moreland
Searcy, Berry vs. The State
Seats, Anderson vs. Banks, Davidson and Kelly
Seats, Sam vs. The State
Seats, Thomas vs. The State
Semore, Richard H. vs. Robert Semore
Shannon, Henry vs. The State
Shavers, Sam vs. Charping and Chaffin
Shaw, Ezell vs. The State
Shaw, Gilbert W. and John Hines vs. Sherrod H. Gay
Shells, Rob vs. The State
Shephard, John M. vs. Melissa H. Shephard
Shepherd, B. U. vs. The State
Shepherd, E. W. vs. A. A. Trammel
Shepherd, J. M. vs. H. J. Wyatt and J. W. Wyatt
Shepherd, Welden vs. S. P. Smith
Shepherd, Weldon vs. A. O. Johnson
Shepherd, William L. vs. Rufus Howel
Sherman, Sam (col) vs. The State
Sherrell, Robert (alias Roy Ray) vs. The State
Shropshire, John vs. The State
Shropshire, William vs. C. W. McElhenney
Shy, Frank vs. The State
Shy, S. G. vs. H. C. Hill
Sigman, F. O. and M. Sigman vs. W. W. Allen
Sigman, Fannie vs. W. B. Lee
Sigman, M. vs. Charles Ellis

Sigman, M. vs. A. L. Sluder
Sigman, Manson, C. B. Lovejoy and Sidney Lovejoy vs. Fannie E.
  Lovejoy
Simms, Henry vs. The State
Simpson, Croff vs. The State
Simpson, Thom vs. The State
Sims, Alford vs. G. W. McElhenney
Singleton, Lee vs. John R. Davidson
Singleton, Willie vs. The State
Slack, Mary vs. The State
Slaughter, Isaac H. vs. John C. Madoux and Co.
Slaughter, Wilkins vs. S. C. Lawrence
Smartt, Littleberry and Robert R. Minter vs. Garland Dawkins
Smith, Aaron and Cade Malone vs. L. O. Benton and Bros.
Smith, Aaron vs. W. R. Smith
Smith, Aaron vs. The State
Smith, Aaron vs. P. H. Warren
Smith, Alex vs. J. T. Pitts and J. W. Pitts
Smith, Alex vs. W. R. Smith
Smith, Alex and Louisa Smith vs. Walton County Guano Co.
Smith, Alex and Louisa Smith vs. S. M. Whitney
Smith, Betsy vs. Wellington and Hickman
Smith, Boykin (col) vs. W. W. Allen
Smith, Boykin vs. Banks, Davidson and Kelly
Smith, Charley (col) vs. The State
Smith, Charlie vs. The State
Smith, Cleveland (col) vs. The State
Smith, Dick vs. N. G. Childs
Smith, Elbert vs. Banks, Davidson and Kelly
Smith, Elbert vs. Robert Childs
Smith, Elbert vs. W. A. Kelly and Bros.
Smith, Elbert vs. N. P. Smith
Smith, Elbert vs. Walton County Guano Co.
Smith, Ellie (col) vs. The State
Smith, Eugene vs. R. L. Furse
Smith, Guy vs. Colbert Jeffries
Smith, Hinto vs. Charles D. Jordan
Smith, J. H. vs. Dr. S. P. Downs
Smith, J. H. vs. Georgia Chemical Works
Smith, J. H. vs. J. D. Tucker
Smith, J. W. A. vs. Baldwin Fertilizer Co.
Smith, Mrs. J. W. A. vs. Kelly and Phillips
Smith, J. W. A., Jr. vs. Asheepoo Phosphate Co.
Smith, J. W. A., Jr. and S. R. Smith, Jr. vs. Georgia Chemical
  Works
Smith, James vs. Abehu (?) Sowel
Smith, Joe Henry vs. The State
Smith, John W. A. vs. James T. Corley
Smith, John W. A., Jr. vs. N. A. Hardees, Son and Co.
Smith, Larry vs. The State
Smith, Liza vs. The State
Smith, Lona vs. Joe Boykin
Smith, Lot vs. James Smith
Smith, Mandy vs. Robert Childs
Smith, Orilious vs. McDade and Paschal
Smith, Percy (col) vs. The State
Smith, Pomp vs. Banks, Davidson and Kelly
Smith, R. L. vs. Baldwin Fertilizer Co.
Smith, R. L. and W. G. Smith vs. J. P. Harris
Smith, R. L. vs. J. D. Tucker
Smith, Raymond vs. The State
Smith, Relious vs. P. W. Warren
Smith, S. R. vs. Ramspeck and Green

Smith, S. R., Jr. vs. W. H. Rogers
Smith, Sam (col) vs. J. R. Mobley and Co.
Smith, Sam Elbert vs. S. A. Lovejoy
Smith, Sam Luke (col) and Nester Smith vs. Robert Childs
Smith, W. G. vs. M. F. Malsly
Smith, W. G. and S. P. Smith vs. M. N. McKinly
Smith, W. G. vs. Willington and Hickman
Smith, W. R. vs. D. J. Hallock and Sons for use of J. W.
  Henderson
Smith, W. R. and John Briant vs. Kelly Brothers, J. L. Porter
  and S. M. Whitney
Smith, W. R. vs. Mobley, Smith and Co.
Smith, W. R. vs. C. S. Thompson
Snell, Wesley S. vs. Oliver E. Maltby and Nathan Starr
Spans, Charlie vs. The State
Sparks, Carden vs. The State
Spearman, Jackson vs. The State
Spearman, John F. vs. W. A. Kelly and Bros. and Fleming Jordan
Spears, A. M. vs. A. L. Sluder
Spears, John B. vs. Tolefree, Harris and Tolefree
Spears, T. L. vs. Banks, Davidson and Kelly
Speights, Doogin vs. The State
Spiller, Henry vs. The State
Spiller, Uleces vs. The State
Spivey, Thomas C. vs. O. O. Banks
Spralding, Tom vs. The State
Spraulding, Jerry vs. The State
Stafford, Willie (col) vs. The State
Stallings, Sanders vs. William Penn
Standefur, Denis vs. J. D. McElhenney
Standifer, Archibald vs. J. R. Godwin
Standifer, Curn and Benjamin Barron, Jr. vs. Jonas H. Holland
Standifer, Luke vs. The State
Standifer, Sherod vs. The State
Standifer, Will vs. The State
Stanford, Lucy (col) vs. The State
Stanford, Manervis vs. The State
Stanley, Albert vs. The State
Stanton, Tom (col) vs. The State
Steadham, John vs. The State
Stedman, Frances (Fanny) vs. The State
Steed, A. S. vs. C. H. Connors
Steel, W. H. vs. M. S. Benton and L. O. Benton
Stevens, Alf vs. The State
Stevenson, John vs. William Penn and William C. Penn
Stewart, Ellie vs. G. W. McElhenney
Stewart, Henry vs. The State
Stewart, Miley Ann vs. Willis Little for use of L. Dwelly and Co.
Stewart, Will vs. The State
Stone, M. P. vs. G. R. Dozier and Speights and Dozier
Stone, M. P. vs. S. J. Kelley and Bro.
Stovall, Richard and Scott Digby vs. The State
Strong, Burney vs. The State
Strong, Johnson and Hiram Glazier vs. John Hendrick
Strong, Robert vs. The State
Strong, Roony vs. The State
Stubbs, James vs. The State
Suttles, George W., Joseph C. Post and William B. Stone vs.
  George W. Holland
Swift, Bart vs. The State
Swift, Berry vs. Frank Goolsby

Taylor, William H. vs. Samuel Goggins

Teasley, Vira vs. The State
Terry, Frank (alias Frank Terrell) vs. The State
Thomas, Augustus vs. The State
Thomas, Bess vs. The State
Thomas, Edna vs. C. H. Jordan
Thomas, Hattie vs. The State
Thomas, James A. vs. The State
Thomas, Martha vs. McClure Merchandise Co.
Thomas, Reese vs. The State
Thomason, Andrew J. vs. James A. Turner
Thomason, Clark vs. J. P. Clark Cunard
Thomason, Jackson C. vs. John Powell
Thomason, William vs. William Askew
Thompson, Delia vs. W. W. Allen
Thompson, Ed vs. The State
Thompson, Frank and Leverett Thompson vs. The State
Thompson, Harrison vs. Wellington and Hickman
Thompson, Henry vs. M. S. Benton
Thompson, Henry vs. C. R. Hodge
Thompson, Henry vs. J. W. Kelly
Thompson, Henry and Pink Thompson vs. W. A. Kelly and Bros.
Thompson, Henry vs. Robinson Brothers
Thompson, Joe vs. Banks, Davidson and Kelly
Thompson, Leo vs. The State
Thompson, Loss vs. The State
Thompson, T. B. vs. W. A. Aiken
Thompson, T. H. and Idella Thompson vs. A. H. Burney
Thunderburk, Joseph and F. E. Thunderburk vs. J. T. Goodman
Thurman, C. D. vs. John H. Kelly
Thurman, Charles and Edward Thurman vs. J. H. Kelly
Thurman, Elizabeth vs. Walton Guano Co.
Thurman, Man vs. E. A. Greene
Thurman, Sarah vs. R. L. Fews
Thurmond, Aaron vs. M. A. McDowell and Mary J. McDowell
Tillman, R. T. vs. Walton Guano Co.
Tilmon, C. B. vs. John McCullough
Tinsley, Allvance R. and Joseph P. Williams vs. Maxey, Jordan
  and Co.
Tinsley, James vs. William Burney
Tinsley, Will vs. The State
Tinsley, Wily vs. The State
Tolen, Adam vs. G. W. McElhenney
Tompkins, Lucius (alias Bug Tompkins) vs. The State
Towns, J. D. vs. M. W. Spearman
Trussell, James D. vs. Charles Cargile
Tucker, J. L. and A. S. Florence vs. J. T. Bowden and J. C.
  Durden
Tucker, J. L. and J. W. Dostor vs. Berry Humphries and Lucy
  Humphries
Tucker, Nath vs. The State
Tuggle, Annie and E. D. Tuggle vs. E. B. Malone
Tuggle, E. D. vs. Dr. J. T. Smith and Mary B. Smith
Tuggle, Edgar vs. The State
Tuggle, F. W. and J. A. Tuggle vs. W. A. Kelly Bros. and Porter
Tuggle, Henry vs. The State
Tuggle, Mrs. J. A. vs. Georgia Chemical Works
Tuggle, J. A. and N. F. Tuggle vs. O. E. Ham
Tuggle, J. A. vs. J. E. Pitts
Tuggle, Mose and Thomas C. Minter, Jr. vs. L. O. Benton & Bros.
Tuggle, W. R. vs. C. M. Spears
Tuggle, Wash vs. S. M. Whitney
Turk, J. W. vs. Harvie Jordan and Brooks Turner
Turk, L. L. vs. State Mutal Agency

Turner, Charles, M. B. Key and O. G. Roberts vs. Mayor and
    Council of Monticello
Turner, George Ellis vs. The State
Turner and Hickman vs. John W. Wyatt
Turner, John vs. Alf Cunard
Turner, Tom vs. The State
Tyler, A. H. vs. The State
Tyler, Marion vs. The State
Tyson, H. F. vs. Byars and Mallett
Tyus, Thomas vs. The State

Universal Brotherhood vs. J. H. Marks
Ushery, J. T. (col) vs. The State
Ushery, Jessee (col) vs. The State

Varner, Edward vs. John Thurmond
Varner, Samuel D. vs. John R. Dickin
Varner, Samuel D. vs. Fielding Flemister
Varner, Samuel D. vs. Jonas H. Holland
Varner, Samuel D. vs. Hurd and Hungerford
Vaughn, Eli vs. The State
Veal, B. W. vs. The State
Vickrum, Charles vs. R. W. Mays
Victrum, Starling (col) vs. The State
Vincent, John vs. The State
Vincent, Ranse vs. The State
Vincent, Robert vs. The State
Vincent, Turner vs. The State
Vinson, James vs. O. P. Hickman
Vonner, Pearce vs. The State

Waddill, Marshall H. vs. Anthony Dyer
Wagner, J. C. and James T. Lewis vs. L. O. Benton and Bro.
Watner, J. U. vs. Hearn and Green
Wagner, J. U. vs. A. H. Jordan
Waits, Agnes and Robert W. Dukes vs. Ann E. Cross
Waits, James vs. J. W. Moran
Waits, Levi vs. James L. Maddux
Walden, Elisha vs. Stephen H. Gilmore and John S. Fall
Walker, Auther (col) vs. The State
Walker, Berry vs. Banks, Davidson and Kelly
Walker, Berry vs. B. W. Cook
Walker, Berry vs. S. A. Lovejoy
Walker, Berry vs. J. H. Smith
Walker, Berry vs. The State
Walker, Crawford vs. The State
Walker, Frank (col) vs. The State
Walker, Jack vs. The State
Walker, Jerry vs. J. J. Clegg
Walker, Jesse (col) (alias Jesse Sincey) vs. The State
Walker, John vs. Samuel Oxford
Walker, John vs. William P. White
Walker, Reese vs. Banks, Davidson and Kelly
Walker, Sid vs. Joe Maddux
Walker, Vince vs. Smith Brothers
Walker, Warren vs. Sallie W. Thomason and A. J. Thomason
Walker, William, Charles Whitehead, Mandy Whitehead and Peter
    Whitehead vs. The State
Wall, W. V. vs. The State
Wallace, Ruth vs. The State
Walton, Joseph vs. Thomas Curtis
Walton, R. I. vs. Robert Taylor
Ward, George vs. G. W. Grubbs

Ware, Robert vs. The State
Washington, Frank vs. A. O. Johnson
Washington, Fred vs. The State
Watson, Aron vs. The State
Watson, Charles vs. Lucian Benton
Watson, Ed vs. The State
Watson, Enie vs. G. W. McElhenney
Watters, Dick vs. Wiley Phillips
Watters, Richard vs. Elihue Waldrop
Watters, William D. vs. Samuel H. Banks
Watters, William D., A. J. Watters and John C. Key vs. James P.
  Boynton
Weaver, Bery vs. The State
Weaver, Howard vs. The State
Weems, George vs. The State
Welch, Jack vs. The State
Welch, Wallace vs. The State
Weldon, Moses vs. George Whitton
Whatley, Michael vs. David Henderson and John G. Colbert
White, A. J. vs. J. W. Brown
White, Aaron vs. E. A. Green
White, Jackson (col) vs. The State
White, P. C. vs. The State
White, Sallie vs. The State
Whitehead, Lucy vs. Lewis Watson (col)
Whitehead, Tom vs. The State
Whitehead, Willie Ann vs. The State
Whitfield, Henry (col) vs. The State
Whitfield, Joe vs. The State
Whitfield, Reubin vs. Robert Whitfield
Whitten, W. C. vs. P. S. Burney
Wilburn, S. C. vs. Georgia Farmers Oil and Fertilizer Co.
Wilcox, Thomas S. vs. John Cubbage
Wilkes, Steve vs. Webb and Coile
Wilkinson, Simeon and Byron Shell vs. Samuel Johnson and Charles
  Forbes
Williams, Ada and Mary Lee Clay vs. The State
Williams, Addie E. vs. The State
Williams, Asbury vs. The State
Williams, Bud vs. The State
Williams, Charlie vs. The State
Williams, Dorsey (col) vs. The State
Williams, James M. and T. B. Williams vs. James K. Polk
Williams, Jim (alias Jim Burke) vs. The State
Williams, Monroe vs. Obe Stanford
Williams, N. M. vs. Clayborne Herring
Williams, N. M. and R. J. Minter vs. Swan, Stewart and Co.
Williams, N. M. vs. Wood and Rogers
Williams, Prince vs. J. H. Holland
Williams, Robert vs. The State
Williams, Smalley vs. The State
Williams, Squire (col) and Amanda Williams (col) vs. The State
Williams, Thomas vs. Robert Russell
Williams, Thomas and Joseph Williams vs. The State
Williams, Tommie (col) vs. The State
Williams, W. S. vs. Mrs. E. A. Waits
Williams, William S. vs. James M. Williams
Willson, Lowry vs. The State
Wilson, Abel P. vs. David Moore
Wilson, Andrew J. vs. Cooley and Robinson
Wilson, Andrew J. vs. Fielding Flemister
Wilson, Andrew J. vs. Robert Minter
Wilson, Andrew J. vs. Stoddard, Miller and Co.

Wilson, Fred vs. The State
Wilson, G. S. vs. Pritchett Bros.
Wilson, James E. vs. Simeon Scales
Wilson, James W. vs. William S. McHenry
Wilson, James W. vs. John Truit
Wilson, Joseph vs. Green McMichael
Wilson, R. W. vs. James Benton
Wilson, R. W. and Annie Wilson vs. S. P. Smith
Wilson, V. A. vs. James Benton
Wilson, V. A. and S. J. Wilson vs. Farmer, Douglas and Co.
Wilson, William S. and Joseph C. Little vs. John M. Beavers
Wimbush, Samuel vs. J. W. Porter
Winbush, Elbert vs. G. W. McElhenney
Winfrey, John vs. Jackson Chaney
Wise, David (col) vs. The State
Wise, George vs. The State
Wood, Jack vs. The State
Wood, Joshua J. vs. Thomas Blann
Woods, John L. G. vs. J. H. Kelly
Woods, John L. G. vs. Rodgers, Worsham and Co.
Woods, Otis vs. The State
Wooton, Riley vs. Robert Coleman and Augustus T. Newsom
Wordsworth, Mrs. Jamie L. vs. The State
Wormack, Sid vs. The State
Wright, Earnest vs. The State
Wright, Henry vs. The State
Wright, James vs. Robert Childs
Wright, James vs. Kelly and Phillips
Wright, Mattie vs. Thomas C. Spivey
Wright, William vs. Ervin Brown
Wyatt, John W. vs. Lawson S. Holland
Wyatt, Otis vs. The State
Wynens, John vs. E. C. Butt

Yancey, Benjamin D. vs. The State
Yancey, J. E. vs. John Merryman and Co.
Yancey, J. E. vs. A. E. Polk
Yancy, J. E. vs. Martha Yancy

Zelkie, Willie (col) vs. The State

CHAPTER IX

PONEY HOMESTEAD (DEBT AND TAX EXEMPTIONS) RECORDS, 1868-1907
Record Group 179-2-11

This series contains unbound original pony homestead exemptions of the Court of Ordinary (now Probate) of Jasper County. The pony homestead exempted from levy and sale $300 worth of household and kitchen furniture and provisions. A person could waive his rights under the constitutional and statutory homesteads, but he could not waive the $300 pony homestead. This was instituted by the Georgia Acts of 1878 and 1879. The records have been flattened, cleaned and placed in folders. They are arranged alphabetically by surname of the person applying for the exemption.

NAME	DATE	NAME	DATE
Aaron, Mitchel	1868	Fears, William T.	1870
Aaron, Richard A.	1868	Freeman, Bob	1875
Aikins, J. J.	1872	Freeman, George	1874
Alexander, George	1875	Freeman, Isaac H.	1868
		Funderburk, J. C.	1876
Bacon, Sumner W.	1874		
Banks, Mrs. Mary	1868	Gaston, Fanny F.	1870
Barber, Augustus	1875	Geiger, H. H.	1868
Barber, Samuel	1875	Geiger, Randal C.	1876
Belcher, O. R.	1869	Glover, Dennis (col)	1872
Berry, A. T.	1868	Goggans, Madison	1869
Binford, Henry	1870	Goolsby, Charles	1877
Binford, Joseph P.	1869	Goolsby, Clayton D.	1873
Blackwell, James	1869	Goolsby, James B.	1869
Blackwell, John H.	1874	Goolsby, Levi	1869
Blackwell, R. M.	1874	Goolsby, W. B.	1876
Bozeman, Henry	1875	Gordon, Clate	1874
Bridges, Charles	1873	Gordon, George D.	1877
Brooks, James H.	1874	Gordon, George D.	1903
Burney, Charles C.	1872	Green, William M.	1869
Burney, J. H.	1874	Greer, Aaron (col)	1871
Burney, John W.	1872	Greer, Griffin	1875
Burns, Henry T.	1876	Greer, Thomas L.	1869
		Grier, George	1873
Campbell, Bill	1875		
Campbell, Martha A.	1872	Hardy, Alfred D.	1869
Cheeek, John W.	1868	Hart, Martha	1875
Cheney, W. R.	1868	Henderson, Charles	1868
Clack, Thomas R.	1870	Henderson, Isaac	1869
Clay, James	1869	Hickman, W. S.	1876
Collier, Isaac	1877	Holloway, Newton	1870
Cook, John W.	1877	Holsenbeck, Alexander	1874
Cunard, Newton	1876	Horton, James A.	1875
		Howard, A. B.	1871
Darden, Martin	1874	Howard, James B.	1871
Davis, George L.	1876	Huff, Henry B.	1876
Davis, S. W.	1874	Hutchison, M. H.	1871
Davis, Samuel	1875		
Dawkins, George W.	1868	Johnson, Allen	1876
Dillard, Mary	1876	Johnson, Eli	1875
Dixon, Sandy	1875	Johnson, M. L.	1873
		Johnston, Martha M.	1869
Edwards, John W.	1868	Jones, Andrew J.	1878
Elder, Edward A.	1872	Jones, James M.	1873
Elder, John G.	1877	Jordan, James (col)	1876
Ezell, B. R., Jr.	1873	Jordan, Lillie	1874
Ezell, Braxton R., Sr.	1869		
Ezell, John H.	1869	Kelly, Anthony	1876
Ezell, Robert	1869	Kelly, Henry	1875
		Kelly, Jack	1877

King, B. G.	1875	Ramey, Anderson	1875
King, George W.	1869	Reeves, Joseph	1878
Kitchen, Joel	1868	Reid, Elizabeth W.	1870
		Reid, Samuel T.	1874
Lane, Augustus	1869	Rivers, Allie	1868
Lane, L. A.	1873	Roby, Thomas L.	1877
Lane, W. D.	1869		
Laurence, Steward	1892	Sanders, Pleasant	1875
Lawrence, Nancy	1868	Seymore, A. H.	1874
Lawrence, Seaborn	1871	Shaws, Edmund	1878
Letson, Robert	1871	Shy, Charles	1876
Lewis, Phillip	1870	Shy, Clem	1875
Lovejoy, John D.	1869	Shy, E. J.	1876
		Shy, Frank	1876
Maddox, Washington	1875	Shy, Seaborn W.	1875
Malone, Floyd B.	1868	Simpson, John	1870
Malone, Frank	1869	Slaughter, Randal	1875
Malone, Jarrel	1869	Smith, John	1877
Malone, S. B.	1870	Smith, John W. A.	1868
Malone, William	1869	Smith, Ruff	1876
Malone, Willis	1875	Spear, Harry	1868
Marsh, James W.	1869	Spearman, Gabriel T.	1869
Meriwether, Charles	1871	Spears, Josiah C.	1868
Moseley, Joe	1907		
		Thomason, Jackson C.	1869
McDonald, A. G.	1876	Thomason, Samuel E.	1871
McElhenney, Sampson	1882	Thompson, William D.	1876
Mcgehee, Benjamin	1871	Tillman, Pitman	1880
McKissack, John F.	1869	Tuggle, Daniel	1877
McKissack, Thomas	1869	Tuggle, W. R.	1871
McKissack, William T.	1869	Turner, James	1877
McMichael, Shadrack I.	1870	Tyler, Francis M.	1884
		Tyler, John J.	1875
Newby, Mike (col)	no date	Tyner, R. I.	1869
Newman, Silas	1877	Tyson, Henry F.	1870
Night, M. V.	1875		
Nix, M. T.	1872	Waits, Alexander	1877
Noles, David G.	1875	Waits, Levi	1878
Noles, J. R.	1875	Waldrep, Lescel J.	1870
		Walker, George	1876
Odom, William	1876	Ward, Fleming J.	1870
Odum, Frank	1873	Webb, Thomas P.	1869
		White, Scott	1877
Parks, Daniel	1875	Whitfield, Jacob	1873
Peddy, Frank	1875	Whitten, Levi	1875
Peddy, Wiley	1869	Williams, Addie E.	1873
Penn, Solomon	1862	Williams, Berry	1874
Phillips, John B.M.	1876	Williams, John	1875
Phillips, R. B.	1874	Williams, Steven	1876
Piper, Thomas S.	1869	Wilson, George	1874
Pitts, Nester	1869	Wilson, James	1873
Pope, John C.	1870	Wilson, Mary E.	1874
Pope, Josiah P.	1875	Wommack, John W.	1877
Pope, M. W.	1874	Wooten, Riley	1877
Pope, Miller W.	1869	Wyatt, J. T.	1868
Pope, W. K.	1868	Wyatt, John W.	1868
Pope, W. K.	1868	Wyatt, Nancy	1868
Preston, Charles T.	1869	Wyatt, Sam	1877
Preston, Spencer	1873	Wynens, Elisha S.	1869
Pritchett, Thomas J.	1870		
Pulliam, William B.	1868		
Pye, Thaddeus B.	1869		

CHAPTER X

LAND GRANT RECORDS, 1799-1823
Record Group 179-2-12

NOTE: Georgia land grant records for the whole state, 1755-1908, are in the Georgia Surveyor General Department, on floor 2V of the Georgia Department of Archives and History, 330 Capitol Ave. SE, Atlanta, Ga. 30334.

This series contains unbound original land grants and plats of the Court of Ordinary (now Probate) of Jasper County. These plats give the exact location and a rough diagram of the surveyed land of the early settlers of Jasper. Also included in these records are the original certified deeds to the surveyed land. These records have been flattened, cleaned and placed in folders. They are arranged alphabetically by surname of the land owner.

Atkins, Orville	1821
Austin, William W.	1823
Beavers, Thomas	1807
Carden, William	1799
Davis, Matthew	1808
Denson, John	1807
Freyermuth, John Sr.	1807
Gardner, Stephen (orphans of)	1809
Irwin, Jared	1807
Jones, James	1814
Morgan, Thomas	1808
North, Abraham	1822
Parham, Mathew	1808
Wallace, Benjamin	1808

CHAPTER IX

ORIGINAL (UNBOUND) DEEDS, 1808-1903
Record Group 179-1-6

This series contains deeds from the Jasper County Superior Court with occasional deeds from other counties. The records have been flattened, cleaned and placed in folders. They are arranged chronologically by timespan of considerable length and thereunder alphabetically. There is an index of slaves and cross-references in Box 3 if needed.

GRANTOR	GRANTEE	DATE RECORDED
Abercrombie, Leonard	Henry Stovall	6/23/1814
Abernathy, William F.	Martin Cochran	12/18/1823
Adams, David	Jonathan Clowers	2/26/1816
Akens, Seaborn J.	Julia A. Akens	3/31/1862
Alewine, David (Alowine)	Isaac Moore	8/3/1821
Alexander, Albert	Turf Club	10/8/1832
Alexander, Charles T.	Albert Alexander	2/14/1835
Alford, Jeptha	William H. Taylor	1/26/1831
Allen, David	Isaac Stricklin	12/17/1816
Allen, John	Willis Breazeal	10/30/1819
Allen, Mark J.	John Robertson	1/17/1813
Allison, James	Robert Allison	5/7/1819
Allison, John	James Pye	3/7/1821
Allum, John	Edward Flowers	8/2/1814
Anderson, Brazor C.-heirs of	Whitmil Hill	12/12/1811
Anderson, William W.	George T. Bartlett	4/22/1857
Arnold, O. H., Jr.	Ella May France	12/3/1892
Ascue, John	Abba Benton	4/2/1824
Austen, William W.	Lemuel Dean	2/21/1825
Avery, Harbert-heirs of	Stephen Beasley	11/17/1838
Aylor, Anthony	John Aylor	4/12/1816
Bailey, Moses P.	Simeon Wilkerson	10/7/1824
Baldwin, John	Joseph Johnson	4/8/1819
Baley, Joel	Thomas Cargile	12/22/1823
Baley, Joel	James S. Weekes	9/4/1821
Balflour, Robert	Moses Mulkey	12/29/1819
Ball, Jesse	James Akins	5/22/1838
Ball, Jonathan	Samuel Thomas	12/5/1833
Banks, Pleasant E.	Crayton A. J. Flemister	6/1/1866
Barber, William	Moses Milton	5/6/1812
Barefield, Abraham	William Harvey	3/2/1818
Barnes, William E.	William Cook	1/19/1810
Barrow, James	Martin Kendirck	2/11/1815
Baskin, Thomas	Thomas Steen	3/13/1818
Bass, Thomas	Lewis C. Holland	9/17/1817
Bass, Thomas	Lewis C. Holland	no date
Batchelor, William	John Simmons	3/19/1821
Baxley, Aaron	Thomas Morris	11/20/1824
Bean, Walter	Stephen Potts	1/17/1822
Beard, Edmund	Joshua Hames	no date
Beasley, Jarrel	Stephen W. Beasley	11/19/1838
Beasley, John	David McCoy	8/2/1809
Beekeom, Allen	Edward B. Brooking	11/30/1811
Beeland, John M.	John Spearman	12/4/1835
Beeland, William	Warren Ambers	10/28/1820
Beeland, William	Benjamin Beeland	12/9/1819
Belcher, Mary	Obadiah R. Belcher	12/20/1838
Belcher, Obadiah	Obadiah R. Belcher	1/15/1839
Belcher, Obadiah R.-heirs of	Robert J. Minter	4/25/1898
Belcher, Wiley	Hiram Glazier	no date
Bellah, Samuel	Joseph Williams	9/5/1822
Benton, James T.	William P. Hardy	1/31/1883

Benton, John	Otis M. Benton	copy 1/5/1883
Berg, Ph. M.	Commissioners of Roads & Rev.	no date
Berry, Augustus T.	Ebenezar T. White	3/12/1861
Bettey, Joseph	Thomas Barren	8/7/1810
Black, Thomas	William B. Hardy	3/8/1820
Blackwell, Fannie	E. B. Malone	1/3/1900
Blair, James	Benjamin Cleveland	7/30/1814
Blake, Joseph	Henry Morris	8/23/1819
Bland, Lucind	Jones Temples	4/30/1811
Board of Education	Crawford H. Kelly	3/10/1900
Bohannon, Kentchen	Andrew Boyd	8/8/1825
Bolles, Eber M.	John Willson	2/9/1819
Bond, Edward	Susanna Cochran	8/17/1815
Bonnell, William	George Merriwether	12/10/1827
Bonner, Whitmill-heirs of	Alsea Holifield	3/29/1822
Bonner, Whitmill-heirs of	Daniel Saffold	11/26/1828
Borum, George-heirs of	Hudson Kirk	9/30/1829
Boswell, Levi	Joseph White	11/24/1811
Bowden, James	William A. Slaughter	5/7/1828
Boyd, James	James Walden	2/1/1814
Boyd, Richard	John Robinson	7/26/1838
Boyd, Richard, Sr.-heirs of	Fanny Bond	4/23/1833
Boykin, Francis	John T. Boykin	6/11/1824
Branan, James	William Penix	7/9/1814
Brannon, Harris	Boley Conner	10/19/1808
Brantley, Greene D.	Thomas Hairston	5/16/1829
Brantley, John H.	Gilbert Ansley	9/8/1826
Brantley, John H.	Reuben Dawkins	10/27/1828
Brazzelle, Benjamin	Aser Allen	4/6/1811
Brewer, George	William Hutcheson	10/28/1818
Bridges, John	Matthew Hogg	6/3/1817
Briers, Lawrence	William Penix	7/9/1814
Briers, Lawrence	William Sharp	3/28/1815
Brinkley, Simeon	Harris Allen	no date or signature
Broach, George	Charles Williams	11/22/1814
Broddus, Thomas	Samuel Walker, Jr.	12/1/1828
Broddus, Thomas C.	Charles G. Chambers	4/8/1881
Broddus, Thomas C.	W. A. Paul	10/10/1873
Brown, Amos	Ezekiel B. Kelly	2/10/1836
Brown, Bartlett	Charles Eagerton	11/3/1824
Brown, Dempsey	Richard Roberts	5/1/1816
Brown, James-heirs of	Irvine Lawson	4/3/1827
Brown, James E.	George W. Holland	8/24/1825
Brown, John	Bouth Fitzpatrick	12/30/1809
Bryant, Artemus	John W. McGehee	11/17/1835
Buchanan, George H.	Amos Brown	12/29/1831
Buchanan, James	Joseph Harreld	11/18/1818
Buchanan, John	Robert Chafin	copy, no date
Buchanan, John W.	Amos Brown	7/15/1833
Buchanan, Michajah	Joshua B. Spears	1/30/1840
Buis, Nancy	Elbert Buis	7/11/1820
Bullard, Jesse	John Knight, Sr.	7/15/1831
Bullard, Tapley	James Davis	2/24/1818
Burgess, James	Joseph Scott	2/7/1809
Burks, James L.	John Willson	4/27/1821
Burnam, William	Jonathan Phillips	8/8/1810
Burney, Arthur	John W. Compton	8/10/1818
Burney, John W.	William H. Reese	10/4/1866
Burney, William V.	William Deadwilder	5/20/1839
Burney, William V.	Obadiah Echols	7/16/1832
Burney, William V.	Lucas Powell	6/20/1839

Burney, William V.	Cornelius Robinson heirs of	5/7/1836
Burton, Abraham	Edward Flowers	6/28/1811
Bush, Mary	Thomas Dean	9/25/1817
Butler, Edward	Nathaniel Deane	3/12/1817
Butler, Partrick	Claburn Martin	9/30/1810
Butrum, James	Joseph Harrel	2/20/1824
Buttrell, Thomas	Jeremiah Pearson	7/8/1834
Buttrell, William	John Willson	12/9/1823
Butts, Samuel-heirs of	John Willson	10/12/1824
Byrom, John	John Rivers	1/7/1819
Byrom, John-heirs of	John Willson	5/23/1821
Byrom, Seymour S.-heirs of	John Farley	2/27/1819
Cabaness, Harrison	Jarrell Beasley	3/8/1811
Calffrey, Lewis	Arthur Burney	2/9/1824
Calhoun, Jordan W.	Carden Goolsby	copy, no date
Callaway, Jabez G.	Drury Wilkins	2/11/1828
Callaway, James	Drury Wilkins	2/17/1828
Camp, Thomas	David Miller	4/28/1818
Camp, Thomas	David Miller	8/4/1815
Campbell, John	Ellemander Warbington	2/13/1822
Campbell, William	Washington Loyd	8/14/1839
Campbell, William	Caleb Spears	11/1/1833
Campbell, William	Joshua B. Spears	11/11/1839
Canant, Jerry	Benjamin Greer	4/20/1831
Candler, Allen D.	Board of Education	3/10/1900
Carden, William	James B. Goolsby	no date
Carel, Benjamin B.	James A. Greer	10/31/1820
Cargile, Charles, Jr.	Lawson S. Holland	1/2/1835
Cargile, John	William Cargile	5/5/1823
Cargile, John	Alston H. Greene	11/28/1822
Cargile, John-heirs of	John Hill	10/23/1827
Carrol, William-heirs of	John Towns	1/28/1814
Carter, John	Henry Hateley	4/28/1821
Carter, Littleton	Daniel Lowe	1/2/1811
Castalow, Amy	James McLendon	7/16/1836
Castello, Amy	David A. Reese	11/9/1823
Castello, John-heirs of	Amy Castello	11/8/1825
Castleberry, Edward	Nathaniel G. Slaughter	5/18/1822
Cellars, Silas	William Cogswell	12/3/1835
Chafin, Joshua	John Chafin	2/16/1831
Chambers, Charles G.	Jasper County Commissioners	no date
Chambers, Robert	Cristofer Dreadwilder	1/26/1810
Champion, Moses-heirs of	Edward Y. Hill	1/22/1842
Chance, Allen	Zachariah White	8/11/1820
Chapman, Abner, Jr.	Woody Dozer	12/31/1816
Childs, Thomas M.	James Scroggins	5/11/1829
Clackly, Jacob-heirs of	Ansalem L. Early	12/2/1828
Clark, Thomas E.	Susan Fulton	7/26/1837
Clark, William	Whitton Keith	10/11/1819
Clay, Jesse	Samuel Clay	11/17/1821
Clay, Samuel	Thomas Clay	11/8/1832
Clayton, Richard C.	Beasley and Weeks	4/13/1830
Clements, Mary	John Knight	5/23/1837
Clower, Jacob	Hillery Phillips	8/2/1821
Coats, James-heirs of	Elizabeth Compton	3/28/1835
Cochran, Alfred	Fields Wilson	9/9/1817
Cochran, James	David Flennekin	11/8/1813
Cochran, John M.	John R. Cargile	9/11/1821
Cochran, Martin-heirs of	Reuben Jordan	8/10/1841
Cochran, Martin	Andrew Willden	2/23/1838

Coffman, Amos	John Coffman	5/12/1827
Cogburn, Moses H.	David Kelly	3/5/1811
Cole, Kenne-heirs of	Robert Humber	5/20/1818
Coleman, John	Jeremiah Thompson	2/7/1841
Collier, Jack	Irvey Wilder	12/19/1823
Collins, Henderson	Nelson Jennings	8/7/1817
Colwell, Edward	John Payne	6/30/1821
Comer, Thomas T.	Thomas H.B. Rivers	2/9/1838
Compton, Elizabeth	Thomas Blair	3/28/1835
Compton, John W.	Alexander Berryhill	2/22/1819
Compton, John W.	Burton Rucker	11/13/1815
Compton, Kate	Drape Compton	3/28/1891
Conger, Eli	John White	7/12/1838
Connel, John	Isaac Moore	8/3/1821
Connell, William	Felix Hardman	9/10/1834
Coogler, J. L.	Jickinias Yancy	no date
Cook, Augustin	Dread Warren	3/5/1818
Cook, Augustus	Bray Warren	3/5/1818
Cook, Augustus	John Wilson	no date
Cook, James	James McMichael	8/10/1815
Cook, William	James Crawley	1/19/1810
Cook, William	John Moore	1/4/1825
Cook, William	John McKenzie	6/24/1818
Cooley, Hollis	Jeremiah Pearson	11/25/1837
Corbett, James	Joshua Chaffin	10/10/1816
Cowles, Asbury	Robert C. Beasley	6/3/1828
Cox, Jess-heirs of	John Griggs, Sr.	3/13/1835
Cox, Wiley J.	Sarah Cox	3/3/1831
Crabb, Enoch	William Stewart	12/29/1818
Craft, Pleasant	James Turner	6/25/1817
Crain, Jeremiah	Isaac Hill	11/12/1811
Crain, Spencer	William Cardin-heirs of	no date
Crain, Spencer	Thomas Gaston	no date
Crawford, Bennet	Benjamin Hammock	10/22/1827
Crawley, James	James Jarrow	12/8/1818
Creel, Jordan	Jeremiah Canant	7/19/1822
Crenshaw, Joseph	James McKemie	1/15/1832
Crockett, James W.	Judah McClendon	7/3/1826
Crockett, Joseph	William Hitchcock	5/12/1828
Crockett, Samuel	James E. Brown	7/8/1824
Crockett, Samuel	John Hill	4/13/1824
Crockett, Samuel	Joel McClendon	3/21/1829
Cross, George	Hiram Glazier	12/27/1811
Cross, George-heirs of	Welcom Parks	4/29/1826
Cross, Harris	James Littlejohn	2/27/1833
Dale, Simon	John Robertson	3/9/1811
Daniel, Beverly	David A. Reese	2/7/1824
Darnell, James J.	William McCane	11/17/1812
David, Isaac	John W. Shackleford	no date
Davidson, Thomas	James K. McCorkle	12/17/1835
Davis, Benjamin	John Beck	7/28/1820
Davis, Ishmael	Joseph Westmoreland	4/22/1816
Davis, Jeremiah	John Willson	11/22/1824
Davis, Robert H.	Hackey Walker	10/13/1819
Davis, Turner A.	John Flemister	2/15/1857
Davis, William	Abraham Heard	11/1/1813
Deadwilder, Christopher	David Watkins	10/30/1811
Dean, Thomas-heirs of	Jepthah Clements	11/24/1832
Deane, Burkett	Burton Rucker	9/30/1816
Deane, Nathaniel	Burkett Deane	5/1/1816
Deane, Nathaniel	James Godley	1/11/1819
Deane, Nathaniel-heirs of	Magers Henderson	2/19/1829

Deen, Drury	Elijah Miles	10/27/1820
Deering, Simeon	Lewis C. Holland	6/14/1824
Denham, James	Levi Boswell	11/26/1814
Dennis, Samuel P.	Richard Brasele	5/17/1812
Denson, Eleanah	Hubbard Holloway	5/5/1819
Dewberry, John	Mary Dewberry	12/10/1827
Dewberry, John	Nancy Dewberry	12/10/1827
Dewberry, Thomas	Thomas Smith	3/17/1830
Dickson, James	Solomon Strickland	1/30/1818
Digby, Berry T.	Ellis Cheek	5/14/1866
Digby, John	John W. Compton	1/15/1818
Dillard, John A.	William Johnson	6/14/1836
Dingler, William	Nancy Dingler	11/30/1822
Dingler, William	Martin Milner	9/7/1812
Dodson, E.	John Porter	9/27/1834
Dodson, Elijah	Baptist Church	9/8/1826
Donaldson, John	John Willson	11/22/1824
Dowdell, Lewis	Smith Davenport	11/11/1836
Dozier, Woody	Abel Diamon (Dimon)	10/31/1821
Dozier, Woody	John Price, Jr.	3/12/1835
Dozier, Woody	John Wilson-heirs of	10/22/1827
Drew, John L.	Arthur Smith	1/5/1825
Driskell, Christopher	James H. Roberts	9/23/1837
Driskell, Jacob	James Davis	3/25/1823
Duke, John	William Walker	9/16/1817
Duke, Joseph	William W. Walker	3/10/1825
Duke, Stephen	Francis Boykin	7/11/1822
Durham, Abner	Benjamin Lassiter	12/8/1818
Durham, Simeon	William Johnson, Sr.	11/20/1821
Durham, Simeon	Thomas B. White	5/10/1832
Dyche, Isaac R.	Elijah Brooks	2/8/1821
Dyer, Anthony	Richard D. King	5/13/1828
Dyer, John	James Glenn Sims	7/10/1810
Early, Ansalom L.	Abraham Key	7/28/1821
Early, Anslem L.	James F. Robinson	12/2/1828
Echols, Obadiah	Lewis C. Holland	8/17/1820
Edge, John	Edmund Bradford	9/28/1815
Edge, John	Benjamin Marshall	10/9/1823
Edge, Obadiah	Marshall Stevens	10/8/1830
Edwards, Robert	Elizabeth L. Wade	8/16/1839
Edwards, William	Absolom Stewart	7/17/1817
Edwards, William Henry	William Morris	2/4/1819
Ellis, Daniel	William Glass	7/8/1811
Evans, David	John McLean	3/13/1818
Evans, James	Sherwood Gay	11/8/1813
Evans, Jesse	Eli Strickland	12/13/1824
Ezell, Braxton R.,Sr.	Braxton R. Ezell,Jr.	10/29/1868
Ezell, L. D.	Commissioners of Roads & Rev.	7/6/1907
Fagin, Mrs. Carrie L.	C. T. Powers	7/13/1904 no signature
Farley, John	Robert Shearman	12/1/1842
Farley, John	Union Academy	4/9/1823
Farmer, Asael	Richard Odom	11/7/1810
Featherston, Richard	Jinney Featherston	2/8/1821
Few, Ignatius-heirs of	Avington Williams	6/7/1816
Fincher, Joshua	Edmon Wamack	9/11/1826
Fitzpatrick, Jackson	John Freeman	9/5/1832
Fitzpatrick, Joseph	Zachariah Philips	10/11/1814
Flanagan, Philip	James S. Weekes	9/5/1822
Fleming, James	George Cunningham	1/1/1822

Flemister, Lewis	Lewis Phillips	5/11/1829
Flewellen, Lovewell C.	Edward A. Broddus	7/17/1841
Fluker, John	Peter Grinnell	12/4/1833
Fluker, John	Justices of Inferior Court	5/14/1822
Ford, John	Edward Flowers	2/2/1811
Ford, William	John Ford	2/2/1811
Foreman, Edmond	Francis B. Smartt	2/22/1819
Foreman, Isaac	Robert Owen	1/21/1819
Foster, John	Obadiah Belcher	8/2/1822
Fowler, John	Allen Bass	5/19/1811
Freeman, Henry H.	William Spears	5/28/1838
Freeman, Isaac	E. B. Annis	6/1/1866
Freeman, Isaac H.	Berry T. Digby	5/15/1866
Freeman, John	Robert Shearman	2/10/1836
Freeman, John	Robert Sherman	12/2/1842
Freeman, Theophilus	Richard Holeman	1/30/1819
Fretwell, Richard	Robert Woods	11/22/1814
Freyermuth, John	Daniel McNiel	3/3/1818
Fudge, Benjamin	William Hitchcock	10/22/1827
Gantt, John	Robert F. Ezell	4/14/1865
Gardner, Samuel	Allen Bass	3/25/1811
Garner, Richard	John Moore, Sr.	10/13/1819
Garner, Richard	Joseph Murdock	4/9/1811
Gaston, Thomas-heirs of	Philip Thurmond	1/4/1832
Gautier, Peter W.	Nathan Warner	10/25/1827
Gay, Jorden	James Cate	2/21/1811
Geiger, Harman H.	Aris Newton	9/12/1835
Geiger, Harman H.	William Spears	1/20/1865
George, Jesse	Hiram Glazier	2/25/1818
Gibbs, Elhanon	John Buchanon-heirs of	2/2/1822
Gibson, John C.	John Willson	12/5/1822
Gilbert, William G.	William Wilkins	3/20/1816
Gilmore, John	Allen Bass	12/23/1823
Gilmore, William	Bartley Pearce	2/2/1811
Gilstrap, Lewis	Lesle I. Waldroup	10/31/1833
Glass, James	Levi Martin	2/2/1818
Glazier, Adam	Hiram Glazier	12/31/1811
Glazier, Hiram	John Donaldson	5/4/1813
Glazier, Hiram	John Willson-heirs of	10/24/1827
Glen, Little P.	Henry Glover	6/10/1834
Glover, Eli	Jasper Corning	6/4/1827
Goddard, Daniel	Thomas Greer	10/10/1817
Godley, James	John Willson	2/10/1819
Golden, William	John Ward	11/7/1816
Goodman, Barney	Commissioners of Roads & Rev.	no date
Goolsby, C. R.	T. A. B. Turner	no date
Goolsby, M. C.	F. C. Goolsby	4/20/1903
Goolsby, M. C.	F. C. Goolsby	5/9/1903
Goolsby, Richard	William M. Marks	9/18/1863
Goolsby, William	William Strozer	10/22/1824
Gordon, Alexander	George Alexander	2/23/1818
Gordon, Charles	Thomas T. Napier	4/25/1822
Gordon, George D.	Oliver Shorter	11/29/1899
Grant, Thomas	John Willson	1/25/1819
Gravenstein, John	Jarell Beasley	3/8/1811
Graves, Lewis	Woody Dozier	10/3/1829
Green, Alston H.	Alston H. Greene	11/29/1822
Greene, Burrell	Phillip Thurmond	10/10/1818
Greene, Edmund	John Abercrombie	1/29/1814
Greer, James A.	Thomas Fletcher	10/31/1820

Greer, Lucie	Commissioners of Roads & Rev.	no date
Greer, Thomas	Isaac Downs	2/23/1813
Gresham, David	Charles Eagerton	11/3/1824
Gresham, William	Charles Eagerton	11/3/1824
Grier, Robert, Jr.	Edward Harper	5/5/1823
Griffin, John	James Jackson	7/17/1817
Griggs, James	Fleming Jordan	7/2/1821
Griggs, John	Sarah Cox	1/21/1833
Grinage, Joshua	John Grinage	7/23/1811
Grisham, John	Zachariah Pendleton	7/28/1821
Gunter, Isham	Patrick Butler	10/17/1810
Hagin, Malachi	Asael Farmer	11/11/1810
Hall, Benjamin	Mackey Walker	12/18/1816
Hames, Joshua	Jarrel Beasley	2/1/1828
Hames, Joshua	Daniel B. Willis	6/3/1817
Haraway, Judith	John Freeman	11/24/1814
Harper, Edward	Joseph Prince	5/6/1823
Harper, Everett	John Willson	3/11/1820
Harrel, Samuel	Samuel Barber	5/6/1835
Harrell, Isaac	Charles McMichael	9/20/1825
Harress, Cuzza	William Pritchett	10/4/1871
Harris, Britain-heirs of	Thomas Morris	2/28/1826
Harris, Isham	Tyre Kelley	11/13/1815
Harris, John	John S. Weems	2/6/1824
Harris, Thomas W.	James G. Sims	4/10/1815
Harris, Walton	David Adams	5/29/1820
Harris, Walton	William Diamond	3/28/1815
Hartsfield, Allen	John W. Compton	6/2/1817
Hartsfield, Warren	Baptist Church	7/12/1813
Harvey, Evan	James Berryhill	4/9/1816
Harvey, William	David Russell	4/3/1820
Hascall, Elijah N.	John Hill & Co.	3/3/1819
Hascall, Elijah N.	Welcom Parks	1/10/1823
Haskins, James	Thaddeus Beall	11/7/1810
Hatcher, Archibald	Edmond Lloyd	3/9/1820
Hatcher, Josiah	William Payne	11/29/1817
Hawk, Harriett	Oliver H. Newton	10/3/1874
Hawk, Seaborn J.	Sallie H. Hawk	7/10/1869
Hay, Gilbert	Gilbert D. Taylor	2/5/1818
Hay, William	Thomas P. Webb	5/17/1847
Heard, Hubbard P.	William B. Buchanan	7/24/1829
Heard, John-heirs of	William Scott	4/11/1825
Heard, Stephen G.	John Heard	3/30/1820
Henderson, James	Robert Kellam	6/25/1839
Henderson, Magers	John Willson	10/31/1821
Henderson, Richard	Doctor H. Beall	5/1/1832
Henderson, Samuel	James Buchannon	11/25/1809
Henley, William	Samuel Lovejoy	6/2/1813
Henry, George W.	John Hall	5/17/1825
Hester, Robert	Jonathan Bonner	3/20/1821
Hester, Robert	James Head	7/26/1820
Hewes, George	William Tedley	5/20/1838
Higgason, P. C.	Richard Higgason	2/13/1818
Hightower, Presley	Robert Trippe	10/17/1811
Hill, Clarence	Emily F. Adams	5/30/1876
Hill, Edward Y.	Wiley Phillips	3/19/1835
Hill, John	Robert C. Beasley	1/4/1832
Hill, John	Lavina W. Cargile	1/26/1825
Hill, John	Samuel Crockett	6/11/1824
Hill, John	William B. Stokes	1/19/1832
Hill, John	William B. Tinsley	5/23/1833

Hill, Miles	James A. Hill	7/21/1825
Hingston, Thomas	James Mercer	6/4/1833
Hitchcock, William	Benjamin Fudge	3/11/1827
Hitchcock, William	Evan J. Harvey	3/14/1842
Hitchcock, William	John Hill	12/2/1828
Hitchcock, William	George Stovall	3/7/1818
Hitchcock, William	John Willson	12/13/1824
Hodnett, John	James Hodnett	2/8/1821
Hoge, Stephen	Hackey Walker	1/6/1819
Holcomb, Joshua	Robert Peerman	8/25/1819
Holifield, Alsea	Lewis Conner Holland	5/8/1816
Holifield, Alsea	James Richards	1/13/1818
Holifield, Alsea	Philip Thurmond	1/23/1815
Holifield, Alsea	John Willson	1/1/1822
Holland, James A.	C. W. McMichael	12/30/1869
Holland, Lewis C.	Obadiah Echols	8/18/1820
Holland, Lewis C.	Phillip Thurmond	5/28/1816
Holley, Martha	Willis Roberts	1/21/1809
Holloway, James	Ralph Huff	7/27/1835
Holloway, Jesse-heirs of	Felix Stanley	12/6/1827
Holmes, Richard	Monticello Academy	3/3/1819
Holt, Simon, Jr.	Jonathan Philips	5/11/1808
Holt, William	Cassandra S. Alexander	3/6/1832
Horton, Lott	Joshua Hames	8/27/1815
Howard, Hezekiah	Clement Lanier	1/13/1817
Howell, Nathaniel	Hardy Lasiter	1/30/1811
Hudson, Richard	Philip Thurmond	6/30/1828
Hudson, Rowland-heirs of	Thomas S. Bailey	8/11/1819
Huff, Ralph-heirs of	Martin Dedwilder	5/20/1838
Hughs, Thomas	Mason Harvill	8/7/1817
Humphries, George W.	Jeremiah Canant	3/9/1820
Hunt, John	Turner Hunt, Sr.	5/15/1812
Hunt, John	Nathan Johnson	10/9/1823
Hunt, Tames	William Green	3/7/1816
Hunt, Turner, Jr.	Turner Hunt, Sr.	5/6/1823
Hunter, James	Jarrel Beasley	2/23/1835
Hust, Henry	Caleb Touchstone	3/7/1811
Huston, John	Samuel Huston	3/1/1826
Huston, John	Howel Tatum	4/8/1814
Huston, John	Joel Towns	6/24/1814
Hutchison, Maximillian	Berry T. Digby	5/18/1866
Hutson, Zadoc	Joseph Mallett	8/17/1809
Hutts, James	David Poole	11/5/1824
Hyde, Thomas	Williamson Roby	3/1/1811
Ingram, Edmund	John K. Simmons	1/19/1820
Irwin, Benjamin	Snelling Johnson	2/10/1818
Ivy, Benjamin	Haynes Pain	5/2/1814
Ivy, Winifred	John Ivy	2/6/1813
Jackson, Celia	William H. Traylor heirs of	no date
Jackson, James	John West, Sr.	5/5/1819
Jackson, James	Nathan Williams	11/1/1809
Jackson, James	Clifferd Woodruff	11/1/1819
Jackson, Samuel	Jesse Cox	6/12/1825
Jackson, Samuel	Sarah Cox	4/5/1830
Jackson, Thomas, Sr. heirs of	Selah Jackson	2/17/1831
James, David	Charles McMichael	7/12/1827
Jasper County Commissioners	John Byrom	2/26/1817
Jasper Co. Commissioners	Moses Champion	4/15/1833

Jasper Co. Commissioners	James Garlington	8/4/1817
Jasper Co. Commissioners	Paschal Murphy	8/7/1817
Jasper Co. Commissioners	James S. Weekes	9/11/1821
Jasper Co. Commissioners	Fields Wilson	4/29/1818
Jean, Jesse	John Lang	9/18/1813
Jeffries, William	William Evan	2/22/1819
Jenkins, Robert-heirs of	William Peel	12/3/1813
Johnson, Andrew	Alfred Cuthbert	5/6/1837
Johnson, Joseph	Philip Flanagan	10/26/1821
Johnson, Joshua	James Barron	2/10/1815
Johnson, Robert	Peter William Gautier	11/20/1810
Johnson, Samuel	James Glenn Sims	8/2/1815
Johnson, William, Sr. heirs of	Sanders Stallings	2/9/1826
Jones, Abner	William B. Hardy	3/8/1820
Jones, David	David Neal	3/5/1811
Jones, John	William Duke	3/28/1821
Jones, John A. C.	George Griffin	1/31/1826
Jones, Joshua	Thomas Key	2/5/1812
Jones, Richard	William Keeling	10/3/1811
Jones, Wilie	James Mercer	10/26/1818
Jordan, Charles	Joseph Key	11/7/1810
Jordan, Fleming	William Hitchcock	1/26/1825
Kelley, Allen	David Meriwether	12/2/1809
Kelley, Beershaby	William Johnson	5/28/1810
Kelley, Charles	Thomas Stamps	no date
Kelley, John	William Kelley	1/3/1810
Kelly, David	Mason Harvell	5/14/1812
Kelly, James	Hannah Sisson	10/10/1833
Kelly, Michael	Jane Vincent	1/24/1866
Kelly, Tyre	Willoughby Hammack	3/2/1818
Kelly, W. A. & Bros.	James Benton	12/20/1899
Kelly, W. A. & Bros.	John B. Webb	1/22/1901
Kennedy, Robert	Benjamin Blanton	8/2/1821
Kennedy, Thomas	Shadrach McMichael	3/12/1835
Key, Joseph	Isaac Benham	5/5/1826
Key, Thomas	Davenport Graves	3/1/1820
Keyton, Benjamin	Lewis T. Wynn	11/18/1818
Kilby, William	Charles Forbes	2/2/1832
Kindrick, Martin	Seymour L. Byrom	2/10/1815
King, Benjamin	John Willson	12/10/1821
King, Jane	Henry Jones	1/28/1814
King, John, Sr.	Milledge Roby	2/9/1831
King, John M.	Burwell Greene	6/2/1819
King, Lewis	Simeon Brinkley	no date
Kinman, John	Briges Pare	9/13/1816
Kinman, Samuel	Zorobable Williamson	9/10/1817
Kirk, Hudson	William Egnew	9/30/1824
Kitchens, Benjamin	Thomas Davisson	12/17/1835
Knight, Calvery F.	John T. Banks	4/6/1825
Knox, Samuel, Sr.	William B. Hardy	3/8/1820
Lamar, John	Lewis Gregory	9/5/1813
Landon, Daniel	Joseph King	11/10/1809
Landrum, Timothy	Baptist Church of Christ	3/6/1811
Lands, John	John Jones	2/21/1812
Lane, Shepherd G.	Lewis Phillips	6/3/1833
Lang, John	David Miller	5/4/1818
Lang, John, Jr.	William White	6/11/1814
Lang, Robert	James Glass	8/17/1820
Langham, William	Solomon Stricklin	3/11/1815

Langley, Osey	James Knowles	2/6/1813
Langston, David M.	Annie Laura Langston	2/13/1901
Lanier, Clement	Lodowick Lard	1/13/1817
Lard, Lodowick	Isaac Coe	1/13/1817
Lassiter, Elisha-heirs of	David A. Reese	1/10/1831
Lassiter, Hardy	Benjamin Lassiter	11/20/1821
Lassiter, Jacob	Daniel Knowles	2/10/1825
Lassiter, John	Susanah Cochran	5/3/1815
Lassiter, John	Thomas Ward	10/8/1812
Lawrence, George W.	Jonas H. Holland	10/15/1831
Lawrence, Malachi	Basset Northern	12/29/1830
Lawrence, Thomas	Hardiman Wellingham	11/26/1819
Lawson, Irvine	Benjamin Garrett	8/15/1840
Leak, Samuel	John Porter	9/27/1834
Lee, William	William H. Morrow	4/12/1816
Leverett, Robert-heirs of	Warner Lewis Kennon	7/30/1811
Lewis, Exum	Baxter Smith	12/10/1807
Lindsey, Samuel	William Patrick	3/10/1831
Locke, James	William Brown	2/2/1811
Lockett, Benjamin	Charles Egerton	11/20/1824
Lockett, Benjamin	Daniel W. Pearson	2/18/1823
Lockett, Cullen	John G. Slappy	no date
Lockwood, William	Richard Johnson	12/30/1833
Lovejoy, Edward	Joel Lane	11/28/1822
Lovejoy, Samuel	Jeremiah Benton	3/3/1820
Lovejoy, Samuel	Felix Hardman	10/29/1827
Lovejoy, Samuel	John Moate	2/7/1828
Lovejoy, William	Edward Lovejoy	1/18/1822
Lowe, John	William Beeland	10/22/1817
Lowe, John B.	Robert Owen	1/16/1819
Loyd, Thomas	Richard S. Loyd	10/23/1820
Lumpkin, Dickerson	William Phelps	11/7/1825
Lumpkin, Harrison	Sherrod Malone	no date
Lumsden, Jeremiah	John Lumsden	11/25/1817
Lumsden, Jeremiah, Jr.	Jeremiah Lumsden, Sr.	6/10/1822
Mallett, Jesse	John Codey	7/6/1809
Malpass, John	John Willson	11/22/1824
Manson, James	Joseph Murdock	11/12/1810
Marks, Hastings	John Hill	10/13/1830
Marks, John H.	Jesse Stanley	8/20/1818
Marsh, William	Charles McMichael	9/13/1825
Marshall, James	Isaac Bryan	8/29/1825
Martin, Bartin	John Kinard	4/13/1841
Martin, Francis S.	Isaac Benham	5/5/1828
Martin, William W.	Reuben Rainey	3/10/1825
Massingale, Daniel	Jacob Boon	5/8/1811
Mathews, James	Joseph White	3/7/1811
Maxey, William	E. T. White	no date
Mayo, Menoah	John Stevens	copy, no date
Melear, Lution	Bradberry Teal	5/23/1881
Mercer, James	Matthew Whitfield	6/4/1833
Mercer, James	Reuben Williamson	4/7/1819
Mercer, William, Sr. heirs of	John Mercer	11/2/1818
Meriwether, David	John Hill	5/12/1856
Meriwether, David	Richard Sansom	3/6/1816
Merritt, Thomas	Snellen Johnson	5/5/1823
Messer, John	James Messer	1/14/1822
Messer, Samuel	Starkey Perry	11/25/1828
Messer, William	James Messer	10/30/1820
Messer, William	James Messer	11/25/1828
Messer, William-heirs of	Thomas Rivers	2/2/1825

```
Miles, Ebenezer                   Cullen Thornton         3/4/1820
Miller, David                     Allen Chance            11/18/1820
Miller, George D.                 Mary Sauls Miller       no date
Milner, John                      Airs Hudspeth           1/28/1819
Milner, John                      Hillery Phillips        5/6/1819
Milner, Marlin                    John Milner             5/5/1819
Milner, Pitt                      John Hammel             10/14/1811
Minter, Robert R.                 James Henry             1/1/1833
Minturn, Benjamin G.              Bolling Hall            4/19/1813
Mitchell, Joel                    Caleb Wilkerson         4/28/1828
Mitchell, Joshua S.               Irwin Lawson            12/22/1827
Mize, Frederick                   John Huston             3/8/1820
Mize, Henry                       Samuel Huston           3/1/1826
Mize, Stacy                       Samuel Huston           2/28/1826
Mobley, Eleazer                   Lee Tuggle              2/10/1827
Mobley, Jethro                    Abel Pennington         1/29/1810
Mobley, Jethro                    John Willson            6/25/1824
Moncrief, Elizabeth               James Akins             2/2/1841
Monk, Thomas                      Benjamin Watts          6/11/1824
Montgomery, David-heirs of        George Weems            6/2/1834
Montgomery, John                  John C. Patrick         2/23/1813
Monticello Commissioners          Joseph Crocket          8/21/1818
Monticello Commissioners          Martin Nalls            no date
Moore, John                       Charles Kitchings       2/14/1818
Moore, John-heirs of              Jeremiah Phillips       12/21/1825
Moore, Martha-heirs of            Benjamin H. Moore       2/27/1900
Moreland, Robert                  Francis Moreland        9/15/1817
Morgan, John                      Charles Morgan          8/2/1830
Morgan, Thomas-heirs of           Philip Thurmond         10/1/1811
Morris, Thomas                    James Hunter            12/1/1830
Morris, William                   John Willson            1/2/1821
Morrow, Robert-heirs of           Andrew Reid             8/27/1818
Morton, Joel                      Isham Berry             3/21/1809
Moseley, Alamon                   Josiah Flournoy         7/16/1823
Moseley, Elisha                   John Hodge              10/10/1823
Moseley, Henry                    William Sharp           3/22/1815
Moses, Joshua                     Noah Ramsey             no date
Mulkey, John                      Pleasant Heeth          12/7/1827
Mulkey, Ruth                      Thomas Worthy           10/22/1817
Mullally, William                 John Robinson           5/1/1832
Murphy, Paschal                   Fields Wilson           2/14/1818
Murray, Stephen                   James Kimball           12/18/1815
Myles, Joshua                     Josiah M. Bonner        2/12/1820
Myles, William H.                 Joseph Johnson          12/28/1818
Myrick, David                     Joseph Buchannon        10/13/1824

McAfee, Green                     Robert McAfee           1/29/1810
McClendon, Jacob                  John Moore              11/15/1815
McClendon, Joel                   Smith Davenport         11/21/1836
McClendon, Thomas                 Asa Crabb               3/7/1820
McClure, James M.                 George Clark            7/11/1828
McCorkle, James K.                Felix Hardman           9/10/1834
McCoy, David                      Allen Beckeom           8/2/1809
McCoy, David                      John Farley-heirs of    10/23/1826
McCoy, Neely                      Selby Hearn             1/14/1822
McCullars, Faithey                Philip Thurmond         1/6/1818
McDougal, Mary (Robinson)         Henry Ware-heirs of     5/18/1821
McDowell, Daniel                  John Price, Jr.         3/12/1835
McDowell, Michael A.              J. M. Byars             1/5/1813
McDowell, William                 Daniel McDowell         12/14/1823
McDowell, William                 Henry Slappy            5/21/1818
McElhenny, V. H.                  Robert V. McElhenny     12/15/1894
McElhenny, Vincent H.-heirs   Mrs. Mary E. McElhenny 1/7/1898
```

McEncroe, William	James E. P. Hunnicut	8/2/1830
McGehee, Jacob	Rice Knowles	9/1/1828
McKemie, James	Thomas Clay	2/5/1833
McKigney, George	Stokeley Morgan	4/25/1809
McLemore, Katharine-heirs of	William McDowell heirs of	6/25/1824
McMichael, Elijah	Alfred Shorter	6/5/1832
McNair, James S.	Benjamin Fudge	10/24/1827
McNeil, Daniel F.	John Robinson	4/28/1818
Napier, Thomas	Herbert Avray	2/21/1826
Newton, Mary F.	William C. Leverett	copy, no date
Newton, Moses	Hack Walker	4/4/1811
Noble, Stephen	Garland Hardwick	8/15/1816
Nolan, Thomas F.	George M. Merriweather	9/21/1825
Norwood, John	Smith Davenport	11/21/1836
Oden, Alexander	Joshua Hames	6/3/1817
Oden, Alexander	Joshua Hames	6/26/1817
Odum, Celia	Isaac Phillips-heirs of	3/20/1811
O'Kelly, James	Isham Alford	8/4/1819
Oliver, Caleb	Abel Pennington, Jr.	5/27/1811
Orr, Allen	John H. Brantley	11/15/1825
Ousley, Points	James K. T. Walton	7/8/1824
Overton, Henry	Cullen Thornton	3/23/1820
Owen, Hardaman	Peyton Clements	10/18/1830
Paine, John	Thomas Dillon	9/14/1819
Parks, Clark D.	Thomas Smith	2/10/1833
Parks, Garrett W.	Philip Thurmond	1/23/1809
Parks, Welcom	James Perry	10/23/1826
Patey, Elijah	Henry Patey	7/12/1827
Patey, Miles	Andrew Johnson	1/19/1837
Patrick, John M.	Thomas Hooks	12/18/1815
Patterson, David	Rice P. Knowles	9/10/1828
Patterson, Mary	Daniel Godard	6/1/1819
Pearce, Bartlet	John Lang	9/27/1816
Pearce, Bartley	Obediah Saterwhite	10/28/1818
Pearson, Jeremiah	Edward Y. Hill	11/12/1830
Peavy, Allen	Robert Owen	2/9/1821
Peddy, Henry	James Mulkey	copy, no date
Peek, Henry	David Phelps-heirs of	5/6/1824
Pemberton, Joshua	Allen Bass	5/19/1811
Pendergrass, Hariett E.	Jasper Co.Commissioners	no date
Penn, William	Jesse Harper	5/5/1823
Penn, William	Daniel McDowell	5/14/1832
Penn, William	James S. Weeks	9/11/1821
Pennington, Ephraim	Aris Newton	9/12/1835
Pennington, Henry	Harris Cross	2/28/1833
Perdue, Daniel	Bradberry Teal	5/23/1887
Perkins, Paul W.	James G. Andrews	4/4/1859
Perry, Starky	James Messer	11/25/1828
Pettyjohn, Jacob	Harrison Cabeness	3/8/1811
Peugh, Jehu-heirs of	H. B. Stuart	2/23/1839
Phelps, Aquilla	Common School of 364th District	8/14/1839
Phelps, Thomas	Shadrick Turner	11/15/1835
Phillips, James	Jesse Cox	3/28/1822
Phillips, John	Hackey Walker	9/17/1817
Phillips, Lewis	Nathan Phillips	2/10/1857
Phillips, Matthew	John Baldwin	1/14/1829
Phillips, Matthew	Elisha G. Crawford	5/4/1831
Phillips, Nathan	Lewis Phillips	6/14/1833

Phillips, Nathan	Thomas H. Tuggle	2/15/1857
Phillips, Reuben	Bynum Alford	1/29/1819
Phillips, William	John Robinson	5/21/1811
Phillips, Zachariah, Jr.	Zachariah Phillips, Sr.	2/11/1815
Phipps, Isaiah	John Duke	12/18/1815
Pickens, Marcus	Joseph Johnson	10/26/1821
Pickens, Marcus	John Willson	4/25/1821
Pilcher, Edward	Stephen Pilcher	5/2/1810
Pinckard, James	Moses Matthews	9/11/1815
Pinckard, James, Sr.	James Pinckard, Jr.	7/4/1829
Pittman, William A.	Theopholus Freeman	12/7/1824
Poland, Thomas	John T. Skelton	10/29/1821
Pon, Lewis W.	William C. Leverett	copy, 4/11/1876
Pon, Lewis W.	Lucien B. Newton	copy, 1/25/1869
Pope, William	Aaron Parker	11/13/1835
Porter, Anthony	William Hutchison heirs of	9/16/1817
Porter, John	Elijah C. Belcher	9/8/1835
Pounds, Alex	Board of Education	3/11/1899
Powell, Allen P.	Zachariah Simms	2/14/1812
Powell, Christopher W.	Thomas Blann	3/28/1835
Powell, Evan H.	Moses Powell	3/13/1820
Powell, Norborne B.	Edward Y. Hill	1/21/1842
Powers, Francis	Bartlett Brown	4/28/1821
Presley, Moses	Silas Barren	3/4/1820
Presley, Moses	Richard Featherston	2/8/1821
Price, Edward	Jarrel Beasley	2/22/1830
Price, Joseph	William Cook	2/4/1819
Pridgen, James	Micajah Sansom, Jr.	2/27/1817
Prince, John	John McMichael	8/12/1810
Pugh, Robert	William Hamilton	3/1/1810
Pye, James-heirs of	Theophilus Pye	no date
Pye, Lewis	Shadrach McMichael	4/14/1838
Pye, Theophilus	Isaac Barr	7/27/1835
Pyle, Abraham	Matthew Whitfield	1/19/1841
Rainey, Ann	John Folds	7/8/1829
Rainey, Mary	Jacob Pettyjohn	3/8/1811
Rainey, Matthew	William Rainey	6/21/1828
Rainey, Reuben M.	John Freeman	5/13/1829
Ramsey, Noah	John Willson	4/8/1822
Ramsey, Randal	Alsea Holifield	6/25/1817
Randolph Co.Commissioners	Samuel Butts	6/1/1812
Randolph Co.Commissioners	Absalom Hammet	no date
Randolph Co.Commissioners	Joseph McBride	9/18/1811
Randolph Co.Commissioners	Nathan Williams	3/21/1811
Randolph, Jeremiah	Joshua Chaffin	4/21/1825
Ray, Mark	John Willson	10/31/1823
Ray, Mary	Lewis Conner Holland	6/14/1824
Ray, Samuel	George Ray	3/24/1819
Reaves, Joshua	William Sprading	3/10/1823
Reese, Cuthbert	Robert Masters	1/25/1827
Reese, Cuthbert	James Wade	12/9/1826
Reeves, Green	William Green, Jr.	3/7/1816
Reeves, James	John Reeves	8/3/1814
Reeves, Joel A.-heirs of	Joel L. Terrell	4/5/1889
Reeves, Joel Avery	John Willson	7/30/1817
Reeves, Jonathan	William Hood	4/23/1821
Reeves, Prier	Thomas H. Everitt	12/10/1835
Reid, Joseph	Martin Cochran	1/30/1819
Rhodes, James	James Jackson	1/5/1810
Richards, James	James Mercer	12/17/1816
Richards, Thomas	Edward Castleberry	5/18/1822

Richards, William B.	Samuel Blackwell	6/21/1842
Richerson, George-heirs of	Robert C. Beasley	4/13/1830
Ricketts, R. S.	W. A. Kelly & Bros.	1/22/1901
Ridley, Charles L.	Charles T. Alexander	2/7/1833
Rimes, Little John	John Lassiter	6/26/1824
Rivers, James	Thomas Rivers	12/6/1827
Rivers, Milly	James Kindrick	2/4/1835
Rivers, Thomas	James S. Maddux	8/4/1842
Rivers, Thomas	Union Academy	4/8/1823
Rivers, Thomas H. B.	Anthony Dyer	4/2/1840
Rivers, Thomas H. B.	Anthony Dyer	11/20/1840
Roberts, O. G.	E. B. Smith	5/6/1899
Roberts, O. G.	E. B. Smith	5/8/1899
Roberts, Richard	David Keath	5/2/1816
Robinson, Abel S.	John White	7/12/1838
Robinson, Benjamin	Reuben Edwards	5/4/1813
Robinson, Benjamin	Greene Reeves	2/5/1812
Robinson, Cornelius	Silas Grubbs	6/17/1823
Robinson, Cornelius	Lot Smith	6/9/1821
Robinson, James T.	Amos Ward	1/6/1832
Robinson, Reden	Henry Ware	2/12/1821
Robinson, Temperance	Henry Ware	9/5/1821
Rogers, George	James Duncan	4/11/1816
Rogers, George	James Rogers	7/14/1813
Rosser, Isaac	William Callaway	12/9/1822
Rosser, Isaac	Jeremiah Canant	2/11/1824
Routon, William	John Luckie-heirs of	7/7/1824
Rucker, Burton	Levinia Kirtley	2/23/1819
Rucker, Burton	Mary Morgan	6/2/1817
Runnels, Howel W.	William P. Culbertson	10/30/1811
Rushing, Bryant	Gilbert Gay	7/29/1816
Russell, William R.	Isaac Bailey	12/9/1823
Salsbury, John R.	Isaac Walker	8/21/1811
Samford, Thomas	Wesley Forbes	10/10/1823
Sanders, John	James K. McCorkle	9/10/1834
Sansom, Archibald-heirs of	Eli Strickland	12/31/1822
Sapp, James	James Kimbel	10/23/1809
Satterwhite, Stephen	Baptist Church of Christ	9/28/1815
Sauls, Patience	James Augustus Tippins	12/11/1807
Saunders, Isiah	James K. McCorkle	9/10/1834
Scarborough, Niles	James Bowden	1/6/1818
Scott, Archibald	John Wyatt, Sr.	11/13/1812
Scott, William-heirs of	Wiley Belcher	3/1/1816
Sharman, James	Francis Moreland	10/15/1810
Sharman, Robert	Judith Harraway	12/6/1813
Shaw, William	William Carroll	1/26/1814
Ship, Richard	William Ruling	10/20/1811
Shorter, Alfred	Thomas C. Garrett	6/2/1838
Shorter, Mary	Jacob Shorter	12/31/1810
Shorter, Reuben C.	Stephen Howard	11/11/1836
Shorter, Reuben C.	Andrew Johnson	5/1/1857
Shorter, Reuben C.	Alexander Walden	4/25/1822
Shy, Seaborn J.	Mary Belcher	12/20/1838
Sims, Zachariah	Andrew Woodley	2/25/1812
Sisson, Richard W.	John Willson	5/12/1828
Skaggs, James	Burwell P. Key	12/6/1827
Skaggs, James	Abel Wilkerson	1/2/1819
Slagle, Jacob	Jeptha V. Dismukes	1/19/1833
Slappy, H.-heirs of	Josiah M. Bonner	2/20/1824
Slappy, Henry-heirs of	George M. Meriwether	9/23/1824
Slappy, Henry-heirs of	David A. Reese	2/5/1824

Slappy, John G.	James Hunter	5/1/1828
Sleigh, Mary	Peter B. Terrell	12/1/1812
Smartt, Francis B.	James Cowan	9/2/1825
heirs of		
Smith, Baxter	Samuel Jackson	4/22/1823
Smith, Benjamin	Joshua Pemberton	5/19/1811
Smith, David	Allen Bass	6/26/1824
Smith, Emanuel S.	Lucian W. Malear	5/22/1837
Smith, James	William Hitchcock	5/11/1829
Smith, Joel	Marlin Towns	7/19/1813
Smith, John	Baptist Church of	9/28/1815
	Christ	
Smith, Jonathan	Joel Towns	1/28/1814
Smith, Joseph	John F. Weathersbee,Jr.	6/9/1870
Smith, Rolen	Fleming Jordan	1/30/1837
Smith, Samuel	Masen Harvill	2/19/1824
Smith, William	Thomas Gaston	12/11/1826
Sorrel, Needham	Moses Melton	10/8/1814
Sowell, Abihugh	Seymour S. Byrom	2/10/1815
Spears, C. M.	Josephine Jeffers	5/1/1877
Spence, John	Woody Dozer	10/22/1827
Spencer, William	Benjamin Carrol	2/4/1811
Spradlin, William	John Lumsden	2/26/1825
Spradling, James	James Buchanon	1/5/1810
Spurgin, Thomas R.	William Routon	no date
Spurlin, William	Marshal H. Waddill	4/14/1829
Stanford, David	Daniel Sharp	4/5/1814
Stanley, Jesse	William Worthy	5/3/1822
State Commissioners	Isaac McLendon	2/28/1818
Stevens, James	John Rivers	10/18/1810
Stevens, Pearce	Thomas F. Nolan	1/28/1825
Stewart, James	Keneard (?) Morgan	3/20/1835
Strickland, Solomon	William Taylor	6/20/1825
Sturdevant, Edwin	Walter Mitchell	1/4/1825
Sullivan, Obadiah	Jane King	1/27/1814
Sutton, Jesse	Allen Beckham	9/23/1808
Tankersley, Carter	William Campbell	1/8/1839
Taylor, Frances N.	Michael M. Toland	6/2/1858
heirs of		
Taylor, Gilbert D.	William B. Hardy	2/5/1818
Taylor, Henry R.	Jesse Stratton	4/28/1828
Taylor, Jacob	Seymore S. Byrom	2/11/1815
Taylor, William F.	Thomas Wilson	12/16/1825
Tedders, Samuel	Wiley Stroud	11/24/1829
Teddlie, William	John Kinard	5/28/1838
Temples, Frederick	David White	11/7/1810
Terrell, Luis	Caleb W. Spears	12/13/1858
Terrell, Peter B.	Robert Sharman	12/2/1842
Thomas, David L.	Milton Clayton	4/5/1829
Thomas, John	David Adams	3/3/1820
Thomas, William	William W. Martin	7/14/1823
Thompson, Edward	Jeremiah Thompson	12/20/1838
Thompson, James	James Reeves	1/24/1827
Thompson, James	Archibald York	10/19/1816
Thompson, John S.	James A. Thompson	8/16/1839
Thompson, William H.	Benjamin W. Cook	no date
Thornton, Cullen	Patrick H. Gardner	11/22/1824
Thornton, Cullen	Josiah G. Lewis	11/2/1823
Thornton, Henry	Alexander Urquhart	1/9/1836
Thornton, Jordan	Joel Lane	12/24/1822
Thurmond, Benjamin	Samuel Crockett	2/10/1821
Thurmond, Phillip	Susan Rivers	12/7/1835

Tie, Henry	Reuben Radford	9/13/1816
Todd, John	James Richardson	2/4/1814
Tomlin, John Harris	William Davies	10/31/1811
Tompkins, Giles	Lemuel Skaggs	7/10/1822
Touchstone, Caleb	William Person	3/1/1811
Towns, Joel	John Huston	1/31/1814
Towns, John	William Gill	12/18/1822
Towns, John G.	Henry Butts	7/27/1824
Towns, John G.-heirs of	William Hitchcock	4/22/1825
Towns, John T. C.	Bartley Towns	3/10/1825
Towns, Marlin	Morey Easters	2/10/1821
Trainer, James	Celia Culbertson	8/16/1824
Tramem, Clement	Phillip Fitzpatrick	1/24/1813
Traweek, Robert C.	Jonathan Nichols	8/11/1818
Traweek, Robert C.	John Willson	2/6/1819
Traylor, C. T.	John Connal	8/2/1821
Traylor, C. T.	Josiah Horton	2/27/1817
Traylor, C. T.	Joseph J. Williams	11/26/1819
Traylor, William H. heirs of	Robert Sherman	12/3/1842
Truit, Nancy (Callaway)	Drury Wilkins	1/14/1828
Tuggle, Lee	Thomas H. Tuggle	2/13/1857
Tuggle, Robert	Richard M. Cisson heirs of	2/12/1821
Turner, Manson	Bardwell Billings	11/22/1825
Tyler, F. M.	Thomas G. Blackwell	1/20/?
Tyler, F. M.	William C. Leverett	4/18/1878
Tyner, R. J.	John McCollough	no date
Tyner, Stephen	Nathan Johnston	10/9/1823
Urquhart, Alexander	Jarrel Beasley	1/11/1836
Vann, Joseph	Wyatt Reeves	4/8/1829
Vann, Joseph	Samuel Weems	12/13/1823
Vickers, Elijah	Felix Stanley	1/1/1825
Waits, Benjamin	Blewford M. Walton	10/21/1834
Waits, Benjamin	Ellemander Warbington	1/1/1822
Waits, Mark	Benjamin Waits	10/21/1834
Walden, Charles	Airs Hudspeth	12/8/1818
Walden, Charles	Thomas Hutson	1/3/1819
Walden, Critia	Jonas Temple	4/20/1811
Walden, Henry	Tomas Barnes-heirs of	10/8/1814
Walden, James	William Green, Jr.	3/7/1816
Walden, James	John Ragan	3/11/1816
Walden, James	John Ragan	3/4/1816
Waldriff, John	Henry Walden	10/21/1810
Walker, Hackey	Green Walker	3/9/1825
Walker, Henry	Baker Hobson	5/4/1813
Walker, Isaac	Phillip Thurmond	5/28/1816
Walker, James-heirs of	Amos Welborn	8/23/1819
Walker, John	Thomas Rivers	2/2/1825
Walker, William	Edward Colwell	4/3/1827
Waller, Charles	Samuel Penington	11/3/1812
Waller, D. F.	Waller Academy	5/22/1896
Waller, Samuel	Robert Owin	8/15/1811
Walthall, Edward-heirs of	Charles F. Walthall	3/2/1841
Walthall, Turman	Wiles N. H. Everett	12/10/1835
Walton, Blewford M.	Benjamin Waits	2/14/1835
Ward, Thomas	Cheadle Cochran	6/29/1812
Ware, James	Silvanus Walker	7/12/1813
Warner, Nathan-heirs of	George L. Holmes	12/18/1834
Warren, Bray	Dread Warren	3/5/1818

Warren, Dread	Henry C. Towns	2/1/1828
Warren, Etheldread	Bradberry Teal	5/20/1857
Weathers, Jesse, Sr.	Abner Bartlett	no date
Webb, Catherine	Stephen Nolen	5/23/1838
Webb, Clinton	John Robinson	3/9/1811
Webb, J. F.	H. V. B. Allen	no date
Webb, James F.	Augustus J. Webb	11/18/1828
Weekes, James S.	James Garlington	no date
Weems, George	Ivy Hill	6/11/1834
Weems, Samuel	Burwell Ragland	1/11/1828
Welborn, Jonathan	Amos Welborn	5/27/1818
Welch, James	James Hamrick	1/3/1822
Welding, Isaac	Randolph Co.Commissioners	3/24/1809
Weldon, John	Cheadle Cochran	2/12/1821
West, Jeremiah	Joseph Williams	9/5/1822
West, John, Sr.	Zielpha Sansom	4/9/1823
Whatley, John B.	John Turk	11/3/1819
Whitaker, West	Amos Welborn	5/26/1818
White, David	Peter W. Gautier	4/14/1812
White, David	John Moore	6/11/1814
White, David	William Smith	11/13/1815
White, John	Thomas Ward	1/27/1812
White, Valentine	Dickerson Lumpkin	12/9/1822
Whitfield, Holling	Willis Newton	11/20/1825
Whitfield, James	Green Holifield	11/11/1824
Whitfield, John B.	Indiana C. Whitfield	9/27/1869
Whitfield, Matthew C.	Clarence Hill	copy, no date
Wicker, Benjamin	James Mills	2/4/1819
Wiggins, Martha	Daniel Wiggins	2/26/1812
Wilkerson, Simeon	William Holloway	10/8/1824
Wilkey, James-heirs of	Cordy Weaver	6/25/1817
Wilkins, Allen	Hartwell Ezell	7/12/1833
Wilkinson, Alexander	Notley Maddux	1/25/1836
Wilks, Georgia A.	R. C. Greer	11/5/1825
Wilks, John, Sr.	Stephen Stephens	3/18/1839
Williams, Aaron	Church of Falling Creek	9/30/1824
Williams, Aaron	Thomas Hairston	9/2/1819
Williams, Aaron	Thomas Ward	4/27/1811
Williams, Charles	John Lang, Sr.	11/24/1814
Williams, Daniel	John Freeman	2/9/1821
Williams, John	William McCorkle	2/14/1818
Williams, Joseph	John Williams	10/9/1823
Williams, Luke	James Thompson	1/26/1827
Williams, Nathan	John Robinson	5/29/1811
Williams, Peter	Thomas Shields	7/17/1817
Williams, T. R.	J. J. Dearing	2/6/1895
Williamson, Benjamin	John Law	8/15/1811
Williamson, Reuben	Levi Newton	6/18/1825
Willis, Daniel H.	Joshua Hames	10/18/1820
Willson, B. H.	Warren T. Castleberry	2/1/1823
Willson, James	Hephzehah Baptist Church	12/9/1823
Willson, John	William Hitchcock	4/5/1820
Willson, John	Ephraim Pennington	3/8/1820
Willson, John	Robert Tuggle	2/10/1821
Willson, John-heirs of	Nathan Warner	10/25/1827
Willson, Leroy M.	Edmund I. Walton	3/5/1851
Willson, Leroy M.	Isaac L. Walton	3/5/1851
Wilson, Abel P.	John Price	3/2/1849
Wilson, Fields	Paschal Murphy	2/11/1818
Wilson, John	Seymore S. Byrom	2/11/1815
Wilson, John S.	John Saunders	6/16/1823

Wilson, Joshua	William Connaway	5/6/1837
Wilson, Leonard	John S. Wilson	5/17/1823
Wilson, Mary	Leonard Wilson	5/7/1823
Winchester, Jonathan	Carden Goolsby	1/1/1836
Wise, Riley	Allen McClendon	3/7/1826
Womack, Edmond	Mordecai Shackleford	9/8/1826
Wood, Aristarchus	William Whitfield	1/28/1823
Woodlwy, Caleb	Francis McClendon	2/22/1826
Wooton, Joseph	William Routon	6/28/1824
Wright, William	Allen Tomson	12/6/1841
Wyatt, John, Sr.	Henry J. Williams	9/28/1815
Yancey, Lewis	William Richards	4/10/1816
Yancey, Lewis D.	Nealey D. Johnson	1/2/1828
Yancey, Lewis D.	William Richards	5/30/1822
Yancy, J. E.	W. H. Pickett	no date
Yarbrough, Jeptha	Solomon Everett	6/30/1821
Young, Greene	Jonathan Phillips	8/14/1809
Young, John	John Robinson	5/20/1811
Young, Maryan	Robert Trippe	no date
Young, Matthew-heirs of	Jesse Cox	copy, no date
Young, Thomas	Eleanah Denson	12/20/?

CHAPTER XII

MISCELLANEOUS UNBOUND RECORDS, 1808-1935
Record Group 179-12-10

This series contains bound and unbound original papers involving, but not limited to:

(1) Deeds	(9) Internal Revenue
(2) Estrays	(10) Merchants' invoices
(3) Affidavits	(11) Liquor records
(4) Bankruptcy	(12) County matters
(5) Bench warrants	(13) Election records
(6) Corporations	(14) School records
(7) Correspondence	(15) Tax records
(8) Insurance	(16) Jurors' lists

Although some of these records rightfully belong in already existing sub-groups, a special sub-group was created due to the fact that most of these records are miniscule in number or are filed regardless of office or origin. All the papers are parts of other matters and in some cases are merely fragments or estrays. The records have been flattened, cleaned and placed in folders according to subject matter. The folders have been arranged in a rough chronological or alphabetical sequence under the various headings and most have surname and/or date listings included outside the respective folder.

Contents

1808-1935

Advertisements
Affidavits (miscell.)
Agreements and contracts
Amnesty oaths (separate index)
Apprentice indentures (separate index)
Auto license records
Bankruptcy
Bench warrants
Bonds (miscell.)
Census, 1860
Church records
Citizenship oaths (separate index)
Corporations
Correspondence (part) (separate index)
Correspondence (continued) (separate index)
Estrays (separate index)
Miscellaneous county matters
Inquests (separate index)
Insurance
Liquor records
Doctors Lawyers
Merchants' invoices (separate index)
Organizations
County matters (part)
County matters (continued)
Health Department
State hospital
Election records
School records
Board of Education, bonds, oaths of office
Public office - oaths and bonds
County police reports
Acts, resolutions, proposed legislation
Penitentiary records
Tax records (part)
Tax records (continued)

Tax records (continued)
Paupers
Jurors (part)
 -Defaultors (separate index)
 -Jurors (separate index)
Jurors (continued (separate index)
Jurors (continued) (separate index)
Court of Ordinary (separate index + cross-reference)
Deeds (slaves) - (separate index + cross-reference)
Deeds (miscell.) - (separate index + cross-reference)
Mortgages, notes (separate index + cross-reference)
Court records, Miscellaneous
 -Defaulting administrators, executors & guardians
 -Court correspondence
 -Correspondence, Superior Court
Court records, Miscellaneous (continued)
 -Court costs
 -Court dockets
 -Court orders
 -Court orders to sheriff
 -Fi Fas received for collection
 -Grand Jury presentments
 -Interrogatories
 -Ordinary's report
 -Registration - free persons of color
 -Road defaultors
 -Subpoenas
Board of County Commissioners records
Tax Commissioner's Office records

JASPER COUNTY - AMNESTY OATHS

Five oaths, signature not legible.

Aaron, John L.	Burns, W. I.
Aaron, R. A.	Byars, O.
Acree, W. B.	Campbell, E. E. F. W.
Akens, James	Cardell, P. D.
Akins, R. S.	Cardell, William
Allen, H. N.	Chaffin, Thomas P.
Allen, O. C.	Chapman, H. H.
Ambroes, Martha E.	Childs, N. G.
Ambroes, Warren	Clark, Henry
Annis, C. S.	Clay, J. J.
Annis, Jesse M.	Clay, Jesse
Bailey, Z.	Comer, Thomas J.
Barr, B. O.	Cook, D. N.
Barr, J. W.	Cook, G. S.
Barr, Willi L.	Cook, J. W.
Beall, John	Cook, L. E.
Belcher, John M.	Cornwell, D. L.
Binford, Henry W.	Cornwell, O.
Binford, Joseph L.	Cornwell, W. D.
Blackman, J. H.	Couch, Mary
Blackwell, T. G.	Couch, N. H.
Bowdoin, James H.	Cranford, John W.
Brandon, William T.	Cunard, Jumina
Brewington, W. J., Jr.	Darden, J. M.
Brown, R. G.	Davis, D. M.
Bryant, Bird	Davis, T. C.
Bryant, J. E.	Dawkins, B. F.

Dawkins, G. W.
Dawkins, W. J.
Deason, Bengaman N.
Digby, B. T.
Digby, John B.
Dillard, George
Doughity, William
Edwards, R. M.
Edwards, R. S.
Edwards, S. B.
Edwards, S. H.
Elder, E. A. (?)
Ezell, Cullen R.
Faulkner, M. R.
Faulkner, Zachariah
Fears, W. M.
Fears, W. T.
Fiacher, S. C.
Fish, N. C.
Fish, Sarena
Fish, William T.
Franklin, John C.
Freeman, A. C.
Freeman, Alemand
Freeman, Floyd
Gann, James A.
Gay, W. F.
Gilstrap, John B.
Goodman, J. T.
Goodman, Richard
Goolsby, C. B.
Goolsby, James B.
Green, T. A.
Greer, Arny (?)
Greer, C. H.
Greer, G. L.
Greer, Thomas S.
Griffin, G. A.
Grubbs, C. M.
Grubbs, J. W.
Grubbs, R. S.
Grubbs, Silas
Hardy, Benager
Hardy, Joseph J.
Hariss, J. S.
Harris, Milton
Hawk, Seaborn I.
Henderson, Charles
Henderson, David
Henderson, S. J.
Hincy, T. J.
Hodge, D. R.
Hogan, A. J.
Hogan, A. J.
Holland, J. H.
Holloway, M.
Homer, Jesse
Horton, Elisha
Howard, J. P.
Howard, S. N.
Howard, S. R.
Huff, G. W.
Huff, T. Thomas

Hutchinson, M. H.
Ivy, R. W.
Johnson, A. L.
Johnston, Martha
Jones, B. F.
Jones, J. R.
Jones, John J.
Jones, M. P.
Kelly, Seaborn J.
Kelly, W. G.
Key, M. D. L.
Key, W. H.
Kinard, Michael
King, A. S.
King, John M.
Lane, Joel
Lane, L. A.
Lane, William D.
Langston, Matilda
Langston, T.W.P.
Lawson, Wm. L.
Lawyer, Rube
Lazenby, J. G.
Leverett, ?
Leverett, Berrel
Leverette, Jesse
Leveritt, T. S.
Lewis, James T.
Linch, P. T.
Lindsey, John
Lindsey, L. F.
Litron, G.A.D.
Loyd, Francis
Maddux, S. H.
Maddux, Wm.
Malone, Franklin
Malone, S. B.
Malone, William H.
Martin, Hugh M.
Millen, H.L.
Minter, John L.
Minter, R. A.
Morgan, E. P.
Morgan, I. H.
Morgan, Isaac N.
Morgan, J. H.
Murphy, J. H.
McAfee, Morjan A.W.
McElhenney, B. F.
McElhenney, John
McElland, J. D.
McGinnis (?), Fleming
McLendon, W. J.
McMelon (?), William
Nall, W. E.
Newton, Aris
Ozburn, B. S.
Oaburn, Charles
Paker (?), S. R.
Park, J. T.
Parks, William W.
Penn, S. A.
Perry, Mat

Phillips, Mary E.
Pinckard, Lemuel C.
Piper, T. M.
Portwood, John
Preston, William H.
Price, R. W.
Pritchett, G. W.
Pye, Theophilus
Rainey, Mathew
Ramey, Mary M.
Ranay, J. W.
Reynolds, J. J.
Rhodes, J. D.
Roberts, O. G.
Robinson, John L.
Roby, H. W.
Roby, W. H.
Rowe, J. C.
Satterwhite, W. D.
Shropshire, W. W.
Shy, S. C.
Smith, Thomas J.
Spear, Elizabeth (2)
Spear, Isabella
Spear, Mary A. H.
Spearman, G. T.
Spears, J. B.
Spears, S. C.
Speers, J. E.
Steel, John W.
Steele, Samuel W.
Steele, William
Strickland, N. M.
Talmadge, John H.
Thomerson, J. C.
Thompson, Aaron P.
Thompson, J. M.
Tomlinson, John T.
Tomlinson, W. M.
Tucker, Jesse M.
Turk, A. T.
Turk, John
Turner, S. W.
Tyler, F. M.
Tyler, J. L.
Varnom, William
Waits, Alexander
Waits, Levy
Waits, Richmond
Waits, W. B.
Waldrep, L. L.
Walker, Henry
White, W. P.
Williams, James M.
Williams, Joseph P.
Williams, S. C.
Williams, W. T.
Willingham, Theophilus
Wise, Joseph A.
Wooten, Riley
Wyatt, J. T.
Yancy, J. E.
Yancy, L. D.
Zachry, W. L.

Name	Apprenticed
Allen, John (col)	
Laura (col)	
Lucy (col)	
(Infant) (col)	to George Davis
Allen, Lucy (col)	to Dick Davis (col)
Arrington, Nancy I.	to J. T. Franks
Banks, Georgia Ann (col)	to Henry D. Banks
Bridges, Anna (col)	
Mary Jane (col)	
Scott (col)	to Mary Appling (col)
Jordan, Washington (col)	to Mary Appling (col)
Broddus, George (col)	
Valentine (col)	to Thomas C. Broddus
Compton, Cathorn	
Charity	
Oliver	
Richard	to William P. Persons
Compton, Phillis	to S. H. Johnston
Darden, John	
Turner	to James M. Williams
Digby, Anderson (col)	
Rhody (col)	to James H. Digby
Digby, Angeline (col)	
Floyd (col)	
Frances (col)	to John B. Digby
Ezell, Marcus (col)	to Robert F. Ezell
Farrer, Will	to A. Newton
Freeman, George (col)	
Sam (col)	to Isaac H. Freeman
George, Lucius (col)	to Americus George (col)
Goolsby, Easther Alberta (col)	to Mrs. Millie Kelly
Goolsby, Samual (col)	to Lula & Alex Rooks
Harriet (col	to Thomas McKissack
Henry (col)	to Edward A. Elder
Isham (col)	to N. G. Childs
Jackson, Andrew	to C. M. Hardy
Jim (col)	to Beverly A. Kelly
Jordan, Lexis	to Percy W. Malone
Jungstrom, Emelia S.	to E. S. Glover
Leverette, James Henry	to Oliver Holloway
McMichael, Lucy (col)	to Pollard B. McMichael
Pearson, John	to Austin Pearson
Penn, Betsey (col)	
Jasper (col)	to Pollard B. McMichael
Pou, Albert (col)	
Ellen (col)	to Elizabeth W. Reid
Price, Ora	to James M. Williams
Ramey, Eugene	to Adaline Barnes
Roberts, Cotes (?) (col)	to Louis Head (col)
Stephens, Ben	to Thomas W. Pope
Strom, Alida Sophia	to A. M. Robinson
Tedders, Susie Elizabeth	to Samuel J. Steel
Thompson, Gilbert	
Henrietta	to W. H. Thompson
Vickrum, Edmond	to William P. White
Willson, Sarah	to Edward L. Elder
Wilson, Flem (col)	
Martha (col)	to Charles Wilson (col)
Wilson, Samuel	to George Owen

Anderson, Aaol E.
Bergstrom, Oscar
Briscoe, Henry
Ericson, Solomon
Garden, Alexander
Ginn, Arthur

Johnson, John
Johnson, Samuel
Kellam, Robert
Looser, John Conrad
Molliere, Clement
Moore, Samuel

McCloskey, John
McDonald, James
McKavitt, Henry
McLaughlin, James
McLea, John
Treynor, Hugh

JASPER COUNTY - CORRESPONDENCE
Campaign Correspondence

Adgate, H. C.
Alfriend, A. H.
Atlanta Banking Co.
Baer, D. I.
Banks, O. O.
Bartlett, George T.
Benton, J. B.
Blackwell, John H.
Bostick, C. D.
Brandon, James L.
Bullard, Dr.
Burney, ?
Burney, C. C.
Burney, J. W.
Campbell, Doyle
Capers, H. D.
Cogburn, L. E.
Cohen, S.
Constitution
Cook, J. W.
Davis, ?
Davis, R. L.
Davis, Richard
Davis, S. C.
Dearing, J. J.
Dennis, R. S.
Digby, ?
Digby, T. E.
Dorsey, E. R.
Dozier, Dr. George R.
Dyer, John P.
Dyer, John R.

Flemister, John
Fletcher, Sallie
Florence, A. S.
Florence, Shed
Florence, W. S.
Franklin Printing
 & Publishing Co.
Fulton, S.
Goolsby, C. L.
Goolsby, C. R.
Goolsby, F. C.
Grier, Crawford & G.
Hardiman & Hambleton
Holsenbeck, D. J.
Jacobson, C. A.
Jessup, Homer
Jones, J. R.
Jordan, E. H.
Kelly, J. H.
Key, John C.
Lane, C. Q.
Leach, John W.
Leverett, W. C.
Lewis, George (col)
Lewis, Grey (?)
Lockwood, T. F.
Lovejoy, Sid
Malone, T. S.
Malone, W. B.
McDowell, F. D.
McMichael, E.
Niblett, J. I.

Parks, J. B.
Person, G. W.
Personsy, George W.
Phillips, Monroe
Phillips, W. H.
Preston, W.J.M.
Robinson, Gordon
Robinson, H. V.
Searcy, W. E. H.
Smith, E. B.
Smith, N. P.
Smith, W. G.
Speairs, S. P.
Swanson, F. M.
Talmadge, Robt.
Taylor & Bolling Co.
Turner, J. A.
Turner, Mrs. J. W.
Walker, Henry
Walker & Walker
Warren, R. J.
Webb, J. B.
Webb & Kelly
Whitfield, Bolling
Winburn, J. J.
Winburn, W. A.
Wingfield, W. B.
Woodruff, James
Wright, Wm. A.
Zachry, W. L.

Correspondence-
 unidentified

JASPER COUNTY - ESTRAYS

Allen, Nancy
Atkins, Joseph C.
Avary, James C.
Bowen, Uriah
Bowers, Enoch T.
Braselton, Jacob
Bullard, James, Sr.
Capes, T. C.
Christian, Ira
Clark, Samuel
Crawford, Elisha G.
Dennis, Catharine
Dunn, E. A.

Evans, William
Foster, Ludwell
Garrett, Daniel
Hairston, Thomas
Hammond, Jackson
Hattaway, B. M.
Hatton, Thomas
Henslee, John P.
Jones, Hilliard G.
Kelly, Owen
Kinard, John
King, Mary
Lett, Hugh

Mills, John
Minter, Andrew J.
Moore, Thomas
Morgan, Stokely
McMichael, John
McMichael, W. S.
Shelton, Joseph
Smith, Washington
Stocks, John
Sturdivant, Jesse
Thompson, Mark
Thurmond, Joe

Estrays - 1824, 1825, 1826, 1827, 1828, 1829, 1875-1880, 1881-1904

Unidentified persons (2)
Aiken, Kimball
Alfred (col)
Amy (col)
Banks, Bob (col)
Banks, Viola
Barber, Wiley
Barnes, Mary
Bradford, Edmund
Brown, Bartlett
Brown, Maria
Bryant, Rena
Bruce, Sary
Bullard, Mary
Carter, Landon
Chapman, Patience
Clayborn (col)
Cogswell, Hiram
Coon (col)
Cullins, Charles (col)
Daniel (col)
Daniel, John
Davis, Thomas B.
Dick (col)
Dickinson, Henry A.
Dixon, Thomas
Donally, James
Easter (col)
Fagan, Ceasor

Fanny (col)
Faulkner, H. D.
Flournoy, Francis
Freeman, Mark Anna
George, Elizabeth
Green (col)
Green, Joe
Hardin, Silas
Harvell (infant)
Henderson, David
Hicks, Arthur
Jenkins, John
Julia (col)
Kelly, John C.
Kendall, David
Lawrence, Jeff (col)
Leverett, Reid
Lewis, (col)
Lewis, John
Luke (col)
Mat (col)
Maxey, Millie
Middlebrooks, Joseph
Mitchel (col)
McClendon, Isaac
McCollum, Elias
McGaha, ?
McGinnis, Jarret
Parker, Zeal

Parnell, John W.
Peter, (col)
Petit, Carry
Phillip (col)
Puckett, Martin
Ridley, Antony
Roberts, Bartholo-
  mew G.
Robertson, William
Roby, Walter
Rockmore, John
Russel, David
Samson, Sarah
Simpson, John J.
Smith, Alexander
Stokes, Allen
Stone, Martha
Thomason, Dick
Trippe, Emanuel
Turner (col)
Turner, Miles
Waits, Alexander
Waters, David
White, Clarence
Whitfield, Amy
Williams, ?
Williams, Joanna
Willis, Jency
Willis, Jonathan
Wooton, Sarah

JASPER COUNTY - MERCHANT'S INVOICES

A. K. Company - oil
Allen & Turner - blacksmith
Allen, W. W. - groceries, dry goods
Amason, J. W. - groceries, liquor
Auto Supply Company - repair
Ballard, W. E. - groceries, general merchandise
Banks, Davidson & Kelly - general merchandise
Banks, I. T. - shoes
Barrett & Barnes - building, tabulating & book writing machines
Bartlett, George T. - lawyer
Battelle, Jonathan - general merchandise
Benton, D. B. & Son - general merchandise
Benton, L. & D. B. - general merchandise
Benton, Lucian - general merchandise
Benton, M. - general merchandise
Benton, M. S. & Sons - livestock, buggies, waggons, general
                      merchandise
Benton Supply Company - department store
Berckman, P. J. & Company - nurseries
Blackwell Brothers - groceries
Blanchard, K. & L. - general merchandise
Brooks, B. - groceries, liquor
Bryson, D. G. - lumber
Burney & Terrell - meat
Butler, G. D. - fertilizer
Buttrill, Gresham & Company - horses, Wagons, buggies
Camp, William J. - upholsterer, cabinet work, undertaker

Campbell, S. R. - undertaker supplies, vehicles
Carhart & Curd - hardware, iron & steel products
Carter, W. M. & Son - ammoniated phosphate
Cary, R. Frank - doctor
Cohen Dry Goods Co. - clothing
Cohen, Sam - general merchandise
Collier, P. F. & Son - publishers
Commercial Nurseries - shrubs and trees
Corley, J. T. - general merchandise
Cornwell, Roberts & Company - Buick and Overland autos
Cox, J. M. & Company - groceries
Davis, Leverett & Company - general merchandise
Driskell, B. W. - meat
Farmers Supply Company - general merchandise & farm supplies
Farmers Union Warehouse
Farrar & Pegg - doctors
Fears, J. W. & Company - wholesale grocers
Fears & Pritchett -
Flatan, M. - department store
Franklin Printing & Publishing Company
Frederick Disinfectant Company
Fuller & Rose - dry goods
Furse Drug Company
Glover, Eli & Company - dry goods
Goolsby, C. E. - groceries
Goolsby, Frank - general merchandise
Goolsby's Garage -
Goolsby, J. W. - groceries
Goolsby, W. L. - groceries
Greer Brothers - general merchandise
Hammond, D. F. & W. R. - lawyers
Hardeman & Sparks - cotton
Harris & Thurmond - dry goods
Harvey Hardware Company -
Harvey, J. D. - hardware, tinware, etc.
Hascall, J. A. & D. - dry goods
Hecht, J. E. - jeweler
Howard, J. T. -
Hungerford, A., Jr. -
Hunt, Rankin & Lamar - wholesale druggists
Jasper Trading Company - general merchandise
Jones, W. N. & Son - leather goods
Jordan & Co. - general merchandise
Jordan, Chas. D. - druggist & apothecary
Jordan Manufacturing Co. - lumber, building supplies
Jordan, Reuben - furniture
Kelly, J. H. - general merchandise
Kempton, E. L. - shoes
Lee, W. B. - general merchandise
Leverett, E. T. - groceries
Leverett, O. Euell - dray line
Levy, Asher - general merchandise
Loyd, G. P. - general merchandise
Malone & Downs - groceries
Malone, Ezell & Beaton - fire insurance
Malone, J. P. - groceries
Marshall & Bruce Co. -
May & Lewis - dry goods
Monticello Auto Co. - repair
Monticello Cafe & Market -
Monticello Cleaning Concern - dry cleaning, pressing, dyeing
Monticello Garage -
Monticello Grocery Co. - wholesale grocers

Monticello Hardware Co. -
Monticello Hotel -
Monticello Lights & Water Works
Monticello Meat Market -
Monticello News -
Moon Mercantile Co. - dry goods, undertakers
Morrison, Bain & Co. - foreign & domestic hardware
Moseley, W. R. - doctor
McMichael, W. S. & Co. - groceries
Oxford, W. C. - pipe
Pearman, Robert - dry goods
Penn Brothers - Monticello News, job & book printing
Penn, John Alex - dry goods
Persons, J. B. - meats
Persons, Phillips, Oxford - dept. store
Pitkin & Pearson - books
Pope, Hollis T. - insurance
Powell Brothers - groceries
Powell & Ellis - general merchandise
Powell, R. R. - bicycle shop, auto repairs
Powell, W. R. - groceries
Pye, D. T. - groceries
Read House - boarding house
Reese, W. H. - shoes
Richards, J. J. & S. P. - books, stationery, music
Roberts, O. G. -
Roberts & Peurifoy - groceries, miscellaneous merchandise
Robinson, A. M. & Co. - general merchandise
Robinson, Kelly Co. - general merchandise, farm supplies
Roby, P. M. - druggist
Ross, B. F. - furniture, carpets, etc.
Sharman, John -
Shaw, A. - furniture
Smith, L. C. & Brothers - typewriters
Smith, S. J. - dentist
Southern Bell Telephone & Telegraph Co. -
Spearman, Wesley -
Stewart & Fain - general merchandise
Talmadge, S. C. - general merchandise
Talmadge & Tolleson - wagons, buggies
Taylor, J. A. - prescription druggists
Teddards, C. M. - cotton
Thompson, Aaron P. - cotton
Thompson, C. F. - sheep
Thompson, Wm. H. - general merchandise
Tolleson, J. G. - general merchandise
Tucker, J. D. - repairs
Turk, W. R. - groceries
Turner, Mrs. M. A. -
Vaughn, William - ferry
Warlick, J. & Son - stoves, mantels, etc.
Warren, Wallace & Co. - cotton
Webb, J. B. & Co. - liquor
White, N. B. & Co. - dry goods & clothing
Whitfield & Brown - general merchandise
Wyatt, George W. - cotton

JASPER COUNTY - DEFAULTING JURORS

Adams, George W.
Adams, James
Alexander, George
Avant, Henry
Avera, Alexander
Bailey, William H.
Barnwell, Henry
Barr, Isaac
Bartlett, James C.
Baynes, John H.
Beall, Doctor H.
Bearden, William
Benton, Abba
Benton, John
Blackwell, James F.
Blankenship, Reuben
Bostick, Charles D.
Broddus, Thomas C.
Burney, Charles C.
Callaway, James R.
Calvert, John M.
Campbell, C.E.F.W.
Carr, Samuel
Carter, Landon
Chaffin, John
Chafin, Moses
Chapman, Abner
Cheek, John W.
Cheek, W. R.
Cisson, Richard M.
Cook, John W.
Cornwell, Elijah, Jr.
Cornwell, Obadiah
Crabtree, John W.
Crawford, B.
Cunard, John
Curry, Thompson
Cuthbert, Alford
Davis, Thomas C.
Dawkins, George
Dawkins, Reuben
Daws, Joel
Faulkner, Maston
Fears, Robert
Fincher, Christopher
Flemister, John
Flemister, William L.
Gay, Sherrod H.
Gibson, John C.
Glover, Henry, Sr.
Glover, John E.
Goolsby, Kirby
Green, Bowling
Greer, Crawford H.
Gross, Ellison
Hardy, William P.
Harvell, Ransom
Hatcher, Uriah
Henderson, Samuel L.
Hines, Littleberry
Holsenbeck, Alexander

Huff, Hamlin
Hungerford, Anson, Jr.
Hurd, William S.
Johnson, David
Johnston, Thomas
Jordan, Fleming
Kelly, Beverly A.
Kinard, John
Kinard, George W.
Kirkpatrick, William
Kitchens, Joel
Lane, Augustus W.
Lane, Matthew P.
Lassiter, Brown
Latson, Robert
Lawrence, Leroy
Lewis, Thomas
Lindsey, John
Lindsey, Lemuel
Lindsey, Lewis F.
Long, George
Lynch, Grief
Lynn, William
Maddux, William D.
Malone, Cader
Miller, John
Minter, William S.
Mize, Joseph
Moye, Thomas W.
McDonald, William A.M.
McKissack, Isaac
McKleroy, Jacob
McMichael, John
Newton, Aris
Ogletree, Edwin
Osborn, James
Pain, John
Parker, Aaron
Parker, Zeal
Patterson, Job C.
Peacock, Merrell
Pennington, William B.
Persons, Benjamin
Persons, William P.
Phillips, Richard B.
Phillips, William
Phillips, William D.
Polk, Archibald L.
Post, G.
Powell, William R.
Price, Leroy M.
Price, Sterling
Reese, Cuthbert
Roberts, Henry
Roberts, L. W.
Ryan, Lewis
Shepherd, Abraham
Shy, Seaborn J.
Smith, Harrison J.
Smith, Samuel R.
Spear, Jesse

Spears, J.A.J.
Spears, John
Spears, Joshua B.
Spears, Robert
Stephens, Stephen
Stewart, J.L.
Sturdivant, Joel
Taylor, Richard
Thompson, Joseph
Trawick, Robert
Tucker, Warren J.
Varner, William
Vaughn, ?
Waldrop, Aaron
Walker, James R.
Walthall, Milton
P.
Warren, Bray
Warren, Thomas
Watters, A.J.
Wilburn, Samuel
J.
Wilkerson,
Eldred
Wilkes, Reuben
Williams, Daniel
Wilson, John S.
Wilson, John W.
Wilson, Leroy M.
Wommack, Elberry
Wynens, Elisha S.

Aaron, J. C.
  J. L.
  James C.
  John L.
  Mitchel
Abels, S. L.
Acree, W. B.
Adams, E. H.
Aiken, J. M.
  O. P.
  Ransom H.
Akens, R. H.
Akins, B. H.
Alexander, G. W.
  J. F.
  J. J.
  N. O.
  Newton
  R. W.
Alfriend, A. H.
Allen, A. J.
  Albert
  H. N.
  H. V. B.
  Harris
  Harris N.
  J. A.
  J. K.
  J. S.
  John S.
  R. C.
  Robert C.
  W. W.
Anderson, J. L.
Andrews, D. K.
  J. O.
  W. H.
  William
Annis, Jesse
Arnold, O. H.
  William H.
Atkinson, H. A.
Avington, Levi
Bailey, B.
  B. P.
  Clark
  R. L.
  W. C.
  William C.
  Z.
  Zachariah
  Zack
Ballard, Charles E.
  W. E.
Banks, H. D.
  O. O.
  Olinious
  Olinious O.
Barker, J. R.
  John R.
Barnes, Ed

Barnes, G. A.
  Homer
  John
  R. C.
  Robert C.
  T. G.
  T. H.
  Thomas H.
Barr, James W.
Barron, Ben
  Benjamin
  J. H.
  James H.
  T. C.
Bartlett, Charles L.
Bartley, W. T.
  William
Baxley, W. D.
Baynes, E. W.
  R. A.
  S. R.
  W. E.
Bearden, S. E.
Beckwith, W. A.
  W. B.
  William
Belcher, John M.
  O. R.
  Obadiah
  Obadiah R.
  Richard
  Russell
  W. D.
Benford, C. S.
  Cicero
  Joseph
  W. L.
Benton, A.
  Abbey (Abbie)
  D. B.
  Daniel B.
  H. C.
  J. B.
  J. Ben
  J. L.
  J. T.
  James
  James T.
  L.
  L. O.
  Lucien
  M.
  M. S.
  Marcellus
  Milton
  O.
  O. M.
  Ossian
  Otis M.
  W. C.
Berner, Robert S.

Berner, W. R.
  William R.
Berry, A. T.
Bickers, J. T.
Binford, B. W.
  Benjamin W.
  E. A.
  Ike W.
  Porter
  S. W.
  T. S.
  Thad
Blackwell, C. D.
  C. Q.
  D. C.
  H. C.
  H. F.
  Hensley
  J. H.
  J. M.
  J. W.
  Jack
  John H.
  S. S.
  Samuel S.
  T. G.
  Thomas
  Thomas G.
  W. F.
  Walker
  William F.
Bogan, C. P.
  Caswell P.
Gonner, A. J.
  T. R.
Boon, John A.
Bowden, D. H.
  J. T.
  R. B.
Braddy, W. E.
Bradley, J. L.
  Louie
  Mat
  W. M.
Bridges, F. M.
Brittain, J. R.
  Jack
Broddus, ?
  T. C.
  Thomas C.
Brooks, H.
  Hiram
  Joseph
Brown, C. D.
  Henry L.
  Russel J.
  T. J.
  W. D.
  W. J.
Bryant, C.
  C. N.

Bryant, Columbus
  D. W.
  H.
  H. J.
  J. L.
  Jefferson L.
  L. P.
Bullard, H. W.
  J. H.
  S. H.
  W. M.
Burks, B. M.
Burner, Bobie
Burney, A. H.
  C. C.
  C. R.
  Charles C.
  G. W.
  George W.
  J. H.
  J. L.
  J. W.
  John W.
  Joseph
  Joseph H.
Burton, H. W.
Bussey, C. L.
Byars, G. W.
  J. M.
Campbell, Ashley
  C. C.
  C. H.
  E. D.
  E. G.
  E. H.
  E. L.
  Elbert
  Frank
  J. F.
  J. J.
  J. L.
  James
  James H.
  James L.
  John
  John J.
  M. O.
  Oscar
  R. D.
  S. R.
  W. C.
Cardell, J. B.
  J. C.
  J. J.
  J. L.
  John
  John C.
  Otis
  W. J.
  William
Cargol, J. W.
Carrell, Redman
Carter, W. M.

Cary, Charles A.
  D. T.
  J. A.
  Job A.
Chaffin
  (Chafin), H.F.
  H. Lee
  J. J.
  J. T.
  R. G.
  T. L.
  T. P.
  Thomas P.
  V. A.
  Virgil
Chambers, C. G.
Chapman, B. W.
Charping, F. H.
  Preston
  S. C.
Chatman, H. H.
  Henry
Cheek, Ellis
  N. H.
  T. J.
  Thad
  W. R.
  William R.
Childs, Green
  N. H.
  Robert
Claiborn, T. B.
Clark, Robert W.
Clay, F. M.
  Jesse
  O. J.
Clements, W. M.
Cochran, J. W.
  John W.
  W. A.
  W. B.
  W. D.
Cofer, Robert
Cohen, S.
  Sam
Comer, George W.
  J. S.
  Lewis
Coile, J. G.
Conley, James
Cook, B. W.
  Bogan
  David
  George
  Hardy
  J. B.
  J. W.
  John B.
  John L.
  L. E.
  P. B.
  R. D.
Cornwell, C. L.

Cornwell, D. L.
  Davis L.
  G. H.
  Gip
  J. C.
  James L.
  W. D.
  William D.
Couch, G. W.
  J. P.
  N. H.
  N. J.
Cox, W. S.
Craine, Marcus L.
Crawford, M. N.
Crutchfield, Ben
  Henry
Cunard, A. C.
  Elbert
  J. S.
  Jewey (?)
  John
  Jumina
  Newton
Curry, Robert
Daniel, Fredrick
Darden, James M.
Davidson, B. M.
  J. R.
  John
  John R.
Davis, D. M.
  Drew M.
  Fletcher
  G. H.
  G. M.
  J. M.
  J. W.
  R. L.
  Sam
  T. F.
  Wm. W.
Dawkins, G. W.
  George W.
Dawson, W. R.
Deason, Benjamin
Dennis, J. H.
  T. P.
  W. E.
Dewberry, T. D.
Dick, Levi W.
Digby, B. T.
  Clinton
  J. B.
  J. H.
  J. M.
  James
  James H.
  John
  John B.
  Lawrence
  W. B.
Dillard, George

Dooley, B. F.
  T. W.
Doster, J. W.
  T. P.
Dozier, A. A.
  Abner C.
  George B.
  W. B.
Driskell, B. W.
  Henry
  J. T.
  James
  James T.
Duke, B. H.
Dyer, John R.
Edwards, C. M.
  Edwin
  H. V.
  John
  John W.
  R. R.
  R. S.
  Robert
  Robert L.
  Robert S.
  S. B.
  Samuel
Elder, B. F.
  C. N.
  J. E.
  James
  James E.
  P. M.
Ellis, A. W.
  Allen
  Allen W.
  C. E.
  E. C.
  G. B.
  J. H.
  John H.
  Joshua
  O. L.
  R. M.
  S. W.
  Samuel
  W. F.
  Whit
  William F.
Eskew, S. B.
Evans, Pat
Ezell, B. R.
  B. R., Jr.
  Braxton
  C. T.
  E. H.
  Frank
  H. E.
  H. H.
  J. H.
  J. R.
  John H.
  L. D.

Ezell, Lee D.
  Levi D.
  Powel
  R. F.
  R. P.
  Robert F.
  Robert P.
  W. B.
  W. P.
  William B.
  Willie
Farrar, Abel
  B. K.
  Benjamin
  Otis
Faulkner, C. M.
  Charles
  H. D.
  J. H.
  J. P.
  John H.
  P. M.
  Persens
  Peter
  Peter M.
  Purse
Fincher, J. J.
  Jack
Fish, N. C.
  Nathan C.
  W. T.
  William T.
Flatan, Morris
Florence, Adial S.
  F. A.
  T. S.
Flournoy, S. A.
  Samuel
  Samuel A.
Floyd, A. S.
Folds, Basil
  Bascom
  Baswell
  G. W.
  J. F.
  James
  W. L.
  William
Franklin, Carter
  Dewitte
  F. H.
  Felix
  Hartwell
  J. C.
  John C.
  R. S.
  Rufus
Freeman, E. A.
  George
  I. H.
  Isaac H.
  M. L.
  Sam

Freeman, W. P.
Fullerton, G. E.
  S. M.
  Samuel
Fulton, Samuel
Funderburk, J. I.
Furse, R. L.
Garland, J. T.
  N. C.
  W. J.
Gay, E. H.
  Elbert H.
  J. W.
  John W.
Geiger, R. H.
  R. L.
  Randal
  Richard
Gilmore, J. H.
Gilstrap, J.
  J. M.
Glawson, A.
Glover, D. R.
  Eli S.
  H. S.
  Henry S.
  Lewis
Goggins, G. T.
  J. S.
  John S.
  Mat
Golden, J. O.
Goodman, G. T.
  J. T.
  J. W.
  James T.
  Jim T.
  John T,
  R. H.
Goolsby, A.
  Alfred
  B. E.
  C. D.
  C. J.
  C. K.
  C. L.
  C. R.
  C. Reese
  Cardin J.
  Cardin R.
  Clayton
  Cullen
  Ezell S.
  F. C.
  Franklin
  Harol
  Hartwell
  J. B.
  J. C.
  J. K.
  J. R.
  James B.
  John K.

Goolsby, Levi
  M. C.
  R. H.
  R. P.
  Rick
  Roswell
  W. B.
  W. T.
  Wade
Gordon, John
  W. R.
Grant, J. C.
  W. T.
Gray, A. T.
  Albert T.
Green, E. A.
  Joseph
Greer, A. C.
  C. H.
  Crof H.
  J. L.
  Jasper
  John R.
  N. H.
  R. C.
  R. J.
  R. J. J.
  W. G.
  Wm. G.
Gregory, J. T.
  John T.
Griggs, R. C.
  Wesley
Grubbs, J. W.
  John W.
  Thomas E.
  W. B.
Hales, A. O.
Hall, G. W.
Hancock, W. H.
  William
Hardeman, Charles
  S. F.
Harden, J. M.
Hardy, A. D.
  Alfred D.
  Aquila
  Benaja
  C. H.
  C. M.
  Cornelius
  H.
  J. D.
  J. G.
  J. J.
  J. L.
  J. P.
  J. T.
  James D.
  James P.
  John L.
  N. H.
  W. G.

Hardy, W. P.
  Wm. P.
Harper, R. L.
Harris, D.
  David
  Milton
Harrison, J. W.
Harvey, Davis
  H. H.
  J. D.
Hartwell, H. D.
Harwell, W. H.
Hatfield, J. B.
  Joe
  W. B.
  W. B. M.
Hays, H. C.
Hearn, C. C.
  F. L.
  W. S.
Hecht, J. E.
  S. A.
Henderson, C. G.
  C. L.
  Charles L.
  Clarence
  I. W.
  Isaac
  Isaac W.
  J. W.
  James
  Joe
  L.
  M. F.
  S. F.
  S. J.
  S. L.
  Samuel
  Samuel J.
  Samuel L.
  W. H.
  W. P.
  Wallace
Hickman, H. W.
  Hull W.
  O. P.
  Oliver
Hicks, W. A.
Hill, H. C.
Hitchcock, E. A.
Hoard, R. K.
Hodge, C. L.
  D. R.
  Duke R.
  J. D.
Holland, B. C.
  E. G.
  J. A.
  J. H.
  J. W.
  J. Washington
  James W.
  O. F.

Holland, Thomas R.
Holloway, D. P.
  Dabney P.
  J. M.
  James M.
  John
  M.
  Maston
  Newton
  Oliver
  W. L.
Holsenbeck, Alex
  Dan
  J. D.
  Marshall
Holstein, Alex
Honeycut, J. E.
Hooks, F. M.
Hooper, N. W.
Hoeton, H. A.
  Harries A.
  Seaborn
  Seaborn A.
Howard, J. B.
  J. T.
  James
  James B.
  W. S.
  William
Huff, Davis
  James
  T. J.
Hunnicutt, J. T.
Hunter, A. A.
  Alexander A.
Hutchings, R. E.
  Robert E.
Hutchins, E.
Hutchison, T. A.
  T. L.
  Thomas L.
Hyatt, L. P.
Ivey, James
  R. W.
Ivy, James
  R. L.
  Robert
  Robert W.
Jeffries, J. H.
Jenkins, F. E.
  J. H.
  W. E.
Johnson, Alfred
  B. D.
  J. H.
  J. Mon
  M. L.
  R. L.
  Reese L.
  S. A.
  S. H.
  Snelling

Johnston, Alfred
  R. L.
  S. H.
  Snelling
  Stephen
  Stephen H.
Jones, A. J.
  J. A.
  J. R.
  J. W.
  James
  James W.
  John W.
  Oscar
  R. A.
  W. C.
  W. N.
  Wiley
Jordan, A. H.
  Bonner
  C. H.
  C. Harvie
  Charles S.
  E. H.
  Erasmus H.
  H. B.
  H. J.
  H. S.
  Henry B.
  Hunter
  J. F.
  R.
  Rubin
  T. M.
  Thomas M.
  W. F.
  W. F., Jr.
  W. H.
  W. J.
Kelly, B. A.
  B. C.
  B. G.
  Beverly A.
  C. H.
  E. D.
  E. H.
  E. Harvey
  G. W.
  I. T.
  Ike T.
  J. A.
  J. B.
  J. H.
  J. R.
  J. T.
  John
  John A.
  John H.
  John R.
  John T.
  John W.
  Julian
  L. S.

Kelly, Lucius
  M. C.
  P. P.
  S. C.
  S. J.
  W. A.
  W. B.
  W. G.
  William G.
Kennon, T. H.
Key, Burrel
  John H.
  L. H.
  M. B.
  T. C.
Kilgore, James
  James E.
Kinard, J. J.
  M.
  M. J.
  Martin J.
  Michael
  Mike
Kinard, W. W.
King, B. G.
  B. P.
  Burrel G.
  G. N.
  Richard
  W. H.
  William H.
Kitchens, Joel
Lancaster, J. A.
  O. E.
Lane, A. G.
  A. W.
  C. Q.
  C. T.
  E. D.
  J. D.
  J. F.
  J. H.
  J. L.
  J. M.
  J. O.
  James M.
  John F.
  L. A.
  P. H.
  T. B.
  T. Ben
  W. A.
  W. D.
  Walter
  William L.
Langston, D. M.
  David M.
  Isaac
Lawrence, A. T.
  Allen T.
  H. C.
  H. P.
  J. L.

Lawrence, S. C.
  S. L.
Layfield, J. M.
Lazenby, Jeff
  Jefferson
  R. G.
Letson, George A. D.
  John
  Robert
Leverett, A. J.
  B.
  B. F.
  D. D.
  E. T.
  Eli
  J. H.
  Jack
  N. H.
  Nathan H.
  William C.
Lewis, H. C.
  Henry C.
  J. T.
  James T.
  W. O.
  W. W.
  William O.
Lindsey, L. F.
  Lewis F.
Lloyd, G. P.
  P. B.
Long, David
  John
  William E.
Lovejoy, J. D.
  John D.
  Sidney A.
Loyd, E. L.
  G. P.
  G. W.
  George P.
  J. M.
  P. B.
  R. L.
  Robert
  W. S.
  William A.
Lumsden, C. A.
Lunceford, John W.
Lunsford, J. M.
Lynch, Fleetwood
  Greif
  W. H.
  William
Maddux, A. B.
  Abram
  E. H.
  Emory
  J. C.
  J. L.
  James L.
  John C.
  S. H.

Maddux, Whitfield
Malone, A. B.
  A. L.
  A. M.
  C. O.
  C. W.
  Clarence O.
  E. B.
  E. T.
  Eli
  F.
  F. J.
  Floyd
  Frank
  Franklin
  Isham
  J. B.
  J. P.
  J. S.
  John B.
  L. A.
  P. C.
  P. W.
  R. A.
  S. B.
  S. F.
  S. H.
  S. J.
  Steve
  Stith B.
  T. J.
  T. R.
  T. S.
  Thomas
  Thomas S.
  W. B.
  W. F.
  W. H.
  W. W.
  William
  William H.
Marks, F. C.
  J. J.
Marsh, A.
  Alfred
  R. L.
Marshall, A. J.
Martin, H. M.
  Hugh M.
  J. B.
Mason, H.
Maxey, William
Mayo, R. D.
Mercer, A. L.
  Andrew
  Lee
  W. A.
  Whit
  Will
Meriwether, C. M.
  Charles
  David
  George F.

Meriwether, T. M.
  Thomas
  W. T.
Middlebrooks, C. F.
  J. A.
  S. H.
  Silas
  W. H.
  W. P.
  William H.
Millen, A. C.
  A. D.
  H. D.
  Henry D.
  R. E.
  Reuben
Minne, S. I.
Minter, A. J.
  A. P.
  J. W.
  John
  John W.
  O. J.
  P. W.
  R. A.
  Richard
  Robert
  T. C.
  Thomas C.
  W. R.
  W. S.
Mobley, R. M.
Moore, W. H.
  W. R.
Moseley, A. F.
  J. H.
  John H.
  Pleas
Murphy, J. F.
Murrell, R. D.
McCart, C. M.
McClelland, John
  T. B.
  Thomas
McClendon, J. A.
  J. C.
  J. H.
  Joel
  Joel A.
  John
McClure, A. P.
  H.
  H. C.
McCullough, E. B.
  John
McDowell, F. D.
  Frank D.
  J. C.
  Joel C.
  M. A.
McElhaney, John
McElhenny, B. B.
  B. E.

McElhenny, B. F.
  B. T.
  F. M.
  George W.
  Herbert
  J. H.
  Jefferson
  M. J.
  M. T.
  Martin
  Martin J.
  S. O.
  V. H.
  W. G.
  W. H.
  W. O.
McGahee, Ridley
McGaughey, R. W.
  W. A.
McGee, T. W.
McHenry, William S.
McIntosh, W. J.
McKinley, E. B.
  W. T.
McKison, William O.
McKissack, Isaac
  Thomas
  William
McMichael, B. E.
  Bedford
  C. O.
  Earnest
  G. G.
  G. L.
  Green
  J. F.
  J. G.
  J. M.
  Monroe
  P. B.
  Pollard B.
  S. E.
  S. L.
  Vines
  W. J.
McMillen, G. A.
McMullen, L. W.
McNair, H. S.
Newton, Aris
  C. A.
  E. E.
  G. T.
  G. W.
  George W.
  James
  L.
  Lucien B.
  O. H.
  Oliver
  Richard
  Willis
Niblett, Charles
  J. H.

Niblett, James
  James H.
  John H.
  Robert
  S. J.
  Tilmon
Noles, D. G. G.
  David
Osborn, E. C.
  Elbert
Osburn, Burney
  Thomas
  Thomas O.
Oxford, C. W.
  Charles W.
  E. J.
  Ed
  Edward
  R. L.
  T. B.
  Thomas J.
Parker, A. J.
  C. R.
  J. M.
  S. R.
Patrick, T. W.
Paul, W. E.
Payne (Paine),
  J. A.
  John
  T. M.
  Tomas
Peacock, W. C.
Pearson, J. W.
  John W.
  W. A.
Pendergrass, H. N.
  N. H.
Penn, Alex J.
  R. J.
  S. A.
  T. R.
  Thomas R.
  W. C.
  William C.
Pennington, A. F.
  J. L.
Perry, Dwin
  E. F.
  Ed F.
  J. R.
  James R.
  O. H.
Persons, B.
  Benjamin
  G. W.
  George W.
  J. B.
  L. M.
  R. F.
  Randolph
  T. B.
  W. F.

Persons, W. P.
  William P.
Peurifoy, B. W.
  Benjamin
  Benjamin W.
  F. W.
  J. B.
  J. W.
  James
  McCarrol
  R. L.
Phillips, J. B. M.
  J. M.
  J. M. B.
  Monroe
  N. H.
  Oscar
  R. B.
  R. F.
  Richard
  W. H.
  W. J.
  Wiley
Pinnell, John O.
Piper, E. W.
  T. L.
  Thomas
  W. E.
  Zadock
  Zed
Pitts, C. C.
  C. N., Jr.
  Carrington
  Nestor
  Owlin
Polk, C. W.
  H. A.
  J. K.
  J. T.
  James K.
  T. W.
  T. W. O.
  Thomas
  Thomas W.
  W. H.
Pope, C. W.
  Charles
  Charles W.
  Clarance
  Clark
  D. W.
  E. C.
  Edgar C.
  J. C.
  J. J.
  J. L.
  James
  James C.
  James J.
  John C.
  L. L.
  M. W.
  R. C.

Pope, S. M.
  T. C.
  Thomas C.
  W. K.
  W. R.
  W. Ross
  William K.
  William R.
Porter, F. R.
Post, J. W.
Potter, A. C.
Potts, S. P.
Pound, T. G.
Powell, A. W.
  Augustus W.
  E. H.
  Evan H.
  W. R.
Powers, G. T.
Preston, C. T.
  Charles T.
  T. C.
  W. B.
  W. J. M.
Price, L. M.
  L. R.
  Leroy M.
  O. D.
  Robert W.
Pritchett, E. H.
  George
  Thomas J.
Pullam, J. W.
Pyars, G. W.
Pye, Durwood
  Hannan
  J. E.
  John
  John E.
  T. W.
  Thomas W.
  W. H.
Rainey, John W.
Redd, B. A.
Reese, Lucius L.
Reeves, Joseph
Reid, S. T.
  Samuel T.
  W. A.
  William A.
Rhea, D. A.
Ricketts, T. O.
Ridley, C. L.
  H. B.
  W. T.
Rigdon, H. J.
Roberts, Charles
  E.
  E. R.
  J. A.
  J. H.
  J. W.
  James H.

455

Roberts, John W.
  L. A.
  L. W.
  Leonidas A.
  O. G.
  P. A.
  Paul
  S. J.
  Sam J.
  W. O.
  W. V.
Robinson, A. M.
  H. V.
  Hershell V.
  J. B.
  J. L.
  James C.
  John L.
  W. M.
Roby, P. M.
  W. A.
  William A.
Rosser, C. B.
Rowe, J. G.
Russell, George
Sanders, Brown
  S. B.
  W. E.
Seymore, John R.
Shaw, J. S.
  Joseph S.
  R. A.
  Robert A.
  W. A.
Shipp, G. V.
Shockley, G. W.
Shropshire, C. H.
  J.
  J. W.
  John
  W. D.
  W. W.
Shy, J. M.
  Mallard
  P. R.
  Peter
  Peyton R.
  S. C.
  S. J.
  T. P.
  W. N.
  W. V.
Sigman, M.
Sluder, J. H.
Smith, A. C.
  A. D.
  A. H.
  Abram
  Abram H.
  Allen C.
  B. R.
  Boykin R.
  Durell

Smith, Edward B.
  Guy
  H. J.
  H. T.
  Henry T.
  Idus
  J. R.
  J. W. A.
  Jefferson
  M. R.
  N. L.
  N. P.
  Niles L.
  R. H.
  R. L.
  Rufus
  S. R.
  Samuel, Jr.
  Samuel R.
  T. J.
  W. R.
Spearman, Fletcher
  George C.
  J. F.
  John F.
  M. W.
  Mathew W.
  W.
  William
  William F.
  William H.
Spears, A. F.
  A. M.
  Alonzo
  C. M.
  Caleb
  J. A.
  J. A. J.
  J. B.
  J. M.
  J. N.
  Joshua
  Joshua A.
  Joshua B.
  Mixon
  Nathan
  S. P.
  T. L.
  W. H.
  William
  Willie
Speights, J. C.
  James
  John
  John C.
  Joseph
Spivey, T. C.
Steel, J. W. J.
  John N.
  S. J.
  S. W.
  Samuel W. J.
  W. H.

Stokes, Columbus
Stone, H. P.
  J. A.
  James
  M. P.
  W. M.
Swanson, E. Y.
  F. J.
  F. M.
  Walker
Talmadge, A. J.
  Albert J.
  C. A.
  H.
  Herbert
  J. E.
  J. H.
  J. M. H.
  John
  John H.
  R. S.
  S. C.
  Stephen C.
  W. J.
  William
Taylor, George
Tedders, G. W.
  George W.
Thomason, A. J.
  D. C.
  J. C.
Thompson, A. P.
  C. F.
  C. S.
  Charles F.
  E. H.
  Hamlin
  J. H.
  J. M.
  J. M., Jr.
  Joseph M.
  L. F.
  M. H.
  Matthew
  S. L.
  T. W.
  Thomas W.
  W. H.
  W. L.
  William H.
Thomson, M. H.
Thornton, H. A.
  J. D.
  J. W.
Tillmon, George
Tilman, E. L.
  J. H.
  John H.
Tingle, W. A.
  William A.
Tolen, J. W.
Tolleson, J.
  J. G.

Tolleson, J. J.
  Joe
  Joseph
Tomlinson, J. D.
  J. J.
  John B.
  S. D.
  W. M.
  William
Tucker, A. L.
  Crayton
  Elmer
  W. A.
  W. J.
  W. R.
Turk, E. B.
  T. J.
Turner, J. W.
  John D.
  R. F.
  S. W.
  T. A.
  T. A. B.
  W. T.
Tyler, A. A.
  Albert
  B. F.
  F. M.
  Francis M.
  G. W.
  George
  J. J.
  J. J., Jr.
  J. M.
  Job
  Job, Jr.
  Job M.
  John J.
  M. D.
  Martin
  Mike B.
  Will
Tyner, H. F.
  R. J.
Tyson, H. F.
Varnum, William C.
Vaughn, J. N.
Vining, J. A.
  J. F.
Wagner, J. W.
Waits, Alex
  Flem
  J. R. W.
  J. W.
  Joshua
  Levi
  W. B.
  W. J.
  William
  William B.
Waldrep, A. J.
  E. N.
  J. A.

Waldrep, John D.
  Kirby
  Oscar
Waldrup, G. W.
  J. L.
  J. S.
  J. T.
Walker, A. S.
  Felix
  J. F.
  James F.
  W. H.
Waller, D. F.
  J. M.
  J. S.
  R. D.
Wamack, James
Ward, F. J.
  Fleming J.
Warren, W. C.
Waters, J. T.
  T. J.
Watters, A. J.
Weaver, R. J.
  Robert
Webb, G. G.
  J. B.
  J. F.
  John B.
  P. A.
  Samuel J.
  Thomas
Weems, Freeman
Weights, William
Wellington, C. E.
White, A. B.
  A. J.
  G. W.
  J. B.
  J. F.
  J. M.
  J. P.
  James F.
  Lucien
  N. B.
  Nehemiah B.
  W. A.
  W. P.
Whitten, H. W.
  Henry
  Levi
  W. C.
Wilburn, L. C.
  S. C.
  Sam, Jr.
  Samuel J.
Williams, D. M.
  G. P.
  George
  George P.
  J. E.
  J. M.
  J. P.

Williams, J. S.
  J. W.
  James M.
  John
  Milton
  P. M.
  Pleasant M.
  T. R.
  Thomas K.
  Thomas R.
  W. L.
  W. S.
  Willie
Willingham, Taylor
  Theophilus
Willis, O. B.
Wilson, C. T.
  Gus
  J. B.
  James
  M. S.
  T. S.
  V. A.
  Vines
Womack, Seaborn
  Sid
Wood, J. L. G.
Wyatt, I. T.
  Isaac T.
  W. H.
Wynens, E. L.
  Elisha L.
  Robert
Wynn, A. L.
  Asa
  Ed
  J. W.
  W. D.
Yancey, Jekonias
  T. J.
Zachry, W. L.

Aaron, Clarissa vs. Horace Vann and Dianna Vann
Banks, Henry D. vs. Drew M. Davis
Baynes, John H., Elbert W. Baynes, James Y. Baynes and Arrington
  Turk vs. James Barrett and Drusilla Barrett
Bridges, Bennet, Mary Bridges and William H. Head vs. Thomas
  Bridges
Brooks, Hiram vs. John Watters
Buckner, William vs. Alice Buckner
Bullard, John W. vs. Matilda Bullard
Cary, Job A. vs. Allen Goolsby
Clark, Amanda vs. Martha Gilstrap
Clark, Ellen vs. Officers of Court
Cook, John S. vs. J. W. McDade
Darden, James F. and B. F. Watkins vs. W. T. McElmurry
Dawkins, George W. vs. Campbell and Jones
Digby, B. T. vs. W. L. McMichael
Dodds, James vs. Rollin Smith and Harriet Smith
Ezell, Lucy Grace vs. William B. Ezell
Finney, Caroline vs. Mary Dozier
Folds, Boston vs. Elvira Driskell
Freeman, William vs. R. A. Shaw
Gibson, Martha, Abraham H. Smith, Samuel Ellis, Karon H. Ellis,
  Glen B. Ellis, John Ellis, Joshua Ellis, Mary Hawk, Thomas H.
  Hawk, Josephine Hawk, James Hawk and William F. Ellis vs. John
  C. Gibson and James M. Williams
Goolsby, Sarah (col) vs. Allen Goolsby (col)
Hardy, Phoebe (col) vs. William Broddus (col)
Harris, Milton vs. Frank Aaron (col)
Hay, William T., George D. Johnson and David H. Johnson vs.
  William H. Stone and Thomas Stone
Holland, Eunice A. vs. Georgia H. Whitfield
Johnston, Nathan and William M. Johnston vs. James M. Clower,
  Lucy (Johnston) Clower, Madison Goggins, Biddy (Johnston)
  Goggins, Thomas W. Moy and Frances E. (Johnston) Moy
Key, George M. and John Key, Jr. vs. Stephen Nolley (col)
Key, Mikajah B. vs. George D. Gordon
Lawrence, Leroy, Seaborn Lawrence and William K. Pope vs. William
  R. Lawrence
Lazenby, J. G. vs. C. C. Layson
Lazenby, William and Francis M. Swanson vs. M. A. Lazenby and
  M. E. Lazenby
Letson, Robert vs. Wilcox, Gibbs and Co.
Malone, Floyd vs. R. J. J. Greer
Meador, A. D. vs. Officers of Court
Meriwether, Louise and G. T. Meriwether vs. F. M. Tyler
Middlebrooks, Aaron (col) vs. Officers of Court
McMichael, Burton J., Shadrack J. McMichael and Clark W.
  McMichael vs. P. B. McMichael, Emily R. McMichael, Mary A.
  McMichael, Clementine N. McMichael, Caroline S. McMichael,
  Alice C. McMichael, John W. Chambers and Sarah A. Chambers
McMichael, Green vs. Caroline McMichael
McMichael, John L. and Fleming Mobley vs. James J. Johnston
Penn, Thomas R. vs. William C. Penn and William F. Jordan
Penn, William C. vs. Salina Penn
Penn, William C. and W. F. Jordan vs. T. R. Penn
Phillips, William and Richard B. Phillips vs. Ellen C. Middle-
  brooks and William S. Phillips
Pye, Florrie E. and Thomas W. Pye vs. R. F. Persons
Ramey, Clarissa (col) vs. Charles Meriwether (col)
Roby, Walter and M. S. Benton vs. Addie L. Roby
Shaw, William vs. John M. Allen

Slaughter, Thomas K. and Matilda Slaughter vs. Leroy Waits and
    William B. Waits
Smith, Felix vs. Adam Nix
Spiller, Rosetta vs. Sophia Hester
Standifer, Curn and Benjamin Barron, Jr. vs. J. H. Holland
Stewart, James and John S. Stewart vs. George T. Pursley
Taylor, Wiley vs. Officers of Court
Thomas, Lewis vs. Warren Daniel
Thomason, J. C. vs. Samuel A. Flournoy
Vining, E. H. vs. Officers of Court
Wagner, H. Lee vs. W. A. Wagner
Williams, Thomas B. vs. Thomas G. McDowell
Williams, Thomas R. vs. Sooky Falkner
Willingham, William and William Johnson vs. Isaac Willingham
Yancy, Lewis D. and Phebe Yancy vs. John Horton and Mary Horton

JASPER COUNTY DEEDS - SLAVES

NOTE: In Record Group 179-12-10 there is a register of Free
Persons of Color (Box 13). The deeds listed in Chapter XI have
a special index to slaves in Record Group 179-1-6 (Box 3).

GRANTOR	GRANTEE	DATE RECORDED
Beall, Jeremiah	John Wood	2/23/1813
Bugg, Anselm	Norborne B. Powell	2/10/1821
Callaway, Elizabeth	Jonathan Callaway	3/3/1823
Cobb, John	Milledge M. Gay	no date
Crawford, Hinton	Mary B. Shy	2/6/1862
Deane, George	Nathaniel Deane	8/7/1817
Deane, George	Nathaniel Deane	10/19/1816
Deane, Nathaniel	Polly Deane	6/22/1816
Edmondson, John	Moses Hairston	no date
Freeman, Josiah	John R. Dickes	no date
Glenn, Simeon G.	Matthew H. Glenn	1/11/1833
Godley, James	John Willson	5/14/1821
Godwin, Mary H.	Algornon G.A. Godwin	10/26/1831
Graybill, Henry	Hubbard Reynolds	1/25/1823
Hampton, George	Harriett McBride	5/3/1822
Hill, John	John Willson	no date
Hill, Mordecai	James Hill	2/1/1814
Hill, Mordecai	John Richeson	5/15/1818
Hill, Whitmell	James Harrison Hill	11/13/1815
Hornbuckle, Solomon	George Hornbuckle	1/28/1818
Johnson, Minor W. S.	Henry Walker	2/19/1809
Jones, William	George Dawkins	5/3/1841
Knight, John, Sr.-heirs	David A. Reese	3/2/1842
Loyd, Thomas	Richard J. Loyd	10/24/1820
Malone, Jarrett-heirs	Nancy Malone	no date
Miles, William	Jonathan Phillips	8/10/1812
Mitchell, Joshua	Martin Cochran	3/3/1819
Mitchell, Joshua	Henry Mitchell	2/25/1819
Mitchell, Joshua S.	John Willson	no date
McNeill, Archey	Sanders McNeill	10/9/1823
O'Kelly, Francis	Abihugh Sewell	3/1/1816
Potts, James, Sr.	Mary A. Crawford	2/25/1842
Powell, Archie	John Wood	6/12/1812
Smith, Fanny	Mary Banks	copy, no date
Smith, Stephen	James Smith	4/9/1823
Thompson, Joseph	Abihu Sewell	7/15/1817
Thurman, Philip	Susan Rivers	12/7/1835
Tilery, Thomas	Margrate Tilery	10/12/1819

Waits, Sarah-heirs	Benjamin Waits	no date
Wilson, Joseph	Micha Wilson	12/5/1822
Wynn, R. W.	P. A. Lewis	10/29/1821
McDonald, Alexander	Samuel Crockett	8/17/1824

JASPER COUNTY - MISCELLANEOUS DEEDS

Listed below in order is Grantor, Grantee, Item and Date recorded

Abbett, Ezekiel - William T. Smith - furniture - 6/2/1820
Avery, James - Abner Eason - cattle - 1/29/1812
Brantley, John W. - Ann Virdell - furniture, misc. - 6/19/1837
Dewberry, John - Mary Dewberry - furniture, stock - 12/8/1827
Dewberry, John - Nancy Dewberry - furniture, stock - 12/8/1827
Dewberry, John - William G. Dewberry - horse - 12/8/1827
Duke, David - William Patrick - horse - 5/3/1811
Farrow, Finch - Elijah Ray, etal - furniture, cows, horses,
  crops - 12/15/1819
Goolsby, C. R. - Annie E. Goolsby - horse - 3/16/1896
Morris, Nimrod - John Edwards - furniture - 12/18/1815
McLeroy, Mary - Nancy McLeroy - furniture, cattle, horses -
  8/2/1821
Porter, William - Nancy Alewine - furniture, notes - 11/14/1837
Smith, Fanny - James M. Trammel - furniture, note - no date
Smith, Leroy - Robert Johnston - crops - 11/20/1897
Steedman, Thomas - Nancy Worsham - furniture, cow - 5/16/1810
Terrell, Elizabeth - Louisa Gordon - furniture - 12/8/1827
Thompson, Nancy - John S. Thompson, etal - estate - 1/6/1836
Townsend, Samuel - Betsey Townsend - furniture, misc. stock -
  4/30/1811
Tucker, J. L. - So. Cotton Oil Co. - house - 3/3/1899
Wynn, Richmond W. - Pearce A. Lewis - crops - 10/29/1821
Wynn, Richmond W. - Pearce A. Lewis - furniture - 10/29/1821
Wynn, Richmond W. - Pearce A. Lewis - misc. stock - 10/29/1821

JASPER COUNTY - NOTES, MORTGAGES, ETC.

Listed below in order is: From, To, Document and Date

No name - Jasper County Bank - Note - 1907
Aaron, Richard A. - Mitchel Aaron - Security Deed - 1861
Aaron, Sarah A. T. - Swan, Stewart, Thompson - Note - no date
Adams, Jonathan, Sr. - William Laurence - Mortgage Deed - no date
Adgate, H. C. - Georgia Ann Hunter - Warranty Deed - 1898
Alford, Collin - Daniel Meadows - Promisory Note - no date
Alfriend, Cornelia L. - Edward H. Noyes - Warranty Deed - 1901
Alfriend, Cornelia L. - Edward H. Noyes - Real Estate Note - N.D.
Alfriend, Cornelia L. - Edward H. Noyes - Extension Agreement -
  no date
Allen, Dennis - Alexander Carter - Note - no date
Allen, John - Milton Harris - Lien - no date
Allen, Ned - Mrs. M. A. B. Crawford - Lien - no date
Allen, Orbie - W. F. Jordan - Mortgage - 1910
Allen, Square - W. F. Jordan - Mortgage - 1908
Andrews, Jerry - James Goolsby - Note - no date
Annis, Mrs. J. M. - Benton Supply Co. - Mortgage - 1903
Annis, Mrs. J. M. - Benton Supply Co. - Mortgage - 1903
Annis, Mrs. J. M. - Benton Supply Co. - Mortgage - 1902
Annis, Mrs. J. M. - Benton Supply Co. - Mortgage - 1902
Appling, William - Benton Supply Co. - Mortgage - 1905
Armstrong, John - Peter Brooks - Note - no date

Banks, Lee - S. H. Pope - Note - no date
Banks, Thomas - Robert Childs - Mortgage - 1886
Banks, Thomas - Robert Childs - Mortgage - 1888
Barnes, Berry - G. P. Loyd - Note - no date
Barnett, John L. - John K. Powell - Mortgage Deed - 1838
Barnett, Sion - Samuel Wilson - Note - no date
Barron, B. - H. P. Smith - Mortgage Lien - 1891
Baynes, John - John Amos Baynes - Mortgage - 1857
Baynes, R. A. - Jasper County Bank - Mortgage - 1904
Baynes, R. A. - Jasper County Bank - Mortgage - 1904
Baynes, R. A. - Liddell Co. - Note - 1906
Baynes, R. A. - Milledgeville Oil Mills - Mortgage Lien - 1903
Beavers, Joshua - Wm. D. Maddux - Mortgage - 1873
Bebee, Rube - Mont. V. Coffin Co. - Mortgage - no date
Benton, Boss - Milton Harris - Lien - no date
Benton, Eldred C. - Taylor Mosley - Warranty Deed - 1900
Benton, James - W. F. Jordan - Mortgage Deed - 1896
Benton, Stephen - W. A. Kelly & Bros. - Note - no date
Binford, Mitchell - Wynn & Clack - Note - no date
Blackwell, Elbert - E. P. Blackwell - Mortgage - 1882
Blackwell, H. C. - Monticello Vehicle Co. - Mortgage - 1905
Blackwell, J. C. - J. D. Persons & Bros. - Mortgage - 1909
Blackwell, John H. - Warren & Wallace Co. - Note - no date
Blackwell, N. E. - Armour Fertilizer Works - Mortgage - 1903
Blackwell, N. E. - Bank of Monticello - Mortgage - 1902
Blackwell, N. E. - Benton Supply Co. - Mortgage - 1903
Blackwell, N. E. - Home Trading Co. - Mortgage - 1907
Blackwell, N. E. - W. F. Jordan - Mortgage - 1902
Blackwell, Wesley - J. L. Tuggle - Mortgage - 1898
Bogan, Bell - E. B. Turk - Note - no date
Boykin, Joe - W. A. Kelly & Bros. - Note - no date
Boykin, Joe - W. A. Kelly & Bros. - Mortgage - 1888
Bradford, Edmond - Isaac Hill - Note - no date
Brandon, Carrie A. - H. J. Rigdon - Mortgage Deed - 1903
Brandon, Carrie A. - H. J. Rigdon - Mortgage - 1903
Brandon, Carrie A. - Martha E. Rodgers - Mortgage - 1905
Braziel, William - H. B. Ridley - Mortgage - 1866
Broddus, E. S. - Ebb Freeman - Lien - 1892
Broddus, E. S. - M. E. Rodgers - Mortgage - 1905
Brooks, James - George Lewis - Promisory Note - 1820
Brown, A. H. - William Bennett - Promisory Note - 1822
Brown, Andrew M. - John Crawford - Promisory Note - 1816
Brown, B. W. - Temple Lea - Promisory Note - 1807
Brown, Willis - Zacheus Averet - Promisory Note - 1817
Burk, W. P. - The Cable Co. - Mortgage - 1906
Burney, J. H. - J. M. Brabson - Promisory Note - 1885
Cable Co. - W. A. Epps - Quit Claim Deed - 1906
Campbell, Bill - J. S. Dumas - Mortgage - 1870
Cardell, Peter D. - Wm. C. Leverett - Mortgage - 1869
Cargile, Sallie - J. D. Persons - Mortgage - 1908
Cargile, Sallie - J. D. Persons - Mortgage - 1908
Cargile, Thos. - John T. Howard - Promisory Note - 1819
Carter, John W. - Augustus Hayward - Mortgage Deed - 1824
Childs, John A. D. - Parham P. Mabry - Note - no date
Childs, N. G. - Franklin Malone - Promisory Note - no date
Clements, Willie - The Hutchinson Co. - Mortgage - 1904
Cogswell, William - Edward Hill - Mortgage - 1857
Cohen, Sam - Dannenberg Co. - Mortgage - 1894
Cohen, Sam - Abe Cohen - Mortgage - 1899
Cohen, Sam - Abe Cohen - Mortgage - 1899
Cole, Robert - Anthony Dyer - Mortgage - 1827
Compton, John W. - Reuben Shorter - Note - no date
Connell, Wm. - William Askew - Note - no date

Cook, B. W. - R. L. Davis - Mortgage - 1899
Cook, B. W. - H. W. Doster - Note - no date
Cook, J. B. - Bank of Monticello - Mortgage - 1902
Cook, J. B. - L. O. Benton - Mortgage - 1901(2)
Cook, J. B. - Ike W. Brown - Mortgage - 1901 (2)
Cook, J. B. - L. O. Benton - Mortgage - 1902
Cook, J. B. - W. F. Jordan - Mortgage - 1902
Cook, J. B. - The Middle Georgia Bank - Mortgage - 1901
Cook, J. B. - The Middle Georgia Bank - Mortgage - 1902
Cook, Thomas L. - Persons, Phillips, Oxford Co. - Mortgage - 1913
Cordell, C. E. - J. D. Shaw - Lien - no date
Cornwell, W. D. - Dempsey & Manley - Security Deed - 1885
Coswell, W. C. - Benton Supply Co. - Mortgage - 1914 (2)
Crabb, H. A. - John Rowlin - Note - no date
Crabtree, Ezekiel - Silas Grubbs - Mortgage - 1854
Dawkins, George - Garland Dawkins - Mortgage - 1828
Digby, Berry T. - William F. Jordan - Security Deed - 1878
Digby, George - S. C. McMichael - Lien - no date
Digby, Isaac - Childs & Bailey - Note - no date
Digby, Isaac - Childs & Bailey - Mortgage - 1896
Digby, John B. - James M. Williams - Note - no date
Dingler, William - John Willson - Note - no date
Dismukes, John F. - Henry T. Smith - Note - no date
Driskell, William, Jr. - F. C. McCullugh - Mortgage - 1903
Dumas, William - Annie Goolsby - Security Deed - 1907
Edwards, John - Talmadge & Tolleson - Note - 1879
Elder, Monroe - Thomas J. Tyler - Mortgage - 1900
Epps, Edom - Madison Epps - Mortgage - 1899
Epps, Joe - Lucian Benton - Mortgage - 1898
"   "   "   "   "   "
"   "   "   "   "   "
"   "   "   "   "   1902
"   "   "   "   "   no date
"   "   "   "   "   1903
"   "   "   "   "   1896
"   "   "   "   "   1904
"   "   "   "   "   "
"   "   "   "   "   1905
Epps, Joe - J. W. Cannon - Mortgage - 1895
Epps, Joe - Jasper County Bank - Mortgage - no date
Etheridge, Janie - L. O. Benton - Security Deed - no date
Evans, Charlie - J. H. Campbell - Mortgage - no date
Farr, W. A. - J. M. Thompson - Landlord's Lien - 1900
Faulkner, Mary O. - Georgia Loan & Trust Co. - Warranty Deed - 1904
Fears, Claiborn - The Guano Co. - Note - no date
Ferguson, Neil - David Urquhart - Note - no date
Flemister, J. M. - G. W. Garrett - Security Deed - 1891
Flemister, J. M. - G. W. Garrett - Security Deed - 1890
Flennikon, Sam - Thomas Kennedy - Lien - no date
Flournoy, Callie - J. D. Persons - Mortgage - 1909
France, William C. - James W. Zuber - Lien - 1892
Freeman, W. M. - Chesapeake Guano Co. - Note - no date
Freeman, William - N. B. White - Note - no date
Gaither, H. C. - Pickney Kelly - Mortgage - 1888
Gaither, Robert - J. E. Pickett - Note - 1857
Garland, Mary Liza - Greene F. Johnson - Mortgage - 1905
Gaston, T. - Thos. C. Spivey - Mortgage - 1897
Gibson, John C. - Jesse Boon - Note - no date
Gibson, John C. - Henry Walker - Mortgage Deed - 1842
Gibson, John C. - Henry Walker - Mortgage Deed - 1840
Gilmore, J. G. - Jas. T. Benton - Security Deed - 1911
Glass, Henry - Chesapeake Guano Co. - Note - no date

Glover, Aaron - Walton Guano Co. - Lien - 1891
Glover, Charlie - H. N. White - Lien - no date
Glover, Charlie - J. M. Allen - Mortgage - 1898
Glover, Mary - M. C. Goolsby - Security Deed - 1899
Godly, James - Peter Johnson - Note - no date
Godwin, Samuel - Harris & Thurmond - Note - no date
Goolsby, A. - Emma Powell - Note - no date
Goolsby, Burgess - Cardin Goolsby - Security Deed - 1854
Goolsby, C. R. - Bank of Hillsboro - Mortgage - 1913
Goolsby, C. R. - Jasper County Bank - Mortgage - 1912
Goolsby, C. R. - Jasper County Bank - Mortgage - 1913
Goolsby, C. R. - Security Investment Co. - Escrow Deed - 1899
Goolsby, H. L. - J. S. Malone, Jr. - Mortgage - 1908
Goolsby, James - Cardin Goolsby - Mortgage Deed - 1853
Goolsby, James - Cardin Goolsby - Mortgage Deed - 1854
Goolsby, Marshall C. - Francis C. Goolsby - Warranty Deed -
  1898
Gordon, Joe - L. O. Benton - Mortgage - 1903
Grant, Alonzo - William T. Stone - Security Note - 1888
Gray, A. T. - W. B. Ezell - Note - 1909
Green, Thomas - T. P. King - Note - no date
Greer, Ida M. - T. L. Greer - Security Deed - 1901
Gregory, Mathew - Jarrel Beasley - Mortgage - 1820
Griggs, George - E. B. Ezell - Security Deed - 1912
Grubbs, Silas - John Edwards - Security Deed - 1840
Grubbs & Waits - Fears & Pritchett - Note - no date
Grubbs, Wiley B. - John R. Greer - Mortgage Deed - 1867
Hardy, James P. - Martha Spears - Note - no date
Hardy, C. M. - Warren & Wallace - Note - no date
  "   "   "   "   "   "   "   "
Harrell, Charles - James McKemie - Mortgage Deed - 1833
Harwell, Western - Green B. Walker - Note - no date
Hascall, Elijah - Peters & Harrison - Note - no date
Hawkins, C. R. - Benton Supply Co. - Note - 1914
Henderson, C. W. - Pendleton Guano Co. - Note - no date
Henderson, C. W. - Glidden & Curtis - Note - no date
Henderson, Hester - John Tillman - Warranty Deed - 1901
Hicks, Efrom - James Holloway - Note - no date
Hill, H. C. - T. L. Greer - Security Deed - 1905
Hill, H. C. - Augusta H. Lester - Security Deed - 1899
Hillard & Anderson - J. F. Malone
Hitchcock, William - William Biscoe - Security Deed - 1836
  "   "   "   "   "   " 1835
Hodge, Aaron - Milton Harris - Lien - no date
Holland, Henry J. - Obadiah Echols - Note - no date
Holloway, R. B. - Bank of Monticello - Mortgage - 1907
Holloway, R. B. - R. A. Malone - Mortgage - 1907
Holmes, Genus - A. T. Small & Sons - Mortgage Deed - 1914
  "   "   "   "   "   "   " 1913
  "   "   "   "   "   "   " 1914
  "   "   "   "   "   "   " 1915
  "   "   "   "   "   "   " 1914
  "   "   "   "   "   Note - no date
  "   " - R. E. Small - Security Deed - 1915
Holmes, James - A. J. Small & Sons - Mortgage Deed - 1915
  "   "   "   "   "   "   " 1913
  "   "   "   "   "   "   " 1914
  "   "   "   "   "   "   " 1913
  "   "   "   "   " - Note - no date
  "   "   "   "   "   "   "   "
Holmes, James - R. E. Small - Security Deed - 1915
Holoway, A. L. - John M. McElhenney - Lien - 1897
Holoway, Mittie D. - R. B. Holoway - Mortgage - 1895

Hudspeth, Airs - William C. Ware & Co. - Security Deed - 1818
Humber, Robert - Harris & Thurmond - Note - no date
Humphries, Milton - L. O. Benton Bros. - Security Note - no date
Hunnicutt, Jas. E. - E. Harvey - Note - No date
Jackson, William - John Jackson - Mortgage Deed - 1841
Jerots, Yarborough - Thomas J. Wray - Promisory Note - no date
Jinks, Mathew - Thomas Williams - Mortgage - no date
Johnson, Andrew - George W. Scott Mfg. Co. - Note - no date
Johnson, Burrel - Shady Dale Trading Co. - Mortgage - 1914
Johnson, H. G. - H. G. Webster - Promisory Note - no date
Johnson, Hugh G. - Hugh Stevens - Security Deed - no date
Jones, Georgeann - M. L. Bullard - Warranty Deed - 1900
Jones, Robert - John Hill & Co. - Mortgage - 1836
Jordan, Bonner - Farmers Bank - Security Deed - 1908
Jordan, Chris - W. B. Digby - Lien - no date
Jordan, E. H. - J. D. Harvey - Note - no date
Jordan, E. N. - Robert S. Talmadge - Note - no date
Jordan, J. F. - E. J. Jordan - Mortgage - 1895
Jordan, J. F. - Mary B. Jordan - Mortgage - 1900
Jordan, Jack - J. M. Campbell - Mortgage - 1894
Jordan, Jane - J. T. Williams - Promisory Note - no date
Jordan, Lott - A. H. Burney - Mortgage - 1896
Jordan, Lot - Madison Epps - Mortgage - 1900
Jordan, Ordelia - S. C. Clements - Mortgage - 1913
Jordan, Robert - H. B. Jordan - Note - 1878
Jordan, W. F. - John J. Campbell - Promisory Note - no date
Jordan, W. F. - Joseph Penn - Note - no date
Keeley, Jessie - Johnnie Broughton - Note - no date
Kelley, Marvel - Harris & Thurmond - Promisory Note - no date
Kellie, Pinkney - H. C. Gaither - Mortgage - no date
Kelly, Anna - J. L. Pitts - Mortgage - 1898
Kelly, J. F. - Avery & Co. - Note - 1905
Kelly, Pinkney - J. T. Aaron - Note - no date
Kelly, S. J. - F. A. Perry - Warranty Deed - 1895
Kello, S. B. - William & James Wommack - Mortgage Deed - no date
Key, Manerva - J. D. Hardy - Mortgage - 1900
Kimbrough, Shadrack - C. W. Rockwell - Mortgage Deed - 1833
Kinard, M. - Richard H. Goodman - Mortgage Deed - 1905
Langston, D. M. - L. O. Benton - Mortgage Deed - 1895
Langston, David M. - British & American Mtg. Co. - Warranty
    Deed - 1899
Lawrence, Lemuel O. - Lawson S. Holland - Mortgage Deed - 1827
Lawson, Thomas J. - A. V. Mann - Note - no date
Lovejoy, J. D. - James T. Corley - Note - no date
Lovejoy, Welcom C. - John W. Wyatt - Mortgage Deed - no date
Maddux, E. M. - Green C. Tucker - Note - no date
Malone, A. M. - Michigan Carbon Works - Note - no date
Malone, A. M. - Walton Co. Guano Co. - Lien - 1891
Malone, E. B. - Bank of Monticello - Mortgage - 1903
Malone, E. B. - British & American Mtg. Co. - Warranty Deed -
    1905
Malone, E. B. - I. W. Brown - Mortgage - 1901
Malone, J. F. - Avery & McMillan - Note - 1901 (2)
Malone, J. F. - Bank of Monticello - Mortgage - 1901
Malone, J. F. - Bank of Monticello - Mortgage - 1903
    "   "   "   "   "   Note   "
    "   "   "   "   "   "   "
    "   "   A. Benton   "   1906
    "   "   J. T. Benton   "   no date
    "   "   Ossian Benton   "   1904
    "   "   J. D. Harvey   "   1905
    "   "   Jasper County Bank - Mortgage - 1900
    "   "   "   "   "   "   1904

Malone, J. F. - Jasper County Bank - Mortgage - 1899
"   "   "   "   "   "   "
Malone, J. H. - J. A. Kelly - Note - 1903
Malone, J. R. - Branch & Smith - Note - 1895
Malone, Joe - Amos Kelly - Note - no date
Malone, John F. - N. E. Blackwell - Lien - 1907
Malone, L. B. - R. J. Minter - Mortgage - 1899
Malone, W. F. - Jas. H. Campbell - Mortgage - 1897
Malone, Will - Dooley & Nash - Mortgage - no date
Malone, Willie - H. P. Almand, Sr. - Note - no date
Marshall, William - Reuben Hill - Mortgage - no date
Martin, P. K. - H. L. Blackwell - Mortgage - no date
"   "   "   "   "   "   1920
Mashburn, Joseph - John L. Bender - Mortgage Deed - 1826
Mason, I. W. - Jacob Odom - Note - no date
Minter, R. J. - Wellington & Anderson - Note - no date
Moore, John - William Cook - Note - no date
Moore, W. R. - A. L. Johnson - Mortgage - no date
Morgan, James H. - David M. Langston - Note - no date
Moseley, A. F. - Avery & Co. - Note - 1905
"   "   "   "   "   "
Murphy, J. H. - H. P. Smith - Mortgage - 1891
McClendon, Allen - William Couch - Note - no date
McClendon, Jacob - James Adams - Mortgage - 1834
McClure, James - Jefferson Adams - Mortgage - 1829
McCorkle, James - Felix Hardman - Mortgage - 1833
McDowell, Joel C. - Richard Mitchel - Note - no date
McDowell, Joel C. - Mary Salter - Warranty Deed - 1882
McKinley, E. B. - Harris & Baer - Note - no date
McLendon, Amos - Wm. Holbrooks - Note - no date
McMichael, Green L. - Elhannan Gibbs - Note - no date
McMichael, Jas. S. - C. A. Talmadge - Mortgage - 1897
Nelson & Knight - Lund Weathers - Note - no date
Newby, Wm. E. - J. B. Newby - Mortgage - 1882
Newton, G. W. - I. W. Brown - Mortgage - 1903
Niblett, T. V. - Wynn & Clack - Note - no date
Nichols, Thos. J. - J. S. Scofield - Mortgage - 1903
Nichols, Thos. J. - G. W. Stinson - Mortgage - 1903
Norton, Thomas - Lucas Powell - Mortgage Deed - 1839
Parker, J. H. - Anna E. Wynn - Mortgage - 1903
Parker, John G. - S. S. Holland - Mortgage - 1830
Parker, Mattie H. - Jasper County Bank - Mortgage - 1903
Parker, William H. - Willis Reeves - Note - no date
Parks, Thomas - W. P. White - Mortgage - 1886
Paul, W. E. - W. L. Lampkin & Co. - Mortgage - no date
Peacock, Aaron - Lewis Walker - Mortgage - 1897
Pearson, W. A. - Eugene Benton - Mortgage - 1902
Pellom, Edward - Simon Easterwood - Note - no date
Penn, A. A. - J. J. Cardell - Mortgage - 1898
Penn, A. P. - E. S. Rogers - Mortgage - no date
Penn, J. A. - Clark, Rosser & Co. - Mortgage - 1881
Penn, W. C. - G. T. Bartlett - Note - no date
Pennington, Abel - John Wilson - Note - no date
Perry, Morris - W. W. Allen - Note - no date
Peteet, J. C. - Middle Georgia Bank - Mortgage - 1902
Phillips, J. B. M. - Dumas & Allen - Mortgage - 1876
Pinnell, L. N. - James Benton - Mortgage - no date
Piper, J. O. - Bailey & Jones - Mortgage - 1906
Plummer, John R. - Thomas J. Dunam - Mortgage Deed - 1836
Plummer, Samuel - William S. Minter - Mortgage Deed - 1845
Pope, Edgar C. - R. W. L. Rasin - Note - no date
Pope, S. H. - J. S. Malone - Mortgage - 1903
Porter, J. W. - Bank of Monticello - Note - no date

Porter, Wess - S. A. Hecht - Lien - 1899
Posey, Squire - Gibbs I. Adams - Note - no date
Potts, James - C. Keenon & Co. - Note - no date
Pounds, Tommie - A. S. Reid - Mortgage - 1899
Powel, John - Thos. Blan - Mortgage - 1842
Powell, John G. - Edward A. Broddus - Mortgage - 1842
Powers, G. T. - L. O. Benton & Co. - Note - 1911
Preston, Ada - Mary A. Preston - Warranty Deed - 1897
Preston, Ida B. - Mary A. Preston - Warranty Deed - 1897
Preston, Runnels - Obadiah Echols - Note - no date
Price, E. C. - D. B. Benton & Co. - Lien - 1892
Pritchett, E. N. - J. O. Shepherd - Note - no date
Pritchett, Mat - Stephen H. Johnston - Note - no date
Pritchett, T. J. - S. Boynton - Note - no date
Pritchett, T. J. - R. L. Loyall - Note - no date
Pritchett, Thomas J. - H. W. Belcher & Co. - Promisory Note -
   no date
Pritchett, Thos. J. - J. W. Fears - Note - no date
Pritchett, Thos. J. - Shadrack McMichael - Note - no date
Pritchett, William - Micajah Samson - Note - no date
Pye, Harmon W. - Thos. C. Garrett - Note - no date
Ragan, John - John Daniel - Mortgage - 1816
Rainey, Daniel M. - Coleman, Ray & Co. - Note (4) - no date
Rainey, Daniel M. - Coleman, Ray & Co. - Mortgage Deed - 1890
Ramey, D. M. - H. J. Lamar - Chattel Mortgage - 1887
Ramey, D. M. - C. B. Standard - Mortgage - 1891
Reeves, Absalom E. - John Willson - Deed of Mortgage - no date
Reid, George - John Lucas - Note - no date
Reid, Mary - John Wilson - Note - no date
Reynolds, W. P. - L. O. Benton & Bros. - Mortgage - 1891
Rivers, T. H. B. - T. J. Comer - Note - no date
Robey, Robert - James G. Sims - Note - no date
Robey, W. B. - James Sharman - Note - no date
Robinson, Emma Z. - J. L. Pitts - Mortgage - 1900
Robinson, J. L. - J. W. Turner - Mortgage - no date
Robinson, Sol - First Nat'l Bank of Mont. - Mortgage - 1909
Robinson, Solomon - J. H. Kelly Co. - Mortgage - 1909
Robinson, William - Simeon Easterwood - Note - no date
Roby, Dink - Arthur Clark - Warranty Deed - 1896
Roby, P. M. - J. B. Cook - Mortgage - 1906
Ross, Dick - J. Y. Howard - Note - no date
Ross, Harry & Co. - Eliza N. Murrell - Mortgage - 1889
Scales, Gilbert - L. C. Bradley - Lien - 1899
Scottish American Mtg. - Bank of Monticello - Warranty Deed -
   1901
Seymour, Leroy P. - Holland & Kirkpatrick - Mortgage Deed - 1842
Showers, Elridge - J. H. Kelly - Note - no date
Shy, A. G. - H. H. Hawk - Note - 1893
Shy, W. V. - L. O. Benton & Bro. - Mortgage - 1903
Shy, W. V. - Greer Bros. & Garland - Mortgage - 1904
Shy, W. V. - W. F. Jordan - Mortgage - 1903
  "   "   "   "   "   "

Sigman, M. - Clark's Cove Guano Co. - Note - no date
Slaughter, H. G. - Joshua Driskill - Note - no date
Slaughter, Joseph W. - Moses B. Hairston - Mortgage Deed - 1842
Slaughter, Wm. A. - Miles Scarborough - Note - no date
Smartt, Elisha - George Alexander - Mortgage - 1822
Smith Brothers - Reuben Johnson - Lien - 1904
Smith Brothers - W. A. Kelly - Note - no date
Smith, Chas. J. - Selia Jackson - Note - no date
Smith, Chas. S. - Jas. T. Standifer - Note - no date
Smith, Elbert - W. A. Kelly & Bros. - Mortgage - 1880
Smith, Guy - J. C. Burton - Note - no date

```
Smith, Guy - Sanders Stallings - Mortgage - no date
Smith, Guy - Warren & Wallace - Note - no date
Smith, Jas. H. - Georgia Chemical Works - Note - no date
Smith, James H. - Scottish American Mtg. Co. - Warranty Deed -
   1890
Smith, John W. A. - John Merryman & Co. - Note - no date
Smith, John W. A. - Warren & Wallace - Note - no date
Smith, Orillous - Robert Whitfield - Mortgage - no date
Smith, S. B. - Deleon Guano Co. - Note - no date
Smith, S. R., Jr. - Ramspeck & Green - Note (2) - no date
Spearman, John - A. W. Gump & Co. - Chattel Mortgage - 1893
Spearman, William - Barrett & Caswell - Note - no date
Spears, Henry - B. T. Lowe - Note - no date
Spears, John - Elijah Page - Note - no date
Spears, W. M. - W. F. Jordan - Note - 1902
Stewart, George W. - George W. Dillard - Note - no date
Stone, Man - N. M. Williams - Lien - 1887
Stovall, George - John Hunt - Mortgage Deed - 1822
Strickland, Barnabas - Joseph Betts - Mortgage Deed - 1840
Swann, T. C. - A. J. Wilson - Fee Simple Deed - 1892
Swanson, E. Y. - F. M. Jordan - Mortgage - 1901
Swanson, E. Y. - W. H. Wilburn - Warranty Deed - 1902
Swanson, F. M. - H. C. Hill - Mortgage - 1879
Swanson, S. E. - Security Investment Co. - Warranty Deed - 1899
Talmadge, C. A. - Farmers National Bank - Mortgage - 1909
Taylor, William - J. M. Willis - Mortgage - 1881
Tedders, G. W. - W. D. Elliott - Mortgage - no date
Thomas, Augusta - L. O. Benton - Mortgage - 1918
Thomas, R. C. - British & American Mtg. Co. - Warranty Deed -
   1907
Thurman, A. S. - Green F. Johnson - Security Deed - 1912
Tucker, G. A. - Columbus Bank - Title Bond - 1911
Tuggle, E. D. - J. H. S. Smith - Note - no date
Tuggle, Phillip - Banks, Davidson & Kelly - Mortgage - 1890
Tuggle, Thomas - David A. Reese - Mortgage - 1830
Tuggle, W. R. - Swann, Stewart & Co. - Mortgage - 1886
Turk, E. B. - Bank of Shady Dale - Mortgage (2) - 1915
Turk, L. L. - J. H. Jackson - Note - no date
Vance, Marcus D. - Bailey Bell - Note - no date
Varner, Cynthia H. - T. J. Pritchett - Note - no date
Varner, Joe - R. H. Goolsby - Mortgage - 1896
Vickers, Elijah - John A. Broughton - Mortgage Deed - 1837
Wagner, J. C. - Jordan Brothers - Mortgage - 1892
Waits, A. M. - L. O. Benton - Note - 1911
Waits, A. M. - B. E. Goolsby - Note (2) - 1814
Waits, Wm. B. - James Langston - Note - no date
Walker, Crofford - W. W. Allen - Mortgage - no date
Walker, Emly - John A. Kelly - Mortgage - 1897
Walker, John - Coleman M. Roberts - Note - no date
Walton, J. L. - James A. Wade - Note - no date
Ward, James D. L. - A. C. Standifer - Security Deed - no date
Waters, Lizzie - J. D. Tucker - Mortgage - 1892
Weatherly, Leven - John Wilson - Note - no date
Weathersbee, James - John A. Broughton - Note - no date
Webb, Ammy K. - Eugene Benton - Mortgage - 1901
Webb, P. A. - S. R. Campbell - Mortgage - 1905
  "      "          "        "        "      1903
  "      "     Farmers Bank           "      1907
  "      "          "        "        "      1906
  "      "     1st Nat'l Bank of Monticello - Mortgage - 1909
  "      "     W. S. Florence                "      1908
  "      "     Jasper County Bank            "      1900
  "      "          "        "        "      "      1904
```

Webb. P. A. - Jasper County Bank - Mortgage - 1904
    "   "   - W. F. Jordan   "   (11) - 1901-1908
    "   "   - J. H. Kelly & Co. - Note - 1909
    "   "   - J. S. Malone, Jr. - Mortgage (3) - 1905
    "   "   - Monticello Merchandise Co. - Mortgage - 1901
    "   "   - Monticello Vehicle Co. - Mortgage - 1909
    "   "   "   "   "   "   1905
    "   "   - W. F. Persons - Mortgage (3) - 1901-1902
    "   "   - G. T. Powers - Mortgage (9) - 1903-1908
    "   "   - Roberson, Kelly & Co. - Mortgage (4) - 1901-1905
Wells, William - Hugh McDonald - Note - no date
Whaley, Charles - Norris Thurmond - Note - no date
Whitfield, J. B. - H. J. Dennis - Note - no date
Whitfield, James - Bud Newton - Note - no date
Whitfield, James - John H. Whatley - Deed of Conveyance - 1828
Whitfield, John B. - John F. Thompson - Note - no date
Whitfield, Matthew - John Carter - Mortgage - 1820
Whitten, H. W. - 1st Nat'l Bank of Monticello - Mortgage - 1910
Wilburn, Samuel V. - James H. Robinson - Note - no date
Williams, T. R. - J. J. Dearing - Note - no date
Williams & Winburn - Lewis & Pritchett - Note - no date
Wilson, J. - Jacob Adams - Note - no date
Wilson, Lessie - Hodge Mercantile Co. - Mortgage - 1906
Wilson, Monroe - C. H. Jordan - Mortgage - 1900
Wilson, Thomas - Elhanan Gibbs - Note - no date
Wilson, V. A. - Georgia Chemical Works - Note - no date
Winans, W. C. - F. W. Gano - Mortgage - 1892
Wommack, J. T. - E. V. Cary - Note - no date
Wright, C. W. C. - Jarrott B. Kelly - Mortgage Deed - 1839
Wynens, E. L. - Jas. H. Johnson - Note - no date
Yancy, B. D. - J. L. Herring - Mortgage - 1907
Yarborough, James - Stephen Noble - Note - no date
Zimmerman, Charlie - E. D. Kelly - Mortgage - 1893

The following document is the sole content of the file of defaulting administrators, executors and guardians:

A list of Defaulting Admrs., Exrs. & Gurds. to March Term 1843

1. Ann C. Wilkins, Exrs., Drury Wilkins
6. Mary Beckwick, adm., Israel Beckwick
7. Davis R. Andrews, guard., J. G. Andrews
11. Armsted Dodson, guard., Josiah & Mary Allen
12. Elbert W. Baynes, adm., Williamson B. Roby
14. Cardin & Kirby Goolsby, adm., James B. Goolsby
15. Cardin Goolsby, guard., Sarah Goolsby
16. "   "   "   Leathy Goolsby
17. "   "   "   Jacob Goolsby
18. Kirby Goolsby, guard., Richard Goolsby
19. Robert Brown, guard., Jacob McDonald (minor) (this line
     crossed out)
20. Obadiah R. Belcher, admr., G. B. Belcher
26. George Folds, admr., John Folds
28. D. R. Anderson, guard., Narcissa Andrews
31. Baily Bell, admr., Joseph Barbee
33. Daniel McDowell, guard., Wm. S. Wilbburn
36. N. W. Gorden, guard., Mary Ann Doggett
37. N. W. Gorden, guard., Elizabeth Doggett
38. N. W. Gorden, guard., Nancy G. Doggett
40. Daniel McDowell, exr., M. A. McDowell
41. Daniel McDowell one of the administrators of the estate of
     William McDowell
    W. R. Marchman, guard., Edmund (?) J. McMichael

The following is a list of the interrogatories (questionings of
witnesses unavailable to the court) found in the interrogatories
file in box 13:

concerning Joe Bartlett, n.d.
concerning John F. Patterson, n.d.
concerning Richard Allen, 1812
Wm. Owsley in Putnam County, concerning James McMichaels, 1817
  mentions James, Mary, and Jane McMichaels
John Carney (Josiah Carney of Clark County, Ala.), 1817,
  concerning James Graham
Joseph Grant and William Dennagee (?), 1818
Wilas Hoskins of Jackson County, 1811, concerning Thomas Haynes
Jesse Sanford, 1812
George W. Foster, 1811
Joseph L. Ingles of Philadelphia, Pa. (age 59), on the
  Methodist Church, 1831
William Woodroof, Benjamin Gorring (? Gowing?), and Tamlin Avent
  of Greenville Co., Va., 1833
John and William Rutherford of Lebanon, Washington Co., 1816
Robert Taylor, Andrew Taylor, Adam Wademan, and Milly Wademan,
  1811
James C. Terondet and Samuel McDonald, 1817
Robert White and Samuel Wilson, 1813
Tandy Walker, 1818
Warren West, 1818

The following is a list of the contents of the file of
registrations of free persons of color:

Jenny Cozens, 1846   Thomas Cozens, age 53, 1846
John Cozens, age 51, blacksmith, 1847

CHAPTER XIII

BOUND ORIGINAL RECORDS AT THE GEORGIA ARCHIVES
(Various Record Groups)

NOTE: Also see Chapters XII and XIV

MISCELLANEOUS BOUND VOLUMES OF SUPERIOR COURT
Records of Jasper County
Record Group 179-1-14

This series contains bound Superior Court records involving,
but not limited to:

(1) Appeals
(2) Court appearance
(3) Minutes
(4) Declarations
(5) Fi fas
(6) Jury lists
(7) Subpoenas
(8) Slave imports

The volumes are in general decay, uncleaned and in the same
condition as they were taken from the courthouse. The volumes
are generally arranged chronologically by date or case or
numerically by case number. Please see the following shelf list
for a complete listing:

1808 - 1898

    Appeals Docket, 1822-60
    Bar Docket, 1809
    Bond Book, 1817-19
    Court Appearance Docket Index, 1808-15
    Court Cases & Jury List Docket, 1894-98
    Court Minutes, 1813-17
    Declarations - Book H, 1815-18
    Execution Docket, 1844
    Fi Fa Docket, 1816-18
    Jury List Docket (Grand & Traverse), 1879-88
    Motion Docket, 1849-162
    Slave Import Oaths, 1818-32
    Subpoena Docket, 1867

    Appeal Docket, 1841-42
    Declarations
      -1818-20, Book R
      -1819-25
    Executions Dockets
      -1822-24
      -1824-28
      -1828-35
      -1835-42

MISCELLANEOUS DOCKET BOOKS OF THE SUPERIOR COURT OF JASPER COUNTY
Record Group 179-1-21

This series contains bound Superior Court records consisting of dockets. These dockets are lists of legal decisions
made by the Superior Court. They are in general decay, uncleaned
and in the same condition as they were taken from the courthouse.
They are arranged chronologically by court term.

    1810 - 1857
      Dockets
        -No date   -1819-22   -1845-66 (2 volumes)
        -1810-12   -1821-23   -1856-57

BOUND MORTGAGE RECORDS OF THE SUPERIOR COURT OF JASPER COUNTY
Record Group 179-1-26

This series contains bound mortgage records of the Superior Court of Jasper County. To be found within these volumes are the legal procedures a person had to take in order to pledge his property to a creditor for the payment of a debt. Most often the security for the payment of the debt consisted of a person's crop and his horse, mule or other farm animal. The volumes are in general decay, uncleaned and in the same condition as they were taken from the courthouse. They are arranged chronologically by date the mortgage was registered with the clerk's office.

VOL.	1808 - 1924
BB-2	1901-03
CC	1903-07
20	1912
21	1912-13
22	1912-13
23	1913-14
24	1913-14
25	1914-15
26	1914-16
27	1915 (To be restored - unavailable for research)
28	1916-17
29	1916
30	1917-18
31	1917-19
32	1917-19
33	1918 (To be restored - unavailable for research)
34	1918-19
35	1918-24
36	1919-20

MISCELLANEOUS BOUND VOLUMES OF INFERIOR COURT - RECORDS OF JASPER COUNTY
Record Group 179-2-15

This series contains bound Inferior Court (now Probate) records involving, but not limited to:

(1) Surveyor's records
(2) Dentists
(3) Estrays
(4) Liquor retailers
(5) Minutes of court
(6) Motions of court
(7) Paupers
(8) Marks and brands

The volumes are in general decay, uncleaned and in the same condition as they were taken from the courthouse. The volumes are generally arranged chronologically by court proceeding, or date of administration, or court term, or numerically by case number. Please see the following shelf list for a complete listing.

1836 - 1911
County Surveyor's Book, 1858-61
Dentists Registry, 1884-97

Estray Book, 1819-1900
Liquor Register, 1882
Minutes, etc., 1850-67
Motion Docket, 1858-67
Pauper's List, 1877-78, (2nd half)
Road Hands Book, 1897-1907, (first half)
Samual Varner's (Clerk of Ordinary Court) Receipt Book,
   1846
Those Entitled to Draw in the Lottery of 1825

Day Book, 1820-32
Execution Docket, 1829-44
Marks and Brands Licenses, 1808-23
Petitions, 1812-18
Receipt Book, 1811
Registration Books
   -1909
   -1911

MISCELLANEOUS DOCKET BOOKS OF THE INFERIOR COURT OF JASPER COUNTY
Record Group 179-2-22

     This series contains bound Inferior Court records consisting
of dockets. These dockets are lists of legal decisions made by
the Inferior Court. They are in general decay, uncleaned and
in the same condition as they were taken from the courthouse.
They are arranged chronologically by court term.

     1836 - 1868
       Dockets
         -1836-49
         -1841-44
         -1858-68

BOUND LISTS OF REGISTERED VOTERS OF JASPER COUNTY
Record Group 179-2-3

     This series contains bound lists of registered voters filed
with the Court of Ordinary of Jasper County. The lists contain
the (1) name, (2) age, (3) race, (4) occupation and (5) district
of the registered voter in Jasper. The volumes are in general
decay, uncleaned and in the same condition as they were taken
from the courthouse. They are arranged chronologically by date.

     1891 - 1910
       List of voters
         -No date (2 volumes)
         -1891
         -1892-93
         -1896
         -1896-97
         -1898 (2 volumes)
         -1910

TRIAL DOCKET INDEX OF COUNTY COURT OF JASPER COUNTY
Record Group 179-3-18

This series contains unbound copies of a trial docket index for County Court. The location of the volume to which this index refers is unknown. The index contains the case number, the parties in litigation and the page number on which the cases might be found within the volume. The index is uncleaned and in the same condition as it was taken from the courthouse. The cases are arranged numerically by case number.

1915

MISCELLANEOUS BOUND VOLUMES OF COUNTY COURT - RECORDS OF JASPER COUNTY
Record Group 179-3-4

This series contains bound County Court records involving, but not limited to:

(1) Court costs
(2) Criminal cases
(3) Subpoenas
(4) Minutes of court
(5) Motions of court

Although these volumes have been erroneously labeled City Court on their spines, their contents actually fall under County Court jurisdiction because in the earlier days of county administration, city court as it is known today did not exist. The volumes are in general decay, uncleaned and in the same condition as they were taken from the courthouse. They are arranged chronologically by term of court.

VOL.	1900 - 1920
	Cash Book, 1900-06
	Criminal Dockets
1	-1906-14
2	-1914-15
	Criminal Subpoena Dockets
1	-1907-15
1	-1907-15
	Execution Dockets
1	-1906-13
2	-1913-20
	Declaration Dockets
	-1906-07
	-1912-15
1	Issue Docket, 1906-15
	Minutes
	-1906-15
	-1915-16
	Motion for New Trial & Forfeiture of Criminal Bond, 1906-11

MISCELLANEOUS DOCKET BOOKS OF THE JUSTICE COURT OF JASPER COUNTY

Record Group 179-4-17

This series contains bound Justice Court records consisting of dockets. These dockets are lists of legal decisions of the Justice Court. They are in general decay, uncleaned and in the same condition as they were taken from the courthouse. They are arranged either numerically by case number or chronologically by court term.

Contents

1859 - 1873
   Attachment Docket, 1873
   Justice Court Docket, 1859-71

MISCELLANEOUS BOUND VOLUMES OF THE COUNTY COMMISSIONER'S OFFICE OF JASPER COUNTY

Record Group 179-5-16

This series contains bound records of the County Commissioner's Office consisting of (1) dockets, (2) appearance books, (3) bond books and (4) receipt books. The volumes are in general decay, uncleaned and in the same condition as they were taken from the courthouse. They are arranged chronologically by term of commissioner

Contents

1848 - 1895
   Cost Docket, 1879-83 (first half)
   County Board of Commissioners, 1874-76
   County Officers Appearance Book, 1849-74
   County Officers Bonds, 1848-69
   Revenue Receipt Book, 1883-95

MISCELLANEOUS BOUND VOLUMES OF THE TAX COLLECTOR OF JASPER COUNTY

Record Group 179-7-19

This series contains bound records of the Tax Collector's Office which consist of tax payers and tax defaulters. The volumes are in general decay, uncleaned and in the same condition as they were taken from the courthouse. They are arranged chronologically by year and thereunder alphabetically by surname of the defaulter or payer.

Contents

1885 - 1980
   Tax defaulters, 1885
   Tax payers, 1900-08 (2nd half)

MISCELLANEOUS BOUND VOLUMES OF SHERIFF'S OFFICE - RECORDS OF
JASPER COUNTY

Record Group 179-9-25

This series contains bound Sheriff's Office records involving the execution of cases and the sale of property to satisfy
debts.   The volumes are in general decay, uncleaned and in the
same condition as they were taken from the courthouse.   They are
arranged chronologically by date of case.

Contents

1880 - 1904
   Execution Dockets
     -1880-93
     -1893-99
     -1898-10-4
   Sale Record, 1880-97

UNBOUND RECORDS OF THE COUNTY TREASURER'S OFFICE OF JASPER COUNTY

Record Group 179-10-8

This series contains unbound original county treasury
records which include, but are not limited to:

(1) Clerk's accounts
(2) Receipts
(3) Disbursements
(4) Taxes paid
(5) Oaths on reports
(6) Reports of clerks to Grand Juries
(7) Reports of jail committees
(8) Reports of clerks to Superior Court
(9) Lists of liabilities
(10) County treasurer's reports
(11) Commissioner of Roads & Revenues reports
(12) Court house expenditures
(13) Court fees
(14) County expense vouchers
(15) Checks to county treasury from General Fund

The records have been flattened, cleaned and placed in folders.
They are arranged chronologically by year. Please see the
following shelf list for a complete listing of dates and shelf
locations.

Contents

No dates, 1819-1880
1881-1889
1890-1899
1900-1903
1904-1919
1920-1926
1927-1935

MISCELLANEOUS BOUND VOLUMES OF THE COUNTY TREASURER'S OFFICE OF
JASPER COUNTY
Record Group 179-10-20

This series contains bound records of the County Treasurer's
Office which consist of account books, receipt books and vouchers.
They are in general decay, uncleaned and in the same condition
as they were taken from the courthouse. They are arranged
chronologically by year.

Contents

1864 - 1884
    Treasurer's Account Books
      -1847
      -1868-71
      -1871-73
      -1893-98
    Treasurer's Book, 1866-68
    Treasurer's Receipt Book, 1864
    Vouchers, 1871-80

CHAPTER XIV

OTHER RECORDS (INCLUDING MICROFILM) AT THE GEORGIA ARCHIVES: AN
INVENTORY

The following inventory lists the Jasper County records on microfilm at the Georgia Department of Archives and History.

Drawer/Box   Description

ORDINARY

36/62   Confederate Records. Pensions and licenses,
             miscellaneous dates. (Note: The Georgia Archives
             has also microfilm of many other Confederate
             pension records, for the whole state.)

36/74   Execution Dockets
             1826-1859 Book B
             1831-1837

             Estate Records--Administrators & Guardians Letters
                and Bonds.
35/43   1808-1844 Vols. A-C Not indexed.
35/44   1844-1891 Vol. D (in two parts) Not indexed.
35/45   1872-1896 Vol. 1   Indexed.
35/46   1888-1902 Vol. 2   Indexed.
35/47   1891-1920 Vol. E   "
71/31   1808-1821 Vol. A-AA   "   (Administrators bonds)

             Estate Records--Annual Returns.
35/51   1823-1833,   1850-1854
35/52   1653-1859
35/53   1858-1859
35/54   1858-1860
35/55   1868-1878
35/56   1877-1890
35/57   1889-1899
35/58   1898-1905

             Estate Records--Docket
35/42   1826-1859,   1831-1837   (Book B)
36/74   (same)

             Estate Records--Index
36/7   1812-1941   A-Z
35/51   1809-1894   Chronological (docket?)

             Estate Records--Inventories & Appraisements.
35/49   1852-1858   Indexed
35/50   1861-1902   "

             Estate Records--Miscellaneous.
36/10   1797-1819   Vol. C
71/29   1809-1815   Vol. A
36/10   1813-1817   Vol. 1
             1815-1820   Vol. 2
71/29   1818-1833   Vols. 4-H
36/11   1821-1833   Vols. 5-7
36/13   1828-1849   Vols. 9-10
36/14   1836-1844   Vols. 11-12
36/15   1841-1845   Vol. 13
36/8   1845-1855   Vol. 2
36/16   1846-1910   Vol. 14
36/12   1849-1852   Vol. 8
36/9   1850-1866   Vol. 13

```
                   Estate Records--Sales Bills.
36/10              1797-1819      Vol. C      Not indexed.
35/48              1809-1815                   "      "
36/10              1813-1817      Vol. I       "      "

(Wills are recorded in Estate Records--Miscellaneous and
  Ordinary Minutes.)

                   Estate Records--Years Support.
36/59              1875-1912      Vol. A

                   Estrays.
36/61              1876-1920                  Not indexed.
71/29              (same)

                   Homesteads.
36/58              1866-1924
36/60              1873-1905    (pony homesteads included)

                   Pony Homesteads
71/30              1873-1898        Book A

                   Inferior Court Declarations.
35/39              1826-1838
35/40              1837-1845
35/41              1820-1823,   1845-1851

                   Inferior Court--Land Lottery List (1827).
186/41             1825 listof eligibles

                   Inferior Court--Minutes
35/38              1820-1868
71/30              1821-1839,   1840-1868

                   Inferior Court--Petitions.
166/2              1812-1818

                   Marks, Brands, and Licenses.
165/7              1808-1823

                   Marriages
36/4               1808-1869        Indexed
36/5               1869-1886          "
36/6               1885-1900          "

                   Ordinary Minutes
71/31              1812-1832      Vols. I, A-C
36/3               1872-1902      Vol. A      Indexed
36/17              1812-1872      Vols. I, A-C
36/18              1878-1901      Vol. 2

                   Tax Records
61/60              1866-1868
36/64              1871-1878
36/65              1879-1886
36/67              1887-1891
36/68              1895-1899
```
For microfilm of tax records for 1906-1952 and 1960, ask the
desk attendant. The Georgia Department of Archives and History
has original tax records beginning c1872 for Jasper and all
Georgia counties.
```
                   State Census Records
10/65              1852 (partial)
```

	Declarations to Secure Debt	
35/67	1807-1815	not indexed
35/68	1812-1820	"
35/69	1820-1824	"
35/70	1824-1828	"
35/71	1828-1843	"
35/71	1843-1847	"
35/73	1846-1851	"
35/74	1852-1855	"
	1852-1861	" "
35/75	1861-1873	" "
	1874-1882	"
36/1	1884-1897	"
36/2	1897-1908	"

	Deeds (and Mortgages prior to 1880).	
36/22	1807-1810	Vols. 1-2
36/23	1810-1811	Vols. 3-4
36/24	1811-1815	Vols. 5-6
36/25	1815-1818	Vols. 7-8
36/26	1817-1827	Vol. A
36/27	1817-1822	Vol. B1
36/28	1823-1835	Vol. B2
36/29	1834-1842	Vol. C
36/30	1842-1852	Vol. D
36/31	1852-1866	Vol. E
36/32	1866-1875	Vols. F-G
36/33	1876-1887	Vols. H-I
36/34	1886-1892	Vol. J
36/35	1892-1897	Vol. K
36/36	1896-1901	Vol. L

	Deeds and Mortgages General Index.	
36/19	1808-1835	Grantor and Grantee
36/20	1837-1938	Grantor
36/21	1837-1938	Grantee

	Docket, Subphoena.	
71/30	1873-1883	
36/56	1873-1921	(civil cases)

	Land Plats.
36/57	1844-1863

	Lien Record Book
36/54	1886-1923

	Minutes	
71/31	1807-1811	not indexed
35/59	1808-1832	" "
35/60	1832-1850	" "
35/61	1851-1859	" "
	1859-1870	"
35/62	1870-1878	"
35/63	1875-1885	"
35/64	1885-1897	"
35/65	1898-1905	"
35/66	1879-1906	"

	Miscellaneous Records
36/75	Court expenses and names of jurors, 1889-1909.

	Mortgages.	
36/38	1880-1884	Vols. I-J
36/39	1884-1886	Vols. K-L
36/40	1886-1888	Vol. M
36/42	1888-1889	Vol. N
36/41	1889-1890	Vol. O
36/43	1890-1891	Vols. P-Q
36/44	1891-1892	Vol. R
36/45	1892-1894	Vol. S
36/46	1894	Vol. T
36/47	1894-1895	Vol. U
36/48	1895-1896	Vol. V
36/49	1896-1897	Vol. W
36/50	1897-1898	Vol. X
36/51	1898	Vol. Y
36/52	1898-1899	Vol. Z
36/53	1899-1900	Vol. AA

	Mortgage General Index.	
36/37	1890-1900	Grantor and Grantee

	Physicians Register.
36/55	1881-1911

PRIVATE RECORDS ON MICROFILM: CHURCHES

57/65	Bethlehem Baptist Church.	
	1821-1879	lists of members
	1833-1879	minutes
	1896-1904	membership list
	1904-1916	minutes and membership lists
74/72	1821-1897	typescript membership list and some deaths through 1904; brief history

	Bethel Baptist Church.	
36/71	1854-1887	minutes and members
	1896-1900	minutes and members

	Calvary Methodist Church.	
19/1	1860-1888	sunday school and church members list
	1879-1888	minutes

	Concord Baptist Church	
74/72	1808-1958	history

	Concord Primative Baptist Church.	
187/72	1808-1954	history and list of charter members
242/29	1812-1917	minutes and membership
242/30	1923-1955	minutes

	Enon Baptist Church.	
74/72	1847	history

	Fellowship Primative Baptist Church.	
74/72	1832-1954	history

	Hillsboro Baptist Church.	
74/72	1889-1954	history
232/60	1889-1969	history, minutes, and membership

74/72	Hillsboro Methodist Church. 1889-1954 history
146/24 74/72	Hopewell Baptist Church. 1847-1921 records 1847 history
74/72	Liberty Methodist Church. 1827-1862 history
74/72	Midway Methodist Church. 1819-1894 history
74/72 36/70	Monticello Baptist Church. 1836-1851 history 1868-1906 minutes 1880-1907 minutes 1868-1906 history and list of members 1865-1936 church record books
36/72	Monticello Methodist Church. 1878-1924 church records
36/60	Monticello Presbyterian Church. 1829-1905 church record book
19/1	Mt. Zion (or Mountain) Methodist Church. 1857 sunday school class record book
49/79 74/72 223/30 218/2	Providence Baptist Church. 1810-1860 history 1810-1841 minutes and members 1810-1905 history and members 1851-1882 minutes and members 1893-1975 minutes and members
74/72	Shady Dale Methodist Church. 1861-1900 history
74/72 36/73	Shiloh Baptist Church. 1808-1858 history and list of members 1870-1931 minutes

PRIVATE RECORDS ON MICROFILM: CLUBS, SOCIETIES, & LODGES

74/76	Miscellaneous on Masonic Lodges, 1849-1920
74/74	Elizabeth Marlowe Chapter, DAR, Monticello (1941). (Includes list of Jasper County Revolutionary War Soldiers)
74/74	Monticello Chapter, UDC
36/63	Sons of Temperance, 1848-1898, record book, list of members and occupations.
194/3	United Confederate Veterans, Camp Key #483, 1897, membership roll.

PRIVATE RECORDS ON MICROFILM: DIARIES

227/63   Mrs. John Baldwin, 1831

PRIVATE RECORDS ON MICROFILM: HISTORY

81/24   Mrs. A. S. Thurmond, "A History of Jasper and
                Monticello," n.d., 47 pp.

74/73   History of Jasper County and Shady Dale
                (Includes 1821 land lottery list)

PRIVATE RECORDS ON MICROFILM: PLANTATIONS

18/20   Seaborn Hawks, journal 1854-1862, 1868

PRIVATE RECORDS NOT ON MICROFILM

Fears-Minter Family Genealogical Papers, 1922-1961. AC 69-419

Physicians Account Book, 1837-1841, 1851-1855. AC 00-214

Thomas Butler King Papers, 1838-1858. AC 72-331

Willis Newton Business Papers, 1887-1895. AC 73-004

Ogletree Family Papers, 1810-1890. AC 60-103

Jesse Stephens Slave Bills of Sale, 1825-1847. AC 65-104

F. M. Swanson Store and Personal Account Book, 1851-1873.
  AC 00-222

Meshack Turner III Genealogical Papers, 1709-1712, 1732, 1751-
  1860, 1870-1976. AC 77-220

MISCELLANEOUS CHURCH AND CEMETERY FILE

Also see Ted O. Brooke, Georgia Cemetery Directory & Bibliography
of Georgia Cemetery Reference Sources (Marietta: The Author,
1986).

Confederate Graves Marked by the Monticello Chapter, UDC.

Concord Primative Baptist Church.

Providence Baptist Church, Shady Dale.

Shiloh Baptist Church, Farrar.

United Methodist Church, Monticello.

Shiloh Baptist Church--History.

? (2): 062

AAPAUT: Mitchel, 086

AAPON: Brooks, Jr., 272; Clarissa, 086, 458; Clasey, 328; Exie, 014; Frank 458; Green, 086, 328; J. C. 086, 328, 449; J.L. 378, 384, 449; J. T. 384, 402, 464; James A., 002; James C., 062, 068, 086, 310, 324, 334, 349, 365, 449; James G., 086; James I., 384; James J., 002, 068, 086, 135; John L., 328, 355, 384, 441, 449; John M., 002, 068, John, 086, 363; Lula, 040; M., 370; Mary F. 025; Mitchel, 064, 068, 086, 261; 310, 322, 328, 384, 414, 449; 460; Mitchell, 086, 103, 261;

AARON: Nancy E., 015; Nancy, 058; Paul S., 002; R.A., 086, 441; P.L., 002; Richard A., 086, 414, 460; Richard, 086; Robert, 002; S. A. F., 328; Sallie, 041; Sarah A. F., 384; Sarah A. T., 460; Sarah F., 328, 384; Sarah M., 060; Sarah, 086; W. A., 002, 086; William H., 002; William M., 086

ABBET: Goodwin W., 086
ABBETT: Elizabeth, 050; Ezekiel, 086, 119, 460; Goodwin W., 263; Goodwin, 086; Peter I., 086
ABBOTT: Ezeliel, 068; Goodwin W., 086; Goodwin W., 275; Peter A., 086; Peter I., 002, 086
ABEL: Gordon, 189, 230, 265
ABELL: Gordon, 228, 301
ABELS: S. L., 449
ABERCROMBEE: Leonard, 132
ABERCROMBIE: Abner, 184; Brewer A., 208; James, 170; John, 090, 110, 125, 170, 304, 425; Leonard, 420; Wiley, 111; Willie, 160
ABERNATHY: Caleb, 090; William F., 420
ABERNETHY: Caleb, 086, 122, 123, 292, 305
ABOTT: Jordan, 177
ACADEMY: Union, 424
ACPE: M. L., 384; W. B., 384; William B., 328
ACPEE: W. B., 002, 086, 328, 352, 441, 449; William B., 328; William, 328
ACRES: Sterling, 098
ADAIP: A. D., 335, 343; Hiram, 086; Jones, 152
ADAMS: Ann, 033; Anna, 293; B. F., 098, 328; Betsey, 159; Caleb B., 086, 087, 119, 172, 310, 384; Catherine F., 038; David L., 087, 293; David P., 289; David, 087, 216, 255, 295, 420, 426, 434; Davis R., 104; Davis S., 087; E. H., 449; Edward H., 328; Elizabeth L., 068; Emily F., 203, 426; Eugenia, 016; George Ann, 033; George W., 068, 087, 188, 448; George, 087, 272; Gibbs I., 466; H. D., 364, 376; ADAMS: J. A., Mrs., 342; Jacob, 468; James, 064, 068, 102, 191, 207, 320, 448, 465; Jefferson, 087, 171, 190, 202, 302, 465; John M., 112, 155, 167, 215, 227; John O., 363; John, 087, 351; Jonathan, Sr., 087, 460; Julia A., 328, 347; Lawson, 168; Leaven, 328; Lura, 068; Martha M., 036; Mary F., 024; Mer(cith, 068, 087; Pauline Pou, 404; Richard, 087, 088, 384; Ropert, 191, 202, 331; Sallie Lee, 037; William H., 289; William L., 167; William M., 320; William P., 155, 215; William T., 112; William, 207
ADGATE: C. F., 328; C. L., 393; Caro L., 007; Fred, 384; H.C., 384, 444, 460; S. J., 177; Sarah L., 328
ADKINSON: William F., 088
ADLEP: H., 374
AIKEN: ?, 088; A.F., 043; A.M., 384; A.S., 068; C. P., 088, 328; C.W., 220; Charles A. F., 088; Charles E., 153; Charles P., 068, 347; Delilah, 039; E. H., 088, 347; E. S., 328; Hamp, 088; I. A., 328; J. J., 088, 328; J. M., 449; Jeff T., 088; Jeff, 328; Jefferson F., 328; Jefferson J., 328; Jefferson, 214, 328, 332; John C., 002, 068, 170; Johnie, 029; Kimball, 002, 384, 445; AIKEN: Lillie, 014; O.P., 449; R. H., 088, 328; R. S., 328; Ransom H., 449; S. J., Mrs., 328; Sarah, 088; T.A., 328; T. A., Mrs., 328, 408; Thomas J., 088; W. A., 088, 408
AIKENSE: Carrie, 088; David, 384; Emms, 016; James, 068, 088; Marla (Sheeparg), 088; Seaborn S., 088; T. A., 328, 385
AIKIN: J. J., 329; J. Jeff, 329; Jeff J., 329; Jeff, 329; Jefferson, 329; Pansom H., 350
AIKINS: J. J., 414; Ransom, 366
AKEN: Daniel, 002; Eliza A., 058; Isaac, 002; J. J., 212; James,

064; Jefferson, 329; Sarah, 104
AKENS: Daniel, 068; Ella, 049; J. J., 329; James, 441; Julia A., 420; P. H., 329, 449; Pansom H., 002; Samuel S., 088; Seaborn J., 420; Thomas J., 329
AKERIDGE: Moses, 088; William, 364, 401
AKIN: Emiline, 010; Jefferson, 329; Mary K., 007; Pobert S., 002
AKINS: B. H., 449; James, 420, 430; John C., 088, 170; Patrick H., 002; P. A., 010; R. S., 441; Samuel S., 002; William B., 088; Thomas J., 002, 088; Thomas, 064, 068, 143
AKRIDGE: Dysey, 014; William, 353
ALDEN: Silas, Jr., 088
ALEP: John, 229
ALEWINE: David (Alowine), 420; David, 090; Nancy, 460
ALEXANDER: A. W., Mrs., 329; Abden, 068, 088, 119, 196; Abcon, 196; Abner, 420; Abraham, 240; Adam, 088, 167, 184, 193, 254, 255, 266, 287, 310; Albert, 088, 089, 133; 273, 283, 420; Alfred, 329; Buck, 088; C. W., 183; Casandra, 088; Cassandra S., 427; Charles T., 088, 420, 433; Eliza, 054, 068, 088; Ella, 088; Ephrain A., 223; Ezekiel, 165; Floid, 384; Florida, 046; G. W., 088; George T., 002; ALEXANDER: George, 068, 088, 114, 183, 272, 274, 304, 329, 337, 384, 400, 414, 425, 448, 466; Green, 002, 329; Henry, 088; Ike, 088; J. F., 449; J. W., 449; J. P., 165; James T., 002; James, 102; Jane, 064; Jeff, 002; Jerry, 329; Jesse, 384; John, 002; John J., 002, 088; Joseph, 002; Lawrence P., 088; Lawrence T., 089; Leila, 089; M. Gertrude, 053; Major, 002, 329; ALEXANDER: Martha, 039, 089; 136; Matilda, 027, 328; Mattie, 050; Moses, 154; N.O., 329, 449; Nealy, 019; Newton O., 330; Newton, 089, 449; Paul, 089; R. W., 329, 449; Robert J., 068; Robert W., 002; Rose, 343; Samuel, 117, 215; Simon, 002; Sylvia, 009; T.J., 329; Thomas 019, 120, 329; Will, 002; William, 002
ALFORD: Bynum, 432; Collin, 460; Halcut, 092; Holcut, 089; Isham, 431; Jeptha, 089, 420; Willie, 303
ALFRIEND: A. H., 089, 329, 444, 449; A. H., Mrs., 329; Cornelia, 367; Edmund, 329
ALISON: Clayton, 089; Creasy, 015
ALLEN: A. J., 089, 329, 384, 449; Abner, 384; Addie, 020; Albert, 449; Alexander M., 089, 292; Alexander, 089, 107; Andrew I., 089; Artexas C., 011; Arthur, 089; Aser, 421; Aubie, 002; Ben, 089; Berthie, 009; Betsy Ann, 041; Beverly, 171, 269; Bob, 002; Bryant, 134; Byran, 284; Charles, 002; Charly, 002; Clark, 002; Colman, 094; Columbus, 089; Corine, 003; Dan, 089; Daniel, 002; ALLEN: David E., 340; David, 068, 192, 420; Dennis, 002, 089, 271, 310, 460; Drury, 002; Ebben E., 089; Edmund, 089; Edward M., 089, 115; Eliza, 134, 205; Elizabeth, 090, 256; Essie, 008; Frank, 449; Frazier, 047; Freeman, 273; Froman, 275; George W., 134; George, 089; Georgia, 018; Green, 002, 090, 254, 384; Greene, 089; H. A., 387; H. N., 441, 449; H.V. B., 328, 436, 449; Harris N., 002, 449; Harris, 064, 068, 096, 421, 449; Haseltine, 024; Herschel W.B., 003; Howard, 384; Infant, 441; ALLEN: J. A., 449; J.C., 332, 342, 351; J. D., 089; J. H., 335; J. K., 449; J. M., 463; J. S., 384, 449; J. Shadric, 003; Jack, 003, 329; Jane, 089; Jeff, 089; Jefferson D., 003; Jesse, 191; John A., 090, 128, 312, 329, 377; John C., 352, 376; John J., 254; John, 003, 369, 458; John S., 449; John, 003, 068, 089, 101, 115, 255, 261, 303, 384, 420, 443, 460; Jordan, 089; Josephine, 024; Josiah, 469; Julia A., 002; Kittie Ann, 037; Laura, 443; Lela Florence, 024; ALLEN: Lemuel, 089; Lottie, 054; Lou L., 012; Love, 018; Lovie, 059; Lucinda, 059; Lucy, 037, 443; Mack, 089, 156; Macon, 069; Margarett, 038; Mark J., 420; Martha Ann, 031; Martha S., 029; Mary P., 029, 256; Mathew, 089; Mathew, 256; Matilda, 032; Nancy, 256, 444; Nathaniel, 091; Ned, 089; Nelly, 384; Nora, 060; O. C., 089, 441; Orbie, 460; P.A.S., 032; Penelope,

089; Penny, 055; Phoebe, 068; ALLEN: Polly, 010; R. C., 089, 329, 384, 449; R. L., 348, 349, 367; R. S., 349; Pichard, 292, 469; Robert A., 068, 089, 090, 138, 293; Robert C., 090, 329, 449; Robert T., 256; Pobert, 089, 164; Sam, 003, 090; Samuel I., 120, 147; Samuel, 064, 068, 090, 096, 312, 313; Sarah P., 045; Sarah, 090, 384; Sid, 090; Sophia, 256; Square, 460; Squire, 005; Thomas, 090, 384; W. W., 068, 090, 132, 134, 329, 350, 358, 369, 384-386, 391, 394, 397-399, 404-406, 408, 445, 449, 465, 467; Wadie, 048; Walker C., 090; Walker W., 329, 340; Walker, 090, 329; Welcome, 260; Wiley, 003; William F., 003; William, 064, 068, 090; Willie, 384; Young D., 262
ALLING: E. T., 329
ALLISON: Abraham K., 263; Alex, 394; Alexander H., 090, 402; Alexander, 090; David, 267; Hamp, 003; Isham L., 090; Isham S. F., 090; James, 420; John, 234, 420; Robert, 206, 220, 420; Smallwood P., 149; Smallwood, 263; William B., 263
ALLISTON: Charles W., 003
ALLMOND: Burwell, 090, 101; Moses, 090; Polly, 101
ALLRED: William B., 144
ALLUM: John, 420
ALMAND: H. P., Sr., 465; John W., 400; Zilla A., 329
ALMON: H. P., 397, 399, 404
ALMOND: Burrell, 379; Burwell, 289; H. P., Sr, 356; J. W., 385
ALMONDS: William, 003
ALMUND: William, 003
ALSTON: Drew, 204
AMASON: J. W., 445
AMBERS: Hance, 384; Warren, 420; William, 177
AMBLER: David A., 220
AMBROES: Martha E., 441; Warren, 441
AMBROSE: Delia, 329; George, 329; Martha, 090, 350; Warren, 384, 090, 111, 282
AMES: Horace, 279
AMMIS: Sam, 384
AMOS: Benjamin B., 248, 292; Benjamin, 292; John, 329; Milton, 090; Savannah, 090
ANCHOPS: J. D., 345; Joseph B., 003
ANDERSON: Aaol E., 444; Anthony, 003; Antony, 329; Berta, 159; Brazor (heirs of), 420; B. F., 449; David, 172; George, 003, 090, 384; Henry, 324; J.L., 449; J.T., 384; J. W., 368; James, 090, 150; John F., 003; John R., 270, 287, 304; John T., 329, 384; John, 090, 310, 325; John, Jr., 090; Jonathan, 090, 092, 164, 169; Joseph S., 203, 290, 296; Joseph, 110; L.M., 368; Lelia, 027; Lucy, 020; Mary, 329; Mittie Mozella, 056; Newton J., 003; S.M., 068, 368; S. M., Dr., 338; S. W., 398; Samuel, 068; Stephen, 172; Thomas, 270; W.P., 356; W. W., 209; William P., 275, 310, 312, 345, 367; William W., 090, 091, 134, 329, 420, 260, 303
ANDREWS: C. H., 329; Cal, 270; D.K., 449; D. R., 329; David R., 329; David, 329; Davis R., 068, 091, 246, 310, 329, 360, 469; Davis R., Jr., 202; Davis, 091; Doris R., 329; Garnett, 122; Greene, 068; J.G., 449; J.H., 342; J. O., 349, 449; James G., 091, 310, 384, 431; Jerry, 460; John, 168, 184, 205; Lottie, 040; Lucius, 384; Nancy C., 091; Narcissa, 469; Pauline, 091; P. R., 329; Rebecca P., 329, 360; Pobert, 068; Sallie, 002; Samuel P., 091; Samuel P., 091, 219; Samuel, 091; Susie, 052; T.P., 329; Thomas G., 091, 310; Thomas P., 329; Thomas, 003; W. A., 329; W. H., 449; William A., 329; William P., 003; William, 003, 091, 205, 302, 310, 311, 338, 340, 341, 347, 350, 367, 379, 381, 384, 449
ANGLIN: Samuel, 003
ANIS: J. M., 384
ANNISE: Barbara, 329; C. S., 441; Charles S., 003; Charles, 091, 149; E.B., 425; Emerson B., 068; J. M., 384; J.M., Mrs, 460; J. P., 091; Jane P., 149; Jesse M., 003, 091; 329, 441; Jesse, 091, 149, 329, 449; Martha G., 068; W. J., 003, 384
ANSLEY: Gilbert D., 091; Gilbert P., 106, 421; Jesse, 228; Rebecca, 003
ANTHONY: Anne, 091; James, 255; John, 091; Joseph, 091; Milton, 091, 106, 258; Nancy, 112
ANTONY: Milton, 087, 091, 103, 122,

123, 128, 129, 133, 137, 141;
169, 179, 193, 234, 267, 270, 312
APPLING: Flora, 091; Henry, 330, 338;
John Henry, 364; Mary, 040, 443;
Mollie, 059; Otho H. 068, 167;
William, 091, 122, 330, 460
ARINGTON: William, 003
ARMES: Dennis, 123; Erastus, 123
ARMOR: James, 068, 097, 091, 092,
128; James, 164, 296, 310;
William, 128, 178, 226, 298
ARMS: Dennis, 310; Erastus, 310;
Lewis, 310; Lucien, 315; Lucius,
092, 137, 263, 391;
Seth, 092, 231, 310
ARMSTRONG: Ajax, 092; John, 068,
092, 142, 173; John, 303, 391, 460;
William, 064, 068, 092, 117, 125,
163, 221, 270, 301, 319, 401
ARNOL: O. H. 203
ARNOLD: Fielding W. 154; John, 246;
O. H. 281, 334, 368, 385, 449; O.
H. Jr. 326, 336, 337, 342, 347,
350, 355, 368, 371, 372, 378, 420;
Sena, 004; Susie, 027; T. J. 385;
W. H. 385, 390; Will, 092; William
H., 341, 449; William W., 068;
Zachariah, 188
ARON: James, 348; John L., 092
ARONHIMER: J. 147
ARRINGTON: Elizabeth, 068; Frances,
059; Nancy I., 443; Thomas, 101;
William, 092
ARTHUR: James, 092
ASCUE: John, 420; Perry, 092
ASHBY: J. W. 332
ASHFIELD: Alfred, 128, 197
ASHMORE: John, 092, 131, 262;
Pointon, 003; Pointun, 154; Sally,
131; Sarah, 092; William, 092
ASHURST: John E., 087; John, 087;
Josiah J. 068; Martha, 126;
Robert, 126, 288
ASEW: Benjamin, 102; David, 092;
James E., 003; John, 092; Patsey,
092; Perry, 092; William H., 092;
William, 068, 092, 124, 140, 146,
149, 236, 248, 267, 276, 408, 461
ASLIN: Croenia, 040
ASPINALL: John, 124;
George, 092, 252, 292
ASPINWALL: John, 216, 310, 318
ATCHESON: Hamilton, 293;
James A. 068, 110, 254
ATCHINSON: Arnold, 092; James A.,
092, 099, 388; Martha, 092;
Samuel C. 092
ATCHISON: Hamilton, 116, 138, 250,
402; James A. 275
ATHENS: Joe Mat. 385
ATHON: Terrell, 003
ATKINS: A. 405; Joseph C. 444;
Orville, 272, 418; R. 405
ATKINSON: Alexander, 093; Armstead,
168; Cornelius, 145, 169; H. A.,
330, 449; Napolean B. 102; Samuel
J., 216; William F. 003; William, 330
ATKISSON: Jesse N. 003; Job, 092
ATTAWAY: Harly, 195; John W., 253
AULTMAN: K. 328
AUSBERN: George, 003, 041
AUSTEN: William W., 420
AUSTIN: William W., 418
AUSTON: Joe, 092
AUTER: Peter W. 094
AVANT: Eli, 092; Eliza, 092; Henry,
064, 068, 448; Lissie, 030;
Mary Ann, 021
AVARY: Asa G., 092; James C., 092,
251, 444
AVEN: E. K., Mrs., 008
AVENT: Alvas, 330; Henry, 003;
Louisa, 039; Tamlin, 469
AVERA: Alexander, 448
AVERET: Zacheus, 461
AVERETT: James, 068, 092
AVEREHART: John W. 003
AVERY: Alexander, 173; Asa G. 068,
092; Ella, 036; Harbert (heirs of),
420; Herbert, 068, 092, 093; James C.,
093, 249; James, 093, 460; Joe, 003;
Mariah, 060; Orpha, 093; Rose
Ann, 068; Samuel, 003, 064, 068;
William, 068, 093
AVERYT: Henry, 093
AVINGTON: Levi, 449; William, 158
AVRAY: Herbert, 431
AWFREY: Ann, 014
AYCOCK: William, 296
AYER: J. C., 341
AYERS: Simeon M. 367
AYLOR: Anthony, 420; John, 420
AYRE: Asher, 262
AYRES: Asher, 324; Ashur, 315
BABB: Mercer, 228
BACHELOR: Nathaniel M., 130
BACKUM: Richard, 003
BACON: Joseph, 104, 177, 182; S. W.,
093, 330, 354; S. W., Mrs., 330;
Sarah J., 093; Summer W., 003,
414; Sumner W., 158, 330
BADGER: Caroline, 047

BAER: ?, 093; D.I., 444; D.J., 157,
353, 392; David J., 330; M.J., 332
BAGGET: James, 268
BAGGETT: James, 203
BAGLEY: Moore, 093; Robert A., 093
BAGWELL: Winkfield, 304
BAILEY: Annie, 058; Azariah, 255;
B. P., 276, 330, 333, 449; B., 449;
C. A., 330; C. J., 410, 449; C. T., 330;
Charles, 093, 163, 171, 314; Clark,
449; Elisha, 330; Elisha, 003,
385; Henry W. 230; Henry, 188;
Isaac, 092, 093, 143, 168, 175,
191, 215, 229, 275, 276, 285, 291,
302, 310, 311, 317, 319, 321, 323,
433; J. J. 385; J. Z. L. 330; J.
L., Mrs., 385; James, 003; Jane,
038; Jane J. 093; Joe, 003,
093; Joel, 093, 258, 281; John M.,
093; John R. 093; John W. 003,
385; John, 003, 093, 168, 171, 180,
247, 317; Jud, 171; Judson, 093;
BAILEY: Lancy, 244; Lee, 003; Lenora
M., 019; Levicy, 294; Lucinda, 009;
Mary Ann, 310; Mary Lou. 010; Moses
P., 420; Nancy, 248; Press, 093; R.
E., 385, 449; R. S., 329, 385;
Richard W. 091, 211, 274; Robert
L., 003; Robert, 093; S. B., 183,
330, 359; Sallie B. 010; Stephen,
111; Thomas S. 427; W. C. 212,
330, 334, 359, 360, 449; W.M. 385;
W. T. 003, 330; William C. 333,
367, 449; William H., 064, 068, 310,
448; William Harrison, 003; William,
093, 094, 112, 147, 199, 219, 220,
231, 232, 269-291, 303, 305, 317,
318, 385; William Williamson, 064, 068,
093, 094, 131, 147, 182, 194, 199,
231, 232, 310, 385; Willis, 003;
Z. Clark, 330; Z.L. 385; Z. 441,
449; Zachariah, 003, 094, 310,
330, 349, 449; Zack, 449
BEVEN: Joseph, 199
BEVENS: Thomas H., 102
BEVERS: Joseph, 102
BIAS: Joe, 006; Leona, 031;
William, 006
BIBB: B. C., 379; Thomas, 140
BICKERS: J. T. 449
BICKERSTAFF: Andrew R. 265; Jane,
025; Robert W. 318; Robert, 102,
103, 311
BIDWELL: Abner, 206, 321
BIELEY: Robson, 119
BIERS: James S. 319
BIGELOW: Alonzo B., 254
BIGGS: Aaron, 133
BILLINGS: Bardwell, 103, 164, 259,
292, 435; Christoper, 103;
Elvira, 012
BILLINGSLEA: Cyrus, 091; Eugene, 386;
James, 146; Mary A., 023
BILLINGSLEY: Norvell, 161, 249;
Urban, 249; Urbun, 161
BILLINGSLY: Josie, 020; Patsy, 042
BILLUPS: J.A., 092, 296; Joel A., 133
BILLUPS: J.A., 088, 099, 236; John,
162; James, 253; Robert P., 091;
Susannah, 162; William, 162
BINFORD: Amanda, 049, 053; Augustus,
006, 333; B.W., 449; Baker S., 400;
Cicero S., 006, 069; Cola, 012;
E. A., 064, 333, 449; Elbert, 006;
Emma, 077, 030; H. W., 333; Henry
W. 069, 441; Henry, 414; Ike W.,
333, 449; J.S., 333; John K., 289,
304; Joseph L., 441; Joseph P.,
414; Joseph T. 069, 331; Josephine
S., 069; Julia, 029; Kate, 007;
BINFORD: Mary (Ware), 289; Mary A.,
049; Mattie, 052; Meeksie, 006;
Mitchell, 333, 461; Mollie P., 007;
Nancy, 030; Oliver, 103; Porter,
449; S. W., 449; Sarah, 026; Seab,
333; Sylvia, 029; T. S., 006, 449;
Thad, 449
BINGES: Thomas, 231
BINNS: Burwell, 069
BIRCH: James A., 006; John N.,
159; Morton N., 182
BIRD: Anna, 045; Carrie, 049; Edward,
302; George, 082, 118, 192; Harvey,
103; Hiram, 258; Irwin, 217; Isaiah,
103; Isiah, 103; James, 217; Job,
303; Joe, 006; John G., 175; John,
006, 111; Richard, 255; Richard,
Sr., 255; Thomas, 103; William,
006, 255, 272
BIRDSON: George L. F., 103
BIRDSONG: Anna Ann, 213;
Benajah, 069, 201, 282
BISCOE: William, 103, 129, 135,
150, 154, 155, 173, 208, 216,
217, 218, 225, 463
BISHOP: James B., 137, 259, 275;
Joseph, 296; Philip, 103;
Phillip, 103
BIUS: Miles, 333
BIVENS: Christopher H., 103;
Thomas, 285

BLACK: E. R., 350; James A., 229;
241; James, 089, 104; J. R., 199;
71, 191, 227, 294, 313, 386; John,
103, 130, 293; Joseph, 104;
Richardson, 182; Sally, 103; Thomas
J., 159; Thomas, 089, 097, 103,
191, 294, 421; William A., 142
BLACKBURN: Benjamin, 103; Martha,
259; Sidney W., 259
BLACKMAN: J. J. 441
BLACKWELL: Ad, 339; Adaline, 040;
Adeline, 333, 364; Alfred, 006,
333; Alice, 007; Amanda, 334; Annie,
004, 011; Ben, 006, 103, 333;
Benjamin, 006; Betsey, 103; C.D.,
333, 449; C. I., 006; C. Q., 449;
Carrie, 047; Charles, 369, 404;
Cornelia, 024; D.C. 006, 333, 449;
Dee, 051; E. R. 461; Ed, 006;
Edward, 006; Elbert, 006, 333, 334,
461; Emel, 386; Emuel, 103; F.,
334; Fannie, 421; Francis, 104;
BLACKWELL: Frank, 386; Franklin J.,
006; G.T. 386; Greene, 006; H.C.,
347, 449, 461; H. E. 103, 334,
354, 386, 449; H. L., 465; Henry
F., 006, 334; Henry, 334; Hensley,
449; India, 036; Isaac, 006, 007,
103, 334, 386, 390, 391; J.C. 461;
J. F. 386; J. H. 007, 069, 334,
449; J. M., 334, 449; J. Madison,
334; J. W. 449; Jack, 104, 449;
James F., 103, 134, 302, 334, 448;
BLACKWELL: James M. 007; James, 414;
John H. 104, 239, 334, 335, 414,
444, 449, 461; John P. 007; John
Warren, 007; John, 007, 103; Julia
Hunter, 008; Kate, 023; Lella, 044;
Litha Ann, 015; Lizzie, 050; Mack,
007; Malissa, 015; Manda, 386; Mary
A. 044; Mary K., 088; Mary Lizzie,
010; Mary, 355; Matilda, 014;
Mattie, 002, 036; Minnie, 040;
Mollie, 032; N.E., 461, 465; N.N.,
015; Nancy, 051; Pate, 386; R. M.,
334, 414; R.W., 104; Randolph, 312;
BLACKWELL: Robert M. 007, 104, 334,
353; Robert, 334; Rosie, 006; S.
F. 334, 386; S.H. 104, 334, 386;
S. S. 088, 104, 334, 449; S. W.
334; Sallie Kate Smith, 004; Sallie
Ophelia, 051; Samuel E., 007; Samuel
H., 064, 069, 103, 334, 253, 269,
334, 335, 397; Samuel H. Sr., 335;
Samuel J. 007, 069, 082, 335, 380,
449; Samuel, 007, 135, 373, 433;
Sarah, 103, 335; Susie, 006; T.G.
104, 441, 449; T.L., 335; T.S. 334;
Thomas G. 007, 335, 338, 435, 449;
Thomas S., 335; Thomas, 104; W.F.
W. F. 386, 449; W. Frank, 335; W.
S., 007, 386; Walker, 449; Wesley,
007, 335, 386, 380, 386, 461; Wess,
335; Will, 335, 386; William F.,007,
449; Willie, 007; Willis, 007, 335
BLAIN: Hosea B. 298
BLAIR: James, 421; Thomas, 300, 423
BLAKE: Anson, 253, 287;
Joseph, 104, 218, 421
BLAKELEY: Malessa Ann, 068
BLAKELY: Robert, 223, 272
BLAKEY: Reuben, 221, 225;
Reubin, 091
BLAN: Melvina, 004; Thomas, 126,
258, 311; Thos., 466
BLANCHARD: Frederick, 104; K., 445;
M., 445
BLAND: Lucind, 421
BLANKENSHIP: Daniel, 104;
Reuben, 104, 448
BLANKINBAKER: Cornelius, 242
BLANN: Thomas, 411, 432; William, 104
BLANTON: B. P., 361; Benjamin, 104,
428; James A., 088
BLAYLOCK: James, 205, 213
BLEAKLY: Robert, 275
BLEDSOE: J. J., 104; Jesse, 161;
Richmond, 106; Robert, 115, 125,
227, 284
BLISS: Elias, 116, 213, 231;
William W., 189
BLIZZARD: G. W., 386; Henry, 069;
James, 007, 111; William, 007
BLOCK: Frank E., 328, 372, 376;
M., 104
BLODGETT: Foster, 243
BLOODWORTH: John D., 104; John,
104; Junius, 104; Thomas F., 104
BLOSSOM: D.R., 389; Simon G., 104;
Simon G., 116, 178, 294, 386
BLOSSOMGAME: William, 296
BLOSSON: Simon G., 104
BLOUNT: Alfred G. P., 104; Alfred
W. G. T., 104; Frances (Kelly),
194; James G., 194; James, 194;
John, 069; Lucinda, 104; Susan,
069; William, 254, 255
BLOW: Frank, 365; Luticen, 365;
Will, 104
BLOWER: Sarah, 043
BLUNT: Alfred W. G. P., 104; Alfred,
386; Henry G., 231; John, 104

BLURTON: John, 104
BOEN: John, 104
BOGAN: Bell, 461; C. P., 339, 449;
  Caswell P.,104, 223, 449; Charles,
  104; Comfort, 335; Ellen H., 023;
  John, 064, 069, 194, 248, 319, 339;
  M.B., 335; Mary J., 040; Roae Ann,
  003; Shadrach, 093; Shadrack, 310;
  Thomas, 007; Tom, 007, 104
BOGGERS: Jeremiah, 315
BOGGS: Archibald, 094
BOGGUS: Jeremiah, 095
BOGGUSS: Jeremiah, 126
BOHANAN: Alexander, 105
BOHANNAH: John, 105
BOHANNON: J. A., 335; James B.,
  007; Kentchen, 421
BOISCLAIR: Peter F., 088, 134,
  192, 204
BOISSEAN: James E., 121
BOLAM: Lula Bell, 386
BOLING: Albert, 007
BOLLES: Eber M., 421
BOLTON: Charles L., 175; Curtis,
  198; John, 198, 199
BOND: Edward, 105, 421; Fanny, 421;
  Henry, 393; William L., 169;
  William S., 069, 105, 270, 311
BONES: John, 145, 249, 302, 308;
  Samuel, 145, 308
BONNELL: William, 421
BONNER: Alex, 402; Alexander, 229;
  Ally, 105; Bethany, 052; Edward,
  105; Eli, 007; George W., 105, 227;
  George, 105; Giles, 007; Gordon L.,
  007; Gordon Lee, 007; Jerry, 105,
  335; Jonathan, 105, 181, 243, 426;
  Jones, 105; Jourdan, 096; Josiah M.,
  105, 430, 433; Matilda, 151; Mattie
  H., 025; O. H., 091; Oliver H.
  P., 091, 310; Pleasant, 138; R. W.,
  091; Richard W., 091, 310; Richard,
  243; T. R., 362, 387, 389, 396;
  Thomas C., 105; Thomas L., 160;
  Thomas R., 007, 105; Thomas S., 132;
  Whitmell (heirs of), 421; Whitmell,
  105; Whitmill, 069, 105, 226;
  William, 007
BONNETT: Joe, 386
BONUEP: Roman, 028
BOOKER: John H., 258; John, 286
BOON: Exum, 069; Henry, 153; J.,
  142; Jacob, 069, 429; James, 105,
  389; Jesse, 462; John A., 313,
  449; John U., 288; Thomas, 007;
  William M., 254, 259
BOONE: George W., 007; James, 219;
  Spencer, 105; William M., 292
BOOTE: William R., 264
BOOTH: Zachariah, 234
BOOZER: O. P., 105
BORAM: George, 069; John, 069, 105
BOREN: Alfred, 135
BORISS: I. D., 007
BOPLAND: Abram, 105; Andrew, 105
BORN: John, 105
BOROUGH: James, 007
BORUM: Benjamin, 105; Benjamine, 105;
  George (heirs ot), 421; George,
  064, 105; Margaret, 105;
  Nathaniel, 105
BOSSTICK: Isaac, 007
BOSTIC: Dave, 105
BOSTICK: C. D., 259, 444; Charles
  D., 096, 105, 106, 219, 254, 300,
  312, 448; Charles O., 190; David
  D., 321; Isaac, John, 248;
  Littleberry, 192, 205; Thornton
  P., 106; Thornton, 300;
  William, 249, 312
BOSTON: John H., Jr., 007
BOSTWICK: Henry, 335; Robert P.,
  255; William, 257
BOSWELL: Elizabeth, 254; Henry, 069,
  168, 172, 231, 282; J., 256; Jerry,
  335; John W., 251, 253; Levi, 421,
  424; Lucius T., 253; William John
  W., 254; Williamson, 213
BOUGHTON: David H., 127, 143, 178
BOWDEN: Aigle, 106; Amanda M., 069;
  Caleb, 335; D.H., 335, 449; Daniel
  H., 007; Dawson, 386; Dumas, 106,
  335; Elizabeth, 043; Fannie, 335;
  I., 106; J., 016, 408, 449;
  James H., 007; James, 421, 433;
  Jesse, 106; Joe, 007; John W.,
  106; Martha E., 090; Martha Jane,
  061; Mattie Lou, 106; N. T., 365;
  Nancey, 064; Nancy, 069; Nathan
  T., 007; R. B., 449; Robert T.,
  007; Robert, 007
BOWDIN: James, 106; John T., 335
BOWDOIN: James H., 441; John Thomas,
  007; Josiah, 270; Julia, 043;
  Robert L., 226
BOWEN: Charles B., 293; Christopher
  C., 106; Horatio, 236; Josiah M.,
  311; Uriah, 444; William, 102,
  112, 122, 185, 197, 273
BOWERS: Enoch T., 444; Giles, 113;
  J. N., 106; Lessie, 335; Martha,
  113; Will L., 335

BOWIE: John, Jr., 278
BOWLES: John, 099
BOY: New, 386
BOYCE: Ker, 314, 322
BOYD: Andrew, 421; Clarisa C., 150;
  David J., 314; Elias, 106; George,
  106, 402; Henry, 270; James, 421;
  John, 106, 311; Nancy, 276; Richard
  Franklin, 007; Richard, 064, 230,
  421; Richard, Sr.(heirs of), 421;
  Samuel, 069
BOYED: J. C. R., 328; John, 384
BOYEP: W. H., 083
BOYET: John, 106; William, 106
BOYETT: Eli E., 007; William W., 288
BOYKIN: C. M., 106, 305; Charity,
  386; Dave, 335, 375, 386; David,
  007; Dilly, 021; Ellen, 106;
  Francis, 069, 106, 192, 421, 424;
  Henry, 007, 106, 386; Jesse W.,
  069; Joe, 007, 386, 406, 461; John
  M.V., 090, 106, 202, 421; Julia, 055;
  M. V., 106, 305; Minnie, 046;
  William P, 069
BOYLES: Elijah, 403; Thomas W., 106
BOYNTON: Elijah, 254; James P., 410;
  James S., 205; S.,466; Stewart, 069
BOZEMAN: Henry, 414; Leonard, 007;
  Samuel, 069
BPABSON: J. M., 461
BRACKN: John, 261, 322
BPADDY: Sarah, 039; W. E., 449;
  William E. 007
BRADFORD: Charley, 387; Edmond, 141,
  461; Edmund, 069, 106, 424, 445;
  Fielding, 105, 226, 271, 277, 317;
  John, 106, 386
BRADLEY: Bunk, 106; Ella, 021; J.
  L., 449; James, 106, 300; John A.,
  257; John W, 007; John, 283; L.
  C., 335, 466; Lee, 335; Louie, 449;
  Mat, 449; Mattie, 013; May Agnes,
  015; Mollie, 106; W. F., 335; W.
  M., 449; Willard, 168; William,
  106, 028, 313, 36
BRADSHAW: Elijah, 221
BRADY: James, 421; Thomas, 069
BPANAN: James, 421
BPANCH: Annie Kate, 028; Lessie,
  041; Mamie, 012; Robert, 335;
  Taylor, 106; Titt, 04?
BPANCHE: John, 106
BRANDON: A. M., 007, 335; Annie M.,
  057; Carrie A., 461; Frances A.,
  035; Green H., 007; Green V., 007,
  106; J. P., 106; James L., 106,
  444; James, 007, 069, 106; John
  J., 007; John, 064, 069; Lucy J.,
  007; Rebecca J. (Dawkins), 106;
  Thomas J., 007; William J., 007;
  Sam, S., 007; William T., 441
BPANHAM: Edmund, 106; Henry, 106,
  121, 182, 211, 218, 338, 401;
  Horace, 106; Joe, 007, 008; Joel,
  225; Mary Jane, 010; Mary, 003;
  Sid, 335; Wesley, 008; Willis, 375
BPANNAN: Russell, 106
BRANNOM: Horace, 335
BRANNON: Harris, 421; Willis, 008
BRANON: Charlie, 387; Hugh G., 390
BRANSFORD: John, 245
BRANSON: Will, 335
BPANT: Dink, 387; Isaac, 283, 304,
  421; Lillilan, 387
BRANTLEY: Benjamin, 279; Green D.,
  069; Greene D., 106, 320, 421; John
  H., 106, 107, 142, 189, 222, 255,
  302, 311, 387, 421, 431; John W.,
  107, 227, 400, 460; Joseph, 387;
  William M., 335
BRANTLY: John H., 107, 308
BRANUM: Harris, 069; Russell, 117
BRASEAL: Ely, 344
BRASELE: Richard, 424
BRASELTON: Jacob, 444; Reubin, 097
BRASWELL: Allen, 205; Anthony, 335;
  Caeser, 107; Candy, 051; Eselene,
  107; John, 107; New Raq, 107;
  Roxy Ann, 052; Samuel, 210
BPAWNER: Charlie, 008; Hattie J.,
  051; William, 133
BRAY: Henry, 107, 335; Katie, 042;
  Peter, 192; Thomas H., 107, 185
BRAZEAL: Kate, 152; William, Jr., 107
BRAZEL: Annie, 012; Bertha, 031;
  Frances, 033; Lawson H., 107;
  Lizzie, 009; Martha, 107; Mary, 045
BRAZIEL: William, 461
BRAZIL: Little, 352; Mose, 107;
  Samuel, 069; Wesley, 008;
BRAZILLE: Barbara, 107; Bettie, 107;
  Green, 008
BRAZILL: William, 105
BRAZILLE: Susie A., 033
BPAZWELL: Aaron, 069
BRAZZELLE: Benjamin, 421
BPEAZEAL: Willis, 420
BPEAZEAL: Green H., 265
BPEED: Thomas, 348
BREEDLOVE: Ann, 069
BPEHM: Henry, 147

APETT: Theodore F., 121
BREWER: Alford, 107; Alfred, 158;
  Benjamin W., 107; Benjamin, 107;
  Clark, 107, 198; Cofe, 107;
  Drewry, 107; Elisha W.,069; Elisha,
  107, 313; Ella J., 107; Emily W.,
  010; Ethan, 107, 198; George, 421;
  Henry, 008; John J., 107, 273;
  Mary, 107, 226; Nathan, 274;
  Nelson, 335; Oliver, 107; Oscar,
  008; Robertson, 149; Susanna, 107;
  Susannah, 107, 363, 387; Thomas A.,
  252, 292; W. J., 107; William, 387
BPEWINGTON: W. J., Jr., 441;
  William I., 188
BREWOR: Minnie, 387
BPEWSTER: Ulysses B., 257
BRIAN: T. J., 102
BRIANT: George, 311; John, 292, 407
BRICE: P. Y., 008
BRICSOE: J. M., 343
BRIDGES: Anna, 443; Bennet, 458;
  Bennett F., 064; Bennett, 069, 097,
  107; Charles, 414; Cooper, 008,
  107; Daniel, 107, 230; F. M., 449;
  Frank M., 008; Frank, 107; Henry,
  107; Herod, 277; John M., 008; John
  W., 159, 188, 190, 192, 218, 220,
  242, 246, 283, 295; John, 107, 421;
  Jonathan F., 108; Mary A., 169;
  335; Mary Ann, 018, 097; Mary Jane,
  443; Mary, 458; Mollie, 030; Scott,
  443; Thomas J., 169; Thomas, 387,
  458; Wiley J., 273; William, 008,
  108; Wiseman, 069, 106, 387
BPIDON: James, 216; Peggy, 216
BPIEN: William L., 142
BRIEPS: Elizabeth, 011; John, 069;
  Lawrence, 421
BRIGGS: Jesse F., 008
BRIGHTWELL: Moses, 093; W. B., 289
BRINKLEY: Simeon, 421, 428
BRINLEY: Frank, 387
BRISCOE: Henry, 444; J. M., 335;
  Waters, 148
BRITAIN(BRITTON): Sanford, 008
BRITT: David J.,219, 384; Willis, 069
BRITTAIN: Benjamin L., 294; J. R.,
  449; Jack, 449; Josie, 042;
  William, 316
BRITTON: George, 108; Jane, 024
BROADDUS: Thomas, 258
BROADNAX: John H., 295
BROADUS: Charley, 108; Liddy, 050;
  Neal, 387; Robert, 108; Thomas,
  108, 137, 151, 228, 355
BRODDUS: ?, 108, 449; Aggie, 022;
  Beatrice, 046; Catherine, 022;
  Charley, 008; Charlie, 008, 108;
  E. S., 108, 275, 341, 344, 353,
  354, 461; Earnest, 387; Edmund M.,
  335; Edward A., 069, 090, 108,
  109, 111, 113, 149, 172, 194, 225,
  231, 232,259, 314, 425, 466; Edward
  S., 069; Edward, 008; Elbert S.,
  008, 108; Elizabeth, 047; George,
  443; Isaac, 008; Janie L., 108;
  Joanna, 045; Lizzie, 335; Luke,
  008, 387; M. C., 335, 341; Mary,
  022, 030; Mollie, 048; Nelson, 008;
BRODDUS: Sallie, 046; Susan, 020; T.
  C., 223, 449; Thomas C., 090, 108,
  234, 259, 321, 335, 338, 341, 354,
  357, 362, 374, 421, 443, 448, 449;
  Thomas, 008, 064, 069, 109, 120,
  197, 215, 321, 421; Tom, 108,
  Valentine, 443; William M., 089,
  097, 104, 108, 152, 188, 194, 219,
  284, 300, 301, 306; William, 387,
  458; Willis, 280
BRODUS: Thomas C., 387
BROGDEN: Peterson O., 108, 387
BROGDON: Telitha Ellen, 058
BRONSON: Sim, 335; Zeno, 192; Zenos,
  089, 108, 116, 126, 228,
  238, 268, 28?
BROOKE: Joseph, 108; Tru O., 485
BROOKES: Allende(?), 387; Bailey
  C., 260; Parker, 273; William, 108
BROOKING: Edward B., 223, 420
BROOKS: Aaron, 108, 277; Aaron, Jr.,
  108; Adaline, 052; Allace, 037;
  Amma, 026; Aron, 196; Ashley, 108;
  B., 445; Bailey, 311; Baley C.,
  108; Bivings, 108; Caroline, 042;
  Delilah, 023; Elijah, 424;
  Elizabeth, 042; Emily, 028; Eugenia
  A., 335; George, 108, 387; Green,
  008; Greene, 108; Guss, 108; H.,
  449; Hattie, 045; Hiram, 108, 311,
  319, 336, 378, 381, 449, 458;
  BROOKS: Iverson L., 138; Iverson S.,
  069, 248; Jacob R., 135; James H.,
  414; James, 108, 311, 461; James,
  Sr., 069, 108; John H., 008; Joseph
  H., 343; Joseph, 449; Lafayett,
  008; Maxey, 204, 214; Moly, 271;
  Moses, 108; Nancy, 266; P. B., 336;
  Pascal, 246; Paschal, 108; Peter,
  460; R.P., 359, 375; Robert, 008;
  Russell, 069; S.I., 008, 108, 381,

387; S. J., 030; 336; Samuel W., 118; Sarah, 003; Shade, 336; Sidney 008; Silas, 108; Thomas J., 008, 109; Thomas, 008; Walker I., 138; William, 069
BROOM: Rufus, 089, 108, 158, 161, 392, 394; William, 109
BROSWELL: Teat, 109
BROTHERS: Elisha, 159
BROTHERS?: Bernd, 338; Daughtry, 340; Jordan, 329
BROUDIS: Nelson, 387
BROUDUS: Thomas 311
BROUGHTON: ?, 088, 109; Anderson, 008; Belitha, 069, 109; Charles, 069; David H, 137; Dock, 109; Ed, 336; J. A., 104, 370; J. B., 387; J.H., 103; John A., 107, 109, 239, 282, 291, 297, 305, 331-333, 366, 382, 467; John J., 329; John, 008, 288; Johnie, 387; Johnnie, 464; Joshua, 129, 227; Josie, 007; Liney, 049; Sarah, 069; W.A. 108, 305, 307, 332, 382; W.H. 331; Wash, 336; William, 107, 109, 244, 276, 300
BROWN: A.H., 461; Ada, 012; Adolphus, 387; Agnes, 109; Alfred H., 109; Amos, 109, 404, 421; Anderson, 109; Andrew M, 109, 244, 461; Anna Lou, 011; Annie, 035; Austen, 008; Austin, 109; B. W., 461; B, 133, 210, 258; Bartlett, 069, 109, 120, 151, 421, 432, 445; Bedford, 109, 115, 127, 140, 273; Benjamin, 109; C. D., 449; Charles D., 008; Christopher, 109, 130; Daniel C., 109; David, 109, 248; Dempsey, 421; BROWN: Dinah, 005; Dink, 109; Doc, 008; Drewcilla, 109; Dunk, 008, 387; Edmond T., 374; Edward, 069, 109; Ellen, 020, 045; Emma, 008, 036; Ervin, 311, 395, 411; Erwin, 120, 388; Eugenia J.,293; Fielding, 109; Francis, 109; Frank, 008; Genie, 047; George A., 069; George F., 008; George Y., 336; George, 008; Georgia, 288; Hamilton, 093, 100, 117, 123, 126, 138, 151, 164, 174, 177, 182, 185, 189, 198, 213, 225, 234, 266, 283, 293, 303, 308; Henry L., 449; Henry, 008, 109, 262; Hiram, 230; Hugh, 109, 275; I.W. 208, 464, 465; Ike W. 398, 462; Irwin W., 008; Isbel, 109;
BROWN: Isham, 109; J.H., 336; J. H., Mrs., 110; J.W., 336, 410; James (heirs of), 421; James E., 109, 110, 331, 421, 423; James L., 240; James Richard, 008; James Wesley Davis, 008; James, 069, 109, 297; Jeremiah, 069; Jim, 069, 109; John A., 008; John G. W., 110, 311; John G., 110; John H., 255; John T., 334; John W., 069; John, 008, 109, 110, 164, 167, 171, 245, 265, 421;
BROWN: Jonas R., 109; Jonas R., 178; Joseph E., 010, 110, 199; Joseph E., Gov., 197; Joseph, 173, 273, 278; Josiah R., 213, 217; Josiah, 069; Josias R., 109, 237; Julia, 059; Kitt, 110; Levi., 336; Levy, 110; Lina, 031, 052; Lizzie, 032, 052; Louisa, 058; Louisiana, 053; Lucinda A., 261; Lucinda, 025; M. E., Mrs., 010; Malinda, 037; Margaret, 022, 043; Marla, 445; Martha B., 157, 379; Martha M, 020; Martha, 034; Mary, 027, 028, 336; Mat, 045; Myrna (Gordon), 275;
BROWN: N. B., 109; Otis, 336; R. G., 441; R.J., 132, 157; Rachael, 029; Richard, 336; Richmond, 110, 191, 281, 387; Robert C., 110; Robert, 069, 089, 110, 152, 160, 197, 220, 229, 232, 237, 292, 311, 469; Rufus, 218; Russel J., 069, 096, 135, 194, 212, 233-235, 261, 269, 291, 374, 449; Russel 200; Russell B, 269; Russell J., 210, 290, 307, 314, 315, 322, 345, 361; 382; Russel J, 354, 367; Salle, 056;
BROWN: Sally, 133; Sanders, 133; Sarah Jane, 059; Seaborn S., 008; Selina, 024; Sim, 008; Simeon N., 288; Simon, 110; Sucky, 069; Susan, 013; Sylvia, 022; T.J., 110, 336, 387, 449; T. W., 110; Tekoah J., 008; Thomas A., 114, 132, 218; Thomas, 069, 110, 155; Thomas Jr., 110; Thomas, Sr., 318; Tucker, 336; W. D., 008, 449; W. J., 449; W. N., 373; William, 110, 200, 271, 296, 297, 387, 429; Wills, 110, 461; Woodie 008
BROWNFIELD: John, 094, 110, 180, 295
BROWNING: Andrew F., 220; Isaiah, 092
BROWNSFIELD: John, 244
BRUCE: B.F., 387; John M., 187; John, 018; Sary, 445
BRUNSON: Willie, 008
BRYAN: Alexander, 167; Bartram, 110; Bartrum, 110; Felise, 237; Felix,

159, 259, 287; Isaac, 429; J. M., 352; James, 198; R. G., 390; Travis, 387; Willis, 008
BRYANT: A.G., 394; Addie, 019; Alice, 387; Amanda, 002; Artemus, 069, 421; Barberella, 336; Bird, 110, 152, 441; C. N., 008, 335, 449; C., 449; Cody C., 372; Cody, 336, 349; Columbus, 11, 450; Cornelia, 058; D.W., 450; E.L. 110; Edmund, 397; Fannie, 056, 111; Fanny Lou, 057; H. J., 450; H., 450; Henry, 111; Hilliard, 111; J. E., 441; J. H., 394; J. J., 450; James H. 291; James, 069; James, 111; Jarrott, 111; Jefferson E, 110; Jefferson, 450; Jim Henry, 397; Jim, 387; BRYANT: Joe, 387; John E., 243; John, 069, 111, 318, 336; Johnie, 069; Joseph C.,132; L.P., 450; Lee, 009, 111; Lovie, 048; Lum, 111; Margaret, 010; Mary Ann, 048; Mattie, 025; N. J., 054; Nancy, 111; Needhah, 111; Rena, 445; Susan, 336; Temp, 111; Tilda, 047; William, 111; Willie, 111
BRYCE: William, 238
BRYOM: John, 244
BRYSON: D. G., 445; Harper, 202; I., 329; William, 202
BUCHANAN: Alexander N., 261; Benjamin B., 111; Benjamin, 069; George F., 105; George H, 090, 421; James E., 111; James, 237, 263, 421; John W., 411, 421; John, 421; MichaJah, 421; William B. 426
BUCHANNAN: Alexander N., 069, 111, 395; Alexander, 392; George, 111; Henry, 212; James, 166, 212; Joseph, 092, 094, 129, 131, 141, 156, 168, 172, 179, 204, 207, 233, 244, 265, 270, 304
BUCHANNON: Alexander N., 111; Alexander R., 126, 141; E.C., 365; George F., 111; George H., 111; Henry, 115, 131, 142; J. W., 365; James P., 111; James, 111, 086, 263, 426; James, Sr., 069; John, 069, 142, 153, 299; Joseph, 089, 091, 093, 095, 103, 104, 109-111, 123, 124, 127, 129, 145, 152-153, 167, 168, 173, 174, 180, 191, 200, 208, 216, 223, 227, 229, 230, 244, 246, 252, 260-262, 264, 269, 272, 275, 280, 292, 299, 313, 316, 322, 324, 402, 430; Pleasant, 153; Priscilla, 299; Robert, 184
BUCHANON: James, 111, 434; John (heirs of), 425
BUCK: John, 111, 199
BUCKHANNON: John, 111
BUCKLEY: Justus R, 318
BUCKNER: Alice, 458; Daniel, 111; John, 111; Lucy, 026; William, 387, 458
BUGG: Anselm, 267, 459
BUIAS: Eliza, 023
BUICE: John, 111
BUIS: Elbert, 009, 111, 421; John, 069, 097, 111, 162; Nancy, 421; William P., 100, 198; Zachariah, 111
BULKELEY: Justus R., 319
BULKLEY: Horace, 178; John T. 305, 320; Justus R., 094, 119; William H., 305, 320
BULLARD: Dr. 444; Elizabeth, 027; Francis, 336; H.W. 203, 372, 450; H., 469, 111, 203, 223, 271-272, 344, 371, 372, 380, 450; James M. 311; James M... Jr., 336; James, 111; James, Jr., 111; James, Sr., 069, 111, 181, 283, 444; Jarmoney G., 283; Jesse, 421; John W., 458; Leona, 041; M. L., 464; Mary, 445; Matilda, 458; Nancy Ann, 111; S. H., 203, 344, 371, 450; Samuel, 336; Tapley, 421; Thomas, 111, 159, 271; Uldine, 053; W. M., 009, 450; Wiley W. 108, 111, 311; Wiley, 069; William J., 445
BULLOCK: Richard, 111; Uriah I., 218
BUNN: Warren, 165
BUNYARD: James, 158
BURDETT: Henry, 399; Samuel L. B., 111, 387
BURDETTE: Samuel L. B., 387
BURDICK: Lysander, 224
BURFORD: Boss, 387; Leonard, 158
BURG: John, 111
BURGAY: John M, 311
BURGE: Hamilton, 191, 267, 296; John, 111, 265, 322, 387, 401; Wylle, 255
BURGESS: James, 421; John, 258, 311; Thomas, 111
BURK: David G., 009; W. P., 461; Walter, 336
BURKARD: John Christian, 297
BURKE: Francis, 111, 157; Jim, 410; Wallace, 253; William B. 112
BURKES: William, 112
BURKS: B. M., 450; James L. 102, 421; James S., 112; Robert, 212;

William, 112, 154, 242
BURNAM: William, 421
BURNER: Alford, 251; Boble, 450; William, 009
BURNES: Birdsong, 107; Elizabeth, 011; William H., 009
BURNETT: Anthony, 112; Charles A., 130; John, 112; Julian D. 009; Peter, 009; William M., 120, 344; William, 112
BURNEY: (?), 444; A. H., 269, 385, 400, 408, 450, 464; Alice (Faulkner), 342; Arthur, 009, 421, 422; Augustus H., 009; Bob, 112; Buck, 112; C. C, 112, 336, 366, 387, 444, 450; C. R., 009, 450; Carrie, 043, 050; Catherine T.,034; Charles C., 069, 112, 387, 414; 448, 450; Elbert, 009; Ella, 112; Eugene, 112; G. W., 112, 450; George, 009; George W., 450; Gilbraith, 120; Harrison 387; Ida, 055; J. H., 009, 069, 082, 387, 414, 450, 461; J. L., 450; J. W., 203, 336, 444, 450; J. W., Jr., 142, 953, 388; Jack, 009, 336; BURNEY: James L., 009, 094, 131; James S., 384; James, 112; Jeff, 112; Jim, 009, 112, 336; John W. 082, 090, 108, 112, 115, 116, 132, 135, 206, 222, 231, 241, 245, 274, 285, 297, 293, 307, 336, 387, 414, 421, 450; John W., Jr. 112, 190, 217; John W., Sr. 069; John, 112, 279; 323; Joseph H, 009, 112; 450; Joseph, 009, 336, 450; Katie, 006; Lola, 034; Man, 336; Martha L., 112; Mary, 026; P.S. 328, 329, 410; Patrick S., 365; S. A., 329; BURNEY: Samuel; 365; Silvanus W.,112; Sylvanus, 009; Thomas J., 115, 112, 160, 260; Tom, 069; Vora, 053; William, 009, 112; William A., 009; William V., 087, 093, 107, 112, 116, 119, 120, 127, 136, 142, 154, 162, 199, 207, 208, 216, 229, 239, 303, 302, 421; William, 009, 112, 122, 336, 408; Zeb, 112
BURNS: Cornelius, 112; Henry T., 414; Martha, 360; Nancy A., 054; Thomas H., 112; W.J., 441; W.J., 112; William J., 394
BURR: S. B., 112
BURRIS: Taylor, 256
BURROW: Phillip, 009
BURTON: Abraham, 422; H. W., 450; Henry W., 009; Henry, 336; Isaih, 009; J.C., 466; J.O., 369; Martha, 037; Patsey W., 113; Pleasant, 265; Sarah (Foreman), 160; Sarah, 113; William, 113
BUSBY: M. A., 336; M. C., 336, 387; Susanna, 387
BUSE: Joseph, 279
BUSH: H. D., 347, 357; John, 113; Mary, 422
BUSICK: Samuel A. 243
BUSSEY: C. L., 450; Charles L., 113; Hezekiah, 144; Jim, 009; Moses, 009
BUSSY: Charles L., 113; Jim, 387
BUTLER: David, 113; Dennis, 009; Edward, 422; G.D., 445; James, 113; John, 113, 325; Laura, 058, 096; Lewis, 009, 336; Partrick, 422; Patrick, 426; Samuel W., 274, 275; Samuel, 298; Thomas, 069, 087, 112, 113, 125, 254, 264; Umphry, 336; William, 260
BUTNER: C. A., 336, 387; Charles A.,336
BUTRAM: Andrew, 113; James, 113, 227
BUTRELL: Burwell, 113
BUTRUM: James, 422
BUTT: E.C., 411; Eldridge, 190; John D., 226, 354; John, 136, 220; Joshua R., 354; Joshua W., 226; Moses, 122; Noah, 123, 190
BUTTER: Jack, 336
BUTTRELL: Thomas, 089, 422; William, 260
BUTTS: Bell, 113; Bill, 336; Charles, 336; Clara, 035; Dumas, 387; Henry, 113, 311, 435; James, 091; Mat, 336; Moses, 320; Redic, 387; Samuel (heirs of), 422; Samuel, 069, 092, 109, 114, 117, 121, 124, 140, 143, 146, 153, 164, 169, 172, 175, 206, 217, 270, 272, 294, 298, 303, 304, 312, 432; William, 387
BYARS: Alice, 004; Angeline, 011; Frances B., 038; G.W., 450; Gabe, 336; J. M., 430, 450; John, 069; Kittie Ann, 019; Leah, 336; Levina, 018; Miles, 009; O., 441; Obadiah, 064, 069; Richard D., 170; William, 238
BYAS: John, 009; Walker, 113
BYBEE: J. A. 379
BYERS: Haddle, 387; Miles, 336
BYINGTON: Bud, 009; Joshoway, 336; Joshua, 009
BYRAM: Harriet, 029; Mat. 113; Silas,

336; Josephine, 045
BYRNE: T., 234
BYROM: Cynthia, 113, 253; Eliza P., 113; Eliza, 113; Henry C., 113; Henry, 009, 313, 387; Jennie, 336; John (heirs of), 422; John L.D., 113, 207, 246, 266, 288, 315, 319, 321, 324; John S. D., 113, 150; 191, 209, 221, 234, 245, 313; John, 069, 113, 116, 148, 150, 253, 321, 422; Manuel, 009; Mat, 336; Matt, 009, 336; Seymore S., 069, 113, 436; Seymour L., 428; Seymour S. (heirs of), 422; Seymour S., 434; William A., 324; William H., 113, 269, 284, 320, 323, 387, 402; William, 113, 150
BYRON: John, 284; William H., 284
BYRUM: Tobe, 387; William H., 172; William, 113, 393
CABANESS: E.G., 204; George A., 332; George, 230; Harrison, 230, 422, 431; Henry B., 113, 230; Palatier, 230; William, 241
CABANISS: George A., 332, 333, 399
CABINESS: Elbridge G., 190; Harrison, 316; Henry B., 090, 113, 387; Henry H., 101; Sally, 139
CADWELL: Lucius T., 159
CAIN: Elisha, 230
CALAWAY: Elmore, 311
CALDWELL: Creed, 113; David, 113, 213; Ebenezer, 275; Edward, 387; John, 250; William D., 069; William, 221
CALFFREY: Harrison, 422
CALHOUN: John L., 242; Lewis, 422
CALLAHAN: Jeremiah, 154
CALLAWAY: Elizabeth, 113, 143, 144, 163, 194, 196, 231, 252, 267, 299, 459; Elmore, 113, 254; J. C., 009; Jabez C., 113, 422; James C., 069, 113; James J., 173, 191; James R., 448; James, 009, 097, 113, 136, 166, 178, 267, 293, 299; Jobe, 114; John, 069; Jonathan, 114, 458; Jordan W., 422; Joshua, 069, 089, 113, 114, 144, 163, 231, 252, 267, 280, 299; Noah, 114; Thomas H., 290; Tobe, 114; William W., 114; William, 433
CALLIS: Otho W., 275, 298
CALLOWAY: Edward, 114; Elizabeth, 118, 296, 299; Elmore, 114, 313; James, 202; Peter, 114
CALVERT: J. F., 329, 388; John M., 114, 448; John, 114; S. W., 329, 388; Susan E., 069
CAMERON: David, 300; James H., 114; James, 114, 136, 286, 306, 311; William H., 009; William, 105, 114, 183
CAMERSON:(?) William, 311
CAMPA: Benjamin, 287
CANFIELD: Abial, 213; Robert B., 137, 144, 278, 293
CAMMERON: James, 136
CAMP: Arch, 114; Carlton, 009; Charles, 268, 291; Harry, 090; Henry, 147; James B., 135; John P., 291; Joseph T., 175, 228; Lucinda, 268; Siller, Mrs., 364; Thomas, 114, 225, 338, 339, 341, 344, 350, 357, 363, 370, 378, 403, 422; William J., 445
CAMPBELL:
336; Andrew G., 114; Angie, 060; Ashley, 450; Beulah M., 012; Bill C., 009; Bill, 009, 115, 336, 414, 461; C. C., 450; C. E. F. W., 448; C. G., 114, 336, 337, 368, 379, 381; C. H., 450; C. L., 364; C. L., Mrs., 114; Calvin, 009; Charles A., 114; Charles E. F. W., 069, 114, 153, 186; Charles E.F., 114; Charles G., 009, 069, 114, 240, 331, 337; Charles, 114, 324, 366;
CAMPBELL: Clementine, 337; Clemmie, 337; Cooley, 069, 114, 242, 337; Dora, 090; Dorcas, 069, 150; Doyle, 444; Duncan, 114; E.D., 009, 450; E. E. F. W., 441; E.G., 450; E.H., 450; E. L., 114, 357, 389, 450; Ednie, 020; Elbert, 450; Elvira, 114; Evan, 009; Frank, 450; George, 009, 337; Gus, 364; India, 336; J. F., 450; J. H., 344, 355, 384, 391; 452; J. J., 450; J. L., 337, 343, 345, 353, 354, 363, 976, 384, 450;
CAMPBELL: J. M., 337, 374, 388, 464; James A., 402; James C., 169, 264; James H., 114, 210, 337, 343, 345, 348, 349, 352, 365, 367, 375, 378, 388, 450; James L., 069, 330, 334, 347, 347, 350, 366, 367, 396, 450; James M., 114, 388; James, 114, 450; Jane, 020; Jarrett, 069; Jas. H., 465; Jasper, 337; Jeff, 114; Jennie B., 014; John J., 009, 450, 464; John V. E., 009; John, 009, 114, 128, 181, 188, 191, 226, 262,

272, 311, 321, 337, 388, 422, 450;
CAMPBELL: Johnie, 009; Kate, 336; Leroy, 388; Lewis, 009; Lucius T., 306; Lum, 114; M.C., 262; M.E., 156; M. O., 337, 450; Martha A., 027, 414; Martha J., 016; Mat, 010; Mattie Lou, 043; Maud, 004; Nellie, 115; Nettie, 053; Oscar, 450; P.D., 010, 450; P.S., 337, 388; Richard S., 069, 115; Richard, 010, 064, 069, 115; Robert, 388; Pubin, 388; S. R., 344, 345, 359-361, 371, 374, 375, 378, 388, 391, 446, 450, 467; Sarah Jane, 011; Sarah, 157; Thomas, 272; W.C., 354, 450; William C., 069, 337, 354; William, 010, 088, 114, 115, 261, 267, 337, 422, 434; Willie Ann, 004; Willie, 388; Zimma, 053
CANANT: Jeremiah, 423, 427, 433; Jerry 115, 260, 422; William L., 115
CANATT: William, 115
CANDE: David, 125, 143
CANDLE: James, 115
CANDLER: A. D., 333, 352; Allen D., 337, 422
CANE: John, 403
CANNAFAX: Benjamin, 115
CANNANT: Chesley, 149
CANNON: Henry, 115; J.W., 462; James, 104, 115; Mureler (Tomlin), 115; Nathaniel, 115; Samuel G., 151; Thomas L., 010; W. F., 350
CANON: John, 010
CANTELOU: Lewis C., 198
CAPE: William B., 115
CAPERS: Amos, 388; Dora, 388; H.D., 444; S. E., 337; William H., 153
CAPES: T. C., 444
CAPS: Eli, 115
CAR: Cely, 010
CARBINE: P. V., 337, 365
CARD: Ada, 050; Annie, 055; Anthony, 352; Florence, 018; Josie, 054; Noah, 010; Peter, 115, 388; Preston, 010; Rachael, 021; Sylla, 021
CARDEL: John C., 069
CARDELL: Aaron, 115, 337; Annie E., 009; Annie L., 033; C. E., 337; Calvin C., 024; E. W., 244; Ed W., 337; Elizabeth, 060; Fannie E., 043; Fannie, 337; J.B., 450; J.C., 450; J. J., 337, 450, 465; J., 450; Janie L., 020; John C., 450; John J., 010; John, 115, 337, 347, 450; Joseph B., 010; Lillie, 040; M.A., 058; M. B., 034; M. F., 337; Mary P., 337; Nettie, 012; Otis, 450; P.D., 337, 441; Peter D., 337, 461; Peter, 010, 069, 115, 337, 356; Sarah Ann, 007; Virginia L., 040; W.J., 450; William J., 010; William, 010, 115, 337, 441, 450
CARDELLF: Peter, 115, 388
CARDEN: Elizabeth, 016; James, 088; John, 086; William, 418, 422
CARDIN: John, 115; Sarah, 367; William (heirs of), 423; William, 069
CAREL: Benjamin B., 422
CAREY: E. V., 337, 389; Edward J., 010; Henry, 010; J. A., 337; Job A., 337
CAPGALL: John P., 389
CARGEL: Lucius, 010
CARGIL: Carrie, 115; Ozroe, 115; Rachael, 388
CARGILE: Augustus, 115; Benjamin M., 179, 285; Brisco, 337; Carrie, 023; Charles, 069, 110, 115, 116, 119, 142, 152, 158, 167, 171, 210, 220, 222, 235, 249, 299, 311, 316, 317, 396, 408; Charles, Jr., 115, 422; Charlotte, 049; Cinda, Mrs., 019; Clayton, 089; Dan, 115; Dave, 115; Easter, 022; Eliza, 021, 030; Eugenia T., 116; Feb, 333; Geor. B., 005; Henry N., 010; Howard, 256;
CARGILE: James, 115, 141, 181, 299, 311, 316, 318, 322; Jason, 115, 311; John (heirs of), 115, 311; John R., 116, 115, 126, 133, 240, 317, 422; John W., 010; John, 010, 069, 089, 113-116, 141, 168, 221, 222, 299, 316, 318, 319, 322, 338, 422; John, Sr., 116; Joseph H., 223; Joseph J., 116, 299, 317, 388; Kelly, 010, 116; Lavina W., 116, 422; Lavinia M., 299; Lavinia W., 221; Lavinia, 116, 141, 318;
CARGILE: Lizzie, 059; Margaret, 010; Mary, 231, 250, 305; Micajah, 010, 115; Monroe B., 116; Munroe B., 388; Rufus, 116; Punno B.M., 116, 177, 299; Sallie George, 053; Sallie, 461; Shade, 388; Susan, 028; Thomas, 069, 096, 116, 199, 226, 296, 300, 311, 420; Thos, 461; William H., 115, 116, 175, 276, 307, 311; William, 115, 116, 141, 221, 299, 300, 316, 318, 422;

2eo, 010; 2ep, 010
CARGILL: Charles, 272; Emeline, 045; John, 138
CARGLE: Anna, 058; Berta May, 046; John, 010
CARGOL: J. W., 450; Oliver, 388
CARGYLE: John, 329, 337, 338
CARHART: Elijah H., 284; Elijah, 115; Elison E., 189; George W., 107; James B., 284; James D., 115, 157, 159, 228; Whitfield D., 105; William B., 115, 159, 284; William, 157, 228
CARIL: Thomas, 116
CARLETON: Charles G., 164
CARLILE: George N., 142; John R., 116, 253
CARLISLE: George M., 388; George W., 116, 388; Mary, 070
CARMAN: J. Q. M., 010
CARMICHAEL: J. C., 375; J. R., 337, 351, 360; John, 070, 181, 204, 248
CARMON: Bell, 024; John Q. A., 117; Laura V., 117
CARNES: Thomas P., 086, 158, 388
CARNEY: John, 469; Josiah, 469
CAROL: David, 117
CARR: Calvin George, 388; Cathrien, 020; Dock, 010; George T., 235, 290; John, 010, 338, 370, 391; Josie, 061; Lizzie, 043; Lynn, 388; Peggy, 033; Samuel, 010, 133, 448; Willie, 388
CARREL: Susan, 100; Thomas, 100
CARRELL: Jesse, 117; John, 293; Redman, 450; Richmond, 117; Spencer, 148; William, 311
CARPIEL: Grief, 258
CARPINGTON: John J., 198; John, Sr., 198
CARPOL: Abner, 388; Benjamin, 434; David, 175; E. H., 330; Susannah, 117; William (heirs of), 422
CARROLL: Benjamin, 208; E. H., 341; E. W., 010; Joseph T., 010; M. J., 388; Redman, 117; Thomas, 117; W. J., 433
CARPY: Doyle, 388
CARSBY: James, 388
CAPSELL: Jim, 117
CARSON: Adam, 121; David, 184
CARSTARPHEN: Oren D., 115
CARSWELL: Neal, 117
CARTER: ?, 117; Abraham, 010; Adolphus, 010; Alex, 338; Alexander, 338, 460; Amanda, 117; Anderson, 010; Andrew, 388; Ann, 035; Armstead, 313; Armsted, 391; Beir(?), 006; Berry Lee, 010; Berry, 010; Booker B., 388; Burke, 010; Carrie, 029; Easter, 033; Eli, 338; Elisha M., 117; Ellis, 010; Farish, 117; Frank, 010, 388; George, 338; Grant D., 151; Hector, 338; Iga, 012; Indiana, 048; Isaac, 154, 192, 259; Jacob, 136; John A., 117, 177; John N., 302; John W., 461; John, 117, 255, 279, 422, 468;
CARTER: Joseph, 113, 117, 122, 123, 145, 184, 236, 255, 257, 298; Josiah, 117; Judy, 040; Kate, 010; Kissiah, 070; Landon, 070, 117, 445, 448; Langdon, 117; Lawson, 010, 338; Lillie, 042; Littleton, 422; Louiza, 036; Marcus E., 010; Martha E., 047; Martha, 377; Martin, 010; Narcisa, 015; Nathan, 098; Ophelia, 041; Randol, 010; Richard V., 117, 118, 311; Richard, 070, 096, 104, 117, 118, 140, 141, 165, 255, 299; Richard, 305, 311; Sarah, 053; Temperance, 064, 117; Thomas Hector, 010; Thomas, 117, 118, 148, 164, 173, 206, 257, 266, 267, 288; Thomas, 300, 347; Thornton, 214; W. M., 010, 338, 388, 446, 450; William B., 099, 115, 388; William, 162; William H., 117
CARTWRIGHT: John, 263; Martha, 263
CARY: C. A., 338; Charles A., 450; D.T., 338, 450; E.V., 468; Emily V., 379; J.A., 118, 338, 373, 450; Job A., 118, 338, 450, 458; Job, 353; Jobe A., 118, 338; P. Frank, 446; Tom, 118, 338
CASE: Midleton W., 118; Wiley J., 070
CASEY: Thomas G., 168; Thomas J., 106, 110, 302
CASH: Jim, 010
CASHIN: John, 091, 118, 122-124, 133, 138, 139, 143, 169, 175, 181, 183, 196, 243, 302, 303, 413
CASHING: Isaac T., 291
CASILS: Absalom, 243
CASTALOW: Amy, 422
CASTELLO: Amy, 422; John (heirs of), 422
CASTELLOW: Amey (Hill), 174; John B., Sr., 070; John, 118, 174; William H., 118

CASTELOW: John, 219
CASTILLOW: Amy, 118; John B., 118; John, 118, 388
CASTILOW: Edward, 109, 118, 136, 286, 422, 432; Thomas, 070; Warren T., 436
CASTON: Asia M., 234; Eliza (Mason), 234; James, 215
CASWELL: Theodore D., 382; W.C., 118
CATCHINGS: Asperry, 118; Asbury, 118, 338, 352; Bart, 010, 118, 338; Barton, 010; Charles, 010, 118; Dave, 338; David, 010, 118; Elbert G., 070, 086; Eliza, 338; Josephine, 118; Mattie, 012; Mitchell, 118; Stephen, 338
CATE: James, 118, 425
CATER: Hezekiah W., 092
CATES: Charles, 297
CATHCINGS: Elbert G., 091
CATHEY: J. A., 356
CATHY: James, 118
CATLIN: John, 172, 267
CATREL: Milley, 051
CAUBLE: Peter, 139
CAVENDER: Barbara, 037; Frances, 281; Obediah E., 281
CAY: Wilson H., 388
CELLARS: Silas, 422
CHAFFIN/CHAFIN: H. F., 450; H. Lee, 450; J.J., 450; J.T., 450; R.G., 450; T.L., 450; T.P., 450; Thomas P., 450; V. A., 450; Virgil, 450
CHAFFIN: Ada, 052; Beulah Kate, 034; Beverly, 070, 169; Cassie, 037; Cinthia Clara, 034; Florence, 017; Green, 118; Greene, 338; Harriet A., 043; Henry, 010, 338; Hiram F., 010; J.M., 388; J. W., 010; Jeptha J., 118; John T., 070; John W., 010; John, 118, 150, 448; Joshua, 388, 423, 432; Mary, 240; Moses, 118, 311, 312; T.L., 388; T.S., 338; Thomas L., 010; Thomas P., 118, 288, 399, 441; Thomas Percy, 118; Thomas, 118; V. A., 338, 388; Virgil, 338; William F. ..., 118; Zachariah, 133
CHAFIN: Beverly, 136; John D., 118; John O., 312; John, 422; Joshua, 118, 422; Moses, 118, 301, 322, 448; Nathan, 118, 119; Patsey, 048; R. G., 010; Robert, 421; Thomas P., 119, 312; Tyre, 010
CHAIPES: Thomas P., 293
CHALIN: Moses, 263
CHAMBERLAIN: Annie, 029; Benjamin V., 249; Benjamin, 119; Charles V., 094, 099; Elliott R., 153
CHAMBERLIN: Robert, 011
CHAMBERS: Alexander, 264, 293; Balzona, 038; C. G., 119, 336, 338, 450; Charles G., 421, 422; Edwin, 154; J. W., 338; John W., 458; John, 011; Mattie A., 039; Robert, 422; Sarah A., 458
CHAMBLISS: Lawson G., 105
CHAMPION: Elizabeth G., 119, 388; Elizabeth, 119; J.W., 011; Jesse, 011, 119; Littleberry, 251; Moses (heirs of), 422; Moses, 070, 119, 151, 244, 295, 404, 427
CHANCE: Allen, 119, 388, 422, 430
CHANDLER: C. B., 388; Elizabeth, 247; Henry, 247; Job, 164; John, 119
CHANEY: Earvin, 011; Jackson, 238, 411
CHANNEL: Sarah, 038
CHANY: Jackson, 305
CHAPMAN: Aaron, 011; Abner, 011, 070, 091, 105, 109, 111, 113, 119, 122, 123, 128, 137, 143, 145, 148, 157, 167, 169, 172, 224, 235, 244, 248, 261, 262, 303, 308, 312, 397, 448; Abner, Jr., 119, 158, 206, 286, 422; Abner, Sr., 119, 128, 186, 316; Adaliza, 052; Allen, 338; Amelia, 054; Andrew, 011; Annie, 023; Asa W.F., 064, 070, 388; Asa W., 388; Asa, 119, 235, 312, 388; B. W., 235, 450; Benjamin, 105; Betsey Ann, 017; Betsey, 109; Britain, 105; Brittain, 119; Britton W., 119; Britton, 262; Crawford, 011; Crof, 388; Cynthia, 235; Dora, 011; Edmond, 070; Emily C., 056; H.H., 441; Henry H., 226, 246; John, 070; Lucy, 009; Patience, 445; Queen, 055; Solomon, 119; Turner, 228; W. W., 194; Will, 011, 119; William W., 202, 304; William, 119, 126
CHARLES: Richard, 011; Willie, 011
CHARPING: P. H., 450; Preston, 011, 450; S. C., 338, 352, 366, 380, 388, 450; Samuel C., 336, 342
CHARTER: George, 116
CHATHAM: Henry, 011; Bobbie, 338; Eli, 011; Frank, 011; H. H., 011, 450; Henry, 388, 450; James, 011;

Janie, 338; Lewis, 011, 338; Lucius, 011; Sallie, 009, 388; Sudie, 055; Walter, 011; William, 011; Willie, 388
CHEAK: Elise, 219
CHEATHAM: W. D., 388
CHECK: John W., 106
CHEEK: Angeline, 032; Anna, 002, 050; Ellis, 424, 450; Frank, 011; John W., 011, 070, 294, 414, 448; Lafayett, 011; Lafayette, 070; Lizzie, 061; Lucy, 006; Mallory S., 011; Mattie E., 021; Moses, 011; N.H., 450; Nancy, 045; Rebecca Ann, 009; T.J., 450; Temperance, 371; Thad, 450; W. R., 405, 448, 450; Walter P., 011; William R., 450; William, 064, 070, 388
CHEESMAN: Oscar, 374
CHEEVES: Thomas, 100
CHENEY: Jackson, 205, 260; John, 388; Linton, 086, 295; W. R., 388, 414; William R., 070
CHENY: J., 388
CHEPPY: David S., 196; James, 338; Jesse, 070, 089, 185, 204, 250, 283, 307; Jim, Jr., 389; John Henry, 011; L. H., 011
CHICHESTER: Thomas W., 211, 234
CHILDEPS: E. D., 388; Mattie F., 046; Stephen, 226
CHILDS: Charley, 011; Elizabeth, 23?; Felix, 257; Green, 450; Henry, 011, 070; Jack, 070; Jacob, 011; John A.D., 461; John L., 324; John, 011, 338, 389; Lizzie, 225; Mary Lou, 007; N. G., 011, 225, 406, 441, 443, 461; N. H., 450; Nannie, 052; Otis, 295, 304; Robert, 125, 262, 328, 332, 338, 340, 368, 380, 390, 406, 450, 461; Thomas M., 237, 422; Walter W., 011
CHILES: Felix, 335
CHIPON: Andrew I., 201
CHISOLM: William, 094; Willis P., 295
CHISSAM: Frances, 023
CHISSON: Andrew J., 201
CHOICE: Tully, 144
CHOVEY: Charles L., 404
CHRISTIAN: Henry, 346; Ira, 444; Johnnie, 054; R. T., 346; William, 113
CHRISTIE: William, 125
CHUGS: Louisa, 047
CHUNN: H. F., 011
CHUPP: J. C., 399
CHUPCH: M. E., 359
CHURCHFIELD: Alford, 389
CHURCHILL: Isaac, 011
CHURCHWELL: A. P., 389
CIMBPOUGH: John, 227
CINQUEFIELD: William, 389
CISSON: Richard M. (heirs of), 435; Richard M., 448
CLACK: Henry, 378; J. J., 357; Thomas R., 414
CLACKLY: Jacob (heirs of), 422
CLAIBORN: T. B., 450
CLAIBORNE: T.B., 011; Thomas B., 011
CLARK: Ada, 031; Alex, 011, 338; Alf, 338; Alfred, 011; Alice, 269; Allen, 011, 064, 338; Amanda, 458; Arter, 389; Arthur, 466; Bannie(?), 020; Burrel C., 088; Burrell C., 261; Cintha, 055; Clara, 014; Daniel, 389; David, 011, 216; Edmond, 011; Edward, 223; Elijah, 278; Elizabeth, 021; Ella, 021; Ellen, 458; Emily, 070; Emma 2, 039; Emma, 269; Essemon, 016; Eula, 021; Francis A., 070; Garret, 141;
CLARK: Garrett, 279; George W., 070; George, 011, 064, 201, 213, 256, 282, 312, 430; Gilbert, 064, 070; Green, 011; H.W., 288; Harriet E., 043; Henry, 441; J. C., 341, 346; J. C., Dr., 346; J. R., 087; James B., 261; James, 239; Jeremiah, 100, 166, 189, 249, 250, 307; Joe, 389; John W., 135; John, 011, 064, 070, 181, 290, 312, 389; Jonas, 196; Joseph, 070; Josephus, 231, 312; Joshua B., 248; Joshua L., 218; Joshua, 070; Kate, 033; Larkin, 303; Leama, 064; Lewis, 119; Lindsey, 011; Lula, 006; Mack, 389; Martin, 011, 119, 338, 389; Matt, 389; Micajah, 119; Mollie, 061; Robert W., 450; Robert, 011; Sallie, 038; Samuel, 119, 444; Sanford, 107; Sarah Martha, 022, 025; Susan, 024; Thomas, 070; Thomas E., 422; Thomas F., 011; W. C., 158, 238, 334, 366, 374, 390, 403; W. W., 253; Warren, 011; Will, 258, 389; William D., 389; William W., 211, 305; William, 011, 091, 119, 150, 239, 338, 422; Willie B., 389
CLARK: George, 119, 120; Jeremiah H., 107; John, 389; Josephus, 120;

Thomas M., 236; Will, 120
CLARKSON: Shotwell B., 096
CLAY: Ada, 022, 060, 120; Charles Augustus, 011; Chris, 011; Dave, 011, 120; Ed, 150; F. M., 450; Frances, 036; Francis, 009; Hezekiah, 070, 120, 130, 160, 227, 389; J. J., 338, 441; James C., 070; James, 120, 312, 338, 414; Jane (Jenny), 008; Jefferson, 120; Jesse F., 120; Jesse, 120, 227, 422, 441, 450; Jesse, Sr., 070; Jessy, 011; Lawton, 338, 389; Maggie Lee, 053;
CLAY: Martha S., 070; Martha, 064, 120; Mary Lee, 120, 338, 410; Mattie, 060; Millie, 034; O.J., 450; Pleasant G., 120; Pleasant, 278; Royal, 159, 173, 267, 315; Royall, 120, 174; Sally, 010; Samuel, 106, 107, 120, 142, 163, 169, 178, 221, 222, 257, 389, 422; Thomas, 120, 178, 422, 431; W.C., 011; William, 120; Willie (Buck), 389
CLAYTON: Charles, 120; Charlie, 011; George R., 120; Milton, 434; R. C., 199; Richard C., 120, 147, 158, 182, 221, 269, 422; Robert, 121; Thomas, 121, 159; Wiley, 159;
CLEALAND: Gilbert, 174
CLEAVLAND: Early, 012, 204
CLEAVLAND: William, 312
CLECKLEY: Jacob, 070
CLEELAND: Gilbert, 132, 278
CLEGG: J.J., 409; Jonathan H., 121; Narcis W., 121; Narcissas M., 121
CLELAND: Gilbert, 128, 300;
CLEM: Henry, 211
CLEMENT: W. C., 187
CLEMENTS: A. E., 193; Aggie, 046; Alex, 389; Allen, 070, 121; Bennie H., 012; Bula, 047; Calvin, 389; Charlie, 121; Cinda, 121; Dave, 338; Davie Jane, 014; Evan, 012, 338; G. C., 121; George C., 333, 364, 389; George, 012; Harvey, 012; Ida L., 012, 121; Isaac, 012; J. H., 121; Jacob, 012, 121; Jeptha H., 121, 278; Jeptha, 121, 190, 218, 312, 338; Jephah, 423; Lizzie, 027, 193; Major, 121;
CLEMENTS: Mariah, 121; Martha, 037; Mary Jane, 014; Mary, 121, 278, 422; Mose, 012, 102, 121; Moses, 012; Oliver, 121; Payton R., 312; Peggy Ann, 014; Peyton R., 121, 202, 230-231, 258; Peyton, 070, 121, 193, 230, 431; Phineas, 338; Polly, 230; Riley, 121, 389; S. C., 464; Simon, 121, 339, 389; Simon, Jr., 012; Thomas, 193; W. C., 193; W. M., 450; Walter M., 012, 353; Wiley L., 121; Wiley S., 214; Wiley, 121, 230; Will, 102, 121; Willie, 339, 389; Zadie, 047
CLEMM: James, 183; Joseph E., 184, 198; Joseph, 243
CLEMMONS: Evelina, 024; Mose, 121; Moses, 278
CLEMONS: David, 339; Jeptha, 121; Mose, 212, 339; Will, 212
CLEMONTS: Isaac, 121; Wilson, 012
CLENDING: John, Jr., 178
CLEVELAND: Benjamin, 421; Early C., 357; Edna (McClendon), 177; Eli, 210; Emma, 022; Fouche, 172; George, 100, 156, 184, 225; Jesse F., 175; Larkin, 121; Mary, 013; Robert M., 175; Washington C., 117, 143, 221; William, 121, 140, 319
CLIATT: Jesse, 086, 121; Thomas H., 203
CLIFTON: George, 234
CLINE: T. A., 011
CLISBY: T. J., 341
CLOPTON: Alford, 289; David, 175
CLOWER: George, 098, 121, 164, 221, 232; George, 247; Jacob, 121, 238, 422; James M., 190, 458; Jonathan, 121, 183; Lucy (Johnston), 458; Stephen, 247, 249
CLOWERS: Jonathan, 420; Miram, 045
CLUB: Turf, 420
CLUTE: John H., 104, 116, 122; John H., 294, 386, 389
COACH: Sam, 012
COAL: Jane, 016
COATES: A. H., 345
COATS: Earnest, 012; J. F., 012; James (heirs of), 422; James, 070; John, 122
COBB: Britt, 122; John, 459; Lee, 122; Martha (Hill), 174; Seth, 174; Silla, 122; Thomas, 389; Tom, 389
COCHRAN: Alfred, 422; Benjamin, 012; Berry, 122, 339, 349; Canthia, 048; Catharine, 011; Chadlea, 174; Charles, 012; Cheadle, 070, 174, 395, 435, 436; Dock, 389; Dudley, 012, 122, 389; J. W., 450; James, 122, 339, 422; Jeff, 122; Jenes,

122; Joe Frank, 389; Joe, 012, 122, 339; 349; John L., 221; John M., 422; John S., 122, 299; John W., 349, 450; John, 070, 122, 339;
COCHRAN: Jubal, 142; Jubel 182; Jubll C., 163; Jubll, 070, 087, 090, 282; Louis, 122; M. A., Mrs., 391 M.E., Mrs., 157; Marion, 122; Marshall, 122; Martin (heirs of), 422; Martin 087, 088, 120, 122, 178, 188, 220, 237, 248, 275, 277, 299, 389, 420, 422, 432, 458; Mary, 005; Mildred, 090, 142; Milford A., 282; Nelson, 122; Oren, 389; Pocert, 122; Simeon, 012; Susanah, 429; Susanna, 421; Thomas 339; W. A., 391, 450; W.B., 450; W.D., 012, 450; William, 012, 122, 139
COCHRANE: Corbin, 122
COCHRON: Bell,389
COCKE: Jack F., 133; Nathaniel, 314
COCKRAN: Allen, 122; Jubal, 122
COCRAN: Monroe,389
CODBETH: Joseph, 270
CODEY: John, 429
CODINGTON: M., 361
CODWISE: James M., 228; James N., 137, 189, 230, 265, 301, 308
CODY: Jeptha M., 235, 290; W.C., 012
COE: Isaac A.,429; R. D., 398
COFER: Anna C., 033; Hattie L., 088; J.E., 012; J.T., 012; J. Thomas, 339; James A., 012; John L., 339; M. J., 359; Mollie, 053; Robert, 012, 450; Susie, 027
COFFMAN: Amos, 423; John, 423
COGBURN: L. E., 444; Moses H., 423
COGGERSHALL: James C., 321; Nathaniel, 127, 321
COGGESHALL: N., 367; Nathaniel, 315
COGGESHELL: Nathaniel, 143, 221, 223
COGGIN: Polly, 025; William, 173
COGSWELL: Hiram, 445; Matilda, 122; William, 422, 461
COHEN: Abe, 461; E. H., 328, 332, 339, 362, 372; H., 122; L., 122; Leopold, 220; Lewin, 116, 170; Lewis, 197; Nathan A., 220; R., 122; S: B., 359, 362; S., 347, 450, 444; Sam, 122, 213, 339, 446, 450, 461; Samuel, 339; Solomon, 337; W. G., 122
COILE: J. G., 450
COKES: Pleasant, 185
COLBERT: Elizabeth, 061; John G., 230, 410; Michael L., 305; Thomas, 122, 228; William, 122, 222, 297
COLE: Carleton B., 307; Delia, 023; Elizabeth L., 070; Emma, 088; George, 012; James D., 313; John P., 122; John, 293; Kenne (heirs of), 423; Rene, 070; Robert, 122, 312, 461; William, 122, 070, 183
COLEMAN: Allen W., 171, 288, 297; Cheney, 042; Daniel, 154, 389; Fannie, 059; Frances, 141; Francis, 389; Frank, 122; James, 122; John, 423; Levie, 339; Polly, 060; Robert, 161, 344, 411; Thomas, 012; William, 318
COLES: Adeline, 026; John P., 101, 104, 115, 122, 256, 312; Patsy,122
COLLEY: Gabriel, 094; Gabriel 122, 164, 192, 218, 318, 322; Hollis, 207, 389; Nelson, 094, 123
COLLIAR: Nelson, 094, 123
COLLIER: Alice, 028; Bryant W., 205; Charles P., 123; Edward W., 188, 263; Howard, 012; Isaac, 339, 414; Jack, 123, 423; John W., 117; John, 070, 123, 245; Lucy, 007, 123; P. P., 446; Robert, 123; Sallie, 023; Temperance A. (Faith), 117; Thomas W., 123; Thomas, 123; Vines, 012; William Jan, 123; William, 070, 123
COLLINGS: John M., 123
COLLINS: Alice, 185; Benjamin S., 250, 312, 315, 316; George B, 250; Gibson, 123; Henderson, 423; Henry, 123; James, 123; John, 012; Joseph B, 312, 315, 316; Jonathan, 240, 298; Lucius, 012; Moses, 123; Robert A., 323; Robert, 120, 250; Stacy B., 250; Thomas, 287; William B., 250
COLLY: Joel, 231
COLORED: Alfred, 445; Amy, 445; Bill, 103, 386; Clayborn, 445; Clem, 338; Coon, 445; Daniel, 445; Dick, 445; Easter, 445; Emily, 356; Fanny, 445; George, 393; Harriet, 445; Henry, 443; Isham, 443; Jim, 443; Julia, 445; Lewis, 356, 445; Luke, 445; Marion, 400; Mat, 445; Mitchel, 445; Peter, 445; Phill, 403; Phillip, 445
COLQUIT: A. H., 122; John T., 123; John Terry, 070; Walter T., 135
COLQUITT: Safronia, 058
COLTON: Julia A., 008
COLVERT: John M., 123

COLWELL: Edward, 123, 124, 423, 435; Sally, 043; William, 123
COMB: George, 291
COMBS: John, 124, 306; Nathan, 012
COMER: Allen, 012; Anderson, 132; Francis, 171; G. W., 219; George W., 124, 190, 450; Ida, 367; J.S., 450; Jere, 012; Jim, 012; John Allen, 389; John F., 301; Juliet A., 062; Lara, 055; Leila, 011; Lewis, 339, 381, 450; Lydia, 070; Lydie, 339; Mary B.,064, 070; Mary, 207; Matilda, 042; Mitchell, 012; Nancy, 132; Pheobe, 389; Sarah, 036; T.J., 466; Thomas B., 131; Thomas J., 012, 064, 070, 095, 124, 187, 217, 254, 265, 282, 441; Thomas J., Jr, 124; Thomas J., Sr., 295; Thomas T., 423; Wash. 012, 124; Wiley, 012; William, 012, 124
COMLY: James C., 121
COMPTON: Alice, 019; Betsey, 047; Cathron, 443; Charity, 443; Cresey, 015; Doctor F., 290; Dora, 339; Drape, 012, 423; Draper, 012; Easter, 010; Elizabeth, 238, 422, 423; John W. 070, 090, 098, 116, 124, 158, 159, 163, 216, 234, 255, 264, 288, 312, 323, 360, 421, 423, 424, 426, 461; John, 092, 238, 264; Jordan, 064, 070, 124; Jorden, 124; Jourdan, 124, 312; COMPTON: Kate, 124, 423; Marv C., 163; Mary, 124, 163; Medora Eberhart, 031; Oliver, 443; Phillis, 443; Pleasant M., 086, 124, 137, 145, 152, 199, 264; Pleasant, 064, 070, 238; Polly Ann, 070; Pichard, 443
COMPTON: Tilda, 368
CONAWAY: Curtis, 170; J. H., 398; William, 203
CONDUIT: John, 110
CONE: Ashbael, 094; Benjamin, 124, 140; Francis H.,125, 153, 219, 236
CONGER: Eli, 124, 423
CONLEY: Augustus, 124; Benjamin, 153, 220, 243; Emmet, 012, 124; James, 124, 450
CONNAL: John, 435
CONNALLY: J. H., 198; J. T., 095; Samuel, 192
CONNAWAY: William, 134, 437
CONNEL: John, 124, 423; William, 124
CONNELL: William, 124, 140, 312, 389, 42; Wm., 461
CONNELLEY: James, 462
CONNELLY: G.H., 339, 341; Gustavus H., 012, 367, 368; H. E., 339; J. H., 341; J. 341; James, 339, 367, 368; Susan, 012
CONNER: Boley, 200, 255, 421; Boly, 124; Charles D., 125, 312; Davie Richard, 012; George, 012; Henry W., 173, 263; Jesse, 294; John W., 070; Mary J., 004; Susie F., 044; W. S., 404; William, 012
CONNOP: Lula G., 058
CONNORS: C. H., 407
CONSTITUTION: --.444
COOGLER: A. C., 125; Auborn E., 012; Endie, 012; J. L., 402, 423; Jesse, 012; Sidney, 384
COOK: ?, 125; A.J., 040; Aaron, 339; Althea Ophelia, 035; Asstadge, 125; Auble, 389; Augustin, 137; Augustus, 125, 312, 423; B. W., 389, 409, 450; 462; Ben, 125; Benjamin W., 012, 070, 434; Benjamin, 206, 295; Bogan, 450; Braz, 012; Callei F., 012; D. N., 441; David P., 125; David, 083, 450; Dawson, 125; Elisha, 264; G. S., 441; G. W., 246; George A., 012; George W., 196; George, 012, 125, 223, 450; Green, 125; H. E., 125; Hardy, 125, 193, 203, 251, 339, 350, 352, 450; Harriet, 004; COOK: Henry H, 105, 114, 115, 125, 135, 154, 168, 213, 240, 252, 254, 266, 279; Henry, 131, 250; Henry O, 206; Henry, 218; Inles, 032; J. B., 339, 396, 403, 450, 462; 466; J. D., 012; J. M., 125, 389; J. W., 339, 441, 444, 450; James C., 091, 105, 240, 252, 279; James W., 012; James, 125, 126, 312, 423; Jim, 125; John B., 450; John S., 013, 458; John W., 013, 070, 094, 125, 129, 234, 339, 389, 414, 448; COOK: John W.,Sr., 013; John Wesley, 339; Johnny, 013; L.E., 339, 441, 450; Lawrence C., 352; Lawrence E., 339, 375; Lucien P., 320; Lula, 003; M. R., 021; Madison, 013; Margaret, 060; Martha, 002; Martin, 125, 312; Mary Ann, 184; Mary J., 039; Mary, 029, 389; Mattie, 010; N.G., 013, 125, 389; Nancy, 060; P.B., 450; P.D., 450; Pobert L.,

013; Sandy, 013; T. L, 352, 356; COOK: Thomas L., 339, 462; Thomas, 339; William A., 126; William M., 125, 126, 389; William, 091, 094, 119, 122, 125, 126, 126, 130, 133, 138, 139, 141, 151, 153, 154, 156, 172, 173, 184, 188, 200, 211, 216, 220, 222, 225, 248, 255, 312, 314, 317, 323, 388, 420, 423, 432, 465; Zadock, 101, 233, 257
COOKE: Martin, 126; William, 175
COOLEY: Briant, 126; Bryant, 126, 171, 402; Charles, 389; Hollis, 113, 114, 119, 120, 126, 130, 131, 135, 171, 178, 187, 189, 191, 208, 210, 230, 244, 245, 250, 272, 280, 284, 291, 294, 305, 306, 308, 423; Milton A., 091; Orpha, 389
COOLY: Bryant, 126; Eli O., 323; Hollis, 170; Ransom, 290
COOP: Willie, 049
COOPEP: Betsey, 238; Charles H., 126; Eli, 013; Elizabeth, 040; Ellen, 057, 354; Howel, 126; Howell, 126; India, 126; James, 127; Lou, 050; Mark A., 237, 292; Nathaniel, 314; Prince, 013; Rhoda, 009; Robert, 126; Sally, 176; Sylvester, 044; Terrill, 046; Thomas, 183, 254, 292, 298; William H., 126, 144; Willis, 126, 399
COOPPER: Benjamin, 126
COOTS: John, 126
COPELIN: Thomas, 175
COPLAND: William, 230
COPPAGE: Oliver H., 126
CORBETT: James, 423
CORBIN: John, 126
CORBIT: Charles, 013
CORDELL: C. E., 195, 462
COPLEY: J. J., 335; J.T., 231, 328, 344, 385, 406, 446; James J., 335, 365, 344, 385, 406, 464; James, 329; John J., 277
COPLY: James T., 387
CORMICK: John, 175, 222
CORNELS: Alexander, 126
CORNEWELL: Gipson H., 291
CORNING: Jasper, 087, 093, 105, 137, 139, 170, 186, 192, 198, 204, 244, 283, 287, 425
CORNWALL: Catherine J., 005; Eli, 126; Kitty, 126
CORNWELL: ?, Mrs., 126; Alice L., 053; C. L., 450; Carrie D., 024; D. L., 013, 441, 450; Davis L., 450; E.C., 013; Elijah, 013, 070, 126; Elijah, Jr., 448; Franklin, 013; G. H., 013, 185, 204, 344, 356, 450; G. L., 013; G. W., 389; George C., 013; George W., 064, 070, 126, 252, 312; George, 126; Gibson H., 312; Gibson, 013, 070, 126, 231; Gibson, 291; Gip, 450; H. M., 389; Henry, 339; Hiram, 126, 312; Hugh M., 013; J.C., 339, 450; James L., 450; L.C., 126; Lee, 389; Lenora, 013; Lon, 389; Lonie, 013; Lorena S., 024; Marv E., 243; Marv T., O., 441; Obadian, 070, 448; Obediah, 126, 231; Odis, 389; Sallie B., 041; Sallie V., 012; W. D., 126, 298, 339, 441, 450, 462; William D., 013, 070, 339, 450; William, 013
CORSEY: George, 126; Marcus, 013; Moses, 389; S. T., 013; Thomas H., 099; W. P., 335; Will, 389
COSGROVES: George, 012
COSNARD: Henry, 267
COSWELL: W. C., 462
COTTON: Abner, 126
COUCH: Albert, 359; Alice, 055; Bessie, 126; Charles, 389; Charley, 013; Charlie, 126; Crawford, 013; Dora Kate, 055; Drury, 126, 127; Ebenezer, 013; Ede, 339; Emma, 047; Florence, 043; G. W., 389, 450; George, 013, 127, 389; Groff, 339; Hilliard, 127; J. P., 450; James P., 162; James, 127; Jeff, 127; Jefferson, 013; John, 126, 127; Joseph, 013; Judson, 040; Mary, 126, 441; Mattie, 020; Mollie, 339; Moses, 070; N. J., 064, 070, 339, 441, 450; N. J., 450; Nancy, 064, 070, 127, 188; Nannie, 127; Nathaniel H., 127; Rebecca, 007; William, 465
COULTER: ?, 205
COURCEY: Monroe D., 127
COUPSEY: Charles, 174; Edmond, 127; Monroe D.,013; Vinson R.,127, 269
COURTNEY: James, 127; William C., 102
COUSBY: Johnnie, 127
COUSINS: Betsy, 127; John, 070; Thomas, 070
COUTHON: John, 389
COWAN: Edwin, 339; James, 100, 108, 110, 114, 127, 139, 143, 145, 146,

165, 184, 185, 215, 218, 230, 234,
246, 255, 262, 264, 277, 278, 282,
283, 286, 312, 434; John, 196, 312
COWEN: James, 127, 190, 218, 221,
230; William A., 104
COWLES: Asbury, 423; Ebenezer M.,
173; Henry, 206; Jerry, 211;
W., 127
COWTHPON: Minnie, 127
COX: A.L., 082; Anna, 258; Cary, 127;
Charles D., 013; Drury M., 194;
Hannah, 050; Henry, 013, 105; Hugh,
254; J.M., 329, 362, 367, 446; Jess
(heirs of), 423; Jesse, 070, 127,
128, 148, 255, 280, 427, 431, 437;
John, 091, 287; Middleton W., 127,
161; Presley, 013; Pressley M.,
127; Rube, 127; Sallie T., 019;
Sarah, 064, 127, 166, 280, 423,
426, 427; Tom, 127, 339; W.M., 339;
W. O., 392, 450; Wiley J., 064,
070, 127, 423; Will, 127; William
M., 082; William S., 013; William,
339; Zachariah, 117, 127, 279
COXE: Edward, 109, 131; Jesse, 239;
M. F.; Mrs., 056
COZART: Hubbard W., 108
COZENS: Jenny, 469; John, 469;
Thomas, 469
CRABB: Asa, 127; Burton, 127;
Samuel, 127
CRABB: Asa, 430; Burton, 256; Enoch,
423; H.A., 462; John, 389; Samuel,
013, 255; Sillia, 389
CRABTREE: Ezekiel, 163; Ezekiel, 127,
162, 291, 304, 312, 315, 390, 462;
James, 390; John W., 304, 315, 448;
Malachi, 127; Maliciah, 013; Mary
A.(Trussell), 312; Thomas M., 127;
Thomas, 013, 165, 312
CRADDOCK: John, 127
CRADRICK: John, 236
CRAFT: Pleasant, 423
CRAGG: Andrew, 279
CRAIG: Andrew, 127, 208
CRAIN: Annie, 042; Edward, 148;
George, 127, 128; Jeremiah, 423;
Lula Viola, 026; Spencer, 127,
232, 264, 423; Spencer, Sr.,
070; Stephen D., 093; 127;
William, 127, 128, 230
CRAINE: Marcus L., 082, 450
CRALL: James, 070
CRANE: Abraham, 087, 249; Abram,
221; Burrel, 013; Burrell, 128;
Lee, 336, 339; Nathan, 013, 339;
S. D., 393; Spencer D., 128;
Spencer, 128; Stephen C., 140;
Stephen D., 093, 135, 192, 230;
Stephen, 092; Susan, 043; William
H., 087, 102, 115, 131, 139, 148,
149, 171, 178, 183, 206, 221,
245, 249, 301; William, 128, 129
CRANFPDI: John W., 441; L. H., 248
CRANGE: Eliza, 128
CRASKEY: Thomas W., 205
CRAVER: Andrew, 114
CRAWFORD: A. W., 390; Abednego J.,
344; Amy, 128; Andrew J., 185;
Andrew, 064, 070; Ann, 128; B.,
186, 448; Bennet, 116, 123, 128,
166, 296, 423; Bennett, 128, 141,
149, 170, 401; Berry, 013; Charles,
116, 128, 134, 150, 159; Dora, 035;
Ebeheart, 013; Eberhart, 128;
Elias, 128; Elisha G., 128, 282,
344, 431, 444; George M., 217;
CRAWFORD: George W., Gov., 232; Hardy,
089, 103, 164, 178, 180, 210, 913;
Hinton, 459; Hugh N., 131; Humphrey,
340; Janie, 036; Jefferson, 013;
Jeremiah, 013; Jesse, 184; Joel,
128, 294; John S., 128; John, 461;
Julia, 020; Leonard, 128, 390; M.
A. B., Mrs., 460; M. N., 013, 450;
Marshall, 128; Mary A., B., 401;
CPAWFORD: Mary A., 458; Mary H., 128;
Meshach N., 128; Meshack N., 144,
312, 325; Meshanc N., 128; Milly
010; Peter, 188; Queen, 053, 340;
Samuel, 128; Samuel, 070; Sarah,
009; Susan, 097; Thomas, 251;
Umphrey, 013; Walter, 128; Will,
013; William A., 344; William H.,
128, 206, 304; William, 097, 128,
253, 267
CPAWL: Elizabeth, 128; Mary, 128;
Samuel, 128
CRAWLEY: J. H., 013; James, 128,
137, 258, 423; V. H., 096, 305
CRAWMAN: Mary, 064, 070, 129, 144
CRAYTON: William L., 179;
William S., 175
CRAZ: Scott, 251
CREAGH: Thomas B., 070, 129
CREEL: Jordan, 423
CRENSHAW: Jarrel W., 101, 129;
Jarrel, 070; Joseph, 129, 423;
MicaJah, 129; Robert, 197; Walter,
193, 211; William F., 129; William
H., 218, 304; William, 197
CPEWS: James W., 128; Joseph, 129;

T. A., 372, 377
CPISWELL: David, 313
CRITCHFIELD: Nichols, 129, 141
CRITTENDEN: George, 013
CPOCKEP: W. J., 390
CROCKET: Joseph, 430;
Samuel, 129, 186, 278
CPOCKETT: James W., 129, 423; Joseph,
248, 423; Joseph, Jr., 129; Joseph,
Sr., 129; Samuel, 092, 103, 119,
129, 134, 135, 141, 151, 423,
426, 434, 460
CPOLL: James, 129; Mary, 129
CPONEP: Samuel, 390
CROSS: Ann E., 409; Ann Easter, 217;
George (heirs of), 423; George,
070, 124, 129, 423; Harris, 126,
423, 431; John, 064, 070; Paleman
P., 390; Palemon, 129; Perlemon,
129; Pleasant P., 129, 268; Pollev,
038; Richard, 129
CROSSPCPONW?: George W. S., 129
CROSSLEY: R. J., 340, 390
CROSSLY: R. J., 129
CPOSSON: James, 320
CROUCH: George, 129; John, 129
CROW: Elisha, 070, 129, 152, 311,
313, 340; Henry, 129; Isaac, 129;
J. W., 344; John M., 070, 277,
313; Martha M., 054; Mary M., 005;
Stephen, 233, 257; William D., 129,
255, 257, 277, 298; William L. D.,
313; William, 390
CROWDER: George W., 129; James, 307;
Thomas, 307
CROWELL: Alfred H., 013;
John, 124, 163, 264
CPOWW?CROSS: George W. S., 129
CROXTON: Gideon H., 129
CRUCE: Catharine, 129
CPUM: J. W., 373
CRUMBY: Judge, 013
CPUTCHFIELD: Annie L., 022; Ben, 450;
Ebbeheart, 013; H., 122; Henry,
450; Jefferson, 013; Jerry, 013;
William, 129
CUBAGE: J., 129
CUBBAGE: John, 130, 340, 410
CULBEPSON: John P., Jr., 013
CULBERTSON: Celia, 435; Robert,
199; Samuel, 070; William P.,
229, 309, 433
CULLEN: Eliza, 034; George, 013;
Lina, 037; Mary, 049
CULLENS: Charles, 013; Panda, 020;
Robert, 013, 014; Will, 130
CULLIN: Will, Jr., 490
CULLINS: Charles, 445
CULUM: James J., 014
CULPEPPEP: Daley, 232; Lemuel,
232; Ronert, 130
CUMMING: Joseph, 272; Thomas, 125
CUMMINGS: Joseph, 225;
Luther, 180, 263, 294
CUMMINS: Ebenezer H., 169
CUNARD: A. C., 450; Alf., 409; Alfred
C., 014; Alfred, 274; C. Zippoah,
903; Charles, 014; E., 384; Elbert,
014, 397, 450; Emily, 195; J. C.,
130, 390; J. P. Clark, 408; J. S.,
328, 390, 450; James Clark, 014;
Jane, 015; Jewev(?), 450; John C.,
014; John, 064, 070, 448, 450;
John, Jr., 064; Jumina, 328;
Jumina, 064, 070, 441, 450; Lella
Estell, 038; Lucindy, 390;
CUNARD: Marthena, 041; Mary Ann, 019;
Mary B., 002; N., 340, 390; Newton,
414, 450; Ople, 053; Pebecca F.,
002; Susan A., 044; William, 390
CUNNINGHAM: Benjamin F., 199; George
M., 147; George, 130, 365, 424;
Horace, 167; James, 143, 299; John,
173, 181; Robert, 299; Sarah L.,
199; Thomas, 181; William, 104,
130, 178, 257, 390
CUPD: John C., 105
CURETON: John, 130
CUPLEE: James, 215; Jesse, 296
CURRY: Dennis, 130; Eliza, 130; Fanny,
130; James, 130; John, 070; Mary,
130; Margaret Eliza, 018; Mose,
130; Nora E., 043; Robert, 405, 450;
Sallie, 033; Thomas, 261; Thompson,
064, 070, 144, 293, 448;
Willie, 130
CURTIS: Peter, 321; Thomas, 409;
Tom, 390
CUTHBEPT: A., 390; Alford, 448;
Alfred, 070, 130, 279, 428
CUTPBELL: Joshua, 014
D ANTIGNAC: William, 173
D ANTIGNAD: William M., 131
DABNEY: A., 391; Anderson, 070, 130,
180; Elizabeth, 094; Garland, 130;
Hannah, 070, 130, 140, 180, 391;
Tyre G., 094, 130, 180, 252
DAILEY: Joel, 279
DALE: Abraham B., 135, 189; Alexander,
244; Andrew C., 130; Robert C.,
149; Robert O., 199, 251; Samuel,
130; Simon, 423

DALTON: E. W., 130
DAMOUR: James A., 112
DANCE: John S., 369
DANFORTH: Jacob, 247, 254, 270
DANIEL: Alexander, 070; Allice, 032;
Anna, 026; Annie, 340; Anthony,
130, 340; Beverly, 102, 105, 126,
130, 220, 423; Dan, 014, 340;
Daniel, 130, 340, 374, 379; David,
014; Echols, 166; Edna, 130;
Egbert P., 136; Egbert, 130; Emma,
037; Ephraim, 130; Frederick, 014,
130, 450; George W., 201; Hopkins,
130; Isaac, 014, 064, 070; James
G., 130; James J., 131; James K.,
154, 263; James K., Sr., 280;
DANIEL: James L., 148; James, 187, 191,
210, 305; Jerry, 014; Jim, 014;
John B., 364; John O., 123, 131;
213; John W., 070; John, 014, 131,
445, 466; Lee, 014, 131; Levi,
070, 128, 208; Levy, 173; Martha
A., 021; Mollie, 131; Moses, 070,
166; Obadiah E., 131; Pig, 131;
Rebecca, 028; Pichard, 014, 131,
255; Robert H., 131, 284, 307,
315; Robert, 014, 340; Sallie,
019; Steth, 165; Susie, 061;
Thomas, 070; Viney, 131; Warren,
014, 340, 458; Will, 131, 366;
William, 014; Wilson, 192
DANIELLY: Nancy, 070; Thomas F.,
014, 114, 131, 228, 259, 285,
318-319; Thomas, 161
DANIELS: Anthoney, 014; John, 390;
Lee
DANNEL: Levi, 148
DARDEN: Anderson, 014; Augustus,
131; Bedford H., 131, 270, 317;
Bedford M., 271; Clark, 014; Delia,
045; Edmung B., 122, 131, 163, 203,
232, 245, 270; Eugene, 131, 014; George
W., 131, 135, 221; George W., Jr.,
131; George, 131; J. M., 441; James
F., 458; James H., 087; James M.,
070, 131, 450; John B., 070; John,
070, 443; Martha, 042; Martin, 414;
Richmond, 131, 339; Turner, 443;
W.W., 340; Wiley, 340; William, 340
DARDIN: James W., 131
DAPDY: William, 014
DARING: William, 170
DARNALL: Benjamin, 101, 183; David,
209; James J., 226; Thomas M.,
099, 131, 152, 208, 282
DARNELL: Benjamin, 314; James J.,
131, 225; John J., 233
DASHER: Thomas J., 131
DAUGHEPTY: Bettie, 005; Joe, 390;
Mat, 131
DAUGHEPTY: H. L., 361; J. G., 361;
R. E., 361
DAVENPOPT: John, 131; Raymond, 140,
252; Smith, 204, 424, 430, 431;
William, 298
DAVID: Isaac, 423; Josiah, 280
DAVIDSON: Alfred, 014; Annie, 050;
B.M., 014, 398, 404, 450; Benjamin,
014; Dick, 215, 339, 340, 342;
Dora, 060; Elijah, 131; Elizabeth,
131; Emma G., 015; F. M., 330;
Hilyaro, 014; J.F., 450; John P.,
014, 349, 406, 450; John, 131,
228, 295, 450; John, Jr., 131;
John, Sr., 070; L.W., 331; Martha
C., 059; Nancy, 007; Rea, 340;
Reid, 131; Richard, 132, 229;
340, 361; Robert, 070, 131, 214;
Sallie, O., 015; T.M., 340; Thomas
M., 340, 350; Thomas, 390, 423;
W. T., 132
DAVIES: Francis B., 342; William, 435
DAVIS (?), 444; Abner, 344; Aggie,
056; Amelia, 021; Anderson, 014,
340; Arthur, 132; Baby, 132; Belle,
053; Benjamin, 132, 324, 423; C.
M., 348, 366, 367, 369; Calvin,
390; Charlott, 046; D. M., 095,
132, 171, 441, 450; David, 132;
132; Dick, 443; Dora, 033; Drew M.,
450; 456; Drew, 340; Drury M.,
014; Drury, 190; Early, 337; Elbert,
288; Emiline, 008; Eshmel, 277;
DAVIS: Finch, 132; Fletcher, 014;
450; Florence, 061; Foster, 014;
Frank, 014; G.H., 450; G.L., 390;
G.M., 450; George B., 132; George
H., 014; George M., 414;
George B., 132; George, 014, 340,
348, 390, 390, 443; Gordon, 232;
Hannah, 132, 210; Henry, 014, 132;
Ishmael, 423; J. M., 450; J. T.,
367, 369; J. W., 052, 357, 450;
DAVIS: J., 390; James A., 130; James
T., 328; James, 014, 132, 272, 421,
423; Jennett, 026; Jeremiah, 123,
127, 132, 137, 154, 161, 198,
272, 314, 423; Joe, 192, 340; Joel,
099, 132; John Abner, 014; John
B., 291; John C., 255; John, 014,
092; John, Jr., 132; John, Sr.,
132; Joseph E. F., 014; Joseph,

308; Josephine, 010; Josiah, 188;
Kate, 132; Lizzie, 053; Marion A.,
340; Martha, 132; Mary Kate, 046;
DAVIS: Mary Lou, 132; Matthew, 132,
418; Mattie. 038; Michael, 313;
Mollie, 340; Nancy T., 151; R. L.,
343, 369, 400, 444, 450, 462;
Richard I, 369; Richard, 014, 444;
Robert H. 132, 210, 423; Robert,
132; S.C. 444; S.E. 051; S.W.
340, 414; Sallie, 340; Sam, 450;
Samuel, 414; Sarah E., 340; Sarah,
132, 340; Savanah, 024; Squire,
390; Susan F., 025; T. C., 441; T.
F., 450; Thomas B, 132, 325, 445;
DAVIS: Thomas C., 254, 340, 310, 448;
Thomas I., 120, 175, 220, 224, 244,
267, 278; Thomas J., 117, 127, 150,
170, 177, 221, 225, 237, 298, 300,
302; Thomas, 070, 094, 113, 132,
210, 222; Turner A., 423; W. C.,
340; W. P., 350; W. R., 372, 401,
W. W., 340; Wiley, 132; Will, 340;
William A., 255, 260; William C.,
263; William F., 307; William G.,
313; William L., 014; William O.,
132; William P., 014; William, 014,
390, 423; Willie, 014; Wink, 132,
192; Wm. W., 450; Woodson, 014
DAVISSON: Thomas, 428
DAWES: Joel, 132, 269
DAWKINS: Annie, 042; B. F., 441;
Daniel, 126, 132, 172, 240, 259,
295; David, 256; G. W., 442, 450;
Garland, 115, 123, 152, 174, 181,
234, 256, 312, 316, 406, 462;
George W., 132, 340, 414, 450,
458; George, 070, 132, 191, 192,
390, 448, 458, 462; Lula, 024;
Martha C., 020; Mary (Mollie), 027;
DAWKINS: Mary Virginia, 036; Partheny,
070; Parthney, 339; Rebecca J.,
007; Reuben, 189, 190, 228, 421;
448; Samuel A., 014; Samuel, 340;
Thomas, 390; Uriah G. 014; W. J.,
442; William H. 132
DAWS: Joel, 133, 156, 313, 340, 372, 448
DAWSON: Andy, 014; Ann, 159; Armstead
B., 133; George, 099; J.M., 335,
374; James M., 330; John, 133,
159, 160; Martha, 026; Thomas, 133,
229; W.R. 340, 450; Warren, 340;
William C., 133, 238, 250, 319;
William J., 311
DAY: Joseph, 104, 224;
William M., 296
DEADWILDER: Chrisley, 133; Christopher
I, 133; Christopher, 133, 297,
423; Eva, 070; William, 133, 421
DEAL: William, 070
DEAN: Lemuel, 276, 420; Martha J.,
019; Robert, 313; Samuel H., 156;
Thomas (heirs of), 423; Thomas,
422; Unice, 103
DEANE: Burket, 133; Burkett, 257,
423; George, 133, 459; Nathaniel
(heirs of), Nathaniel, 070,
133, 156, 189, 255, 270, 271, 313,
422, 423, 458, 459; Polly, 458;
Robert, 313; Thomas, 070;
Unicey, 103, 133
DEARING: Annie, 018; J.J., 401, 436,
444, 468; Simeon, 133; William, 254
DEARMOND: William P., 188
DEASON: Ben, 390; Bengaman N., 442;
Benjamin, 460; Elmina S., 024;
Joseph, 133; Maria C., 003; Mary
J., 061; Michael, 133; William, 133
DEDWILDER: Christopher, 133;
Martin, 427
DEEN: Drury, 424
DEENS: Edmond, 241
DEEPING: Abner T., 195; Simeon, 424
DEES: John, 255
DEGRAFFENREID: Thomas, 318
DEGRAFFENREIDT: Boswell B., 097
DEITER: A. W., 340
DELANO: Edwin, 249; Joel B., 249
DELAY: James, 252
DELEON: P. M., 369; Perry M., 382;
T. M., 399
DELK: Joseph, 233
DELL: J. S., 333, 334, 371
DELOACH: J. M., 243; Simeon, 135
DELONA: Edward, 140
DENHAM: D. B., 014; Dumas, 133;
James C., 133, 247, 346, 359;
James, 424; Josiah C., 247; Laura
J., 340; Willy, 340
DENIER: Clement, 133
DENIS: Wilse, 133
DENNAGEE: William, 469
DENNIS: Annie E., 340; Carrie, 014;
Catharine, 444; Celestia E., 041;
D.W., 014; Frank, 340; G.W., 340;
G. Wesley, 340; George W.,
133; H. J., 468; Harriet, 340;
Harry J., 099; J.H., 014, 450;
J.T., 390; Jesse, 070; John M.,
082; John T., 014; John, 014, 340;
Jordan, 014; Michael, 106, 268;
Nat, 133; R. S., 444; Samuel P.,

424; T. P., 450; Tom, 133, 207;
W. E., 133, 340, 450; William,
015, 278
DENSON: Edmond, 133; Eleanah, 424,
437; Ell, 130, 133, 180; Elkanah,
133; James M., 225, 289, 340, 313;
James, 390; John H., 134; John W.
C., 134; John, 134, 418; Lee Ann,
225; Obediah, 134; Rebecah, 225;
Sarah, 225
DENT: Elizabeth, 016; John, 156;
Nathan S., 213; Willis, 127
DEOMATARIE: John, 135
DERBY: L. A., 390
DERDEN: H. W., 402
DERICA: Dock, 340
DERICE: Eliza, 005
DERICO: Dock, 015; Eliza, 134;
Lina, 028; Lucien, 340
DERRING: Abner F., 133, 239
DESHAZO: Wilins, 134; Wilkins, 134
DEUPREE: Drury, 146; Giles, 134
DEVANEE: Patrick S., 015
DEVANEY: Cornelia S., 061
DEVANT: R. P., 015
DEVANY: John S., 015; William, 134
DEVEREAUX: John W., 167; Samuel, 167
DEVEPEUX: John W., 091
DEWALD: Solomon, 310
DEWBERRY: Giles, 134; Hopson, 134;
John, 134, 424, 460; Mary, 424,
460; Nancy, 424, 460; Richard,
134; T. D., 134, 450; Thomas,
134; William G., 460
DIAMON (DIMON): Abel, 424
DIAMOND: Abel, 135; H. M., 015;
Henry M., 015; William, 134,
424, 426
DIBBLE: Caleb C., 098, 124, 134,
178, 324
DICK: James, 286; Levi W., 450; Levi,
015; R.F., 248, 400
DICKEN: John R., 097, 131, 134,
208; Richard, 184
DICKENS: Charles A., 156; Charles,
134; J. L., 356; John R., 134
DICKENSON: Colonel M., 121; Henry
A., 097, 134, 199; John, 251
DICKES: John R., 458
DICKEY: J. B., 369, 401; John P.,
980; Mary, 057; Raymond, 390
DICKIN: John H., 388; John P., 116,
177, 179, 201, 249, 260, 298,
299, 392, 409
DICKINSON: Henry A., 070, 097, 098,
134, 147, 251, 272, 294, 303, 321,
395, 445; Sarah A., 097, 251;
Sarah, 099
DICKSON: Capers, 184; David, 229;
Elbert, 102, 134; James, 107, 117,
125, 143, 161, 183; Thomas, 134, 168;
William, 107, 117, 143, 183, 336
DIEMEP: Clement, 134, 390
DIGBY (?), 444: Abe, 340: Abraham,
015: Alex, 134; Amos, 015;
Anderson, 443; Angeline, 443;
Annie, 134; B.T., 089, 134, 156,
235, 241, 264, 329, 340, 341, 364,
366, 370, 374, 384, 442, 450, 458;
Belinda, 125, 129, 134, 243;
Benjamin, 015, 340, 341, 390; Berry
M., 015; Berry T., 064, 070, 095,
096, 104, 112, 135, 166, 177, 184,
198, 209, 219, 225, 231, 235, 240;
259, 261, 263, 268, 280, 284, 285,
319, 330, 331, 338, 358, 370, 377,
401, 402, 424, 425, 427, 462;
DIGBY: Berry, 145; Bum, 134; Caroline,
018; Charles, 134, 195, 390;
Charley, 015; Charlie, 015, 386;
Clinton, 134, 450; Dennis, 015,
341, 390; Easter, 022; Eleoge, 390;
Ellodae, 015; Emaline, 390; Everett
W., 015; Floyd, 443; Frances, 443;
George, 015, 341, 462; Ike, 015,
390; Isaac, 390, 462; Isnam, 390;
J.B., 450; J. Clinton, 390; J. H.,
450; J. M., 341, 450; James H.,
015, 134, 341, 390, 443, 450;
DIGBY: James M., 134, 341; James,
112, 134, 160, 341, 424, 450; John
B., 070, 135, 341, 390, 442, 443,
450, 462; John C., 135; John, 070,
125, 129, 134, 243, 341, 390, 424,
450; Lawrence, 015, 333, 450; Lee,
015; Lou, 014; Louisa, 392; Martha,
034, 046; Mary, 052; Mollie, 058;
Ora, 032; Rhody, 443; Saby, 053;
Sallie, 054; Sarah, 016, 032;
047; Sawrence, 341; Scott, 135,
407; T. E., 341, 444; Talitha, 007;
W. B., 135, 341, 450, 464; W.
Berry, 390; W.L. 341, 390; Wesley,
015; Whit, 135; William B., 015,
341; William B. (alias Dash), 135;
William Berry, 015; William, 135, 341
DIKE: Isaac R., 135
DILLARD: Arthur, 391; E. F., 028;
George W., 086, 467; George, 015,
442, 450; John A., 070, 086, 135,
321, 424; Mary, 135, 414; Nancy,
050; Thomas, 015, 070, 086, 092,

135; W. C., 015; Will, 341
DILLON: Amanda, 002; Henry, 116,
135, 192, 285, 299; John, 070;
N. H., 031; Nancy (Cargile), 299;
Robert, 266; Thomas, 129, 220,
313, 391, 431
DIMON: Abel, 135, 206
DINGLER: Jonathan B., 135; Nancy,
135, 424; T. P., 135; Thomas B,
135; Thomas P., 313; William, 070,
135, 424, 462
DIOMATARIE: John, 135
DISBOW: Deborah M., 161
DISMUKE: Jeptha V., 141
DISMUKES: James, 135; Jeptha V.,
136, 433; Jepthah V., 015; John
F., 136, 198, 217, 240, 300, 301,
319, 462; Martha D., 070
DISSOWAY: Israel, 139
DIXON (DICKSON): David, 184
DIXON: Angelina, 035; Capers, 101.
386; D., 142; David, 101, 363,
386; G. H., 343; Henry, 136; Jane,
017; Joseph, 257; Sandy, 015, 414;
Seaborn, 341; Thomas, 445;
William, 125, 336
DLLIS: Samuel, 147
DOBBINS: Jacob, 015; Sealey, 343;
Warren, 015, 136
DOBY: Durrell, 136; John, 133;
Waitus, 136
DODD: James, 136
DODDS: Caroline E., 313; James,
196, 268, 313, 458
DODRIDGE: Noe, 159
DODSON: Armstead, 194; Armstead, 089,
110, 160, 310, 469; Armsted, 136,
247, 317; Armstid, 242; E., 424;
Elijah, 070, 089, 136, 139, 170,
275, 292, 294, 300, 306, 424;
Hannah, 023; James, 139; Joel W.,
136, 139, 306; Joe; 136; John P.,
136; Leah, 136, 139, 306; Leroy,
015; Presley, 098, 136, 305; Sarah
A. V. Mrs. 025; Sarah Ann, 023;
W. A., 136
DOE: John, 255, 256
DOGGET: Matilda G., 269
DOGGETT: Elizabeth, 156, 469; Garner
(Orphans of), 158; Garner, 070,
256; John, 064, 070; Mary Ann, 256,
469; Nancy G., 469
DOLES: Thomas, 165
DOMENEY: J. E., 391
DONALDSON: John, 093, 110, 132, 136,
153, 158, 196, 286, 424, 425;
Peter, 155
DONALLY: James, 445
DONALSON: Clatie Bell, 391;
Lola Butts, 391
DOOLEY: B. F., 451; John M., 196,
221, 304; T. W., 451
DOOLITTLE: Eureal H., 112;
Burial H., 122
DOOLY: John M., 282, 311; Maggie
May, 014; T. W., 38
DOREMUS: Francis, 121
DORITZ: William, 264
DORSATT: James, 221
DORSETT: Andrew, 136; James, 097,
136, 157, 162; P.W., 097, 157, 353;
Palemon W., 071; Palemon, 156;
Pleaman W., 180, 367; Sarah E., 023
DORSETTE: James, 136
DORSEY: E. R., 444; Henry W., 283;
John, 237
DOSIER: E. V. 015
DOSS: Azariah, 015; Claborn, 136
DOSSEY: Daniel, 163
DOSTER: Addie Belle, 038; Burney,
136; Georgia, 007; H. W., 462; J.
W., 408, 451; James C., 015, 064,
071, 136; James W., 015, 071, 255,
258, 341; James, 190; John, 015,
095; L.P., 341; Luvana, 048; Mary,
044; P.W., 341; Pleas, 015; Sarah
J., 033; T. A., Mrs., 341; T. P.,
451; Tabitha A., 255; Thomas, 015;
William, 137
DOSURE: Dinwodda, 127
DOUGHERTY: Annie, 041; Clark, 015;
E. C., 137; Ed, 137; Elizabeth,
017; Grover, 137; James Madison,
015; Jim, 015; Joe, 015; John,
137; Joseph, 298; Katie, 015;
Maggie, 050; Nannie, 048; P. H.,
341; Sarah E., 039; William, 071,
137, 317, 341; Willie, 015
DOUGHTY: William, 442
DOUGHTIE: Louanga, 014
DOUGHTRY: H. L., 342; J. G., 342;
R., 342
DOUGLAS: Martin, 137; Rachael, 059
DOUGLASS: John, 303; Peter, 303
DOW: John, 255
DOWDEL: James, 161; Lewis, 137
DOWDELL: James, 100, 137, 174, 242;
Lewis, 137, 232, 313, 424
DOWDLE: Pierce, 015, 137
DOWNEY: Calvin, 137, 164; Charles C.
P., 137; Charles P., 137; James,
137, 210, 235; Peter, 137, 264;

Phebe (McAfee). 164; Polley, 049;
  Sally, 235; Samuel, 110, 137, 264;
  Sarah, 002
DOWNING: H. B., 353
DOWNS: Clifford E., 035; Ella C.,
  036; Isaac, 426; James A., 015;
  James, 137, 173, 181; James, Jr.,
  137; John S., 364; John, 064, 137;
  Mark, 391; Hattie C., 032; S. P.,
  071, 372, 386; S. P. Dr., 406;
  Shelly F., 155; Shelly P., 015,
  137, 149, 345; Skelly, 071;
  Thomas P., 015
DOYLE: Francis, 143, 174; Hardy, 316
DOZER: Woody, 422, 434
DOZIER: A. M., 015, 451; Abner C.,
  064, 071, 157, 314, 451; Abner,
  242; Adaline B., 064; Addie P.,
  024; Ed, 137; G. P. 341, 346,
  368; G. R., 371, 398, 403, 407;
  G.W., 347; George B., 451; George
  R., 015, 071, 186, 235, 341, 366;
  George R., Dr., 444; John P., 097,
  118; Katie, 003; Mary, 458; S. J.,
  052; Sallie, 381; Thomas J., 119,
  137; Tom, 137; W. B., 015, 331,
  356, 371, 374, 381, 393, 398,
  451; Warner, 341; Warren, 261;
  Washington, 015; Woody B., 363;
  Woody, 071, 092, 127, 136, 137,
  166, 170, 196, 237, 282, 299,
  313, 320, 323, 424, 425;
  Woody, Jr., 087
DREADWILDER: Cristofer, 422
DREGHORN: John, 264
DREW: Franklin, 341; John G., 208;
  John L., 137, 175, 424; John M.,
  015; John S., 154, 179, 204, 268,
  294, 299; John, 223
DREWERY: Samuel, 182
DREWEY: Samuel, 101
DRICHAL: Thomas, 015
DRIGGERS: John, 391
DRIGGONS: John, 137
DRISCAL: Laza, 027
DRISCHAL: Anceline, 057; Julia,
  012; Rebecca, 023
DRISCOL: Alex, 015
DRISCOLL: Alex, 341; Dolly, 050;
  Queen, 030
DRISKEL: Meridy, 341; Mollie, 341
DRISKELL: B. W., 446, 451; Bob, 391;
  C. W., 391; Carrie T., 037;
  Christopher, 138, 206, 424; Ellen,
  054; Elvira, 343, 458; Henry H.,
  015; Henry, 451; J.T., 451; Jack,
  341; Jacob, 424; James B., 071;
  James L., 341; James T., 138, 341,
  451; James, 015, 451; Jennie,
  009; John Thomas, 015; John,
  071; Joshua, 466; Julia G., 064,
  071; Kate, 034; Lou Ella, 016;
  Mary A., 038; Mary, 003; N. N.,
  138; Reese, 016; Susan, 009;
  Thomas, 391; Tilla, 012; Tom, 016;
  W.J., 391; William, 016, 341;
  William, Jr., 462
DRISKILL: Christopher, 138
DROWRY: Samuel, 279
DRUMMER: Sam, 016
DRUMMOND: Noah S., 120
DUBERRY: Thomas, 341
DUCK: Timothy, 138, 143, 292
DUDLEY: Adaline, 022; Bithy, 379;
  Edward, 149, 189; James, 016;
  Joe, 341
DUESAN: George, 221, 265
DUFFY: Pearl, 016
DUGGER: Sampson, 138
DUKE: B. H., 451; Bartholomew H.,
  138; David, 460; Eldridge, 016;
  Frederick, 138; Genie Elizabeth,
  011; Hardy, 138; Henry, 229; Isham,
  071; Jane, 138; John, 273, 424,
  424, 432; Joseph G., 138; Joseph
  T., 016; Joseph, 016, 138, 424; M.
  L., 258, 355, 370; Marion, 016;
  Mordecai, 016; O. M., 016; Polly,
  297; Richard, 016; Robert G., 240,
  242; Robert L., 207, 262; Stephen
  H., 016, 138; Stephen, 138, 424;
  Thomas M.016; William, 016, 186, 428
DUKES: F. M., 341; Frederick, 083,
  124, 138, 313; Hardy H., 138; J.L.,
  391; Joseph T., 082; Joseph, 391;
  Louvora, 049; Mary L., 391; Mary,
  391; Ransom H., 138; Ransom, 391;
  Robert W., 138, 391, 409; Sarah
  Ann, 042; Sarah, 138; Stephen H.,
  138; Stephen, 138; Thomas M., 016;
  Tobe, 391; William, 096, 124, 131,
  134, 138, 161, 285, 290, 318, 391
DUMAS: Cincinattus, 016; Cincinatus,
  138, 341; Cincinnatus, 016, 338,
  341; Cooley, 016, 138; Eula C.,
  391; Frank, 341, 391; Henry, 016;
  J. S., 461; Jack, 138; James, 138;
  Jeness, 391; John C., 138, 310;
  John, 391; Medora, 341; Nettie,
  027; Nora, 005; Richard, 016;
  Sibilitie, 053; Steve, 138; Susie,
  038; Weyman, 016; William, 016, 462

DUNAM: Thomas J., 465
DUNCAN: Elizabeth, 139; James, 138,
  166, 199, 244, 433; Joseph, 175,
  197; Mathew, 128, 139; Matthew,
  126, 139, 205, 228;Thomas, 071, 178
DUNLAP: Daniel, 139, 144, 391;
  Samuel, 254
DUNN: Albert G., 071, 391; Albert,
  139; Alice, 004; Barney, 016, 199;
  Byron, 016; Byron, 139, 391; E.A.,
  444; Ed, 139, 267; Gatewood, 071,
  139, 169, 391; Gatwood, 391; James
  M., 165, 307; James, 257; John,
  149, 255; John, Jr. 255; Josie,
  273; Larkin, 199, 315; Martha L.,
  A., 005; Pauline, 009; Penny, 025;
  Samuel C., 220; Stephen, 256;
  Uriah, 257; William G., 016, 064,
  071, 139, 310; William J., 324;
  William, 139
DUNNING: Calvin, 278
DUNOM: Thomas J., 139; Thomas J., 139
DUNSEITH(?): J. C. 395
DUNTON: Hollis, 242
DUPEE: James, 230
DUPPEE: Drury, 391; James, 114, 160
DURDAN: Stephen, 281
DURDEN: Bill Graft, 139; J. C., 341,
  345, 387, 402, 408; Joe C., 139;
  John, 096, 139, 319, 325, 233,
  298; L. W., 016; Leontine, 030;
  Martin, 370; O. J., 261; Oliver,
  385; Rona, 139; Stephen J., 071,
  325; W. D., 139, 341; Wiley, 341;
  Will, 391
DURDIN: John, 155, 231, 261, 314,
  402; Sllie, 053; W. D., 342; Walt,
  016; Walter B., 016; Wiley T., 016
DURHAM: Abner, 256, 424; Averilla
  R., 222; Genie, 018; Kindsay H.,
  121; L. H., 311; Lindsay H., 308;
  Lindsey A., 219; Lindsey H., 086,
  094, 108, 139, 161, 210, 214, 245,
  253, 291, 321; Lola, 139; Sanders
  W., 256; Simeon, 096, 121, 139;
  209, 313, 391, 424; Singleton,
  256; W. M., Dr., 374
DURK: William L., 258
DURP: Michael, 139, 279, 391
DUSENBERRY(?), Richard, 284
DUSENBERRY: Mollie, 355, 358
DUVALL: W. L., 361
DWELLY: L., 407
DYAP: Hallie C., 043
DYCHE: Isaac P., 424
DYEP: Anthony, 064, 071, 086, 089,
  091, 092, 094, 103, 105-107, 109,
  111, 112, 114-117, 121, 123, 124,
  129, 132-134, 136, 137, 139, 141,
  145, 147, 149, 152, 153, 155, 156,
  160, 165, 168, 169, 176-178, 182,
  185-187, 189, 192, 205, 208, 215,
  217, 218, 222, 226, 232, 234-236,
  242, 245, 247, 250, 251, 253, 255,
  257, 264, 267, 271, 273, 292, 294,
  300, 304, 313, 318, 322, 396, 401,
  404, 409, 424, 433, 461; Corydon,
  102; Edmund Walker, 139; Elisha, 168;
  DYEP: Henry, 016, 341; John P., 071,
  444; John P., 094, 095, 097, 105,
  114, 132, 154, 153, 155, 157, 165,
  171, 205, 208, 210, 226, 251,
  260, 289, 291, 307, 310, 311, 314,
  317, 318, 384, 342, 444, 451; John
  Randolph, 112; John, 424; Marie H.,
  025; Otis, 110, 139, 147, 160, 171;
  216, 217, 234, 242, 271, 304, 313
DYFES: Tom, 342
EAGERTON: Charles, 421, 426; Mary,
  139; Zachariah B., 139
EARLEY: L. A., 139; Ansalum, 322;
  Anslem L., 139, 188, 194; Caleb,
  139, 140, 194, 313; Comber, 342;
  Joseph, 140
EARPLY: Ansalem L., 422; Ansalom L.,
  424; Anselem, 140; Anslem L.,140,
  391, 424; Anslem, 140; Caleb, 140,
  252, 313, 391; Columbus, 016;
  Comer, 229; Eleazar, 287; Jacob,
  260, 272; Joseph, 140, 290;
  Melissa (Hay), 260, 272
EARNEST: L. W., 314
EARSBY: Jim, 016
EASCO: Nancy M., 140; Nancy, 140
EASCOE: John, 140
EASON: Abner, 460; Allen, 016, 346;
  Henry, 016; Rosa, 011; Whitmel, 140
EASTER: Baxter, 140; Catharine, 140;
  Champion, 140, 160, 215; John C.,
  140; John, 140; Richard J., 206
EASTEPS: Elbert J., 140; John A.,
  395; Morey, 435
EASTERWOOD: Gideon, 214; Gldian, 206;
  John, 214; Lawrence, 214; Simeon,
  466; Simon, 465
EASTES: Nancy M., 140; Zachariah, 140
EASY: William, 391
EAVENS: A. L., 391
EAVES: Bartlet, 143; Bartlett, 140;
  Buckner, 140
EBEPHAPDT: George W., 342
EBEPHART: George W., 122

ECHELBERGER: William, 184
ECHOLS: Absalom, 122, 140, 313;
  Benjamin, Sr., 183; Edward, 163,
  246; Elizabeth, 071, 107, 166; John
  T., 341; John, 126, 140, 257; Levi
  H., 170; Melinda, 028; Obadiah,
  141, 173, 182, 241, 421, 424, 427,
  463, 466; Obediah, 218, 244;
  Richard, 141; Robert M., 301;
  Robert, 264; Simeon, 170; William,
  141, 170, 235, 391
ECKLES: J. T., 355; John T., 305,
  353; John, 208; Thomas, 164
ECKLEY: Levi, 209
ECKOLS: J. T., 404
ECTOR: Amanda, 323; Hugh W., 121,
  124, 151, 158; Hugh W., 173, 178,
  323; Hugh, 233; Java L., 323; John,
  124, 151, 158, 173, 178, 233;
  Martha, 141; William B., 355;
  Wylie B., 111, 222
EDDY: Samuel, 016
EDELMAN: David, 141; Moses, 141
EDGAR: John, 089, 238
EDGE: Allen, 141; Jake, 141; James,
  016; John, 141, 424; Obadia, 141;
  Obadiah, 141
EDGER: Robert, 224
EDGGER: Robert, 224
EDMONDS: Amos, 141; James, 151;
  John, 141; Kethrin, 211; Mary,
  012; Rachel, 064, 071
EDMONDSON: Benjamin C., 071, 091,
  141, 312, 323, 391; Benjamin, 155;
  Crawford, 071, 103, 123, 124, 140,
  141, 182, 207, 216, 227, 233, 277;
  Francis, 140; Hannah, 141; Henry D.,
  C., 141, 142; Humphrey, 141, 253;
  Humphry, 302; John, 245, 312, 459;
  Martha, 099, 141, 142; Richard,
  120, 142; Samuel, 071, 141, 314;
  Thomas, 142; William A., 141;
  William D., 391; William O., 141,
  142, 152, 163, 232, 313, 321
EDWARD: James, 142; John, 142
EDWARDS: Anna, 023; Bethia O., 013;
  C. L., 016; C. M., 016, 451;
  Columbus, 342; E.F., 364; Ed, 342;
  Edwin, 451; Eliza, 254; Elizabeth,
  013; Emaline, 013; H.L., 142; H.
  V., 451; Henrietta, 036; Henry F.,
  016; Herbert, 071, 142; James B.,
  016; James, 071, 142, 174, 182,
  269, 303, 391; Joel J., 071, 356;
  Joel, 403; John W., 142, 313, 324,
  358, 414, 451; John, 016, 071, 142,
  197, 300, 312, 338, 342, 451, 460,
  462, 463; Joseph B., 016; L. D.,
  391, 393; Lawrence, 016; Leander,
  391; Lee, 016; Lena M., 059; Lizzie,
  031; Lou, 056; M. L., 040; Mamie,
  055; Mariah, 342; Martha E., 009;
  EDWARDS: Martha Jane, 040, 056; Mary
  M., 053; Mattie, 054; Nancy A.,
  353; R. M., 442; R. R., 451; R. S.,
  442, 451; Rebecca, 059; Reuben,
  064, 071, 142, 161, 291, 433;
  Richard M., 016; Richard, 016, 342;
  Robert L., 451; Robert S., 071,
  451; Robert, 016, 354, 424, 451;
  S. B., 342, 391, 442, 451; S. D.,
  390; S.H., 442; S.J., 342; Samuel,
  016; Samuel, 016, 451; Sarah,
  024; Susan, 142; W. A., 016; W.C.,
  016, 342; W. M., 391; W.S., W. S.,
  390; Walter C., 451; William C.,
  016; William Henry, 424; William
  J., 071; William S., 016;
  William, 142, 150, 424
EEDS: John, 313
EGERTON: Charles, 429; Zachariah
  B., 391
EGNEW: Francis, 142; Mattox, 303;
  Susan, 315; William, 071, 142,
  303, 428
EICHELBERGER: William O., 198;
  William, 243
ELDER: Ada, 040; Augustus, 142; B.
  F., 342, 391, 403, 451; Benjamin
  F., 017, 142, 342, 361; C.N., 451;
  Charles H., 017; Dave, 342; David,
  142, 359; E.A.(?), 442; Edward A.,
  071, 142, 259, 302, 342, 381, 391,
  395, 414, 443; Edward L., 443;
  Edward, 142; Edward, Sr., 142;
  Eliza, 036, 334; Elizabeth, 049;
  Eva E., 044; G.B., 348; George B.,
  142; Harnett B., 142; Hattie, 018;
  Henry, 017; Herbert B., 142;
  313; J. E., 451; J. G., 254, 334,
  335, 337, 342, 350, 364; J. G.,
  Mrs., 365; James E., 017, 142, 451;
  James, 142, 291, 451; John F., 354;
  John G., 142, 342, 352, 364,
  414; John Henry, 017; Lucy, 013;
  Mary, 142; Monroe, 462; Mynona
  030; P.M., 451; Polly, 142; Salina
  C., 342; Selina, 014; Susan, 071;
  Turner, 017, 071, 142, 143; W.
  A., 142; W.S., 342; Walter, 391;
  William A., 142; William S., 017
ELIAS: S., 385

ELLIOT: John, 128; Mattie Fannie,
031; W. D., 467
ELLIOTT: Abram B., 248; J. H., 142;
James H., 082; Patsey, 142; Ross,
017; Samuel C., 295
ELLIS: A. W., 451; Allen W., 451;
Allen, 451; C.R., 451; Charles,
214, 222, 405; Daniel, 142, 424; E.
C., 451; Edgar C., 017; Elizabeth,
143; Elmyra C., 033; G. B., 451;
Glen B., 458; Glen, 398; Henry,
064, 071; J. H., 451; James, 071,
143, 154, 311; John A., 148, 228,
231, 252-253; John B., 071; John
H., 451; John, 017, 458; Jonathan,
Jr., 158, 200; Joshua, 451, 458;
ELLIS: Karon H., 458; O.L., 451; Ora
Bay, 061; Phebe W. (Cheatham), 228;
R.M., 451; Radford, 064, 071, 143;
Radford, Sr., 143; Ruby, 032; S.
W., 451; Samuel W., 017; Samuel,
017, 451, 458; Sarah Ann, 015;
Thomas H., 266; Thomas M., 120; W.
F., 451; Whit, 451; William A.,
210; William P., 451, 458;
William, 143
ELY: Horace, 092; John, 092
EMERSON: James, 168
EMMERSON: John, 286
EMMONS: John, 127, 143
EMORY: Amanda, 019; Samuel, 143
ENGLISH: Augustus, 071, 143;
Elizabeth, 007; J. B., 342
EPPS: Ab, 391; Alf, 017; Alfred, 143;
Andrew, 143, 150, 342; B.J., Jr.,
342; Benjamin, Jr., 342; Benjamin,
Sr., 017; Berry, 143; Burrell, 017,
143; David, 087, 218, 244; Edom,
017, 342, 462; Elizabeth, 342; Emma,
051; Eugene, 017; Hattie, 391;
James L., 308; Jimmie L., 143;
Jimmie Lee, 017; Joe, 391, 462; John
Clark, 017; Joseph, 071; Josiah B.,
308; Juno, 050; Loudell, 041;
EPPS: Madison, 143, 337, 341, 342,
344, 347, 350, 351, 353-355, 360,
362-364, 367, 375, 377, 386, 391,
462, 464; Matt, 342, 391; Millie,
031; Mollie, 032; Morgan, 017, 342;
Penda, 019; Sallie, 019; Sophia,
008; Thomas, 017; Took, 143; W.A.,
461; Zachariah, 017
ERICSON: Solomon, 444
ERVIN: Andrew, 193; Andrew, Jr.,
193; James, 193
ERWIN: Andrew, 211; James, 211; Thomas
B., 087, 108, 110, 114, 127, 139,
143, 145, 164, 165, 178, 185, 184,
190, 198, 218, 221, 225, 230, 234,
246, 249, 250, 255, 262, 265, 283,
286, 307, 387; Thomas E., 277, 278,
282; Thomas, 100; William, 143
ESKEW: Jim, 143; S. B., 451
ESTERS: James, 143; John A., 143;
Mary, 280; Philip, 143
ESTES: Baxter, 129; Elliott, 337,
369; J. T., 340; John A., 143;
Mary, 319; Robert, 143; William M.,
230; Winston C., 143; Winston, 143;
Zachariah, 143, 227
ETHRIDGE: Coswell, 097; James A.,
219; Janie, 462; William D., 145
EUBANKS: Amie B., 039; Elizabeth,
325; Magers, 071; Majers, 143
EVAN: William, 428
EVANS: A. Y., 017, 392; Ann Eliza,
057; Asbury T., 263; Asbury, 144;
Augustus W., 296; Carl, 397;
Charles, 143, 365; Charlie, 017,
462; Corer, 038; David, 143, 197,
313, 424; Drury P., 195; Drury, 107;
Francis, 144; Henry W., 071, 143,
153, 255; Henry, 017; James, 424;
Jesse, 120, 124, 138, 139, 143, 146,
191, 206, 275, 276, 313, 424; Jesse,
Jr., 143, 144; Jesse, Sr., 071, 143,
144; Jim, 392; John F., 089; John
M., 144, 241, 274, 306, 402; John,
36; Joseph M., 241, 274, 306;
EVANS: Josiah J., 071; Luella, 004;
Mary, 371; Mathew B., 238; Matthew
R., 106; Pat, 451; Patrick, 017;
S. C., 144, 342; Sallie A., 038;
Samuel, 372; Thomas, 274, 305; W.
V., 332, 340, 343, 352; Walter,
017, 144; William, 017, 144, 132,
192, 305, 444; Zou Ella, 054
EVANSON: William C., 251
EVELETH: Joseph, 156
EVERETT: R. M., 369; Solomon, 437;
Wiles N.H., 435; Wiley N.H., 144
EVERITT: R. M., 388; Thomas H., 432
EVERS: Jasper, 144
EVERSON: Henry P., 367
EVES: Bartlet, 144
EWING: Samuel B., 086
EXUM: John, 178
EZEL: Braxton R., 284
EZELL: ?, 356; Anna L., 061; B. R.,
385, 451; B. R., Jr., 414, 451; B.
R., Sr. 357, 381; Braxton R., 071,
144, 153, 218; Braxton R., Jr.,

144, 424; Braxton R., Sr., 373.
414, 424; Braxton, 294, 451; C.T.,
017, 099, 346, 451; Cullen R., 017;
E.B., 340, 347, 355, 365, 385, 463;
E. H., 451; E. W., 376; Emma, 017;
Evan B., 379; Frank, 451; H. E.,
451; H.H., 176, 451; Hartwell, 436;
Henry G., 144; Henry L., 017; J.
H., 451; J. R., 451; James P., 017;
EZELL: John H., 017, 144, 212, 241,
318, 342, 414, 451; John, 071, 286,
342; L.D., 144, 342, 381, 424, 451;
Lee D., 451; Levi D., 144, 451; Lucy
Grace, 458; Marcus, 443; Mattie P.,
035; Powel, 451; R. F., 451; R. P.,
451; Robert F., 133, 144, 148, 334,
342, 347, 425, 443, 451; Robert P.,
451; Robert Y., 103; Robert, 071,
414; W. B., 017, 359, 451, 463; W.
P., 342, 451; William B., 451, 458;
William P., 017; Willie, 451;
Cullen R., 442
EZZARD: William, 115
EZZARD: William, 115
FAGAN: Aron, 167; Ceasor, 445;
Grace Ann, 048
FAGIN: Carrie L., Mrs., 424
FAILS: Arthur, 144; Peuben, 144
FAIN: William, 203
FAIR: Miranda, 029; Neg, 017
FAIRCHILD: John A., 219; John, 130;
William, 130, 266
FALKNER: James, 144; John H., 144;
John, 144; Sooky, 458; Z.W., 355
FALL: John H., 144; John N., 144;
John S., 404
FALLEN: William, 017
FALLEY: Abe, 392
FAMBROUGH: Allen G., 183, 265;
Angelina P. (Smartt), 183, 265
FANNIN: Abraham B., 173; Catharine,
306; Isham S., 234; John H., 121;
John, 112
FANNING: Frederick D., 159, 192,
224, 264; Isham S., 235
FARGO: James C., 155, 215; John
C., 167; Joseph C., 112
FARLER: David, 017
FARLEY: James, 144, 194, 392; James,
Jr., 144; James, 144; John (heirs of),
490; John J., 313; John, 017, 144,
192, 222, 231, 422, 424; Mathew,
387, 395; Matthew C., 126; Nancy,
009; Russ, 144
FARMER: Asael, 424, 426; Jimie,
144; M. E., 404
FARR: J.M.P., 342; W.A., 392, 462
FARRAR: Abel, 017, 451; Abselem,
246; B. K., 451; Benjamin, 451;
Charlie, 144; Elizabeth, 040; G.
W., 144; George W., 451; George,
144; Otis, 017, 451; Peter, 142;
Samuel M., 170; Samuel S., 163;
Will, 145, 443; William W., 071;
William P., 118; William, 144
FARRER: Amos, 276; Benjamin K., 145
FARRILL: Erasmus W., 017
FARRINGTON: William, 180, 263, 294
FARRIS: J. P., 390; Willie C., 054
FARROW: Absalom, 145; Bell, 012;
Finch, 145, 460; Jane (Ray), 145;
Nich, 145; Tinch, 017
FARTHING: Joe, 145; Maud, 020
FAULKNER: Allice V., 009; C.M., 451;
Carrie, 039; Charles M., 017;
Charles, 451; Charlotte E., 043;
Claudie M., 041; Elizabeth R., 034;
Floyd, 145; H.D., 445, 451; Hartwell
P., 017; Hilton James, 017; Homer,
017; J. H., 451; J. P., 017, 145,
342, 392, 451; Jacob, 131, 190,
249, 258, 283; James Hilton, 017;
James W., 210, 242; Johm M., 145;
John H., 082, 145, 451; John P.,
017; John T., 017; John, 064, 071,
145, 323, 392; Luther, 088, 273;
FAULKNER: M. P., 442; Mary O., 442;
Mastin R., 145; Maston R., 017;
Maston, 064, 071, 145; Maud, 046;
Melissie, 035; Nannie Kate, 028;
P.M., 451; Persens, 451; Peter M.,
451; Peter, 451; Purse, 451;
Ruckner, 145; Thomas H., 145; Z.
M., 360; Zachariah, 071, 122,
123, 145, 313, 442; Zacherish, 292
FAVER: John, 298
FAVERS: J. P., 342
FAVORS: Joe T., 343; Joseph, 071,
203; Nisbet, 314
FEAGIN: William H., 145
FEAPS-MINTEP: Family, 485
FEAPS: Allsey, 064; Albert, 392;
Alsea, 071; Alsey, 145; Benjamin
Franklin, 071; Berry, 374; Buster,
343; Charity, 019; Clabe, 343,
392; Claborn, 145, 392; Claborn,
017, 392, 462; Claiborne, 343;
Clara, 392; Colsby, 145; Easter,
029; Edgar, 017; Elizabeth, 343;
Ellen, 404; Ephraim, 343; Ezekiel
P., 145, 288; Ezekiel, 071, 237,
311; Fannie L., 015; Fannie, 034;
FEAPS: Frances E., 292; Freeman,

017; Georgia Ann, 052; Georgia,
047; Green, 392; Hannah, 010; J.P.,
329; J.W., 446, 466; James S., 145,
215; James, 099; Jesse R., 017;
Jesse W., 095, 231; John P., 145,
245, 262, 314; John, 102, 282, 343,
387; Jonah, 017, 145; Lela, 041;
Lonnie, 392; Lou, Mrs., 012; Lucy
Ann, 023; Lucy, 039, 049; Lyda,
013; Mary Frances, 046; Matilda,
350, 061; Mattie, 042; Mike, 343;
FEARS: Milly, 025; Mollie, 005;
Nancy, 002, 012; Ollie, 006; Peter,
017; Pleas, 392; Rans, 392; Rhoda,
343; Riley S., 114, 145m 201, 206,
312, 320; Riley, 318; Robert, 017,
448; Sallie, 031; W. M., 442; W.
T., 442; Wesley, 017; Wiley M.,
082; Wiley, 145, 277; Will, 017,
145; William G., 071; William T.,
145, 297, 414; William, 018, 145;
Willie, 392; Wyly, 071
FEATHERSTON: Jinney, 424;
Pichard, 071, 424, 432
FEE: Jobe (Shy), 145
FELKER: Stephen, 250, 279
FELL: F., 331
FELLOWS: Cordy, 095; James, 304;
Pichard S., 304
FELPHS: Eliza Jane, 051
FERGASON: Neal, 145
FERGERSON: Alfred W., 145; Joseph,
270; Neil, 145; Neill, 145
FERGUSON: Beulah G., 026; J.E., 368;
John, 111; Joseph, 230; Neil, 462;
Neill, 201; P. H., 018
FERNANDEPS: James, 221
FERNDON: Michea C., 232
FERREL: Albert, 392; William, 145;
John, 110; William, 112, 145
FERRELL: Cuthbert, 145; J.M., 364;
John, 110; William, 112, 145
FERRILL: John J., 242
FESSENDER: Stephen, 272
FESSET: Drucilla, 055
FEW: Ignatius (heirs of), 424;
James M., 305; Odessa, 023;
Sidney, 146
FEWS: R. L., 408
FIELD: Benjamin H., 251;
Willis, 358, 374
FIELDER: Franklin O., 230; James M.,
145, 146; Obadiah M. B., 145,
146, 273; Thomas B., 146
FIELDS: Lemuel H., 146; Martin, 146;
William B., 146; Willis, 330
FINCH: Charles, 270; Mose, 146;
Thomas, 120
FINCHER: Angeline (Angelira), 146;
Christopher, 146, 203, 259, 290,
307, 448; Herman, 018; Isaac, 170,
206; Isabel, 041; J.J., 451; Jack,
451; James D., 018; James, 099,
146, 224; Joe, 018; John E., 018;
John L., 018; Joshua, 424; Leonard
C., 071; Mary (McCurdy), 146; Moses,
146; Sarah M., 012; William A.,
018; William, 308
FINDLAY: Mary, 101
FINDLEY: Alfred, 212
FINLEY: Celia, 146; Cullen, 146;
George W., 320; Harriott, 146;
Jacob, 146, 227, 282; James M.,
089, 240, 267; John, 146;
Murchison, 290; Quinton, 146;
Riley, 146, 205, 392
FINLY: Tyree G., 134
FINNEY: Caroline, 458; Ed, 392;
Janie, 052; William, 018
FIPPS: Lewis, 144; Patsey
(Faulkner), 144
FISCHER: S. C., 442
FISH: Aaron, 018, 345, 357; Addie,
016, 058; Ann, 022; Annie, 055;
Bernhard, 146; Calvin, 064, 071;
Charles, 146; Charlie, 018; Corine,
042; Emily B., 064; Gena, 023; Gim,
392; Henry, 343; Isaac, 146; James,
392; John, 018, 343; Julia, 023;
Liza Ann, 039; Louisa, 010; Lucy,
014; Maggie Lee, 042; Martha, 003;
FISH: Mary, 056; N.C., 442, 451; N.N.,
018; Naomy, 146; Nathan C., 018,
149, 201, 371, 451; Nathan, 071,
146, 161, 201; Prior, 392; Pryor,
018; Rejes, 018; Ridges, 146;
Russell, 018, 146; Sarena, 442;
Thomas G., 325; Vines, 095, 205;
Vinis, 232; W.T., 359, 451; William
P., 018, 082, 239, 343, 354, 367,
378, 442, 451
FISHER: Ann Eliza, 057; Nancy E.,
043; Sarah J., 060; W. W., 189,
298, 356
FITCH: Thomas, 143, 169, 170, 287;
W. F., 336
FITSIMONS: O. P., Jr., 374
FITZGERALD: George, 142
FITZPATRICK: Benjamin, 287; Bennett,
286; Bird, 238; Booth W., 146;
Booth, 146; Bouth, 017, 421; Hugh
P., 314; Jackson, 113, 146, 167,
225, 233, 253, 255, 263, 284, 306,

307, 314, 319, 424; Joseph, 109,
146, 392, 424; Mary L., 049; Mary,
003; Philip, 132, 146; Phillip, 146,
435; Phillips, 146; Rene, 126, 146,
191, 201, 314; Richard, 018; W.B.,
278, 355; William B., 235; William
W., 314; William, 071, 146, 288;
Y., 350
FITZSIMMONS: Emma, 071; O. P., 018,
342, 346, 381
FITZSIMONS: O. P., 335
FLAKE: William, 147, 266
FLANAGAN: Philip, 424, 428
FLANDERS: Benjamin W., 211; David, 131,
194, 211, 250, 285, 310, 319;
Davis, 200; Kate Ann, Mrs., 031
FLANEGIN: Joel, 147
FLANNAGAN: James, 147
FLANNEPY: John, 328
FLANNIKEN: David, 147
FLANNINGHAM: Lucy, 204
FLAT: John, 147
FLATAN: M, 341, 354, 365, 446;
Moris, 229; Morris, 333, 334,
336, 343; 354, 358, 367, 451
FLATAU: Moris, 147
FLEMING: James, 230, 424; John, 272,
315, 394; Mary, 272; Miller, 272;
Portec, 232, 302, 306; William, 314
FLEMISTER: Adaline, 036; Aley A.,110;
Alse, 147; Alsy, 147; C.A.J., 230,
392; Craton A. J., 093, 147, 202;
Craton A. J., 289, 290; Crayten A.
J., 147, 162, 194, 303; Crayton A.
J.,305, 306, 317, 318, 420; Crayton
A., 314; Creighton A. J., 147;
Eliza, 060; Elleanor, 147; Ellender
G., 071; Elsie, 314; Emelina J.,
199; Fielding, 120, 210, 272, 280;
388, 392, 409, 410; George M., 343;
FLEMISTER: Georgia M., 343; Georgia
M., Mrs., 341, 343; Horace, 147,
343; 352, 360; Indiana, 343; Isaac,
018; J.C., 343; J.M., 343, 392,
462; James C., 071, 136, 147, 174,
261; Jeff, 147, 392; Jim, 147;
John M., 147; John, 147, 395, 423,
444, 448; Lewis W., 147, 203;
Lewis, 147, 425; Mandy, 017;
Martha, 343; Richard, 120, 141,
147, 152; Richard, 208, 217, 245,
402; William A., 147; William L.,
147, 148, 301, 448; William S.,
148, 301; Willson L., 148, 199
FLEMMING: James, 148; John, 269
FLENNEKIN: David, 147; Joel, 175
FLENNIKEN: Samuel, 148
FLENNIKON: Sam, 462
FLETCHEP: Charles, 148; John, 283;
Sallie, 444; Thomas, 148, 266, 425
FLEWELLEN: Louzia C., 139; Lovewell
C, 148, 304, 425
FLINT: Charles C., 088
FLOOD: William, 088
FLORENCE: A. S., 071, 271, 397, 408,
444; Adial S., 451; Annie, 392;
F. A., 451; Mattie Lou, 036; Shed,
444; T. S., 451; W. S., 333, 372,
381, 444, 467; William A., 018;
William H., 148
FLOURNOY: Dock, 392; Joseph, 148
FLOURNEY: Annie Kate, 003;
Josiah, 173
FLOURNOY: Anna, 011; Callie, 462;
Elizabeth G, 148, 228; Florine,
047; Foy, 392; Francis, 445; Frank,
018; George, 148; Green, 018; J.
E., 343; Josiah, 071, 121, 430;
Lizzie, 050; Lucy, 026; Mary, 054;
Mickey, 343; Otis, 018; Robert,
099, 387; S.A., 343, 374, 375, 451;
Sallie F., 053; Sallie M., 015;
Sam, 392; Samuel A., 071, 181, 304;
451, 458; Samuel, 018, 148, 343,
451; Will M., 343; William B., 294;
William F., 071, 210, 294; William,
148, 294; Willie, 006; Willis,
148, 333, 343, 392
FLOWERS: Benjamin, 233; Edward, 128,
148, 314, 420, 422, 425; James M.,
322, 324; Lillie, 011; Theophilus,
148; William, 176, 215, 314
FLOYD: A.S., 451; Bell, 012; Georgia
A., 026; J.M., 384; Jim, 148; John
J., 253, 296; John, 148, 229; Mary,
007; Nancy J., 382, 392; Richard,
148; Thomas, 239; William, 148
FLUELEN: Lovewell C., 148
FLUELLEN: Eaton, 239
FLUKER: Baldwin, 120; John, 111,
125, 141, 148, 183, 191, 227,
248, 272, 273, 304, 317, 386, 425
FOALDS: George, 198
FOARD: Thomas, 150
FOLDS: Annie M., 014; Bascom, 451;
Basil, 451; Baswell, 451; Boston,
343, 458; Camilla, 016; Charles J.,
071; Eli, 392; Fannie, 040; G. W.,
451; George W., 082; George, 163,
469; Grandason, 071; J. F. 343
451; Jacob, 071; James, 343, 451;
Jane, 343; John J., 148; John, 071,

163, 432, 469; Martin, 096; Mary
G. 011; Mary, 148; Mattie, 007,
339; Sarah, 028; Thomas, 163; W.
L., 343, 392, 403, 451; William,
148, 451; Z. K., 148
FOLK: William, 08?
FON: Pichard W., 218
FONTS: Oliver P., 230
FOOSHEE: Jepthah, 148
FOOT: Shuback, 102
FORBES: Charles, 099, 148, 149,
189, 256, 260, 314, 310, 428;
Wesley, 149, 433
FORBS: Charles, 149
FORCE: Benjamin W., 175, 220; John
P., 099, 149, 175, 220;
Lewis M., 175
FORD: John, 425; Richmond, 392;
Mary, 038; Moses, 278; Neal, 343;
Washington, 071; William P., 131,
136, 176, 188, 192, 196, 210,
426, 268; William, 425
FOREMAN: Edmond, 425; Edmond, 149;
Eli, 265; George, 234; Ira, 113;
Isaac, 111, 149, 160, 319, 425;
Jacob, 071, 149; Jesse, 149
FORMBY: Aaron, 161
FORSYTH: John, (Governor), 277
FORT: Angeline, 061; Henry, 107;
Robert W., 107, 173; Robert, 121;
Sam, 343; Samuel, 343; Tomlinson,
154; William, 183
FORTE: Alexander, 149; Robert, 392
FOSTER: A. G., 178, 262, 305; A.W.
333, 334, 357, 359, 363, 371, 369,
370; Abe, 343; Albert W., 366;
Andrew, 149; Claborn, 223; Doe,
392; Edward C., 291; F. C., 178,
305; Frank, 343; George W., 469;
Granville W., 149; Jake, 149, 333,
343; Jemiha, 392; John L. S., 177;
John, 147, 425; Ludwell, 444;
Martha, 149; Nathaniel G., 234;
Polley, 149; Pichard, 149; Thomas
A., 278; Thomas F., 288; William,
149, 230, 290; Young, 343
FOWLER: John, 425; Stephen, 343;
Theophilus, 265, 314; William
P., 149, 283
FOXEY: William, 279
FOXIL: William, 234
FRANCE: Ella May, 420; William C., 462
FRANCOISE: Peter, 150
FRANK: Leo, 346
FRANKLIN: A.S., 343; Alfred S., 149,
297, 351; Bedney, 248; Carter, 451;
Dewitte, 451; Effie, 058; Ernest,
149; F. H., 398, 451; Felix, 451;
Floyed, 392; Hartwell, 451; Hattie,
343; Henry, 392; J. C., 089, 451;
John C.,071, 442, 451; John Carter,
064; Lewis, 323; Marcus A., 392;
Mary J., 042; Mary Jane, 006; R.
S., 362, 392; Robertine, 003;
Rufus, 451; Theodore, 147;
Victoria, 017
FRANKS: Britton J., 149; J.T., 443;
Minnie, 026; William B., 149
FRASIEP: Andrew, 280
FRASER: Ely, 149
FRAZIER: Andrew, 071; Eli, 149;
John, 392
FREEMAN: A. C., 305, 343, 442; A.
J., Mrs., 038; Ada, 038, 343;
Alemand, 442; Alsey, 051; Andrew
J., 314, 344, 358, 375; Andrew,
358, 379; Andy, 365; Ann, 043;
Anna, 031; Annie M., 027; Augustus
C., 133; B. B., 149; Bailey, 071,
138, 149, 259, 400; Benjamin P.,
071, 107, 149, 233, 343; Bob, 149,
414; Brown, 149, 343; C., 344; Carl
Lee, 392; Catharine B., 042;
FREEMAN: Charles, 149; Cinth a
(Wyatt), 314; Corey, 338; Cynthia
A., 064, 343; Daniel, 071, 149,
284, 290, 299; Dora, 044; E. A.,
343, 392, 451; E., 343; Ebb, 461;
Ed, 149, 150; Edmund, 344; Edward
A., 242; Eliza, 150, 343, 392;
Elizabeth H., 003; Elleck, 305;
Ellie, 343; Emily C., 010; Floyd,
064, 343, 442; Frances A., 013;
Frances, 007; Frank, 343, 344, 392;
Frederick, 199; Fulton, 125; George
H., Jr., 149; George, 071, 149,
150, 194, 344, 414, 443, 451;
FREEMAN: George, Sr., 344; Georgia
Ann, 048; Georgia C., 008; Hamlin,
093, 193, 212, 314; Hartwell, 149;
Hartwell W. B., 071, 152, 314;
Hawkins, 149; Henry H., 149, 425;
Henry, 344; Hopson, 071, 149, 284;
Horse, 344, 392; I. H., 103, 340,
344, 451; India V., 036; Indiana,
024; Isaac H., 018, 071, 091, 149,
149, 150, 185, 259, 314, 319, 329,
334, 343, 344, 352, 414, 425, 443,
451; Isaac T., 343; Isaac, 149,
425; J. H., 103, 342, 370; J. W.,
388, 392; Jabez, 150, 392; James,
064, 071, 149, 150, 149, 194, 284,

290; Jane, 007, 032; Jesse, 018,
150; Joe, 150; John F., 150, 344;
FREEMAN: John J., 392; John, 150,
158, 160, 344; John, 424-426, 432,
436; Josiah M., 392; Josiah, 064,
071, 459; Julia P., 034; Julia,
037; King, 018; L. E., 392; Lee,
018, 344, 354, 392; Levi, 150,
314; Linda, 036; Louisa, 013;
Lucky, 344; M. A., 343; M. L.,
451; Mariah, Mrs., 036; Mark
Anna, 445; Martha, 016; Mary Ann,
048; Mary C., 064, 071; Mary, 093;
Matilda, 014; Mollie, 344; Mose,
018; N. B., 393; Nannie, 050;
FREEMAN: Phillip, 150; Reuben, 149;
Richard, 018; Robert, 018, 124,
132, 151, 158, 173, 178, 188, 233,
375, 323; Rose Ann, 006; Sallie,
015, 052, 059; Sam, 150, 344, 443;
Samuel, 018, 393; Sarah Ann, 057;
Silla, 344; Tabitha, 356;
Theophilis, 111, 125, 150, 210,
314, 391, 425; Theopholus, 432;
Thomas, 018, 150, 231, 344; Timothy,
150, 197, 205, 323; Tom, 018, 150;
Turner, 393; Virginia, 031; W.M.,
344, 462; W. P., 451; Warner, 018;
Wesley, 018, 344; William M., 018;
William, 018, 087, 120, 121, 148,
182, 198, 236, 267, 293, 344,
393, 458, 462
FPENCH: M. C., 039
FRETWELL: James, 113, 150, 229;
Micaiah H., 150, 167, 255, 314,
393; Micajah N., 162; Richard,
150, 425
FPEYERMUTH: John, 425; John, Sr., 418
FRITH: Francis Marion, 117; John W.,
117; Mary F., 117; Thomas, 150
FPOST: Philemon, 251
FPY: Dave, 150; Jean Lodowick, 150
FUDGE: Benjamin, 129, 151, 175,
425, 427, 427, 431
FULFOPD: O. L., 393
FULLER: Annie, 027; Catherine, 008;
Joanna, 045; S.R., 400; Sam, 151;
Simeon, Jr., 025; Step, 018;
Stephney, 151; Stepney, 256; Thomas,
018, 151; William, 018, 151
FULLERTON: Aurie 1., 037; G.E., 451;
James, 151; S. M., 451;
Samuel, 151, 451
FULTON: S, 444; Samuel, 125, 135,
150, 151, 244, 283, 300, 451;
Susan, 422
FULWOOD: W. Andrew, 391
FUNDERBUNK: Bettie, 023
FUNDERBURG: J. C., 344
FUNDERBURK: Addie Jane, 027; Alice
A., 027; G.R., 151; J. C., 414;
J. I., 451; Joseph, 255, 393; M.A.,
056; Mattie L., 036; Thomas B.,
018; William A., 018, 071
FURGASON: Julius, 150
FURLOW: Charles M., 108, 288;
William, 270
FUPSE: R. L., 406, 451; Robert L.,
018; T. L., 337
GAFFORD: James, 222
GAINES: George G., 161
GAITHER: Beckie, 047; Bob, 151;
Charley, 018; Eli E., 175; Emma,
019; Georgia, 151; H. C., 462, 464;
Harris, 393; James, 018; Jim, 393;
Josephine, 393; Morris, 344;
Ophelia, 393; Rob, 151; Robert,
151, 393, 462; Wodin, 393
GALIAGAN: Lawrence, 108
GALLAWAY: James M., 018
GALLEY: Robert, 169
GALLMAN: James, 018; Jesse, 087,
254; John C., 071
GALLOWAY: William, 122
GAMAGE: Martha, 061; Thomas, 244
GAMBLE: Israel, 225
GAMBOL: Israel, 284
GAMMON: Sarah (Smith),151; Silas, 151
GANN: James A., 442
GANNT: John Wesley, 018
GANO: F. W., 468
GANT: Cornelia P., 058; Ellie, 393;
Elmira, 344; Georgia Ann, 031;
Henry, 018; James, 393; Jefferson,
018; Jim, 018; John, 344; Levi,
018, 151; Lewis, 018, 344, 393;
Louis, 344; Mima, Mrs., 032; Oliver,
151; Ridley, 018, 151; Singleton,
018; Sylvania, 005; Tabitha, 151;
Victoria, 012
GANTT: Bob, 344; Cicero, 344, 393;
Dora, 393; Eula, 393; Henry, 344;
Jim, 344; John, 384, 425
GAPDEN: Alexander, 131, 149, 444
GARDEN: Cain, 019
GAPDNEP: Asa, 242; Ben, 019; Benjamin,
019; Charlotte, 045; Cornelia, 005;
Dennis, 019; Ethelred, 071, 233;
Harriet, 393; James P., 118; James,
019, 151; John E., 151; Ned, 019;
Patrick H., 151, 434; Samuel, 425;
Stephen (orphans of), 418

GARISON: James D., 019
GARLAND: Crawford, 019, 151; Darkis,
010; Edward, 151, 275, 386; Eugene,
393; Harry, 019; Hastings, 151; J.
T., 384, 451; Janie, 055; John,
071, 151, 190; John, Jr., 151;
Lucy J., 027; Mary Liza, 462; N.
C., 451; Thomas, 151; W. J., 451;
William D.,114, 300; William J.,019
389, 428, 436
GARLINGTON: Albert C., 324; James,
124, 151, 159, 218, 317-318,
389, 428, 436
GARMANY: Robert, 222
GARNER: John W., 019, 151; John, 114,
151; Nancy (Smith), 151; Richard,
151, 215, 217, 248, 285, 298, 425;
Stephen, 151; Vincent, 204
GARNETT: Ell, 097
GARRET: Miles, 151
GARRETT: Benjamin, 094, 151, 429;
Blount L., 151; Blount S., 237;
Blunty, 071; Daniel, 444; Eleazer,
151; G. W., 389, 462; George S.,
071, 151; George, 151; Jefferson,
152; Jesse H., 151; Jesse, 151;
John B., 089; Jonathan, 152; Joshua
C., 108; Mary Ann, 045; Mials, 314;
Miles, 151, 152; P. M., 344; Robert
M., 019; S. W., 335, 344; Tabitha
J., 360; Tabitha, 214; Talitha, 151;
Thomas C., 152, 177, 259, 433;
Thomas, 152; Thos. C., 466; W. W.,
393; William, 152, 257
GARTEN: Nathan H., 101
GARTRELL: Horatio, 196; William, 100
GARY: Matthias E., 314; Mattias G.,
152; William, 152, 314
GASSET: Henry, 091, 211
GASSETT: Henry, 230, 274
GASTON: C. A., 019; Catharine, 071;
Charles B., 152; Charles R., 152;
Charles, 344, 330, 375; Charley
A., 344, 349; Charlie, 152;
Elizabeth, 152, 344; Fannie P.
(Powell), 366; Fanny F., 414; George
M. T., 152; Henry W., 152, 314;
Henry, 178; Hudson, 152; James, 152;
Kate, 152; Lizzie, 152; M.P., Mrs.,
374, 380; Mary, 013, 354, 381;
Mattie Clyde, 032; Nancy A., 008,
071; P.F., 071; T.G., 344; T. 462;
Thomas (heirs of), 425; Thomas,
071, 087, 150, 152, 260, 264, 389,
423, 434; Tom, 344; W. T., 393
GATES: Bettie, 014; Carney, 152;
Charles, 019; Daniel, 019; Emma,
023; Fannie, 043; Harriet, 051;
Henry, 019; Ida, 046; John,
019; Lewis, 019, 344; Major, 019;
Milledge, 019; Sameul, 019;
William, 019
GATHRIGHT: Nelson, 194; William C.,
095; Wilson, 152
GAULT: Robin, Jr., 019
GAUTHER: Peter, 152
GAUTIER: Fannie, 344; Peter W., 019,
209, 239, 425, 436; Peter W. Sr.,
277; Peter William, 202, 428;
Peter, 152
GAY: A. O. M., 336, 344; Augustus O.
M., 344; Charles, 344; E.H., 153,
355, 451; Elbert H., 152, 310, 344,
451; Elbert, 130, 152; Ellen, 019;
Elvira, 130; F. H., 152; Franklin
H., 114, 152; Freeman, 356; Gilbert,
126, 152, 177, 257, 293, 433;
Gilbert, Jr., 019; Henry, 019;
Hilliard H., 153, 314, 393; Ida,
029; J. W., 153, 451; Jane, 050;
Jerry, 019; John W.,153, 451; John,
019; Jordan, 153; Jorden, 425;
Lavice, 015; M. Louisa, 152; Mattie,
002, 029; Milledge M., 153; Sherod
Milledge, 130; Sarah, 130; Sherod
H., 137, 153, 158, 166, 167,
175, 229, 236, 293; Sherrod H., 064,
071, 106, 153, 186, 236, 290, 296,
307, 389, 405, 448; Sherwood H.,
153, 174; Sherwood, 424; Thomas
A., 153, 442; William, 311,
316; Willis, 395
GAYER: George, 254
GEARPETT: Jesse, 153
GEASLAND: Hiram, 127; Matilda Ann,
127; Matilda, 127
GEIGER: Elizabeth, 064, 071; Ester
M., 044; Freeman, 019, 153; H. H.,
414; Harman H., 064, 071, 153, 277,
288, 425; Harman, 187; Harmon H.,
191; Hattie E., 041; J. S., 051;
James M., 019; James W., 153; Jere,
019; John H., 019; M. L., 031; Man,
153; Margaret C., 153; R. C., 344;
R. H., 451; P. L., 451; Randal C.,
153, 414; Randal H., 019, 071;
Randal, 451; Richard, 451; Tony,
019; Washington, 071
GEORGE: America, 153, 344; Americus,
443; Anna, 032; Berry, 344;
Elizabeth, 445; F., 347; Francis M.,
292; Franklin, 019, 149, 153, 159,
186, 314, 329, 332, 337, 340, 366,

375, 376, 380; Harriet, 344; Henry,
120, 139, 152, 153, 155, 359;
Hilliard, 344; James H., 134; James,
071, 123; Jeptha V., 153; Jepthah,
271; Jesse, 425; Lawson E., 380;
Lucius, 443; Lucy Jane, 057; Martha,
054; Marv, 003, 046; Merina, 153;
Patience, 002; Thomas P., 123;
Tunstall B., 237, 260; Whitson H.,
094; William, 153, 257
GERALD: George F., 317
GEPDING: Benjamin F., 331; Charles,
328, 331, 332, 335, 352, 354, 370.
380; Julius, 235
GERMAIN: William, 153, 393
GERMANY: James, 107, 179; Nancy, 049;
Robert, 107, 116, 226, 296, 300,
301, 303; William, 107, 166
GEROLD: George F., 318
GERRETT: Tabitha, 356
GHANT: Dora, 344
GHASTON: Charley P., 019
GHOLSTON: Anthony, 071; James S., 311
GIBBS: Achsah P., 153; Achsah, 322;
D. A., 343; Elhanan, 127, 153, 468;
Elhannan, 465; Elhanon, 425; Leonard
G., 267; Leonard Y., 305, 335, 372;
Phebe, 322; Pheolus, 153; Zacheous,
297; Zachery, 153
GIBSON: Abe, 344; Adolphus H., 299;
Eliza, 154; J. C., 266; John C.,
071, 087, 108, 131, 140, 147, 154,
156, 195, 238, 244, 264, 304, 307,
311, 314, 393, 425, 448, 458, 462;
John, 188; Jonathan, 184, 252;
Lewis, 158, 266, 283; Martha, 458;
Robert B., 314; Thomas, 188;
William, 166
GILBERT: Felix H., 130, 156, 167,
204, 299; Felix, 143, 167, 302,
323; George, 168; Hiram, 280;
William G., 130, 143, 167, 174,
204, 275, 299, 425; William, 156,
167, 299, 323; Wilson, 155
GILES: Bud, 248; Catharine, 043;
Felix, 019; Jettie, 019; John J.,
154; John, 154, 344; Johnson, 393;
P. C., 154; Robinson, 154; Thomas
J., 019; Thomas, 154; Thomas, Jr.,
154; Tommie, 393; William, 130
GILL: Callie, 042; Delia, 059;
George, 154, 343; John, 163;
William, 123, 127, 37, 154, 161,
163, 208, 264, 314, 393, 435
GILLAM: John, 154
GILLCOAT: Azariah, 154; Hannamah, 154
GILLCOATT: Hananiah, 124
GILLEDAND: George W.,146; Thomas, 154
GILLESPIE: James, 109; John, 154
GILLIAM: John, 019
GILLILAND: William H., 132
GILLIS: Kenneth, 154
GILLSTRAP: Rubin, 019
GILMORE: Amanda, 007; David, 155;
Eliza J., 007; Elizabeth, 155; J.
G., 462; J. M., 451; James
(Thames), 275; John H., 170; John,
155, 425; Mary (Thames), 275;
Natley, 155; Notley, 155; Robert,
155; Rosa, 010; Samuel, 155; Sanford
M., 155; Stephen H., 409; Stephen,
176, 210, 275; Thomas, 155, 344; W.
E., 393; Willie, 155; William, 425;
Willis, 155

GILSTRAP:
Jr., 019; Bill, 393; Clemle, 051;
David, 019; Davis, 019; Emily C.,
394; George, 019; Hattie, 018;
Indianna, 004; J.M., 345, 451; J.,
451; James, 019, 393; Jane, 047;
Jeremiah M., 147, 155, 307, 314,
345; John B., 019, 071, 442; John,
155; Lee, 155; Lewis, 286, 425;
Love, 155; Mariah, 011; Martha,
337, 458; Mattie Lou, 050; Nealie,
057; Otis, 019; Reuben, 019, 345;
Sallie Lou, 011; William, 019, 365
GINC: Noma, 039
GINN: Arthur, 294, 444
GIVENS: J. P., 376
GLASCOCK: Thomas, 155
GLASS: Henry, 345, 462; Hubeard, 155;
James, 155; James P., 019; James,
191, 155, 296, 314, 425, 428;
Thomas, 019, 314, 345; Tom, 019;
William W., 019; William, 142, 424
GLAWSON: A., 451; Caroline, 017;
Carrie, 031, 047; Genus, 345;
Gertrude, 021; James L., 392, 402;
Jasse, 052; Jesse, 181; Joseph, 155,
204; L. C., 155; Lou, 058; Martha
Ann, 061; Mary E., 345;
Mary Eliza, 052
GLAZER: Hiram, 092
GLAZIER: Adam, 425; Hiram, 116, 137,
142, 232, 293, 407, 420, 423, 425;
Marnoch, 142; Marnock, 154, 206;
Wesley, 132, 155, 224, 299, 304
GLEN: Little P., 425
GLENN: Drucilla, 036; Joseph C., 157;
Little P., 155; Matthew H., 155,
171, 458; Simeon G., 173, 459;

Thornton I., 071
GLISSEN: John, 155
GLOVER: Aaron, 019, 463; Ada, 022;
Adaline, 155; Aggie, 022; Allen,
155; America, 345; Anderson, 020,
345; Angeline, 024; Anna, 030;
Augustus L., 155; Benjamin, 324;
Bill, 155, 289; Blute, 156; Bob,
155; Brack, Jr., 345; Catharine,
027, 047; Celia, 020; Charles, 155,
393; Charlev, 020; Charlie, 020;
463; Christopher, 155; D.P., 192,
335, 348, 359, 362, 367, 378, 451;
GLOVER: David R., 020; Dealey, 333;
Della, 028, 341; Dennis, 020, 155,
345, 414; Diana, 036; Dinah, 035;
E. S., 443; Ebenezer I., 155;
Ebenezer, 155; Edenborough, 020,
155; Elbert, 020, 393; Ell S., 071,
155, 219, 235, 451; Ell, 071, 091,
107, 108, 116, 118, 122-125, 129,
133, 137-139, 143, 145, 152, 155,
160, 169, 175, 179, 181, 183, 184,
191, 196, 210, 213, 214, 216, 218,
226, 238, 243, 270, 288, 302-304,
310, 314, 315, 323, 393, 402, 425;
446; Ell, Sr.,064; Eliza, 071, 030;
GLOVER: Elizabeth, 016; Ellen, 029;
Emily, 014, 030, 345; Eugene, 020;
Evaline, 002; Eveline, 155; Fannie,
027, 041, 056, 393; Frances, 155,
345; Frank, 155; Gena, 155, 345;
George Ann, 009; George, 020, 155;
H. S., 345, 451; Hannah, 057;
Harriet, 014; Henry S., 155, 156,
345, 451; Henry S. Jr., 393;
Henry S., Sr., 071; Henry, 020,
092, 155, 345, 425; Henry, Sr., 448;
Indianna, 016; Isaac, 020; J. H.,
345; J. J., 345, 393; Jake, 020;
GLOVER: James P., 136, 156, 217;
James, 156, 393; Jefferson, 020;
Jenette, 156; Jessie, 345; Jim,
020; John E., 071, 100, 110, 169,
179, 250, 252, 292, 448; John J.,
020, 156, 314; John, 020, 071, 148,
156, 393, 397; Jonah, 393; Joseph,
020; Jossie, 035; Julia, 055;
Katie, 015; Lewis, 020, 156, 342,
345, 451; Louis, 156; Madora, 016;
Margaret, 019; Mary Jane, 156;
Mary, 045, 054, 393, 463; Mathew,
156, 345, 363; Matthew, 345;
GLOVER: Mattie Lou, 006; Mattie, 156;
Milley, 345; Millie, 345; Milton
P., 156; Mitch, 345; Mitchel, 020;
Mitchell, 156; Mollie, 041; N. S.,
098; Nancy, 027; Nannie, 059;
Nathaniel S.,268; Nelson, 343, 379;
Orange, 345; Peter, 020, 156, 345;
Rebecca M., 031; Peese, 156; Rich.,
156; Richard, 020, 156; Robert,
020, 156; Roberta, 012; Roy, 156;
Sallie B., 054; Sarah, 009, 030;
155; Sidney, 042; Silvie, 032; Sol,
156; Solomon, 020; Stewart, 345;
Tom E., 020; Tom, 156; W. P., 020,
360, 402; Walter, 020; Wash, 020;
Will, 156; William Henry, 156;
William, 020, 345, 393
GOBEL: Luther, 020
GOBLE: Luther, 174, 188, 252, 254
GODARD: David, 431; Joseph, 196;
William, 362
GODDARD: Austin, 156, 244; Bailey,
183, 277, 283; Daniel, 425; Ira,
019, 229, 270; James, 260; W.T., 020
GODFREY: James, 167; William, 168, 188
GODKIN: John R., 156, 162, 261,
314, 345
GODLEY: James M., 156; James, 156,
423, 425, 459, 463; John, 295
GODWIN: Algornon G. A., 458; Edward,
236; J.R., 407; Mary H., 156, 459;
Samuel, 156
GOEN: Robert, 198
GOFF: Garlin, 156; Nathaniel, 083, 320
GOGANS: Samuel, 367
GOGGANS: J.M., 156; J.S., 393; Lucy
E., 008; Madison, 393, 414;
Middleton, 020; Samuel, 047, 156;
Washie, 012; William M., 020
GOGGINS: Abraham G., 275; Biddy
(Johnston), 458; G.T., 451; J.S.,
451; John S., 451; Madison, 071,
458; Martha, 010; Mat, 451;
Samuel, 275, 407
GOINS: Cora, 022
GOLDEN: J. O., 451; William, 425
GOLDIN: S., 122
GOLDSBOROUGH: Charles, 294
GOLDSLEY: William, 020
GOLLSBY: Willie, 347
GOOD: Sterling, 071
GOODDAPD: Ira, 121
GOODE: James H.,071; James Henderson,
064; Jesse, 064, 071; John C., 064,
071, 245; Macerniss, 158;
William, 072
GOODHUE: N., 091
GOODIN: James A., 399

GOODMAN: Andrew, 020; Annie, 026;
Barney, 072, 345, 425; C. L., 057;
Caroline, 393; Creacy, 006; Daley
Ann, 016; Daniel, 237; E.N., 348;
Elisha N., 020; Elizabeth, 061; G.
L., 451; George W., 020; H. A.,
393; Isaac, 156, 232; J. T., 361,
408, 442, 451; J. W., 451; James
E., 020; James T., 345, 451; James,
345; Jane, 023; Jerry, 020; Jim T.,
451; John F., 329; John, 156,
451; John W., 020; John, 020, 312,
315, 317, 323, 324; Louisa E., 034;
GOODMAN: Martha Lilian, 028; Mary C.,
037; Mattie, 018; Mollie, 008, 156;
345; P. H., 451; Rebecca, 050;
Richard H., 156, 464; Richard H.,
Jr., 020; Richard, 442; Richard,
Jr., 282; Wiley, 156
GOODRICH: William H., 086
GOODRUM: Juda, 049; Tom, 020
GOODSON: Mary E., 331
GOODWIN: Randall, 345; William H., 156
GOOLSBY: A. L. Mrs., 451,
463; Abe, 020; Ada, 037; Adaline,
047; Addie B., 039; Addie May, 039;
Adelphia, 058; Albert, 020; Alex,
345; Alfred, 020, 183, 195, 241,
345, 451; Alick, 020; Allen, 156,
316, 458; Amanda, 056; Amarintha,
156; Anderson, 020, 056; Angerona,
045; Annie E., 460; Annie, 037,
053, 462; Artemas, 175; Artemus,
142, 156, 157, 158, 234, 276, 303,
305, 317; B.E., 451, 467; Bart, 393;
GOOLSBY: Ben, 393; Benjamin, 393;
Bird, 106; Bob, 020; Braxton E.,
157; Braxton, 345; Burgess, 250,
463; C. B., 442; C. D., 345, 451;
C. E., 446; C.J., 354, 451; C. K.,
451; C. L., 345, 444, 451; C. R.,
020, 021, 345, 393, 425, 444, 451,
460, 463; C. Reese, 451; Caleb,
021; Caliss, 393; Carden J., 157;
Carden, 021; Carden R., 157, 345;
Carden, 064, 142, 157, 290, 307,
319, 422, 437; Cardin J., 451;
GOOLSBY: Cardin P., 451; Cardin P.,
Sr., 157; Cardin, 072, 138, 157;
158, 163, 175, 235, 241, 251, 260,
307, 356, 391, 463, 469; Caroline,
036, 393; Carrie Lee, 017; Carrie,
030; Charity, 007; Charles, 157,
346, 393, 414; Charley, 157, 346;
Charley, Jr., 021; Charlie, 021;
Cincinnattus J.,072, 157; Cincinnatus
L., 064, 152, 232, 346; Cincinnatus
S., 295; Cincinnatus, 319; Clark,
021, 393; Clayton D., 346, 414;
Clayton, 021, 451; Coot, 346; Cora,
009; Corl, 021; Crit, 021, 157, 393;
GOOLSBY: Cullen, 451; Dan, 157;
Daniel, 021; Davis L., 021; Dee,
021; Dennis, 021, 072; Eadie, 006;
Easther Alberta, 443; Eberhart,
157; Edenboro, 157; Edenborough,
021; Elizabeth, 038, 157; Ellen,
025; Emma K., 039; Ezell S., 451;
F.C., 157, 296, 346, 425, 444, 451;
Fannie Kate, 049; Fannie Lou, 055;
Fanny, 030; Florence P., 057;
Francis C., 463; Francis, 346; Frank
Walker, 021, 346; Frank, 021, 346,
407, 446; Franklin, 451; Freeman,
346; Gabe, 021; General, 021;
GOOLSBY: Genus, 021; George, 021,
393; Georgia, 038; Grant, 021, 157,
302; Gus, 278, 346; H. L., 346, 463;
Harol, 451; Hartwell, 451; Hastie,
026; Ida M., 056; Ira, 021; Irene,
021; J. B., 157, 393, 451; J. C.,
346, 451; J. K., 157, 346, 451; J.
P., 451; J. W., 346; Jacob, 064,
072, 469; James B., 021, 072, 142,
157, 160, 180, 191, 346, 351, 367,
391, 404, 414, 422, 442, 451, 469;
James, 157, 346, 460, 463; Jane,
011; Jennett, 020; Jennie May, 021;
GOOLSBY: Jennie, 015; Jim, 021, 393;
Jinnie, 024; Jodie, 394; Joe, 394;
John Henry, 021, 157; John K., 157,
212, 346, 451; John N., 157, 235,
314; John Walker, 021; John, 021,
157, 394; John, Sr., 072; Johnie,
021; Johnnie, 394; Joshua, 157;
Julia E., 157, 375; Julia, 011;
Katie, 019, 036; Kirby, 157, 391,
448, 469; Leathy, 469; Lee, 021;
Leman, 346; Lemon, 021; Levi, 021,
072, 120, 379, 394, 414, 452; Litha,
002; Lizzie, 041, 047; Lorena, 036;
GOOLSBY: Lou Zella, 052; Lou, 010;
Lucy Ann, 005; Lucy Jane, 045;
Lucy, 021; Lula, 026, 027; M.A.,
333, 346; M. C., 021, 346, 425,
452, 469; Manda, 009; Mariah, 031;
Marshall C., 398, 463; Martha P.,
003; Mary A., 224; Mary E., 012;
Mary Frances, 021; Mary, 346, 347,
394; Mason, 346; Mat Lou, 053; Mat,
157, 335; Matilda, 047, 048;
Mattie, 054; McClendon, 021; Meredy,

346; Merida, 394; Merridy, Jr.,
021; Milledge, 021; Miranda, 055;
GOOLSBY: Mitchel, 021; Mollie, 014,
157; N. B., 021, 330, 346; Nancy,
026; Nat Jr., 346; Ned, 157;
Nelson, 021, 394; Obe, 394; Oliver,
157; Peter E., 021; Peter, 021;
Pleasant, 157; R. A., 345, 347, 394,
452, 467; P. P., 021, 452; Rachael
Mrs., 037; Rachel, 004; Rebecca,
031; Peese, 112; Reuben, 021, 128;
Phoda, 031; Pich H., 021; Richard,
021, 157, 228, 425, 469; Rick, 157,
462; Ross, 157; Poswell, 452;
GOOLSBY: Rufus, 021, 346; Sallie, 053
Samual, 157, 443; Sarah A., 003;
Sarah J., 054; Sarah, 458, 469;
Scott, 021; Seely, 157; Sherman,
157; Silvey, 057; Simon, 157;
Spencer, 021, 394; Squire, 347;
Stephen, 021; Tabitha, 345; Thomas
H., 021; Thomas, 394, 103, 157;
Tom Alf, 158; Tom, 157, 347; Trump,
158; W. B., 021, 347, 394, 378,
414, 452; W. H., 394; W., 446,
W.T., 452; Wade B., 021, 072, 158,
347, 371; Wade, 393, 452; Wesley,
180; Wiley J., 021; Will, 158;
William J., 152, 158, 202, 232, 395
William, 021, 065, 072, 083, 094,
126, 158, 163, 165, 157, 347, 395,
425; Willie, 347; Winny, 020;
GOOPE: Thomas, 158
GOPDAN: G. O., 158; John, 158;
Juvver, 158
GOPDEN: N. W., 469
GOPDON: Aaron, 021; Ada, 003; Agella,
005; Alexander, 425; Andrew, 314;
Annie, 021; Arthur, 158; Charles
P., 021, 111, 119, 139, 172, 187,
186, 196, 278, 303; Charles, 425;
Clate, 414; Clayt, 158; Clayton,
347; David, 021; Delphia, 053;
Edman J., 021; Edmond J., Jr., 022;
Elizabeth, 005, 022; Emily, 010;
Ephraim, 235; Fannie, 048; Frances,
Mrs., 006; D. L., 341; G. O., 347;
George D., 394, 414, 425, 458;
GORDON: George Dyer, 158; George M.,
172; George O., 022, 347; George
W., 394; George, 347; Georgia Ann,
022; Hugh, 022; Isaac, 022; J. W.,
347; James H., 172, 199, 278, 290;
Jim, 022; Joe, 463; John B., 157,
242; John J., 022; John Wesley,
022; John, 022, 251, 358, 452;
Lizzie, 035; Louisa, 072, 151,
275, 460; Louise, 065; Louis, 021;
Malissa, 052; Mary D., 072; Mary,
010; N. W., 158; Nathaniel G., 190;
Nathaniel W, 158, 219, 238, 256;
Nathaniel, 303; Rebecca, 051;
Peuben, 022; Reuben, Sr., 158;
Robert, 022, 158; Sallie F., 046;
Sallie, 059; Susie, 026; Thomas
A., 072; Thomas G., 159; Thomas,
158; Victoria, 021; W. R, 347,
452; Zachariah, 278, 323
GORE: Thomas, 121, 158
GORMAN: H. D., 394; John B., 256
GORPING(GOWING?): Benjamin, 469
GOSS: Benjamin, 158; Churchwill C.,
158; Hamilton, 191; Zachariah H.,162
GOTFEPP: Lula, 032
GOTELL: Lucy, 051
GOTIEP: Fannie, 347; Hattie, 005; J.
C., 394; Laura, 043, 050; Maria,
022; Martin, 022; Wesley, 022;
William, 022, 394
GOULD: Ada, 347; Artemas, 094, 119,
172, 208, 270, 318-320; Artemous,
305; Artemus, 090, 092, 137, 188,
273; H. S., 158, 34
GPACE: James, 158, 317; Jared E.,
193; John, 072; Joshua, 158, 201,
314; Mary (Bollinger), 158
GRADY: Willis, 103, 304
GPAHAM: Alexander, 093, 115, 181;
Alexander, 206, 228, 301; Isaac
G., 251; Jackson, 153; James, 072,
159, 276, 469; Richard, 339;
William M., 72
GPAINGER: Robert, 216
GPANGEP: Robert, 268
GPANT: Alonzo, 022, 158, 463; Annie
Lee, 056; Brittain, 279; Charley,
022; Cornelius, 158; Daniel, 093,
145, 152, 164, 173-175, 177, 178,
183, 186, 197, 199, 204, 205, 211,
221, 229, 244, 258, 277, 281;
Earnest, 158; Fannie, 158; J.C.,
452; James, 314; John, 022;
Joseph, 469; Lewis, 347; Nathaniel,
158; Pidiey, 158; Popbin, 148;
Samuel, 072, 158, 394; Talitha, 158;
GPANT: Thomas, 072, 093, 100, 106,
118, 128, 145, 146, 157, 158, 164,
170, 173-178, 182, 183, 186, 187,
189, 192, 204, 205, 208, 210, 211,
221, 223, 224, 229, 234, 244, 248,
253, 254, 258, 271, 277, 281, 313,
318, 325, 400, 425; Thomas, Sr.,

223; W. T., 452; William, 314
GRANTHAM: William R., 082
GRAVENSTEIN: John, 425
GRAVES: Charlie, 347; Davenport, 158,
428; Edwin, 175, 190, 203; Erastus,
092, 109; Floyd, 022; J. B., 158;
John, 105, 124, 153, 158, 159,
288, 291; John, Sr., 233; Lewis,
072, 425; Minton, 124; Rufus L.,
314; Rufus B., 109, 175
GPAY: A.T., 072, 159, 347, 452, 463;
A.T., Mrs., 159; Adaline, 114, 159;
Adam, 022, 347; Albert T., 452;
Annie C., Mrs., 159; Annie S., 347;
Chester, 022; J. T., 391; James A.,
380; James R., 126; John F., 171;
John, Jr., 159; Katie, 347; L.
C.,022; Matthias S., 159; Richard,
294; Sherrod H., 232
GPAYBILL: Henry, 113, 159, 459;
Henry, 159; James S., 159, 221
GRAYSON: Spence M., 295
GREAR: Thomas, 159
GREAVES: Joseph D., 159
GREEN: --,445; Aaron, 394; Allen,
160; Alston H., 103, 105, 110, 114,
115, 199, 209, 244, 425; Andrew J.,
022; Angie, 007; Ann, 347; Annie,
061; Austin, 022; Bolden, 159;
Bowling, 448; Burrel, 159; Burrell,
159, 214; Burwell, 159; Burwell,
Jr., 129; Clifford G., 023;
Crawford, 022; E. A., 291, 347;
398, 404, 410, 452; Edmond, 155;
Edmund, 323; Elizabeth Jane, 049;
Elizabeth, 347; Frances, 037;
Franklin, 022; Frederick, 202;
GREEN: G.F., 159, 347; Gabriel, 228;
Gilbert, 159, 394; Ira, 394; J.A.,
347; J. M., 159; James A., 347;
370; James H., 290; James M., 159,
347; James, 159; Joe, 022, 387,
394, 445; John C., 203; John H.,
183; Joseph B, 307; Joseph, 347,
452; Lizzie, 058; Lucinda, 159;
Moris C., 290; N.H., 394; Nancy J.,
347; Nancy, 166; Nona, 017;
Pleasant, 072; R. Jasper, 347;
Raleigh, 159; Randal, 347; Randel,
394; Robert, 347; Samue, 022; T.
A., 442; Thomas, 159, 463; Virginia,
051; Wayman, 159; Will, 159; William
M., 159, 221, 314, 414; William
435; William, Sr., 072
GPENE: Allen, 159, 247; Alston H.,
080, 091-093, 095, 104, 109, 110,
123, 124, 127, 129, 131, 141, 145,
151, 152, 154, 166-168, 172-174,
179-181, 200, 204, 207, 208, 216,
223, 227, 229, 230, 233, 246, 252,
260-262, 264, 265, 268, 270, 272,
276, 280, 292, 301, 313, 316, 322,
324, 402, 422, 425; Amos, 211;
Bowling, 159; Burrel, 425; Burwell,
072, 159, 166, 231, 274, 428; E.A.,
347, 387, 408; Edmond, 138; Edmund,
092, 123, 159, 425; G. F., 347;
GREENE: George, 159; James, 159, 347;
Jessie, 394; John C., 296; John,
159, 258; Joseph P., 176; Lemuel,
091; Pleasant, 189; Raleigh, 159;
Pobert, 159; Thomas B., 274;
Thomas, 159; William M., 159;
William P., 160; William, 159, 163
GREENLEE: Samuel, 253
GREENWALD: David, 339; Samuel, 339
GREENWOOD: John, 160
GREEP: Alice, 022; ? 239; A. C., 347,
452; Aaron, 022, 072, 347, 414;
Abraham, 072, 348; Abram, 345; Adam,
022; Andrew, 160, 348; Anna A.,
056; Annie J., 013; Annie Lee, 052;
Annie, 057, 348; Arlee, 012; Arny?,
442; Arthur, 394; Benjamin, 160,
394, 442; Ben, 394; Bettie, 017;
Biana, 055; Bill, 348; C.H., 089,
097, 160, 256, 351, 354, 442, 452;
Cannon, 022; Charles, 348; Clark,
160, 348; Crafford H., Sr., 398;
GREEP: Crawford H., 092, 110, 112,
126, 135, 157, 171, 200, 201, 226,
238, 240, 246, 280, 292, 306, 312,
377, 448; Crawford H., Jr., 022;
Crawford H., Sr., 072; Crawford,
091; Crof H., 452; Daisy, 059; Dick,
022, 348; Ebenezer C., 348; Emily,
039; Emma, 029, 061; Felix, 022;
Frances, 348; Frank, 160, 348; G.
D., 160, 348; G. L., 442; George,
022, 160, 348; Gilbert D., 022,
160, 348; Gilbert, 022, 149, 339;
GREEP: Giles, 348, 349; Green, 348;
Greene, 022; Griffin, 022, 391;
Hamp, 348; Hannah, 026, 042; Hattie,
072; Henry, 348; Ida M., 463; Ida,
Mrs., 160; J. C., 348, 394; J. L.,
348, 398, 452; J. P., 394; Jack,
160, 348; James A., 160, 198, 314.
348, 425; James, 022, 160; Jasper,
348, 394, 452; Jefferson, 072;

Jlles, 394; Jim, 160; Joe, 160, 359; John Anderson, 022; John C., 348; John L, 348; John R., 022; 072, 099, 112, 113, 160, 197, 200, 229, 306, 340, 342, 345, 347, 348, 354, 379, 393, 394, 452, 463; John, 139, 149, 184, 189, 202, 274; Jonas, 160; Joseph, 022; K. P., 213, 339, 340, 347, 371, 399; Kittie, 030;
GREER: Leroy, 160; Lewis, 022; Lou, 026; Lowell, 160; Lucie, 426; Lucinda, 348; Madison, 022; Manuel, 394; Margaret Jane, 032; Mary Jane, 331; Mat, 160; Missouri, 017; Mollie, 007; 045; N. H., 348, 362, 394, 452; Natan H., 022; Nathaniel H., 348; Otis, 122; Pep, 160; Polly, 027; R.C., 348, 436, 452; R. J. J., 268, 377, 452, 458; R. J., 452; Richard, 348; Robert S., 072; Robert, 160, 348; Rufus, 022; Sallie R., 348; Sallie, 059; Sarah Mrs, 058; Womack, 023
GREER: Susan, 033; T. L., 463; Thomas F., 022; Thomas L., 072, 393, 414; Thomas S., 442; Thomas, 116, 149, 152, 160, 174, 206, 212, 232, 238, 272, 289, 425, 425; W. C., 089; W. G., 022, 452; Washington, 022; Will, 160, 348, 436, 452; 023, 160, 348; William, 022; 023, 160, 348; William, G. Jr., 023; Willie, 348; Wilmoth, 018; Wm. G., 452; Womack, 023
GREGG: Jacob, 160
GREGORY: Elizabeth, 160; Hardy, 127; J. T., 452; James M., 160; John T., 452; Lewis, 065, 072, 159, 160, 266, 315, 428; Mathew, 160, 299, 463; Matthew, 072, 160; Richard V., 111, 160; Richard, 245; William B., 140, 160
GRESHAM: Barnett, 093; Benjamin, 222; David, 161, 426; Ellison, 315; Isham, 161; James, 161, 202, 203; John, 127, 316; Lemuel, 238; Sellers, 161; William, 023, 296, 426; Young, 101
GREY: Addam, 394
GRICE: Garry, 179; Jesse, 229
GRIENER: Charles A., 144; Frederick B., 144
GRIER: Aaron W., 072; Benjamin, 161; Crawford, 444; Crawford H., 248; G. D., 161; G. 444; George, 161, 414; Gilbert D., 348, 378; Giles, 160, 348; Haly, 348; J. L., 394; James A., 165; James, 302; John Anderson, 161; John R., 201, 274, 388; John, 161, 190; Nathaniel H., 161; Robert L., 426; Sue, 161; Thomas, 065, 086, 318
GRIERSON: Robert, 103, 161
GRIFFIN: Alonzo, 348; Benjamin, 161, 394; Bettie, 348; D.R., 161; David, 161; Dick, 023; E.H., 348; Everett, 348; G.A., 442; George, 428; Harvey, 394; I.L.P., 023; J. J., 023, 348; J.I.P., 348; James, 091, 266; John, 161, 289, 291, 426; Larkin, 105; Lela, 039; Lydia, 161; Maggie, 348; Mattie, 014; Milledge, 161; Missouri, 348; Morris, 023; Parker, 394; Richard, 161; Sally, 161, 259, 289; Thomas B., 381; W. A., 348; William, 017; Willie, 348
GRIFFINS: Dick, 161
GRIFFITH: Jonathan, 161, 185
GRIPPITTS: N. A., 350
GRIGGS: Adaline, 052; Albert, 023; Anna, 014; Augustus, 023; Bettie, 023; Bob, 161; Bully, 394; Charles, 328; Cincinnattus W., 315; Cincinatus W., 161, 170, 315; Cincinnattus W., 315; Cincinnatus W., 161; Cincinnatus, 161; Cora, 022; Edward Y., 286; Elbert, 348; Elisebeth, 017; Ella, 394; Felix, 023; Field, 023; Frances, 018; Frank, 161; Frederick, 023, 161; Gene, 161; George, 394, 463; Gus, 160, 348; Guss, 394; Hal, 367; Hugh, 240; J. W., 161, 230, 348; James, 023, 086, 123, 131, 138, 177, 225, 241, 278, 284; 387, 426; John I., 161; John J., 072, 161, 279; John, 127, 161, 426; John, Jr., 138; John, Sr., 423; Jullous, 394; Katie, 008; Lee, 158; Levy, 161; Lizzie, 003; Mark, 348, 369; Melia, 351; R. C., 452; Robert, 161; Sack, 023; Sallie, 059, 061; Simmons, 348; Viola, 024; Warren, 023, 394; Wesley, 100, 138, 161, 337; Wesley, 348, 357, 452; Wiley, 242; William, 160
GRIGS: Hugh, 224, 240; Hughs, 162
GRIMES: Bishop, 348; Clarence, 394; Minnie M., 015; Peter, 348; Thomas W., 297; William C., 023; William D., 187, 215
GRIMET: Seaborn B., 162
GRIMMETT: James T., 072; Sarah E., 072; Seaborn B., 162, 253, 260; William, 072, 189

GRINAGE: John, 426; Joshua, 426
GRINNET: Peter, 145, 173
GRINNELL: Benjamin, 072, 247; Charles, 072; Peter, 093, 152, 162, 164, 174, 175, 177, 183, 186, 187, 189, 203-205, 211, 221, 223, 244, 258, 277, 281, 296, 425
GRISHAM: David, 162; John, 426; Joseph, 162
GRISWOLD: Abraham, 023; Giles, 307; Samuel, 175, 203, 232, 276, 301, 332, 345, 366
GRITS: Sam, 348, 363
GROATHOUSE: Archibald, 162
GROCE(?): Jane, 211
GROMET: Joseph, 162
GROMET: Joseph, 162
GROODZUISKI: H. M., 348
GROSS: Ellison, 137, 162, 448; John, 072, 162; Polley, 023
GROSSMAYER: Henry, 146
GROVES: Jasper B., 162, 349; Joseph B., 214
GRUBB: Conrad, 162; William, 162
GRUBBS: Annie, 029, 031; C. M., 442; E., 361; Edney D., Mrs., 034; Edvin, 349; Eliena C., 072, 162, 323, 394; Elisha, 195, 162; Elizabeth, 048, 162; G. W., 409; Ida M., 022; J. W., 349, 953, 357, 371, 374, 442, 452; James, 315; John W, 162, 315, 349, 452; Joseph S., 023; Joseph, 023, 162; Lilie Belle, 008; M. A., Mrs, 349; M. T., 041; Mary Jane, 059; Mildred A., 162; Missouri, 394; R. S., 442; GRUBBS: Richard J., 315; Richard L., 224; Richard S., 023, 091, 377; Richard T., 262; Richard, 023, 162; Sarah E., 057; Silas, 136, 141, 152, 162, 229, 232, 262, 304, 312, 315, 433, 442, 462; 463; Thomas E., 162, 452; Thomas, 394; W. B., 452; Wiley B., 023, 072, 135, 162, 339, 349, 394, 463; Wiley, 349; William B., 023, 105; William W., 162; William, 315
GRUHN: A., 346, 349
GUIN: John, 162, 270
GUINN: Daniel, 114; Franklin, 072; T. D., 381
GUMP: A. W., 467
GUN: Gabriel, 162
GUNALDS: Aley, 162
GUNN: D. P., 277; Daniel, 132, 218, 219, 232; David, 283; Gabriel, 072, 162, 233, 280, 307; James, 158, 162; John T, 349; John W. H., 262; John, 219, 283, 316; Thomas, 023, 162; Tom, 394; William, 232
GUNNELLS: Thomas, 023
GUNNELLS: Alsea, 162, 394; Joseph, 161, 162, 182; Pittman, 162; W. T., 349
GUNTER: Isham, 426; M. A., 162
GUTHRIE: Robert, 296
GUY: Charles, 023, 162, 257, 349; Charley, 023; Emily, 018; Lewis, 023; Miles, 023; Mollie, 061
GWATHNEY: Humphrey B., 225
GWINN: Franklin, 087; William L., 230
GWYN: Bailey, 162, 275; James, 089, 100, 126, 132, 134, 151, 174, 177, 185, 189, 213, 219, 225, 234, 266, 283, 303, 308; Payton, 177; Peyton, 126, 138, 151, 174, 185, 189, 225, 234, 266, 303, 308; Thomas P., 089, 119, 132, 213, 219, 283, 293, 303
GWYNE: John, 187
GWYNN: James, 138; Thomas P., 091, 100, 134
HACKANESS: Bill, 023
HACKNEY: Ben, 023; Davd, 023; Emmett, 163; James B., 163; Jasper, 023; Sarah S., 163; Stephen, 087, 163, 229; Steven, 149
HADAWAY: George W., 163; Lizzie, 163; W. T., 349
HADDOCK: Henry, 120; Robert, 120
HADLEY: Anderson, 023, 163; Patsey, 006; Simon, 163; Thomas J., 143, 163; Thomas, 072, 124, 163
HADLY: Simon P., 098
HAFNER: Adam, 023
HAGAN: John, 298
HAGERTY: Joshua, 121
HAGGERPTHY: Joshua, 315
HAGGIN: John, 150
HAGIN: Malachi, 426
HAGOOD: Benjamin, 257
HAIL: Jonas, 305
HAILE: Hosea, 242; Joel, Jr., 242; Lydia, 242
HAITES: Lucious, 349
HAINES: Ione, 021; William, Jr., 263
HAIRSTON: Carter V., 265; Charles A., 163; Charles C., 163, 322; Eliza M. C., 110, 163; Eliza, 163; Elizabeth, 163; Hugh B., 163; John, 163, 315; Lucretia, 163; Moses B., 072, 110, 118, 127, 132, 163, 285; Moses, 317, 458, 466; Thomas, 072, 107, 163, 172, 182, 221, 234, 286,

315, 395, 421, 436
HAITLEY: John, 023
HAITLY: Henry, 023
HALBEPT: James H., 223
HALE: Amanda, 046; Josev, 072; Samuel, 103, 271, 272; T. H., 349
HALES: A. O., 452; J. F., 349; John R., 023; Mandy, 038; Thomas, 163
HALL: Benjamin, 426; Bolling, 430; Durham T., 198; Elizabeth D., 163; Elizabeth N., 163; G. W., 452; Henry B., 257; Isaac R., 187; James N., 072, 103, 129, 141, 150, 163, 173, 208, 216, 225, 234, 251, 395; John H., 163; John T., 072, 092, 315, 426; Samuel, 111, 157; Seaborn L., 163; Wiley, 023; Will, 349; Zachariah, 090, 392
HALLMARK: John, 163
HALLOCK: D. J., 407; George B., 144, 171, 180, 207, 212, 225; George P., 201
HAM: John, 163; O. E., 408; Stephen, 163; William, 163
HAMEL: Hugh, 163, 246; James, 163; John, 163
HAMES: Comfort, 163; Henrietta, 349; Joshua, 163, 164, 420, 426, 427; 431; Kitty Ann, 349; Liddie, 019; Louisiana, 349; Margarette, 026; Wesley, 023
HAMETT: William, 238
HAMIL: Hugh, 164; John, 123, 164
HAMILL: Hugh, 096
HAMILTON: Amos, 164; Andrew M., 110, 164; Anna, 035; David, 164, 253; Duke, 187, 222; Everard, 284; Everard, 121, 221; George P., 254; George, 164; James, 023, 164; John, 023, 164, 252; Julius A., 023; Sallie J., 002; Thomas P., 072, 125, 164, 257; Walter, 150, 229; William, 432; Winney, 072; Zeb, 165
HAMLIN: Robert D., 148
HAMMACK: Willoughby, 428
HAMMEL: G. A., 072; John, 430; Simeon, 164
HAMMER: Richard, 315; Richardson, 164; Wingfield, 164, 315
HAMMETT: Absalom, 432; William, 152, 164, 169, 319; William, 143, 184, 316, 403
HAMMOCK: Asa C., 164; Benjamin, 164, 165, 423; Jeptha J., 161; John G., 315; John, 165; William, 023; Willoby, 089; Willoughby, 165
HAMMOND: Amos W., 227; D. F., 446; Mortimore L., 165; Nancy W. (Puckett), 165; Thomas C., 165; Thomas S., 339; W. R., 446
HAMMONS: Jesse J., 165; John, 023
HAMP: Zeb, 165
HAMPTON: George, 165, 255, 459; Wille, 023
HAMPICKY: James, 165, 315, 436; Seburn, 023, 165; William, 239
HAN: Mitchell, 394
HANCOCK: A. H., 291; Antony, 165; Isham, 165; J. H., 311; James W., 023; Janie, 044; John H., 161; John, 023; Kittie, 058; Levina, 016; Lum, 349, 394; Tom, 349; W. A., 452; William H., 165; William, 072, 452; 452
HAND: Daniel, 306; John C., 023; John, 093; William, 023
HANDCOCK: Mary, 020
HANFORD: Jennett, 004
HANKS: John, 394; Thomas, 315, 394
HANLY: C., 023
HANN: James, 165; John, 165
HANNAH: George, 101; Samuel, 315, 316; Thomas, 243; William, 167, 285
HANNAHAN: Henry, 253
HANNAY: Samuel, 312
HANSFORD: Elmina, 020; George W., 165; John M., 165; Simeon, 349
HANSON: Edward, 023; J. B., 384; John, 288
HARALSON: V., 301
HAPAWAY: Judith, 426
HAPDAGE: William, 023
HAPDAWAY: Bubber, 360; John W., 088, 175
HAPDEES: N. A., 405, 406
HAPDEMAN: Charles, 452; Daniel, 165, 349; Henry, 165; Hunter, 023; Isaac, 368; Jim, 165; John, 165; Mattie, 375; Maud, 018; Robert V., 119; S. F., 452; Thomas, 091, 105, 118, 182, 185, 220, 234, 242, 281, 290, 301, 314, 322; Will, 165; William P., 024
HAPDEN: J.M., 452; Lucy, 019; M. F., 056; Peter, 024; S. A., 349; Sallie H., 029; Silas, 087, 165; Susan, 023; Susie, 165; William B., 165; William, 277
HAPDIMAN & HAMBLETON: --, 444
HARDIN: Henry, 126, 165; J. M., 349; John S., 072; Mattie, 050; Monroe, 394; Nancy, 005; Patsey, 050; Silas M., 072; Silas, 445; W. S., 349;

William R., 165
HARDING: Atkinson T., 258;
Parthena, 048
HARDMAN: Alice, 394; Allis, 394; Alp,
349; Alphonso, 065, 104, 349;
Alphonzo, 072; Amanda J., 011;
Amanda, 349; C. A., 394; Charles,
394; Charley, 024; Daniel, 349;
Elizabeth, 019; Felix, 318, 423,
429, 430, 465; Mollie, 349;
Samuel, 165
HARDON: Virgil O., 359
HARDRICK: Annis, 012; Ella, 019;
Reuben, 024
HARDWICK: Ben, 165; Charity, 065;
Clara, 061; Cornelius, 100; Elijah,
094; Elisha, 094; Frizell M., 094;
Frizzell W., 258; Garland, 165, 166,
196, 396, 431; George W., 255;
George, 166, 222; H. V., 394; John
W., 024, 315; John, 024, 100, 154,
166, 321, 349; Rachel, 010; Robert
M., 094; Thomas, 349; William, 072,
166, 201; Winny, 060
HARDY: A.D., 349, 452; Alfred D., 124,
414, 452; Alfred H., 349; Aquila,
452; Aquilia, 166; Araminta, 166;
Benager, 442; Benaja, 452; Benajah,
072, 166; C. H., 452; C. M., 024,
349, 360, 394, 395, 443, 452, 463;
Carrie, 044; Cora D., 013; Cornelius
M., 242; Cornelius, 024, 072, 082,
166, 223, 242, 355, 452; D., 166;
Dora A., 166; Elizabeth, 017; Elmina
S., 013; Florence N., 053; Gertrude
N., 054; H., 452; J. D., 452, 464;
HARDY: J. G., 166, 349, 452; J. H.,
373; J. J., 452; J. L., 452; J. P.,
345, 452; J.T., 452; James D., 024,
349, 452; James G., 024; James P.,
024, 265, 349, 452, 463; James, 166,
242; John H., 024; John L., 024,
452; John P., 024; John T., 166;
Joseph J., 442; Josiah, 224; Julia
F., 019; Lewis, 024; Lou, 043;
Louisa S., 056; Martha E., 016;
HARDY: Miles, 166; N. H., 452; Nannie
L., 018; Phoebe, 458; Robert M.,
166; Sallie B., 013; Sophia C., 044;
Susan, 166; W. G., 373, 452; W. P.,
340, 349, 369, 384, 452; William B.,
166, 194, 206, 297, 315, 319, 421,
428, 434; William G., 024; William
P., 072, 166, 315, 349, 355, 420,
448; Wm. P., 452
HARFIELD: Will, 168
HARGRAVES: George, 117, 125, 132,
188, 191, 211, 216, 219, 237, 252,
295, 317, 319, 325
HARGROVE: Robert T., 166
HARISS: J. S., 442
HARKNESS: James, 128; Jonathan, 166;
Thomas M., 096
HARMAN: John, 166; William M., 275
HARMON: William, 166
HARP: Luke, 259
HARPER: Alexander T., 149, 166;
Edward, 426; ella, 349; Eluno, 253;
Everett, 426; Florence, 046; James,
119; Jesse, 431; R. C., 376; R. L.,
452; Samuel, 143, 166, 176, 308;
Sarah, 166; Thomas L., 024; William,
097, 119, 166, 194, 242
HARPAL: James, 072, 120, 147, 403;
James, Jr. 403
HARPALE: Elvira, 015
HARPAWAY: Judith, 433
HARREL: Samuel, 248; Jethro, 166;
Joseph, 422; Samuel, 145, 166, 426
HARRELD: Joseph, 421
HARRELL: Charles, 463; Cuthbert, 266;
Gethro, 024; Henry K., 194; Isaac,
426; Jethrow, 166; Joseph, 166;
Lewis P., 183; Mary, 153, 166;
Samuel M., 024; Samuel, 166, 283;
Western, 463
HARRESS: Cuzza, 426
HARREY: William, 166
HARRINGTON: Bert, 314; Jepthah, 273;
Young J., 221
HARRIS: Adeline, 051; Albus, 298;
Anna, 016, 027; Azariah, 024; Baker,
298; Benjamin, 305; Britain (heirs
of), 426; Buck, 024; Buckner, 301;
Butler, 349; Carrie, 059; Claudia,
376; Cora, 018; Cross, 153; D., 452;
David, 072, 166, 241, 279, 366, 452;
Early, 123; Early, 141, 201, 246,
272, 301, 312; Esco, 024, 395;
Frank, 349; George, Jr., 192; Ida,
051; Indianna, 018; Isham, 072,
167, 426; J. P., 332, 371, 376,
396, 399, 406; Jack, 167; James,
1, 349; Jesse, 167; Joel N., 167;
HARRIS: John G., 024; John P., 332,
367; John, 072, 167, 203, 426;
Joseph H., 024; Lara, 298; Leah,
167; Leila, 014; Lena, 042; Lessie,
002; Lewis F., 268; Lewis M., 242;
Lizzie, 034; Lucinda, 004; Marina,
052; Martha E., 005; Mary A., 041;
Mary Ann, 036; Mary Jane, 051;

Mary, 072, 153; Medora, 376; Melton
024; Micajah, 162, 167; Milton, 349;
442, 452, 458, 460, 461, 463;
Mollie, 006, 036; Monroe, 024; Nels,
395; Nelson, 024; Peter, 167, 228;
HARRIS: Pon, 024, 095, 167; Pugh, 167;
Rilious, 349; Samuel, 342; Sarah H.,
124, 213, 236, 299; Shade, 349;
Shedrack, 024; Simeon, 024, 228,
349; Solomon, 024; Stephen W., 124,
213, 235, 246; Stephen W., 229, 287,
299; Thomas W., 086, 128, 129, 172,
175, 176, 197, 275, 316, 323, 426;
Thomas, 143, 167; Walton 255, 426;
Wesly, 024; West, 220; Wilery, 298;
Will, 167; William as, 167; William
094, 128, 167, 236, 239, 279;
315; William, 094, 132, 137, 164,
178; Winney, 049
HARRISON: Adeline, 056; Augustus W.,
024; Benjamin, 286, 290; Carter B.,
126, 158, 279; Epthpatha, 072;
Gabriel, 144, 145, 237; Henry, 072;
J. W., 452; Jacob, 167; James, 024,
122; Jeremiah, 245; Richard, 024;
Sarah, 043; Sterling, 119;
HARRY: John, 167; William, 167
HART: Adam, 350; Alvarez, 320; Isaac,
300; Martha, 414; Robert, 284;
Vine, 008; Will, 024
HARTFIELD: Moses, 092
HARTRICK: Dicie, 036
HARTRIDGE: Charles, 254
HARTSFIELD: Allen, 167, 426;
Middleton, 065, 072, 315; Moses,
167, 313; Warren, 167, 426
HARTWELL: H. D., 452
HARVEL: Frank, 350; Mason, 167
HARVELL: Infant, 445; James, 350;
Mason, 167, 428; Ransom, 448
HARVEY: Benjamin, 264; Charles F.,
102; Davis, 452; E., 351, 464;
Elizabeth, 167; Evan, 167, 175; Evan
J., 167, 176, 395, 427; Evan P.,
167; Evan, 050, 352, 376, 426;
Florence, 058; Franklin, 116;
George W., 285; H. H. 167, 452;
Isaac, 101; J. D., 369, 400, 446,
452, 464; James D., 024; James P.,
167; James, 344; Jeremiah, 106,
268; Laura J., 003; Lily, 002;
Nehemiah, 129, 167, 315, 395; Viny,
009; William, 420, 426; Willie P.,
010; Zenepheniah, 167; Zepheniah, 072
HARVILL: Frank, 373; John T., 024;
Masen, 434; Mason, 427
HARVILLE: Dotson, 243
HARWELL: Amos, 167, 350; Armor, 024;
C. A., 352, 371; Elmyra, 029;
Ernest, 167; Frank, 024; Isaac,
167; J. C., 399; J. L., 167; Janie,
008; Joe, 024, 167; John, 350;
Launie, 019; Lewis P., 133, 175,
253; Littleton T., 188; London,
024; Marcus, 350; Mason, 072;
Matilda, 012; Ransome, 101; Robert,
024; Sarah, 364; Thomas B. 161,
167, 249; Thomas, 306; W. H., 452;
William, 250
HARWILLIA: John, 395
HASCAL: Elijah N., Jr., 119
HASCALL: D., 090, 168, 266, 446; David
N., 088; David, 097, 105, 106, 113,
115, 124, 132, 159, 162, 167, 168,
182, 184, 196, 211, 220, 266, 275,
287, 294, 315, 321, 616, 090, 265;
Elijah N., 088, 097, 106, 113, 115,
128, 132, 137, 159, 162, 167, 168,
173, 182, 190, 196, 211, 212, 220,
221, 266, 286, 287, 289, 292, 305,
310, 315, 426; Elijah, 463; J. A.
168, 446; James A., 128, 167, 168,
220, 275, 315; James S., 270;
James, 168, 266
HASCHAL: Cornelia, 350
HASELTINE: William H., 275
HASKINS: James, 167
HASS: Jacob, 139
HASTON: Rodah, 149
HATAWAY: G. W., 024
HATCHER: Archibald, 205, 426;
Caroline, 065; Josiah, 168; Lucy L.,
007; Martin, 168; Mary L.,
055; Mary, 205; Mastin, 168;
Maston, 168; Samuel C., 168; Susan,
060; Uriah, 024, 072, 168, 315, 448
HATFLEY: Henry, 422
HATFIELD: J. B., 452; Joe, 452; W.
B., 452; W. B., 452
HATHCOCK: John, 168
HATHHORN: Sarah, 061
HATTAWAY: Frank, 168; W. H., 024
HATTERWAY: Martin, 350
HATTON: Thomas, 444
HAVILAND: Daniel G., 092, 197; David
G., 128; David, 134; Edmond, 134;
Fleming J., 205; James C., 120, 128,
147, 197, 211, 254; Robert B., 092,
120, 128, 147, 196-197
HAWK: Andrew, 168; Anthony, 024;
Calhoun, 024; Genia, 007; H. H.,

466; Harriett, 339, 426; Henry, 065,
353; Isaac, 350; Jacob, 168; James,
458; John, 168, 295; Josephine,
458; Mary, 458; Peter, 168, 169;
350; Sallie H., 426; Sarah, 019,
203; Seaborn I., 442; Seaborn J.,
072, 426; Thomas H., 458; Wade,
024; Will, 169
HAWKINS: Alexander, 169; Aray, 046;
Benjamin, 137; C. R., 463; Callie,
056; Exey, 169; Frances, 024; J.A.,
384; John W. H., 024; John I., 024,
072, 169, 196; John, 116, 395;
Juliann, 047; Mathew, 143; Matthew,
299; Stephen, 308; Thomas, 169
HAWKS: Jacob, 169; Peter, 169;
Seaborn, 485
HAWTHORN: Benjamin, 169; Elizabeth,
169; James, 169; James, Sr., 105
HAWTHORNE: James, Sr., 311
HAY: Chesley, 169; Edmond, 072;
Gilbert, 426; Leonard B., 169;
Stephen, 072, 169; Thomas H., 024;
Washington, 072; William T., 072,
458; William, 260, 426
HAYDEN: Nathaniel, 264; Sylvester, 024
HAYES: Albert C., 169; Henry, 169;
Hyram, 266; James T., 140, 169,
253; John R., 284; Martin, 169
HAYGOOD: Benjamin, 233, 257
HAYNES: Albert G., 259; G. W., 024;
George W., 350; Henry, 156, 169,
287; Ione, 036; Moses, 222; Robert,
237; Thomas, 169, 466
HAYS: ?, 169; Chesley, 350; H.C., 452;
Henry C., 024; Henry, 099, 268;
Hyram, 322; James T., 099, 159, 210,
252; James, 169; John K., 163; John
R., 221; John, 202, 203; Nancy,
169; Rebecca, 072; Stephen, 169;
Thomas L., Jr., 403
HAYWARD: Augustus, 140, 204, 218, 461;
Munford W., 207; T. C., 319;
Thomas C., 125, 146
HAZELIP: John, 160
HAZELTINE: William, 090
HAZLEHURST: William, 348
HEAD: Carrie, 048; George, 169; Henry,
089, 169; J. G., 350; J. H., 350;
Jack, 024; James D., 104, 113, 116,
165, 175, 208, 241, 244, 250, 296;
James, 173, 426; John H., 350, 395;
John, 100, 156, 169, 395; L. W.,
013; Lee, 169; Louis, 443; Richard,
169; Samuel B., 278; ?, 395;
W. H., 907, 169, 251, 363, 366;
William B., 024; William H., 170,
212, 240, 341, 349, 350, 353, 355,
356, 397, 458; William R., 024;
William, 025; Wilson, 350
HEALD: Henry, 160; Jeremiah, 170;
Samuel, 170
HEARD: Abraham, 257, 322, 423; Abram
A., 104; Aggie, 034; Anna, 268;
Annis, 170, 299; Bartlett, 395;
Clark R., 395; Clark, 025, 350,
395; Daniel C., 239; Daniel, 025;
Elizabeth, 140; Frank lin, 266;
Franklin, 213, 254; George, 395;
Hubbard, 426; Ida, 043; James, 180;
John (heirs of), 426; John, 094,
134, 166, 170, 204, 268, 299, 314,
426; Joseph, 101, 158, 170; Lee,
025; Lizzie, 043; Nancy, 025;
Nettie, 060; Samuel, 170; Spencer,
268, 299; Stephen G., 123, 128, 170;
Stephen J., 315, 318, 426; Stephen
J., 321; Stephen, 121, 170, 289,
299; Thomas, 170; W. M., 025;
Wesley, 025
HEARN: Asa, 170; C. C., 170, 350,
452; Christopher C., 170; Columbus
C., 170; Eleazer M., 260; F. C.,
Mrs., 350; F. L., 452; Ferdinand
L., 170; George, 170; Guss, 395;
Isaac, 170; James C., 191; John,
170; Legare, 170; Oscar, 170;
Mattie, 033; Oscar, 170; Priscilla,
170; Robert L., 025; Samuel, 025;
Selby, 170, 430; Thomas, 238; W. A.
J., 350; W. S., 350, 452; W., 350;
William, 170, 170, 366; Zabad, 170;
Zabed, 170
HEARNE: Absalom, 158; Ebenezer T., 108
HEARNTON: Mack, 395
HEAPS: Abraham, 405
HEARTFIELD: Moses, 170
HEAPTWELL: James P., 218
HEATH: Abel F., 170; H. H., 395;
Richard, 025, 072; Van, 170
HECHT: J. E., 446, 452; J. J., 025;
Mary, 170; S. A., 396, 452, 466;
S. Alexis, 981; Sadie, 007;
Samuel, 170
HEETH: Allen, 289; Pleasant, 430
HEFLIN: James S., 025; John, 170
HEIGHT: Amanda, 170; Matthew, 025;
Phoebe, 170
HEITH: Chappel, 091
HELDEBRAND: David, 170, 315
HELMS: Lloyd, 170

HEMPFIELD: Kate, 035; Lena (Laura),
037; Sarah, 350
HEMPPIEL: Jacob, 365
HENDERSON: ?, 170; A.R., 395; Albert,
350; Allie, 034; Andrew, 165; Berry,
026, 395; Bessie e, 061; Brockman We.,
170; C. G., 452; C. C., 341, 346,
352, 361, 373, 452; C.W., 350, 463;
Carrie, 015; Charles L., 025, 344,
393, 452; Charles, 065, 072, 102,
171, 350, 414, 442; Charles, Sr.,
350; Charley, 025; Clarence, 452;
Cynthia, 235; David, 168, 243, 260,
410, 442, 445; Della, 025; Dubon,
171; Elizabeth, 237; Flem, 171;
HENDERSON: Frances, 023, 031, Francis,
171; Frankie, 072; G. B., 025;
George, 171; Hester, 463; I. W.,
452; Isaac P., 203; Isaac W., 072,
171, 350, 414, 452; Isham, 025;
Isiah, 395; J. P., 352; J. P., 025,
130, 395; J. T., 352; J. W., 025,
407, 452; Jake A., 025; James P.,
025, 171; James, 025, 065, 072, 157,
171, 177, 178, 225, 257, 289, 332,
354, 426, 452; James, Jr., 025; Jane
072; Joe, 452; John P., 025;
HENDERSON: John T., 171, 291; John,
025, 072, 171, 308, 311, 395; Joseph,
025, 072, 095, 159, 171, 294, L.,
452; Leah, 038; Lewis, 025, 171,
350, 395; Lizzie, 025; Lou, 025; M.
F., 452; M. G., 350; Magers, 025; M.
128, 141, 170, 171, 192, 244, 245,
255, 289, 423, 426; Majers, 133,
170, 171, 300; Manda, 042; Margarett
A., 009; Martha A., 004; Mary, 008,
165; Matilda, 004; Mattie, 350;
Milly, 028; Minnie M., 057; P.D.,
350; Reed, 336; Richard W., 025,
171, 199, 232; Richard, 373, 426;
HENDERSON: Robert Jr 153, 203; S. P.,
171, 452; S. J., 171, 442, 452; S.
L., 452; Sam, 192; Sam, Jr., 171;
Sam, Sr., 171; Samuel J., 025, 452;
Samuel L., 171, 315, 334, 350, 390,
448, 452; Samuel, 065, 072, 093,
136, 171, 350, 426, 452; Sarah, 038;
Susan Elizabeth, 051; Thomas, 171;
Tony, 171; Virginia, 171; W.H., 452;
W. P., 350, 452; Wallace, 452;
Wesley, 171; William P., 379;
HENDRICK: Gustavus, 166, 297; Henry,
108, 387; James, 433; John, 120,
145, 217, 407; Mary Magdaline, 172;
Mastin D., 273; Micajah, 089, 172,
255; Nancy, 172, 256; S. J., 315;
Seaborn J., 086, 172, 234
HENDRICKS: John H., 172; Seaborn I.,
172; Seaborn J., 172
HENEY: George W., 221;
HENLEY: Micajah, 221; William, 426
HENLY: Abijah, 072, 255
HENRY: Daniel, 150; E. H., 351;
George W., 165, 172, 426; James,
103, 172, 316, 430; John P., 206;
Maria, 058; William P. 256, 269
HENSEY: Nancy, 039, 172, 227; Richard,
025, 172; Susan, 058
HENSLEE: John F., 444
HENSLEY: Thomas, 172
HENSLY: Thomas, 025
HENSON: James, 329; Joe, 172;
Robert, 172
HEPBURN: Henry, 188, 210
HERBERT: William, 172
HERD: Dorah, 005; Lucinda, 014
HEREFORD: John W., 218
HEPMAN: Isaac, 363
HEPPAGE: Benjamin, 172
HEPMEN: Alexander, 152, 172, 260, 395
HEPPIDGE: John, 025
HEPPIN: Alexander, 172; James, 172
HERRING: Alexander, 224; Arthur, 169,
172, 194, 315; Clayborne, 410;
Cyril, 169; Ephraim, 318; J.L., 468;
James, 111; John Henry, 350; John,
025, 288; Moses, 318; Sallie, 012
HEPPINGTON: J. C., 395
HEPRON: David, 172
HEPSHFIELD: Jacob, 172
HEPVEY: Franklin, 099, 172, 234, 267
HESTEP: Abraham, 103, 313; Albert,
395; Augustus, 025; George, 025;
Henderson, 025, 350; Henry, 173;
Laura, 374; Michal, 025; Obadiah,
025; Obediah, 350; Robert, 173,
426; Sophia, 458; Sophy, 336;
Thomas, 190, 398; William, 072
HETCH: Harriett, 381
HEWES: George, 426
HEYER: Cornelius, 284

414; Walter H., 025
HICKS: Arthur, 445; Cella, 047;
Charlie, 395; Edward, 099, 116,
173-175, 179, 187, 222, 225, 258,
282, 300, 308, 391; Effom, 463;
Eliza, 019; Ephraim, 173; John J.,
072; John Kennady, 173; John, 072;
Joseph, 072, 173, 174, 289, 316;
Marcus, 174; Mark, 174; Moze, 350;
Oliver H., 315; Rich, 174, 184;
Richard, 025; Susanah, 132; W.A., 452
HICKSON: Thomas, 130, 174, 316;
HIDE: John E., 119; Samuel, 174, 292;
Thomas, 147
HIGDON: Terrel, 119
HIGGASON: Larkin, 174; P. C., 426;
Philemon C., 173; Philemon, 025;
Phillemon C.,181; Richard, 173, 426
HIGGINBOTHAM: Burras, 173; Elizabeth,
254; Ephraim, 173; Ephram, 197;
Jacob, 072; Joseph, 072, 173, 316;
Robert, 072, 197; Thomas, 155, 223;
William, 173
HIGGINS: Joe 173; Palmer A., 173;
Wiley I., 173
HIGH: Clem, 350; J.R., 328, 329; John
T., 321; John, 179; Joseph R., 118,
120, 146, 186, 314, 315, 322; W. G.,
104; W. L., 357; Wiley W., 247,
312; William L., 334, 366, 371
HIGHT: Phebia, 036; Stephen, 025
HIGHTOWER: Daniel, 119, 173;
Elizabeth, 173; J. R., 347;
Margarett, 040; Presley, 426;
Thomas, 164; Tony, 350; William, 146
HIGHTS: Mathis, 173
HIGINBOTHAM: Jacob, 292
HILDEBRAND: David, 173
HILL: Angle, 008; Anthony, 350; Asa,
127, 173, 218, 316; Ashley, 174;
Augustus, 350; Belle, 050; Benjamin,
173, 174, 221, 264; Burton B., 156;
Charles B., 296; Charley, 025;
Clarence, 426, 436; Edward D., 111;
Edward Y., 096, 139, 164, 172, 237,
258, 311, 422, 426, 431, 432;
Edward Young, 097, 217, 262; Edward,
174, 461; Elizabeth, 039; George
F., 174; Gordon, 174; Green B., 174;
HILL: Green, 242; Greene B., 124, 132;
H.C., 337, 343, 354, 363, 405, 452,
463, 467; Henry, 025, 174; Iby, 192;
Isaac, 072, 108, 115, 135, 141, 160,
170, 174; Isaac, 190, 192, 220
247, 254; 259, 264, 297, 299, 307,
311, 395, 423, 461; Isaac, Sr.,
174; Ivy, 134; James A.,
427; James Harrison, 458; James,
072, 281, 458; Jeptha, 218; Jesse,
174, 265; Jim, 350;
HILL: John, 088, 090, 091, 094, 096,
098, 103, 105, 116, 123, 124, 127,
129, 131, 134, 137, 139, 150, 154,
156, 157, 160, 167, 168, 173, 174,
178, 183, 187, 189, 191, 196, 200,
213, 214, 217, 218, 220, 226, 224,
225, 236, 237, 243, 250, 252, 254,
255, 257, 260, 263, 265-268, 272,
273, 276, 278, 281, 282, 284, 295,
300-302, 307, 308, 313-315, 323,
324, 379, 422, 423, 426, 427, 429,
459; Joseph, 173, 174, 210;
HILL: Joshua, 086, 099, 108, 112,
120, 129, 131, 136, 139, 142, 148,
163, 164, 174, 195, 210, 214, 232,
240, 246, 247, 251, 277, 284, 301,
302, 310-313, 317, 318, 322,
323, 349, 350, 375, 395, Katie, 018;
Lawrence, 072, 167; Lucinda, 174;
Lydia, 174, 395; Mary, 031;
Middleton, 174; Miles, 270, 427;
Mordecai, 459; Moses, 196;
HILL: Nathaniel, 289; Peter, 174, 360,
395; Phinea, 174; Reuben, 465;
Ruth, 045; Sam, 350; Samuel, Sr.,
278; Shadrach, 395; Starkey, 137;
Susan, 171; Susanna, 174;
Theophilus, 072, 174, 225; Thomas,
233, 257; W. C., 350; Whitmell, 316,
322, 459; Whitml, 420; William,
072, 308, 395; Winifred, 030;
Wright, 096, 174, 305
HILLARD: William, 124
HILLSMAN: Henry St. J., 151;
Margaret Ann J., 029
HILLYER: Shaler, 320
HILTON: Julia B., 039
HINCY: T. J., 442
HINDMAN: William, 115
HINDSLEY: Michael, 174
HINES: Catherine, 026; Elias, 072,
175; J. R., 025; James, 065, 113,
172, 175, 182; 191, 221, 292, 316;
James, Sr., 072; John, 072, 162,
175; 187, 190, 219, 247, 262, 316,
405; Lamech, 113; Lamech H., 184;
Littleberry, 175, 448; Maramla (?),
175; Nancy, 226, 395
HINGSTON: Thomas, 427
HINSEY: James A., 025; Mary, 016;
Nancy, 175

HINSON: John, 200
HINTON: Jacob, 216; John, 208
HIRL(?): Catharine, 122
HITCHCOCK: Belle, 028; E. A., 452;
Jesse, 175, 316; John, 175; Laney,
042; Matthew, 072, 175, 179;
Overton, 175; William, 072, 108,
110, 116, 126, 137, 139, 147, 162,
174-176, 178, 196, 202, 203, 213,
217, 218, 237, 238, 272, 395, 401,
423, 425, 427, 428, 434-436, 463
HITT: Charles B., 203
HIX: Amanda, 012; George, 025;
Julia, 008; Rick, 176
HIXON: Thomas, 128
HOADLEY: Hervey S., 268
HOARD: J. E., 403; Lewis H., 144,
198; R. K., 357, 452
HOBBS: Robert, 083; Thomas, 219
HOBBY: Alfred M., 198, 198, 213;
William J., 294
HOBSON: Baker, 170, 176, 435, 236;
Christopher, 072, 103, 124, 153,
176, 200, 210, 216, 220, 231, 238,
240, 268, 270, 273, 293, 294, 299,
316, 318, 319, 322, 402; Francis,
178, 179, 202, 222; Hardy, 176;
Harriet H., 103, 153, 200; Joel, 231;
John, 072, 103, 124, 135, 176, 178,
179, 199, 202, 210, 215, 220, 222,
238, 240, 268, 270, 273, 278, 294,
299, 316, 319, 322, 402; John, Sr.,
176; Matthew, 316; William H., 176
HOCK: Eli, 025
HODGE: Aaron, 463; Alice, 026;
Alsey, 303; Amos, 025; Andrew S.,
203; Andrew, 176; C. L., 025, 452;
C. R., 396, 408; Cincinnatus L.,
026; D. R., 065, 442, 452; David,
264; Dessa C., 061; Duke P., 072,
452; Easley, 026; Frances, 005; J.
D., 452; James D., 026; James, 072;
Janie, 012; Jesse, 176; Jesse, 026,
395, 430; Lee, 026, 176; Lon L.,
176; Mary (Polley), 048; Mollie,
035; Nathaniel, 176; Paul, 177;
Phebe (McClendon), 176; Richard,
026; Vera, D18; Viola, 010;
William, 072; Willis, 177
HODGES: Addie, 177; Andrew, 177; F.
J., 043; Harvey, 177; J. J., 350;
James J., 026; John, 259; Susan,
222; William, 196, 212, 229, 303
HODNETT: Benjamin, 072, 177; Henry
177; James, 427; John, 427
HOETON: A. N., 452; Harries A., 452;
Seaborn A., 452; Seaborn, 452
HOFF: William, 177
HOFFMAN: Charles F., 306
HOGAN: A. J., 350, 442; Andrew J.,
177; Cimeon, 026; Dave, 177; David
E., 026; Ellis, 026, 177, 351;
Frances, 031; Loftin, 351; Lofton,
062; Lucy, 041; Malissa, 043;
Mansfield, 026, 351; Squire, 026
HOGANS: Carrie Bell, 038;
Sylva A., 035
HOGE: Stephen, 427
HOGG: Lewis, 317; Matthew, 421
HOIL: William B., 026
HOLAND: Mat, 351
HOLBROOK: Ephraim, 105, 137, 139,
170; Ephraim, 186, 191, 287; J. M.,
343; William, 177
HOLCOMB: Joshua, 196
HOLCOMBE: Joshua, 275; Thomas, 091
HOLDER: John H., 026
HOLDERFIELD: Daniel, 266
HOLEBPOOKS: William, 104
HOLEMAN: Isaac, 026; Mamon, 316;
Richard, 425
HOLIFIELD: Alsea, 106, 141, 143, 165,
177-179, 202, 216, 222, 224, 244,
244, 301, 305, 421, 427, 432; Andrew
J., 177, 395; Green, 244, 436; James
B., 395; James, 141; Mary, 395;
Polly, 072; Thomas R. L., 395;
Thomas P. S., 143, 201; Thomas P.,
395; Thomas, 395; Wiley, 072, 258;
William, 395
HOLLAND: A. S., 329, 330, 343, 349,
351, 362, 368, 369, 373, 376, 377;
Aaron, 351; Abe, 395; Abraham, 026;
Alexander L., 350; Alexander S.,
026, 113, 316; Alexander, 177;
Alexander, Dr., 351; Allice, 057;
Amew, 031; Andrew, 026; B. C., 452;
B. L., 329; B. W., 177; Bus, 177;
C. C., 026; Carrie, 023; Charley,
026; Charlotte, 178; Dave, 026, 177;
Delile C., 177; E. A., 177; E. G.,
452; Ed, 026; Elizabeth A., 313;
HOLLAND: Emily Frances, 019; Emma,
044; Eunice A., 218, 280, 289, 335,
458; Eunice, 108; F. B., 026; Frank
B., 398; Genie, Mrs., 013; George
T., 177; George W., 178; George
W., 098, 135, 152, 177, 178, 182,
188, 198, 206, 208, 223, 232, 244,
249, 268, 396, 400, 407, 421;
George, 351; Georgia V., 008;

Harfery, 241; Harvy, 177; Henry J., 072, 177, 178, 316, 463; J. A., 026, 177, 452; Jo H. 177, 224, 226, 278, 331, 350, 360, 368, 380, 410, 442, 452, 458; J.L., 072, 329;
HOLLAND: J. B., 135; J. W. 026, 399, 350, 355, 452; J. Washington, 452; Jack, 026; Jackson, 026; James A., 177, 351, 427; James Adolphus, 026; James C., 120; James H., 214, 397; James W., 072, 177, 293, 375, 376, 452; James, 026; Jane N., 177, 358; Jesse, 026; Jim, 177, 354; John, 106, 351, 395; Jonas H., 257;
HOLLAND: Jonas H., 090, 093, 103,108, 110, 116, 118, 120, 126, 133, 135, 142, 147, 154, 156, 163, 177-179, 181, 183, 193, 200, 201, 204, 211, 218, 219, 226, 229, 243, 246, 249, 250, 265, 274, 279, 280, 289, 294, 298, 304, 305, 310, 314, 316, 319-321, 345, 346, 351, 354, 387, 407, 409, 429; Jonas H. Sr., 072; Jonas N., 221; Jonas W., 152; Jonas, 279; Joseph A., 285; Joseph L., 116, 119, 134, 151, 165, 177, 178, 244, 316; Joseph S., 295, 298, 312, 404; Joseph, 190; Judge, 178, 351; L. Mrs., 108; L., 325;
HOLLAND: Lawson S., 072, 116, 136, 140, 168, 171, 172, 174, 177-179, 208, 211, 214, 224, 238, 244, 256, 257, 272, 261, 293, 296, 301, 306, 316, 404, 411, 422, 464; Lawson, 173, 202; Levinia, 072; Lewis C., 072, 116, 124, 131, 172, 178, 179, 187, 201, 294, 316, 388, 395, 420, 424, 427; Lewis Conner, 427, 432; Lewis R.,179; Littleton, 026; Lona, 015; Louis C., 389; Louisa, 012;
HOLLAND: Louisiana, 041; Margaret, 179, 180; Margarett, 072; Mary A., 073; Mary Ann, 244; Mary, 180; Neal, 107; D. P., 452; P. L., 180; Rhoda, 023; Ruby, 048; S. S., 465; Sallie, 011; Scott, 026; Seymore, 180; Silva, 033; Silvey, 053; Stephen, 209, 316; Thomas R., 026, 180, 298, 361, 452; Thomas, 251, 318, 378; Tom, 180; W., 152, 158, 180, 378; W. A., 156, 280; Walter (Walton) F., 026; Walter J., 026; Wiley, 003; William M., 156; William T., 073; William W., 108, 218, 235, 274; Z. E., 384; Zeltner, 180
HOLLAWAY: Isham, 297; James, 106; Judith, 297; Maston, 180; William, 214
HOLLEY: Martha, 427
HOLLIFIELD: Mary, 157
HOLLIMAN: William, 180
HOLLINGSWORTH: J. H., 261, 323; Jacob J., 308; James H., 147, 306, 311; T. D., 261, 323; Thomas D., 107, 213, 311; William H., 358
HOLLIS: James, 180; Thomas, 128, 180; William, 180, 240
HOLLOWAY: Ada, 021; Alonzo, 026, 180; Alsey, 073; Anna, 031; Chelsey D., 180; P., 180; P., 065, 073, 452; Dabney P., 065, 073, 452; Dan, 180; Daniel, 180, 396; Eliza, 022; Elizabeth, 073; Emily, 048; Emma, 360; Eugenia, 024; Frances C., 057; Francis E., 180; Harriet, 041, 047; Hubbard, 424; Irine, 012; Isam, 073; J. M., 452; James M., 073, 452; James, 427, 463; Jesse (heirs of), 427; Jesse, 065, 073, 180; Joe, 026, 180;
HOLLOWAY: John W., 180; John, 026, 351, 395, 452; Joseph, 026, 180; Josephine, 037; Lenaan, 040; M. A., 039; M., 395, 442, 452; Martin, 180; Maston, 026, 452; Mattie, 039; Newton, 351, 414, 452; Oliver, 351, 353, 443, 452; Patsey, 014; R. B., 026, 344, 351, 463; R. S. 026; Randal, 026; Robert W., 180; Rosalea, 026; Rosalie (Cook), 180; Samuel, 073, 180; Sarah, 022; Thomas, 173, 191; W. L., 452; William, 026, 180, 436
HOLLY: Lucy I., 279
HOLMES: Cyrus, 189; Elbert, 351; Eliza, 044; Genus, 463; George L., 133, 222, 435; James P., 180, 214, 249, 316; James, 026, 463; John, 180, 199, 316; Jonathan T., 224; Liberty, 086; Norman, 180; O.L., 362; Pleas, 180; Plumer, 026; Richard, 266, 291, 427; Sam, 026; Thomas, 180, 225; Warren, 026; Will, 180; William, 026
HOLMS: Elbert H., 026; Genie, 041; Howard, 026; Isham, 026
HOLOWAY: A. L., 463; Clarra, 048; M. D., 395; Madison S., 312; Mittle D., 463; R. B., 463; Ran, 395
HOLSENBACK: Alex, 452; Alexander, 180; Dan, 452; J. D., 452; Marshall, 180, 452
HOLSENBAKE: Alexander, 351

HOLSENBECK: Alex, 351, 396; Alexander, 026, 082, 351, 414, 448; Alfred, 073; Alice, 030; D. J., 341, 385, 444; J. E., 351; M. J. 026; Marshall, 180, 351; P. R., 026; R.L., 180; W.A., 180; W.H., 376; Will, 351
HOLSEY: George, 073; James, 187
HOLSOMBACK: Nancy A. E., 055
HOLSTEIN: Alex, 452
HOLSTIN: Alexander, 026
HOLSTON: Christianna, 059
HOLT: Asa, 180; Billie, 026; Caroline, 023; Carrie, 031; D. S. 180, 273; Dave, 180; David, 026, 351; Davie, 396; Eli, 026; Ella, 351; Fannie, 005; Frank, 026; Gus, 180; Henry, 180; James, 165, 195, 316, 396; John Wesley, 026; Laura, 015; Malinda, 016; Mariah, 048; Matilda, 004, 181; Owen, 027, 351; Peter, 027, 181; Peyton, 293; Phebee, 026; Richard, 027; Russel, 181, 351; Russell, 351; Simon, Jr., 427; Susan, 351; Thaddeus G., 158; Thaddeus, 158; Wes, 351; Will, 027, 351; Will Jr., 181; William Alex, 027; William, 180, 181, 255, 280, 427
HOLTS: Edney, 396
HOMER: Jesse, 442
HOMES: Richard, 396
HONEYCUT: J. E., 452; James E., 351; John, 181; Solomon, 181
HONEYCUTT: Annie Ella, 049; Lee, 012; Thomas J., 027
HOOD: Ichabod, 181, 222; Lucea, 012; Wiley, 073, 181, 233; William, 181, 432
HOOKS: Charles D., 027; David I., 027; F. M., 452; Farra M., 027; John W., 073; L. J., Mrs., 024; Madora A., 024; Mary J., 043; Rhoda A., 059; Robert, 396; Thomas, 206, 320, 431
HOOPER: John, 115; N. W., 452; N. W., Jr., 181; N. W., Sr., 181; Nannie Lee, 016; Thomas, 181
HOOTEN: Amos, 181; D. W., 027; James, 073
HOOTON: D. W., 181; James, 181; Sidney L. (Anderson), 181
HOPE: James, 146, 219, 308
HOPKINS: Lambeth, 210
HOPPER: William, 027
HOPPING: Ephraim S.,147; Theodore, 404
HOPSOM: Warren, 181
HOPSON: Berry, 027; Hardy, 181, 240; Rosetta, 053; Warren, 111, 181; William, 316
HORN: Amanda J., 252; Charles N., 252, 288; Henry, 290; James J., 288; Joseph, 181; Thomas, 181, 193, 311; Richard B., 181; Solomon, 459
HORNE: Amanda J., 253; Charles N., 253; James W., 232; Joseph, 181
HORSELEY: Morris, 396; Robert (Bob), 351; W. G., 351; William G., 337; William, 181
HORSLEY: James, 027; Thomas, 181; William C., 102; William G., 027, 181, 351
HORTER: Eli S., 209
HORTON: A. J., 351; A., 334; Caroline 2, 018; Columbus, 027; Elisha, 065, 073, 442; Elizabeth, 060; George, 295; Hal, 351; James A., 181, 316, 351, 414; James P., 027; James, 073, 181, 351; Jerrie, 351; John, 142, 181, 232, 316, 458; Josiah, 435; Lizzie, 060; Lott, 427; Mary Ann (Thompson), 181; Mary Jane, 073; Mary, 458; Nancy, 027; Peter, 351; Proser, 246; Robert, 027; Saban, 195; Sarah M., 018; Seaborn R., 073; Stephen, 181; Tressa, 058; Turner, 181; Wesley, 027
HOSKINS: Wilas, 466
HOUGH: A. L., 371; A. S., 370, 371; John, 123, 233
HOUGHTON: John W., 088, 092; Josiah, 065, 073; W. A., 329, 332
HOUSE: James, 181, 184; William H., 167, 181
HOVATER: Jacob, 182
HOWARD: A.B., 414; Alexander H., 251; Allie, 028; Annie, 182; Coradon H., 182; Coredon (?) H., 182; Coryden H., 182; Corydon H., 182, 316, 396; Cresie, 038; Fed, 351; Frances, 047; Henry, 182, 226; Hezekiah, 427; J. B., 065, 212; J.P., 442; J. T., 446, 452; J.Y, 466; James B., 027, 073, 155, 171, 178, 285, 351, 414, 452; James, 268, 345, 452; Jessie, 396; John T., 226, 251, 461; John, 027, 090, 172; Joseph, 182, 261; HOWARD: Judith Ragene, 030; Nancy 351; Martha, 060; Mary Jane, 050; Mattie, 026; Ophelia, 032; Pleas, 182; S. N., 351, 442; S. R., 442;

Samuel, 073; Stephen, 065, 073, 171, 212, 433; Tell, 396; Thomas J., 219, 319; Thomas T., 027; W. H., 369; W. S., 452; Will, 182; William H., 096, 118; William S., 027; William, 182, 216, 452; Willis, 027
HOWE: Robert, 325
HOWEL: Byrum, 182; Mason, 212; Rufus, 261, 405
HOWELL: Nancy, 182; Nathaniel, 427; Vines, 316; Weston, 182
HOXEY: Thomas, 149, 189
HOYT: Eli T., 127, 137, 178; Eli, 143; Rullel, 143; Russel, 127; Russell, 137; Tolbert, 370; William J., 243; William S., 260, 263; William, 176
HOZEY: James, 182
HUBBARD: Cinetta, 350; John R., 146; Margarett Jane, 030; Roy, 396; Samuel, 073; Sarah, 052
HUBERT: John, 150
HUCKABY: Charles, 182; David, 182; Isham, 182; William, 266
HUCKEBY: Isham, 187, 285, 316; John, 108; Nancy, 215
HUDDLESTON: J. H., 342; John F. M., 182; John, 108; Nancy, 215
HUDSON: Charlie, 027; Ephraim, 192, 193; Erby, 104; Irby, 100, 148, 176, 234, 276, 286, 292, 314, 322; Isum, 182; Jane, 056; John F., 027; John, 095, 129, 182; Lessie, 054; Lewellen W., 292; Lewellyn W., 315; Lewis, 182; Love, 006; Nelson, 027; Richard, 182, 222, 232, 233, 427; Robert, 129, 260; Rolan, 182; Rowland (heirs of), 427; Samuel P., 095; Thomas, 182, 316; William, 111, 181, 182
HUDSPETH: Airs, 138, 181, 182, 222, 225, 316, 319, 321, 430, 435, 464; Ares, 182; Aris, 182; John, 239; Mark, 182; Polly, 025; Richard, 224; Thomas, 224
HUES: Bob, 027
HUFF: Adda, 182; Andrew, 182; Bart, 396; Bartlett D., 027; Clayton W., 027, 073; Davis, 182, 452; Elizabeth A., 018; Emaliza, 032; Faithey, 090; Frank, 182; G. W., 442; George W., 027; Hamblin, 182, 396; Hamllin, 448; Hawkins, 169; Henry B., 182, 298, 414; J. D., 182; J. P., 351; J. T., 027; James D., 027; James, 182, 452; John, 027, 351; L. E., 351; Lucinda E., 182; Lundy, 182, 244, 272; Oscar G., 027; Ralph (heirs of), 427; Ralph, 073, 182, 396, 427; Suiervin, 396; T. J., 452; T. Thomas, 442; Tabitha, 183; Thomas, 073; Thomas, 027; Whitfield, 183
HUGHES: Ann, 045; Isaac, 115, 261; Jack, 027; Jerry, 183; Peter M., 176, 183, 245, 316; Polly, 031; Ras, 351; Robert, 261; Susan, 022; Willie, 396
HUGHS: Allen, 027; George, 164; John W., 096; Peter M., 271; Thomas, 427; Wesley, 027; Wilson, 027
HUGSPETH: Airs, 248
HULBERT: James, 172
HULING: James, 268
HULL: Francis M., 183
HULME: George H., 365, 372, 377
HUMBER: Mary E., 091; Robert, 091, 183, 423, 464
HUMBURG: Sabra, 183
HUMPHREY: Carrie, 007; Charlotte, 002; Edmond, 027, 351; Evan, 027; Howard, 027; Joshua, 027; Katie, 011; Marshall, 351; Milton, 352; Sallie, 040; Thomas, 183, 243
HUMPHREYS: Charles, 314; Edmund, Jr., 183; George, 299; Hardy T., 117; Lucy, 061
HUMPHRIES: Berry, 408; Emma, 011; George W., 183, 427; George, 352; Isaac, 122; Lucy, 408; Martha, 041; Milton, 183, 352, 464; Uriah, 183
HUMPHRY: Anderson, 352; Edmond, 183; Lucy, 408; Nancy, 045
HUNGERFORD: A. Jr., 446; Anson, 086, 093, 095, 108, 113, 117, 126, 136, 147, 163, 179, 192, 197, 207, 213, 215, 223, 241, 246, 249, 261, 265, 274, 281, 284, 290-292, 301, 303, 307, 308; Anson Jr., 073, 090, 147, 155, 210, 226, 227, 267, 305, 448; Dana, 114
HUNICUTT: Thomas, 316
HUNNEYCUT: Thomas, 183
HUNNICUT: Callie, 057; James E. P., 431
HUNNICUTT: Carrie Lou, 015; E. P., 183; J. T., 452; Jas. E., 464; Lee, 058; Thomas, 183
HUNPHRIES: Uriah, 405
HUNT: A. J., 027; Aaron, 183; Abe, 352; Appleton, 183; W., 340, 355; Betsey, 090; Catharine, 183, 352; Ed, 027; Elbert, 027; Eliza (Smartt), 265, 322; Eliza, 012; George, 379; Harrison, 352; Henry,

183; Jack, 183; James, 073, 094,
183; Jesse, 073; John R., 183; John,
027, 101, 129, 138, 183, 219, 234,
280, 322, 427, 467; Judkins, 183;
HUNT: Maggie, 049; Mary Ann, 183; Obie
Dias, 396; Randal, 352; Randall,
Robert Henry, 027; Roberta,
022; Sarah, 059; T. J., 380; Tames,
427; Thomas, 130, 246; Turner, 175;
Turner, Jr., 427; Turner, Sr., 427;
W. H., 073; William H., 183;
William, 027
HUNTER: A.A., 452; Alexander A., 065,
452; Alexander, 183; Anderson V.,
373; Annie, 183; Asbury, 352; Bud,
396; Cleve, 352; Cornua, 027; David,
089; Georgia Ann, 460; Glp, 027;
Green, 027; Henry, 027, 073, 183,
352; Ida, 031; Idus, 183; Jackson,
027; James F., 183; James T., 065,
073; James, 183, 221, 270, 427,
430, 434; John, 317; Joseph, 037;
Mary, 046; Matilda, 038; Mollie E.,
043; Nicholas P., 275, 310, 312;
Quince, 352, 396; Reuben, 027, 337;
Reubin, 183; S. A., 073; Samuel B.,
116, 138, 250; Silla, 343; Sylla,
183; T. P., 073; Will Frank, 352;
Will, 352; William A., 027;
William, 138, 183
HUNTINGTON: Alfred I., 281; Alfred
J., 208; Alfred S., 281
HURD: Celia, 017; Charity, 028; Clark,
027; Jack, 280; Maggie, 006; William
L., 117, 182; William S., 086, 090,
108, 113, 117, 126, 147, 155,
163, 179, 190, 207, 210, 213, 215,
223, 226, 227, 241, 246, 249, 261,
265, 267, 274, 281, 284, 290-292,
301, 303, 305, 307, 308, 311, 318,
448; William, 093, 095, 147
HURST: John N., 027; John, 138
HURSTON: John, 183
HURT: Catharine, 029; Cornelia, 030;
Emily, 352; Fannie, 003; Fronie,
032; Lillian, 396; Mason, 183, 352;
Vena, 024; William C., 316;
William, 073, 145, 150, 183
HURTS: Blanche, 029
HUSON: Alexander, 241; David, 073,
183; John, 183; Judith, 256; Judy,
183; O. S., 363; Thomas W., 212;
Thomas, 094
HUSSON: A., 170
HUST: Henry, 427
HUSTING: John, 183
HUSTON: David, 317; George, 088;
John, 146, 184, 220, 246, 274,
287, 299, 427, 430, 435; Judy, 317;
Oliver, 222; Samuel, 184, 213,
239, 294, 427, 430; Thomas 240
HUTCHENS: Nathan L., 289; William, 184
HUTCHESON: Henry C., 184, 223, 271,
293, 317; John C., 184; William,
184, 421
HUTCHINGS: Charles, 236; Cornelia,
335; Phillip P., 027; R. C., 352;
R. E., 332, 352, 452; R. H., 335;
Richard S., 073; Robert E., 352,
452; Walter, 027, 396
HUTCHINS: E., 452; George, 352; Isaac.
135; John, 135, 153; P. P., 352; R.
E., 352; Robert E., 352
HUTCHINSON: Alfred, 184; Henry C.,
125, 133, 184; M.H., 073, 184, 363,
442; Mamie, 055; Maxamillian H., 232;
Maximilian H., 090, 108, 110, 222;
Maximillian H., 152, 232; R. W.,
333, 334, 346; Sallie, 006; T. A.,
028, 333, 334, 346, 347, 351, 357,
371, 394, 452; T. L., 452; Thomas
L., 028, 073, 452; William (heirs
of), 432; William, 396
HUTCHISON: Henry C., 257, 271, 299;
Lula, 047; M. A., 232; M. H., 232,
414; Maximillian H., 090; Maximillian
H., 200, 205, 290, 291; Maximillian
231; Maximillian H.147,; Maximillian
H., 153, 200, 205, 225, 276;
Maximillian H., 027; Richard, 184;
William, 184
HUTSEL: James, 099
HUTSON: John, 184; Thomas, 236,
286, 435; Zadoc, 427
HUTTS: James, 427
HYATT: H. C., 184; L. P., 184, 396,
452; Lelia, 007
HYDE: Samuel, 184; Simeon, 100, 156,
184, 191, 225; Thomas, 427
HYSLOP: Robert, 295
IKE: Joe, 183; John, 028, 399;
Joseph, 184; Lewis, 183, 184
ILSLEY: Stillman, 253
INGLES: Joseph L., 469
INGOLDSBY: Felix, 121
INGRAHAM: William, 156
INGRAM: Andrew, 028; Edmund, 427;
Elizabeth, 101; George, 101;
Nimrod D., 261; Presily, 184;
Thomas, 097; W. R., 257;
William P., 261
INMAN: H. T., 351; Hugh T., 349,

364, 381, 394
IRBY: Anthony, 184
IRVEN: John, 184
IRVIN: Absalom, 184, 275; Benjamin,
184; Christopher, 184, 317;
Francis, 125, 246; James, 184,
199, 292; John, 184; William, 184
IRVINE: Benjamin, 103, 292;
Christopher, 255
IRWIN: Benjamin, 184, 292, 427;
Charles, 028; Christopher, 184;
Francis, 100, 175, 184, 246, 307;
James, 159, 287; Jared, 418
ISAAC: Dennis, 028; Frances, 027;
Reese, 028; Robert, 103, 117,
126, 184
ISAACS: Dennis, 028; Robert, 163
ISHAM: Christian, 096; Robert, 396
IVERSON: Alfred, 209, 254
IVEY: Ephralgen (Ephraim), 215;
Ephraim, 181; Fannie, 184; H.H.,
352; James, 452; Jesse, 216; L.
M. Mrs., 053; Lot, 073; R. W.,
452; Robert W., 184; Sam, 184
IVINS: John, 184; Josiah, 028
IVORY: Sam, 028; Will, 382
IVY: Benjamin, 427; Ella, 049;
Flournoy, 028; Henry, 073; James,
452; Jordan, 176; Littleton, 243;
R.L., 452; R.W., 442; Reese, 028;
Robert W., 073, 452; Robert S., 355,
452; Robert, Sr., 363, 382; Sarah
(Williams), 176; Wenney, 073;
William H., 028; Winifred, 427
JACKSON: Aaron, 352; Ada, 031;
Albert, 396; Alfred, 028; Alice,
045, 185; Amanda, 028, 038;
Andrew, 443; Andy, 352; Ann, 048;
Anthony, 185; Arthur, 352; Ben,
028; Berry, 028; Bethany, 013;
Bettie, 023; Bose, 028; Boss, 396;
Buddy, 185; Bunk, 185; Burwell,
251; Caroline, 026; Carrie, 021;
Charley, 028, 185, 427; Charlie,
028; Charlie, 185; Cilla, 031; Cinda,
027; Clarence, 185; Clark, 028;
Claud, 028; Claude, 185, 396; Coby
R., 281; Comfort, 007; Corine
035; Dave, 396; Delle, 185; Diana,
030; Doc, 028; Dock, 185; Dora,
016; Eliza Ann, 044; Eliza, 073;
Ellen, 044; Essie, 021; Fed, 028;
Frank, 352; Garfield, 185, 396;
JACKSON: George, 028; Gordon, 396;
Grady, 396; Green, 028; Greene B.,
185; Greene, 352; Hattie, 029;
Henry, 028, 352, 396; Hester, 006;
Hiram, 028; Ida, 048; Isaac R.,
185; Isaac, 073; Isham, 352; Ivy,
352; J.H., 467; Jack, 352; James,
028, 311, 426, 427, 432; Jeanette,
028; Jim, 028; John F., 082; John
Henry, 352; John, 028, 073, 185,
234, 259, 464; Julia Ann, 352;
JACKSON: Julia, 053; Katie, 061;
King, 028; Laura, 053; Levie, 032;
Lewis, 028; Lottie, 352; Lucy
013, 185; Luke, 185; Lula, 033;
Maggie, 059; Martha, 047; Mary
Jane, 054; Mary, 024, 045, 046,
396; Mason, 068; Mattie May, 017;
Mattie, 011, 024, 061; Melissa
Jane, 050; Mose, 352, 396; Nancy,
020, 281; Nettle, 352; Pauline,
028; Penney, 041; Peter L., 310;
Peter, 028, 352; Pless, 185; Pleas.
352; Pleasant, 065, 073, 185, 314,
352; Polly (Hill), 174; Price, 028,
352; R.P., 028; Ran, 396; Reuben
292; Richard, 028; Robert Lee, 028;
JACKSON: Robert, 028, 396; Rosa, 016;
Samuel, 256, 427, 434; Selah, 427;
Selia, 466; Seneca, 185, 352;
Senica, 329; Spencer, 028; Stephen
D., 185; Stoby, 352; Sudie, 028;
Susie, 028; Thomas, 028, 073, 185,
352; Thomas, Sr.(heirs of), 427;
Tildy, 030; Wade, 028, 396;
Wallace, 185; Warren, 185; Wilkins,
185, 270; Will, 028, 185; Willey,
028, 174, 185, 464; Willie Flem, 028
JACOB: Jack, 028; Nathan, 028
JACOBS: John, 185; Joshua, 185
JACOBSON: Annie, 026; O. A., 444;
C., 396; Charlie, 028, 185, 352
JAILLET: Peter F., 086; Peter, 086
JAMES: Andrew, 028; Charlie Lee,
028; David, 427; Dovie, 185; Jesse,
159; Jim, 185; John P., 185; John,
028, 162; Lula, 061; Marshall,
029; Michel, 029; Minnie, 035;
Mitchel, 396; Rachael, 049; Scott,
185; Sidney, 008; Wash, 352;
Wesley, 029, 185; West, 185; Willie
William, 226; Willie Lee, 185;
JAMISON: Arthur, 185; H., 396
JAQUES: R. S., 347
JARRATT: Deveraux, 133
JARREL: Leroy F., 157, 186, 256;

Leroy, 250
JARRELL: Leroy F., 215
JARRETT: William D., 216
JARROW: James, 423
JARVIS: James, 184
JASPER: Academy, 186
JASTERS: Martha, 045
JAY: William, 186
JEAN: Jesse, 428
JEFFERIES: A. L., 352; C., 352;
William, 428
JEFFERS: Berry, 186, 352; Bolin L.,
153; Colbert, 396; Cordy, 029;
Frank, 186; Gella, 195; Grady,
186; Josephine, 434; Lee, 186;
Lela, 195; Rans, 396; Thomas, 352
JEFFERSON: Hattie, 042; Thomas, 029
JEFFRIES: Albert, 186; Alice L.,
396; Alice, 111, 186, 396; Amanda,
052; Amelia, 059; Anna, 049; Annie,
004; Aurelius, 029; B. S., 073;
Beatrice, 062; Belle, 050; Berry,
396; Betsie, 052; Betsy, 038;
Bill, 396; Billy, 029; Bolin S.,
186; Boling L., 317; Boling S.,
186; Boling, 186; Bolling S.,
186; Bolling, 186; Burket, 187;
Burkett M., 186, 246; Burkett,
396; C., 396; Calvin, 029; Cenl,
353; Charley, 396; Charlie, 396;
JEFFRIES: Clarissa, 026; Col., 186;
Colbert, 029, 073, 186, 187, 195,
268, 323, 352, 353, 376, 396, 397,
406; Coos, 353; Cordial D., 073;
Cordial, 186; Dan, 029; Dilley,
353; Easter L., 052; Elijah, 029;
Elizabeth M., 015; Ella, 004;
Emily, 017; Epsie, 004; Everett,
397; Florence, 020; Frank, 029;
Geary, 186; George, 186, 267, 281,
297; Georgia Ann, 073; Grady, 186;
JEFFRIES: Harriett, 012; Henry, 029;
186, 353, 397; Henry, Jr., 029;
Hill, 186; Hilliard, 386, 397; J.
H., 452; J. P, 186, 397; J. R.,
397; James, 029, 186, 397; Janie,
015; Jeanie, 397; Jennie, 049;
Jessie, 029; John, 029, 186, 397;
Katie, 021; Lane, 186; Lee, 029,
186; Leila, 017; Lelar, 186;
Lissie, 025; Lizzie, 050; Mahala,
017; Manda, 029; Margaret, 045;
JEFFRIES: Mary Jane, 012; Mary, 055,
397; Matilda, 397; Milton, 029;
Mollie, 047, 186; Murf, 186; Nancy,
051, 204; Nat, 397; Naz, 029;
Norman, 186; Oscar, 029; Payton,
029; Pearl, 029; R.S., 392; Raney,
012; Ransom, 330; Richard, 186,
397; Rollin, 029; Rowland, 029;
397; Samuel, 029; Sarah J., 330;
Sarah, 186; T. J., 186; Thomas
J., 029; Thomas, 029, 073, 186,
187, 397; Tom, 029, 187, 397;
Tooms, 029; Vinie, 026; Wesley,
029; Will, 029; William R., 073;
William, 029, 099, 133, 178, 186,
187, 220, 296, 297; Zach, 029
JELKS: Ethelred, 191
JENKINS: Annie D., 156; Loften, 397; M.
112; B. W., 029; Benjamin, 167,
187, 317; Charlie, 317; Clem, 187;
Cora, 033; Cyrus R., 073; Edmond,
121, 187, 225; Edmund, 086, 187;
Elizabeth, 058; Emma, 016; F. E.,
187, 353, 452; F.S., 099; Frances,
397; Francis, 029, 073, 110,
135, 187, 265, 317, 353; Frank F.,
029; Hattie Ann, 048; Henry, 029;
Isham, 187, 353; J. H., 452; James,
110; John R., 073, 187, 353; John
P.,233, 317; John, 445; L.O., 187;
JENKINS: Lelia, 056; Loften, 397; M.
B., 029; Robert (heirs of), 428;
Robert, 397; Sarah J., 049;
Sterling, 287; W. E., 452; W. F.,
281; William, 065, 073, 096,
187, 397; Willie, 187
JENNINGS: Anna (Lovejoy), 187; David
C., 187; Norman, 423; Yarborough, 464
JEROTS: Yarborough, 464
JESSUP: George R., 184; Homer, 444;
William C., 101, 110, 190, 312
JESTER: Dorah, 058; Thomas, 202
JETER: Andrew, 135, 166, 177, 187,
272; Eleazer, 316; James, 154
JETTON: Bennedick, 109
JEWEL: Diamond, 029; Dimond, 029;
Lula, 025
JEWETT: Abram, 121, 160; Abram, 292;
Jonathan, 124, 137 189, 228, 230,
265, 301, 308; Martha, 073;
William, 109, 123
JILES: R. E., 187
JINKS: John, 186; Mathew, 187, 464
JOHN: E. D., 029; Enoch D., 042
JOHNS: Thomas, 073
JOHNSON: A.E., 353; A.I., 337, 442,
465; A. O., 182, 388, 395, 405,
410, 417, 397; Aaron, 029; Abel,
260; Ahab P., 187; Ahab, 185;
Albert, 187; Alexander, 073, 187;

Alfred, 029, 073, 187, 189, 190,
200, 224, 289, 452; Alice, 030;
Allas, 029; Allen, 187, 353, 372,
414; Allis, 353; Alonzo, 029;
Anderson, 397; Andrew, 029, 179,
187, 428, 431, 433, 464; Andrews,
397; Annie, 031, 037; Annis T.,
073; Anthony, 187, 283; Arnold,
190; Arthur, 317; B.C. 314;
JOHNSON: B.D. 452; B.F. 335, 351;
Benjamin, 029, 320; Bennie D. 029;
Bill, 287, 397; Brice C. 187;
Bryant, 029, 187, 339, 353; Bryce
C., 295; Burrel, 029, 464;
Caroline, 018, 037, 357; Carrie,
049; Cartley, 161; Catharine, 353;
Charley, 029; Charlie, 029;
Chelsea, 320; Chenney, 018; Cicero,
030; Cleavland, 187; Cornelius,
187, 317, 397, 267; Corrina, 023;
JOHNSON: Cortley, 185; Daniel, 188,
253; David H. 458; David, 099,
148, 188, 303, 448; Doctor, 339;
Ed, 188; Eddie, 029; Eli, 030,
188, 353, 397, 414; Elizabeth,
353; Ellick, 329; Emiline, 195;
Emma, 025; Ephraim, 030, 397;
Ervin, 030; Fannie, 019, 028;
Felix, 073; Fleming, 188; Frances
S., 224; Francis S., 180; Frank,
188; Gabriel, 188, 230, 243;
JOHNSON: George D., 458; George, 030,
189; Georgia Ann, 353, 397; Gip,
188; Green F., 360, 467; Greene
F., 462; H. G., 464; Haney, 073;
Hannah, 021, 188; Harriet, 058;
Hattie, 030; Henry, 030, 188, 252;
Herschel V. Gov., 232; Hiram,
186, 188; Hosea, 152; Hugh C., 184;
Hugh G. 138, 188, 215, 317, 397,
464; Hugh P., 188, 283; Hugh, 106;
Hungerford J. 316; Ida, 068;
JOHNSON: India, 022; Isaac N., 211;
J. C., 030, 329; J. H., 353, 452;
J. T. M., 099; J. Mon.,
354, 367, 452; Jack A., 164, 188,
317; Jack, 030; Jackson A. 317;
James C., 188; James D., 290; James
H., 030, 091, 188, 397; James M.,
030, 073; James S., 301; James W.,
317; James, 030, 086, 130, 186,
188; Jas., 468; John C. 030;
John R., 097; John W., 030; John,
030, 073, 171, 188, 367, 444;
JOHNSON: Johnnie, 030; Jonas, 030;
Jonas, Jr., 397; Joseph A., 353;
Joseph H., 030; Joseph S., 030;
Joseph, 103, 108, 133, 148, 154,
168, 171, 172, 184, 188, 196, 216,
221, 223, 226, 252, 264, 265, 272,
274, 299, 302, 315, 317, 320, 420,
428, 430, 432; Joshua, 428; Julia,
038; LaFayette, 187; Lee Ann, 035;
Legree, 188; Lemma Anne J., 043;
Lemma, 055; Lesle, 397; Lewis,
188; Lizzie, 008; M.F., 030; M.L.,
401, 414, 452; Margaret, 005;
JOHNSON: Margarett, 353; Martha,
353, 357; Martin L., 397; Martin,
030; Mary Eliza, 019; Mary J.,
057; Mary M., 013; Mary, 149, 357;
Matilda, 010; Mattie, 043; Melvin,
397; Minnie, 045; Minor W.S., 188,
459; Missouri Ann, 024; Molle,
018, 034, 047; Moses, 030, 353;
Nancy A., 016; Nancy, 052; Nathan,
427; Nealey D., 437; Ned, 030;
Nicholas, 188, 189, 271, 303,
317; Oliver H., 030; Oliver, 030;
JOHNSON: Onie, 048; Patsy, 004; Paul,
397; Peter, 189, 397, 463; Polly
O., 189, 271; Polly O. 197; R.
L., 452; Reese L., 452; Reuben,
030, 466; Rich, 380; Richard, 429;
Robert, 428; Rosser M., 030; S.A.,
353, 452; S. H., 353, 374, 452;
Sallie, 004; Sam, 189; Samuel, 030,
107, 150, 175, 189, 199, 410, 428,
444; Sarah Jane, 034; Sarah, 019;
Sithy (Dukes), 189; Snellen, 073,
145, 189, 190, 215, 429; Snelling,
030, 087, 111, 121, 125, 127, 136,
172, 188, 189, 225, 228, 231, 245,
271, 278, 293, 297, 312, 313, 317,
353, 424, 428, 458; William, Jr.,
189, 295; William, Sr. (heirs of),
428; William, Sr., 073, 189, 424;
Willie Ann, 022; Willis, 186, 190
JOHNSON:
Ann G., 007; Cornelius, 308;
Elisabeth, 011; Eliza, 055; Ella,
353; Emily, 030; Fleming, 190,

353; Frances, 304; Francis, 317;
Georgia Ann, 057; Gip, 387; Henry,
030; Hiram E., 215; Hiram, 199;
Isaac, 030, 190; Jack A., 190;
James H., 030, 190, 200, 295, 317;
James J., 190, 373, 458; James M.,
065, 163; James S., 030; James,
089, 157, 183, 190, 194; James,
053; John, 065, 190, 219;
JOHNSTON: Joseph H. 030; Kittie, 032,
355; Lancetor, 165; Launcelot
306; Letha, 059; Littleton, 190,
265, 321, 384; Margaret, 190;
Martha Jane, 358; Martha M., 065,
073, 442; Martha, 190, 442; Mary
N., 353; Mary, 060; Mattie, 004;
Minnie, 030; Mittie, 002; Nancy,
052; Nathan, 073, 190, 219, 435,
458; Nettle, 034; Patsey Marla,
190; Peter, 397; Pollard, 030;
JOHNSTON: Puss, 056; R. L., 453;
Reese, 190; Richard, 190, 277;
Robert A., 148; Robert, 460; S. H.,
190, 443, 453; Snelling, 190, 212,
073, 442; Martha, 190, 200, 340
353, 453, 466; Stephen, 199, 353,
453; Thomas, 065, 073, 312, 448;
W.S., 353; William A., 030, 073;
William B., 121, 267; William G.,
280; William L., 190; William N.,
073; William M., 190, 353; William
M., 190, 219, 458; William S., 190,
353, 397; William, 145, 165
JOHNSTONE: Fleming, 190; James H., 190
JOICE: Telitha, 224
JONES: A. D., 397; A. D. Mrs., 397;
A.J., 453; A. L., 030; Abner, 428;
Abraham D., 397, 401; Abraham, 119;
Abram D., 190, 397; Absalom, 178;
Ada, 013; Adaline, 002; Adam W.
226, 305; Albert, 145; Amos, 145,
190, 255; Andrew J., 414; Anna,
036; Annie, 036; B. F., 386, 442;
Ben L., 400; Benjamin, 258, 353;
David C., 065, 073; David, 428;
Edward, 073; Eford H., 190;
JONES: Elbert, 216; Elijah C., 234;
Elijah E., 306; Emma, 021, 037;
Ephraim, 190; Evans, 190; Francis
P., 190; George, 243;
Georgeann, 464; Gideon L. 317;
Ginie, 145; Goodrich, 191, 278;
Green, 030; H. H., 341; Hardy,
190; Harold, 190; Harry Hill,
030; Hartwell, 129, 190, 191,
247, 282, 397; Hartwell, Jr.,
191; Hartwell, Sr., 191; Hattie
E. 018; Henry W., 090; Henry,
191, 253, 428; Henry, Sr., 173;
JONES: Hilliard G., 444; Ida, 020;
Ike, 353, 397; Isaac 030; J.A.
453; J. J., 030; J. R. 191, 442,
444, 453; J. W., 453; Jack, 191;
James H., 098; James M., 030, 349,
353, 386, 414; James P., 030, 145,
197; James S., 150; James W., 453;
James, 191, 283, 287, 418, 453;
James, Jr., 397; Jane, 229; Jeff,
191; Joel, 191; John A. C., 428;
John A., 119, 271; John D. 030;
JONES: John, 030; John W., 030; John
L., 092; John P., 272; John R.,
298; John W. 108, 453; John, 164,
184, 185, 191, 198, 206, 219, 317,
397, 428; Joseph W., 191; Joseph,
073, 353; Joshua, 255, 428; Lilla,
060; Lucy, 019; M. P., 442; Mary
Ann, 060; Mary, 191, 213, 215,
246, 252, 277, 295, 299; Shack,
191; Susan E., 381; Susan, 003;
JONES: Thomas B., 191; Thomas P.,
030; Thomas, 162, 163 191, 297;
319; Tomerlane, 150; Tommie, 017,
030; Tuck, 397; Vincent, 073, 191;
W.C., 453; W. T. 191, 353; W. N.
446, 453; Walter, 353; Weaver, 398;
Wesley, 031; Whit, 191; Wiley
Oscar, 031; Wiley R., 031; Wiley,
168, 453; Wille, 428; William B.,
192, 249, 283; William C., 031;
William H. 031; William, 264;
William, 030, 190, 191, 213, 140,
145, 165, 191, 192, 228, 234, 459;
William, Jr., 192; William, Sr.,
073; William, 030; Wood, 192;
JORDAN: ?, 192, 353; A.H., 192, 335,
341, 346, 348, 352, 359, 361, 367,
373, 378, 409, 453; Aaron, 031;

Abram, 192; Adaline, 353; Addie
Joe, 005, 192; Alex Hunter, 031;
Anna, 005, 192; Augusta, 045;
Benjamin, 073, 103, 110, 152, 192,
312, 317, 358; Bessie C., 037;
Betsy, 353; Bill, 073, 192; Bob,
192; Bonner, 453, 464; Burwell,
201; C. D., 369, 385; C.H. 353,
364, 368, 398, 408, 453, 468; C.
Harrey, 364; C. Harvie, 453; C.
S., 247; C. W., 192, 202, 209,
328; 349, 353, 354, 356;
JORDAN: Caroline M., 354; Caroline,
020; Carrie Lee, 044; Charles A.,
031; Charles D., 406; Charles H.,
031; Charles Lee, 031; Charles S.,
095-097, 103, 105, 106, 112, 114,
118, 132, 161, 171, 177, 180, 182,
192, 197, 205, 209, 211, 224, 229,
247, 259, 260, 280, 285, 289, 291,
303, 310, 312-315, 317, 318, 323,
324, 453; Charles S. Jr., 192,
297, 317; Charles S. Sr., 311,
314, 315,317-319, 321-323; Charles,
031, 099, 305, 354, 428; Charley
Scott, 192; Charley, 354; Charlie,
031, 192; Chas. D., 446; Chris,
031, 352, 354, 464; Christopher,
031; Cora, 005; Daniel, 031;
JORDAN: Dick, 229, 353; Doll, 192;
E. H., 192, 193, 240, 335, 359;
362, 367, 378, 444, 453, 464; E.
J., 464; E. N., 444; E. T. Mrs.,
351, 369, 377; Edmond, 354; Edward,
031, 169; Elizabeth, 053, 054, 354;
Ellen, 010, 354; Emily, 181, 193,
352, 354; Emma, 018, 053; Erasmus
H., 031, 453; F. C., Mrs., 193,
353; F. C., 191, 374, 467; F.,
360, 379; Fannie, Rebecca, 346;
JORDAN: Fannie, 038; Fleming B., 031;
Fleming, 095, 104, 115, 116, 131,
134, 137, 138, 142, 149, 153, 154,
183, 187, 192, 193, 196, 232, 233,
246, 247, 252, 255, 266, 269, 276,
280, 293, 300-302, 317, 353, 388,
407, 426, 428, 434, 448; Fleming,
Jr., 031; Fleming, Sr. 065, 073,
193; Floyd, 193, 354, 398; Frances
C., 354; Frances M., 354; Francis
C., 093, 355; Genie, 017; Gentry,
193; George, 031, 193, 354; Georgia
Ann, 011; Gus, 031, 193; Gussie,
056; H. B., 192, 335, 338, 348,
359, 362, 367, 378, 453, 464;
JORDAN: H.H., 3621 H.J. 354; 453;
H. S., 453; Hardy, 193, 354;
Harriet, 012; Harry, 193; Harvie,
408; Hattie, 010, 013, 033; Henry
B., 354, 373, 453; Henry, 031; 086,
114, 123, 192, 193, 315; Hilliard,
031; Howard, 031; Hunter, 453;
Ione, 022; Irene, 030; Isaiah, 354,
362, 375; J. F., 193, 453, 464;
Jack, 031, 073, 193, 354, 464;
Jacob, 193; James 031, 414; Jane,
338, 464; Janry, 031; Jeanette H.
032; Jeff, 398; Jenty, 399; Jewell,
398; Jewett, 031, 342, 354; Jim,
031; Jimmie, 031; Joe, 031, 398;
JORDAN: John F., 193; John, 031
193; Johnnie, 398; Johnnie, 125;
Josie, 026; Julia, 047; Kate, 013;
Katie, 012; L., 031; Laura, 025;
Lexis, 443; Liddie, 354; Lillie,
414; Lizzie (not, 031; Lot,
354, 464; Lott, 193, 464; Louis,
354; Lovice P. 150; Lucinda, 011;
Lucy, 015, 020, 023, 048; Lula,
015, 019; Lutisa, 026; Margaret,
010; Martha, 031; Mary B., 464;
Mary Davis, 044, 047; Mary Frances,
058; Mary, 002; Mattie Lou, 009;
JORDAN: May, 031; Medora J., 022;
Medora, 058; Mille, 046, 398;
Missiouri, 008; Mollie, 054;
Mortimer, 177, 193; Moses, 031;
Nathaniel W.,178; Nathaniel, 193;
O.G., 193; O. I. Mrs., 040;
Ordelia, 464; Patience, 051;
Pitman, 193; Polly, 266; P., 335,
340, 354, 372, 375, 453; Randal,
031, 354; Randall, 193, 354;
Randol, 354; Randolph, 354;
JORDAN: Rebecca J.,025; Reuben, 065,
106, 193, 209, 246, 251, 299, 337,
422, 446; Reuben, Sr., 073, 290;
Robert, 031, 464; Rosa, 052; Rubin,
453; Rufus L. 031; Sallie J.
003; Sallie, 026; Sam, 354; Sarah,
193; Scott, 031; Seneca, 193;
Shine, 398; Sim T., 031; Sim, 333;
Singleton, 031, 192; Spencer, 073,
354; Starling, 193; Sterling, 073;
JORDAN: Susie A., 054; Susie, 022; T.
M., 159, 193, 354, 453; T., 256;
Thomas M., 031, 073, 112, 142, 193,
203, 354, 453; Thomas, 031; Thompson,
149; V. A., 031; Vic., 194; W.
157, 160, 223, 227, 258, 329, 333,
337, 340, 341, 343, 345, 347, 351,
354, 358, 361, 367, 370, 374, 375,

378, 394, 453, 458, 460-462, 464,
466-468; W. F. Jr., 453; W. F.
Mrs., 337; W. H., 193, 344, 354,
359, 453; W. J., 193, 398, 453;
JORDAN: Warren, 398; Wash, 194;
Washington, 443; Wesley, 031; Wiley
H.,194; Will, 194; William F., 151,
193, 341, 343, 354, 458, 462;
William F. Jr., 031; William P.,
Sr., 073; William, 031, 192, 193,
343, 354; William, Jr., 031;
Willie, 194; Wyatt, 032; Zach,
032; Zachariah, 130
JORDAN?: Sally, 333
JOSEPH: Alex, 032
JOURDAN: Burwell, 160; Warren, 307
JOURDEN: Fleming, 305; Mose, 354
JUMSTROM: Amelia, 003
JUNGSTROM: Emelia S., 443
JUNIOR: Polly, 138
KAIGLER: Alexander, 032
KANGLETON: William, 145
KANNARD: Blount (?), 099
KEATH: David, 433; James, 177
KEATON: Benjamin, 165, 214
KEELAND: Ike, 032
KEELEY: Jessie, 464
KEELING: Leonard, 194; William,
073,194, 428
KEEN: Madora, 343
KEENE: Ann T., 065, 073; Ann, 170;
B. F., 121; B. K., 194; Benjamin
F., 073, 120, 152, 194; Benjamin
J., 194
KEENER: Bastiti, 153
KEENER: William, 107, 153
KENNON: C., 464
KEESE: John, 250; Theodore, 120, 147
KEITH: Jeremiah, 194; John, 194;
Whitten, 032; Whitton, 422;
William F. T., 032
KELER: Oscar, 398
KELLAM: Henry, 302; Robert, 113, 116,
119, 125, 133, 148, 158, 181, 194,
217, 224, 232, 246, 248, 274, 284,
306, 316, 426, 444
KELLER: Everett, 194, 354, 398;
Henry, 094; Robert, 398
KELLEY: Allen, 428; Beershaby, 428;
Beverly A., 194; Bill, 398;
Charles, 428; Croft, 194; Henry,
317; J.R., 328; Jacob, 194; James,
239, 354; Jarrett B., 095, 194;
John R., 194; John, 194, 428;
Lewis, 194; Lizzie Lee, 042; Lona,
050; Marvel, 464; Tyre, 426;
William O., 109; William, 428
KELLIE: Pinkney, 464
KELLO: Robert, 032; S. B., 464;
Samuel B., 073, 227
KELLOGG: Andy, 194L Edward, 174,
266, 277
KELLOR: Everett, 032
KELLUM: Henry, 194
KELLY: A. J., 194; Aaron, 348, 398;
Adaline, 022; Addie D., 026; Addie
Kate, 035; Alfred, 088, 194, 291,
354; Alice, 029, 397; Allen, 073,
194, 195, 321; Alley, 024; Amos,
032, 195, 333, 354, 398, 465; Ann,
004; Anna, 006, 060, 354, 454;
Annie, 027, 035, 043; Anthony,
195, 354, 414; Archie, 032; B.A.,
195, 453; B.C., 239, 354, 369,
453; B.G., 453; B.,195; Bee, 195;
KELLY: Betsy, 037; Bettie, 055;
Beverly A., 091, 194, 241, 280,
399, 443, 448, 453; Beverly, 195;
Bill, 398; Buddie, 195; Bundy A.,
091; Burney, 032; Burt, 195;
Burton, 032, 398; C.B., 354; C.H.,
195, 453; Caroline, 036; Carrie,
035, 051; Catherine, 034; Celia,
053; Charity Ann, 032; Crawford
H., 032, 421; Crawford, 195, 373;
Daniel, 073, 195; David, 423, 428;
KELLY: Davis, 004; Digby, 398; E.
D., 354, 453, 468; E. Digby, 354;
E.H., 269, 355, 369, 398, 453; E.
Harvey, 453; Eaton Digby, 032;
Eaton H., 032, 195, 342, 369; Eaton
S., 073; Eaton, 355; Edin H., 195;
Eden H., 195, 355, 373; Eden H.,
Jr., 195; Eden, 195; Elizabeth,
013; Elmira, 042; Elmyra F., 018;
Emily, 354, 398; Emma, 027, 051;
Ephraim, 032; Erbin H., 355;
KELLY: Everett, 032; Ezekiel B.,
195, 421; F. M. O., 355; Fannie,
050; Francis O., 195; G. W., 453;
Geila, 195; Genie, 039; George W.,
270; George, 195, 398; Ginnie,
008; Hamp, 195; Helon, 032; Henry,
032, 100, 211, 355, 380, 385,
391, 398, 414; I.T., 453; Ida,
044; Ike T., 453; Ina Maud, 042;
India, 015, 044; Isaac T., 032;
KELLY: Isham, 130; J.A., 348, 369,
395, 453, 465; J. B., 195, 453;
J. F., 464; J. H., 160, 195, 213,
251, 273, 281, 331, 337, 338, 342,
343, 345, 348, 349, 354-356, 361,

367, 368, 373, 379, 385, 396, 393,
399-401, 410, 410, 444, 446, 453,
466, 468, J. R., 195, 453; J. T.,
334, 349, 355, 453; J. W., 408;
Jack, 398, 414; Jacob, 032, 195,
398; Jake, 355, 393; James, 032,
102, 195, 314, 428; Jane E., 073;
KELLY: Jane, 398; Jarrell B., 095;
Jarrett B., 073, 091, 095, 195;
Jarrott B., 280, 398, 468; Jennie,
022; Jim, 032, 398; John A., 032,
289, 453, 467; John C., 073, 195;
445; John H., 032, 184, 195, 202,
335, 346, 355, 357, 362, 365, 367,
381, 396, 408, 453; John H., Sr.,
073; John R., 065, 073, 094, 195,
453; John R., Jr., 032; John T.,
453; John Thomas, 195; John W.,
065, 073, 262, 371, 453; John, 032,
398, 453; Julian, 032, 453; L. S,
373, 390, 397, 398, 453; Lee P.,054
KELLY: Lela, 195; Lewis, 032, 195;
Lillian, 017; Lit, 398; Littleton,
355; Lizzie, 048, 056; Lou, 018;
027; Lucius, 453; Lucy, 016, 196;
Lula, 003; M.C., 032, 453; M. K.,
398; Maggie, 053; Margaret, 035;
Martha, 035; Marvin, 195; Mary A.,
042; Mary E., 005; Mary I, 031;
Mary Lou Ella, 056; Mary, 014, 073;
Matilda, 052; Mattie L. Mrs., 035;
Mattie, 008, 027; Michael, 195,
355, 428; Mille, 443; Minnie,
054; Mollie, 029; Murry, 398; Owen,
444; P.P., 355, 453; Pickney, 462;
KELLY: Pink, 195; Pinkney, 398, 464;
Pleasant P., 335, 357; S. C., 103,
453; S. H., 197; S. J., 195, 355,
385, 392, 407, 453, 464; Sallie H.,
331, 361; Sallie, 028, 049, 331,
Sally H., 348; Samuel, 032; Sarah
A., 036; Seaborn C. 073, 195,
354; Seaborn J., 032, 195, 442;
KELLY: Seaborn, 185; Serena C., 048;
Stephen, 355; Thomas, 195; Tipe,
398; Tire, 195; Tom, 032; Type,
195; Tyre, 428; W. J., 159, 195,
211, 328, 330, 331, 333-335, 338,
345, 350, 351, 353-355, 359, 370,
382, 428, 433, 453, 461, 466; W.
R., 453; W. G., 032, 195, 355,
442, 453; W. H., 195, 355, 390,
398, 407, 408; Wallis, 032; Walter,
032; Will, 195; William A 196,
208, 333, 357, 368, 378, 390;
William G., 371, 453; William M.,
196; William, 195, 453; Willie,
036
KELSEY: Charles W., 197; Charles,
178, 189, 198, 213, 292; George
A., 292; George N., 119; H.H., 401
KELTON: B. T. 196
KEMP: Annie, 006
KEMPTON: E. L., 446
KENAN: Augustus H., 131; Hardy H.,
196; Owen H, 115, 148, 196,
216, 255, 264, 298, 304; Owen W.,
233; William H. 233
KENDALL: David, 445; Paul, 032;
Whit, 355
KENDRICK: Benjamin B., 196; Burks,
196; Isaac, 131, 134, 217, 249;
280, 292; Isham, 194; James, 196,
199; John W., 271; John, 116, 136,
178, 257; Jones, 249; Martin, 420;
Shadrack, 073
KENDRICK: Willis E., 032
KENDRIX: Angie, 073
KENIMORE: Michael, 297
KENNADY: John, 275; Thomas, 196, 240
KENNAN: Owen H., 388
KENNEDAY: Agnes, 003
KENNEDY: Absalom, 155, 317; David,
073, 255, 288; Elias, 246; H.P.,
388; Jane, 065; John, 196, 398;
Robert, 428; Thomas, 130, 132,
196, 428, 462; William, 117
KENNON: Annie E., 021; Charles L.,
144, 218; Charles, 117, 175, 196;
Howell, 144; Isham, 196; James,
196; Lula, 046; Richard, 196; T.
H., 355, 453; Thomas, 310; Warner
L., 117, 196; Warner Lewis, 429;
William W, 196, 304, 398
KENNYMORE: Byrum P., 120, 196, 227;
Michael, 155, 196
KENT: Charlie, 347; George, 347;
Richard, 347
KERLING: David, 264
KERLING: David, 130
KERNOCHAN: Joseph, 087, 093, 105,
137, 139, 170, 186, 191, 198,
204, 244, 283, 287
KERR: Alfred D., 198, 208; Andrew,
093, 115, 146, 181, 206, 301, 308;
John, 099, 115, 146, 181, 206,
211, 228, 301, 308
KETCHENS: Neise, 355
KETCHINGS: Charles, 355
KETCHUM: Ralph, 168
KETTNER: Mary, 033
KEY: Abraham, 196, 237, 317, 424;

Asa, 032; B.P., 065, 073, 223;
Burney, 032, 196; Burrell, 453;
Burrell P., 196, 223, 255, 256,
325, 433; Burrell, 196; Burwell
P., 196, 197, 216, 242; Caleb W.,
164; Ell, 032; F.C., 197; Freeman,
032; George M., 197, 339, 348, 351,
355, 356, 359, 366, 394, 458; Ida,
051; India A., 051; Jacob, 355;
Jane Zelemer, 003; Jerrie, 398;
John C., 032, 090, 197, 253, 313,
357, 372, 410, 444; John H., 453;
KEY: John, 242; John, Jr., 458;
Joseph, 197, 428; L. H., 453;
Lawrence, 032; Loney, 048; M.B.,
082, 197, 255, 356, 364, 409,
453; M. D. L., 355, 442; Manerva,
464; Mary G., 073; Mary, 040, 355;
MicaJah B., 197, 277; MicaJah B.,
458; Osh, 032; Pearl, 036; S. M.,
043; Sallie, 058; T. C., 453;
Tandy W., 158, 197; Thomas C.,
032; Thomas F., 255; Thomas, 196,
197, 317, 428; W.H., 442; William
H., 197; Willie, 197
KEYTON: Benjamin, 428
KIBBEE: John M., 203
KIDD: Anderson R., 197; James H., 197
KIGHT: Samuel, 197; Samuel, Sr., 197
KILBEE: Sarah, 13°
KILBURN: Joseph K., 115, 137, 188;
Joseph K., 259, 267
KILBY: William, 073, 428
KILCHRIST: Daniel, 298
KILCREASE: Daniel, 185
KILCRISE: Daniel, 220
KILEY: M. J., 355
KILGO: Will, 355
KILGORE: Absalom, 099; Charles,
355; Clara, 040; E.C., 032; Isaac
C., 033; J.A., 398, 399; James A.,
033; James E., 453; James, 386,
398, 453; John, 197; Joseph, 197;
Lewis, 099; Matthew, 099; S. P.,
Mrs., 023; W.C., 033; William I.,
033; William Isaac, 398; William,
073, 292, 398
KILL: Phineas, 100
KILLBEE: Christopher, 199
KILLGO: Will, 398
KILLGORE: John, 197
KILPATRICK: George L., 284; J. D.,
171, 281, 388; James, 197
KIMBALL: Benjamin, 073; James, 430
KIMBEL: James, 433
KIMBELL: J. H., 033; Lucy A., 045;
M. V. 033
KIMBLE: David, 073
KIMBRO: John, 197
KIMBROUGH: Shadrack, 197; Shadrack,
464; Shadrick, 197; William H.,197
KINARD: America T., 026; Barney C., 197; Catharine,
146; Barney C., 197; Catharine,
039; F. M., 387; Francis M., 073;
George W., 448; J.J., 453; J., 197;
Jesse, 197; John H., 073; John J.,
355, 365; John, 115, 200, 429,
444, 448; Joseph C., 033; M. J.,
197, 453; M.K., 348; M., 348, 453;
464; Martha Ann M., 048; Martin J.,
197, 312, 453; Michael, 197, 442,
453; Mike, 370, 453; T. J., 348;
T. L., 355; W. W. 453; John, 434
KINCAID: W. C., 329
KINDALL: Elisha, 141; Whit, 398
KINDRICK: Major W. E., 033; Martin,
428; W. E., 398
KINEBREW: Shadrack, 073
KING: A. S., 442; Ada, 039; Alford,
163; Amelia, 015; B. G., 073, 355,
415, 453; B.P., 453; Benjamin, 088,
197, 267, 428; Burl G., 355; Burrel
G., 355, 453; Butler B., 238;
Cattel, 073; Dock, 197; Dolly, 065,
073; Edward D., 197; Edward, 197;
Elizabeth, 398; Ellen, 052;
Frances, 025; G.N., 453; George W.,
415; George, 033; Ida, 011; J. E.,
355; J. M., 219; Jacob, 197, 355;
KING: Jake, 033; James, 105, 294,
316, 355; Jane, 021, 428, 434;
Jesse, 316; Jim, 033, 197; Joe,
033, 400; John A., 267; John M.,
104, 124, 189, 197, 198, 250, 428,
442; John M., Jr., 197; John
Mitchel, 073; John, 033, 197, 242,
398; John, Sr., 428; Joseph, 428;
Josiah, 302; L. A., 037; Lewis,
144, 428; Lizzie, 049; M.T., 034;
Mamie B., 016; Mamie E., 009;
Martha A. E., 013; Martin, 139;
KING: Marv, 398, 444; Mattie C.,
009; Mitchel, 074; Nancy, 197;
Richard D., 074, 198, 228, 424;
Richard, 197, 198, 216, 291, 310,
319, 379, 453; T.P., 463; T. P.,
353, 355, 378, 385; T.R. Jr., 355;
Tabitha, 018; Tandy D., 104, 115,
198, 225, 247, 248, 259, 283, 317;
Thomas Butler, 485; Thomas B.,
190, 198, 219, 319; Thomas S., 252;
Thomas V., 319; Thomas, 198; W.H.,

453; Wiley King, 057; William H.,
453; William, 033, 074
KINGSLEY: Joseph, 176
KINMAN: John, 428; Samuel, 198, 428
KINNARD: Barney, 198
KINNON: Richard, 198
KIRBY: Henry, 153, 242, 251, 308;
Horace, 321; Jesse, 198; Sarah
A., 197
KIRK: Hudson, 119, 198, 421, 428;
Stephen, 174
KIRKPATRICK: Alice P., 026; H. P.,
398; High P., 110, 177; Hugh P.,
098, 128, 136, 142, 147-148, 152,
162, 177, 182, 198, 204, 207,
208, 223, 224, 232, 238, 244, 249,
253, 260, 263, 268, 280, 284, 290,
295, 300, 319; James H., 317;
James, 154; John D., 101; William
N., 131, 177, 180, 260, 311, 313,
317; William, 134, 448
KIRKSEY: Elisha S., 198, 256, 398;
Elisha, 198; William, 198
KIRTLEY: Lemma, 198, 317;
Levinia, 433
KISER: J. F., 338, 355, 379; M. C.,
338, 355, 379; Newt, 198
KISSINGER: John, 186
KITCHEL: Aaron W., 174
KITCHEN: Charles, 198; Joel, 415;
William K., 241; William R., 235
KITCHENS: Asberry, 355; Asbury, 355;
Barthenia, 290; Benjamin, 033,
104, 284, 428; Brant, 198; Charles,
065, 074, 198, 217, 240; E.C., 049;
Elizabeth, 198, 302; George, 033;
Henry, 198, 231; Joel, 033, 198,
231; 448, 453; M.L. Mrs., 011;
Martha Ann, 041; Martha, 062;
Nelson, 033, 198, 231; Oscar, 198;
Thomas J., 329; W. H., 198;
William, 198
KITCHINGS: C. W., 033; Charles,
430; Winney C., 030
KNAPP: George H., 157; Nathan B., 127
KNEELAND: Solomon, 122, 125, 313
KNIGHT: Calvery F., 428; Carey
Frances, 329; Carrington, 160, 198;
Elisha, 198; James M., 145; James
P., 198; James, 181, 199, 376;
John, 033, 107, 156, 159, 181,
198, 199, 286, 294, 422; John, Jr.,
199, 292; John, Sr. (heirs) 459;
John, Sr., 074, 199, 421; Richard,
222; T.P. 199; Thomas J. 158;
Warren, 033, 199, 355; Wiley, 199;
William, 088, 090, 162, 196, 199,
228, 266
KNOTT: David, 295; Reuben, 095
KNOWLES: Benjamin E., 199; Charles,
199; Daniel, 429; James P., 307;
James, 429; Laura, 010; Morris,
090; Rice F., 115, 158, 199, 283,
431; Rice, 431; W. J., 355
KNOX: Andrew, 125, 297; Benjamin,
136; Samuel, 128; Samuel, Sr.,
126, 428
KOLB: David, 199; Richard, 161
KOPMAN: Joseph, 102, 172, 178, 191,
227, 301
KUNZE: George W., 134
LABUZAN: Charles, 096, 103, 105,
109, 111, 113, 123, 124, 129, 130,
150, 154, 155, 157, 160, 162, 167,
168, 176, 179, 183, 189, 200, 217,
218, 220, 222, 224, 225, 236, 252,
260, 264, 272-275, 278, 281, 293,
294, 307, 308, 313
LACE: Allen L., 087
LACEY: Philemon, 074
LACIE: John S., 247
LACKEY: Albert, 033, 355; W.T., 364
LACY: Thomas, 398; William, 199
LAINE: John, 110
LAIRD: Lodowick, 233
LAKE: Elisha, 137, 165
LAMAR: Bob, 199; Easter, 010;
Gasaway D., 105; Gazaway B., 178,
179, 268; George, 183; H.J., 243,
329, 341, 349, 356, 361, 367, 466;
Henry G., 313; Henry J., 284, 360;
Jenry J., 142; John D., 183; John
P., 199, 201, 249, 250, 269, 321;
John T., 137; John, 428; Robert,
033; Thomas, 146
LAMBACK: Frederick, 144
LAMBERT: Elizabeth, 053; Stokeley,
199; Stokely, 198, 218; William, 199
LAMBERTH: Eden, 199; Edwin, 199;
John, 199
LAMBETH: James, 199; Jesse, 203;
W. M., 149; William M., 150
LAMBRIGHT: William, 199, 317
LAMKIN: James, 141, 220, 268, 281,
284; Robert, 198
LAMPKIN: W. L., 142, 465
LAMSDEN: Jeremiah C., 199
LANCASTER: Clayton, 376; Emma, 027;
J.A., 433; James, 033; Kitty, 355;
O.E., 453; Samuel, 166, 315;
Theron, 175
LANCER: Nathan S., 199

LAND: A. W., 298; Andrew J., 247;
Hiram, 199, 398; James, 105
LANDERS: J. M., 367
LANDON: Daniel, 428
LANDRUM: Dony, 398; Elias, 090, 199,
297; Thomas, 074; Timothy, 199, 428
LANDS: John, 428
LANDWORTHY: John, 260
LANE: A. E., 028; A. G., 453; A. W.,
199, 381, 453; Alexander, 199;
Alice, 017; Annie, 038; Augustus G.,
033; Augustus W., 033, 074, 105,
137, 157, 199, 200, 210, 246, 448;
Augustus, 415; Ben, 033; Benjamin,
226; Biddle, 033; Bobbie, 016;
Burnetta, 054; C.D., 355, 444, 453;
C.T. 453; Carlton, 199; Charles
Q., 033, 355; Cynthia M., 048; D.,
356; Davis 074, 090, 096, 134,
166, 180, 190, 192, 199, 223, 286,
312, 317, 318, 324; E.D., 355, 453;
Edward W., 199, 271; Elbert,
033; Elijah D., 033; Emma J., 035;
Emma, 007; Fannie A., 006; Floyd,
033; Georgia E., 012; Gussie, 056;
Henry, 165, 172, 199; J. D., 453;
J. F., 453; J. H., 281, 339, 355,
453; J. I., 453; J. Jr., 398;
J. M., 453; J. O., 453; James M.,
199, 355, 453; James O., 033;
James, 199; Jennie F., 055; Jennie,
038; Jesse, 199, 172, 287; Joel,
429, 434, 442; John B, 199; John
033, 199, 453; John T., 074;
Lane: John, Jr., 204; L.A., 033, 074,
381, 415, 442, 453; Laura V., 010;
199, 200, 317; Lewis, 188, 199;
Louisa J., 027; Lucy, 060; Martha
M., 056; Martha P., 045; Martha,
345; Mary Ann, 005; Mary M., 056;
Mary, 042; Matthew P., 448; Mattie
Lou, 013; Mollie P., 015; P. H.,
453; Pearl, 054; R. J., 033; Rhoda
A., 003; Rhoda, 058; Robert M.,
033; S. P., 346, 355; Sampson,
200, 255, 256; Samuel, 200, 233,
315, 317; Shepherd G., 428;
LANE: T.B., 453; T. Ben, 453; T.J.,
356; Thomas J., 180; Thomas P.,
292; Victoria A., 040; W.A., 453;
W. B., 201; W. R., 200, 415, 453;
Walter, 453; William A., 188, 199,
259; William D. 033, 065, 074,
200, 356, 442; William G. 155,
255, 307; William L., 033, 453;
William P., 358
LANEAR: James, 182
LANFORD: Jesse, 187; William, 187
LANG: John, 184, 200, 288, 428,
431; John, Jr. 428; John, Sr.,
256, 436; Robert, 256, 428
LANGDON: Aman W., 283; Amos W.,
192; Amos, 260
LANGSTON: Anson W., 218, 259
LANGHAM: Elias G., 203; Elias, 200;
James, 200; William, 428
LANGLEY: Osey, 429
LANGSTON: Annie Laura, 429; D. M.,
033, 200, 209, 282, 356, 369, 394,
453, 464; David M., 074, 112, 134,
156, 200, 209, 235, 244, 291, 323,
335, 356, 367, 374, 429, 453, 464;
465; Henry, 398; I. M., 356, 363;
Isaac L., 074; Isaac M., 033;
Isaac W., 296; Isaac, 452;
200, 207, 264, 265, 291, 317, 356,
453; J. E., 291; James, 033;
LANGSTON: James, 200, 467; Jefferson
F., 074; John E. 065, 074, 095,
152, 161, 200, 217, 228, 235, 259,
284, 290, 302, 303, 319, 320, 356,
374; John G., 285, 286; John S.,
356, 363; John, 200, 228, 311;
Matilda, 442; Mattie L., 025; Q.
M., 356; T.W.P., 442; Thomas W.P.,
033; Thomas, 200; Warren A., 033;
Warren, 200
LANIER: Clement, 427, 429; Frances
(Boyd) 200; James, 110, 200, 256,
273, 317; John, 199, 200; Lewis,
125, 236, 245; Nathan S., 200,
290; Nathan, 129, 178; William, 074
LANKEY: John I., 210, 305
LANNIN: S. L. Mrs., 159
LANOS: Charles, 212
LAPD: Adam, 200; Lodowick, 429
LARKIN: James, 280
LARRENCE: William, 321
LASENBY: John, 091
LASETTER: Elisha, 074
LASH: Israel G., 104; Thomas, 104
LASITER: Benjamin, 200; Hardy, 208,
427; W. M., 377
LASON: J. R. 398
LASSETER: John, 294
LASSETTER: V. T. 033
LASSITER: Benjamin, 424, 429; Brown,
448; Elisha (heirs of), 429;
Hardy, 155, 256, 429; Jacob, 200,
252, 429; John, 429, 433; R. M.,
332, 376

LASSITTER: John, 318
LATSON: Robert, 448
LAUGHRIDGE: Jacob, 094, 126, 245
LAURENCE: George, 254; James
033; Jeff, 033; Lemuel O., 201;
Robert, 033; S. C., 268; Steward,
415; Susie E., 011; William, 460
LAURENS: Peter, 158
LAVENDER: David M., 033
LAW: Elijah, 131, 269; John, 436;
John, Jr., 273; Thomas, 398
LAWRENCE: A.T. 453; Abraham, 201;
Allen T., 453; Allen, 135, 251;
Allen, Sr., 208; Anthony, 033,
399; Ben, 033, 399; Bennet, 240;
Bennie, 033; Charles, 033; Clayton,
323; Creasy, 019; Francis C., 033;
Frank, 033, 201, 399; George W.,
200, 267, 429; George, 201; H. C.,
453; H. P., 453; Harvey P., 033;
J. L., 453; J.A.C.S. 033; James,
074, 201, 238, 318, 356; Jeff,
445; John A. C. S., 353; John J.,
168; John T., 154, 238, 287, 316;
LAWRENCE: John, 356; Lee, 399; Lemuel
L., 395; Lemuel O., 176, 199, 201,
265, 318, 373, 464; Leroy, 065,
074, 087, 135, 201, 226, 251, 293,
318, 356, 448; Malachi, 254, 429;
Mary, 028; Mattie M., 201; Mattie,
059; Nancy, 201, 415; Overton, 033;
Richard, 238, 287; Robert, 033; S.
C., 201, 286, 333, 340, 356, 357,
376, 378, 394, 395, 406, 453; S.
L., 453; S. R. 351; Seab, 180;
Seaborn, 033, 074, 201, 240, 277,
286, 356, 362, 376, 415, 458;
LAWRENCE: Stephen C., 201, 332;
Stephen, 117; Stewart, 201, 356;
Susan, 037; Thomas J., 200;
Thomas, 168, 429; W. H., 336;
William R., 458; William, 065,
135, 182, 201, 220, 234, 251, 336,
401; William, Jr., 074; William,
Sr., 074
LAWS: Alexander, 201; Isham, 201;
James M., 222; John, 399; Joseph,
201; Martin, 074; Spencer, 201;
Stephen, 201; Thomas, 201
LAWSON: Arthur, 201, 202, 218, 318;
David, 074, 202; F. M., 329;
Francis, 202, 207; Irvine, 194,
202, 421, 429; Irvin, 430; Ivey,
033; James, 149; John H., 226;
Jonas, Sr., 149; Mary, 074;
Matilda, 202; Munford, 230; Reuben,
086, 202, 399; Reubin, 116; Robert,
218; Sarah A., 074; Sarah Jane,
050; Sarah W., 002; Thomas J., 033,
464; Thomas R., 202; William, 074;
Wm. L., 442
LAWYER: Rube, 442
LAY: Andrew, 399; L. A., 034
LAYFIELD: J. M., 453; James M., 034
LAYLESS: James, 182, 260
LAYSON: Ann N., 202; B. T. 356;
Berry, 202; C. C., 202, 329, 356,
458; C. C. Sr., 202; C. C.,
Sr., 074, 356, 399; Eliza, 399;
J. N., 202, 356, 399; Lum, 399;
William A., 034
LAYTON: Benjamin, 202
LAZENBY: Bob, 202; Dan, 202; Dinah,
037; Ellender, 074; J. G., 114;
202, 346, 442, 458; Jeff, 453;
Jefferson G., 343; Jefferson, 202,
453; John, 074, 202; M. A., 458;
M. E. 458; Martha E., 202; Mary
A., 065; Michael, 034; Paten, 202;
R. G., 453; S. E., 344; Sarah E.,
202; William, 074, 202, 458
LEA: Temple, 464
LEACH: Hiram, 034, 356; J. R., 034,
356; J.W., 356, 398, 399; John W.,
034, 444; Mollie, 202
LEAK: Robert, 108, 115, 149;
Samuel, 429
LEAKE: Robert, 202
LEATH: Emma, 399; Jennie, 004;
Jesse, 034; John, 034, 356,
399; Jordan, 034
LEATHY: Allen, 034
LEDBETTER: Banks, 096, 202; Henry,
074; Joseph, 130; Lucy A., 047;
William, 149
LEE: Adam, 034, 188, 202, 259, 275;
Allen, 034; Annie, 050; Berry, 034;
Bryan, 246; Donald, 356; Edward,
125; George, 285; Green, 285; Henry
H., 188; Ida, 059; Jesse, 034; John,
202, 318; Johnson P., 257; Kate W.,
017; Levi, 221; Lula, 054; Manie,
013; Nathan P., 144; Nathan R.,
399; Oliver H., 306; W. B., 390,
399, 405, 446; William S., 379;
William, 074, 114, 117, 140, 143,
146, 153, 169, 172, 202, 206, 217,
245, 270, 272, 292, 294, 304, 429
LEFFMAN: Lee, 202
LEGGETT: C. R., 074
LEGGON: John Henry, 399
LEITH: Richard, 034

LEMAN: William W., 220
LEMMONDS: Joseph, 086
LEMON: Abraham, 318
LEMONS: Joseph, 086
LENARD: C. V., 331
LEOKOUICZ: I, 122
LEONARD: Reubin, 034; William
H., 202
LEPPER: John, 173
LEROY: Lawrence, 458
LESLIE: Thomas, 090
LESTER: Augusta A., 463; F.M., 328,
329, 335, 337, 339, 344, 350, 368,
372, 377, 381, 392; J. S., 332;
M. F., 351
LESTIN: Levi, 268
LETSON: Cynthia, 009; George A. D.,
034, 453; Henry, 390; John, 453;
Mary H., 058; Ollie, 025; Robert
F., 034; Robert, 074, 202, 356,
415, 453, 458; S. K., 043;
Susan, 038
LETT: Hugh, 444
LEVEN: Edgar Lee, 034
LEVERET: John, 202
LEVERETT: ?, 442; A.J., 453; Addie,
048; Alice, 009; Andrew J., 034;
Anna E., 048; B.F., 360, 453; B.,
356, 453; Bedford F., 105; Bee,
034, 202; Berrel, 442; Burrel,
202; Caroline, 356; Catharine, 033;
Celia Ann, 233; Charles P., 202;
D. D., 453; D. F., 034; David D.,
356; David, 356; E.T., 446, 453;
Edward A., 202; Edward, 203; Eli,
453; Eme[iza, 056; Emma, 039;
LEVERETT: Francis A., 158, 162;
Francis, 269; Frank, 328, 329,
331, 332, 334, 340, 344, 350, 355,
356, 362, 366, 376, 379-381;
Harriet B., 051; Henry, 202; J.H.,
202, 453; Jack, 202, 453; James
H., 034; James, 202, 203, 356;
Jane, 269; Jeremiah, 202, 356;
074, 202; John, 202; Lemna S.,
004; Lizzie, 005; Mancefield, 356;
Martha C., 034; Martha Caroline,
065; Martha J., 059; Mary E., 013;
LEVERETT: Mary I., 033; Mary Kate,
017; Mary M., 030; N. H., 203,
453; Nancy Jane, 203; Nathan H.,
167, 453; O. Duell, 446; Ophelia,
013; Reid, 034, 445; Robert
(heirs of), 429; Sarah, 013; Susie
L., 012; Telitha Clementine, 057;
Thomas G., 034; Thomas J., 356;
Thomas M., 337; Thomas, 203;
Victoria V., 044; W.C., 202, 242,
332, 444; William C., 074, 147,
193, 203, 267, 356, 360, 380,
431, 432, 435, 453; William, 034,
399; Wm. C., 461
LEVERETTE: B. F., 203; E. T., 034;
Francis, 372; James Henry, 443;
Jane, 372; Jesse, 356, 442; N. H.,
203, 356; Nathan, 203; Sallie A.,
044; W.C. Jordan, 203; W.C. 203,
369, 405; William C., 192, 203,
234, 282
LEVERIT: William, 259
LEVERITT: Burrel, 203; T. S., 442
LEVERPETT: Ambros, 203; David, 203;
Em W. Mrs., 203
LEVERPITT: Burrell, 180
LEVINGSTON: Ludwick H., 104
LEVY: Asher, 091, 332, 339, 352,
446; Fisher, 373; Lewis, 203;
S, 342
LEWIS: Adaline, 006; Allice, 016;
Andrew F., 336; Anthony, 195, 282;
Ben, 399; Cara F., 040; Charles S.,
283; Charles, 196; Christian, 192;
Clifford, 343; Cora Lee, 014; E.
F., 034; Emma, 028; Exum, 429;
Felix, 108, 167; George, 034, 108,
203, 387, 399, 444, 461; Grev(?),
444; H.C., 453; H.G., 354; Hattle,
017; Henry C., 453; Henry, 356,
399; Hiram, 175; J.T., 453; J.W.,
203; James B., 074, 203, 232, 245;
LEWIS: James L., 329; James T., 034,
134, 156, 203, 333, 341, 356, 384,
409, 442, 453; James, 158; John,
203, 445; Josiah G., 434; Lessie,
041; Lon, 203; Martha, Mrs., 003;
Mary Ann,074; Mary Frances, 008;
Mattle, 043, 061; Ned, 034; P. A.,
460; Pearce A., 191, 460; Phillip,
203; Phillip, 034, 074, 356, 399,
415; R.W., 034; Rena, 038; Robert
A., 290; Sallie, 203; Sally, 343;
Sarah, 028, 399; Sophia N. M. B.,
057; Taylor, 034; Thomas, 193, 318,
448; W.D., 453; W.W., 453; Walden,
132; William O., 453; William,
196, 314; Willis, 203
LEWY: L., 359; S., 334, 366;
Solomon, 363
LIGHTFOOT: William S., 285; William
T., 161; William, 200, 310, 319
LILLAPD: James W., 166
LIMBRICK: James, 034

LIN: Fergus C., 203; Rees H., 203,
296; Reese H., 203
LINCH: Henry, 356; John, 182;
Jones, 203; Lewis, 171, 298;
P. T., 442
LINDSAY: John L., 323; Parham, 164,
303; Will, 203
LINDSEY: Cornellus, 399; David,
034; E. J., 331; Emanuel, 034, 203;
Frank, 034, 356; Jacob, 231; James
H., 203; John A., 204; John L.,
074; John W., 152; John, 146, 147,
203, 204, 442, 448; John, Sr. 204;
L. F., 442, 453; Lemuel W., 204;
Lemuel, 448; Lewis F., 448, 453;
Lewis, 204; Lula, 007; S.A., Mrs.,
204, 356; Sallie 051; Samuel,
074, 429; Sarah A.(Jeffries), 204;
Sarah, 204; Thomas, 034;
Will, 034, 357
LINN: Lula, 015
LINSEY: Milly, 032; Piram, 303
LINZIE: E. J., 357
LINZIE: Will; 399
LITRON: G. A. D., 442
LITTLE: Dan, 399; Emma, 060; John,
204; Joseph C, 105, 403, 411;
Reuben, 034; Sid, Jr., 034;
Sidney, 034, 204; Sydney, 204;
William, 118, 155, 204; Willie,
240; Willis, 162, 237, 407
LITTLEJOHN: James, 423; Thomas,
074, 204, 318
LIVINGSTON: A., 401
LLOYD: Daniel M., 204, 276; Daniel,
160; Edmond, 204, 318, 426; Edmund,
074, 179, 204, 208, 294; Emily,
233; G. P., 453; John T., 257; P.
G., 453; W. D., 034; W. H., 372;
William H., 392
LOCHRANE: Osburn S., 313
LOCKE: James, 230, 429
LOCKET: Abner, 283; BenJamin, 204
LOCKETT: BenJamin, 204, 429; Cullen,
214, 429; Henry, 235; Reuben, 170;
Solomon, 235; Winfrey, 218, 248
LOCKHART: Joel, 117
LOCKWOOD: James, 074; T. F., 444;
William, 204, 429
LOFTEN: Ann, 014
LOFTIN: E. M., 082; Nettie, 040;
Riley, 204; W. A., 143, 357
LOFTON: Antoinette, 092; Eva, 049;
John, 209; Sarah, 031; William
A., 034, 162, 198, 204; William
H., 204
LOGAN: James, 170; John, 137, 181,
248; Riley, 399
LONG: Alexander, 204; Coulbron, 204;
D. T., 204; David, 204, 256, 453;
Elizabeth, 204; George, 065, 074,
311, 448; H. H., 204; J. C., 399;
J.W., 399; James, 034, 105, 139;
Jesse L., 194; John J., 034; John,
453; L.A., 011; L.B., 204, 399;
Lizzie, 043; Thomas, 357; Tom,
357; Tommie, 034; William E., 453
LONGSTREET: Augustus B., 119, 179;
208; Gilbert, 159, 160, 172, 207,
213, 229, 256, 271, 275, 287, 298;
William, 213
LONGWORTH: Joseph, 245
LOOSER: John C., 204
LORD: Daniel, 199, 169, 185, 199;
Elizabeth, 215; Lodowick, 214;
Rufus, 188; Thomas, 315
LORDAN? Sally, 333
LOSSER: John Conrad, 444
LOSSON: Eliza Ann, 058
LOTT: Elizabeth, 151; Sanders, 151;
Susan, 151; William, 151
LOUGHRIDGE: Jacob, 204
LOUIS: Henry, 399
LOURY: William W. J., 159
LOVALL: Jesse, 204
LOVE: Catharine, 040; Ed, 204;
Jackson, 204; James, 204;
John, 034, 204, 305, 399
LOVEJOY: Addie E., 059; C.B., 204,
357, 399, 406; Coleman B., 034;
Colman B., 074; Colman, 399;
Crawford, 204, 205; Edward, 074,
205, 214, 452, 453; Elizabeth, 074,
205; Emily, 013; F.A., 357; Fannie
E., 406; Fannie, 357, 399; Hampton,
205; J.D., 357, 399, 400, 453, 464;
John D., 074, 156, 205, 318, 443,
347, 353, 357, 377, 399, 415, 453;
LOVEJOY: John, 205, 453, 399; Mary
E., 040; Nora, 399; P.P., 156,
182, 196, 205, 209, 214, 348, 357;
Pleasant P., 074, 205, 219, 220,
254, 311, 343, 377; Pleasant T.,
097; Pleasant, 318; S. A., 204,
205, 357, 392, 399, 407, 409;
Samuel, 102, 166, 205, 222, 257,
314, 318, 426, 429; Sarah, 047;
357, 444; Sidney A., 357, 399
453; Sidney, 406; Simeon L., 123;
LOVEJOY: Simon, 301; W. C., 232;
Welcom C., 109, 205, 318, 464;
Welcome C., 232, 240, 322, 323;

William C., 205, 264; William H.,
205; William, 205, 252, 316,
399, 429
LOVELL: John, 325
LOW: Alexander, 103; Andrew, 092,
095, 103, 117, 126, 163; Edmond,
399; Elizabeth, 175; George, 246;
John H., 226; John, 095; Robert,
092; Tom, 205
LOWE: Andrew, 184; B. T., 376, 467;
BenJamin T., 099; Daniel, 422;
Druclla, 044; John B., 429; John
H., 164; John, 429; Thomas, 285
LOWELL: Richard, 156
LOWERY: Adeline N., 026; Ann, 074;
Charles, 129; Elisha, 205; James,
347; Kirby D., 074; R. J., 398;
W. M., 398; William W. J., 159
LOWRY: Ann, 065; Elizabeth, 065,
074, 205; Kirby D., 205; William
W. J., 205
LOWTHER: Elizabeth (Billingslea),
218; Samuel, 218, 287
LOYAL: Jesse, 098, 304
LOYALL: Ann, 134; Jess, 242; Jesse,
074, 087, 120, 132, 149, 152, 168,
174, 184, 191, 201, 205, 207, 217,
234, 238, 240, 241, 249, 252, 264,
269, 285, 301, 304, 311, 312, 315,
316, 321, 322, 324, 385, 390-392,
394, 396, 404; R.L., 466; Richard
J., 095, 096, 105, 161, 205, 259,
286, 302, 310, 311, 318-320, 324;
Richard, 171, 179, 199, 213, 279;
William, 205
LOYD: Ada, 009; E. L., 453; Edmond,
154; Edmund, 175, 205; Francis,
442; G. P., 034, 331, 446, 453;
461; G. W., 453; George P., 453;
J. M., 453; James I., 034; James
M., 034; John D., 034; John T.,
104; John, 034, 236; Lewis, 034;
Lucy M., 039; M.A., 357; Mary O.,
057; Nancy, 205; P. A., 453; Peggy,
040; Pleasant B., 034; R.L., 453;
LOYD: R.W., 205; Richard J., 185,
458; Richard Jay, 205; Richard S.,
429; Richard T., 205; Robert, 453;
Thomas, 205, 211, 236, 318, 429,
459; Thomas, Jr., 034, 205; W. S.,
Sr., 205; W. S., 453; Washington,
422; William A., 453; William P.,
206; William, 379
LUCAS: Duffy, 399; John, 074, 091,
092, 109, 114, 115, 117, 121, 140,
143, 146, 150, 153, 154, 164, 169,
172, 175, 206, 217, 245, 270, 272,
278, 287, 289, 292, 294, 298, 303,
304, 312, 466; John, Jr., 124;
Mary Frances, 008; Mary, 004;
Walter, 289
LUCKETT: George H., 316; Maria, 206;
Thomas H., 206
LUCKEY: James, 321
LUCKIE: Champion T., 129; Hezekiah,
129; John (heirs of), 433; John,
102; Phoebe, 042; William D.,
229, 296; William F., 074
LUCUS: James, 110
LUKE: Thomas M., 034
LUKER: Joseph, 127; Polly, 023
LUMMUS: Cornelius, 324;
William M., 035
LUMPKIN: Dickerson, 429, 436;
Dickinson, 206; Drusilla, 123;
Frances, 026; George, 206;
Harrison, 119, 206, 429; James,
303, 325; John, 074; Judge, 035;
Lucy, 011; Mary, 074; Robert, 206,
399; Robert, Jr., 206; W., 206;
Walter, 206
LUMSDEN: C. A., 453; Charles T.,
035; Jeremiah C., 269; Jeremiah,
074, 200, 293, 429; Jeremiah, Jr.,
429; Jeremiah, Sr., 429; John G.,
096, 115, 233; John, 179, 356,
429, 434; Laney, 058; Mary M., 056
LUNCEFOPD: John W., 453
LUNDY: Joshua, 307; Thomas, 283
LUNSFORD: Ally B., 453; Harris, 129;
J.P., 398; J.M., 453; J. R., 035;
J. W., 035; Leonard L., 074;
Leonard, 065, 206; Nancy, 013
LUSK: Sylvester G., 096
LUSON: Marcus L. D., 180
LUSTER: F. M., 331, 380
LUTHER: David W., 211
LYLE: James G., 175; Noah, 206
LYNCH: Alberta, 013; Ben, 035,
357; Benjamin, 035; Charles C.,
035; Charles, 357; D. F., 206;
Dealy, 039; Elizabeth, 206;
Ephraim, 240; Fleetwood, 035, 453;
Genus, 357; Greif, 206, 453; Gried,
035; Grief, 162, 206, 318;
381, 399, 448; Grief, Sr., 359;
Henry, 357; James N., 206; James,
035; Jarratt, 074; Jarrett, 035,
265, 300; John, 035, 206, 318;
LYNCH: Josie, 206; Lemma, 006; Lewis,
155, 212, 345, 351; Lizzie, 053;
Maggie, 018; Margarett, 009;

Martha E. 027; Melle, 357; Monroe,
035; Nelile, 035; Philip, 035;
Phillip, 035; Pleasant T., 035;
Sackville, 206, 223, 318; Sacville,
210; Seab, 357; Thomas, 097, 206;
399; W.H., 453; Wilkins, 203;
William H., 035; William, 453
LYNES: Edward, 243
LYNN: Asa, 206; David, 087, 099,
179, 206, 318; William, 094,
206, 448
LYON: Harford, 194; James M., 206;
John, 074; Josiah M., 101; Nathan,
278; Rufus M., 035; Thomas, 092
LYTTE(?): Thomas, 206
M?: Harriet, 011
MABEE: George J. W., 251
MABRAY: Polley, 056; Rezin, 035
MABRY:
Daniel, 206; Elizabeth, 024;
Lizzie, 061; Louiza, 206; Parham
P., 101, 115, 135, 179; 181, 206,
223, 461; Reason E., 102, 196;
Reazen E., 123; Rezin E., 301;
Thornton, 206
MACARTHY: David, 162
MACARTHY: C. E., 357
MACDONALD: Hugh, 166, 206, 207
MACEY: William, 317, 321
MACHEN: E. C. 207
MACMAHAN: William, 399
MACK: Carrie, 057; Golan, 357;
Will, 357
MACKEY: Alexander, 139
MACKIE: Thomas, 320
MACMURPHY: W.G., 267; William C., 335
MACON: Edwin H., 106; Martha
Williamson, 065; Nathaniel G., 074
MACY: Henry M., 209, 358
MADDEN: David, 207; Toliver, 207
MADDERA: Henry, 280
MADDERS: Henry, 259
MADDOX: Abraham B., 332; Annis, 399;
Billie, 207; Charley, 035; Ellen,
357; Green, 035; Harriett, 060; J.
C., 399; James Henry, 035; John,
035, 207, 230, 266, 332, 400;
Joseph, 035; Maria, 047; Minnie,
399; N. C., 399; N. R., 399;
Richard D., 233; Samuel, 108;
Theresa, 197; Tillman, 035; Troy,
207; W. D., 190; Wash. Jr., 207;
Washington, 415; Will, 207;
William D., 170, 233; Willie, 014
MADDUS: James L., 311; John, 323
MADDUX: A.B., 453; Abe, 035; Abram,
035, 453; Ambrose, 035; Annie, 357;
Arter, 357; Arthur, 035; Barney
F., 035; Benjamin W., 207; Billie,
035; Callie, 038; Catharine A.,
027; Cora, 060; Dennis, 035;
E. H., 453; E.M., 357, 400, 464; Eady,
010; Ellen, 033, 207; Emery M.,
335; Emma, 060; Emocy, 453; Green,
400; J. Kate 020; J. C., 453;
MADDUX: J.D., 135; J.L., 240, 453;
James L., 100, 119, 130, 148, 154,
157, 199, 200, 236, 243, 250, 268,
274, 286, 295, 335, 354, 357, 367,
373, 391, 409, 453; James S., 366,
388, 433; Joe, 409; John C., 035,
065, 090, 136, 148, 200, 220, 235,
280, 303, 316, 322, 453; John,
035, 065, 074, 239, 319; Leonard,
183; Maggie, 017; Margarett A.,
041; Martha, 207; Minnie, 060;
MADDUX: Notley, 436; Phil, 357; S.
H., 442, 453; Sawney, 035; Simeon
D., 210; Sol, 400; Tex, 046; Troy,
357; W. D., 135, 339; W. G., 398;
Wash, 357; Washington, 035, 207;
Whitfield, 454; William D., 065,
074, 091, 103, 104, 154, 207, 220,
233, 240, 261, 303, 305, 322, 323,
335, 448; William T., 200;
William, 035, 400; Wm. D., 461;
Wm., 442; Zachariah, 183
MADOCKS: Richards, 277
MADOUX: John C., 406
MAGAVIRK: James, 219
MAGBY: Hiram, 035
MAGRUDER: William, 223
MAHON: John Henry, 035; Susan, D61
MAHONE: Boling, 207
MAHONEY: Dennis, 242; William, 242
MALAY: James, 074
MALDEN: Henry, 207
MALDINI: Benjamin F., 139
MALEAR: Lucien W., 434; Matilda, 092
MALLARY: E. Y., 332; F. L., 332
MALLET: W. M., 380
MALLETT: Jesse, 429; Joseph, 427
MALLORY: John H., 158
MALONE: A. B., 454; A. L., 365, 454;
A. M., 357, 400, 454, 464; Allen
M., 035; Amos, 035, 357, 400;
Anna B., 065, 358; Anna, 025;
Annie B., 074; Annie Kate, 050;
Augustus, 357; Berta, 042; Bessie,
044, 207; Biddle S., 037; Biddy,
190; Bill, 400; C.O., 454; C. R.,
357; C. W., 454; Cade, 035, 207,
400, 406; Cader, 074, 207, 250,
448; Charity, 006; Charles R.,
035; Charles, 035, 357; Charley,
400; Clarence O., 035, 454;
MALONE: Clarence, 207; Cora L., 009;
Cornelia, 023; Dee, 400; Dora, 050;
E. B., 207, 335, 355, 400, 408,
421, 454, 464; E.T., 454; Edward
D., 260, 272; Effie Liela, 011;
Eli T., 035; Eli, 207, 454;
Elizabeth(Hay), 260, 272; Elizabeth
C.A., 014; Elle J., 030; Emaline,
049; Emma Kate, 054; Eugene B.,
035; Eula, 032; F., 035, 454; F.,
454; Felix, 207; Floyd B., 415;
MALONE: Floyd, 035, 074, 207, 250;
454, 458; Francis, 074, 207, 250;
Frank, 035, 207, 226, 415, 454;
Frank, Sr., 074; Franklin, 190,
207, 317, 357, 358, 442, 454, 461,
George, 035, 207, 208, 318, 358,
380, 400; Gilbert, 207, 210; Gus,
358; H. E., 035; Hannah, 046;
Harriet E., 190; Henry, 035, 102,
207; India, 022; Isaac, 334; Isham
P., 035; Isham A., 454; J. B., 207,
400, 454; J. F., 463-465; J. H.,
465; J. P., 281, 329, 446, 454;
MALONE: J. R., 358, 465; J. S., 035,
454, 463, 465, 468; James D., 178,
208, 232, 400; James, 135, 207,
208; Jarrel, 074, 208, 415;
Jarrell, 208, 314; Jarrett (heirs),
459; Jarrett, 074, 135, 208;
Jeptha, 074; Jesse, 006, 208; Jim,
358; Jimmie Lee, 400; Jinnie K.,
002; Joe, 465; John B, 036, 454;
John F., 465; John, 036, 250, 400;
Jordan, 036, 358; Josiah P., 036;
MALONE: Kittie, 041; L.A., 454; L.B.,
465; Lizzie, 006, 022; Louisa, 004;
Lucinda, 020; Lush, 208; Mariah,
018; Martha V., 045; Mary Lucy,
074; Mat, 400; Matt, 208, 400;
Mattie Lou, 195; Mattie, 049, 358,
388, 399; Nancy, 208, 232, 400,
458; Obe, 358; P. C., 358, 454;
P. W., 454; Pearla V., 035; Percy
W., 443; Persey W.,036; Pete, 400;
MALONE: Peter, 036; R.A., 143, 454;
453; R. W., 281; Reubert, 154, 264,
272; S. B., 358, 415, 442, 454;
S.F. 454; S.H., 358, 454, 513;
454; Sallie, 025; Sarah, 006, 036,
358; Sheroa, 358; Sherod, 074,
118, 208; Sherrod, 207, 208, 429;
Sidney, 036, 267, 400; Stephen
F., 036; Stephen, 208; Steth, 190;
Steve, 454; Stith B., 142, 208,
358, 454; T. J., 454; T. S. 357, 400,
444, 454; Thomas L., 358; Thomas
S., 036, 208, 358, 454; Thomas
Jr., 358; Thomas, 036, 207,
208, 358, 370, 400, 454; Vallie
D., 042; W. B., 074, 444, 454;
MALONE: W. F. 400, 454,465; W. H.,
203, 208, 355, 358, 454; W. W.,
454; Walker B, 036, 208; Wash, 036;
West, 208; Wills, 400; Will, 208,
385, 400, 465; William P., 036;
William H., 442, 454; William, 074,
207, 208, 226, 334, 358, 369, 400,
415, 454; Willie B, 400; Willie
E., 060; Willie, 026, 465; Willis,
036, 415; Zipporah, 050
MALPASS: John, 123, 127, 132, 137,
154, 161, 208, 264, 314, 393, 429
MALPRIS: John, 272
MALSLY: M. F., 395, 407
MALTBY: Oliver E. 407
MANAGE: Lucinda, 025
MANELL: Buster, 400; Davis, 400;
Ed, 400
MANES: Mary, 046
MANGHAM: John G., 086; Thomas,
149, 208, 209
MANING: Ada, 036; Bert, 036; Mary
Lou, 013; Simeon, 036; William, 036
MANINGS: Siman, 036
MANINGS: Simon, 036
MANLEY: John L., 388
MANN: A. V., 036, 464; Americus V.,
209, 291, 318, 379; Claiborne S.,
036; John, 209, 223; Polly, 209;
Zifford, 243
MANNING: Aaron, 036; Berry, 036;
Billy, 036; Dick, 358; Dock, 036;
George, 400; Gus, 036; James, 114,
209; Jemes, 209; John, 176, 260,
263; Pink, 400; Richard, 036;
Rufus, 365; Silas, 358; Troy, 209;
Will, 209
MANNINGS: George, 036; James, 036;
John, 400
MANSFIELD: Lucas, 209; Lucias, 036;
Lucius, 14, 209, 217, 385
MANSON: James, 429
MANTZ: Philip M., 134
MANUEL: Dennis, 358; Ed, 036, 209;
Harriet, 050; Mack, 209; Walter, 209
MAPP: B. H., 358; Benjamin H., 036,

358; Jeremiah, 074, 209; John L.,
381; Julia, 358; William F., 104,
129, 166, 178, 388; William, 400
MARABLE: Erasmus, 121; Robert, 209;
Thomas C., 209
MARBERRY: James Newton, 036
MARCHMAN: John, 036; W. R., 469;
William R. 320, 321
MARCUS: Williamson Aquilla, 241
MARE: James, 233
MARKS: Amaringha P., 200; Arnold,
036; Billy, 036; Brack, 036; Brock,
177, 209, 388; C.H., 209; Charlie,
336; Clara, 026; Clarra, 209;
Dozier, 036, 209; E. H., 356;
Easter, 005, 054; Edenboro, 358,
400; Edenborough, 036, 358;
Edinbourough, 036; Elia, 031;
F. C., 180, 209, 358, 400, 454;
Fannie, 055; Fernando C., 209;
George, 209; Harvey, 400; Hastings,
217, 429; Henry, 036, 209; Horace,
036, 209, 358; I. H., 036, 358;
MARKS: J. H., 209, 409; J. J., 454;
James K., 074, 209; James, 036,
358; Jeff, 036; Jennie, 209; Jim,
B., 209; Job, 209; John H., 194,
209, 429; John T., 036, 209, 209;
John, 209; Lena, 010; Letha, 057;
Levi, 036; Lige, 036; Lucius, 036;
Mary Jane, 027; Mattie, 018; N.T.,
358; Nathan T., 200, 209; Nelson,
036; R. C., 180; Samuel J., 036;
MARKS: Sarah, 023, 028, 209; Scott,
036, 209; Sherman, 209; Susan Ann,
028; Susie, 050; Thomas, 100, 209,
276, 385; Tom, 036; W. A., 209;
Wade, 400; Wallace, 036, 209; Will,
036, 209; William M., 425;
William, 036, 323
MARLOWE: Elizabeth, 484
MARONEY: Benjamin, 180
MARROW: John, 300
MARSH: A., 454; Alfred, 454; Collins,
168; Hanah, 168; James W., 415;
John, 284; Joseph J., 403; Joseph,
209; Moses, 168; R. I., 036, 358,
454; Sarah L., 051; William, 209
MARSHALL: A.J., 454; Amos, 226, 288;
Andrew J., 036; Benjamin, 100,
154, 173, 178; Benjamin, 187, 209,
424; Charles, 120, 147, 266;
Daniel, 223; Edward W., 220; Hattie
H., 267; Henry J., 282; James F.,
230; James, 429; John R., 223;
John, 209; Stephen B., 124, 163;
William, 400, 465
MARTEN: L. F., 400
MARTIN: Allen, 131, 209, 234, 264,
316, 358; Amos, 108, 229; Ananias
D., 285; Angus, 166, 205; Bartin,
429; Ben, 358; Claburn, 422; Edy
(Steedman), 227; Edy, 256; Elijah,
209; F. P., 209; Felix B. 091,
112, 250; Felix, 093; Francis S.,
209, 399, 429; George W., 209; H.
M., 454; Henrietta, 009; Hugh M.,
074, 385, 442, 454; Isaac N. D.,
209, 226, 227, 256; J. B., 209;
359, 454; J.H., 384; James L., 210;
MARTIN: James S., 210; James, 108,
210; Jerry P., 036; John B., 400;
John F. 275, 400; John, 113, 204,
210, 223; John, 276; Joseph, 274;
R., 210; Joshua D., 253; Julia E.,
034; Levi, 183, 428; Lucy, 200;
Mahalah, 210; Martha, 210; Mary,
207; Moses, 142; Oliver H., 210;
P.K., 210, 465; Perk, 400; Robert
D., 288; Robert, 130; Roman, 400;
3.L., 359; S.L., Mrs., 090; Susan
E., 012; Thomas, 037, 210;
Toilefair, 296; Toliver, 210; W.
P., 104; William A., 210; William
W., 210, 429, 434; William, 200,
209, 291; Yearby, 210, 314, 318, 400
MARTON: Joel, 146
MARVIN: Aaron B., 164
MARYE: Robert V., 105, 172
MASCEY: William, 305
MASHBURN: Jefferson, 400; John H.,
037; Joseph, 465
MASON: A. M., 210; Alfred, 210;
Araminta, 234; Churchill, 130;
Dempsey, 037; Francis, 359; H.,
454; Henry Turner, 037; I.W., 465;
James, 037; Lottin, 359; Lotton,
210; Mary, 026; Retta, 035; Richard,
238; Thomas, 234; Turner, 037;
Wiley M., 249; William, 037,
158, 243
MASSEY: Enos, 065, 074; Nathan, 232,
261, 281, 301, 306; O. W., 274;
Orren W., 124; Orrin W., 311; Susan
L. C. (Ware), 281; Susan, 261
MASSINGALE: Daniel, 429
MASTERS: Robert, 400, 432
MASTERSON: C., 347; Wallace, 347
MATHEWS: Elizabeth, 013; George G.,
125; George, Jr., 162; James, 429;
Jefferson, 074; Jesse, 245, 268;
Moses, 218

MATHEWSON: J. C., 346
MATHIS: Davis, 037; E.T., 332, 352;
  Elisha, 197; Evan T., 351, 376; J.
  C., 400; James, 210; William H.,
  097, 103, 114, 144, 166, 170, 193,
  200, 203, 240, 241, 268, 269, 351;
  William R., 165; William, 102,
  194, 207, 237, 258, 262
MATON: Joe, 210
MATTHEWS: Charles L., 136; Edgar,
  037; Fannie, 011; James, 210;
  Jesse, 203, 216; Lear, 057; Moses,
  432; Rebecca, 248; W. F., 340
MATTHEWSON: J. P., 351
MATTHIS: John T., 037
MAULDIN: Henry, 321, 405
MAXCEY: Garland, 137, 261; Moses,
  210; Thomas, 210; Walter, 210;
  William, 129, 210; Yelverton, 210
MAXCY: Moses, 094; Randy, 359;
  Yelverton (Yerton), 210
MAXEY: Ada, 046; Adolphus, 037;
  Babe, 210; Boze, 153, 210; Della,
  044; Dock, 037; Emma, 061; Garland,
  074, 087, 108, 116, 173, 210, 245;
  Green, 359; Greene, 210; Hattie,
  011; Isham, 037, 359; James E.,
  210, 400; James, 037; Jim, 037;
  John, 134, 141, 210; Kage, 400;
  Kenan, 211; Kinion, 210; Lawson,
  Jr., 359; Lawson, Sr., 359; Lizzy,
  026; Lonnie, 400; Mabe, 037, 210,
  359; Mabron, 037; Mayburn, 211;
MAXEY: Millie, 445; Pink, 029;
  Pouncey, 151, 211, 244; Pouncy,
  259; Robert, 211; Sld, 037, 211;
  W. H., 359; W., 401; Will, 194,
  211; William, 065, 074, 095-099,
  105, 107, 108, 110, 111, 113, 114,
  116, 118, 125, 131-133, 135, 142,
  147, 148, 152, 161, 163, 167, 171,
  172, 175, 177, 180-183, 195, 197,
  205, 209-211, 213, 217, 224, 227,
  229, 231, 232, 236, 241, 242, 246,
  248, 249, 251, 259, 260, 280, 284,
  285, 289, 291-293, 298, 301-303,
  306, 310-319, 322, 323, 387, 395,
  398, 401, 429, 454; Yelverton,
  211, 318
MAXWELL: John, 143; Nathan, 211;
  William B., 211
MAY: Benjamin, 283; Charles F., 037;
  James, 211; Joseph, 107, 125;
  Rebecca, 013
MAYBERRY: Adam P., 074
MAYE: Jeremiah P., 094
MAYES: Samuel, 247
MAYFIELD: Lewis, 211
MAYNARD: W. T., 348; William, 400
MAYO: J. M., 359; John, 314;
  Menoah, 429; R. D., 454
MAYS: Abney, 074; Drury, 236; John
  W., 144; John, 167, 211, 282;
  Martha, 303; Moses I., 218; Moses
  J., 211; R. W., 409; Robert, 323;
  Rutherford, 120; Seaborn J., 179
MCACKENZIE: Alexander, 135
MCAFEE: Abraham, 169; Green (minor),
  092; Green, 092, 220, 256, 268,
  301, 430; Greene, 075, 164; Morian
  A. W., 442; Nancy G., 092; Robert,
  075, 092, 165, 170, 220, 230,
  268, 430
MCALISTER: Ellander, 236; James C.,
  246; John, 236
MCALLISTER: Charles, 275; Frances,
  010; Henry, 360; John, 102, 220;
  Margaret, 220
MCARTHUR: John, 220, 324
MCARTHY: Charles E., 220
MCBEAN: Daniel, 220; Henry L., 075;
  William, 214, 221, 423
MCBRIDE: Andrew, 220, 221; Harriett,
  458; Joseph, 146, 155, 323, 432
MCBRYDE: James, 107, 116, 126, 179,
  217; John, 107, 116, 126, 179,
  217; Andrew, 111
MCCAIN: Hugh, 221
MCCALISTER: Henry, 221
MCCALL: John H., 093, 172
MCCANE: Alexander, 319;
  William, 214, 221, 423
MCCAPT: C. M., 384, 454
MCCARTEN: Thomas, 154, 233
MCCARTER: John B., 221; John, 165
MCCARTHY: A., 357; Arthur, 360;
  C. E., 221, 251, 399, 401;
  Roger, 098
MCCAY: Benjamin, 216
MCCLELAND: A. P., 221, 360
MCCLELLAN: T. B., 360
MCCLELLAND: A.P., 360; David, 075;
  J.J., 350, 366; James J. M., 357;
  James J., 241; John, 454; Pearce,
  401; T. B., 454; Thomas, 454
MCCLENDON: Adam, 086; Allan, 110;
  Allen, 098, 108, 109, 112, 125,
  132, 148, 155, 166, 170, 178,
  184, 187, 186, 191, 202, 211,
  221, 234, 243, 245, 257, 269,
  277, 281, 282, 294, 301, 313, 315,
  317, 320, 323, 394, 437, 465; Amos,
  221, 222; Caroline, 227; Charlie,

  221; Ethelred, 075; Fill, 401;
  Frances, 221; Francis, 174, 221,
  227, 299, 437; Freeman, 104, 247;
  Isaac, 065, 075, 140, 148, 174,
  191, 209, 242, 293, 445; J.A.,082,
  360, 384, 401, 454; J. C., 454;
  MCCLENDON: J. H., 454; Jacob, 087,
  092, 221, 230, 237, 292, 319, 401,
  430, 465; James, 219, 221; Jeptha,
  221; Jesse, 221; Joel B., 454;
  Joel, 075, 221, 222, 227, 278, 313,
  321, 401, 404, 423, 430, 454; John,
  454; Jonathan (minor of), 221;
  Jonathan, 075; Joseph, 222; Judah,
  222, 423; Lola, 026; Moses J.,
  075; Nancy, 313; Nanie, 014; P.T.,
  401; Pheba E., 222; Rebecca, 132;
  S., 360; Stephen W., 065, 075,
  107, 110, 152, 397, 401; Stephen,
  123, 221, 222, 319; Susan, 227;
  Thomas, 222, 430; Washington, 075;
  Wiley, 075; Wiley, 313
MCCLOSKEY: John, 444
MCCLOUD: Daniel, 229; Donald, 117
MCCLURE: A. P., 454; Georgia Ann,
  038; H. C., 151, 214, 222, 227,
  266, 294, 328, 348, 351, 357, 358,
  364, 454; H, 454; Henry C., 345,
  346, 390; Henry, 365; India, 040;
  James, 146; James H., 430; James
  S., 145, 146; James, 095, 166, 291,
  465; Mattie E., 040; T. A., 360;
  Thomas A., 222; W. J., 222
MCCOLLISTER: Margaret, 268
MCCOLLOUGH: John, 435
MCCOLLUM: Ben, 401; Elias, 445;
  Mary, 144
MCCOMBS: R. A., 222; W. S., 114
MCCOMBS: Otis, 360; Robert A., 295
MCCOMMONS: John, 360
MCCOOK: Daniel, 208
MCCORD: H. Y., 328; James R., 094,
  145; Rebecca, 279; Robert, 279;
  William, 222
MCCORKLE: James E., 222, 423, 430,
  433; James, 465; William, 222,
  319, 436
MCCORMACK: James, 075
MCCORMICK: Edward, 222; John, 222
MCCOWEN: John W., 254
MCCOY: Daniel, 401; David, 117, 146,
  222, 227, 256, 420, 430; Davis,
  154; James, 397; Jonn, 118; Nealey,
  222; Neely, 430; Sarah, 016
MCCRARY: John, 098
MCCRAY: Charity, 224
MCCREE: William, 278
MCCROY: David, 272
MCCULLARS: Burwell, 134; Falthey,
  430; Nancy Ann, 051
MCCULLERS: Bradford, 222; Burwell,
  401; Culpepper, 282; Freeman, 222;
  Henry, 282
MCCULLOCH: John, 302
MCCULLOUGH: Bradford, 222; E. B.,
  454; Freeman, 261; Hugh, 165;
  John C., 247; John, 160, 205,
  222, 282, 356, 408, 454; Loyal, 226
MCCULLUGH: F. C., 462
MCCUNE: Jane, 222; Thomas B., 075,
  222; William, 222
MCCURDY: John S., 162; John, 233
MCDADE: J. J., 038, 222, 454
MCDANIEL: Adam, 038; Araminta J.,
  024; Benjamin F., 038; Daniel,
  223; Ednie, 027; George F., 075;
  George T., 110, 222; George, 222,
  401; Henry, 360; Jacob (Minors of),
  292; Jacob, 075, 222, 283; John
  B., 107; Martha A., 223; Martin R.,
  127; Nancy Ann, 223; Nancy, 223;
  Polly, 041; S. C., 380; Samuel,
  223, 283, 307; W.S., 223; W. T.,
  038; William T., 254
MCDAVID: John, 223
MCDONALD: A. G., 415; Alec G., 361;
  Alex, 038; Alla, 319; Alexander,
  087, 184, 223, 279, 296, 460;
  Daniel, 401; Henry, 361; Hugh, 166,
  253, 299, 468; Jacob, 469; James,
  132, 444; Jane, 016; Nancy Ann, 055;
  Sally, 032; Samuel, 469; Sarah A.,
  009; Thomas, 125, 222, 404; W. A.,
  223; William A. M., 448; William
  A., 075, 096, 222, 260, 319;
  William, 188, 256
MCDONNEL: Hugh, 223
MCDONNELL: Rachael, 401
MCDONOUGH: Sallie, 008
MCDOUGAL: Jonathan, 223, 296; Mary
  (Robinson), 289, 430; Samuel, 289
MCDOUGALL: Andrew, 124; Jonathan,
  207; Kendrick, 264; Thomas, 223
MCDOWELL: Ann, 010; Brady, 401;
  Charles, 223, 228, 260; Daniel,
  065, 075, 097, 123, 159, 178, 206,
  223, 240, 255, 318, 319, 324, 430,
  453, 454; George, 223; Hattie Kate,
  005; Isaac, 361; J. C., 223, 454;
  James M., 075, 223; Joel C., 098,

  212, 223, 305, 318, 333, 361, 401,
  454, 465; John M., 075, 223, 319,
  320; Levi, 223; Lucy, 026; M. A.,
  099, 223, 295, 342, 348, 353, 354,
  362, 366, 368, 408, 454, 467;
MCDOWELL: Mack, 361; Mamie J., 005;
  Margaret R., 223; Margarett A.,
  003; Martha C., 223; Mary Ann,
  075; Mary E., 042; Mary J., 408;
  Michael A., 075, 361, 366, 430;
  Michael, 332; Starling, 038; Susan
  C., 005; Thomas G., 458; Thomas,
  166, 236; Wallace, 361; William
  (heirs of), 431; William T., 223,
  311; William, 075, 123, 150, 223,
  238, 356, 430, 469; William, Jr.,223
MCELHANEY: G. W., 387; John M., 361;
  John, 454; R. V., 361; Samps, 361;
  V. H., 361
MCELHANY: John, 223
MCELHENEY: Barney F., 038; Edward,
  402; J. D., 361; John, 361; Judge,
  038; Sarah, 014
MCELHENNEY: Albert, 039; Alice, 026;
  Allen, 361; B. F., 442; Barney F.,
  082; Caroline, 029; Frances R.,
  024; C. W., 075, 223, 361; George
  W., 361; Georgia Ann, 053; Greene,
  039; H. C., 361; Hezekiah, 039; J.
  D., 384, 387, 390, 393, 407; J. M.,
  039; James W., 039; John H., 039;
  John M., 039, 463; John, 075, 223,
  442; Katie, 060; Lee M., 039; Lucy
  E., 060; M. T., 039; Mariah, 045;
  Martin, 039; Mary J., 056; Maud,
  013; Rebecca, 057; Robert V., 039;
  Sampson, 415; Vincent H., 039 075;
  William H., 039; William J., 039;
  William, 039
MCELHENNY: B. B., 454; B. E., 454;
  B. F., 454; B. T., 454; F. M., 454;
  G. W., 384, 388-390, 392-395, 397,
  399-408, 410, 411; George W., 039,
  454; Herbert, 454; J. H., 454;
  Jefferson, 454; Lula, 049; M. J.,
  454; M. T., 454; Martin J., 454;
  Martin, 454; Mary E., Mrs., 430;
  Robert V., 430; S.D., 454; V.H.,
  430, 454; Vincent H.(heirs), 430;
  W. G., 454; W.H., 454; W.O., 454
MCELHENY: J. D., 361
MCELLAND: J. D., 442
MCELMURRY: W. T., 458
MCELROY: Andrew, 202, 224; Henry,
  224; Isaac W., 224; Isaac, 224;
  James, 224; John J., 224
MCELVANY: J. J., 368
MCENCPOE: William, 075, 431
MCENTIRE: John, 154
MCEVOY: Robert P., 144
MCFALL: Fleming, 142, 224
MCFALLS: W. P., 224
MCGAHA: (?), 445
MCGAHEE: Benjamin, 075; Edward,
  075; Lucy F., 038; Ridley, 454;
  W. H., 039
MCGAR: William, 231
MCGAUGHEF: William R., 039
MCGAUGHEY: Benjamin F., 039; Benjamin,
  224; R. W., 454; Robert, 402; W.
  A., 454; William R., 224
MCGEE: Allie, 361; John, 224; Robert,
  224; T. W., 361, 454; William, 277
MCGEHEE: Abner, 141; Augustus, 278;
  Benjamin, 415; E. W., 378; Edward,
  200, 224, 291; Isaac, 165, 185,
  248, 271; Jacob, 224, 431; James
  W., 122; James, 189, 231, 255,
  278; John W., 224, 283, 421;
  Mahaley, 248; Robert, 216, 224;
  Thomas J., 248; Thomas, 114, 165,
  210, 218, 224, 232, 275, 299, 307;
  Thomas, Jr., 224; Thomas, Sr.,
  224; William V., 197, 296;
  William, 121
MCGHEE: Nannie, Mrs., 011; T. W.,
  039; Thomas, 218
MCGINNIS: (?), Fleming, 442
MCGINNIS: Emily, 035; Jarrett, 445;
  Thomas, 402; Tom, 361, 402;
  Will, 224
MCGINTY: Robert, 173
MCGLAUGHLIN: James, 065
MCGOUGH: Jane, 039; Robert, 230;
  W., 361
MCGOWEN: Robert, 139, 311
MCGREGOR: Alexander, 096
MCGRIGOR: Alexander, 210
MCGRUDER: Zadoc, 151
MCGUIRE: Amanda, 043; Jane, 043;
  Rich, 039; Robert, 361; Timothy, 125
MCGUIRK: John, Jr., 224;
  John, Sr., 224
MCHENRY: James, 117, 126, 163; John
  G., 228; John, 092; William S.,
  387, 388, 401, 404, 411, 454
MCHUTCHINS: John C., 359
MCINIS: A., 039
MCINTIRE: Charles, 189, 197, 198,
  213, 292; George, 178; Ralph, 178;
MCINTOSH: W.J., 454; William, 224, 319

MCINTYRE: J. W., 039
MCINVALE: James, 229
MCKAVITT: Henry, 444
MCKAVITTE: Henry, 163
MCKAY: George, 336; Henry R., 098
MCKEE: James P., 218; John F. M.,
  065; John, 168, 176; Lewis W.,
  075; Lewis, 118, 170, 224, 261,
  263, 277; Robert, 319
MCKEEN: Hugh, 224; P. 289
MCELROY: Andrew, 191; James, 224
MCKEMIE: James, 075, 109, 177, 224,
  229, 431, 463
MCKENZIE: John, 075, 092, 108, 125,
  166, 187, 204, 221, 234, 236, 268,
  310, 312, 319, 321, 324, 423;
  Kenneth, 126; William C., 319
MCKEY: George, 353; John C., 361;
  Lewis C., 146
MCKIBBEN: M. V., 333, 349, 385
MCKIGNEY: George, 431
MCKINLEY: Annie Lee, 402; Annie, 020;
  E.B., 224, 402, 454, 465; E.C., 039;
  Eli B., 039; 224; Francis C. 250;
  Lula V., 038; Lula, 075; M.M., 039,
  339; M., 361; Merchant M., 127;
  Miranda J., 011; Nannie L., 008;
  Rufus 402; W. T., 454; William
  039
MCKINLY: Elvada, 057; M. N., 373,
  407; W. P., 023
MCKINNE: John, 128, 142, 143, 164,
  183, 219, 220, 227, 256, 270, 284;
  Joseph P., 126; Joseph, 125
MCKINNEY: David, 125, 179; Eli, 283;
  Joseph Pope, 105
MCKINNIE: John, 187; John, 322
MCKISON: William O., 454
MCKISSACK: Archy, 143; Catherine,
  039; Duncan, 075; Dunkin, 224;
  Isaac C.W.T. 089, 189, 224, 284,
  293; Isaac, 039, 352, 361, 393,
  402, 415; Isabella, 048; John F.,
  224, 415; John, 075, 224, 293, 361,
  402; Julia, 004; Lucy, 143; Polly,
  060; Susan, 008; Thomas, 065, 075,
  224, 415, 443, 454; W. T., 358, 361;
  William T.,075, 224, 361, 377, 415;
  William, 361, 454
MCLANCKING: James, 224
MCKLEHANEY: George W., 338
MCKLEROY: Jacob, 448
MCKRAVIN: Adam, 097
MCKREE: William, 206, 225
MCLAMORE: Franklin, 225
MCLANE: John, 306
MCLAUGHLIN: James, 075, 225, 288,
  319, 444
MCLEA: John, 167, 204, 225, 233,
  263, 268, 319, 444
MCLEAN: Allen, 161, 225; Alsey, 226;
  John T., 351; John, 424
MCLEAR: Robert H., 225;
  Robert Hardwick, 233
MCLELLAN: William, 217
MCLELLAND: Elijah, 225
MCLEMORE: Catherine, 075; Charles,
  139, 148, 221, 225, 283, 319, 402;
  Clark, 217; Franklin, 225, 319;
  James, 137, 225, 319; John, 223;
  Katharine (heirs of), 431
MCLENDON: Amos, 225, 465; Francis
  M., 075; Francis, 225; Isaac, 434;
  James, 237, 422; Joel, 225; Stephen
  W., 190, 225, 287; Stephen, 087,
  225; W. J., 442
MCLEDDY: Donald, 107, 125; Norman, 240
MCLEROY: Andrew, 225; James, 075,
  144, 225, 246, 280, 319; Mary P.,
  225; Mary, 460; Nancy, 460; William
  H., 225; William T., 225, 340
MCMAHAN: William, 225
MCMANUS: Richard, 094
MCMATH: John H., 225; William,
  198, 196, 198
MCMELON: William, 442
MCMICHAEL: Addie L., 047; Alice C.,
  458; Alice, 027; Angie, 057; B.E.,
  454; B.H., 225; B.J., 225, 361;
  Bedford, 454; Betsey (Carter), 117;
  Brown, 225; Burton J., 146, 225,
  245, 361, 458; C. C., 361; C. G.,
  454; C.J.(?), 226; C.O., 454; C.W.,
  099, 225, 427; Caroline S., 032,
  458; Caroline, 458; Carrie, 028,
  041; Catharine, 225, 343, 402;
  Charles, 120, 225, 321, 426, 427,
  429; Charlie, 039; Clark W., 226,
  212, 458; Clementina L., 004;
  Clementine N., 458;
  Cleminy, 013; Clemmie L., 034; D.,
  226; David, 075, 226, 227, 319;
  Delphie, 026; E.H.S., 226; E., 444;
  Earnest, 403, 454; Ed. 039; Edmund
  (?) J., 469; Elijah H.L., 065, 075;
  Elijah, 075, 105, 226, 227, 244,
  431; Eliza A., 118; Elizabeth, 096,
  114, 227, 305; Ella, 361; Emily P.,
  227, 458; Emmit, 039; Fish, 158;
  G., 226, 454; George Ann, 361;
MCMICHAEL: George, 226; Gittie, 054;
  Green L. (children of), 361; Green
  L., 039, 226, 257, 320, 361, 362,
  465; Green, 186, 226, 244, 411,
  454, 458; Greene L., 075, 226;
  Griffin, 039, 361; J. F., 454; J.
  G., 454; J. H., 039; J. M., 361,
  454; J. S., 361; James M., 333,
  361; James S., 391; James, 075,
  226, 423; Jas. S., 465; Jeanette,
  361; Jennie, 048; Joe, 039; John
  B., 226; John G., 039; John L., 039,
  075, 180, 207, 226, 227, 232, 245,
  324, 361, 458; John Lee, 039, 226,
  245, 404; John S, 226, 251, 265;
  John, Jr., 226; John, 226; John,
  Sr., 226; Joseph, 117, 118, 226; L.
  Lily, 362; Lizzie, 039; Lucy, 443;
  Margaret (Peggy), 226; Mary A.,
  458; Mary Elizabeth, 011; Mathew,
  227; Merina, 227; Mollie, 034;
MCMICHAEL: Monroe, 454; N.A., 227;
  N.D., 227; 362; Nancy(Hinsey), 227;
  Nancy D., 362; Nancy (Penn), 227; P. B.,
  227, 362, 454, 458; P.B.Jr.,039;
  P. Brown, 227; P.J. 232; P.W.
  227; Peter, 227, 362; Pollard B.
  114, 120, 225, 227, 362, 443, 454;
  Pollard, 227; Robert, 227; S. C.,
  462; S.E., 454; S.I., 337; S.I.,
  Sr., 227; S.J. 039; 152, 227, 333;
  S.L., 227, 362, 402, 454; S., 099;
MCMICHAEL: Sallie, 060; Sally, 227;
  Sarah M., 011; Seaborn L., 362;
  Seaborn, 362, 363; Shade, Jr.,227;
  Shadrach G., 303; Shadrach I.,243;
  Shadrach I.,Jr., 039; Shadrach J.,
  197, 243; Shadrach 065, 094, 104,
  105, 122, 152, 217, 226, 227, 260,
  274, 280, 310, 311, 428, 432;
  Shadrack I., 227, 415; Shadrack J.,
  175, 243, 361, 458; Shadrack, 075,
  227, 232, 466; Shadrick I., 226;
  Shadrick, 103, 226; Shadwick, 152;
MCMICHAEL: Shasrick I., 227; Susan
  C., 380; Susan, 331; T., 362;
  Telitha, 061; V.F. 196, 338, 362;
  Vines Fish, 039; Vines, 454; W.G.,
  039; W.J., 227, 362, 454; W. J.,
  Jr., 039; W. L., 458; W., 039,
  362, 393, 444, 447; Walter, 227;
  Warren, 039; William, 039, 286,
  289; William S., 157; William F.,
  075; William, 075, 096, 141, 217,
  305; Willie Ann, 020; Willis, 348;
  Zachariah W., 039, 321; Zachariah,
  075, 227
MCMICHAELS: James, 469; Jane,
  469; Mary, 469
MCMICHAL: John, 227; Emily R., 011
MCMILLAN: Alexander, 146
MCMILLEN: G. A., 454; L. W., 454
MCMULLINS: Willie, 057
MCMURPHY: William C., 305
MCMURRAIN: John, 206, 214;
  John, Sr.,172
MCMURRAY: John, 227; John, Jr., 227
MCMURRIN: John, 075
MCMURRY: John, 075, 227
MCMURY: John, 065
MCNAIR: Alma J., 044; E. Caroline,
  011; E. S., 051; Eileen, 045;
  H. S., 454; I. L., 039; James S.,
  431; Julia, Mrs. 362
MCNEAL: Alfred, 039; Archibald,
  104; Charley, 362; Fred, 227;
  Jacob, 362
MCNEEL: James, 150
MCNEIL: Alfred, 227, 228; Daniel
  F., 075, 431; James, 229;
  John, 284
MCNEILL: Archey, 459; Archibald,
  228; Sanders, 458
MCNIEL: Daniel, 425
MCQUEEN: John, 197
MCREE: David W., 118
MCWILLIAMS: Mary A., 025
MEACHAM: John, 245
MEADOR: A. D., 458
MEADOWS: Daniel, 460; P. W. L., 037
MEALER: Thompson, 211
MEDARIS: John S., 211; John W., 211
MEDFORD: George, 074, 211
MEDLOCK: Charles, 211; George D. F.,
  287, 304; George D. Lafayette,
  211; George DeLafayette, 211;
  George F., 211; George George D.
  F., 211; George, 211, 238; J.O.,
  364, 396; R., 364
MEEKS: B. B., 359; Benjamin, 367;
  Bennie B., 037; Ella, 025; J. H.,
  204; Joseph, 155
MEGRUDER: Zadoc, 401
MELEAR: Lution, 429
MELISS: Andrew, 270; John, 270
MELROSE: William, 156
MELSON: Daniel, 109; John, W. 307
MELTON: Jonathan, 233, 257; Moses,
  434; Robert, 295; Timothy, 074
MELVIN: Joseph B., 318
MENDENHALL: Marmaduck, 173;
  Marmaduke T. 186
MENEFEE: Thomas H., 037
MERCER: A.L., 359, 454; Andrew, 454;
  Charles, 23, 235; D.T., 037, 118,
  364; Daniel F., 037, 118, 211;
  Jacob, 098, 121, 211; James, 093,
  248, 253, 427-429, 432; John, 216,
  429; L.A., 037, 157, 359; Lee, 454;
  Levi, 256; Luke B., 037; Thomas W.,
  037; W. A., 359, 454; Whit, 454;
  William, 454; William B., 037;
  William, 037, 074, 211; William,
  Sr. (heirs of), 429
MERCHON: Enos, 283
MEREDITH: Fannie Lou, 038
MERIDY: Annie, 052
MERIWETHER: Aaron, 228, 349; Alcy,
  386; Anna, 028; C. M., 234, 355,
  359, 377, 454; Charles W. 349,
  379; Charles, 037, 074, 211, 212,
  268, 330, 353, 359, 390, 415, 454,
  458; David, 065, 134, 163, 181,
  204, 211, 263, 279, 295, 308, 395,
  428, 429, 454; David, Jr., 156;
  David, Sr., 074, 156, 211; Dawson,
  037, 211, 359; Doner, 211; Dorman,
  211; Dorse, 359; Ed. 359; F. P.,
  458; G. T., 458; George F., 211,
  212, 325, 380, 454; George M., 074,
  134, 433; George, 037; Humphry,
  037; James A., 156, 212, 254, 285;
MERIWETHER: James 037, 205; Joe,
  212; Julius, 037; L.G., 017; Letha,
  009; Louise, 458; Lucy Jane, 041;
  Lucy M., 034; Lula, 074; Matilda
  A., 074, 211; Matilda Ann, 308;
  Matilda, 156; Mila, 022; Nelson,
  037; Prince, 298, 359; Queen, 212;
  Rosetta, 019; Sallie A., 065, 074;
  Sallie, 029, 045; Sarah, 055; T.M.,
  454; Thomas, 037, 359; 379, 454;
  W. T., 454; Walter, 037; William,
  176, 220, 222, 366; Willie Flem, 037
MERK: Howard, 212
MERRIETT: Sarah, 040
MERRIMAN: Charles P., 133
MERRIT: Madrick, 037; Thomas, 212
MERRITS: Thomas, 212
MERRITT: Benjamin, 212; Thomas, 429
MERRIWEATHER: George M., 431
MERRIWETHER: Aaron, 212, 359; Charles,
  114, 212, 359, 400; David, 156,
  212, 300; George F., 212, 330;
  George, 421; James A., 121; M. A.,
  212; Thomas, 359; William, 400
MERRYMAN: John, 099, 359, 340,
  346, 359, 411, 467
MESON: William B., 170
MESSER: James, 429, 431; John, 212,
  429; Samuel, 429; William (heirs
  of), 429; William, 074, 429
MEYERS: A., 376
MICHAEL: Arther, 400; David, 127;
  John, 117, 152; Lou Genie, 031;
  Sallie, 059; Sylvia, 027
MICHELL: David, 274
MICKELBERRY: Mark H., 310; W.H.C., 087
MICKEN: Silvia Ann, 022
MIDDLEBROOKS: Aaron, 212, 458; Alfred,
  212; Alonza, 359; Anderson J., 341;
  Ann G., 021; Aron, 400; Batch, 037,
  329; C. F., 037, 359, 454; Clark,
  037; E. C. Mrs., 359; Ellen C.,
  333, 458; F. G., 359; J. A., 454;
  Jacob, 037; James, 037; Joe, 212,
  359; John, 160; Joseph A., 074;
  Joseph, 445; Kittle, 042; L.H.,
  037; L.I., 019; L.L., 335; Leila,
  048; Mary L., 020; Mattie M., 022;
  Mattie, 018; Nannie, 017; Oda, 042;
  Rhoda,055; Robert L., 037; Robert,
  037; S. H., 454; Sarah M., 020;
MIDDLEBROOKS: Silas, 359, 454; Thomas
  J., 165; Thomas, 190; W. H., 212,
  360, 454; W. P., 359, 454; Walter
  P., 037; Walter, 359; William H.,
  037; William, 454; William H., Jr.,
  037; William, Jr., 224; William P.,
  180; William S., 286; William, 201;
  Williamson P., 212
MIKE: Monroe, 037
MILAM: Benjamin, 212; Dudley, 401;
  Samuel, 401; Thomas F., 212;
  Thomas, 212; Wiley, 212;
  Willie, 284
MILBURN: Samuel J., 203;
  William B., 212
MILES: Ebenezer, 430; Elijah, 212,
  424; John, 140, 212; Lewis, 212;
  William H.,230; William, 212, 459
MILLBROOK: Joe Bell, 408
MILLEN: A.C., 454; A.D., 454; Alfred
  C., 212, 371; Charlotte C., 007;
  Cornelia M., 212; Cornelia, 044;
  Cornelius M., 093; Elizabeth, 212;
  Genie, 008; George D., 074, 093,
  198, 212, 311, 401; H. D., 454; H.
  L., 442; Henry D., 037, 212, 454;
  Henry, 074; John, 074; Lucy, 118;
  Mary S., 212, 318; Mary Sauls,
  093, 212; Mary, 212, 359; R. E.,

454; Reuben, 454; Samuel, 038
MILLER: A. J., 038; Aaron, 238;
Abner, 401; Andrew J., 161;
Andrew, 090; Brice, 155, 284;
Cornelia M., 387; Cornelius M.,
094; Daniel, 074, 206; David, 212,
422, 428, 430; Edwin W., 212;
Elijah, 120, 212; Elizabeth, 227;
Ephraim, 094, 099; George D., 430;
George, 212; Georgia, 359; Harris,
102, 212; Harrison, 102, 212;
Horation, 212; Ike, 213; Jacob,
038; Jake, 213, 359; James H., 086,
213, 227, 318, 401; James, 083;
MILLER: Jeremiah, 155, 204; John,
038, 179, 213, 401; 448; Joseph,
295; Mark, 213; Martha, 051; Mary
Sauls, 430; Nathan, 117; Nettie,
143; Priscilla, 016; S. R., 367;
Sam, 213; Stephen T., 199; Stephen,
213; William H., 304; William L.,
093; William S., 172; William, 074,
213, 236, 359
MILLON: Mary, 213
MILLS: Claiborn, 108; Claiborne,
116, 287; Henry C., 359, 380;
Isaac, 286; James, 436; John,
444; William, 213
MILNER: Dudley, 213; Hopson, 213;
John, 212, 430; Marlin, 430;
Martin, 424; Matilda, 213; Pitt, 430
MILTON: Moses, 420
MIMMS: Seaborn S., 171
MIMS: Henry, 300, 323
MINES: Isaac, 206
MINION: Victoria, 022
MINNE: S., 454
MINTER: A.J., 213, 359, 454; A. P.,
454; Ada, 213; Andrew J., 038,
213, 359, 444; Andrew, 038; C. O.,
238; Calhoun, 213; Carrie, 042;
Collins, 038; Cordella, 375;
Edmond, 038; Ednie, 036; Eliza,
004; Emma J., 359; Emma, 359, 360;
Evaline, 042; F.B., 074; Fleetwood,
359; Frances Caroline, 043;
Gideon G., 213; J.C., 401; J. P.,
213; J.W., 213, 348, 374, 454;
MINTER: James R., 356; Jane E., 213;
Jane, 359; Jeremiah P., 098, 065,
074; Joe, 074; John H., 272; John
L., 442; John W., 038, 074, 213,
454; John, 213, 454; Judson R.,
401; Judson, 359; Lee, 117, 359;
Lella, 030; Leroy, 359; Maggie,
045; Marier, 049; Mary A., 213;
Mary Jane, 213; Mattie, 359;
Nancy, 052; Nannie, 359; O.J.,
454; Olin J., 038, 394; P.W., 454;
MINTER: Pat, 213; R. A. 020, 038,
401, 442, 454; R. J., 213, 359,
410, 465; Rachel, 213; Richard A.,
038; Richard, 074, 359, 454; Robert
J., 074, 379, 420; Robert R., 122,
213-214, 219, 273; 312, 387, 401,
406, 430; Robert, 038, 119, 213,
401, 410, 454; Rufus, 214, 359;
S. E., 060; S., 190; Sam, 360;
Samuel, 038; Sol, 214; Stewart,
150; T. C. 360, 401, 454; Thomas
C., 074, 214, 355, 360, 401, 454;
MINTER: Thomas C., Jr., 408; Thomas,
038, 284; Thomas Jr., 401;
Vincent, 038; W. R., 454; W. S.,
214, 355, 360, 400, 454; Wallace,
038, 360; Warner 038, 214; William
L., 355, 360; William S., 074, 089,
151, 204, 214, 237, 243, 294, 298,
333, 354, 355, 360, 448, 465;
William, 214
MINTON: James D., 319
MINTOR: Gideon G., 149
MINTURN: Benjamin G., 430
MIRACK: Bill, 401
MIRES: William S., 239
MISER: Joseph, 074
MISON: Francis, 206
MITCHAL: Wess, 401
MITCHEAL: Richard, 038
MITCHEL: Daniel, 074; Davis, 038;
Henry, 038; Lula, 029; Melvin, 214;
Mira, 214; Richard, 465; Robert,
038; Tom, 038; Walter H., 249
MITCHELL: Americus C., 185; Bob, Jr.,
214, 360; Charles, 360; Charlie,
038; David, 279, 360; Dick, 360,
379; Elizabeth, 214; George, 038,
214; Hala, 017; Henry, 038, 098,
153, 360, 458; Homer, 038, 214;
Isaac, 038; Isham, 104; James,
098, 133, 191, 248, 267; Jefferson,
214; Joel, 214, 430; John F. M.,
214; John, 236, 248, 293, 302;
Joshua S., 175, 214, 430, 459;
Joshua, 459; Julius C. B., 164;
MITCHELL: Levin, 214; Lillie, 028;
Mary, 049; Mathew, 303; Matthew,
133, 202; Melvin, 360; Molley,
132; Richard, 065, 074, 214, 360;
Robert, 151, 152, 214, 233; Sam,
214, 257; Shatteen C., 136; Thomas
J., 214; Tomie, 044; Uriah G.,164;
Walter H., 164; Walter, 434; Wess,
038; Will, 038; William, 131,
214, 215
MITCHEM: Byron E., 038
MIXON: A. C., 088; Georgia E., 266;
Georgia, 269; Jesse F., 266, 269;
Noel, 114
MIZE: Elizabeth, 054; Frederick,
430; Henry, 430; James B., 214;
James, 074, 099, 214; Joseph, 448;
Stacy, 214, 430
MOATE: John P., 275; John, 429
MOATS: John P., 300; John, 214
MOBLEY: Albert, 214; Alexander, 125;
Eleazer, 214, 227, 281, 430;
Fannie Rebecca, Mrs., 018; Fleming,
157, 189, 226, 361; 458; Fleming,
118, 264; Harrison, 142; J.R., 171,
343, 385, 407; Jackson, 188; James,
224; Jethro, 137, 210, 301, 430;
Ledford, 206; Lucy, 215; Nathan,
214; N. M., 454; Stephen D., 101,
332, 333, 364; Stephen H., 215,
318; Stephen, 074, 087, 215, 267,
271; William, 215
MOBLY: Jackson, 199
MOFFIT: Thomas, 106
MOHON: Dorah, 052
MOHORN: Henry, 038
MOOR: L., 392
MOLEMAN: Stephen, 038, 215
MOLLIER: Clement, 215
MOLLIERE: Clement, 094, 097, 155,
206, 215, 286, 318, 444
MOLYNEUX: Edmund, Jr.,130
MONCRIEF: Elizabeth, 430
MONDAY: Andrew J., 235
MONK: Thomas, 215, 430
MONKS: P. C., 385
MONROE: John, 388; Madison, 038;
Thomas, 401
MONTGOMERY: Agatha, 231; B.T., 132;
Benjamin H., 074; David (heirs
of), 430; David F. P., 038; David,
074, 111; Effie, 014; Flora, 023;
Henry, 360, 360; James, 075;
James N., 065; John, 360, 430;
Lizzie, 252; Rachel, 023
MOODY: P.M., 038; Greene, 215; Joel,
215; Littleberry, 251
MOON: Bud, 038; Emma, 002; Eva, 192;
James, 137; John, 5c., 215; Mary,
215; William H., 215
MOONEY: Isack, 319; Snelling S.,
360; Valentine, 215
MOONEYHAM: Charles, 360; Charley
Lee, 038; Charlie, 215; Mattie, 037
Andrew, 396; Archelaus, 182; Aron,
252; Asa, 216; Augustus C., 075;
B. A., 360; B. H., 401; Benjamin
H., 430; Benjamin L., 215; Benjamin
S., 215; Burnet, 255; David, 410;
E.B., 360; Elbert, 215; Elisabeth,
030; Ella, 035; Elmer, 215;
Franklin, 204, 215, 318; George W.,
130; George, 138, 215; Georgia
Ella, 027; Hiram, 075; Horace, 360;
MOORE: Ignatious, , 216; Isaac C.,
204; Isaac, 111, 215, 420, 423;
Isaac, Jr., 256; Isaac, Sr., 256;
J. B., 038; Jack, 038; Jackson,
215; Jacob, 215, 256; James B.,
216; James T., 170; James, 183,
215, 216; Jane, 216; John (heirs
of), 430; John, 075, 116, 120, 258,
178, 215, 216, 222, 237, 256, 262,
308, 318, 423, 430, 436, 465; John,
Sr., 425; Jonas, 216; Joshua G.,
253; Joshua, 216; Josiah J., 216;
MOORE: L. D., 130; Leila, 016; Lela
A., 043; Martha (heirs of), 430;
Martha S., 401; Michael, 139, 143,
148, 191, 216, 287, 302, 303,
305, 308; Michel, 216; Moring,
268; Morning, 216; Moses, 124,
216; Newton, 401; Odus, 215; Owens,
401; Palatine, 075; Polly, 216;
Prudence, 216; Robert, 215; Sallie,
005; Samuel, 444; Sebron, 101;
Seth H., 216; Thomas, 094, 124,
171, 444; W. H., 454; W. R., 401,
454, 465; William M., 132, 153,
216, 302; William H., 038; William
P. 232; William, 215, 216
MOORHORN(?): Henry, 401
MOORHON: Lula, 047
MORAN: J. M., 378, 409
MORE: Consale, 216; Lilly, 216;
Sallie, 058
MORELAND: Amanda, 032; Emma, 009;
Frances, 065; Francis, 075, 216,
430; 433; G. W. 038, 360; George,
360; Ginsie Kitte, 020; Gus, 216;
Henry, 216, 360; Isaac T., 197;
Jane B., 164; John F., 190; John,
075, 150, 216; Joseph, 405; Joseph
T., 280; Lizzie, 055; Mattie, 021;
Rebecca, 028; Robert, 430; Salena,
216; Susan T., 027; Thomas, 075,
138, 230, 246, 396; Turner, 176;
Wesley, 216; William, 216;
Wood, 216, 230
MORETON: Ben, 344
MORGAN: A.H., 216; Aaron, 159, 218,
266; Alice, 004; Allen, 126; Asa,
H., 216, 217, 242, 318, 319, 322,
401; Asa, 216; Barthenia, 290;
Berry, 038, 401; Bethena(Kitchens),
217; Charles S., 248; Charles, 075,
088, 160, 217, 219, 299, 319, 430;
Clark, 360; E. P., 442; Elizabeth
L., 033; Frank, 217; Grady, 401;
H. A., 360; Henry, 092, 401; I.
H., 442; Isaac N., 217, 442; Isham,
340, 360; J. C., 364; J. H., 349,
442; J. W., 377; James E. 038,
087; James H., 217, 465; James W.,
099, 107, 160, 176, 217, 318, 401;
MORGAN: James, 217, 360; Jefferson
P., 038; Jim, 038; John E., 107,
129, 181, 231, 248; John H., 176;
John W., 331, 332, 337, 339-341,
343, 344, 347, 351, 352, 360,
362, 366, 368, 375, 379-381, 395,
John, 038, 217, 319, 430; Jumima,
217; Keneard (?), 434; Leila, 055;
Lena, 046; Lorrissa, 015; Lou, 046;
Luke I., 319; Luke J., 139, 176,
217, 240, 355; Luke L., 240; Maggie,
017, 038; Martha J., 040; Mary Lou,
002; Mary, 038, 433; Matilda, 033;
MORGAN: Milton, 075; Mineard, 217;
Miniard, 217; Minyard, 217; Mollie,
039; Newton Charles, 038; Nicholas,
256; Nix, 038; Richard, 158; Sally,
217; Sarah F., 047; Sarah N., 217,
319, 401; Sarah, 217; Stokeley,
196, 217, 431; Stokely, 113, 128,
137, 141, 202; Stokely, 206, 218,
242, 219; Stokely, 286, 319, 324,
387, 444; Stokeley, 075; Stokly,
100; Thomas (heirs of), 430;
Thomas, 418; W. L., 401; W.T. 348;
Will, 218; William J.,075; William,
038, 105, 119, 129, 160, 213, 218,
260, 271, 277, 317, 319, 359, 401;
Wooddie, 218
MORRIS: Alexander, 218, 273; B. F.,
218; Benjamin F., 075, 248;
Benjamin, 218; Burrell, 218, 360;
Cyrus, 218; Edmund, 218; F.M., 379;
Fannie, 018; George, 218; Henry,
218, 421; Henrietta, 209; Isham,
218, 401; James, 181, 255, 297;
John G., 075, 101, 118, 138, 250,
260; John, 127; Lou, 054; Madison,
279; Martha, 212; Mary, 060; Nimrod,
460; Rebecca, 127; Robert, 114;
Sarah M., 075, 274; Stephen, 075,
209, 358; Thomas, 218, 420, 426,
430; Uriah C., 218; Uriah, 096;
W. I., 360; William, 075, 424, 430
MORRISON: A. C., 121; A. J., 218;
Alexander C., 215, 218; Alexander
G., 121; Alexander, 218, 278, 401;
Angus C., 219; Angus G., 218, 278;
Angus, 167, 218, 395; M.A.E., 360
MORROW: Alexander, 098; J. H., 265;
James H., 088, 184, 192, 213, 214,
218, 219, 249, 255, 262, 266, 283,
287, 307, 310; James, 218, 265;
Rebeckah, 219; Robert (heirs of),
430; William H., 219, 429; Zoro, 060
MORTON: Alice, 360; Beatrick, 401;
Ben, 360, 401; Bob, 360; Cora,
357; Erotas, 219; Joe, 360; Joel,
430; Levi, 401; M.H. 118; Robert,
401; Roxie, 023; Sallie, 041;
Sarah, 360; Thomas, 161, 172
MOSELEY: A. F., 219, 454, 465;
Alamon, 430; Alansom, 219; Augustus,
337, 351; Benjamin, 160, 389;
Elisha, 219, 430; Henry, 065, 430;
J. H., 454; James B., 319; Jesse,
093; Joe, 415; John H., 454; Peter,
140; Pleas, 454; Sally, 140;
Thomas, 176; W. R., 184, 398, 447;
William R., 219
MOSELY: Alansom, 430; Aug, 339;
Augustus, 328, 347; Daniel, 122;
Elisha, 219; Henry, 075; Joe, 268,
360; Joseph, 364; Peter, 115, 127,
258; Polly, 025; Sally (Brown),
115; 128; W. R., 075, 392;
William, 282
MOSES: --, 219; Ann, 129, 167; John,
075, 129, 167; Joshua, 430;
Samuel, 129, 167, 296
MOSLEY: Taylor, 461; Thomas, 148
MOSS: Amanda, 043; Archibald, 075;
Emma, 004; Henrietta, 041; Henry,
319, 401; John H., 230; Joseph,
108, 140, 151, 171, 181, 271, 283,
313, 322, 205; Lucy, 030;
Susannah C., 075
MOSSY: Nathan, 195
MOSTELLER: Jacob, 295
MOTEN: Ben, 257; Emma, 018; Joe, 257
MOTHERSHED: Eleanor, 219; Elleanor
F., 219; Ellen F., 285; William
H., 219, 285, 319; William, 219
MOTON: Nancy, 018

MOTT: William B., 261
MOULTON: Charles F., 137
MOUNCE: Moses, 388; Urban D., 388
MOY: Frances E. (Johnston), 458;
  Thomas W., 458
MOYE: J.P., 311; Jeremiah P., 219;
  Thomas W. 075, 219, 335, 448;
  Wiley, 219, 335; Wille, 219
MOYNIHAN: Thadeus, 109, 182, 325
MUCKELROY: James S. 219
MUCKLEROY: Andrew, 219; Jacob,
  219; James, 219
MULKEY: James, 431; John, 430;
  Madison J., 219; Moses, 143, 420;
  Ruth, 430; William, 089
MULKY: Moses, 125; Phillip, 132
MULLALLY: William, 430
MULLEN: Arbella, 015
MULLENS: Burton, 300; Elizabeth A.,
  059; James, 219, 299; Mary, 015;
  Pleasant I., 219; Pleasant J., 219,
  311, 319; Blandina E., 046; Burton,
  320; Fed, 401; George, 401; James,
  161, 225, 266, 299; Mary Jane, 058;
  Mattie, 005; Pleasant J., 219;
  Pleasant J., 118, 219; Pleasant
  P., 219
MUMFORD: John, 098
MUNROE: Annie, 023; Nathan C., 291;
  Precious, 014
MURDOCK: Charles G., 156, 274, 275;
  Charles, 304; Joseph, 219, 220,
  425, 429
MURELL: G. W., 386
MURPHEY: Mary E., 025; Mastin W.,
  220; Pascal, 178; Paschal, 133, 220
MURPHY: J.F., 454; J.H., 360, 442,
  465; James F., 082; James S., 083;
  James, 361; John S., 117; L.A.,
  390; Mastin, 220; Pascal, 120,
  389; Paschal, 105, 146, 220, 231,
  233, 242, 293, 311, 319, 428, 430,
  436, R.A., Mrs., 360; R.G., 360;
  Sis, 056; Solomon B., 127;
  W.R., 360
MURRAH: Charles, 220
MURRAN: Charles, 191
MURRAY: Henry, 220, 275; Stephen,
  430; William, 202
MURRELL: E. N., Mrs., 332; Eliza
  A., 466; J. W., 346, 364, 365; John
  T., 224; Joseph H., 216, 217;
  R. D. 454
MURPELLE: Eliza N., Mrs., 220
MURRIL: Samuel, 266, 322
MURROW: John, 302
MUSGROVE: Robert H., 131, 264, 316
MYGATI: A., Mrs., 347
MYGATT: Ann E., 330, 342; George,
  075, 320; William G., 220, 324;
  William, 322
MYLES: Elijah, 220; Isham, 220;
  Joshua, 430; William H., 075,
  220, 319, 430
MYRICK: David, 110, 148, 176, 220,
  259, 430; Eliza, 046; James, 165;
  Mattie, 030; Nannie, 017; Robert,
  131, 148, 176; William, 220
NALL: Frances, 284; James, 228, 243;
  John P., 103, 133, 228, 274, 315,
  316, 402; Martin, 177, 228, 284;
  Nathan, 075; W. E., 442;
  Willis B., 228
NALLS: Martin, 430
NAPER: John, 362
NAPIER: James, 039; Jesse, 228;
  John, 362; Leroy, 139, 140, 173,
  176, 280; Mose, 039; Skelton, 239;
  Thomas T., 167, 204, 425; Thomas,
  092, 098, 104, 110, 115, 117, 164,
  173, 174, 192, 196, 199, 214, 228,
  250, 257, 262, 283, 287, 302, 303,
  315, 401, 431
NAPPER: Dock, 040
NASH: Boston, 040; Dan, 228, 349;
  Ed, 402; Georgia Ann, 040; Hanna,
  050; Hannah, 054; James F. 040;
  Jef, 400; King, 228, 362; Lee,
  040; Mariah, 038; Martha, 060;
  Matilda, 228, 362; Ollie, 040;
  Peter, 040; Salle, 028, 034;
  Silla, 057; T.J., 281, 362, 386,
  402; Tempe, 040; Tempy, 042;
  Titus, 040; Valentine, 153, 215
NEAL: David, 228, 428; John, 122,
  228, 290; McCormick, 217, 333,
  334, 358, 359, 381
NEALEY: Thomas, 323
NEELY: Henry, 209
NEIL: David, 402
NELAMS: John 109
NELSON: A. B., 402; Adline, 046;
  Andrew, 362; Jennie C., 223; John
  G, 164; John, 040; King, 040;
  Lula, 027; Riley, 228; Sou, 402;
  Thomas, 228; Walter, 040; William,
  088, 090, 115, 136, 157, 162,
  196, 228, 256, 266
NESBIT: John, 230, 292, 304
NEWBY: Hiram, 040; J. B., 402, 465;
  John, 075, 191; Mike, 228, 415;
  Pearl, 011; Rena, 022; S. M., 402;

Sylvia, 029; Will, 228; Wm E., 465
NEWCOMB: Lemuel, 173
NEWELL: Isaac, 149; James, 243;
  Leonard, 228; William E., 243;
  William M., 243
NEWHALL: Cheeves, 156; Chervir(?), 270
NEWLAND: James, 162; Joseph, 203, 296
NEWMAN: Josiah, 218, 303, 307, 308,
  322; M., 354; S., 362; Silas,
  335, 415; William Frank, 040
NEWSOM: Augustus T., 411; Joel, 169
NEWTON: ?, 228; A. 358, 362, 380,
  443; A. Jr., 282; Alrs, 396;
  Alice C., 014; Anna, 048; Aris,
  040, 075, 092, 099, 103, 122,
  144, 148, 228, 254, 260, 262,
  320, 331, 342, 352, 363, 402,
  425, 431, 442, 448, 454; Aris,
  Jr. 228, 243, 334, 350; Aristachus,
  228; Aristarchus, 055, 203; Arthur
  R., 040; Bud, 468; C. A., 454;
  Charles Aris, 040; Charles
  F., 087; Cornelia, 330, 374; E.
  454; E., 328, 373; Eliza L.,
  112; Emett, 040; G.T., 454; G.W.,
  454, 465; George W., 040, 228,
  280, 362, 454; George, 372; Isaac,
  362; Jake, 362; James M.,131, 214;
  James, 454; Josiah, 167, 219;
  Julia, 075; L. B., 228, 362; L.,
  454; Levi, 253, 436; Levy, 169;
  Lucian B., 228; Lucien B., 075,
  201, 432, 454; Lucien, 361; Lucius,
  340; Mark L., 075; Mark S., 114;
  Martha B., 075; Martha, 028;
  Mary F., 075, 133, 228, 362, 431;
  Mary J., 381; Minnie G., 046;
  Mollie F., 362; Mollie I., 362;
  Moses, 431; Neal, Mrs., 362;
  O.H. P., 075; O. H. 040, 362,
  454; Oliver H., 075, 426; Oliver,
  454; Peter, 040; R. W., 362;
  Richard, 108, 183, 228, 363, 454;
  Seaborn, 228; Sid C., Mrs., 203;
  Sidney, 363; Willis, 075, 167,
  228, 337, 362, 363, 377, 380,
  436, 454, 485
NIBLET: T.S., 363; Tilman, 186, 219,
  228; Tilomn, 138, 228, 290, 302,
  311, 319
NIBLETT: Alice, 025; Ann Elizabeth,
  056; Annie L., 033; Charles, 454;
  Charlie, 040, 361, 362; Ed, 229;
  Eli, 040; M. H., 040; J. H., 040,
  454; J.I. 444; J.V. 363; James
  E., 040; James H. 040, 229, 363,
  455; James I. 040; James L., 040;
  James M., 040; James, 040, 455;
  John H., 455; Lucy F. 007; Lula,
  023; M. A. 040; Mattie I, 061;
  Mattie, 061; Mollie, 034; Pearl
  039; Robert, 455; S.A., 013; S.J.,
  455; Sarah F., 033; T. V., 465;
  Tilman, 083, 228, 290; Zno,
  228; Tilomn, 138, 229, 284, 286,
  303, 319, 455; Virginia Lee, 010
NICHOLS: Barack P., 040; Barkar F.,
  110; Basak, 190, 312; Catherine,
  229; Charles, 245; Cheney, 044;
  Elijah, Jr., 168; Frederick, 245;
  George, 102; Henry, 363; Jeff,
  229, 400; John, 229; Jonathan,
  435; Joseph, 245; Mary, 056;
  Patsey, 098; Richard I., 316;
  Richard, 040, 363; Simon W., 229;
  Starr, 281, 292; T.J., 363; Thomas
  363; Thos., 465; Tom Jeff,
  040; Tom, 229; Travis, 229
NICHOLSON: Gilliam, 259
NICKOLS: Jeff, 363; Lizzie, 009
NICKS: Frank, 040
NIGHT: M. V., 415; Wiley, 040
NILES: Ambrose, 229
NILMS: Mary Jane, 026
NIMS: Seth, 164, 172; Theodore,
  274, 297; Theodus, 275
NISBET: Alfred M., 287; John, 090,
  151, 183, 256; Milus C., 287
NISBIT: James L., 394
NIVENS: Charlie, 402
NIX: Ada, 058; Adam, 040, 458;
  Berry, 040, 363; David, 229, 260;
  Jacob, 229; Joe D. 364; Julius,
  040; Lula, 056; M.T. 415; Martha,
  019; McKendin T., 229; McKendrick
  T., 363; Mittle, 006; Nora, 058;
  Richard, 040; Sarah A., 229; Sofa,
  016; Thomas L., 229; Thomas, 311;
  Tucker, 363; Wash, 363;
  Washington, 229, 363
NIXON: Joseph, 150, 229
NOBLE: Stephen, 229, 431, 468
NOLAN: Agnes, 021; Cynthia M.,
  046; Elizabeth C., 065; Emma, 017;
  John E., 395; John, 288; Thomas
  B., 086, 151, 160, 222, 229, 240,
  314, 320, 431, 434; Thomas P.,
  402; Thomas T., 142; Thomas, 040
NOLAND: Thomas P., 222
NOLEN: Anna M., 046; Ellen, 046;
  John W., 040; Stephen, 436;
  Thomas, 195

NOLES: A.P., 402; Ada, 010; Alfred,
  040; D.G.G., 455; David G., 040,
  063, 363, 415; David, 455; Elender,
  040; Elinor, 075; Ellander, 363;
  Ellen, 363; Ellender, 338, 363;
  Emeliza, 027; Georgia A. 013;
  J.H. 040, 075; J.R. 415; John
  W. 075, 229; John, 040; M. E.,
  027; Martha, 028; Mary, 010;
  Micha A., 012; Morris, 229, 322,
  363, 402; Nancy Jane, 037; W.A.J.,
  402; William A. 402; William
  A. 040; William D., 040, 075;
  Zachariah, 229
NOLIN: Stephen, 399
NOLLEY: Ada, 229; Alfred, 040;
  Daniel, 320; Emma Liza, 043;
  George, 040; John, 229; Nathan,
  229, 320; Otis, 040; Stephen, 458
NOLLY: Claudie, 013; Fed, 229;
  Georgia, 061; Isaac, 040; John,
  040; Martha, 009; Mary R., 024;
  Nathan, 229; Nora, 009; Troy, 040
NOOSO: Gust, 402; John, 402
NORMAN: Charley, 040; Gideon, 216;
  Stephen, 215, 229, 363; Sue, 282;
  Susan, 004
NORRID: Eli, 040
NORRIS: Benjamin F., 065; Francina,
  014; James, 040; Joel D., 040;
  John, 320; Needham, 229; Rigdon,
  229; Robert, 300; Samuel G., 040;
  Samuel S., 236; Saran M., 065;
  Stephen, 198, 236; Thomas P.,
  223; William, 229
NORSWORTHY: James, 040, 229;
  Samuel, 229
NORTH: Abraham, 418; John, 176,
  219, 260, 263
NORTHERN: Basset, 429
NORTON: Charles C., 205; Robert S.,
  229; Thomas, 176, 229, 465
NORWOOD: James, 229, 040, 127, 154,
  175, 179, 204, 208, 215, 229,
  233, 276, 294, 431; Margaret
  (Loyd), 154; Margaret, 179, 294;
  Mary Jane, 040; Ned, 229
NOSWORTHY: D., 363
NOTTINGHAM: W. D. 102
NOVA: William, 229
NOWELL: Sarah E., 053
NOWLAND: George, 229
NOWLES: Rice B., 303
NOYES: Edward H., 460
NUBIE: Nancy, 022
NUNNALLY: Archelas, 297; Moses, 229
NUTE: Jeremiah, 153
NUTT: Andrew, 229; Samuel, 229;
  Charles H., 242
NUTTING: Charles A., 246;
O'CONNER: Patrick B., 230;
  Patrick, 229
O'DANIEL: Alexander, 134, 217, 230;
  John, 230, 289, 292; Wilson, 230
O'HARA: Charles, 230, 320;
  Mary Jane, 402
O'KELLY: F. M., 363; Francis M.,
  041; Francis, 459; James, 431
O'NAIL: Jesse, 230
O'NEAL: Jesse, 402; Osborn R., 188;
  Thomas W., 202; William W., 260
O'REAR: Claudia May, Mrs., 018
OABURN: Charles, 442
OAKMAN: William H., 181, 198, 211
OATS: James D., 247; William H., 247
ODELL: Aura, 010
ODEN: Alexander, 161, 230, 431
ODER: D. B., 363
ODOM: B. B., 091, 230, 315, 348,
  380, 405; Dock, 040; Eliza, 019;
  Eva, 005; Gus, 230, 363; Hester,
  016; Honor, 156; Jacob, 465; John
  Wes, 363; Luke, 041; Richard, 424;
  Roland, 230, 402; S.E., 230, 348;
  Taylor, 041; William, 415; Winborn,
  234; Winburn, 145, 197
ODOMS: S. B., Mrs., 075
ODOY: J. B., 381
ODUM: Augustus, 363; Celia, 431;
  Cora, 014; Frank, 415; Harriet,
  042; Jim, 402; Louraney, 047;
  Rainy, 403; Wesley, 363;
  Winburn, 075, 219
OGDEN: Elisha, 127
OGETREE: Osborne G., 149
OGLESBY: James, 230
OGLETREE: Edwin, 448; Family, 485;
  Joseph H., 230
OLIVER: Burrell, 041; Caleb, 431;
  Charles, 236; J. S., 248; James,
  133; John, 041; Love, 230
OLMSTEAD: George B., 211; Ralph,
  171, 188; Timothy, 093
OLMSTED: Ralph, 139, 144
ONAIL: Jesse, 230, 320
ONEAL: Bartlet, 230; Edmund, 230;
  Jesse, 148; Osban, 230;
  Thomas W., 230
ORANGE: Eliza, 230; Ella, 020;
  Titus, 041, 402
OREAR: James F., 041
ORGAN: Matthew, 075, 230

ORR: Allen, 075, 207, 230, 263, 313, 320, 402, 431; Christopher, 241; J.K., 330; James T.I., 307; James T.J., 114; James, 230; John, 127; Kiziah, 191; Nathan, 320; Sample, 230
OSBERN: George, 194
OSBORN: Benjamin, 230; Charles, 230; E. C., 455; Elbert, 455; J., 230; James, 230, 448; Jesse H., 363; Lazerous, 230; Thomas O., 230
OSBORNE: Elisha, 259; Thomas J. N., 147; William, 075, 215
OSBURN: Burney, 455; Charles, 230; Elias, 320; J. M., 041; Thomas O., 320, 455; Thomas, 455
OSBURNE: Rebecca, 002
OSGOOD: John, 165
OTIS: John, 144
OUSLEY: Newdevate, 118; Points, 431
OVERTON: Henry, 431; Mary Lou, 021
OWEN: Augustus, 088; Bracket, 230; George W., 294; George, 181, 443; Hardaman, 230, 254, 431; Hardeman, 230, 231; Hardiman, 402; Jacob (orphans), 120; Jacob, 092, 098; John, 086, 104, 116, 135, 165, 184, 188, 221, 252, 275, 299, 314; Mary, 120; Philemon, 123, 128; Polly, 231; Robert, 092, 123, 128, 162, 231, 425, 429, 431, 435
OWENS: Anderson, 041; Elijah M., 231, 270; George W., 215; Hardaman, 231; Hardeman, 107, 231; Hardiman, 231; J. M., 041; Jacob, 075; Jesse, 363; John N., 231; Robert P., 041; Robert, 231; S. C., 393; Stewart, 075; Susannah C.(Spencer), 270; Susannah C., 075, 231, 259; William, 231
OWENSBY: Francis, 231
OWSLEY: Wm., 469
OWSLY: Robert, 197
OXFORD: Annie B., 024; Bernice, 026; C. W., 455; Charles W., 455; E. J., 455; Ed, 455; Edward I., 041; Edward, 455; J.W., 231, 338; James W., 075, 146; James, 338; M. L., 033; Otelia, 056; P. L., 075, 455; Samuel,409; T.B., 455; Thomas J., 455; Tilman D., 145, 320; Tilmon D., 099; W.C., 447; W.J., 108; Washington, 065
OZBORN: Charles, 222; E.J., 402; James, 075; Matilda, 003; N.B., 402
OZBURN: B. S., 363, 442; Charles, 231; E.C, 041; E. J., Mrs, 402; Elias, 199, 231; Fannie, 015; Hattie Lou, 056; J.E., 363; Lizzie, 059; M.E., Mrs, 402; Martha, 027; Mary, 016; Matthew, 180, 231; William M., 041
PABODIE: Albert, 102, 116, 231, 239, 263; William, 102, 109, 140, 213, 231, 267, 293
PACE: C. D., 390; Lucretia J., 027; Mary, 028; Noel, 268; Stephen, 231; W. H. C., 235, 290; William H.C., 217; William T., 231, 320, 402; William, 231
PAGE: William, 467
PAIN: Haynes, 427; John, 448
PAINE: Edward, 101, 133, 170, 183, 226; Henry D., 169, 231; John, 118, 123, 124, 231, 238, 431; Randal, 231; Randolph, 188; T.M., 041; Thomas, 075
PAINTER: Samuel, 173
PAKER(?): S. R., 442
PALMER: Chaney, 231; David E., 231; Elizabeth, 259, 378; Hezekiah, 245; Mary Ann, 174
PANE: John, 231; Randolph, 231
PARAMORE: James, 114
PARDU: Leverett, 320
PARE: Briges, 320
PARHAM: Mathew, 418; Polly, 075
PARISH: Daniel, 087, 093, 100, 105, 137, 139, 170, 186, 191, 198, 204, 223, 283, 287; David, 244; Henry, 105, 137, 139, 170, 186, 191, 198, 223, 287; Jonathan, 232, 287; Polly, 005; Thomas, 087, 093, 100, 198, 204, 223, 244, 283
PARK: Emily, 010; F.M., 372; Henry, 363; J. T., 442; Jeanette, 017; Mary E., 033; Melissa, 007; Quedalious S., 041; William, 092
PARKER: A.J., 041, 455; Aaron, 198, 231, 432, 448; Andrew J., 231; Ann Eliza, 075; Ashley, 214; C.R., 455; Carrie, 023; Charles W., 314; Charles, 232; Chris, 041; Clara C., 007; Ed, 231; Elizabeth, 054; Emeline, 058; Isaac H., 231; Isaac L., 075, 093, 110, 139, 147, 152, 153, 169, 194, 200, 211, 217, 222, 231, 232, 240, 241, 263, 265, 320, 363, 400, 401; Isaac, 204, 320; J.H., 465;

J.M., 455; Jacob, 041; James M., 041; James, 041, 232; Jesse, 041; Jodie, 402; John, 232, 465; Johnnie, 402; L.B., 363; Landford, 232; Lewis S., 075; Mary Ann, 040; Mattie H., 465; Mitchell, 145; Nancy J., 033; Nancy, 013; Robert, 214; Rowe, 232, 363; S. R., 455; Sidney P., 041, 363; T. L., 301; Thomas M., 041; Urania Elizabeth, 065; W.C., 363; William C., 075, 232, 363; William H., 083, 232, 179, 232, 233, 320, 465; William R., 102, 402; William S., 233; William, 083, 232; Zeal, 445, 448
PARKS: Abraham, 363; Clark D., 294, 301, 431; Clayborn, 233; Daniel, 415; Dolphus, 381; Elizabeth, 038, 202; Fannie Kate, 022; Garrett W., 431; J. B., 444; Jack, 041; John B., 075, 169, 200; John, 206; Labora, 040; Luther, 233; Mary Jane, 013; Mattie, 015; Samuel, 179; Thomas, 041, 233, 465; Welcom, 169, 172, 194, 200, 206, 233, 257, 294, 301, 423, 426, 431; Welcome, 325; William W., 041, 442;
PARMALEE: Thomas I., 144; Thomas J., 172, 176
PARMELEE: Albert O.,146, 227; Thomas I., 289; Thomas J., 090, 093, 131, 134, 137, 138, 201
PARMER: Jesse, 233
PARNALL: Cyrus, 320; Daniel, 320
PARNELL: Cyrus, 184; James, 233; John W., 041, 445; John, 075
PARR: Jasper N., 041
PARRISH: Jonathan, 111, 251
PARROT: George, 233, 286; Henry, 075; William H., 233
PARPOTT: William H., 233, 320
PARSHALL: James O., 273
PARSONS: C. M., 135; John, 117; Pinckney, 210
PASCHAL: Betsey, 274; Mahala, 027; Nancy, 055; Samuel, 274; Scott, 402
PASCHALL: Elizabeth, 305; William, 075, 305
PASS: Arthur, 402; Nathaniel B., Jr, 221
PATE: James, 086; William, 121
PATEN: Fannie, 233
PATEY: Elijah, 238, 245, 431; Henry, 431; Miles, 431
PATILLO: David, 402
PATILLOE: David, 402; Delilah, 233, 402
PATON: Levi, 041
PATRICK: Anthony, 041; Charlie, 233; Charly, 041; D.L., Jr, 170; John C., 430; John M., 200, 211, 233, 251, 255, 431; John W., 233; Jonathan, 233; T. E., 455; William, 151, 233, 429, 460
PATTERSON: Alexander, 222; Carrie, 019, 049; David, 431; Drury S., 132, 192; Drury, 207; Elizabeth, 022; Henry, 233; J.F., 382; James B., 176; James, 111, 122, 126, 137, 146, 153, 166, 266; Jesse, 075; Job C., 448; John C., 233; John F., 090, 097, 102, 103, 114, 130, 144, 150, 153, 159, 166, 170, 190, 193, 194, 199, 200, 203, 207, 223, 233, 237, 240, 241, 258, 261, 262, 268, 269, 306, 312, 317, 318, 351, 361, 469; John G., 170; John L., 286; John R., 192; PATTERSON: John, 176, 193, 220, 221; Lina, 012; Mary Jane, 039; Mary, 431; Polly, 017; Rich, 041; Wade, 041; William, 233
PATTILLO: David, 233
PATTON: Matthew, 041
PATY: Elijah, 234, 258; Henry, 234; John, 126; William, 174
PAUL: W. A., 421; W. E., 234, 279, 363, 376, 455, 465; William B., 346, 363, 364, 379
PAYNE(PAINE): J.A., 455; John, 455; T. M., 455; Thomas, 455
PAYNE: Henry D., 234; John, 075, 107, 234, 286, 423; William, 426
PEACE: Barnabas, 141
PEACOCK: ?, 091; Aaron, 041, 465; Aden, 402; Alice, 234; Charly, 403; Cora, 364; Daniel, 075; Dub, 403; Dudley, 041, 364; Emma, 020; Frank, 364; Gil, 364; Gilbert, 234, 364; Gill, 041, 442; Hattie, 057; Joe, 041; John, 075, 108, 234; Lewis, 086, 108, 301; Louisiana, 052; Luiza, 005; Merrell, 448; Scot, 403; W. C., 455; William, 075, 108
PEAL: Eleanor, 012
PEARCE: Bartlet, 431; Bartley, 425, 431; James, 234; John, 320
PEARMAN: Robert, 180, 234, 447; Weekly I., 094

PEARSON: Abbie, 025; Abel, 207; Austin, 041, 076, 364, 443; Auston, 037; Charles D., 133, 345; Charles, 141, 234, 301, 314, 322; Daniel W., 429; Edwin W., 172, 234; Elira, 214; Ellis, 041; Flora, 039; Francis, 234; George, 041; Green, 234; Henry, 094; Henry, Jr., 130, 156, 167, 234; J.W., 455; Jeremiah, 065, 076, 087, 092, 094, 102, 104, 107, 110, 113, 123, 124, 132, 137, 138, 148, 150, 152, 155, 156, 164, 165, 168, 173, 176, 177, 181, 191, 198, 205, 209, 210, 214, 219, 222, 225, 226, 234, 237, 244, 245, 248, 258, 260, 264, 272, 275, 275, 278, 280, 293, 297-299, 301, 302, 304, 308, 313, 317, 318, 422, 423, 431; PEARSON: John M., 169, 237, 270; John W., 041, 076, 234, 280, 356, 370, 455; John, 321; Mollie, 051; Reese, 041, 076; Rhoda Ann, 058; Rhoda, 045; S. S., 234; Samuel W., 180; Simeon, 234; Simon, 322; Thomas G., 234; W. A., 234, 331, 455, 465; William W., 403; William, 041; John, 443
PEARSONS: Andrew J., 041
PEAVY: Allen, 234, 431; Benjamin, 302; David, 234; Eli, 303
PECK: David, 231; Elam, 231; Elma, 019; Thomas B., 239
PEDDIE: Moses, 041
PEDDY: Francisco B., 020; Frank, 415; Henry, 119, 174, 234, 275, 431; James, 151, 234, 151; Jeremiah, 174; Millie, 054; Morris, 041; Mort, 041; Moses, 370; Penny (Hill), 174; Wiley, 076, 089, 091, 118, 142, 187, 200, 224, 234, 248, 271, 280, 282, 292, 320, 351, 361, 397, 415; Willie, 155; William, 139, 191, 231, 234; Wily, 224
PEEBLES: Henry, 215
PEEDE: James, 097
PEEK: Henry, 431
PEEL(PEALE): John, 234; William, 234, 428
PEELER: Anthony, 076; Jacob, 144
PEEPLES: Benjamin M., 159, 288; Thomas B., 234
PEEPMAN: Robert, 427
PEET: Thomas B., 140, 168
PEEVY: David, 272
PEGG: William H., 234, 235, 320
PEFENS: William, 112, 125
PELLOM: Edward, 465
PELOT: J. J., 235; S. C., 076
PEMBERTON: Alton, 159; J. S., 361; Jane, 235; Joshua, 235, 431, 434
PENDARVIS: James, 320
PENDEPGRASS: H.E., 364; H.N., 041, 364, 455; Harlett E., 431; N.H., 455
PENDLETON: Zachariah, 426
PENICK: Joseph P., 154
PENINGTON: Samuel, 435
PENIX: William, 421
PENMAN: Wess, 235
PENN: A.A., 041, 235, 347, 364, 465; A.P., 465; Aaron, 041; Alex J., 455; Alfred A.,364; Andrew Jackson, 041; Anna, 053; Annie P., 235; Annie W., 015; Berta, 048; Betsey, 443; Bill, 235, 364; Celina, 364; Daniel, 235, 364; David, 211; Delphy, 347; F. L., 041; Frances, 044; Giles, 403; Harral, 031; Henry, 041; 364; Henry R., 269; Henry, 041, 235, 364, 378; J. A., 041, 235; 364, 465; Jasper, 443; John A., 364; John Alex, 447; Joseph, 065, 076, 223, 235, 313, 464; L.A., 364; PENN: Louis, 364; Lula, 031, 235; M.A., 364; M.A., 364; M.T., 364, 403; Martha A., 065, 076; Martha, 119, 269; Patience, 013; Peter, 235; Phoebe, 024; R.J., 455; Renda, 012; Russel J.,181, 235, 266; Russel, 269; Russell J., 041, 279, 364; Russell, 364; S.A., 442, 455; Salina, 041, 364, 458; Selina, 235; Selma, 269; Solomon, 338, 364, 415; Stephen A., 076, 235; T.P., 235, 364; Thom, 403; Thomas R., 065, 210, 235, 282, 364, 370, 455, 458; PENN: Thomas R., Mrs., 364; Thomas 041; 269; West Tom, 235; W. C., 235, 353, 364, 455, 465; W.J., 364; William C., 076, 090, 135, 211, 235, 236, 250, 260, 266, 269, 274, 279, 281, 330, 341, 354, 364, 372, 407, 455, 458; William J., 042; William, 076, 119, 123, 129, 134, 164, 210, 218, 222, 226, 235, 243, 252, 255, 272, 281, 292-294, 296, 316, 321, 403, 407, 431
PENNAMON: Morris, 042
PENNELL: Green, 102; John O., 042
PENNIMAN: Joshua S.,254; Morris, 042

PENNIMON: Anthony, 371
PENNINGTON: A. F., 455; Abel, 430,
465; Abel, Jr., 431; Abel, Sr.,
143, 144; Abraham, 236; Belle,
050; Ephraim, 133, 281, 431, 436;
Floyd, Mrs., 328; Frederick, 140;
G. F., 042; Henry, 125, 150, 153,
210, 236, 431; Isaac, 235, 236;
J. C., 236, 333, 364, 370; J. L.,
455; James, 144; John C., 364;
John L., 107, 236; John, 236, 321;
M.F., 364; Mary F., 008; Richardson,
112, 127, 236; Samuel S., 042;
Thomas, 076, 118, 236, 259, 282;
William B. R., 236; William B.,
042, 076, 448
PENNYMAN: George, 236;
John Wesley, 042
PENSON: James, 076
PENTECOST: William, 236
PENTON: John, 042; William, 236
PEOPLES: James D., 249; James, 254
PERDELL: Jackson, 236
PERDUE: Daniel, 431; Eliza E., 039;
Penelope, 236
PERKINS: Abraham, 141, 187, 240;
Alexander, 141,187, 240; Archibald,
141, 187, 240, 320; Charity, 016;
David A., 076; Frances, 187;
Francis, 236; J.O., 042; John, 042,
236; John, Sr., 236; Lelia B., 002;
Moses, 065, 076, 129, 146, 167,
236; Paul W., 431; Paul, 076, 091,
236, 246, 306; Phebe, 055;
William J., 042
PERMINTER: Susannah, 308
PERNELL: Green, 403; Greene, 195
PERRY: A. C., 344; A. F., 355;
Anna, 037; Annie, 025; Bose, 042;
Burrel, 277 Burrell, 236; Cora,
006; Daniel, 042; Dwight B., 251;
Dwin, 455; E.F., 455; Ed F., 455;
Edward N., 236; Edward, 214, 236,
401; Elvira, 076; F. A., 464;
Frances, 055; Green, 042, 117;
Hardy, 089; J. R., 455; James R.,
455; James, 076, 199, 236, 273,
431; Jerry, 042, 236; Joe, 042,
403; Joseph, 042, 403; Josiah,
126, 172; Maggie I., 051; Malvina
(Trammel), 236; Mary A. B., 013;
PERRY: Mat, 442; Mattie Lou, 046;
Miles W., 236; Miles, 199; Morris,
403, 465; Moses, 042; Nathaniel,
214, 401; Nep, 364; O. H., 455;
Rhoda, 030; Starkey, 246, 275,
429; Starky, 431; Susan Ann, 047;
Thomas, 042; Tom, 236; Wayman W.,
042; William A.,296; William, 076
PERRYMAN: David B., 117;
Elisha, 113, 202
PERSLEY: Crawford, 236; George T.,
042; J.S., 392
PERSON: G. W., 444; George W., 397,
390, 401; William, 435
PERSONS: A. J., 364; Amanda, 044;
Amos J., 176; B., 455; Benjamin,
076, 298, 448, 455; Bud, 150;
Burrell, 042; Clara, 035; E. E.,
365; Easter, 058; G. W., 455;
George W., 176, 236, 455; J. B.,
236, 364, 447, 455; J. C., 034;
J. D., 236, 461, 462; James, 365;
Jeff, 042; John, 042; L. M., 455;
Lovick, 101; Marinda, 060; Matilda,
227; Mollie E., 037; Nannie, 041;
R. F., 042, 455, 458; Randolph,
455; Sallie Beck, 037; T.B., 455;
Thomas B., 042; Thomas, 236; W.F.,
365, 403, 455, 468; W. F., 455;
William P., 042, 336, 365, 443,
448, 455; Willie F., 042
PERSONSY: George W., 444
PERTEET: Solomon, 237, 258
PERTEIT: Solomon, 236, 173,
176, 181, 301
PERTELL: J. C., 281, 465
PETERS: George, 365
PETERSON: Jake, 236; kartsten, 297
PETIT: Carry, 445
PETRIE: C. B., 042
PETTER: Anson L., 237
PETTIE: Anson L., 237, 365;
George, 403; W. B., 237
PETTIY: John, 237, 369; Lillie, 021
PETTYJOHN: Jacob, 431, 432
PEUGH: Jehu (heirs of), 431
PEURIFOY: Alice, 237; Annie R.,
050; Arrington, 076; Avaline,
065; Avoline, 076; B.W., 065,
076, 362, 455; B. W., Jr., 237;
Benjamin W., 320, 455; Benjamin,
455; Bragg, 042; Eliza Jane, 002;
F. W., 455; Gus, 042, 237; Henry,
042; J.B., 455; J.W., 455; James,
042, 455; John, 320; Kitty Ann,
047; Manerva, 025; Mary, 053;
McCarroll, 365, 455; McCarroll, 076;
S. L., 455; Silas M., 076, 320
PHAGIN: Randa, 058
PHARR: A., 208; M. A., 208;
Marcus A., 119, 305

PHELPS: Aquilar, 237; Aquilla, 065,
087, 088, 100, 113, 127, 136, 223,
237, 245, 260, 265, 275, 293, 300,
304, 312, 313, 431; Aquilla, Jr.,
076, 237; Aquilla, Sr., 076;
Aquilla, 401; Aquilia, 287, 288,
291; Carter, 403; Charly, 042; David
(heirs of), 431; Elizabeth J., 223;
Laura, 042; Morgan, 253; Oliver,
042, 237; Robert, 117; Tabitha,
237; Thomas, 237, 431; Warren,
091, 132, 164, 176; 209, 219, 318;
Washington, 076, 117, 237, 311,
397; William N., 042; William,
169, 237, 429
PHENESEE: William, 237
PHENY: Josie, 006
PHILLIPS: John B. M., 313; Jonathan,
427; Joseph, 157; Pobert B., 237;
Robert C., 281; Solomon, 289;
William,102, 316; Zachariah, 424
PHILLIPS: ?, 237; A. L., Mrs., 365;
Alice, 351; Ambrose A., 131, 262;
Ambrose, 162, 237, 253; Amy (Ann,
Nancy), 146; Angeline, 052; Annie,
021; Annis, 036; Augustus C., 076;
Bill, 365; Blewford, 237; Bryant
G., 076; Carrie, 045; Carry, 052;
Charles, 237; Charley, 042; Clem,
042; Daisie, 021; Daniel, 161;
Dempsey, 237; Demsey, 257; Edmund,
237; Edney E., 037; Elbert, 237;
PHILLIPS: Elijah, 119; Fell, 365;
Floyd, 042, 237; Frand, 365; Frank,
237; George, 206, 304; Ginnie, 033;
Green M., 344, 358, 375; H. N.,
269, 330; Henrietta, 018; Henry,
042; Hillery, 076, 237, 422, 430;
Isaac (heirs of), 431; Isaac, 076,
152, 184, 241; J.B.M., 237, 365,
455, 465; J.M.B., 365, 455; J.M.,
455; James, 112, 192, 233, 237,
431; Jenny, 184; Jeremiah, 237,
430; John B. M., 042, 076, 205,
237, 358, 365, 370, 415; John B.,
344, 358, 375; John H., 322; John
P., 237; John W., 042; John, 237,
365, 431; Jonathan, 212, 421, 437,
458; Joseph, 146, 250; Levi O.,
291; Lewis I., 042; Lewis Q., 237;
Lewis, 065, 076, 237, 425, 428,
PHILLIPS: Littleberry, 237; Mary B.
(Smart), 265; Mary E., 068, 076,
442; Mary, 042; Mathew, 139, 237;
Matthew, 174, 175, 216, 237, 431;
Mattie, 004; Maud, 041; Minor, 402;
Monroe, 237, 365, 444, 455; Monrow,
400; N. A., 238; N. H., 455; Nancy
A., 190; Nancy, 004, 024; Nathan,
146, 238, 431, 432; Nimrod, 238;
Oscar, 365, 455; Palmer R., 238;
Phil, 238; Polly (Medlock), 211;
PHILLIPS: John B., 118, 199, 238, 365,
403, 415, 455; R.F., 455; Reuben,
265, 432; Richard B., 238, 348, 448,
458; Richard, 076, 365, 455; Rufus
W., 298; Scott, 042, 238; Solomon,
174, 224; Stephen J., 042; Sue,
037; W. H., 365, 372, 400, 444,
455; W. J., 373, 390, 455; W.S.,
365; Webster, 042; Wiley H., 042,
076, 365; Wiley J., 421; Wiley P.,
259; Wiley, 065, 094, 141, 152,
154, 182, 238, 246, 253, 320, 344,
358, 364, 375, 410, 426, 455;
William D., 237 448; William L.,
076, 190, 238, 365, 455; William R.,
114, 219; William S., 042, 458;
William, 091, 118, 174, 184, 190,
238, 256, 259, 316, 365, 432, 448,
458; Willie, 042; Z., 238, 303;
Zaccheus, 303; Zachariah, 125, 198,
211, 238, 287, 297; Zachariah, Jr.,
138, 238, 303, 432; Zachariah, Sr.,
238, 432; Zacheus, 117, 164,
238, 259, 403
PHILPOT: Elhannon Thomas, 153
PHINEZY: C. H., 228; P. B., 228
PHININEX: J. P., 262
PHINISE: William, 238
PHINISE: C. H., 238; Hiram, 403;
John H., 403; William J. P., 403;
William, 238, 256; William, Jr.,403
PHINIZEE: William, 076, 238
PHINLTY: Ferdinand, 114, 191, 229
PHINNISEE: William, 238
PHIPP: Charles, 365
PHIPPS: Isaiah, 432
PHIPS: Jeremiah, 216, 268
PHROPHITT: O. S., 185
PICKENS: Marcus, 432; Rosetta, 031;
Thomas, 042; Tillman, 342; Tilman,
042, 359; Tilmon, 042; William,
209, 238
PICKETT: J.E., 462; James, 293; John
B., 308; Leroy, 042; W.H., 238, 363,
385, 398, 432; William H., 398
PIE: Eli, 365; Elizabeth, 365;
Kitty, 365; Ruby Lee, 365
PIEPCE: Banley, 042; John, 043;

Lucy, 034
PIERSON: Jeremiah, 139, 169, 185, 199
PILCHER: Edward, 432; Stephen, 432
PILES: Abraham, 238
PINCHARD: James, 076, 391, 432
PINCKARD: James, 268; James, Jr.,
432; James, Sr., 432; John, 263;
Lemuel C., 442; Peyton, 391; Thomas
043, 092, 094, 238, 263
PINKARD: James, 139; John, 222, 238;
John, Jr., 257; Thomas C., 200;
Thomas, 392
PINKERTON: Davis, 238
PINKEY: James, 403
PINKINSTON: Joshua, 126, 238
PINNELL: Eula, 016; Green, 238,
403; Hattie, 237; J. O., 365;
John O., 365, 455; L. N., 465;
Lee, 043; S. C., 365
PINSON: Aimey, 089; James, 255
PIOER: J. O., 043
PIPER: E. W., 455; J.C., 365, 465;
Jane, 226; John, 043, 226, 238,
365; Lilian, 046; T. L., 455; T.
M., 442; Thomas L., 076, 239, 365,
403; Thomas R., 043; Thomas S.,
415; Thomas, 455; W.E., 239, 365,
455; Zadock, 043, 365, 455; Zed,
455
PITCHEP: Annie, 040
PITKIN: John R., 134, 192, 214,
276; John, 087
PITMAN: Barns, 239; Jeremiah, 143;
Jess, 239; Jesse, 239; Joe, 379;
Micajah, 186; William A., 239;
William, 239
PITMON: Dudley, 043; Ezell, 043
PITTARD: Jim, 239
PITTMAN: Jeremiah, 176; Joseph, 212,
239, 247; William A., 432
PITTS: Amanda I., 104; C. A., 246;
C.C., 455; C.N., 365; C.N., Jr.,
455; Carrington, 455; Carrinton,
082; Chaney, 043; Charles N., 043;
Corine, 032; Coy, 403; Dicky, 239;
Eugene, 043; Evaline, 058; Georgia
Ann, 038; Henry, 043; Isaac, 239;
J. A., 043; J. E., 043, 330, 343,
389, 404, 408; J.L., 171, 397,
464, 466; J. T., 386, 390, 406;
J. W., 386, 390, 406; James, 043;
Jetrey, 221; Jesse, 106, 188, 212;
PITTS: John C., 076; John W., 089,
155, 165, 238, 243, 267; Joseph
A., 076; Joseph C., 365; Julius,
239; M. W., 043; Manse, 403;
Manson, 043, 350; Martha, 040;
Nancy A., 279; Nester, 076, 296,
415; Nestor, 455; Owlin, 455;
Permelia, 076; Pleas, 043; Sally,
047; Sarah, 059; Thomas, 043;
Wesley, 043; Will, 043; William,
043, 279
PLATT: George, 076, 239
PLOWMALE: Thomas, 043
PLUM: Isaac No., 251
PLUMMER: John R., 465; M. S., Mrs.,
002; Samuel, 076, 111, 213, 239;
265, 395, 465
PLUNCKET: J. F., 239
PLYMAIL: Michael, 239
PLYMALE: Andrew, 212; Clem, 365;
Mike, 365; T. W., 043; W.,043
POARCH: Vera, 057
POE: John, 255; Washington, 096
POGG: William H., 145
POINDEXTER: Susannah, 194
POINTS: James W., 366
POLAND: Thomas, 432
POLHILL: Benjamin M., 122;
Mary J. (Cochran), 122
POLF: A. E., 411; Archibald L.,
198, 448; Betsey, 004; C.W., 455;
Charles E., 076; Clara, 051; Dan,
239; Frank, 043; G.W., 365; George
W., 403; George, 403; Grover C.,
403; H.A., 455; J.A., 043; J.K.,
043, 455; J. T., 455; James K.,
339, 410, 455; James T., 043;
Jemimah C., 041; John, 043; Joshua
F., 076; Julian B., 403; Kizzie
E., 010; Laura, 002; Lucy, 042, 043
055; Mollie, 034; Nannie, 056; P.
A., 403; Sarah M., 018; T.W.O.,
455; T. W., 455; Thomas G., 265;
Thomas W., 455; Thomas, 455; W.H.,
455; Will H. A., 403; William H.
A., 043; William O., 043
POLLARD: James, 154; Major A.,239;
Richard, 076, 140, 239, 320
PON: Caroline, 335, 343, 354, 359,
369; Caroline, Mrs., 359; Dixie,
368; E., 239; Edgar, 365; Giles,
239; John T., 076; L. W., 335,
343, 344, 354, 465; Lewis W., 153,
279, 377, 379, 380, 432; Nuck, 043;
Pauline, Mrs., Rebecca C.,239, 347,
351, 359, 365; Taylor, 076
PONCE: Dimas, 135
PONDER: Posco, 239; S.M., 043; Sallie,
027; Tom, 403

PONDS: Vera, 057
PONE: Zell, 403
POOL: Abram, 127; Elizabeth, 236
POOLE: Abram, 076; Adam, 239; David, 427; Frederick, 239; Thomas, 076
POPE: ?, 239; A. H., 043; Adaline, 004; Alsa, 234; Andrew, 043, 239; Annie J., 076; Annie M., 239; Burwell, 043; C.H., 239; C.M., 033; C.W., 201, 239, 354, 403, 455; Cary W., 297; Charles W., 043, 455; Charles, 455; Clarance, 239, 455; Clark, 455; Cohen, 239, 254, 365; D.W., 455; Dan, 239; Daniel, 043, 239; Danniel W., 365; Doc, 043; Dock, 239; E.C., 239, 289, 365, 366, 379, 455; Easter, 004;
POPE: Edgar C., 239, 344, 365, 366, 403, 455, 465; Ever Gene, 057; Fannie M., 020; Florence E., 059; Frances E., 033; Gideon, 105, 189; Gidion, 301; Gim, 403; Henry, 264; Hollis T., 447; Hopson J., 043; Ida, 011; J. C., 455; J. E., 043; J. G., 337; J. J., 239, 381, 391, 455; J.L., 455; J. Otis, 455; Jack, 366; James C., 455; James J., 043, 083, 297, 455; James, 366, 455; Jane, 299; Jefferson, 142; John C., 076, 115, 239, 282, 415, 455; John F., 167; John H., 271; John, 091;
POPE: Josiah P., 043, 239, 313, 320, 415; Josiah, 076; Josias, 172, 234; Kate, 038; Katie, 012; L. L., 043, 455; Laurance L., 043; Leroy, 167; Lucius, 043, 240, 267; M.W., 336, 415, 455; Mary Ann, 011; Mary Jane, 014; Mary Virginia, 017; Mary, 240; Miller W., 043, 076, 148, 223, 240, 246, 366, 415; Nancy, 047, 297; Nathan, 366;
POPE: Nicie, 022; Ophelia, 008; R. C., 455; Robert, 270; Rufus, 043; S.H., 239, 461, 465; S.H., Mrs., 239; S. M., 043, 344, 366, 455; Sallie H., 364; Sarah H., 366; Sarah J., 041; Sherod, 254, 365; T. C., 455; Tannis, 043; Thomas C., 043, 366, 455; Thomas W., 443; W.K., 415, 455; W.M., 403; W.R., 356, 366, 455; W. Ross, 455; Wash, 043; Washington, 119; William R., 076, 148, 201, 240, 356, 455, 458; William R., 455; William W., 144, 194, 198, 225, 240, 402, 432; Willie, 043; Wilson, 301; Wilson, 105, 189; Zachary, 104, 266, 270, 283; Zachery, 153; Zachry, 200
PORTER: Anthony, 432; Archibald, 240, 388; Catharine, 076; Cornelia, 003; Dennis, 240; Edward R., 240; Elizabeth, 076, 123, 128; Ernest, 287; F.R., 152, 455; Fannie, 366; Henry, 043; Hugh, 091, 153; J.C., 152; J. L., 407; J. W., 411, 455; James H., 288; John Henry, 043; John W., 154, 306; John, 424, 429, 432; Lula, 057; Matilda M., 065, 076; Oliver S., 379; Robert B., 094, 141, 148; Wess, 466; William, 076, 214, 246, 251-253, 260, 293, 460
PORTWOOD: Benjamin, 240; Catharine, 076, 298; Dempsey, 187; Howard, 043, 403; John R., 043; John, 139, 240, 391, 442; Lucy, 403; Manda A., 059; Montgomery, 043; Sam, 240; Thomas J., 043
POSEY: Francis, 240; John, 121; Squire, 466
POST: G., 448; J. W., 455; Jim, 403; Joseph C., 162, 240, 407; Joseph M., 180, 200, 240, 320; Joseph S., 366; Joseph, 240; Marian, 240; Mary J., 366; Samuel B., 240; Samuel G., 240; Samuel M., 240; Samuel, 065, 076, 106, 189, 240; Thomas, 168; William M., 240
POTT: Gideon, 125
POTTER: A. C., 185, 241, 366, 455; Adam C., 076, 366; Pleasant, 076, 240; Riley, 211, 240, 317; Robert D., 197
POTTS: James, 240, 466; James, Sr., 311, 459; Moses, 160, 237, 241, 256; S.P., 455; Stephen, 044, 076, 160, 240; Stephen, Jr., 320; William L., 256
POU: Albert, 443; Angeline N., 044; Carey, 044; Carle, 044; Edmond, 044; Ellen, 443; Hardy, 204; Ida, 011; James, 263; Jennie, 036; John T.,065; John W., 044; Kattie, 038; Lewis W., 153, 241, 297; Mahala, 006; Pearler, 028; Rena, 014; Sarah, 059; Syna, 056; Turner, 044; Wesley, 044
POUND: Ell E., 044; Nelson, 363; Paul P., 044; Sol, 363; T.G., 455
POUNDS: Alex, 432; Annie, 048; Bill, 241; Callie, 193; Frank, 241; Herriman, 217; John, 044; Lizzie, 009; Lula, 041; Merriman, 241;

Sallie, 015, 403; Sarah Bell, 403; Tommie, 044, 466
POWEL: John, 466; Wilkin, Sr., 177; William R., 318; William, 223; Zacheus, 241
POWELL: A. L., 065; A. L., Mrs., 335; A. W., 403, 455; Albert, 044, 241; Allen P., 432; Allie Laura, 076; Allis L., 404; Anna Cora, 021; Archie, 459; Augustus W., 044, 455; Barnet R., 241; Barnet(t), 127, 191; Benjamin W., 044; Carrie, 366; Charity, 039; Charles, 250; Charlie, 366; Christopher W., 241, 432; Cordelia, 058; Cornelius, 044; Davis, 044; E.H., 455; Eliza, 366; Elizabeth, 031, 241; Emily G., 017; Emma, 241, 463; Evan H., 044, 065, 076, 114, 129, 167, 267, 286, 290, 301, 432, 455; Evan, 241;
POWELL: Fannie, 019; Frances, 031; George, 164, 234, 314; Harriet, 051; James T., 366, 398, 401; James, 044; Jeremiah, 201; John G., 076, 241, 466; John K., 461; John, 044, 105, 172, 193, 241; John, 300, 366, 408; Johnson, 241; Lewie, 241; Lewis, 044; Lilie, 020; Louis, 366; Lucas, 087, 134, 135, 232, 233, 403, 421, 465; Marla, 011; Martha, 013, 021; Moses, 076, 229, 321, 432; Norbin B., 241; Norborn B., 263, 268; Norborn, 310;
POWELL: Norborne B., 149, 152, 196, 233, 241, 245, 432, 458; Norborne P., 175; Norborne, 044; Pompey, 366; R.F., 354; R.R., 447; Rachel, 065; Reuben, 241; Sallie, 006; Sammy Davis, 241; Sarah, 020; Simeon, 241; Thomas, 135, 241; Tom, 241; W.R., 241, 366, 447, 455; Whit, 076; William C., 250; William R., 044, 076, 286, 448; William, 241; Woody, 044, 241; Zacheus, 215
POWER: Charles G., 044
POWERS: Butler, 366; C. T., 424; Eliza Jane, 021; Francis, 241, 432; G. T., 338, 349, 352, 366; G. T., 386, 403, 455, 466, 468; J. B., 403; James, 115; John H., 194, 241; Robert, 241; Thomas, 366
POYNTS: J. W., 366
PRESLEY: Joe, 241; Moses, 432
PRESSLEY: William, 247
PRESTON: Aaron, 044, 366, 403; Ada, 466; Amanda, 049; Amarintha, 048; Amos, 241, 344, 403; Archibald, 241, 242; C-T-, 241, 366, 455; Charles F.,205, 322; Charles T.,076, 320, 366, 415, 455; Charles, 242; Charley, 044; Charlie, 403; Childs, 403; Elbert, 044, 366; Essick, 242; Essie Hall, 052; Fannie, 022; Gilliam, 241; Harriet, 044; Ida B., 466; O. F., 366; U. W., 366, 372;
PRESTON: James A., 333; James M., 112; John, 044; Johnnie, 044; Joseph W., 044, 086, 197, 331, 366; Lee, 242, 366; Leila, 366; Lonie, 054; Lony, 242; Lucy, 035; Magnolia, 051; Major, 366; Mamiee, 005; Mandy, 025; Manuel, 366; Maria, 036; Mattie O., 014; Mollie G., 509; Ola Lee, 226 Patcy, 386; Pauline, 035; Pearl, 013; Riley, 044; Punnels, 466; Salina V., 009; Sarah, 039;
PRESTON: Spencer, 399; Spencer, 103, 334, 366, 403, 415; T.C., 455; T. G., 044, 366; Teluia J., 053; Thomas G., 242, 366; Thomas, 236; Tildy, 242; Victoria, 033; W. B., 366, 455; W.H., 242, 366; W.J.M., 044, 228, 242, 337, 340, 342, 366, 380, 444, 455; W.J., 360; William H., 065, 097, 112, 153, 209, 223, 333, 442; William H. Jr., 076; William H. Sr., 205, 320; William J.M., 044, 332; William S., 366
PREWITT: John, 283
PRICE: A.W., 367; Althea, 054; Ann, 242, 401; Annie J., 018; Calhoun, 044, 403; Charles, 188, 242; Clara J., 027; Crawford, 242; E.C., 466; Edward, 076, 113, 118, 129, 143, 232, 242, 250, 256, 259, 284, 432; Eliza A., 024; Estelle V., 061; Florence, 062; Isaac, 044; James, 093; Jane L., 030; Jane, 060; John U., 290; John W., 083; John, 044, 076, 218, 242, 436; John, Jr.,430;
PRICE: John, Sr., 381, 424; Joseph, 144, 203, 205, 224, 242, 304, 432; L. M., 242, 336, 337, 367, 387, 455; L. M., 367, 387; Leonidas R., 152, 365, 367; Leroy M., 090, 232, 242, 448, 455; Leroy R., 196, 390; Leroy, 242, 356; Lucinda, 032; Maggie, 006, 282; Margarett, 095; Mary (Morgan), 218, 242; Mary J., 002, 014; Mary Jane, 041; Mary,

065, 242; Mattie Lou, 010; Nancy, 048; O. D., 371, 455; Ora, 443;
PRICE: Oscar D., 044; R. W., 242, 367, 395, 442; Rebecca, 033; Richard W.,367; Rindy, 053; Robert W., 044, 242, 455; Robert, 044, 076, 242, 367; Stephen, 044; Sterling, 242, 448; Thomas R., 242, 318, 367; Turner, 044; W.B., 403; Wash, 044, 242; Will, 242
PPICHARD: P. E., 390
PPICKETT: David, 242
PRIDGEN: James, 242, 432; William, 320
PRIE(PPYE): James, 242
PRIGDEN: James, 123
PRIGIN: James, 129
PRIMROSE: Peter, 137
PRINCE: Charles H., 243; Charles, 210; John, 432; Joseph, 242, 260, 320, 426; Mary, 293; Reuben, 044; Sarah, 293; William, 242
PRIOR: John, 242
PRITCHARD: John, 395
PRITCHET: Dora, 020; William, 242
PRITCHETT: Abraham, 044, 242; Abram, 367; Alexander, 044; Alfred M., 044, 290, 323; Alfred, 108, 109, 118, 119, 152, 214, 239, 276, 277, 282, 286; Burman, 016; Burney, 028; Druscilla, 177; E. P., 242, 243, 367, 455; E. N., 466; Edward H., 243, 367; G. W., 442; George W., 243, 323; George, 108, 109, 119, 152, 277, 282, 286, 455;
PRITCHETT: Jeanette, 035; Lethe, 035; Lizzie, 011; Lovall J., 243; Mary, 243; Mat, 367, 466; Matt, 190, 367; Moses, 367; Patience, 041; Philip B., 292; S. L., 243, 367; Sarah L. (Comer), 367; Sarah L., 242, 367; S. L., 076, 243, 320, 367, 391, 403, 466, 467; Thomas L., 118, 299; Thomas J., 108, 109, 119, 152, 214, 239, 243, 276, 277, 282, 286, 289, 290, 323, 325, 358, 367, 377, 404, 415, 455, 466; Thomas L., 243; Thomas, 044, 243; Thos. J., 466; William H., 076, 184, 204, 242, 243, 246, 297, 316, 320, 325; William S.,103; William, 044, 093, 243, 257, 367, 404, 426, 466
PROCTOR: Brad, 185; Cresa, 059; Henry, 044, 243; Joseph J., 044; Laura, 056; Martha Ann, 049
PROFFIT: O. S., 352
PROFFITT: O. S., 246
PROPHET: A. L., 121; Susan, 053
PROPHIT: George, 243, 367; O.S., 195, 281; Oglesby S.,270; Oglesby S., 401; Oglesby, 243; Oldby S., 132; Robert, 208
PROUDFIT(?): Alexander, 262
PROW: Peter, 127
PRTCHETT: Alfred M., 076
PPUDDEN: Samuel, 223
PPUDHOMME: Lewis, 313
PRUIT: Fields, 224
PPYER: William, 243
PPYOR: Marlow, 191; William B., 097; William, 226, 243
PUCKET: Martin, 242
PUCKETT: Edmund, 131; John C.I.A.W., 243; Martin, 076, 093, 136, 148, 163, 195, 243, 245, 253, 300, 445; Nancy W., 243; Nancy, 243; Robert L., 243, 285
PUGH: Robert, 432
PUGHE: Edward, 243
PUGSLEY: John, 193, 313
PULLEY: Emma E., 042; Mary T., 044
PULLIAM: Susan, 002; William B., 415
PULLY: N. E., 015
PURCELL: Robert, 404
PURCY: John L., 243
PURIFOY: Aaron, 202; Benjamin, Sr., 243; McCarrol, 241
PURINGTON: Dee, 025; William, 044
PURKINS: Daniel, 076
PURSE: Emma S., 023; Isiah, 101
PUPSLEY: G.T., 350; George T., 458; J.S., 330, 343, 373; S.C., 350
PUTMAN: Hosea, 294
PYAPS: G. W., 455
PYE: Andrew, 217; Asa, 124, 212, 243, 404; B. W., Mrs., 390; H., 357, 401; Barthena, 367; Bartheny, 076; Benier, 221; Berner, 315; Burrell J., 045; D. T., 447; Durwood, 455; Edward H., 045; Eli, 243; Elizabeth, 029, 243; Emily, 055; Emma, 014; Florrie E., 458; Georgia Inez, 058; Griffin L., 076, 226, 243; H.W., 282, 357;
PYE: Hannah, 455; Harman W., 244; Harman, 244; Harmon W., 076, 137, 320, 367, 466; J. E., 455; James (heirs of), 432; James, 065, 076, 109, 137,215, 224, 244, 320, 420; Jefferson, 242, 320; Jesse, 258;

John E., 244, 340, 455; John, 455;
Jordan, 065, 076, 100, 191, 244,
320; Kittle, 055; Lewis H., 121,
244 Lewis, 212, 244, 243, 432;
PYE: Lottie L., 244; Lucy, 021;
Lumpkin, 244; Mary, 034, 149;
Nannie O., 038; Pete, 404; Rina,
367; Scipio, 342; Stephen, 045; T.
W., 197, 360, 455; Thad B., 367;
Thaddeus B., 367, 415; Thadeous,
320; Thadeus B., 367; Thadeus,
076; Theophilus, 065, 076, 104,
160, 244, 248, 321, 432, 442;
Thomas W., 045, 076, 339, 455,
458; Thomas, 244, 367; Tom, 244;
W.A., 221, 289; W.H., 455; W.T.,
367; W. Tom, 244; Wade, 045;
William A., 379; William H., 045;
William, 045, 105
PYLE: Abraham, 188, 253, 391, 432;
Abram, 194, 260
PYLES: Abraham, 237
QAPFERMAN: Florence, 404
QUAKER: Alexander, 045
QUARTERMAN: Dave, 367
QUEEN: Will, 404
QUIN: Edward, 176, 181, 188, 191, 272
QUINN: J. P., 346, 358
RABUN: William, 231
RADCLIFF: Moses, 076
RADDEN: Abner, 321
RADDEN: Abner, 198, 244;
David, 076, 321
RADFORD: Charles, 045, 244; Mose,
045; Reuben, 200, 435
RAFF: Aaron A., 189
RAGAN: Asa, 076, 113, 244, 321; Berry,
045; John, 139, 435, 466
RAGLAND: Alexander M., 119, 151;
Alexander, 090; Burrel, 223;
Burwell, 138, 213, 320, 436;
Drayton, 244, 367; Ferderick W.,
244; Fererick, 244; John A., 244;
John, 244; Mary R., 065; Milledge,
045; Pettus, 076, 107
RAGLIN: George, 127, 161; Jack, 045
RAGSDALE: Sarah, 022
RAIFORD: Baldwin, 192; John S.,
192; John, 192; Lucry, 192
RAINES: Josiah, 244; Nathaniel, 185
RAINEY: Ann, 244, 432; Daniel M.,
466; Elizabeth, 244; John W., 455;
John, 198, 159, 244; Mary E., 244;
Mary, 432; Mathew, 442; Matthew,
076, 094, 244, 321, 432; Nathaniel
H., 076; Reuben M., 244, 245;
Reuben, 429; William H., 244;
William, 076, 245, 432
RAINY: Ike, 367
RALSTON: David, 146
RAMBLE: Henry, 249
RAMEY: Absalom, 076; Allice, 076;
Anderson, 415; Brazoria T., 056;
Charles D.,145, 153, 203, 210, 214,
216, 239, 245, 252, 253, 284, 285,
321, 404; Clarissa, 076, 458; D.M.,
466; Daniel M., 076; Elizabeth P.,
076; Eugene, 443; Frances, 034;
Ike, 045; John C., 245; John D.,
145, 239, 252, 253, 284; Mary A.,
004; Mary M., 442; Mary, 039; N.H.,
245; Nathanle H., 045, 321;
Nathaniel, 245; Sarah, 020; William
P., 264, 321; William, 096, 104,
120, 136, 226, 245, 265, 300,
321, 390
RAMSAY: Alexander, 245; George, 128,
271; Noah, 202; Thomas, 245
RAMSEY: Elizabeth, 050; Henry,
321; Noah, 245, 430, 432; Randal,
432; Thomas, 245; W. A., 245
RAMY: Alice, 367; D. M., 367;
Ike, 245; John, 136
RAMY: Lizzie, 367
RANAY: George, 245; J.W., 442; John
W., 245, 315; Mary E., 245;
Mathew, 245, 387
RANDAL: Richmond, 045
RANDALL: Annie, 404; J. C., 367;
James B., 140, 205, 245; John
Henry, 245; Richmon, 367
RANDEL: Anderson, 367
RANDLE: Benjamin J., 245; James G.,
236; James, 184; John S., 249;
John, 097; Newton, 245;
Washington, 184, 238; Willis, 260
RANDOLPH: Jeremiah, 432; Joel F.,
238, 257; Joel, 193; Peter, 139,
200, 233, 257, 322
RANEY: Elizabeth, 245; George,
245; Harriet, 245; John, 257;
Lucy, 329; Mathew, 394
RANKIN: Andrew, 094, 154; Robert
C., 107, 245
RANSOM: James B., 245; Joseph,
245; Reuben, 140
RANY: Mathew, 378; Matthew, 357
RAPELYEA: Daniel, 154, 316
RASBERRY: William, 245
RASIN: R. W., 465
RASSETER: White, 245
RATCLIFF: Moses, 065

RATHBONE: William P., 150, 162, 266
RATLIFF: Elizabeth, 245
RAVENAL: James, 142, 210
RAVENEL: James, 118
RAVENS: James H., 262
RAWLS: B. H., 369
RAY (WRAY): Jane, 017
RAY: B. H., 330: Bolivar H., 344;
Clark, 245; Claxton, 248; David,
297; Elijah, 460; G. A., 344;
George, 432; Jane, 100; Jeremiah
W., 155, 238; Joseph, 045; Mark,
245, 289, 432; Mary, 432; P.J.,
245; Roy, 405; Sally, 297; Samuel,
432; Thomas, 245; William, 245
PAYMOND: Oliver C., 263
RAYNOR: Savannah, Mrs., 007
REA: David A., 045; James, 125, 168
PEAGAN: Kissiah, 045
REASE: Sarah, 008
REAVES: John, 302; Joshua, 432;
Warner, 404; William, 321, 367
REDD: B. A., 445; Mary Jane, 016;
Matilda(Kelly), 195; William A.,163
REDDICK: Allen, 367; Delia, 008;
George, 076, 246, 367; Henry, 076
REDDING: John, 349; Thomas, 152;
William C., 257; William D., 170
REDFIELD: Charles, 173
REDICK: Dave, 404
REDMAN: Charles, 045; Charlie, 246;
Stephen, 246
REDMOND: Josie, 060; Lula, 032
REECE: William, 045
REED: Benjamin H., 131, 176;
Benjamin, 171; Dixie, 368; Elias,
248; Elliot, 277; Elsi, 060; Image,
368; James, 167, 190; John T.,
273; John, 287; Joseph, 122;
Lizzie, 404; Lou, 060; Mathew,
106; Peter, 246; Robert, 109;
Samuel, 132; Will, 404; William, 142
REES: David A., 245; John, 118;
Jordan, 246; Thadeus B., 132
PEESE: A.W., 341; Albert, 045; Allen,
045; America, 045, 246; Charles M.,
134; Charlie, 045; Cuthbert, 065,
076, 090, 108, 138, 147, 246, 278,
284, 292, 432, 448; David A., 087,
097, 100, 110, 116, 134, 137, 139,
141, 147, 163, 175, 176, 187, 196,
201, 217, 234, 246, 251, 252,
260, 266, 276, 297, 293, 300-302,
321, 401, 422, 423, 429, 433, 458,
467; Davie Jane, 027; Ela, 011;
REESE: Hamp, 246; Harriett, 246; J.
B., 351; Jim, 404; John C., 145,
184, 255; John, 236, 246; Jordan,
145, 246; Joseph, 090, 108, 246,
251, 266; Josephine, 022; Louise
C., 013; Lucian, 231; Lucien L.,
246, 312; Lucius L.126, 455; Lucy
(Meriwether), 134; Martha, 344;
Peter, 045, 368; Sam, 045; Sam,
Jr., 368; Samuel, 045, 368; Samuel,
Jr., 045; Seaborn, 368; T.W., 364;
T.W., Mrs, 343; Thadeus B., 246;
Thornton, 045; Titus, 045; W. H.,
447; William H., 368, 361, 421;
William, 045; Williamson H., 246
REEVE: Charles F. V., 223
REEVES: Absalom E., 466; Allie H.,
404; Allie Jane, 024; Allie, 368;
Asa, 246; Avery, 223, 246, 398;
B. F., 356, 368, 386, 387, 404;
Ben, 045, 246, 367, 404; Benjamin
F., 368; Benjamin, 045; Cap, 246;
Charles F. V., 302; G. V., 246;
Green, 432; Greene, 432; James M.,
325; James, 246, 294, 432, 434;
Joel A. (heirs of), 432; Joel A.,
076, 185, 246; Joel Avery, 432;
REEVES: Joel, 404; John W.L., 246,
316, 321; John W. S., 246; John,
246, 432; Jonathan, 163, 179, 242,
244, 246, 247, 432; Joseph, 045,
076, 246, 415, 455; Joshua, 246,
270; Littice W., 052; Martha C.,
007; Mary Francis, 330; Minnie,
007; P. W., 246; P. Wyatt, 321;
Pleasant W., 247, 321; Prier, 432;
Prior, 247; Robert T.,247; Sherman,
404; Thomas K., 247; Warner, 045,
247, 368; Wiatt, 257; Wiley, 247;
404; Willev, 247; William, 244,
247; Willis, 465; Wyatt, 246,
247, 435; Zeb, 247
REID: A.S., 466; Alexander S., 280;
Alfred, 045; Allie, 055; Andrew,
247, 430; Augustus, 045; Ben, 045;
Charles, Jr., 368; Charlie, Jr.,
045; Comfort, 007; Cunningham D.,
136, 247; David, 249; Dennis, 045,
404; Dora, 050; E. W., Mrs., 192;
Elizabeth W., 415, 443; George W.,
045, 247; George, 466; Gus, 247;
Harriet, 247; James L., 099; James,
223, 247, 266; John (heirs), 247;
REID: John C. H., 154, 198, 208, 263,
315; John C., 104; John T., 088;
John, 045, 153, 182, 222, 234,
247, 302, 321; Joseph, 368, 432;

Joshua, 368; Katie, 005; Lilburn
H., 045; Lish, 247; Luke, 174, 188,
211, 252, 254, 275; M. A., 263;
Mandy, 032; Mary Jane, 368; Mary,
037, 466; Minnie, 404; Nathan, 045;
Patsev, 005; Rachael, 023; Richmond
A., 295; Richmond H., 361; Robert
A., 371; Robert Robinson, 045; S.
T., 335, 368, 404, 455; Sam, 404;
REID: Samuel T., 192, 247, 368, 415,
455; Samuel, 065, 076, 247, 368;
Virgil, 076; W. A., 207, 247, 368,
455; Washington, 247; Will, 368;
William A., 065, 076, 145, 153,
247, 341, 368, 404, 455; William
M., Sr., 192; William, 247, 268;
Willie, 045
REILLY: Philip, 268
REISON(PASCHAL): Betsey, 202
REISON: Benjamin, 202
RELAFORD: Susan, 029
PEMSEN: Simeon, 287
PENFOE: James T., 045, 368
RENFROE: Elisha, 247; James F.,
090; James W., 190;
Stephen, Jr., 247
REPASS: Churchwell, 076
PEPASS: W. T., 289
RESPASS: Churchvill, 314
RESPESS: Saulsburv, 223
RESSAN: Evan, 045
RESSEAN: George M., 045
PEVEPE: Richard, 313
REVES: Ella, 029
REYNOLDS: Benjamin H., 255; Coleman
F., 307; Frances, 019; Hubbard,
458; Hubert, 150; J.J., 442; James,
264; John, 247, 368; Jordan, 264;
Jule, 045, 368; Larkin, 283; Mary,
045; Minnie L., 061; Patrick, 045;
Permecus, 296; Robert, 274; Sarah,
039; Thomas P., 105; Thomas, 096,
247; W. P., 466; Willie, 368
RHEA: D. A., 455
RHEMES: Littlejohn, 045
RHODES: Absalom, 150; J. D., 442;
James, 432; Samuel P., 076; Samuel
T., 248; Samuel, 248
RHODS: Lula, 404
RHYMES: Jesse J., 270; John, 314
RICE: Allen P., 092; B., 328, 342,
366, 362; Berien, 331; Charles
N., 170; James, 248; John M.,
243; William, 223
RICH: George, 248
RICHARD: John, 045; Robert E., 119
RICHARDS: Aurie, 056; Burrel, 094;
Carrie, 053; Duke, 045; Gabriel,
045; George, 045; Green M., 248;
J. J., 447; James, 093, 094, 098,
113, 119, 122-124, 129, 132-134,
140, 142, 168, 169, 172-174, 186,
195, 199, 206, 214, 225, 230, 236,
248, 253, 259, 280, 282, 285, 286,
287, 293, 299, 303, 304, 311, 313,
321, 404, 427, 432; Jerre, 045;
RICHARDS:John, 046; Malbary, 013;
Robert, 046, 132, 404; S.P., 447;
Seaborn, 046; Thomas C., 398;
Thomas, 229, 432; William B., 248,
433; William, 046, 232, 248, 437;
Willis, 119, 133, 168, 169, 172,
186, 199, 206, 248, 259, 280,
282, 286, 293, 404
RICHARDSON: Armstead, 194, 204;
Cliff, 368; Daniel, 248; George,
076, 248; Harman, 046; Jacob, 248;
James E., 111; James, 046, 165,
173, 404, 455; John H., 266; John,
209, 252, 270; Jonathan, 165, 234,
248; Jordan, 248; Moses, 248;
Peter B., 248; Pichard, 198; Robert
E., 248; Thomas, 202, 321; William
G. W., 248; Woodmoreland, 111
RICHESON: George (heirs of), 433
PICHESON: John, 458
RICHEY: E. J., 368; Edward J., 076;
Nannie, 368; Spencer, 368
PICHIE: Temple, C12
RICKEPSON: B. A., 248; Benjamin,
248, 368; Ed, 248; J. C., 404;
Janis, 004; Mary Wills, 006; Neel,
368; R. A., 248
RICKERSON: William, 368
RICKET: Dolphus, 368
RICKET: Laura, 054
RICKETT: C. A., 046
RICKETTS: Ellen, 016; John M., 046,
368; R. S., 433; Richard S., 076;
RICKS: Jesse, 174, 257
RIDGEWAY: Havs, 248
RIDGLEY: Nicholas G., 184
RILEY: Anthony, 445; Archibald B.,
076, 145; C. L., 368, 388, 455;
Charles B., 248; Charles L., 248,
270, 433; Charles S., 202; Charles,
046, 248; Charlie, 404; Corine,
051; Crissy, 248; 368; Delphy, 020;
Drucilla, 051; Elisebeth, 030;
Eliza, 134; Ella, 055; Francis M.,
248; Frank, 046; Gus, 248; H. B.,

342, 357, 363, 404, 455, 461;
RIDLEY: Hamilton B., 095, 248; Hamp, 368, 098; Hannibal, 248, 368; Howard, 248, 368; Jesse, 368; John, 248; Jomima, 044; Julia, 046; Jumima, 368; Lavina, 046; Lucy, 008; Mariah, 012; Marshall, 046; Melvina, 017; Patience, 023; Peter, 248; Robert A. F., 248; Robert A.T., 145, 218; Robert A., 199, 279; Robert, 248; Stephen, Jr., 248; Steve, 046; Sue Lee, 028; Tom, 404; W.T., 455; William Thom, 046; William, 046, 404; Willie, 046
RIDLY: Hannah, 040
RIDNOUR: D. C., 329; Silas, 329
RIECE: Sam, 248
RIEVES: John, 201
RIGDON: H. J., 455, 461
RIGGINS: John, 046; Scott, 046
RIGHT: Frances, 003
RILEY: Edward S., 224; Joseph, 245; William, 241
RIMES: Little John, 433
RINES: Joseph, 249
RIPLEY: ?, 212; Miller, 292
RISBY: Mary, 008
RISLEY: C. T., 403; H. W., 403; Hubbel W., 120; Hubbell W., 147
RITCHEY: E. J., Jr., 249; Edward J., 082; Edward, Jr., 046; Minnie, 043; Will, 368
RITCHIE: E. J., 249; Spencer, 046; Will, 392
RIVERS: Allie, 415; Benjamin, 065, 076; Burwell G., 250; C. K., 046, 368; Cary, 046; Charley, 046; Claude, 249; Dock, 368; Elijah, 206, 249; Fred, 076; James, 076, 225, 249, 250, 433; John F., 116, 249, 251, 404; John W. L., 249; John, 116, 146, 146, 249, 250, 308, 422, 434; Lee, 046; Milly, 250, 433; Mollie, 020; Nathaniel A., 250; Patience, 045; Poggie, 061;
RIVERS: Robert T., 249, 250, 321; Sallie, 041; Sam, 250, 404; Susan (Thurmond), 249; Susan, 201, 249, 250, 321, 434, 458; T.H.B., 466; Thomas A., 251; Thomas H. B., 138, 165, 249-251, 272, 300, 321, 404, 423, 433; Thomas H., 250; Thomas, 101, 239, 249-251, 279, 321, 404, 429, 433, 435; Thomas, Sr., 249-251; William W., 250, 251, 321; William, 046; Willis, 046
ROACH: David K., 251; Elizabeth, 057; Floyd, 404; James, 251; John Lee, 046; Martha, 003
ROAN: Jesse J., 207; Leonard, 251; Willis J., 207
ROBBINS: Elisha, 088
ROBENETT: Jesse, 251
ROBERSON: Duffy, 251; Elbert, 046; Gellia, 020; George, 046; John H., 046; Margaret D., 019; S. A., 046; Sam, 046
ROBERT: Lawrence Wood, 076; Minnie N., 368
ROBERTS: Abbie, 041; Alice S., 039; Annie Mae, 010; Anthony, 368, 369; Augustus, 369; Bartholomew G., 076, 445; Beatris, 031; Brown, 046; Caroline, 028; Carrie, 047; Charles, 251, 455; Charley, 046; Coleman M., 172, 467; Cornelia, 053; Cotes(?), 443; Daniel A., 046; Daniel, 077, 369; Delphy, 052; Dora, 404; E. D. (children of), 369; E. R., 251, 355, 455; E., 455; Elias W., 046;
ROBERTS: Emma, 045; Eugenius R., 046; Gulford, 046; Harvey, 046; Henry, 046, 369; 448; Hyder, 369; J. A., 046, 455; J. H., 115, 336, 397, 455; J. R., 046, 338, 369; J. W., 046, 251, 369, 455; J. Willie, 369; James H., 077, 094, 126, 138, 143, 165, 187, 190, 219, 237, 242, 251, 254, 265, 273, 311, 317, 321, 325, 364, 368, 424, 455; James, 046;
ROBERTS: John M., 139; John W., 456; John, 046, 404; Jordan, 251, 360, 369; Joseph, 046; Julia, 017; L. A., 196, 456; L. H., 369; L. W., 448, 456; Laurence W., 046; Leah, 020; Leander, 046; Leonidas A., 456; Lex, 251; Lucious, 046; Lucius, 251; Ludie, 010; Lydia, 251; Malinda, 038; Mariah, 037; Marsh, 251; Mary A., 026, 369; Mary E., 059; Mary, 009, 351;
ROBERTS: Michael A., 260; Michael, 160; O. G., 196, 197, 251, 281, 357, 362, 363, 369, 381, 409, 433, 442, 447, 456; P. A., 456; Paul, 251, 456; Peyton, 046; Richard, 251, 421, 433; Rufus, 404; S. J., 456; Sam J., 456; Samuel M., 251;

Sarah, 077, 251; Spencer, 369, 404; Sue, 251; T. A., 251; Thomas H., 147, 228; Thomas J., 138; Thomas, 093; Tilman W., 251; W. O., 456; W. V., 046, 456; Walter, 125; Will, 251; William S., 093, 138, 47, 209, 228; William, 137, 404; Willis, 427
ROBERTSON: Albert, 369; Clarissa, 055; George B., 251; Isaac E., 077; Isaac, 251; James, 137, 175, 178, 179, 214, 297; Jesse, 251; John, 077, 166, 174, 300, 420, 423; Mary Eliza, 060; Nancy, 021; Samuel, 046; Susan, 031; William, 155, 270, 445; Willis, 046
ROBEY: Aquilla Marcus Delayfayette, 176; D'Lafayette, 241; DeLafayette, 249; Eliza Jane, 077, 252; Eveline, 241; James R., 251; James, 252; Maria, 249; Mariah, 176, 241; Mary E., 154; Mary Evaline, 176; Mary Eveline, 249; Milledge B., 251; Milledge R., 242; Nathan, 065, 252; Robert, 109, 111, 168, 209, 220, 252, 263, 280, 293, 304, 315, 466; Timothy, 065, 109, 164, 168, 252, 263, 293, 315; W. B., 466; William P., 251; Williamson B., 113; Williamson, 173, 176, 231, 241, 249, 252, 300,
ROBINETT: Allen, 252; Jesse, 252, 318
ROBINSON: A. M., 330-332, 335, 337, 339, 341, 345-347, 350, 351, 354, 362, 368, 372, 373, 377, 378, 443, 447, 456; Aaron, 369; Abel L., 256; Abel S., 433; Aggie, 057; Alan, 234; Alex, 046, 369; Allen, 234; Annie Belle, 019; Annie, 043; Augustus M., 135, 350, 363, 364, 380; Benjamin, 433; Berry, 252, 369, 386, 404; Bert, 252; Burt, 046; Burton, 404; C. C., 171; Caroline, 013; Carrie, 054; Cary, 046; Charles, 046;
ROBINSON: Clark S., 046; Cornelius (heirs of), 422; Cornelius, 077, 095, 234, 252; 267, 268, 321, 433; Delia, 049; Earnest, 046; Eliza, 004; Elizabeth, 022; Eliza, 007; Ellen, 032, 252; Emma 2, 466; Frank F., 253; George, 252; Gordon, 444; Grace, 046; H. V., 296, 444, 456; Hartwell, 046, 404; Henry Jeff, 252; Henry, 229, 252; Hershell V., 456; Hillard, 046; Ike, 046, 369;
ROBINSON: India E., 057; Indianna, 057; Isaac E., 252; Isaac T., 200; Isaac, Jr., 046; Isaac, 046; J.B., 171, 350, 378, 456; J.H., 369; J.L., 186, 456, 466; J.R., 346; J. S., 247; James C., 091, 185, 252, 253, 296, 358, 404, 456; James F., 077, 131, 140, 169, 243, 252, 253, 260, 261, 313, 391, 424; James H., 113, 116, 126, 135, 194, 210, 245, 250, 266, 290, 294, 310, 363, 364, 380, 468;
ROBINSON: James M.C., 090; James T., 077, 253, 433; James, 118, 174, 186, 194, 201, 252, 350, 353; Jep, 047; Jerry, 047, 077, 253; Jess, 047; Jesse J., 253, 260, 300; Jesse, 253; John I., 047, 091, 128, 240, 253, 269, 319, 334, 344, 355, 358, 369, 442, 456; John S., 096, 180, 253, 312, 369; John, 047, 077, 112, 114, 118, 128, 131, 147, 154, 166, 169, 194, 231, 232, 240, 253, 260, 288, 299, 421, 430-432, 436, 437; John, Sr., 235; Josiah, 047;
ROBINSON: Kinion, 047; L. J., 051; Lancy, 018; Lemma, 062; Lex, 251; Lonie, 369; Lydia, 260; Mariah, 004; Mary, 050; Mason, 253; Matilda, 006; Mellie, 032; Mima, 003; Mollie, 003; Monroe, 364, 404; Nancy R., 169, 253; Nancy, 042; Osborn, 253; Parthene, 006; Perry, 047; Peter, 047; R. M., 404; Randal, 145; Reden, 433; Richard, 169, 253; Sallie, 020; Sam, 253; Sherman, 047; Sallie F., 253; Seth, 253; Sherman, 047;
ROBINSON: Sol, 253, 466; Solomon, 047, 466; Susan, 058; Temperance, 433; Thomas, 077, 124; Tolitha, 404; W. M., 171, 279, 333, 346, 350, 359, 456; Wallace, 047, 253, 404; Willia, 047; William C., 047, 065, 077, 099, 119, 217, 253, 319, 358; William O., 217; William T.L., 236, 253; William, 102, 110, 116, 139, 140, 192, 239, 253, 260, 275, 300, 323, 369, 377, 466; Willie, 047, 234, 369; Willis, 234, 404
ROBNETT: Elizabeth, 260; John, 094,
ROBSON: Cornelius, 321; John, 094, 122, 204, 224, 247, 306; Robert C., 136; Sean B., 136; Sion B., 321
ROBY: ?, 228; Addie L., 458; Addie, 057; Adel, 253; Annis, 033; Augustus, 369; Charles W., 253.

254; Dink, 466; Dora, 007; Eddie, 254; Eliza Ann, 253; Eliza Jane, 016; Elizabeth, 100, 207, 208; Emily, 022, 392; Florence, 047; Frank, 254; George, 047, 254; Gus, 254; H. W., 442; Henry R., 311; Henry W., 254; Henry, 200, 254, 369; Hill, 404; James R., 047; James, 047; John N., 254; John, 047, 404; Malachi, 253; Marian, 254; Mary E., 057, 253; Milledge Bartlett, 097; Milledge, 077, 254, 405, 428; Milton T., 269; Milton, 114; Mollie, 042; Nancy, 171, 332; Nathan, 077, 253; P.M., 254, 337, 369, 447, 456, 466; Parthena, 033; Paul M., 255; Richard P., 253; Robert, 146, 155, 164, 197, 279; T. S., 369; Thomas L., 077, 415, 405; Timothy, 077, 279; Tom, 405; W. A., 369, 456; W. H., 442; W. L., 253, 254, 358, 447, 456; Walter, 047, 077, 369; Walter, 254, 369, 445, 458; William A., 254, 321, 456; William B., 207; William P., 170; William, 047, 253L Williamson A.L.D., 253; Williamson A., 142, 190, 254, 321; Williamson B., 077, 102, 254, 447, 456, 466; 077, 110, 134, 140, 168, 208, 209, 254, 275, 282, 427; Willie, 047
ROCK: Frank, 254; Philip, 047; Shade, 254
ROCKMORE: John, 445; Ziek, 405
ROCKWELL: C. W., 464; Charles W., 125, 146, 178, 197, 231, 292; Charles, 107; Samuel, 214, 254, 388
ROCQUEMORE: Lee, 371
RODDEN: Nancy Jane, 027
RODGERS: B., 254; Benjamin W., 168, 176; Bud, 082; Cathren, 254; Charles, 047; Emily, 049; J. F., 384; James H., 077, 255, 321; John C., 090, 246, 248, 254, 255, 287, 321; John, 047; Lizzie, 040; M. E., 461; Martha E., 254; 347, 461; Rhoda, 011; Robert Y., 047; Thomas E., 248, 254, 255, 321; Vincent, 047; William R., 273; William, 319; Wyley, 255
ROE: Charles, 133; Early, 255; J.G., 276; James, 255; John, 167; Matilda O., 256; Richard, 255, 256; L. (Minor children of), 190; Zachariah, 188, 190, 256
ROFF: Aaron A., 307
ROGERS: Benjamin W., 125; Charles, 091; Dread, 065, 256; E.S., 465; Eliza, 061; Ellis, 256; Enoch, 077; George J., 144; George T., 091; George, 047, 245, 433; James A., 256; James H., 090; James, 433; John C., 231, 256, 405; Mattie, 028; Robert, 077, 197; Thomas E., 113; W.H., 407; W., 256; Wiley S., 256; William, 047; Wiley, 135, 298
B., 256; William, 144; Wiley, 135, 298
ROLAND: A. P., 047; Charles, 369; D. P., 369
ROLL: Jacob, 107; Luther, 102, 172, 250
ROLLINS: Samuel, 152
ROLLS: Isaac, 318
ROOKS: Aggie, 021; Alex, 047, 443; Alexander, 047; Dudley, 047; Frances, 061; George, 405; Hilard, 405; Jesse, 151; Jim, 405; Joe, 047; John Ben, 256; Johnnie, 047; Lula, 443; Mattie, 020; Pearia, 256; Pope, 008; S. T., 405; Simon, 047; Tom, 256; Will, 369; William, 047, 256, 369, 405; Willie Ann, 051
ROON: Leonard, 215
ROOSEVELT: Henry L., 093; Henry N., 198
ROSE: Alexander, 143; L., 257
ROSEBERRY: L. A. J., 088
ROSEL: Anderson, 369; Phillis, 369
ROSELL: Anderson, 369; Phillis, 369
ROSENFIELD: Jacob B., 229
ROSS: B. F., 447; Benjamin F., 247; Berny, 047; Caleb, 131; Caroline, 058; Dick, 466; Emma, 024; George Jr., 047; George W., 285, 310; George, 405; Harry, 369, 466; Henry, 047, 369; Ida, 036; James J., 087, 151, 244; James, 257; Jane, 060; John B., 256, 310; John, 047, 369, 405; Mattie, 046; Rachael, 054; Rich, 047; Richard, 257; Thomas E., 138, 249; Thomas, 047, 357; Tom, 335, 369; Washington, 207; William A., 194, 202, 285, 304, 310; William, 047, 065, 077, 087, 126, 151, 197, 234, 244, 252, 257, 306
ROSSEL: Lucy, 046
ROSSER: Ada S., 257; Benjamin, 257; C.B., 369, 456; Charles B., 400; Elizabeth, 317; Isaac, 257, 297.

433: Moses, 110
ROSSETER: Appleton, 289
ROSWELL: Bob, 257; Carrie, 046;
  Fredrick, 257; John, 047, 369,
  405; Martha, 045; Mary, 044;
  Robert, 047
ROUNTREE: Solomon, 117
POUSSEAU: James, 191
POUTON (ROUDON): John, 241
ROUTON: John, 257; John, Sr., 257;
  Talbot, 257; William, 257, 433,
  434, 437
ROWAN: Albert, 306
ROWDEN: Laban, 257; Lot, 257
ROWE: Adna, 116; Annie E., 009;
  J. C., 047, 442; J.G., 369, 456;
  John C., 077, 369; Matilda G.,
  405; Mattie W., 053
ROWLAND: Charlie, 377; Eliza N.,
  257; Emma, 014; G. W., 047; John
  , 173; O. P., 047, 369
ROWLEY: Ansel, 257
ROWLIN: John, 462
ROZELL: Joe, 047
RUARKS: William, 257
RUCKER: Benton, 313; Burton, 165,
  257, 423, 433; Fielding, 257; John
  , 321; John, 193; Mastin, 257
RUDISILEE: John, 113
RULING: William, 433
RULLAS(?): Randolph, 229
RUMBLE: Henry, 161
RUMLEY: Smith, 303
RUNNELLS: Preston, 322, 405;
  Sophia, 257
RUNNELS: George, 257; Harmon, 105,
  139, 233, 257; Howel W., 259,
  322, 433; Howell W., 109, 257
RUSH: Christopher, 181
RUSHIN: Bryant, 257
RUSHING: Bryant, 257, 433
RUSSEL: Ben, 047; Bill, 257; David,
  077, 445; Eleanor, 257; Henry T.,
  252; Henry, 047; Ignatius, 257;
  Jesse, 047; John R., 245; Monroe,
  047; Rich, 405; Richard, 047;
  Robert, 236; William P., 102, 257,
  258, 276; William, 211
PUSSELL: Albert, 047; Alexander,
  228; Benjamin, 268; David, 426;
  Ellender, 322; George, 456;
  Ignatius, 265, 322; John R., 258;
  John, 258; Jordan, 048; Lee, 258;
  Major, 048; Mary Bell, 059; Mary,
  008, 013; Mittie, 003, 016; Pete,
  405; Robert, 298, 410; Thomas C.,
  108, 179; Wiley, 258, 370; William
  H., 112, 433; William, 048, 258;
  Willie, 258; William, 300
RUTHERFORD: John, 469; Robert, 264;
  William, 469
RUTLAND: Randolph, 150;
  Shadie Ann, 025
RUTLEDGE: Alvah H., 258; James, 133,
  146; Mary J., 045; Robert, 405
RUTLIN: Lewis, 405
RUTTER: William C., 176
RYAN: Ann, 215; Hiram, 258; Hulda
  Ann, 236; Lewis, 077, 091, 148,
  215, 236, 284, 448; Sarah, 258;
  William, 322
PYE: Buss, 405; Lawrence, 370
PYLAND: Allen H., 094; Allen, 202
SADDLER: Pat, 022; Sam, 048; Samuel,
  048; Willie, 048
SADLER: Bartley, 123;
  Charles W., 130
SAFFO: Ben, 370; Eberhart, 370
SAFFOLD: Adam G., 167, 251, 253,
  279, 288; Ben, 048; Daniel, 258;
  Cooley, 258; Daniel, 230, 258,
  274, 421; David, 258; Deck, 405;
  Dexter, 048, 405; Eberhart, 048;
  Ellen, 258; Heard, 258; Polly,
  293; William, 239
SAILOR: Ernest, 405; Sally, 037
SALINGER: L., 367; Julius, 258;
  Levi, 258
SALSBURY: John R., 433
SALTER: Benjamin, 258; Mary, 465
SAMFORD: Thomas, 433
SAMMONS: J. W., 338
SAMPLE: Newton H., 097
SAMPLES: Eli, 258, 370
SAMSON: Micajah, 466; Sarah, 445
SANDEFER: Isaac, 048; T.B., 370;
  Thomas B., 048
SANDERS: Addeline, 405; Albert, 258,
  370; Allen, 048; B.H., 048; Brown,
  258, 456; Cheney, 333; Claborn,
  405; Clifford B., 048; Daniel, 258,
  405; Dave, 405; David F., 250;
  Eliza, 041; Ephraim P., 077; Ephraim,
  092, 135, 387; Eveline, 032; Hardy,
  048; Hattie A., 255; James, 258;
  Jeanette, 035; Jim, 048; John, 433;
  Kesiah, 258; Kiziah, 128; Laura,
  060; Martha, 059; Mary A., 258;
SANDERS: Mattie A., 258; Mattie, 055,
  258; Moses, 258, 370; Nancy, 059; P.
  P., 368, 405; Pleas, 340, 370, 405;
  Pleasant, 048, 415; R. W., 048;

Reuben T., 159, 259; Richard W.,
  258; Robert, 048, 258; Rossie,
  258; S.B., 258, 370, 404, 456;
  Sallie, 021; W.E., 456; Walter,
  405; Wash, 048; Wesley, 370;
  William, 303; Wyatt E., 258
SANDFORD: Presley, 258; Vincent, 318
SANDS: Frances, 035; James, 048;
  Joe, 348; Ophelia, 022;
  Tom, 048, 370
SANDUSKY: Emanuel, 170
SANFORD: A. C., 374; Benjamin, 096,
  173, 220, 221, 233; Bushead W.,
  284; Daniel, 220, 221; Jesse, 469;
  Presley, 255; Thomas G., 301;
  William, 087
SANKEY: John T., 130
SANSOM: Archibald (heirs of), 433;
  Elizabeth C., 003; Jacob, 199;
  James, 102, 258, 273; Martha, 057;
  Micajah, Jr., 432; Peter, 258;
  Richard, 077, 258, 429; Robert,
  258, 322; William, 258; Zielpha, 436
SAPP: James, 433
SATERWHITE: Obediah, 431
SATTEPWHITE: Andrew, 259; Carrie,
  370; Dawson, 065, 077; Stephen,
  218, 258, 322, 433; W.D., 048, 442
SAULS: Patience, 433
SAUNDERS: Alexander, 258; Charles,
  148; Clifford B., 048; Isiah, 433;
  John, 436; Nancy, 258; Pobert T.,
  130; Simon H., 160, 258; Tony,
  259; Troy S., 405
SAVAGE: Eliza A., 002
SAWYER: King, 048; P. C., 332, 350;
  Peter C., 380
SAXON: Benacer, 252
SAYPE: Nathan C., 290; Robert S.,
  239; William H., 287
SCALES: Gilbert, 466; Joe, 259, 470;
  Pompey, 405; Simeon, 096, 120,
  131, 163, 172, 214, 220, 226, 228,
  245, 259, 260, 264, 290, 300, 304,
  312, 313, 320, 322, 324, 401, 404,
  411; William, 259
SCARBOROUGH: Miles, 466; Niles, 433;
  Thomas, 291
SCAPBPOUGH: William, 130, 165
SCARVER: Amanda, 046
SCHOGIN: Nehemiah, 200, 256
SCHOGIN: Nehemiah, 288
SCISSON: Edwin S., 322; Lucy, 322
SCIXAS(?): Jacob L., 258
SCOFIELD: J. S., 465
SCOGAN: Gilum, 170
SCOGGIN: Gilliam, 259; Gilliam, 259;
  Nehemiah, 259; Philip, 259
SCOGGINS: Fielding, 259
SCOGIN: Benjamin, 259; Nehemiah, 259
SCOTT: Adam T., 275; Archibald H.,
  094, 120; Archibald, 433; Arthur,
  370; Benjamin C., 259; Daniel,
  094; G. W., 345, 374, 389; George
  W., 331, 343, 385, 396, 400, 464;
  Isaac, 157, 228; Jacob, 048; John
  S., 283; Joseph, 421; Levi, 048,
  370; Robert A., 259; Sandy, 259;
  Stephen P., 259; Thomas W., 174,
  185; Thomas, 143; Victoria, 043;
  Walter, 098; William (heirs of),
  433; William R., 048; William,
  115, 143, 215, 238, 242, 244, 259,
  302, 303, 426; Wilson, 259, 370
SCOVILL: Hezekiah M., 128;
  Hezekiah W., 189, 236
SCRANTON: Joseph J., 147, 306;
  Lucy, 176
SCROGGIN: George, 259
SCROGGINS: Anderson, 259; Fielder,
  048; Fielding, 259; James, 089,
  422; Phillip, 259
SEABORN: Dolly, 048; Lizzie, 054
SEAGO: George, 203
SEAGRAVES: Esteli, 016
SEARCY: Berry, 405; W.E.H., 444
SEATS: Lucy, 320; William V., 305
SEATS: Anderson, 370, 405; Andrews,
  370; Ann, 259; Harriet, 029;
  Sam, 405; Thomas, 370, 405
SEAVORS: Henry, 259
SEGAR: Hiram, 365
SEGPEESE: Walter, 259
SEGUP: John D., 129
SEIFT: Lucy, 379
SELF: William, 259, 370
SELFFRAGE: Robert, 259
SELFRIDGE: John, 256
SELL: Jonathan, 091
SETLAPS: Silas, 259
SELLBECK: Graham, 086
SELLECK: George N., 119, 263;
  George, 312; Gresham, 101, 104,
  111, 115, 135, 241, 247
SELLEMAN: Gold S., 284
SELLEPS: Sue, 047
SELMAN: John, 151, 242; Minor, 151
SELY: Edward R., 134
SEMORE: James, 259; Richard H.,
  259, 405; Robert, 405
SENTELL: Joseph, 259, 260, 295
SESSIONS: Elizabeth, 256; John, 142;

Joseph, 256; Robert F., 119, 260
SETTLE: J. B., 359; John, 242
SETZE: John P., 151
SEWELL: Abinu, 260, 458; Abihugh,
  260, 311, 458; Abyhugh, 116,
  166, 260
SEXTON: Thomas, 287; Yancy, 260;
  Zadock, 260; Zadocke, 260
SEYMORE: A.H., 048, 415; H.C., 181;
  Henry C., 087, 228, 260, 298, 370;
  Henry, 260; Isaac G., 300; John
  P., 077, 456; L.P., 048; L. V.,
  370; Leroy M., 202; Leroy P., 260,
  292; Martha, 077; Richard H., 260;
  Sarah C., 010
SEYMOUP: A. H., 330; Alice, 370;
  Harriet, 277; Henry C., 182, 210,
  252, 284, 285; Henry, 199, 351;
  Isaac G., 300; John R., 277; Leroy
  P., 466; Richard, 260; Robert, 260;
  William A., 260; William H., 260
SEYMOUPE: William H., 260
SHACKELFORD: Mordecai, 184; Mordica,
  203; Richard D., 211; Collin, 048,
  166; Edmund, 322; James, 128, 260;
  John W., 423; Mordecai, 288, 437;
  Susannah H. (Medlock), 211
SHAFFER: James L., 319
SHAHAN: James H., 285
SHAMTITLE: William, 260
SHANNON: Beula, 053; Henry, 405;
  James M., 048, 149, 150; John,
  260; Josia, 029; Mary E., 149
SHARD: Cornelius, 077
SHARMAN: James, 077, 433, 466; Jesse
  H., 244; Jesse S., 120; John A.,
  166, 260; John, 113, 260, 471;
  Robert, 092, 249, 257, 260, 271,
  391, 433, 434
SHARP: Augustus B., 251, 305; Daniel,
  434; George, 251; Henry, 169;
  James, 077, 260; John, 094, 238;
  Lucrecy, 120, 260; Robert, 220;
  Samuel, 261; Thomas, 261;
  William, 109, 261, 421, 430
SHAPPE: Augustus, 261; William, 077
SHARPIN: Sam, 370
SHAVEP: Henry, 405; Sam, 370
SHAVEPS: Sam, 405
SHAW: A., 333, 382, 447; Alfred,
  116, 262; C. A., 048; Caleb T.,
  261; Cathren, 261; Eli D., 261;
  Eli, 261; Ezell, 405; G.W., 152;
  Gilbert H., 261; Gilbert W., 086,
  131, 175, 205, 261, 307, 308, 316,
  322, 405; Gilbert, 261; Horace T.,
  114; J.D., 462; J.L., 370; J. S.,
  048, 456; J.W., 261; James H., 048;
  James W., 261; James, 176, 261,
  369, 370; Joe, 261; Joel, 261; John, 065,
  077, 129, 261; Joseph S., 048, 456;
SHAW: Joseph, 228; L. A., 032;
  Margaret, 200, 322; Martha Ann
  (Loveloy), 316; Mary Ann, 131;
  Milus, 370; Nedd, 048; R. A., 456,
  458; Robert A., 261, 456; Robert,
  360; Salina W., 007; Sarah M.,
  015; Solona, 002; Sophia W., 032;
  Viola, 047; W. A., 456; Watson,
  077, 131, 280, 306; William, 110,
  111, 181, 280, 310, 315, 322,
  433, 458; Willie E., 048
SHAWS: Edmund, 415
SHEAP: William, 230
SHEARER: Gilbert, 103, 271; James,
  133, 146; William, 134, 146
SHEARMAN: Robert, 424, 425
SHECUT: John F., 370
SHEETS: Tarlton, 127, 166;
  William, 162
SHEFFELD: Barnabee, 077
SHEFFIELD: John, 095, 128, 322; Mary
  Lizzie, 015; Patsev, 215
SHEHEE: Cal, 370
SHEILDS: Augustus, 048; Emma, 036;
  Laura, 052
SHELDON: Erastus, 243; Henry K., 243
SHELL: Byron, 410
SHELLS: Rob, 405
SHELTIN: Hamilton S., 211
SHELTON: Hamilton L., 234; Joseph, 444
SHELVEPTON: H. N., 370
SHEPHARD: Melissa H., 405
SHEPHERD: Abraham, 077, 261, 448;
  Abram, 322; Alford, 112; Alfred,
  164, 188, 212, 224, 261, 386;
  Andrew, 161, 394; B. U., 405;
  Carter, 140, 235, 261, 405; David,
  136, 206, 214, 261; E. W., 322,
  405; Eleazer W., 066, 077, 261;
  322; Eleazer, 282; F. J., 363; G.
  A., 024; Hence, 048; J.A., 269;
  J. M., 261, 405; J. O., 184, 335,
  341, 348; J. O., 361, 364, 367,
  370, 378, 389, 396, 466; James,
  405; John C., 261; John M., 048,
  404, 405; John, 261, 370; Malissa
  Ann, 261; Minerva E., 048; Minerva,
  370; Nancy, 296; Sarah, 066;
  Sevesta, 035; T.J., 329, 384; Thomas
  J., 349, 405; Thomas, 261; W. K.,
  261; Wash, 048; Weldon K., 048;

Weldon, 261, 405; William L., 077,
186, 261, 405; William, 322, 349;
Winburn R., 077
SHEPPERD: Lula, 061
SHERMAN: Edgar, 101, 110, 190, 312;
Jefferson, 370; Lizzie, 020;
Robert, 425, 435; Sam, 405;
Wiley, 048
SHERRELL: Robert, 405
SHERWOOD: Adiel, 178
SHI(SHY): James H., 306
SHI: Augustus C., 261; James H.,
136, 264, 269, 302
SHIELD: Milas C., 396
SHIELDS: Anna, 031; Evaline, 012;
Harvey, 048; Jermina, 370; Mary,
006; Samuel, 114, 154; Thomas,
048, 436; William T., 262;
William, 282
SHINGLETON: Jason, 139
SHIP: Richard, 433
SHIPP: C.H., 261; G.M., 390; G. V.,
261, 322, 341, 370, 456; Gustavus
V., 077, 261; Gustavus, 135;
Mary A. M., 033
SHIRLING: Isom W., 262
SHIVERS: Barney, 229; James, 181;
Thomas W., 236; William, 091
SHOATS: Allen, 404
SHOCKLEY: G. W., 370, 456; George
M., 135; George W., 048, 077,
162, 394
SHOLAR: Edward, 262
SHOLDERS: David, 257
SHONERS: Elias, 048
SHORES: Elijah, 229
SHORT: Jesse, 136; William T., 048,
161, 262, 276
SHORTER: Alfred, 107, 120, 122, 128,
130, 155, 169, 179, 201, 217, 221,
262, 265, 275, 296, 318, 324, 431,
433; Bedford, 104, 115, 129, 160,
229; Eli S., 092, 100, 108, 113,
119, 123, 124, 137-140, 163, 178,
179, 181, 184, 213, 219, 224, 230,
235, 236, 246, 252-255, 277, 291,
297, 299; Ell, 103, 136, 221;
SHORTER: Jacob, 048; Mary, 433;
Oliver, 077, 425; Reuben C., 109,
116, 146, 156, 165, 170, 172, 179,
182, 186, 191, 205, 211, 220, 249,
253, 262, 264, 271, 274, 277, 283,
286, 288, 296, 304, 310, 316, 320,
433; Reuben, 197, 278, 461
SHOTWELL: Harvey, 120; Jacob, 120
SHOULDERS: David, 124, 178
SHOWERS: Addie, 055; Carry, 049;
Clara, 017; E. S., 370; Eldridge,
048; Elias, 370; Ella, 012;
Elridge, 077, 466; Jeremiah, 370;
Lucius, 262, 370; Mollie, 023;
Paschal, 066, 077, 370; Paschall,
370; Randa, 049; Roxie, 015;
Tibetny, 371
SHROPSHERP: Julia W., 370
SHROPSHIRE: Annie, 027; C.H., 456;
Charles H., 048; H.C., 262; Henry
C., 262; J.W., 456; J., 456; James
E., 077, 262, 390; James W., 066,
077, 093, 262, 284; James, 092;
John H., 048, 083, 262, 364; John,
405, 456; Julia W., 331; M.G., 077;
Martha G., 370; Mattie, 044; Olivia
J., 066; Rebecca E., 370; W. D.,
048; W. W., 442, 456; Walter, 255,
262; Wiley, 048; William W., 048,
082; William, 141, 262, 405;
Wingfield, 105, 111
SHROPSY: Leah, 009
SHULT2: Henry, 187
SHUMAN (SCHUMANN): Theo, 387
SHURLOCK: Sam, 262
SHY: A. G., 466; A. V., 047; Alfred,
370; Anderson, 048, 370; Blakeley
S., 046; C. F., 370; Caroline C.,
371; Caroline F., 262; Caroline
034, 051; Charles, 370, 415;
Charlott, 034; Chess, 048; Clem,
415; Della, 006; E.J., 415; Elvira,
060; Ephraim, 049; Evalyne, 051;
Frank, 049, 077, 370, 405, 415;
SHY: Freeman, 049; George, 370;
Georgia, 014; Iverson, 062; J. M.,
370, 371, 456; Jack, 370; Jackson,
370, 371; James H., 101, 156; James
M., 371; Jennie, 007; Job, 237;
Joe, 049, 262, 337; John Wesley,
262; John, 049; Joseph, 049; Julia
Ann, 009; Laney, 043; Lessie, 061;
Lewis, 049; Lucinda, 051; Lucius,
049; Mallard, 456; Maranda, 370;
Marla C., 009; Mary Ann, 025; Mary
B., 458; Mary C. (Kirby), 101, 156;
SHY: Milas W., 005, 029; P.
R., 262, 370, 456; Peter, 049, 370,
456; Peyton R., 049, 262, 371, 456;
Peyton, 077; Pleas, 049; R.L., 371;
Reese, 370; Robert L., 049; S. C.,
371, 442, 456; S. G., 340, 371,
404, 405; S. J., 371, 456; S. W.,
371; Sallie, 040, 371; Samuel C.,
262, 353, 371; Samuel, 077, 154,

264; Seaborn J., 066, 262, 371,
433, 448; Seaborn W., 195, 262,
415; Seaborn, 077, 262; Sebron W.,
371; Sidney, 049; Smaley, 262;
SHY: Sophronia, 032; Susan, 013;
Susie, 008; T.P., 365, 369, 371,
456; Thad, 371; Thaddeus P., 262;
Thaddeus, 049; Thomas W., 370;
Vila, 056; W.N., 371, 456; W.V.,
049, 456, 466; William N., 371;
William R., 049; William V., 049;
William, 049, 262; Willie, 049;
Wyatt, 049
SIBLEY: Amory, 105, 310, 312
SIBLY: Amory, 230; Royal, 230
SIDWELL: William A., 304
SIGMAN: F. O., 405; Fannie, 405;
Lee Idus, 033; M., 405, 406, 456,
466; Manson, 371, 399, 406
SILDEN: David, 168, 301
SILEP: William D., Sr., 077
SILLIMAN: Gold L., 090
SILLIVANT: George, 049; Johnson, 049
SILVEY: John, 355, 377
SIMENS: Dock, 049
SIMMONS: Allen G., 049; Allen, 262,
322; G.M., 049; George, 193, 268;
Greenesville, 100; Henry F., 098;
Henry, 117; James, 123, 138, 262;
John K., 168, 262; John, 049,
173, 262, 420; Jones, 371; Lissie
Ann, 052; Lou, 029; Sanders W.,
077; Savanah, 030; W. S., 375;
William E., 328; William, 113,
158, 179, 262, 279, 391
SIMMS: Arthur L., 155; Henry, 406;
John, 197; Joshua, 262; L. H.,
354, 364; Lucy H., 392; Reddick
P., 263; Richard S., 077, 296;
Sarah L., 012; Thomas, 263;
William, 263; Zachariah, 432
SIMON: Carrie, 027; Frank, 049;
Mary, 056
SIMONS: Kittie, 043
SIMONS: James G., 263; James T.,
256, 263; John, 261; Nancy, 324;
Pleas, 263; Thomas, 263
SIMONTON: Absalom, 230; Agnes I.,
232; Agnes J., 263, 295; Agnes
I., 142; G., 315, 402; Gilbraith,
077, 093, 116, 126, 127, 142, 225,
232, 249, 263, 264, 280, 295, 300,
325; Gilbreath, 136, 301; Robert,
263; W., 402; William, 126, 225,
263, 264, 325
SIMPSON: Charles Robert, 049; Croft,
406; Jack, 263; John F., 090;
John J., 077, 263, 445; John P.,
263; John, 077, 263, 415; Pete,
263; Thom, 406; Thomas, 263;
William, 263; V. A., 371
SIMS: Alford, 406; Allen J., 263;
Benjamin, 287, 298; David, 105;
Emma, 021; James G., 257, 263,
322, 426, 466; James Glenn, 424,
428; John M., 105; John T., 253;
Josie, 036; Little, 283; Perry,
263; Redick, 167; Thomas W., 263;
William, 154, 236, 257, 263, 273,
284, 298, 315; Zachariah, 243,
261, 270, 433
SINCEY: Jesse, 409
SINCLAIR: Elias, 201
SINGER: John, 162
SINGLETON: Anna, 008; Bob, 263;
Charley, 049; D. T., 339, 346,
348; David, 263; Elisha, 049; Emma
Kate, 017; Henry, 049; Jane, 027;
Julius, 357; Lee, 049, 406; Lizzie,
050, 057; Lucy, 016; Mary, 058;
Monroe, 049, 103, 368; Owen, Jr.,
263; Rebecca Louise, 016; Robert,
371; T. M., 102; T. W., 263; Tom,
049; Willie, 406
SINGUEFIELD: William, 117
SISSION: Edwin B., 263; Hannah,
428; John B., 134; Richard M.,
263; Richard W., 433; Richard,
118, 263; William, 118, 263
SISTRUNK: Samuel, 077
SIZMOUR: Henry C., 148
SKAG: John R., 180
SKAGGS: Henry M., 263; James, 433;
Lemuel B., 125; Lemuel P., 167;
Lemuel, 272, 435
SKEGGS: John R., 302
SKELTON: John T., 263, 432;
Martha E. (Abernathy), 263
SKILLMAN: William G., 130
SKINNER: Callie F., 209; Ebenezer,
131; Elizabeth, 042; Henrietta M.
B.A., 016; Jonas, 317;
Robert, 049, 263
SLACK: Ambrose, 049; Georgia, 050;
Henry, 263; Joseph B., 264, 050;
Seaborn, 263, 264; Mary, 406;
William, 049, 264; Willie Mary, 034
SLADE: Daniel, 219, 278; Dave, 247;
L.C., 291, 370
SLAGLE: Harriet R., 002;
Jacob, 264, 433
SLAPPY: Anne, 264; H. (heirs of),

433; Henry (heirs of), 433; Henry,
180, 264, 430; Jacob, 264; John
G., 264, 429, 434; John, 091
SLATON: Obadiah, 264
SLATTER: Hope H., 293;
Shadrick F., 251
SLAUGHTER: Andrew G., 077; Andrew
J., 264; Augustin, 096, 103, 105,
109, 111, 113, 123, 124, 129, 130,
150, 154, 156, 160, 162, 167, 168,
176, 178, 183, 189, 200, 217, 218,
220, 222, 224, 225, 236, 252, 260,
264, 272, 273, 275, 278, 293, 294,
307, 308, 313; Augustine, 274,
295; Augustus, 304; Della, 371;
Elizabeth T., 077; Frances (033;
Fed, 371; Frances (Fanny), 264;
SLAUGHTEP: Francis, 264, 265, 297,
322; Frederick, 265; H.G., 466;
Henry P., 264; Henry, 049, 077,
111, 191, 271, 272; Isaac H., 226,
264, 265, 309, 308, 322; John G.
Isaac, 265; Jacob, 049; John
B., 077, 108, 195; John G., 103,
119; John, 264; Joseph W., 163,
265, 466; Joseph E.; Lawrence
S., 211; Martha L., 005; Mason,
265; Matilda, 265, 297, 322, 458;
Moses B., 265; Moses, 303; Nathan
T., 077, 152; Nathaniel B., 218,
240, 265, 422; Randal, 415;
SLAUGHTER: Reuben, 168; Robert,
265; Robin, 049; Sallie E., 017;
Sarah, 077, 182, 265, 293, 307;
Sopha, 265; T.K., 265; Thomas K.,
077, 087, 136, 163, 200, 240, 241,
262, 265, 312, 322, 323, 458;
Thomas P., 322; Thomas, 086; Tom
Allen, 049; Wilkins, 049, 265,
406; William A., 219, 226, 265,
279, 293, 322, 421; William, 303;
Wm. A., 466
SLAYTON: Obediah, 136
SLEDGE: Alexander, 322; Chappel,
287; Charles M., 112; Shearly, 191
SLEIGH: Mary, 434
SLICKHEEL: Jim, 049
SLOAN: Alexander, 283; Henry, 369, 373
SLOCUM: Angeline D., 054
SLOCUMB: R. V., 371; John E., 049;
W. S., 371
SLUDER: A.I., 341; A.L., 187, 240,
265, 281, 341, 355, 365, 371, 373,
406, 407; Augustus L., 265, 330;
J. H., 456; John H., 049, 330;
John, 077; Parthie, 029
SLUTZ: W.A., 371
SLUTER: A. L., 049
SLUTTER: Ed., 371
SMALL: A. B., 049, 161, 248, 265,
328, 332, 365, 372, 377, 378; A.
J., 463; A. T., 463; Andrew E.,
088; Archie, 265; F. E., 463
SMART: Elisha, 077, 100, 265, 322;
Francis B., 077; Osborne, 265
SMARTT: Elisha, 234, 246, 265, 266;
466; Eliza, 088, 090, 266, 324;
Francis B. (heirs of), 434; Francis
B., 088, 221, 265, 266, 322, 324;
425; Henry T., 145, 221, 255, 265;
266, 322; Henry, 265; Littleberry,
266; Osborne, 466; Osborn, 265;
266; Osborne, 266; Thomas B., 265
SMELL: Wesley A., 156
SMITH: ?, 339; A.C., 456; A.D., 456;
A.F., 049; A. H., 266, 456; Aaron
M., 127; Aaron, 049, 108, 174,
406; Aaron F., 049; Abraham
H., 066, 077, 458; Abraham, 166;
Abram H., 456; Abram, 361, 456;
Aaaline, 008, 016; Albert W., 307;
Albert, 147, 266, 306; Alex, 049,
266, 267, 371, 406; Alexander,
077, 090, 141, 195, 210, 255, 276,
445; Alice, 034; Allen C., 456;
SMITH: Allen Eugene, 049; Allen,
049; Alonzo, 049; Amanda, 024,
049; Amarintha, 021; Anderson, 050;
Andrew, 077, 256; Ann R., 266;
Ann, 066; Anna, 004, 047; Annie
C., 014; Annie, 003, 040, 048,
373; Anthony, 371; Antony W., 266;
Arthur, 424; Asa, 147, 148, 151;
179, 219, 388, 283; B. L., 050;
B. P., 371, 374, 456; Basil, 050;
Baxter, 429, 434; Bazil, 266;
Beckle, 050; Benjamin, 153, 266,
284, 434; Berry, 050; Betsy, 046,
406; Bettie, 050, 055; Bill, 266;
SMITH: Bittie, 266; Bowline, 266;
Boyken, 266; Boykin R., 050, 266,
266, 339, 456; Boykin, 050, 266,
371, 406; Bunk, 050; C.E., 050;
Carl E., 050; Caroline, 371;
Carrie, 003, 044, 266; Cart, 050;
Casand, 045; Caught, 050; Cell;
266; Chandler, 092; Charity, 050;
Charles, 077, 185; Charles S.,
066, 185; Charles W., 196;
Charles, 133, 140, 266, 322,
406; Charlie, 256; Chas. J., 466;
SMITH: Chas. S., 466; Chatman, 050;

Chyde, 050; Cinda, 030; Cindy,
036; Clara (Clary). 266; Clara
Bel, 049; Cleveland. 406; Cooley.
050; Cora, 006, 049; Cornelia,
040, 371; Cornelius, 050; Coy, 050;
Cynthia, 033, 151; Dan. 050; David,
050, 066, 077, 097, 225, 255, 266,
267, 322, 434; Davis, 102; Della
Ann, 267, 371; Dick, 268, 405;
Doc, 050; Dock, 385; Drury, 267;
SMITH: Dudley, 267; Durell, 456;
Durrell, 050; E.B., 365, 433, 444;
E. B., Jr., 394; Earl, 050; Ed.
050, 267, 371; Edgar T., 077;
Edward B., 077, 267, 456; Edward,
267, 294; Elbert, 050, 267, 392,
406, 466; Elizabeth, 039, 045, 281;
Ella, 009, 029; Ellie, 406;
Emanuel S., 434; Emma, 014; Enley,
055; Ernest, 267; Eugene, 371, 406;
Ezekiel F.,211, 304L Ezekiel, 211,
304; Fannie, 040, 460; Fanny
(Frances), 269; Fanny, 077, 142,
267, 269, 459; Farrar, 267, 393;
SMITH: Felix, 458; Frances, 056;
Francis (Fanny), 267; Francis B.,
090; Francis, 077, 267; Gardner,
372; Gene, 267; George Ann, 044;
George W., 088; George, 050, 176,
267, 371; Georgia A., 049; Georgia
Ann, 038; Georgia Kate, 031;
Georgia, 007, 031, 040; Ginnie,
044; Grant, 050; Green, 050; Grief,
108; Guy, 266, 267, 269, 271, 306,
371, 406, 456, 466, 467; H.J.,
456; H.P., 343, 371, 461, 465;
SMITH: H. T., 371, 456; Hampton S.,
248; Hampton, 050, 087, 181, 384;
Hannah, 040, 313; Hanniah, 268;
Hansford, 088; Harriet, 458;
Harrison J., 077, 267, 448;
Harrison, 109, 220, 228, 389;
Hattie W., 354, 371; Henrietta,
004, 046; Henry O., 269; Henry
T., 050, 266, 077, 094, 145, 205,
266, 267, 269, 297, 372, 381, 456,
462; Henry W., 267; Henry, 267,
269, 371; Hezekiah, 201, 290;
SMITH: Hinto, 406; Hollis, 050;
Homer, 050, 266, 267; Horace, 050,
372; Ida, 006; Idus, 384, 456;
J.H.S., 267, 348, 350, 356, 372,
395, 467; H., 332, 342, 371,
372, 390, 397, 400, 405, 406,
409; J. Henry, 372; J. Hinto, 372;
J. L. K., 354; J. R., 456; J. T.,
337, 340, 372; J. T. Dr., 408;
J. W. A., 232, 247, 267, 372, 406,
456; J.W.A., Jr., 371; J.W.W., Jr.,
456; J.W.A., Jr., 371; W., 332, 377;
SMITH: J. Y., 396; Jacob B., 077;
Jacob, 118, 263; James H., 467;
James J., 050, 267, 372; James L.,
267; James M., Gov., 381; James
T., 050; James Thomas, 338, 345,
347, 360; James, 050, 093, 110,
144, 148, 155, 167, 169, 171, 181,
183, 204, 208, 215, 221, 232, 243,
245, 260, 267, 273, 279, 283, 303,
324, 389, 406, 434, 458; Jane L.,
095; Jane, 015, 054; Jas. H., 467;
SMITH: Jeff, 077; Jefferson, 267.
456; Jeremiah, 118, 258; Jesse H.,
077; Jesse, 077; Jim Bolden,
050; Jim, 050; Joe Henry, 406;
Joe, 050; Joel, 239, 434; John C.
C.,082, 372; John C.,109, 147-149,
179, 219, 238, 267, 283, 304, 306,
372; John D., 287; John H., 077,
166; John Henry, 050, 268; John
J., 119, 282, 267, 283; John J.,
111, 121, 126, 155, 182; John J.,
207, 228, 231, 268, 271, 322; John
L., 277; John T., 077; John W. A.,
066, 077, 090, 147, 189, 229, 242,
268, 290, 322, 330, 372, 395, 406,
415, 467; John W.H., 242; John W.,
268, 281; John Wesley, 050; John,
050, 066, 136, 151, 155, 177, 211,
267, 269, 372, 390, 415, 434;
SMITH: John, Sr., 151; Johnie, 050;
Jonathan, 268, 322, 434; Joseph H.
S., 050, 363; Joseph H., 050;
Joseph Henry S., 050; Joseph, 050,
151, 191, 266, 268, 291, 434; Julia
Ann, 020; Julia, 019; Keziah, 266,
269; L. C., 447; Lany, 029; Larry,
406; Laura, 004, 018; Lean, 372;
Lela, 051; Lema, 032; Leroy, 460;
Levi, 050, 268; Lewis D. M., 322;
Lewis, 050, 171, 234, 268; Linsey,
118; Liza, 406; Lizzie, 056; Lon,
331; Lona, 406; Lonie, 010; Lot,
268, 324, 406, 433; Lou, 268;
SMITH: Louisa, 037; Louise, 343;
Louvinia, 053; Loy, 052; Lucius,
051, 268; Lucy Ann, 036; Lucy B.,
077, 376; Lucy, 291, 372; Lucy,
Mrs., 372; Lugene, 023; Lula J.,
014; M. R., 456; Manch, 372; Mandy,
406; Maneb, 372; Marcus, 051;
Margaret, 035; Margarett, 029,

032; Marshall, Jr., 271; Martha
(Appling), 268; Martha E., 200;
Martha, 035, 042; Martin, 051;
SMITH: Mary B., 337, 408; Mary E.,
058; Mary Jane, 010; Mary Lou, 335;
Mary, 003, 034, 062, 267; Mason,
015; Masoury, 032; Matilda, 003;
Matt, 051, 372; Mattie A., 012,
077; Mattie Lou, 019, 034; Mattie.
004, 032, 045, 047, 050, 058;
Maud, 018; Maxey, 268, 291; Millie.
022; Minerva, 186; Miranda, 044;
Missouri, 212, 268, 372; Mitta,
049; Monroe, 051, 268; Moses, 244;
SMITH: N. L., 456; N. P., 406, 444,
456; Nancy R., 268, 322; Nancy T.,
029; Nancy, 035, 268; Nannie B.,
007; Nathan, 119, 268; Nazro, 129;
Nester P., 051; Nester, 407; Nevel
G., 268; Nevel, 277; Nezro, 268;
Niles L., 051, 456; Nola Mae, 024;
Oney, 002; Orb, 259; Orellous.
372; Orillous, 051, 372, 406;
Orillous, 467; Ossie Pearl, 051;
Percy, 406; Peyton Thomas, 268;
Peyton, 268; Pollie, 268; Pomp,
406; Ponder, 372; Presley W., 137,
311, 314, 402; Presley Wheeler, 268
SMITH: R. H., 456; R. L. 406, 456;
Ranisome, 051; Ransom H., 116, 142,
253, 268, 306; Ransom R., 288;
Ransom, 144, 268; Raymond, 406;
Rebecca, 011, 015; Reddick, 273;
Reid, 256; Rhoda Ann, 372; Rhoda
Ann, Mrs., 372; Rich, 268; Richard
B., 077; Richard, 051, 146, 266,
268; Pillous, 353, 406; Robert,
219; Rolen, 184; Rolin, 077, 173.
268; Rollin, 268, 313, 458; Rony,
051; Rose, 034, 047; Ruff, 415;
SMITH: Pufus H., 051; Rufus, 456;
S.B., 467; S.D., 159; S.J., 447;
S.P., 332, 372, 376, 405, 407,
411; S. R., 372, 406, 456; S. R.,
047, 456; Alonzo, 456; S. R.,
R., Sr., 330; Sal, 119, 372;
Sallie, 013, 047; Sally, 023;
Sam Elbert, 407; Sam Luke, 407;
Sam, 051, 269, 372, 407; Samuel
P., 316; Samuel R., 096, 171,
247, 269, 322, 330, 448, 456;
SMITH: Samuel R., Jr., 269, 330, 368,
372; Samuel R., Sr., 077, 269;
Samuel, 051, 222, 269, 434; Samuel,
Jr., 456; Sarah A., 033, 268; Sarah
Cornelia, 047; Sarah, 017, 018;
Scott, 051; Sheldon, 090; Sherman.
051; Shop, 269; Sidney, 269, 372;
Soloman, 367, 372; Sophronia B.,
024; Stephen, 240, 269, 459;
Sterling W., 092; Sterling, 269,
372; Sultana, 053; Susan E., 008;
Susan M., 159; Susan, 005; Susie
Ann, 042; Swanson, 051; T.A., 051;
SMITH: T. C., 028; T.J., 338, 343.
456; T. Jeff, 368; T.P., 372;
Telitha, 004; Thomas E., 051;
Thomas Edgar, 051; Thomas G., 108;
Thomas I., 171, 194, 292, 249, 301,
306; Thomas J., 077, 089, 091-093,
097, 098, 102, 104, 112, 136, 148,
152, 188, 190, 219, 221, 235, 245,
260, 269, 280, 283, 284, 290, 292,
300, 316, 320, 324, 335, 372, 391,
392, 396, 401, 442; Thomas R., 077,
269, 295; Thomas S., 229; Thomas
W., 077, 223, 269; Thomas, 051,
077, 107, 125, 144, 147, 148, 159,
175, 179, 181, 209, 219, 269, 283,
299, 385, 424, 431; Tom, 269, 372;
SMITH: Turner, 269; Uriah, 306;
Viola J., 053; W. F., 366; W. G.,
269, 372, 399, 406, 407, 444; W.H.,
403; W. R., 269, 343, 372, 390,
397, 402, 407, 456; Walton, 051;
Warner, 268; Washington, 444; Wes.
269; Wesley, 183; Will, 051, 269;
William (Buck), 269; William B.,
269; William F., 051; William
G., 066, 077, 095, 267, 269, 401;
William G., Sr., 240; William H.,
051, 077, 282; William Henry, 051;
William R., 154, 295, 316; William
T., 460; William W., 087, 098, 267,
269, 294; William, 051, 051, 159,
209, 235, 246, 304, 379, 386, 434,
436; Willie, 051, 269; Willis, 373;
Woodie, 051; Wyatt B., 269; Wyatt
R., 077, 089, 183, 210, 260, 270,
395; Wyatt, 051, 165, 402;
Zachairah P., 051; Zachariah A.,
077; Zipporah A., 077
SMITHSON: Henry G., 319
SNEED: Archibald H., 109, 268
SNELL: Wesley A., 214, 236, 285,
310, 324; Wesley S. 407
SNELLING: Henry D., 305
SNELLINGS: Henry D., 119;
Madison B. 306
SNOWDEN: Gilbert T. 230
SNYDER: Edwin, 156
SOLOMON: Henry, 105, 206; Jane, 020

SOLOWAY: Abe, 373
SORREL: Needham, 434
SOWEL: Abehu(?), 406
SOWELL: Abihuah, 434
SPAIN: Drury, 091; William, 051
SPAINWELL: John, 220
SPANS: Charlie, 407
SPARADLIN: William, 206
SPARKS: Alex M., 300; Alex, 051;
Carden, 407; , 380; J. R.,
211, 362; John, 193; Leathy, 004;
Maranda, 025; Mattie, 007; Nap,
051; O.G., 118, 220, 242, 350;
Texas, 381; Thomas, 214, 294; W.
B., 134, 339; William, 051
SPEAIRS: Caleb W., 066; S. P., 335,
444; Thomas E., 373
SPEAR: A.M., 307; Charles, 193;
Elizabeth, 442; Elizabeth A., 373;
Francis M., 051; Francis, 101;
Harry, 077, 415; Isabella, 442;
Jane, 056; Jesse, 448; John, 257;
Kittie T., 025; Lewis, 298; Mary
A., H., 442; Mary Jane, 014;
William H., 373; William T., 051
SPEARMAN: Albert, 051; Amos M., 051;
Andrew, 373; Bessie, 024; Fleming,
051; Fletcher, 456; G. C., 352;
G. T., 066, 442; Gabriel T., 077,
415; George C., 456; J. C., 051;
J. F., 456; J.S., 373; J. T., 356;
Jackson, 407; James, 051; Jennie
M., 049; John F., 077, 222, 262,
354, 372, 407, 456; John, 051,
066, 098, 101, 142, 208, 246, 306,
313, 373, 387, 420, 467; Julia A.,
390; Lizzie, 048; M.W., 051, 390,
408, 456; Martha, 056; Mary W.,
456; Mattie, 007; Nancy Ann C., 007;
Sallie V., 037; T., 334; Toombs,
404; W. S., 051, W., 456; William
F., 456; William H., 456; William,
051, 373, 376, 456, 467
SPEARS: A. F., 456; A. M., 051, 373,
407, 456; Alonzo, 456; Alphonsus
F.,341; Annie C., 034; Annie Lee
055; Aug, 111; Augustus, 077, 373;
Bessie, 035; Betsey, 373; C. E.,
340, 363; C. M., 408, 434, 456;
Caleb P., 052; Caleb W., 434;
Caleb, 422, 456; Catharine, 373;
Cicero M., 052, 088, 196, 270;
Cicero, 270; Columbus E., 052,
066, 077; Creed A., 066; Creed
E., 077, 203, 320, 372; Della,
054; Eaton, 077, 270; Francis,
232, 306; Henry, 373, 456;
SPEARS: Hezekiah, 097; Indiana, 011;
J.A.J., 448, 456; J. A., 373, 456;
J. B., 052, 442, 456; James J.,
270; James F., 077; James,
270, 273; Jane, 373; Jefferson C.,
270; Jefferson E., 237, 241, 270,
306, 403; Jesse, 077; John B., 407;
John N., 052; John W., 052; John
Wesley, 077; John, 066, 077, 132,
191-192, 270, 448, 467; John, Jr.,
170, 270; John, Sr., 192; Joseph,
052, 270; Joshua A., 456; Joshua
B., 077, 421, 422, 448, 456; Joshua
C., 270; Joshua, 456; Josiah C.,
077, 415; Liza, 042; Louisa, 020;
SPEARS: Mahala, 373; Martha A., 265,
270, 373; Martha, 463; Mattie Lou,
306; Mittie, 026; Mixon, 456;
Moses, 270; N.A., 066; Nathan, 456;
Oscar H., 052; Robert, 270, 448;
S.C., 373, 442; S. P., 456; Sarah
Josephine, 029; Sarah, 014; Sidney,
052, 077, 373; Susannah C. (Moss),
203-204; T.A., 009; T. L., 407, 456;
Thomas J., 077; Thomas L., 373;
Thomas, 270; W. H., 456, 467; Wash.
270; Welcome, 270; William H., 066,
077, 262, 370; William, 077, 170,
200, 270, 425, 456; Willie, 456;
Zipporah, 046
SPEEAR: Isabella, 043
SPEER: A. M., 331, 382; H. M., 332;
J. E., 306; John P., 307; John W.,
199; Lessie, 305; Moses, 248, 270,
395; Nancy, 199; Sarah F., 052;
Thomas Eugene, 052; William H., 235
SPEERS: Amanda I., 016; Hezekiah,
270, 404; U.E., 442; Sabrina, 006
SPEIGHT: Dave, 270; George, 270;
Jutson, 270
SPEIGHTS: Dave, 052; Delia, 010;
Dooglin, 407; J. C., 456; James,
066, 077, 102, 456; John C., 052,
456; John, 456; Joseph, 456;
Surania, 373
SPEIR: James, 159, 190, 192, 218; John
P., 130, 252, 293, 294; Moses, 257
SPEIRS: Moses, 154
SPELLER: Dave, 052; Frank, 052;
Lewis, 052; Oliver, 052
SPELLERS: Joshua, 052;
Oliver, 052, 373
SPENCE: Horatio N., 270; I.N.B., 343;
John, 434; Malachi, 270; Nathan,
182; Paul, 077; William, 105, 167,

170, 270; Haratio, 286; Horatio N.,
121, 135, 185, 270; Horatio R.,
229; Horatio, 199, 219; Jesse M.,
077, 270; Joseph J., 197; Thomas
F., 270; William, 434
SPIER: James, 218; John P., 206
SPIKES: Ananias, 052
SPILLARDS: Priscilla G., 061
SPILLER: Frank, 052, 373; Henry,
407; Ike, 270; Rosetta, 458;
Uleces, 407
SPIRES: Hezekiah, 321; Martha, 321
SPIVEY: L.C., 395, 397, 400; T. C.,
361, 371, 456; Thomas C., 096, 278,
331, 356, 407, 411; Thomas, 203;
Thos. C., 462
SPIVY: Joab, 270; Thomas, 052
SPLAWN: James, 200, 270
SPOFFORD: Enoch W., 134
SPON: James, 270
SPRADING: William, 432
SPRADLIN: James, 270; William, 434
SPRADLING: James, 434; William, 270;
Tom, 407
SPRATLIN: William, 223, 279
SPRAULDING: Jerry, 407
SPRINGER: Job, 170; Johnson, 089,
185, 224; McCullars, 270, 275
SPRINGFIELD: Aron, 245
SPRINGFIELD: Thomas R., 434
SPURLIN: James M., 138, 145, 270,
273; John, 270; William, 434
SPURLOCK: Drury, 105; James, 105
SQUIRE: Charles, 090, 284;
Jonathan, 188
ST. JOHNS: Isaac R., 087
STACY: Robert, 166
STAFFORD: Willie, 407
STAGNER: Daniel, 312; James, 270,
291; Rachel, 190
STALLINGS: J. P., 270; Jeremiah W.,
270; Jeremiah, 323; Jesse, 270;
John E., 093; Sangers, 103, 133,
270, 271, 323, 407, 428, 467;
Simeon W., 052
STALNAKER: Gacriel, 257
STAMPS: Martin W., 290; Thomas,
256, 305, 428; Timothy, 271
STANCIL: L. E., Mrs., 375
STANDARD: C. B., 466
STANDEFUR: Denis, 407
STANDEFER: Milley, 373
STANDFORD: Sallie, 057
STANDIFER: A. C., 467; A., 118;
Adolphus, 052, 271, 373, 405;
Aggie, 018; Allen, 052; Amanda,
047; Amey Ann, 058; Angeline, 020;
Archibald C., 289, 323; Archibald,
066, 077, 407; Boby, 052; Byrom,
052; Curn, 407, 458; Currin, 373;
Eliza, 031; General, 052, 271;
Georgia Ann, 031; H.V., 118, 271;
Jack, 052; James L., 280, 282,
306; Jane, 061; Jas, T., 466;
STANDIFER: Jennie, 009; Joel, 271;
John, 052, 271; John, Jr., 052;
Jonas, 345; Julia, 046; Lidia,
021; Lollie, 052; Lucy, 033; Luke,
271, 407; Martha, 271; Mary Ann,
014; Matilda, 011; Milly, 271;
Pres, 271; Robert, 052; Sallie,
052; Sam, 052, 271; Sherod, 407;
Silas, 052, 271, 373; Tabitha,
026; Thomas, 271; Tisshy, 021;
Tomie, 271; Walker, 052, 373;
Will, 407; Willie, 005; Willis
W., 052; Zachairah, 052
STANDIFORD: Archibald, 271
STANDIFUR: William, 052
STANFORD: David, 179, 188, 434;
Fanny, 004; Joe, 052; Joel, 078,
218, 265, 271; Jordan, 078; Jordon,
202; Lettie, 021; Lucy, 407;
Manervis, 407; Mary A., 004;
Nehemiah, 102; O. A. W., 365;
Obadiah, 052, 271; Obe, 373, 410;
Phillip, 271; Thomas J., 251;
Thomas, 096
STANLEY: Albert, 407; Caleb, 052,
271; Felix, 427, 435; James, 271;
Jesse, 429, 434; Lewis, 245;
Martin, 066, 271, 271; Nancy, 018;
Samuel G., 124, 232, 271
STANLY: Martin, 297
STANTON: H. D., 269; Henry T., 388;
Minton, 026; Tom, 407; William
D., 162, 262
STARK: James A., 204; John W., 112;
Joseph, 130, 193; W. H., 374
STARKE: Mary, 373
STARKS: Tom, 271
STARR: Marcus A., 173; Nathan, 407;
R. E. A., 039; S. H., 052, 392;
Silas B., 344
STATTHAM: Nathaniel, 283
STAYNER: John, 216
STEADHAM: John, 052, 407
STEAGALL: Samuel, 165
STEDEVENT: John, 271
STEDMAN: Frances (Fanny), 407
STEED: A. S., 271, 373, 407;
Alexander, 303

STEEDMAN: Cyntha, 256; Frances, 166;
Mary, 271; Thomas, 227, 256,
271; 323, 460
STEEL: A., 238; Alexander, 308;
Francis M. W., 078; Hutson, 143;
J.N., 373; J.W.J., 456; John J.,
456; John W., 442; Margarett A.,
053; S. J., 456; S. W., 456;
Samuel J., 443; Samuel S., 167;
Samuel W. J., 456; Sarah A., 034;
Sarah Jane, 038; W. H., 373, 407,
456; William F. M., 078; William
F., 397
STEELE: G. A., 052; J. N., 373;
James, 261, 271, 273, 323; John
A., 213; John N., 367; John, 373;
Jonas, 052; Mary A., 021; Mollie
A., 373; Polley, 308; S. J., 204,
344, 356; Samuel W.J., 236; Samuel
W., 442; Tom M., 052; W. H., 271,
373; William F., 164, 196, 248;
William M., 052; William, 271, 442
STEEN: Thomas, 420
STEENE: Thomas, 271
STEGALL: Samuel, 271
STEPHEN: Peter, 052
STEPHENS(STEVENS): Anne Jane, 059
Andrew, 271; Ben, 271, 443; Burl,
052; Genie, 373; George, 189, 283;
Green, 176; Henry, 158, 271, 317;
James, 146; Jesse, 146, 159, 485;
John M., 090; John, 160, 271, 299;
Mary, 018, 255; Pierce, 271;
Sherman, 373; Stephen, 116, 144,
436, 448; Steven, 189, 283;
William, 111, 189, 271, 283
STEPHENSON: John, 144, 323
STERLING: Whitmel L., 289;
Wiley G., 052
STEVENS: Alf, 407; Henry, 188, 271,
397; Hugh, 464; James, 434; John,
271, 429; Marshall, 424; Patrick
M., 284; Pearce, 189, 271, 434;
Pierce, 271; Richardson R., 167;
Sherman, 271; T. L., 271; T. L.,
397; Tucker I., 018; William,
163, 272
STEVENSON: John, 272, 407;
Willington, 211, 294
STEWARD: Absalom, 272; John, 181
STEWART: Absolom, 424; Andrew J.,
091, 310; Andrew G., 091; Ardelle,
042; Asa, 256; Ben, 272; Betsey
Ann, 016; Charles D., 124, 125,
188, 201, 211, 216, 219, 252, 317,
325; Charles, 086, 181, 272;
Charlotte, 035; Elizabeth, 272;
Ellie, 407; Emily J., 039; Floyd,
052; Francis M., 078; George W.,
467; Georgia, 041; Henry, 373, 407;
Hugh B., 272; Hugh, 272; Ishmael,
216; J. A. B., 387; J. King, 387;
STEWART: J. L., 448; James T., 052;
James, 078, 272, 434, 458; John
P., 272; John S., 380, 458; John,
052, 159, 165, 181, 272; Joseph,
373; Leroy, 052; Levin 284; Levin
J., 284; Martha, 033; Miley Ann,
407; Phillip, 272; R. S., 328;
Richard, 272; Robert, 117; Susan,
373; Sylvanus, 272; Will, 407;
William H., 164; William, 423
STILES: Amos J., 254; Benjamin, 173;
William, 268
STILL: John, 272
STILLWELL: John F., 233; John, 270
STILWELL: Charles H., 152, 158;
John, 200
STINSON: Burrel, 272; G. W., 465;
George, 257; Micaiah, 181
STOCK: William, 140
STOCKHOUSE: Samuel H., 125
STOCKS: John, 444; William, 258
STODDARD: E. B., 102
STODGHILL: William F., 217
STOKES: Allen, 988, 445; Archibald,
128, 287, 292; C.M., 373; Columbus,
456; Edward, 052; Ignatius, 078,
221, 272; J. W., 359, 360, 373;
Levi, 106; Mary, 103; Munford, 133;
Nancy, 015; Pheby (Gordon), 272;
William B., 078, 237, 426;
William, 260
STONE: Addie, 044; Alpheus H., 094,
119; Edmund, 237; Elvira A., 004;
Gus, 053; H. P., 456; Henry N.,
272; J. A., 272, 347, 363, 374,
456; James A., 143, 343; James,
373, 456; Jeff, 053; John W., 078,
272; Julia A., 058; L. E., 373;
Lucinda E., 272; Lucinda, 213;
M. D., 053, 359, 373, 407, 456;
Mahala Ann, 078; Man, 467; Martha,
445; Mary, 040; Nancy, 035; Philip,
053; Rhoda, 034; S. H., 385; Sarah
C., 042; Susan J., 272; Thomas,
162, 272, 458; W.M., 053, 456;
William M., 407; Willie M., 053;
William H., 458; William M., 053;
William T., 463
STONEWALL: Walter, 053

STOODLY: Robert, 236
STOREY: Hannah, 016
STORR: Anthony, 163; John B., 159, 284
STORRS: Hiram, 272, 132, 314;
James, 053; Prudy, 008
STOUT: Aquila G., 121
STOVALL: Betsy, 196; G.B., 371;
George B., 306; George, 125, 133,
141, 148, 187, 196, 272, 292, 323,
427, 467; Henry, 204, 272, 420;
Joseph, 100, 131, 137, 298;
Pleasant, 090, 092, 100, 109, 131,
136, 148, 153, 176, 179, 182, 184,
188, 192, 196, 219, 226, 268, 280,
292; Richard, 053, 407
STOW: John B., 115
STPAHAN: Neal, 112
STRAITON: Ginnie, 037; John, 225
STRATON: John I., 227
STRATTEN: Asa E., 272; Asa O., 308
STRATTON: A. E., 272; Acee E., 272;
Andrew, 272; Asa E., 088, 138, 140,
150, 168, 171, 266, 272, 273, 297,
304, 311; Asa F., 175; Asa, 273;
James, 138, 150, 168, 171, 175,
273, 297; Jesse, 273, 434
STPAUS: Ferdinand, 137; Joseph, 110,
137, 279
STREET: George, 278
STRICKLAND: Barnabas, 194, 224,
273, 467; E. S., 053; Eli, 053,
424, 433; Fly, 124; Henry S., 187;
Henry, 308; Isaac, 089, 273; J. W.,
374; James, 273; Joshua, 087;
Kinchin, 235; Kissie, 057; N. M.,
442; Nathan M., 053; Solomon, 113,
116, 139, 150, 236, 243, 273, 323,
424, 434; Solomon, Sr., 078;
Thomas C., 267, 297, 310
STRICKLIN: Isaac, 420; Solomon, 428
STRINGFELLOW: George W., 078, 114,
145, 181, 273; George, 141, 153,
201; James, 078; John, 273
STROCHACKER: E. S., 180
STROHICKEP: E. S., 134
STROM: Alida Sophia, 443
STRONG: Bagger, 053; Burney, 407;
Charles, 107, 176, 273; Grant,
374; Johnson, 143, 144, 206, 273,
407; Robert H., 283; Robert, 407;
Poony, 407; Sherwood, 133, 322;
William E., 374; William, 374
STPOTHEP: John, 233, 257; Richard, 153
STROUD: Philip, 273; Phillip, 183,
248, 273; Wiley, 273, 434;
William, 167, 221, 224, 273
STRUZER: William, 273, 425
STPOLIER: Fannie, 041; James W.,
053; John W., 273; William, 135,
189, 273
STUART: H. B., 431; James, 273
STUBBS: James H., 323; James, 273,
407; James, Sr., 078; John W.,
323; Thomas B., 165; Thomas P., 323
STUDDARD: Augustus, 355
STURDEVANT: Edwin, 273, 434; Joel,
087; Robert, 177; James, 273;
Jesse, 444; Joe, 448; John, 280
STURGES: Nathaniel J., 193, 198, 257;
Nathaniel S., 266; Nathaniel, 181,
188; Oliver, 317; Samuel, 181,
188, 193, 198, 257, 266
STURTA: Alfred, 198
STYLES: William, 268
SULLIVAN: A. S., 374; L. E., 328,
374; Mary Ann, 061; Obadiah, 434;
Otis H., 053; William, 053, 273
SULLIVANT: Isaac, 166; Thomas, 405
SUMMERLIN: Henry, 197, 392
SUMMERS: John T., 374
SUMTEP: James M., 273; James, 198
SUNGERFORD: Anson, 311
SUSONG: George W., 114
SUTTILE: Bill, 273; George, 273;
Isaac, 144
SUTTLES: George W., 273, 407;
George, 273
SUTTON: Jesse, 053, 273, 434;
Joseph, 122, 273
SUYDOM: Richard, 314
SWAIN: George, Jr., 293
SWAN: John T., 221; Joseph B., 279
SWANN: John T., 140, 149, 274, 274;
Joseph B., 323; T.C., 359, 393,
467; Thomas C., 356; William, 274
SWANSON: E. T., 377, 378; E. Y., 374,
456, 467; F.J., 456; F.M., 019,
078, 102, 142, 199, 271, 274, 330,
332, 333, 336, 341, 346, 350, 351,
354, 358, 362, 366, 372, 374, 376,
382, 444, 456, 467, 485; Frances
J., 242, 366; Francis M, 086, 091,
095, 110, 112, 118, 131, 144, 152,
161, 187, 202, 205, 214, 217, 219,
239, 254, 264, 265, 274, 276, 277,
282, 291, 292, 303, 321, 325, 331,
334, 341, 342, 344-347, 350, 353,
354, 359, 362, 363, 368, 374,
376-379, 458; Francis, 290; Frank
J., 053; James F., 095, 231; S.E.,
467; Susan, 374; Thomas J., 235,
320; Walker, 456; William G., 178,

179, 210, 215, 274, 302; William, 305
SWEENEY: E. Ray, 274
SWEET: John, 092, 129, 274, 323
SWENNEY: Pansom, 211
SWIFT: Adam, 274; Bart, 053, 407;
Berry, 053, 407; Eudoxcess, 324;
Hiram, 053, 274; James, 053; Jim,
374; Jim, Jr., 053; Lucy, 056;
Millie, 274; Sam, 053; Thomas L.,
331; Will, 053; William, 053;
Willis, 107, 374
SWINNEY: John, 274; Polly, 274;
Ransom, 078, 274; Zeno D. E., 296
TAFT: Orray, 230
TALBERT: John, 111, 181
TALER: Armsted, 110
TALIAFERRO: Lewis B., 166;
Benjamin, 157
TALMADGE: A. J., 118, 148, 171, 235,
243, 274, 331, 332, 334, 336, 342,
344, 350, 352, 353, 359, 364, 366,
373, 376, 377, 380, 384, 389, 456;
Aaron, 160; Albert I., 274; Albert
J., 121, 217, 335, 336, 344, 456;
Albert L., 237; Albert, Jr., 359;
C.A., 374, 456, 465, 467; Clovis
A., 053, 274; Emily C., 274; H.J.,
232, 361; H., 456; Harriet N.,
025; Henry, 374; Herbert, 053, 194,
233, 274, 456; Indiana, 043;
TALMADGE: J. E., 053, 456; J. H.,
456; J.M.H. 456; John H., 078,
329, 374, 442, 456; John, 078, 366,
456; L.C., 096; Mary F., 059; R.
S., 395, 456; Robert S., 374, 464;
Robt., 444; S. C., 134, 148, 232,
240, 243, 324, 334, 338, 345, 373,
374, 447, 456; S. Flourine
(Flournoy), 274; Stephen C., 066,
078, 091, 095, 105, 110, 111, 116,
118, 121, 136, 151, 162, 170, 171,
199, 206, 217, 224, 229, 235, 237,
240, 244, 246, 247, 254, 259, 262,
264, 274, 306, 314, 319, 323,
290-292, 394, 456; W. J., 456;
William, 456
TALMAGE: J. H. 245
TANKERSLEY: Carter, 434
TANKERSLY: Richard, 307; Carter, 274
TANNEP: A.W., 374, 381; Arch W., 286;
Arch, 243; Archibald W., 292;
Carrie, 300; John, 267; Link, 053;
Mary, 049; William, 274
TAPE: Clay, 370
TARVA: Henry, 274
TATNALL: Josiah, 130
TATOM: Howell, 230
TATUM: Howel, 158, 427; Howell, 274;
James, 232; Organ, 274; Parthenia,
276; Peter, 274; Thomas, 239
TAYLOR & BOLLING CO.: --, 444
TAYLOR: Absalom, 274; Alfred, 274;
Andrew, 469; Benjamin F., 187,
274; C., 346; David, Jr., 231,
270; Evan P., 160; Frances N.
(heirs of), 434; Frances, 276;
Francis N., 078, 274, 397; George
A., 053; George, 456; Gilbert D.,
426, 434; Hardy, 274; Henry R.,
274, 275, 434; Hugh, 087, 117,
280, 288; J. A., 373, 447; J. P.,
372; Jack, 275; Jacob, 434; James
J., 053; James, 053, 095, 183,
312, 323, 364; Jefferson, 264;
TAYLOR: John M., 214, 259, 263; John,
053, 322; Jordan, 053; Leonard,
066, 078, 274; Lewis, 053;
Margaret, 046; Mariah Jane, 055;
Mark, 374; Richard, 448; Robert,
238, 409, 469; Rolan, 288; Samuel,
374; Sarah, 012; Stephen S., 275,
323; Thomas C., 146, 160, 217,
387; Uriah, 158, 275; Wiley, 458;
William B., 275, 290; William F.,
434; William H., 078, 194, 198,
274, 275, 323, 400, 407, 420;
William, 275, 434, 467
TEAL: Bradberry, 429, 431, 436; Henry,
275; Jesse, 275; Jordan, 318;
Lodowick, 275, 318; William, 275
TEASLEY: Vira, 408
TEDARD: Samuel, 275
TEDARDS: Masey, 009
TEDDARDS: C. M., 447
TEDDARDS: C. M., 078; G. W., 374
TEDDERDS: Walker, 053
TEDDERS: G. W., 456, 467; George W.,
053, 456; Lola, 034; Samuel, 078,
275, 434; Susie Elizabeth, 443
TEDDLIE: William, 434
TEDDY: Samuel, 094
TEDLEY: William, 426
TEEL: Henry, 053, 246; Meshack, 275;
Meshic, 275; Mellev, 275; Penny,
060; Thomas, 275
TELLER: James, 053
TEMPLE: Jonas, 435
TEMPLE: Frederick, 434; Jones, 421
TENNET: Gilbert B.,102
TERHUNE: C. D., 380; Cornelius D.,
092, 099, 160, 172, 188, 211, 275,
283, 404; Cornelius, 258, 374

TERONDET: James C., 469
TERREL: David, 273
TERRELL: David, 169; Elizabeth, 275,
460; Frank, 408; Hezekiah, 130,
196; J. M., 342; James M., 348,
371; Joel L., 275, 340, 432; Joel
S., 363; Luis, 434; Nancy, 025;
Peter B., 434; Thomas, 078, 191,
238; William D., 114;
William, 117, 187
TERPY: Frank, 408; Garland B., 275;
Jeremiah, 275, 323; Jerry, 135,
275, 323; William, 222, 293
THADAWAY: Jackson, 190
THAMES: Joseph, 275; William, 197
THAXTON: John, 053
THAYER: Henry, 220
THERMAN: Robert, 141
THERMON: John, 275
THIGPEN: Gilbert E., 107
THOMAS (THOMSON): Cora, 019
THOMAS: Albert, 053; Amanda, 011,
029; Angeline, 050; Augusta, 467;
Augustus, 408; B. A., 380; B.F.,
370; Beckie, 051; Ben, 053;
Benjamin, 053; Bess, 408; Buck,
275, 374; C. C., 275; Carl, 043;
Caroline, 023, 031; Carrie, 028;
Charles, 053; Charley, 053; David
L., 434; David S., 218, 275, 276;
Dily, 008; Douglas, 276; Edna,
408; Egnev, 378; Ednie, 374;
THOMAS: Edward, 123, 134, 193, 286;
Elbert, 276; Eli, 053; Eliza, 035;
Ella, 024, 041; Ellen, 012, 051,
378; Emaline, 045; Emily, 016,
037; Emma, 056, 378; Eugene, 010;
Fleetwood, 053; Florence, 006;
Franc, 276; Frederick L., 408;
Frederick S., 174, 254, 275; G.
Wash, 276; Gabriel R., 100;
George, 277; Georgia, 043; Govenor,
276; Gus, 276; Harper, 276;
Hattie, 010, 408; Henrietta, 046;
THOMAS: Henry, 291; Hilliard, 053;
Hiram, 374; Ida E., 025; Ida, 036;
Jack, 276; James A., 408; Jane,
012; Jeff, 374; Jim, 053; Joe,
053, 192, 276; John H., 053; John,
053, 093, 170, 276, 292, 307, 434;
Jonas, 235; Joseph, 053; Larcenie,
058; Laura, 061; Lena, 006; Lewis,
276, 374, 381, 458; Lewis, Jr.,
053; Lizzie, 004, 016; Louisa, 059;
Lucinda, 044; Lucius, 054; Marian,
034; Martha, 157, 408; Mary Ann,
023; Mary, 275, 374; Mat, 374;
THOMAS: Matilda, 028, 345; Matthew
Anderson, 176; Mattie, 012, 031,
057; Mittie, 017; Mollie, 024;
Olin, 276; Oliver, 054, 276;
Oliver, Jr., 054; Onie, 011;
Parthenia, 004; Pennie, 031; P.
C., 467; Reese, 408; Rich, 374;
Richard, 054; Safrona, 276;
Sallie, 020; Samuel, 053;
Samuel, 420; Scott, 054, 276,
374; Silvia, 019; Stephen, 216;
Stevens, 144, 183, 228; Susan,
043; Susie, 030; Tobe, 054; Wash,
374; Wiley, 276; Will, 374;
William T., 054; William, 054,
Wyatt, 054
THOMASON: A. J., 374, 409, 456;
Amelia, 276; Andrew J., 054, 409;
Clark, 276, 408; D. C., 456; Davis
Clark, 054; Delona S., 057 Dick,
445; Isaac, 276, 374; J. C., 054,
204, 232, 276, 374, 456, 458;
Jackson C., 078, 121, 276, 374,
404, 408, 415; James, 054; Jennie
B., 017; Joe, 054; Katie L., 017;
Lilie, 033; Louangie, 056; Martha
M., 276; Martha, 276; Martin A.,
276; Oscar, 054, 380; P. P., 352,
388; Permenius R., 145; Permenus
R., 305; Richard S., 276; Richard,
276; S. E., 276; Sallie W., 409;
Samuel E., 054, 415; T. J., 276,
374; Thomas, 066, 078, 276; Usher,
352; W., 374; William J., 054;
William S., 276; William, 247,
276, 408
THOMASSON: Aaron, 276; William S.,276
THOMASTON: Elizabeth, 024; Jackson,
276; P. R., 262; Permemus R.,
213; William L., 276
THOMPSON: Jackson, 054
THOMPKINS: Mason, 054
THOMPSON: ?, 042; P. P., 456; Aaron
P., 442, 447; Abraham, 374;
Alexander, 078; Amarintha A., 269;
Anderson F., 147, 232, 246, 249;
Annie F., 032; Boot (John Henry),
276; Brookling, 276; C. F., 371,
447, 456; C.S., 407, 456; Charles
F., 374, 456; Charles C., ...
247; Charles H., 269; Charles J.,
269; Christopher, 269; Cora, 004;
Daniel, 276; David, 054, 145;
THOMPSON: Delia, 408; Dora, 061; E.

H., 456; E. I., 374; Ed N., 054;
Ed, 054, 276, 408; Eddar, 124;
Edmund B., 176; Edward J., 054,
277; Edward, 434; Edwin J., 054;
Elbert, 054; Elijah, 311;
Elizabeth, 048; Emma, 034, 042;
Evan, 054; Frank, 408; Frederick,
316; G. M., 277; Genie, 039; George
M., 054; George, 054, 165, 277;
330; Gilbert, 443; H. T., 054;
Hamlin, 456; Hannah, 078; Harriet,
259; Harrison, 054, 408; Henrietta,
443; Henry B., 323; Henry T., 054;
THOMPSON: Henry, 054, 066, 277, 374,
408; Hezekiah, 251, 272; Hiram,
277; Idella, 408; Isham, 181, 220,
241, 248, 250; J. C., 374; J. F.,
374, 375; J. H., 2; J. I.; J. H.,
456; J. M., 281, 375, 382, 442,
456, 462; J. M., Jr., 054, 456;
..Mat, 062; J. Matt, 277; J. P.,
277; J. R., 054; J. W., 33; 350;
Jackson P., 375; Jacob M., 078,
277, 323, 375; Jacob, 295; Jake,
281; James A., 434; James S., 289;
THOMPSON: James, 078, 277, 434, 436;
Jannie, 277; Jeramiah, 078, 277,
423, 434; Jim, 054; Joe, 054, 277,
404, 408; John, 054, 277, 468;
John F. Jr., 277; John S., 434;
460; John, 277, 375; Joseph M.,
375, 456; Joseph R., 375; Joseph,
277, 372, 375, 448, 459; Katie,
013; L. F., 456; L. L. 375;
Leo, 408; Leverett, 408; Lewis,
162, 277; Lizzie, 007; Loss, 408;
THOMPSON: Louis, 332; Lucy May, 032;
Luia, 046; M. A., 026; M. H., 277,
456; Mandy, 021; Mariah, 050; Mark,
444; Martha, 384; Mary S., 003;
Mary, 018, 375; Mat, 375; Matthew
J., 054; Matthew, 375, 456; Mattie,
054; Nancy, 460; Pink, 054, 277,
372, 408; Robbie A., 002; Robert
277; Robert, 140, 248;
277; S.E, 277; S.I., 456; Sallie,
078; Samuel, 054, 089, 233, 277,
316, 375; Sarah Ann, 035; Stephen,
277; T. B., 408; T. H, 408; T.
W., 242, 456; Tete, 277; Thomas
W., 054, 456; Thomas, 277; Thommy,
W., 054, 456; Tom, 054; Turner M.,
W. D., 375; W. H., 153, 370, 375,
443, 456; W. L., 456; William C.,
104; William D., 054, 375, 415;
William E., 150; William F., 054;
William H., 144, 171, 237, 277,
344, 356, 375, 385, 434, 456;
William L., 054, 277, 375; William,
054, 141, 277, 375; William, Jr.,
375; Wm. H., 447; Zaydee, 054
THOMSON: Agelia, 045; Anna, 181;
Etta, 035; M.H., 456; Parminas, 107
THORNTON: Anthony, 054; Archibald,
277; Carrie, 145; Cullen, 054, 430,
431, 434; Frank, 277; Georgia Ann,
004; H. A., 456; Handy, 054, 375;
Haney E., 038; Henry, 434; Isham,
104; J. D., 108, 362, 374, 456;
J.J., 349; J.W., 456; James, 054,
277; Jordan, 115, 179, 180, 293,
434; Joseph D., 375; Lula, 054;
THORNTON: Mahala, 277; Mark, 289;
Mary Ann, 014; Meahalah, 277;
Ninnie, 060; Noble, 277; Solomon,
054; Thomas, 277; Wiley, 277;
Yancy, 160, 265, 277
THOPP: Cicero A., 098; Green, 277
THPASH: Carrie, 055; David, 121;
Jacob, 210; Martin, 278, 323, 390
THRASHER: Earley W., 095;
Early W., 336, 374
THPOWER: Thomas, 278
THUNDERBURK: F.E., 408; Joseph, 408
THURBER: H. K., 243
THURMAN: A. S., 339, 340, 345, 370,
381, 467; Aaron, 055, 278, 375;
Aaron, Jr., 342; Arnel, 278;
Arnold, 278; Augustus, 055;
Benjamin, 278; Edward, 278, 408;
408; Cass Ann, 055; Charles, 408;
Charlie, 278; Edward, 278, 408;
Elizabeth, 408; Fannie, 356; Frank,
375; George, 352; James, 278, 375;
Joe, 055, 375; John, 278; Nan, 408;
Mary Jane, 022; Mary, 005; Matilda,
046; Mitch, 055; Mitchel, 278;
Mitchell, 375; Moody, 339, 375;
Peter, 052; Philip, 176, 272, 278,
459; Phillip, 055, 078, 125; Primus,
375; Rich, 375; Sarah, 375, 408;
Stephen, 122; Wilkes, 278;
Wilks, 375
THURMOND: Lilie, 057
THURMON: Aaron, Sr., 375; Fountain
M., 278; James, 278; Philip, 204
THURMOND: A. S., Mrs., 485; Aaron,
055, 369, 375, 408; Benjamin, 055,
323, 434; Betsy, 050; C. D., 361,
375; Carrie, 011; Charles Crawford,

150: Charles H., 375; Charles, 278; Clint, 278; Ed H., 375; Edmond, 278; Fountain M., 078, 103, 277, 278; Jack, 278; James, 278; Jesse, 109, 141, 278; Jim, 055; Joe, 444; John, 113, 121, 131, 218, 222; 232, 246, 249, 251, 278, 284, 294, 311, 318, 409; Mannie, 055; Mattie, 046; Norris, 468; Philip, 219, 249, 250, 299; Phillip, 154, 278, 425, 427, 430, 431, 434, 435; Phoebe, 012; Richard, 297; Rowland, 141, 312; Stephen, 055; Sydney, 055; Thomas, 278; William, 278; Willie, 055; Wilson, 055
TIDWELL: Benjamin F., 223; John G., 278
TIE: Henry, 435
TIGNOR: Young F., 118
TILERY: Margrate, 458; Thomas, 459
TILLER: Ephraim E., 278; Ephraim, 278; Mason, 278; Paul H., 278; Sam, 278
TILLERY: Hudson, 055; John, 278
TILLETT: George, 278
TILLMAN: Bob Lee, 278; C.B., 375; Dan, 278; Dave, 278; George, 278; Henry, 055; James, 278; John, 055, 078, 463; Lizzie, 052; Mary Ann, 022; Penelope, 278; Phoebe, 078; Pitman, 415; R.T., 408; Robert Lee, 375; Robert, 055; Walter, 278
TILLMON: George, 456
TILMAN(TIGLMAN): Malissa, 052
TILMAN: Betsy, 032; Bob, 278; E. L., 456; Edny, 375; Elijah L., 055; Fannie Kate, 008; Frances, 038; George I., 375; George, 055; Henry, 278; J. H., 456; John H., 456; John, 197, 276, 277
TILMON: C. B., 408; Caroline, 033; John, 055; Martha A., 022; Martha, 021; Mary L., 025; Nancy, 018; Richard, 055; William H., 055
TINDALL: Henry W., 170
TINDILL: Jonathan, 078
TINDOL: Samuel, 279
TINDSLEY: Annie Kate, 023; Frank, 055; Homer, 055; James, 055; Lewis, 055
TINER: David, 378; Reuben, 279
TINGLE: Joseph, 279; Steven G., 055; W.A., 279, 375, 456; William A., 456
TINNAN: David, 279
TINSELEY: Charles, 375
TINSLEY: Allancen R., 279; Allvance R., 408; Arch, 055; Bill, 391; Charles, 055, 118; Charlie, Jr., 375; Cheney, 038; Daniel, 055, 375; Easter, 015; Emma, 020, 279; Henry, 055; James, 055, 408; Joe, 055; Lewis, 055; Martha, 034; Mary, 279, 375; Sarah, 002; Wiley, 055; Will, 375, 408; William B., 426; William, 055, 279, 375, 386; Wily, 408
TINSLV: Anaka, 009; Annie, 021
TIPPINS: James Augustus, 433
TISON: John, 247; Kinchen P., 324
TITTS: J. E., 375
TODD: Ed, 375; Ira D., 055; John, 435
TOLAN: Emeline, 035
TOLAND: Adam, 127, 279; Asa P., 110, 279; Bob, 055; C.M., 059; Celia P., 051; Charlotte, 005; E. H., 291; Emma, 007; Iverson L., 279; Lewis, 055; M.M., 397; Mariah, 279; Matilda, 375; Mattie, 048; Michael M., 066, 078, 279, 434; Michael, 223, 279; Richard, 279; Sally, 078; Samuel, 078; Sylvia, 048; T. L., 279; Thyers J., 055, 110; Thyus J., 279
TOLEFREE: Robert, 094, 104, 147, 212, 251; Robert, 279, 301, 306, 308; William, 111, 279
TOLEN: Adam, 408; U. W., 456
TOLES: Addie, 027
TOLLERSON: J. G., 279
TOLLESON: J. G., 344, 347, 348, 352, 353, 362; J. G., 366, 376, 377, 447, 456; J. J., 457; J., 456; Joe, 457; Joseph G., 336, 342, 380, 381; Joseph, 457; Lula M., 025
TOMASON: P. R., 371
TOMERSON: J.C., 442; Martha M., 276; Seliency, 047
TOMES: Francis, Jr., 304; Francis, Sr., 304
TOMKINS: John, 166
TOMLIN: Dave, 279; John Harris, 435; Matilla A., 010; Polly Ann, 030; Rufa, 279
TOMLINSON: Amanda Melvina, 176; Daniel, 111; Humphrey W., 176; J. D., 055, 457; J.J., 457; J. T., 376; Jack J., 055; Jack, 376; James Lee, 055; John B., 457; John D., 078; John T., 442; John, 376; John, Jr., 279; Lucy F., 019; M. W., 376; Mitchael, 158; S.D., 457; Stephen D., 055; W.J., 376; W.M.,

376, 442, 457; William, 457
TOMMERSON: William, 127
TOMPKINS: Bug, 408; C.H., 403; Ed, 055; Eubanks, 279; Fannie, 029; Giles, 225, 279, 435; John, 279; Lewis, 349; Lucius, 408; Lucy Ann, 066, 078; Mary T., 024; Mason, 376
TOMPSON: John F., 279
TOMSON: Allen, 437
TONEY: Lucy, 009
TORRENCE: George W., 055
TOUCHSTONE: Caleb, 427, 435; Christopher, 279
TOUGGLE: W. R., 376
TOURNEY: Jesse, 279
TOWLES: Moses G., 175
TOWNS: Ann (Lankey), 210, 305; Ann, 158; Anna, 279; Bartley, 279, 280, 435; Drury, 210, 305; George W.B., 263, 279; Henry C., 279, 280, 436; J.D., 408; J.T.C., 279; Jarrel O., 308; Joel, 105, 158, 261, 279, 289, 294, 427, 434, 435; John G. (heirs of), 435; John G., 066, 078, 113, 279, 435; John T.C., 078, 140, 158, 189, 219, 270, 279, 280, 323, 435; John, 100, 252, 259, 263, 279, 422, 435; Lewis, 280; TOWNS: Marlen, 280; Marlin, 280, 323, 434, 435; Moses, 280; William, 244
TOWNSEND: Betsey, 460; George, 280; Isaac, 186; Jesse, 280; Robert C., 173, 186; Samuel, 228, 460; Samuel, Sr., 400; William H., 173, 186, 237; William S., 104, 144, 171; William, 280
TOWNSON: Nathaniel F., 261
TOWSON: John, 149
TRAILER: William, 216
TRAINER: James, 435
TRAMEN: Clement, 435
TRAMMEL: A. A., 280, 405; Augusta A., 280, 298; James M., 460; Mark D., 323
TRAMMELL: Amanda, 061; Augustus H., 095
TRAPP: Levi, 189
TRASK: Alanson, 121
TRAVIS: Jesse, 294
TRAWECK: Robert, 280
TRAWEEK: Robert C., 435
TRAWICK: Robert, 280, 448
TRAYLER: Francis, 282; Harriet, 024; Thomas G., 280
TRAYLOR: Averilla B. (White), 106; C. T., 435; Champion T., 066, 078, 090, 124; George H., 119, 220; John W., 280; Lucy, 125; Mark, 055, 280, 376; Mason, 280; Milamin B., 280; Thomas G., 280; Thomas, 066, 302; William H. (heirs of), 427, 435; William H., 078, 087; William, 164, 303; Wylv, 284
TRAYNEP: James, 323
TRAYWICK: Maggie E., 023
TREADWAY: George T., 298
TREADWELL: David, 174
TREDWELL: A. H., 357; James, 280
TREMBLE: Moses, 245
TREYNOR: Hugh, 444
TRICE: Thomas C., 280
TRIGG: George P., 367
TRIMBLE: Charlie, 055; Henry, 280; James S., 160
TRIP: Emanuel, 055
TRIPLETT: John N., 389; John, 280
TRIPP: Robert, 280
TRIPPE: Emanuel, 445; Henry W., 280; Henry, 230, 280; James, 280; Robert, 127, 255, 256, 280, 308, 426, 437; William, 078, 280
TRITTLE: James N., 251
TROUTMAN: Hiram B., 322; Hiram P.,313
TRUESDALE: Nathaniel, 184
TRUESDELL: Nathainiel, 285
TRUIT: Amanda, 050; Jack, 280; John, 306, 411; Nancy (Callaway), 435; Riley, 078
TRUITT: Henry T., 166; J.T., 055, 376; John, 078, 280; William P.,171
TRUMAN: Hamlin, 108
TRUSSEL: Daniel, 280
TRUSSELL: Charles H., 078; Claborn, 162; Daniel, 162; Green B., 055, 280; Green, 147; James D., 408; James L., 280; James, 280, 294; Mary A., 110; William H., 055, 280
TUCKER: A. L., 457; Alfred, 376; Allen, 055, 078, 315; Annie J., 007; B. H., 376; Benjamin P., 128; Florence, 049; G. A., 467; G. C., 376; George A., 055; George, 280, 285; Green C., 280, 376, 464; Green, 376; Greensville, 280; J. D., 395, 406, 447, 467; J. L., 363, 408, 460; J. S., 381; James L., 129, 340, 343, 387, 398; Jesse M., 442; Jesse, 274; Joel, 280; TUCKER: John B., 457; John, 280; Mattie I., 041; Nancy, 315; Nath,

408; Pinton, 142; Pointon, 297; Reddick, 280; Robert T., 088; Robert, 321; Susan E., 356; Susan, 006; T. C., 376; Tabitha, 061; Thomas, 280; W. A., 457; W. E., 280, 329, 342, 347, 352, 355, 362, 363, 375, 392, 395; W.J., 386, 457; W. R., 457; W.T., 177; Warren J., 279, 281, 448; Warren, 281; William E., 351; William G., 281; William, 281, 376, 457
TUCKERMAN: Gustavius, 214; Gustavus, 156, 276; William, 156, 214, 276
TUFTS: Gardner, 315
TUGGLE: A.F., 376; Alf, 281; Alfred F., 055; Anna, 061; Annie, 013, 408; Benjamin F., 281, 313; Berry W., 386; Berry, 376; Bob, 281; Carlton, 055; Carrie, 006, 032, 281; Carry H., 049; Catherine, 281; Cathrin, 004; Charlie, Jr., 376; Crayton, 055; Daniel, 415; Dora, 048; E. D., 343, 376, 399, 408, 467; Earnev, 376; Eq, 281; Edgar, 408; Eliza, 051; Elizabeth, 066, 078, 281; Elmore D., 055; TUGGLE: Emma, 056; F.M., 281; F.N., 281, 376; P.W., 408; Flawainer(?) N., 329; Florence N., 376; Frank, 055; Harry, 376; Henry, 056, 376, 408; Hugh, 281; J. L., 281, 408; J.A. Mrs., 408; J.L., 461; James, 056; John, 281; Joseph, 056; Junie A., 078; L.S., 376; Lee, 281, 430, 435; Leonard, 281; Lewis, 281; Lizzie, 056; Lodowick, 281; Lou S., 281; Martha, 052; Mose, 408; TUGGLE: N.F., 408; Otis, 376; Phil, 281; Phillip, 056, 467; Robert, 078, 128, 244, 281, 376, 435, 436; Samuel, 056; Selina C., 017; Silla, 029; Thomas H., 169, 281, 301, 432, 435; Thomas, 135, 281, 467; W.J.L., 366; W. J. S., 335; W. R., 281, 330, 373, 374, 376, 381, 408, 415, 467; Wash, 376, 408; Washinaton, 056; William J. L., 066, 078, 137, 166, 211, 281, 301; William R., 056, 078, 368, 376; William, 281; Willie, 078
TUGLE: Lee, 083
TURK: A.A., 376; A.T., 442;Adolphus Arrinaton, 458; Avinaton, 056, 099, 376; Callie, 030; Charles, 056; Claudius, 337; E. B., 212, 281, 376, 457, 461, 467; Edward B., 056, 376; Elizabeth, 099; Emeliza, 054; Fanny, 034; Frank, 056; Henry, 260; J.W., 408; Jeff, 056; Jennie, 060; Joe, 056; John, 066, 078, 099, 212, 277, 281, 341, 358, 363, 373, 436, 442; Jonathan, 056, 078; Julia, 036; L. L., 408, 467; Lucian L., 147; Lucius, 281; TURK: Marv J., 017; Mary, 050; Medina, 337; Medora, 376; Oscar, 056; Sarah, 008; Swan, 056; T. J., 281, 376, 377, 457; Thomas L.,377; Thomas J., 377; W. C., 339, 341, 358; W. R., 447; Will R., 281; Will, 056; William C., 078, 277; William, 056, 125, 363, 373
TURKE: John, 377; Thomas, 377; W. C., 277
TURNBALL: George, 260
TURNELL: ?, 117; W.W., 332, 376, 377
TURNER: A.J., 281, 377; Abner, 106, 238; Allen, 281, 377; Anderson, 056, 281; Annie L., 048; Archibald, 281; B.S., 281; Benjamin H., 056; Brooks, 408; Charles, 197, 281, 332, 342, 409; Colored, 445; Crawford, 281; Easum, 206; Elizabeth, 025; Esom, 056, 115, 281; Frances, 003; George Ann, 281; George Ellis, 409; George, 282; Gertrude, 041; Green B., 225, 236, 281, 305, 306; Greenburg H., 281; Greene B., 169; Greene R., 219; Henry G., 281; J. W., 282, 377, 457, 466; James, 056; James F., 282, 323; James H., 399; James N., 282; James, 099, 140, 146, 212, 222, 282, 312, 336, 346, 375, 377, 415, 423; Jennie, 030, 040; Joel, 456; John D., 056, 457; TURNER: John G., 078; John W., 056; John, 056, 117, 282, 377, 409; Joseph, 204; L. W., 056; Larkin, 172, 282; Lucy, 029; Lula, 043; M. A. Mrs., 447; Malissa, 013; Mamsom (Manson), 282; Manson, 188, 259, 282, 435; Martha S., 056; Martha, 301; Mary L., 002; Mason, 189; Mattie, 025; Meshack III., 485; Metal, 389; Miles, 445; Nettie, 025; Newton, 095; Nick, 377; Owen, 377; P. F., 377, 457; R. Newton, 282; Reuben, 192; TURNER: Richard, 136, 179, 282;

Roberson H., 282; Roxie Ann. 002;
S.W. 442. 457; S. W., Jr., 066;
Samuel. 282; Sarah. 026; Shadrach.
282; Shadrick. 431; T.A.B. 377.
382. 425. 457; T.A. 457; Thomas
M.. 078; Thomas. 056. 377; Thomas.
Jr. 377; Toliver A.. 078. 377;
Toliver B.. 292; Tom. 282. 409;
W.L., 345; W.T., 377. 457; Wade
.. 179; Willie. 056
TURNEY: Jesse. 282. 296; P. F., 078
TURPIN: William H.. 088. 173. 184. 252
TWEEDELL: Alexander W. H. 282
TWIGGS: Abraham. 192; George. 192;
John. 192
TWITTY: George. 184
TYE: Daniel. 236
TYLER: A.A., 457; A.H., 409; Ada.
016; Albert A. 056; Albert. 282.
457; Andrew L.. 056; B. F. 282.
457; Barney F.. 282. 367; Barney.
282. 377; C. E. 057; Ed. 282;
Ella. 026; F. M.. 056. 282. 377.
435. 442. 457; F. Marion. 377;
Frances M.. 360; Francis M.. 056.
078. 415. 457; G.W.. 457; George.
282. 457; Ida. 015. 017; J. J..
282. 457; J.J., Jr. 457; J. L..
442; J. W. 457; Jane. 361; Job
M.. 457; Job. 056. 078. 217. 457;
TYLER: Job. Jr.. 282. 457; John J..
056. 332. 377. 382; John J.. 415.
457; John J7. Jr.. 056; John. 078.
377; Joseph. 374; Kate. 039; M.
D.. 457; Marcus H.. 078; Marion.
409; Martin. 377. 457; Mary J..
223; Mike B.. 457; Mike. 377;
Nora. 055; Ollie. 057; Rachel.
021; Samuel B.. 056. 078; Samuel.
282; Sarah Jane. 036; T.M.. 377;
Thomas J.. 462; Thomas. 282; W.
E.. 364; Will. 457; William P..
282; William. 199. 282
TYNER: Charles J.. 056; D. M.. 377;
David M.. 056. 282. 367. 377;
David. 056; H. F. 457; J. M..
249; M. A.. 377; M. V.. 331. 358.
377; Martin V..056. 138. 334. 358.
363; Martin. 226; Matilda D.. 040;
R. 1.. 415; R. J.. 056. 282. 435.
437; R. John. 078; Reuben J.. 282.
377; Reuben. 282; Reubin J.. 138;
Rheuben J.. 335; Sallie. 046;
Sarah M.. 020; Stephen. 194. 282.
295. 435
TYSON: H. F.. 409. 457; Henry F..
078. 282. 415; Roxy Ann. 015
TYUS: John. 283; Lewis. 283; Thomas.
391. 409; William G.. 122. 256.
282. 283
UMPHREY: Milton. 377
UNDERHILL: Charles. 138. 214;
William. 138. 214
UNDERWOOD: Addie. Miss. 008; Agnes.
026; Cordelia. 058; John. 230;
Mary. 012; William S.. 230;
William. 289
UNIDENTIFIED PERSONS: (2), 445
UPSON: Ransalier. 324
URQUHART: Alexander. 078. 283. 434.
435; David. 145. 462; Henry. 283.
323; Kenneth M.. 227; M. V.. 203;
Neil. V.. 078; Neill. H.. 289
URQUHEART: Alexander. 283
URSERY: Irene. 039
URSRY: Mose. 377
USERY: Jackson. 056
USHER: Carrie. 036; Robert O.. 203.
295. 296. 310; Sarah A.. 283
USHERY: J. T.. 409; Jessee. 409
USRY: Jordan. 056; Mollie. 023;
Mose. 056; Nettie. 028;
William. 177
USSERY: Caroline. 026
VAIL: Amos S.. 101
VALENTINE: Thomas. 283
VAN ANWEER: William. 135
VAN WAGENIN: John. 166. 175
VAN: Sanders. 283
VANANTWERP: William. 323
VANBIBBER: Henry. 283
VANCE: Marcus D.. 136. 283. 284.
467; Marcus. 197. 199. 204. 282
VANCROFT: Dyer C.. 139
VANDEGRIFT: John. 284
VANDERGRIEF: John. 284
VANN: Dianna. 458; Horace. 458;
Joseph. 435; Sanders. 099. 207
VANNERSON: J. H.. 056
VANWAGENEN: Jonathan. 130. 214. 315
VARDEMAN: Henry W.. 284;
William. 078. 284
VARNAM: W. C.. 284
VARNER: Alex. 377; Amos. 284; Andrew
J.. 092. 138. 262. 284. 285. 291.
323; Caroline. 234; Clinton L..
284. 285. 291; Clinton. 284; Cynthia
H. (Byron). 284; Cynthia H.. 284.
467; David. 056; Earley. 284;
Early. 284; Edward. 092. 113. 130.
194. 249. 269. 284. 285. 323. 324.
409. 291; Frederick A.. 284. 285.

323; George. 117. 206; Harvey.
056; Hendley. 285; Henley. 285;
VARNER: Ida. 038; Jefferson N.. 138.
284. 285; Jefferson. 285; Joe. 467;
Joseph W.. 323; Milas. 056; Pierce.
284; Reuben. 056; Samuel D.. 157.
202. 216. 234. 245. 284. 285. 324.
409; Samuel. 323. 474; William G..
285; William. 078. 206. 260. 284.
285. 448
VARNOM: Margaret J..033; William. 442
VARNUM: Margarett. 285;
William C.. 457
VASON: David A.. 153. 311. 312. 322;
Davis A.. 290; Joseph. 305
VASSER: Jonathan. 169
VAUGHAN: ?. 448; Albert B.. 110. 133.
300; Albert. 056; Andrew. 056.
285; Aurie. 060; Benjamin T.. 078.
285; Berry. 285; Bill. 377;
Chaney. 024; Dora. 171; Eli. 409;
Ella Carv A.. 015; Frederick. 239;
Georgia (Missie). 285; Harriet.
055; Henry. 110. 127. 202. 246.
301; Horace. 285; Isham. 285;
VAUGHN: J. N. 457; James M.. 078;
James W.. 093. 105. 133. 135. 136.
148. 163. 195. 239. 243. 245-247.
285. 300. 302. 306. 324; James.
093; Jane. 045; Jeff. 377;
Jefferson. 377; John. 285; Josie.
040; Lizzie. 017; Mary. 049;
Matilda. 026; Mattie. 005. 060;
Mila. 016; Milton. 285; Stephen
H. 066. 078; Thomas J. 078;
Tom. 331; Will. 285; William H..
147. 182; William. 056. 078. 087.
253. 285. 447; William. Sr.. 320
VAWN: William. 285
VEAL: B. W. 409; Joseph E.. 296;
Joseph. 285; Thomas C. 296
VEGAL: George. 175
VENTERS: Stephen. 215. 285
VICKERS: Elijah. 078. 285. 435. 467;
H. H.. 057; John. 285; Lucinda.
050; Mary C.. 013; William. 303
VICKERSON: Wash. 057
VICKERY: Middleton. 285
VICKRAM: Caroline. 005; William. 057
VICKRUM: Adolphus. 057; Charles.
409; Edmond. 443; Homer. 377;
Reese. 057; Walter. 285
VICRAM: Thomas L.. 057
VICTORY: Thomas. 133
VICTRUM: Andrew. 057; Carrie. 285;
Mary Jane. 039; Starling. 409;
Woody. 057
VINCENT: Anna. 021; Caroline. 285;
E.. 378; Florence. 026; Henry. 285.
324; James. 377; Jane. 428; Jim.
057. 285; John. 409; Minnie. 045;
Nathaniel. 285; P. P.. 201. 205;
Powel P.. 285; Rance. 057; Ranse.
409; Ransom. 057; Rebeca A.. 039;
Robert. 409; Thomas G.. 285;
Thomas. 285; Tom. 057; Turner. 057.
409; W.T.. 376; William L.. 286
VINCIENT: James. 057
VINEABLE: ?. 286
VINES: Joe. 333
VINING: E.H. 458; J.A.. 457; J. F..
390. 457; James F.. 057. 324;
Shadrach. 286
VININGS: John. 282
VINSON: Elisha. 099; J. W.. 057;
James. 409; John. 377; Leona. 040; .
Nimrod. 155; Turner. 336
VIPDELL: Ann. 460
VIRGIN: J. A.. 388
VONNER: Pearce. 409
WACHOB: Joseph F.. 292
WADDILL: Marshal H.. 434;
Marshall H.. 286. 409
WADE: Allah H.. 045; Benjamin. 066.
078. 206; Elijah. 057; Elizabeth
L..078. 424; Gus. 057; H.. 078;
James A.. 288. 467; James. 078.
156. 286. 432; Jennie. 010; Joe.
378; Joel. 057; Manda. 005; Mary
A. E..078; Mary. 008. 019; Medora
(Cochran). 122; Reuben. 092;
Richard. 156; Sam. 057;
William E.. 149; William L.. 209;
William. 199
WADEMAN: Adam. 469; Milly. 469
WADFORD: Alexander. 378
WADLEY: Henry. 378
WADSWORTH: John. 259. 304
WAGGONER: Mattie. 041; Nicholas. 146
WAGNER: Benjamin. 191; Cora. 014;
H. Lee. 378. 458; J.C.. 378. 409.
467; J.H.. 378; J.C.. 409; J. W..
378. 457; James. 286; Jeremiah.
286; John W.. 286; Minnie. 024;
Narcissa L.. 052; Nicholas. 216;
Nora B.. 037; Sampson. 078; Susan.
015; T. L. 057; W. A.. 062. 458
WAGONER: Hiram. 078; Jerry. 286
WAIT: Marv. 435
WAITS: A. M.. 467; Addie. 286;
Agnes. 409; Alex Milton. 057;
Alex. 457; Alexander. 057. 078.

176. 286. 415. 442. 445; Alexander.
Jr. 378; Amy. 078; Annie E.. 024;
Assian. 057; Benjamin. 066. 078.
290. 435. 460; Berta L.. 021? C.
L.. 378; Charles. 057; Clara. 056;
E.A. Mrs.. 410; Edgar. 057; Ella.
043; Emma. 055; Flem. 457; G.W.T..
286; Georgia. 003; Gurley. 286;
WAITS: Harvey. 057; Henry. 057. 286;
Isaac N.. 057; J.P.W.. 457; J.W..
457; James. 148. 164. 378. 409;
Jefferson. 378; Jennie. 044; John
A. C.. 057; John R.. 057; John.
078. 116. 286; Joshua. 057. 278.
286. 378. 457; Julia Frances. 027;
Leroy. 057. 066. 250. 286. 458; Levi
Fleming. 057; Levi. 057. 286. 378.
409. 415. 457; Levy. 442; Lucinda.
378; Lucy T.. 038; Mittie. 378;
WAITS: Nathaniel. 057; Rebecca. 048;
Richmond. 150. 392. 442; Sallie.
037; Sally Ann. 345; Sarah(heirs).
460; Sarah A.. 227; Sarah C.. 054;
Susie. 057; T. L.. 378; Thomas. 057.
378; Tobe. 378; W. B. 378. 442.
457; W.J. 057. 378. 457; Wade.
378. 404; William B.. 286. 457.
458; William W.. 286; William.
057. 286. 378. 457; Wm. B.. 467
WALBURG: Jacob. 094
WALBURG: Jacob. 093
WALDEN: Alexander. 286. 433; Charles.
211. 248. 286. 435; Critia. 435;
Daniel. 286; Elisha. 409; Henry.
286. 435; James. 211. 286. 421.
435; William H.. 286
WALDEON: Henry. 104
WALDIN: Charles. 286
WALDON: Alexander. 297
WALDREP: A. J.. 457; E. N. 457;
Elihu N. (Elisha). 057; J.A.. 457;
James. 057; John D. 457; John S..
057; Kirby. 457; L.L.. 442;
Leecel. 078; Leecil J.. 066;
Leesol J.. 286; Lescel J.. 415;
M. M.. 023; Matilda B.. 018;
Mittie L.. 040; Mollie. 05?;
Nancy S.. 035; Nannie J.. 039;
Oscar. 457
WALDPIFF: John. 435
WALDROP: Aaron. 442; Abraham. 145.
212; David. 286; Delphia A.. 078;
Elihue. 410; Jacob. 387; John S..
083; John W. (Isaac). 286; John
W.. 057. 286; Johnson. 078;
Solomon. 078. 286; W. R. 352
WALDROUP: Leslie I.. 425
WALDPUP: Clifford. 378; E. N. 342;
Elihu V.. 138; G. W. 057. 457;
J.A.. 457; J.S.. 378. 457; J. T.
057. 457; K.J.. 378; Kirby. 286;
O. W.. 378; Oscar. 378
WALKER: A. S.. 457; Adaline. 006;
Albert Sidney. 057; Allen. 057;
Amanda. 019; Ann. 054; Annie. 042;
Asa. 286; Auther. 409; Bartley.
057. 154. 287. 358; Bastley. 177;
Benjamin. 274; Berry. 057. 287.
384. 409; Burney. 287; C. B.. 034;
Chaney. 046; Charity. 287; Charles.
287. 397; Charlie. 287; Cornelius.
287; Crawford. 409; Crofford. 467;
David. 199. 287; Delia. 044. 053;
WALKER: E. H.. 118; Eady. 287; Edee.
286; Edmund. 395; Ell H.. 130. 135.
163. 312; Elige. 057; Elijah C..
179. 287; Elijah. 057. 286. 467;
Emily. 037; Emily. 467; Emma. 409;
378; Ernest. 287; F. Elijah. 287;
F.. 329; Fec. 057; Felix. 157. 457;
Ferebee. 304; Fereby (Medlock).
238; Ferrebee (Medlock). 211;
Florence Mozelle. 003; Frank. 409;
Frea. 287; G. W.. 288; Genie. 028;
George W.. 226; George. 256. 365.
415; Green B.. 463; Green. 057. 435;
WALKER: Hack. 431; Hackey. 066. 078.
423. 427. 431. 435; Hattie O..
036; Henry B.. 177; Henry H.. 057;
Henry. 057. 066. 078. 126. 128.
138. 139. 141. 143. 145. 148. 154.
155. 161. 176. 191. 200. 204. 216.
225. 266. 287. 289. 240. 246. 302.
353. 305. 308. 378. 398. 435. 442.
458. 462; Isaac. 433. 435; J. B..
057; J.F. 457; J. W.. 378; Jack.
378. 409; James (heirs of). 435;
WALKER: James F..289. 457; James R..
448; James S.. 198; James. 057.
178. 210. 216. 287. 324; Jeff.
287; Jeremiah S.. 287; Jerry. 409;
Jesse. 409; Jim. 058. 287; Joe.
287; John H.. 296; John. 110. 117.
165. 245. 287. 324. 378. 409. 435.
467; Joseph. 058; Lewis. 058. 102.
287. 378. 465; Lizzie Kate. 056;
Lucy. 032. 049. 052; Mackey. 426;
Magers. 078; Margaret. 009;
Margarett. 029; Mary Jane. 055;
WALKER: Mary. 021. 378; Mattie. 008.
042. 061; Miranda. 037; Mollie.
029. 353; Moses. 078; N. S.. 337.

340, 346, 347; Nick, 378; Nix,
058; Rebecca, 378; Reese, 058;
287, 378, 400, 409; Rhoda, 029;
Rhody, 127; Richard S., 086;
Roland, 378; Rowland, 058; Ruth
Pearl, 008; Samuel, 143, 216, 287,
324, 366; Samuel, Jr., 287, 421;
WALKER: Sanders, 210, 216, 271, 287,
289, 324; Sarah, 048, 054; Scott,
287, 378; Sid, 378, 409; Silvanus,
435; Simeon, 287; Simon, 287;
Squire, 215, 229; Susan (Smith),
139; Susan, 378; Sylva, 287;
Sylvanus, 312; Tack, 048; Tandy,
469; Taswell, 058; Thomas L., 211;
Thomas T., 146, 152, 211, 231,
238, 287, 288, 304, 320; Thomas,
058, 130, 135, 213, 287; Tobe,
288; Tom, 058; Troup, 058; 378;
WALKER: Trudie, 020; Vince, 409; Viney,
051; W.H., 378, 457; Warren, 287,
409; Westley, 378; Wesly, 378;
Wilkes, 351; Wilks, 102; Will,
288; William F., 126; William W.,
078, 171, 424; William, 124, 137,
166, 175, 178, 179, 214, 288, 289,
297, 409, 424, 435; Willie, 058;
Wilson, 288; Winfield, 378
WALL: Charles F., 216; Evan, 288;
John, 171, 293; W. V., 409
WALLACE: Alexander, 116, 179;
Benjamin, 200, 288, 378, 418; John,
247; John, Jr., 297; Norman, 246;
Ruth, 409; Warren, 088, 093, 098,
288, 357, 358; William C., 288;
William W., 288; William, 143,
166, 256
WALLEN: Elias, 105, 126, 220;
Jarratt L., 058
WALLER: Arnold Winkelried, 058; C.C.,
288; Charles, 435; Christopher C.,
058; D.F., 435, 457; David L., 288;
David S., 288; David, 288; Handy,
103, 216; J. M., 457; J. S., 082;
457; James B., 288, 324; Jonathan
S., 058; Mason, 288; Nancy P., 060;
Nat, 288; Nathaniel G., 288;
Nathaniel, 288; R.D., 457; Robert
D., 058; Samuel, 435
WALLIS: Polly, 060; William C., 288
WALLS: Conrad, 313; John, 288
WALLTHRALL: Edward, 087
WALTERS: Warren, 378; William, 288
WALTHAL: Richard, 288
WALTHALL: Charles F., 288, 321, 435;
Edward (heirs of), 435; Edward,
078, 140, 288, 321; Mary, 240;
Milton P., 094, 113, 217, 448;
Turman, 321, 435; William P.,
240; William, 324
WALTON: Alfred Y., 224; Blewford
M., 249, 435; Bluford M., 078,
163, 250; C. W., 378; Columbus,
058; E. J., 378; E. J., 379;
Ed., 379; Edmond J., 288; Edmund
L., 436; Edmund J., 288; Edward
J., 288; Edward P., 288; Harris,
134; Henry B., 078, 288; Hiram,
078, 288, 295; Isaac L., 153, 224,
225, 270, 288, 395, 306, 436;
Isaac R., 317; I.J., 467; James
J., 431; James W.Y., 130, 157;
WALTON: John H., 268, 312; John W.
Y., 224; John, 128, 188, 205,
308, 312; Joseph W., 169, 253;
Joseph, 409; Martha A., 059;
Mason, Mrs., 046; Peter W., 288;
R. L., 409; Robert J., 078, 094;
Robert, 168; Salina H. J., 027;
Serena R., 288; Serina R., 288;
Thomas J., 307; Thomas, 125, 146,
268, 312; Washington L., 134
WALTZ: Elsworth, 058; Emma, 018;
James L., 058
WAMACK: Edmon, 424; Edmond, 288;
Edmund, 288; James, 457; John E.,
288; John, 275
WAMMACK: Alameda, 263; Almeda, 144;
Amanda J., 025; E. H., 379; James
T., 379; James, 058, 078, 379;
John W., 058; Linton, 058, 379;
Nancy, 272; T. K., 379; Thomas K.,
058; Williamson L. B., 058;
Sid, 058
WARBINGTON: Allemander, 289;
Elemander, 288; Ellemander, 157,
212; Ellemander, 422, 435;
Ellimander, 289; Jacob B., 289;
Jacob, 289, 305
WARD: Amos, 269, 281, 289, 433;
Benjamin F., 136, 179, 289, 324;
Benjamin, 379; Bradley, 034;
Charlie, 289; Davis, 058; Diana,
009; E., 340, 368; Ed, 058;
Edmond, 058; F.J., 289, 379, 457;
Fleming J., 193, 289, 379, 415,
457; Fleming, 152, 289, 379; Francis
M., 058; Francis, 193, 289;
Franklin, 289; Frederick, 173;
George, 058, 409; Georgia Ann, 027;
WARD: James D. S., 078, 289; James

D., 467; John E., 078, 289; John,
092, 425; Lucretia, 023; Mador,
012; Martha, 193; Mayroe, 005;
Moses, 226; Nathan B., 289; Nathan,
219; R.C., 193; S.B., 193; Sarah
H., 225; Seth, 171; Thomas, 058,
289, 429, 435, 436; Tommie, 058;
Willie, 058
WARDLOW: M.C., 379; Margaret, 153, 289
WARDWELL: G. W., 366
WARE: Allen, 289; Bennet M., 104,
187; Bennett M., 196, 201, 258;
Bennett W., 141; Clifford, 289;
George, 379; Henry (heirs of),
430; Henry, 066, 078, 289, 433;
James, 289, 301, 435; John, 289;
Joseph A., 301; Joseph H., 078;
Nicholas, 315; Oscar, 058; Robert,
203, 410; Susan L.C., 261; William
C., 181, 248, 464; William, 260;
Willis, 058
WARES: John, 289
WARLICK: J., 447
WARNEP: Amos, 298; Edward, 285;
Effingham H., 249; Jason, 126;
N., 289; Nathan (heirs of), 435;
Nathan, 116, 128, 136, 179, 192,
289, 324, 425, 436; Thomas, 289
WARREN: Abraham, 106; Adaline F.,
033; Benjamin H., 198; Bray, 078,
289, 423, 435, 448; Dread, 220,
423, 435, 436; E.B., 333; Edmond,
078; Edward, 078; Eliza Ann, 284;
Etheldread, 436; James, 289; John
H., 058; John, 058, 106, 162, 179,
237, 279; Mattie, 058; P.H.,
406; P. W., 354, 406; R.J., 372;
Robert J., 058, 348; Thomas, 448;
W.C., 457; William, 058, 247
WARPILL: Sanford C., 223
WASHBURN: Joseph, 134, 290
WASHINGTON: Adaline, 049; Frank,
058, 410; Fred, 410; George, 058,
289; Georgia Ann, 015; Lucy, 051;
Richard, 289
WASLEY: Isaac, 378
WASSON: Robert, 102
WATER: William B., 082
WATERS: Bill, 289; David, 445;
Ernest, 058, 246, 379; Fred, 379;
Hudson, 058; J.T., 457; John C.,
324; John C., Sr., 324; John G.,
097; Lane, 289, 379; Lizzie, 046,
058, 457; Nancy, 280; Richard,
058; Robert P., 078; Rosa, 039;
Susie, 040; T.J., 457; Tom, 403;
Warren, 058; William, 058, 289
WATES: Benjamin, 259
WATKINS: Alexander, 078; Anderson,
220; B. F., 458; Charity, 289;
David, 423; Joseph, 239; Kinman,
058; Mary, 355; Moses, 229
WATLEY: Alice E., 009; Richard, 307;
Willis, 278
WATNER: J. U., 409
WATSON: Aron, 410; Charles, 379,
410; Charley, 058; Charlie, 289;
Douglas, 297; Ed, 410; Emma Kate,
008; Enie, 410; Farrar, 058;
Farrer, 379; Genie, 013; Gideon,
289; Harriet, 044; Henry, 058;
J.F., 273; James H., 289; James,
079, 157, 289; John, 100, 136, 181;
Kate, 289; Lewis, 410; Martin, 058;
Nannie, 289; Pharrer, 343; Pip,
379; Robert (Bob), 289; P. Thomas,
100; W., 391; William C., 139;
William D., 110, 133; Willie, 379
WATT: William, 325
WATTEN: John, 238
WATTERS: A. J., 284, 410, 448, 457;
Aaron, 379; Amanda, 006; Andrew J.,
086, 289-291, 324, 379; Andrew,
289; Delia, 023; Dick, 379, 410;
Georgia E. E., 036; J. C., 284;
Jane, 079; John C., 066, 079, 086,
094, 140, 169, 195, 223, 232, 233,
242, 290, 291, 307, 324; John C.,
Jr., 291; John C., Sr., 291; John
E., 139; John, 290, 458; Joseph,
203, 222, 268, 302; Lane, 379;
WATTERS: Lizzie, 044, 056; Martha,
042; Mary C., 079; Mattie, 042;
Richard, 410; Robert P., 066, 090,
290, 291; Sarah J., 095, 290, 291,
324; W. D., 324; Warren, 291, 379;
William D., 324; William, 324, 410;
William, 058, 291; Wyatt, 059
WATTS: No. 291; Benjamin, 430;
Gassard S., 205; John, 289; L.B.,
180; Littleberry, 168, 317; Ludwell
291; Pleasant, 168, 180, 237, 317;
Seaborn B., 139; Thomas, 230, 233;
Wade, 059
WAXELBAUM: S., 345; Solomon, 374
WAYNE: William, 209, 409
WEATHERLY: Leven, 467
WEATHERS: Jenkins D., 109, 111, 228;
Jesse, Sr., 436; Lund, 465; Mary
G., 059; S. R., 059
WEATHERSBEE: Charlotte M. (Toland),
291; Charlotte, 291; James H., 109,

191; James, 467; John F., 059; John
F. Jr., 291, 434; John G., Jr.,
291; Owen, 079, 167; Sarah, 167
WEATHERSBY: ?, 192; James, 379;
John F., Jr., 324; James, 274;
Owen, 291
WEAVER: Bery, 410; Cordy, 436; George
A., 120; George, 059, 291; Howard,
410; Isham, 296; James J., 247;
John S., 097, 230, 291, 305, 379;
Mary Thomas, 010; P. J., 457;
Robert, 457; W. M., 059; Wesley,
059; Will, 379
WEBB: Agnes K., 044; Ammy K., 467;
Annie J., 079; Augustus J., 436;
Austin, Jr., 059; Catherine, 436;
Charles H., 300; Charles, 141,
244; Clinton, 436; Columbus H.,
335; Deeprew S., 291; Eliza, 079;
F. G., 277; Frank G., 059; G. G.,
379, 457; George G., 379; George
W., 059; George, 379; Isaac H.,
119; J. B., 341, 357, 379, 387;
447, 457; J. F., 194, 392, 436,
457; James F., 059, 436; James,
079, 312; Jefferson, 356; John B.,
091, 197, 291, 334, 345, 351, 355,
357, 361, 362, 366, 375-378, 390,
398, 428, 457; John G., 107, 199;
WEBB: John P., 348; John, 152, 198,
291, 350, 391; Lane, 059; Maggie
H., 025; Minnie L., 015; Nancy,
024; P. A., 079, 291, 379, 457;
467, 468; Samuel J., 457; Thomas
P., 079, 291, 292, 324, 379, 415,
426; Thomas, 204, 256, 457, 458;
William W., 059; Wyatt P., 292
WEBSTER: Edward, 205; Edwin B.,
144; George W., 247; George, 139,
188, 189, 215, 233, 257, 272, 280,
288; H. G., 272, 464; Hosea, 093,
131, 134, 137-139, 144, 172, 176,
188, 189, 201, 215, 227, 233,
257, 272, 280, 288, 289; J.R., 332
WEDDINGTON: Charity, 207; Robert,
207; Zeno, 207
WEED: Daniel A., 292; Joseph B.,
224, 264; Luraney (Green), 292;
Lurany (Weed), 292
WEEK: Joseph B., 195
WEEKES: James L., 108, 158, 159,
165; James S., 092, 104, 172,
204, 241, 278, 292, 420, 424, 428,
436; James, 233, 292; Joseph C.,
250, 292; Palemon L., 100, 163,
182, 228, 292; Palemon S., 100,
292; Palemon, 101, 129, 244, 246,
288, 292; Palomon S., 106;
William, 219, 292
WEEKS: James S., 110, 431; James,
059; Palemon L., 088, 093, 100,
249, 283
WEEMS: Annie E., 149; Freeman, 457;
George, 410, 430, 436; John S.,
426; John, 292; M. E., 218; Samuel
C., 112; Samuel, 233, 292, 435, 436
WEICHSELBAUM: E., 330; Ed, 292; 346;
S., 330
WEIGHTS: John, 079; William, 067
WEIL: D., 376
WELBORN: Amos, 257, 435, 436; John
P., 260; Jonathan, 436; Samuel J.,
253, 292; William J., 253
WELBURN: Samuel J., 292
WELCH: Gus, 292; Jack, 292, 410;
James R., 292; James, 436; John,
292; Wallace, 410; William, 292
WELD: J. D., 335
WELDEN: John W., 292; Joseph, 139
WELDING: Isaac, 436
WELDON: A. W., 059; Abraham, 379;
Abram, 059; Andrew, 079, 243,
292; Asa, 292; Catharine, 292;
Isaac, 079; James, 059;
Jane, 293; John W., 293; John,
058; Mary, 079, 293; Moses, 410
WELLBORN: Johnson, 288, 291;
Sanford, 128; Thomas, 300;
William T., 079
WELLINGHAM: Hardiman, 429
WELLINGTON: C.E., 457; Charles E., 059
WELLS: Isaac, 240; James, 172; John
D., 293; John, 324; Matthew, 153;
William H., 293; 324;
William, 293, 468
WELTCH: James B., 293
WEMPLE: James, 134
WESBY: Jim, 059
WESSON: James M., 251
WESSONS: Andrew, 121; David, 121
WEST: Andrew, 066; J. A. A., 293;
J. A. J., 079; Jeremiah D., 324;
Jeremiah, 059, 324, 436; John,
138, 293; John, Sr., 222, 436; L.
W., 293; Lucius, 059, 379; Lush,
379; M. P., 373; Warren, 460
WESTER: Edward, 209; Robert P., 293
WESTMOPELAND: James H., 198; John,
293; Joseph, 174, 396, 423
WETHERSBEE: Charlott M., 079
WETHERSBY: Charlotte, 258;
Victoria, 020

WEYMAN: Taylor, 059
WHALEY: Charles, 293, 468
WHANN: Walton, 239
WHATLEY: Allen J., 021; Green, 225;
Hiram, 189; John B., 293, 436;
John H., 293, 468; Michael, 293,
410; Michael, Jr., 088; Mollie F.,
039; Phineas, 116; Ransom, 124,
255; Rebecca, 215; Richard, 154;
Seaborn J. I., 112; William B.,
293; William, 090; Willis, 079,
293, 302, 324; Wilson, 289
WHATLY: Priscilla, 275; Willis, 293
WHEALAS: Joab, 293; Hardy, 184
WHEATLEY: Jesse, 293; Lucy, 293
WHEDBEE: Joseph, 253, 293
WHEELER: Amos, 405; Emma, 004; M.
J., 394; Richard D., 271, 273;
Richard, 256; William, 293
WHEELES: Isam, 293; Littleberry,
293; William R., 158
WHEELESS: Drury, 293
WHEELUS: Isem, 324; Isom, 293, 324;
William R., 293
WHIPPLE: James O., 110; William, 110
WHITAKER: John B., 059, 196, 293,
294; John P., 079; Martha Fannie,
024; Rachel(Douglas), 294; Thomas,
258, 260; West, 109, 436
WHITE: A. B., 457; A. F., 059, 156;
A. J., 410, 457; Aaron, 059, 410;
Ada C., 224; Adda C., 334; Albert,
059, 294; Alford, 059; Andrew, 059;
Ann H., 066, 079; Anna, 047; Anne,
294; Annie S., 032; Archa B., 059;
Austin A., 165, 379; Benjamin,
142; Cato, 059; Charlie, 059;
Cindy, 331; Clarence, 445;
Clifford, 294; Cyrus, 206, 268,
294, 300, 324; David L., 255, 265;
WHITE: David S., 255; David, 294,
434, 436; Dennis, 059; E.G., 311;
E. T., 091, 291, 294, 429; Eben
T., 089; Ebenezer J., 273; Ebenezer
T., 112, 161, 170, 172(1), 199,
247, 294, 307, 421; Edward S.,
273; Edward, 161, 294; Elizabeth
A., Mrs., 036; Elizabeth B., 251;
Emma, 011, 051; Frances, 044;
Francis M., 215; G.W., 457; George
B., 279; George, 059, 294; H.N.
Mrs., 193, 360; H.N., 222, 294,
370, 463; Hattie N., 031; Henry
B., 294; Henry, 294; Hugh, 095,
324; Ida, 022; J.A., 059; J.B.,
457; J.E., 379; J.F., 457;
WHITE: J.M., 457; J.P., 457; Jackson,
410; Jacob, 294; James F., 059,
457; Jimmie, 059; Joanna, 005;
Joe, 379; John J., 059; John
Walton, 059; John, 066, 079,
204, 294; John, 423, 433, 436;
Joseph C., 116, 224; Joseph B.,
294; Joseph, 079, 106, 209, 215,
222, 294, 421, 429; Joshua, 294;
Jugar Ann, 021; L., 103, 213,
333, 345, 349, 359, 361, 371;
WHITE: Laura E., 024; Levora E.,
053; Linda, 052; Lizzie Kate,
031; Lizzie, 050; Lucien, 457;
Lucinthia C., 057; Lucius, 079,
086, 090, 101, 112, 205, 207,
208, 213, 235, 240, 247, 269,
292, 294, 308, 333, 345; Lucy,
048; Martha, 003; Martin, 294;
Mich, 294; Miranda, 042;
Monroe, 059; Moses D., 294; N.B.,
150, 151, 180, 182, 193, 213,
214, 222, 227, 294, 328, 330,
332-334, 339-341, 344-346, 348,
349, 352, 354, 355, 358-362, 365,
367-375, 379, 381, 382, 387, 388,
393, 403, 447, 457, 462; Nancy E.,
033; Nehemiah B., 079, 086, 090,
101, 112, 205, 208, 213, 235, 240,
247, 269, 308, 333, 345, 346, 377,
378, 457; Nehemiah, 292; Nicey, 052;
WHITE: P. C., 410; Rebeccah, 022;
Robert, 469; Roney D., 013; S.,
180; Sallie, 021, 045, 410; Samuel,
079; Sarah, 003, 021; Scott, 380,
415; Susan, 044; T.A., 380; Thomas
B., 121, 242, 251, 424; Thomas,
079, 106, 209, 222, 246; V. B.,
103; Valentine, 294, 436; W. A.,
457; W. B., 333; W. P., 442, 457,
465; William A., 059; William H.,
119, 251, 285, 294, 295, 324;
William M., 277; William P., 144,
166, 355, 409, 443; William, 059,
260, 428; Zachariah, 116, 172,
185, 189, 260, 295, 311, 317, 324,
422; Zifford, 295
WHITEFIELD: B., 209
WHITEHEAD: Addie E., 357; Charles,
409; Eugene S., 357; F.M., 357;
F. N., 008; Jack, 059, 336; Leonard
J., 295; Leonard T., 295; Leonard,
295; Lucinda, 295; Lucy, 274, 410;
Mandy, 409; Peter, 409; Richard,
158; Robert, 059; Samuel, 059;

Thomas, 295; Tom, 410; William
A., 059, 357; William, 274, 275;
Willie, 410
WHITEN: Aida, 021; Anna, 008;
Mary Lizzie, 019
WHITFIELD: Alfred, 380; Amy, 445;
Angviline, 055; Anna, 008; B. W.,
235; B., 114, 202, 380; Bettie,
059; Bolling, 112, 177, 183, 243,
295, 332, 337, 347, 349-351, 353,
356, 358, 360, 368-370, 373, 375,
377, 380, 381, 385; Charles, 380;
Clifton, 152, 295; Clovis, 059;
Delia, 028; Diamond, 295; Emma,
051; Eugene, 380; Gaston, 295, 339,
380; George, 059; Georgia H., 248,
458; Georgia, 295, 380; Henry,
059, 295, 410; Holling, 436; India
C., 295, 380; India, 380; Indiana
C., 436; Indiana, 380; Indie C.,
380; Indie, 380; Ione, 015; J.B.,
380, 468; Jacob, 059, 295, 340,
375, 415; Jake, 059, 380;
WHITFIELD: James W., 285; James, 087,
088, 097, 100, 102, 103, 107, 108,
117, 120, 122, 124, 127, 133, 135,
141, 149-151, 163, 164, 169, 174,
175, 177-179, 187, 189, 190, 199,
201, 202, 219, 221, 222, 225, 229,
233, 236, 240, 244, 245, 248-250,
252, 254, 257, 271, 273, 274,
279-281, 284, 287, 289, 292, 295,
300, 307, 316, 317, 380, 389, 436,
468; Jane, 045, 060; Jim, 367;
WHITFIELD: Joe, 410; John B., 079,
295, 380, 436, 468; John P., 295;
Jordan, 059; Julia, 037, 041;
Lara, 054; Lena E., 061; Lewis,
059, 277, 295, 380; Linie, 005;
Louis, 059; Lucinda, 044; M.C.,
295; M., 236, 295, 296; Martha,
335; Mat, 139, 262; Mathew C.,
295; Mathew, 152, 153, 155, 172, 178,
185, 191, 194, 200, 237, 244, 262,
272, 273, 276, 295, 311, 315, 317,
361; Matilda J. (Henderson), 171;
WHITFIELD: Matthew C., 079, 235, 436;
Matthew, 059, 066, 079, 088, 096,
097, 099, 100, 103, 104, 114, 117,
118, 120, 133, 140, 144, 150, 151,
159, 164, 166, 170, 178, 192, 193,
198, 200, 203, 207, 214, 219, 229,
240, 241, 246, 247, 252, 253, 256,
258, 260-262, 268, 269, 272, 274,
277, 281, 285, 291, 295, 306, 313,
339, 429, 432, 468; Nancy, 020,
380; Rachel, 027; Reuben, 352,
380, 410; Robert, 243, 286, 338,
340, 352, 356, 358, 362, 367, 375,
380, 410, 467; Sam, 380; Samuel,
059, 362, 380; Susan, 061; W.H.,
222; West, 296; William H., 276;
295, 296, 317, 324; William,
109, 169, 171, 437;
WHITEHEAD: Leonard P., 274
WHITING: Fannie, 051; Kizzie, 019;
Moses, 296; Shade, 059
WHITLEY: William, 195
WHITLOCK: John M., 274; W., 384
WHITNEY: Giles, 127, 154; Joseph,
182, 275; S. M., 406, 407, 408
WHITSLEY: Daniel, 274
WHITTEN: George F., 059; H.W., 349,
457, 468; Henry W., 060; Henry,
457; James A., 060; Levi, 380, 415,
457; M. F., 013; Scott, 060;
W. C., 410, 457
WHITTLE: Joseph L., 060
WHITTON: George, 410
WHOPTON: William, 269
WHYTE: Oliver, 191
WIATT: Samuel, 296
WICKER: Benjamin, 436
WIDEMAN: Henry, 060
WIGGINS: Daniel, 436; James, 123;
Lemuel G. P., 296; Martha, 436;
Wade, 079
WIGINS: Peter, 192
WILBERN: T. R., Jr., 296
WILBORN: Amos, 296; S.J., 295; Sam,
305; Thomas, 182
WILBOURN: James P., 296
WILBURN: Clark, 380; Elizabeth,
296; H. H., 296; Herman H., 079;
Jack, 296; John, 060; L.C., 457;
Leonidas C., 060, 079, 296; M. A.,
Mrs., 398; Martha, 369, 380;
381; Martha, 380; Polk, 380; S.
C., 380, 398, 410, 457; S.J., 296,
380; Sam J., 380; Sam, 296; Sam
Jr., 457; Samuel C., 296, 369,
380; Samuel J., 203, 324, 380, 448,
457; Samuel V., 468; Samuel, 296,
380, 381; Thomas, 403; W. Eugene,
296; W. H., 380, 381, 467; William
H., 296, 380, 381, 393, 398;
Wm. S., 469
WILBURNE: Thomas, 296
WILCOX: D. A., 267; D. H., 345;
Daniel H., 267, 292, 305, 335,

372; Thomas S., 410; William, 204
WILD: J. D., 346
WILDER: Dred, 079; Irvey, 423;
Isaac, 079; John R., 290; John,
296; Joseph, 296; Larken, 296;
Larkin, 060, 296; Solon F., 403;
W. M., 302
WILDING: James, 296
WILDMAN: Nathaniel H., 281, 292
WILEY: A.C., 380; B. F., 380; James
H., 153; Laird H., 107, 121; Leroy
M., 100, 155, 158, 159, 196, 219,
243, 244
WILIE: Adam, 116
WILKERSON: Abel, 433; Alexander, 279;
Caleb, 430; Edmond, 099; Eldred,
196, 448; Harmon, 079; J., 189;
Jeptha, 189, 213, 296; John, 279;
Lemuel, 296; Matilda, 213; Samuel,
398; Simeon, 296, 420, 436
WILKES: Georgia A., 348; Osborn,
169; Osborne, 296; Reuben, 296,
448; Steve, 410
WILKEY: James (heirs of), 436
WILKINS: Aladin, 296; Allen, 436;
Ann C., 469; Cynthia (Youngblood),
296; Drury, 060, 079, 206, 296,
297, 315, 324, 422, 435, 469; F.
P., 297; James C., 066; Warren,
391; William M., 213; William, 079,
124, 235, 246, 299, 425
WILKINSON: Alexander, 122, 436;
Archibald, 297; J.P., 364; John,
297; John, Sr., 297; Maurice, 250,
286, 314; Mauris, 162; Simeon, 410
WILKS: Emmie Lee, 039; Georgia A.,
436; John, Sr., 436; Lizzie, 014;
Osborne, 247
WILL: Saran, 024
WILLARD: Roswell, 079, 297
WILLBORN: Thomas, 134
WILLBURN: Samuel J., 203
WILLDEN: Andrew, 422
WILLIAM: James M., 284
WILLIAMS(WILSON): Almey, 029
WILLIAMS: (?), 445; A. M., 156;
Aaron, 297, 317, 436; Ada, 410;
Adaline, 009, 039; Addie E., 410,
415; Alfred, 079; Alice, 036, 061;
Alonzo, 060; Amanda, 410; Ammi(?),
116, 120; Anderson, 060; Aron, 240;
Arthur, 297; Asberry, 297; Asbury,
410; Augustus L., 079; Avington
P., 149; Avington, 117, 118, 129,
160, 220, 297, 424; Berry, 381,
415; Beverly, 060; Bud, 410; Cage,
060; Charles D., 154, 197, 273,
284, 315; Charles, 060, 150, 171,
297, 421, 436; Charlie, 297, 410;
WILLIAMS: Clinton, 297; Cora, 014;
Crisie, 030; D. M., 060, 457;
Daniel, 297, 436, 448; David M.,
297; David, 060; Delie, 051;
Dick, 060; Dilia, 445; Doratha,
059; Dorsey, 410; Durham, 060;
Edmund S., 981; Edward, 215;
Elizabeth, 297, 298; Ellen, 038;
Elmira, 028; Elvira, 034; Emma,
040, 045; Esquire, 060; Evan, 060;
025; Francis H., 297; Francis M.,
079; G. P., 297, 457; George D.,
457; George W., 241; George, 276,
457; Georgia Ann, 036; Grady, 381;
Hampton, 060; Handy, 381; Harriet,
036; Hattie, 030, 054; Henry J.,
437; Henry, 060, 297, 348; Hugh,
150; Ida, 029; Isaac, 288, 297;
J. B., 457; J. M., 457; J. P.,
457; J. S., 381, 457; J. T., 464;
WILLIAMS: J. W., 335, 379, 457; J.
Westly, 381; Jack, 060; Jacob, 297;
James E., 060; James H., 296;
James M., 066, 079, 096, 137, 152,
156, 166, 190, 197, 208, 214, 246,
253, 297, 365, 286, 296, 298, 310,
322, 410, 442, 443, 457, 458, 462;
James, 381; Jane, 060; Jeems, 381;
Jefferson D., 060; Jennett, 028;
Jesse, 297; Jim, 381, 410; Joanna,
445; Jock, 060; John Dempsy, 297;
WILLIAMS: John P., 060; John S.,
060; John, 060, 133, 196, 297,
381, 415, 436, 457; Joseph J.,
435; Joseph P., 297, 366, 408,
442; Joseph, 131, 196, 297, 324,
331, 410, 420, 436; L. H., 381;
Lena, 014; Lilly, 034; Lou T.,
017; Lou, 056; Luke, 128, 136,
175, 256, 297, 298, 436; Lydia,
010; M. N., 371; Mancy, 060; Mark,
298; Mary Jane, 044; Mary Lou,
022; Mary, 017, 273; Matthew, 210,
304; Melford, 297; Milton, 457;
WILLIAMS: Missie, 298; Mollie, 040;
Monroe, 410; Moses, 271, 298;
N. B., 296; N. W., 079, 101, 137,
298, 337, 371, 381, 410, 467;
Nannie, 032; Nathan H., 134;
Nathan, 128, 139, 140, 252, 271,
297-299, 324, 427, 432, 436; Ned,
298; Nicholas B., 166; Obadiah,

271. 371: Oblire. 060: P.M.. 457:
Peter. 436: Pilgrim. 291: Pleasant
M.. 060. 457: Polley. 042. 210:
Pony. 381: Prince. 298. 381. 410:
WILLIAMS: Rachael. 013: Rebecca.
027: Reese. 060. 381: Rhoda Ann.
050: Richard. 060. 183: Robert.
029. 298. 410: Roe. 060: Rose.
020: Rowland. 298: S. C.. 442:
Sam. 381: Samuel. 060. 210. 298:
Sarah. 059: Senetta. 009: Silva
Ann. 041: Smalley. 410: Solomon.
060: Squire. 381. 410: Steven.
415: Susan. 059: T.B.. 223. 410:
T. R.. 298. 436. 457. 468: Thomas
B.. 240. 458: Thomas K.. 457
WILLIAMS: Thomas M.. 401: Thomas R..
079. 298. 374. 381. 457. 458:
Thomas P.. Sr.. 060. 218. 274.
275. 298. 324. 404. 410. 464:
Thomas. Sr.. 182: Tommie. 410:
Vesta. 043: W.L.. 457: W.S. 060.
298. 410. 457: W. T.. 442: Wesley.
060. 298: William D.. 105. 189:
William L.. Sr.. 079: William S..
060. 298. 410: William T.. 130.
298: William. 060. 106. 130. 163.
251. 254. 257. 259. 298. 303. 324:
Willie. 060. 457: Zachariah. 079.
299. 314
WILLIAMSON: A. M.. 249: Benjamin.
197. 207. 436: Charles. 154: Green
B.. 196: Green. 111. 114. 300:
Isaac B.. 280. 285: Isaac. 079.
299. 324: James H.. 299: James.
115. 250. 299: John N.. 191: John.
247: Mary. 100. 168. 171. 183.
299: Micajah. 162. 299: Reese.
160. 299: Reuben. 299. 429. 436:
Richard. 299: Robert. 100. 114.
115. 131. 141. 142. 150. 209. 221.
263. 299. 302. 314. 316. 318. 322.
323: Sallie. 022: Thomas J.. 060:
William T.. 299: William W.. 275.
299. 300: William. 111. 114. 313.
299. 300: Willis. 100. 299:
Zarobabel. 114: Zorobabel. 111.
300: Zorobable. 428
WILLIFORD: Adaline. 031: David. 300
WILLINGHAM: Archer. 112: Archibald.
300: B.L.. 345: George W.. 283:
Isaac. 190. 217. 300. 458: Jeremiah.
300: Joe. 300: Mollie. 039: Nancy
J.. 039: Sallie. 055: T.. 401:
Taylor. 457: Theophilus. 060:
Theophilus. 381. 442. 457: Thomas.
231: W. N.. 060. 381: William.
079. 110. 300. 321. 458
WILLINGTON: C. E.. 381
WILLIS: Arthur. 079. 100: Daniel
B.. 426: Daniel H.. 174. 250. 436:
Hosea. 184L J. M.. 467: Jack. 110:
Jency. 445: Jimey (June). 100:
John C.. 257. 300. 387: John G..
126: Jonathan. 060. 445: Jonathon.
079: Louden. 285: D. B.. 457:
Robert L.. 197. 300. 301. 325:
Robert. 300
WILLIAM?(WILLIAMS): Richard J.. 324
WILLS: Matthews. 125: William H..220
WILLSON: Abel P.. 136. 147. 300:
Alford G.. 300: Annie M.. 043:
Archillis. 300: B.H.. 436: Benjamin
H.. 111. 114. 300: Benjamin. 300:
C.T.. 388: Charles T.. 306: Colonel
John. 300: Elijah. 181: Fields.
182. 300: Frank. 300: George. 079.
300: Hiram. 300: James E.. 079.
300: James. 134. 137. 187. 196.
265. 276. 294. 300. 301. 436: John
(heirs of). 425. 436: John. 079.
103. 112. 113. 116. 126. 134. 137.
141. 149. 153. 156. 164. 176. 187.
196. 200. 204. 216. 241. 244. 248.
266. 276. 278. 297. 299- 301. 304.
314. 316. 325. 421-430. 432. 433.
435. 436. 458: John. 462. 466:
WILLSON: Joseph. 301: Lawrence L..
301: Lerov M..102. 103. 144. 166.
170. 193. 200. 203. 207. 240. 241.
258. 268. 269. 301. 306. 351. 436:
Lerov W.. 114: Lerov. 153: Lowery.
410: Pleasant. 102. 103. 114. 144.
153. 166. 170. 193. 200. 203. 207.
240. 241. 258. 268. 269. 306. 351:
Sally. 301: Sarah. 443: Talitha.
016: William L.. 301
WILLY: Thomas. 216. 235
WILLYFORD: Hartwell. 279
WILSON: A.B.. 056: A.J.. 079. 467:
Abe. 301: Abel P.. 135. 141. 147.
148. 195. 301. 302. 386. 391. 392.
410. 436: Abraham V.. 060: Adel
L.. 047: Adel S.. 079: Alfred G..
149: Allen. 060: Alvah. 191:
Andrew J.. 301. 302. 410: Annie.
411: Arkiles. 120: Arkillis. 066.
079. 302: Augustus. 060: Barthena.
196: Ben. 381: Benjamin H.. 172:
Benjamin J.. 207. 301. 302:
WILSON: Bethenia. 302: Bill. 186:
C.M.. 400: C.T.. 457: Caroline.

003: Charles John. 302: Charles
M.. 060: Charles. 060. 302. 335.
348. 381. 443: Daniel. 111. 123:
Dave. 060. 302: David. 061:
Dawson. 061: E. A.. 041: Eaton
P.. 302: Elick. 061: Elijah. 061.
079. 325: Eliza. 041: Ella. 017:
Fields. 206. 222. 268. 270. 302.
422. 428. 430. 436: Flem. 443:
Fred. 411: Fulton. 061: G.S.. 411:
WILSON: George I.. 325: George J..
079. 302. 347: George. 061. 381:
415: Graves E.. 186: Graves S..
120. 302: Graves. 142. 302: Gus.
457: Harriet. 060: Henry. 381:
Hiram. 381: Hugh. 302: Irvin W..
061: J.B.. 457: J.W.. 352. 381:
J.. 468: James D.. 325: James E..
217. 313. 411: James H.. 061. 381:
James W.. 302. 357. 381. 411:
James. 061. 142. 252. 276. 302.
415. 457: James. Jr.. 381: Jane.
WILSON: 014. 061: Jenkins. 079. 149.
241: Jim. 186. 302. 381: Jimmie.
400: John (heirs of). 424: John
H. L.. 061: John L.. 302: John
P.. 302: John S.. 436. 437. 448:
John W.. 448: John. 061. 110. 125.
164. 236. 302. 316. 361. 423.
436. 465-467: Joseph A.. 079. 205.
291: Joseph. 066. 129. 238. 302.
325. 411. 460: Joshua. 437:
Larkin. 302: Lawrence L.. 302:
WILSON: Leola. 003: Leonard. 119.
182. 302. 437: Lerov M.. 150. 159.
237. 262. 295. 448: Lerov. 097.
194: Lessie. 468: Lillie. 036:
Lizzie. 055: Lucious. 061: Lula.
019: Lum. 061: M.S.. 457: Martha.
031. 061. 302. 443: Mary E.. 045.
302. 415: Mary Jane. 059: Mary.
334. 358. 437: Mattie. 038: Micha.
460: Milly. 381: Mintie. 040:
Monroe. 378. 468: Munroe. 381:
WILSON: Nancy S.. 325: Nancy. 025.
208. 226. 302. 381: Nelson. 302:
Pat. 302: Pleasant. 097. 150. 159.
194. 237. 262: R. W.. 381. 411:
Rachael. 066. 079. 205: Rachel
(Lowry). 302: Randol P.. 302:
Robert. 061. 302: Rufus. 061: S.
J.. 411: Samuel. 443. 461. 469:
Sarah. 079. 301. 302. 325: Sopha.
021: Sophia. 059: T. S.. 437:
Texas. 381: Thomas B.. 079: Thomas.
132. 302. 434. 468: V.A.. 377. 381.
411. 457. 468: V. H.. 380: Vines
A.. 381. 403: Vines. 457: Wiley.
164: William L.. 123. 302: William
S.. 079. 411: William. 165. 243.
302. 325: Willie. 302
WIMBERLY: Elijah. 061
WIMBISH: Sam. 061
WIMBUSH: Elbert. 411: Lizzie. 005:
Mary Jane. 079: Samuel. 061. 411:
411: Sarah. 061: 302
WINANS: ?. 062: C. A.. 381: John.
321: W. C.. 468
WINBURN: George W.. 297: J.J.. 444:
Martha A.. 380
WINBUSH: Mollie. 005
WINCHESTER: Jonathan. 437
WINDBUSH: Julia. 302
WINDHAM: Elias. 191
WINFREY: John. 238. 302. 411:
Margaret. 003
WINGFIELD: Alfred M.. 275: Alfred
W.. 306: J.. 397: John. 133. 140.
275. 293. 306. 312. 320. 402:
Marcellus A.. 312. 320: S.. 117:
W. B.. 444: Ella. 050
WINN: Francis. 255. 303:
Hartwell. 061
WINNE: Francis. 303
WINSHIP: Joseph. 236. 246
WINSLETT: John C.. 303
WINSTED: Samuel. 303
WINSTELL: John C.. 303
WISBORN: Eliga. 061
WISDOM: Elenor. 303: Francis. 109.
300. 303: Hamilton. 303
WISE: Augustus. 303: Barnabas. 290.
303: Barney. 079: Betsey. 303:
Creed T.. 095. 264. 399: Cyntha.
108: Dave. 061: David. 411:
Elizabeth. 164. 303: Emily. 108:
Fannie. 048: George. 411: Green.
351: Henry. 061. 381: Hugh. 111.
125. 153. 290. 303: Isaiah. 079:
J. M.. 348: James C.. 079. 108:
James. 061: Joel. 303. 397: John.
303: Joseph A.. 061. 303. 442:
M.F.. 039: Mary E.. 039: Matilda.
033: Patton. 061. 079. 164. 238.
303: Riley. 437: William. 108. 303
WISEMAN: William. 303
WISENERS: Thomas. 079
WITT: Anna Olivia. 031: David. 204.
302: Savannah. 028
WODDEY: Lucy. 019
WOLEF: S. B.. 376
WOLF: George W.. 375: Jacob. 088. 371

WOLFE: J.. 328: Jacob. 333. 334.
353. 363.Jacob. 381. 382. 396.
404: William. 079
WOLLSEY: Abraham M.. 132
WOMACK: Edmond. 437: Eva. 381:
Georgia. 015: James T.. 381: James.
303: John H.. 061: Josephine. 013:
Seaborn. 061. 457: Sid. 171. 457:
Sidney. 061: T. T.. 381
WOMMACK: Edmond. 437: Edward. 303:
Elberry. 448: J. T.. 468: James.
464: John W.. 415: S. W.. 395:
Thomas K.. 376: William. 381. 464
WOOD: A.. 391: Amasa. 256. 303:
Aristarchus. 437: Asa. 088. 100:
Carrie. 034: Cary. 174. 210. 300.
306: Charles. 302: E.. 391:
Earnest. 183: Ezelie. 100:
Georgianna. 303: J. L. G.. 457:
Jack. 411: James B.. 061: James
E.. 220. 303. 322. 324: James M..
303: Jim. 061: John. 079. 104.
176. 283. 303. 388. 458: Joshua
J.. 303. 411: Lucinda. 303:
Stephen. 231: Tabitha. 218: Thomas.
203. 303: William. 303: Woody. 303
WOODALL: John. 154L Robert. 224. 279
WOODARD: Owen. 297
WOODFIN: Moses. 304
WOODLEY: Andrew. 433: Caleb. 156.
192. 221. 302. 393. 437: Josie.
033: William. 061
WOODLY: Andrew. 215: Caleb. 099
WOODREW: James. 126
WOODROOF: William. 469
WOODROW: James. 184
WOODRUFF: Agatha. 304: Clifford. 427:
Clifford. 061. 304: Clifford. Jr..
304: David. 221. 252. 304. 322:
Davis. 283: James. 238. 252. 304.
325. 444: Joseph. 304: Philo D..
283: Philo. 088: W. W.. 346:
Worsham W.. 290
WOODS: J. L. G.. 061: John L.. 411:
Otis. 411: Robert. 425: William.
110. 130. 140. 230. 231
WOODWARD: Isham. C.. 304: John. L. 321
WOODY: James. 061
WOOLLEY: Zadock. 299
WOOLSEY: Abraham M.. 154. 273. 304:
Abraham. 197: Abram M.. 241: John
C.. 241: John M.. 132. 154. 273.
304: William C.. 132. 154. 304:
William M.. 154. 241. 304. 314
WOOLSEY?(WOLLSEY): Abraham M.. 132
WOOTEN: Bartley. 145: Bartly. 304:
Elizabeth. 066. 079: James. 079:
John. 183. 304: Joseph. 257: M.
F.. 061: Mattie. 061: Nancy
Elizabeth. 061: Richard J.T.. 061:
Riley. 304. 351. 415. 442:
Susannah. 035: Thomas. 191. 270:
William. 304
WOOTON: James. 061: John. 248. 304:
Joseph. 437: Nancy. 303: Riley.
WOOTTEN: Richard B.. 239: Thomas. 219
WOPDSWORTH: Jamie L.. Mrs.. 411
WOPMACK: Sid. 411
WORMLEY: Cora. 046: Will. 381
WOPMLY: Eliza. 381
WOPRILL: Solomon. 283
WORSHAM: Cannon. 261. 290: James C..
090. J.. S.. 365: Nancy. 460
WOPTEN: Lewis. 163
WORTHY: Ardena. 044: George. 381:
Leonard. 233. 304: Ose. 381:
Thomas. 194. 430: William. 434
WOSSHUM: John. 304
WRAY: Thomas J.. 464
WRIGHT: Abednego. 140: Ada. 004:
Anderson. 061: Anna Jane. 019:
Benjamin (Orphans). 121: Benjamin
H.. 251: Benjamin M.. 304: C.W.C..
163. 468: Charles W.C.. 152. 172.
177. 183. 300. 304. 381: Cora. 048:
David. 218. 304: Eadv. 241:
Earnest. 411: Eliza. 027: Ella.
036: Frank. 344: Franklin. 379: G.
W.. 381: George W.. 061. 079. 226.
270: Henrietta. 029: Henry. 061.
411: James K.. 329. 334. 357:
James. 061. 113. 304. 366. 411:
WRIGHT: John E.. 305: John L.. 329:
John. 083. 258: Mary. 097. 217.
305: Mattie. 411: Michael. 204.
305. 325: Nancy L.. 217: Robert
A.. 096-097. 305: Robert. 061.
194: Thomas. 079. 096. 220: William
B.. 096. 305: William D.. 139:
William. 088. 090. 194. 233. 257.
258. 305. 411. 437: Wm. A.. 444
WRITE: Abraham S.. 283
WYATT: Annie. 034: Asriah. 382:
Azariah. 061: Barton. 061: C..
306: Carrie Belle. 007: Carrie T..
025: Coalman. 061: Cvntha A.. 018:
Cynthia. 325: Eliza. 029: Emma. 052:
Frances. 029. 041: G.W.. 079. 129.
305: George W.. 206. 305. 306.
325. 447: H.J.. 382. 405: Hattie.
006: Henry. 061: Henry J.. 061:

I.T., 382, 457; Ike, 305; Isaac
T., 061, 079, 186, 305, 325, 343,
382, 457; J. O., 382; J. T., 305,
382, 415, 442; J.W., 405; Jeff, 382;
WYATT: Jesse, 061; John H., 306; John
W., 079, 093, 095, 106, 147, 162,
186, 235, 305, 306, 318, 325, 344,
376, 409, 411, 415, 464; John W.,
Jr., 306; John, 061, 305; John,
Sr., 433, 437; Julia, 035; Linda,
009; M. A., 288; M. L., 382;
Margarett, 032; Mary A. F., 079;
Mary Ann, 066; Nancey, 306; Nancy,
415; Otis, 411; Pleas, 061, 306;
Quinn, 382; Sallie, 030; Sam, 382,
415; Sarah, 008; T., 306; Thomas,
066, 079, 107, 128, 302, 306, 325;
W. H., 457; Will, 382; William H.,
079, 095, 104, 144, 231, 232, 263,
264, 301, 306, 325; William H.,
Jr., 167, 306
WYCHE: Henry, 123, 233; Peter, 189
WYLLIE: Hugh, 152
WYLY: A. C., 363; B. F., 363
WYNEN: John, 265, 266
WYNENS: Allen, 265, 306; Almeta M.,
042; E. L., 382, 457, 468; Elisha
L., 306, 457; Elisha S., 079, 180,
214, 306, 307, 415, 448, Elisha,
306; John, 218, 265, 266, 306,
307, 411; Robert, 457
WYNING: John, 307
WYNN: A. L., 457; Anna E., 465; Asa,
457; Dawson B., 091; Ed, 457;
Edward, 061, 397; Green, 252, 269,
283; Hartwell, 267; J. W., 457;
James C., 06l; James, 091; Lemuel,
287, 307; Lewis T., 428; Lewis,
111, 121, 126, 228, 231, 252, 278,
293, 307; Priscilla, 275; R. W.,
307, 460; Richmond W., 269, 283,
307, 460; Richmond Williamson, 158;
Robert B., 307; Robert J., 161;
Rosa, 036; Thomas, 116, 307; W.D.,
098, 156, 307, 334, 335, 337, 347,
358, 363, 370, 375, 379, 382, 457;
William, 079, 283; Williamson,
217, 279, 307
WYNNE: Lemuel, 307
YANCEY: Abram, 266; Benjamin D., 411;
Benjamin, 061; Ellender, 079;
George, 382; J. E., 411; Jekonias,
457; Layton, 307; Lewis D., 079,
099, 437; Lewis, 437; Louis H.,
061; Nancy, 079; Polley, 149;
Richard D., 307; Sarah, 079, 324;
T. J., 457; Thomas, 307, 324
YANCY: B. D., 468; Benjamin D., 307;
Benjamin, 307; Delphi, 033; George,
061, 307; J. E., 382, 411, 437,
442; Jackonias, 325; James, 062,
307; Janie, 034; Jickinias, 423;
L. D., 442; Layton, 079, 307, 325;
Lewis D.,066, 307, 458; Lewis, 307;
Martha, 411; Nancy, 066, 308;
Pheba, 307; Phebe, 458; Polly,
308; Polly, 308, 325; Rebecca L.,
005; Richard D., 307; Richard,
256, 307, 308; Thomas J., 308;
Thomas Y., 308; Thomas, 308, 382
YARBOROUGH: Delilah, 007; James,
468; Martha E., 017
YARBROUGH: James W., 239, 308;
Jeptha, 437; Joseph, 308;
Josiah, 166
YATE: James E., 294
YATEMAN: W. K., 360
YATES: James, 079
YEATMAN: W. K., 382
YEOMANS: Martin, 087, 189, 202, 308
YONGE: Henry, 325; William P.,
112, 308, 325
YORK: Archibald, 434
YOUNG: Earnest L., 107, 308; Earnest
S., 298; Ernest L., 079, 113, 308;
Gasham, 308; George T., 308; Green,
308; Greene, 308, 437; Harrison,
164, 308; Henry F., 285; James W.,
235; John N., 308; John, 308, 437;
Maryan, 437; Matthew (heirs of),
437; Patsey, 053; Pobert, 331,
339; Thomas, 437; W. T., 181, 368;
William P., 308; William T., 164;
William, 062, 308
YOUNGBLOOD: Abemilicn, 308;
Abimeleck, 308
ZABRISKEE: James, 117
ZABRISKIE: Christian, 188
ZACHARY: Abner S., 079
ZACHREY: W. L., 365, 370
ZACHRY: Abner S., 062; W.L., 062,
157, 282, 286, 357, 372, 378, 442,
444, 457; Walter L., 062, 157,
158, 180, 353, 378
ZELKIE: Willie, 411
ZIMMERMAN: Charles, 382; Charlie,
468; James, 235; John F., 390;
R. P., 402; James, 216
ZINN: Edwin, 308; Jacob, 308, 325
ZINNAMAN: Sallie, 028
ZINNAMON: Charles, 308
ZUBER: James W., 462

271. 371; Oblire. 060; P.M.. 457;
Peter. 436; Pilgrim. 291; Pleasant
M.. 060. 457; Polley. 042. 210;
Pony. 381; Prince. 298. 381. 410;
WILLIAMS: Rachael. 013; Rebecca.
027; Reese. 060. 381; Rhoda Ann.
050; Richard. 060. 183; Robert.
089. 298. 410; Roe. 060; Rose.
020; Rowland. 298; S. C.. 442;
Sam. 381; Samuel. 060. 210. 298;
Sarah. 059; Senetta. 009; Silva
Ann. 041; Smalley. 410; Solomon.
060; Squire. 381. 410; Steven.
415; Susan. 059; T.B.. 223. 410;
T. R.. 298. 436. 457. 468; Thomas
B.. 240. 458; Thomas K.. 457
WILLIAMS: Thomas M.. 401; Thomas R..
079. 298. 374. 381. 457. 458;
Thomas P.. Sr.. 060. 218. 274.
275. 298. 324. 404. 410. 464;
Thomas. Sr.. 182; Tommie. 410;
Vesta. 043; W.L.. 457; W.S.. 060.
298. 410. 457; W. T.. 442; Wesley.
060. 298; William D.. 105. 189;
William L.. Sr.. 079; William S..
060. 298. 410; William T. 130.
298; William. 060. 106. 130. 163.
251. 254. 257. 259. 298. 303. 324;
Willie. 060. 457; Zachariah. 079.
299. 314
WILLIAMSON: A. M.. 249; Benjamin.
197. 207. 436; Charles. 154; Green
B.. 196; Green. 111. 114. 300;
Isaac B.. 280. 285; Isaac. 079.
299. 324; James N.. 299; James.
115. 250. 299; John N.. 191; John.
247; Mary. 100. 168. 171. 183.
299; Micajah. 162. 299; Pleasant.
160. 299; Reuben. 209. 429. 436;
Richard. 299; Robert. 100. 114.
115. 131. 141. 142. 150. 209. 221.
263. 299. 302. 314. 316. 318. 322.
323; Sallie. 022; Thomas J.. 060;
William T.. 299; William W.. 275.
299. 300; William. 111. 114. 313.
299. 300; Willis. 100. 299;
Zarobabel. 114; Zorobabel. 111.
300; Zorobable. 428
WILLIFORD: Adaline. 031; David. 300
WILLINGHAM: Archer. 112; Archibald.
300; B.L.. 345; George W.. 283;
Isaac. 190. 217. 300. 458; Jeremiah.
300; Joe. 300; Mollie. 039; Nancy
J.. 039; Sallie. 055; T.. 460;
Taylor. 457; Theophalus. 060;
Theophilus. 381. 442. 457; Thomas.
231; W. N.. 060. 381; William.
079. 110. 300. 321. 458
WILLINGTON: C. E.. 381
WILLIS: Arthur. 079. 100; Daniel
B.. 426; Daniel H.. 174. 250. 436;
Hosea. 184; J. M.. 467; Jack. 110;
Jency. 445; Jimey (June). 100;
John C.. 257. 300. 387; John G..
126; Jonathan. 060. 445; Jonathon.
079; Louden. 285; O. B.. 457;
Robert L. 197. 300. 381. 325;
Robert. 300
WILLIAM?(WILLIAMS): Richard J.. 324
WILLS: Matthews. 125; William H..220
WILLSON: Abel P.. 136. 147. 300;
Alford G.. 300; Annie M.. 043;
Archillis. 300; B.H.. 436; Benjamin
C.T.. 388; Charles T. 306; Colonel
John. 300; Elijah. 181; Fields.
182. 300; Frank. 300; George. 079.
300; Hiram. 300; James E.. 079.
300; James. 134. 137. 187. 196.
265. 276. 294. 300. 301. 436; John
(heirs of). 425. 436; John. 079.
103. 112. 114. 116. 126. 134. 137.
141. 149. 153. 156. 164. 176. 187.
196. 200. 204. 216. 241. 244. 248.
266. 276. 278. 297. 299- 301. 304.
314. 316. 325. 421-430. 432. 433.
435. 436. 458; John. 462. 466;
WILLSON: Joseph. 300; Lawrence L.
301; Leroy M..102. 103. 144. 166.
170. 193. 200. 203. 207. 240. 241.
258. 268. 269. 301. 306. 351. 436;
Leroy W.. 114; Leroy. 153; Lowery.
410; Pleasant. 102. 103. 114. 144.
153. 166. 170. 193. 200. 203. 207.
240. 241. 258. 268. 269. 306. 351;
Sally. 301; Sarah. 443; Talitha.
016; William L.. 301
WILLY: Thomas. 216. 235
WILLYFORD: Hartwell. 279
WILSON: A.B.. 056; A.J.. 079. 467;
Abe. 301; Abel P.. 135. 141. 147.
148. 195. 301. 302. 386. 391. 392.
410. 436; Abraham V.. 060; Adel
L.. 047; Adell S.. 079; Alfred G..
149; Allen. 060; Alvah. 191;
Andrew J.. 301. 302. 410; Annie.
411; Arkiles. 120; Arkillis. 066.
079. 302; Augustus. 060; Barthena.
198; Ben. 381; Benjamin H.. 172;
Benjamin J.. 297. 301. 302;
WILSON: Bethenia. 302; Bill. 186;
C.M.. 400; C.T.. 457; Caroline.

003; Charles John. 302; Charles
M.. 060; Charles. 060. 302. 335.
348. 381. 443; Daniel. 111. 123;
Dave. 060. 302; David. 061;
Dawson. 061; E. A.. 061; Eaton
P.. 302; Elick. 061; Elijah. 061.
079. 325; Eliza. 041; Ella. 017;
Fields. 206. 222. 268. 270. 302.
422. 428. 430. 436; Flem. 443;
Fred. 411; Fulton. 061; G.S.. 411;
WILSON: George 1.. 325; George J..
079. 302. 347; George. 061. 381.
415; Graves E.. 186; Graves S..
120. 302; Graves. 142. 302; Gus.
457; Harriet. 060; Henry. 381;
Hiram. 381; Hugh. 302; Irvin W..
061; J.B.. 457; J.W.. 352. 381;
J.. 468; James D.. 325; James E..
217. 313. 411; James H.. 061. 381;
James W.. 302. 357. 381. 411;
James. 061. 142. 252. 276. 302.
415. 457; James. Jr.. 381; Jane.
WILSON: 014. 061. 079. 149; Jenkins. 079. 149.
241; Jim. 186. 302. 381; Jimmie.
400; John (heirs of). 424; John
H. L.. 061; John L. 302; John
P.. 302; John S. 436. 437. 448;
John W.. 448; John. 061. 110. 125.
164. 236. 252. 302. 316. 361. 423.
436. 465-467; Joseph A.. 079. 205.
291; Joseph. 066. 129. 238. 302.
325. 411. 460; Joshua. 437;
Larkin. 302; Lawrence L. 302;
WILSON: Leola. 003; Leonard. 119.
182. 302. 437; Leroy M.. 150. 159.
237. 262. 295. 448; Leroy. 097.
194; Lessie. 468; Lillie. 036;
Lizzie. 015; Lucious. 061; Lula.
019; Lum. 061; M.S.. 457; Martha.
031. 061. 302. 443; Mary E. 046.
302. 415; Mary Jane. 059; Mary.
334. 358. 437; Mattie. 038; Micha.
460; Milly. 381; Mintie. 040;
Monroe. 378. 468; Munroe. 381;
WILSON: Nancy S.. 325; Nancy. 025.
208. 226. 302. 381; Nelson. 302;
Pat. 302; Pleasant. 097. 150. 159.
194. 237. 262; R. W.. 381. 411;
Rachael. 066. 079. 205; Rachel
(Lowry). 302; Randol P.. 302;
Robert. 061. 302; Rufus. 061; S.
J.. 411; Samuel. 443. 461. 469;
Sarah. 079. 302. 325; Sopha.
021; Sophia. 059; T. S.. 457;
Texas. 381; Thomas B.. 079; Thomas.
132. 302. 434. 468; V.A.. 377. 381.
411. 457. 468; V. H.. 380; Vines
A.. 381. 403; Vines. 457; Wiley.
164; William L.. 123. 302; William
S.. 079. 411; William. 165. 243.
302. 325; Willie. 302
WIMBERLY: Elijah. 061
WIMBISH: Sam. 061
WIMBUSH: Elbert. 411; Lizzie. 005;
Mary Jane. 079; Samuel. 061. 411;
William. 061. 302
WINANS: ?. 062; C. A.. 381; John.
321; W. C.. 468
WINBURN: George W.. 297; J.J.. 444;
Martha A.. 380
WINBUSH: Mollie. 005
WINCHESTER: Jonathan. 437
WINDBUSH: Julia. 062
WINDHAM: Elias. 191
WINFREY: John. 238. 302. 411;
Margaret. 303
WINGFIELD: Alfred M.. 275; Alfred
W.. 306; J.. 397; John. 133. 140.
275. 293. 306. 312. 320. 402;
Marcellus A.. 312. 320; S.. 117;
W. B.. 444; Ella. 050
WINN: Francis. 255. 303;
Hartwell. 061
WINNE: Francis. 303
WINSHIP: Joseph. 236. 246
WINSLETT: John C.. 303
WINSTED: Samuel. 303
WINSTELL: John C.. 303
WISBORN: Eliga. 061
WISDOM: Elenor. 303; Francis. 109.
300. 303; Hamilton. 303
WISE: Augustus. 303; Barnabas. 290.
303; Barney. 079; Betsey. 303;
Creed T.. 045. 264. 309; Cyntha.
108; Dave. 061; David. 411;
Elizabeth. 164. 303; Emily. 108;
Fannie. 048; George. 411; Green.
351; Henry. 061. 381; Hugh. 111.
125. 153. 290. 303; Isaiah. 079;
J. M.. 348; James C.. 079. 108;
James. 061; Jane. 303. 381; John.
303; Joseph A.. 061. 303. 442;
M.F.. 039; Mary E.. 039; Matilda.
033; Patton. 061. 079. 164. 238.
303; Riley. 437; William. 108. 303
WISEMAN: William. 303
WISENERS: Thomas. 079
WITT: Anna Olivia. 031; David. 204.
302; Savannah. 028
WODDFY: Lucy. 019
WOLEF: S. B.. 376
WOLF: George W.. 375; Jacob. 088. 371

WOLFE: J.. 328; Jacob. 333. 334.
353. 363.Jacob. 381. 382. 396.
404; William. 079
WOLLSEY: Abraham M.. 132
WOMACK: Edmond. 437; Eva. 381;
Georgia. 015; James T.. 381; James.
303; John H.. 061; Josephine. 013;
Seaborn. 061. 457; Sid. 171. 457;
Sidney. 061; T. K.. 381
WOMMACK: Edmond. 325; Edward. 303;
Elberry. 448; J. T.. 468; James.
464; John W.. 415; S. W.. 395;
Thomas K.. 376; William. 381. 464
WOOD: A.. 391; Amasa. 256. 303;
Aristarchus. 437; Asa. 088. 100;
Carrie. 034; Cary. 174. 210. 300.
306; Charles. 302; E. 391;
Earnest. 183; Ezelle. 100;
Georgianna. 303; J. L. G.. 457;
Jack. 411; James B.. 061; James
E. 220. 303. 322. 324; James M..
303; Jim. 061; John. 079. 104.
176. 283. 303. 388. 458; Joshua
J.. 303. 411; Lucinda. 303;
Stephen. 031; Tabitha. 218; Thomas.
203. 303; William. 303; Woody. 303
WOODALL: John. 154L Robert. 224. 279
WOODAPD: Owen. 297
WOODFIN: Moses. 304
WOODLEY: Andrew. 433; Caleb. 156.
192. 221. 302. 393. 437; Josie.
033; William. 061
WOODLY: Andrew. 215; Caleb. 099
WOODREW: James. 126
WOODROOF: William. 469
WOODROW: James. 184
WOODPUFF: Agatha. 304; Clittera. 427;
Clifford. 061. 304; Clifford. Jr..
304; David. 211. 252. 304. 329;
Davis. 283; James. 238. 252. 304.
325. 444; Joseph. 304; Philo D..
283; Philo. 089; W. W.. 346;
Worsham W.. 290
WOODS: J. L. G.. 061; John L.. 411;
Otis. 411; Robert. 425; William.
010. 130. 140. 230. 231
WOODWARD: Isham. 247; John L.. 321
WOODY: James. 061
WOOLLEY: Zadock. 299
WOOLSEY: Abraham M.. 154. 273. 304;
Abraham. 197; Abram M.. 241; John
C.. 241; John M.. 132. 154. 273.
304; William C.. 132. 154. 304;
William M.. 154. 241. 304. 314
WOOLSEY?WOLLSEY: Abraham M.. 132
WOOTEN: Bartley. 145; Bartly. 304;
Elizabeth. 066. 079; James. 079;
John. 183. 304; Joseph. 257; M.
F.. 061; Mattie. 021; Nancy
Elizabeth. 061; Pichard J.T.. 061;
Riley. 304. 351. 415. 442;
Susannah. 035; Thomas. 191. 270;
William. 304
WOOTON: James. 061; John. 248. 304;
Joseph. 437; Nancy. 303; Riley.
411; Sarah. 445; William. 304
WOOTTEN: Pichard B.. 239; Thomas. 219
WODSWORTH: Jamie L.. Mrs.. 411
WORMACK: Sid. 411
WORMLEY: Cora. 046; Will. 381
WORMLY: Eliza. 381
WORRILL: Solomon. 283
WORSHAM: Cannon. 261. 290; James C..
304; C.. 363; Nancy. 460
WORTEN: Lewis. 163
WORTHY: Ardena. 044; George. 381;
Leonard. 233. 304; Ose. 381;
Thomas. 194. 430; William. 434
WOSSHUM: John. 304
WRAY: Thomas J.. 464
WRIGHT: Abedneao. 140; Ada. 004;
Anderson. 061; Anna Jane. 019;
Benjamin (Orphans). 121; Benjamin
H.. 251; Benjamin M.. 304; C.W.C..
163. 468; Charles W.C. 152. 172.
177. 183. 300. 304. 381; Cora. 048;
David. 218. 304; Eadv. 244;
Earnest. 411; Eliza. 027; Ella.
036; Frank. 344; Franklin. 370; G.
W.. 381; George W.. 061. 079. 226.
270; Henrietta. 029; Henry. 061.
411; James K.. 329. 334. 357;
James. 061. 113. 304. 366. 411;
WRIGHT: John E.. 457; John L.. 329;
John. 083. 258; Marv. 097. 217.
305; Mattie. 411; Michael. 204.
305. 325; Nancy L.. 217; Robert
A.. 096-097. 305; Robert. 061.
194; Thomas. 079. 096. 220; William
A.. 096. 305; William D.. 139;
William. 088. 090. 194. 233. 257.
258. 305. 411. 437; Wm. A.. 444
WRITE: Abraham S.. 283
WYATT: Annie. 034; Asriah. 382;
Azariah. 061; Barton. 061; C..
306; Carrie Belle. 007; Carrie T..
025; Coalman. 061; Cyntha A.. 018;
Cynthia. 325; Ella. 029; Emma. 052;
Frances. 029; G.W.. 061. 079. 129.
305; George W.. 206. 305. 306.
325. 447; H.J.. 382. 405; Hattie.
006; Henry. 061; Henry J.. 061;

I.T., 382, 457; Ike, 305; Isaac
T., 061, 079, 186, 305, 325, 343,
382, 457; J. O., 382; J. T., 305,
382, 415, 442; J.W., 405; Jeff, 382;
WYATT: Jesse, 061; John H., 306; John
W., 079, 093, 095, 106, 147, 162,
186, 235, 305, 306, 318, 325, 344,
376, 409, 411, 415, 464; John W.,
Jr., 306; John, 061, 305; John,
Sr., 433, 437; Julia, 035; Linda,
009; M. A., 288; M. L., 382;
Margarett, 032; Mary A. F., 079;
Mary Ann, 066; Nancey, 306; Nancy,
415; Otis, 411; Pleas, 061, 306;
Quinn, 382; Sallie, 030; Sam, 382,
415; Sarah, 008; T., 306; Thomas,
066, 079, 107, 128, 302, 306, 325;
W. H., 457; Will, 382; William H.,
079, 095, 104, 144, 231, 232, 263,
264, 301, 306, 325; William H..
Jr., 167, 306
WYCHE: Henry, 123, 233; Peter, 189
WYLIE: Hugh, 152
WYLY: A. C., 363; B. F., 363
WYNEN: John, 265, 266
WYNENS: Allen, 265, 306; Almeta M.,
042; E. L., 382, 457, 468; Elisha
L., 306, 457; Elisha S., 079, 180,
214, 306, 307, 415, 448, Elisha,
306; John, 218, 265, 266, 306,
307, 411; Robert, 457
WYNING: John, 307
WYNN: A. L., 457; Anna E., 465; Asa,
457; Dawson B., 091; Ed, 457;
Edward, 061, 397; Green, 252, 269,
283; Hartwell, 267; J. W., 457;
James C., 061; James, 091; Lemuel,
287, 307; Lewis J., 428; Lewis,
111, 121, 126, 228, 231, 252, 278,
293, 307; Priscilla, 275; R. W.,
307, 460; Richmond W., 269, 283,
307, 460; Richmond Williamson, 158;
Robert B., 307; Robert J., 161;
Rosa, 036; Thomas, 116, 307; W.D.,
098, 156, 307, 334, 335, 337, 347,
358, 363, 370, 375, 379, 382, 457;
William, 079, 283; Williamson,
217, 279, 307
WYNNE: Lemuel, 307
YANCEY: Abram, 266; Benjamin D., 411;
Benjamin, 061; Ellender, 079;
George, 382; J. E., 411; Jekonias,
457; Layton, 307; Lewis D., 079,
099, 437; Lewis, 437; Louis H.,
061; Nancy, 079; Polley, 149;
Richard D., 307; Sarah, 079, 324;
T. J., 457; Thomas, 307, 324
YANCY: B. D., 468; Benjamin D., 307;
Benjamin, 307; Delphi, 033; George,
061, 307; J. E., 382, 411, 437,
442; Jackonias, 325; James, 062,
307; Janie, 034; Jickinias, 423;
L. D., 442; Layton, 079, 307, 325;
Lewis D.,066, 307, 458; Lewis, 307;
Martha, 411; Nancy, 066, 308;
Pheba, 307; Phebe, 458; Phoebe,
308; Polly, 308, 325; Rebecca L.,
005; Richard D., 307; Richard,
256, 307, 308; Thomas J., 308;
Thomas Y., 308; Thomas, 308, 382
YARBOROUGH: Delilah, 007; James,
468; Martha E., 017
YARBROUGH: James W., 239, 308;
Jeptha, 437; Joseph, 308;
Josiah, 166
YATE: James E., 294
YATEMAN: W. K., 360
YATES: James, 079
YEATMAN: W. K., 382
YEOMANS: Martin, 087, 189, 202, 308
YONGE: Henry, 325; William P.,
112, 308, 325
YORK: Archibald, 434
YOUNG: Earnest L., 107, 308; Earnest
S., 298; Ernest L., 079, 113, 308;
Gasham, 308; George T., 308; Green,
308; Greene, 308, 437; Harrison,
164, 308; Henry P., 285; James W.,
235; John N., 308; John, 308, 437;
Maryan, 437; Matthew (heirs of),
437; Patsey, 053; Robert, 331,
339; Thomas, 437; W. T., 181, 368;
William P., 308; William T., 164;
William, 062, 308
YOUNGBLOOD: Abemilicn, 308;
Abimeleck, 308
ZABRISKEE: James, 117
ZABRISKIE: Christian, 188
ZACHARY: Abner S., 079
ZACHREY: W. L., 365, 370
ZACHRY: Abner S., 062; W.L., 062,
157, 282, 286, 357, 372, 378, 442,
444, 457; Walter L., 062, 157,
158, 180, 353, 378
ZELKIE: Willie, 411
ZIMMERMAN: Charles, 382; Charlie,
468; James, 235; John F., 390;
R. P., 402; James, 216
ZINN: Edwin, 308; Jacob, 308, 325
ZINNAMAN: Sallie, 029
ZINNAMON: Charles, 308
ZUBER: James W., 462